Owen Hood Phillips
1907-1986

O. HOOD PHILLIPS'
CONSTITUTIONAL
AND ADMINISTRATIVE LAW

AUSTRALIA AND NEW ZEALAND
The Law Book Company Ltd.
Sydney : Melbourne : Perth

CANADA AND U.S.A.
The Carswell Company Ltd.
Agincourt, Ontario

INDIA
N. M. Tripathi Private Ltd.
Bombay
and
Eastern Law House Private Ltd.
Calcutta and Delhi
M.P.P. House
Bangalore

ISRAEL
Steimatzky's Agency Ltd.
Jerusalem : Tel Aviv : Haifa

MALAYSIA : SINGAPORE : BRUNEI
Malayan Law Journal (Pte.) Ltd.
Singapore and Kuala Lumpur

O. HOOD PHILLIPS'
CONSTITUTIONAL
AND ADMINISTRATIVE LAW

Seventh Edition

BY

THE LATE O. HOOD PHILLIPS
Q.C., D.C.L., M.A.(OXON.), J.P.

*Formerly Emeritus Professor of Jurisprudence
and sometime Dean of the Faculty of Law
in the University of Birmingham*

AND

PAUL JACKSON
LL.D. (LIVERPOOL), B.C.L. (OXON.), M.A. (DUBLIN)

*of Gray's Inn, Barrister;
Professor of Law, University of Reading*

LONDON
SWEET & MAXWELL
1987

First edition	.	. 1952
Second edition	.	. 1957
Third edition	.	. 1962
Fourth edition	.	. 1967
Fifth edition	.	. 1973
Sixth edition	.	. 1978
Seventh Edition	.	. 1987

Published in 1987 by
Sweet & Maxwell Limited of
11, New Fetter Lane, London
Computerset by Promenade Graphics Limited, Cheltenham
Printed and bound in Great Britain by
Richard Clay (The Chaucer Press) Limited, Bungay, Suffolk

British Library Cataloguing in Publication Data
Phillips, Owen Hood
    O. Hood Phillips Constitutional and
    administrative law.—7th ed.
    1. Great Britain—Constitutional law
    2. Administrative law—Great Britain
    I. Title   II. Jackson, Paul
    344.102   KD3989
    ISBN 0–421–35030–X
    ISBN 0–421–35040–7 Pbk

PREFACE TO THE SEVENTH EDITION

This new edition of *Constitutional and Administrative Law* is somewhat lengthier than its predecessor. That growth reflects both the activity of the legislature and the courts in the period between the two editions and the decision to expand the treatment of various topics, for example freedom of the person (Chapter 25). At the same time it is hoped that due attention has been given to the process of pruning the redundant and the out-dated. To be distinguished from those is historical matter without which the current constitution cannot be understood. "The study of the fundamental principles of our unwritten Constitution can hardly be separated from that of their history. We must at least go back to cases of the early and late Stuarts for explanation of the Bill of Rights in 1688, if not to the emergence of Parliament in the time of Edward I." (O. Hood Phillips, "Dicey: A Personal View" [1985] P.L. 587, 589.) The putting into commission of the office of the Treasurer in 1714 retains a present significance in the law on such a thoroughly modern topic as value added tax; Value Added Tax, 1983, section 9; Treasury Signature Act 1849; *post* p.329.

To readers in Scotland it will be perfectly obvious that this book is written in England with English law largely in mind. Nonetheless a deliberate effort has been made to avoid obscuring the existence of a separate legal system on the other side of the border. I have tried to avoid referring to the Constitution of the United Kingdom as the English constitution. (Dicey has much to answer for.) In some places, for example in the chapters on administration of justice and freedom of expression, there are attempts to draw attention to variations between English and Scottish law. In others, reference to Scottish works may at least help readers to remember that there are differences between the systems and to pursue their own researches further. Where statutes are applicable to England and Scotland, for example, the Representation of the People Acts and the Crown Proceedings Act 1947, helpful Scottish cases have been cited. The absurdity of unconsciously extending English law to Scotland by statute is referred to in connection with the Extradition Act 1870. (The extension of the law of treason in an earlier century was a conscious act of political expediency; *post* p.475).

In Part I (General Part) important developments include decisions such as *Re Amendment of the Constitution of Canada* (1981) 125 D.L.R. (3d) 1 and *Manuel* v. *Attorney-General* [1983] Ch. 77. Chapter 5, The United Kingdom and the European Communities, has been largely rewritten and the discussion of the European Communities Act 1972, section 2 transferred to Chapter 4 where it seems logically to belong. No doubt in any future edition further thought will have to be given on the best way to incorporate the European element into a book on the constitutional law of the United Kingdom.

Part II (Parliament) has taken account of recent legislation such as the various Representation of the People Acts and the Parliamentary Constituencies Act 1986. The chapters on parliamentary procedure, national finance and parliamentary privilege have been revised and in many places largely rewritten by Mrs. Patricia Leopold, my colleague at Reading. Both Hood Phillips and I were very pleased to have her assistance.

In Part III (The Central Government) perhaps the most important judicial contribution is to be found in the House of Lords decision, *Council of Civil Service Unions* v. *Minister for the Civil Service* [1985] A.C. 374. References have been made to such celebrated events of recent years as the Westland imbroglio—to quote Geoffrey Marshall [1986] P.L. 184. (Whether that remarkable story has any lasting constitutional significance remains to be seen.) The scope of two historic royal prerogatives came into question in *Attorney-General for the Duchy of Lancaster* v. *G. E. Overton (Farms) Ltd.* [1982] Ch. 277 and *Pierce* v. *Bemis* [1986] Q.B. 384.

Part V (Rights and Duties of the Individual) has seen considerable rewriting and rearrangement of the chapters into what is hoped is a more logical order—although in this area there are inevitable overlaps between chapters. In the chapter on nationality account has been taken of the British Nationality Act 1981. The chapter on freedom of person and property has inevitably been expanded to take account of the Police and Criminal Evidence Act 1984. (At what stage, however, do the detailed provisions of such legislation cease to be of *constitutional* significance?) New sections in the chapter include those on the rights of mental patients and prisoners, privacy and freedom of religion. It has also been thought appropriate to remove to this chapter, and expand, the account of the law on obstructing constables, formerly to be found in the chapter on police. The chapter on freedom of speech has become an expanded and re-written chapter on freedom of expression. Mrs. Leopold again kindly undertook primary responsibility for freedom of assembly and association where the Public Order Act 1986 required extensive rewriting.

It is possible to argue that there has been more change and development in the law falling within Part VI (Administrative Law) than in any other sphere of the law since the previous edition. An Introduction now seeks to put modern developments in an historic setting. The chapter on Local Government takes account of a succession of statutes affecting the structure and powers of local authorities. To do more than provide a framework in a book of this scope is practically impossible and, perhaps, unnecessary as local govenment becomes an increasingly fashionable area of study which has generated a number of books, monographs and articles. The chapter on public corporations can similarly offer little more than an introduction. A brief section takes account of the major development in the area, privatisation. The chapter on administrative jurisdiction has been considerably re-written and the section on the Parliamentary Commissioner removed to a new chapter on non-judicial remedies. The two chapters on judicial review have been revised to take account particularly of Order 53 and the plethora of cases following *O'Reilly* v. *Mackman* [1983] 2 A.C. 237. The time must be approaching when it will no longer be possible to continue to pour new wine into these old bottles. In Crown proceedings the most rapid development has been in the area of public interest immunity. For the lawyer, if not the serviceman, it is tantalising that the Government has agreed to repeal section 10 of the Crown Proceedings Act 1947 just when it has provoked such interesting cases as *Brown* v. *Lord Advocate* 1984 S.L.T. 146; *Bell* v. *Secretary of State for Defence* [1986] Q.B. 322 and *Pearce* v. *Secretary of State for Defence* [1987] 2 W.L.R. 782.

In Part VII (The Commonwealth) important legislative developments include the Canada Act 1982, the Hong Kong Act 1985 and the Australia Act 1986—measures which will enable this Part to be still further compressed in the future. Nonetheless, the Privy Council retains an active jurisdiction as the number of new decisions cited in this edition show.

In preparing a new edition one is acutely aware of how many errors and shortcomings in the previous edition reviewers have mercifully failed to point out. For the constructive suggestions on the Sixth edition I am grateful and I hope it appears that an attempt has been made to take account of them where, at least, I agreed with them. Professor R. F. V. Heuston very kindly wrote with comments and to point out a howler at page 21, particularly unforgivable on the part of two graduates of T.C.D. Even he, however seemed to have overlooked the remarkable statement to be found at page 155 n. 29 of the previous edition. On various matters Professor C. Munro, of the University of Manchester, has taken the trouble to reply at length to my inquiries. Apart from my specific debt to Mrs. Leopold mentioned above I owe a more general debt for help with advice and information. Mr. P. R. Ghandhi and Mr. P. Schofield, also of this department, have patiently answered my questions on areas within their special knowledge. As always I must mention the cheerful help given by Mr. Ian Sainsbury, of the University Library: nor would it be right to fail to mention Mary Blake of Birmingham's Harding Law Library. Without my secretary Mrs. Hutton-Penman the whole task would have been impossible.

To Sweet and Maxwell, my obligations go far beyond those which any author owes to his publishers. The production of this edition was unduly delayed for various unhappy reasons. At all times they showed sympathy and understanding. They also showed professional expertise of the highest order by producing a printed text from a bundle of annotated pages and typed sheets which could hardly be called a manuscript.

I have attempted to take account of legal developments up to November 7, 1986 and it proved possible to take account of certain later developments when correcting proofs.

Although Hood Phillips died before this edition could be published he had seen and approved, before his death, the major part of the revised text. In preparing the rest I relied heavily on the detailed notes which he continued to make until almost the end of his life. I had, too, the advantage of having worked with him in preparing the previous edition. I hope this is not too unworthy a memorial.

April 1987   P.J.

OWEN HOOD PHILLIPS

Owen Hood Phillips was born on September 30, 1907 and died in his seventy-ninth year on May 25, 1986. He read law at Oxford between the Wars—retaining always an affection for his old college, Merton—and in 1931 began his long and distinguished career as an assistant lecturer in laws at King's College, London. After four years he moved to Trinity College, Dublin, that unique nursery in earlier times of great English judges.[1] Two years later he returned to King's as a Reader in Laws, a post he held until being called to war service at the Ministry of Aircraft Production. In 1946 he was appointed Barber Professor of Jurisprudence at Birmingham. The Faculty of Law then was still under the direction of its legendary founding dean, C. E. Smalley Baker, assisted in his duties by the Faculty Secretary the equally remarkable Miss K. M. Tyndall (Cooey) who died in her mid-nineties only a few months before Hood Phillips. Smalley Baker's reign of twenty-two years ended in 1949 (when he returned to his native Canada to a second career as Dean of Osgoode Hall Law School) and Hood Phillips succeeded to a post which he was to hold for nineteen years: a burden in these days almost unimaginable when deanships and headships of departments are generally accepted for three or four years at most. Those nineteen years were years of expansion, the Faculty quadrupling in size and moving ultimately from its original site in the centre of town, via a variety of prefabricated buildings into its present accommodation in the middle of the Birmingham campus, close to the great campanile. From 1972 until 1975 he was Vice Principal and Pro-Vice Chancellor, playing an important role in the drafting of the University's new charter. Outside the University his distinction was recognised by his appointment as Queen's Counsel in 1970 and the conferment in 1971 of the degree of Doctor of Civil Law by the University of Oxford. The esteem and affection in which he was held inside the Faculty was shown by the publication of a commemorative volume of the Holdsworth Law Review in 1982, composed of contributions from members and former members of the Faculty, to mark his seventy-fifth birthday.

One of his last public functions was to address the seminar organised by *Public Law* at All Souls College in 1985 to mark the centenary of the publication of Dicey's *Law of the Constitution*. Participants were delighted and amused by an after lunch speech which revealed a less reverential view of Dicey than they had probably expected. ("Dicey: A Personal View" [1985] P.L. 587). If it was disappointing to learn that the two constitutional lawyers had never met—Dicey died four years before Hood Phillips went up to Oxford—it was a surprise to learn of the undergraduate who had written on his copy of the *Law of the Constitution*, "This chapter is tripe" against Chapter 13 where Dicey sought to reconcile his doctrines of Parliamentary Supremacy and the Rule of

---

[1]   R. F. V. Heuston, "Hugh McCalmont Cairns," (1975) 26 N.I.L.Q. 269.

Law. (The pencilled inscription is still legible. Subsequent private comments on later writers continued to display equally uncompromising brevity.)

While still Reader at King's College, London he wrote his first major book, *The Principles of English Law and the Constitution*, which appeared in 1939. It ran to more than six hundred pages. An introductory part dealt with theories of law and of the state; subsequent parts with the English legal system, the constitution of the United Kingdom and the constitution of the British Empire. The preface explained that "[this] book is intended primarily for those who have to take examinations in law. . . But the attempt has been made to make the book readable by the 'intelligent layman' whose intelligence is manifested by his avoiding examinations in law altogether." In words which defined the principle underlying his subsequent writings the author added, "As this is a law book, emphasis is naturally placed on the legal aspects of the constitution." *The Principles* was the ancestor of two books which, after the war, were to occupy much of Hood Phillips's time; the *First Book of English Law*, of which the first edition appeared in 1948, the seventh in 1977, with the assistance of Professor A. H. Hudson who is currently editing an eighth edition; and *The Constitutional Law of Great Britain and the Commonwealth* which appeared under that title in 1952, when Hood Phillips was assisted by G. Ellenbogen. That book had been preceded in 1946 by *Chalmers and Hood Phillips on Constitutional Law* which was itself based on the fifth edition of an earlier textbook, *Chalmers and Asquith's Constitutional Law*. Readers of *Chalmers and Hood Phillips* learned from the preface that the writing of the book had been done in the time spared from "my work in a Government Department, and not seldom it was accompanied by the sound of air-raids, flying bombs or rockets". *Constitutional Law* became *Constitutional and Administrative Law* in 1962, the year of the third edition. The preface explained, "The change in the title of this book . . . reflects the fact that Britain has lost an Empire and gained a Council on Tribunals." Subsequent editions followed regularly. In the preparation of the sixth edition, which appeared in 1978, he was assisted by the present writer who, sadly and unexpectedly, has had to assume responsibility for completing the current, seventh edition. Since its inception the textbook has been accompanied by a collection of leading cases, currently *Leading Cases in Constitutional and Administrative Law*, 5th ed., 1979). In 1970 Hood Phillips published *Reform of the Constitution* where he discussed many of the issues which have continued to be controversial subjects for debate such as the desirability of adopting a written constitution or enacting a new bill of rights and the election of Parliament for a fixed term.

Hood Phillips, in manner and appearance, could only be described as formal and reserved, qualities partly innate and partly, perhaps, adopted as being in his view appropriate to his public position. He presided at Faculty Board in a way not calculated to encourage dissent or even discussion. He was of a generation and background where use of surnames was far commoner than indiscriminate resort to first names after one meeting and colleagues were inclined to think long before concluding that they were entitled to address him as Owen. But the new lecturer who blithely invited the, by then, ex-Dean to a party for students discovered that the invitation was happily accepted and the students were charmed by his kindliness and dry sense of humour. To take at face value any remark he made was unwise; nothing delighted him more than to realise that a listener had been misled into thinking that some outrageous expression of opinion represented Hood Phillips's own view. It was at home, whether in Edgbaston or in the country, first at Henley-in-Arden and later at Clee St. Margaret—in the company of his wife, Lucy, that he gave full vent to his sense of fun. A guest who professed an interest in baking might well be taken to the kitchen, given the raw materials and required to provide a loaf as proof of his culinary ability.

Apart from the law Hood Phillips had a lifelong interest in the works of Shakespeare, as evidenced by his articles in the Law Quarterly Review to mark the quatercentenary of the playwright's death in 1964 and later his book, *Shakespeare and the Lawyers*, published in 1972. (He liked to point out to visitors that there was no reason why Shakespeare should not have walked in the orchard of his cottage at Henley-in-Arden.) Only after retirement did he feel that he had time enough to tackle Proust, which he did with the care and thoroughness he brought to everything he undertook. In due course Terence Kilmartin, after the appearance of his new translation of *A la Recherche* in 1981, received a letter of the kind with which, in earlier years, anyone who had written on constitutional law would be familiar, full of points, questions, comments, criticisms and suggestions which had occurred to Hood Phillips. While not addicted in the manner of some, it should be added that for country reading he recommended the works of P. G. Wodehouse.

O.H.P.—it is hard not to think of him by that signature which appeared invariably on memoranda, at the bottom of letters, on post-cards from around the world—professed that *Love's Labour's Lost* was his favourite Shakespearian play. That may have been one of his remarks made to tease. But, if true, it was an apt choice. He had spent almost all his life in universities. The King of Navarre, his lords, the Princess and her ladies are eternal undergraduates with all the gaiety and enthusiasm of youth. The royal park is an ideal university, in a term that is always summer with the sun always shining. And Don Adriano and Holofernes? They are colleagues from other faculties, to be encountered regularly at university meetings.[2]

P.J.

---

[2] I am glad to acknowledge my indebtedness to Professor L. Neville Brown's obituary of Professor O. Hood Phillips which was published in The Times on May 29, 1986, to his address at the funeral service on June 4, 1986, and the obituary which he wrote for The University of Birmingham Bulletin, June 16, 1986, copies of which were kindly supplied to me.

CONTENTS

PART V: RIGHTS AND DUTIES OF THE INDIVIDUAL

22. *RIGHTS AND DUTIES GENERALLY*   423

23. *NATIONALITY, CITIZENSHIP, IMMIGRATION AND EXTRADITION*   446

PART VI: ADMINISTRATIVE LAW

35. *CROWN PROCEEDINGS* 702

PART VII: THE COMMONWEALTH

36. *DEPENDENT TERRITORIES* 727

TABLE OF CASES

TABLE OF STATUTES

Foreign Statutes

PART I

GENERAL PART

CHAPTER I

THE NATURE OF CONSTITUTIONAL AND ADMINISTRATIVE LAW

The constitutional law of a state is the law relating to the constitution of that state. It is therefore desirable at the outset to discuss briefly the terms "Law," "State" and "Constitution."

Law

Many attempts have been made to define this apparently simple term, and for these the reader is referred to books on legal theory which English writers commonly call jurisprudence. We are concerned with state law (municipal law), and it will be sufficient for our present purpose to define the law of a state as consisting of those rules of conduct which are enforced by the duly constituted courts of that state. This would not be an adequate definition for the student of jurisprudence, or the science of law in general; for it does not explain whence the courts derive their authority to lay down the law, nor why the courts in administering justice look to certain sources and not to others, and look to those sources in a certain order and in a certain way. To say that the law is the law because the courts declare it to be so would be like defining an acid as that which turns litmus paper red. Litmus paper provides a convenient working test whereby the chemist determines whether a given liquid is acid or alkali, but it does not explain what acids and alkalis are in themselves. Similarly, enforcement by the courts is a sort of litmus test which may be used to distinguish between legal and non-legal rules of conduct. Enforcement by the courts does not necessarily mean specific enforcement, but usually takes the form of punishment or some other treatment (in criminal law), or an order to pay damages or to deliver up property (in civil law).

This criterion is admittedly imperfect when applied to constitutional and administrative law. In the first place, many decisions in English administrative law are made by tribunals other than the ordinary courts. These tribunals, however, are created by Acts of Parliament; their jurisdiction, composition and powers are defined by statute, and their decisions—whether subject to appeal to the courts or not—are recognised and enforced by the courts. Again, law cannot be enforced against the government, though it can be enforced against members of the government individually. Nor can law be enforced against Parliament or either House of Parliament, although the courts may make a declaration as to the law in relation to either of the Houses, and law may be enforced against members of either House personally. Actions in tort or contract may be brought against a government department representing the Crown, but the judgment cannot be enforced by execution.[1] The law is not enforceable against the Queen in her personal capacity, but this is not of practical importance. Statutory "duties" may be declared by Parliament to be unenforceable in the courts, such as the

[1] Crown Proceedings Act 1947.

3

duty of the Railways Board to provide railway services under the Transport Act 1962; and the performance of certain functions by the Speaker under the Parliament Acts may not be questioned in the courts. Moreover "the law and custom of Parliament," although it is recognised by the ordinary courts, is enforced by the Houses of Parliament through their officers, and is both historically and analytically a distinct branch of British constitutional law.[2]

Some writers, however, find the essential element of legal rules to be their recognition as obligatory, by legislative and executive as well as by judicial officers.[3] But the question remains, what would happen (or what ought to happen) if a given rule were broken? We still need the formal distinction between rules which the courts enforce and rules which they do not enforce. If constitutional conventions were called laws, then we should have to distinguish between judicially-enforced laws and non-judicially-enforced laws.[4]

Legal rules, with these modifications, are thus distinguished from rules of public morality which are not enforced by the courts, although they may in some cases, e.g. constitutional conventions (such as the responsibility of members to Parliament), be recognised as existing by the courts. Although constitutional conventions are not laws as here defined, a study of them is essential to the understanding of a constitution—especially the British Constitution—and a description of the more important conventions is always included in books on British constitutional law.[5]

Legal rules are also distinguished from rules of private morality or ethics which are not enforced by the courts, e.g. the moral obligation to carry out a freely made bargain which is not unlawful but which for some reason (such as absence of consideration) lacks legal sanction. The contents of ethics and law overlap to a great extent, e.g. murder, theft and slander; but there are many rules of ethics which the law does not seek to enforce, such as the commandment to honour our parents; and many legal rules which are not intrinsically moral, such as the husband's general liability to pay tax on his wife's income.

Law includes not only the sum total of particular laws, whether statutory or otherwise, but also the complex interrelations between those laws, as well as the technique—judicial precedent, statutory interpretation and so on—by which the law is administered.

The state

This is another very difficult term to define,[6] and a full discussion of this question also falls within the province of jurisprudence or political theory. For present purposes, however, we may define a state as an

---

[2] See Chap. 12; and for Standing Orders, Chap. 10.
[3] See e.g.A. L. Goodhart, *English Law and the Moral Law* (1955), pp. 46–65.
[4] See further, O. Hood Phillips, "Constitutional Conventions: A Conventional Reply" (1964) 8 J.S.P.T.L. 60; and *post*, Chap. 6.
[5] See Chap. 6; also Chaps. 7, 16 and 37.
[6] For judicial attempts see *Chandler* v. *D.P.P.* [1964] A.C. 763; *post*, p. 484. See also the reference, without explanation, to "the State" by Lord Templeman in *Ross* v. *Lord Advocate* [1986] 3 All E.R. 79, 92.

independent political society occupying a defined territory, the members of which are united together for the purpose of resisting external force and the preservation of internal order. No independent political society can be termed a state unless it professes to exercise both these functions; but no modern state of any importance contents itself with this narrow range of activity. As civilisation becomes more complex, population increases and social conscience arises, the needs of the governed call for increased attention; taxes have to be levied to meet these needs; justice must be administered, commerce regulated, educational facilities and many other social services provided.

A fully developed modern state is expected to deal with a vast mass of social problems, either by direct activity or by supervision or regulation. In order to carry out these functions, the state must have agents or organs through which to operate. The appointment or establishment of these agents or organs, the general nature of their functions and powers, their relations *inter se* and between them and the private citizen, form a large part of the constitution of a state.

The constitution of a state[7]

The word "constitution" is used in two different senses, the abstract and the concrete. The constitution of a state in the abstract sense is the system of laws, customs and conventions which define the composition and powers of organs of the state, and regulate the relations of the various state organs to one another and to the private citizen. A "constitution" in the concrete sense is the document in which the most important laws of the constitution are authoritatively ordained. A country, such as our own, which has no "written" constitution as explained below, has no constitution in the concrete sense of the word. It should be clear from the context which meaning is being employed.

Written and unwritten constitutions[8]

A constitution is said to be "written" when the most important constitutional laws are specifically *enacted*. Probably all civilised states, except the United Kingdom, New Zealand[9] and Israel[10] now have mainly written or enacted constitutions. Those who attain power in a state, whether as a result of revolution (*e.g.* France), war of independence (*e.g.* United States), federation or confederation of existing units (*e.g.* Switzerland), or emergence of a new independent nation (*e.g.* former British colonies and protectorates), put into the form of legislative enactment the manner in which the state is to be organised, government carried on and justice administered, and this arrangement is commonly approved by a referendum of the electorate. The most important

[7] See Colin Munro, "What is a Constitution?" [1983] P.L. 563.
[8] Political scientists suggest other ways of classifying constitutions: see S. E. Finer, *Comparative Government* (1970); L. Wolf-Phillips, *Constitutions of Modern States* (1968), pp. ix–xxvi, and *Comparative Constitutions* (1972).
[9] The Constitution of New Zealand is still largely unwritten: J. L. Robson, *New Zealand: The Development of its Laws and Constitution* (2nd ed., 1967), Chap. 1; K. J. Scott, *The New Zealand Constitution* (1962), Chap. 1.
[10] H. E. Baker, *The Legal System of Israel* (2nd ed., 1968); E. Likhovski, *Israel's Parliament* (1972): there are "basic laws," but no constitution has been drawn up yet.

laws constituting the basis of the state are specified in one formal document or a series of formal documents which are binding on the courts and all persons concerned.[11]

It is not practicable for a written constitution to contain more than a selection of constitutional laws. It is invariably supplemented, within the limits prescribed in the constitution, by amendments passed in the prescribed manner; by organic laws, and other legislation passed in the ordinary way from time to time to fill in gaps; usually also by judicial decisions interpreting the written documents; and by customs and conventions regulating the working of the machinery of government.[12] Organic laws are a special class of laws for the passing of which a constitution prescribes some special procedure, but which do not amount to constitutional amendments.

Flexible and rigid constitutions

A more significant classification of the types of constitution is that into "flexible" and "rigid," metaphors given currency by Bryce.[13] A flexible constitution was defined by Dicey as "one under which every law of every description can legally be changed with the same ease and in the same manner by one and the same body." Dicey defined a rigid constitution as "one under which certain laws generally known as constitutional or fundamental laws cannot be changed in the same manner as ordinary laws."[14] The distinction is of great importance in relation to constitutional amendment.

Where the constitution is rigid, certain provisions are distinguished from others in that some special procedure is necessary for their alteration, if they are legally alterable at all. Most European and American constitutions are rigid. The method of amending "fundamental" or "constitutional" laws varies in different constitutions: it may be the legislature sitting in a special way (as in France) or with a prescribed majority or a prescribed quorum (as in Belgium), the convention of a special constituent body (as in the United States), the consultation of the component members of a composite state (as in the United States and Swiss Federations), or a referendum of the electorate (as in Switzerland and Australia). Amendment of the United States Constitution, for example, requires either initiation by two-thirds of both Houses of

---

[11] Compilations of texts include A. J. Peaslee, *The Constitutions of the World* (3rd ed., 1977). A. P. Blaustein and G. H. Flanz, *Constitutions of the Countries of the World*. For particular constitutions outside the Commonwealth, see E. S. Corwin, *The Constitution and What it Means Today* (12th ed.); B. Schwartz, *American Constitutional Law* (1955); Max Beloff, *The American Federal Government* (1959); C. Hughes, *The Federal Constitution of Switzerland;* P. Campbell and B. Chapman, *The Constitution of the Fifth Republic* (1958); Dorothy Pickles, "The Constitution of the Fifth French Republic" (1959) 22 M.L.R. 1; Wm. Pickles, "The French Constitution of October 4th, 1958" [1960] P.L. 228; Maurice Duverger, *Les Institutions françaises* (1962), pp. 144–147.

[12] Wheare, *Modern Constitutions*, Chaps, 3, 7 and 8. See *e.g.* Munro, *The Constitution and Government of the United States* (4th ed.), pp. 76–88; Dawson, *The Government of Canada*, pp. 69–72; H. W. Horwill, *Usages of the American Constitution* (1925).

[13] *Studies in History and Jurisprudence*, Vol. 1, Essay 3. Other descriptive names considered by Bryce were moving and stationary, or fluid and solid (crystallised); *op. cit.* pp. 131–132. Lord Birkenhead L.C. preferred "controlled" and "uncontrolled": *McCawley* v. *The King* [1920] A.C. 691 (P.C.). *Cf.* Wheare. *op. cit.* Chap. 6.

[14] Dicey, *Law of the Constitution* (10th ed.), pp. 126 *et seq.*, and 146–150.

Congress and ratification by the legislatures of three-fourths of the states (the usual method), or initiation by two-thirds of the states and ratification by conventions in three-fourths of the states (*e.g.* repealing 18th Amendment on prohibition).

A subdivision of rigid constitutions can be drawn according to whether the special amending procedure is within the sole power of the legislature, or whether some outside agency has to be brought in. In the latter case the constitution may be said to be supreme over the legislature.

Sometimes a constitution or part of it may not be legally alterable at all, as certain articles of the Constitution of the German Federal Republic (1949), the "basic articles" of the Constitution of the Republic of Cyprus (1960) and the representation of a state in the United States Senate (unless that state consents); or it may be unalterable before a certain time, *e.g.* certain provisions of the United States Constitution before 1808. In such cases any alteration would legally amount to revolution.

It is unnecessary and it may be confusing to draw a distinction, as Dicey does in the first definition quoted, between the relative ease and difficulty of amending a law; this is not a distinction of which lawyers can take account, for it depends on political and psychological factors. It may be more difficult to pass a British statute amending the law relating to the sale of intoxicating liquors or the opening of shops on Sunday than to pass a French statute reducing the period of office of the President of the Republic from seven to five years.

Unwritten constitutions are in practice flexible, but written constitutions are not necessarily rigid. The Constitution of Singapore is written but entirely flexible, while the constitutions of the Australian states are written and largely flexible.[15]

Fundamental laws and judicial review of legislation

Those who frame a rigid constitution seem to be placed in a dilemma. They may give the power to interpret the constitution and to declare legislation invalid *ex post facto* as being repugnant thereto, to the ordinary courts, or to a special constitutional court. Here the final and supreme power would appear to be vested in the courts, which would usually be contrary to the intention of the framers of the constitution. Why should judges, whose function is primarily judicial, set up their own views in opposition to the will of a popularly elected legislative assembly? Two answers may be suggested: first, the judges may be appointed by the executive which initiates legislation and presumably keeps in touch with public opinion; or, alternatively, the "will of the people" is supposed to be embodied in the constitution in a more permanent way than it is represented in the legislative assembly of the day.

On the other hand, if the legislature itself is given authority to interpret the constitution, what guarantee is there that it will ever hold itself to be wrong? In other words, how can the constitution in this case be

---

[15] R. D. Lumb, *The Constitutions of the Australian States* (Brisbane, 2nd ed., 1965).

rigid at all? Dicey saw this difficulty and stated the paradox that the "fundamental laws" in the continental type of "rigid" constitution placing restrictions on the authority of the ordinary legislature, without giving power of judicial review, so far from being laws of a particularly sacrosanct character are found on analysis not to be laws at all. When the courts are not given and have not assumed authority to declare legislation unconstitutional, the constitutional restrictions on legislative activity—though in fact they may be carefully observed—appear on Dicey's view to be merely constitutional conventions resting on the force of public opinion.[16]

It is comparatively rare for the courts to have jurisdiction to review legislation ("constitutional adjudication") except in federal states, such as Switzerland[17] and the federal members of the Commonwealth, where some check is necessary to preserve the respective rights of the federation and its component members.[18] The United States is the classic example of a federation in which each state as well as the federation has a completely rigid constitution. Here the state courts have jurisdiction to declare state legislation repugnant to the state constitution; and the federal courts have jurisdiction to declare provisions of state constitutions, state legislation and federal legislation repugnant to the Federal Constitution. It is not strictly accurate to say that the courts declare legislation void: when cases are brought before them judicially, they may declare that an alleged right or power does not exist or that an alleged wrong has been committed because a certain statute relied on is unconstitutional. Under the influence of Chief Justice Marshall the American Supreme Court first assumed the power of declaring Federal legislation unconstitutional in *Marbury* v. *Madison* (1803),[19] and the power of declaring state legislation repugnant to the Federal Constitution in *Fletcher* v. *Peck* (1810).[20] It may be added by way of further justification that, not only is the United States a federation, but the executive is not responsible to the legislature and so there is not the same reason for the will of the legislature to prevail. The Republic of Ireland, on the other hand, is a unitary state, with an executive legally as well as conventionally responsible to the legislature, whose Constitution gives the Supreme Court and High Court some power of review.[21]

The modern alternative to review of legislation by the ordinary courts is not necessarily the complete absence of any review of constitutionality. A special constitutional court may be set up for such cases, as in the

---

[16] *Cf.* Bryce, *op. cit.* pp. 193–198.

[17] C. Hughes, *The Federal Constitution of Switzerland*; Geoffrey Sawer, *Modern Federalism* (1969), Chap. 10.

[18] Judicial review obtains in dependent territories of the Commonwealth, however, because their legislatures are regarded as subordinate to the British Parliament; *post*, Chap. 36.

[19] 1 Cranch 137.

[20] 6 Cranch 87.

[21] By Article 26 the Supreme Court may rule on the constitutional validity of legislation before it receives the President's assent.

By Article 34.3.2.° both the High Court and Supreme Court have jurisdiction to declare unconstitutional legislation after it has been enacted.

Constitutions of the Republic of Cyprus (1960), West Germany,[22] and Italy.[23]

Another device is to establish a constitutional council to which Bills may be referred *before* being submitted to the Head of State for his assent. Thus the Constitution of the Fifth French Republic (1958) provides for a *Conseil constitutionnel* composed of former Presidents of the Republic and nine other members, three being appointed by each of the President of the Republic, the President of the National Assembly and the President of the Senate. Before organic laws are promulgated, the Council must examine them to ensure that they do not conflict with the constitution. The President of the Republic, the Prime Minister or the President of either House may also submit ordinary laws to the Council before they are promulgated. If a provision is declared unconstitutional it cannot be promulgated or come into force.[24] There is no appeal against decisions of the Constitutional Council, which are binding on all public, administrative and judicial authorities. This device differs from judicial review in that the *Conseil* is not a court, and judicial review operates *ex post facto*.

The Constitutions of the Irish Republic and India expressly recognise the distinction between fundamental rights safeguarded by the courts against amendment otherwise than by the appropriate procedure, and "directive principles of social (or state) policy" for the general guidance of the legislature but which are not cognisable by any court. Such directive principles of state policy are morally binding on the legislature, but can scarcely be called laws.

The scope of constitutional law

The constitutional law of a state is the law relating to its constitution. Where the constitution is written, even though it may have to be supplemented by other materials, it is fairly easy to distinguish the constitutional law of a state from the rest of its legal system; but where, as in Britain, the constitution is unwritten, it is largely a matter of convenience what topics one includes in constitutional law, and there is no strict scientific distinction between that and the rest of the law. It follows from what has been said that constitutional law deals, in general, with the distribution and exercise of the functions of government, and the relations of the government authorities to each other and to the individual citizen. It includes the rules—though the nature of these is difficult to define—which identify the law-making authorities themselves, *e.g.* the legislature and the courts.[25]

More specifically, constitutional law embraces that part of a country's laws which relates to the following topics, among others: the method of choosing the Head of State, whether king or president; his powers and

[22] E. McWhinney, *Constitutionalism in Germany and the Federal Constitutional Court* (1962).

[23] Malcolm Evans, "The Italian Constitutional Court" (1968) 17 I.C.L.Q. 602. The Italian Constitutional Court has been concerned with the effect of community law on government agencies and with the secondment of regional civil servants.

[24] The French Constitutional Council has been concerned with Bills relating to the financial resources of the European Community, budgetary control by the European Assembly and direct elections to the European Assembly. See further, Barry Nicholas, "Fundamental Rights and Judicial Review in France," [1978] P.L. 82, 155.

[25] See H. L. A. Hart, *The Concept of Law* (1961), pp. 107–108.

prerogatives; the constitution of the legislature; its powers and the privileges of its members; if there are two Chambers, the relations between them; the status of Ministers and the position of the civil servants who act under them; the armed forces and the power to control them; the relations between the central government and local authorities; treaty-making power; citizenship; the raising and spending of public money; the general system of courts, and the tenure and immunities of judges; civil liberties and their limitations; the parliamentary franchise and electoral boundaries; and the procedure (if any) for amending the constitution.

Administrative law

A distinction is commonly drawn in continental countries between constitutional law and administrative law, but because English law is not codified or officially systematised English jurists have found difficulty in determining the distinction. Sir Ivor Jennings contended that administrative law, like other branches of law, ought to be defined according to its subject-matter, namely, public administration. Administrative law then determines the organisation, powers and duties of administrative authorities.[26] This description is in accordance with continental and American usage,[27] and is now generally accepted in this country.

What specially distinguishes administrative authorities from private individuals is the extent of their powers. An important aspect of administrative law is the control exercised by courts or tribunals over those powers, especially in relation to the rights of citizens. The remedy of the citizen may be left to the jurisdiction of the ordinary courts, or the matter may be regulated by special rules and adjudicated by special courts or by administrative tribunals. A system of administrative courts or tribunals is not essential for the existence of administrative law, as is shown by the experience of Belgium, which did not set up a *Conseil d'Etat* until 1946; but the fact that France has long possessed special administrative tribunals—notably the *Conseil d'Etat*—which in appropriate cases oust the jurisdiction of the ordinary civil courts, has no doubt helped towards the systematisation of administrative law in that country.[28]

Where there is a written constitution, as in France and the United States, it is easier to demarcate administrative law from constitutional law, although neither the French *droit administratif* nor American administrative law is codified. Where the constitution is unwritten, as in this country, it is largely a matter of convenience where the line is drawn.[29]

[26] Jennings, *The Law and the Constitution* (5th ed.), p. 217.
[27] L. Neville Brown and J. F. Garner, *French Administrative Law* (3rd ed., 1983); B. Schwartz, *American Administrative Law; French Administrative Law and the Common-Law World.*
[28] L. Neville Brown, "The Reform of the French Administrative Courts" (1959) 22 M.L.R. 357; M. Letourneur and J. Méric, *Conseil d'Etat et Juridictions Administratives* (1955); Maurice Duverger, *Les Institutions françaises* (1962) Part IV. For an earlier period, see C. J. Hamson, *Executive Discretion and Administrative Control* (1954).
[29] *Post*, Chap. 2; and Part VI. For a statutory recognition of the term "administrative law" see the State Immunity Act 1978, s.3(2).

Public law

A convenient descriptive term for both constitutional law and administrative law is public law. Many legal systems, influenced by Roman Law,[30] draw a clear distinction between public law and private law. Public law matters may be dealt with in separate courts. The rights and remedies of parties may depend on whether a claim raises a question of public law or private law. As Lord Wilberforce has explained,

> "The expressions 'private law' and 'public law' have recently been imported into the law of England from countries which, unlike our own, have separate systems concerning public law and private law. No doubt they are convenient expressions for descriptive purposes. In this country they must be used with caution . . . The principle remains intact that public authorities and public servants are, unless clearly exempted, answerable in the ordinary courts for wrongs done to individuals."[31]

The reasons for this development and its significance will be discussed later.[32]

The functions of government

Montesquieu in *L'Esprit des Lois* (1748),[33] following attempts by Aristotle[34] and Locke,[35] divided the powers of government into: (i) the legislative power; (ii) the executive power in matters pertaining to the law of nations, and (iii) the power of judging; and so we get the first statement of the modern classification to which we are now accustomed, *viz*: (i) legislative, (ii) executive, and (iii) judicial.

We may attempt a general description of the various governmental functions in the modern state on the following lines:

(i) *The legislative function* is the making of new law, and the alteration or repeal of existing law. Legislation is the formulation of law by the appropriate organ of the state, in such a manner that the actual words used are themselves part of the law: the words not only contain the law, but in a sense they constitute the law. Legislation may take the form of the decree of a personal ruler, whether king or dictator; or it may be issued by an autocratic body or by a democratic assembly wholly or partly elected by the people. Without a legislative body of some sort a state could not provide law readily enough to meet modern conditions.

Two methods of direct lawmaking are found in some states: the *refer-*

---

[30] Public law was that part of the law which concerned the State; private law that which concerned individuals; D.1.1.1.2; *Institutions* 1.1.4. (In this sense criminal law must be regarded as part of public law.) A similar distinction had been drawn by Aristotle, *Rhet* i.13.3. Scots law distinguishes public right and private right (Stair, *Institutions* 1.1.23). See, Article XVIII of the Union with Scotland Act; *Gibson* v. *Lord Advocate* 1975 S.L.T. 134; *infra*, p. 64.

[31] *Davy* v. *Spelthorne B.C.* [1984] A.C. 262.

[32] *Post*, Part VI, Introduction.

[33] Bk XI, Chap. 6.

[34] Aristotle, *XXX*, Vol. IV (transl. Jowett).

[35] John Locke, *Second Treatise of Civil Government* (1690) Chap. 12.

endum by which certain measures have to be submitted for approval to the electorate before being enacted by the legislature; and the *initiative* by which certain kinds of measures may be proposed by a specified number of the electors for enactment.[36] The referendum is usually a method for amending federal constitutions.[37]

(ii) *The executive or administrative function* is the general and detailed carrying on of government according to law, including the framing of policy and the choice of the manner in which the law may be made to render that policy possible. In recent times, especially since the industrialisation of most civilised countries, the scope of this function has become extremely wide. It now involves the provision and administration or regulation of a vast system of social services—public health, housing, assistance for the sick and unemployed, welfare of individual workers, education, transport and so on—as well as the supervision of defence, order and justice, and the finance required therefore, which were the original tasks of organised government.

(iii) *The judicial function* consists in the interpretation of the law and its application by rule or discretion to the facts of particular cases. This involves the ascertainment of facts in dispute according to the law of evidence. The organs which the state sets up to exercise the judicial function are called courts of law or courts of justice.

Although the above classification of the functions and corresponding powers of government, based on a material or functional analysis, may be useful in helping to arrange the facts and to think about the problems of government, the categories are inclined to become blurred when it is attempted to apply them to the details of a particular constitution. Some hold that the true distinction lies not in the nature of the powers themselves, but rather in the procedure by which they are exercised. Thus legislation involves a formal and instantaneous act designed to establish general rules by which all disputes shall be settled; administration is a continuing and mainly informal process aimed at preventing disputes in classes of cases and does not create rights by establishing precedents; adjudication pre-supposes an existing dispute in a particular case, is governed by strict rules of procedure and evidence and tends to create rights by establishing precedents.

Others hold that the distinction is organic or formal. Thus administration consists of the operations, whatever their intrinsic nature may be, which are performed by administrators; and administrators are all state officials who are neither legislators nor judges.[38] This last doctrine seems to be as difficult to apply as the functional or material conception of governmental functions. Thus in the Constitution of the Fifth French Republic not only has the Parliament other powers than the strictly

---

[36] Wheare, *op. cit.* Chap. 6; A. B. Keith, *British Cabinet System* (2nd ed., Gibbs), pp. 256–260; H. J. Laski, *Introduction to Politics*, pp. 66–68; Philip Goodhart. *Referendum* (1971). And see *post*, p. 74.

[37] It has however been used on a number of occasions in the United Kingdom since 1972: Northern Ireland (Border Poll) Act 1972; Referendum Act 1975; Scotland Act 1978, Wales Act 1978. There is a continuing provision for resort to a referendum in the Northern Ireland (Constitution) Act 1973.

[38] Jennings, *op. cit.* pp. 24–25. For a contrast between the conceptual and the functional approach, see Griffith and Street, *Principles of Administrative Law.* (4th ed., 1967).

legislative, but the law-making power is divided between the Parliament (*loi*) and the government (*règlement*), so that the Parliament may only make laws dealing with matters enumerated in article 34, while all others matters fall within the province of ministerial regulation.[39]

Doctrine of the separation of powers[40]

The doctrine of "the separation of powers" as usually understood is derived from Montesquieu,[41] whose elaboration of it was based on a study of Locke's writings[42] and an imperfect understanding of the eighteenth-century English Constitution. Montesquieu was concerned with the preservation of political liberty. "Political liberty is to be found," he says, "only when there is no abuse of power. But constant experience shows us that every man invested with power is liable to abuse it, and to carry his authority as far as it will go . . . . To prevent this abuse, it is necessary from the nature of things that one power should be a check on another . . . . When the legislative and executive powers are united in the same person or body . . . there can be no liberty . . . . Again, there is no liberty if the judicial power is not separated from the legislative and the executive . . . . There would be an end of everything if the same person or body, whether of the nobles or of the people, were to exercise all three powers."

A complete separation of powers, in the sense of a distribution of the three functions of government among three independent sets of organs with no overlapping or co-ordination, would (even if theoretically possible) bring government to a standstill. What the doctrine must be taken to advocate is the prevention of tyranny by the conferment of too much power on any one person or body, and the check of one power by another. There is an echo of this in Blackstone's *Commentaries* (1765): "In all tyrannical Governments . . . the right of making and of enforcing the laws is vested in one and the same man, or the same body of men; and wheresoever these two powers are united together there can be no liberty"; and this doctrine was taken over by the fathers of the American Constitution.

The question whether the separation of powers (*i.e.* the distribution of the various powers of government among different organs), in so far as is practicable, is desirable, and (if so) to what extent, is a problem of political theory and must be distinguished from the question which alone concerns the constitutional lawyer, namely, whether and to what extent such a separation actually exists in any given constitution. As a matter of fact the doctrine has not received much acceptance either in its country or origin or in other European countries.[43] Governmental powers are co-ordinated by the effective part of the executive—the Council of Ministers or Cabinet— which is created by, but in fact con-

---

[39] B. Nicholas, "Loi, Règlement and Judicial Review in the Fifth Republic" [1970] P.L. 251.
[40] W. B. Glyn, *The Meaning of the Separation of Powers* (1965); M. J. C. Vile, *Constitutionalism and the Separation of Powers* (1967); G. Marshall, *Constitutional Theory* (1971), Chap. 5. Colin Munro, "The Separation of Powers" [1981] P.L.19.
[41] *L'Esprit des Lois*, Chap. XI, pp. 3–6.
[42] Locke, *Second Treatise of Civil Government*, Chaps. 12–13.
[43] See, *e.g.* L. Neville Brown, "The Participation of the French Conseil d'Etat in Legislation" (1974) 48 *Tulane Law Review*, 796.

trols, the legislature in which its members sit. The executive in some democratic countries is made responsible to the legislature; but in totalitarian states the executive has acquired complete domination over both the legislature and the judiciary. The doctrine may be said to have received its main application in democratic countries by securing the independence of the courts from the control of the executive.[44]

The United States Constitution goes further than any other in applying the doctrine. Thus the federal executive power is vested in the President, the federal legislative power is vested in Congress, and the federal judicial power is vested in the Supreme Court. The President and his Cabinet are not members of Congress (except that the Vice-President presides over the Senate), and they are not responsible to Congress. The President holds office for a fixed term and he is not necessarily of the same political party as the majority in either House of Congress. The President and Cabinet cannot initiate Bills or secure their passage through Congress, but he may recommend legislation in a message to Congress. But the separation of powers is by no means complete, the three branches of government being connected by a system of "checks and balances." Madison's theory was that one branch must not have the whole of another branch vested in it, nor obtain control over another branch. The chief danger in a republic with a representative legislature was, he thought, that the legislature (rather than the executive) would encroach on the other departments.[45] Thus the President may veto measures passed by Congress, though his veto may be overridden by a two-thirds vote of both Houses. The President has the power to negotiate treaties, but they must be ratified by a two-thirds vote of the Senate. The Supreme Court, asserting the continued significance of the separation of powers, has held that Congress has no power to veto executive acts of the President.[46] The Senate may refuse to confirm certain appointments made by the President, notably that of judges of the Supreme Court; and the judges of that court, although appointed for life, may be removed by impeachment. The power of judicial review of legislation was assumed by the Supreme Court, and was not expressly conferred—although it may perhaps be implied—by the constitution. The three branches of government are therefore interrelated; they act as checks on each other. The problem that may have to be faced before long is whether the draftsmen of the constitution, in their zeal to prevent too great a concentration of power, did not provide restraints that unduly hamper the working of government.[47]

Fundamental Rights

Rights which are regarded as possessed by human beings prior to their recognition by a legal system—or despite their denial by a legal

---

[44] The doctrine of the separation of powers in its earlier history had no true application to judicial matters, and had nothing to do with the independence of judges: C. M. McIlwain. *Constitutionalism: Ancient and Modern* (1940) (revised ed., 1947), pp. 141–142.

[45] *The Federalist*, Nos. 47 and 48 (1788).

[46] *Immigration and Naturalisation Service* v. *Chadha* (1983) 51 U.S. Law Week 4907; B. Schwartz, (1984) 100 L.Q.R.9.

[47] See, *e.g. Youngstown Sheet & Tube Co.* v. *Sawyer*, 343 U.S. 579 (1952) (the "Steel Seizure Case"): B. Schwartz, *American Constitutional Law*, Chap. 7.

system—can conveniently be described as human rights or natural rights. Formulations of natural rights date from the second half of the eighteenth century, the revolutionary period in America and France.[48] Both countries borrowed largely from English experience and thought, especially as embodied in the writings of Locke[49] and, in the case of America, Coke's commentary on Magna Carta and Blackstone's *Commentaries* (1765). For Blackstone the absolute rights of Englishmen were the rights of personal security, personal liberty and private property.

Such rights when recognised in a constitution and guaranteed protection against curtailment (except by legislation passed by special procedure) can be distinguished as "fundamental rights." In this sense the British Constitution does not recognise "fundamental rights," although the phrase was used by Lord Scarman in *Morris* v. *Beardmore*[50] to describe the right of privacy because of the importance attached by the common law to the privacy of the home[51] and because of its recognition under the European Convention of Human Rights which the United Kingdom has ratified and under which the United Kingdom permits the individual right of petition.

Many modern constitutions incorporate certain "fundamental rights" such as personal freedom, equality before the law, freedom of property, free elections, freedom of speech, freedom of conscience and worship, freedom of contract, the right of assembly, the right of association and family rights. They are always restricted, expressly or impliedly, by some such concepts as "public order" or "due process of law"; and the courts may or may not have jurisdiction to review legislation that infringes such rights.

The American Declaration of Independence (1776) states that all men are created equal, and among their inalienable rights are life, liberty and the pursuit of happiness. The American "Bill of Rights" consists of 10 amendments added in 1791 to the Federal Constitution of 1787.[52] These rights include free exercise of religion, freedom of speech and the press, peaceable assembly, petition for redress of grievances (1st Amendment); security of persons, houses, papers and effects from unreasonable searches and seizures (2nd Amendment); no deprivation of life, liberty or property without due process of law[53] (5th Amendment); and freedom from excessive bail or fines and from cruel or unusual punishments (8th Amendment). The American Constitution had already provided that the writ of habeas corpus should not be suspended, that no *ex post facto* law should be passed, and that the trial of all crimes, except in cases of impeachment, should be by jury.[54] Later

---

[48] See further D'Entreves, *Natural Law* (2nd ed., 1970) especially Chapter 4. For the translation of the political theory of natural rights into positive laws in the constitution of modern states and in international treaties see F. E. Dowrick (ed.) *Human Rights: Problems, Perspectives and Texts* (1979).

[49] *Two Treatises of Civil Government* (1690); see Bk. II, "Of Civil Government."

[50] [1981] A.C. 446.

[51] *Entick* v. *Carrington* (1765) 19 St. Tr. 1029.

[52] A Bill of Rights was intentionally excluded from the original United States Constitution for the reasons given by Hamilton in *The Federalist*, No. 88.

[53] "Due process of law" may be traced back to (1354) 28 Edw. III, c.3.

[54] The Statute of Provisors 1351–52, c.4, required for a criminal charge indictment or presentment of good and lawful people of the neighbourhood.

amendments abolished slavery, and preserved the franchise from discrimination on grounds of race, colour or sex. The constitutions of individual American states also contain Bills of Rights.

A Declaration of the Rights of Man was prefaced to the French Constitution of 1791, and was confirmed by the preambles to the Constitutions of 1946 and 1958.

A Universal Declaration of Human Rights was adopted by the General Assembly of the United Nations in 1948,[55] and this was followed by the European Convention for the Protection of Human Rights and Fundamental Freedoms drawn up at Rome in 1950.[56] The Convention came into force in 1953. The European countries which have signed the Convention, including the United Kingdom,[57] guarantee to all persons within their jurisdiction a number of rights and freedoms. In so far as these do not already exist in their laws, the countries which have signed the European Convention are under an obligation to introduce the necessary legislation. The rights concerned are a more detailed version of those contained in the Universal Declaration of 1948. They are still expressed in very general terms, and the limitations are not fully stated. There is an enforcement machinery, partly adoptive, through the European Commission of Human Rights, the Committee of Ministers of the Council of Europe and the European Court of Human Rights.

Declarations of Rights in various forms have been incorporated into a number of constitutions of Commonwealth countries in recent years, including Canada, India, the Federation of Malaysia, Malta, Nigeria, and other African countries.[58]

[55] H. Lauterpacht, *International Law and Human Rights*. The Declaration is set out at pp. 428–434. See *post* p. 424.
[56] F. G. Jacobs, *The European Convention on Human Rights* (1975); A. H. Robertson, *Human Rights in Europe* (1963); *European Institutions* (3rd ed., 1973).
[57] Cmd. 8969 (1953).
[58] Sir Kenneth Roberts-Wray, "Human Rights in the Commonwealth" (1968) 17 I.C.L.Q. 908.

CHAPTER 2

GENERAL CHARACTERISTICS OF THE BRITISH CONSTITUTION

Unitary constitution: the United Kingdom

The United Kingdom constitution is unitary as opposed to federal or
confederal. The United Kingdom is a union of England, Wales, Scotland
and Northern Ireland.[1] The state for the purpose of international relations is the United Kingdom, although it is often popularly but inaccur-
ately referred to as "Britain," "Great Britain" or "England." The words
"United Kingdom," when used in a statute or public document, mean
Great Britain and Northern Ireland, unless the contrary intention
appears.[2]

Wales[3]

The *Statutum Walliae*, passed in 1284 after Edward I had defeated
Llewelyn ap Griffith, declared that Wales was incorporated into the
Kingdom of England. Henry VIII completed the introduction of the
English legal and administrative system into Wales. This union was
effected by annexation rather than treaty. The Laws in Wales Act 1536
united Wales with England, and gave to Welshmen all the laws, rights
and privileges of Englishmen. Welsh constituencies received representation in the English Parliament. An Act of 1542 covered land tenure,
courts and administration of justice. References to "England" in Acts of
Parliament passed between 1746 and 1967 include Wales.[4] The judicial
systems of England and Wales were amalgamated in 1830.

Scotland[5]

Scotland and England were separate kingdoms with their own rulers
until 1603, when James VI of Scotland succeeded Elizabeth I as James I

---

[1] The status of the Isle of Man and the Channel Islands is discussed in Chap. 36.

[2] Interpretation Act 1978, s.5 and Sched. 1. For an express intention to the contrary see
the Crown Proceedings Act 1947 where references to the United Kingdom (*e.g.* in
s.40(2)(c)) have to be read in the light of s.52.

[3] See William Rees. *The Union of England and Wales* (University of Wales Press, 1938); J. F.
Rees, *Studies in Welsh History* (Cardiff, 1947); *Welsh Studies in Public Law* J. A. Andrews
ed. 1970).

[4] Wales and Berwick Act 1746; Welsh Language Act 1967. It may be objected that this statute—like many others—has a singularly inapt short title; H. W. R. Wade, *Constitutional
Fundaments* (1980), p. 19.

[5] See T. B. Smith, *Scotland: The Development of its Laws and Constitution* (1962); J. D. B.
Mitchell, *Constitutional Law* (2nd ed., 1968); *The British Commonwealth: Development of
its Laws and Constitution: I The United Kingdom*, pp. 603 *et seq.*; T. B. Smith, "The Union
of 1707 as Fundamental Law" (1957) P.L. 99; G. M. Trevelyan, *Ramillies and the Union
with Scotland*, Chaps. 12–14; D. Daiches, *Scotland and the Union* (1977); D. N. MacCormick, "Does the United Kingdom have a Constitution?" (1978) 29 N.I.L.Q.I.
The name "Great Britain" was suggested by Francis Bacon: "Brief Discourse Touching
the Happy Union of the Kingdoms of England and Scotland."

of England. This was merely a personal union, and was followed in 1707 by a union of the two Kingdoms into a United Kingdom of Great Britain.[6] The Treaty was ratified by both the English and Scottish Parliaments, which ceased to exist on the transference of their powers to the Parliament of Great Britain. The Union with Scotland Act 1706 provided for the succession of the Crown of Great Britain in accordance with the English Act of Settlement. There was to be a Parliament of Great Britain. Any law in force in either Kingdom inconsistant with the terms of the Union was to be void. Conventions of constitutional government were coming into being in England, but there was no constitutional tradition in Scotland and so the development of conventions after the Union continued on the English lines.[7] Scots law was to continue in force unless altered by the Parliament of Great Britain. Public law might be assimilated, but Scots private law was not be changed "except for evident utility of the subjects within Scotland." The preservation of the established Presbyterian Church in Scotland ("Church of Scotland") is an essential term of the Union.[8] Scotland has its own system of courts, with final appeal in civil, but not criminal, cases to the House of Lords.[9]

Northern Ireland[10]

For centuries before 1800 Ireland had been a subordinate Kingdom of the English (British) Crown. It had a Parliament of its own on the English model, though how far it was subordinate to the English (British) Parliament was a matter of controversy. Ireland also had a system of courts on the English model, but again doubts were expressed from time to time whether final appeal lay to the English or the Irish House of Lords. The executive in Ireland was definitely under the control of the English Government through the Lord-Lieutenant. The Union with Ireland Act 1800 united the two Kingdoms of Great Britain and Ireland into the United Kingdom of Great Britain and Ireland, under provisions similar to the Union of 1707. Again a personal union was turned into a legislative union. However, the union with Ireland, unlike that with Scotland, was not based on a treaty negotiated by commissioners representing each country, but was brought about by Acts of the British and Irish Parliaments following parallel resolutions passed by each Parlia-

---

[6] There was also a personal union of Great Britain and Hanover from 1714 to 1837, and the Act of Settlement 1700 provided that England should not be obliged to engage in any war for the defence of Hanover without the consent of Parliament. As to allegiance, see *Isaacson* v. *Durant (Stepney Election Petition)* (1886) 17 Q.B.D. 54.

[7] *Cf. MacCormick* v. *Lord Advocate* 1953 S.C. 396; *post,* p. 65.

[8] See R. King Murray, "The Constitutional Position of the Church of Scotland" [1958] P.L. 155. And see further, *post,* pp. 64 *et seq.*

[9] *Greenshields* v. *Magistrates of Edinburgh,* Robertson, App. 12. See Dicey and Rait, *Thoughts on the Union between England and Scotland,* pp. 194–195; Turberville, *The House of Lords in the Eighteenth Century,* pp. 94–95, 139–141. *Cf.* Scottish Episcopalians Act 1711.

[10] See H. Calvert, *Constitutional Law in Northern Ireland* (1968); *The British Commonwealth: Development of its Laws and Constitutions: I The United Kingdom* (1955), pp. 411 *et seq.* (by L. A. Sheridan); A. S. Queckett. *The Constitution of Northern Ireland* (1928–46); V. T. H. Delaney, *The Administration of Justice in Ireland* (2nd ed., 1965); Claire Palley. "The Evolution, Disintegration and Possible Reconstruction of the Northern Ireland Constitution (1972). 1 *Anglo-American Law Review* 368.

ment in response to messages from the Crown.[11] The greater part of Ireland ceased to form part of the United Kingdom in 1922[12] and after a period of "Dominion status" similar to that of Canada at the time, it became in 1949 an independent republic outside the Commonwealth.[13] Northern Ireland, consisting of six[14] of the nine counties of Ulster, remained within the United Kingdom, and for half a century from 1920 considerable legislative and executive powers were devolved on it, so that it had its own subordinate Parliament and government departments.[15] The Province also had (and still has) its own system of courts, with final appeal in both civil and criminal cases to the House of Lords.

In 1969 the United Kingdom government concluded that it was necessary to deploy troops in Northern Ireland to assist the civil authorities in maintaining law and order. Existing constitutional arrangements were suspended in 1972 by the Northern Ireland (Temporary Provisions) Act 1972. A Secretary of State for Northern Ireland became responsible for governing the Province. Legislation in 1973[16] was aimed at establishing a new legislature and executive enjoying widespread support among all sections of the community. For that reason elections to the newly created Assembly were, contrary to the normal practice in the United Kingdom, to be by a system of proportional representation (the single transferable vote). The provisions of the 1973 Act conferring powers on the new authorities were only to come into effect when the Secretary of State for Northern Ireland was satisfied that an Executive could be formed which was "likely to be widely accepted throughout the community."[17] The new experiment in "power-sharing" was short lived. The Assembly was prorogued and provision made for government by Order in Council.[18]

A subsequent attempt at devolving some powers of government was made by the Northen Ireland Act 1982 which envisaged a gradual process of transfer of functions to an elected Assembly and Executive. The Assembly could submit proposals to the Secretary of State relating to the resumption by the Assembly of some or all of the powers which it had been intended to possess under the Constitution of 1973. Such proposals were to have the support of 70 per cent. of the members of the Assembly or of a majority of the members in cases where the Secretary of State was satisfied that a particular proposal was likely to command

---

[11] It is generally accepted that duress and bribery were employed to induce the unrepresentative Irish Parliament to pass the Act: see, e.g. Edmund Curtis, A History of Ireland (1936), Chap. 17.

[12] Irish Free State (Agreement) Act 1922.

[13] Ireland Act 1949.

[14] Antrim, Armagh, Down, Fermanagh, Londonderry and Tyrone.

[15] Government of Ireland Act 1920, as amended from time to time.

[16] Northern Ireland Assembly Act 1973; Northern Ireland Constitution Act 1973; Northern Ireland Constitution (Amendment) Act 1973.

[17] Further measures intended to secure widespread general support for the new Constitution were the anti-discrimination provisions, the Northern Ireland Constitution Act 1973, s.17, and the establishment (by s.20 of the same Act) of the Standing Advisory Commission on Human Rights.

[18] Northern Ireland Act 1974. One consequence of "direct rule" was the increase in the number of Northern Ireland M.Ps allowed to sit at Westminster from 12 to 17: House of Commons (Redistribution of Seats) Act 1979; infra, p. 191.

widespread acceptance throughout the community. The Secretary of State was required to lay before Parliament any proposals submitted to him and, if approved by both Houses, effect would be given to them by Order in Council. The Assembly was, however, dissolved in the summer of 1986 as a result of the refusal of Unionist members to participate in its work.[18a]

In addition to these constitutonal measures, legislation has been passed with a view to defeating terrorism which confers special powers on the police and members of the armed forces, creates a number of new crimes, provides for trial without jury and confers jurisdiction on the courts of Northern Ireland over certain acts committed in the Republic of Ireland.[19]

In practical and political terms any solution to the problems of Northern Ireland must obviously involve the Republic of Ireland—as the United Kingdom has recognised at least since the ill-fated conference held at Sunningdale in 1973. In 1981, both governments agreed to establish an Anglo-Irish Inter-Governmental Council, and further developments were envisaged in the White Paper which preceded the Northern Ireland Act 1982.[20–21] In November 1985, the Governments of the United Kingdom and the Republic of Ireland concluded an agreement (the "Hillsborough Agreement") which established an Inter-governmental Conference to consider, on a regular basis, matters relating to Northern Ireland and relations between the two parts of the island of Ireland. The Conference will meet at ministerial or official level as required. The Secretary of State for Northern Ireland and a Minister of the Irish Government will jointly chair meetings at Ministerial level. The main provisions of the Agreement, which was subsequently approved by the British and Irish Parliaments, are set out in Appendix I.

Applications to challenge the legality of the Agreement by way of judicial review were made by four Ulster Unionist Members of Parliament within a few days of its signing. The appellants did not challenge the powers of the Government to enter into the Agreement, but they argued that the Agreement would fetter the statutory functions of the Secretary of State for Northern Ireland; that it would infringe the rights of Northern Ireland citizens and conflict with the provisions of the Northern Ireland Constitution Act 1973; that it handed over partial sovereignty to the Irish Republic; and that it would be in breach of the Union with Ireland Act 1800, which provides that in all treaties British citizens living in Ireland shall have the same privileges as citizens living in Great Britain. Taylor J., assuming without deciding that the applicants had *locus standi*, dismissed the application. He said the Agreement was in the field of international relations and was "akin to a treaty" and that he could find "no arguable case."[21–22]

[18a] As a protest against the Anglo-Irish Agreement. Dissolution was effected by the Northern Ireland Assembly (Dissolution) Order 1986 and direct rule restored by the Northern Ireland Act 1974 (Interim Period Extension) Order 1986.

[19] See *post*, Chap. 24.

[20–21] *A Framework for Devolution* Cmnd. 8541.

[21–22] *Ex p. Molyneaux* [1986] 1 W.L.R. 331.

The Unionist Members representing 15 of the 17 Ulster constituencies subsequently resigned their seats in the House of Commons to produce something approaching a referendum on the terms of the Hillsborough Agreement.[23]

Devolution

A revival of Scottish and Welsh nationalism in the 1960s led to the setting up of a Royal Commission on the Constitution, which reported in favour of a measure of devolution to Scotland and Wales (Kilbrandon Report).[24] Legislation was eventually enacted (Scotland Act 1978; Wales Act 1978) but failed to come into effect because the required degree of support was not forthcoming in referendums held under the provisions of the two Acts.

This topic is further discussed in Appendix II.

Unwritten constitution

The British Constitution is described as "unwritten"[25-26] because it is not embodied, wholly or mainly, in any enactment or formally related series of enactments.[27] At the time of the Norman conquest, constitutions were of a customary nature. After the civil war of the seventeenth century, Cromwell drew up an Instrument of Government (1653)[28]—the only written constitution the English[29] have had; but this came to an end in 1660 with the restoration of the monarchy. Recent suggestions for a written constitution for the United Kingdom put forward on wide grounds[30] have attracted little general support hitherto, as distinct from support for the proposal of a Bill of Rights.

The laws of the British constitution comprise three kinds of rules: statute law, common law, and custom (especially parliamentary custom). To these we must add constitutional conventions if we are to understand modern developments and the manner in which the constitution works. The sources of the legal rules are the same as for private law, namely, statutes, judicial precedents, customs and books of authority,[31] except that under the third head we must include parliamentary custom. Treaties are not in themselves sources of municipal (i.e. national) law, as they are in some countries.

[23] The difficulties of co-ordinating 15 resignations are described by Clifford Boulton, "The Almost-General Election in Northern Ireland, 1986," [1986] P.L. 211.

[24] Cmnd. 5460 (1973).

[25-26] Or "not written," "part-written," "uncodified" or "evolutionary": L. Wolf-Phillips, *Comparative Constitutions* (1972), pp. 46–47. Sir Kenneth Wheare prefers to say that Britain "has no written Constitution": *Modern Constitutions*, p. 19.

[27] *Ante*, p. 5.

[28] S. R. Gardiner, *Constitutional Documents of the Puritan Revolution, 1625–1660* (3rd ed., 1906), p. 405.

[29] Cromwell also incorporated Scotland and Ireland into the Protectorate.

[30] *e.g.* Lord Hailsham, *The Dilemma of Democracy* (1978); O. Hood Phillips. Reform of the Constitution (1970); *British Government in an Era of Reform* (ed. W. V. Stankiewicz, 1976), pp. 78–93. Lord Scarman, Constitutional Reform, A Legal Possibility?" (Holdsworth Club Address 1979); D. C. M. Yardley, "Constitutional Reform in the United Kingdom" [1980] Cur.Leg.Prob. 147.

[31] See O. Hood Phillips, *A First Book of English Law* (7th ed., 1977), Part II.

Statutes

These consist of Acts of Parliament and subordinate legislation.

Some of the principles and detailed rules of the British Constitution are contained in formally unrelated Acts of Parliament, such as the Act of Settlement 1700; the Parliament Acts 1911 and 1949; the Crown Proceedings Act 1947; the Supreme Court Act 1981 and the British Nationality Act 1981. Laws intended to bind both Houses of Parliament are put into the form of Acts, *e.g.* Provisional Collection of Taxes Acts, the Laying of Documents before Parliament (Interpretation) Act 1948 and the Royal Assent Act 1967. There are also a few important documents of a quasi legislative nature, such as Magna Carta 1215 (and subsequent reissues and confirmations by King and Parliament[32]), and the Bill of Rights 1688 (passed by a "convention" Parliament, but deemed to have the force of statute)[33] and at least two Acts of Parliament which have a peculiar status—the Union with Scotland Act 1706,[33a] based on a treaty negotiated by the English and Scottish Parliaments, and the Statute of Westminster 1931, based on conventions agreed between the United Kingdom and the British Dominions at that time.

Subordinate legislation consists mainly of legislation made by persons or bodies to whom the power has been delegated by Parliament. Parliament confers on the Queen in Council the power to legislate by Orders in Council, a method which is useful for filling in the more important details giving effect to the principles of the enabling Act, and also valuable in times of emergency when Parliament may not be in session. Legislative powers are also frequently delegated by Parliament to individual Ministers, local government authorities and public corporations. Delegated legislation issued by Ministers usually takes the form of orders, rules or regulations, and these in appropriate cases are mostly published as Statutory Instruments. Delegated legislation made by local authorities is known as byelaws, and is published by the local authority concerned.

Judicial precedents

Many of the principles of British constitutional law are to be inferred from decisions of the courts in particular cases, such as the extent of the liberties of the citizen, determined in disputes between individuals and the executive. Such cases arise incidentally, as it were, in the ordinary course of litigation. They will most commonly be found in the decisions of the Queen's Bench Division (previously the Court of King's Bench), which not only grants damages for breach of legal rights but also has a special jurisdiction in proceedings for habeas corpus, certiorari, prohi-

[32] The version of Magna Carta that became law for subsequent times was that of Henry III (1225); and the authoritative text was that of (1297) 25 Edward I, later understood as expounded by Coke in his Second Institute. Obsolete provisions—not including Cap. 14 (forbidding excessive fines) and Cap. 29 (Caps. 39 and 40 of 1215)—were repealed in the nineteenth century by Statute Law Revision Acts. See *The Great Charter* (New York, 1965 Griswold ed.;) Alec Samuels, "Magna Carta as living law" (1969) 20 N.I.L.Q. 49. Confirmations by Edward I (1297) and Edward III (1324) were largely repealed by the Statute Law (Repeals) Act 1969.

[33] Crown and Parliament Recognition Act 1689.

[33a] The argument that some of the terms of the Union with Scotland constitute fundamental rules of the British Constitution is discussed later; p. 63.

bition and mandamus; in the decisions of the Court of Appeal and the House of Lords on appeal therefrom, and the Judicial Committee of the Privy Council in appeals from British overseas territories.[34]

Examples of judicial precedents laying down important principles of constitutional law, chosen from hundreds of cases that might be cited, are: *Ashby* v. *White* (1703)[35] (*ubi jus ibi remedium*); *Att.-Gen.* v. *Wilts United Dairies* (1922)[36] (no power to levy money without authority of Parliament); *Campbell* v. *Hall*[37] (no prerogative power to legislate for colony with representative assembly); *Entick* v. *Carrington*[38] (general warrant illegal); *Johnstone* v. *Pedler*[39] ("act of state" no defence in tort as regards act committed in relation to a friendly alien in this country); *Case of Proclamations*[40] (the King cannot create offences by proclamation); *Stockdale* v. *Hansard*[41] (Commons cannot change law by claiming new privileges); *Wason* v. *Walter*[42] (defence of qualified privilege extends to unauthorised reports of parliamentary debates); *Ridge* v. *Baldwin*[43] (*audi alteram partem*); *In re Mc.C* (*A Minor*)[44] (immunity of judges; privileged position of superior courts).

Custom

A custom in private law is a rule of conduct which has not been adjudicated upon by the courts, but which would be recognised and enforced by the courts if the matter came before them. It is based on usage, but in order that it may be recognised by the courts as law, a custom must be: (i) regarded by those subject to it as obligatory; (ii) certain; (iii) reasonable; (iv) of immemorial antiquity; and (v) it must have been in existence continuously. These are the main tests which English courts apply to an alleged local custom, and they would presumably apply the same tests to an alleged general custom not hitherto adjudicated upon. The traditional doctrine was that the common law of England consisted of the general "customs of the realm." It is true to a certain extent that the early common law consisted of general immemorial customs; but it is almost certain that general customs are no longer a creative source of English private law, as they have all become embodied by judicial recognition and enforcement in the system of case law or else have been displaced by legislation.

Custom (largely feudal in origin) has been a source of important parts of our constitutional law, for example, the royal prerogative and parliamentary privilege.[45] As Plucknett said: "Feudal custom includes the

---

[34] The influence of equity on constitutional law has been comparatively slight, although the remedies of injunction and declaration were equitable in origin: see Hanbury, "Equity in Public Law" in *Essays in Equity* p. 80.

[35] Ld.Raym. 938.

[36] 91 L.J.K.B. 897. And see *Congreve* v. *Home Office* [1976] 2 Q.B. 629 (C.A.).

[37] (1774) 1 Cowp. 204; Lofft 655.

[38] (1765) 19 St.Tr. 1029, 1066.

[39] [1921] 2 A.C. 262.

[40] (1610) 12 Co.Rep. 74.

[41] (1839) 9 Ad. & E. 1.

[42] (1868) L.R. 4 Q.B. 73.

[43] [1964] A.C. 40 (H.L.).

[44] [1985] A.C. 528.

[45] But much of paliamentary privilege is not of "immemorial antiquity": Parliament itself may be said to have originated with Edward I.

relationship of Crown and nobles until the moment when this body of custom separates and becomes, first, the law of the prerogative, and then later still combines with the custom of the King's High Court of Parliament to form modern constitutional law."[46] The royal prerogative is now regarded as part of the common law. The law and custom of Parliament, including parliamentary privilege, is a special kind of customary law—recognised, but not developed, by the ordinary courts—which is not of immemorial antiquity. There may still be some customary constitutional laws which have not had occasion to be recognised by the courts but which would be so recognised if the question came before them, for example, such rules (not being statutory or merely conventional) as prescribe the forms according to which acts of the Crown are to be performed. If so, customs of this kind would hardly require immemorial antiquity, but would rest rather on the necessity of there being some form (such as sealing and counter-signature) by which the Crown's acts can be authenticated.

Books of authority

The general rule applied by English courts is that textbooks, however eminent their authors, and whether or not they were judges, are not authoritative.[46a] Between later authors and some of the earlier writers, however, there is a difference of authority so great as virtually to amount to a difference in kind. Some of the earlier textbooks are treated by the courts as authoritative statements of the law of their time, and therefore of present law if it is not shown to have been changed, which may be quoted and relied on in court on the authority of their authors. The statements of such writers are presumed to be evidence of judicial decisions that have been lost, and they are therefore accepted if not contrary to reason. This is chiefly to be explained by the difficulty of ascertaining the law of early times, and of course it only applies in the absence of statutes and reported decisions on the point. Whether a textbook will be treated as authoritative in this special sense is determined by the tradition of the legal profession and the practice of the courts, and depends on such factors as the reputation of the author and the date when the book was written.

Among the books of authority that are most important as sources of English constitutional law are Fitzherbert's *Abridgment* (1516), Brooke's *Abridgment* (1568), Glanvill's *Tractatus de Legibus et Consuetudinibus Angliae* (c. 1189), Bracton's treatise of the same name (c. 1250),[47] Littleton's *Tenures* (c. 1470), Fitzherbert's *Natura Brevium* (1543), Coke's *Institutes of the Laws of England* (1628–1644), Hale's *History of the Pleas of the Crown* (published in 1736, 60 years after the author's death),[48] Hawkins' *Pleas of the Crown* (1716), Foster's *Crown Cases* (1762),[49] and Blackstone's *Commentaries on the Laws of England* (1565–1769).[50] Of these Blackstone's

---

[46] T. F. T. Plucknett, *A Concise History of the Common Law* (5th ed.), p. 309.
[46a] *Cordell* v. *Second Clanfield Properties Ltd.* [1969] 2 Ch. 9, 16 *per* Megarry J.
[47] See *Case of Prohibitions (Prohibitions del Roy)* (1607) 12 Co.Rep. 63.
[48] See *R.* v. *Casement* [1917] 1 K.B. 98, 141–142.
[49] See *Joyce* v. *Director of Public Prosecutions* [1946] A.C. 347.
[50] See *e.g. Thomas* v. *Sawkins* [1935] 2 K.B. 249; *R.* v. *St. Edmundsbury and Ipswich Diocese (Chancellor)* [1948] 1 K.B. 195.

Commentaries, being the most general and elementary as well as the most recent, have not such a high authority on points of detail as Hale, Hawkins and Foster.

Flexible constitution

The British Constitution is described as "flexible" because any principle or rule of the constitution can be altered by the same body and in the same manner as any other law. In other words, there is no formal distinction between laws that are specifically "constitutional" or "fundamental" and that are not. The body which has the power to alter the constitution, or any other rules of law, is the Queen in Parliament, and the procedure is the same as for any other legislation. The legislature is supreme over the Constitution. There are no laws that cannot be repealed or altered in this way, that is to say, none that are "entrenched."[51] The flexibility of the British Constitution is a corollary of the fact that there is no written constitution or "higher law" binding on Parliament, and the consequent legislative supremacy of Parliament (*infra*). The courts therefore have no power to "review" parliamentary legislation and to declare it unconstitutional.[52]

It follows also that the distinction drawn between British constitutional law and administrative law or other branches of English law, and the selection of the contents of each, are matters of convenience, guidance being sought from tradition and comparison with other constitutions.

Legislative supremacy of Parliament[53]

The most important characteristic of British constitutional law is the legislative supremacy (sometimes called "sovereignty") of the United Kingdom Parliament. Positively this means that Parliament can legally pass any kind of law whatsoever: negatively it means that there is no person or body whose legislative power competes with it or overrides it. We may call it the one fundamental law of the British Constitution,[54] which may itself be unalterable by Parliament.[55]

Constitutional or limited Monarchy

The British political system is in form monarchical. But it is a limited or "constitutional" monarchy, as opposed to an absolute or strong monarchy.[55a] That is to say, the governmental powers which as a matter

---

[51] *Cf. McWhirter* v. *Att.-Gen.* [1972] C.M.L.R. 882 (C.A.) (summons for declaration that accession to EEC would be contrary to the Bill of Rights, struck out as an abuse of the process of the court); *R.* v. *Jordan* [1967] Crim.L.R. 483 (Race Relations Act restricts "freedom of speech").

[52] A written and entrenched constitution for this country is advocated in Lord Hailsham, *The Dilemma of Democracy* (1978) and O. Hood Phillips, *Reform of the Constitution* (1970).

[53] See further, Chaps. 3 and 4.

[54] Taken with the Parliament Acts 1911 and 1949 and the convention that the Queen will not refuse the Royal Assent to Bills, this virtually means the supremacy of a majority of the House of Commons. "That is really all the British Constitution that there is": Kenneth Pickhorn, M.P. (1956) 550 H.C.Deb., col. 1821.

[55] *Post*, Chap. 4.

[55a] O. Hood Phillips, "A Hundred Years of Constitutional Monarchy," (1978) 75 L.S. Gaz. 64.

of legal form are vested in the Queen are in practice exercised according to the laws, customs and conventions of the constitution; and they are exercised either by the Queen on the advice of her Ministers or by the Ministers in her name.[56] This principle applies both to the Queen's common law ("prerogative") powers[57] and to her statutory powers. It is a product of English political history from the seventeenth century, when the monarch ceased to govern either himself directly or through delegates limited only by the law. The modern principle is secured by means of constitutional conventions.[58] "Constitutionalism" involves both legal limits to arbitrary power and also political responsibility of the government to the governed.[59]

Responsible parliamentary government

Parliamentary government

Parliament itself does not govern, nor is it capable of doing so. The expression "parliamentary government" is somewhat misleading, and means government by the executive in and through Parliament. Parliament exercises supreme control over all branches of government. Besides its supreme law making power, Parliament supervises the general conduct of the executive. It makes and unmakes state offices and government departments, controls their finances, asks questions concerning the carrying out of their duties, and debates motions of confidence. Parliament also reorganises the system of courts, though it does not in practice interfere with the conduct of litigation. All this is a matter partly of law, partly of custom and partly of convention.

Responsible government

Ministers are responsible to Parliament—more particularly to the House of Commons. They defend their conduct there, and continuance in office depends on retaining the confidence of the Commons. This is mainly a matter of constitutional convention.[60] The key to responsible parliamentary government lies in the Cabinet system, which ensures that Ministers are members of the legislature, that they must retain the confidence of the Commons, and that they can appeal to the electorate to return an assembly that will support their policy.

Responsible parliamentary government of this kind may be found in a republican régime, as in India. It is in marked contrast to the presidential system that exists, for example, in the United States, where the executive power is vested in the President, who is not a member of Congress and whose continuance in office does not depend on the support of the House of Representatives.[61]

---

[56] *Post*, p. 762 for the position with regard to the Queen as Head of the Commonwealth.
[57] *Post*, Chap. 14.
[58] *Post*, p. 28 and Chap. 6.
[59] McIlwain, *op.cit.* p. 146.
[60] See *post*, Chaps. 6 and 16.
[61] In addition to the "executive" type of President (*e.g.* U.S.A.) and the "parliamentary" type of President (*e.g.* India), there are other varieties of the presidential system, *e.g.* in South America and Africa.

Representative government

It is implied in what has been said of the British Constitution that the legislature "represents" the people in a general way. Responsible government involves representative government, though the converse is not necessarily true. A general election nowadays is in effect the election of a prime minister, the leader of a political party with a certain programme. Political parties are a development since 1688. They rest almost entirely on convention or merely political fact, though their existence was assumed by the Ministers of the Crown Act 1937, which defined the Leader of the Opposition and granted him a salary.[62]

Representative government presupposes that the electors are free to organise themselves in political parties, and (within the limits imposed by the requirements of public order and peaceful change) to express their views and to criticise the government. The party system is inevitable in a democratic country, since men disagree about political ends and means. It is "a convenient device to enable the majority to have their way and the minority to have their say."[63] Party organisation exists both in the constituencies and in Parliament. Parties are voluntary associations, subject to the general law.[64] Although, as George Tierney said, it is the duty of the Opposition[65] to oppose, the responsible aspect of the party system is brought out in the expression "His Majesty's Opposition," which was coined—originally as a joke—by J. C. Hobhouse early in the last century.

Following the Report of the Houghton Committee[66] public funds have been made available to opposition political parties, according to a formula which takes account of the number of seats held by each party and the number of votes cast.[67]

Representative government is now assisted also by secret ballot, universal adult suffrage,[68] independent Boundary Commissions, and a strict limitation of the powers of the House of Lords as against the House of Commons.[69]

In contrast to other forms of political system the British system is described as a liberal democracy. It is a qualified democracy for the activity

---

[62] See now, Ministerial and other Salaries Act 1975. For a further reference see House of Commons (Administration) Act 1978, s.1(4).

[63] S. D. Bailey, *The British Party System* (Hansard Society, 1952), p. xii. For the political parties, see also Sir Ivor Jennings, *Party Politics*, Vol. II; *The Growth of Parties* (1961); I. Bulmer-Thomas, *The Growth of the British Party System* (1965); Robert McKenzie, *British Political Parties* (2nd ed., 1963); C. S. Emden, *The People and the Constitution* (2nd ed.); S. E. Finer, *The Changing British Party System, 1945–1979* (1980); V. Bogdanor, *People and the Party System* and *Multi Party Politics and the Constitution* (1983).

[64] See *Conservative and Unionist Office* v. *Burrell* [1982] 1 W.L.R. 522 (C.A.); *Re Grant's Will Trusts* [1980] 1 W.L.R. 360.

[65] *Post*, p. 127.

[66] *Report of Committee on Financial Aid to Political Parties* (1976) Cmnd. 6601.

[67] The legal authority for such payments is to be found in the annual Appropriation Act (*infra* p. 220), *e.g.* Appropriation Act 1985, Sched. (B) Pt. 15, Class XIII, Vote 2.

[68] *Post*, Chap. 8. Direct "participation" of the people at the national level is not practicable, even if it were thought desirable; see Bernard Crick, " 'Them and Us': Public Impotence and Government Power" [1968] P.L. 8; and see Crick, *In Defence of Politics* (1962; Pelican, 1964), Chap. 3 ("A Defence of Politics Against Democracy").

[69] *Post*, Chap. 7.

of government is limited; society is recognised as being pluralistic, that is to say, government is not in the interest of any one group or groups but in the common interest; the majority opinion prevails but minorities are given a chance to become the majority.[70]

Importance of constitutional conventions[71]

The word "conventions," as used by constitutional lawyers, refers to rules of political practice which are regarded as binding by those whom they concern—especially the Sovereign and statesmen—but which would not be *enforced* by the courts if the matter came before them. The lack of judicial enforcement distinguishes conventions from laws in the strict sense. This is an important formal distinction for the lawyer, though the politician may not be so interested in the distinction. Privileges enforced by each House are also excluded from the definition of conventions.

Conventions are found to a greater or less extent in most countries that have written constitutions. This is so not only in the Commonwealth countries[72] but also, for example, in the United States. There the method of electing the President and the manner of choosing the President's Cabinet are governed largely by convention.[73] What is characteristic of the British Constitution is the extremely important part played by conventions. Not only do the British have no written constitution, but they have been reluctant to stereotype their rules of government in the form of statutes. Many important political developments have been effected since 1688 without recourse to legal forms at all. It is constitutional conventions that describe and explain how the constitution works, how it lives and grows. Their general purpose is to adapt structure to function. In this way the strong monarchy of 1688 has become a limited monarchy with responsible parliamentary government.

Independence of the judiciary from the executive[74]

The justices of the Royal courts, which grew up in Norman and Plantagenet times, were the King's servants: down to the time of the Stuarts they usually held office during the King's pleasure and, like other Crown servants, could be dismissed by the King at will.[75] This fact doubtless affected some of the judicial decisions given in the reigns of James I and Charles I. After the revolution of 1688, judges of superior courts were appointed "during good behaviour," but there was doubt whether at common law this referred merely to good behaviour in relation to the King. Eventually the Act of Settlement 1700 provided that "'Judges commissions be made *quamdiu se bene gesserint*, and their salaries ascertained and established, but upon the address of both Houses of Parliament it may be lawful to remove them." The first and

---

[70] S. E. Finer, *Comparative Government* (1970).
[71] See further, *post,* Chap. 6.
[72] On Conventions in Australia, see George Winterton, *Parliament, The Executive and the Governor General* (1983).
[73] W. B. Munro, *The Government of the United States* (4th ed., 1936) pp. 80–83.
[74] See further, *post,* Chap. 20.
[75] Blackstone discusses the independence of the judiciary in a chapter on the King's Prerogative: Bl. Com. I. 269.

third of those provisions have been substantially re-enacted by the Judicature Acts and are now to be found in the Supreme Court Act 1981, s.11. The security of tenure of Lords of Appeal is protected by section 6 of the Appellate Jurisdiction Act 1876. Their effect is that judges of the *superior* British courts may not be removed except for misbehaviour in their office or (probably) conviction of some serious offence. Removal is by the Crown. Removal may be on an Address by both Houses of Parliament, but it is not certain whether such an Address is necessary.[76]

There are now statutory retiring ages for all judges (except the Lord Chancellor) and magistrates. Circuit judges and magistrates are removable at the instance of the Lord Chancellor on the grounds of incapacity or misbehaviour under various statutes.[77]

The provision as regards the ascertainment and establishment of salaries is secured by the practice of passing permanent Acts[78] defining judicial salaries and charging them on the Consolidated Fund. The executive, therefore, cannot bring pressure to bear on the judges by threatening to reduce their salaries, nor do their salaries come up for annual review (with opportunity for discussion of their conduct) by the House of Commons as do most estimates of public expenditure.

As the body of Ministers or 'the Government" has in practice come to play the part in public affairs formerly played by the Sovereign, the modern significance of the independence of the judges is that they are free from control or influence by the Government in the administration of justice. Even the Houses of Parliament do not seek to interfere in the conduct of current litigation; not only are the judges' salaries charged on the Consolidated Fund, but it is a parliamentary custom that questions should not be asked in the House about the decisions of the courts in particular cases.

A different, though relevant, principle is the immunity of judges from legal proceedings taken against them in respect of the discharge of their judicial functions, in order that the law may be administered freely and without fear or favour.[79]

No strict separation of powers

There is not, and never has been, a strict separation of powers in the English constitution in the sense that legislative, executive and judicial powers are assigned respectively to different organs, nor have checks and balances between them been devised as a result of theoretical analysis.[80] Development of our public institutions has been mainly empirical.

The Crown has always been an element in the exercise of all three kinds of powers—executive (the Queen's government, Her Majesty's ministers), legislative (the Queen in Parliament, throne in the House of

---

[76] See S. Shetreet, *Judges on Trial* (1976) and *post*, Chap. 20.

[77] *Post*, Chap. 20.

[78] Strictly, there are no *permanent* Acts, *i.e.* Acts which Parliament cannot repeal or amend. The expression here refers to Acts passed for an indefinite period, as contrasted with Acts passed for some definite period, *e.g.* Annual Acts.

[79] *Sirros* v. *Moore* [1975] Q.B. 118 (C.A.); *In re McC* (*A Minor*) [1985] A.C. 528 (H.L.).

[80] For the eighteenth century, Holdsworth finds Montesquieu's analysis inadequate and misleading: *History of English Law*, Vol. X, pp. 713–724.

Lords, royal assent to Bills), and judicial (Royal Courts of Justice, Her Majesty's judges, indictment in the name of the Queen). The Cabinet and other ministers are members of the legislature. Most notably, the Lord Chancellor presides over the Second Chamber, is the head of the judiciary and is a Cabinet Minister. The Home Secretary exercises the prerogative of mercy, and the Attorney-General may enter a *nolle prose-qui* to a prosecution on indictment. Ministers and government departments have powers of delegated legislation, while ministers and administrative tribunals have power to make decisions affecting private rights, and local government authorities may make byelaws for the good rule and government of their area.

The Houses of Parliament do not act exclusively as parts of a legislature but also set up select committees of inquiry and committees to scrutinise the administration. The House of Lords, besides being the Second Chamber, acts in another capacity as the final court of appeal. Early Parliaments, indeed, were concerned as much with judicial matters and the receiving of petitions and remedying of grievances as with actual law making.[81]

Courts must have some executive powers to prevent interference with their proceedings and to secure enforcement of their decisions. Final appeal from certain overseas courts, as well as in certain kinds of cases in this country, lies to the Judicial Committee of the Privy Council, technically an advisory executive organ of the Crown.

The absence of judicial review of Acts of Parliament may look like a separation of powers, though it is not based on a theory of that kind but expresses the doctrine of the sovereignty of Parliament.

From that doctrine it follows that while the power of making law belongs to Parliament, the duty of the judges is to apply it—interpreting it where necessary—whatever their views about the wisdom, justness or morality of the legislation at issue. Nor are the courts concerned, in interpreting the law, with the wishes and views of the Government[82] or the likelihood of the Government finding the courts' interpretation unwelcome.[83] It is doubtful whether it is helpful or necessary to attribute that clear distinction of roles to a theory of the separation of powers, as Lord Diplock did in *Duport Steels Ltd.* v. *Sirs.*[84]

The "basic concept of separation of legislative, executive and judicial power as it had been developed in the unwritten constitution of the United Kingdom" was also relied on by Lord Diplock as a guide to the interpretation of the constitution of Jamaica in *Hinds* v. *The Queen.*[85] In that case the Privy Council held that vesting the power to vary sentences in certain cases in a Review Board, the majority of members of which were not judges, was an unconstitutional attempt to vest judicial powers in a body not entitled to exercise such powers. A written constitution may enshrine the doctrine of the separation of powers, explicitly or by implication. To borrow it from the United Kingdom seems, how-

---

[81] *Post,* pp. 123–124.
[82] *Abse* v. *Smith* [1986] Q.B. 536, 554 *per* Sir John Donaldson M.R.
[83] *Sherdley* v. *Sherdley* [1986] 1 W.L.R. 732, 736 *per* Sir John Donaldson M.R.
[84] [1980] 1 W.L.R. 142, 157. Similarly, *Chokolongo* v. *Att.-Gen. of Trinidad and Tobago* [1981] 1 W.L.R. 106, 110 *per* Lord Diplock.
[85] [1977] A.C. 195.

ever, dangerous: a country where not merely the Home Secretary[86] but even the Commissioners of the Customs and Excise[87] can release prisoners from jail. By contrast in *Liyanage* v. *R*[88] the Privy Council, in striking down legislation as an improper interference with the judicial power rejected any analogy drawn from the British Constitution. "The British constitution is unwritten whereas in the case of Ceylon their lordships have to interpret a written document from which alone the legislature derives its legislative power."[89]

No distinct system of administrative law

Administrative law, as we have seen,[90] determines the organisation, powers and duties of administrative authorities. It is the law relating to public administration. English and Scots law contain both general principles and detailed rules relating to the structure of administrative authorities, their functions and powers, and the supervision of the relations between them and the private citizen. Administrative authorities include Ministers and central government departments, local government authorities, public corporations, and their officers and servants. There are numerous statutes establishing their structure, and conferring the powers (including powers of delegated legislation and administrative jurisdiction) necessary for the exercise of their functions relating to such matters as public health, education, transport, planning, housing, national insurance, electricity supply and so on. Administrative Tribunals deal with a wide range of matters ranging from social welfare and employment to mental health and immigration, from which appeal may lie to the courts on questions of law. But until recently it could not be said that there was a *system* of administrative law in this country— and there is still no *system* of administrative courts.

The topics covered by administrative law in the United Kingdom have to be picked out, as a matter of choice, from the general body of our constitutional law. They comprise, roughly, the topics covered by Part VI of this book. The rest of our constitutional law would then deal with the monarchy and the royal prerogative, the conduct of foreign affairs, and control of the armed forces and the civil service; Parliament; nationality, citizenship aliens and immigration; offences against the State and public order; the general principles relating to the rights of the individual; the administration of justice; and the Commonwealth.

This view has slowly gained ground among academic lawyers. At first, English writing on administrative law tended to deal mainly with the delegation to the executive of legislative and judicial powers,[91] not

---

[86] See, for example, Imprisonment (Temporary Provisions) Act 1980; a statute which passed through all its stages in both Houses and received the Royal Assent within a mere two days.

[87] Customs and Excise Management Act 1979, s.152(d); note, [1984] P.L. 2.

[88] [1967] 1 A.C. 259, 288 *per* Lord Pearce. See G. Marshall, *Constitutional Theory*, p. 120. ("The strong and surprising adoption of the separation of powers doctrine").

[89] See further, O. Hood Phillips, "A constitutional myth: separation of powers" (1977) 93 L.Q.R. 11.

[90] *Ante*, p. 10.

[91] *e.g.* Carr, *Delegated Legislation; Concerning English Administrative Law*; Robson, *Justice and Administrative Law* (3rd ed.); Allen, *Law and Orders* (3rd ed.); *Administrative Jurisdiction*.

because administrative law is confined to these topics but largely because the great influence of Dicey[92] made them controversial ground and they revealed tendencies that were resented by the more conservative and individualist members of the legal profession.[93] Dicey's attitude was due not only to his political predilections in favour of individual liberty as against government "interference," but also to a misunderstanding of the French *droit administratif* which led to the false conclusion that there could be no administrative law without a separate system of administrative courts.[94] Since Dicey's day, however, English authors have produced textbooks covering a much wider field and monographs on specific aspects.[95]

In *Ridge* v. *Baldwin*[96] Lord Reid said: "We do not have a developed system of administrative law— perhaps because until fairly recently we did not need it." Developments since then[97] have been such that Lord Diplock has claimed that

> "The extension of judicial control of the administrative process has provided over the last 30 years the most striking feature of the development of the common law in those countries of whose legal systems it provides the source; and although it is a development that has although it is a development that has already gone a long way towards providing a system of administrative law as comprehensive in its content as the droit administratif of countries of the civil law, albeit differing in procedural approach, it is a development that is still continuing."[98]

Important elements in that development were the introduction in 1977[99] of a new, simplified procedure (application for judicial review) by which to challenge the legality of administrative acts and the decision of the House of Lords in 1983[1] that actions involving administrative bodies must now be categorised as raising questions of "public law" or "private law." In the former case the new procedure must be

---

[92] Dicey, *Law of Constitution* (10th ed.), Chap. 12.
[93] See Lord Hewart, *The New Despotism*; Cmnd. 4060 (1932), *Report of the Committee on Ministers' Powers.*
[94] See, however, Dicey's article, "*Droit Administratif* in Modern French Law" (1901) 17 L.Q.R. 302, on changes in French administrative law after 1872. Dicey did not deny the existence of any administrative law in England, but the existence of anything like the French *droit administratif* as he understood it.
[95] *e.g.* Griffith and Street, *Principles of Administrative Law* (4th Ed., 1967); H. W. R. Wade, (4th ed., 1980); D. Foulkes, *Administrative Law* (5th ed., 1982); P. P. Craig, *Administrative Law* (4th ed., 1967); (5th ed., 1982); S. A. de Smith, *Judicial Review of Administrative Action Administrative Law* (1983); S. H. Bailey, (6th ed., 1985) D. C. M. Yardley *Principles of Administrative Law* (2nd ed., 1986); S.H. Bailey, C. A. Cross and J. F. Garner, *Cases and Materials in Administrative Law.* And see H. W. R. Wade, "Anglo-American Administrative Law: Some Reflections" (1965) 81 L.Q.R. 357; J. D. B. Mitchell, "The Causes and Effects of the Absence of a System of Public Law of the United Kingdom" [1965] P.L. 95.
[96] [1964] A.C. 40, (H.L.).
[97] See *post*, Part VI, Introduction.
[98] *Mahon* v. *Air New Zealand* [1984] A.C. 808.
[99] The reform was initially effected by amendments to the Rules of the Supreme Court. Subsequently legislative effect was given to the new procedure (contained in R.S.C. Ord. 53) by the Supreme Court Act 1981, s.31.
[1] *O'Reilly* v. *Mackman* [1983] 2 A.C. 237.

used. Only where questions of private law are involved can a plaintiff sue a public authority without having recourse to the application for judicial review. There may not yet be a separate *system* of Administrative Law but there are now separate procedures for enforcing public rights and private rights.

The rule of law

Introductory

The "rule of law" is an ambiguous expression, and may mean different things for different writers. Only when it is clear in what sense the phrase is being used is there any value in asking whether the rule of law exists in a particular legal system.

Historically, the phrase was, perhaps, first used with reference to a belief in the existence of law possessing higher authority—whether divine or natural—than that of the law promulgated by human rulers which imposed limits on their powers. It was probably in this sense that Aristotle expressed the view that "the rule of the law is preferable to that of any individual."[2] Bracton, writing in the thirteenth century adopted the theory generally held in the Middle Ages that the world was governed by law, human or divine; and held that "the King himself ought not be subject to man but subject to God and to the law, because the law makes him king."[3] The same view is also expressed in the Year Books of the fourteenth and fifteenth centuries.[4] Such superior law governed kings as well as subjects and set limits to the prerogative. On that ground Fortescue, in the middle of the fifteenth century, based his argument that there could be no taxation without the consent of Parliament.[5] During the conflict between King and Parliament in the reigns of the early Stuarts, the doctrine propounded by Coke was the superiority of the traditional common law over King and executive; but the common lawyers (including Coke in his later life) were in alliance with Parliament, and this theory had to be combined with the new doctrine of the supremacy of Parliament. What was supreme, therefore, was the law for the time being; that is to say, the common law subject to such changes as King in Parliament might make from time to time.[6] This view eventually prevailed with the revolution of 1688, although the law now regarded as supreme was not the common law (subject to parliamentary change) in the narrow sense, but the whole of English law, both statute law and case law, in whatever courts it was administered.

Thus it could be said that the British Constitution does not know of

---

[2] *Politics,* Vol. III, P. 16. He goes on to define law as "reason unaffected by desire." Commentators point out that Aristotle is not necessarily expressing his own view in this chapter; he may be reporting views held by others.

[3] "Ipse autem rex non debet esse sub homine sed sub Deo et sub lege, quia lex facit regem": *De Legibus et Consuetudinibus Angliae,* f. 5 b.

[4] See *Report of Committee on Ministers' Powers* Cmnd. 4060, (1932) pp. 71–72.

[5] *De Laudibus Legum Angliae,* Chap. 18; *The Governance of England,* Chap. 3.

[6] Holdsworth, *History of English Law,* Vol. II, pp. 441–442; Vol X, pp. 647–649. See also F. W. Gough, *Fundamental Law in English Constitutional History* (1955); *cf.* Roscoe Pound, *The Development of Constitutional Guarantees of Liberty* (1957); McIlwain, *The High Court of Parliament,* Chap. 2.

any rule of law since no superior law puts limits to what Parliament may legislate.[7] In this sense it would be appropriate to describe those legal systems which recognise a judicial power to hold legislation unconstitutional as being subject to the rule of law.

A second sense in which the phrase may be used is that the Crown (or Executive) must be able to demonstrate a lawful authority for its actions, whether common law, statutory or prerogative. A search warrant is not lawful merely because issued by a Secretary of State: *Entick* v. *Carrington*.[8] Taxation can be levied only by, or under, an Act of Parliament; hence the Crown cannot lawfully demand taxes on the basis of a resolution of the House of Commons.[9] Thus the rule of law can be said to be a characteristic of the British Constitution which precludes arbitrary action on the part of the Crown or members of the Government.[10]

The importance of this limit on the activities of the Executive must not be over-estimated. It does not have to show express authority for every action; "England . . . is not a country where everything is forbidden except what is expressly permitted: it is a country where everything is permitted except what is expressly forbidden"; *Malone* v. *Metropolitan Police Commissioner*.[11] In the absence of statutory provisions or judicial precedent to the contrary, the Home Secretary was not precluded from authorising the tapping of private telephones.[12] Where statutory authority is required, the Government can generally secure the passing by Parliament of such laws as it wants.[13]

In many instances governments, of whatever political hue, prefer to achieve their objectives by "extra-legal" means, rather than introduce legislation with the possible embarrassment of Parliamentary criticism and, subsequently, the risk of challenge in the Courts. Employers are "persuaded" to follow government guidelines on pay, under the threat of losing grants and government contracts.[14] A "voluntary" system of censorship relating to matters of defence and security insulates decisions taken by the responsible officials from any form of review.[15] In some instances particular sections of the community may be prepared to reach informal agreements with a government in order to

---

[7] See *post*, p. 63, for possible limits arising from the Union with Scotland, membership of the EEC, and adherence to the European Convention on Human Rights.

[8] (1765) 19 St. Tr. 1029, 1066. See, too, discussion of the "right" of a condemned prisoner to insist on being executed: Martland, *The Constitutional History of England*, p. 476; P. Brett "Conditional Pardons and the Commutation of Death Sentences," (1957) 20 M.L.R. 131; R. F. V. Henston, *Essays in Constitutional Law* (2nd ed. 1964) pp. 69–70.

[9] *Bowles* v. *Bank of England* [1913] 1 Ch. 57. *Cf.* Provisonal Collection of Taxes Act 1968.

[10] See *infra* Chap. 33 for the supervisory jurisdiction of the High Court under which decisions of Ministers may be invalidated if they have failed to exercise their discretionary powers properly.

[11] [1979] Ch. 344, 357 *per* Sir Robert Megarry V.-C.

[12] But see now, Interception of Communications Act 1985; *infra*, p. 518.

[13] For example, *Burmah Oil Co.* v. *Lord Advocate* was followed by the War Damage Act 1965; *R. (Hume)* v. *Londonderry Justices* [1972] N.I. 91 by the Northern Ireland Act 1972.

[14] G. Ganz, [1978] P.L. 333.

[15] E. Barendt, "Prior Restraints on Speech" [1985] P.L. 253, 273. See also E. Barendt, *Freedom of Speech* 1985, p. 135. (Informal rules regulating publication of ministers' memoirs).

avoid being subjected to what they fear will be still stricter control by legislation.[16]

The rule of law may, again, be used to refer to those formal character- istics which rules of a legal system must possess before citizens can take them into account in determining their future conduct.[17] The law must, for example, as far as possible, be clear; "Absence of clarity is destruc- tive of the rule of law."[18] Retrospective legislation is, generally, to be avoided.[19]

A system of law which complied with the "rule of law" in the two senses just discussed might, nonetheless, be a system which most people would regard as grossly unjust. The Executive might wield only powers given to it by law; the individual laws of the system might be admirably clear and possess every other desirable formal quality but their aim might be, for example, to maintain one group in power in that state and to deny, on racial or religious grounds, all rights to members of other groups. It is for this reason that some writers and jurists have used the phrase "rule of law" to refer to a minimum material or sub- stantive element in a legal system. Perhaps the most important example of this approach is to be found in the Declaration of Delhi, 1959[20] accord- ing to which the rule of law implies, inter alia:—a right to representative and responsible government; certain minimum standards or principles for the law, including those contained in the Universal Declaration and the European Convention, in particular, freedom of religious belief, assembly and association, and the absence of retroactive penal laws; that a citizen who is wronged should have a remedy against the state or government; the certainty of the criminal law, the presumption of inno- cence, reasonable rules relating to arrest, accusation and detention pending trial, the giving of notice and provision for legal advice, public trial, right of appeal, and absence of cruel or unusual punishments; the independence of the judiciary.

Admirable though the sentiments contained in the Delhi Declaration may be, it can be argued that to equate them with the rule of law is con- fusing and misleading; indeed, in the words of one writer is a "perver- sion of the doctrine."[21] The objection to attempting to equate the phrase with a particular set of political beliefs is that it involves the use of a term which seems to imply the objective existence of certain qualities in

---

[16] Richard Lewis, "Insurers' Agreements not to enforce strict legal rights: Bargaining with Government and the Shadow of the Law." (1985) 48 M.L.R. 275.

[17] J. Raz, "The Rule of Law and Its Virtue" (1977) 93 L.Q.R. 195.

[18] Merkur Island Shipping Corpn. v. Laughton [1983] 2 A.C. 570, per Lord Diplock.

[19] Infra, p. 55. In R. v. Kirk [1985] 1 All E.R. 453 the European Court described non-retroac- tivity of criminal legislation as a general principle of law observed by the Court and common to all the legal orders of member states. See also Article 7 of the European Con- vention of Human Rights. (Retroactive legislation is not, however, entirely precluded in the European Community: Staple Dairy Products v. Intervention Board for Agricultural Produce [1984] 1 C.M.L.R. 238.)

[20] "Declaration of Delhi" (1959) 2 Jo.Int.Com. of Jurists; pp. 7–32 "The Rule of Law in a Free Society" in Report of International Congress of Jurists (New Delhi, 1959). See further, N. S. Marsh, "The Rule of Law as a Supra-National Concept" in Oxford Essays in Juris- prudence (ed. A. G. Guest 1961), Chap. 9; N. S. Marsh, "Civil Liberties in Europe" (1959) 75 L.Q.R. 530; A. H. Robertson, Human Rights in the World (1972).

[21] Raz. See note 17, at p. 196. See also T. D. Weldon, The Vocabulary of Politics op.cit. (1953), p. 61.

the structure of a legal system as a covert political slogan to give approval to a particular system which the speaker or writer considers satisfactory.

Yet another sense in which "rule of law" may be used is to refer to the general duty binding "all citizens in a Parliamentary democracy to obey the law, unless and until it can be changed by due process."[22] A similar duty binds the judge: unless he applies the law laid down by Parliament, whatever his own views, "public confidence in the political impartiality of the judiciary, which is essential to the continuance of the rule of law" will be endangered.[23]

The "untrammelled power" of the courts to regulate their own proceedings in cases where they are not regulated by ancient usage or statute has been claimed to be essential for "the maintenance of the rule of law": *Abse* v. *Smith*.[24]

For students of the British Constitution however the rule of law preeminently means Dicey's doctrine of the rule of law.

Dicey's doctrine of the rule of law

Dicey first published his *Law of the Constitution*, based on lectures he gave as Vinerian Professor of English Law at Oxford, in 1885. His purpose was to deal "only with two or three guiding principles which pervade the modern constitution of England."[25] The three distinguishing characteristics of the English Constitution that he chose to explain and illustrate were "the Sovereignty of Parliament, the Rule of Law, and the Conventions of the Constitution."[26] A large part of the book was devoted to an exposition of his doctrine of the "rule of law,"[27] and this has had a profound influence among those who think and write about the constitution, as well as those who work it.

For Dicey the expression "the rule of law" included three distinct though kindred conceptions.

(i) The absence of arbitrary power. No man is above the law. No man is punishable except for a distinct breach of law, established in the ordinary legal manner before the ordinary courts.

(ii) Equality before the law. Every man, whatever his rank or condition, is subject to the ordinary law and the jurisdiction of the ordinary tribunals. This Dicey contrasted with the French *droit administratif*,

---

[22] *Francome* v. *Mirror Group Newspapers Ltd.* [1984] 1 W.L.R. 892, 897 *per* Sir John Donaldson M.R. The Master of the Rolls recognised that in some cases the citizen might feel a moral obligation to disobey the law—on which see Geoffrey Marshall, *Constitutional Theory* Chap. IX.

[23] *Duport Steels* v. *Sirs* [1980] 1 W.L.R. 142, 157 *per* Lord Diplock.

[24] [1986] Q.B. 536, 555 *per* May L.J.

[25] Preface to 1st ed. (1885). A recent biography and analysis of Dicey's work and thought is R. A. Cosgrove, *The Rule of Law: Albert Venn Dicey* (1981).

[26] Dicey, *Law of the Constitution* (8th ed., 1914), p. xvii.

[27] Dicey, *Law of the Constitution* (10th ed.), Part II. H. W. Arndt, "The Origins of Dicey's Concept of 'The Rule of Law' (1957) 31 A.L.J. 117, points out that Dicey elaborated and expanded the ideas of W. E. Hearn in *The Government of England* (1867), to which Dicey made a general reference in the Preface to his first edition. Dicey first used the phrase in 1875; "Stubbs' Constitutional History of Great Britain," *Nation* 20 (March 4, 1875) 154; Cosgrove, *op. cit.* p. 67.

under which the responsibility of public officers for their official acts is decided by a distinct system of administrative courts.

(iii) The general principles of the British Constitution—especially the liberties of the individual, such as personal liberty, freedom of speech and public meeting—are the result of judicial decisions in particular cases. The constitution is judge-made.

Dicey's doctrine has been chiefly criticised with regard to the notion of equality before the law and the topic of administrative law.[28]

The first principle ("No man is punishable," etc.) applies generally in criminal law. Criminal courts usually have a wide discretion with regard to punishment, but this favours the citizen as it is a discretion downwards from a statutory maximum. The principle excludes, as a general rule, preventive detention, compulsory acquisition of goods and direct enforcement of administrative decisions, although preventive detention by order of the Home Secretary was authorised by Parliament during the two World Wars.

Whether discretionary powers conferred on Ministers by Parliament should be described as "arbitrary" or not is, largely, a matter of judgment. To the extent that Dicey objected to any discretion being conferred on ministers he was, it has been pointed out, attempting to turn particular political and economic theories into a constitutional doctrine. Certainly, the granting of wide powers to ministers is now a settled feature of legislation.[29]

To the doctrine that all persons have equal rights and duties before the law, however, so many exceptions have now to be made that the statement is of doubtful value. Ministers and other public authorities have many powers that the ordinary person has not got. Thus local authorities have statutory power under certain conditions to buy land compulsorily, and the police have special powers of arrest and search by common law and statute, and ministers have wide powers of delegated legislation. Immunity from the general law of tort may attach to acts done "in contemplation or furtherance of a trade dispute."[30] Rights and obligations of the individual are now decided in many cases not by the ordinary courts but by special or administrative tribunals. Judges and ambassadors have immunity from being sued in the courts, although the immunity of judges actually favours "the rule of law" to the extent that it helps secure the independence of the Judiciary from control by the Executive. In one important respect we are paradoxically nearer to Dicey's "rule of law" than when he wrote, for the common law immunity in tort of the Crown (in effect, the government) was largely

---

[28] See, e.g. E. C. S. Wade in Dicey, Law of the Constitution (10th ed.), pp. xcvi–cli; Jennings, op. cit. Chap. 2, s.1 and Appendix II; "In Praise of Dicey" (1935) 13 Public Administration 123; B. Schwartz, French Administrative Law and the Common-Law World, Chap. 10. For a re-appraisal of Dicey's doctrine, see F. H. Lawson, "Dicey Revisited" (1959), Political Studies, Vol. VII, pp. 109, 207. See also A. L. Goodhart, "The Rule of Law and Absolute Sovereignty" (1958) 106 Univ. Pennsylvania Law Rev. 943.

[29] Quite exceptional powers may be delegated to ministers in times of emergency: see post, Chap. 19.

[30] The width of the immunity tends to vary with the political complexion of the government. For the present position see B. Perrins, Trade Union Law (1985) Chaps. 18 and 19.

removed by the Crown Proceedings Act 1947.[31] Nonetheless the government retains legal immunities and privileges not possessed by the private citizen.[32]

With regard to administrative law[33], its existence does not necessarily involve special administrative courts, as is shown by the fact that Belgium before 1946 had a *droit administratif* without such separate courts. The essence of administrative law is that different principles should apply in relation to the official acts of public authorities and officers. These are not confined to liability to pay compensation for injury caused to private individuals. In any event, *droit administratif* is looked upon by the French as a protection for the individual, not as a privilege for public officials.[34] If French administrative law provides compensation for excess or abuse of power *ex post facto*, English administrative law might be said to seek to deter public officials from exceeding their powers in the first instance.

Whatever Dicey's initial distrust of a separate system of administrative law it should be remembered that the development of such a system has been claimed as one of the judicial achievements of the last thirty years.[35]

It is not easy to see how Dicey's treatment of the "rights of the subject" in British constitutional law is related to the other parts of his doctrine. It is true that the rights of the individual are mostly to be inferred from judicial decisions[36] and are therefore part of the common law, especially if such enactments as the Bill of Rights 1688 be regarded mainly as declaratory. That such rights are *part* of the ordinary law is a necessary consequence of the fact that the British Constitution is unwritten; but the fundamental principle both in the ordinary English law and in British constitutional law is the legislative supremacy of Parliament, so that it cannot be said with exactness that either the principles or the decisions are *derived* from the others.

In so far as Dicey's general statement of the rule of law may be taken to involve the existence in the English Constitution of certain principles almost amounting to fundamental laws, his doctrine is logically inconsistent with the legislative suspremacy of Parliament. Dicey attempted to reconcile the two notions by saying that parliamentary sovereignty favors the rule of law because the will of Parliament can be expressed only in the form of an Act, which must be interpreted by the courts; and that the rule of law favours parliamentary sovereignty, as any additional discretionary powers that the government needs can only be obtained

---

[31] An anomalous exception was the exemption of the Post Office and its employees under section 9 of that Act, which was substantially re-enacted in the Post Office Act 1969. See now the British Telecommunications Act 1981, s.23 (immunity of British Telecom) and s.29 (immunity of Post Office).

[32] G. Zellick, "Government beyond Law" [1985] P.L. 283.

[33] Dicey, *op. cit.* Chap. 12; *cf.* A. V. Dicey, "*Droit Administratif* in Modern French Law" (1901) 17 L.Q.R. 302; "The Development of Administrative Law in England" (1915) 31 L.Q.R. 148 (based on the case of *Local Government Board* v. *Arlidge* [1915] A.C. 120).

[34] L. Neville Brown and J. F. Garner, *French Administrative Law*, (3rd ed., 19XX, Chap. 11).

[35] *Ante*, p. 32.

[36] But statutes have curtailed some (*e.g.* Public Order Act 1986) and modified others (*e.g.* Habeas Corpus Acts). See further, *post*, Chaps. 25–27.

from Parliament.[37] His doctrine is a political theory, in some of its aspects connected with the doctrine of the separation of powers. From another point of view it implies moral restrictions on the legislative activity of Parliament, its juridical nature resembling the "directive principles of state policy" found in the Constitutions of the Republic of Ireland and India.

Conclusion

Despite the supremacy of Parliament, theories of the rule of law may be significant in at least three ways. First they may influence legislators. The substantive law at any given time may approximate to the "rule of law," but this only at the will of Parliament. Secondly, their principles may provide canons of interpretation which give an indication of how the law will be applied and legislation interpreted. English courts lean in favour of the liberty of the citizen, especially of his person: they interpret strictly statutes which purport to diminish that liberty, and presume that Parliament does not intend to restrict private rights in the absence of clear words to the contrary.[38] But Parliament could pass an Act requiring the judges to interpret social legislation freely in favour of the administration. Thirdly, the rule of law may be a rule of evidence: everyone is prima facie equal before the law. A person, whether an executive officer or not, may have peculiar rights, powers, privileges or immunities; but, if so, he must prove them. In this sense, the government is subject to law.

The British Constitution and human rights[39]

The British Constitution contains no fundamental rights in the strict sense. Being unwritten and flexible, the constitution in any of its parts can be changed in the same way as any other part, namely, by ordinary Act of Parliament. The legislative supremacy of Parliament means that there is no legal limit to the extent to which Parliament can abridge or abolish rights that in other countries may be regarded as "fundamental."[40] The practical checks are the influence of public opinion, the vigilance of the Opposition, and the restrictive interpretation of the courts. The rights of the individual in English law are the *residue* of freedom that is left after legislative and executive powers have been defined, and their extent can only be determined by examining the restrictions placed on the activity of the individual and the enjoyment of his property.[41]

The traditional view in this country has been that statements of the "rights" of the individual are very misleading unless they are properly qualified, and when qualified they almost amount to truisms. A citizen's person or property may not be interfered with—unless it may. A

---

[37] Dicey, *op. cit.* Chap. 13.
[38] See, *e.g. Allen v. Thorn Electrical Industries Ltd.* [1968] 1 Q.B. 487 (C.A.). This aspect of the importance of the rule of law is developed by T. R. S. Allen "Legislative Supremacy and The Rule of Law" [1985] C.L.J. 111.
[39] See further, *post,* Chap. 22.
[40] But see *Morris v. Beardmore* [1981] A.C. 446, *per* Lord Scarman.
[41] See *post*, Chaps. 22–27.

person is not liable for what he speaks or writes—unless he is. No liability attaches to one who takes part in a public meeting—unless it does. The British attitude is much more concerned with judicial enforcement, with the provision of effective remedies administered by an independent and incorruptible judiciary, than with the formulation of general principles on paper.

Nevertheless, there has been a strong movement since the War—both within the Commonwealth and outside—to define fundamental or human rights, and such definitions or declarations have come to form an important part of a new international concept of "the rule of law."[42] The United Kingdom has ratified the European Convention on Human Rights, accepted the compulsory jurisdiction of the European Court of Human Rights, and recognised the right of individuals to bring petitions against her before the European Commission of Human Rights. The European Convention is not incorporated into British constitutional law, though it is binding on her morally and in international law, and it is beginning to impinge on Community law.

---

[42] *Ante*, p. 33.

Chapter 3

PARLIAMENTARY SUPREMACY I: HISTORY AND NATURE

I. Historical Introduction

In the nineteenth century the prevailing juristic theory in this country was Austin's doctrine of sovereignty, which supposed that in every mature legal system there was some person or body—the "Sovereign"[1]—vested with unlimited power to make law.[2] Austin himself did not apply his own doctrine consistently to the British Constitution. Dicey's treatment, in which he ascribed sovereignty to the United Kingdom Parliament, was more consistent.[3]

The doctrine of sovereignty in the theory of municipal law as opposed to international law, however, is now out of fashion, and the continued use of the term "sovereignty" in the present context tends to prejudice discussion of the lawmaking power of the United Kingdom Parliament, with which legislature we are here concerned. A body may have supreme (highest) power without necessarily being sovereign (unlimited) in Austin's sense, nor do we need to assert or imply here that there must be a sovereign authority in every legal system.

The establishment of parliamentary supremacy was a product of the revolution of 1688. Before then the chief rivals were, first, the King or King in Council, and then the common law courts. Later the House of Commons acting by resolution occasionally threatened a breach in the authority of the Parliament as a whole.[4]

---

[1] The doctrine of sovereignty was derived by Austin from Bodin, Hobbes, Blackstone and Bentham. Coke's description of the "transcendant and absolute" power and jurisdiction of Parliament for making of laws in proceeding by bill (4 Inst. 36) was thought by Sir Ivor Jennings to refer to the jurisdiction of the High Court of Parliament (*The Law and the Constitution* (5th ed., 1959), App. III). Sir Thomas Smith's discussion in *De Republica Anglorum* (1589), Bk. 2, Chap. 1 (Alston ed.), of the "absolute" power of Parliament probably referred to Parliament as the highest court, "absolute" here meaning "not subject to appeal." In the Middle Ages the King ruled (subject to custom and advice) and was called the Sovereign, but "the Sovereign" as applied to the modern constitutional monarch is a courtesy title.

[2] John Austin, *The Province of Jurisprudence Determined* (1832). There are many editions and commentaries, notably H. L. A. Hart's edition (1954) and Jethro Brown's *The Austinian Theory of Law* (1906). Most English textbooks on jurisprudence contain criticisms of Austin's theory; and see H. L. A. Hart, *The Concept of Law* (1961). Bentham's work, inadequately published until recently, would no doubt be known to Austin; see H. L. A. Hart, "Bentham on Sovereignty" (1967) 2 Ir. Jur. (N.S.) 327; J. H. Burns, "Bentham on Sovereignty: an Exploration" in *Bentham and Legal Theory* (M. H. ed. James, p. 133 (re-printed from (1973) 24 N.I.L.Q.).

[3] *Law of the Constitution*, (10th ed., 1959) Chaps. 1–3, *cf.* E. C. S. Wade's Introduction, pp. xxxiv–xcvi. Dicey suggests indeed that Austin's general theory of sovereignty was a deduction from the position of the British Parliament.

[4] *Stockdale* v. *Hansard* (1839) 9 Ad. & E. 1; *Case of the Sheriff of Middlesex* (1840) 11 Ad. & E. 273; *post*, Chap. 12.

The King as lawmaker

Parliament emerged as an effective body in the fourteenth century.[5] In the reign of Henry VI the Lords and Commons framed the statutes and the King assented in much the same fashion as at the present day. Nevertheless it would seem that the King continued to legislate on matters of lesser or temporary importance. Whether there was a significant distinction between the terms "statute" and "ordinance," the former applying to Parliament and the latter to royal legislation, has long been a matter of controversy, but Plucknett thought these terms were synonymous.[6]

Proclamations

The Statute of Proclamations 1539,[7] which gave the King power, with the advice of the Council, to make proclamations that would have the force of statutes, was of very limited scope and short-lived. Intended for emergencies, it provided that proclamations might not impose the death penalty (except for cases of heresy), take away a subject's property or conflict with existing statutes, customs or common law. This Act was repealed in the first year of Edward VI.[8] Notwithstanding its repeal, Mary and Elizabeth I continued to make and enforce proclamations concerning imports and also certain religious matters.

In the reign of James I the Commons complained of the abuse of proclamations. The opinion of Chief Justice Coke and four of his colleagues was sought and given in the *Case of Proclamations* (1610),[9] when James I wanted to prohibit by proclamation the building of new houses in London in order to check the over-growth of the capital, and the manufacture of starch from wheat so as to preserve wheat for human consumption. The opinion was to the effect that no new offence can be created by proclamation; the only prerogative possessed by the Crown is that which is conferred by the law of the land; but that to prevent offences the King can by proclamation warn his subjects against breaches of the existing law, in which case a breach would be the more serious.

The suspending and dispensing powers

By virtue of the *suspending* power the King claimed to postpone indefinitely the general operation of a given statute; by virtue of the *dispensing* power he relieved particular offenders or classes of offenders from the statutory penalties they had incurred. In the reign of Henry VII it was held that the King could at common law dispense with *mala prohi-*

---

[5] See E. B. Fryde and E. Miller (eds.) *Historical Studies of the English Parliament: Origins to 1399* (1970); Sir Goronwy Edwards *The Second Century of the English Parliament* (1979); R. G. Davies and J. H. Denton (eds.), *The English Parliament in the Middle Ages* (1981).

[6] T. F. T. Plucknett, *Statutes and their Interpretation in the Fourteenth Century*, p. 34. See also S. E. Thorne, *Introduction to a Discourse upon the Exposition and Understanding of Statutes* (Huntington Library, 1942); H. G. Richardson and G. O. Sayles, *Law and Legislation from Aethelberht to Magna Carta* (1966); "The Early Statutes" (1934) 50 L.Q.R. 201, 540.

[7] 31 Hen. VIII, c. 8. The Act was debated by Parliament for 15 days, the Commons rejecting the first Bill sent down by the Lords.

[8] (1547) 1 Edw. VI, c. 12.

[9] 12 Co.Rep. 74; 2 St.Tr. 723.

bita but not *mala in se*.[10] Subject to this restriction, both the suspending and dispensing powers were accepted as part of the prerogative in the sixteenth and seventeenth centuries. The Stuarts used these prerogatives to subvert established laws. James II issued a proclamation that a Declaration of Indulgence, suspending the operation of all laws against Roman Catholics, should be read in all the churches; but in the *Seven Bishops' Case* (1688)[11] the Primate and six bishops were acquitted by a jury on a charge of seditious libel for signing a petition claiming that to read the declaration would be illegal and against their conscience. The right of the subject to petition the King was also confirmed.

In *Thomas* v. *Sorrell* (1674)[12] the plaintiff claimed a penalty for selling wine without a licence contrary to a statute of 12 Charles II. The jury returned a special verdict that they had found a patent of 9 James I incorporating the Vintners Company and granting them permission to sell wine without a licence, *non obstante* an Act of 7 Edward VI forbidding such sale. The judges decided that the King might dispense with an individual breach of a penal statute by which no man was injured, or with the continuous breach of a penal statute enacted for the King's benefit. In *Godden* v. *Hales* (1686)[13] a collusive action was brought to test the King's *dispensing* power. Sir Edward Hales accepted appointment as colonel of a regiment, and was sued for a penalty for neglecting to take the oaths of supremacy and allegiance and to receive the Sacrament according to the Test Act of 25 Charles II. Hales pleaded a dispensation of James II. The court held that the dispensation barred the right of action, as the King had a prerogative to dispense with penal statutes in particular cases for reasons of which the King was the sole judge.

The Bill of Rights 1688 declared: "That the pretended power of *suspending* of laws or the execution of laws by regal authority without consent of Parliament is illegal; that the pretended power of *dispensing* with laws or the execution of laws by regal authority *as it hath been assumed and exercised of late* is illegal."[14] Projected legislation, stating in what cases dispensation should be legal, was never passed.[15] It is by virtue of the words "as it hath been assumed and exercised of late" in relation to the dispensing power that the prerogative right to pardon was retained. These words were also relied on as legalising a dispensation granted by Elizabeth I in 1566 in the *Eton College* case (1815)[16] where, owing to their insertion, a fellow of Eton College was allowed to hold a living in conjunction with his fellowship.

The prohibition on the suspending and dispensing powers might be thought to give rise to doubts about the legality of the practice of the

---

[10] Y.B.Mich. 11 Hen. VII, no. 35 (1495) *per* Fineux C.J.; see Holdsworth, *History of English Law*, Vol. VI, pp. 218–219.

[11] 12 St.Tr. 371.

[12] Vaughan 330.

[13] 11 St.Tr. 1166; 2 Shower 275.

[14] For a purported attempt to suspend legislation in New Zealand, see W. A. McKean, "The Suspending Power Exhumed," [1978] P.L.7. An example of a dispensing power conferred by statute is to be found in s.134 of the Army Act 1955 under which a superior officer may "condone" an offence committed by a soldier; see *R*. v. *Bisset* [1980] 1 W.L.R. 335 (Ct–M.A.C.); *post*, p.350.

[15] Holdsworth, *op. cit.* Vol. VI, pp. 215–225, 240–241.

[16] *King's College, Cambridge* v. *Eton College*, P.Wms. 53; Broom, *Constitutional Law*, p. 503.

Inland Revenue of making extra-statutory concessions to tax payers. The practice is not new and certainly existed in the nineteenth century. By 1944 it was so well established that a list of agreed concessions was published.[17] Sir Stafford Cripps said in 1947 that such concessions had come into existence "without any particular legal authority under any Act of Parliament but by the Inland Revenue under my authority."[18] Judicial concern about the powers claimed by the Revenue was voiced in *Vestey* v. *I.R.C.* (No 2).[19] In that case a taxpayer claimed that the construction of the relevant statute urged by the Revenue could not be correct because, *inter alia*, of the absurdly wide liability it would impose on beneficiaries under a trust. The Revenue's response that there was no risk of any individual being harshly treated; in its discretion particular beneficiaries would be assessed for reasonable sums. Walton J. and the House of Lords held that the beneficiaries were not liable to tax under the statute. Walton J. went on to indicate very clearly his belief that the power of dispensing claimed by the Revenue was contrary to the Bill of Rights. In the House of Lords Lord Wilberforce similarly emphatically repudiated any such power, although the Commissioners must act with administrative common sense, so that they were under no duty to expend a large sum of taxpayers' money in attempting to collect a small amount of tax, and they could bring humanity to bear in hard cases.[20] The problem arose in another way in *Furniss* v. *Dawson*[21] where the House of Lords abandoned the principles laid down in earlier cases and, in wide and vague terms, indicated that elaborate schemes designed to minimise tax liability might in future be at risk of being set aside at the instance of the Revenue. To allay alarm the Inland Revenue issued a draft statement of practice indicating what schemes would continue to be acceptable. As the result of concern expressed that the Revenue was claiming a dispensing power, the statement was withdrawn—and a similar one, in the form of a written answer to a parliamentary question, was issued by the Chief Secretary to the Treasury.[22]

Monopolies

Formerly the granting of monopolies by the monarch was presumed to inflict a hardship on the public. In the *Case of Monopolies* (1602)[23] Darcy, a servant of Elizabeth I and grantee of the sole rights of importing and making playing-cards, sued Allein for interfering with his grant. The court held that the grant was a monopoly and void, and that the Queen could not exercise her dispensing power to confer private gain on an individual contrary to statutes of Edward III and Edward IV,

---

[17] The latest list was published in 1985: see N. L. J. May 31, 1985, p. 534.

[18] See D. W. Williams, "Extra Statutory Concessions" [1979] B.T.R. 137, 140.

[19] [1979] Ch. 177; [1980] A.C. 1148.

[20] Administrative commonsense is exemplified in *R.* v. *I.R.C. Ex p. National Federation of Self Employed and Small Businesses Ltd.* [1980] A.C. 952. ("Amnesty" to Fleet St. casuals).

[21] [1984] A.C. 474.

[22] Dawn Oliver, "Tax Planning and Administrative Discretion" [1984] P.L. 389. The case for the legality of the Revenue's practice of making concessions is argued by John Alder, "The Legality of Extra-Statutory Concessions," 180 N.L.J. 1980, 180.

[23] *Darcy* v. *Allein*, 11 Co.Rep. 84b. For the background of this case, see D. R. Seaborne Davies, "Further Light on the Case of Monopolies" (1932) 48 L.Q.R. 394.

which imposed a penalty on the importation of certain goods and were enacted for the public good. The grant of monopolies is now governed by Patent Acts.[24]

Taxation

It was supposed to have been settled by Magna Carta and by legislation in the reigns of Edward I and Edward III that taxation beyond the levying of customary feudal aids required the consent of Parliament. One of the central themes of English constitutional history was the gaining of control of taxation and national finance in general by Parliament, and in particular the Commons; for this control meant that the King was not able to govern for more than short periods without summoning Parliament, and Parliament could insist on grievances being remedied before it granted the King supply. This applied at least to *direct* taxation. With regard to *indirect* taxation different considerations might apply. Down to the early seventeenth century import duties, for example, were regarded rather as licences or concessions than as taxes and, further, the royal prerogative relating to foreign affairs—and hence the regulation of foreign trade in the national interest—was relevant. Issue was joined in two famous cases in the reigns of James I (the "Case of Impositions") and Charles I (the "Case of Ship-Money").

In *Bate's Case* (*Case of Impositions*) (1606)[25] Bate, a Levant merchant, refused to pay a duty imposed by letters patent of James I on the import of currants, contending that the imposition was contrary to a statute of Edward III which declared that such taxation required the consent of Parliament. The Court of Exchequer gave judgment unanimously for the King. Their reasons were that foreign affairs, and therefore foreign commerce, were within the absolute power of the King; as the King could prohibit the importation of goods, still more could he tax imported goods; and the court must accept the King's statement that the purpose of the tax was to regulate foreign trade. Coke and Popham C.JJ. thought this decision was right.[26] The judgment has been condemned by some modern historians, but it may well have been warranted by the law of that time in so far as it rested on the prerogative power to regulate foreign trade. This power, however, was liable to be abused, and danger also lay in dicta treating the matter as a question of revenue within the "absolute" (*i.e.* inalienable) powers of the Crown. It was in the debate on impositions in 1610, says Holdsworth,[27] that the supremacy of the King in Parliament over the King out of Parliament was first asserted by James Whitelocke.

The Petition of Right 1628 was occasioned largely by *Darnel's Case* (*The Five Knights' Case*) (1627),[28] where the defendants were imprisoned

---

[24] The Crown's right to make use of patents is preserved by the Crown Proceedings Act 1947, s. 3 (see *Pfizer* v. *Ministry of Health* [1965] A.C. 512.) and the Patent Act 1977, ss. 55–59.

[25] 2 St.Tr. 371. See further Holdsworth, *History of English Law*, Vol. VI, pp. 42–48; G. D. G. Hall, "Impositions and the Courts 1554–1606" (1953) 69 L.Q.R. 200.

[26] 12 Co.Rep. 33.

[27] *Some Lessons from our Legal History*, pp. 124–125.

[28] 3 St.Tr. 1.

for refusing to pay a forced loan. The Petition of Right was assented to by Charles I, and has always been regarded as having statutory force although largely superseded by the Bill of Rights. It forbad tallages, aids, forced loans, benevolences, taxes and suchlike charges "without common consent by Act of Parliament."[29]

While this document was still fresh in men's minds, Charles I (after consulting the judges) imposed under the Great Seal a direct tax known as ship-money, to be used to furnish ships for the navy. The tax was charged first on the seaport towns, which had the primary responsibility for finding ships and men for the national defence, and then on the inland counties. In *R. v. Hampden (Case of Ship-Money)* (1637)[30] proceedings were taken against John Hampden, a Buckinghamshire gentleman, for refusing to pay the amount of £1 assessed on him. The majority of the judges in the Court of Exchequer Chamber gave judgment for the King. The gist of their decision was that the King's prerogative to defend the realm in time of danger overrode the general principle that taxation required the consent of Parliament, and that the King was sole judge both of the existence of an emergency and also of the steps to be taken to meet the danger. It is difficult to criticise this decision in the light of the law at that time. The precedents were conflicting, and Hampden's counsel did not place much reliance on the Petition of Right. The verdict of most historians has been against the correctness of the decision, which they put down to the subservience of the judges to the King. Even if the decision was right in law, it had implications that were politically dangerous. The judgment itself was declared void by the Long Parliament in 1641.

The eventual solution was political rather than legal, for the revolution of 1688 meant that Parliament henceforth controlled the King. The Bill of Rights 1688 accordingly settled the matter for the future, as regards both direct and indirect taxation, by declaring that "levying money for or to the use of the Crown by pretence of prerogative without consent of Parliament for longer time or in other manner than the same is or shall be granted is illegal." It may be noted that the Tenures Abolition Act 1660 had confirmed the abolition of military tenures, and no revenue was derived from that source after 1645.[31]

An attempt by the government (which in modern times represents the Crown) to levy money without express statutory authority was *Att.-Gen. v. Wilts United Dairies.*[32] The Attorney-General sought to recover £15,000 from Wilts United Dairies, representing a fee of 2d. a gallon on milk purchased by them under licence from the Food Controller, which was granted under statutory orders made in virtue of Regulations issued under the Defence of the Realm (Consolidation) Act

---

[29] Tallages were imposts set by the King as landlord on his own demesne lands, aids were free-will offerings by tenants to their lord in time of need, and benevolences were extorted free-will offerings. These methods of raising money were not invented by the Stuarts, but were known in the fourteenth and fifteenth centuries.

[30] 3 St.Tr. 825. See further Holdsworth, *History of English Law*, Vol. VI, pp. 48–54; D. L. Keir, "The Case of Ship-Money" (1936) 52 L.Q.R. 546.

[31] For the "sovereignty" of Parliament in the eighteenth century, see Holdsworth, *op. cit.* Vol. X, pp. 526–531.

[32] (1922) 37 T.L.R. 884; 91 L.J.K.B. 897.

1914. The House of Lords unanimously upheld the decision of the Court of Appeal that the charge was *ultra vires* as a levy of money for the use of the Crown without the authority of Parliament. Lord Buckmaster stated that neither the Act creating the Ministry of Food, nor the Regulations issued under the Defence of the Realm Act, directly or by inference enabled the Food Controller to levy payment. The charges to the extent of £18,000,000 were validated retrospectively by the War Charges (Validity) Act 1925. Parliament can, of course, expressly delegate the power to levy such charges, and did so in the Second World War.[33]

In 1954 it was discovered that the Post Office had for many years been inadvertently charging licences for wireless sets without the power to do so, since no regulations with the consent of the Treasury had been issued as required by the Wireless Telegraphy Act 1904. The Post Office repaid the plaintiff's licence and costs,[34] and the charge for wireless licences was validated retrospectively by the Wireless Telegraphy (Validation of Charges) Act 1954. In *Congreve* v. *Home Office*[35] the Home Secretary gave notice of his intention to increase the fees for television licences. Some licence holders, in order to forestall the increase, took out new licences at the existing rate before their licence had expired. The Home Secretary, who had a statutory discretion to revoke television licences, proposed to revoke such overlapping licences unless the increased fee was paid. The Court of Appeal held that the Minister's discretion must be exercised reasonably,[36] and that this was an attempt to levy money without authority of Parliament.[37]

The Judges and a Higher Law[38]

Medieval judges, though appointed by the King, had inherent authority to declare and apply the law, which was mainly feudal and customary, even against the King[39]; and they could develop the law, within the limits set by a narrow range of sources, to meet new situations. But judges had no jurisdiction to change the direction of the law by introducing novel provisions or to abolish law already established: these functions fell within the province of legislation. A fundamentally new and written constitution like that of the United States would be required to give British courts coordinate authority with that of the legislature, involving jurisdiction to review primary legislation and to test its validity against the supreme law of the constitution. Judges cannot confer such authority on themselves.

There are dicta in the common law courts, however, down to the seventeenth century to the effect that there is a law of nature or reason

---

[33] Emergency Powers (Defence) Act 1939, s.2.

[34] *Davey Paxman & Co. Ltd.* v. *Post Office* (action settled) *The Times*, November 16, 1954.

[35] [1976] Q.B. 629.

[36] *Padfield* v. *Ministry of Agriculture, Fisheries and Food* [1968] A.C. 997 (H.L.). The Parliamentary Commissioner had strongly criticised the Home Secretary's action: *Seventh Report of Parliamentary Commissioner for Administration*, Sess. 1974–75. p. 680.

[37] Citing *Att.-Gen.* v. *Wilts. United Dairies, supra.* The Home Secretary later obtained statutory power to alter television licence fees without advance notice.

[38] J. W. Gough, *Fundamental Law in English Constitutional History*; Roscoe Pound, *The Development of Guarantees of Liberty* (1957); E. S. Corwin, *The "Higher Law" Background of American Constitutional Law* (reprint 1955).

[39] Bracton, *De Legibus et consuetudinibus Angliae*, f. 5b.

superior even to Acts of Parliament. The most celebrated example is *Dr. Bonham's Case*,[40] in which Coke C.J. presided over the King's Bench. The question was whether Dr. Bonham was liable to pay a fine, half to the Crown and half to the Royal College of Physicians, under the charter of the College which had been confirmed by Act of Parliament. The Court gave judgment for Bonham on the ground that the College had no jurisdiction over those practising outside London; but Coke's report of the judgment goes on to say that "when an Act of Parliament is against common right and reason, or repugnant, or impossible to be performed, the common law will control it, and adjudge such act to be void." This statement was obiter, and is also inconsistent with what Coke says in his *Institutes*.[41]

In *Day* v. *Savadge*[42] the question was whether Day, as a freeman of the City of London, was exempt from wharfage duty on a bag of nutmegs. On behalf of the Corporation it was contended that by a statute of 7 Ric. II disputes as to the customs of the City were to be decided on the basis of a certificate of the mayor and aldermen. Hobart C.J., giving the judgment of the Court of Common Pleas, held that the custom in this case was to be tried by jury and not by certificate, and added obiter: "even an act of parliament, made against natural equity, as to make a man judge in his own case, is void in itself; for *jura naturae sunt immutabilia*, and they are *leges legum*." This dictum may be taken as illustrating a logical impossibility or moral limitation, or merely as traditional rhetoric. Again in *City of London* v. *Wood*,[43] where the Court of Common Pleas gave judgment for Wood on a writ of error from the Mayor's Court in an action for the recovery of a forfeiture to the City of London under a byelaw made by virtue of an Act of Parliament, Holt C.J. is reported to have approved Coke's dictum in *Dr. Bonham's Case*, saying: "an Act of Parliament can do no wrong, though it may do several things that look pretty odd," and adding that an Act of Parliament may not make adultery lawful, though it may dissolve the marriage of A and his wife and make her the wife of B.

These cases concerned the privileges of corporations under royal charters confirmed by Parliament, and the dicta may be taken to express a presumption of interpretation that Parliament does not intend to confer on a corporation or its officers jurisdiction to determine its own legal rights in disputes between the corporation and other persons. Blackstone's statement that no human laws are of any validity if contrary to the "law of nature"[44] was a relic of traditional rhetoric. On the type of case cited above he is more explicit. If Parliament gave a man power to try all causes arising in his manor, Blackstone explains,[45] the courts would construe this as not intending to extend to causes in which he

---

[40] (1610) 8 Co.Rep. 114, 118; *cf.* T. F. T. Plucknett, "Bonham's Case and Judicial Review" (1926) 40 *Harvard Law Review* 30; S. E. Thorne, "Dr. Bonham's Case" (1938) 54 L.Q.R. 543.

[41] 4 Inst. 36. Coke as a Law Officer supported the prerogative, as a judge the supremacy of the common law (which he equated with reason), and as a parliamentarian the sovereignty of Parliament.

[42] (1615) Hobart 85, 97.

[43] (1710) 12 Mod. 669, 687–688. This report is, however, considered to be unreliable.

[44] Bl.Comm., I, 41.

[45] Bl.Comm., I, 91.

himself is a party; but if Parliament should clearly and expressly enact that he might try his own causes as well as those of other persons, no court would have power to defeat the intent of the legislature.

The modern view was expressed by Willes J. in *Lee* v. *Bude & Torrington Ry.*[46]: "It was once said that if an Act of Parliament were to create a man judge in his own cause, the court might disregard it. That dictum, however, stands as a warning rather than an authority to be followed. . . . Are we to act as regents over what is done by Parliament with the consent of the Queen, lords and commons? I deny that any such authority exists." In *Pickin* v. *British Railways Board*[47] Lord Reid said "In earlier times many learned lawyers seem to have believed that an Act of Parliament could be disregarded in so far as it was contrary to the law of God or the law of nature or natural justice but since the supremacy of Parliament was finally demonstrated by the revolution of 1688 any such idea has become obsolete."

II. The Nature of Parliamentary Supremacy[48]

The "Legislative Supremacy of Parliament" means that Parliament (*i.e.* the Queen, Lords and Commons in Parliament assembled) can pass laws on any topic affecting any persons, and that there are no "fundamental" laws which Parliament cannot amend or repeal in the same way as ordinary legislation. Dicey[49] was following the tradition of Coke[50] and Blackstone[51] when he said that Parliament has "the right to make or unmake any law whatever," and further that "no person or body is recognised by the law of England as having the right to override or set aside the legislation of Parliament." Once a document is recognised as being an Act of Parliament, no English court can refuse to obey it or question its validity; *Manuel* v. *Att.-Gen.*[52] per Sir Robert Megarry V.C. In that case, presented with the text of the Canada Act 1982, the learned Vice Chancellor held himself obliged to recognise its validity once satisfied that it had been passed by the House of Commons and the House of Lords; had received the Royal Assent and there was no suggestion that the copy was not a true copy of the Act.[53]

Legislative supremacy as thus defined is a legal concept. The supremacy of Parliament, being recognised and acted on by the courts, is a principle of the common law. It may indeed be called the one fundamental law of the British Constitution, for it is peculiar in that it could not be altered by ordinary statute, but only by some fundamental

---

[46] (1871) L.R. 6 C.P. 576, 582.

[47] [1974] A.C. 765, 782.

[48] Dicey, *Law of the Constitution* (10th ed.), Chaps. 1–3; H. W. R. Wade, "The Basis of Legal Sovereignty" [1955] C.L.J. 172, and review in [1954] C.L.J. 265; O. Hood Phillips, *Reform of the Constitution* (1970), Chaps. 1 and 7.

[49] Dicey, *op. cit.* pp. 39–40; quoted by Wild C.J. in *Fitzgerald* v. *Muldoon* [1976] 1 N.Z.L.R. 615, 622.

[50] 4 Inst. 36.

[51] Bl.Comm., I, 160–162.

[52] [1983] Ch.77, 86. The reference to an English court is explicable by the fact that the learned Vice–Chancellor is an English judge and was clearly not meant to imply that a different rule applies in Scotland: but see *post*, p. 65.

[53] On the definition of Act of Parliament, see *post*, pp. 83–84.

change of attitude on the part of the courts resulting from what would technically be a revolution. Parliament could not, of course, confer this authority on itself. Thus the first Acts passed by the Convention Parliaments of 1660[54] and 1689,[55] legalising their own authority, confirmed the result of revolutions; and the American Colonies Act 1766,[56] asserting the full power and authority of Parliament to make laws binding on the American colonies, was merely declaratory.

On the other hand a state may be a sovereign state and yet have a legislature which is not unlimited and courts with jurisdiction to review its legislation. Thus the 1947 Constitution of Ceylon (an independent sovereign state within the Commonwealth) required for its amendment the Speaker's certificate that not less than two-thirds of the members of the House of Representatives voted in favour. It was held by the Privy Council in *Bribery Commissioner* v. *Ranasinghe*[57] that the Bribery Tribunal by which the respondent had been convicted was not lawfully appointed, because the Act under which it was appointed was passed by the ordinary legislative procedure, whereas it required a constitutional amendment relating to the appointment of judicial officers. This is also the principle that emerges from the South African case *Harris* v. *Minister of the Interior* ("the Cape coloured voters case"),[58] in so far as that case is relevant to the present context. The question in issue was the validity of the Separate Representation of Voters Act 1951, which was passed by the two Houses sitting separately and thus infringed section 152 of the South Africa Act 1909, which Act formed the basis of the Constitution. This section provided that no repeal or alteration of section 35 (qualification of Cape coloured voters) should be valid unless the Bill was passed by both Houses sitting together and the third reading was agreed to by not less than two-thirds of the members of both Houses. It was held by the Appellate Division of the Supreme Court of South Africa that the Separate Representation of Voters Act was invalid as the South Africa Act was a superior law to the Union Parliament, which it created. Whether the Union Parliament was called a "sovereign" legislature was a matter of definition: the Parliament functioning bicamerally was restricted in certain respects, but anything it could not do in that way could be done by a two-thirds majority in the Parliament functioning unicamerally.[59]

The legislative supremacy of the British Parliament, as well as being a legal concept, is also the result of political history and is ultimately based on fact, that is, general recognition by the people and the courts. It is therefore at the same time a legal and a political principle.[60]

The doctrine of the legislative supremacy of Parliament has been so

---

[54] Parliament Act 1660.
[55] Crown and Parliament Recognition Act 1689.
[56] Repealed by the Statute Law Revision Act 1964.
[57] [1965] A.C. 172. Ceylon is now called Sri Lanka and has a new constitution.
[58] [1952] (2) A.D. 428; *sub nom. Harris* v. *Dönges* [1952] 1 T.L.R. 1245. See D. V. Cowen, *Parliamentary Sovereignty and the Entrenched Sections of the South Africa Act* (1951).
[59] The desired legislation was eventually passed by changing the composition of the Senate; see *Collins* v. *Minister of the Interior* [1957] (1) A.D. 552.
[60] Professor H. L. A. Hart calls it "the ultimate rule of recognition," which may be regarded both as an external statement of fact and as an internal criterion of validity; *The Concept of Law*, p. 108.

firmly established that it has scarcely been challenged in the courts. When Canon Selwyn made an application questioning the validity of the Royal Assent to the Irish Church Disestablishment Act 1869 as being inconsistent with the Coronation Oath and the Act of Settlement, Cockburn C.J. and Blackburn J. in refusing the application said: "There is no judicial body in the country by which the validity of an act of parliament can be questioned. An act of the legislature is superior in authority to any court of law . . . , and no court could pronounce a judgment as to the validity of an act of parliament" (*ex p. Selwyn*).[61] In *Vauxhall Estates Ltd.* v. *Liverpool Corporation*[62] and *Ellen Street Estates Ltd.* v. *Minister of Health*[63] counsel unsuccessfully argued that a later Act could not repeal the provisions of an earlier Act, with which it was inconsistent, except by express words. That contention, said Scrutton L.J. in the latter case, "is absolutely contrary to the constitutional position." In *Hall* v. *Hall*[64] the plaintiff claimed that the Probate Act 1857, on which the defendant based the title to a house, had not really received the Royal Assent as he challenged the Royal Succession from the days of James II. The county court judge said he could not ignore a statute that had been acted on for more than eighty years, and that in any event Parliament could validate all titles by passing an Indemnity Act.

In *R.* v. *Jordan*[65] J, who had been sentenced to imprisonment for offences under the Race Relations Act 1965, applied for legal aid to enable him to apply for habeas corpus on the ground that the Race Relations Act was invalid as being in curtailment of free speech. The Divisional Court, dismissing the application, held that Parliament was supreme and there was no power in the courts to question the validity of an Act of Parliament, adding that the ground of the application was completely unarguable. In *Cheney* v. *Conn*[66] a taxpayer contended that the Finance Act 1964 conflicted with the Geneva Conventions incorporated in the Geneva Conventions Act 1957, and that it was contrary to international law that part of his tax should go to the construction of nuclear weapons. Ungoed-Thomas J. held that there was no conflict between the two Acts; the Finance Act prevailed over international convenions, which are an executive act of the Crown; and that what Parliament enacts cannot be unlawful.

In *Martin* v. *O'Sullivan*[67] Nourse J. and the Court of Appeal refused to consider a claim that proceedings in the House of Commons during the passage of the bill which became the Social Security Act 1975 were invalid because the members of the House were all disqualified from sitting. There was, according to the judges, a fundamental answer to this case, namely, that a court could only look at the parliamentary roll of statutes and if it appeared that an Act had passed both Houses of Parliament and had received the Royal Assent it could look no further.

[61] (1872) 36 J.P. 54.
[62] [1932] 1 K.B. 733 (D.C.) *post*, p. 61.
[63] [1934] 1 K.B. 590 (C.A.) *post*, p. 62.
[64] (1944) 88 S.J. 383 (Hereford C.C.). The judgment as reported appears to beg the question.
[65] [1967] Crim.L.R. 483; 9 J.P.Supp. 48.
[66] [1968] 1 W.L.R. 242.
[67] [1982] S.T.C. 416; [1984] S.T.C. 258 (C.A.).

In an appeal to the House of Lords in *Edinburgh and Dalkeith Ry.* v. *Wauchope*,[68] where it had been suggested in the Scottish court below that a private Act might not be applicable against a person whose rights were affected but who had not been given prior notice, Lord Campbell pronounced the following dictum: "All that a Court of Justice can do is to look to the Parliament roll: if from that it should appear that a Bill has passed both Houses and received the Royal Assent, no Court of Justice can enquire into the mode in which it was introduced into Parliament, nor into what was done previous to its introduction, or what passed in Parliament during its prgress in its various stages through both Houses." In another case concerning a private Act, *Lee* v. *Bude and Torrington Ry.*,[69] Willes J. said: "Acts of Parliament are the law of the land and we do not sit as a Court of Appeal from Parliament."[70]

The matter was fully reviewed again in relation to a private Act of Parliament by the House of Lords in *Pickin* v. *British Railways Board*,[71] where Pickin pleaded that the British Railways Act 1968 (c. xxxiv) contained a false recital, that the Board had misled Parliament by obtaining the Act *ex parte* as an unopposed Bill, and that it was therefore ineffective to deprive him of his land. Their Lordships held unanimously that the courts could not go behind private Acts to show that a provision should not be enforced, or examine proceedings in Parliament to show that the Board by fraudulently misleading Parliament, caused him loss. Lord Reid said that the law was correctly stated by Lord Campbell in

[68] (1842) 8 Cl. & F. 710; cited and followed, *Sillars* v. *Smith* 1982 S.L.T. 539; *post*, p. 66.
[69] (1871) L.R. & C.P. 576.
[70] Other judicial dicta that may be cited are: "The supremacy of Parliament. . . . That sovereign power can make and unmake the law": *per* Lord Denman C.J. in *Stockdale* v. *Hansard* (1839) 9 Ad. & E. 1; "Whereas . . . you may canvass a rule and determine whether or not it was within the power of those who made it, you cannot canvass in that way the provisions of an Act of Parliament": *per* Lord Herschell L.C. in *Institute of Patent Agents* v. *Lockwood* [1894] A.C. 347, 359; "For us an Act of Parliament duly passed by Lords and Commons and assented to by the King, is supreme and we are bound to give effect to its terms." *per* Lord Dunedin (Lord Justice General) in *Mortensen* v. *Peters* (1906) 8 F.(J.C.) 93, 100; "Parliament is omnipotent": *per* Vaughan Williams L.J. in *R.* v. *Local Government Board, ex p. Arlidge* [1914] 1 K.B. 160, 175–176; "Nothing we do or say could in any degree affect the complete power of the legislature by Act of Parliament to carry out the present scheme, or any other scheme": *per* Atkin L.J. in *R.* v. *Electricity Commissioners* [1924] 1 K.B. 171; "Parliament is supreme. It can enact extraordinary powers of interfering with personal liberty. If an Act of Parliament . . . is alleged to limit or curtail the liberty of the subject or vest in the executive extraordinary powers of detaining a subject, the only question is what is the precise extent of the powers given"; *per* Lord Wright in *Liversidge* v. *Anderson* [1942] A.C. 206; "Parliament has absolute sovereignty and can make new legal creatures if it likes"; *per* Scott L.J. in *National Union of General and Municipal Workers* v. *Gillian* [1946] 1 K.B. 81; "Parliament could do anything . . . being omnipotent": *per* Harman J. in *Hammersmith Borough Council* v. *Boundary Commission, The Times*, December 15, 1954. "The supremacy of Parliament . . . it is not for the Court to say that a parliamentary enactment, the highest law in this country, is illegal; *per* Ungoed—Thomas J. in *Cheney* v. *Conn* [1968] 1 W.L.R. 242, 247; "That central feature of our constitution, the sovereignty of Parliament." *per* Lord Simon of Glaisdale in *Jones* v. *Secretary of State for Social Services* [1972] A.C. 944: "The supremacy of Parliament was finally demonstrated by the revolution of 1688"; *per* Lord Reid; "parliamentary democracy. Its peculiar feature in constitutional law is the sovereignty of Parliament," *per* Lord Simon of Glaisdale.: *Pickin* v. *British Railways Board, supra.*
[71] [1974] A.C. 765. See P. Wallington, "Sovereignty Regained" (1974) 37 M.L.R. 686; and Chap. 10, *post*, for procedure in Private Bills.

Edinburgh v. *Dalkeith Ry.* v. *Wauchope* (*supra*): although that was *obiter* [*semble*, as regards public Acts] no one since 1842 had doubted it. The court had no concern with the manner in which Parliament, or its officers in carrying out its standing orders, performed their functions.

Examples of subject-matter

Examples of the positive aspect of the legislative supremacy of Parliament as regards subject-matter are the Septennial Act 1715, extending the maximum duration of the existing and future Parliaments from three to seven years; the Parliament Acts 1911 and 1949, restricting the power of the House of Lords to withhold its assent to public Bills (especially money Bills), and reducing the maximum duration of a Parliament to five years; the prolongation of its own life by annual Acts to eight years by the Parliament that passed the Act of 1911,[72] and annual prolongations during the last war of the life of the Parliament that was elected in 1935[73]; the Act of Settlement 1700, which regulated the succession to the throne on the failure of Queen Anne's issue, and His Majesty's Declaration of Abdication Act 1936, which varied that succession; the Union with Scotland Act 1706, by which the English Parliament extinguished itself and transferred its authority to the new Parliament of Great Britain; the Government of Ireland Act 1920 and the Irish Free State Agreement Act 1922, dissolving the union between Great Britain and Ireland (which had been created by the Union with Ireland Act 1800), setting up a subordinate legislature in Northern Ireland[74] and giving Dominion status to the Irish Free State[75]; the Defence of the Realm Acts and Emergency Powers (Defence) Acts of the two World Wars, conferring extremely wide—though temporary—powers on the government.[76] Parliament may legislate with retroactive effect if it wishes. Although it is presumed that legislation is not intended to be retrospective[77] "If Parliament wishes to enact retrospectively it can do so, provided it uses sufficiently plain words. The intention to legislate retrospectively need not be expressed provided that there is a very clear implication to that effect."[78] Acts of Indemnity may legalise, for example, acts which when they were done were illegal, such as the Housing Finance (Special Provisions) Act 1975, removing further surcharges arising out of the failure of the Clay Cross councillors to implement the Housing Finance Act 1972 and terminating any local electoral disqualification arising from such surcharges.[79] Invalid delegated legislation may be retrospectively validated.[80] Other notable

---

[72] Parliament and Local Elections Acts 1916, 1917 and 1918.
[73] Prolongation of Parliament Acts 1941, 1942, 1943 and 1944.
[74] *Ante* p. 18.
[75] Recognised as the independent Republic of Ireland by the Ireland Act 1949.
[76] See especially, Emergency Powers (Defence) No. 2 Act 1940, authorising Defence Regulations to make provision "for requiring persons to place themselves, their services and their property at the disposal of His Majesty."
[77] *Waddington* v. *Miah* [1974] 1 W.L.R. 683 (H.L.)
[78] *Tracomin S.A.* v. *Sudan Oil Seeds Co. Ltd.* [1983] 1 W.L.R. 1026, 1030 *per* Sir John Donaldson M.A. See also *Azam* v. *Secretary of State for the Home Dept.* [1974] A.C.18.
[79] J. E. Trice, "Rule of Law: Clay Cross," *New Law Journal*, April 4, 1974.
[80] National Health Service (Invalid Direction) Act 1980.

examples of retrospective legislation are the War Damage Act 1965,[81] and the Northern Ireland Act 1972 legalising retrospectively to 1920 the use of troops in Northern Ireland for certain civilian purposes.[82]

The absence of "fundamental" laws means, as we have seen in Chapter 2, that the courts have no jurisdiction to declare an Act of Parliament void as being *ultra vires* or "unconstitutional."

Composition

Parliament is also free to alter its own composition. The composition of the House of Commons may be affected by redistribution of seats, alteration of the franchise or changes in the disqualifications for membership. The composition of the House of Lords has been affected by extending the qualification of Scottish peers, and the creation of life peerages and Lords of Appeal. Parliament could confine membership of the House of Lords to life peers. Indeed, Parliament could abolish the House of Lords, perhaps without its own consent under the provisions of the Parliament Act[82a] and it could abolish the monarchy, though that would require the Royal Assent. It would be idle to speculate on the abolition of the House of Commons, as such an event postulates a completely different kind of constitution.

Persons and areas

With regard to persons and areas, since Parliament is the Parliament of the United Kingdom its Acts are presumed to apply to the United Kingdom and not to extend further. If an Act is not intended to apply to Wales,[83] Scotland or Northern Ireland, or if it is intended to apply outside the United Kingdom, *e.g.* to a colony, this must be expressly stated.[84] Thus the European Communities Act 1972 includes the United Kingdom, together with (for certain purposes) the Channel Islands, the Isle of Man and Gibraltar. Parliament can define the country's territory,[85] fishery limits,[86] and continental shelf.[87] It can penalise offences of an international or Community character,[88] the broadcasting of elec-

---

[81] Reversing the decision of the House of Lords as regards war damage in *Burmah Oil Co. v. Lord Advocate* [1965] A.C. 75.

[82] Other examples of retrospective legislation include Marriage Validation Acts, the War Charges (Validity) Act 1925, the Truck Act 1940, the Charitable Trusts (Validation) Act 1954, the Wireless Telegraphy (Validation of Charges) Act 1954, the Finance Act 1960, s.39(5) ("the foregoing provisions of this section shall be deemed always to have had effect"); Finance Act 1984, s.8 (increase of surtax rates for 1972–1973). The Social Security (Miscellaneous Provisions) Act 1977, s.14(8); noted [1979] P.L.58. The Representation of the People Act 1981, s.1, the Employment Act 1982, s.2 and the London Regional Transport (Amendment) Act 1985. And see A. L. Goodhart, "Ex Post Facto Penal Offences," in *United Nations Year Book on Human Rights* (1955).

[82a] But see Peter Mirfield, "Can the House of Lords Lawfully be Abolished?" (1979) 95 L.Q.R. 36; George Winterton, "Is the House of Lords Immortal?" (1979) 95 L.Q.R. 386.

[83] References to "England" in Acts of Parliament after 1967 no longer include Wales: Welsh Language Act 1967.

[84] *R. v. Martin* [1956] 2 Q.B. 272, *per* Devlin J.

[85] Island of Rockall Act 1972.

[86] Fishery Limits Act 1976, extending British fishing limits to 200 miles from the territorial sea baselines of the United Kingdom.

[87] Continental Shelf Act 1964.

[88] Aviation Security Act 1982; European Communities Act 1972, s.11.

tion propaganda from abroad,[89] the operation of private radio stations outside territorial waters,[90] and the destruction of animals and plants in Antarctica.[91]

The general principle, however, is expressed in the words of Donaldson L.J. in *R.* v. *West Yorkshire Coroner ex p. Smith*,[92]

> "Every Parliamentary draftsman writes on paper which bears the legend, albeit in invisible ink, 'This Act shall not have extra-territorial effect save to the extent that it expressly so provides.' The court knows this and they read it into every statute."

The presumption against a parliamentary intention to make acts done abroad by aliens triable as criminal offences by British courts is particularly strong.[93]

For obvious reasons Parliament does not generally attempt to legislate with regard to acts done in foreign territory.[94] Under the Foreign Jurisdiction Acts 1890–1913, however, the Crown has power to make laws for overseas territories over which it has acquired jurisdiction. Criminal jurisdiction may be exercised over British citizens for acts committed abroad, for example, in the cases of murder, manslaughter and bigamy, under the Offences Against the Person Act 1861, ss. 9 and 57 and in the case of any crime under the Merchant Shipping Act 1894, s. 686(1).[95] Increasingly it is necessary to have resort to legislation with extra-territorial effect to deal with terrorism and give effect to international convenions aimed at its eradication.[96] An unusual example of legislation with extra-territorial effect is the Protection of Trading Interests Act 1980 under which British firms trading abroad may be guilty of criminal offences if, contrary to a direction of the Secretary of State, they comply with instructions from foreign courts or officials when to do so would in the Secretary of State's view damage the trading interests of the United Kingdom.[97]

The application of legislation passed by the British Parliament to independent members of the Commonwealth is discussed later in Chapter 37.

Practical limitations
There are in practice, of course, factors which limit Parliament's ability to pass any laws it likes, or, rather, which limit the choice of

---

[89] Representation of the People Act 1983, s.92.

[90] Marine etc. Broadcasting (Offences) Act 1967; passed as a consequence of *R.* v. *Kent Justices, ex p. Lye* [1967] 2 K.B. 153 (D.C.); *Post Office* v. *Estuary Radio* [1967] 1 W.L.R. 1396 (C.A.).

[91] Antarctic Treaty Act 1967. Acts of this kind are usually based on international treaties.

[92] [1983] Q.B. 335. For other presumptions of constitutional importance in the interpretation of Acts of Parliament, see O. Hood Phillips, *A First Book of English Law* (7th ed.), Chap. 11.

[93] *Air India* v. *Wiggins* [1980] 1 W.L.R. 815 (H.L.).

[94] With regard to independent members of the Commonwealth see *post*, Chap. 37.

[95] *R.* v. *Kelly* [1982] A.C. 665.

[96] Aviation Security Act 1982; Suppression of Terrorism Act 1978; Internationally Protected Persons Act 1978; Taking of Hostages Act 1982.

[97] See further, *British Airways Bd.* v. *Laker Airways Ltd.* [1985] A.C. 58.

measures that the government puts before Parliament for approval. These factors are the concern of the political scientist rather than the student of constitutional law, but it is convenient to mention some of the more important ones briefly here.

The mandate or party manifesto

The government is expected to carry out the policy (if any) indicated at the last general election and is not expected to act contrary to that policy, according to the general and rather vague doctrine of the "mandate," which seems to have been invented in the latter part of the nineteenth century. But a government acts for the whole people, not only those who voted for their party. Ministers are servants of the Crown and members of Parliament are not delegates.[98] The government must remain flexible and deal with emergencies, so that it may be its duty to ignore or even to act against the mandate. In any case, a government that has been in power for some time must meet changing circumstances in all fields of the national life such as defence and the state of the economy, and is not expected to mark time because it has exhausted its "mandate," which may have been expressed in very general terms and which few electors (except professional politicians) read. In Sir Ivor Jennings's words: "The doctrine of the mandate is part of the political cant. It is a stick used by the Opposition to beat the Government. . . . The doctrine is, however, of importance. Though it must necessarily be vague and its operation a matter of dispute, it is recognised to exist."[99] (A fortiori a local authority cannot rely on the terms of its manifesto to avoid exercising discretionary powers vested in it in a reasonable manner.[1])

Public opinion

Parliament must also take account of the even vaguer concept of "public opinion." Public opinion expresses itself through the press, radio, television, trade unions, industrialists, local councillors, party organisations and in countless other ways. The manner in which it is interpreted by the government and other members of Parliament must obviously affect Parliament's activities, including the passing of legislation. The moral ideas and ideals of the community, especially as expressed through the leaders of the Churches, make their influence felt. The strength of the Opposition—although ex hypothesi a minority in the Commons—is a variable factor, but in our system of parliamentary government the official Opposition must always be taken into respectful account. The government's legislative proposals must stand up to debate, the debates will be reported in the press or be available in Hansard, and the government must remember that within a few years at most it will have to face another general election.

---

[98] Labour Prime Ministers have so far successfully resisted the claim of the National Executive Committee that a Labour Government is bound by the party manifesto.

[99] Jennings, Cabinet Government (3rd ed.), p. 505. See also C. S. Emden, The People and the Constitution (2nd ed.); G. H. L. Le May, "Parliament, the Constitution and the 'Doctrine of the Mandate' " (1957) 74 South African Law Journal 33.

[1] Bromley L.B.C. v. G.L.C. [1982] 2 W.L.R.62 (C.A.); [1983] 1 A.C. 768.

Consultation of organised interests

In modern times the government does not in practice introduce legislation affecting well-defined sections of the community without first consulting organisations of the groups specially concerned or interested ("pressure groups"). In matters affecting industry or trade, for example, the Minister proposing to initiate legislation would consult the employers' associations, chambers of commerce and the trade unions, notably the officers of the Trade Unions Congress[2] and the Confederation of British Industry. The National Farmers Union would be consulted in matters affecting agriculture. Any reorganisation of local government would involve discussions with the associations representing the different kinds of local authorities. Professional associations would expect to be consulted in any matter that concerned their professions. Thus the introduction of the National Health Service would have been impossible without the co-operation of the General Medical Council, and reforms in legal procedure would be preceded by discussions with the Bar Council and the Law Society. Societies promoting causes, such as the Howard League for Penal Reform and the R.S.P.C.A., would also be consulted where appropriate.[3]

There is no general legal duty to consult. Still less is the Minister bound to accept the advice given, which will often be conflicting anyway. The practice is to discuss the general principles of the proposed legislation, rather than the draft Bill.[4]

International Law

The principles of International law are said to be part of the law of England,[5] but treaties do not automatically become part of English law.[6] International law as such does not bind Parliament, although the activities of Parliament are in fact restrained by considerations of international law and the comity of nations.[7] There is a presumption that Parliament does not intend to legislate contrary to the principles of international law, and a statute would be interpreted as far as possible so as not to conflict with them[8]; but the legal power of Parliament to make laws contrary thereto remains,[9] and redress would have to be sought by diplomatic action and not through the courts. Where a statute is clear and unambiguous the "comity of nations" is irrelevant (per Lord Porter in Theophile v. Solicitor-General[10]), its provisions must be fol-

---

[2] Ross M. Martin, T.U.C. The Growth of a Pressure Group 1868–1976 (1980).

[3] See F. E. Finer, Anonymous Empire (2nd ed.).

[4] Sir Ivor Jennings, Parliament (2nd ed.), Chap. 7.

[5] For a discussion of the doctrines of "incorporation" and "transformation," see per Lord Denning M.R. in Trendtex Trading Corp. v. Central Bank of Nigeria [1977] Q.B. 529 (C.A.).

[6] McWhirter v. Att.-Gen. [1972] C.M.L.R. 882; (C.A.) per Lord Denning M.R.

[7] See Cheney v. Conn [1968] 1 W.L.R. 242, ante, p. 52, Chung Chi Cheung v. The King [1939] A.C. 160, 167–168 (P.C.) per Lord Atkin; Holdsworth, "The Relation of English Law to International Law" Essays in Law and History, p. 260; History of English Law, Vol. XIV, pp. 22–33.

[8] The Zamora [1916] A.C. 77 (P.C.); Co-operative Committee on Japanese Canadians v. Att.-Gen. for Canada [1974] A.C. 87, 104 (P.C.); cf. Polites v. The Commonwealth (1945) 70 C.L.R. 60 (High Ct. Austr.).

[9] Cf. Sovereignty within the Law, by Arthur Larson, C. Wilfred Jenks and Others (1966).

[10] [1950] A.C. 186, 195.

lowed even if they are contrary to international law (*per* Viscount Simonds in *I.R.C.* v. *Collco Dealings Ltd.*),[11] for the sovereign power of Parliament extends even to breaking treaties (*per* Diplock L.J. in *Salomon* v. *Customs and Excise Commissioners*[12]).

This principle is well illustrated by the case of *Mortensen* v. *Peters*.[13] Mortensen, a Danish citizen and captain of a Norwegian trawler, was convicted by the High Court of Justiciary of infringing the Herring Fishery (Scotland) Act 1889, which forbad trawling in the Moray Firth, although the acts done took place outside the three-mile limit. Diplomatic representations were made to the Foreign Office, and the Crown remitted the fine, although it recognised that the Court was right to apply the Act of Parliament. Shortly afterwards an Act was passed[14] providing that prosecutions should not be brought under the Act of 1889 for trawling outside the three-mile limit, but that fish caught by prohibited methods might not be landed or sold in the United Kingdom. And in *R.* v. *Secretary of State for Home Department, ex p. Thakrar*,[15] where an Asian British protected person, who had been expelled from Uganda, claimed the right to enter the United Kingdom, the Court of Appeal held that any rule of international law requiring a state to receive its nationals expelled by another State was expressly excluded by the Immigration Act 1971.

The special aspects of Community law are discussed in the following two chapters and the European Convention on Human Rights in Chapter 22.

---

[11] [1962] A.C. 1 (H.L.).
[12] [1967] 2 Q.B. 116 (C.A.).
[13] (1906), 8 F 93, *per* Lord Dunedin, Lord-Justice General. The ship was in fact British owned, but was given a foreign master and registration with a view to evading the Scottish fishery regulations.
[14] Trawling in Prohibited Areas Prevention Act 1909.
[15] [1974] Q.B. 684: anyway, such a rule between states could not be invoked by an individual.

CHAPTER 4

PARLIAMENTARY SUPREMACY II: PROBLEM OF
SELF-LIMITATION[1]

The problem of self-limitation

The problem raised in this chapter is that known to logicians as self-referring or reflexive propositions. The view put forward here is that it is impracticable for a legislature to limit itself as to the laws it shall make[2] or repeal unless it is empowered, expressly or impliedly, so to limit itself by some "higher law," that is, some (logically and historically) prior law *not laid down by itself*.[3] If our courts were to recognise any limitation on the power of Parliament to pass statutes applicable within the United Kingdom, dealing with (say) the constitutional status of Northern Ireland or Community law or civil rights, there would have to be some juridical reason for such decision. In British constitutional law, what could be such a reason?

One of three possible higher laws might be suggested: (i) a supreme Constitution, that is, a written Constitution (not enacted by Parliament itself) containing provisions entrenched against alteration by (ordinary) Act of Parliament; (ii) the primacy of International law, including Community treaties, or (iii) natural law. However, we have seen in Chapter 2 that the first (a written Constitution with entrenched provisions) does not exist. As Lord Pearce said in *Bribery Commissioner* v. *Ranasinghe*[4]: "in the Constitution of the United Kingdom there is no governing instrument which prescribes the lawmaking powers and the forms which are essential to those powers." In Chapter 3 we have seen that

---

[1] Dicey *Law of the Constitution* (10th ed.), pp. 64–70; Anson, *Law and Custom of the Constitution*, Vol. 1 (5th ed. Gwyer), pp. 7–8; H. W. R. Wade, "The Basis *of Legal Sovereignty* [1955] C.L.J. 172, and review in [1954] C.L.J. 265; Hood Phillips, *Reform of the Constitution* (1970), pp. 151–156; "Self-Limitation by the United Kingdom Parliament" (1975) 2 *Hastings Constitutional Law Quarterly*, 443.
   Cf. Sir Ivor Jennings, *The Law and the Constitution* (5th ed.), Chap. 4; D. V. Cowen, "Legislature and Judiciary: Reflections on the Constitutional Issues in South Africa" (1952) 15 M.L.R. 282; (1953) 16 M.L.R. 273; B. Beinart, Parliament and the Courts" [1954] *South African Law Review* 135; G. Marshall, *Parliamentary Sovereignty and the Commonwealth* (1957), Chap. 4, and *Constitutional Theory* (1971) Chap. 3; R. F. V. Heuston, *Essays in Constitutional Law* (2nd ed., 1964), Chap. 1; J. D. B. Mitchell, *Constitutional Law* (2nd ed., 1968), Chap. 4; George Winterton, "The British Grundnorm: Parliamentary Supremacy Re-examined" (1976) 92 L.Q.R. 591.
[2] The Taxation of Colonies Act 1778, for removing all doubts and apprehensions, provided, that after the passing of the Act Parliament would not impose any taxes on the colonies in North America and the West Indies, except such duties as might be expedient for the regulation of commerce and for the use of the colony concerned.
[3] See Alf Ross, "On Self-Reference and a Puzzle of Constitutional Law" (1969) 78 *Mind*; Hans Kelsen, *General Theory of Law and State* (1945), pp. 124–128. *Cf.* H. L. A. Hart, *The Concept of Law* (1961) pp. 144–148 *et seq.* distinguishing between *continuing* omnipotence (sovereignty) and *self-embracing* omnipotence (sovereignty): "it is clear that the presently accepted rule is one of continuing sovereignty so that Parliament cannot protect its statutes from repeal."
[4] [1965] A.C. 172 (P.C.).

judicial authority is strongly against the second (primacy of International law, including treaties),[5] and there is no judicial decision in favour of the third (natural law).

The question may be illustrated in relation, first, to the subject-matter of legislation, and, secondly, to the "manner and form" of legislation.

I. Subject-Matter of Legislation

Repeal or amendment

The Treason Act 1495, which was passed to protect subjects who had served a *de facto* king from being impeached or attainted for treason under some future *de jure* king, either by the course of law or by Act of Parliament, provided that if any such Act of Attainder were to be passed, it should be void and of no effect. Bacon wrote[6] that the latter provision was illusory. "For a supreme and absolute power cannot conclude itself, neither can that which is in its nature revocable be made fixed"; and Coke wrote[7] that the Act would be applicable to ordinary prosecutions for treason, but would not restrain any parliamentary attainder. Henry VIII procured an Act in 1536[8] enabling future kings to revoke any Acts passed while they were under the age of 24 years. This Act was repealed in the first year of Edward VI,[9] when he was 10 years old, the royal assent being given by the Protector, Somerset, and the Council consisting of Henry's executors.

Coke introduces a section of his *Institutes* with the heading: "Acts against the power of the Parliament subsequent bind not . . . for it is a matter in the law of the Parliament, *quod leges posteriores priores contrarias abrogant.*"[10] In *Godden* v. *Hales*[11] Herbert C.J. said: "if an Act of Parliament had a clause in it that it should never be repealed, yet without question, the same power that made it may repeal it." It is true that Parliament apparently thought it necessary in 1705 to pass two Acts[12] in order to naturalise Princess Sophia, Electress of Hanover (who was abroad), without her having to take the oath of allegiance at Westminster as required by the Naturalisation Act 1609; but it is submitted that one Act would have been sufficient, the Act of 1609 being regarded not as binding Parliament itself until repealed or amended but as being directed towards petitioners and officials. The Meeting of Parliament 1694 provided: "That from henceforth no Parliament whatsoever . . . shall have any continuance longer than for three years only at the farthest." Yet at the time of the Jacobite rising Parliament enacted in the

---

[5] For an argument in favour of the primacy of International law, see Hans Kelsen, *The Pure Theory of Law* (2nd ed., transl. Max Knight, 1967), Chap. 7.

[6] *History of Henry VII* (1622), p. 133.

[7] Co. Inst. 43.

[8] 28 Hen. VIII, c.17.

[9] 1 Edw. VI, c. 11. The repealing Act still allowed the king to revoke statutes passed while he was under 24 years of age, but such revocation was not to have retrospective effect.

[10] 2 Co. Inst. 685: "Later laws abrogate prior laws that are contrary to them"; and *Dr. Foster's Case* (1615), 11 Co.Rep. 56b, 62b.

[11] (1686) 11 St.Tr. 1165, 1197.

[12] 4 & 5 Anne, c. 14 and c. 16. See *Att.-Gen.* v. *Prince Ernest Augustus of Hanover* [1957] A.C. 436, *per* Viscount Simonds.

Septennial Act 1715[13]; "That this present Parliament and all Parliaments that shall at any time henceforth be called assembled or held shall and may have continuance for seven years and no longer" unless sooner dissolved by the Crown. This extension of the life of the existing Parliament as well as future Parliaments did in fact meet considerable opposition in both Houses, and the controversy over it outside Parliament continued for many years.

Blackstone, who quoted Coke's statement (*supra*), says[14]: "Acts of Parliament derogatory from the power of subsequent parliaments bind not. . . . Because the legislature being in truth the sovereign power, is always of equal, always of absolute authority: it acknowledges no superior upon earth, which the prior legislature must have been, if its ordinances could bind a subsequent parliament. And upon the same principle Cicero, in his letters to Atticus, treats with a proper contempt these restraining clauses, which endeavour to tie up the hands of succeeding legislators. 'When you repeal the law itself,' says he, 'you at the same time repeal the prohibitory clause, which guards against such repeal.' " Dicey[15] followed this tradition. Many readers have formed the view that it is an exception to what these writers called the "sovereignty" of Parliament; but the apparent paradox is verbal only, as will be seen if the proposition is expressed the other way round: "Parliament is not bound by its predecessors." Indeed the marginal note in Coke's *Institutes* reads: "Subsequent Parliaments cannot be restrained by the former."

As has been suggested in the previous chapter, it is preferable to use the expression "legislative supremacy" rather than "sovereignty" in relation to Parliament's lawmaking power. In either event the power of *express* repeal is so well established that it has never been contested in the courts. "It is good constitutional doctrine," said Lord Reid extrajudicially,[16] "that Parliament cannot bind its successors."

There are two cases, however, in which it has been argued by counsel that a provision in an earlier Act precluded *implied* repeal in a later Act. The Acquisition of Land (Assessment of Compensation) Act 1919, s.7(1), stated: "The provisions of the Act or order by which the land is authorised to be acquired . . . shall . . . have effect subject to this Act, and so far as inconsistent with this Act those provisions shall cease to have or shall not have effect . . . ." The marginal note (which is not binding) to section 7 reads: "Effect of Act on existing enactments." In *Vauxhall Estates Ltd.* v. *Liverpool Corporation*[17] the plaintiffs claimed that compensation for land compulsorily acquired from them should be assessed on the basis of the Act of 1919 and not on the less favourable terms provided by the Housing Act 1925. The Divisional Court held that even if the Act of 1919 could be construed as intended to govern future as well as existing Acts assessing compensation, which construction was doubtful, yet the relevant provisions must be regarded as impliedly

---

[13] Amended by Parliament Act 1911, s.7, reducing the maximum life of Parliament to five years.
[14] 1 Bl. Comm. 90–91.
[15] *Loc. cit.*
[16] "The Judge as Law Maker" (1972) 12 J.S.P.T.L. 22, 25.
[17] [1932] 1 K.B. 733.

overridden by the inconsistent provisions of the Act of 1925. In *Ellen Street Estates Ltd.* v. *Minister of Health*[18] a similar argument on the relation between the provisions for compensation contained in the Act of 1919 and the Housing Act 1925 and 1930 was raised in the Court of Appeal. Here the decision that the Housing Acts impliedly repealed the Act of 1919 in so far as they were inconsistent with it was part of the ratio. "The Legislature cannot, according to our constitution," said Maugham L.J., "bind itself as to the form of subsequent legislation, and it is impossible for Parliament to enact that in a subsequent statute dealing with the same subject-matter there can be no implied repeal. If in a subsequent Act Parliament chooses to make it plain that the earlier statute is being to some extent repealed, effect must be given to that intention just because it is the will of the Legislature."

Three topics call for special treatment in this context, namely, Acts of Union, Independence Acts conferring independence on countries that formerly came under the authority of Parliament, and the European Communities Act 1972. A fourth, the question of enacting a new "Bill of Rights" and whether it could be entrenched against repeal or amendment by ordinary Act of Parliament, is more conveniently discussed in Chapter 22.

Acts of Union

Union with Ireland

The Union with Ireland was negotiated by commissioners,[19] and based on Acts of the British and Irish Parliaments[20] in response to messages from the Crown. The Union with Ireland Act 1800, passed by the British Parliament, provided that the Kingdoms of Great Britain and Ireland should be united "for ever" into one Kingdom, by the name of the United Kingdom of Great Britain and Ireland; and that the United Kingdom should be represented in one and the same Parliament. It further provided that the government and doctrine of the United Church of England and Ireland should be and should remain "for ever" assimilated to those of the existing Church of England, and that the continuance of the United Church should be deemed "an essential and fundamental part" of the Union of the two Kingdoms. Nevertheless, the Church of Ireland was disestablished by the Irish Church Act 1869,[21] some 50 years before the political Union itself was partly dissolved by the creation of the Irish Free State. Although there was much opposition in this country to the disestablishment of the Church of Ireland, it does not seem to have been based on the theory that the union of the Churches was legally indissoluble. Similarly, the difficulties preceding the separation of the Irish Free State from the United Kingdom by the Irish Free State (Constitution) Act 1922 were political and not legal. The

---

[18] [1934] 1 K.B. 590; approving *Vauxhall Estates Ltd.* v. *Liverpool Corporation supra*, *Cf.* F.M. Auburn, "Trends in Comparative Constitutional Law" (1972) 35 M.L.R. 129.
[19] There was no formal treaty between Great Britain and Ireland.
[20] Union with Ireland Act 1800.
[21] *Ex p. Selwyn* (1872) 36 J.P. 54; *ante*, p. 51.

main part of section 5, constituting the United Church of England and Ireland, was repealed in 1953.[22]

When the secession of Eire (the Republic of Ireland) from the Commonwealth was recognised by the United Kingdom Parliament in the Ireland Act 1949 the following declaration was inserted in section 1(2): "It is hereby declared that Northern Ireland remains part of His Majesty's dominions and of the United Kingdom, and it is hereby affirmed that in no event will Northern Ireland or any part thereof cease to be part of His Majesty's dominions and of the United Kingdom without the consent of the Parliament of Northern Ireland."

This provision was confirmed by the Northern Ireland (Temporary) Provisions Act 1972, which suspended the Parliament of Northern Ireland. Then the Northern Ireland Constitution Act 1973 abolished the Northern Ireland Parliament and replaced it by an Assembly, declaring and affirming in section 1 that in no event would Northern Ireland or any part thereof cease to be part of His Majesty's dominions and of the United Kingdom without the consent of the majority of the people of Northern Ireland voting in a poll held for this purpose.[23] The Northern Ireland Act 1974 then abolished the Assembly, provided for the holding of a constitutional Convention (now extinct), and preserved the declaration in the 1973 Act with the provision for a referendum.[24] It appears that: (i) if the requirement in the 1949 Act for the consent of the Northern Ireland Parliament were binding on the United Kingdom Parliament, the provisions of the 1973 Act could not have been passed in the proper form; (ii) if the declaration in the 1949 Act were binding on Parliament, there would be no need to confirm it in 1972; and (iii) if the declaration in the 1973 Act were binding there would be no need to confirm it in 1974.

These declarations, it is submitted, should be regarded as expressions of intention and establishing a constitutional convention, based on agreement and analogous to that applying to self-governing colonies.[25]

Union with Scotland[26]

The Union was preceded by a treaty negotiated by the Parliaments of England and Scotland through commissioners. The Articles of Union

[22] Statute Law Revision Act 1953.

[23] A referendum was held in Northern Ireland in 1973 and a large majority of those voting favoured staying in the United Kingdom.

[24] Northern Ireland has been governed by "direct rule" from Westminster since 1974.

[25] Cf. Lord MacDermott, "The Decline of the Rule of Law" (1972) 23 N.I.L.Q. 474, 493, who suggests that the constitutional Acts relating to (Northern) Ireland from 1800 may together constitute a fundamental law, and it is arguable that the United Kingdom Parliament has no power to alienate the allegiance or reduce the status of the people of Northern Ireland. And see H. Calvert's "very tentative" arguments in Constitutional Law of Northern Ireland (1968), Chap. 1.

[26] Dicey and Rait, Thoughts on the Union between England and Scotland (1920) G.M. Trevelyan, Ramillies and the Union with Scotland, Chaps. 12–14. Cf. T.B. Smith in The British Commonwealth, Vol. 1, Part II, Scotland, pp. 641–650; "The Union of 1707 as Fundamental Law" [1957] P.L. 99; British Justice: The Scottish Contribution (1961), pp. 201–213. J.D.B. Mitchell, "Sovereignty of Parliament—Yet Again" (1963) 79 L.Q.R. 196; Lord Kilbrandon, "A Background to Constitutional Reform" (Holdsworth Club, University of Birmingham, 1975).

were ratified first by the Scottish Parliament ("Estates") which also passed Acts for securing the Presbyterian Church government and concerning the election of Scottish representatives to the Parliament of Great Britain, which Acts were to be part of the terms of the Union. Then the English Parliament ratified the terms approved by the Scottish Estates, together with an Act for the security of the Church of England. While Englishmen refer to the English Act of Union, Scotsmen tend to refer to the "Treaty."

The Union with Scotland Act 1706, passed by the English Parliament, provided that the two Kingdoms of England and Scotland should for ever after be united into one Kingdom by the name of Great Britain (Art. I); the United Kingdom of Great Britain should "be represented by one and the same Parliament" to be styled the Parliament of Great Britain (Art. III); that (subject to a common public law) Scots law was to remain as before but alterable by the Parliament of Great Britain, except that no alterations should be made "in laws which concern private right except for evident utility of the subjects within Scotland" (Art. XVIII). Article XIX preserved the Court of Session and Court of Justiciary as superior Scottish courts in all time coming, subject to regulations made by the Parliament of Great Britain for better administration of justice. The Act incorporated an Act for securing the Protestant religion and Presbyterian Church governments in Scotland, paragraph 2 of which required professors of Scottish universities to subscribe to the Confession of Faith (a religious test), and paragraph 4 of which states that this Act with the establishment therein contained "shall be held and observed in all time coming as a fundamental and essential condition of any treaty or union to be concluded betwixt the two Kingdoms without any alteration thereof or derogation thereto in any sort for ever."

It was clearly intended that the Union itself should be permanent, and that certain provisions—concerning, or mainly concerning, the Scottish Church—should be unalterable. The Church Patronage (Scotland) Act 1711,[27] repealing a Scottish Act and restoring lay patronage in Scotland, has been described as "the chief and almost the only example of an Act of the British Parliament passed in violation of the Act of Union," and is said to have been "opposed to the spirit, and probably the letter, of the Act of Union."[28] As early as 1713 a Bill to repeal the Union Act was introduced and nearly passed in the House of Lords.[29] The provision requiring professors at Scottish universities to subscribe to the Confession of Faith was repealed by the Universities (Scotland) Act 1853. With regard to changes in Scots private law, it is not certain whether Parliament or the Scottish courts are supposed to have the power to determine whether they are for the "evident utility" of Scottish citizens.

In *Gibson* v. *Lord Advocate*[30] G. sought a declaration that section 2(1) of

---

[27] 10 Anne, c. 21.
[28] Dicey and Rait, *op. cit.* pp. 280–281.
[29] Dicey and Rait, *op. cit.* pp. 298–300.
[30] 1975 S.L.T. 134; [1975] 1 C.M.L.R. 563 (Outer House, Court of Session); *post*, p. 110. And see J.M. Thomson "Community Law, the Act of Union, and the Supremacy of Parliament" (1976) 92 L.Q.R. 36; A.W. Bradley, "Scots Private Law—'Evident Utility,' " in *Devolution* (Essays, ed. H. Calvert, 1975), p. 101.

the European Communities Act 1972 was contrary to Article XVIII of the Act of Union, and therefore null and void, in so far as it purported to enact as part of the law of Scotland certain Community Regulations providing for equal treatment of Member States with regard to fishing in maritime waters. He argued that, immediately before the Act of Union, Scottish subjects had exclusive fishing rights in Scottish coastal waters; that the laws conferring these rights concerned "private right," and that the Community Regulations were not "for the evident utility of the subjects within Scotland." Lord Keith dismissed the action on the grounds, first, that the action was incompetent in seeking consideration of the utility of an Act of Parliament and, secondly, that Community Regulations operate in the field of public and not private law. His Lordship stated that the question whether an Act purporting to alter a particular aspect of Scots private law was for "evident utility" of the subjects within Scotland (Art. XVIII) is not justiciable in the courts; but he reserved his opinion on the question whether the court would have jurisdiction where an Act purported to abolish the Court of Session or the Church of Scotland, or to substitute English law for the whole body of Scots private law.

The most significant question is whether Parliament has power to repeal or radically amend the provisions relating to the Presbyterian Church in Scotland. The orthodox view, at any rate among English writers, is that at the Union the English and Scottish Parliaments extinguished themselves and at the same time transferred their powers to the new Parliament of Great Britain, and it is assumed that the Parliament of Great Britain inherited and developed the characteristics of the English Parliament, including sovereignty.[31] If so, this means that the United Kingdom Parliament, although morally bound by the terms of the Union with regard to the Scottish Church, might legally repudiate them.[32] In the Scottish courts, however, doubt has been expressed whether this view is sound. *MacCormick* v. *Lord Advocate*[33] (the "Royal Numeral Case") arose out of the official use in Scotland of the title "Elizabeth II," which was adopted by royal proclamation under a power conferred by the Royal Titles Act 1953. The Court of Session held that the Treaty did not prohibit the use of the numeral, and that the petitioners had no legal title or interest to sue. Either of these reasons would have been sufficient for the decision, but the Court added obiter that it was not satisfied that the Royal Titles Act would be conclusive if it had been repugnant to the Treaty, although in any event the court would have no jurisdiction to review a governmental act of this kind. "The principle of the unlimited sovereignty of Parliament," said Lord Cooper, "is a distinctively English principle which has no counterpart

---

[31] It is commonly said that the Scottish Parliament was not recognised as having sovereignty; but *cf.* Erskine, *Inst.* i, 1, 19; Bk. 1, Tit. IV, 61.

[32] So Blackstone, *Commentaries,* Introduction, para. 4 note; Austin, *The Province of Jurisprudence Determined* (ed.Hart) Lecture 6, pp. 256–257; Maitland, *Constitutional History,* p. 332. Dicey and Rait, *op. cit.* 252–254 thought that the declaration concerning the Scottish Church, though not a legal limitation represented a moral restriction and a warning.

[33] 1953 S.C. 396; 1953 S.L.T. 255. See T.B. Smith, "Two Scots Cases" (1953) 69 L.Q.R. 512–516.

in Scottish constitutional law. . . . I have difficulty in seeing why it should have been supposed that the new Parliament of Great Britain must inherit all the peculiar characteristics of the English Parliament but none of the Scottish Parliament, as if all that happened in 1707 was that Scottish representatives were admitted to the Parliament of England." Here we have Scottish obiter dicta to the effect that Parliament is bound by the fundamental terms of the Treaty (or Act of Union), although the effect of the dicta is considerably reduced by the admission "that there is neither precedent or authority of any kind for the view that the domestic courts of either Scotland or England" have jurisdiction to review governmental acts done under unconstitutional legislation, and *a fortiori* (presumably) to review the unconstitutional legislation itself.

In *Sillars* v. *Smith*,[34] where the validity of the Criminal Justice (Scotland) Act 1980 was challenged, the Lord Justice-Clerk (Wheatley) cited both *Edinburgh and Dalkeith Ry. Co.* v. *Wauchope*[35] and *MacCormick* v. *Lord Advocate* before concluding that the appellants' plea should be rejected, "based as it is on a submission that the Act of 1980 which had gone through all the parliamentary processes and received the Royal Assent is invalid."

But to hold that Parliament is bound by certain articles of the Union—whatever that may mean in the absence of a judicial power of review—raises difficulties that appear to be insoluble in legal terms. It implies that there is a fundamental law to which Parliament is subordinate. Then what happens if this subordinate Parliament infringes the fundamental law? To say that the Union would be terminated involves the assumption that England and Scotland are still separately identifiable nations. If Parliament cannot alter these fundamental terms, who can? There might come a time when the Presbyterian Church was no longer a majority church in Scotland. How can the wishes of the Scottish people be known? The Members of Parliament for Scottish constituencies are a minority in the Commons and they are not necessarily Scotsmen. There is no provision in the Treaty for appointing commissioners to negotiate a revision, or for holding a plebiscite in Scotland. As a matter of legal theory the conclusion must be that the doctrine of sovereignty or legislative supremacy has developed since the Union as a characteristic of the United Kingdom Parliament.[36] It is highly probable that the House of Lords in its judicial capacity would hold this view if the matter came before it, although there is no appeal from Scottish courts to the House of Lords in criminal cases.[37]

---

[34] 1982 S.L.T. 539.

[35] (1842) 8 Cl. & F. 710.

[36] D.G.T. Williams, "The Constitution of the United Kingdom," [1972B] C.L.J. 266, 270.

[37] Professor T.B. Smith ([1957] P.L. 99) argues that the twofold ratification constituted both a treaty *jure gentium* and a fundamental law for the Union, whereas the Acts of Parliament of each country bound the subjects within that country alone as ordinary legislation. The Treaty *qua* Treaty ceased to exist by merger of the parties at the Union. What is left, Professor Smith contends, is the "fundamental law" which cannot be altered except by (technical) revolution. On the question of judicial review, he admits that a private individual would seldom have a title to sue, and the Lord Advocate would presumably agree with the government of which he was a member.
Lord Kilbrandon, in "A background to Constitutional Reform," *loc. cit.* says the Treaty

Grants of Independence

Statute of Westminster 1931

Another problem (though scarcely of practical importance) is whether Parliament can continue to legislate for members (or former members) of the Commonwealth which have been granted independence. After the growth of conventions relating to self-governing colonies, the next legislative stage was section 4 of the Statute of Westminster 1931. This provides that an Act of the United Kingdom Parliament passed there-after shall not extend, or be deemed to extend, to a Dominion (as therein defined) as part of the law of that Dominion unless it is expressly declared in the Act concerned that that Dominion[38] has requested, and consented to, its enactment. The definition of "Dominion" for this pur-pose now covers Canada, Australia and New Zealand.[39] This provision enacted what was already an established convention, which was also recited in the preamble to the Statute. It is a statement of Parliament's intention, and also a direction to the courts, which are concerned only with the presence or absence of a declaration in the Act of a Dominion's request and consent. The Statute did not purport to terminate Parlia-ment's power to legislate for the Dominions altogether. It was contem-plated that such request and consent might still be forthcoming in particular cases, as happened, for example, in connection with Austra-lian and New Zealand emergency powers during the war and with the Cocos Islands Act 1955, which transferred the Cocos Islands to Austra-lia. Further, reservations were made with regard to the power of consti-tutional amendment in some of the Dominions, which they would otherwise have had under section 2, so that in 1964 Parliament amended the Canadian Constitution at Canada's request.[40] (Canada's legislative dependence on the United Kingdom was formally deter-mined by the Canada Act 1982, s.2.[41])

Lord Sankey L.C. in *British Coal Corporation* v. *The King*[42] said obiter that as a matter of "abstract law" Parliament could repeal this Statute either expressly or by passing legislation inconsistent with it; but he added, "that is theory and has no relation to realities." More recently, in *Blackburn* v. *Attorney-General*[43] Lord Denning M.R. went so far as to say obiter; "We have all been brought up to believe that, in legal theory, one Parliament cannot bind another and that no Act is irreversible. But legal theory does not always march alongside political reality. Take the

---

is now defunct since the independent countries of England and Scotland have ceased to exist, and its functions have been superseded by the Union Acts of the two Parlia-ments. If it is wrong to accept the unlimited sovereignty of the Parliament of Great Britain, he asks, where is the lawful machinery for putting the matter right?

[38] The request and consent required are those of the government of the Dominion con-cerned, and in the case of Australia those of its Parliament also.

[39] The Statute originally applied also to Newfoundland (now a province of Canada), and to South Africa and the Irish Free State (later Eire or the Republic of Ireland), which are no longer within the Commonwealth.

[40] British North America Act 1964, empowering the Canadian Parliament to legislate with regard to old age pensions.

[41] *Post*, p. 752. See also, *post* p. 754 for the Australian Act 1986.

[42] [1935] A.C. 500, 520; the case concerned Canadian legislation passed before the Statute of Westminster.

[43] [1972] C.M.L.R. 882 (C.A.).

Statute of Westminster 1931, which takes away the power of Parliament to legislate for the Dominions. Can anyone imagine that Parliament could or would reverse that Statute? Take the Acts which have granted independence to the Dominions and territories overseas. Can anyone imagine that Parliament could or would reverse these laws and take away their independence? Most clearly not. Freedom once given cannot be taken away.[44] Legal theory must give way to practical politics." But Salmon L.J. was content to remark; "As to Parliament, in the present state of the law, it can enact, amend and repeal any legislation it pleases."

The meaning and effect of section 4 of the Statute of Westminster was considered in *Manuel* v. *Attorney General*.[45] The plaintiffs sued on behalf of themselves and certain Indian "bands." They sought declarations to the effect that the United Kingdom Parliament had no power to amend the Canadian Constitution so as to prejudice the Indian Nations of Canada without their consent, and that the Canada Act 1982 was therefore *ultra vires*. Indian rights had been confirmed by a Royal Proclamation made in 1763, subsequently confirmed under a number of "treaties" made with the Indian bands and entrenched under the British North American Acts. The plaintiffs argued that the amendment of certain entrenched Indian rights still required United Kingdom legislation even after the British North America (No. 2) Act 1949 conferred on the Canadian Parliament a limited power of constitutional amendment. At first instance Sir Robert Megarry V.-C. held that once he was satisfied that the document before him was an Act of Parliament it was his duty to apply it. The Vice-Chancellor went on to consider the dictum of Lord Denning in *Blackburn* v. *Attorney General*, quoted in the previous paragraph. He commented that it was clear from the context that Lord Denning was using the word "could" in the sense of "could effectively," and not "could as a matter of abstract law." His Lordship added:

> "I have grave doubts about the theory of the transfer of sovereignty as affecting the competence of Parliament. In my view it is a fundamental of the English constitution that Parliament is supreme. As a matter of law the courts of England recognise Parliament as being omnipotent in all save the power to destroy its omnipotence. On the authority of Parliament the courts of a territory may be released from their legal duty to obey Parliament, but that does not trench on the acceptance by the English courts of all that Parliament does. Nor must validity in law be confused with practical enforceability."[46]

In the Court of Appeal, Slade L.J., delivering the judgment of the Court,

---

[44] An echo of the words of Stratford A.C.J. in *Ndlwana* v. *Hofmeyr* [1937] A.D. 229, 237, "Freedom once conferred cannot be revoked."
[45] [1983] Ch. 77. See O. Hood Phillips, "Statute of Westminster in the Courts" (1983) 99 L.Q.R. 342.
[46] [1983] Ch. 77, 89.

held that the Canada Act 1982 complied with the requirements of section 4 which

> "does not provide that no Act of the United Kingdom Parliament shall extend to a Dominion as part of the law of that Dominion unless the Dominion has in fact requested and consented to the enactment thereof. The condition that must be satisfied is a quite different one, namely, that it must be 'expressly declared in that Act that that Dominion has requested, and consented to, the enactment thereof.' . . . If an Act of Parliament contains an express declaration in the precise form required by section 4, such declaration is in our opinion conclusive as far as section 4 is concerned."[47]

The Court of Appeal did not therefore have to consider the effect of a failure to comply with the provisions of section 4.

If section 4 of the Statute of Westminster is regarded primarily as a rule of construction addressed to the courts,[48] it seems probable that British courts (if the question could be brought before them) would continue to regard Parliament as unrestricted by it, at least as far as the monarchies are concerned.[49] Section 4 refers to alteration of *the law of a Dominion*, not to alteration of *the law in this country*. As Lord Reid stated with reference to the Statute of Westminster in *Madzimbamuto* v. *Lardner-Burke*[50]: "It is often said it would be unconstitutional for the United Kingdom Parliament to do certain things, meaning that the moral, political and other reasons against doing them are so strong that most people would regard it as highly improper if Parliament did these things. But that does not mean that it is beyond the power of Parliament to do such things. If Parliament chose to do any of them the courts could not hold the Act of Parliament invalid." However, the courts of the country (former "Dominion") concerned (in so far as they could not construe such Act as not being intended to infringe the section) would presumably decline to apply an offending British statute, and an appeal to the Privy Council could be prevented or nullified by local legislation where such appeals have not already been abolished. And appeals from that country to the Privy Council would very soon be abolished. Such a divergence of judicial decisions in other parts of the Commonwealth from decisions in this country would be a reflection in the courts of a (technical) revolution that had already taken place in the political sphere.[51]

It has been suggested above that the local court would, if possible, construe an Act of Parliament as not being intended to apply to the

---

[47] At p. 106.

[48] See K. C. Wheare, *The Statute of Westminster and Dominion Status* (5th ed.), Chap. 6, s.3. And see further *post*, Chap. 37.

[49] A republic is not one of Her Majesty's dominions, and it may be that on this ground an Act of Parliament would not be construed as extending to it.

[50] [1969] 1 A.C. 645, 723 (P.C.).

[51] s.2(2) of the Statute of Westminster allows the Dominions to pass laws repugnant to United Kingdom legislation, but to say that this would enable the Dominions to nullify a repeal of the Statute begs the question.

Dominion, unless passed at its request and with its consent. This is borne out by *Copyright Owners Reproduction Society* v. *E.M.I. (Australia) Pty Ltd.*,[52] where the High Court of Australia held that Copyright Acts of 1928 and 1956 did not apply to Australia. Dixon C.J. said that even before 1931 there was a strong convention that the United Kingdom Parliament would not legislate for a Dominion without its consent: there was therefore in Australian courts a rule of construction that, in the absence of evidence of such consent, a United Kingdom Act was not intended to apply to that Dominion.

Independence Acts

The "Dominion status" of 1931, by the further development of constitutional conventions in relation to the countries concerned, has in effect become independence within the Commonwealth. The grant of independence to a number of former dependent territories from 1947 onwards has been done by separate Acts of Parliament. As regards legislative powers, the Independence Acts for Ceylon (1947) and Ghana (1957) followed the Statute of Westminster,[53] but the Act for Nigeria (1960) and those that followed did not contemplate that the country concerned would in future request the United Kingdom to legislate for it. The post-war Independence Acts have gone further than the Statute of Westminster by expressly divesting the United Kingdom Government of any responsibility for the government of those countries.

A distinction might be drawn between the mere transfer of the *legislative* powers of Parliament under the Statute of Westminster and the transfer also of the *governmental* powers of the United Kingdom under the post-war Independence Acts. Where in relation to a particular territory the sovereignty of the Crown as head of the United Kingdom Government has been transferred to a sovereign state, or in such a way as to make the transferee a sovereign state—recognised as such by other countries, and becoming a member of the United Nations—it seems absurd to say that Parliament can still legislate for such territory. Could Parliament cancel the cession of Heligoland to Germany,[54] or even repudiate the independence of the United States.[55] Nonetheless in the words of Sir Robert Megarry V.-C.

"Plainly once statute has granted independence to a country the

---

[52] (1958) 100 C.L.R. 597. The Acts concerned were the Copyright Order Confirmation (Mechanical Instruments: Royalties) Act 1928, and the Copyright Act 1956. The draftsmen of the 1956 Act indicated that the repeal of the Copyright Act 1911 was not intended to affect the law of any country other than the United Kingdom. And see H.R. Gray, "The Sovereignty of the Imperial Parliament" (1960) 23 M.L.R. 647.

[53] The Indian Independence Act 1947 followed the Status of the Union Act 1934 (South Africa) in providing that Acts of the United Kingdom Parliament would not extend thereto unless adopted by its own legislature.

[54] Anglo-German Agreement Act 1890. This Act was repealed by the Statute Law Revision Act 1953.

[55] An Act of 1782 (22 Geo. III, c.46) authorised the Crown to negotiate a truce with America, and by the Treaty of Paris 1783, signed between Great Britain and the United States, Britain acknowledged the United States to be free, sovereign and independent states; and relinquished all claims to the government of the same. Statutes of 1782 relating to trade with America and American loyalists (23 Geo. III, c. 26, 39, 80) implied that the United States were no longer British colonies: *Doe* d. *Thomas* v. *Acklam* (1824) 2 B. & C. 778.

repeat of the statute will not make the country dependent once more; what is done is done, and is not undone by revoking the authority to do it. Heligoland did not in 1953 again become British. But if Parliament then passes an Act applying to such a country I cannot see why that Act should not be in the same position as an Act applying to what has always been a foreign country, namely, an Act which the English courts will recognise and apply but one which the other country will in all probability ignore . . . "[56]

The distinction between the method used in 1931 and the method used after 1947, however, is probably no longer significant. When the courts recognise the political fact that territory formerly under the authority of Parliament has become independent of that authority, then Parliament can no longer alter the law in that territory; although it may pass laws in relation to persons or acts in such territory as in any other "foreign" country, which may be enforceable in the courts of this country.[57]

The legislative supremacy of Parliament, then, is a concept of British public law. It is recognised by the Courts of the United Kingdom[58] and its dependencies,[59] and is enforced by these courts in relation to persons and property which are or which come within their jurisdiction.

European Communities Act 1972[60]

The Treaties whereby the United Kingdom agreed to join the European Communities (the "Common Market") were executive acts, affecting the relations between the United Kingdom and the other member States. In order to provide for the consequent changes of law in this country an Act of Parliament was necessary.[61] This was the European Communities Act 1972, which is discussed more fully in the next chapter. Its main provisions are briefly as follows. Section 2(1) gives effect to rights and obligations created by or arising under the Treaties, *i.e.* created by the Treaties themselves and by existing and future Community Regulations which take effect directly as law in the Member

---

[56] *Manuel* v. *Att.-Gen.* [1983] Ch. 77, 88.

[57] *Ante*, pp. 54–55.

[58] But as to Scotland, *cf. ante*, p. 63.

[59] *i.e.* colonies and other dependencies from whose courts appeal lies to the Privy Council.

[60] *Legal and Constitutional Implications of United Kingdom Membership of the European Communities* Cmnd. 3301 (1967); *The United Kingdom and the European Communities* Cmnd. 4715 (1971): *Membership of the European Community: Report on Renegotiation* Cmnd. 6003 (1975).

Lawrence Collins, *European Community Law in the United Kingdom* (3rd ed., 1984) (But see also 1st ed. at pp. 1–21); D. Lasok and J. W. Bridge, *Introduction to the Law and Institutions of the European Communities* (3rd ed. 1982); T. Hartley, *Foundations of European Community Law* (1981); Geoffrey Howe, "The European Communities Act 1972 (1973) 49 *International Affairs*, 1; O. Hood Phillips, "Self-Limitation by the United Kingdom Parliament" (1975) *Hastings Constitutional Law Quarterly*, 443.

For different approaches see: S.A. de Smith "The Constitution and the Common Market" (1971) 34 M.L.R. 597; Mitchell, Kuipers and Gall, "Consitutional Aspects of the Treaty and Legislation relating to British Membership" (1972) C.M.L. Rev. 134; J.-P. Warner, "The Relationship between European Community Law and the National Laws of Member States" (1977) 93 L.Q.R. 349.

[61] *Case of Proclamations* (1610) 12 Co.Rep. 74; Bill of Rights 1688, art. 4.

States. (Enforceable Community Rights). With regard to future Community Regulations this was a constitutional innovation, introducing a new and special kind of secondary legislation.[62] Section 2(2) confers a limited power to give effect by Statutory Instrument to Community Directives. Section 2(4) provides, in effect, that delegated legislation made under section 2(2) may make any such provision as might be made by Act of Parliament, and that existing and future enactments are to be construed and have effect subject to the provisions of section 2. It should be emphasised that the Act contains no provision purporting to exclude or limit the power of Parliament to repeal or amend the Act itself. Section 3 provides that for the purpose of legal proceedings, the meaning of the Treaties and the validity or meaning of any Community Instrument are questions of law which, if not referred to the European Court of Justice at Luxembourg for a preliminary ruling, are to be determined in accordance with the principles laid down by that Court. The general effect of the European Communities Act is to override *existing* domestic law so far as is inconsistent therewith, and to impose a presumption of interpretation that *future* statute law is to be read subject to Community law for the time being in force. Parliament is expected to refrain from passing legislation inconsistent with Community law.

It was widely objected that Parliament, by passing the European Communities Act, would surrender a large part of its "sovereignty" to the Community institutions, and that as there is no time limit in the Treaties Parliament would be binding itself for ever. In *Blackburn* v. *Attorney-General*[63] the plaintiff sought a declaration that the government, by signing the Treaty of Rome, would surrender in part the sovereignty of Parliament and would surrender it for ever, which would be in breach of law. The Court of Appeal decided that the statement of claim disclosed no cause of action and should be struck out. The Treaty of Accession to the EEC was a prerogative act, and the question with regard to Parliament was hypothetical. Lord Denning M.R. after stating that "in theory Mr. Blackburn is quite right in saying that no Parliament can bind another, and that any Parliament can reverse what a previous Parliament has done," added: "nevertheless so far as this court is concerned, I think we will wait till that day comes;" but he did so (it is submitted) not because he doubted the soundness of Mr. Blackburn's proposition, but because courts do not answer hypothetical questions that have not yet arisen. In *McWhirter* v. *Attorney-General*[64] the Court of Appeal held that the plaintiff might not argue that joining the EEC would be contrary to the Bill of Rights, which declared that full powers of government are vested in the Crown. The exercise of the prerogative could not be impugned in the courts, either before or after a treaty is signed. "Even though the Treaty of Rome has been signed," said Lord Denning M.R. "it has no effect, so far as these Courts are concerned, until it is made an Act of Parliament. Once it is implemented by an Act of Parliament, these Courts must go by the Act of Parliament."

Successive Lord Chancellors, both in the House of Lords and extra-

---

[62] *Post*, Chap. 5.
[63] [1971] 1 W.L.R. 1037 (C.A.).
[64] [1972] C.M.L.R. 882 (C.A.).

judicially, denied either that Parliament would surrender its sovereignty or that the Act would be irreversible—Lord Kilmuir and Lord Dilhorne in the House of Lords in 1962, Lord Gardiner in the House of Lords in 1967, and Lord Hailsham of St. Marylebone in 1971.[65] Lord Gardiner[66] pointed out that the United Kingdom had accepted restraints on its legislative power to take account of obligations arising out of such treaties as the United Nations Charter, the European Convention on Human Rights, NATO and GATT. The treaty obligations are reciprocal: all the members remain sovereign States: the United Kingdom would take part in the making of new Regulations (which in practice is done unanimously),[67] and also in the judicial work of the EEC tribunals. Lord Hailsham[68] further pointed out that there were "stacks" of treaties designed to last for an indefinite period, some designed to last for ever, and most peace treaties fall under one of these heads. He saw membership of the Community not as a derogation from sovereignty, but as sovereignty plus the advantages of membership. Lord Gardiner also said: "Under the British constitutional doctrine of Parliamentary sovereignty no Parliament can preclude its successors from changing the law . . . . There is in theory no constitutional means available to us to make it certain that no future Parliament would enact legislation in conflict with Community law"; but he added that repeal of the Act would be a breach of *international obligations*, unless it was justified by exceptional circumstances and had the approval of the other member States.[69]

Again, Lord Diplock has expressed the opinion extrajudicially that: "If the Queen in Parliament was to make laws which were in conflict with this country's obligations under the Treaty of Rome, those laws and not the conflicting provisions of the Treaty would be given effect to as the domestic law of the United Kingdom."[70] And Lord Justice Scarman (as he then was) has written: "The European Communities Act preserves, of course, the *de jure* sovereignty of Parliament. Community law has the force of law because Parliament says so . . . . The European Communities Act cannot be read as limiting the sovereignty of Parliament. No British court could, I suggest, go so far as to hold that Parliament today had limited the freedom of action of Parliament tomorrow without a constitutional reform that is in fact beyond the power of Parliament by statute to effect."[71]

The attitude of leading statesmen and responsible political parties is also relevant in considering the fundamentals of the Constitution. Mr. Harold Wilson, then Leader of the Opposition, is reported to have said

---

[65] H.L.Deb., Vol. 322, cols. 195–208.

[66] H.L.Deb. cols. 1202–1204 (May 8, 1967).

[67] The unanimity principle is used in important matters, and could not be abrogated without the agreement of the United Kingdom, whose Ministers depend on Parliamentary support: see letter from Lord Gladwyn to *The Times*, January 9, 1975.

[68] At the Mansion House: *The Times*, July 14, 1971, Lord Hailsham also said: "either Dilhorne or Kilmuir got every leading lawyer . . . to discuss this very question and they came to the same conclusion": *The Listener*, July 13, 1972, p. 40.

[69] See note 66, *ante*.

[70] "The Common Market and the Common Law" (1972) 6 *Law Teacher*, 3, 5.

[71] "The Law of Establishment in the European Economic Community" (1973) 24 N.I.L.Q. 61, 70–72.

in a speech at Bonn in February 1972[72] that a future Labour Government would withdraw from the EEC if it could not satisfactorily renegotiate the terms for British membership: it would recognise "the British constitutional doctrine that one Parliament cannot bind its successors." Again, in February 1974, he announced that if Labour won the pending general election (which it did) it would renegotiate the terms of Britain's entry (sic) into the EEC, and if these negotiations did not succeed then the existing treaty obligations would not be regarded as binding.[73] It was publicly known that the Labour Government, formed in 1974, was sharply divided on the question of Britain's continued membership of the EEC. Renegotiation of the terms of membership attracted little attention, but in order to preserve the unity of their party in the Commons, the Government (advocating continued membership) adopted the unprecedented and controversial device of a referendum.[74] The passing of the Referendum Act 1975, under the authority of which the referendum was held,[75] implied that the Government and members of Parliament generally presumed that, if the result of the referendum in the United Kingdom as a whole went against continued membership, this country would withdraw from the EEC and Parliament would pass legislation repealing the European Communities Act and disentangling our domestic law from Community law. The Government conceded that Parliament would not be bound by the result of the referendum, but indicated that the Government itself would abide by it. In the event a large majority in England and smaller majorities in Scotland, Wales and Northern Ireland voted in favour of the United Kingdom remaining in the EEC.

Conflict between United Kingdom law and Community law

Two provisions of the European Communities Act 1972 deal with the relationship between Community Law and the domestic law of the United Kingdom. Section 2(4) provides:

> "The provision that may be made under subsection (2) above includes, subject to Schedule 2 to this Act, any such provision (of any such extent) as might be made by Act of Parliament, and any enactment passed or to be passed, other than one contained in this Part of this Act, shall be construed and have effect subject to the foregoing provisions of this section, but, except as may be provided by any Act passed after this Act, Schedule 2 shall have effect in connection with the powers conferred by this and the following sections of this Act to make Orders in Council and regulations."

Section 3(1) provides:

---

[72] *The Times*, February 5, 1972.

[73] *The Times*, February 13, 1974.

[74] *Referendum on United Kingdom Membership of the European Community* Cmnd. 5925 (1975).

[75] The question was: "Do you think that the United Kingdom should stay in the European Community (the Common Market)?" Votes were counted in England and Wales by counties, in Scotland by regions and in Northern Ireland as a whole. Courts were precluded from entertaining any proceedings for questioning the numbers of ballot papers counted or answers given in the referendum. And see R. E. M. Irving, "The United Kingdom Referendum, June 1975" (1975) 1 *European Law Review* 3.

"For the purposes of all legal proceedings any question as to the meaning or effect of any of the Treaties, or as to the validity, meaning or effect of any Community instrument, shall be treated as a question of law (and, if not referred to the European Court be for determination as such in accordance with the principles laid down by and any relevant decision of the European Court."

Section 2(4) is a complex piece of draftsmanship which is best regarded as consisting of three parts. The first (from the beginning to "as might be made by Act of Parliament") deals with the making of delegated legislation to implement Community obligations (under section 2(2)), and provides that such subordinate legislation has the effect of an Act of Parliament or that it may not merely change the common law but may amend or repeal Acts of Parliament. The third part (from the words "but, except as may be provided" to the end) protects Schedule 2 from amendment by delegated legislation made under the Act. Thus it imposes a limit to the wide powers conferred by the first part of the subsection.

The second part of the subsection—and any enactment passed or to be passed, other than one contained in this Part of this Act, shall be construed and have effect subject to the foregoing provisions of this section—can only be described as obscure. It would not be surprising if it were dealing only with delegated legislation; the other two parts of the subsection are, unarguably, so confined.[76] If "enactment to be passed" includes future Acts of Parliament, as is generally assumed, what becomes of the reference to "in this Part of this Act." Is "enactment" being used to mean both statute and section? No explanation of these cryptic words is entirely satisfactory. Probably the least unsatisfactory is that they lay down a rule of construction or a presumption of interpretation in the absence of a clear express intention in a later Act.[77] With regard to existing legislation, section 2 confers power to make such amendments as may be necessary to give effect to Community law. With regard to future legislation, subsection (4) expresses a rule of construction that would have to give way in a British court to a contrary expressed intention.[78] Parliament did not even purport to entrench this provision which, at most, attempts[79] or, better, pretends to secure the supremacy of Community law.

In *Garland* v. *British Rail Engineering Ltd.*[80] Lord Diplock, with whom the other members of the House concurred, clearly treated section 2(4)

---

[76] See J.M. Thomson, "The Supremacy of European Community Law?" [1976] S.L.T. 273.

[77] There is no problem about conflict between United Kingdom statutes passed before January 1, 1973 and Community Law. The European Communities Act itself resolves any such conflict in favour of Community law: sub. ss.2(1) and 2(2). In such cases it is true to say that the Act "enacted that relevant Common Market law should be applied in this country, and should, where there is a conflict, override English law." *per* Graham J. in *Aero Zipp Fasteners* v. *Y.K.K. Fasteners (U.K.) Ltd.* [1973] C.M.L.R. 819, 820. (Interpretation of pre-1973 rules of court).

[78] The words "shall be construed" surely supply the answer to the argument that s.2(4) cannot be "a mere rule of construction"; de Smith, *Constitutional and Administrative Law* (5th ed. 1985), p. 91.

[79] H.W.R. Wade, *Constitutional Fundamentals* (1980) pp. 25–27 and 31–34.

[80] [1983] 2 A.C. 751, 771. See further, O. Hood Phillips, "A Garland for the Lords: Parliament and Community Law Again," (1982) 98 L.Q.R. 524.

as establishing a rule of interpretation. He envisaged that an English (*semble*, Scottish also) court would have to apply "an express, positive statement in an Act of Parliament passed after January 1, that a particular provision is intended to be made in breach of an obligation assumed by the United Kingdom under a Community Treaty." The only question was what, if anything, short of an express, positive statement would justify a court in the United Kingdom applying domestic law which conflicted with Community law.

It might be thought that there is little likelihood of *implied* conflicts[81] because of the presumption of construction contained in section 2(4) and the judicial ingenuity exercisable in the construction of statutes. This has been exhibited in a number of cases relating to equal pay legislation.[82] In *O'Brien* v. *Sim-Chem*[83] the House of Lords managed to reach a conclusion compatible with Community law while unable to explain how it reached that conclusion. Lord Russell, who delivered the only speech, could do little more than say that he was happy "to echo the words of Lord Bramwell in *Bank of England* v. *Vagliano Brothers* [1891] A.C. 107, 138: 'This beats me' and jettison the words in dispute as making no contribution to the manifest intention of Parliament."

When a court is faced with a statutory provision which is alleged to conflict with Community law, the correct approach, it is suggested, is first to ascertain the relevant rule of Community law—if necessary by a reference to the European Court—and then to interpret the United Kingdom statute. That was the procedure followed by the House of Lords in *Garland* v. *British Rail Engineering Ltd.*[84] where, in the view of Lord Diplock, the statutory provision in question could without any undue straining bear either a narrow or a wide meaning and could easily be construed to take account of the view of the European Court. A similar process is followed when a court is faced with other presump-

---

[81] Any unintended conflicts could be remedied by amending Acts, either *ad hoc* or (if such conflicts should become frequent) by an annual Communities Act: H.W.R. Wade, "Sovereignty and the European Communities" (1972) 88 L.Q.R. 1. See also F.A. Trindale, "Parliamentary Sovereignty and the Primacy of European Community Law" (1972) 35 M.L.R. 375. See also, on implied repeal and conflict, Evelyn Ellis, "Supremacy of Parliament and European Law" (1980) 96 L.Q.R. 511; "Parliamentary Supremacy After a Decade of EEC Membership," (1982) 7 *Holdsworth Law Review* 105.

[82] See, for example, *Shields* v. *E. Coomes (Holdings) Ltd.* [1978] 1 W.L.R. 1408; *Clay Cross (Quarry Services) Ltd.* v. *Fletcher* [1978] 1 W.L.R. 1429; *Rainey* v. *Greater Glasgow Health Board* [1986] 3 W.L.R. 1017 (H.L.). On Social Security legislation see *Re an Absence in Ireland* [1977] 1 C.M.L.R. 5. (EEC regulation provided that one Member State should take into account insurance periods under the legislation of any other Member States. Later, the Social Security Act 1975 provided that a person should be disqualified from receiving any benefit for any period during which he was "absent from Great Britain." The applicant had been absent for a period in the Republic of Ireland, but the National Insurance Commissioner held that he was not disqualified during his absence because the EEC Regulation of 1971 "overrode" the provision in the 1975 Act. The report does not explain what the Commissioner meant by "overrode": there appears to have been no legal argument or citation of judicial authority on this point. The decision may be taken to mean that the Act was construed in such a way as not to conflict (not to be intended to conflict) with Community law).

[83] [1980] 1 W.L.R. 1011, 1017; noted (1981) 97 L.Q.R. 5.

[84] [1983] 2 A.C. 751.

tions of interpretation. It is the reading into a statute of the presumed requirement of *mens rea* or the presumption against extra-territorial effect that makes a formerly unambiguous statute ambiguous and requires the court to determine whether in that particular Act, Parliament has manifested an intention to exclude the requirement of *mens rea* or to legislate for foreign territories.[85]

In *McCarthys* v. *Smith*,[86] however, the majority of the Court of Appeal first construed the provisions of the Equal Pay Act 1970 and the Sex Discrimination Act 1975, and then sought a ruling of the European Court on the relevant rule of community law. The question before the Court was whether the principle of equal pay for equal work applied only where a male and female worker had been employed contemporaneously or whether it sufficed that the woman was employed in succession to the man.[87] Lawton L.J. construed the Equal Pay Act in accordance with the "ordinary" English canons of construction, finding that it applied only to a woman in the same employment at the same time as a man, and not to a woman working in succession to a man. Turning then to Article 119 he found it doubtful whether the Article applied to the case where the woman was employed on the same work in succession to a man. Cumming–Bruce L.J., following the same method as Lawton L.J., agreed with his conclusions both as to the interpretation of the Equal Pay Act taken by itself and the doubt as to the meaning of article 119. As the majority of their Lordships were doubtful whether article 119 covered the facts of the case, the Court of Appeal unanimously decided to ask the European Court to give a preliminary ruling. The European Court held that article 119 was not confined to situations in which men and women were contemporaneously doing equal work for the same employer. The reasoning of the majority is expressed in the dictum of Cumming Bruce L.J.; "I do not think that it is permissible, as an aid to construction, to look at the terms of the Treaty. If the terms of the Treaty are adjudged in Luxembourg to be inconsistent with the provisions of the Equal Pay Act 1970, European law will prevail over that municipal legislation. But such a judgment cannot affect the meaning of the English statute."[88] Lord Denning M.R., in his dissenting judgment, first construed article 119 and the (explanatory, if not directly applicable) directive, then the Act, and finally looked at both the Treaty and the Act together. He found no conflict. Both the Community law and the Equal Pay Act, he thought, extended the principle of equal pay to cases where the woman is employed on like work in (close) succession to a man. This, it is submitted is the preferable approach. Subsequent proceedings in the Court of Appeal related only to the question of costs.[89] Cumming Bruce L.J. re-affirmed what he had

---

[85] See, generally, Sir Rupert Cross, *Statutory Interpretation* (1976) Ch. 7. On the presumption against extra-territoriality see *ante*, p. 55.

[86] [1979] I.C.R. 785. See O. Hood Phillips, "High Tide in the Strand? Post-1972 Acts and Community Law" (1980) 96 L.Q.R. 31.

[87] S.2(1)(*a*) applied where "the woman *is* employed on like work with a man." The E.A.T. had found no difficulty in interpreting the words to cover the situation where the woman was employed on like work with that formerly done by a man: *McCarthys* v. *Smith* [1978] 1 W.L.R. 849.

[88] [1979] I.C.R. 785, 798.

[89] [1981] Q.B. 180.

said formerly about interpretation but emphasised that his dictum related to unambiguous statutes. It would, he thought, have been proper to look at Community law had the statute been ambiguous.[90] Lord Denning M.R. expressed further views about the relationship between United Kingdom law and Community law. Earlier in the litigation he had said,

> "Thus far I have assumed that our Parliament, whenever it passes legislation, intends to fulfil its obligations under the Treaty. If the time should come when our Parliament deliberately passes an Act—with the intention of repudiating the Treaty or any provision in it—or intentionally of acting inconsistently with it—and says so in express terms—then I should have thought that it would be the duty of our Courts to follow the statute of our Parliament."[91]

In the second proceedings Lord Denning M.R. said,

> "The provisions of art 119 of the EEC Treaty take priority over anything in our English statute on equal pay which is inconsistent with art. 119. That priority is given by our own law. It is given by the European Communities Act 1972 itself. Community law is now part of our law; and whenever there is any inconsistency, Community law has priority. It is not supplanting English law. It is part of our law which overrides any other part which is inconsistent with it. I turn therefore to the decision given by the European Court. Community law is part of our law by our own statute, the European Communities Act 1972. In applying it, we should regard it in the same way as if we found an inconsistency between two English Acts of Parliament; and the court had to decide which had to be given priority."

It should be borne in mind that the legislation in *Macarthys* v. *Smith* was silent on the question of consecutive—as opposed to contemporaneous—work and so left open the field for the application of directly effective Community law. No question of "conflict" or "priority" or "supremacy" arose. The more generous Community rule no more conflicted with the narrower United Kingdom rule than a generous United Kingdom rule could be said to conflict with a more restrictive Community rule; *Jenkins* v. *Kingsgate Ltd.*[92]

In *Worringham and Humphreys* v. *Lloyds Bank Ltd.*[93] the plaintiffs con-

---

[90] At p. 201.

[91] [1979] I.C.R. 785, 789. The difficulty of establishing Lord Denning M.R.'s views on the relationship between United Kingdom and Community Law is further illustrated by dicta in *Felixstowe Docks Railway Co.* v. *British Transport Docks Board* [1976] 2 C.M.L.R. 655, 664, ("It seems to me that once the Bill is passed by Parliament and becomes a statute, that will dispose of all this discussion about the Treaty. These courts will then have to abide by the Statute without regard to the Treaty at all"); and *Shields* v. *E. Coomes (Holdings) Ltd.* [1978] 1 W.L.R. 1408, 1415 ("Suppose that the Parliament of the United Kingdom were to pass a statute inconsistent with Article 119: as for instance, if the Equal Pay Act gave the right to equal pay only to unmarried women. I should have thought that a married woman could bring an action in the High Court to enforce the right given to her by Article 119.")

[92] [1981] 1 W.L.R. 1485, 1491 *per* Browne Wilkinson J.

[93] [1979] I.R.L.R. 440 (C.A.). See Frank Wooldridge and Joseph M. Thomson, "Equal Pay, Pensions and European Law" (1981) 97 L.Q.R. 357.

ceded that they were precluded by earlier decisions of the Court of Appeal from arguing that a pension scheme which favoured male employees was contrary to United Kingdom legislation; they argued that it was contrary to article 119, and the Court of Appeal referred the question to the European Court which held that the contributions to the pension scheme made by the employer on behalf of male employees constituted "pay" within article 119 and hence male and female employees were not receiving equal pay. Lord Denning M.R. in the initial proceedings in the Court of Appeal, spoke of directly applicable law taking "priority" over the United Kingdom legislation. Shaw L.J. asked "Does Article 119 of itself override . . . domestic legislation . . . or does such legislation survive and operate [until amended by domestic procedures]?" Neither dictum adverts to the distinction between legislation prior and subsequent in date to entry into the EEC. Nor, if the procedure in *Garland* is followed in the future, is the Court of Appeal likely to find itself in the dilemma of having to choose between domestic and Community law.

The possibility of conflict between national and community law was raised in another context in *Prince* v. *Secretary of State for Scotland*,[94] where a group of S.D.P.—Liberal Alliance voters applied to the Court of Session for a declarator that the pursuers had an "enforceable Community right" in terms of section 2 of the European Communities Act 1972, to a system of election which was not discriminatory and which gave equal weight to all votes cast so far as practicable in the forthcoming election for membrs of the European Parliament. The pursuers' argument was that the European Elections Act 1978, in so far as it did not provide for proportional representation, was *ultra vires* the Treaty of Rome. Lord Cameron refused to grant interim relief to the pursuers. In one place in his judgment, however, he referred to statutes retaining their legal effect until "repealed or otherwise deprived of [their] validity and force." Later, in criticising the suggestion that the 1978 Act was *ultra vires* the Treaty of Rome his Lordship said, " . . . I should have thought that [the] question . . . is whether the statute was *ultra vires* the United Kingdom Parliament because of its conflict with Community law."

In contrast to the *dualistic* approach of the British courts the European Court of Justice, in considering conflicts between national and community law, has adopted a *monistic* theory according to which both laws are part of one legal system in which Community law has primacy.[95] In the *Van Gend en Loos*[96] case the Court said that the Community constituted a new legal order, for the benefit of which the member states have limited their sovereign rights, albeit within limited fields. In *Costa* v.

---

[94] 1985 S.L.T. 74; noted, J.M.T. (1985) 101 L.Q.R. 149; *post*, p. 99.
[95] Gerhard Bebr, "Law of the European Communities and Municipal Law" (1971) 34 M.L.R. 48; Advocate-General J.P. Warner, "The Relationship between European Community Law and the National Laws of Member States" (1977) 93 L.Q.R. 349. *Cf.* Collins, *European Community Law in the United Kingdom*, Chap. 1; Hood Phillips, "Self-limitation by the United Kingdom Parliament," *loc. cit.* Distinctions between Community Law and International Law are drawn by P. Pescatore, "International Law and Community Law—a Comparative Analysis" (1970) 7 C.M.L. Rev. 167.
[96] *Van Gend en Loos* v. *Nederlandse Administratie der Belastingen* [1963] E.C.R. 1, 12.

E.N.E.L.[97] the Court clearly affirmed the primacy of Community law which, it said, stemming from the Treaty, an independent source of law, could not, because of its special and original nature, be overridden by domestic legal provisions. In so far as the Court relied for proof of the primacy of Community law on a provision of the Treaty (Article 189) it could be said to have been relying on a circular argument. The member states may accord primacy to rules made under the Treaty—as the inhabitants and courts of a state may accord primacy to a document which they recognise as their constitution—but the Treaty can no more give itself primacy than a constitution can. The Court went on to say that the transfer by member-States, from their national order in favour of the Community order, of the rights and obligations arising from the Treaty, carries with it a clear limitation of their sovereign right against which a subsequent unilateral law incompatible with the aims of the Community cannot prevail. That appears to confuse State sovereignty and internal legislative supremacy. In a sense, every treaty to which a State is a party involves some loss of State sovereignty (freedom of action) in international law and as a matter of politics, but in British constitutional law this does not affect the supreme authority of Parliament to make law *for the United Kingdom.*

In the *Internationale Handelsgesellschaft* case[98] the European Court of Justice stated that under article 189 of the Treaty a directly-applicable Community regulation overrode even fundamental rights declared in the Constitution of the German Federal Republic. In the *Simmenthal*[99] case the Court, on a reference by an Italian court (the Pretore di Susa), ruled that:

> "A national court which is called upon, within the limits of its jurisdiction, to apply provisions of Community law is under a duty to give full effect to those provisions, if necessary refusing of its own motion to apply any conflicting provision of national legislation, even if adopted subsequently, and it is not necessary for the court to request or await the prior setting aside of such provision by legislative or other constitutional means."

Under Italian Law, legislation contrary to EEC regulations may be held unconstitutional but only by the Constitutional Court. The view of the European Court, however, was that any court, acting within its jurisdiction, is bound to refuse to apply national legislation which is incompatible with Community law.

The emphasis on the primacy of Community law has been accompa-

---

[97] [1964] E.C.R. 585.

[98] *Internationale Handelsgesellschaft m.b.H.* v. *Einfuhr-und Vorratsstelle für Getreide und Futtermittel* [1970] E.C.R. 1125, 1134. The German administrative court then referred the matter to the Federal Constitutional Court, which decided that it was competent to rule on the application of Community Law in relation to the Federal Constitution, but that the Community regulation concerned was not inconsistent with the basic rights guaranteed by the Constitution.

[99] *Amministrazione delle Finanze dello Stato* v. *Simmenthal* [1978] E.C.R. 629. See O. Hood Phillips, "Has the "Incoming Tide Reached the Palace of Westminster?" (1979) 95 L.Q.R. 167.

nied by insistence on the direct applicability of some rules of the Community system within the territories of the Member States and the creation of directly effective rights, enforceable by individuals before municipal courts. This aspect of Community law is recognised and given effect to by section 2(1) and 2(2) of the European Communities Act 1972. Section 3(1) of the European Communities Act directs United Kingdom courts to determine questions of Community law according to the principles laid down by the European Court. Thus, in deciding whether a provision of the Treaty or a piece of Community legislation is directly applicable within the United Kingdom, a court would apply the tests laid down by the European Court or seek a preliminary ruling from the Court under Article 177 of the Treaty.[1] So far as the primacy of Community law is concerned, however, section 3 must yield like any other legislation to a later Act of Parliament. What has been said about the effect of subsequent legislation in regard to section 2(4) applies equally here.

The Constitutions of the various member states differ as to the legal effect of treaties in general and of Community law in particular within their respective countries. Many European states accord primacy to treaty obligations over the provisions of their municipal legal systems. Article 55 of the 1958 French Constitution, for example, provides that treaties duly ratified have authority superior to domestic laws. The Irish Constitution, specifically amended to give effect to Community law, lays down in Article 29.4.3 that

> "No provision of this Constitution invalidates laws enacted, acts done or measures adopted by the State necessitated by the obligations of membership of the Communities or prevents laws enacted, acts done or measures adopted by the Communities, or institutions thereof, from having the force of law in the State."

Nothing, however, in the European Communities Act 1972 even pretends to affect the fundamental principle of the Supremacy of the United Kingdom Parliament. Where conflicts between domestic law and Community law have arisen they have been resolved by the passing of sub-ordinate legislation under the European Communities Act. It may be argued that the position has now been reached where it can be said to be a constitutional convention that the government of the day will initiate the steps necessary to pass amending legislation in such circumstances. So far as United Kingdom courts are concerned, constitutional law—notably the legislative supremacy of Parliament—is supreme, and Community law can take effect in this country only by force of Act of Parliament.[2] Although decisions and opinions of the European Court of Justice on Community law are required to be followed in United Kingdom courts by section 3 of the European Communities Act, the European Court cannot (even by Community law)

---

[1] *Post*, p. 102.
[2] See *e.g. Rustomjee* v. *R.* (1876) 1 Q.B.D. 487; 2 Q.B.D. 69; *Att.-Gen. for Canada* v. *Att.-Gen. for Ontario* [1937] A.C. 326, 347; *Chung Chi Cheung* v. *R.* [1939] A.C. 160; *Salomon* v. *Customs and Excise Commissioners* [1967] 2 Q.B. 116, 173.

overrule a decision of a national court.[3] As has been stated, Parliament *can* legislate contrary to treaties,[4] though there is a *presumption* that Parliament does not intend to legislate contrary to international law,[5] and this common law presumption is reinforced in relation to Community law by sub-section 2(4) of the European Communities Act.[6] But a presumption of interpretation is a different matter from a limitation on the power of Parliament to legislate.

The question has been discussed here in the light of the probable attitude of the British courts at the present time and in the near future. It is possible, as has been suggested,[7] that our courts might change their attitude towards the lawmaking power of Parliament in the future with regard to express[8] conflicts between later Acts of Parliament and Community law or with regard to legislation implementing the executive act of withdrawing from the EEC. This speculation supposes judicial recognition of the supremacy of international law, or at least of Community law, which would be a reversal of long-established judicial thinking amounting to a revolution in our constitutional history. But revolutions, or changes in the basis of the Constitution, are made by popular movements following political leaders. It is for judges to acknowledge revolutions, not to make them. Meanwhile, the attitude of our political leaders and of members of Parliament generally has been noticed. Our judges, not possessing the coordinate authority with the legislature accorded to the Supreme Court by the American Constitution, are liable to be dismissed from office on an address from both Houses of Parliament. Incidentally, the House of Lords, which would be the final court of appeal in such constitutional matters, is itself strictly a part of that Parliament whose authority would be challenged. In any event, Parliament by statute can nullify decisions of the courts, and has done so on many occasions.

If membership of the EEC does not involve a fundamental change in the legal basis of the British Constitution, it has raised the questions of ensuring ministerial responsibility for Community decisions affecting this country and the parliamentary scrutiny of Community instruments, both regulations having direct effect in this country and delegated legislation implementing Community directives.[9-10]

---

[3] Lord Mackenzie Stuart, *The European Communities and the Rule of Law* (Hamlyn Lectures, 1977), pp. 38, 68. See also F.G. Jacobs and A. Durand, *References to the European Court: Practice and Procedure* (1975), pp. 153, 169, 194. On application by the Commission or another member State the European Court of Justice may declare that a State has, in adopting or maintaining in force a law, failed to fulfil its obligations under the Treaty.

[4] *I.R.C.* v. *Collco Dealings Ltd.* [1962] A.C. 1; *Cheney* v. *Conn* [1968] 1 W.L.R. 242.

[5] *Salomon* v. *Customs and Excise Commissioners* [1967] 2 Q.B. 116.

[6] *Ante* p. 75.

[7] Sir Leslie Scarman, "Law and Administration: A Change in Relationship" (1972) 50 *Public Administration* 253; S.A de Smith, "The Constitution and the Common Market: A Tentative Appraisal" (1971) 34 M.L.R. 597, at pp. 612 *et seq.*; D. G. T. Williams, "The Constitution of the United Kingdom" [1972 B] C.L.J. 266, at pp. 289, *et seq.*; F. M. Auburn, "Trends in Comparative Constitutional Law" (1972) 35 M.L.R. 129.

[8] Implied conflict is a matter of interpretation, *ante*, p. 76.

[9-10] *post*, pp. 106–107.

II. "MANNER AND FORM" OF LEGISLATION

The next question is whether Parliament can bind its successors as to the "manner and form"[11] of legislation, that is, as regards its own procedure.

Authentication of Acts of Parliament

There must be some rules logically prior to Parliament by which an act can be recognised as the act of Parliament.[12] This is not a matter of limiting Parliament, but of identifying its enactments. The principle applies to all legislatures, and is not a problem relating specifically to "sovereignty." For many centuries, except during the revolutionary Commonwealth period in the seventeenth century, "Parliament" has meant the Monarch, the Lords and Commons in Parliament assembled. "There is no Act of Parliament," says Coke,[13] "but must have the consent of the Lords, the Commons and the Royal Assent of the King, and as it appeareth by Records and our Books, whatsoever passeth in Parliament by this threefold consent, hath the force of an Act of Parliament." And in *Middleton* v. *Croft*[14] Lord Hardwicke L.C., said: "As to the general nature, and fundamentals of our constitution, no new law can bind the people of this land, but what is made by the King and Parliament; nor any law made by the King alone, nor by the King with consent of any particular number or body of men." It has been a custom since the reign of Edward III for the Lords and Commons to deliberate separately,[15] but Parliament's formal acts until 1967 were always done by one body in the Parliament chambers.[16] An Act of Parliament then, is a measure enacted by these three elements acting together in a way customarily prescribed by themselves, namely, by a simple majority of the members present and voting in each House separately, and assented to by the Queen. The legislative formula for ordinary Acts of Parliament has long been established as follows: "Be it enacted by the Queen's most Excellent Majesty, by and with the advice and consent of the Lords Spiritual and Temporal, and Commons, in this present Parliament assembled, and by the authority of the same, as follows. . . ."[17] It will be noticed that this formula does not refer to the Houses of Lords and Commons.

The chief original sources for Acts of Parliament before 1849 are the

---

[11] The expression is taken from the Colonial Laws Validity Act 1865, s.5 and ultimately from the Foreign Jurisdiction Act 1843.

[12] These rules are both common law and fact.

[13] 4 Inst. 25. And see *The Prince's Case, post.*

[14] (1743) Cas. T. Hard. 326 (Eccls. Ct.).

[15] A.F. Pollard, *Evolution of Parliament* (2nd ed.), pp. 120–123.

[16] Pollard, *op. cit.* p. 123. And see Chitty, *Prerogatives of the Crown*, p. 75: "That which constitutes law is the concurring assent of all the branches of the legislature, wherever it may originate, whatever may happen to be the form of it." For the giving of the Royal Assent, and the Royal Assent Act 1967, see *post*, p. 135.

[17] Different formulae are used for Finance and Appropriation Acts, private Acts, and Acts passed under the special procedure of the Parliament Acts.

Statute Rolls and Parliament Rolls, consisting of inrollments in Chancery and proceedings in Parliament. We also have most of the original Acts since Henry VII, *i.e.* the drafts from which the Clerk of the Parliaments made up the inrollments. Since 1849 the Queen's printer has made two vellum prints authenticated by the proper officer of each House, one of which is kept in the House of Lords and the other deposited in the Public Record Office. Except in rare cases of doubt, printed copies of the statutes are sufficient—the King's (Queen's) printer's copies for Acts passed since 1713, and Statutes of the Realm for statutes passed down to that year.

It appears from *The Prince's Case*[18] that it was sometimes difficult to determine the authenticity of earlier Acts, and that a charter (recited as coming from the King and apparently having the authority of Parliament) would be accepted as an Act of Parliament if it was entered on the Parliament Roll and had always been allowed as an Act. In *Heath* v. *Pryn*[19] counsel challenged the Parliament Act 1660 on the ground that the Lords and Commons were not summoned by the King's writ, but the Court of King's Bench said: "the Act being made by the King, Lords and Commons they ought not now to pry into any defects of the circumstances of calling them together." The recital of the assent of the Monarch, Lords and Commons is generally taken to be conclusive, and it is doubted whether a *litigant* would be allowed to attempt to prove that one of these assents had not in fact been given. On the other hand, *either House* may have the privilege of asserting by reference to its journals that it had not agreed to the Bill, or that amendments proposed by one House had not been agreed by the other. A House of Lords amendment to the Bill that became the Rent (Agriculture) Act 1976 was agreed to by the Commons under the guillotine procedure without discussion: but through the inadvertance of the House of Lords officials who prepare Bills for the Royal assent, the amendment was not inserted. Parliament consequently passed the Rent (Agriculture) Amendment Act 1977 in order to give effect to the amendment.

Although the question of the authentication of Acts is sometimes brought into discussions about the legislative supremacy of Parliament, it is more appropriately described by Erskine May as "Subsidiary Points in connection with Legislative Procedure."[20] Under the Parliament Acts, however, the Speaker's certificate is stated to be conclusive.[21]

Courts not concerned with procedure in Parliament

Centlivres C.J. in *Harris* v. *Minister of the Interior*[22] suggested that a Bill passed by both Houses of British Parliament sitting together would

---

[18] (1606) 8 Co.Rep. la., 13b, 18a–19b, 20b, 28a. The Court included Lord Ellesmere L.C., Coke C.J. and Fleming C.B.

[19] (1670) 1 Vent. 14.

[20] Erskine May, *Treatise on the Law Privileges Proceedings and Usage of Parliament* (20th ed. 1983), p. 605. See Craies, *Statute Law* (7th ed. 1971), pp. 37–38.

[21] *Cf. post*, p. 144.

[22] (1952) (2) S.A. (A.D.) 428, 470. And see R. T. E. Latham, "The Law of the Commonwealth," in *Survey of British Commonwealth Affairs*, Vol. 1, ed. Hancock, pp. 523–524.

not be an Act of Parliament, as otherwise a Conservative Prime Minister who had lost his majority in the Commons could get a Bill passed by the Lords and Commons sitting together. But Centlivres C.J. took as his example a particular case which would be constitutionally objectionable. It may be replied, conversely, that it would be absurd for a court to deny validity to an Act passed unanimously by both Houses sitting together. There seems to be no strictly legal objection to the Lords and Commons debating and voting in a joint sitting. The matter seems now to be one of the Commons' privileges and of constitutional convention. If it is one of the Lords' privileges also, both Houses would have to agree before a joint sitting could be held. It is submitted that the courts would not wish to involve themselves in these procedural matters.

The decision of the Court of Appeal in *Ellen Street Estates Ltd.* v. *Minister of Health*[23] is a precedent for saying that Parliament cannot bind its successors as to the form of subsequent legislation by providing that there shall be no *implied* repeal of an Act.

The judgment of the House of Lords in *Pickin* v. *British Railways Board*[24] may be relied on in relation to public as well as private Acts (although as to public Acts the considered statement was strictly *obiter*), to the effect that the courts will not concern themselves with the *procedure* by which a Bill passed through either House. Suppose that when a Labour Government was in office Parliament had passed an Act providing that no Bill to implement Britain's joining the EEC should have effect unless approved by the electorate in a referendum.[25] If Parliament under a subsequent Conservative Government passed a European Communities Act without a referendum being held, it is submitted that no court would hold the latter Act void. Again, suppose that an Industrial Relations Act contained a provision that it might not be repealed or amended unless the Bill for that purpose was approved by the votes of not fewer than two-thirds of the members of the House of Commons.[26] It is submitted that if Parliament under a future Conservative Government passed an Act purporting to repeal or amend that earlier Act, the courts would hold the subsequent Act valid even though it could be shown that it had received fewer than two-thirds of the votes of the members of the Commons. Similarly, with an Act to alter the status of Northern Ireland as part of the United Kingdom.[27]

It is submitted that the courts would regard these as procedural matters. This does not mean that if Parliament made such statutory provisions they would be "void." Steps taken under them to hold a national referendum or a plebiscite in Northern Ireland would be lawful. What we are saying is that the same Parliament, or a subsequent

---

[23] [1934] 1 K.B. 590; *ante*, p. 62.

[24] [1974] A.C. 765; *ante*, p. 52.

[25] A requirement of a referendum as a condition precedent to constitutional reform was classified as a matter of procedure by the Privy Council in *A.G. for N.S.W.* v. *Trethowan* [1932] A.C. 526, *per* Lord Sankey L.C.

[26] Such a provision would require a government to have the unusual majority of more than 200 in the Commons.

[27] *Ante*, p. 53.

Parliament (probably of a different political complexion), could repeal these provisions or simply ignore them. There is no reason why a later Act should be accorded less authority than an earlier one.

Contrary arguments

It has been argued by Sir Ivor Jennings[28] and others that the requirement of a referendum or the approval of some outside body such as the Parliament of Northern Ireland would constitute, not a procedural requirement, but a change in the *composition* of Parliament (which for this purpose would include the electorate or the Northern Ireland Parliament, as the case might be) and so be binding on the legislature. This view, if followed through to its logical conclusion, would lead to absurd results, for by the law and custom of Parliament all the elements constituting Parliament must be summoned to Westminister by Royal Writs to deliberate, vote and hear the Royal Assent. The application of this argument to the repeal of the European Communities Act 1972, implementing withdrawal of the United Kingdom from the EEC, would require us to regard the governments or legislatures, or even the electorates, of the other Member States (although aliens) as forming part of the composition of Parliament of this purpose. Again, a change in the composition of Parliament has been classified as a matter of procedure rather than subject-matter, and so (it is argued) binding on Parliament.[29] But if this were so the members of the Commons elected for three years under the Triennial Act 1694[30] who took part in passing the Septennial Act 1715 would not have been qualified to sit for the extra four years, with incalculable consequences for the validity of subsequent legislation.

Alternatively it has been argued by followers of D.V. Cowen[31] that a requirement such as a special majority of (say) two-thirds in either House or both Houses would constitute a *redefinition* of "Parliament" for this purpose, so in that case "Parliament" would mean the Queen, Lords and the Commons approving by a majority of not less than two-thirds. This *"redefinition,"* it should be noticed, would be done not by some higher law as in the South African case of *Harris v. Minister of the Interior*[32] but by Parliament itself. To say that Parliament (while retaining its existing composition) can redefine *itself* in this way begs the question. It is a fiction or formula designed to avoid classifying the matter as "procedural," and so not within the ambit of the courts. The argument applied to the Triennial Act would mean that Parliament in 1694

---

[28] *e.g.* Jennings, *Constitutional Laws of the Commonwealth* (1957), pp. 124–125; R. F. V. Heuston, *Essays in Constitutional Law* (2nd ed., 1964); and see Jennings, *The Law and the Constitution* (5th ed., 1959), pp. 151–163.

[29] G. Marshall, *Constitutional Theory*, p. 42; G. Winterton, "The British Grundnorm: Parliamentary Supremacy Re-examined,' *loc. cit.*

[30] Now entitled the Meeting of Parliament Act.

[31] D. V. Cowen, *Parliamentary Sovereignty and the Entrenched Sections of the South Africa Act* (1957).

[32] D. V. Cowen's original argument referred to the meanings of "Parliament" in different sections of the constituent South Africa Act.

redefined itself in such a way that a future Parliament was not competent to legislate after three years. In so far as this argument differs from the "composition" argument, also, it would lead to the consequence that the word "Parliament" as applied to the United Kingdom Parliament could have an indefinite number of meanings.

The unicameral New Zealand Parliament is similarly not limited by a higher law,[33] and an "uncontrolled"[34] constitution can be amended by implication by an ordinary statute.[35] The Electoral Act passed by the New Zealand Parliament in 1956 included section 189 which states that certain provisions relating to such matters as the life of Parliament, the franchise and secret ballot, may not be repealed or amended except by a majority of 75 per cent. of all the members of the House of Representatives or by a simple majority of votes in a referendum. Section 189 did not itself require this special procedure for its own repeal or amendment. It has been argued, first, that in any event in order to alter these electoral provisions it would be necessary to repeal section 189 (*semble* by a simple majority); but, secondly, that section 189 is probably binding on the New Zealand Parliament as a "redefinition" of the legislature for this purpose.[36] Most New Zealand lawyers and politicians at the time, however, admitted that the sanction provided by section 189 was merely moral and conventional,[37] and it is submitted that this is the correct view. The reason why the legislature did not try to "entrench" section 189 itself was that it recognised that such an attempt would be ineffectual.

The arguments concerning "manner and form" or "redefinition" in relation to the United Kingdom Parliament have also prayed in aid cases concerning legislatures that are subordinate to a higher law, or "controlled" constitutions. The first and best known of these is *Attorney-General for New South Wales* v. *Trethowan*.[38] The New South Wales legislature had passed an Act in 1929 providing that no Bill to abolish the Legislative Council (the Upper House) should be presented to the Governor for his assent unless it had been approved at a referendum, and that this provision should also apply to any Bill to repeal or amend the Act. After a change of government in 1930 two Bills were introduced, one to repeal the Act of 1929 and the other to abolish the

---

[33] New Zealand Constitution Amendment Act 1973 (N.Z.). *Cf.* the dictim of Moller J. at first instance in *R.* v. *Fineberg* [1958] N.Z.L.R. 119.

[34] See *McCawley* v. *R.* [1920] A.C. 691 (P.C.) per Lord Birkenhead L.C.

[35] *Kariapper* v. *Wijesinha* [1968] A.C. 717 (P.C.); *cf. Ibralebbe* v. *R.* [1964] A.C. 900 (P.C.); no implied repeal of entrenched provisions. And *cf. R.* v. *Drybones* (1969) 9 D.L.R. (3d) (S.C. Canada) on Canadian Bill of Rights.

[36] See *e.g.* Aikman, *New Zealand, its Laws and Constitution* (2nd ed. Robson), pp. 66–69.

[37] See *e.g.* K.J. Scott, *The New Zealand Constitution* (1962), pp. 6–9.

[38] [1932] A.C. 526 (P.C.) on appeal from the High Court of Australia in *Trethowan* v. *Peden* (1931) 44 C.L.R. 394. The case could have been argued on the question whether an injunction would lie to prevent the Bills from being presented to the Governor for the Royal Assent, but the Australian High Court allowed special leave to appeal to the Privy Council only on the question of "manner and form." The use of the case in this context is largely due to the fact that it was "a recent decision" when Jennings published the first edition of his *The Law and the Constitution* in 1933.
See also O. Hood Phillips, "Ryan's Case" (1936) 52 L.Q.R. 241.

Legislative Council. The Privy Council held that if they received the Governor's assent without being approved at a referendum the Acts would be void, because they would not have been passed in the "manner and form" required by the law in force in New South Wales. It is clear from the judgment of the Privy Council, and has been confirmed since by the Australian High Court,[39] that the decision in *Trethowan's* case was based on the ground that New South Wales (although no longer a "colony") was still subject to the Colonial Laws Validity Act 1865, which recognises the lawmaking power of a representative colonial legislature provided that its laws are passed "in such manner and form as may from time to time be required by an Act of Parliament . . . or colonial law for the time being in force in the said Colony." "The answer depends," said Lord Sankey L.C. in that case, "entirely upon the consideration of the meaning and effect of section 5 of the Act of 1865." The limitation placed on itself by the New South Wales legislature in 1929 was therefore binding on it in 1930 *by virtue of the Colonial Laws Validity Act*, a "higher law" passed by a legislature to which it was legally subordinate. The case is no authority whatsoever for saying that the United Kingdom Parliament can bind itself in this way.

The application of the "manner and form" argument to the United Kingdom Parliament appears to have been initiated by an obiter dictum of Dixon J., as he then was, in the Australian High Court in *Trethowan's* case.[40] His lordship suggested that if the United Kingdom Parliament passed legislation concerning the abolition of the House of Lords similar to that passed by the New South Wales legislature in 1929, it would be unlawful to present a repealing or abolition Bill for the Royal Assent; and if it was found possible (*sic*) to raise the question for judicial decision the court would be bound to pronounce it unlawful to do so; further that, if such Bill did receive the Royal Assent without being submitted to a referendum, the courts might (*sic*) be called upon to consider whether the supreme legislative power in respect of the matter had in truth been exercised in the manner required for its authentic expression and by the elements in which it had come to reside. He concluded that the answer was "not clear." In a later Australian case,[41] however, Dixon C.J. (as he had become) said that in Australian law an injunction ought not to be granted in connection with the legislative process,[42] that therefore *Trethowan's* case was probably wrongly decided, and the remedy was judicial review after the Royal Assent had been given. He implied that it was unlikely that such a case could be brought before the courts in the United Kingdom. The disinclination of English courts to

---

[39] *Clayton* v. *Heffron* (1960) 105 C.L.R. 214; G. Sawer in [1961] P.L. 131. Dixon C.J. and the majority of the court said the case had no analogy to *Trethowan*, where there was a definite statutory prohibition against presenting the Bill to the Governor: here the ground was that the procedure was not correctly followed. And see *per* Dixon C.J. in *Hughes and Vale Pty. Ltd.* v. *Gair* (1954) 90 C.L.R. 203. *Cf.* W. Friedmann, "Trethowan's Case, Parliamentary Sovereignty and the Limits of Legal Change" (1950) 24 A.L.J. 103.

[40] 44 C.L.R. 426. The dictum seems to have been inspired by counsel's argument.

[41] *Hughes & Vale Pty. Ltd.* v. *Gair* (1954) 90 C.L.R. 203.

[42] It might be regarded as a breach of privilege: *Clayton* v. *Heffron* (1960) 105 C.L.R. 214.

intervene by injunction in the process of private Bill or delegated legislation is shown in several decisions.[43] *A fortiori* they are unlikely to intervene in the process of public Bill legislation, which is a matter within the cognisance of Parliament, apart from the fact that an injunction cannot be brought against an officer representing the Crown.[44] In *Harper* v. *Home Secretary*,[45] where an injunction was refused to restrain the Home Secretary from presenting a draft electoral boundaries order (approved by both Houses) to the Privy Council, Lord Evershed M.R. pointed out that *Trethowan's* case was concerned with a strictly limited legislature, and said: "That seems to me quite a different case from the present. We are here in no sense concerned with a Parliament or legislature having limited legislative functions according to the constitution."

In *Rediffusion (Hong Kong) Ltd.* v. *Attorney-General of Hong Kong*[46] the Privy Council held that no declaration or injunction lay to restrain the colonial legislature of Hong Kong from debating, passing and presenting to the Governor a copyright Bill, although it might, if enacted by the Governor's assent, be void under the Colonial Laws Validity Act 1865, s.5, as being repugnant to United Kingdom statute. The principle of this decision would clearly rule out declaration or injunction as ways of preventing the presentation of a Bill to the Queen for the Royal Assent.

What we have said about cases concerning subordinate legislatures applies also to two appeals to the Privy Council from Ceylon, which are sometimes cited in this context. The reason for the invalidity of the Bribery Tribunal in *Bribery Commissioner* v. *Ranasinghe*[47] and of the special court in *Liyanage* v. *R.*,[48] was that the setting up of these judicial institutions had not been done by the special legislative procedure of constitutional amendment required by the written[49] Constitution of Ceylon, although that country was a sovereign state. In the *Ranasinghe* case Lord Pearce said that there was no analogy to the British Constitution, which has no instrument governing the forms of the lawmaking power.

Attempts have been made to suggest drafting formulae by which Parliament might bind itself, but none of them would be effective to

---

[43] *Bilston Corporation* v. *Wolverhampton Corporation* [1942] 1 Ch. 391 (statutory obligation not to oppose application for private Bill); *Hammersmith Borough Council* v. *Boundary Commission for England, The Times,* December 15, 1954 (forwarding of Boundary Commission's report to Home Secretary); *Merricks* v. *Heathcoat-Amory* [1955] Ch. 567 (ministerial marketing scheme); *Harper* v. *Home Secretary* [1955] Ch. 238 (C.A.). And see W.S. Holdsworth (1943) 59 L.Q.R. 2 (denying jurisdiction of courts in such cases); Z. Cowen, "The Injunction and Parliamentary Process' (1955) 71 L.Q.R. 336.

[44] Crown Proceedings Act 1947, s.21. But see *R.* v. *Governor of Pentonville Prison, ex p. Herbage,* [1986] 3 W.L.R. 504; *post* p. 715.

[45] [1955] Ch. 238, *ante.*

[46] [1970] A.C. 1136; O. Hood Phillips, "Judicial Intervention in the Legislative Process" (1971) 87 L.Q.R. 321. *Cf.* G. Sawer, "Injunction, Parliamentary Process, and the Restriction of Parliamentary Competence" (1944) 60 L.Q.R. 83: suppose an Act expressly authorises the citizen and the courts to intervene by injunction.

[47] [1965] A.C. 172. *Cf.* G. Marshall, "Parliamentary Sovereignty: A Recent Development" (1966–67) 12 McGill L.J. 523.

[48] [1967] 1 A.C. 259.

[49] The Ceylon Constitution of 1947 was not merely "written," but contained entrenched clauses subject to judicial review.

prevent repeal or amendment by a later Act.[50] (The European Communities Act 1972 does not, it should be remembered, contain any provision purporting to bind future Parliaments.)

Parliament Acts[51]

Public Acts (with one specific exception) may, in certain circumstances, be passed by the Queen and the Commons without the consent of the Lords under the Parliament Acts 1911 and 1949. It has been argued that by the Parliament Acts Parliament has bound itself for the future as to the manner and form of legislation, or that for this purpose "Parliament" now consists of the Queen and the Commons. It is submitted that both arguments are unsound. In the first place, the Parliament Acts do not limit the powers of Parliament. All Bills (including Money Bills) must be sent to the Lords, and the Lords have the opportunity of agreeing to them all if they wish. What the Parliament Acts do is to alter the usual procedure for public Bills by limiting the time during which the Lords may deliberate: after that time a Bill may be sent for the Royal Assent although the Lords have not agreed to it. This is an alternative permissive procedure, which only comes into play after the prescribed period if the Lords do not consent to a Bill in the form approved by the Commons. Again, the five-year maximum life of Parliament is effective in that, if Parliament is not dissolved by prerogative by the end of five years, it would be dissolved automatically by the Parliament Act 1911; but Parliament can during the five-year period pass an Act in the ordinary way extending or reducing its life.[52]

Secondly, the Parliament Acts do not alter the composition of Parliament.[53] When an Act is passed by the Queen and the Commons under the provisions of the Parliament Acts, the enacting formula must state that this is done in accordance with the provisions of those Acts (which include the sending of the Bill to the Lords),[54] and so it may best be regarded as a kind of subordinate or delegated legislation.[55]

Indeed, we may doubt whether the measure calling itself "the Parliament Act 1949" is valid.[56] The Parliament Act 1911, of course, received

---

[50] *e.g.* Keir and Lawson, *Cases in Constitutional Law* (4th ed., 1954), p. 7: an Act providing that no Bill to repeal it should have effect unless approved by a referendum (passage omitted from later editions); J. L. Montrose, *Precedent in English Law and other Essays* (1968) and J. D. B. Mitchell, *Constitutional Law* (2nd ed., 1968), p. 89, cite the National Insurance Act 1965, s.116, which reproduced certain departmental regulations but provided that their validity might be determined as though they remained delegated legislation. Montrose, *op. cit.* pp. 283–284, also suggested the application of Interpretation Acts and the maxim *generalia specialibus non derogant* as possible limitations on the doctrine that Parliament cannot bind itself.

[51] See further, *post,* Chap. 7.

[52] Parliament in fact extended its life during both World Wars.

[53] *Cf.* Jennings, *Constitutional Laws of the Commonwealth* (1957), pp. 124–125.

[54] A number of procedural provisions must be complied with, as to which the Speaker's certificate is stated to be conclusive: Parliament Act 1911, s.3. *Cf. Akar* v. *Att.-Gen. of Sierra Leone* [1970] A.C. 853 (P.C.).

[55] H. W. R. Wade [1954] C.L.J. 265; [1955] C.L.J. 193.

[56] Hood Phillips, *Reform of the Constitution,* pp. 18–19, 91–93; letter from O. Hood Phillips to *The Times,* July 15, 1968; Graham Zellick, "Is the Parliament Act *Ultra Vires?*" (1969) 119 New L.J. 716. See further, *post,* Chap. 7.

the consent of the House of Lords; but the "Parliament Act 1949"—designed to reduce still further the period during which the Lords might delay a public Bill other than a Money Bill—did not receive the consent of the Lords but purported to be passed in accordance with the provisions of the Parliament Act 1911. It therefore offended against the general principle of logic and law that delegates (the Queen and Commons) cannot enlarge the authority delegated to them. We are not, of course, arguing—as it is impossible in English law to argue—that an Act of Parliament is invalid; what we are questioning is whether the measure called "the Parliament Act 1949" bears the character of an Act of Parliament. In other words we are contending that the Parliament Act 1911, as an enabling Act, cannot itself be amended by subordinate legislation of the Queen and Commons. At the time of writing no Act has purported to be passed without the consent of the Lords "in accordance with the provisions of the Parliament Acts 1911 and 1949," and so no legislation yet stands in jeopardy as depending on the doubtful effectiveness of the "Act" of 1949.

Regency Acts[57]

The Regency Acts 1937–53 provide that if the Sovereign is under 18 years of age, the royal functions shall be exercised by a Regent appointed under the provisions of the Acts. The Regent may assent to Bills, except Bills altering the succession to the throne or repealing the Acts securing the Scottish Church. It is clear that the Regent and the two Houses could not repeal these exceptions, not because Parliament has bound its successors, but because legislation passed with the Regent's assent is a kind of subordinate or delegated legislation which must keep within the limits prescribed by the Regency Acts. On the other hand, it seems that a Sovereign under the age of eighteen could assent to Bills, including Bills excepted from the Regent's authority and Bills to repeal or amend the Regency Acts themselves,[58] for a Sovereign is never an infant at common law and Parliament is not bound by the procedure provided by the Regency Acts. This does not mean that these provisions of the Regency Acts are "void." They are valid and effective so long as they remain unrepealed in that, if a Regent is appointed, Bills assented to by him (subject to the two exceptions) will be recognised as valid statutes.

Conclusion

It appears that the only way by which the legislature of this country could become legally limited would be for the United Kingdom Parliament to extinguish itself, after surrendering its powers to a new written constitution,[59] with entrenched provisions (e.g. as to abolition of the Second Chamber, the life of Parliament, membership of EEC, and a Bill of Rights) and judicial review—a constitution limiting the powers of the

---

[57] See further, post, Chap. 13.
[58] H. W. R. Wade [1955] C.L.J. 193n.
[59] Cf. A. V. Dicey. England's Case against Home Rule (3rd ed., 1887), pp. 241–245; could Parliament merely transfer its powers to another legislature?

new legislature *and to which the new legislature would owe its existence.*
The new constitution could either be drafted by the existing Parliament,
or its drafting could be entrusted to a constituent assembly, the new
constitution perhaps receiving the extra moral sanction of an inaugural
referendum. In either case there would be a *breach of continuity* between
the old and the new constitutions.[60]

---

[60] Hood Phillips, *Reform of the Constitution*, pp. 156 *et seq.* For another suggestion, see
Lord Hailsham, *The Dilemma of Democracy*, Chap. 36.

CHAPTER 5

THE UNITED KINGDOM AND THE EUROPEAN COMMUNITIES[1]

I. THE EUROPEAN COMMUNITIES

In the previous chapter the constitutional implications of membership of the European Communities were considered in the light of the supremacy of Parliament and section 2(4) of the European Communities Act 1972. In this chapter it is intended to consider more generally the impact on United Kingdom law of the 1972 Act and Community law.

In 1951 France, the German Federal Republic, Italy, Belgium, Holland and Luxembourg established, by the Treaty of Paris, the European Coal and Steel Community (ECSC). The same six States in 1957, established by two Treaties of Rome, the European Economic Community (EEC) and the European Atomic Energy Community (EURATOM). The three Communities remain distinct entities although the organs of the three bodies have been merged so that there is now a single Court, Assembly, Council of Ministers and Commission for all three. The United Kingdom first applied to join the Communities in 1961, when Mr. Macmillan was Prime Minister and Mr. Heath led the negotiations on behalf of the Government. This attempt to join was frustrated in 1963 by France. Mr Wilson's Government renewed the application in 1967, and negotiations were continued after the general election of 1970 by Mr. Heath's Government. With the approval of Parliament a Treaty of Accession was signed at Brussels in 1972, to take effect from January 1, 1973. Denmark and the Republic of Ireland also acceded. Subsequently Greece became a member in 1980 and Spain and Portugal in 1986.

The main institutions common to the three European Communities are the Council of Ministers, the Commission, the Assembly and the Court of Justice. *The Council* is made up of one representative of the government of each of the Member States. General Council meetings are attended by Foreign Ministers; specialised Council meetings are attended by ministers responsible for a particular subject, *e.g.* agriculture, industry or transport. The President of the Council holds office for six months and rotation between the member states is in alphabetical sequence. The Council makes general policy decisions and adopts formal legal acts, nearly always based on proposals made by the Commission. Proposals are normally transmitted by the the Council to the Assembly for its opinion. Although the Treaty lays down a rule requir-

[1] L. Collins, *European Community Law in the United Kingdom* (3rd ed., 1984); D. Lasok and J. W. Bridge, *Introduction to the Law and Institutions of the European Communities* (3rd ed., 1982); A. Parry and J. Dinnage, *Parry and Hardy EEC Law* (2nd ed., 1981); Lord Mackenzie Stuart, *The European Communities and the Rule of Law* (Hamlyn Lectures, 1977); L. Neville Brown and F.G. Jacobs, *The Court of Justice of the European Communities* (2nd ed., 1983); T. C. Hartley, *The Foundations of European Community Law* (1981); M. P. Furmston, R. Kerridge and B. E. Sufrin (eds.), *The Effect on English Domestic Law of Membership of the European Communities* (1983).

ing the taking of most decisions by a qualified majority vote[2] the Council has normally sought to reach agreement without using the formal voting procedures prescribed by the Treaty.

Following bitter disagreement between the then members of the Council a compromise was reached (*the Accords de Luxembourg*) in 1965 under which unanimity was required before a decision could be taken where a member state felt that an important national interest was involved. Whether the *Accords* has any legal validity is open to doubt. Nor has it been always adhered to. In May 1982, for example, the Council approved an increase in the price of agricultural products against the opposition of the United Kingdom, supported by Denmark and Greece.

The Commission consists of 17 Commissioners appointed by agreement among the governments of the Member States. Commissioners are required to act independently in the interests of the Community and not as representatives of their national government. Each of the five larger member states, France, Germany, Italy, Spain and the United Kingdom, has two Commissioners, and the smaller members have one each. The Commission acts as a collective body by majority vote. It makes policy proposals to the Council and drafts legislative acts for adoption by the Council, as well as itself adopting certain formal acts.[3] As guardian of the Community Treaties the Commission has power to initiate action against a member state for violation of the Treaty, and eventually to take proceedings against a member state before the Court of Justice.

The Assembly (or "European Parliament") represents the peoples of the Member States. The powers of the Assembly so far are deliberative and consultative rather than legislative, though since 1975 it has had control over part of the Community budget, a power which it has increasingly used.[4] A government is not formed from its members. The Council usually consults (and in some cases is required to consult) the Assembly on proposals submitted to it by the Commission. The Assembly comments on the proposals and may put forward amendments, which the Council is not obliged to accept. Questions may be asked in the Assembly about the work of the Council and the Commission, and the Commission may be required to resign and to be replaced if the Assembly passes a motion of censure against it by a two-thirds majority of the votes, constituting a majority of the members of the Assembly.

Until 1978 the members of the Assembly were chosen by the national legislatures from among their own numbers. In 1976 the governments of the member states agreed that from 1978 the members of the European Assembly should be directly elected by universal suffrage. The size of the constituencies varies from state to state to secure that there is not too great a variation in the number of representatives of each state. Lux-

---

[2] Each member state has a weighted vote: France, Germany, Italy and the United Kingdom have ten votes each; Spain has eight votes; Belgium, Greece, the Netherlands and Portugal have five votes each; Denmark and Ireland have three; Luxembourg has two. The qualified majority is 54 votes, out of a possible 76.

[3] The Treaties avoid the word "legislation" and speak of "acts" of the Council and the Commission.

[4] See *Council of the European Community* v. *European Parliament, The Times*, 4 July, 1986.

embourg, at one extreme, has six representatives; France, Germany, Italy and the United Kingdom have 81 representatives.[5] As a result of the accession of Spain and Portugal, the total number of seats in the Assembly is now 518.

The Court of Justice, which sits at Luxembourg, consists of 13 judges appointed by agreement among the governments of the member states.[6] The President of the Court is elected from among the judges. The Court is assisted by six advocates-general, an office to which there is no precise parallel in common law or Scottish legal systems.[7] The Court has jurisdiction to decide disputes between member states concerning the application of the terms of the Treaties or relating to the general object or purpose of the Communities, and to hear proceedings brought by Community institutions against member states, including power to determine the validity of acts of the Council and Commission. In addition to its contentious jurisdiction, the Court is empowered by Article 177 of the EEC Treaty to give preliminary rulings, in particular cases arising in the courts of the member states, on the interpretation of the Treaty and of acts and statutes of Community organs. This advisory jurisdiction is discussed below.

The aims of the EEC

The treaty which established the Common Market referred specifically to "four freedoms," the freedom of movement of goods; the freedom of movement of persons; the freedom to provide services and the freedom of movement of capital. A further fundamental principle of the Common Market is the development of a common agricultural policy among the member states.[8] The law of the EEC has developed on the basis of these underlying foundations; its effect on the domestic laws of the United Kingdom will be considered in the following sections of this chapter.

Political, economic and institutional reform of the EEC

A major step to future reform of the EEC was taken when the Treaty, known as the Single European Act 1986, was adopted by the heads of state or government of the member states. This treaty has to be ratified by all the member states before it can take effect. In accordance with the requirement of British law the European Communities (Amendment) Act 1986 gives internal effect to the Treaty in the United Kingdom.

The Treaty refers in the preamble to the will to continue the work

---

[5] Spain has 60 representatives; the Netherlands has 25, Belgium, Greece and Portugal have 24; Denmark has 16 and Ireland has 15.

[6] In practice each member has a judge of its nationality on the court. The thirteenth judgeship is held in rotation by a national of France, Germany, Italy and the United Kingdom.

[7] A. A. Dashwood, "The Advocate General in the Court of Justice of the European Communities" (1982) 2 Leg. Stud. 202; Sir G. Slynn, "The Court of Justice of the European Communities" (1984) 33 I.C.L.Q. 409.

[8] The development of the common agricultural policy has been one of the most controversial features of the EEC. For an introduction, see Francis G. Snyder, *Law of the Common Agricultural Policy* (1985).

towards a European Union, and a variety of political and economic steps are provided to move towards this goal. These include an expansion of the scope of Community competence into new areas including social policy, research and technological development and the environment; the adoption of measures aimed at progressively establishing the internal market[9]; the coordination of foreign policies in matters such as security; and the establishment of regular formal meetings within the framework of European political cooperation.

The most significant institutional change concerns decision-making in the Community. A new "Cooperation procedure" is introduced for certain categories of Community legislation which will increase the influence of the European Parliament (as it will now officially be known), and the Commission, although the last word will remain with the Council of Ministers. There is also to be an extension of qualified majority voting in the Council, which is aimed at speeding up the completion of the internal market of the Community by 1992. The extent to which the Luxembourg compromise will affect the new areas of majority voting remains to be seen. Other institutional changes are the official recognition of the "European Council,"[10] although it is not given any specific powers or functions; and provision for the future establishment of a court of first instance to hear "certain classes of action or proceedings brought by natural or legal persons." The latter proposal aims to ease the existing workload of the Court of Justice.

The Treaty is of constitutional significance for all the member states. It represents a movement towards greater collective action in the Community and will effect the amount of influence national governments and parliaments can hope to exert on future Community laws.[11]

II. The United Kingdom Legislation

Effect was given inside the United Kingdom to the treaties establishing and regulating the European Communities by the European Communities Act 1972. The holding of elections to select representatives to sit in the European Assembly is mainly governed by the European Assembly Elections Acts 1979.

European Communities Act 1972

Section 1 is a deceptive section which appears to do no more than provide a short title for the Act (sub s.1) and define certain terms such as "the Communities" and "the Treaties" which are used later in the Act (sub s.2). "The Treaties" include various specifically named treaties[12] and *inter alia* any treaty ancillary to any of "the Treaties" entered into by the United Kingdom. Additions to "the Treaties," as defined, may be

---

[9] The internal market refers to an area without internal frontiers where there is free movement of goods, persons, services and capital.

[10] *i.e.* Heads of State or Government of the member states meeting from time to time.

[11] Several reports have been made by committees on the implications of the single European Act. See *e.g.* 1985–86; H.C. 264; 1985–86; H.C. 400; 1985–86; H.C. 442 and government reply Cmnd. 9858; 1985–86; H.L. 149.

[12] The list has been extended by the European Communities (Greek Accession) Act 1979 and European Communities (Spanish and Portuguese Accession) Act 1985.

made by Order in Council, subject to the approval by resolution of both Houses of Parliament, if the treaty was entered into by the United Kingdom after January 22, 1972. (sub s.3) The significance of that sub-section became clear in *R. v. H.M. Treasury, ex p. Smedley*,[13] where the applicant sought to challenge the legality of a draft Order in Council which purported to recognise as an ancillary treaty an agreement to make payments to cover expenditure required under the budget which had been agreed by the Community. The importance of such recognition is to be found in section 2(3) of the 1972 Act which provides the Treasury with authority to charge on and issue out of the Consolidated Fund or, as the case may be, the National Loans Fund, the amounts required to meet any obligation created or arising under "the Treaties." From which it follows that once an international agreement has been declared to be one of the Community Treaties the Treasury is, without further authority, entitled to make any payments called for by that agreement. Although the Court of Appeal could not express a view on a draft Order in Council, it indicated that an Order in Council in the terms of the draft would have been *intra vires*. Sir John Donaldson M.R. thought that the concept of one treaty being "ancillary" to another was not one of precision and it was no doubt for that reason, amongst others, that Parliament has provided in section 1(3) of the 1972 Act for a system whereby an Order in Council should be conclusive of what treaties were to be regarded as Community treaties. The Master of the Rolls added that in his view nothing could be more ancillary to the Community treaties than the provision of funds to enable the Community to fulfil its essential functions. Slade L.J. similarly thought that the phrase was deliberately "an imprecise expression of wide and somewhat uncertain import."

Section 2(1) provides that all such rights and obligations from time-to-time created or arising under the Treaties, and all such remedies and procedures from time to time provided for by or under the Treaties, as in accordance with the Treaties are without further enactment to be given legal effect or used in the United Kingdom shall be recognised and be available in law, and be enforced, and followed accordingly; and the expression "enforceable Community right" shall refer to one to which this subsection applies. This subsection provides for the recognition and enforcement in the United Kingdom of directly effective or applicable Community rights and obligations enjoyed by or imposed on member states or private individuals. This means Community law as interpreted in accordance with the Treaties. It covers rights and obligations created by the Treaties themselves, by existing and future Community *Regulations* which take effect directly in the member states[14] and by *Directives* to the extent that they are directly effective or applicable.[15] It is a constitutional innovation to give effect to *future* Community Regulations and Directives which constitute a new source of law in this

---

[13] [1985] Q.B. 657 (C.A.) For a statutory increase in the United Kingdom's financial obligations to the Community see the European Communities (Finance) Act 1985.

[14] Art. 189(2) of the Treaty of Rome provides that a Regulation shall be binding in its entirety and directly applicable to all Member States.

[15] Art. 189(3).

country. The expression "remedies and procedures" appears to provide for references under Article 177 to the European Court of Justice. Community law that is not directly applicable is dealt with elsewhere in the Act, notably in section 2(2) and Schedule 2, or in other Acts such as the Finance Act 1972 (dealing with VAT).

Section 2(2) confers power by Order in Council or ministerial regulation (subject to Sched. 2) to give effect to existing and future Community laws that are not directly effective or applicable, especially Community *Directives* (which set out the objects to be achieved while leaving it to each member state to choose the method of achieving them). This power includes power to deal with supplementary matters, probably including references to the European Court of Justice. The person exercising any statutory power or duty is empowered to have regard to the objects of the Community and to any rights and obligations of the United Kingdom under the Treaties.[16]

Schedule 2 provides that the power to make subordinate legislation under section 2(2) does not include power:

(a) to impose or increase taxation; or
(b) to legislate with retroactive effect; or
(c) to confer power of sub-delegation,[17] except rules of court; or
(d) to create any new criminal offence punishable with imprisonment for more than two years or (on summary conviction) three months, or with a fine up to the maximum figure on level 5 or *per* day at level 3.[17a]

The power of subordinate legislation conferred is to be exercised by statutory instrument; and any such statutory instrument, if made without a draft having been approved by each House, is subject to annulment by resolution of either House.

Section 3, which was discussed in Chapter 4, provides for the reference to the European Court of questions relating to Community law and directs the courts of the United Kingdom to determine disputes involving Community law according to the principles laid down by the European Court. Any question of the meaning of a provision of European law is to be treated as a question of law, that is it is to be determined by the judge, not the jury, and in the light of argument from counsel not on the basis of evidence by expert witnesses.[18]

The remaining sections of the Act effect specific amendments to the laws of the United Kingdom. In particular, section 6 provides for the creation of an Intervention Board to enable the United Kingdom to participate in the Common Agricultural Policy.

European Assembly Elections Act 1978

The European Assembly Elections Act 1978 makes provision for the direct election to the European Assembly of "representatives of the

---

[16] In practice delegated legislation giving effect to Community law is often made under general enabling provisions in other statutes, *e.g.* Agriculture Act 1970.

[17] Sub-paragraph (c) does not apply to a power to legislate conferred otherwise than under s.2(2), or to a power to give administrative directions.

[17a] Criminal Justice Act 1982.

[18] See *R.* v. *Goldstein* [1982] 1 W.L.R. 804 (C.A.).

people of the United Kingdom" (s.1). Of the total number of 81 representatives, 66 are to be elected to represent England, eight to represent Scotland, four to represent Wales and three to represent Northern Ireland. The determination of the boundaries of the constituencies is entrusted to the Boundary Commissions which are responsible for keeping under review constituency boundaries for the purpose of general elections.[19] As a general principle, persons disqualified for election to the House of Commons are disqualified for election to the European Assembly. Peers, however, other than Lords of Appeal in Ordinary, and ordained clergymen of any religious denomination are eligible for election to the Assembly.[20] For elections to the European Assembly the francise is extended to include peers.[21] The method of voting in England, Wales and Scotland is the traditional British simple majority system. In Northern Ireland—where the three representatives are returned by one constituency—the method is the single transferable vote system.[22]

The legality of the simple majority system under Community law was unsuccessfully challenged in *Prince* v. *Secretary of State for Scotland*[23] in which a group of S.D.P. Liberal Alliance voters applied to the Court of Session for a declarator "that the pursuers had an "enforceable Community right" in terms of section 2 of the European Communities Act 1972, to a system of election which is not discriminatory and which gives equal weight to all votes cast so far as practicable in the forthcoming election for members of the European Parliament." The pursuers' argument was that the European Elections Act 1978, in so far as it did not provide for proportional representation, was *ultra vires* the Treaty of Rome. While Article 138(3) of the Treaty had envisaged that the Council would lay down a uniform system of voting throughout the Community, no scheme had been adopted as a result of the United Kingdom's veto. However, Article 138(3) had nevertheless provided that direct elections were to be "by universal suffrage." Like other provisions of the Treaty, Article 138 fell to be interpreted in accordance with fundamental principles of Community law which included the right of equality or non-discrimination. The right to equality of voting was thus "an enforceable Community right" in terms of the European Communities Act 1972: this had been infringed by the 1978 Act, which, by endorsing the first-past-the-post system, was unequal and discriminating. As important issues of Community law were inevitably involved in their declaratory conclusions, the pursuers maintained that a reference to the European Court of Justice was necessary under Article 177. In refusing the reference, Lord Cameron held that on the pleadings as they stood, a reference would be premature because no attempt had been made to formulate with sufficient precision the questions which were to be put to the European Court, which, in his Lordship's view did *not* exist "for the purpose of determining academic questions." More-

---

[19] Parliamentary Constituencies Act 1986. *Post*, p. 191. See also European Assembly Elections Act 1981.
[20] *Post*, p. 198.
[21] *Post*, p. 190 for the rules applicable to elections to the House of Commons.
[22] *Post*, pp. 198–199.
[23] [1985] S.L.T. 74.

over, there were serious issues in the case which were still uncertain and had to be clarified before a reference could be made. For example, there were doubts whether the pursuers had title to sue merely because they were on the electoral list, whether Article 138(3)—which *prima facie* gives no rights to individuals—could be the basis of enforceable Community rights and, finally, whether the principle of equality in Community law could be invoked outside commercial matters. In view of the fact that the other members of the Community use various forms of proportional representation and that it is used in Northern Ireland even in domestic elections, it is unlikely that the last has been heard of the issue.

Section 6 provides that no treaty which is intended to increase the powers of the Assembly shall be ratified by the United Kingdom unless it has been approved by an Act of Parliament. Normally treaties are ratified by the Crown (or executive) although legislation is required subsequently if they are to have effect within the United Kingdom. In this instance the Executive is precluded from even concluding an agreement without legislative approval.[24]

Provisions for the payment of salaries, allowances and pensions to Representatives elected to the Assembly is made by the European Assembly (Pay and Pensions) Act 1979.

III. Community Law as a Source of Domestic Law

Community law is a direct source of law in this country in the case of matters having a "European element,"[25] if it is "directly applicable" to individuals, and if such law is either self-executing or implemented under section 2(2) of the European Communities Act 1972 or by any other Act of Parliament.

Enforceable Community rights

Section 2(1) of the 1972 Act gives effect in British courts to rights and obligations which, under Community law, are to have effect within member states without further enactment. Provisions which are not directly applicable or effective are not part of the law of the United Kingdom until legislation has made them so under section 2(2). Hence it is not true to say that Community law is part of domestic law "lock, stock and barrel" as Lord Denning M.R. said in *Re Westinghouse Uranium Contract*.[26] Whether a rule of Community law requires domestic legislation to become part of the law of the Member States or is law *proprio vigore* is itself a matter of Community law. In the case of the litigant seeking to rely on Community law in a British court, it is necessary to show that the rule in question creates a directly enforceable individual right (direct effect). Rules of Community law may, however, be

---

[24] See further, *post* p. 285.
[25] *R. v. Saunders* [1980] Q.B. 72 (E.C.J.) (Freedom of movement of workers: Art. 48 inapplicable to purely domestic provisions of criminal law which do not involve discrimination between nationals of different Member States). Followed, *In re Narinder Singh Virdee, The Times*, March 13, 1980 (Div. Ct.).
[26] [1978] A.C. 547, 564.

directly applicable within member states without creating individual rights.[27]

To be directly effective, a rule of Community law—whether a provision of the EEC Treaty or of a Regulation or Directive or Decision made under the Treaty—must be clear and unconditional; capable of being implemented without legislative intervention by the member states and by its nature indicate that it does not only concern the member states in their relations *inter se*.[28] In the *Van Gend en Loos case*[29] the European Court held that Article 12 of the Treaty which forbade the introduction of new customs duties or any increase in existing duties, had direct effect so that an individual could rely on its terms in a natural court. In *Belgische Radio en Televisie* v. *SABAM*[30] the European Court gave direct effect to Articles 85 and 86 of the Treaty which forbid practices which unduly reduce competition or amount to an abuse of a dominant trading position. In *Defrenne* v. *Sabena (No. 2)*[31] the European court held that the principle of equal pay for equal work, laid down by Article 119, was directly effective.[32] Article 52, which recognises the freedom of establishment, was held by the European Court to have direct effect in *Patrick* v. *Minister of Cultural Affairs*.[33] Regulations are explicitly recognised under Article 189 as being directly applicable. Direct effectiveness, without the need for further legislation was attributed by the European Court to two Regulations providing for the payment of premiums in respect of slaughtered dairy cows in *Orsolina Leonesio* v. *Minister for Agriculture and Forestry of the Italian Republic*[34] Directives may have direct effect as shown by *Van Duyn* v. *Home Office*,[35] the first reference to the European Court by an English Court. More usually they require implementation by municipal legislation before they take effect.[36]

The question of direct effectiveness or applicability has arisen in a

---

[27] The distinction remains valid, even if the European Court is not always consistent in its terminology. See J. Steiner, "Direct Applicability in EEC Law—A Chameleon Concept" [1982] 98 L.Q.R. 229; M. Friend, "Judicial Review, Private Rights and Community Law" [1985] P.L. 21.

[28] See G. Bebr, "Directly Applicable Provisions of Community Law: the Development of a Community Concept" (1970) 19 I.C.L.Q. 257; J.A. Winter, "Direct Applicability and Direct Effect" (1977) 9 C.M.L. Rev. 425; E. Easson, "The 'direct effect' of EEC Directives" (1979) 28 I.C.L.Q. 319; "Can Directives impose obligations on Individuals?" (1979) 4 E.L. Rev. 67. See also, *European Law and the Individual* ed. F.G. Jacobs, (1976).

[29] [1963] E.C.R. 1.

[30] [1974] E.C.R. 51; cited by the Court of Appeal in *Application des Gaz S.A.* v. *Falks Veritas Ltd.* [1974] Ch. 381.

[31] [1976] E.C.R. 1. See *Snoxell and Davies* v. *Vauxhall Motors* [1978] Q.B. 11.

[32] The Court ruled that direct effect was to be limited to the future so its decision could not open the floodgates to claims based on facts occurring before its judgment in that case.

[33] [1977] 2 C.M.L.R. 523 (English architect with qualifications recognised by French law; entitled to practise in France).

[34] [1972] E.C.R. 287.

[35] [1974] E.C.R. 1337; [1975] Ch. 338 (Implementation of Art. 48—free movement of workers—by Directive). See too *Marshall* v. *Southampton and South West Hampshire Area Health Authority (Teaching)* [1986] 2 All E.R. 584 (E.C.J.).

[36] *e.g. Hugh-Jones* v. *St. John's College, Cambridge* [1979] I.C.R. 848 (EAT); *Farrall* v. *Dept. of Transport* [1983] R.T.R. 279 (Q.B.).

number of cases before the English Courts. The Court of Appeal supposed they were following Community law in *Schorsch Meier GmbH.* v. *Hennin*,[37] where S was a motor manufacturer in Munich and H a motor dealer in England. Article 106 of the EEC Treaty requires that a creditor in one Member State shall receive payment for goods in the currency of the country in which he resides. The Court of Appeal held that the common law rule that judgment for a sum of money could be awarded only in sterling had been superseded by the EEC Treaty and there was no need to refer the case to the European Court. The House of Lords in *Miliangos* v. *George Frank (Textiles) Ltd.*,[38] however, doubted whether Article 106 was directly effective, but gave a decision to the same effect on the different ground of the changes in the foreign exchange situation generally and the position of sterling in particular.

Reference to the European Court of Justice[39]

Article 177 of the EEC Treaty gives the European Court of Justice jurisdiction to give preliminary rulings on Community law at the request of the courts of member states. This Article provides that:

(1) The European Court has jurisdiction to give preliminary rulings concerning:
  (a) the interpretation of the Treaty;
  (b) the validity and interpretation of acts of Community institutions;
  (c) the interpretation of the statutes [*i.e.* constitutions] of bodies established by the Council.

(2) Any court or tribunal of a member state *may*, if it considers that a decision thereon is necessary to enable it to give judgment, request the Court to give a ruling.

(3) A court or tribunal of a Member State [in which such a question arises] against those whose decision there is no judicial remedy under national law, *shall* bring the matter before the European Court.[40]

Where the national court has a discretion under (2), the principles on which a British court should exercise that discretion were indicated by Lord Denning M.R. in *Bulmer* v. *Bollinger*.[41] The question was whether English firms might continue to describe their products as "champagne cider" and "champagne perry," or whether under Community law the word "champagne" might be used only for wine produced in the Champagne district of France. The French company wanted the English judge to refer the question to the European Court for preliminary rulings, but the Court of Appeal held that an English judge or court below

---

[37] [1975] Q.B. 416; [1975] C.M.L.R. 20.
[38] [1976] A.C. 443.
[39] F.G. Jacobs, "When to refer to the European Court" (1974) 90 L.Q.R. 486; J.W. Bridge, "Community Law and English Courts and Tribunals" (1975) 1 E.L.Rev. 13; J. Forman and T. Stevens, "The Attitude of British Courts to Community law" (1976) 13 C.M.L. Rev. 388; P.D. Dagtoglou, "The English Judges and European Community Law" [1978] C.L.J. 76.
[40] R.S.C., Ord. 114 deals with references by the High Court to the European Court and appeals from the High Court in such cases to the Court of Appeal. Rules of Court have also been made with regard to references to the European Court in criminal appeals, and from the Crown Court and County Courts.
[41] *H.P. Bulmer* v. *J. Bollinger SA* [1974] Ch. 401; *cf. per* Stephenson L.J.

the House of Lords has a complete discretion whether to refer to the European Court a question of the interpretation of the Treaty. Lord Denning M.R. said that:

(a) the decision of the question must be *necessary* to enable the English court to give judgment;

(b) the decision of the question must be *conclusive* of the case;

(c) if the court decides a decision is *necessary* it must still in the exercise of its discretion consider such circumstances as the delay involved, the difficulty and importance of the point, the expense, and the burden on the European Court. In order to exercise its discretion properly the court should decide the facts before considering whether to make a reference to the European court.[42]

Lord Denning M.R.'s guidelines have been criticised as unduly restrictive, in particular his requirement that the point in question is conclusive of the case only if whichever way it is decided by the European Court, it will determine the outcome of the case. It may be that a point decided in one way would be conclusive of a case: judges should surely be entitled to seek a ruling from the European Court in such circumstances. Doubts were also expressed about Lord Denning M.R.'s suggestion that it is not necessary to refer a question where the law is clear and the national court has merely to apply the law (the *acte clair* doctrine).

The European Court itself had the opportunity to consider the meaning of Article 177 in *C.I.L.F.I.T.* v. *Italian Ministry of Health*,[43] where it was asked to consider the meaning of the third paragraph of the Article (which relates to a national court against whose decision there is no judicial remedy under national law). The European Court concluded that there is no duty to refer a question where the question is irrelevant, that is if the answer to that question, regardless of what it may be, cannot affect the outcome of the case. Secondly, there is no duty to refer a question which is materially similar to one already decided by the Court.[44] Thirdly, there is no need to refer where there is no real doubt about the law. Before, however, a national court comes to the conclusion that such is the case, it must be convinced that the matter is equally obvious to the courts of the other member states and to the Court of Justice.[45] *A fortiori*, it might be thought, a court with a discretion to refer questions to the European Court will be entitled not to do so in these three cases.

The third paragraph of Article 177 applies not only to the House of Lords, from whose decisions there can never be an appeal, but to any court in the United Kingdom against whose decision in particular proceedings there is no further judicial remedy. There may be doubt as to what constitutes a judicial remedy. Thus a tribunal against whose decision there is no appeal may be said to fall within the third paragraph although in certain circumstances its decision could be set aside

---

[42] See further *Customs and Excise Cmrs.* v. *ApS Samex* [1983] 1 All E.R. 1042.

[43] [1983] 1 C.M.L.R. 472.

[44] See, for example, *R.* v. *Secretary of State for Social Services, ex p. Bosmore Medical Supplies Ltd., The Times*, December 16, 1985.

[45] See, for example, *Re Sandhu The Times*, May 10, 1985 (H.L.).

on an application for judicial review.[46] Similarly the Court of Appeal should perhaps be included within the third paragraph if, for any reason, no further appeal is available.[47]

The desirability of establishing the facts of a case before referring a question to the European Court is, as a matter of general principle, obvious and has been emphasised in *R. v. Henn*.[48] It is not, however, an invariable rule: *R. v. Plymouth Justices ex p. Rogers*.[49] In both cases, too, emphasis was placed on the need for caution on the part of magistrates and judges at first instance in referring cases to the European Court.[50] Appellate courts are better placed to assess the need for a reference and to formulate questions.

References by United Kingdom courts and tribunals

The first reference from the House of Lords was in *R. v. Henn*[51] where the appellants had been convicted of offences in connection with importing obscene or indecent articles. The House asked the European Court whether a statutory prohibition on the importing of a type of article constituted a "quantative restriction on imports" within Article 30 and, if so, whether it could none the less be justifiable within Article 36 as a restriction imposed on the "grounds of public morality, public policy or public security." In *Garland* v. *British Rail Engineering*[52] the House of Lords sought the opinion of the European Court on the meaning of "pay" in Article 119, before construing the Sex Discrimination Act 1975. References from the Court of Appeal (Civil Division) have also often been concerned with equal pay and sex discrimination: *e.g. Macarthys* v. *Smith*[53]; *Worringham* v. *Lloyds Bank Ltd.*[54] The Court of Appeal (Criminal Division) in *R. v. Thompson*[55] inquired whether the prohibition on the quantitative restriction of imports under Article 30 applied to gold and silver coins; and, if it did, whether a restriction on the importing of such coins might be justified on the grounds of public policy under Article 36.

The deportation of EEC nationals convicted of criminal offences gave rise to a reference by the Divisional Court in *R. v. Secretary of State for Home Affairs, ex p. Santillo*.[56] The applicant had been convicted on

---

[46] *Post*, p. 661.

[47] *Hagen* v. *Fratelli D. and G. Morretts S.N.C.* [1980] 3 C.M.L.R. 253, 255 *per* Buckley L.J.

[48] [1981] A.C. 580 (H.C.) See too, *Church of Scientology of California* v. *Customs and Excise Cmrs.* [1981] 1 All E.R. 1035, (C.A.).

[49] [1982] Q.B. 863.

[50] A caution demonstrated, for example, by Dillon J. in *MacMahon* v. *Department of Education and Science* [1983] Ch. 227.

[51] [1981] A.C. 580; *post*, p. 108.

[52] [1983] 2 A.C. 751; *ante*, p. 75. Patent law was the subject of the reference in *R. v. Comptroller Patents Ex p. Gist-Brocades* [1986] 1 W.L.R. 51 (H.L.).

[53] [1981] Q.B. 180; *ante*, p. 77.

[54] [1981] 1 W.L.R. 950; [1982] 1 W.L.R. 841; *ante*, p. 78.

[55] [1980] Q.B. 229; 69 Cr.App.R. 22.

[56] [1981] Q.B. 778 (Div. Ct. and C.A.); [1980] 2 C.M.L.R. 308 (E.C.J.) Templeman L.J. commented, "The Divisional Court was obliged to turn its back on reality and to propound certain questions to the European Court of Justice. Immersed in the cloudy generality of its functions under article 177 of the E.E.C. Treaty, the European Court was also obliged to ignore reality but furnished replies which enable this court now to approach the moment of truth"; [1981] Q.B. 778, 797.

charges of rape and buggery. The Home Secretary made an order for deportation as the end of Santillo's period of imprisonment approached. The prisoner sought judicial review of the order on the ground that the procedure by which it was made did not comply with Community law, in particular Directive (64/221/E.E.C.). The Divisional Court sought the guidance of the European Court and in the light of its ruling the English courts were able to conclude that the deportation order had been properly made. In *R.* v. *National Insurance Commissioner, ex p. Warry*[57] the Divisional Court in proceedings for judicial review of a decision of the National Insurance Commissioner referred a question relating to entitlement to social security benefits to the European Court.

Reference to the European Court of Justice from the High Court is illustrated by *Van Duyn* v. *Home Office.*[58] Miss D, of Dutch nationality, had been offered employment as secretary with the Church of Scientology at a college in England, but the immigration officer refused her leave to enter under the Immigration Act 1971 (exclusion conducive to the public good), and the question arose whether this infringed Article 48 of the EEC Treaty (freedom of movement of workers). The Vice-Chancellor held:

(i) that issues of fact and of national law should in general be determined before reference is made to the European Court; and

(ii) that the question of whether Article 48 of the Treaty of Rome confers on individuals *rights* enforceable in the courts of member states should properly be determined by reference to the European Court before trial of the action. His Lordship therefore stayed the proceedings and requested a preliminary ruling from the European Court which ruled that:

(a) Article 48 and the Council Directive on the movement and residence of foreign nationals confer on individuals rights (qualified by the Directive) which national courts must protect; but

(b) a member state may impose restrictions justified on grounds of public policy, and may take into account the conduct of the individual concerned and his association with some organisation considered by the State as socially harmful, even though it is not an unlawful association and no similar restriction is placed on its own nationals against taking employment with that organisation.

The Employment Appeal Tribunal (which, despite its name is a superior court of record[59]) has referred various questions to the European Court relating to pay and discrimination.[60]

The application of the criminal law in magistrates' courts may have a European element and require reference being made to the European Court, for instance with regard to the deportation of EEC nationals (*R.* v. *Bouchereau,*[61]) offences under the Immigration Act 1971 (*R.* v.

---

[57] [1978] Q.B. 607.

[58] [1974] 1 W.L.R. 1107; subsequent proceedings [1975] Ch. 385; [1975] 1 C.M.L.R. 1.

[59] Employment Protection (Consolidation) Act 1978, s.135 and Sched. 11.

[60] See *Jenkins* v. *Kingsgate (Clothing Productions) Ltd.* [1981] 1 W.L.R. 972; [1981] 1 W.L.R. 1485; *Burton* v. *British Railways Board* [1981] I.R.L.R. 17; [1982] Q.B. 1080; [1983] I.C.R. 544.

[61] [1978] Q.B. 732.

Pieck[62]) or the enforcement of United Kingdom fishing legislation (*R.* v. *Plymouth Justices, ex p. Rogers*[63]).

Tribunals, as well as courts, are within the terms of Article 177. References have been made by the National Insurance Commissioner[64] and the Special Commissioners for Income Tax.[65]

A reference from Scotland was made by the High Court of Justiciary in *Gewiese* v. *Mackenzie*[66] to establish whether the making of a statutory instrument restricting fishing complied with procedural requirements laid down by Community law.

The jurisdiction of the European Court to give preliminary rulings on points of Community law at the request of national courts and tribunals must not be confused with its jurisdiction directly to enforce Community law. The Commission or a member state may bring an action in the Court against any state which is alleged to be in breach of its Treaty obligations (EEC Treaty Articles 169 and 170). A State which is found to be in breach of Treaty obligation is under a duty to take the necessary measures to comply with the judgment of the Court. The Commission, for example, after lengthy negotiations with the United Kingdom about the latter's failure to implement a Regulation relating to the use of tachographs in lorries finally brought proceedings in the European Court. A judgment against the United Kingdom[67] resulted in domestic legislation to give effect to Community law. Similarly the United Kingdom only took steps to reduce the discriminatory levels of excise duty on imported wines after the Commission had successfully brought proceedings in the European Court.[68] The Act of Accession which embodies the terms on which the United Kingdom joined the EEC limited the rights of member states to regulate fishing in their national waters (Articles 100–103) and in a number of cases the United Kingdom has been held to be in breach of these provisions.[69]

Secondary legislation

The European Communities Act 1972 did not give effect to a static body of rules—as is usually the case when a statute makes a treaty part of the law of the United Kingdom. The law of the Community continues to grow, through decisions of the European Court and legislation in the form of Regulations, Decisions and Directives. Accession to the Treaties and their enactment in the European Communities Act 1972 means that bodies outside the United Kingdom may by their decisions and legislation affect domestic law. Apart from debates and questions in both

---

[62] [1981] E.C.R. 2171 (Reference from Pontypridd Magistrates' Court).
[63] [1982] Q.B. 863.
[64] (Since 1980, the Social Security Commissioners). See *Kenny* v. *National Insurance Officer* [1978] E.C.R. 1489; *Re Search for Work in Ireland* [1978] 2 C.M.L.R. 174.
[65] *Lord Bruce of Donnington* v. *G. Aspden* [1981] E.C.R. 2205.
[66] [1984] 2 All E.R. 129 (E.C.J.) *Cf. Prince* v. *Secretary of State for Scotland* [1985] S.L.T. 74 (Pursuer's title to sue doubtful; questions not sufficiently focused on the pleadings: therefore it was not "necessary" to make a reference).
[67] *Commission* v. *United Kingdom* [1979] E.C.R. 419.
[68] *Commission* v. *United Kingdom, The Times,* July 14, 1983.
[69] *Re Fishing Net Mesh Sizes: France* v. *U.K.* [1980] 1 C.M.L.R. 6; *Re Fishery Conservation Measures: E.C. Commission* v. *U.K.* [1981] C.M.L.R. 219; *R.* v. *Tymen* [1982] 2 C.M.L.R. 111.

Houses of Parliament on EEC matters, particular concern has been felt about control over the making of legislation by the Council and Commission—secondary legislation as opposed to the primary legislation of the Treaties. Both Houses have established Select Committees to scrutinise proposals for European legislation. They examine legislation to be made by the Council for which ministers in their role as members of the Council can be regarded as having direct responsibility. Conversely, they do not examine secondary legislation made by the Commission, which forms the bulk of Community legislation. The Committees consider draft texts and explanatory memoranda supplied by the Government. In addition to reports on particular proposals the Committees make, from time to time, general reports on aspects of Community policy: for example the House of Commons Committee has expressed dissatisfaction with the adequacy of its opportunities to comment on and influence draft community legislation in two special reports.[70] In 1981 the House of Lords' Select Committee on the European Communities published a report on the proposals that the EEC should adhere to the European Convention on Human Rights.[71] The House of Lords' Committee has appointed a number of sub-committees which deal, *inter alia*, with finance, economics and regional policy; education, employment and social affairs; agriculture, food and consumer affairs and environment. Particularly important is the sub-committee on the legal aspects of community legislation which is chaired by a Law Lord. Its terms of reference are:

> "to consider and report to the Committee (a) whether any draft regulation or draft directive would, if adopted, impliedly repeal or amend existing UK legislation; (b) whether any draft regulation, if adopted, would render legislation in the UK necessary or desirable to facilitate its operation; (c) whether any draft directive, if adopted, would necessitate any legislation in the UK to give effect to it; (d) upon the merits of such proposals as are referred to them by the Select Committee; (e) whether any important developments have taken place in Community Law; (f) any matters which they consider should be drawn to the attention of the committee, concerning (i) the form which legislation found to be necessary under paras. (b) or (c) above, should take; (ii) the vires of any proposal."

IV. THE IMPACT OF COMMUNITY LAW

In earlier parts of this chapter the relationship between Community law and the laws of the United Kingdom was discussed with particular reference to the ways in which Community law becomes enforceable as part of domestic law. In this part it is intended to look, in outline, at the substantive effect of Community law in those areas where it has already played a particularly important role and where it may be important in the future.

---

[70] H.C. 527 (1983–84); H.C. 400 (1985–86).

[71] 71st Report of the House of Lords Select Committee on the European Communites (1979–80) H.L. 362. See Lord Fraser of Tullybelton "Scrutiny of Community Legislation in the United Kingdom Parliament," in *In Memoriam—J.D.B. Mitchell* (1983), p. 29.

From *Van Duyn* v. *The Home Office*[72] onwards, the right of freedom of movement of workers (Art. 48) has been involved in many cases before the domestic courts. EEC workers may not be refused admission to the United Kingdom except within the limits laid down by Directive 64/221, which allows states to exclude an individual on grounds of public policy or of public security but only on the basis of the individual's personal conduct. In *R*. v. *Bouchereau*[73] the European Court considered the circumstances in which an EEC national could be deported after a criminal conviction, and concluded that deportation was only justified where the infringement of the law posed a genuine and sufficiently serious threat affecting one of the fundamental interests of society which went beyond the threat to public order which is inherent in any crime.

In *R*. v. *Secretary of State for the Home Department, ex. p. Dannenberg*[74] the Court of Appeal pointed out that Community law now requires that reasons must be given when a judge recommends that an EEC national should be deported. To attempt to impose on an EEC national who is entitled to enter the United Kingdom a time limit on his stay under the Immigration Act 1971 is a breach of Community law: *R*. v. *Pieck*.[75] Rules requiring a qualifying period of residence before an EEC national is eligible to apply for a local education award were held to constitute discrimination in breach of Article 48 in *MacMahon* v. *Department of Education and Science*.[76]

Serious impediments to the free movement of goods, in the sense of the normal range of imports and exports, are likely to be challenged directly in the European Court. Thus restrictions by the United Kingdom on the importing of potatoes[77] and poultry[78] were referred to the Court by the Commission, as were restrictions by France on imports of lamb from the United Kingdom.[79] A rather different example of the United Kingdom being found to be in breach of Article 30 is provided by *Commission* v. *U.K.*[80] where the Court held that a Statutory Instrument which required certain categories of goods sold by retailers to be marked with an indication of the countries of origin was a quantitative restriction on the movement of goods. It is not entirely surprising that resort to Article 30 in domestic courts should be made in cases where, at first sight, Community law has little relevance. In *R*. v. *Henn*,[81] for example, the only hope of the accused importers was to argue that the United Kingdom's prohibition on the importing of obscene or indecent

---

[72] [1974] E.C.R. 187; [1975] Ch. 358.
[73] [1978] Q.B. 732. *Cf*. *R*. v. *Secchi* [1975] 1 C.M.L.R. 383 (Met. Magistrate): (Italian in London not a worker; even if he were, convictions for theft and indecency justified recommendation for deportation).
[74] [1984] Q.B. 766. See further on the compatibility of U.K. deportation law with EEC law, *R*. v. *Secretary of State for the Home Department, ex p. Santillo* [1981] Q.B. 778.
[75] [1981] E.C.R. 2171.
[76] [1983] Ch. 227. See also *R*. v. *ILEA, ex p. Hinde, The Times*, November 19, 1984.
[77] *Re Imports of Potatoes. E.C. Commission* v. *U.K.* [1979] 2 C.M.L.R. 427 (E.C.J.).
[78] *Re Imports of Poultry Meat: E.C. Commission* v. *France* [1982] 3 C.M.L.R. 497 (E.C.J.).
[79] *Re Restrictions on Imports of Lamb: E.C. Commission* v. *France* [1980] 1 C.M.L.R. 418 (E.C.J.).
[80] [1985] 2 C.M.L.R. 259 (E.C.J.).
[81] [1981] A.C. 580.

articles was contrary to Community law. The European Court held that such a prohibition could be justified in the light of Article 36 which refers to "public morality, public policy or public security," and that the question of public morality was to be determined by each state in accordance with its own scale of values. The Court did not discuss the fact that the test of obscenity or indecency applied to imported books[82] was wider than the test applied for example, under the Obscene Publications Act 1959, to books published in England, although Advocate General Mr. J. P. Warner referred to the complexities of the laws of the United Kingdom which arise: first because the laws of the different parts of the United Kingdom, namely England and Wales, Scotland, Northern Ireland, and the Isle of Man, are different, and, in each case, derived from a variety of sources rather than from any coherent scheme; and secondly because nowhere in the United Kingdom is pornography treated quite as strictly internally as on its importation.

The importers of various articles of an erotic nature were however more successful in *Conegate Ltd.* v. *Customs and Excise Commissioners.*[83] The European Court held that the United Kingdom was not entitled to prohibit the import of goods under Article 36 where the manufacture of such goods was not prohibited in its own territory under its domestic law.

The first judicial consideration of the effect of the EEC Treaty on English law involved Articles 85 and 86 which are designed to ensure free competition: *Application des Gaz S.A.* v. *Falks Veritas.*[84] Later cases in which these Articles have been relied on have shown the difficulties that may arise in finding the appropriate domestic remedy to protect a Community right. In *Garden Cottage Foods Ltd.* v. *Milk Marketing Board*[85] the appellants sought an injunction to prevent the Board from acting in a way which constituted a breach of Article 86. The House of Lords took the view that an injunction ought not to have been granted on the facts and also, contrary to the view expressed in the Court of Appeal, indicated that contravention of Article 86 could be remedied by an award of damages by analogy to a breach of statutory duty. It has, however, been argued that there is considerable doubt about the appropriate remedy under Community law for a breach of Article 86 and that the House of Lords should have referred the issue to the European Court.[86]

In *Bourgoin S.A.* v. *Ministry of Agriculture Fisheries and Food*[87] the Court of Appeal was concerned with the remedies available where a ministerial order had been held by the European Court to be in breach of Article 30 of the Treaty. Parker L.J., who delivered the judgment of the majority, held that a *mere* breach of the Treaty was remediable by judicial review, declaring the minister's order to be invalid and order-

---

[82] Customs Consolidation Act 1876, s.42; Customs and Excise Act 1952, s.304.
[83] [1987] 2 W.L.R. 39. The articles were described by the Advocate General (Sir Gordon Slynn) as "love love" dolls "Miss World specials," "rubber ladies" and "sexy vacuum flasks."
[84] [1974] Ch. 381 (C.A.).
[85] [1984] 3 W.L.R. 143 (H.L.).
[86] M. Friend and J. Shaw, "Damages for Abuse of Dominant Position" (1984) 100 L.Q.R. 188.
[87] [1986] Q.B. 716.

ing the officials concerned to permit the landing of the goods. The *Golden Cottage Foods* case, in the opinion of the learned Lord Justice, established that there is a right to damages where there has been a breach of law which also amounts to an abuse of power. In *An Bord Bainne Co-operative Ltd. (Irish Dairy Board)* v. *Milk Marketing Board*[88] the English Courts had to decide whether rights arising under competition provisions of the EEC Treaty fell within the sphere of private law or public law for the purpose of determining the appropriate forms of procedure and remedies[89]: the Court of Appeal decided that the rights were private law rights and the plaintiff could, by writ, seek damages for their breach. (The desirability of seeking the view of the European Court was, again, not raised).

Article 119, as was obvious from the earlier discussion of references to the European Court under Article 177, has been a fruitful source of litigation. In a number of cases initiated by the Commission the United Kingdom has been held by the Court to be in breach of its obligations under Community law relating to equality between the sexes. Following the decision of the Court in *E.C. Commission* v. *U.K.*[90] that the provisions of the Equal Pay Act 1970 failed to comply with the EEC Equal Pay Directive (75)/117), the United Kingdom Statute was amended by the Equal Pay (Amendment) Regulations, under section 2(2) of the European Communities Act 1972.[91] That is the procedure which in practice is likely generally to be followed where there is a discrepancy or conflict between domestic and Community law. At least where Community law is not directly effective it must be true that "It is a misunderstanding that any statute can be regarded as null and void because of the European Treaty. What is required is that the Member State shall introduce regulations or legislation which shall give effect to decisions which are binding because of the Treaty"; *per* Stephen Brown J., in *Farrall* v. *Department of Transport*.[92] Even where a provision of Community law is directly effective it may be of limited value until Member State has passed detailed legislation as, for example, in the case of the right of establishment. The European Court in *Patrick* v. *Minister of Culture*[93] recognised that the fundamental right of establishment was of limited importance until a system of mutual recognition of qualifications awarded in the various member states had been adopted in domestic legislation.

A problem peculiar to Scots law was raised in *Gibson* v. *Lord Advocate*.[94] G. sought a declaration that section 2(1) of the European Communities Act 1972 was contrary to Article XVIII of the Union Act, and therefore null and void, so far as it purported to enact as part of the law

[88] *The Times*, May 22, 1984.
[89] *Post*, p. 578.
[90] [1982] I.R.L.R. 33, [1982] I.C.R. 578. See too *Drake* v. *Chief Adjudication Officer* [1986] 3 All E.R. 65 (E.C.J.); *Johnston* v. *Chief Constable of the R.U.C.* [1986] 3 All E.R. 135 (E.C.J.).
[91] Equal Pay (Amendment) Regulations 1983, S.I. No. 1794. See further R. Townshend-Smith "The Equal Pay (Amendment) Regulations" (1984). Similarly, effect has been given to *Marshall* v. *Southampton and South West Hampshire Area Health Authority (Teaching)* [1986] Q.B. 401 (*supra*, n.35) by the Sex Discrimination Act 1986.
[92] [1983] R.T.R. 279, 291.
[93] [1977] 2 C.M.L.R. 253.
[94] [1975] 1 C.M.L.R. 563; 1975 S.L.T. 136.

of Scotland certain Community Regulations providing for equal treatment of member states with regard to fishing in maritime waters. He
argued that immediately before the Act of Union, Scottish subjects had
exclusive fishing rights in Scottish coastal waters; that the laws conferring these rights "concerned private right," and that the Community
Regulations were not "for the evident utility of the subjects within Scotland." Lord Keith dismissed the action, not only on the ground that
action was incompetent in seeking consideration of the utility of an Act
of Parliament[95] but also on the ground that Community Regulations
operate in the field of public law and not private law.

In assessing the possible future significance of Community law it
must be remembered that apart from the provisions of the Treaties and
subsequent secondary legislation, the European Court has developed a
concept of general principles of Community law with which it supplements and completes the written texts which it has to interpret and
apply. Thus the principles known in common law countries as "natural
justice" have been applied by the European Court as general principles
of law.[96] From the provisions of Article 119 and other Articles the Court
has fashioned a general concept of "equality." The principle of "proportionality" which has been referred to by the Court on a number of
occasions has been cited by Lord Diplock in *Council of Civil Service
Unions* v. *Minister for Civil Service*[97] as a possible new ground on which
ministerial and administrative decisions may be subject to review
under domestic law. The recognition by the Court that the general principles of law include respect for fundamental human rights[98] provides a
point of contact between the EEC and the European Convention on
Human Rights.[99] Two attempts by litigants in English and Scottish
cases to make use of this link have been unsuccessful. In *Allgemeine Gold
und Silberscheideanstalt* v. *Cmrs. of Customs & Excise*[1] the German plaintiffs claimed that the forfeiture of smuggled krugerrands was contrary to
the European Convention and therefore contrary to Community law.
Donaldson J. held that, while the EEC Treaty might have been drafted
against a background of the recognition of human rights, it did not
incorporate them by unwritten, implied Articles. The proper remedy, if
the plaintiffs thought that the United Kingdom legislation infringed the
European Convention on Human Rights, was to complain to the European Court of Human Rights. The Court of Appeal affirmed Donaldson
J., without adverting to the matter of the European Convention,

---

[95] *Ante*, p. 64.
[96] *Transocean Marine Paint Association* v. *E.C. Commission* [1974] E.C.R. 1063.
[97] [1985] A.C. 374; *post*, p. 265. Cf. *R.* v. *Barnsley Metropolitan Borough Council, ex p. Hook*
[1976] 1 W.L.R. 1052 where Lord Denning M.R. suggested that judicial review was
applicable on the ground of natural justice where an administrative body had imposed
a punishment out of proportion to the offence.
[98] *Internationale Handelsgesellschaft* [1970] E.C.R. 1125, 1134; *Nold* v. *E.C. Commission* [1973]
E.C.R. 491. See *The Protection of fundamental rights in the European Community* (Bulletin
of the European Communities, Supplement 5/76); U. Scheuner, "Fundamental Rights
in European Community Law and in national constitutional law" [1975] 12 C.M.L.R.
171; A. Drzemczewski, "EEC and Human Rights" (1975) 91 L.Q.R. 311.
[99] *Ante*, p. 14 and *post*, p. 433.
[1] [1978] 2 C.M.L.R. 292; [1980] 1 C.M.L.R. 488 (C.A.). This case was the sequel to *R.* v.
Thompson [1980] Q.B. 229; *ante*, p. 104.

although Lord Denning M.R. remarked briskly that there is no rule of International law which prohibits the forfeiture of smuggled goods.

In *Kaur* v. *Lord Advocate*[2] an attempt was made to rely on the Convention as part of Community law to challenge the legality of a deportation order. The Lord Ordinary (Ross), while appreciating that the European Court has accepted that the fundamental human rights recognised by member states are an integral part of Community law, held that the European Court could only deal with fundamental rights when these arose and had a bearing upon issues of Community law. No such issue arose in this case since neither of the deportees was an EEC national.[3] Three children had been born to the deportees while they were living in the United Kingdom and were entitled to reside in the United Kingdom although their parents, not surprisingly, took them with them when they were deported. It might be argued that Lord Ross's conclusion overlooked the fact that the children were nationals of the United Kingdom. There is a principle of EEC law that the nationals of a member state enjoy the same rights under EEC law as nationals of other member states: accordingly, the children in this case should have the same rights under EEC law as children of EEC nationals who have entered the United Kingdom as a result of the freedom of movement of workers within the Community. But it is generally agreed that a child's right to enter and remain in a member state is dependent on his parent's right of entry. The parents in this case had no such right because they were not EEC nationals. Moreover, as the Lord Ordinary pointed out, the deportation orders were made against the parents, not the children who remained entitled to live in Scotland: the 1971 Act had envisaged that families might have to be split up in certain circumstances. The children's rights to remain in the United Kingdom had, therefore, not been infringed when their parents decided to take them to India.

---

[2] [1980] 3 C.M.L.R. 79; 1981 S.L.T. 322; noted, J.M.T. (1982) 98 L.Q.R. 183.
[3] Cf. R. v. *Saunders* [1980] Q.B. 72 (E.C.J.); *ante*, p. 100.

CHAPTER 6

CONSTITUTIONAL CONVENTIONS[1]

I. THE NATURE AND PURPOSE OF CONSTITUTIONAL CONVENTIONS

Nature of constitutional conventions

Some study of constitutional conventions is necessary in order to understand the working of the British Constitution. In drawing the distinction between the laws and conventions of the Constitution, Dicey was anticipated by a number of nineteenth-century writers, notably by E. A. Freeman in his *Growth of the English Constitution* (1872)[2]; but the significance of conventions in the working of the British Constitution, and therefore the importance of their study for an understanding of our constitution, were brought out by the emphasis Dicey placed upon them. Dicey's discussion of the distinction between the laws and conventions of the Constitution was not designed to exclude the latter from the purview of law students. On the contrary, his purpose was to insist that the student of constitutional law ought not to neglect to study the conventions as well.

Conventions are sometimes called "unwritten laws," but this is very confusing because according to the generally accepted doctrine they are not laws at all. "Unwritten law" in our system is a term properly applied to the common law. Again conventions are sometimes called "customs." This is liable to cause confusion with customary law, which not only is law in the strict sense but requires for its validity (as conventions do not) immemorial antiquity.

The working definition of consitutional conventions suggested here is: *rules of political practice which are regarded as binding by those to whom they apply, but which are not laws as they are not enforced by the courts or by the Houses of Parliament.*

This definition *distinguishes* constitutional conventions from:

(i) *mere practice, usage, habit or fact*, which is not regarded as obligatory, such as the existence of political parties (fact) or the habit of Chancellors of the Exchequer in carrying from Downing Street to the House of Commons a dispatch case supposed to contain his "Budget" speech.

---

[1] See Dicey, *Law of the Constitution* (10th ed.), Chaps. 14 and 15; *cf.* Professor E. C. S. Wade's *Introduction*, pp. cli–cxci; R. A. Cosgrove, *The Rule of Law, Albert Venn Dicey, Victorian Jurist* (1981), pp. 87–90. Sir Ivor Jennings, *The Law and the Constitution* (5th ed.), Chap. 3; *Cabinet Government* (3rd ed.), Chap. 1; *Parliament* (2nd ed.), Chap. 3; G. Marshall and G. C. Moodie, *Some Problems of the Constitution* (5th ed.), Chap. 2; K. C. Wheare, *Modern Constitutions* (1951), Chap. 8; *The Constitutional Structure of the Commonwealth* (1960); S. A. de Smith. *The New Commonwealth and its Constitutions* (1964), Chaps. 1–3; O. Hood Phillips, "Constitutional Conventions: A Conventional Reply" (1964) 8 J.S.P.T.L. 60; C. R. Munro, "Laws and Conventions Distinguished (1975) 91 L.Q.R. 218; "Dicey on Constitutional Conventions." [1985] P.L. 637; G. H. L. Le May, *The Victorian Constitution* (1979); G. Marshall, *Constitutional Conventions* (1984).

[2] O. Hood Phillips, "Constitutional Conventions: Dicey's Predecessors (1966) 29 M.L.R. 137.

If the persons concerned are not aware that they are under an obligation to act in a certain way, there is no convention. On the other hand, the opinion that they are bound is not conclusive as they may be mistaken. The precise content of some conventions is uncertain, since they must be flexible enough to meet changing circumstances; and as that which is not certain cannot be obligatory, it is sometimes difficult to distinguish between obligatory rules and non-obligatory practice, such as the consultation of outside interests when social welfare legislation is being drafted.[3]

(ii) *non-political rules, i.e.* rules of conduct which are not referable to the needs of constitutional government, *e.g.* ethical or moral rules, or the almost invariable custom of crowning the Queen Consort, which has no constitutional significance.[4]

(iii) *judicial rules of practice such as the rules of precedent.*[5] In *R. v. Knuller (Publishing, Printing and Promotions) Ltd.,*[6] Lord Simon of Glaisdale referred to the current practice under which the House of Lords does not consider itself as bound by its own previous decisions as "one of those conventions which are so significant a feature of the British constitution, as Professor Dicey showed in his famous work." Whatever the status of the rules of judicial precedent, particularly in the House of Lords,[7] to describe them as conventions is probably more misleading than helpful.

(iv) *rules enforced by the courts, i.e. laws.* Judicial enforcement does not necessarily, or indeed usually, imply specific enforcement. In public law it usually involves an action for damages, declaration or injuction, habeas corpus or judicial review of administrative action; or it may involve a criminal prosecution or a defence to a criminal charge.[8] Sir Ivor Jennings,[9] while admitting that there was this formal distinction between laws and conventions, contended that there was no distinction of substance. The distinction may perhaps be comparatively unimportant for the political scientist or the politician, but it is surely of vital importance for lawyers.[10] Mitchell criticised the distinction on the ground that there may be laws with no judicial sanction.[11] It is true, as

---

[3] See E. C. S. Wade in Dicey, *op. cit.* at pp. cliv–clv.

[4] In *Queen Caroline's Claim* (1821) 1 St.Tr.(N.S.) 949, the Privy Council held that the Queen Consort has no legal right to be crowned.

[5] See too the rules relating to rights of audience before the Courts: *Abse* v. *Smith* [1986] Q.B. 536.

[6] [1973] A.C. 435, 484.

[7] See Sir Rupert Cross, *Precedent in English Law* (3rd ed.), pp. 109 *et. seq.*

[8] In *Madzimbamuto* v. *Lardner-Burke* [1969] 1 A.C. 645 the Privy Council held that the convention under which the United Kingdom Parliament did not legislate for Southern Rhodesia without the consent of the government of that colony, although important as a convention, had no effect in limiting the powers of the United Kingdom Parliament.

[9] Jennings, *Law and the Constitution* (5th ed.), p. 117.

[10] The distinction between legal and non-legal rules is recognised outside the field of constitutional law, *e.g.* (formerly) the Judges' Rules, the *Highway Code* and Codes of Practice made under various statutes.

[11] J. D. B. Mitchell, *Constitutional Law* (2nd ed. 1968), pp. 34–39.

Jennings pointed out, that laws cannot be enforced against the government as a body or against either House of Parliament; but they can be enforced against individual Ministers personally,[12] or (subject to parliamentary privilege, which is itself part of the law) against individual members of either House; and judgment may be delivered (though not executed) against a government department.[13] It is also true, as Mitchell pointed out, that Parliament sometimes imposes "duties" on public authorities while going on to say that such duties are not to be enforced by judicial proceedings. For example section 59 of the British Telecommunications Act 1981, provides: "(1) It shall be the duty of the Post Office . . . to provide . . . such services for the conveyance of letters as satisfy all reasonable demands for them . . . . (4) Nothing in this section shall be construed as imposing upon the Post Office, either directly or indirectly, any form of duty or liability enforceable by proceedings before any court."[14] On analysis it appears that from a legal point of view such "duties" are properly classed as powers.[15] The statutory requirement that a Governor-General shall direct the issue of writs has been construed to be directory, not mandatory[16]; and the requirement that a Minister shall lay certain instruments before Parliament would probably be interpreted in the same way.[17]

(v) *rules enforced by the Houses of Parliament* through their officers, *e.g.* the Speaker and the Serjeant-at-Arms, notably parliamentary procedure and privilege (part of "the law and custom of Parliament," which is itself part of the common law in the wide sense). These may, however, overlap constitutional conventions. Thus some parts of parliamentary practice constitute conventions, such as the protection of minorities in debate and the party composition of committees. Standing Orders are often said to be examples of constitutional conventions; but on analysis they will be found to consist partly of law, partly of mere practice, and only to a small extent of convention.[18]

It is also useful to distinguish "conventions" from such distinct, if allied, concepts as " 'traditions,' "principles" and "doctrines.' "[19] The purpose of conventions may be seen as to give effect to these traditions, principles or values.[20] In *R. v. H.M. Treasury, ex p. Smedley*,[21] for example, Sir John Donaldson M.R. referred to the relationship between Parliament and the judiciary in terms of conventions:

---

[12] *Raleigh* v. *Goschen* [1893] 1 Ch. 73.
[13] Crown Proceedings Act 1947.
[14] Subs. (4) means what it says: *Harold Stephen & Co. Ltd.* v. *Post Office* [1977] 1.W.L.R. 1172 (C.A.); *per* Lord Denning M.R. at p. 1177.
[15] Although s.58 enumerates "powers" of the Post Office. The non-performance of "duties" would concern the ultimate authority of the Minister under the Act.
[16] *Simpson* v. *Att.-Gen.* [1955] N.Z.L.R. 271 (C.A. of New Zealand).
[17] *Post,* Chap. 30.
[18] *Post,* Chap. 10.
[19] Geoffrey Marshall, *Constitutional Conventions* (1984), p. 3.
[20] *Reference re Amendment of the Constitution of Canada* (1982) 125 D.L.R. (3d) 1, 84, *per* Martland, Ritchie, Dickson, Beek, Chouinard, Lamer J.J.
[21] [1985] Q.B. 657, 666.

"Although the United Kingdom has no written constitution, it is a constitutional convention of the highest importance that the legislature and the judicature are separate and independent of one another, subject to certain ultimate rights of Parliament over the judicature."

The independence of the judiciary might be described as a *principle* of the Constitution since 1668, enshrined in successive statutory provisions guaranteeing judicial security of tenure.[22]

Judicial recognition of conventions

The fact that the courts do not *enforce* constitutional conventions does not mean that the courts do not incidentally recognise their existence. They may be relied on as an aid to statutory interpretation or to justify non-intervention by the courts in ministerial decisions in areas in which the courts feel that they cannot or should not become involved. Thus the responsibility of the Home Secretary to Parliament was one of the reasons for the decision of the House of Lords in *Liversidge* v. *Anderson*.[23] The Judicial Committee of the Privy Council in *British Coal Corporation* v. *The King*[24] mentioned the conventions regulating what was then called Dominion status, and also the convention that the Crown invariably accepts the Judicial Committee's advice. In *Carltona Ltd.* v. *Commissioners of Works*[25] Lord Greene M.R. referred to the convention of a Minister's responsibility to Parliament for the acts of his officials; in *Att.-Gen.* v. *Jonathan Cape Ltd.*,[26] Lord Widgery C.J. referred to the doctrine of joint responsibility within the Cabinet, Cabinet meetings, the Secretary to the Cabinet and the Prime Minister; and in *Ex p. Hosenball*,[27] Lord Denning M.R. referred to the responsibility of the Home Secretary to Parliament for the exercise of his power to deport persons on grounds of national security. In *Air Canada* v. *Secretary of State for Trade*[28] there were a number of references to the convention which prohibits ministers of one party from having access to the papers of their predecessors of other parties without the agreement of the previous administration.

---

[22] *Post*, p. 386.

[23] [1942] A.C. 206; but the Home Secretary was also required by statutory regulation to report monthly to Parliament. Ministerial responsibility was also referred to in *Padfield* v. *Minister of Agriculture, Fisheries and Food* [1968] A.C. 997, by Lord Reid, and in *Raymond* v. *Attorney General* [1982] Q.B. 839, by Sir Sebag Shaw.

[24] [1935] A.C. 500; W. Ivor Jennings, "The Statute of Westminster and Appeals" (1936) 52 L.Q.R. 173.

[25] [1943] 2 All E.R. 560.

[26] [1976] Q.B. 752; refusing an injunction to restrain publication of Vol. 1 of Richard Crossman, *Diaries of a Cabinet Minister*.

[27] *R.* v. *Secretary of State for Home Department, ex p. Hosenball* [1977] 1 W.L.R 766 (D.C.), 776 (C.A.).

[28] [1983] A.C. 394 (H.L.). See further, Lord Hunt of Tanworth, "Access to a Previous Government's Papers" [1982] P.L. 514. Mr. Callaghan was reported in *The Times*, July 14, 1986 to have agreed to allow Conservative Ministers to examine the papers on which the Labour Government in 1977 had decided to buy the Nimrod airborne early warning system; *post* p. 313.

The case *Re Amendment of the Constitution of Canada*[29] that came before the Supreme Court of Canada in 1981 is of great interest as being a unique discussion of constitutional conventions by a Commonwealth court of the highest standing, especially since a case of this kind could never come before British courts who have no jurisdiction to determine such matters.[30] The Canadian Supreme Court was hearing an appeal from various provincial courts exercising their statutory jurisdiction to consider references from the Executive on matters which included questions that otherwise might not be justiciable. In addition to the legal question whether the consent of the Provinces was required before the Canadian Parliament could request the United Kingdom to amend the Canadian Constitution (British North America Act 1867, as amended), the Supreme Court accepted appellate jurisdiction to determine whether such consent was required by constitutional convention and, if so, whether the convention had been observed in that case. Both the existence and content of the alleged convention being disputed, the Supreme Court's decision involved an analysis of the general nature of constitutional conventions. A majority held in the first place that a constitutional convention cannot crystallise into law. They said[31]:

"No instance of an explicit recognition of a convention as having matured into a rule of law was produced. The very nature of a convention, as political in inception and as depending on a persistent course of political recognition by those for whose benefit and to whose detriment (if any) the convention developed over a considerable period of time, is inconsistent with its legal enforcement. . . . The attempted assimilation of the growth of a convention to the growth of the common law is misconceived. The latter is the product of judicial effort, based on justiciable issues which attained legal formulation and are subject to modification and even reversal by the courts which gave them their birth. . . . No such parental role is played by the courts with respect to conventions."

Conventions, said their Lordships, are not enforced by the courts: if there is a conflict between conventions and law the courts must enforce the law. The sanctions for conventions are political, though the violation of conventions is "unconstitutional." The Supreme Court approved Jennings's criteria for establishing the existence of a convention (*supra*). However, Jennings says "it is sometimes enough to show that a rule has received general acceptance," and goes on to speak of the

---

[29] (1981) 125 D.L.R. (3d) 1. And see O. Hood Phillips, "Constitutional Conventions in the Supreme Court of Canada" (1982) 98 L.Q.R. 194. *Cf.* Rodney Brazier and St. John Robilliard, "Constitutional Conventions: The Canadian Supreme Court's Views Reviewed" [1982] P.L. 28: they go too far in saying "the question of the existence, but not of the precise limits of a convention is now unquestionably a justiciable issue." The jurisdiction of the Canadian Supreme Court in this context was based on certain special provincial statutes, and in any event that Court's opinions, though persuasive, are not binding in this country.

[30] The Judicial Committee of the Privy Council might possibly be called upon to give an opinion on such a matter in relation to the constitution of some other Commonwealth country from which appeals to it have not been abolished.

[31] At p. 22.

assertions of "persons of authority," whereas their Lordships apparently took the view that it is the actors who must have treated the rule as binding.[32] The majority admitted a lack of precision in the convention asserted, but came to the conclusion that "at least a substantial measure" of provincial agreement was necessary, a requirement which was not satisfied in this case. A minority (including Laskin C.J.) had no doubt that the consent of all the Provinces was required, taking the view, which it is submitted is preferable, that a convention must be sufficiently definite to be understandable and understood. They said further that conventions have the unquestioned acceptance not only of the politicians but of the public at large. The precedents on this view were far from conclusive.

Legislation may recognise or presuppose conventions. Thus the Ministers of the Crown Act 1937 implied a knowledge of the existence of the Prime Minister, the Leader of the Opposition and the Cabinet; and later statutes dealing with salaries and pensions acknowledge the existence of leaders of the Opposition and Chief Whips in both Houses.[33] The preamble to the Statute of Westminster 1931 recites several conventions of inter-Commonwealth relations.

Conventions are capable of being formulated in statute, e.g. the Statue of Westminster 1931, s.4, and they have been incorporated (with or without justiciable effect) in various Commonwealth constitutions.[34]

The laws of the constitution could stand alone, although the constitution would then be antiquated and static; but the conventions would be meaningless without their legal context. Every constitutional convention is closely related to some law or laws, which it implies. The conventions forming the Cabinet system, for example, presuppose the laws relating to such matters as the Queen's royal prerogative, the office and powers of Ministers (except the Prime Minister), the constitution of government departments, and the composition of Parliament. There are thus layers, as it were, of laws, conventions and facts (political practice); and any one situation may be governed by a number of layers of this kind, perhaps including a statute which implies the existence of a convention.

On the other hand, constitutional conventions are subject to the processes of growth and transformation. As Baldwin said in the House of Commons at the time of the "agreement to differ" in 1932: "The historian can probably tell you perfectly clearly what the constitutional practice of the country was at any given period in the past, but it would be very difficult for a living writer to tell you at any given period in his lifetime what the constitution of the country is in all respects, and for this reason, that at almost any given moment of our lifetime, there may be

---

[32] Marshall, op. cit. note 19 pp. 11–12, on the obligatory nature of conventions distinguishes bewteen "positive morality" (subjective test) and "critical morality" (objective test), preferring the latter but not stating definitely whose opinion is to be taken.

[33] See now, Ministerial and other Salaries Act 1975. Post, p. 186.

[34] Adegbenro v. Akintola [1963] A.C. 614 (P.C.) per Viscount Radcliffe; cf. Ningkan v. Government of Malaysia [1970] A.C. 379; see de Smith The New Commonwealth and its Constitution (1964), pp. 51–52, 88–90. K.J. Keith, "The Courts and the Conventions of the Constitution" (1967) 16 I.C.L.Q. 542. (British constitutional conventions were not expressly incorporated but were used by the courts to help to interpret the Nigerian constitution.)

one practice called 'Constitutional' which is falling into desuetude and there may be another practice which is creeping into use but which is not yet called 'Constitutional.' "[35]

Purpose of constitutional conventions

Conventions are a means of bringing about constitutional develop-ment without formal changes in the law.[36] This they often do by regu-lating the exercise of a discretionary power conferred on the Crown by the law. It must not be supposed that conventions are peculiar to unwritten constitutions. They are found to a greater or less extent in written constitutions as well. Canada and Australia,[37] for example, observe the main British constitutional conventions, and many conven-tions have been developed in the United States relating to such matters as the method of electing the President, his choice and use of a Cabinet, and "senatorial courtesy" in making appointments to office.[38] This informal method of change is more adaptable than a series of statutes or constitutional amendments. The general tendency is towards democ-racy, due regard being had to the protection of minorities and their right to be heard.

The ultimate object of most conventions is that public affairs should be conducted in accordance with the wishes of the majority of the elec-tors. The reason why the Ministry must be chosen from the party or par-ties enjoying a majority in the Commons is that, on the assumption that the majority of the Commons reflect the views of the majority of the electors,[39] a Ministry so selected will be most likely to give effect to the will of the nation as a whole. And this is also the reason why the Queen should act on the advice of Ministers, why Ministers should resign if they lose the confidence of Commons, and why the House of Commons should have a political ascendancy over the House of Lords, especially in matters of finance.

To ensure that the power of government shall be exercised in accord-ance with the popular will, that will must be ascertained from those best qualified to know it, namely, the elected representatives of the people; hence the convention requiring Parliament to be summoned annually. If the Government no longer retains the confidence of the House of Commons the Prime Minister should ask for a dissolution of Parlia-ment,[40] in order to enable the electorate, through a new Parliament, to obtain a new Ministry more in accordance with its views.

In this way the legal framework of 1688—a strong monarchy limited in certain specific ways—has become a "constitutional" monarchy, that

---

[35] H.C. Deb., Vol. 261, ser. 5, col. 515 (1932).

[36] Conventions therefore change in accordance with the underlying ideas of government: see Holdsworth, "The Conventions of the Eighteenth-Century Constitution" (1932) 17 *Iowa Law Review* 161.

[37] George Winterton, *Parliament, the Executive and the Governor-General* (Melbourne, 1983).

[38] H. W. Horwill, *The Usages of the American Constitution* (1925).

[39] Owing to our "first past the post" electoral system, a majority in the Commons may, however, represent a minority of the voters and a smaller minority of the electorate.

[40] In some circumstances it may be appropriate for the Ministry to resign; *post*, pp. 150 *et seq.*

is to say, a democratic political system with a hereditary Head of State practically bereft of governmental powers and distinguished from the head of the Government (Prime Minister). To meet current political ideas and social needs, conventions have facilitated the growth of the Cabinet system; changed the emphasis on the functions of Parliament, which is now largely occupied in representing the views of the electors by criticising the government's activities and debating their measures; and developed the autonomy of other Commonwealth countries.

Conventions also make the legal constitution work by providing means for co-operation in the practice of government. In particular, the Cabinet system co-ordinates the work of the various government departments among themselves, and promotes co-operation between the departments and Parliament and between the Ministry and the Queen. Similarly, the conventions governing inter-Commonwealth relations enable the members of the Commonwealth, although independent, to co-operate to a great extent in their defence and foreign policy.

How and when do conventions become established?

It is wrong to suppose that constitutional conventions are analogous to customary law in that they must necessarily have existed a long time, or even from time immemorial. A moment's thought will show that this cannot be so, for the conventions of our constitution mostly date from a time later than the Revolution of 1688, and in most cases a good deal later. Many conventions are indeed based on usage, although this is not necessarily of long standing. Some conventions, however—especially among those concerned with Commonwealth relations—are based on agreement,[41] and we know exactly when and how they were formulated.

It is not easy to say precisely how or when conventions based on usage come into existence. Every act by the Queen or a responsible statesman is a "precedent"[42] in the sense of an example which may or may not be followed in subsequent similar cases, but it does not necessarily create a binding rule. For that it must be generally accepted as creating a rule by those in authority. A long series of precedents all pointing in the same direction is very good evidence of a convention, but this is not possible in the case of recent precedents. Thus the fact that no monarch has refused the Royal Assent to a Bill since Queen Anne clearly points to the existence of a convention that the Royal Assent should not be refused; but can we say that the Queen may in no circumstances refuse the Prime Minister's request to dissolve Parliament?

Sir Ivor Jennings suggested two requirements for the creation of a convention: (i) general acceptance as obligatory, and (ii) a reason or purpose referable to the existing requirements of constitutional government. Thus one precedent might create a convention whereas a long series of precedents might not. Owing to Cabinet secrecy, posthumous

---

[41] This is the sense in which international lawyers speak of "conventions."
[42] The word "precedent" is not, of course, used here in the technical sense of a legal (judicial) precedent.

biographies and prejudiced autobiographies, it is often difficult to find out whether the actors thought they were obeying a binding rule.[43]

Why are conventions observed?

What is it that induces obedience to these extra-legal or conventional rules? The answer seems to be that obedience is yielded to the conventions because of the consequences that would plainly ensue if they were disregarded. Thus if Parliament were not summoned annually the army and air force could not lawfully be maintained, an important part of the public revenue, namely income tax, could not be lawfully raised, and even less could be lawfully spent.[44] If the Queen appointed as Prime Minister someone who did not enjoy the confidence of the majority of the Commons, he and his colleagues could be defeated in the lower House. If a government after such defeat in the House declined to resign or ask for a dissolution, the Commons could paralyse the business of government by withholding supplies or refusing to agree to the continuance in force of the Army and Air Force Acts. Even if a government succeeded in carrying on for a time in disregard of Parliament, it would cease to be in touch with the will of the electors and would forfeit their favour, assuming this had not been already lost by the recourse to extra-parliamentary government.

Some conventions are not always observed if special circumstances warrant a departure from established practice, but if they were not regularly observed they would not be, or would cease to be, conventions.[45] It is the reason or purpose for which they stand that both leads to their development and secures their observance. The "agreement to differ" in 1932, whereby certain Liberal members of the Cabinet were permitted by their colleagues to disagree openly on the majority's fiscal policy, was alleged to be justified by the necessity of preserving the National (Coalition) Government in view of the "economic crisis"; but it did not work, and the recalcitrant members soon resigned office.[46] The convention of the collective responsibility of Ministers has shown signs of weakening in the last few years, notably during the EEC referendum campaign in 1975 when the Prime Minister (Mr. Wilson) allowed Ministers to speak against this country's staying in the Community, though this concession did not extend to speaking in Parliament.[47] One Minister who did speak in the Commons against the Government White Paper advocating continued membership of the EEC, was dismissed from office.[48]

Dicey rejected the answer that observance of constitutional conven-

---

[43] *Cabinet Government* (3rd ed.), pp. 5–13.

[44] That is, so long as the practice, itself also a convention, continues of authorising these matters by annual Acts or statutory provisions having force for one year only.

[45] F. D. Roosevelt broke the American convention against standing for the office of President for a third term. He was elected and later re-elected for a fourth term; but an amendment to the Constitution has since been passed limiting the tenure of office to two terms.

[46] Keith Middlemas and John Barnes, *Baldwin* (1969) Chap. 24.

[47] See David L. Ellis, "Collective Ministerial Reponsibility and Collective Solidarity", [1980] P.L. 367; *post* p. 312.

[48] *Post*, p. 312.

tions is secured by "public opinion," on the ground that it begs the question, which is, why does public opinion appear to be sufficiently strong to ensure the observance of the conventions?[49] In the past, respect for conventions was established by the threat of impeachment, greatly influenced by public opinion; but a stronger sanction was needed, and impeachment has in practice become obsolete as being unnecessary in view of the development of ministerial responsibility to Parliament. Dicey concluded that the sanction of constitutional conventions is to be found in the fact that a person who persisted in the breach of convention would inevitably be led into a breach of the law "sooner or later"—in one place he says "immediately." Thus if Parliament were not summoned in any one year, so that the annual Finance and Appropriation and Army Acts[50] expired, the collection of much of the national revenue (especially income tax), the expenditure of most of the public funds and the maintenance of a standing army and enforcement of military discipline would be illegal under the Bill of Rights.

Dicey dealt, however, only with one group of conventions, though admittedly the most important, namely, those that regulate the relations between the executive and Parliament, especially those between the government and the House of Commons. No breach of law would follow if Standing Orders relating to the rights of minorities were not followed in conducting the business of either House, nor (by English law) if the United Kingdom Parliament legislated for an independent member of the Commonwealth without its consent, nor (assuming it to be a constitutional convention, as distinct from the practice of the court, that they should not) if lay peers took part in an appeal before the House of Lords.

Further, certain qualifications must be made even in the case of those conventions to which Dicey's argument applies. If a government that was committing breaches of convention retained the confidence of the Commons it could procure the alteration of the law, as it did with the Provisional Collection of Taxes Act 1913, following the decision of *Bowles* v. *The Bank of England*,[51] or the passage of an Act of Indemnity, thus indicating that the convention in question was considered undesirable or to have lost its purpose. Even if the government lost the confidence of the Commons, it might remain in office for some months without breaking the law owing to the time-lag between the lapsing of the Finance Act (fixing the standard rate of income tax and authorising most of the expenditure) and the Army Act and the beginning of the next financial year when the Commons must be asked for fresh supplies.

For the reasons stated above, however, it is submitted that it is not necessary to go as far as Dicey. The question why conventions are observed is a political or psychological question. One might equally ask what motives induce people to obey the law, since fear of the legal sanc-

---

[49] Dicey, *op. cit.* note 1 Chap. 15.
[50] His argument is not affected by the modern procedure whereby the Army and Air Force and Naval Discipline Acts are continued in force for 12 months at a time by Orders in Council subject to affirmative resolution of both Houses: Armed Forces Act 1976.
[51] [1913] 1 Ch. 57.

tion only operates on some of the people some of the time.[52] As a matter of fact, statesmen probably observe the conventions because they wish the machinery of government to go on[53] and because they hope to retain the favour of the electorate.[54]

II. Classification and Illustration of Constitutional Conventions

This section should be prefaced by a reminder that it is not practicable either to enumerate all the conventions applicable to the working of the British Constitution or to define most of them with any great precision. Subject to this caution, it is proper to ask what non-legal rules we would feel constrained to put into a written constitution if it was decided to have one?[55]

Constitutional conventions may be classified into three main groups:
(1) relating to the exercise of the royal prerogative and the working of the Cabinet system;
(2) regulating the relations between the Lords and Commons, and proceedings in Parliament; and
(3) regulating the relations between the United Kingdom and the independent members of the Commonwealth.

The first group is the most important, and forms the main theme of Dicey's discussion (ante). The second group has lost much of its importance as convention since the passing of the Parliament Acts. The third group has developed almost entirely since Dicey's day.

It is difficult to say to what extent conventions, in the sense in which we have defined them, exist in English local government, e.g. as to the election of chairmen of council and its committees, having regard to the state of the parties on the council. The practice varies greatly from one local authority to another, and is often not consistent over a period within the same authority. Further, political scientists who have examined this question tend to ignore the distinction between rules regarded as obligatory and mere practice.[56]

1. Conventions relating to the exercise of the royal prerogative and the working of the Cabinet system

The Sovereign could legally declare war or make peace; dissolve Parliament at any time, and need not summon another for three years; she could refuse her assent to measures passed by both Houses of Parliament; she could at any time dismiss her Ministers and appoint others, and so on. The exercise of these powers, however, is either restricted

---

[52] See Bryce, *Studies in History and Jurisprudence*, Vol. II, Essay IX.

[53] Marshall and Moodie, *op. cit.* suggest that the sanction for the observance of conventions is that a breach of convention is likely to lead to a *change* of law.

[54] Reciprocity is the chief sanction of Parliamentary conventions; each Government is likely in time to be in opposition.

[55] Mr. Trudeau, Prime Minister of Canada, made a partial attempt to do this in 1969; *The Constitution and the People of Canada* (Ottawa), pp. 64 *et seq.*

[56] See R. S. B. Knowles, "Local Government Practices—or Conventions?" (1958) 122 J.P. 856; E. S. Walker, "Conventions in Local Government" (1959) 123 J.P. 234; H. Maddick and E. P. Pritchard, "The Conventions of Local Authorities in the West Midlands" (1958) *Public Administration* 145; (1959), *Public Administration* 135.

altogether or regulated by conventions, of which the following are some of the most important.

(i) The Queen must invite the leader of the party or group commanding a majority of the House of Commons to form a Ministry. The person so called on is the "Prime Minister." In law the Prime Minister until recently did not exist, and even now is only referred to incidentally in statutes relating to salaries and pensions.[57]

(ii) The Queen must appoint as her other Ministers such persons as the Prime Minister advises her to appoint. Ministers should have seats in either the House of Commons or the House of Lords. The latter convention is illustrated by the appointment by Mr. Harold Wilson of Mr. Cousins and Mr. Gordon Walker to ministerial posts after the Labour victory in the general election in October 1964. Neither was a Member of Parliament: Mr. Cousins was a trade union official, and Mr. Walker (who was appointed Foreign Secretary) had actually been defeated at Smethwick in the recent election. In January 1965 they stood as candidates in by-elections facilitated by the grant of life peerages to two Labour M.P.s. Mr. Cousins was elected, but Mr. Walker was again defeated and resigned office next day. (By law the Queen can appoint and dismiss Ministers at her pleasure).[58]

(iii) The body of Ministers so appointed become the "Government," and an inner ring of them is called the "Cabinet."[59] Cabinet Ministers are always made Privy Councillors, if not such already. The Cabinet is entirely the product of convention, and is unknown to the law except for a few incidental references in statutes relating to Ministerial salaries, the Parliamentary Commissioner Act 1967 and the Data Protection Act 1984.

(iv) The Queen is bound to exercise her legal powers in accordance with the advice tendered to her by the Cabinet through the Prime Minister. She has the right to be kept informed and to express her views on the questions at issue, but not to override ministerial advice. This advice is expected to be unanimous.

(v) The Queen must assent to every Bill passed by the Houses of Parliament, or passed by the House of Commons only in accordance with the provisions of the Parliament Acts. A sovereign has not refused assent to a Bill since Queen Anne refused her assent to the Scottish Militia Bill in 1707, and the exercise of this prerogative today would be unconstitutional.[60] (No Bill has the force of law until the Queen gives her assent, but there is no law requiring her to give it.)

---

[57] *Ante*, p. 118; Even so, to get the salary or pension the Prime Minister must hold, or have held, the legal office of First Lord of the Treasury.

[58] See also *post* p. 304 for the case of Lord Young of Graffham, elevated to the House of Lords in 1984 and appointed Minister without Portfolio before becoming, in 1985, Secretary of State for Employment.

[59] It has been suggested that it has also become a convention that the Opposition leaders should form a Shadow Cabinet; D. R. Turner, *The Shadow Cabinet in British Politics.* (1969).

[60] The Prime Minister might perhaps advise the Queen to refuse assent to a Private Bill passed by both Houses but to which the government objected; and possibly to a Public Bill if there has been a change of circumstances or a mistake has been found in the text; though in the latter case an amending Act would more likely be the appropriate procedure.

(vi) Parliament must be summoned to meet at least once each year. The observance of this convention is secured by the practice (probably itself also a convention) of limiting to one year at a time the statutory authority covering the raising and spending of part of the revenue and the maintenance of the Army and Air Force. (By the Meeting of Parliament Act 1694 Parliament must be summoned at least once in three years.)

(vii) The Government is entitled to continue in office only so long as it enjoys the confidence of a majority in the House of Commons. The Prime Minister is bound to advise the Sovereign to dissolve Parliament, or to tender the resignation of himself and his ministerial colleagues, if the government is defeated on the floor of the House of Commons on a motion of confidence or of no confidence. Owing to party discipline, the defeat of a Government with a party majority in the Commons on a motion of this kind is rare in modern times. Mr. Wilson's government was defeated in the Commons in March 1976 on its policy of cutting public expenditure, but it won a motion of confidence next day. When Mr. Callaghan's government was defeated on a guillotine motion relating to the Scotland and Wales Bill in February 1977, this was not regarded by either side as a question of confidence. Similarly in May 1978 the Government was defeated twice in three days in Committee on amendments to the Finance Bill but did not—and was not expected—to resign.[61] Ramsay MacDonald's minority government was defeated 12 times in 1924 but the Prime Minister had announced that he would not resign or ask for a dissolution unless defeated on a major issue.[62] (By law, subject to the Meeting of Parliament Act 1694 (*supra*) and the Parliament Act 1911, fixing the maximum duration of a Parliament at five years, the Queen has power to summon and dissolve Parliament at her pleasure.)

(viii) The Ministers are collectively responsible to Parliament for the general conduct of the affairs of the country. This collective responsibility requires that on a major question Ministers should be of one mind and voice. If any Minister does not agree with the policy of the majority in the Cabinet, he should resign or, if the matter is a minor one or he is not a member of the Cabinet, at least keep quiet about it.[63] Apart from the dramatic occasions of the "agreement to differ" in 1932 and the EEC Referendum campaign in 1976,[64] there appears to have been some weakening of collective responsibility in Labour Governments since 1974. The old idea was that a Ministry should give collective advice to the Sovereign; but the recent attitude seems to be that, so long as the government can retain its majority in the House of Commons, the main consideration is its popularity among the electorate.[65]

---

[61] Cf. a defeat in the House on Budget resolutions which would lead to resignation. *Post*, p. 223.

[62] Motions other than motions of confidence or no confidence may be treated as matters of confidence, and rather more latitude is allowed to a minority government *i.e.* one that does not hold a party majority in the House. See further, pp. 150–152, See Philip Norton, "Government Defeats in the House of Commons: Myth and Reality," [1978] P.L. 360.

[63] *Post*, Chap. 16.

[64] *Ante*, p. 74.

[65] *Post*, Chap. 16.

(ix) Ministers are also individually responsible to Parliament for the administration of their departments. A Minister must be prepared to answer questions in the House concerning matters for which he is administratively responsible, and if a vote of censure is passed against him he must resign his office. Standing Orders of the House of Commons assume the existence of the former convention by prescribing days and times for questions. (By law, Ministers are individually responsible to the Sovereign.)

(x) Ministers are expected to disembarrass themselves of any company directorships or shareholdings that would be likely, or might appear, to conflict with their official duties.

(xi) A government should not advise the Crown to declare war, make peace or conclude a treaty unless there is ample ground for supposing that the majority of the Commons approve of the policy. (By law the power to make war and peace and to enter into international treaties is vested in the Queen, who is not bound to consult advisers[66] or Parliament, though the Bill of Rights prevents her from imposing taxation to meet financial commitments.)

2. Conventions regulating the relations between the Lords and Commons, and proceedings in Parliament

The House of Commons being the representative assembly, its will ought ultimately to prevail in cases of conflict with the House of Lords, which is mainly hereditary and partly nominated. Since medieval times the Commons have claimed the right to control national finance, that is, the levying of taxation and the supervision of the expenditure of public money.

Each House must have power to control the conduct of its own proceedings free from outside interference, and in course of time the Houses have evolved rules and customs, privileges and practice regulating legislative procedure and the conduct of debate.

The following are some of the most important conventions in this group:

(i) In cases of conflict the Lords should ultimately yield to the Commons.[67] (Perhaps the Parliament Acts 1911 and 1949—by defining the period during which the Lords may delay public Bills, other than a Bill to extend the maximum duration of Parliament—have rendered this convention unnecessary.) Until the Parliament Act 1911 was passed it was legitimate for a Ministry, when an important measure was rejected by the Lords, to advise the Sovereign as a last resort to create a sufficient number of peers to ensure its passage in the Upper House. The Treaty of Utrecht was ratified by this method in 1712; and the Reform Act 1832 and the Parliament Act 1911 were passed by the threat of recourse to it. (The Parliament Act 1911 made recourse to this expedient for the future unnecessary and perhaps improper.)

---

[66] Foreign countries, however, might well be unwilling to enter into a treaty that was not authenticated by the signature or seal of some senior Minister.

[67] See post 147 for a discussion of recent instances of serious embarrassment caused to the Government by the rejection and amendment of legislation by the House of Lords.

(ii) Proposals involving the expenditure of public money may only be introduced on behalf of the Crown by a Minister in the House of Commons. Standing Orders provide that a financial resolution shall only be proposed by a Minister on behalf of the Crown. There may be elements here of parliamentary custom and privilege, as well as constitutional convention. (The Parliament Act 1911 assumes, without expressly stating, that Money Bills will be introduced in the Commons.)

(iii) The business of the House of Commons is arranged informally "behind the Speaker's Chair" between the Prime Minister or Leader of the House and the Leader of the Opposition. The last is a product of convention more recent than the Prime Minister, and fulfils the function of a sparring partner. Charles James Fox is generally regarded as the first Leader of the Opposition, when the younger Pitt became Prime Minister in 1783. (The Ministers of the Crown Act 1937 first gave the Leader of the Opposition a salary payable out of the Consolidated Fund; and the Ministerial Salaries and Members' Pensions Act 1965 gave salaries to the Leader of the Opposition in the House of Lords and the Chief Opposition Whips in both Houses.[68] These salaries are charged on the Consolidated Fund.) A member may, so far as his Chief Whip is concerned, safely absent himself from a debate if he obtains a "pair" from among members of the other party.

(iv) The majority in Parliament must not stifle minorities. It is a duty of the Speaker to protect minorities in debate, and so far as possible he calls on speakers from alternate parties.

(v) The political parties are represented in parliamentary committees in proportion to the number of their adherents in the House. (The Ministers of the Crown Act 1937 indirectly recognised the existence of political parties in its definition of the Leader of the Opposition.)

(vi) Peers who do not hold or have not held high judicial office do not take part when the House of Lords is sitting in its judicial capacity. (The Appellate Jurisdiction Acts provide for the appointment of a certain number of Lords of Appeal in Ordinary, but there is no law that lay peers may not sit as well.) This rule is perhaps rather one of parliamentary practice or the practice of the court than a "convention," as it is not of a political nature referable to the needs of constitutional government.[69]

(vii) We may say that there is a convention that the Houses of Parliament will not entertain, or pass, a private Bill without providing for adequate notice to be given to persons affected and allowing them an opportunity to state objections. The Standing Orders relating to private business, which are alterable in detail, presuppose this convention.[70]

3. Conventions regulating the relations between the United Kingdom and other members of the Commonwealth

A number of conventions have grown up, or have been formulated, regulating the relations between the United Kingdom and the indepen-

---

[68] These provisions are now contained in more recent legislation.
[69] See further, *post*, p. 170.
[70] Cf. *Edinburgh and Dalkeith Ry.* v. *Wauchope* (1842) 8 Cl. & F. 710 (H.L.); *Pickin* v. *British Railways Board* [1974] A.C. 765 (H.L.).

dent members of the Commonwealth, providing methods of co-operation and communication among the members of the Commonwealth
and concerning negotiations between them and foreign countries.
Many of these conventions were formulated as resolutions of Imperial
Conferences between the wars, though that did not give them legal
effect. The following are some of the most important of this group of
conventions:

(i) The Parliament of the United Kingdom may not legislate for a former dependent territory that is now an independent member of the
Commonwealth except at its request and with its consent. (This convention is recited in the preamble to the Statute of Westminster 1931,
and enacted as section 4 of that Act. It has also been enacted in various
Independence Acts.)

(ii) Any alteration in the law touching the succession to the throne or
the Royal Style and Titles requires the assent of the Parliaments of
Canada, Australia and New Zealand as well as of the Parliament of the
United Kingdom. (This convention is recited in the preamble to the
Statute of Westminster 1931.) The same convention may apply to other
members of the Commonwealth of which Her Majesty is Queen.

(iii) The Queen in appointing the Governor-General of an independent Commonwealth country acts on the advice of the Prime Minister of
that country.

(iv) The Governor-General is the representative of the Queen, not of
the British Government, and acts on the advice of the government of the
Commonwealth country concerned.

(v) The governments of the United Kingdom and the independent
members of the Commonwealth keep each other informed with regard
to the negotiation of treaties and the conduct of foreign affairs, and one
of them can commit the others to active participation without their consent.

The Crown or the Governor-General would not be bound by English
law to observe these last three conventions, but such conventions may
be enacted in the constitutions of Commonwealth countries. Convention (iii) and (iv) are not applicable to Commonwealth countries that
have become republics, and is doubtful whether convention (ii) is
applicable to them.[71]

---

[71] See further, *post,* Chap. 37.

Part II

PARLIAMENT

CHAPTER 7

"THE HIGH COURT OF PARLIAMENT"[1]

I. HISTORICAL INTRODUCTION

In origin Parliament was not primarily a lawmaking body, nor are its functions exclusively legislative at the present day. A "parliament" was a council summoned to discuss some important matter, and the name is still appropriate to its present activity of debating policy and questioning and criticising the government. The title given it in the Book of Common Prayer, "the High Court of Parliament," reminds us that Parliament was, and still is, a court—the highest court in the land. The word "court" (*curia*) has a number of meanings. It may mean the place where the Sovereign is, a body of judges appointed to administer the law, or a place where justice is administered. Coke, in his treatment of the jurisdiction of the courts, deals first with "The High and most Honourable Court of Parliament,"[2] and says that "the Lords in their House have power of Judicature, and both Houses together have power of Judicature."[3]

The distant precursor of Parliament was the *Curia Regis*, in which the judicial, executive and legislative powers were fused. Its remotest ancestor, the Witenagemot, also exercised all three functions of government. In the early Middle Ages the common law courts split off from the council, and the latter may be said to have separated from Parliament in the reign of Richard II. Appeal by writ of error passed to what came to be called the House of Lords. Adjudication was one of the essential elements in the early Parliaments, notably those of Edward I.[4] The statutes of the Lords Ordainers (*temp*. Edward II in 1311) ordained that the King should hold a parliament at least once a year in which pleas that had been delayed or about which the judges differed should be recorded and determined.

The medieval King decided whether or not the assembly he had in mind should be a Parliament and whether legislation should be passed, or taxation discussed, or popular representatives summoned. The medieval Parliament was not "democratic." Professor Sayles has suggested that three factors combined to produce the early Parliaments: (i) the King's desire to expedite the processes of administration and law by the

---

[1] The leading reference book on the topics discussed in Chapters 7–12 is Erskine May's *Treatise on the Law, Privileges, Proceedings and Usage of Parliament*, hereafter cited as Erskine May, *Parliamentary Practice*. The first edition appeared in 1844; the twentieth (current) edition in 1983. Although a valuable work of reference it is *not* itself authoritative nor is it necessarily always correct: Mr. Robin Maxwell Hyslop M.P., Letter to *Daily Telegraph* 10 Jan. 1984.

[2] 4 Inst. 3, 4.

[3] 4 Inst. 15.

[4] Maitland, *Memoranda de Parliamento* (1893); McIlwain, *The High Court of Parliament* (1910), Chap. 3; Baldwin, *The King's Council during the Middle Ages*, Chaps. 1 and 12; Pollard, *Evolution of Parliament* (2nd ed., 1926), Chap. 2; Pike, *Constitutional History of the House of Lords*, Chap. 4.

provision of means for resolving difficulties; (ii) the desire of the barons to control the government by establishing a method of proper consultation; and (iii) the popular desire to get abuses removed and grievances remedied through ready access to an institution which could grant the highest justice.[5]

Judicial functions

Before treating of the legislative functions of Parliament, which today are at least of equal importance to its general supervision of the government of the country, we may preserve a historical sense by glancing at its remaining judicial functions. These include:

(1) The appellate jurisdiction of the House of Lords, both civil and criminal.

(2) The judicial functions of the Lords and Commons within the sphere of their privileges.[6]

(3) The jurisdiction of the Lords and the Commons in committees dealing with private Bills.[7]

(4) The judicial functions of the Lords with regard to claims to ancient peerages.[8]

These are discussed later in their appropriate chapters. Here we will mention impeachment and attainder (now in practice obsolete) and trial of peers (abolished)[9] to which we may add a note on Committees and Tribunals of Inquiry.

Impeachment

Impeachment was a judicial proceeding against any person, whether lord or commoner, accused of state offences beyond the reach of the law, or which no other authority in the state would prosecute. The Commons were the accusers, and the Lords were judges both of fact and law.

The first recorded case of impeachment occurred in 1376, when two lords and four commoners were charged with removing the staple from Calais, lending the King money at usurious interest, and buying Crown debts for small sums and then paying themselves in full out of the Treasury. There were no impeachments between that of the Duke of Suffolk for treason in 1449 and that of Sir Giles Mompesson in 1621 for fraud, violence and oppression. In the same year Bacon was impeached for bribery in the office of Lord Chancellor: the large fine was remitted and the King set him at liberty, but he was banned from public office for the rest of his life.[10] Most impeachments took place in the early 1640s.

The Act of Settlement 1700 provides that no pardon under the Great Seal shall be pleadable to an impeachment by the Commons. This pro-

---

[5] G.O. Sayles, *The King's Parliament of England* (1975) covers the period 1258–1377.

[6] *Post*, Chap. 12.

[7] *Post*, Chap. 10.

[8] *Post*, Chap. 8.

[9] For the history of impeachment, attainder and trial of peers, see Stephen, *History of the Criminal Law* (1883), Vol. I, Chap. 5.

[10] See Clifford Hall, "Francis Bacon: The 'Wisest, Brightest, Meanest of Mankind'?" (1976) 7 *Cambrian Law Review*, 38.

vision arose out of *Danby's Case*.[11] Danby was impeached in connection with a letter written by him to the English ambassador at Versailles with the approval of Charles II, who wrote on the letter: "This letter is writ by my Order—C.R." The last two cases of impeachment were those of Warren Hastings, Governor-General of India,[12] and Lord Melville, formerly treasurer to the Admiralty.[13] Both were acquitted.

Impeachment may be said to be now obsolete. So far as Ministers are concerned this is mainly due to the development of the conventions relating to collective ministerial responsibility to Parliament.[14] Further, criminal trial is the proper procedure for trying criminal offences, and the Commons would not now like to admit that they need the help of the Lords to control Ministers. A report of the Select Committee of the House of Commons on Parliamentary Privilege suggested that this procedure should be abolished by legislation.[15]

Acts of Attainder[16]

An Act of Attainder, though it served the same purpose as impeachment, was strictly a legislative and not a judicial act. It was an Act of Parliament finding a person guilty of an offence, usually a political one of a rather insubstantial kind, and inflicting a punishment on him. The subject of the proceedings was allowed to defend himself by counsel and witnesses before both Houses. One of the first Acts of Attainder of which we know was that of the Duke of Clarence in 1477, and from about that time until James I's reign this procedure was commonly used instead of impeachment. Attainder was later used occasionally down to 1715. It has not been used since the early eighteenth century when Cabinet government was beginning to develop. We may therefore describe it as possible but in practice obsolete.[17]

Committees and Tribunals of Inquiry

A *Select Committee of Inquiry* may be set up by either House to investigate any matter of public interest, and such a committee may include

---

[11] (1679) 11 St.Tr. 599.
[12] *Impeachment of Warren Hastings* (1787) Lords' Journals Vol. XXXVII, p. 678; (1795) *Lords' Journals*, Vol. XL, p. 388; P. J. Marshall, *The Impeachment of Warren Hastings* (1965); Keith Feiling, *Warren Hastings*.
[13] *Impeachment of Lord Melville* (1805) 29 St.Tr. 549.
[14] *Cf.* G. W. Keeton, "Legal Responsibility for Political Acts" [1948] C.L.P. 15. Keeton, *The Passing of Parliament*, Chap. 4, suggests that the critical moment was in 1742, when Walpole's opponents failed to impeach him.
[15] *Report from Select Committee on Parliamentary Privilege* (1967) H.C. 34.
[16] Lord Justice Somervell, "Acts of Attainder" (1951) 67 L.Q.R. 306. And see *Kariapper* v. *Wijesinha* [1968] A.C. 717.
[17] The privilege of peers to be tried by the House of Lords for treason or felony, or misprision of either, could be traced back to the *judicium parium* of Magna Carta, c.39, though the law did not become settled until well after 1215. If Parliament was sitting the House was presided over by the Lord Chancellor as the Lord High Steward. If Parliament was not sitting, the Lord High Steward acted as judge, sitting with a jury of peers. The last trial of a peer before the House of Lords was that of Baron de Clifford for manslaughter in 1935 (*R.* v. *Baron de Clifford*, *The Times*, December 13, 1935, pp. 15–16; *Proceedings on the Trial of Lord de Clifford*, H.M.S.O. 1936). The so-called privilege, which could not be waived and entailed great expense, was abolished by the Criminal Justice Act 1948.

persons who are not Members of Parliament. This method was first used in 1689 to investigate the conduct of the war in Ireland, but Parliament is a political body and voting tends to be on party lines.

The Tribunals of Inquiry (Evidence) Act 1921 therefore provides that on a resolution of both Houses on a matter of urgent public importance, a *Tribunal of Inquiry* may be appointed by the Queen or a Secretary of State with all the powers of the High Court as regards examination of witnesses and production of documents. It was under this Act that the Porter Tribunal was appointed in 1936 to inquire into a Budget leakage through J. H. Thomas (Secretary of State for the Colonies); the Lynskey Tribunal was set up in 1948 to inquire into allegations of bribery and corruption arising out of the use of "contact men" to approach Ministers[18]; and in 1957 Parker L.J. presided over an inquiry into allegations of improper disclosure of information relating to the raising of the bank rate. The Vassall spy case was the subject of a Tribunal of Inquiry under Lord Radcliffe in 1963. Allegations of irregularities by the Crown Agents were investigated by a Tribunal of Inquiry under Croom Johnson J. which was set up in 1978 and reported in 1982. If a person refuses to answer relevant and essential questions or to produce documents, the matter may be referred to the High Court to be dealt with as contempt of court. The latter power was invoked at the Vassall inquiry, when two journalists refused to reveal the source of their information, one being sentenced to six months' imprisonment and the other to three months.[19]

An objection to Tribunals of Inquiry is that all sorts of allegations may be made against individuals which are not—and sometimes cannot be—made the substance of criminal or other judicial proceedings.[20] It is an inquisitorial investigation, usually in public without a jury. There are no strict rules of evidence, no right of appeal, no right to legal representation, and no opportunity to meet allegations made by witnesses. A Royal Commission recommended in 1966 that the inquisitorial powers of tribunal should be retained, with certain safeguards (some of which require amendment of the 1921 Act) for persons appearing before or taking part in such inquiries.[21]

II. THE MEETING OF PARLIAMENT

Royal prerogative in relation to Parliament

A "parliament" lasts from the summons of the legislature until its sittings are terminated by dissolution or lapse of time. During a single

---

[18] (1949) Cmd. 7616.

[19] *Att.-Gen.* v. *Clough* [1963] 1 Q.B. 773 (Lord Parker C.J.): Clough never in fact served his sentence as the source revealed itself and he confirmed it: *Att.-Gen.* v. *Mulholland* and *Att.-Gen.* v. *Foster* [1963] 2 Q.B. 477 (C.A.), *post* p. 405. See also *British Steel Corpn.* v. *Granada Television Ltd.* [1981] A.C. 1096.

[20] See G. W. Keeton, *Trial by Tribunal* (1960).

[21] *Royal Commission on Tribunals of Inquiry* (1966) Cmnd. 3121. And see Sir Cyril Salmon, *Triunals of Inquiry* (Lionel Cohen Lectures, 1967); *Report of Interdepartmental Committee on Tribunals of Inquiry and Contempt* (Salmon L.J.) (1969) Cmnd. 4078. *Tribunals of Inquiry set up under the Tribunals of Inquiry (Evidence) Act 1921*, (1973) Cmnd. 5313. See also Z. Segal, "Tribunals of Inquiry: A British Invention Ignored in Britain." [1984] P.L. 206.

parliament there may be a number of sessions—before 1914 generally not more than one a year, since 1918 usually two a year. A session is terminated by prorogation. Within a session there are a number of sittings separated from each other by adjournments, which can be brought about by motion of each House.

The exercise of the royal prerogative is necessary to summon, to prorogue or (before the expiration of the statutory period) to dissolve Parliament. The royal proclamation that dissolves one Parliament also summons the next. Before 1965 the control, use and occupation of the whole of the Palace of Westminster rested with the Lord Great Chamberlain on behalf of the Queen. When the House of Commons was sitting, control of that side of Parliament was delegated by him to the Serjeant-at-Arms acting for the Speaker; but during Parliamentary recesses and at weekends control reverted to the Lord Great Chamberlain. In 1965 the Queen handed over control of the Palace of Westminster to the two Houses themselves, and since then the Speaker has been in control of the House of Commons whether it is sitting or not.

Sovereign's presence in Parliament

The Sovereign, although in constitutional theory present in the High Court of Parliament as in other courts, does not now in practice visit Parliament in person, except to read the speech from the Throne in the Lords' Chamber at the opening of a new Parliament or session. Other royal functions performed in whole Parliament, such as prorogation, dissolution or giving the Royal Assent to Bills, are now done by royal proclamation or commission under the Great Seal.

A convention to ensure freedom of debate forbids the Sovereign to be present in either House sitting separately. As regards the Commons, the Sovereign was not present in the Middle Ages, but occasional intrusions were made in the seventeenth century. The Lords, on the other hand, were the Great Council and the Sovereign's presence was necessary in early times; but the practice of attending was dying out in the Stuart period and ceased on the death of Queen Anne.

Royal Assent to legislation

The Queen may still give the Royal Assent in person in Parliament, but this has not been done since 1854. The Royal Assent Act 1967 provides that the Royal Assent, signified by letters patent under the Great Seal signed with Her Majesty's own hand, may also be: (a) pronounced by commissioners in the presence of both Houses in the House of Lords in the manner customary since George III's reign[22]; or (b) notified to each House separately by the Speaker of that House. The latter method was new and avoids interrupting the proceedings of the Commons by a summons from Black Rod. The customary method (a) is still used at the time of prorogation.

When the Royal Assent is given to a public or local Bill the words "La

---

[22] Under the Royal Assent by Commission Act 1541, which was repealed by the 1967 Act.

Reine le veult" are pronounced by the Clerk of the Parliaments. For a private Bill the words "Soit fait comme il est désiré" are used, and for a Money Bill the following: "La Reine remercie ses bons sujets, accepte leur bénévolence, et ainsi le veult." If the Queen were to refuse her assent, which would now be unconstitutional, the tactful formula, "La Reine s'avisera" (The Queen will think about it) would be used.

Frequency of Parliaments

In early times Sovereigns generally pleased themselves when they would convene Parliament. In the reign of Charles I the Long Parliament passed the first Triennial Act (1640), which enacted that a Parliament should be held in every third year; and made provision for the issue of writs for the election of the Commons if the King omitted to do so for these years. In the reign of Charles II this was repealed by the Triennial Act 1664, which provided that the sitting of Parliament should not be discontinued for over three years; but it laid down no machinery for the summoning of Parliament if the clause were disregarded. The provision that a Parliament should be held once at least in three years was re-enacted in section 1 of the Meeting of Parliament Act 1694, which is still in force.[23] Section 2 provides that within three years after the determination of every Parliament, legal writs shall be issued by directions of the Sovereign for calling another new Parliament.

The Bill of Rights 1688 meanwhile declared (s.13) that for the redress of all grievances and for the amending, strengthening and preserving of all laws, Parliament ought to be held "frequently." The real security, however, for the frequent—indeed annual—meeting of Parliament consists (as we saw in Chapter 6) in the practice of passing annual Finance Acts and annual orders continuing the Army and Air Force and Naval Discipline Acts. In modern times it is necessary to keep Parliament in almost constant session, not only to legislate but to supervise the government of the country, to say nothing of dealing with emergencies.

Summons of a new Parliament

When the Queen accepts the advice of the Prime Minister to dissolve, a proclamation is published dissolving the existing Parliament and fixing the date for the meeting of the new Parliament.[24] The proclamation also announces the making of an Order in Council directing the Lord Chancellor of Great Britain and the Secretary of State for Northern Ireland to issue the necessary writs. The Clerk of the Crown in Chancery then prepares writs, which are sent to the temporal peers and the 26 Lords Spiritual. The judges are also summoned to attend and advise, but (unless they are peers) they do not attend, though they may be asked to advise the House of Lords sitting as the final court of appeal. The returning officers are instructed by writs to cause election to be

---

[23] The Act of 1694 also fixed the maximum life of Parliament at three years; *post*, p. 138.

[24] The former rule that the time appointed for the meeting of Parliament should not be less than twenty clear days after the proclamation summoning it was repealed by the Representation of the People Act 1985, s.28(2).

made of a member to serve in Parliament for the constituency mentioned, and to return the name to the Crown Office.[25]

Meeting of a new Parliament

On the appointed day each House assembles in its own chamber until the Gentleman Usher of the Black Rod requires attendance of the Commons at the bar of the Lords. As many members as space permits, and as have the inclination, then proceed with the Assistant Clerk of the Parliaments (Clerk to the House of Commons) to the "bar," a line which is deemed to mark the boundary of the Lords' Chamber. Unless the Sovereign is present, the commission for opening Parliament is then read by the Lord Chancellor. The Commons are then bidden by him to retire and proceed to the election of a Speaker. The election of Speaker ends the day.

Next day the new Speaker proceeds with the Commons to the bar of the House of Lords. He announces his election, which is confirmed by the Lord Chancellor in the name of the Sovereign. It is not certain whether the Sovereign's approval is required by law; but it is always sought and has only once been refused, by Charles II in the case of Sir Edward Seymour in 1678. After this the Speaker claims certain ancient privileges of the House. The Sovereign, if present, reads the Queen's speech. If she is absent her speech is read by the Lord Chancellor. It is drafted by the Cabinet,[26] and outlines the government's policy with regard to foreign affairs and legislation. After this the Commons retire, and each member of either House proves his right to membership. Then members of both Houses take the statutory oath or affirmation of allegiance. The address in reply to the Queen's speech provides an opportunity for a debate on government policy. Out of courtesy to the Sovereign, it is agreed to without a division, though any amendments proposed may be voted on.

Adjournment

Either House may adjourn its *sittings* for any given number of hours, days, weeks, or months; but the Crown has a statutory power to issue a proclamation ordering resumption of business when both Houses stand adjourned for more than fourteen days. A proclamation may be issued giving one day's notice in an emergency.[27]

Prorogation

Prorogation terminates a *session* of Parliament. It is effected by command of the Queen—acting by convention on the advice, formerly, of the Cabinet but, it seems, in practice in modern times on the advice of

---

[25] Representation of the People Act 1983, s.23 and Sched. 1.

[26] In 1981 the Parliamentary Labour Party introduced a new standing order under which the contents of the Queen's Speech at the opening of Parliament and each succeeding session would be considered at a special meeting of the Party.

[27] Meeting of Parliament Acts 1797 and 1870; Parliament (Elections and Meeting) Act 1943.

the Prime Minister[28]—such command being signified to both Houses either by the Lord Chancellor (in the Queen's presence or by commission) or by proclamation. In either case the date for the new session is stated, but statutes enable the Crown by proclamation to accelerate or defer the next meeting of a Parliament that stands prorogued.[29] The interval between two sessions is called a recess.

The progress of public Bills (including private Members' Bills) is liable to be stopped by prorogation. This rule has been subject to criticism, and has recently been modified.[30] The House commonly pass resolutions allowing private Bills to be proceeded with in the next session. It is probably better that Parliament should have to clear its books, as it were, at the end of the session rather than that the order paper should become cluttered by a number of stale Bills and motions. Prorogation also keeps the government up to the mark in the attempt to complete its legislative programme. A Minister is sometimes content to drop a Bill and bring in an improved version later.

Prorogation may be preceded by the signification of the Royal Assent to Bills that have passed both Houses, and the Queen's Speech surveying the work of the past session.

Beginning of a new session

At the beginning of each session (except the first session of a Parliament) when the Speaker returns from the Lords to the House of Commons, a Bill for the Suppression of Clandestine Outlawries[31] is formally read the first time. This practice preserves the right of the House to initiate Bills not foreshadowed in the Queen's Speech, and in particular the ancient right of the Commons to air grievances before granting the Sovereign supplies. The Speaker then reads a copy of the Queen's Speech to the House, and a loyal address of thanks to Her Majesty for the speech is moved and seconded. On that question amendments may be moved, and a general debate on the address takes place, in which the government programme is discussed and criticised.

A similar debate on the Queen's Speech, in the form of a loyal address, takes place in the House of Lords after the formal first reading of the Select Vestries Bill.

Duration of Parliament

The Meeting of Parliament Act 1694, s.3, provided that no Parliament should last for more than three years. This provision was repealed at the time of the Scottish rising by the Septennial Act 1715, which provided that the existing and future Parliaments could continue for a period not exceeding seven years. The latter provision in its turn was repealed by the Parliament Act 1911, which provides (s.7) that the maximum life of a

---

[28] *Post.* p. 323.
[29] Meeting of Parliament Act 1797; Prorogation Act 1867; Meeting of Parliament Act 1870; Parliament (Elections and Meeting) Act 1943.
[30] *Post*, Chap. 10.
[31] See G.Chowdharay-Best, "The Clandestine Outlawries and Select Vestries Bills" (1974) 124 New L.J. 230.

Parliament shall be five years. This period can, of course, be extended by Act of Parliament,[32] but it has only been done in wartime and the practice has been to extend the period for one year at a time. Thus the Parliament that passed the Parliament Act 1911 survived until after the Armistice in 1918, and the Parliament elected in 1935 lasted until 1945.

The life of Parliament is terminated by lapse of time, *viz.* five years under the provisions of the Parliament Act 1911, or by a dissolution. In practice the government makes an opportunity thought to be favourable to its own interest to advice a dissolution during the fifth (or even fourth) year if no crisis has occurred before then.

Parliament and the demise of the Crown

Formerly Parliament expired when the Sovereign died, but this inconvenient rule was abolished by various statutes. On the demise of the Crown, Parliament (if sitting) is to proceed to act, and if prorogued or adjourned is to meet immediately without the usual form of summons.[33] The duration of an existing Parliament is not affected by a demise of the Crown.[34] All members of both Houses must take the oath of allegiance to the new Sovereign.

When a demise of the Crown occurs after a proclamation summoning a new Parliament has been given it shall have no effect except that if the demise occurs before the date of the poll, the meeting of Parliament shall be delayed by 14 days.[35]

Dissolution

A dissolution by the Sovereign in person is possible, but Parliament has only been dissolved that way once, in 1818, since the reign of Charles II. Parliament is now invariably dissolved by Royal Proclamation, expressed to be issued with the advice of the Privy Council.[36]

III. The Lords and Commons in Conflict[37]

Earlier conflicts

In the reign of Charles II the Commons passed resolutions denying the right of the Lords to introduce or amend Money Bills. They did not specifically deny the right of the Lords to reject a Money Bill, a right which the Lords continued formally to claim, although before 1860 they exercised it extremely rarely. In 1832 there was a serious controversy over the Reform Bill. William IV, much against his inclination, sup-

---

[32] Such a Bill may not be passed without the consent of the Lords under the provisions of the Parliament Act 1911; see *post*, p. 144.

[33] Succession to the Crown Act 1707.

[34] Representation of the People Act 1867.

[35] Representation of the People Act 1985, s.20.

[36] For the exercise of the prerogative of dissolution, see pp. 149 *et seq.*

[37] This section is confined to conflicts over legislation and finance. The two Houses have also on occasion been in conflict on judicial issues (*post*, Chap. 8) and over their privileges (*post*, Chap. 12). Formerly a conference of members of both Houses might be held in an attempt to settle conflicts—as is still the case in the United States. The last resort to this procedure in the United Kingdom was on a private Bill in 1936 and the details of the procedure have been omitted from *Erskine May* since the 1971 edition: K. Bradshaw and D. Pring, *Parliament and Congress* (1972) pp. 299–300.

ported Lord Grey by threatening to use the prerogative power of creating sufficient peers to carry the measure in the House of Lords. This power was actually exercised by Queen Anne in 1712 by the creation of 12 Tory peers to ensure a majority in the House of Lords for approval of the terms of the Peace Treaty of Utrecht.[38]

In 1860 the Lords exercised their legal right of rejecting Money Bills by throwing out a measure for the repeal of the paper duty. Three resolutions to the following effect were carried in the Commons: (1) that the right of granting aid and supplies to the Crown is in the Commons alone; (2) that, although the Lords could legally reject Money Bills, yet the exercise of that power was regarded by the lower House with peculiar jealousy; (3) that the Commons had the power so to impose and remit taxation and to frame Bills of Supply that the right of the Commons as to the matter, manner, measure and time might be maintained inviolate.[39] In the following year, Gladstone being then Chancellor of the Exchequer, the opposition of the peers was overridden by tacking the provision regarding paper duties on to a general financial measure for the services of the year. The House of Lords, therefore, had to face the alternative of passing the provision they disliked, or of rejecting the whole financial provision for the year. They shrank from the latter alternative. There is no constitutional objection to the House of Lords *discussing* the provisions of a Financial Bill. For example in 1978 they considered the propriety of a clause in the Finance Bill of that year which had retrospective effect—but then gave the Bill a second reading.

In 1869 the Irish Church Disestablishment Bill was strongly opposed by the Lords, in spite of the clearly expressed wishes of the electorate, but the difficulty was surmounted by Lord Cairns's influence. Another memorable dispute concerned the rejection in 1872 of a Bill to abolish the purchase of Army commissions. The warrant authorising the purchase of commissions was cancelled by exercise of the prerogative, and so the Government attained their object without a direct conflict between the two Houses. There was considerable friction between the two Houses when the Lords at first rejected the Representation of the People Bill in 1884, but mutual concessions were made by Salisbury and Gladstone. The next dispute was over Gladstone's second Home Rule Bill in 1893, but as the Lords were in this instance supported by the electorate their position was for the time being maintained.

Events leading to the Parliament Act 1911[40]

In 1905–06 the Liberals were returned to power with a gigantic majority, only to find that their principle measures continued to be rejected or drastically amended by the upper House. In 1907 the Commons passed

---

[38] The commercial treaty between England and France, however, was rejected by Parliament.

[39] C.S. Emden, *Selected Speeches on the Constitution*, Vol. I, pp. 141–142.

[40] See Anson, *Law and Custom of the Constitution* (5th ed. Gwyer), Vol. I pp. 304–308; Jennings, *Parliament* (2nd ed.), pp. 408 *et seq.*; Harold Nicolson, *King George V*, pp. 102–104, 125–139, 148–158; Kenneth Rose, *King George V*, (1983) pp. 112–131; Roy Jenkins, *Mr. Balfour's Poodle* (1954); *Asquith*, Chaps. 14 and 15; R.C.K. Ensor, *England 1870–1914*, pp. 422 *et seq*; G.H.L. Le May, *The Victorian Constitution* (1979) Chap. 7.

a resolution to the effect that the power of the Lords to alter or reject Bills passed by the Commons should be so restricted that the will of the Commons should prevail within the lifetime of a single Parliament.[41] This resolution as explained by Campbell-Bannerman, the Prime Minister, afterwards with some expansion formed the basis of the Parliament Act 1911. In 1908–1909 Liberal measures—notably the Licensing Bill—were again thrown out by the Lords.

The climax was reached in 1909 when the Finance Bill, containing Lloyd George's Budget, was thrown out in its entirety. The Commons resolved that this action was "a breach of the Constitution, and a usurpation of the rights of the Commons." Edward VII refused to promise Asquith, the Prime Minister, to create enough peers to swamp the Lords until the government's financial policy had been endorsed by the electorate. Parliament was dissolved. In the general election of January 1910 the government lost many seats, but retained its majority with the help of Irish Nationalist and Labour members. The Lords then passed the Finance Bill, which had been reintroduced by the Commons. The Parliament Bill was introduced in the Commons in April; but Edward VII died, and a conference of party leaders was formed to try to reach a settlement and to preserve King George V from a constitutional crisis at the beginning of his reign. Lord Landsdowne, leader of the Conservative peers, proposed that when an important constitutional Bill dealing with such matters as the Crown or the Protestant succession thereto, or establishing a national legislature in Ireland, Scotland, Wales or England, has been rejected three times by the House of Lords, the matter should be decided by referendum. Balfour, the Conservative leader, moved a clause requiring a referendum also for Bills affecting the Parliamentary franchise, the distribution of Parliamentary seats, or the constitution and power of either House of Parliament or relations between the two Houses.[42] Another suggestion was that deadlock over non-financial Bills should be resolved at a joint sitting of both Houses, with the Speaker of the Commons as chairman. Other Lords' amendments would exclude from the operation of the Parliament Bill certain fundamental or constitutional matters, including Irish Home Rule.

The conference broke down, mainly on the application of the Bill to Home Rule, and in November the Cabinet advised another dissolution. It is now clear that the second general election was embarked on in deference to the wishes of Edward VII expressed shortly before his death. The Cabinet also asked the new King to promise to create a sufficient number of peers to pass the Parliament Bill, and advised that his intention should not be published unless and until the actual occasion should arise. About 400 additional peers[43] would have been needed. The King felt that he had no alternative but to assent to the advice of the Cabinet.

The following general election made little difference to the position of

---

[41] The requirement of the Lords' consent to the grant of self-government to the Transvaal in 1907 was obviated by the use of an Order in Council.

[42] See Philip Goodhart, M.P., Referendum (1971), Chap. 2.

[43] The provisional list of nominees later published shows that most of them had no male issue, so that the number of new hereditary peerages would in fact not have been large.

the parties. The Lords proposed a number of amendments to the Parliament Bill which the Commons rejected, and in the summer of 1911 the Prime Minister divulged the King's promise to create a sufficient number of peers to force the Bill through the Lords. The Parliament Bill was eventually passed by the Lords in August 1911 with the help of a large number of abstentions, a majority of 17 (131–114) voting against the Lords insisting on their amendments.

The Parliament Act 1911[44] in effect abolished the Lords' power to reject Money Bills (as therein defined); and substituted for their power to reject other public Bills a power to delay them (with one important exception) for two years spread over three sessions. The important exception was a Bill to extend the life of Parliament.

Events leading to the Parliament Act 1949[45]

In the general election of 1945 the Labour Party said that they would not allow the House of Lords to thwart the will of the people, but they did not ask for a mandate for its abolition or reform. There was a mandate for the nationalisation of certain industries, not including iron and steel. The House of Lords did not reject the Labour Government's nationalisation measures in 1945–47: they suggested a number of useful technical amendments, but did not insist on any amendments to which the Commons did not agree. It seemed likely, however, that the Lords would reject the Iron and Steel Bill.

In 1947 the Commons passed a Parliament Bill (in the form which eventually became the Parliament Act 1949) designed to reduce the period of the Lords' delaying power in the case of public Bills other than Money Bills from two years to one year, spread over two sessions instead of three. The object of introducing this Bill at that stage was to ensure the passing of the Iron and Steel Bill, and perhaps further nationalisation measures, in spite of the opposition of the Lords in the fourth year of the existing Parliament. The Conservative majority in the Lords opposed the Parliament Bill on the grounds that (*inter alia*) it did not reform the membership of the upper House, the nation had expressed no desire for it, and it would go far to expose the country to the dangers of single chamber government.

A Conference of Party Leaders, representative of the three main parties in each House was convened in 1948.[46] It was agreed that the discussion should treat the composition and powers of the House of Lords as interdependent, but as far as concerned powers the terms of reference were limited to the delaying power. The Conservative leaders regarded twelve months from the third reading in the Commons as the shortest period acceptable. The Labour leaders regarded the maximum period acceptable as nine months from the third reading in the Commons or one year from the second reading, whichever might be the longer in a particular case. The difference between the parties was more

---

[44] *Post*, p. 143.
[45] See Jennings, *op. cit.* pp. 428–434.
[46] (1948) Cmd. 7380.

than a matter of three months, for it revealed a cleavage of opinion as to the purpose of the delaying power. The Labour view was that each House should have a proper time for the consideration of amendments to Bills proposed by the other. In effect this meant that *the Commons* should have time to think again. The Conservative view was that in the event of serious controversy between the two Houses on a measure on which the view of the electorate is doubtful, a sufficient time should elapse to enable *the electorate* to be properly informed of the issues involved and for public opinion to crystallise and express itself. This does not necessarily involve a general election. The Conference therefore broke down, and the Lords then rejected the Parliament Bill at its second reading. The Bill was eventually passed in 1949 *without the consent of the Lords* under the provisions of the Parliament Act 1911, it being necessary to introduce an extra short session for the purpose.[47]

The Parliament Act 1949 was remarkable as being an important constitutional measure that included a retroactive provision (the proviso to s.1) extending to Bills introduced before the Parliament Bill itself. The Iron and Steel Bill was not in fact forced through under these provisions. The Commons compromised[48] on the Lords' amendment to postpone the date of its coming into operation until after the next general election, which the government lost. The 1949 Act made no change with regard to Money Bills as the Lords could scarcely be allowed a shorter period to consider them than the month allowed by the 1911 Act.

The Parliament Acts 1911 and 1949

The provisions of the 1911 Act, as amended in 1949, are to the following effect: After reciting (*inter alia*) that it was eventually intended to substitute for the existing House of Lords a second chamber constituted on a popular instead of a hereditary basis, it is provided that:

Section 1.—(1) If a *Money Bill*, having been passed by the Commons and sent to the House of Lords[49] at least one month before the end of the session, is not passed by the Lords without amendment within one month after it has been sent up, the Bill, unless the Commons direct to the contrary, shall be presented to the Sovereign and become an Act of Parliament on the Royal Assent being signified, notwithstanding that the House of Lords have not consented to the Bill.[50]

(2) A Money Bill means a public Bill which, in the opinion of the

---

[47] The Parliament Act 1949 has been described as anti-democratic in so far as, by reducing the delaying power of the Lords, it reduces the opportunities of the electorate to express their views and correspondingly enlarges the powers of the Ministry: C. S. Emden, *The People and the Constitution* (2nd ed.), p. 307.

[48] The compromise was to reject the Lords' amendment, but to undertake to postpone the appointment of the proposed corporation until a date that would arrive after the general election.

[49] A Money Bill as defined in Standing Orders, which definition is wider than that in the Parliament Act 1911, must be introduced into the House of Commons in accordance with the privileges of the Commons and constitutional convention.

[50] The Parliament Acts assume separate sittings of the House of Lords and the House of Commons.

Speaker of the House of Commons, contains *only* provisions dealing with the following topics:

imposition, repeal, remission, alteration or regulation of taxation (not including local rates);

imposition for any financial purposes of charges on the Consolidated Fund or the National Loans Fund,[51] or on money provided by Parliament, or the variation of such charges;

supply;

appropriation, receipt, custody, issue or audit of accounts of public money;

raising or guarantee of any loan (not including loans by local authorities) or the repayment thereof; or

subordinate matters incidental to the above topics or any of them.[52]

(3) There shall be endorsed on a Money Bill when sent up to the Lords, and when presented to the Sovereign for assent, a certificate signed by the Speaker that the Bill is a Money Bill. Before so certifying the Speaker is to consult, if practicable, two members to be appointed from the Chairmen's Panel[53] at the beginning of the session by the Committee of Selection.

Section 2—(1) If any *public Bill*[54] (*other than a Money Bill or a Bill containing any provision to extend the maximum duration of Parliament beyond five years*)[55] is passed by the Commons in *two*[56] successive sessions (whether of the same Parliament or not),[57] and, having been sent to the Lords at least one month before the end of the session, is rejected by the Lords in each of those sessions, that Bill shall, on the *second*[58] rejection by the Lords, unless the Commons direct to the contrary, be presented to the Sovereign for the Royal Assent and thereupon become an Act of Parliament without the consent of the Lords. But the foregoing provision is not to take effect unless *one year*[58] has elapsed between the date of second reading[59] in the first of the sessions in the Commons and the date of its passing the Commons in the *second*[60] session.[61]

---

[51] National Loans Act 1968.

[52] For a discussion of this definition, see Jennings, *op. cit.* pp. 416 *et seq.*; Lord Campion, *Introduction to the Procedure of the House of Commons* (3rd ed.), p. 293.

[53] Composed of the Chairmen of Standing Committees of the Commons.

[54] Not including a Bill for confirming a Provisional Order, s.5.

[55] See *post*, p. 149. This exclusion from the Parliament Act 1911 was the only Lords' amendment agreed at a late stage of the proceedings on the Bill. Professor Denys Holland, in a letter to *The Times*, June 29, 1968, expressed the view that this exception could be repealed or amended without the consent of the Lords under the provisions of the Parliament Acts. Professor O. Hood Phillips in a letter to *The Times*, July 15, 1968, disputed this view on the ground that delegates (the Queen and the Commons) cannot enlarge their powers.

[56] Amendment made by the Parliament Act 1949.

[57] Prescribing more than one *session* enables both Houses to think again: a compromise is possible, or the Bill may be dropped.

[58] See note 56, *ante.*

[59] The Parliament Acts assume the practice of having three readings.

[60] See note 56, *ante.*

[61] A minimum *time* limit is also prescribed because the government could arrange one-day sessions.

(2) When a Bill is presented to the Sovereign for assent under this section, the signed certificate of the Speaker[62] that the requirements of this section have been complied with shall be endorsed thereon.

(3) A Bill shall be deemed to be rejected by the Lords if it is not passed by them without amendment or with amendments agreed to by both Houses.

(4) A Bill shall be deemed to be the same Bill as a former Bill sent up to the Lords in the preceding session if, when sent to the Lords, it is identical with the former Bill or contains only such alterations as are certified by the Speaker to be necessary owing to lapse of time since the date of the former Bill, or to represent amendments made by the Lords in the former Bill in the preceding session and agreed to by the Commons.

The Commons may, if they choose, in the *second*[63] session suggest further amendments without inserting them in the Bill, and such suggested amendments, if agreed to by the Lords, shall be treated as amendments agreed to by both Houses; but the exercise of this power by the Commons shall not affect the operation of this section in the event of rejection of the Bill by the Lords.[64]

Section 3. The Speaker's certificate *"shall be conclusive for all purposes,*[65] *and shall not be questioned in any court of law."* It may be noticed that the Parliament Acts do not describe the Speaker's functions thereunder as "duties."[66]

Section 4. When a Bill is sent up for the Royal Assent without the consent of the Lords the enacting formula is as follows:

"Be it enacted by the Queen's most excellent Majesty, *by and with the advice and consent of the Commons* in this present Parliament assembled, *in accordance with the provisions of the Parliament Act 1911 and 1949,* and by the authority of the same, as follows."

Section 5. "Public Bill" does not include a Bill for confirming a Provision Order.[67]

Section 6. "Nothing in this Act shall diminish or qualify the existing rights and privileges of the House of Commons."[68]

Section 7. "Five years shall be substituted for seven years as the time fixed for the maximum duration of Parliament under the Septennial Act 1715."[69]

---

[62] It has been suggested that it would be more satisfactory if a certificate of such importance were issued by a Joint Committee of the two Houses or a High Court judge.

[63] See note 56, *ante*.

[64] Questions were raised in the Commons whether the Aircraft and Shipbuilding Industries Bill 1976, in the form it left the Commons after the Lords' amendments had been dealt with, was the same Bill as that originally sent up to the Lords, and so could be passed under the procedure of the Parliament Acts. The Bill was reintroduced in a modified form in the next session and eventually passed.

[65] This expression could cover the Lords and the Sovereign.

[66] *Cf. ante,* p. 115, concerning the argument that there may be legal duties that are not enforceable in the corts.

[67] "Public Bill" is not otherwise defined by Parliament Acts.

[68] This preserves the various privileges of the Commons, especially in relation to financial measures, *e.g.* that they should only be introduced in the lower House, and that the Lords should not amend a Money Bill. See *post,* Chap. 11.

[69] A shorter maximum life of Parliament (three or four years) is advocated: O. Hood Phillips, *Reform of the Constitution,* pp. 52–54.

Measures not covered by the Parliament Acts

These include: (i) a Bill to extend the maximum duration of Parliament (s.2(1)); (ii) Bills to confirm Provisional Orders (s.5); (iii) Finance and other Supply Bills not certified as "Money Bills"; (iv) private Bills[70]; (v) Statutory Instruments[71] or other subordinate legislation; and (vi) Bills introduced into the Lords.

Relations between the two Houses since 1949

Apart from the 1949 Act itself, only two other Acts have received the Royal Assent in accordance with the provisions of the Parliament Act 1911, namely, the Government of Ireland Act 1914 and the Welsh Church Act 1914. The former never came into force as it was postponed by the outbreak of war and eventually superseded by the Government of Ireland Act 1920; the latter became law with some modifications.

Differences between the two Houses can normally be composed without recourse to the Parliament Acts. When the House of Lords sends back a Bill with amendments, a Committee of the House of Commons (if it disagrees with the amendments) sends the amended Bill back with a statement of its reasons for so doing, and a settlement is often reached by conferences between party leaders. If the Lords are opposed to a Bill sent up by the Commons, they generally propose amendments on the Committee stage rather than vote against the second reading. It has been said that there is a convention that amendments at the Committee stage should not reopen matters of principle already accepted by the Commons.[72] Nevertheless, while recognising the convention that the Lords should not oppose the second reading, the Opposition moved a reasoned amendment to the Rates Bill in 1984—which it lost. Most amendments in the upper House are in fact introduced by the government to improve the drafting of their own Bills. Defeats of Labour and Conservative Governments in the Lords have not been uncommon, in the last 20 years; but nowadays the Lords would very rarely insist on their amendments to a Government Bill. In August 1975 the government was defeated in the Commons and a Lords amendment approved, deleting from the Housing Finance (Special Provisions) Bill a clause to remove disqualification from office of the Clay Cross councillors; but the Lords gave way on other provisions of the Bill affecting the disqualification of 400 other councillors not yet dealt with by the courts. The Lords eventually gave way also on their amendments

---

[70] The British Transport Docks (Felixstowe) Bill 1976 was defeated in the Lords, although supported by the government. Jennings, *op. cit.* p. 446, suggests that the Commons could suspend their standing Orders relating to Private Bills or Hybrid Bills so as to bring them within the procedure of the Parliament Act 1949. He also states that a Bill to amend the Parliament Acts can be passed under these Acts but *cf. post.* p. 149. On the question whether the composition and powers of the House of Lords can be altered under the Parliament Act procedure, see Jennings, *op. cit.* pp. 437–439.

[71] If the Lords reject a Statutory Instrument the Minister can introduce a new version, which the Lords are not likely to reject, *e.g.* Statutory Order imposing further economic sanctions on Rhodesia in 1968.

[72] Lord Home of the Hirsel in the House of Lords: May 15, 1985.

to the Trade Union and Labour Relations (Amendment) Bill in 1975–76.[73]

The House of Lords has, of course, no need to give way on their amendments when a Government, lacking an effective majority, is unable to secure their rejection in the Commons. Thus a Labour Government had to accept the enactment of the Dock Work Regulation Act 1976 in the seriously weakened form in which it returned from the Lords. In the case of the Aircraft and Shipbuilding Industries Act 1977, the Lords had excluded from the scope of the Bill, when it was first before them, ship-repairing industries. The Commons restored them to the Bill but on its return to the Lords it was classified as a hybrid Bill.[74] To avoid the delays inherent in the procedure applicable to such Bills, the Government agreed to the deletion of the offending clauses.

Since 1979 the Conservative government has suffered a number of reversals on important matters in the House of Lords. Ten major defeats have been identified in the Parliament of 1979–83 and twelve in the first session of the Parliament elected in 1983. In most cases the Government has accepted the defeat or at least the principle involved despite its Commons majority.[75] In 1980, for example, the Duke of Norfolk led the successful opposition to a clause in the Education Bill which allowed local education authorities to impose transport charges for children travelling to school in rural areas. In 1984 the House forced the Government to compromise on its plans for transitional arrangements pending the abolition of the Greater London Council and the metropolitan councils contained in the Local Government (Interim Provisions) Bill. In the face of threats to introduce amendments to the Telecommunications Bill in 1984 to regulate telephone tapping the Government agreed to introduce later its own legislation on that topic.[76]

In 1985 the Government was defeated at the report stage on a provision in the Prosecution of Offences Bill under which the Attorney General could refer cases to the Court of Appeal for, its opinion on the adequacy of a sentence imposed by the Crown Court after a conviction on indictment. Later in the same year the House rejected at report stage the Education (Corporal Punishment) Bill which had been introduced as a compromise, following a ruling of the European Court on Human Rights.[77] The Bill would have allowed parental choice; the Lords preferred the complete abolition of corporal punishment.

In the debate on the War Damage Bill 1965 the Marquess of Salisbury, a Conservative elder statesman, suggested that the House of Lords should only insist on its amendments: (i) if the question raises issues

---

[73] Mr. Wilson (then Prime Minister) threatened that a sufficient number of peers would be created to override the House of Lords; but the implementation of such a threat would probably be a breach of convention, since the Parliament Acts provide a remedy; would be an unworthy and unnatural way to operate a Constitution; would incite the Leader of the Opposition to do likewise if returned to power, and so on *ad infinitum*; and would still leave open the question of the validity of the "Parliament Act 1949."

[74] *Post*, p. 210.

[75] D. R. Shell, "The House of Lords and the Thatcher Government" (1985) 38 *Parliamentary Affairs* 16.

[76] See now Interception of Comunications Act 1985; *post* p. 518.

[77] Corporal punishment in state schools was ultimately abolished by the Education (No. 2) Act 1986.

important enough to justify such drastic action; and (ii) if the issue is one which can be readily understood by the people and on which the Lords can expect their support, an issue on which the House of Lords would really be acting as the watchdog of the people.[78] The policy of Lord Carrington, when Leader of the Conservative Opposition, was that the Lords should not insist on their opposition to a government Bill for which there is a mandate: but that they may impose delay if the constitution is at risk, or public opinion is so clearly against the government that the electorate ought to be consulted before the proposed law is enacted. Thus the Lords did not insist on their amendment to the War Damage Bill 1965, which (by omitting the *ex post facto* provision) would have frustrated the main purpose of the Bill[79]; but in 1969 the Conservative Opposition moved a number of "wrecking" amendments in Committee to a Redistribution of Seats Bill, which they regarded as gerrymandering and therefore unconstitutional, and the amendments were passed by a majority greater than the number of hereditary peers present. The Lords then rejected a revised Bill, which the government dropped.[80]

In October 1975 Lord Carrington (Leader of the Opposition) said, in relation to Housing Finance (Miscellaneous Provisions) Bill that, although on an issue of grave constitutional importance such as this, the Lords would be entitled to use their delaying powers, they had already achieved their main purpose by making the Government think again and the Opposition should not on this occasion seek to pursue the matter any further. In similar vein, Lord Hailsham said, in March 1976, in relation to the Trade Union and Labour Relations (Amendment) Bill, that the Opposition had exhausted their powers in sending the Bill back once to the Commons, and had discharged their duty. There appears now, therefore, to be almost a convention that the Lords will not return a Government Bill to the Commons for reconsideration more than once.[81]

The 1968 reform proposals[82]

The Parliament (No. 2) Bill 1968, introduced by the Labour Government, would have reduced the period of delay to *six months* from the day on which the House of Lords disagreed in the case of a public Bill sent up by the Commons, other than a Money Bill, a Bill to extend the maximum duration of Parliament or a Bill to confirm a Provisional Order. A resolution of the Commons to present such a Bill for the Royal Assent without the Lords' consent would not be affected by prorogation or dissolution. If the Lords postponed an overt disagreement by delaying tactics, the Commons would have power to resolve that the Bill be treated as having been disagreed by the Lords. There was also pro-

---

[78] H.L. Debs., Vol. 266, cols. 784–785 (1965).

[79] Which was to nullify the decision of the House of Lords as to war damage in *Burmah Oil Co.* v. *Lord Advocate* [1965] A.C. 75, *post*, p. 275.

[80] *Post*, p. 192.

[81] Lord Hailsham has also said that the House of Lords ought not to use its powers in such a way as to frustrate the purposes of executive government, or to prevent the passage of legislation which would be effective only if passed before a given date (letter to *The Times*, November 19, 1975).

[82] For the proposals relating to the composition of the House of Lords, see *post*, p. 167.

vision to the effect that resolutions of the Lords concerning the making, coming into operation or continuance in force of subordinate legislation could be overridden by the Commons. Sections 2 and 5 of the Parliament Act 1911 and the whole of the Parliament Act 1949 would have been repealed.

Is the "Parliament Act 1949" a valid Act of Parliament?[83]

We have already raised doubts on the validity of the measure calling itself the "Parliament Act 1949."[84] It is a mistake to suppose that Parliament in 1911 "conferred" on the House of Lords power to "delay" legislation for certain periods, and that "Parliament" in 1949 reduced this period. At common law the consent of the Lords was essential to the passing of any legislation. In 1911 the power of the Lords to reject Bills was restricted, but the upper House retained thereafter any power that was not expressly abrogated. The Parliament Act 1911 may be said to have delegated a lawmaking power to the Monarch and the Commons under certain specific conditions, and it is submitted that it is not open to them as delegates to enlarge that power as they purported to do in 1949.[85] If this argument is sound in relation to a reduction of the delaying period, it may also apply to a Bill to abolish the Second Chamber (the existence of which is implied by the provisions of the Parliament Act 1911), and possibly also to a Bill to alter the composition of the House of Lords. It may be that the consent of the Lords would be necessary for the validity of any of these measures.

The provision of section 3 of the Parliament Act 1911 that the Speaker's certificate shall be conclusive for all purposes, and shall not be questioned in any court of law, certainly appears to raise a difficulty; but the House of Lords in its judicial capacity has decided that where a statute states that an instrument such as an order or certificate shall be "conclusive evidence" or words to that effect, this implies that the instrument has been properly made, and does not extend to some purported order or certificate which was beyond the power of the maker to make.[86] This principle could be applied to a certificate signed by the Speaker in misconstruction of the power conferred on him by the Parliament Act 1911.

IV. THE PREROGATIVE OF DISSOLUTION[87]

The Queen, the Prime Minister and the Commons

Although in law the Queen may dissolve Parliament when she likes, her conduct would be unconstitutional (*i.e.* contrary to convention) if

---

[83] Hood Phillips, *op. cit.* pp. 91–93; letter to *The Times,* July 15, 1968. And see G. Zellick, "Is the Parliament Act *Ultra Vires?*" (1969) 119 New L.J. 716.

[84] *Ante*, p. 90.

[85] The express exclusion of Bills to extend the maximum duration of Parliament, however, might be taken to imply that no other exceptions are intended.

[86] *Anisminic* v. *Foreign Compensation Commission* [1969] 2 A.C. 147.

[87] Sir Ivor Jennings, *Cabinet Government* (3rd ed. 1959), pp. 412–428, and Appendix III; J.P. Mackintosh, *The British Cabinet* (3rd ed., 1977); B.S. Markesinis, *The Theory and Practice of Dissolution of Parliament* (1972); Anson, *Law and Custom of the Constitution* (5th ed. Gwyer). Vol. I, pp. 325–330; Dicey *Law of the Constitution* (10th ed.), pp. 432–437. See also B.E. Carter, *The Office of Prime Minister* (1956), pp. 273–294; E.A. Forsey, *The Royal Power of Dissolution of Parliament in the British Commonwealth* (1943); H.V. Evatt, *The King and His Dominion Governors*.

she did so without or against the advice of her Ministers. In what circumstances it is constitutionally proper for the Prime Minister (or the Cabinet) to refuse to advise a dissolution, and whether the Queen is necessarily bound by convention to dissolve when advised to do so, are questions discussed in the following paragraphs.

The conventions governing the exercise of the prerogative power to dissolve Parliament are in *normal* circumstances the following:

(a) The Sovereign should dissolve Parliament when requested by the Prime Minister to do so.

(b) The Sovereign should not dissolve Parliament unless requested by the Prime Minister to do so.

(c) The Prime Minister has the power to choose the time of dissolution, within the five-year period prescribed by the Parliament Act 1911. (This power of timing is a weapon of great political importance in the hands of the government, and especially of the Prime Minister.)[88–89]

(d) If the Government party is defeated at a general election, the Prime Minister should tender the resignation of the Government at once, at least where another party has an overall majority, and the Opposition will take over. At one time, before the party unity was as definite as it is now, it was the practice to await defeat in the Commons. If there is in the future a return to a system where no one party has a clear majority this former practice may revive. After the general election called by Mr. Heath in February 1974, Labour were returned with a few more members than the Conservatives (who had the largest number of votes), but neither party had a majority in the Commons. Mr. Heath attempted unsuccessfully to persuade the Liberals to join a coalition. Only after the failure of this attempt did he resign and Mr. Wilson succeeded him as Prime Minister. Some thought Mr. Heath ought to have resigned as soon as the results of the general election were known, but his ministry was still in office and the refusal of the Liberals was not a foregone conclusion.[90]

(e) If the government is defeated in the House of Commons on a motion of confidence or a motion of no confidence, the Prime Minister must either ask for a dissolution or tender the resignation of himself and his ministerial colleagues.[91] Where there is a disolution, which is the usual course, Ministers retain office during the ensuing general election. The Address on the Queen's Speech and the general Budget resolution would be regarded as matters of confidence. In practice also, before a debate on a major item of government policy the Prime Minister may indicate—largely for the information of his followers—that he intends to regard the pending vote as one of confidence. A government with a very small majority in the Commons, or a minority government, allows itself rather more latitude if defeated in the House on important issues that are not specifically motions of confidence or no confidence.

[88–89] In practice general elections tend to be held in the autumn to allow the financial business of the year to be dealt with and to avoid popular holiday times: David Butler, *The Times* February 2, 1983. But cf. June elections in 1983 and 1987.

[90] See further, *post*, 319.

[91] *Ante*. p. 125. See further Philip Norton "Government Defeats in the House of Commons: Myth and Reality" [1978] P.L. 360; S.E. Finer, *Five Constitutions* (1979), pp. 68–69.

Mr. Wilson stated in the House in March 1974 that if the Government were defeated in the Commons it would consider its position and make a definitive statement after due consideration; but the Government would not be forced to go to the country except in a situation where members voted knowing the full consequences of their vote. He added that a snap division, or even a defeat on quite major matters, would not immediately lead to the Government's asking for a dissolution or resigning.

After the general election in October 1974 Labour were returned with a very small majority. The Government were defeated several times in the Commons within 18 months on such subjects as the earnings rule for State pensioners, VAT for rented television sets, a House of Lords amendment relating to disqualification from office of the Clay Cross councillors, and proposals for cutting public expenditure. This last occasion in March 1976 was due to Labour abstentions. Next day Mr. Wilson turned it into a motion of confidence, which the Government won. By the time Mr. Callaghan had succeeded Mr. Wilson as Prime Minister, the Government's party majority in the House had eroded away, and in the period 1976–1978 the Government suffered several defeats on both the Finance Bill and the Trade Union and Labour Relations Bill. Other important defeats were on the Aircraft and Shipbuilding Industries Bill, which was reintroduced in a modified form in the next session; on the Docks Work Regulation Bill, when the Government had to accept Lords' amendments; on the guillotine motion relating to the Scotland and Wales Bill owing to the abstention of Labour members, with the result that the Bill was dropped and replaced by separate and revised Scotland and Wales Bills in the next session; and on an adjournment motion relating to a White Paper setting out the Government's economic policy. Owing to the abstention of all Labour members on that occasion[92] the Government was defeated by the surprising margin of 293–0 votes. Mr. Callaghan declined the challenge by Mrs. Thatcher (Leader of the Opposition) to table a motion of confidence, saying he "had no time." Mrs. Thatcher therefore tabled a motion of no confidence a day or two later, which the Government (having made a deal with the Liberals) won.

Opposition parties do not necessarily want to force a general election at any given time. They may be short of electioneering funds or may think their electoral chances will improve later on. Yet a minority government cannot control the parliamentary timetable, as they cannot guarantee to win guillotine and other time-saving motions. A minority Labour Government also risks having to accept uncongenial Lords' amendments.

Defeats in by-elections do not require a government to resign unless they wipe out its majority in the Commons, though Balfour resigned in 1905 when Parliament was not in session as the loss of a series of by-elections indicated that his party no longer enjoyed the support of the electorate.

---

[92] The procedure of adjournment was chosen because it was thought it would avoid a vote.

Defeats of a government in Committee of the Commons, which are not rare when the government has a small majority, can usually be reversed later on the floor of the House. A minority government may lose its majority membership of committees, where its Bills are subject to amendment. When the Labour Government lost its overall majority in the Commons in the early part of 1976 there was controversy as to the meaning of the Standing Order that directs the Selection Committee to have regard to the composition of the House. Labour members argued that the principle of a Bill is approved by the Commons on second reading, and therefore the government should be assured that it can get its Bills through Committee; but they gave way and agreed to equal numbers of Labour and Conservative members together with third-party representative.[93]

Exceptional situations

The question arises whether there are any exceptional circumstances in which the Sovereign may: (i) dissolve Parliament without, or against, the advice of the Prime Minister; (ii) dismiss a Ministry that refuses to advise a dissolution; or (iii) refuse a dissolution when advised by the Prime Minister to dissolve.

1. *Dissolution without or against advice*

There is no instance in this country, since the Restoration, of a Sovereign attempting to dissolve Parliament without or against the advice of the Ministry. It seems that, apart from convention, the Queen cannot now in practice dissolve Parliament without or against the advice of her Ministers. Dissolution involves an Order in Council made at a meeting of the Privy Council convened by the Lord President of the Council; and the issue of a proclamation and writs of summons under the Great Seal, which is kept by the Lord Chancellor.[94] She might dissolve Parliament orally in the House of Lords, but proclamations and writs would still be required for the holding of elections and the summoning of the new Parliament. The Queen may take the initiative in proposing a dissolution, and then if the Ministers agree with her they adopt her policy as their own; but if Ministers refuse to advise a dissolution, they could only be dismissed.

2. *Dismissal of a government that refuses to advise a dissolution*

The last occasion in this country when a Ministry was dismissed was that of the North-Fox Coalition in 1783. During the Irish Home Rule controversy of 1913, Dicey expressed the opinion that the King might dismiss a Ministry that refused to advise a dissolution if he had reason to think that their policy, although supported by the House of Commons, was not approved by the electorate. On the other hand, although

---

[93] Defeats on the second reading of a Bill used to be regarded as matters of confidence—but Mr. Callaghan ignored a defeat on the second reading of the Redundancy Rebate Bill in 1977; S.E. Finer, *loc. cit. supra*, n. 90.

[94] Great Seal Act 1884; a warrant under the Royal Sign Manual countersigned by the Lord Chancellor, or by a Secretary of State or two Treasury Commissioners, is necessary and sufficient authority for passing any instrument under the Great Seal; but the authority of the Lord Chancellor alone is sufficient in cases where that was so before the Act.

there might be an argument for dissolution if the Sovereign thought the Government had lost its majority in the country,[95] it is very doubtful whether she is sufficiently in touch with public opinion to judge the attitude of the electorate or to anticipate its decision on all items of the government's policy. Only most exceptional circumstances would justify the dismissal of a Ministry, such as unconstitutional conduct like introducing Bills for unnecessary or definite prolongations of the life of Parliament, gerry-mandering of constituencies or fundamental modifications of the electoral system in the interests of one party,[96] or if the government were unable to obtain supply from the Commons.[97]

Dismissal of a Ministry would be a last resort, for the evil to be expected from inaction by the Sovereign would have to be weighed against the evil of bringing the Crown into the political arena. And the Sovereign would have to be satisfied, presumably from the advice of the Leader of the Opposition (which normally cannot be sought unless the Government resigns) that an alternative Government was willing to take office.[98]

3. Refusal of dissolution

Down to the early nineteenth century the defeat of the government at a general election was regarded as a rebuff to the Sovereign. Since the Reform Act 1832 the prestige of the Sovereign has been dissociated from the fate of governments and there has been no instance of refusal to dissolve the British Parliament. George V is said to have refused (at least temporarily) to dissolve Parliament in 1910 and the Cabinet decided to resign; but he later agreed to a dissolution.[99] In 1918 the King only agreed to Lloyd George's request for a dissolution with justifiable reluctance: it is not certain whether Lloyd George would have resigned if the request had been refused.[1]

The question whether the Sovereign could still constitutionally refuse to dissolve Parliament when advised by Ministers to do so was raised in 1923–24 and 1950, and again early in 1974. In 1923 Ramsay MacDonald was appointed Prime Minister of a minority Labour Government which could only count on a majority in the House of Commons so long as it retained the support of a sufficient number of Liberals. Lord Cave, the Lord Chancellor in the previous administration, advised George V's private secretary, Lord Stamfordham, that if no constitutional reason exists for the request of a dissolution the Sovereign may properly refuse

[95] Cf. Adegbenro v. Akintola [1963] A.C. 614 (P.C.). For the background of this case, see B. O. Nwabueze, Constitutionalism in the Emergent States (1973), pp. 74–75.

[96] Jennings, op. cit. p. 412.

[97] The dismissal by the Governor-General of Australia of the Prime Minister (Mr. Gough Whitlam) in November 1975 is an instructive precedent, but it must be studied in the light of the Senate's legal power to refuse to grant supply. See D.P. O'Connell, "The Dissolution of the Australian Parliament: 11, November 1975," (1976) 57 The Parliamentarian, 1–14. The Leader of the Opposition was invited to form a caretaker government (no appointments and no legislation) on the understanding that, when the Senate had approved the grant of supply, he would forthwith advise a dissolution.

[98] The Sovereign can, and will, dismiss individual Ministers on the Prime Minister's advice, but the Prime Minister usually persuades an unwanted Minister to resign.

[99] Jennings, op. cit. pp. 414–415.

[1] Ibid. p. 425.

the request, provided he is assured that other Ministers are prepared to carry on the government. He went on to say that if a statesman is asked to form a government and makes it a condition of accepting office that the Sovereign will grant a dissolution in the event of a new government being defeated in the House of Commons, the Sovereign is under no obligation to give such a promise, and he should not give such an assurance unless it is the only way of securing that the government of the country will be carried on.[2]

Asquith (a former Liberal Prime Minister) said that "the Crown is not bound to take the advice of a particular Minister to put its subjects to the tumult and turmoil of a series of general elections so long as it can find other Ministers who are prepared to give contrary advice. The notion that a Minister who cannot command a majority in the House of Commons . . . is invested with *the right* to demand a dissolution is as subversive of constitutional usage as it would, in my opinion, be pernicious to the paramount interests of the nation at large." When the minority Labour Government was defeated in the Commons in 1924, George V did not want to grant a dissolution but did so after consulting Conservative and Liberal leaders, who were unwilling to combine in the existing House. Lord Attlee thought that the King might legitimately have refused a dissolution to Ramsay MacDonald, but he added: "I fancy it was thought impolitic to refuse the request of the first Labour Prime Minister."[3] The view that a Sovereign is not bound to grant a dissolution when asked for, provided that he can obtain other Ministers to take responsibility for the royal refusal, was supported by Keith, who added: "The right to a dissolution is not a right to a series of dissolutions. The King could not, because a Ministry had appealed and lost an election, give them forthwith another without seeming to be endeavouring to wear out the resistance of the electors to the royal will."[4]

Refusal of a dissolution would be proper if, but only if, there was general agreement inside and outside the House of Commons that a general election should be delayed pending further developments of the situation, for where the view of the people can be gathered without a dissolution it would be absurd to insist upon it. Another possible case would be where a government which is normally supported by a majority in the House of Commons is defeated by a snap vote, the result of which can be rectified or overlooked. As Anson said, the uniform practice for more than a century that the Sovereign should not refuse a dissolution when advised by her Ministers to dissolve has been largely due to the observance of another convention, namely, that dissolutions should not be improperly advised.

The other view is that the Sovereign's right to withhold a dissolution has become obsolete, and that the convention that she must in all circumstances accept the advice of the Prime Minister provides her with a clear and simple rule about which there can be no mistake.[5] Sir Ivor Jennings denied that it is a *convention* that a dissolution may not be

---

[2] R. F. V. Heuston, *Lives of the Lord Chancellors 1885–1940* (1964), pp. 432–435.
[3] "The Role of the Monarchy," *Observer*, August 23, 1959.
[4] Keith, *op. cit.* p. 301.
[5] Lord Chorley, letter to *The Times*, April 26, 1950.

refused, since Victoria, Edward VII, George V and their Prime Ministers all thought there was a right to refuse a dissolution[6]; but he thought that while the Queen's personal prerogative is maintained in theory, there are hardly any circumstances in which it could be exercised in practice. He pointed out, however, that this assumed a continuance of the two-party system. "If the major parties break up," he wrote,[7] "the whole balance of the Constitution alters; and then, possibly, the Queen's prerogative becomes important." Some writers who adopt the "new" doctrine which deprives the Queen of any discretion, would make an exception where a Prime Minister requests a second dissolution immediately after being defeated at a general election, provided that an alternative government could be formed.[8]

The former opinion, which allows a limited personal prerogative to the Sovereign, appears to be the better one. It is more in consonance with the traditions of British parliamentary government, and it has tended to be adopted in other Commonwealth countries. It was supported by Viscount Simon (a former Lord Chancellor) in April 1950[9] when the Labour Government had been returned with a majority of only six in the Commons.[10] Attlee, who was Prime Minister in 1950, later expressed the opinion that if the Government had been defeated in the House at that time, George VI would have been within his rights in sending for the Leader of the Opposition if he thought a working majority in the House could have been obtained by him.[11]

The reason for the general convention that the Sovereign is bound by the advice of her Ministers is not applicable if they do not represent the wishes of the electorate (or the Commons). Among the factors that would have to be taken into account before the Sovereign could properly refuse a dissolution would be the time that had elapsed since the last dissolution, whether the last dissolution took place at the instance of the present Opposition, whether the question in issue is of great political importance, the supply position,[12] whether Parliament is nearing the end of its maximum term, whether the Prime Minister is in a minority in the Cabinet,[13] whether there is a minority government[14] and, perhaps, whether there is a war on.

[6] *Law and the Constitution* (5th ed.), p. 135.
[7] *Cabinet Government* (3rd ed.), pp. 427–428.
[8] G. Marshall and G.C. Moodie, *op. cit.*
[9] Letters to *The Times*, April 24 and 27, 1950.
[10] And see Wheeler-Bennett, *King George VI*, pp. 771–775.
[11] "The Role of the Monarchy," *loc. cit.*
[12] The grant of a dissolution must be dependent on supply having been voted to the Crown for the period that would elapse before the meeting of the new Parliament.
[13] Lord Blake in a letter to *The Times*, October 25, 1974.
[14] Markesinis thinks the practice shows that the Crown cannot refuse a dissolution to a majority government, but it may refuse a dissolution to a minority government (whether defeated or not) provided an alternative government can be formed.

CHAPTER 8

THE HOUSE OF LORDS

Historical introduction

The origin of the House of Lords is to be found in the Great Council
(*magnum concilium*) of Norman times, and even in the earlier
Witenagemot.[1] The *magnum concilium* of the Norman and early Plantagenet Kings was a council of the chief men of the nation, summoned by
the King because of their wealth or skill. Wealth and power went with
the holding of land, which was in the main hereditary. The connection
between summons to early Parliaments and what later became peerage
lies in the confused theory of "baronage." "Baron" was the Norman-
French for "man," "the King's barons" were the King's men. Baronage
was connected in early times both with jurisdiction and with tenure. In
the thirteenth century those who were summoned individually to the
King's Council in Parliament were the holders of a barony (*baronia*),
probably not less than 13 1/3 knights' fees. The lesser barons during the
course of that century ceased to be summoned collectively through the
sheriffs, but were represented in Parliament by the knights of the shire
and thus became commoners.

The next development is the notion of "peerage." A person who had
received a summons to Parliament and had taken his seat, acquired not
only a right to be summoned in future but a hereditary right to be summoned which descended to his heirs. The ordinary meaning of the
word "peer" is simply "equal," and it was a later refinement of "peer"
that gave it the meaning of one who was entitled to be tried for treason
or felony by the King's Council in Parliament.

A peerage has been held to be an incorporeal hereditament,[2] and is
classed as real property.[3] The principles laid down in peerage cases
apply retrospectively and are regarded by the House of Lords as always
having been the law, that is, back to 1290 or 1295.[4]

The older method of creating peerages was by writ of summons to
Parliament, followed by the person summoned taking his seat. Baronies
were created in this way in the reign of Edward I. A peerage by writ, as
it was called, descended to the heirs general, *i.e.* male and female, lineal
and collateral. The usual method of creating peerages in more recent
times has been by letters patent, which give the grantee a right to a
summons. A peerage by patent descends in accordance with the limitation in the patent, which is generally (though not invariably) to the
lineal heirs male. A peerage may not be granted for an estate of inheri-
tance not known to the common law.[5]

---

[1] Pike, *Constitutional History of the House of Lords*, Chap. 4.
[2] *Nevil's Case* (1605) 7 Co.Rep. 33; *Grey de Ruthyn Peerage Case* (1640) Collins' Claims 244;
Lord Cowley v. *Countess Cowley* [1901] A.C. 450.
[3] *Buckhurst Peerage Case* (1876) 2 App.Cas. 1.
[4] *e.g. Fitzwater Barony Case* (1668) Collins' Claims 268; *Clifton Peerage Case* (1763) Collins'
Claims 291; *Norfolk Peerage Case* [1907] A.C. 10; *Berkeley Peerage Case* (1861) 8 H.L.C. 79.
[5] *Wiltes Peerage Case* (1869) L.R. 4 H.L. 126.

In order to establish his right to attend Parliament, a new peer presents his letters patent and writ of summons to the Lord Chancellor at the Woolsack. Other peers present their writs of summons at the table of the House. If a peer is entitled to a writ of summons but does not receive one, he may petition the Crown.[6] A person entitled, however, is under no obligation to apply for the writ if he does not wish to do so, and it is the custom that a writ of summons is only issued to a consenting party (*Re Parliamentary Election for Bristol South-East*[7]).

Peerage claims

The House of Lords, acting on the advice of its Committee for Privileges, can itself and of its own motion determine the validity of the creation of a new peerage and the question whether the grantee is entitled to a writ of summons. An example is the *Wensleydale Peerage Case*.[8] The House also has the privilege of deciding whether anyone other than the original grantee is entitled to sit.[9]

A claim to an *existing* peerage, which is in abeyance[10] or the title to which is disputed, is made by petition to the Crown through the Home Secretary, and is referred by him to the Attorney-General. The Crown may accept or reject the claim on the Attorney-General's report, but if—as is often the case—there is some doubt, it is the practice for the Crown to refer the matter to the House of Lords. The House in turn refers the question to its Committee for Privileges, which hears the arguments of the claimant or his counsel and of the Attorney-General on behalf of the Crown, and reports to the House. The Committee for Privileges consists of 16 peers and four Lords of Appeal. Four Law Lords and five lay peers heard *The Ampthill Peerage* case[11]: Each of the Law Lords delivered an opinion, and the lay peers contented themselves with concurring. Lapse of time is no legal bar to a peerage claim,[12] but it was thought to be the modern practice that a petition would not be entertained if a peerage has been in abeyance for more than one hundred years.[13] However, in *Earldom of Annandale and Hartfell*[14] an earldom was revived after 193 years.

The House of Lords may summon the judges to advise the House on a matter of peerage law.[15]

There is no precedent for proceedings in a peerage claim being taken

---

[6] *Bristol Peerage Case* (1626) 3 Lords' Journals 544.

[7] [1964] 2 Q.B. 257; [1961] 3 W.L.R. 577. Gorman J. described this as a convention, and said there was no constitutional convention to the contrary; but it would be better to describe it as parliamentary custom.

[8] (1856) 5 H.L.C. 958.

[9] *Viscountess Rhondda's Claim* [1922] 2 A.C. 339.

[10] *e.g.* because it descended to two or more females in the same degree.

[11] [1977] A.C. 547 (H.L.): rival claims to the Barony of Ampthill, in abeyance since 1973; declaration of legitimacy (1926) under Legitimacy Declaration Act 1858 binding for all purposes and extends to peerage claims. And see *Russell* v. *Russell* [1924] A.C. 687 (H.L.).

[12] *Hastings Peerage Case* (1840) 8 Cl. & Fin. 144 (peerage unclaimed for 450 years); *Camoys Peerage Case* (1839) 6 Cl. & Fin. 789 (peerage called out of abeyance after 420 years).

[13] Sir Geoffrey Ellis, *Earldoms in Fee* (1963), Chaps. 8, 13.

[14] [1986] A.C. 319.

[15] Palmer, *Peerage Law in England*, pp. 231–235.

in an ordinary court of law, and a court has no jurisdiction to determine even incidentally any question relating to a dignity.[16]

1. COMPOSITION OF THE HOUSE OF LORDS

Lords Spiritual

The 26 Lords Spiritual now consist by statute of the Archbishops of Canterbury and York, the Bishops of London, Durham and Winchester, and 21 other diocesan bishops of the Church of England in order of seniority of appointment.[17] They are summoned on their "faith and love."[18] In the Middle Ages archbishops and bishops could attend Parliament both as holders of important offices of state and as tenants-in-chief or holders of baronies. Their presence was not due to any theory of the "three estates" of clergy, barons and commons.[19] Until the Reformation the Lords Spiritual formed a large part, sometimes a majority, of the House of Lords. It was not certain at the time of Elizabeth I, when Acts of Supremacy and Uniformity were passed, whether a Bill that was opposed unanimously by the Lords Spiritual was valid.[20] The bishops were excluded during the Commonwealth period.

Hereditary peers

The bulk of the Lords Temporal consists of the holders of hereditary peerages of England and Scotland[21] (created before the Union of England and Scotland), of Great Britain (created after the Union with Scotland and before the Union with Ireland) and of the United Kingdom (created since the Union with Ireland).[22] Their ranks in order of precedence are dukes, marquesses, earls, viscounts, and barons, but these distinctions do not affect their rights as Lords of Parliament. There are about 800 hereditary peers, although a relatively small number now attend regularly. Changing ideas and the institution of life peerages

[16] *Earl Cowley* v. *Countess Cowley* [1901] A.C. 450. *Cf.* an election court; see *Re Parliamentary Election for Bristol South-East* [1964] 2 Q.B. 257, *post*, Chap. 9.

[17] The number was fixed by the Bishoprics Act 1878. Although the See of Sodor and Man forms part of the Province of York the Bishop of Sodor and Man is not entitled to set in the Upper House as one of the Lords Spiritual, the Isle of Man not forming part of the United Kingdom.

[18] The summons now omits the *praemunientes* clause: Crown Office (Writs of Summons) Rules 1969.

[19] "Those who pray, those who fight, those who work": Maitland, *Constitutional History*, p. 75.

[20] Maitland, "The Reformation," in *Cambridge Modern History*, Vol. II, p. 571.

[21] The Union with Scotland Act 1707 provided that 16 representative peers of Scotland should be elected by the Scottish peers to each Parliament; but this provision was repealed by the Peerage Act 1963 under which all peers of Scotland may sit and vote in the House of Lords.

[22] The Union with Ireland Act 1800 provded that 28 representative peers of Ireland should be elected to the House of Lords for life by the Irish peers. After the Irish Free State was established in 1922 there was no machinery for the election of Irish peers to replace those who died. The last representative Irish peer died in 1961, and relevant enactments were repealed by the Statute Law (Repeals) Act 1971. See Lord Dunboyne, "Irish Representative Peers" [1967] P.L. 314;' C. E. Lysaght, "Irish Peers and the House of Lords" (1967) 18 N.I.L.Q. 277.

have led to the creation of few hereditary peerages in recent years.[23] After the general election in 1983 Mrs. Thatcher recommended hereditary peerages (Viscountcies) for Mr William Whitelaw, a former Cabinet Minister, and Mr. George Thomas, ex-Speaker of the House of Commons. Neither had direct male heirs. But in 1984 Mr. Harold Macmillan, former Prime Minister, was created an Earl on the occasion of his ninetieth birthday and he had heirs to succeed to the title.

Hereditary peeresses

In *Viscountess Rhondda's Claim*[24] the Committee for Privileges held that a hereditary peeress in her own right was not entitled to a writ of summons to the House of Lords, in spite of the general provisions of the Sex Disqualification (Removal) Act 1919.[25] The Peerage Act 1963, s.6, now provides that the small class of hereditary peeresses may sit and vote in the House of Lords.

Disclaimer of hereditary peerages

The main object of the Peerage Act 1963 was to permit the disclaimer of hereditary peerages.[26] Section 1 allows the holder of a hereditary peerage (other than an Irish peerage) to disclaim the peerage for his life. A peer who succeeded before the passing of the Act had one year in which to disclaim, or, if under age, he could disclaim within one year after attaining his majority. A peer who succeeds after the passing of the Act may generally disclaim within one year of his succession or attaining his majority; but section 2 provides that a member of the House of Commons who succeeds to a peerage has only one month from succession in which to disclaim; and similarly a candidate for election to the House of Commons who succeeds to a peerage has, if he is elected to that House, one month in which to disclaim.

Disclaimer of a peerage is irrevocable. A peer who disclaims is divested of the peerage and any offices or privileges attaching thereto. No other hereditary peerage may at any time be conferred on him. On the other hand, he is relieved of the disqualification from voting for and being elected to the House of Commons. Disclaimer does not affect any rights of property (s.3). It is anomalous that the Act makes disclaimer of a peerage operate for life only: succession on death to the peerage is not affected, though no writ of acceleration may be issued to the heir. The Peerage Act does not deal with courtesy titles, which are matters of the Queen's pleasure and not of law.[27]

---

[23] The former custom in the political field was for ex-Prime Ministers to be created earls, ex-Cabinet Ministers viscounts, and other ex–Ministers barons. For Lord Chancellors, see *post*, p. 160n.

[24] [1922] 2 A.C. 339.

[25] As a matter of fact, during the debate on the 1919 Bill the Lords rejected a Commons amendment declaring that "public function" included sitting and voting in the House of Lords.

[26] *Report of Joint Committee on House of Lords Reform* (1962) H.L. 23 and H.C. 38. And see Lord Hailsham, *The Door Wherein I Went* (1975), pp. 221–223. *Cf. Re Parliamentary Election for Bristol South-East* [1964] 2 Q.B. 257; [1961] 3 W.L.R. 577; *post*, Chap. 9.

[27] *e.g.* Lord Lambton, M.P., who disclaimed the Earldom of Durham. The Commons, however, regarded his mode of address in the House as a matter of privilege.

Life peers and life peeresses[28]

In order to increase the number of those who could be expected in the circumstances of the day to attend and take part in debates regularly—especially those who are not Conservatives—the Life Peerages Act 1958 gave Her Majesty power by letters patent to confer on any person (man or woman) a peerage for life, entitling him or her to rank as a baron and (unless disqualified by law) to receive writs of summons to attend the House of Lords and to sit and vote therein. No limit is set to the number of life peers.

The Conservative Government's case for the Bill was that if a Second Chamber is necessary, it must contain an Opposition. Some life peers might be independent, but in recruiting for the Opposition the intention was that the Prime Minister should consult the Leader of the Opposition and accept his suggestions. There were 334 life peers in 1986.

The Lord Chancellor[29]

The Speaker of the House of Lords is the Lord High Chancellor of Great Britain, who is Keeper of the Great Seal. He may not leave the country without first notifying the Queen in order that Commissioners may be appointed to affix the Great Seal in his absence. He presides over the House from "the Woolsack," a seat traditionally stuffed with wool, the emblem of England's medieval prosperity. The Speaker of the Lords need not be a peer, the Woolsack being notionally outside the limits of the Chamber.[30] As the officer who issues the writs for parliamentary elections and summoning of peers in Great Britain,[31] he is present *ex officio*. Because the Lord Chancellor is appointed by the Crown and not elected, the House of Lords have never delegated to him authority to keep order, to control the order of speeches or to rebuke recalcitrant members. These powers are exercised by the House itself, usually under guidance from the Leader of the House, and in debate peers address the House and not the occupant of the Woolsack. The Lord Chancellor in debate speaks as a politically minded peer, standing

---

[28] O. Hood Phillips, "Lords and Ladies for Life" (1958) 1 *Oxford Lawyer* 21.

[29] See Viscount Hailsham, *The Duties of a Lord Chancellor* (Holdsworth Club, University of Birmingham, 1936); Lord Schuster, "The Office of the Lord Chancellor" (1949) 10 C.L.J. 175; Lord Gardiner, *The Trials of a Lord Chancellor* (Holdsworth Club, University of Birmingham, 1968); "The Role of the Lord Chancellor in the Field of Law Reform" (1971) 87 L.Q.R. 326; Lord Hailsham of St. Marylebone, *The Door Wherein I Went* (1975), Chap. 36; *The Problems of a Lord Chancellor* (Holdsworth Club, University of Birmingham, 1972); R. F. V. Heuston, *Lives of the Lord Chancellors 1885–1940* (1964) Introduction; *Report of the Machinery of Justice Committee* (1918) Cd. 9230.

[30] Before the reign of George III the Speaker of the Lords was sometimes a commoner called Lord Keeper (of the Great Seal), *e.g.* Sir Nicolas Bacon (1558) and his son Sir Francis Bacon (1617); but the latter was a nephew of Lord Burghley, and a year later was appointed Lord Chancellor with a peerage. Modern practice was to make the Lord Chancellor a viscount or baron on appointment, and to promote him to earl or viscount if his period of office continued for some years; but Gerald Gardiner Q.C. was appointed a life peer as Lord Gardiner in 1963 in anticipation of his taking office after the general election of 1964, and Quintin Hogg Q.C. was appointed a life peer as Lord Hailsham of St. Marylebone on taking office in 1970, being disqualified from holding a hereditary peerage after having renounced his viscountcy.

[31] During the Stormont regime these writs were issued in Northern Ireland by the Governor.

a few feet away from the Woolsack.[32] On a division he votes first, and has no casting vote. When the House is in Committee the Lord Chancellor speaks from the Government front bench. He gives preliminary rulings on peerage claims, subject to reference to the Committee for Privileges.

The Lord Chancellor is the senior legal and constitutional adviser of the government, a Minister of the Crown and almost invariably a member of the Cabinet. He has been called the Keeper of the Queen's Conscience since the time of Elizabeth I. The Lord Chancellor (Tenure of Office and Discharge of Ecclesiastical Functions) Act 1974, however, for the avoidance of doubt, declares that the office of Lord Chancellor is tenable by an adherent to the Roman Catholic faith[33]; and if the office is held by a Roman Catholic the Privy Council may provide for his ecclesiastical functions and partronage of livings to be performed by the Prime Minister or any other Minister.

The Lord Chancellor is also the head of the judiciary in England[34] presiding over the House of Lords sitting as the final court of appeal, and over the Judicial Committee of the Privy Council when he is present.[35] He therefore performs legislative, executive and judicial functions of great importance. He is President of the Supreme Court, an ex-officio judge of the Court of Appeal and President of the Chancery Division of the High Court.[36] He does not in practice sit in these latter courts, the senior judge of the Chancery Division now being called Vice-Chancellor; but he is responsible for regulating their business through the Rule Committee. In addition to the salary payable as Speaker of the House of Lords, he receives a judicial salary which is charged on the Consolidated Fund. The Lord Chancellor certifies, in cases of doubt, who is the Leader of the Opposition in the House of Lords for the purpose of the latter's salary.[37]

The Lord Chancellor plays the leading part in the appointment, or recommending the appointment of judges, magistrates and legally qualified chairmen of statutory tribunals in England.[38] He is the patron of some hundreds of benefices in the Church of England. The Land Registry and the Public Trustee Office are under his control, and he has general responsibility for court records.[39]

The Lord Chancellor has the prime responsibility under the Law

---

[32] He moves two paces to the left of the Woolsack, which brings him to the place assigned to him by Henry VIII; Lord Hailsham, *The Door Wherein I Went*, pp. 248–249.

[33] Plowden, who was a Roman Catholic, is said to have declined an invitation from Elizabeth I to be Lord Chancellor, as he would incur that Queen's displeasure if he had charge of Her Majesty's conscience: Richard O'Sullivan Q.C., *Edmund Plowden* (Middle Temple, 1952) p. 20.

[34] In Northern Ireland, the Lord Chief Justice is President of the High Court and the Court of Appeal. The head of the judiciary in Scotland is the Lord President (and Lord Justice General).

[35] *Cf. post*, p. 172.

[36] Supreme Court Act 1981, s.1(2) and s.5(1)(*a*).

[37] Ministerial and other Salaries Act 1975.

[38] For further details and the position in Scotland and Northern Ireland see *post* Chaps. 20 and 31.

[39] Land Registration Act 1925, Public Trustee Act 1906 and Public Records Act 1958. There is an advisory committee on public records under the Master of the Rolls.

Commissions Act, 1965,[40] for keeping law reform and the revision of statute law under constant review, especially by appointing and considering the reports of the Law Commission. The Courts Act 1971[41] assigns to the Lord Chancellor responsibility for the staffing and accommodation of the Crown Court centres. A similar responsibility for magistrates' courts may also be transferred to him in the future.

Proposals for a Ministry of Justice have been considered more than once, but so far the view has prevailed that it is valuable to have the holder of the highest judicial office as a link between the judiciary and the executive, protecting the former from the latter.[42]

The Lord Chancellor's small department has a Permanent Secretary, who is also Clerk of the Crown in Chancery, and a Secretary of Commissions. The Crown Office in Chancery seals and issues writs and other documents.

Lords of Appeal in Ordinary

In the middle of the nineteenth century attention was drawn to the dearth of qualified lawyers in the House of Lords, which in one of its capacities is the highest court of appeal. The only solution, if the appellate jurisdiction of the House of Lords was to be retained, was to make a limited number of judges Lords of Parliament for life, or at least during their tenure of office; and, as at common law a peer could not be created for a term of years, and as the House had ruled that a peer for life would not be allowed by parliamentary custom to take his seat (*Wensleydale Peerage Case*, 1856),[43] two Lords of Appeal in Ordinary were introduced by the Appellate Jurisdiction Act 1876. Their maximum number has been gradually increased to eleven.

As members of the upper House, the "Law Lords"[44] (including retired Lords of Appeal[45] and judges who are peers) take part in debates on legislation affecting the law and the courts; but there has been a convention since the 1920's that when they speak on controversial nonlegal matters they do so in a personal capacity.[46]

Disqualification from membership of the House

The following persons are disqualified from sitting and voting in the House of Lords:

---

[40] See *Proposals for English and Scottish Law Commissions* (1965) Cmnd. 2573. The Home Secretary, however, is concerned with reform of the criminal law.
[41] Based on the Report of the Royal Commission on Assizes and Quarter Sessions (Beeching) 1966–69) (H.M.S.O.) 1969.
[42] Viscount Birkenhead, *Points of View* (1922). And see *Report of Machinery of Government Committee* (1918) Cd. 9230; R.M. Jackson, *The Machinery of Justice in England*, (7th ed., 1977) pp. 580–4; G. Gardiner and A. Martin, *Law Reform Now* (1963), pp. 7–10; Lord Hailsham. *The Door Wherein I went.*; G. Drewry "Ministry of Justice: A Matter of Meaning" (1982) N.L.J. 402; S. Silkin, "The Legal Machinery of Justice", [1984] P.L. 179.
[43] 5 H.L.C. 958. An account of this case is given in Pike, *op. cit.* pp. 372–384.
[44] See generally, Alan Paterson, *The Law Lords* (1982).
[45] Lords of Appeal in Ordinary were at first Lords of Parliament during tenure of office only, but since the Appellate Jurisdiction Act 1887 they are entitled to sit in the House for life with the dignity of baron.
[46] Robert Stevens, *Law and Politics: The House of Lords as a Judicial Body, 1800–1976* (1979), p. 308. And see pp. 262n, 266, 303, 308.

(i) aliens (Act of Settlement 1701, s.3)[47];
(ii) persons under 21 years of age (Standing Order No. 2, 1685);
(iii) a person convicted of treason is disqualified till the expiry of his sentence of imprisonment or the receipt of a royal pardon[48-49];
(iv) bankrupts; the disqualification ceases on the bankruptcy being discharged[49];
(v) a member who has been expelled by sentence of the House acting in its *judicial* capacity (*i.e.* on impeachment), unless pardoned by the Crown.[50]

Members of the boards of public corporations who are peers are not disqualified from sitting but they are subject to the convention (the Addison Rules 1951) that, although they may exercise their right to speak in the House, the parent Minister and the government are alone responsible to Parliament. Members of such boards therefore, should not give information to the House concerning the detailed work of the boards, nor should they answer questions about it.

Standing Orders relating to attendance

The House has power to enforce attendance, although this has not been exercised since 1841; but it is not within the power of the House to exclude members who habitually do not attend.[51] At the time of the passing of the Life Peerages Act 1958, Standing Order No. 20 was amended so as to provide that "Lords are to attend the sittings of the House or, if they cannot do so, obtain leave of absence." They need not apply for leave of absence, however, if they propose to attend as often as they reasonably can. A lord may apply for leave of absence for a session, or the remainder of a session or the remainder of the Parliament. On the summoning of a new Parliament, the Lord Chancellor is to ask every lord whether he wishes to apply for leave of absence. At the beginning of every subsequent session the Lord Chancellor is similarly to ask every lord whose leave of absence has come to an end, or who (though not granted leave of absence) did not attend during the preceding session. A lord who has been granted leave of absence is expected not to attend until the period has expired. If a lord having been granted leave of absence wishes to attend during the period, he is expected to give at least one month's notice, after which the leave comes to an end. About 200 peers apply for leave of absence.

The revised Standing Order relating to attendance ought to be considered together with the Life Peerages Act. Together they should ensure the regular attendance of an adequate number of competent peers, while at the same time discouraging sporadic forays by the "backwoodsmen." The average attendance is currently about 300.

---

[47] This disqualification does not extend to Commonwealth citizens or citizens of the Republic of Ireland: British Nationality Act 1981; s.52(6) and Sched. 7.

[48-49] Insolvency Act 1986, s.427. Forefeiture Act 1870, as amended by the Criminal Law Act 1967.

[50] The House of Lords as a legislative chamber cannot disqualify one of its members. On the application of the Mental Health Act 1983 to Peers, see *post*, p. 249.

[51] *Report by the Select Committee on the Powers of the House in Relation to the Attendance of its Members* (1956) H.L. (7) (66–1) (67).

Expenses of attendance up to a certain amount per day, plus travelling expenses, have been reimbursed since 1957.

Officers of the House

The *Chairman of Committees,* who holds office for the session, takes the Chair when the House is in Committee, and is Deputy Speaker of the House. He also superintends all matters relating to private Bills.

The offices of *Gentlemen Usher of the Black Rod* and *Serjeant-at-Arms of the House of Lords* were amalgamated in 1971. The holder executes warrants of commitment or attachment under the rules of the House, carries the black wand surmounted by a golden lion which is used as the Mace of the Lords, and desires the attendance of the Commons when necessary.[52]

The *Clerk of the Parliaments* is appointed by the Crown, and is removable only on an address from the House. He is head of the staff of the House, keeps the minutes and journals, and pronounces the Royal Assent to Bills.

The terms of service of the staff are similar to those of civil servants but they are servants of Parliament not of the Crown. Although not within the terms of the Employment Protection (Consolidation) Act 1978, s.139, they enjoy similar rights on a non-statutory basis.[53]

II. MODERN FUNCTIONS OF THE HOUSE OF LORDS[54]

Most legislatures contain—in addition to a representative assembly directly elected by popular vote—a Second Chamber, upper House or Senate, elected indirectly or by some different method, or nominated. This in spite of the apparent dilemma propounded by the Abbé Sieyès, that if a Second Chamber dissents from the First, it is mischievous, while if it agrees it is superfluous. In a federation a Second Chamber is regarded as essential in order to preserve the rights of the individual states. In a unitary state a Second Chamber is generally thought desirable in order to admit into the legislature persons with special kinds of experience or representing ethnic, relegous or other minorities, and also to provide opportunity for second thoughts about policy and legislation. As this country has no written constitution, if we had a unicameral legislature our governmental system and laws would be at the mercy of a majority of one in the House of Commons, and moreover the House of Commons could prolong its own life indefinitely. There are, therefore, strong reasons for retaining a Second Chamber of some kind,

---

[52] *Cf. ante,* p. 137.

[53] H.L. Deb. Vol. 369, col. 2035 (April 13, 1976).

[54] K.C. Wheare, *Legislatures* (1963) Chap. 8; Sir Ivor Jennings, *Parliament* (2nd ed., 1957), pp. 395–402; Viscount Massereene, *The Lords* (1973); Sir John A. Marriott, *Second Chambers; The Federalist,* LXII–LXVI; S.D. Bailey (ed.) *The Future of the House of Lords* (Hansard Society, (1954); P.A. Bromhead, *The House of Lords and Contemporary Politics, 1911–1957* (1958); Lord Chorley, "The House of Lords Controversy" [1958] P.L. 216; Janet P. Morgan, *The House of Lords and the Labour Government 1964–1970* (1975); B. Hadfield, "Whether or Whither the House of Lords" (1984) 35 N.I.L.Q. 313. See *Erskine May Parliamentary Practice* (20th ed., 1983), Chap. 21, "Organisation and conduct of business in the House of Lords."

although of course the one we possess came into being for very different reasons. The House of Lords, as we have seen, emerged from the ancient *magnum concilium*, whereas the representation of the Commons was a medieval and novel addition.

The functions of the House of Lords in modern times may be considered under eight headings[55]:—

(1) *Revision of Public Bills sent from the Commons*

The importance of this function arises from the lack of time available in the Commons to debate legislative proposals. In some cases where, for example, discussion has been curtailed by the guillotine, clauses may not have been discussed at all in the lower House. The government is often happy itself to move amendments in the Lords. The usefulness of the upper House in this connection may be illustrated from the fact that the Lords proposed about 1,200 amendments to the nationalisation Bills of 1946–47, of which 95 per cent. were accepted by the Commons. They proposed 300 amendments to the Criminal Justice Bill 1967, all but six of which were accepted; and they passed 341 amendments to the Industrial Relations Bill 1971, about half of them moved by the government to meet proposals made by Opposition peers.

Difficulties arise when, from the point of view of the government, revision becomes interference with the will of the people as expressed in the Commons. Examples of conflicts of this kind between the two Houses were discussed earlier in Chapter 7.

(2) *The delaying of legislation*

The delaying powers of the House of Lords are at present to be found in the Parliament Act 1911 and the "Parliament Act 1949."[56] The delaying power is controversial. Many thought that the power left by the Parliament Act 1911 was still too great; some think that there should be no delaying power at all; and others think that the control gained by the Cabinet over the Commons by reason of the party system makes it all the more necessary that the Lords should have power to prevent a dictatorship by the Cabinet.

(3) *The initiation of non-controversial public legislation and private members' bills*

At the beginning of a session—and later during the passage of the Finance Bill—there may be more pending legislation than the Commons can cope with. The House of Lords provides a convenient place in which to initiate some, at least, of the outstanding bills.

Opinion may differ on the meaning of "non-controversial" but it is likely to be held to cover, for example, law reform measures and consolidation bills, bills giving effect to international agreements to which the United Kingdom has become a party and other issues which do not involve matters of party political controversy.

---

[55] The first seven of these are derived from the Bryce Conference 1917–18, Cd. 9038 and the White Paper of 1968 on *Reform of the House of Lords*; Cmnd. 3799.
[56] *Ante*, Chap. 7.

(4) *Scrutiny of private bills*[57]

(5) *Scrutiny of delegated legislation*[58]

(6) *Scrutiny of the Executive*
This is one of the House of Lords' less important functions.
Their debates do not affect the fate of governments,[59] the practice being to "move for papers" and then to withdraw the motion rather than press it to a vote.
Questions to Ministers are of less significance than in the House of Commons. There are few ministers in the Upper House and their Lordships do not have to concern themselves with the problems of constituents. Four questions only may be asked each day at the start of business, although questions may also be put at the end of the day's business and written answers may also be requested.[60]
The House of Lords has two important standing committees, on Science and Technology and the European Communities (whose work is considered below). From time to time *ad hoc* committees are established, whose work can be said largely to fall within the function of the House to be considered next.[61]

(7) *Full and free discussion of large and important questions*
The House of Lords, by virtue of the wide and varied background of its members, particularly since the introduction of life peerages, and its freedom from the constraints of party discipline provides a place where controversial issues of any kind may be debated. About one-fifth of the time of the House is devoted to such discussions. *Ad hoc* Committees of the House, such as that which considered a proposed Bill of Rights,[62] contribute by their work to this aspect of the House of Lords' function. Public opinion can be informed and educated by debate and the taking of evidence. Government can assess by public reaction the desirability of legislation on controversial matters where considerations of policy and principle are likely to take second place to a fear of offending vocal pressure groups.

(8) *Scrutiny of EEC Proposals*
The work of the Select Committee on the European Communities is discussed above in Chapter 5.

The Lords have several other functions that are not of political importance. They are hereditary advisers of the Crown and have in theory the right of individual audience with the Sovereign; but this

---

[57] *Post*, p. 215.

[58] *Post*, p. 631.

[59] The House of Lords defeated the Government on a motion of confidence in January 1968 concerning the withdrawal of forces east of Suez and defence cuts. This had no practical effect.

[60] In the Session 1982–1983, for example, 356 questions were put at the beginning of business (starred questions); 36 unstarred questions at the end of business and 619 questions sought written answers.

[61] For a full list of House of Lords' Committees, see *Erskine May Parliamentary Practice* Chap. 21.

[62] (1978) H.L. 176; *post*, 436.

right is not now exercised except by Ministers who are Privy Councillors. Being part of the High Court of Parliament, the House of Lords
retains certain judicial functions: it is the court of final appeal, it has the
privilege of determining who is entitled to sit and vote in the House, it
has the power to enforce its privileges and to punish for contempt, and
it would try impeachments if they were still brought.

III. PROPOSALS FOR REFORM OF THE HOUSE OF LORDS[63]

The need to reform the composition of the House of Lords was recognised in the preamble to the Parliament Act 1911 which recited that Parliament intended eventually "to substitute for the House of Lords as it
at present exists a Second Chamber constituted on a popular instead of
hereditary basis." To a large extent how a modern House of Lords
should be constituted depends on what functions it is thought to be
required to perform. At present the Conservative, Liberal and Social
Democratic Parties believe it has a role to play. The Labour Party has,
since 1977, maintained that the House of Lords should be abolished. (In
1968 the case *for* the House of Lords was well put in the Labour Government's White Paper.[64])

Many proposals for reform have been made in this century, including
those of a Select Committee set up by Lord Rosebery in 1908, Lord
Landsdowne in 1911, the Bryce Conference in 1917, the Government in
1922, and the Conferences of Party Leaders on the Parliament Bills of
1947 and 1968.

Reform of the House raises two questions; what powers it should
possess and how should it be composed. With regard to the former,
there can be no doubt that the powers of the House in general should
complement those of the Commons. The main area of controversy
relates to its delaying powers.[65-66] Views on what these should be are,
in turn, likely to be influenced by what powers it is thought proper to
accord the Commons. What is appropriate for a Chamber elected by a
method of voting which gives some rough correspondence between
votes cast and seats won might not be thought appropriate for a
chamber elected under the present British system where the correspondence between votes and seats can be almost fortuitous. Apart from a
general delaying power it may also be thought appropriate to give

---

[63] McKechnie, *Reform of the House of Lords*, Chaps. 6 and 9; Lees-Smith, *Second Chambers
in Theory and Practice*, Chaps. 11 and 12; Jennings, *Parliament* (2nd ed.), pp. 434–453;
Conference on the Reform of the Second Chamber (1918) Cd. 9038; *Agreed Statement on
Conclusion of Conference of Party Leaders* (1948) Cmd. 7380; S. D. Bailey, *The Future of the
House of Lords* (Hansard Society, 1954); Bernard Crick, *The Reform of Parliament* (2nd
ed., 1968), Chap. 6; *House of Lords Reform* (1968) Cmnd. 3799; O. Hood Phillips, *Reform
of the Constitution* (1970), Chap. 4.

[64] Cmnd. 3799. Unicameral legislature would be contrary to the practice in other democracies with large populations. The growth in volume and complexity of legislation strengthened the case for a revising chamber. Abolition of the House of Lords would add to
the burden of the House of Commons.

[65-66] *Ante*, p. 148.

special powers in the case of specific types of legislation, for example, extending the life of Parliament. Other possibilities might include the right to call for a referendum before legislation takes effect. Introduction of devolved powers to Scotland, Wales and Northern Ireland could give the House of Lords a role akin to that of Upper Houses in Federal States.

The composition of a reformed House of Lords raises various issues. Should, for example, the new House retain a link with its historical forbear so that members of the Royal Family and hereditary peers could be members, but without voting powers? Secondly, should the anomalous position of the Archbishops and Bishops of the Church of England be maintained? Should other religious communities be automatically represented and, if so, how should their representatives be chosen? What powers of speaking and voting should the Lords Spiritual possess? Thirdly, how should the members of the Upper House be chosen? If by election, there is a danger of merely duplicating the composition of the House of Commons unless the constitutencies, or the method of selection, or both are different. Should elections for both Houses take place at the same time? If they did not—and particularly if the Upper House were elected for a longer term than the Lower—there might be conflict between the two Houses based on political differences. Another method of selection of some or all of the members might be by nomination, whether for life or a fixed period. The Prime Minister, with or without appointed advisers, might have powers of nomination of a limited number of members while others were selected to represent various professional and cultural interests.[67] Members of the new Upper House, like those of the Commons, would have to be paid a reasonable remuneration. Two other matters would inevitably arise on a comprehensive reform of the Upper House. First, what provisions, if any, should be made to ensure that some members of the government sat in the Upper House? Secondly, what should be the position of the Law Lords. They could cease to sit in the Upper House and a new final Court of Appeal be constituted separately from it, a solution open to criticism as depriving the House of the Law Lords' help on matters of legal importance, or they might continue as members with, or without, voting rights.

The Parliament Bill 1968

The Bill introduced by the Labour Government in 1968, with the substantial agreement of the leaders of each side in both Houses, adopted a two-tier scheme of voting members and other (non-voting) members of the House of Lords. Voting peers would be peers of the first creation, that is, life peers and first holders of hereditary peerages who had made a declaration that they wished to take advantage of this qualification. There would be about 230 voting peers, who would lose their voting right at the age of 72, or by failing to attend two-thirds of the meetings in a session without excuse. Non-voting members would be those peers

---

[67] See the Irish Constitution, Art. 18.7.

by succession who had already received or applied for a writ of summons before the commencement of the Act. Non-voting members would retain the right to move any motion, and to take part (otherwise than by vote) in any proceedings of the House or a Committee. Attendance regulations would be modified for Ministers, Lords of Appeal and Lords Spiritual, the numbers of which last would be gradually reduced from 26 to 16. All peers, including the Lords Spiritual, would be entitled to vote at parliamentary elections, and any peer not entitled to sit in the House of Lords would be qualified to stand for election to the House of Commons.

The problem of the party complexion of a reformed House of Lords brings out two apparently conflicting principles. The first is that an effective Second Chamber must possess a degree of genuine independence of the government; the second is that a government must expect normally to pass its measures without undue delay, though subject to scrutiny. The solution adopted in the 1968 Bill was to ensure that the government would have a majority of (say) 10 per cent. of the *party* membership, but not an overall majority including cross-benchers. These last would in theory hold the balance of power, but they are not organised as a group.

The creation of new peers (presumably life peers) would continue to be done by prerogative, that is, on the advice of the Prime Minister; but the preamble to the Bill referred to the policy expressed in the White Paper, namely, (a) to preserve the balance of parties and non-party members among voting peers, and (b) to include voting peers with knowledge of the various countries, nations and regions of the United Kingdom. The Prime Minister would be expected to consult the leaders of other parties over the choice. An incoming government would achieve its majority of about 10 per cent. over other parties by new creations during its first months of office. A reviewing committee to report periodically on the state of the parties in the House was suggested in the White Paper, though it was not mentioned in the Bill. Who would appoint such a committee? It was implied that the committee would take account of the state of parties in the Commons, which changes over a period as a result of by-elections; but if the total number of voting peers were not fixed there would be nothing to prevent a Prime Minister from threatening to swamp a reformed upper House.

An alliance of backbenchers from the two main parties ensured the defeat of the 1968 Bill. There have been no further legislative efforts to deal with the problem, despite the report in 1978 of a Committee under the Chairmanship of Lord Home which had been set up by the Conservative Party and the recognition in that party's 1979 Election Manifesto of the need for a "strong Second Chamber."

IV. The House of Lords as the Final Court of Appeal

Before the Appellate Jurisdiction Act 1876[68]

The early doctrine was that ultimate jurisdiction in the administration of justice lay with "the King in his Council in Parliament," and in

---

[68] Holdsworth, *History of English Law*, I, Bk, i, Chap. 4.

the fifteenth century it was held[69] that this jurisdiction in error belonged not to Parliament as a whole, but to the House of Lords which had been part of the Council. Error from the equitable jurisdiction of the Court of Chancery was not established until the case of *Shirley* v. *Fagg*.[70]

Since the dispute with the Commons over the case of *Skinner* v. *East India Company*[71] the Lords have not attempted to exercise an original jurisdiction in civil cases. The only criminal jurisdiction exercised at first instance by the House of Lords was the trial of peers for treason and felony, and trial on impeachment.[72]

The House of Lords assumed appellate jurisdiction in civil cases from Scottish courts (the Court of Session) soon after the Union, although this jurisdiction was not expressly conferred by the Union with Scotland Act 1707. The earliest case to attract public attention was *Greenshields* v. *Magistrates of Edinburgh* in 1711.[73]

The Union with Ireland Act 1800 conferred on the House of Lords appellate jurisdiction in civil cases from Irish courts.

Lay peers in the House
Few of the Lords had adequate legal qualifications, and the House discouraged reports of its proceedings,[74] so that the House of Lords was scarcely regarded as a regular and ordinary court of justice before the end of the eighteenth century.[75] The last reported occasion on which lay peers attempted to take part in the strictly judicial proceedings of the House was *O'Connell* v. *The Queen*[76] on a writ of error from the Court of Queen's Bench in Ireland, in which the conviction of Daniel O'Connell for criminal conspiracy was quashed. This case may be said to have established the convention or practice that lay members do not take part when the House of Lords is setting as a court of appeal. The Lord Chancellor, Lord Lyndhurst, ignored the votes of the lay peers. A discussion followed, during which the legally qualified peers emphasised the argument that a peer who had not heard the whole proceedings should not vote. The lay peers eventually withdrew on the ground that only those qualified should vote. It appears, however, that Earl Spencer, a layman,

---

[69] (1485) Y.B. 1 Hen. VII, P. pl. 5.
[70] (1675) 6 St.Tr. 1122.
[71] (1666) St.Tr. 710.
[72] *Ante*, Chap. 7.
[73] Robertson 12; Dicey and Rait, *Thoughts on the Union Between England and Scotland*, pp. 194–195; A.D. Gibb, *Law from Over the Border*, pp. 9–11; A.S. Turberville, *The House of Lords in the Eighteenth Century*, pp. 94–95, 139–141.
[74] Regular reports of House of Lords cases began with the authorised reports of Dow (1812–1818).
[75] Pollock's Preface to Volume 1 of the Revised Reports; Turberville, *op. cit.*; "The House of Lords as a Court of Law, 1784–1837" [1946] 52 L.Q.R. 189.
[76] (1844) 11 Cl. & Fin. 155, 421–426. The legally qualified peers present were Lord Lyndhurst L.C., and Lords Brougham, Campbell, Cottenham and Denman. The lay peers present included Lord Wharncliffe, the Earl of Stradbroke, the Marquess of Clanricarde and the Earl of Verulam. Clarke and Finelly cite previous examples of lay peers taking part in judicial decisions in 1695, 1697, 1703 (*Ashby* v. *White*), 1769, 1773, 1775 and 1783.

sat in about 1860[77]; and that the second Lord Denman (son of the Chief Justice and a barrister of fifty years' standing) sat throughout, spoke and voted in *Bradlaugh* v. *Clarke*,[78] his vote (which was ignored) not affecting the result.[79]

Three is the quorum under Standing Orders of the House of Lords in both its legislative and judicial capacities, and it appears that the leading case of *Rylands* v. *Fletcher*[80] was heard by Lord Cairns L.C. with one other legally qualified peer (Lord Colonsay, former President of the Court of Session) and a lay peer—probably a Lord Spritual—within call to form a quorum.[81]

There was wide criticsm in the last century both of the House of Lords as a court of appeal and of the system of two-tier appeals. The attempt by virtue of the prerogative to create Baron Parke[82] a life peer with the right to sit and vote in the House of Lords had failed.[83] Lord Selborne, Liberal Chancellor, introduced the Supreme Court of Judicature Bill 1873, which in its original form would have given the final appeal in English cases to a new Court of Appeal while retaining the Lords' jurisdiction in Scottish and Irish cases. The opposition to the abolition of the House of Lords' jurisdiction was largely due to the fear that this would undermine the remaining powers of the hereditary House. Also, the Scots and Irish would not want their appeals to go to an English Court of Appeal. This Act, as amended to retain the Lords' jurisdiction, came into force at the beginning of 1876.[84]

From the Appellate Jurisdiction Act 1876[85]

Meanwhile a Bill introduced by the Conservative Chancellor, Lord Cairns, met most of the criticisms that had been made of the House of Lords as an appellate court. This became the Appellate Jurisdiction Act 1876. It provided for appeals in civil cases to be heard by the House of Lords from the new English Court of Appeal, in addition to appeals from the courts of Scotland and Ireland (s.3).

The Act of 1876 created salaried Lords of Appeal in Ordinary, who must either have held high judicial office for at least two years or be practising barristers of not less than 15 years' standing (s.6). Their number, at first two, has been gradually increased by subsequent stat-

---

[77] See *Re Lord Kinross* [1905] A.C. 468, 476.

[78] (1883) 8 App.Cas. 354.

[79] Lord du Parcq. "The Final Court of Appeal" in (1949) C.L.P. 4–6; *cf.* R.E. Megarry in (1949) 65 L.Q.R. 22–24, Lord Denman is not mentioned in the law report: Megarry, *Miscellany-at-law*, pp. 11–13. Lord Denman also attempted to vote in *Bain* v. *Fothergill* (1874) L.R. 7 H.L. 158, but his vote was not counted. It has been questioned whether lay peers sat in *Hutton* v. *Upfill* (1850) 2 H.L.C. 674, 647n., and *Hutton* v. *Bright* (1852) 3 H.L.C. 341; see Lord Denning, "From Precedent to Precedent" (Romanes Lecture, 1959) pp. 26–28.

[80] (1868) L.R. 3 H.L. 330.

[81] R. F. V. Heuston, "Who was the Third Lord in *Rylands* v. *Fletcher*?" (1970) 86 L.Q.R. 160.

[82] He was not a peer, but a baron (*i.e.* judge) of the Court of Exchequer.

[83] *Wensleydale Peerage Case* (1856) H.L.C. 958.

[84] Supreme Court of Judicature Acts 1873–1875.

[85] See L. Blom-Cooper Q.c. and G. Drewry, *Final Appeal: A Study of the House of Lords in its Judicial Capacity* (1972); Robert Stevens, *Law and Politics: The House of Lords as a Judicial Body 1800–1976* (1979).

utes. It provided that there should be present at the hearing of an appeal at least three of the following Lords of Appeal: (1) the Lord Chancellor, (2) the Lords of Appeal in Ordinary, and (3) such peers of Parliament as hold or have held "high judicial office" as therein defined. The last group includes ex-Lord Chancellors (s.5). In important cases the court usually consists of five members.

The Act further provided that the House of Lords may hear appeals during any prorogation of Parliament (s.8), and that arrangements may be made for the hearing of appeals by the Lords of Appeal in the name of the House of Lords during a dissolution of Parliament (s.9).[86] The origin of the court is preserved, however, in the form to be used on an appeal, *viz.* a petition to the House of Lords praying that the matter may be reviewed before Her Majesty the Queen in her Court in Parliament (s.4). The Lords give their opinions in the form of speeches, and an appeal is won or lost on a vote in the House.

One effect of the Appellate Jurisdiction Act 1876 was to increase the importance of the House of Lords as a court of English common law. Previously it had been more important for Scottish appeals, while English appeals had usually been cases in equity.[87]

Appeals to the House of Lords in criminal cases, as distinct from jurisdiction on writ of error, were not introduced until the Criminal Appeal Act 1907, which created the Court of Criminal Appeal. Criminal appeals since 1966 lie from the criminal division of the Court of Appeal.[88]

Appeals from Irish courts since 1922 are confined to Northern Ireland, but include criminal cases.

Lord Cairns had suggested a Judicial Committee of the House of Lords, sitting throughout the year in a separate courtroom. This did not occur until a change of practice at the end of the last war. The court used to sit in the House of Lords debating chamber when the House was not sitting for legislative business. During the last war it was often impossible for peers to get home before the nightly air-raids started, so the House decided to meet at 2.30 p.m. instead of 4.30 p.m. As the House cannot sit in two places at once, it was resolved to refer appeals temporarily to an "Appellate Committee" consisting of Law Lords sitting in a committee room.[89] This arrangement has become permanent.

The Lord Chancellor presides if present. In his absence hearings are presided over, since 1984 by one of two Law Lords nominated by him for that purpose.[90] Formerly the right to preside was determined by seniority by date of appointment as a Lord of Appeal.[91]

---

[86] As in the case of *Race Relations Board* v. *Dockers' Labour Club and Institute Ltd.* [1976] A.C. 285.

[87] Robert Stevens, "The Final Appeal: Reform of the House of Lords and Privy Council, 1867–1876" (1964) 80 L.Q.R. 343.

[88] Criminal Appeal Act 1968, consolidating the Criminal Appeal Act 1966 and other statutes.

[89] Petitions for leave to appeal are referred to an Appeal Committee, consisting of three Law Lords: *Practice Direction (House of Lords: Petitions: Leave to Appeal)* [1979] 1 W.L.R. 497.

[90] H.L. Deb. (1984) Vol. 453. cols. 914–918.

[91] A practice introduced in 1969 when ex-Lord Chancellors lost the right to preside in the absence of the Lord Chancellor: H.L. Deb. vol. 302, col. 469.

After hearing argument the Appellate Committee formerly reported to the House, where the appeal was considered and the vote taken. Since 1963 the opinions of the Lords of Appeal whether in civil or criminal appeals are no longer, as a general rule, delivered orally in the House. When the House meets for the delivery of opinions their Lordships confine themselves to stating that, for the reasons given in their opinions, they would allow or dismiss the appeal. The question is then put from the Woolsack and the answer made. Copies of the opinions are available for counsel an hour beforehand.[92] This practice is similar to that employed by the Judicial Committee of the Privy Council and saves time for both judges and counsel.

The earlier sitting of the House clashes with the sittings of the Appellate Committee. This has meant that since the war it has been very difficult for the Lord Chancellor to sit judicially, except for about a fortnight in January and a fortnight in October when the courts are sitting but Parliament is not.[93] Lord Hailsham had devoted more time to sitting in the Appellate Committee and has appointed Deputy Speakers, from time to time to preside over debates.[94]

In cases of difficulty their Lordships may summon the judges of the Queen's Bench Division (formerly the Court of Queen's Bench) for advice, but this has only been done four times since the creation of Lords of Appeal in Ordinary in 1876. The advice of the judges was usually accepted as in *Mersey Docks and Harbour Board* v. *Gibbs*,[95] but not always, as in *Allen* v. *Flood*,[96] this being the last English case in which the judges were summoned. The last occasion in a Scottish appeal was *Free Church of Scotland (General Assembly)* v. *Lord Overtoun*.[97]

The House had no authority to summon Chancery judges unless they were peers.

---

[92] *Practice Direction (H.L.) (Delivery of Opinions)* [1963] 1 W.L.R. 1382.
[93] Lord Gardiner, *The Trials of a Lord Chancellor* (Holdsworth Club, University of Birmingham, 1968) pp. 2–3.
[94] Lord Hailsham, *The Door Wherein I Went*, pp. 249–250.
[95] (1866) L.R. 1 H.L. 93.
[96] [1898] A.C. 1. See further, R. F. V. Heuston, "Judicial Prosopography," (1986) 102 L.Q.R. 90.
[97] [1904] A.C. 515.

CHAPTER 9

THE HOUSE OF COMMONS

1. MEMBERSHIP OF THE HOUSE OF COMMONS

Historical introduction[1]

Simon de Montfort, leader of the rebel forces against Henry III, may be called the founder of the House of Commons, though not the founder of Parliament. His innovation in 1265 was to summon not only the knights for each shire—there were precedents for this—but also two burgesses from each borough. This action was not based on any theory of representative government (which originated in ecclesiastical organisations before the thirteenth century), but in order to counteract the power of the King.

Edward I revived the idea of summoning the knights and burgesses in 1275 primarily, it is supposed, for financial purposes. Parliament was in a formative stage in his reign, and some of his most important statutes were passed in the absence of the Commons. There was still no clear distinction between Council and Parliament. The Commons became more regularly established during the reign of Edward III, although as a body they were not of much influence before the end of the fourteenth century. The division of Parliament into two Houses may be said to have taken place in the reign of Edward III. Petitions involving judicial decisions were dealt with by the Council and the courts. The elected knights and the burgesses were concerned with common petitions and requests by the King for aids. In time they came to form a House of Commons, meeting in the Chapter House of Westminster Abbey, appointing a Speaker to reply in the parliament chamber to the King's requests and demanding that their common petitions be made statutes.[2]

The knights were elected in the county court by the freeholders. The borough franchise varied according to the customs and privileges of the various boroughs. For centuries members of the House of Commons consisted of knights and burgesses so elected.

Since 1774 a candidate for a parliamentary election need not have any connection with his constituency. In 1858 the property qualification was abolished. From the time of Elizabeth I penal statutes against papists, Protestant dissenters and others, and the requirement of a parliamentary oath that could conscientiously be taken only by Anglicans, virtually excluded non-Anglicans from Parliament for many years. Civil disabilities against dissenters were removed in 1828, and Roman Catholics were admitted to Parliament by the Roman Catholic Relief Act

---

[1] For a survey and guide to the literature, see Taswell-Langmead, *English Constitutional History* (11th ed. Plucknett), Chap. 6.
[2] A.F. Pollard, *The Evolution of Parliament* (2nd ed.), pp. 117–128.

1829. The oath was later made acceptable to Jews.[3] Quakers and others who objected to taking an oath were allowed to make an affirmation.[4] Women were admitted to the House of Commons in 1918.[5]

Offices or places of profit from or under the Crown, and pensions at the pleasure of the Crown

The Act of Settlement 1700, s.6, would have provided that "no person who has an office or place of profit under the King, or receives a pension from the crown, shall be capable of serving as a member of the House of Commons," but this provision was repealed before it came into force. The Succession to the Crown Act 1707, passed at the time of the union with Scotland, provided by section 24 that no person who held any office or place of profit under the Crown *created after 1705*,[6] and no person having any pension from the Crown *during pleasure*, should be capable of being elected or of sitting or voting as a member of the House of Commons. Section 25 provided that if a member of the House of Commons accepted any office of profit from the Crown, his election should become void but he should be capable of being re-elected. One who sat and voted as a member when disqualified was liable to pay a heavy fine at the suit of a common informer, although it seems that no common informer actions were ever brought for this purpose. Section 25, requiring re-election of a member on appointment to office, should probably be taken to apply only to offices existing in 1705.[7]

Pensions from the Crown were a disqualification only if they were held "during pleasure," or (according to the Pensioners Civil Disabilities Relief Act 1869) for any term or number of years. This disqualification by 1957 extended to very few persons, such as those who held small pensions in the Civil List, for it did not apply, *e.g.* to holders of civil or military service pensions.

By the end of the eighteenth century three principles were established: (i) certain non-ministerial offices were incompatible with membership of the House of Commons; (ii) the control of the government over the House through members who were office-holders must be limited; but (iii) a certain number of Ministers must be members of the House in order that Parliament could control the executive. A series of statutes after 1707 therefore converted the distinction between the holders of "old" offices (qualified) and "new" offices (disqualified) into a distinction between the holders of *political* offices (qualified within limits) and *non-political* offices (disqualified), by disqualifying or suppressing many old offices of a non-ministerial nature and providing for

---

[3] Jews Relief Act 1858.

[4] Promissory Oaths Act 1868; Oaths Act 1888 (atheists). *Cf. Bradlaugh* v. *Gossett* (1884) 12 Q.B.D. 271. The current legislation is to be found in the Oaths Act 1978.

[5] Parliament (Qualification of Women) Act 1918.

[6] The date of an intervening Act, the Succession to the Crown Act 1705, which was repealed in order to take account of the Union.

[7] While s.24 refers to offices or places held *under* the Crown, s.25 specifies offices accepted *from* the Crown, which are probably limited to appointments made directly by the Crown and not through the medium of a Minister, *i.e.* senior ministerial offices and Household offices.

the eligibility of the ministerial heads of newly created departments, subject to the necessity for re-election if already members.[8]

Number of Ministers in the House of Commons

A limit was set to the number of Ministers and Secretaries of State, respectively, who might sit in the House of Commons. The Ministers of the Crown Act 1937 abolished the distinction in this respect between Secretaries of State and other Ministers, but limited the total number who might sit in the Commons. There remained a residual number of Ministers who were excluded, and who therefore by convention had to sit in the House of Lords.[9]

Government contractors, i.e. persons who held contracts for or on account of the public service, were disqualified by the House of Commons (Disqualification) Acts 1782 and 1801, the purpose being to exclude those who contracted to supply goods to government departments and who might therefore be under the influence of the government. Actions by common informers were brought under these Acts for the penalty of £500 a day for sitting and voting while so disqualified.[10] The House of Commons Disqualification (Declaration of Law) Act 1931 declared that the scope of the Acts was confined to contracts for furnishing or providing money to be remitted abroad, and wares and merchandise to be used in the service of the public.[11]

The House of Commons Disqualification Act 1957[12] repealed the enactments disqualifying the holders of offices or places of profit under the Crown and of persons holding pensions from the Crown, and instead disqualified the holders of *specified* offices. The disqualification of government contractors was also removed by the Act of 1957, since there was no evidence of corruption in the previous 100 years and it was impracticable to remove anomalies. With one exception, noted below, the right of common informers to sue was abolished and replaced with a right to seek a declaration from the Privy Council.

Miscellaneous existing disqualifications

There are several disqualifications from membership which are not affected by the House of Commons Disqualification Act:

---

[8] Certain offices to which a member was appointed continued to vacate the seat but allowed re-election, until the requirement of re-election was finally abolished in 1926: Re-election of Ministers Act 1919 and 1926. Gladstone inadvertently vacated his seat in 1859 by accepting the post of Lord High Commissioner of the Ionian Islands: Sir Philip Magnus, *Gladstone*, p. 135.

[9] Cf. later House of Commons Disqualfication Acts and Ministers of the Crown Acts.

[10] *Forbes* v. *Samuel* [1913] 3 K.B. 706; *Burnett* v. *Samuel* [1913] 3 K.B. 742. Forbes's original claim for £46,500 was reduced in the statement of claim to £17,500. Judgment was given for the defendant in both cases on technical grounds, the judge clearly disliking common informer actions.

[11] Cf. *Re Sir Stuart Samuel* [1913] A.C. 514 (advisory opinion of the Privy Council).

[12] Repealed and substantially re-enacted by the House of Commons Disqualification Act 1975; *post*, pp. 179 *et seq.*

1. *Aliens*,[13] *i.e.* persons who are not British subjects or Commonwealth citizens, and are not citizens of the Republic of Ireland.[14]

2. *Persons under twenty-one years of age*.[15]

3. *Persons suffering from mental illness*. "Lunatics" and "idiots" were disqualified at common law. The Mental Health Act 1983 s.141, now provides that the Speaker must be notified when a member is detained as a person suffering from mental illness. The Speaker must then obtain a medical report. If the detention is confirmed by this report, and the member is still detailed as a mental patient according to a second medical report six months later, his seat is vacated.

4. *Peers and peeresses* are disqualified by the law and custom of Parliament.[16] except that by statute Irish peers are no longer disqualified.[17] The wives and eldest sons of peers, who have courtesy titles, may sit.

5. *Clergy* who have been episcopally ordained, including clergy of the Church of England and the Church of Ireland (House of Commons (Clergy Disqualification) Act 1801; *Re MacManaway*[18]), and Roman Catholic priests (Roman Catholic Relief Act 1829, s.9); but not clergy of the Church of Wales (Welsh Church Act 1914).

Ministers of the (Presbyterian) Church of Scotland are also disqualified by the Act of 1801.[19]

6. *Treason*. A person convicted of treason is disqualified till the expiry of his sentence of imprisonment or the receipt of a royal pardon.[20]

7. *Other crimes*. The statutory disqualification imposed in the cases of treason by the Forfeiture Act 1870 extended also to a conviction of

---

[13] *R. v. Cassel* [1916] 1 K.B. 595; *R. v. Speyer* [1916] 2 K.B. 858.

[14] Ireland Act 1949. British Nationality Act 1981, Sched. 7.

[15] Parliamentary Elections Act 1695; Family Law Reform Act 1969. It appears that before 1832 several infants sat in the Commons "by connivance," including Charles James Fox and Lord John Russell. See P. Norton "The Qualifying Age for Candidature in British Elections" [1980] P.L. 55.

[16] *Report from the Committee of Privileges: Petition concerning Mr. Anthony Neil Wedgwood Benn* (1961) H.C. No. 142; *Re Parliamentary Election for Bristol South-East* [1964] 2 Q.B. 257; [1961] 3 W.L.R. 577; G. Borrie, "The Wedgewood Benn Case" [1961] P.L. 349. See also *Beresford-Hope* v. *Lady Sandhurst* (1889) L.R. 23 Q.B.D. 69 (C.A.). And *cf.* now, renunciation of peerage: Peerage Act 1963; *ante* p. 159.

[17] Peerage Act 1963 (non-representative Irish peers); *Re Earl of Antrim's Petition* [1967] 1 A.C. 691; Statute Law (Repeals) Act 1971.

[18] [1951] A.C. 161 (P.C.). The Act of 1801 was passed to keep out Rev. Horne Tooke. Section 2 under which a common informer may claim a £500 *per diem* penalty as long as a clergyman disqualified under the Act continues to sit, is still in force. Under the Clerical Disabilities Act 1870 it is possible for any clergyman of the Church of England legally to relinquish the rights and privileges of his office and so become eligible for election to Parliament.

[19] See, further, *Report from the Select Committee on Clergy Disqualification* (1953) H.C. No. 200. The Committee recommended that no change in the law on this topic should be at present made, as did the Select Committee on the House of Commons Disqualification Bill (1956) H.C. No. 349.

[20] Forfeiture Act 1870, as amended by the Criminal Law Act 1967, Sched. 3.

felony and a sentence of imprisonment of more than 12 months. This provision was repealed by the Criminal Law Act 1967 which abolished the distinction between felonies and misdemeanors. Thereafter the position with regard to *any* conviction was that which had formerly applied to convictions of misdemeanours or felonies but with sentences not exceeding 12 months: the person convicted was not disqualified but the House might pass a motion to expel him.[21] This gap in the law was remedied by the Representation of the People Act 1981, section 1, which disqualifies for membership of the Commons anyone found guilty of an offence, whether before or after the passing of the Act, whether in the United Kingdom or elsewhere, and sentenced to be imprisoned or detained indefinitely or for more than one year.[22] If a member becomes disqualified under the terms of the Act his seat is vacated.

8. *Bankrupts.* Formerly, in England and Wales disqualification lasted for five years after discharge. Disqualification now ceases on discharge.[23]

9. *Corrupt and illegal practices.* Various statutes constituted certain kinds of conduct at parliamentary elections "corrupt" or "illegal" practices. These provisions are now to be found in the Representation of the People Act 1983.[24] The consequences so far as disqualification from sitting in the House of Commons is concerned are:

(a) If a candidate who has been elected is reported by an election court personally guilty, or guilty by his agents, of any corrupt or illegal practice, his election is void (s.159(1)).

(b) A candidate is also incapable of being elected for the constituency concerned: (i) for 10 years if reported personally guilty of a corrupt practice; (ii) for seven years if reported guilty by his agents of a corrupt practice or personally guilty of an illegal practice; and (iii) during the Parliament for which the election was held if reported guilty by his agents of an illegal practice (s.159(2)).

(c) A candidate reported by an election court personally guilty of a

---

[21] Miss Bernadette Devlin M.P., who was sentenced to six months' imprisonment in Northern Ireland in 1969 for encouraging petrol bomb attacks against the police, served her sentence, but was not expelled. The imprisonment of Mr.John Stonehouse M.P. in 1976 gave publicity to the Home Office rules resulting from the report of the Select Committee of Privileges *On the Rights of Honourable Members detained in Prison* (1970–71; H.C. 185). A Member should be produced at the House of Commons if the House so desires; he may not take part in parliamentary business but may write to the House; he must not carry on constituency business, but should be granted reasonable facilities to arrange for someone to conduct constituency matters on his behalf.

[22] The statute was given retrospective effect to invalidate the election in April 1981 for the Constituency of Fermanagh and South Tyrone of a prisoner serving a long term of imprisonment for various firearms offences. The principle of the Act is criticised by C.P. Walker, "Prisoners in Parliament: Another View," [1982] P.L. 389.

[23] Insolvency Act 1986, s.427.

[24] For corrupt and illegal practices, see *post*, p. 195 L.M. Helmore, *Corrupt and Illegal Practices* (1967) gives an account of the trial of the Exeter election petition in 1911.

corrupt practice is incapable for five years of being elected to the House of Commons, and if already elected shall vacate his seat (s.160).

(d) A person convicted of a corrupt practice on indictment or by an election court is subject to the incapacities mentioned in (c) above (s.173).[25]

The House of Commons Disqualification Act 1975

From time to time Indemnity Acts were passed to indemnify members who had become disqualified unwittingly through holding certain offices or places of profit from or under the Crown,[26] and usually the election was validated also.[27] A Select Committee was set up in 1941, and recommended the passing of an Act to reform and consolidate the law on this subject.[28] The matter was taken up again after the war,[29] and the House of Commons Disqualification Act 1957 was passed, dealing with a particular range of problems, but not forming an exhaustive code of disqualification from membership.[30] The main provisions of the Consolidating Act of 1975 are as follows:

Section 1. *Disqualification of holders of certain (non-ministerial) offices and places.* A person is disqualified for membership of the House of Commons if he falls into any of the following categories:

(1)(a) *Judicial offices.* The holders of the judicial offices specified in Part I of Schedule 1. These include judges of the Supreme Court, circuit judges[31] and stipendiary magistrates, but not justices of the peace.

(b) *Civil service.* Civil servants, whether established or not, and whether whole or part time. Service regulations require that if a civil servant becomes a candidate for parliamentary election, he must resign his office.[32]

(c) *Armed forces.* Members of the regular armed forces of the Crown. Service regulations forbid members of the regular forces from standing for Parliament.[33] It was discovered that this regulation provided a means of getting service engagements terminated, and the Home Secretary therefore appointed an advisory committee in 1963 to report to the appropriate Service Minister whether they were satisfied that such applications were bona fide.

(d) *Police forces.* Members (*i.e.* full-time constables) of any police force maintained by a police authority.

---

[25] *Cf.* s.174 (mitigation and remission of incapacities).
[26] See *ante*, p. 175.
[27] *Cf.* Charles Beattie Indemnity Act 1956, which did not validate the election because with more care Mr. Beattie would have discovered his position.
[28] *Report of the Select Committee on Offices or Places of Profit under the Crown* (1941) H.C. Pap. 120.
[29] *Special Report from the Select Committee on the House of Commons Disqualification Bill* (1956) H.C. No. 349; Charles Doughty Q.C., M.P., "House of Commons Disqualification" [1957] P.L. 340.
[30] See *ante.* pp. 177–178 as to aliens, minors, peers, clergy, etc.
[31] Courts Act 1971, s.17(5).
[32] Servants of the Crown (Parliamentary Candidature) Order 1960.
[33] In 1963 a large number of service-men applied for release from the forces for the purpose of contesting by-elections, 175 at Colne Valley and 496 at Rotherham.

(e) *Foreign legislatures*. Members of the legislature of any country outside the Commonwealth. Members of such legislatures would generally be disqualified as aliens, but this provision disqualifies those with dual nationality and members of the legislature of the Republic of Ireland.

(f) *Commissions and Tribunals, etc.* Members of the commissions, tribunals, and other bodies specified in Part II of Schedule 1. These include the boards of the nationalised industries, and many other statutory bodies whose members are appointed by the Crown, *e.g.* the various electricity boards, the Gaming Board, the British Railway board, the Post Office, the National Coal Board, the Lands Tribunal, the Council on Tribunals, the Law Commission and the University Grants Committee. The list is constantly being extended or modified by statute. The reason for the disqualification of members of public corporations is that some Minister is in the last resort responsible for them to Parliament and it would impair his responsibility if members of these boards could sit in the House of Commons.

Certain other offices. The holders of various offices specified in Part III of Schedule 1, including British ambassadors and high commissioners, boundary commissioners, the Comptroller and Auditor-General, judge-advocates, Parliamentary Commissioner, chairmen of many statutory tribunals and councils, governors of the British Broadcasting Corporation, and registration officers at elections. These are disqualified either because they are appointed by the Crown or because their office is incompatible with membership of the House of Commons.

Section 1(2). *Offices disqualifying for particular constituencies*. The holder of any office described in Part IV of Schedule 1 is disqualified from membership for any constituency specified in the Schedule in relation to that office. A lord-lieutenant or sheriff, for example, is disqualified in relation to any constituency in the area for which he is appointed.

Section 1(4). *Effect of section* 1(*holders of certain offices*). A person is not disqualified for membership of the House of Commons by reason of holding any office or place of profit except as provided in the Act. Conversely, a person is not disqualified for appointment to any office or place by reason of his being a member of that House.[34]

Schedule 1 containing the list of offices mentioned above may be amended by Order in Council, following a resolution of the House of Commons—a remarkable example of delegated legislation; and Her Majesty's printer is required to print copies of the Act with Schedule 1 as amended from time to time by Order in Council or other Acts (s.5).

Section 2. *Ministerial offices*.[35] Not more than 95 holders of the ministerial offices specified in Schedule 2 may sit and vote at any one time in

---

[34] The latter provision negatives what is called "reverse disqualification."

[35] These statutory provisions should be distinguished from the *convention* that Ministers shall disembarrass themselves of any company directorships or shareholdings which would be likely, or which might appear, to conflict with their official duties.

the House of Commons. It is now permissible for all senior Ministers, except the Lord Chancellor, to sit in the Commons.[36]

Section 4. Stewardship of the Chiltern Hundreds, etc. It was established by the early seventeenth century that a member could not resign his seat. If a member wished to relinquish his seat, therefore, it has been the practice since about 1750 to apply to the Chancellor of the Exchequer for the Stewardship of the Chiltern Hundreds. The office has for long been a sinecure, but it is technically an "office of profit under the Crown" and therefore under the previous law disqualified the holder from further membership of the Commons. In order to preserve this interesting historical relic, the Act provides that the Stewardship of the Chiltern Hundreds and three similar offices, for which application is made to the Chancellor of the Exchequer, shall be treated as included among the disqualifying offices listed in Part IV of Schedule 1.[37]

Section 6. Effect of disqualification, and provision for relief. If a person disqualified for membership is elected, his election is void; and if a member of the House becomes disqualified his seat is vacated. If, however, the disqualification has been removed the House may, if it appears proper to do so, direct that the disqualification shall be disregarded; but such order is not to affect proceedings on an election petition or the determination of an election court.[38]

Section 7. Jurisdiction of Privy Council as to disqualification. Any person who claims that a person purporting to be a member of the House of Commons is disqualified by the Act may apply to Her Majesty in Council for a declaration to that effect. The application is referred to the Judicial Committee in the same way as an appeal from a court under the Judicial Committee Act 1833, s.3. As regards disqualification under the Act, this is an alternative method to an election petition,[39] though without the time limit. The Judicial Committee may direct an issue of fact to be tried in the High Court,[40] whose decision shall be final. A declaration may not be made, however, if an election petition is pending or has been tried, or if the House of Commons has directed that the disqualification shall be disregarded.

It should be noticed that the House itself may resolve that a case be referred by the Crown to the Judicial Committee under section 4 of the Judicial Committee Act 1833 for an advisory opinion on a point of law, and this could include any legal disqualification, whether arising under

---

[36] The 1957 Act limited the number of senior ministers who might sit in the Commons at any one time to 27; but this limit was removed by the Ministers of the Crown Act 1964, for Mr. Wilson, the new Prime Minister, wished to give a large number of members of his party experience of office without creating more peerages.

[37] There are four offices, enabling four members to resign in quick succession, *viz.* Steward or Bailiff of the Chiltern Hundreds, and Steward or Bailiff of the Manor of Northstead. The Chancellor of the Exchequer usually grants them alternately.

[38] *Post,* p. 200.

[39] *Post,* p. 200.

[40] Or the Court of Session or the High Court in Northern Ireland.

the House of Commons Disqualification Act or not. This was in fact done in the case of MacManaway.[41]

Section 8. Relaxation of obligation to accept office. No member of the House of Commons or candidate for a parliamentary election may be *required* to accept any office which would disqualify him from membership. This relaxation does not apply to any obligation, statutory or otherwise, to serve in the armed forces of the Crown. It appears that the office of sheriff is the only other office which is by custom regarded as obligatory. Sheriffs were formerly required to remain in the county during this year of office, and therefore could not sit in the House.[42] In 1626 Charles I excluded Coke and four other members by "pricking" them sheriffs against their will,[43] but the Commons resolved in 1675 that it was a breach of privilege to appoint a member of the House as sheriff.[44] Section 8 was inserted *ex abundante cautela*, in case the government should be able to exclude members of the Opposition by appointing them to disqualifying offices.

A candidate's consent to nomination at a parliamentary election must contain a statement that he is aware of the provisions of the Act, and that, to the best of his knowledge and belief, he is not disqualified from membership of the House of Commons (s.10).

The Act of 1957 repealed all provisions whereby common informers could sue for penalties in respect of parliamentary disqualifications.[45] Apart from the procedure laid down in section 7 (*supra*) the Courts will not examine whether a member of Parliament is disqualified from sitting.[46]

Payment of Members

In medieval times knights, citizens and burgesses received a few shillings a day from their constituencies. This right was balanced by statutory penalties for non-attendance, which are now obsolete. Although called wages, these payments were intended as expenses, and they too became obsolete with the fall in the value of money.

As a result of the decision in *Amalgamated Society of Railway Servants v. Osborne*[47] declaring that a "political levy" by trades unions on their members was illegal, so that trades unions could not pay salaries to M.P.s whom they sponsored, the House of Commons resolved that members who were not Ministers should receive a salary under the annual Appropriation Act payable out of the Consolidated Fund.

---

[41] *Re MacManaway* [1951] A.C. 161; *ante*, p. 177.
[42] 4 Co.Inst. 48.
[43] Holdsworth, *History of English Law*, V, pp. 448–449.
[44] Wittke, *Parliamentary Privilege*, p. 38.
[45] With the exception of that contained in the House of Commons (Clergy Disqualification) Act 1801; *supra*, n. 18. The Common Informers Act 1951, which abolished the common informer procedure generally, did not extend to parliamentary disqualifications.
[46] *Martin v. O'Sullivan* [1984] S.T.C. 258; *ante* p. 51 (Challenge to qualifications of the entire House of Commons).
[47] [1910] A.C. 87 (H.L.). *Cf. post*, Chap. 27 (trade unions).

In order to avoid, or minimise, the embarrassment of members of Parliament having to determine their own salaries, that duty was in 1970 entrusted to the newly-established Review Body on Top Salaries which conducts regular reviews of the salaries of those working in the higher levels of the public service. In 1983 it was agreed that from 1988 the salaries of members of Parliament would be linked to that of the grade of civil servants which was being paid £18,500 in June 1983, provided that such an arrangement is approved within the first three months of each new Parliament.[48] Members are entitled, in addition to their salaries, to secretarial, postal, and travel expenses. Various statutes, of which the latest is the Parliamentary Pensions etc. Act 1984, provide for the payment of pensions to former members of Parliament.

The Speaker[49]

The practice of the Commons having a spokesman arose gradually in the Middle Ages. The first two members who may be regarded as holding a definite office as Speaker were Sir Peter de la Mere and Sir Thomas Hungerford in the years 1376 and 1377. The Commons appear always to have elected their Speaker. For some time he also attended the King's Council, and his position as liaison between the Commons and the King was for long a dangerous one.

The Speaker is elected by the Commons from their own number at the beginning of each new Parliament. Formerly, when a new Speaker was chosen, the Clerk of the House supervised the proceedings. The choice was agreed informally among the leaders of the various parties, and the election—although normally unanimous—was occasionally opposed. In 1971 there was a division on the motion for the election of Mr. Selwyn Lloyd, the objection of the minority being not to Mr. Selwyn Lloyd but the lack of consultation of members by the party leaders. The new procedure adopted on the retirement of Mr. (later Lord) Selwyn Lloyd in 1976 is that the retiring Speaker takes the chair, the "Father of the House" (the senior member in years of service) moves the election of the member (selected from the Government party) whose name has been previously agreed between the party leaders after wide consultations among back benchers, the retiring Speaker formally asks whether there are other nominations and the House then votes in favour of the motion. As we have seen, it is a convention that the Sovereign should be asked for, and should give, consent to the choice of Speaker.[50]

The Speaker of the previous Parliament is usually re-elected unanimously, if he is still a member and willing to stand. Re-election by the House has not been opposed since 1835.[51]

[48] H.C.Deb., vol. 46, col. 329–352.
[49] See Dasent, *The Speaker of the House of Commons* Erskine May, *Parliamentary Practice*; Sir Ivor Jennings, *Parliament* (2nd ed.), pp. 63 *et seq.*; Selwyn Lloyd, *Mr. Speaker, Sir* (1976).
[50] *Ante*, p. 137.
[51] A Select Committee on Procedure recommended in 1972 that the "Father of the House," instead of the Clerk to the House, should preside over the election of the Speaker, and also that he should propose the re-election of a Speaker, and that all candidates for election after the first should be put to the House in the form of an amendment to the original motion.

A Speaker takes no active part in a parliamentary election campaign, and it was thought by some to be a convention that he should not be opposed in his constituency at a general election. However, the Speaker was opposed by Labour and Liberal candidates at the general election in 1964. In 1979 the Speaker (Mr. George Thomas) was opposed in a general election by Plaid Cymru and the National Front and in 1987 Mr. Bernard Weatherill by Labour and Liberal candidates. In order that a constituency may not be virtually disfranchised, it has been suggested that the Speaker should have a fictitious constituency or none at all, so that on a member's election as Speaker there would be a by-election in the constituency which returned him to Parliament. On the other hand, it would be incorrect to say that the Speaker's constituency is disfranchised, because the member who fills that office continues to look after the interests of his constituents.

The Speaker is the channel of communication between the Commons and the Queen, and between the Commons and the Lords. Hence his title of "Speaker" or spokesman. On his appointment he claims from the Sovereign certain "ancient and undoubted" privileges of the House at the beginning of each Parliament.[52]

The Speaker presides over the House, except when it is in Committee.[53] When in the chair he maintains order, and guides the House on all questions of privilege and practice. He is expected to be impartial between political parties, and especially to protect the rights of minorities in the House and to ensure that they have their say. The Speaker does not take part in debate. He does not vote unless there is a tie, in which case, according to the ruling of Speaker Addington (1796), "the Speaker should always vote for further discussion where this is possible." Thus he will usually give his casting vote in favour of the introduction of a Bill, against amendments to a Bill at the report stage, against Lords' amendments to a Bill sent up by the Commons and against a guillotine motion.

The Speaker gives advice and rulings on procedure; signs warrants of committal for contempt, and reprimands members and strangers for misconduct; and signs warrants for the issue of writs for by-elections.

The Speaker has the duty under the Parliament Acts 1911 and 1949 of certifying "Money Bills," and giving his certificate that the procedure for overriding the House of Lords has been complied with. If it were doubtful which was the largest party in opposition to the government in the House of Commons, or who was the leader in the House of such party, the Speaker would issue a certificate for this purpose, which would be binding and conclusive.[54]

The Speaker has an official residence. His salary is charged on and payable out of the Consolidated Fund.[55] This means that it is payable by permanent legislation, and does not come up for annual review and perhaps debate. On a dissolution of Parliament the Speaker retains

---

[52] *Post*, Chap. 12.
[53] Until 1870 he sometimes spoke in Committee.
[54] Ministerial and other Salaries Act 1975, s.2.
[55] Ministerial and other Salaries Act 1975, s.1. This is the culmination of a series of statutes going back to the Speaker of the House of Commons Act 1790.

office until a Speaker is chosen by the new Parliament. In precedence he ranks next after the Lord President of the Council.[56] When he retires, it is customary to bestow on him a peerage[57] and a statutory pension.

The Clerk of the House has custody of all the records of the House, makes entries of what takes place in the House, and from these materials prepares the Journals. He indorses Bills sent up to the Lords. Formerly when the Commons retired to elect a Speaker the Clerk of the House has occupied the chair.

The Serjeant-at-Arms is appointed by the Crown by letters patent under the Great Seal. The present practice is for the Queen to discuss the appointment informally with the Speaker, who sounds the feelings of the party leaders. The Lancastrian Kings first appointed one of the Sergeants-at-Arms (originally royal bodyguards) to attend the Commons, and the Commons came to use him to protect their privileges because through him they could arrest or imprison offenders without having to take proceedings in the courts. During session he attends, with the mace,[58] the Speaker when the latter enters and leaves the House.

It is the duty of the Serjeant-at-Arms to carry out directions for maintaining order, and to arrest strangers who have no business in the House. With the mace in his hands he can arrest without warrant anyone who obstructs the Speaker's procession. He executes the Speaker's warrants for contempt, and when ordered to do so brings persons in custody before the bar of the House. He or his assistants serve processes of the House. When a person is arrested by order of the House, the Serjeant-at-Arms keeps the prisoner in his custody until arrangements are made for his bestowal elsewhere. The Metropolitan Police on duty in the precincts come under his orders when the House is in session.

The Chairman of Ways and Means is a member elected at the beginning of each Parliament to preside over committees of the whole House.[59] He maintains order in Committee and can "name" members, but where a suspension is necessary the Speaker reoccupies the chair. The closure can be applied by the Chairman in Committee.

The Chairman of Ways and Means also acts as Deputy Speaker, and by the Deputy Speaker Act 1855 he can exercise the Speaker's statutory functions. In both capacities he is expected to show the same political

---

[56] Order in Council 1919.

[57] The traditional viscountcy was conferred on Mr. George Thomas in 1983.

[58] The mace, at first both a weapon and the Serjeant's emblem of office, has come to be regarded as the symbol of the authority of the House; but during prorogation the Serjeant-at-Arms reverts to being a member of the royal household, and the mace is returned to the Lord Chamberlain. See article in *The Times*, December 31, 1956, and letter from Edward F. Iwi to *The Times*, December 11, 1961.

[59] And formerly over the Committee of Ways and Means.

impartiality as the Speaker. He also has important duties in conjunction with the Chairman of Committees of the House of Lords relating to private Bills. There is a Deputy Chairman of Ways and Means, who may also act as Deputy Speaker. Neither the Chairman nor the Deputy Chairman of Ways and Means speaks or votes except in his official capacity. Hence their offices, and that of the Speaker, are called the three "non-voting" offices.[60]

House of Commons staff

The appointment and terms of employment of the staff who work in the various departments of the House of Commons—for example, the Administration Department, the Department of the Library, The Department of the Speaker—is subject to the control of the House of Commons Commission, a body established by statute in 1978.[61]

In addition to staff appointed by the Commission the Speaker appoints his own personal staff.

Staff appointed by the Commission and the Speaker's personal staff are entitled to the individual employment rights to which workers generally are entitled.[62]

Government and Opposition Whips[63]

The Government Whips consist of the Chief Whip (the Parliamentary Secretary to the Treasury),[64] the Deputy Chief Whip (the first junior Lord of the Treasury) and the Junior Whips (the other four junior Lords of the Treasury, and the Treasurer, Comptroller and Vice-Chamberlain of the Household). The Government Chief Whip is responsible to the Prime Minister and Leader of the House for fitting the government's programme of business into the time available during the session. He and the Chief Whips of the other parties constitute the "usual channels" through which business communications pass between the parties.

It is the duty of the Whips, whether acting for the government or not, to see that their parties are fully represented at important divisions and to arrange "pairs." They also keep their leaders informed of the state of feeling in the party. Again, they act as intermediaries between the leaders of the party and the constituency organisations, and can often influence the local association in its choice of candidate. The Chief Opposition Whip and Assistant Opposition Whip, nominated by the

---

[60] See Philip Marsden, *The Officers of the Commons, 1363–1978* (H.M.S.O. 1979).
[61] House of Commons (Administration) Act 1978. The Commission consists of the Speaker, the Leader of the House of Commons, a member of the House nominated by the Leader of the Opposition and three other members of the House, appointed by the House, not being Ministers of the Crown.
[62] Employment Protection (Consolidation) Act 1978, s.139.
[63] "Whip," originally "whipper-in," is a term derived from the hunting field.
[64] Formerly known as the patronage secretary, as it was through him that the patronage of the Treasury was administered and appointments to departments under its control were made.

Leader of the Opposition, and the Assistant Government Whip, now have statutory salaries.[65]

II. PARLIAMENTARY FRANCHISE AND ELECTIONS

Modern history of the parliamentary franchise[66]

The modern history of the parliamentary franchise begins with the Representation of the People Act 1832 ("the Reform Act") which extended the franchise by means of property qualifications from the landed gentry and borough caucuses to the middle classes. The indirect consequences of this Act and its successors were immense. The Commons became the predominant element in the government of the country, the Crown became detached from politics, and governments recognised that they depended on the will of the electorate.[67]

The Representation of the People Act 1867, by introducing certain occupation and lodger qualifications in the boroughs, gave the vote to many urban workers. The Representation of the People Act 1884 extended the lodger and householder qualifications to counties, thus giving the vote to many agricultural workers.

The Representation of the People Act 1918 introduced adult male suffrage, and for the first time gave the vote to women,[68] but only at the age of 30. The Act provided for both a residence and a business premises qualification. The Representation of the People Act 1945 assimilated the local government franchise to the parliamentary franchise in so far as every parliamentary elector was to have the local government franchise. The Representation of the People Act 1948 laid down that no elector should have more than one vote at a general election, abolished the business premises qualification and the university franchise[69] and provided that each constituency should henceforth elect only one member.[70]

The Representation of the People Act 1969, s.1, lowered the minimum age of voting from 21 to 18 years, in spite of an almost unanimous recommendation of a Speaker's Conference on Electoral Law in 1968 that the minimum age of voting should be 20 years.[71] This provision added about three million electors.

Qualifications for the franchise

The Representation of the People Act 1983, s.1 provides that a person, in order to qualify as a parliamentary elector in any constituency, must:

---

[65] Ministerial and other Salaries Act 1975.

[66] Sir Ivor Jennings, *Party Politics I: Appeal to the People* (1960); D.E. Butler, *The Electoral System in Britain since 1918* (2nd ed. 1963).

[67] The proportion of the electorate to the population was raised from 3 to 4 per cent. by the Act of 1832, from 18 to 47 per cent. by the Act of 1918, and to 65 per cent. by the Act of 1928.

[68] Women received the vote at the age of 21 by the Representation of the People (Equal Franchise) Act 1928.

[69] The university franchise was granted to Oxford and Cambridge Universities in the reign of James I: the other British universities were added from time to time: see Lord Salter, *Memoirs of a Public Servant* (1961) Chap. 19; Butler, *op. cit.* Chap. 5.

[70] S.1, which is still in force. The list of constituencies as amended from time to time (see *post*, p. 191) is contained in a Schedule to the Act.

[71] Cmnd. 3717, *Departmental Report on the Law relating to Parliamentary Elections.*

(a) be resident in the constituency on the qualifying date (October 10 in England, Wales and Scotland, September 15 in Northern Ireland, subject to the power of the Secretary of State to vary the date under section 13(2));

(b) on that date and on the date of the poll—
  (i) not be subject to any legal incapacity to vote (age apart); and
  (ii) be either a Commonwealth citizen[72] or a citizen of the Republic of Ireland; and

(c) be of voting age (that is, 18 years or over) on the date of the poll.[73]

A person so qualified is not entitled to vote in a constituency unless registered there in the register of parliamentary electors to be used at the election.

No one may vote more than once in the same constituency at any parliamentary election or in more than one constituency.

Residence

Some guidance is given to the courts by section 5 which provides, in particular, that regard shall be had to the purpose and other circumstances, as well as to the fact, of a person's presence at or absence from the address in question.[74] The broad, matter-of-fact approach by the courts to the meaning of residence is shown by the Court of Appeal decision in *Hipperson* v. *Newbury Electoral Officer*.[75] A number of women had lived for some time in tents, vehicles and other makeshift accommodation in the vicinity of Greenham Common United States Air Force Base. Their presence was sufficiently well known for letters addressed to them at the site to be delivered by the Post Office. The Court of Appeal held that they were resident in the constituency where they were living and entitled to register as voters. It was irrelevant that their living accommodation was such that under other legislation they might be described as homeless: "To import considerations based upon the standard of accommodation into qualification for the franchise would be to put the clock back to the days when the franchise depended upon a property qualification."[76] The Court also held that for the purpose of qualifying for the franchise it was irrelevant that the women

---

[72] British Nationality Act 1981, s.37; *post*, p. 452.

[73] For the purposes of the Representation of the People Acts a person attains a given age at the commencement of the relevant anniversary of his birthday, and not (as formerly at common law) at the commencement of the previous day: Representation of the People Act 1983, s.202(1).

[74] s.5(2) expressly deals with various examples of temporary absence, and s.6 provides that a merchant seaman's absence shall not prevent him being regarded as resident at the address where, but for his duties, he would normally live or at any hostel or club which provides accommodation for merchant seamen at which he commonly stays in the course of his employment.

[75] [1985] Q.B. 1060. See also *Fox* v. *Stirk and Bristol Electoral Registration Officer; Ricketts* v. *Cambridge City Electoral Registration Officer* [1970] 2 Q.B. 463 (C.A.) (Students living in college or hall of residence—or, presumably, in lodgings—entitled to be registered in that constituency.) See Susan Maidment, "The Case of the Student Voters" [1971] P.L. 25.

[76] [1985] Q.B. 1060, 1072 *per* Sir John Donaldson M.R.

might be trespassers or even guilty of criminal offences as a result of living where they had chosen to. Only an injunction forbidding a person to remain in a particular place would be effective to prevent presence ripening into residence.[77]

In England, Wales and Scotland it is only necessary to establish residence on the qualifying date. In Northern Ireland a voter must establish residence for the whole of the period of three months ending on the qualifying date, but not necessarily in the particular constituency in which he wishes to vote.[78]

Special rules have been laid down for three classes of voters:—

(1) Service voters[79]

Any of the following persons has the right, on making a "service declaration," to be entered on the register as a service voter in the constituency in which he or she would have been residing if he were not abroad: (a) a member of the forces, (b) any other person employed in the service of the Crown in a post outside the United Kingdom, (c) an employee of the British Council in a post outside the United Kingdom, (d) the wife or husband of a member of the forces, (e) the wife or husband of a person within (b) or (c) who is residing outside the United Kingdom to be with her husband (or his wife).

(2) Overseas electors[80]

A British citizen, otherwise entitled to vote in a parliamentary election, may do so even though not resident in the United Kingdom provided that he satisfies the definition of overseas elector and has made an overseas elector's declaration. An overseas elector must (a) be resident outside the United Kingdom; (b) have been included on a register in respect of residence in a particular constituency; and (c) the date by which residence was determined for inclusion in the register is not more than five years earlier than the qualifying date of the register in which the elector wishes to be included as an overseas elector.

(3) Mental patients[81]

Mental patients compulsorily detained in any place are not treated as being resident there for the purpose of registration as electors.[82] A voluntary mental patient may choose to be regarded as resident at the address other than the hospital in which he is a patient where he would normally be regarded as residing or he may make a declaration (if he is

---

[77] At p. 72.
[78] Representation of the People Act 1983, s.1(2). Before the Representation of the People Act 1949 there had been a general requirement of a qualifying period, fixed at six months by the Representation of the People Act 1918.
[79] ss.14–17.
[80] Representation of the People Act 1985, ss.1–3.
[81] Representation of the People Act 1983, s.7.
[82] *Semble*, nor are they resident anywhere else for the purpose of the Act.

able to do so without assistance) that he wishes to be treated as resident at the hospital.

Voters who, for various reasons are unable to attend in person at the appropriate polling station may apply to be treated as "absent voters" and exercise their franchise by proxies.[83]

The Electoral Register[84]

The Electoral Register is published on February 15, and remains in force for 12 months from February 16. Thus a householder in 1987 should include on the form Commonwealth citizens or Irish citizens resident at that address on October 10 who are 18 or over, or will have their eighteenth birthday during the life of the Register, *i.e.* by February 15, 1989. These latter may vote as soon as they become 18.

The electoral register for each constituency is prepared by the registration officer.[85] It is his duty to determine any claim by a person to be registered or any objection to any registration. Appeal lies to the County Court and then to the Court Appeal from whose decision there is no appeal.[86]

Disqualifications for the franchise

The following are subject to legal incapacity from voting, either under the Act of 1983 or under the pre-existing law:

  (i) Aliens
  (ii) Minors (under 18 years of age).
  (iii) Peers,[87] except Irish peers.[88]

Although it had always been assumed that Lords Spiritual are not eligible to vote, the Archbishop of Canterbury, who had been registered as an elector, voted in the 1983 election. In an ensuing debate in the House of Lords an assurance was given that Lords Spiritual would not attempt to vote in the future. Their legal right to vote is doubtful and the inclusion of the name of a Lord Spiritual on an electoral register could be challenged under section 10 of the Representation of the People Act 1983.[89]

  (iv) Convicted persons while detained in penal institutions or unlawfully at large, having escaped from confinement.[90]

---

[83] Representation of the People Act 1983, ss.19–22. See *Maccorquodale* v. *Bovack* 1984 S.L.T. 328 (Ct of Sess.).
[84] Representation of the People Act 1983, ss.9–13.
[85] s.8; *Post*, p. 193.
[86] s.10 and s.56 (See s.57 for Scottish Appeals). The procedure, in England, is exemplified by *Hipperson* v. *Newbury Electoral Officer* [1985] Q.B. 1060.
[87] *Beauchamp (Earl)* v. *Overseers of Madresfield* (1872) L.R. 8 C.P. 245. The former convention that peers should not take part in parliamentary election campaigns was broken in the general election of 1909–1910, and the sessional order was restricted in 1910 to peers who were lords-lieutenant: Roy Jenkins, *Mr. Balfour's Poodle*, pp. 73–74.
[88] Peerage Act 1963, s.5.
[89] P. Hughes and S. Palmer, "Voting Bishops" [1983] P.L. 393.
[90] Representation of the People Act 1983, s.3, as amended by the Representation of the People Act 1985, Sched. 4.

(v) A person who has been reported by an election court personally guilty, or who has been convicted of a *corrupt* practice is disqualified for *five years* from voting at any parliamentary election. In the case of an illegal practice the five-year disqualification is limited to that constituency.[91]

Conduct of elections[92]

The conduct of elections is now governed mainly by the Representation of the People Acts 1983 and 85 and the Parliamentary Constituencies Act 1986.

Writs for a general election in Great Britain are issued by the Crown under the Great Seal, which is kept by the Lord Chancellor.

By-elections

When a casual vacancy occurs while Parliament is in session the practice is for a by-election writ to be moved by the Chief Whip of the party that previously held the seat. The writ is issued by the Speaker. A Speaker's Conference in 1973 recommended that writs for by-elections should normally be moved within three months of a vacancy.[93] A controversial recommendation is that by convention the writ should continue to be moved only by the late member's party.

During a recess of the House of Commons it is the duty of the Speaker to issue a warrant for a new writ for electing a member when a seat falls vacant.[94]

Constituencies

Four permanent and independent Boundary Commissions for England, Scotland, Wales and Northern Ireland were set up in 1944. By the Parliamentary Constituencies Act 1986 the Commissions are to keep under review the representation in the House of Commons of the part of the United Kingdom with which they are concerned[95] and to submit reports to the Home Secretary as to the redistribution of seats at intervals of not less than ten or more than fifteen years. The criteria to be applied as far as practicable include numerical equality of voters between constituencies, respect for the boundaries of natural local communities, the distance to be travelled between parts of a single constituency, and the balance between the several parts of the United Kingdom.

The reports are to be laid before Parliament by the Secretary of State

---

[91] Representation of the People Act 1983, s.60. For corrupt and illegal practices, see *post* pp. 195–197.

[92] For an historical account, see Jennings, *op. cit.* Chaps. 1 and 3.

[93] *Conference on Electoral Law* (1973) Cmnd, 5000. Suggested exceptions are August (holiday month), April-May (local elections), mid-December to mid-February (new Electoral Register operates from mid-February), but within a maximum of four months. Some relaxation should be allowed in the fifth year of Parliament.

[94] Recess Elections Act 1975.

[95] This responsibility extends also to constituencies for elections to the European Assembly: European Assembly Elections Act 1981; *ante* p. 98.

as soon as may be, together with a draft Order in Council giving effect (with or without modifications[96]) to their recommendation. If the draft Order is approved by resolution of each House, the Secretary of State must submit it to Her Majesty in Council, and the Order will take effect on the dissolution of Parliament.

The number of constituencies allotted is not substantially greater or less than 613 for Great Britain (including at least 71 for Scotland and 35 for Wales) and 17 for Northern Ireland. The number is 650 at present. Parliamentary constituencies are still divided into county and district constituencies. Every constituency is to return a single member. The electorate of each constituency is to be as near as practicable to its "electoral quota," which is about 60,000 at present; but Scotland and Wales, containing large rural areas, are over-represented. Northern Ireland, because it had its own Parliament was under-represented until the passing of the House of Commons (Redistribution of Seats) Act 1979.[97]

Section 4 of the Act of 1986 provides that the validity of an Order in Council when made may not be called in question in any legal proceedings.

The court has refused to grant a mandatory injunction against a Boundary Commission to withdraw its recommendations after they had been reported to the Home Secretary: *Hammersmith Borough Council* v. *Boundary Commission for England*[98]; and the Court of Appeal has upheld the refusal to grant an injunction to restrain the Home Secretary from submitting to Her Majesty draft Orders in Council alleged to be *ultra vires: Harper* v. *Home Secretary*.[99] On the other hand, when in 1969 an elector applied for mandamus ordering the Home Secretary to lay before Parliament draft Orders in Council implementing the report of a Boundary Commission, the court did not disclaim jurisdiction on the ground of parliamentary privilege or otherwise; but the application was dismissed by consent when the Attorney-General assured the court that the Home Secretary undertook to perform this statutory duty.[1]

This last case arose out of the fact that Mr. Callaghan, the Home Secretary, had refrained from introducing draft Orders in Council to give effect to the latest recommendations of the Boundary Commission, on the ground that a major reorganisation of local government was envisaged and it was desirable that parliamentary and local government boundaries should as far as practicable be the same. Instead he introduced a House of Commons (Redistribution of Seats) Bill implementing the Commission's recommendations for Greater London, the government of which had been reorganised in 1963, but not the recommendations relating to the provinces. This Bill failed to pass the House of

---

[96] A statement of the reasons for any modifications must accompany the draft Order.

[97] The Kilbrandon Commission recommended that, on the setting up of Scottish and Welsh Assemblies, the number of Scottish and Welsh members of Westminster shoud be reduced; and the Hansard Society Commission on Electoral Reform (Lord Blake) (1976) recommended that Scotland, Wales and Northern Ireland should be put on the same basis as England for the purpose of delimitation of constituencies. See further, Appendix II; *post* p. 780.

[98] *The Times*, December 15, 1954.

[99] [1955] Ch. 238.

[1] *R.* v. *Home Secretary, ex p. McWhirter, The Times*, October 21, 1969 (D.C.).

Lords, and lapsed.[2] Mr. Callaghan then laid the draft Orders before Parliament, thus avoiding a possible order of mandamus, but moved that they should be *not* approved. The Orders were accordingly rejected by means of the Government's majority, which device made a mockery of the whole procedure.[3] The draft Orders were eventually re-introduced by the new Government and approved by both Houses after the general election of 1970.

In 1983 a number of leading figures in the Labour Party sought, by way of an application for judicial review,[4] to prevent the Boundary Commission for England from presenting their proposals for revising parliamentary constituency boundaries to the Home Secretary: *R. v. Boundary Commission ex p. Foot.*[5] The Court of Appeal held that although no appeal against the Commission's proposals lay to the Courts, judicial review was available to ensure that, like any body entrusted with discretionary powers by statute, the Commission had not exceeded their powers or had not exercised them "unreasonably."[6] The Court of Appeal concluded that it had not been shown that the Commission had exceeded its powers or misinterpreted the statutory guidelines which indicated the factors to be taken into account in revising constituency boundaries. The Court also indicated that had it felt it should interfere, the appropriate remedy would have been a declaration rather than an order for prohibition, which would have precluded Parliament from even considering the Commission's proposals. The House of Lords refused a petition for leave to appeal. Because of the public importance of the case the Appeal Committee consisted of five law lords instead of the normal three. Their decision avoided any risk of an unseemly conflict between the House of Commons and the House of Lords in its judicial capacity. To preclude the possibility of future conflicts it is suggested that legislation should provide that any form of court proceedings relating to the work of the Boundary Commissions the Court of Appeal[7] should be the final court of appeal, as in the cases of disputes relating to the electoral register[8] and decisions of the election court.[9]

Returning and registration officers

The *returning* officers are the sheriffs of counties, the chairmen of district councils and the mayors of London boroughs.[10] Most of their duties, however, are delegated to the *registration* officers of districts and

---

[2] See *ante*, p. 148.
[3] Lord Shawcross Q.C., in a letter to *The Times*, October 16, 1969, said that it seemed to involve "an almost unbelievable cynicism in regard to our legal and constitutional processes."
[4] *Post* Chap. 34.
[5] [1983] Q.B. 600.
[6] For the meaning of "unreasonable" in the context of judicial review see *post*, p. 669.
[7] Or, as appropriate the Court of Session or the Court of Appeal in Northern Ireland.
[8] *Ante*, p. 190.
[9] *Post*, p. 200.
[10] Local Government Act 1972, s.40. Separate provisions apply to Scotland and Northern Ireland.

London boroughs,[11] who are disqualified from membership of the House of Commons.[12]

The principal duty of the registration officer is to prepare and publish each year a register of parliamentary electors for each constituency in his area, and a register of local government electors.[13] He must further keep lists of voters entitled to vote by post or proxy.[14]

Returning officers, registration officers, presiding officers and others who commit breaches of their official duties are liable for penalties under section 63 of the Representation of the People Act 1983[15] but no action for damages now lies against them: *cf. Ashby* v. *White.*[16]

Election campaign

Part II of the Representation of the People Act 1983 as amended by the Representation of the People Act 1985 makes detailed provisions in relation to election campaigns.

Candidates

A candidate must submit a nomination paper to the returning officer within the prescribed time between a dissolution of Parliament and polling day. The nomination must be signed by the proposer and seconder, and eight other electors.[17] To be valid the nomination form must be accompanied by the deposit of £500 which is forfeited if the candidate fails to obtain one twentieth of the votes cast.[18]

The returning officer may declare that a nomination paper is invalid if it fails to satisfy the rules relating to signatures and deposit or if the candidate is disqualified by the Representation of the People Act 1981, (*i.e.* is serving a sentence of imprisonment of more than one year, or of an indefinite period).[19] A candidate disqualified from membership of the House of Commons, on any ground other than that contained in the 1981 Act, may be nominated and stand for election. The validity of his election must be subsequently challenged in the Election Court,[20] as for

---

[11] Local Government Act 1972, s.39. Separate provisions apply to Scotland and Northern Ireland.

[12] House of Commons Disqualification Act 1975. A returning officer is disqualified by parliamentary custom for the constituency for which he acts.

[13] These registers are to be combined, as far as practicable, with "L" marked against the names of persons registered as local government electors only, *ante,* p. 187.

[14] Representation of the People Act 1985, ss.6–7.

[15] As amended, Representation of the People Act 1985, Sched. 4.

[16] (1703) 2 Ld. Raym. 938; *post,* p. 249.

[17] Before the Ballot Act 1872 candidates were nominated by oral declaration to the presiding officer on the public "hustings."

[18] Representation of the People Act 1985, s.13. Under the 1983 Act the deposit was £150 but the candidate had to obtain one eighth of the votes cast if his deposit were not to be forfeited.

[19] Representation of the People Act 1983, Sched. 1, Pt. II, r. 12; *ante* p. 178.

[20] *Post,* p. 200.

example, happened in the case of Viscount Stansgate (Tony Benn)[21] or by way of reference to the Privy Council under the House of Commons Disqualification Act 1975, section 7.[22]

A candidate is required to have an election agent, though he may be his own agent.[23] Stringent limits are set on the permissible amount of election expenses,[24] and the purposes for which they may be incurred. Election expenses must be paid through the election agent, and they must be declared and published.

Every candidate is entitled for the purpose of holding public meetings to the use of a suitable room in a school within the constituency.[25]

Corrupt practices include personation, bribery, treating and undue influence.[26] These were ill-defined offences at common law. Corrupt practices continued after the Reform Act 1832, and a significant improvement only came with the Parliamentary Elections Act 1868.[27] Their virtual elimination followed the Act of 1883,[28] which first set a limit to election expenses.[29]

Illegal practices include false statements as to candidates[30]; corruptly inducing a person's withdrawal from candidature[31]; use of unauthorised premises; broadcasting on radio or television in the United Kingdom items about a constituency pending a parliamentary or local government election without the consent of any candidate who takes

---

[21] *In re Parliamentary Election for Bristol South East* [1964] 2 Q.B. 257.

[22] *Ante*, p. 181.

[23] Most candidates are adopted by the committee of the constituency branch of their party, and sitting Members of Parliament are usually re-adopted in the same way; *cf.* Nigel Nicolson, *People and Parliament* (1958). Party "primaries" have been held by some Conservative constituency associations in recent years, in which the candidate is adopted on the vote of the registered members of the local party present. There is a recent tendency for some Labour constituency associations, captured by a left-wing caucus, to displace the sitting M.P. as candidate for the next general election. The Hansard Society Commission recommended the general adoption of party primaries for choice of candidates.

[24] The Representation of the People Act 1983, s.76 sets the amount at £2700, plus a capitation fee for the number of entries in the register of electors. This does not include postage, broadcasting time or personal expenses. The Secretary of State may by order vary the figures in the section to take account of a change in the value of money: s.76A added by Representation of the People Act 1985, s.14 which repealed s.16(3) of the 1983 Act.

[25] Representation of the People Act 1983, s.95, which defines school as "county or voluntary" in England and Wales, and "not independent" in Scotland. *Webster* v. *Southwark L.B.C.* [1983] Q.B. 698 (Writ of sequestration to enforce right of National Front candidate).

[26] Representation of the People Act 1983, ss.60, 113–115.

[27] *Post*, p. 200.

[28] Corrupt and Illegal Practices Prevention Act 1883.

[29] Cornelius O'Leary, *The Elimination of Corrupt Practices in British Elections, 1868–1911* (1962). In Northern Ireland personation is still regarded as a problem that requires the taking of special measures. By the Election (Northern Ireland) Act 1985, an elector may not vote unless he is able to identify himself by production of one of the documents specified in the Act, *e.g.* a driving licence or passport. This provision was applied for the first time in the by-elections held in January 1986, following the mass resignation of the Ulster Unionists M.P.s in protest at the concluding of the Hillsborough Agreement.

[30] Representation of the People Act 1983, s.106.

[31] Representation of the People Act 1983, s.106.

part in the item[32]; broadcasting on radio or television from outside the United Kingdom in connection with a parliamentary or local government election otherwise than as arranged by the British Broadcasting Corporation[33] or Independent Broadcasting Authority; payment for exhibition of election notices, except to a commercial advertising agent; not printing the name and address of the printer on election publications; employment of paid canvassers; and any other payments contrary to, or in excess of, those allowed by the Acts.[34]

There is scope for difference of opinion as to what exactly constitutes an election expense in the case of issuing publications "with a view to promoting or procuring the election of a candidate at the parliamentary election in the constituency" under section 75 of the Representation of the People Act 1983. In R. v. Tronoh Mines Ltd.,[35] where advertisements had been issued by the sugar industry against nationalisation ("Mr. Cube") McNair J. held that the relevant section of the Act of 1949 (which prohibits expenses not authorised by election agent on issuing advertisements) is intended to prohibit expenditure on advertisements *supporting a particular candidate in a particular constituency*, which, if authorised by the election agent, would form part of the election expenses for that constituency: it is not intended to prohibit expenditure on advertisements supporting the interest of a particular party generally in all constituencies, at any rate at the time of the general election, and not supporting a particular candidate in a particular constituency. In Grieve v. Douglas-Home[36] an action was brought to have Sir Alec Douglas-Home's election at the general election in 1964 declared void, on the ground that he had not included in his return the expenses of party political broadcasts on behalf of the Conservative Party. It was held that no corrupt or illegal practice had been committed by anyone, as the motive of the BBC and ITA in presenting party political broadcasts was to give information to the public, and not to promote Sir Alec's election to Parliament. In D.P.P. v. Luft,[37] where pamphlets had been issued urging voters "Don't vote National Front" and accusing members of the National Front of being liars and fascists, the House of Lords held that an offence could be found by establishing an intention on the part of the person incurring the expense to prevent the election of a particular candidate or candidates.[38]

The statutory restrictions on election expenses in individual constituencies do not apply to the publication of any matter relating to the election in newspapers or other periodicals or in broadcasts by the BBC and I.B.A.[39] (Nor is there any limit at all on expenditure between elections.) A matter of particular concern to the smaller parties is how the BBC and I.B.A. decide to allocate party political broadcasts between and

---

[32] Representation of the People Act 1983 s.93.
[33] s.92. See Marshall v. B.B.C. [1979] 1 W.L.R. 1071.
[34] Representation of the People Act 1949, ss.108–112.
[35] [1952] 1 All E.R. 697; [1952] 1 T.L.R. 461.
[36] 1965 S.L.T. 186 (Scottish Election Court: Lords Migdale and Kilbrandon).
[37] [1977] A.C. 962. Cf. C. Munro, "Elections and Expenditure" [1976] P.L. 300.
[38] C. Munro, "Legal Controls on Election Broadcasting," in Political Communications, The General Election Campaign of 1983 (I. Crewe and M. Harrop, eds., 1986).
[39] Representation of the People Act 1983, s.75(1).

during election campaigns. The task is undertaken, in a manner typical of the British Constitution, by a non-statutory body, the Committee on Party Political Broadcasts which consists of officials from the broadcasting authorities and representatives of the various parties.[40] It does not publish its rules but apparently relies largely on the votes which each party has obtained at the previous election, with weight being given to subsequent by-election results. Thus a party—such as the Social Democratic Party—which appears for the first time between elections—is at a disadvantage.

Apart from party political broadcasts, there may be questions about the fairness with which the broadcasting authorities provide publicity in their news and current affairs programmes for the various parties. In *R. v. Broadcasting Complaints Commission, ex p. Owen*[41] the Leader of the Social Democratic Party sought judicial review of the refusal of the Commission to investigate his complaint that the allocation of time to the various parties was "unjust or unfair."[42] The Divisional Court concluded, after some hesitation, that the Commission had jurisdiction to consider the complaint: the statutory provisions could cover allegations of general unfairness as opposed to unfairness or imbalance in a particular programme. But the Commission was entitled to refuse to adjudicate on the complaint because it raised a question of fairness of editorial policy which could only be settled by expressing a view about a fundamental issue of British politics, *i.e.* the weight to be given to the seats held by parties as opposed to the votes polled. Presumably, in the view of the Court, since the current electoral law allows for a disparity between seats and votes it cannot be unreasonable for broadcasting authorities to allocate time and publicity by seats rather than votes.

The ballot

The Parliamentary and Municipal Elections Act 1872, commonly known as the "Ballot Act," made the vitally important innovation of substituting a secret ballot (by placing a cross on a ballot paper in a polling booth) for open election at the hustings. These provisions are now contained in the Representation of the People Act 1983. Each voter's ballot paper has a number printed on the back, which number is also printed on the counterfoil as it may be necessary in later *judicial* proceedings to discover whether there has been personation or plural voting; but such strict precautions as are humanly possible are made to ensure that no unauthorised person can ascertain, by a comparison of the ballot paper with the counterfoil, for which candidate a given elector voted.

A description of the candidate, not exceeding six words, is allowed if desired in the nomination paper and on the ballot paper.[43] The object is to enable a candidate's party to be shown, which was previously forbidden.

---

[40] Colin Munro, *The Times*, February 12, 1982. Alan E. Boyle, "Political Broadcasting, Fairness and Administrative Law," [1986] P.L. 562.

[41] [1985] Q.B. 1153; *post*, p. 668.

[42] Broadcasting Act 1981, s.54.

[43] Representation of the People Act 1983, s.23 and Sched. 1, r. 6(2) and (3); r. 19.

The voting system[44]

The system of voting at parliamentary elections in the United Kingdom is commonly called "first past the post" (relative majority, plurality), whereby voting takes place in single-member constituencies and the candidate with the highest number of votes is declared elected. But (i) the successful candidate is often elected with fewer than 50 per cent. of the votes cast; (ii) the representation of the parties in the House of Commons does not accurately reflect their strength among the electorate, the party with most votes usually getting a disproportionally large number of seats, while small parties (*e.g.* the Liberals and Social Democrats) are under-represented[45]; and (iii) the result of general election usually depends on the results in a small number of marginal constituencies. The Royal Commission on Electoral Systems in 1910[46] admitted that our electoral system does not profess to provide representation of all parties in proportion to their voting strength. "A general election," they said, "is in fact considered by a large portion of the electorate of this country as practically a referendum on the question of which of two governments shall be returned to power." Proposals for proportional representation or alternative or single transferable vote were decisively rejected by Speaker's Conferences on Electoral Reform in 1944[47] and again in 1968.[48] The Liberal party has naturally called for proportional representation for some years, and support for the proposal has widened recently under the influence of the recommendation of the Kilbrandon Commission concerning elections to Scottish and Welsh Assemblies as well as the ambitions of the Scottish National Party. In Northern Ireland proportional representation was introduced in 1973 for Assembly elections and in 1978 for elections to the European Assembly. The European Commission on Human Rights has rejected a claim by the Liberal Party that the current system of voting in England, Wales and Scotland is in breach of Article 3 of the First Protocol to the European Convention on Human Rights which guarantees "the free expression of the will of the people."[49]

The British system is also adopted by the United States, Canada and New Zealand. A similar system operates in France, except that if in any constituency no one candidate receives an absolute majority over all his opponents a second and final ballot is held in that constituency a week later. The single transferable vote (STV), the method used in the Republic of Ireland, and in Northern Ireland, requires multiple-member constituencies of members.[50] Multiple-member constituencies are also required for the various kinds of "Party List" system used in Belgium, Italy and Scandinavian countries. The candidates are nominated and

---

[44] See Enid Lakeman, *Nine Democracies* (1975).
[45] In the 1983 General Election the Conservative Party obtained 42.4 per cent. of the votes polled and 61.1 per cent. of the seats in the House of Commons. The SDP/Liberal Alliance obtained 25.4 per cent. of the votes and 3.5 per cent. of the seats.
[46] Cd. 5163.
[47] Cmd. 6534.
[48] Cmnd. 3550.
[49] *Liberal Party* v. *United Kingdom*; (1980) 4 E.H.R.R. 106 A. Boyle, "Electoral Fairness and the Liberal Party," [1980] P.L. 168.
[50] The Northern Ireland Act 1982 provides for a minimum of four members in one Assembly constituency and a maximum of ten in another, Sched. 2, para. 11.

placed in order on the List by the parties, and there is proportional representation as between the parties. An elector votes for a party, and the party is allotted in each constituency a share of seats proportional to the votes it obtains. Variations on this theme give electors more or less opportunity to show a preference for particular candidates. West Germany has a mixed system of "first past the post" corrected by the Party List. Proportional representation in its various forms is said to lead to coalitions involving jockeying for position by the parties and resulting in a succession of weak governments, whereas our system is said to favour strong government. Recently, however, the view has been gaining strength in this country that coalitions provide continuity of policy, and discourage that polarisation of the two main parties that we have been witnessing. That still leaves the fact that single-member constituencies are said to foster a personal relationship between the member and his constituents of all parties which members of Parliament value highly.[51]

Disputed elections

The King and Council originally settled election disputes, but as early as the reign of Richard II the Commons began to remonstrate against this practice. James I in the proclamation summoning his first Parliament specifically forbad the choice of bankrupts and outlaws. Sir Francis Goodwin was elected (against his will) for Buckinghamshire, but the Clerk of the Crown refused to receive the return on the ground that Goodwin was an outlaw, and Sir John Fortescue, a Privy Councillor, was elected in his place. The case of *Goodwin* v. *Fortescue* (1604)[52] followed, the real struggle being in the background between the Commons and the King. The Commons disputed Goodwin's outlawry, and contended that in any event outlawry did not disqualify him. The King and the Commons consented to submit the dispute to the judges, but no such reference took place. Finally, James admitted the right of the Commons to judge disputed election returns.[53] The Commons' privilege was confirmed by the Court of Exchequer Chamber and the House of Lords during the protracted litigation in *Barnardiston* v. *Soame* (1674–1689).[54]

---

[51] See further, *Report of Hansard Society Commission on Electoral Reform* (Lord Blake) (1976) recommending for elections to the House of Commons the Additional Member System (AMS) or alternatively STV; H.W.R. Wade *Constitutional Fundamentals* (1980), Chap. 2; S.E. Finer, *The Changing British Party System 1945–1979* (1980); V. Bogdanor, *The People and the Party System* (1981); Dawn Oliver "Reform of the Electoral System," [1983] P.L. 108. See also K.R. Gladdish, A.T.W. Liddell and P.J. Giddings *M.P.'s Perceptions of the British Electoral System* (1984). (Almost 80 per cent. of Conservative and Labour M.P.s approve of the present system, largely because of the link which they consider it fosters between M.P. and voters)

[52] 2 St.Tr. 91.

[53] The Commons later claimed the privilege of settling the rights of electors, and this gave rise to the celebrated cases of *Ashby* v. *White* and *Paty's Case, post,* Chap. 12.

[54] (1674) 6 St.Tr. 1063, 1092; (1689) 6 St.Tr. 1119; Broom, *Constitutional Law* (2nd ed.), pp. 800, 839. This was an action against the sheriff for falsely and maliciously making a double return at the Suffolk by-election in 1672. The Parliamentary Elections (Returns) Act 1689, which subsequently allowed such an action, was repealed by the Representation of the People Act 1949; see Robin L. Sharwood, *"Barnardiston* v. *Soame*: a Restoration Drama" (1964) 4 Melbourne Univ. Law Rev. 502.

After *Goodwin* v. *Fortescue* disputed elections were tried first for a time by Select Committees of the House, then by a committee of the whole House, the decisions tending to be made on party lines, and from 1770 by Select Committees under the provisions of various statutes. Eventually the Parliamentary Elections Act 1868, passed after the very corrupt general election of 1865, handed jurisdiction in disputed elections over to the Court of Commons Pleas, proper safeguards being added to secure to the Commons their privileges. By the Parliamentary Elections and Corrupt Practices Act 1879 this jurisdiction was, with similar safeguards, committed to two judges of the High Court.

Election court

These provisions are now re-enacted in Part III of the Representation of the People Act 1983. An election petition may be presented by: (a) a person who voted or had the right to vote, (b) a person claiming to have had the right to be elected or returned, or (c) a person alleging that he was a candidate.[55] The election court consists, in England, of two judges of the Queen's Bench Division, acting without a jury. They have the powers of the High Court, and may sit in the constituency for which the election was held. Discovery and interrogatories are allowed. If the person elected is found to be disqualified, and if the electors knew the facts on which his disqualification was based, the election court may declare the candidate with the next highest number of votes to have been elected.[56] If the circumstances warrant, an election may simply be held to be void.

Appeal lies on a question of law with the leave of the High Court to the Court of Appeal, whose decision is final, the Commons not being willing that such questions should be decided by the House of Lords.

Corresponding provisions in the cases of Scotland and Northern Ireland confer jurisdiction on two judges of the Court of Session and the High Court or the Court of Appeal of Northern Ireland.

The election court certify their finding to the Speaker. Section 144 of the 1983 Act provides that the House shall order the certificate and report to be entered in their Journals, and shall give the necessary direction for confirming or altering the return, or for issuing a writ for a new election, as the case may be.[57]

---

[55] *Cf.* application to the Judicial Committee of the Privy Council for a declaration under the House of Commons Disqualification Act 1975, s.7; *ante*, p. 181.

[56] See *Re Parliamentary Election for Bristol South-East* [1964] 2 Q.B. 247; [1961] 3 W.L.R. 577; *ante*, p. 177. This case was heard in London. See also *Beresford-Hope* v. *Lady Sandhurst* (1889) L.R. 23 Q.B.D. 79; *Re Mid-Ulster Election Petition, Beattie* v. *Mitchell* [1958] N.I. 143; *Re Fermanagh and South Tyrone Election Petition, Grosvenor* v. *Clarke* [1958] N.I. 151.

[57] The Commons have the privilege, however, of deciding whether a person who has been duly elected shall be allowed to sit in the House; *post*, Chap. 12.

CHAPTER 10

PARLIAMENTARY PROCEDURE[1]

I. THE NATURE OF PARLIAMENTARY PROCEDURE

THE functions of Members of Parliament are not only, or indeed primarily, legislation (including taxation) but cover the discussion of policy and current affairs, and—especially in the Commons—the supervision of national finance and scrutiny of the administration. This chapter deals with parliamentary procedure generally, and the ordinary legislative process; while the next chapter covers national finance and scrutiny of the administration. The emphasis, for obvious reasons, is on the House of Commons.

Content

The content of parliamentary procedure may be divided into the following parts:

1. *Forms of proceedings, e.g.* the various stages in the passing of a Bill the process of debate by motion, question and division; the methods by which the Commons control the administration in supply, questions to Ministers and motions for the adjournment.

2. *Machinery,* including the officers of each House (especially the Speaker of the Commons), committees and "Whips."

3. *Rules of procedure* in the strict sense, *i.e.* directions which govern the working of the forms of proceedings and the machinery of each House; *e.g.* the rule that a public Bill may be presented without an Order of the House; the rule that the principle of a Bill is decided on the second reading; and the rules regulating the powers and duties of the Speaker in the conduct of debate and the maintenance of order.

4. *Parliamentary conventions, i.e.* rules not enforced by the Chair but by the public opinion of the House; for example, the rule that the Government will reply to reports made by Select Committees which touch on the actions of a government department.

Rules of procedure vary considerably in importance, that is to say, in

---

[1] See Erskine May, *Parliamentary Practice* (20th ed., 1983).
See also Anson, *Law and Custom of the Constitution* (5th ed., 1922; Gwyer) Vol. I Chap. 6; Lord Campion, *Introduction to the Procedure of the House of Commons* (3rd ed., 1958); Sir Ivor Jennings, *Parliament* (2nd ed., 1957); C.R. Niven, *Notes on Parliamentary Procedure* (Hansard Society); *Parliamentary Reform, 1933–1960* (Hansard Society, 2nd ed., 1967); K. Bradshaw and D. Pring, *Parliament and Congress* (1972); Bernard Crick, *The Reform of Parliament* (2nd ed., 1968); J. A. G. Griffith, *Parliamentary Scrutiny of Government Bills* (1974); Walkland and Ryle, *The Commons Today* (1981); George and Evans "Parliamentary Reform—The Internal View" in Judge *The Politics of Parliamentary Reform* (1983), Chap. 4, Philip Norton (ed.) *Parliament in the 1980s* (1985).

the extent to which they are essential or useful to the exercise of their functions by each House. At one end of the scale is the Standing Order of the House of Commons that expenditure must be proposed by the Crown, which is of great constitutional importance; at the other end come rules, such as that the "Ayes" divide to the right and the "Noes" to the left, where it does not matter what the rule is so long as there is one.

Historical development

The forms and rules show traces of their origin in various stages of historical development. So far as the development of the Commons procedure is concerned, Lord Campion (a former Clerk of the House of Commons) suggested the following periods:

(i) From the establishment of Parliament to the beginning of the Commons Journals, during which period constitutional forms came to be settled (c. 1300–1547).

(ii) The period of "ancient usage," from the beginning of the Journals to the Restoration (1547–1660).

(iii) The period of later "parliamentary practice," from the Restoration to the great Reform Act (1660–1832).

(iv) The period of modern Standing Orders (from 1833 to the present day).[2]

Sources of parliamentary procedure

The sources of parliamentary procedure may be classified as follows:

(i) *Practice, i.e.* the unwritten part of procedure;

(ii) *Standing Orders;* also Sessional Orders and ad hoc resolutions;

(iii) *Rulings from the Chair, i.e.* by the Speaker or Chairman of Committees;

(iv) *Acts of Parliament* regulating certain aspects of the procedure of both Houses.

The greater part of the procedure of the House of Commons is unwritten and has to be collected from the Journal[3] (made from the Votes and Proceedings[4]), reports of debates[5] and personal experience. Standing Orders are merely appendant to the unwritten part, which they presuppose.[6] The well-known rules that a Bill is "read" three times, and that certain kinds of amendments may be moved on the second or third reading, are not contained in Standing Orders but are part of unwritten practice. In ascertaining what is the practice of the

---

[2] Campion, *op. cit.* p. 5.

[3] The permanent official record of the proceedings of the House, compiled from the minute books of the Clerks at the table, and published annually.

[4] The daily record of the proceedings of the House.

[5] For "Hansard," see *post*, p. 240.

[6] The bulk of House of Commons Standing Orders in fact relate to private business, *i.e.* the procedure on private Bills. For the division of the *content* of Standing Orders into laws, customs and conventions, see *ante*, p. 115. The Standing Orders referred to here, and elsewhere, are those of November 12, 1986 (1986–87, H.C. 1).

House reliance is placed on precedents as recorded in the Journals. The practice before 1832 was evolved mainly in order to facilitate and encourage debate.

Standing Orders are passed in the ordinary way by resolution of the House; but it is expressly provided that they shall last beyond the end of the session, otherwise they would be terminated by prorogation. The main purpose of Standing Orders relating to public business is to enable more business to be done by speeding up debate.[7] Sessional Orders are passed for the session only, and *ad hoc* Orders or resolutions for the particular occasion; the former are often experimental and both are used to regulate the order of business. A Standing Order or a Sessional Order can be set aside by an Order of the same kind, and either can be suspended by an *ad hoc* Order. An express Order of any kind overrides a rule of practice.

The function of the Speaker or Chairman in giving rulings is mainly interpretative and declaratory, and involves the application of practice and Standing Orders in particular circumstances as they arise.

Acts of Parliament modifying parliamentary procedure are few. They are passed in order to bind both Houses, so that one House cannot change the rule without the other. Some of the more important examples are the Exchequer and Audit Departments Act 1866, the Parliamentary Elections Act 1868,[8] the Parliament Acts 1911 and 1949, the Provisional Collection of Taxes Act 1968, the Statutory Orders (Special Procedure) Acts 1945 and 1965 and the National Audit Act 1983. Acts of Parliament, of course, have overriding authority over the Orders of both Houses or either of them.

The House of Lords procedure contains a larger proportion of Standing Orders. Their purpose is rather to declare practice than to accelerate business. About a quarter of the Lords Standing Orders relate to privileges.

The rules relating to private business (*i.e.* private Bills) are mainly contained in a separate set of Standing Orders of each House.

II. PROCEDURE IN THE COMMONS

Order of business

The House meets at 2.30 p.m.[9] on Mondays to Thursdays, and at 9.30 a.m. on Fridays. The usual order of business on Mondays to Thursdays is:

(1) prayers; (2) business taken immediately after prayers, *e.g.* motions

---

[7] See Ilbert, *Parliament* (3rd ed. Carr), pp. 117–118. *Cf.* Lord Chorley, "Bringing the Legislative Process into Contempt" [1968] P.L. 52, 54; "the caterpillar speed of the legislative process is really one of its outstanding values."

[8] Now the Representation of the People Act 1983 Part III.

[9] The mornings are largely occupied by committee work "upstairs," by Ministers in their departments and by lawyers in the courts. Morning sittings were introduced as an experiment in 1966 for less important and non-contentious business, but were abandoned as a failure after a time in exchange for a Standing Order (S.O. No. 10) allowing a Minister to move that a debate continuing after 10 p.m. be suspended until the following morning.

for new writs, and private business; (3) questions for oral answer, and private notice questions[10]; (4) business taken after questions, *e.g.* ministerial statements,[11] proposals to move the adjournment under S.O. No. 20 (urgency motions), consideration of Lords' amendments, raising matters of privilege[12]; (5) business taken "at the commencement of public business," *e.g.* presentation (first reading) of public Bills, and government motions regulating the business of the House; (6) consideration of report of Committee of Privileges; (7) public business, *i.e.* mainly "Orders of the Day" (including the stages of public Bills and Committees of the whole House) and notices of motion; (8) certain business motions by Ministers; (9) business exempted from the 10-o'clock rule (including Finance, Consolidated Fund, and Appropriation Bills); (10) presentation of public petition[13]; (11) adjournment motions. Many of these items are omitted on Thursdays.

If the House has not previously adjourned, it sits until half an hour after the motion for adjournment has been proposed, either at 10 p.m. (Friday 2.30 p.m.) for ordinary business or at the conclusion of exempted business. Sittings on Saturday are rare,[14] and on Sunday are confined to emergencies.

Rules of debate

The rules of debate that have been developed over the years are designed to ensure orderly conduct, the dignity of the House and the right of a minority to be heard. A debate is always on a motion, *e.g.* "that the Bill be read a second time"; and every matter is determined on a question put by the Speaker and resolved by the House in the affirmative or negative. A member who wishes to speak must rise in his place and "catch the Speaker's eye." Privy Councillors have generally a right to priority in being called upon to speak: this gives an advantage to present and former Cabinet Ministers at the expense of back-benchers. A member may only speak once in the House to the same question, except to raise points of order or to correct misrepresentations of fact. All remarks must be addressed to the Chair.[15]

There are rules to ensure relevancy and to avoid repetition, but pro-

---

[10] See post Chap. 11 p. 228.

[11] A class of "ministerial written statements" has been made available at the end of question time since 1972.

[12] Since 1978 a Member may only table a motion relating to a complaint of breach of privilege after he has first made a written complaint to the Speaker and he has decided that the matter should have precedence.

[13] It is an ancient liberty of the citizen to petition Parliament to remedy some grievance; *Chaffers* v. *Goldsmid* [1894] 1 Q.B. 186, although a member cannot be compelled to present a petition. However, few petitions are presented nowadays and they are no longer debated in the House, so that they have lost their importance. Their place may be said to have been taken by members' questions.

[14] The House met on a Saturday during the Falklands conflict see H.C. Deb., Vol. 21, col. 633 (April 3, 1982).

[15] In most assemblies this is an excellent rule as an aid in maintaining order. It is in contrast to the practice in the House of Lords, where it is evidently not needed and peers address the House.

posals to limit the length of speeches have hitherto been rejected. No reference may be made to the House of Lords under that name (it is commonly referred to as "another place"); nor to any matter *sub judice* in a court of law. The name of the Queen must not be mentioned either disrespectfully or in order to influence the House.[16] No treasonable or seditious words are allowed, nor may a person speak to obstruct business. Members must not be referred to by name, but as "the Hon. Member for Camford," etc. nor may any offensive expressions against members be used or personal charges made. If a member refuses to withdraw an objectionable remark, he may be suspended. No allusion may be made to a debate of the same session on any question not at the time under discussion. A member may refer to notes but must not read his speech. It is a rule of the House that a member who has a relevant pecuniary interest, whether direct or indirect, in a question should declare his interest if he speaks, and must not vote on it.[17] This rule applies to all proceedings of the House and its Committees.

Urgency motions

Under Standing Order No. 20 a member who has given proper notice to the Speaker may, at the commencement of public business, propose in an application lasting not more than three minutes, to move the adjournment of the House on *"a specified and important matter that should have urgent consideration."* If the Speaker rules that the matter is proper to be discussed under the Standing Order—having regard to the extent to which it concerns the administrative responsibilities of Ministers and the possibility of the matter being brought before the House in time by other means—and the House gives leave, the motion is usually debated at the commencement of public business next day, but exceptionally at 7 p.m. on the same day. The Speaker does not have to give reasons for his decision. The present content of this Standing Order dates mainly from 1967 when the House agreed to recommendations from a Select Committee[18] which has meant that such debates take place

---

[16] Disraeli when Prime Minister, with Queen Victoria's approval, obtained the permission of the House in 1876 to use the Queen's name in debate, in order to rebut a statement made in a public speech that the Queen had asked two previous Prime Ministers for the title of Empress of India: Robert Blake, *Disraeli* (1966), p. 563.

[17] A Select Committee in 1969 recommended that in any debate, or communication with other members or with Ministers or civil servants, a member should disclose any relevant pecuniary interest or benefit, whether direct or indirect: *Report from Select Committee on Members' Interests* (1969). The House, in 1975, approved the recommendations of a Select Committee on Members' Interests that a Register of Members' Interests should be kept and made available for inspection, in which members should be expected to disclose the source of certain interests that might influence their parliamentary conduct. These include remunerated company directorships, employment or offices, trades, professions or vocations; financial sponsorships as candidate or member; land or property of substantial value; and companies in which a member owns more than 1 per cent. of shares. In 1976 a Select Committee on Members' Interests was established (S.O. No. 128). See Erskine May, *op. cit.* pp. 435–439.

[18] Second Report from Select Committee on Procedure 1966–67 (urgent and topical debates) H.C. 282.

more frequently than before.[19] Examples are the inquiry into losses incurred by the Crown Agents in December 1977 and the policing of the Miners Strike in April 1984.

Suspension of member

When a member contumaciously declines to accept a ruling of the Speaker, *e.g.* by refusing to "withdraw" an offensive remark, or is guilty of misbehaviour or flagrantly breaks the rules of the House, the Speaker may be asked to "name" him. The question is then put that the member be suspended from the service of the House, and if the motion is carried he is suspended on the first occasion until the fifth day, on the second occasion in the same session until the twentieth day, and on a subsequent occasion until further order or until the end of the session. A suspended member must withdraw from the precincts of the House.

Divisions

When the Speaker closes a debate by "putting the question," he first senses the feeling of the House by asking members to say "Aye" or "No," but in any important matter the members challenge the Speaker's opinion and he orders a division. Electric bells are rung, the lobbies are cleared, and after two minutes[20] the Speaker puts the question again. Unless the division is then "called off" the members now present divide by filing through the two lobbies, their names being checked and the numbers counted by two members nominated to act as tellers for each lobby. The figures are then read out to the Speaker by the senior teller for the majority.

The quorum of 40, including the Speaker, was established in 1641. If a division reveals that fewer than that number of members are present the business under discussion stands adjourned and the House proceeds to the next business.[21]

Closure[22]

This is a device (known as "the Gag") for bringing to an end a debate or a speech at any time. A member moves "that the question be now put," and if the Speaker or Chairman accepts the motion and it is carried in a division, not fewer than 100 members voting in its support, further debate on the subject must cease. This is used frequently, but the Speaker has a discretion to refuse the closure where he considers

---

[19] Before 1967 only 15 such debates took place in 20 years. The Select Committee thought that about five emergency debates *each* session would be about right. In the 10 years up to May 1985, there were 21 emergency debates: See First Report from the Select Committee on Procedure: *The Operation of S.O. No. 10* (as it was numbered until November 1986) (1985–86; H.C. 42). The recommendation of this Committee to limit speeches on the application for the adjournment to three minutes was accepted by the House in February 1986.

[20] The Lords have four minutes in which to cover the distance to their Chamber.

[21] The "count" has been abolished. See S.O. No. 40.

[22] S.O. No. 35, 36.

that the rights of the minority would be infringed, or that the motion is an abuse of the rules of the House.

"Guillotine"[23]

An allocation of Time (or "Guillotine") order is a closure by compartments. In order to ensure that the remaining proceedings on a public Bill in the House or in Committee are speeded up, a Minister may move either (a) that specified dates and days be allotted to the various stages of the Bill, or (b) that the Committee shall report the Bill to the House by a certain date, leaving the details to the Business Committee of the House or a business sub-committee of the Committee. This device arouses opposition, and is used sparingly. Voluntary timetabling is usually attempted first, though that often fails. The Guillotine motion for the Scotland and Wales Bill 1976 was defeated,[24] but the motion for the Scotland and Wales Bill 1977 was successful. More recently it has been used for the British Nationality Bill 1981 and the Local Government Bill 1985.

Committees of the Commons[25]

The Commons have long made use of committees for various purposes. Sometimes a matter was committed to a single Privy Councillor, more often the committee was a Committee of the whole House. The main function of Standing Committees has been to consider and amend public Bills, thus doing what the House could do if it had time. Select Committees do the kind of things that the House as a whole could not easily do. Committees of the Commons may be classified as follows:

1. *Committees of the whole House, i.e.* the House itself sitting with a Chairman instead of the Speaker.[26] This procedure is less frequent now that it has been abolished for financial legislation, but it is used for important constitutional measures such as the European Communities Bill, the Canada Bill and the Police and Criminal Evidence Bill.

2. *Standing Committees.* Standing Orders provide for the appointment of as many Standing Committees as may be necessary for the consideration of public Bills, and other business committed or referred to a

---

[23] See John Palmer, "Allocation of Time: The Guillotine and Voluntary Timetabling" (1970) XXIII *Parliamentary Affairs*, p. 232. Cf. "Selection of amendments ('Kangaroo')" *post* p. 213. See Second Report from the Select Committee on Procedure: *Public Bill Procedure* (1984–85; H.C. 49). This recommended the establishment of a Legislative Business Committee which would consider all Government Bills committed to a Standing Committee, and if it considered any bill would require more than 25 hours in committee, it would recommended a maximum number of hours. Such a recommendation should be implemented and decided by the House without a debate.

[24] The only occasion since the war when a guillotine motion was lost.

[25] For a comparison with the committee system of the United States Congress, see Bradshaw and Pring, *op. cit.* Chap. 5, especially pp. 258–262.

[26] The Serjeant-at-Arms places the mace on brackets beneath the table. The Chairman does not sit in the Speaker's chair, but on a chair "at the table" which is ordinarily occupied by the Clerk of the House.

Standing Committee. They consist of 16 to 50 members nominated by the Committee of Selection. The Selection Committee is required to have regard to the qualifications of members, and also to the composition of the House.[27] Their most important function is to consider Bills which, having been read a second time, stand committed to a Standing Committee. As an experiment the House in the 1980–81 session committed three Bills to "Special Standing Committees,"[28] which were entitled to use up to three morning sittings to take evidence from affected outside interests. Other examples of Standing Committees are European Community Documents Committees, Second Reading Committees, and Finance Bill Committees.[29]

3. *Select Committees.* These are Committees composed of a number of members specially named, and appointed from time to time or regularly re-appointed to consider or deal with particular matters. Select Committees have their powers and authority delegated to them by the House of Commons, including the power to send for "persons, papers and records."[30] The power to summon witnesses does not extend to Members of either House, who are therefore invited to attend. Only an order of the House can require an M.P. to attend. A Select Committee may only request their production of papers and records relevant to its work from private or public bodies[31] or individuals. Where documents are in the possession of a government department, a Select Committee may order the production if they are of a public and official nature and not private or confidential. Departments headed by a Secretary of State

[27] A majority Government would therefore expect to get its Bills through Standing Committee unscathed, but *cf.* P. Norton, "Dissent in Committee" (1976) 57 *The Parliamentarian* 15. When, in 1976–79, the Government did not have an overall party majority, it was agreed that the number of members of the government party on Standing Committees should equal the number of members of the other parties, the Chairmen exercising their casting vote against changing a Government Bill.

[28] The suggestion for these committees was made in the First Report of the Select Committee on Procedure (1977–78; H.C. 588). See H.J. Beynon [1982] P.L. 193. Since the 1980–81 session only two Bills have been referred to Special Standing Committees (S.S.C.). The Select Committee on Procedure in its report on *Public Bill Procedure* (1984–85; H.C. 49 had recommended a greater use of S.S.C.'s, and in February 1986 the House passed a S.O. to provide for such Committees (now S.O. No. 91).

[29] The Scottish Grand Committee is a standing committee consisting of all the members for Scottish constituencies. It considers public bills relating exclusively to Scotland referred to it before second reading in relation to their principle, or at report stage; also Scottish estimates and such other matters relating exclusively to Scotland as are referred to it.
The Welsh Grand Committee is a standing committee consisting of all members sitting for Welsh constituencies with five other members, which may consider the principle of public Bills relating exclusively to Wales before second reading, and such other matters relating to Wales as may be referred to it.
There is a similar standing committee for Northern Ireland and one on regional affairs to consider any matter relating to regional affairs in England referred to it.

[30] S.O. 177. See Select Committee on Procedure (1977–78; H.C. 588; K.P. Poole, *The Power of Select Committees of the House of Commons to send for Persons Papers and Records* (1979) XXXII Parliamentary Affairs 268.

[31] Including nationalised industries, although Mr. John Biffen, Leader of the House, has proposed that in future Ministers should be able to stop crucial information demanded by Committees from being released. *The Times* April 26, 1985.

may only be ordered to produce documents by means of moving in the House an Humble Address to the Queen.

There are several types of Select Committee. They include:

(i) Select Committees for considering public Bills (rarely employed), or to make a detailed study of some topic before the preparation of legislation, *e.g.* direct elections to the European Assembly (1976)

(ii) Select Committees on private Bills;

(iii) Sessional Committees re-appointed at the beginning of every session, either under Standing Order or an Order renewed each session, to consider all subjects of a particular nature, or such of them as are referred to it, or to perform other functions of a permanent nature, *e.g.* the Selection Committee, the Standing Orders Committee, the Public Accounts Committee, the Committee of Privileges, the Select Committee on the Parliamentary Commissioner, the Select Committee on Members' Interests, Sound Broadcasting, the Liaison Committee, the European Legislation Committee, the House of Commons Services Committee and Select Committees on Procedure.

(iv) Select Committees related to government departments. Fourteen such committees were established for the first time in 1979. Their main purpose is to scrutinise the administration. The functions of these committees and the Committee of Public Accounts will be examined in the next chapter.

4. *Joint Committees, i.e.* a Select Committee of the Commons sitting with a Select Committee of the Lords, an equal number being chosen from each House. The Chairman may be a member of either House. Joint Committees are set up from time to time to deal with non-political questions that equally concern both Houses, *e.g.* since 1973 there has been a Joint Committee on Statutory Instruments which undertakes the technical scrutiny of Statutory Instruments, and some private Bills are dealt with in this way. There is also a joint Standing Committee to consider consolidation Bills. This Committee was set up to review the form, drafting and amendment of legislation, and the practice in preparation of legislation for presentation to Parliament.[32]

III. Procedure on Legislation[33]

Drafting of Bills

Nearly all government Bills are drafted by Parliamentary Counsel to the Treasury, a staff of barristers or solicitors in the Treasury whose

[32] *Select Committee on Procedure: Process of Legislation* (1970–71; H.C. 538). For consolidation and revision of statute law, see Consolidation of Enactments (Procedure) Act 1949; Viscount Jowitt, *Statute Law Revision and Consolidation* (Holdsworth Club, University of Birmingham, 1951); Law Commission Act 1965, s.3; *Law Commission's Second Programme on Consolidation and Statute Law Revision* (1971) H.C. 338. Rt. Hon. Lord Roskill "The Function of the Joint Committee in the Consolidation Process" [1983] Stat. L.R. 133.

[33] Miers and Page, *Legislation* (1982); Bennion *Statute Law* (1983).

office was constituted in 1869. Parliamentary Counsel also advise on amendments proposed during the passage of a Bill.[34]

The government sometimes lends drafting assistance to a private Member's Bill that has passed its second reading. Otherwise private members are responsible for drafting their own Bills.

Classification of Bills

A project of law during its passage through Parliament is called a Bill, and its subdivisions are called clauses. Bills are classified into three kinds;

1. *Public Bills, i.e.* measures affecting the community at large or altering the general law. A public Bill applies by description to all persons subject to the authority of Parliament or to certain classes of such persons. Strictly, all public Bills are introduced by members in their capacity as members; but in ordinary language those introduced by Ministers are called "government Bills," and those introduced by private (or unofficial) members are called "private members' Bills." Government Bills are far the most numerous, and are assured of the general support of the government's majority. Little time is allotted to private members' Bills,[35] which must be carefully distinguished from private Bills (*post*).

2. *Private Bills, i.e.* measures dealing with local or personal matters, such as a Bill giving special powers to a local authority or altering a settlement. They apply to particular persons or groups who are named or otherwise identified (*e.g.* by locality). They are promoted by petition by interested persons or bodies outside Parliament and are governed by special procedure under separate Standing Orders.[36]

3. *Hybrid Bills, i.e.* Bills which, although they are introduced as public Bills (mostly by the Government, but occasionally by private members), affect a particular private interest in a manner different from the private interest of other persons or bodies of the same category or class, in such a way that if they were private Bills preliminary notices to persons affected would have to be given under the Standing Orders. They are governed by a special procedure before second reading similar to that on private Bills, but which obviates the necessity of allowing objectors to appear one by one before the House. The classification is difficult in some cases[37]: thus the Bill to nationalise the Bank of England, the London Passenger Transport Bill and the Cable and Wireless Bill were held

---

[34] Ilbert, *Mechanics of Law Making* (1913); *Legislative Methods and Forms* (1901); Sir Granville Ram, "The Improvement of the Statute Book" [1951] J.S.P.T.L. 442. See also "The Making and Form of Bills" by one of the Parliamentary Counsel, in (1948–49) 2 *Parliamentary Affairs* (Hansard Society), p. 175; Sir Ivor Jennings, *Parliament* (2nd ed.) Chap. 7. Report of the Renton Committee, *The Preparation of Legislation* Cmnd. 6053 (1975).

[35] *Post*, p. 214.

[36] *Post*, p. 215.

[37] The matter may be referred to the Examiners, two officials appointed by the House of Lords and the Speaker.

to be hybrid Bills; but the Bills to nationalise gas, electricity and the coal industry were regarded as public Bills.[38] A Bill introduced into the House of Commons in 1976 to nationalise the aircraft and shipbuilding industries was classified by the examiners of Private Bills in the House of Lords as hybrid, because it applied to some (but not all) ship-repairing firms. After much controversy the Government accepted Lords' amendments omitting ship-repairing firms, in order, if necessary, to get the rest of the Bill through as a public Bill under the procedure of the Parliament Acts.[39] More recently the Bill to provide for the construction of a Channel tunnel has been introduced under the procedure for hybrid Bills.

It appears that the Commons can suspend their Standing Orders relating to hybrid Bills, but that the Lords could still classify the Bill as hybrid.

We must also notice *provisional order confirmation Bills*. These are Bills confirming orders and schemes made by government departments under statutory powers that would otherwise formerly have to be dealt with by private Bills. The delay and expense of private Bill legislation was thus saved, and local authorities in particular during the latter half of the nineteenth century and the first half of the present century acquired powers in this way by ministerial order under various statutes. A provisional order has no effect until confirmed by Parliament. It is scheduled, along with others, to a Provisional Orders Confirmation Bill introduced by the Minister. This procedure is now virtually obsolete, having been replaced by Special Procedure Orders.[40]

Ordinary procedure on Public Bills[41]

Most kinds of public Bills may originate either in the Commons or the Lords, but there are certain classes of Bills, such as Money Bills and Bills dealing with the representation of the people, which by parliamentary custom or constitutional convention may originate only in the Commons. A relaxation of the privileges of the House of Commons in 1972 has made it possible for financial Bills to be introduced in the House of Lords.[42] In practice many more Bills originate in the Commons than in the Lords, although the latter method is convenient for non-controversial topics that either require little discussion, such as the Australia Act 1986, or that require technical discussion on non-party lines, such as the Crown Proceedings Act 1947. Consolidation measures are another type of Bill which may originate in the House of Lords, for example the Insolvency Act 1986. Where an Act of Parliament is required urgently, Bills may be introduced concurrently in both Houses for example the Northern Ireland (Temporary Provisions) Act 1972.

---

[38] See R.W. Perceval, "The Origin and Essence of Hybrid Bills" (1949) 2 *Parliamentary Affairs* (Hansard Society), p. 139; W. Craig Henderson, "Procedure on Hybrid Bills" *ibid.* p. 148.
The procedure was amended following the Report of the Select Committee on Procedure in Committee (1948) H.C. 191.
[39] In the end this was not necessary.
[40] See *post*, Chap. 30.
[41] For Money Bills and financial clauses, see *post*, Chap. 11.
[42] S.O. No. 78.

Introduction of Bills

A member, whether a Minister or unofficial member, introduces a Bill by presenting it at the table or by motion for leave to introduce it, in either case after giving notice. The former method is usual, as the latter may lead to a debate.

The five stages through which a Bill passes in the legislative process in the Houses are: (i) first reading, (ii) second reading, (iii) committee stage, (iv) report (or consideration of amendments) stage, and (v) third reading.

(i) *First reading.* The Bill is ordinarily presented in "dummy," *i.e.* a sheet of paper on which is the name of the member, and the title of the Bill. The "first reading" is purely formal. The Clerk at the table reads the title only. The Bill is then deemed to have been read a first time, and is ordered to be printed.

(ii) *Second reading.* The member in charge of the Bill moves that it "be now read a second time." The Bill is not actually read, but its main principles are discussed. If no one objects to the Bill, it can be "read" a second time when unopposed business is taken. If it is opposed,[43] it can only come on on one of the days fixed for taking opposed Bills.

Since 1965[44] it has been possible for a Minister, having given ten days' notice, to propose that a public Bill be referred to a *Second Reading Committee* to make a recommendation to the House whether it should or should not be read a second time. The Second Reading Committee is a Standing Committee nominated for the consideration of each Bill referred to it. This experiment, designed to save time, has been successful, and means that a number of non-controversial Bills and unopposed Bills for which the government are not prepared to find time on the floor of the House can be introduced. The procedure may be used unless at least 20 members object.[45] Bills relating exclusively to Scotland may, unless ten members object, be referred to the Scottish Grand Committee, which will consider the principle of the Bill and report back to the House.[46] When the order for the second reading is read a motion may be made by a Minister to commit the Bill to a Scottish Standing Committee. If this is agreed, then the Bill is deemed to have been read a second time. A Minister cannot move such a motion if notice of an amendment has been given by at least six members.[47]

(iii) *Committee stage.* When a Bill has passed the second reading it goes to one of the Standing Committees, unless the House otherwise

---

[43] In 1772 a Bill was rejected, thrown about and kicked out of the House; Anson, *Law and Custom of the Constitution*, Vol. I (5th ed. Gwyer), p. 272.

[44] On the basis of a suggestion by the Select Committee on Procedure (1964–65; H.C. 149); S.O. No. 60.

[45] Such objection is not seldom forthcoming: Select Committee on Procedure: The Process of Legislation (1970–71; H.C. 538).

[46] S.O. No. 93.

[47] A procedure similar to that used for referring a Bill to a Second Reading Committee may be used for Bills relating exclusively to Wales to be referred to the Welsh Grand Committee (S.O. 98).

orders.[48] If the House otherwise orders it may be referred to a Committee of the whole House or (rarely) to a Select Committee, (e.g. the five-yearly Armed Forces Bill) or (for certain purposes) to a Joint Committee of the two Houses. One part of a Bill may be considered by a Standing Committee and another part by a Committee of the whole House, the advantage of the latter being that all members have an opportunity to take part.

The committee stage of public bills relating exclusively to Scotland is taken by one of two Scottish standing committees, including not less than 16 members representing Scottish constituencies. The committee stage of a public bill relating exclusively to Wales will be referred to the Welsh Grand Committee.

The committee stage is the time for discussing details and proposing amendments. The Bill is taken clause by clause, and amendments are moved in the order in which they come in the clause. In the committee stage the procedure is less formal than in the House; a motion need not be seconded, and a member may speak more than once on the same question. When the clauses are finished new clauses and postponed clauses are considered. After that the schedules, if any, are taken.

Selection of amendments ("Kangaroo").[49] In order to save time. Standing Orders give to the Speaker on the report stage, or a Chairman of Committee, the power to select certain new clauses or amendments for discussion. The rest are voted on without debate. A previous announcement is made concerning the selection of amendments.

(iv) *Report stage.* The bill as amended in Committee is then "reported" to the House. It may, with certain restrictions, be further amended as in Committee. If voluntary timetabling fails and the Speaker exercises his power of selection of amendments (*ante*), his reason for not "calling" a particular amendment will often be that it has been fully discussed in Committee.[50]

The Select Committee on Procedure has recommended[51] that the procedure under Standing Order 92 whereby a Bill, whose second reading was in Second Reading Committee or the Scottish Grand Committee, could be sent to a Standing Committee at the report stage, should be repealed. Since its introduction in 1967 this procedure has only been used once.

(v) *Third reading.* After the Bill has been considered on report, it is put down for "third reading." If there is a debate on third reading, it is on general principles and only verbal amendments can be moved.[52] The Bill as a whole can be opposed in principle by the same method as at second reading. If the motion "that the Bill be now read a third time" is

---

[48] For the use of "Special Standing Committees" see *ante* p. 208.

[49] S.O. No. 31.

[50] The criteria for the selection of amendments at Report stage were listed by Mr. Speaker King in a memorandum to the Procedure Committee (1966–67) H.C. 539 p. 87.

[51] *Op. cit.* (1984–85; H.C. 49), para. 20 (formerly S.O. 78).

[52] The Bill may, however, be recommended to a committee to allow the introduction of amendments.

carried—which it almost certainly will be if it is a government Bill—the Bill is deemed to have passed the House. It is now sent up to the House of Lords, endorsed with the words *"Soit baillé aux Seigneurs"* (let it be sent to the Lords).

Procedure in the Lords[53]

The procedure on legislation in the House of Lords resembles generally the procedure in the Commons, although it has greater flexibility. If the Lords propose amendments to a Bill sent up by the Commons, the Bill is endorsed *"A ceste bille avecque des amendemens les Seigneurs sont assentus"* and returned to the Commons for consideration. The Commons may assent to the amendments (*"A ces amendemens les Communes sont assentus"*), or dissent from them, or further amend them (*"Ceste bille est remise aux Seigneurs avecque des raisons"*).

Private Members' Bills[54]

Public Bills may be introduced by private members. Private members do not introduce Bills authorising expenditure, because these require a financial resolution with a recommendation from the Crown. However where a Private Members' Bill proposes an incidental charge on the public revenue, and the Bill has Government support, a Minister may move the necessary resolution.[55] Otherwise private members are free as regards subject-matter. There are a number of procedures under which Private Members may initiate Bills.

The Ballot

There are always more Private Members wishing to introduce Bills than there is Parliamentary time available. At the beginning of each session a Ballot is held and the 20 successful members have priority to introduce a Bill in the time made available.[56]

Ten Minute Rule

A private member who has not won a place in the ballot can take advantage of the *"Ten Minute Rule,"* whereby motions for leave to introduce Bills may be set down at the commencement of public business on Tuesdays and Wednesdays (S.O. No. 19). Members must give three weeks' notice of such a motion. After the mover has briefly explained the objects of the Bill, another member is allowed to make a short speech in opposition, and the question is then put without further debate. This procedure gives early publicity to controversial measures. Bills under this rule are limited to one a day, and a member is limited to one such notice in a period of 15 sitting days.

Standing Order No. 58

This is the way the majority of Government Bills are presented, and it can be used by private members.

[53] For the pocedure under the Parliament Acts see *ante*, p. 143.
[54] For Private Bills see *post* p. 215. See Peter G. Richards "Private Members Legislation" in Walkland and Ryle *op. cit.* Chap. 6.
[55] S.O. No. 48.
[56] The Government agreed in 1972 to grant up to £200 towards drafting expenses of members gaining the first ten places in the ballot.

The difficulty with Private Members' Bills is to find sufficient time to go through their various parliamentary stages. Private Members' Bills have precedence over Government Bills on ten Fridays in the session,[57] and on ten other Fridays they take a similar precedence but after private members' motions. Private Members' Bills may also be discussed until seven p.m. on four days other than Fridays. Members who were successful in the ballot have priority on these occasions and for this reason success in the ballot is the most likely way to success with a Private Members' Bill. To assist members to get Private Members' Bills through their second reading it was agreed in 1979 that provided ten days' notice is given, a sponsoring member can move a motion to refer a Bill to a Second Reading Committee.[58] This can only be done on or after the seventh private members' Friday and one objection can defeat the motion. The chance of a private members' Bill reaching the final stage—or even an advanced stage—by the end of the session (when uncompleted Bills expire) is generally remote, unless the Government give it their active support.[59] About 10 to 12 Private Members' Bills becomes Acts each session.

Procedure on Private Bills[60]

Private Bills are initiated not by Members of Parliament within the House, but by petition from persons or bodies ("promoters") outside Parliament. The procedure on private Bills is complicated and is governed by a special set of Standing Orders. Local Bills[61] deal with the construction of works, such as harbours, or extend the powers of local authorities or public utilities. There has in recent times been a great decline in the number of local Bills, partly because the purposes they served in the eighteenth and nineteenth centuries (enclosure of commons, construction of railways and canals) have been accomplished, and partly because of the increased use of Public General Acts, Provisional Orders and Special Procedure Orders to effect such purposes more conveniently and cheaply. Personal Bills[61] dealing with family estates are sometimes passed, but this class of Bill is now comparatively rare since their purposes—such as settlements, naturalisation and divorce—are now effected under Public General Acts.

Standing Orders require that full notice shall be given, so that persons affected may come in and oppose. A private Bill is usually introduced by being presented at the table by the Clerk of the Private Bill

---

[57] S.O. No. 13.

[58] S.O. No. 90(2).

[59] See A.P. Herbert, *The Ayes Have it: Independent Members* (1937); P.A. Bromhead, *Private Members' Bills in the British Parliament* (1956). It has been suggested that there should be a steering committee, or that private members' Bills should be given priority according to the amount of support they obtain.

[60] May, *Parliamentary Practice*, Part III; Jennings, *op. cit.* Chap. 13; O. Cyprian Williams, *The Historical Development of Private Bill Procedure* (1948); Sir Cecil Carr (1950) 66 L.Q.R. 216. Study of Parliamentary Group "Private Bill Procedure: A Case for Reform" (1981) P.L. 206.
This sketch does not apply to Scottish Bills, for which a special procedure was provided by the Private Legislation Procedure (Scotland) Act 1936.

[61] "Local" and "Personal" is a House of Lords classification.

Office. It is then deemed to have been read a first time. Intricate questions frequently arise as to the *locus standi* of various parties to appear and be heard before the Select Committee. The second reading is the first opportunity the House has to discuss the general principles of the Bill. The Bill usually passes the second reading unopposed or with directions to the Committee to delete or insert certain provisions. When the Bill has passed the second reading it goes either to the Committee on Unopposed Bills or, if opposed at this stage, to a Select Committee. The Select Committee proceeds to hear counsel and witnesses for and against the objects of the Bill, and if it finds that a sufficient case for legislation has been made out, declares the preamble proved. The clauses are then gone through before the contending parties, evidence is taken and arguments of counsel heard, and amendments, if necessary, are made. The Bill, as amended in Committee, is then reported to the House. After third reading, the Bill is sent to the other House.

In *Pickin* v. *British Railways Board*,[62] the House of Lords held unanimously that the plaintiff was not entitled to challenge the private Act obtained by the Railways Board on the ground that the House had been deceived by the preamble reciting that plans and a list of persons affected had been duly delivered to the appropriate local authority, so that the Bill went before the Committee on Unopposed Bills.

Although private Bills are by Standing Orders subject to a number of formalities that do not apply to other Bills, when they come before either House they are read the same number of times and treated at each stage in a similar way to public Bills. If passed by both Houses, a private Bill receives the Royal Assent in the same way as a public Bill, except that a different form of words is used: *Soit fait comme il est désiré.*

---

[62] [1974] A.C. 765; approving *Edinburgh and Dalkeith Ry.* v. *Wauchope* (1842) 8 Cl. & F. 710 (H.L.); *ante*, p. 52, *per* Lord Reid. And see P. Wallington (1974) 37 M.L.R. 686.

CHAPTER 11

NATIONAL FINANCE AND SCRUTINY OF THE ADMINISTRATION

I. National Finance[1]

Introduction

Governments require powers of raising and spending money. In the British system the regulation of national finance is governed by rules of financial procedure concerning the relationship between the Crown and the House of Commons. The functions of the Commons are to control policy by authorising most types of public expenditure (supply services) and most taxation; and to satisfy itself that the expenditure it approved has been properly spent. In addition to its participation in the procedural aspects of finance, the government possesses wide powers of control in the field of financial and monetary matters. For example, by statute[2] and by the use of the economic power and influence of the Bank of England,[3] it can control the supply of money.

Public revenue

The national revenue is not solely derived from taxation. The Exchequer derives a certain revenue from the Crown lands, in respect of which and other hereditary Crown revenues Parliament pays over to the Queen a fixed annual sum called the Civil List. The government will also raise money by borrowing which need only be approved by the Commons in a general way.[4] In modern times, however, the great bulk of revenue is supplied to the Crown by Parliament for the government of the country. It is the practice to impose some taxes by "permanent Acts" which remain in force until repealed or amended, *e.g.* stamp duties and capital transfer tax, value added tax,[5] and to impose others by annual Acts, which remain in force for one year only. Thus the annual Finance Act sets out the rates of income tax, customs and excise

---

[1] Erskine May, *Parliamentary Practice* (20th ed., 1983), Chaps. 27–32; Lord Campion, *Introduction to the Procedure of the House of Commons* (3rd ed.), Chap. 8; Sir Ivor Jennings, *Parliament* (2nd ed.), Chap. 9 and Appendix IX; Sir Alexander Johnston, *The Inland Revenue* (1965); K. Bradshaw and D. Pring, *Parliament and Congress* (1972); Second Report from the Treasury and Civil Service Committee: *Structure and Form of Financial Documents Presented to Parliament* (1984–85; H.C. 110); Seventh Report from the Treasury and Civil Service Committee (1984–85; H.C. 323). Tenth Report from the Treasury and Civil Service Committee (1984–85; H.C. 544).

[2] Borrowing (Control and Guarantees) Act 1946, s.1; Emergency Laws (Re-enactments and Repeals) Act 1964, s.1; Bank of England Act 1946, s.4.

[3] Daintith, "The Law in Short Term Economic Policy" (1976) 92 L.Q.R. 72 *et seq.*

[4] The First Report from the Select Committee on Procedure (Finance) (1983) suggested that the House of Commons should concern itself with both the form and amount of public borrowing. (1982–83; H.C. 241). This report was debated in the House on December 6, 1983: H.C. Deb., Vol. 50, col. 245–293.

[5] This is also subject to the EEC Sixth Directive on VAT. By VAT Act 1983, s.9 the Treasury may, by order, increase or decrease the positive rate of VAT by a percentage not exceeding 25 *per cent.*

duties.[6] These taxes and duties are known as "charges upon the people." All the national revenue of whatever kind goes into the Bank of England, where it is credited to the Exchequer account and is called *the Consolidated Fund*.[7] Withdrawals must be authorised by statute.[8]

Public expenditure

Public expenditure may be of two types: supply services or Consolidated Fund services. The bulk of public expenditure is on the supply services which include the armed forces, the civil service and the general requirements of government departments. These services are described as charges paid out of "moneys provided by Parliament" and are subject to the annual control of Parliament under its supply procedure, and require statutory authorisation.

Consolidated Fund services are charges on the "public revenue" or "public funds" and permanent Acts give continuing authorisation to pay these services out of the Consolidated Fund or National Loans Fund. This means that Parliament does not have to give annual authorisation for their payment. These services include payment of interest on the national debt; the Queen's Civil List; the salaries of judges of the superior courts, the Speaker, the Comptroller and Auditor General and the Parliamentary Commissioner for Administration; and payments to meet European Community obligations.[9] In 1985 the Government backed down in its attempt to pay money required for a supplementary Community budget directly from the Consolidated Fund, and instead inserted the sum as a Supplementary Estimate in the Consolidated Fund (No. 2) Act 1985.[10]

The Crown and the Commons

Erskine May says:

> "The Sovereign, being the executive power, is charged with the management of all the revenue of the State, and with all payments for the public service. The Crown, therefore, acting with the advice of its responsible ministers, makes known to the Commons the pecuniary necessities of the Government; the Commons, in return, grant such aids or supplies as are required to satisfy these demands; and they provide by taxes, and by the appropriation of

---

[6] These are also subject to EEC law; see European Communities Act 1972 (E.C.A.), s.5 which grants a power to the Treasury to use delegated legislation to alter customs duties in furtherance of a Community obligation.

[7] Established in 1787 by the younger Pitt. Before that date the various taxes were charged arbitrarily on particular sources of revenue. In 1968 a new account, the National Loans Fund, was established (National Loans Act 1968) and some of the functions and revenues from the Consolidated Fund were transferred to it.

[8] Either a Consolidated Fund Act or an Appropriation Act see *post* p. 220.

[9] E.C.A. s.2(3).

[10] In *R. v. H.M. Treasury, ex p. Smedley* [1985] Q.B. 657 the Court of Appeal held that an "undertaking" by the Member States to provide the funds to meet the supplementary budget could be specified in an Order in Council as a treaty "ancillary" to the Community treaties (E.C.A., s.1(3)), and thereby entitled the Government to make the payment under E.C.A., s.2(3). However, "for the avoidance of doubt," the Government abandoned this course. See the Third Report from the Treasury and Civil Service Committee (1984–85; H.C. 158).

other sources of the public income, the ways and means to meet the supplies which they have granted. Thus the Crown demands money, the Commons grant it, and the Lords assent to the grant: but the Commons do not vote money unless it be required by the Crown; nor do they impose or augment taxes, unless such taxation be necessary for the public service, as declared by the Crown through its constitutional advisers."[11]

Five general principles should here be noticed:

(1) A proposal affecting supply for the public service or a charge on the public revenue must be recommended by a Minister (royal recommendation) ("the Crown demands money"). This common law principle is now in part embodied in Standing Order No. 46 which dates back to 1713. It demonstrates the control which the Government has over expenditure and taxation since it prevents back-bench M.P.'s from proposing additional expenditure or taxation.

(2) A proposal to raise or spend public money must be introduced in the House of Commons ("the Commons grant it"). This is part of the custom of Parliament and one of the privileges of the Commons, asserted by resolutions of 1671 and 1678, confirmed in 1860 and 1910 and implied by the Parliament Act 1911. So in the Queen's Speech on the opening, prorogation or dissolution of Parliament, the Commons are separately addressed when estimates or supply are mentioned; and the principle appears in the enacting formulae of the annual Finance and Appropriation Acts.

(3) Charges, whether for the raising[12] or spending of money, must be authorised by legislation originating in the Commons. This rule is subject to statutory modifications.[13]

(4) Charges for the raising or spending of money must first be considered by the Commons in the form of a resolution which, when passed, will authorise the charge to be included in a Bill. Consolidated Fund Bills are brought in upon supply resolutions; finance and other taxing bills are brought in upon Ways and Means resolutions.

(5) The Lords may not *alter* Bills of aids and supplies ("the Lords assent to the grant"), although in theory they may reject them, as any other kind of Bill (subject now to the Parliament Acts). Such Bills include (a) supply to the Crown, becoming a Consolidated Fund Bill, or (b) taxation (Finance Bill). This is similarly a privilege of the Commons, included in the resolutions of 1671 and 1668. Section 6 of the Parliament Act 1911, preserving the Commons' privileges, allows the Commons to choose whether to proceed on the Lords' amendments under the procedure of the Act[14]

---

[11] May, *op. cit.* p. 750.

[12] Art. 4, Bill of Rights 1688 " . . . the levying of money for or to the use of the Crown without grant of Parliament is illegal.": *Att.-Gen.* v. *Wilts United Dairies* (1921) 37 T.L.R. 884; *Bowles* v. *Bank of England* [1913] 1 Ch. 57.

[13] Provisional Collection of Taxes Act 1968, *post*, p. 223; Finance Act 1972; Contingencies Fund Act 1974.

[14] The definition of "Money Bill" in the Parliament Act 1911 is narrower than that for the purposes of Commons procedure.

or under their privileges: in the latter case they may waive their privileges and accept the Lords' amendments.[15]

The annual cycle of finance

Each financial year, which runs from April 1 to March 31[16] is treated separately, and money voted for one financial year cannot be applied to a subsequent year. Although, as has been seen, some expenditure and revenue is given permanent statutory authority, most is subject to annual control by Parliament. Since the financial year does not coincide with the parliamentary session, parliament in any one session will consider provisions relating to more than one financial year. The annual cycle of finance will be considered first with regard to expenditure (supply) and then with regard to revenue (ways and means).

The estimates

Every autumn the government departments prepare estimates of their expenditure for the next financial year, based on the policy for each department which has been decided by the responsible Minister with the approval of the Cabinet. The estimates are submitted to the Treasury,[17] which scrutinises them in the interests of economy within the limits of government policy. In particular it will check that they are within the Government's "cash limits,"[18] which will have been published with the Budget the previous April. Cash limits set a limited amount of cash which the Government proposes to spend on certain services during the financial year. The Cabinet, which is the umpire in any dispute between the departments and the Treasury, finally settles the estimates, which are presented to the Commons in the Spring.[19] The estimates are divided into "classes" each of which corresponds to a separate programme as laid down in the Government's annual Public Expenditure White Paper. Classes are divided into units of appropriation known as "votes" for the various departments. The estimates provide the basis for Parliament to authorise specific expenditure by Appropriation Act, and for audit by the Comptroller and Auditor-General.

Supply business

In accordance with principle 4 (*supra*), the estimates are brought in for approval by the Commons upon Supply resolutions, which, if carried, must be embodied in legislation. This is finally provided for in the annual Appropriation Act which authorises the issue of money from the Consolidated Fund and appropriates in detail the application of the

---

[15] As in the case of the Inshore Fishery Industry Bill 1946.

[16] Except the income tax year which runs from April 6 to April 5.

[17] *Post* p. 329.

[18] Cash limits were introduced in 1976. See Cmnd. 6440 (1976); M. Elliot (1977) 40 M.L.R. 569. Cash limits are not subject to separate parliamentary approval, but they are assimilated in the estimates so that Parliament is aware whether or not an estimate is subject to a cash limit. Of the 185 Supply estimates for 1985–86, 120 were subject to cash limits: Cmnd. 9450 (1985).

[19] Important changes in the customary form of the estimates should be first approved by the Committee of Public Accounts and the Treasury and Civil Service Committee.

amounts voted to the departments. This is usually passed in July or August. However money is usually required by departments before this date. Interim statutes called *Consolidated Fund Acts* are therefore passed from time to time, providing votes on account to cover expenditure in the period from April 1 to the time when the Appropriation Act will be passed. These Acts also provide for supplementary estimates to cover unforeseen expenditure in the current financial year and even "excess votes" to provide for excess expenditure incurred by a department in the previous financial year. The Appropriation Act, which is itself a final Consolidated Fund Act, deals with the balances of money voted but so far undisposed of, and confirms retrospectively the appropriations made by the Consolidated Fund Acts.

The theory of the Constitution with regard to supply is shown in the special enacting formula of the annual Appropriation Act: "Most Gracious Sovereign, We, Your Majesty's most dutiful and loyal subjects the Commons of the United Kingdom in Parliament assembled, towards making good the supply which we have cheerfully granted to Your Majesty in this Session of Parliament, have resolved to grant unto Your Majesty the sum hereinafter mentioned; and do therefore most humbly beseech Your Majesty that it may be enacted, and be it enacted . . . " etc.

From the earliest days of Parliament the granting of supply was the basis of the power of the Commons over the executive. Gradually this control became formal only. The 29 Supply days allotted each session for debating supply resolutions were regarded as an opportunity for the Opposition to choose topics to be discussed which did not have to be concerned with the estimates. Supply days became guaranteed parliamentary time available to the Opposition to criticise the Government. By standing order[20] there were three dates each year by which certain estimates had to be voted on, and the use of a Supply guillotine on each occasion ensured that the estimates were approved on time, and the Government had the money it required for its expenditure plans. The subsequent debates on the Consolidated Fund Bills and the Appropriation Bill did not provide scrutiny of expenditure either, since they were regarded as time available to back-bench M.P.'s to choose topics for debate provided they were within the remit of the Estimates. As the system had evolved there was virtually no opportunity for the Commons to discuss any details of the estimates. Growing dissatisfaction resulted in the referral of Supply procedure to a Select Committee in 1980. On July 19, 1982, following the Committee's report[21] the Commons agreed to changes in its supply procedure.

Supply days are abolished. Instead, in each session before August 5, three full days, "Estimate Days,"[22] are set aside for the consideration of such of the estimates as are selected for discussion by the Liaison Committee.[23] Although not all estimates are debated, the role given to the Liaison Committee ensures that an informed back-bench view is taken

[20] Formerly S.O. No. 19, now S.O. No. 52.
[21] First Report from the Select Committee on Procedure (Supply) (1980–81; H.C. 118).
[22] The Select Committee had proposed eight Estimates Days.
[23] *Post* p. 232. S.O. No. 52 and S.O. No. 131.

as to which estimates should be debated. Unlike debates on Supply days, debates on Estimate days are required to be relevant to the need to grant, refuse or reduce an item of expenditure, and not on matters of general policy. At 10.00 p.m. on each Estimate day a vote is taken on the selected estimates and any proposed amendments. As before, the Supply guillotine is used three times a year to ensure the approval of the remaining estimates.[24]

The guarantee of days available to the Opposition for scrutiny of the Government continues with 20 "Opposition Days" available per session.[25] Proceedings on Consolidated Fund Bills and Appropriation Bills have become purely formal and without debate. But on completion of these proceedings the adjournment is moved and a series of private members' debates can take place until 9.00 a.m. the next day.[26]

Despite the formal, legal significance of the Appropriation Act, it must be remembered that a great deal of public expenditure falls outside its terms. Nor does it reflect governmental commitments for the future, so that it has been said that the figures contained in the Act are "in economic terms . . . all but meaningless."[27]

Ways and means business

Taxes which are authorised for one year only,[28] such as the rates of income tax and corporation tax, require annual Parliamentary approval for their continuation. This is also the case for an increase in a permanent tax, such as customs and excise duties, the imposition of a new tax or the extension of the incidence of an existing tax. Proposals for the rates of these taxes are contained in the Chancellor of the Exchequer's financial statement of the year, or "Budget," which is presented near the beginning of the financial year. In an attempt to stimulate advance discussion of Budget options the Government has, since 1982, published an autumn economic statement containing projections for government revenue and borrowing for the next financial year[29] and an indication of proposed tax changes.[30] In addition to tax rates, the Budget contains a financial review of the previous year, an estimate of

---

[24] S.O. No. 53.

[25] S.O. No. 13. The reduction in the number of days available to the Opposition is offset by an agreement that certain topics previously dealt with in Supply Days would be taken in government time *e.g.* the armed forces, Scottish affairs and EEC debates. 17 of the 20 Opposition Days are reserved for the Leader of the Opposition, the other three are allotted to the Leader of the second largest Opposition party.

[26] S.O. No. 54.

[27] Daintith. "The Law in Short Term Economic Policy" (1976) 92 L.Q.R. 62, 71.

[28] Permanent authority for the machinery for collecting these taxes is contained in, for example, Income and Corporation Taxes Act 1970 and Taxes Management Act 1970.

[29] This goes further than the announcement traditionally made by the Chancellor at this time, and was in response to recommendations of the Sixth Report for the Treasury and Civil Service Committee (1981–82; H.C. 137), although it does not go far as suggested by the Select Committee. The Chancellor of the Exchequer described the Autumn Statement as a "pretty good Do-it-Yourself Budget Kit." (1982–83; H.C. 24).

[30] The Government in its reply (1984–85; H.C. 545) to the Report from the Treasury and Civil Service on the 1985 Budget (1984–85; H.C. 306) indicated that it was seriously considering discontinuing giving details of proposed tax changes in the autumn statement. This was described by the Committee as "most retrograde."

probable expenditure for the next year and a statement of the Government's general financial and economic policy.

Budget resolutions

Before the Finance Bill which will give effect to Budget changes can be brought in, the House must approve the Ways and Means resolutions upon which the Bill will be founded.[31] In the case of the Budget this happens in two stages. Immediately after the Chancellor's speech the necessary detailed budget resolutions to allow the continued collection of income and capital transfer tax and for changes in the rates of these taxes or in the rates of any of the permanent taxes or duties, will be introduced. These resolutions will then be provisionally passed by the House. Since there will not at that stage have been an opportunity to debate these resolutions, they will have to be further approved by the House within ten days. This will be in the course of the subsequent four day general debate on all the budget resolutions, at the end of which the House will vote on the resolutions and, if agreed, the Finance Bill will be ordered to be brought in. For more than a century before the case of *Bowles* v. *Bank of England*[32] it had been the practice to anticipate the passing of legislation by collecting certain taxes on the authority of the resolutions. In that case Parker J. declared the practice of deducting tax without the authority of an Act of Parliament to be a violation of the Bill of Rights. The decision resulted in immediate legislation[33] to give temporary statutory effect to the proposals contained in the resolutions. The position is now governed by the Provisional Collection of Taxes Act 1968.[34] This Act requires the resolutions to be confirmed by the second reading of the Bill relating to the tax within 25 days of the House approving the resolutions. It also provides that their statutory effect shall continue only until August 5, if passed in the previous March or April, or for four months if passed at any other time. This then gives the Government a deadline for the passage of its Finance Act.

The Finance Bill

Debates on the second reading of the Finance Bill usually cover a general review of national finance. Amendments may be put forward, but they may not increase the amount or extend the area of incidence of a tax as already authorised in the resolutions.[35] The Committee stage is divided between a committee of the whole House and a standing committee.

The Finance Bill is not usually a "Money Bill" for the purposes of the Parliament Act 1911 since it often includes provisions dealing with subjects other than those enumerated in section 1(2) of the Parliament Act. Therefore, subject to the special privileges of the Commons in relation to finance, it will proceed through the Lords in the usual way.[36]

---

[31] Rule 4 *ante*. p. 219.
[32] [1913] 1 Ch. 57.
[33] Provisional Collection of Taxes Act 1913.
[34] As amended by, for example, Finance Act 1972, s.1(5), Finance Act 1973, s.50, Finance Act 1981, s.128(2), Value Added Tax Act 1983, s.50.
[35] It is possible to propose a decrease in a tax.
[36] *Ante*. p. 214.

The theory of the Constitution with regard to taxation is shown in the special enacting formula of the annual Finance Act:

> "Most Gracious Sovereign, We, Your Majesty's most dutiful and loyal subjects the Commons of the United Kingdom in Parliament assembled, towards raising the necessary supplies to defray Your Majesty's public expenses, and making an addition to the public revenue, have freely and voluntarily resolved to give and grant unto Your Majesty the several duties hereinafter mentioned; and do therefore most humbly beseech Your Majesty, that it may be enacted, and be it enacted . . . " etc.

The Royal Assent is given in the form: *La Reine remercie ses bons sujets, accepte leur bénévolence et ainsi le veult.*

Scrutiny of national finance by Parliament[37]

The annual cycle of finance requires Parliament's authority for the spending and raising of various categories of public money. Parliament has two additional functions to perform in relation to national finance. First, it must be able to scrutinise and comment on the totality of public expenditure, both short and long term. Secondly, it must ensure that the sums of public money voted by it, and no more, have been spent for the purposes for which they were granted.

Total public expenditure

The planning of public expenditure programmes has to be over several years since projects such as the building of roads and hospitals and the provisions of various State benefits have implications for many financial years. In 1961 the Plowden Report[38] emphasised the importance of taking a longer look ahead in planning the economy and estimating expenditure and resources. Its fundamental recommendation was that regular surveys should be made of public expenditure as a whole over a period of years ahead, and in relation to prospective resources. Effect is given to these proposals by an annual inter-departmental spending survey by the Public Expenditure Survey Committee (P.E.S.C.), which is composed of the principle finance officers of the departments and chaired by a member of the Treasury. The P.E.S.C. report is submitted to the Cabinet and enables it to decide on future expenditure in the light of plans by all the spending departments. The result of the Cabinet deliberations is published before the end of the financial year[39] as the annual Public Expenditure White Paper, and represents one of the key features of the Government's economic policy. The White Paper will include information on the Government's planning for the total public expenditure for the next three years and the implications of such expenditure in the two or three subsequent years. There is no definition of public expenditure agreed to by Parliament,

---

[37] See Michael Elliot, "The Control of Public Expenditure" in *The Changing Constitution* (Jowell and Oliver eds. 1985) Chap. 7.

[38] Control of Public Expenditure, Cmnd 1432.

[39] In recent years it has been published in late January or early February rather than, as previously, with the Budget, to give Parliament more time to consider the proposals.

and the figure given is to some extent an arbitrary total dependent on the definition adopted by the Government.[40] However, whatever precise definition is used, it covers a much wider spectrum of public spending than that found in the annual supply estimates. In particular it will include[41] local authority expenditure,[42] the Consolidated Fund Standing Services, National Insurance benefits and the external financing requirements of nationalised industries.[43] The Public Expenditure White Paper forms the basis for review of government expenditure by House of Commons committees and by the House itself.

The Expenditure Committee and its successors

From 1971 until 1979 a Select Committee on Expenditure considered any papers on public expenditure presented to the House of Commons, and such of the estimates as it thought fit. In particular, the Committee considered how, if at all, the policies implied in the figures of expenditure and in the estimates could be carried out more economically. The Committee worked through six sub-committees, each concerned with a particular type of public expenditure. It produced reports and aimed to help keep Parliament better informed about the activities of government. In 1979 this Committee, along with other "subject" and "departmental" Select Committees, was replaced by a new comprehensive system of select committees relating to government departments.[44] All 14 committees established are authorised to examine the expenditure, administration and policy of the principal government departments and associated public bodies.[45] The Public Expenditure White Paper may be examined for its particular departmental implications by any of these committees, but the most significant will be the examination and subsequent report by the Treasury and Civil Service Committee. In recent years it has become the practice for the Commons not to debate the White Paper until after the publication of the Treasury and Civil Service Committee report, to enable a more informed debate to take place. At the end of this debate the House will vote on whether to approve or disapprove the Public Expenditure proposals. However, there is no legal requirement that a Government defeated on this vote should resign or alter its proposals. The role of the House of Commons is to scrutinise, and not to control, total public expenditure.

Securing the legality of public expenditure

Parliamentary scrutiny of the legality of public expenditure is carried out by a Select Committee, the Committee of Public Accounts, which bases its work on reports made by the Comptroller and Auditor General (C. & A.G.). This structure for an external audit of public accounts was

---

[40] The Select Committee on Procedure (Finance) (1982–83; H.C. 241) suggested that a definition should be explicitly agreed to by Parliament.

[41] Expenditure from the Contingencies Fund is not included as public expenditure, since no expenditure from it is planned.

[42] The single largest item of non-supply expenditure, usually representing about 25 per cent. of total public expenditure.

[43] i.e. finance by way of government grant or government or market borrowing.

[44] Post p. 231.

[45] S.O. No. 130.

established at the end of the nineteenth century,[46] and in substance remained little changed until 1983 when the National Audit Act (N.A.A.) was passed.[47] This Act sought to strengthen Parliamentary control and supervision of expenditure of public money by making changes in the status of the C. & A.G. and increasing his power.

The Comptroller and Auditor General[48]

The C. & A.G. is an officer of the House of Commons.[49] He is appointed by the Crown on an address by the House of Commons which is moved by the Prime Minister with the agreement of the Chairman of the Public Accounts Committee.[50] His independence of the executive and Parliament is ensured in several ways: his salary is charged on the Consolidated Fund[51]; he holds office during good behaviour, being removable only on an address from both Houses of Parliament[52]; and, subject to any statutory duties, he has complete discretion in the discharge of his functions, subject to the proviso that he takes into account proposals from the Committee of Public Accounts.[53] The C. & A.G. is head of the National Audit Office[54] (N.A.O.), and is responsible for the appointment and remuneration of such staff as he considers necessary.[55]

The C. & A.G., as his title implies, has two main functions. First, as Comptroller, he controls the issue of money from the Consolidated Fund and the National Loans Fund. The Treasury sends an authority to the C. & A.G. requesting the payment of money to government departments. Before directing the Bank of England to pay, the C. & A.G. has to be satisfied that there is statutory authority for the payment and that all statutory requirements have been complied with.

Secondly, as Auditor General, through his staff at the N.A.O., he audits the accounts of central government departments and various other public bodies, such as Regional Health Authorities and the uni-

---

[46] The Committee of Public Accounts was established in 1861. The Exchequer and Audit Departments Act 1866 created the office of Comptroller and Auditor General.

[47] The background to this Act was several House of Commons papers critical of existing auditing arrangements e.g. (1977–78; H.C. 535), (1977–78; H.C. 588), (1980–81; H.C. 115); and lukewarm Government response, e.g. (1979) Cmnd. 7845, (1981) Cmnd. 8323. See also Barnett *The Extension of Public Spending Auditing in the United Kingdom*, The Parliamentarian LXIII (1982) 79; Pitblado *Proposals for Expanded Scrutiny of Public Spending in the United Kingdom*, The Parliamentarian LXII (1981) 209. The N.A.A. started life as a private members Bill (Parliamentary Control of Expenditure (Reform) Bill) which was taken over and substantially amended by the Government: See Drewry [1983] P.L. 531.

[48] His full title is Comptroller General of the Exchequer and Auditor General of the Public Accounts.

[49] N.A.A. s.1(2).

[50] N.A.A. s.1(1).

[51] Parliamentary and other Pensions and Salaries Act 1976, s.6.

[52] Exchequer and Audit Departments Act 1866.

[53] N.A.A. s.1(3). Certain powers of direction and intervention previously exercised over the C. & A.G. by the Treasury are repealed N.A.A. s.11 and Sched. 5.

[54] N.A.A. s.3. Formerly known as the Exchequer and Audit Office.

[55] N.A.A. s.3(2) (3). The N.A.O. has a staff of more than 800. Each year the C. & A.G. must present estimates for the N.A.O. to the newly established Public Accounts Commission (N.A.A., s.2) which shall examine them and present them, with any necessary modifications, to the House of Commons.

versities. The extent and nature of this audit was reformed by the N.A.A. Now the C. & A.G. has statutory authority not only to conduct a finance and regularity audit, that is to ensure that expenditure was made for the purposes authorised by Parliament, but also to carry out a value for money (V.F.M.) audit. This enables him to examine "the economy, efficiency and effectiveness" of the use of resources to discharge the functions of any of the bodies to which the N.A.A. applies.[56] This is, in fact, a statutory recognition of functions the C. & A.G. had performed for many years. The question, over which bodies the C. & A.G. should have powers, has proved controversial, and the N.A.A. does not greatly extend his jurisdiction. In particular the auditing of public money spent by the nationalised industries continues to be excluded.[57]

To enable him to carry out his work the C. & A.G. has a statutory right of access to documents in the possession of any of the bodies concerned.[58] The C. & A.G. may report to the House of Commons the results of any audits carried out by him.[59] These reports form the basis of the work of the Committee of Public Accounts.

The Committee of Public Accounts[60]

This Committee consists of not more than 15 members appointed at the beginning of each session to examine all appropriation accounts and "such other accounts laid before Parliament as the Committee may think fit."[61] By tradition it is chaired by a member of the Opposition and the C. & A.G. attends all its meetings. It can propose to the C. & A.G. that he should conduct a V.F.M. audit into a body supervised by him. In the light of reports by the C. & A.G. the Committee will examine whether government policy has been carried out efficiently, effectively and economically. In carrying out these investigations it will examine the chief accounting and other senior officers of departments under investigation. In recent years it has identified fraud and corruption in the Property Services Agency[62] (the body responsible for building and maintaining government property); the need for economies in the cost of N.H.S. supplies[63]; and the grave misuse of public resources in the De Lorean car project.[64]

The Committee makes its reports to Parliament, and one day each session is devoted to debating its reports. The importance attached to

[56] N.A.A. s.6(1) and s.7(1).
[57] They would have been included under the original version of the Bill. The auditing of the spending of public money by local authorities which a Report had suggested should be transferred to the C. & A.G. (1977) H.C. 588, had been superseded by the establishment of a statutory Audit Commission for local authorities under the Local Government Finance Act 1982.
[58] N.A.A., s.8.
[59] N.A.A., s.9. See e.g. (1986–87; H.C. 131) which is critical of the use made of the assets of the Defence Estate by the Ministry of Defence; also (1986–87; H.C. 95) on the use of manpower in the N.H.S.
[60] Flegmann, *The Public Accounts Committee; A Successful Select Committee?* XXXIII Parliamentary Affairs (1980), 166; Sheldon, *Public Sector Auditing and United Kingdom Committee of Public Accounts in 1984* LXV The Parliamentarian (1984), 91.
[61] S.O. No. 122.
[62] (1983–84; H.C. 295).
[63] (1984–85; H.C. 280).
[64] (1983–84; H.C. 127).

these reports is shown by the Government undertaking to make a reply to the debate.

An additional function of the Committee is to look at "excess votes"—that is where a department has spent more upon a service in the financial year than the amount granted to it by Parliament. Before Parliament can approve an excess vote, a report will have been made to the Committee by the C. & A.G., which will have to report that it sees no objection to the sums being provided in this way.

II. Scrutiny of the Administration

Party organisation usually ensures that government proposals will be adopted by Parliament, and legislation passed to accord with the wishes of the Government. This increases the importance of Parliament's role in the scrutiny of the working of the administration. Parliament is assisted in this role by the law on parliamentary privilege,[65] which enables M.P.'s to criticise and comment freely on matters of public concern, and the rules whereby it is contempt for a witness to refuse to assist Parliament in carrying out this, and its various other functions.[66]

There are a variety of different ways in which the Commons can participate in the scrutiny of the administration.

Questions[67]

The device of parliamentary questions developed slowly in the eighteenth century, and became increasingly important after the Reform Act of 1832.

Owing to the strictness of party discipline in modern times, debates tend to run on party lines. Question time therefore constitutes an important check on the activities of the executive, and is now one of the most important functions of Parliament. Each year over 40,000 questions are tabled by M.P.'s. Questions are asked in order to focus attention on matters of topical interest either to individual constituents or to the public generally. Owing to the publicity given by the media, the practice is indulged in more for the benefit of the electorate than of the House. "If I want to get something done I write to the Minister," said Sir Austen Chamberlain; "if I want to cause trouble I put down a parliamentary question." It is by asking questions that the private member comes into his own, for he can put forward the grievances of individual citizens who have suffered at the hands of government departments, thereby reinforcing the convention of ministerial responsibility. It is also a useful tool for members of the Opposition for, when used skilfully, the asking of questions may be made a source of considerable embarrassment to the Government.

Questions may be asked and answered orally or in writing. Oral

---

[65] *Post*, Chap. 12.
[66] *Post*, pp. 244–245.
[67] Select Committee on Procedure: Question Time (1969–70; H.C. 198); Select Committee on Parliamentary Questions (1971–72; H.C. 393). See P. Howarth, *Questions in the House* (1956); D.N. Chester and N. Bowring, *Questions in Parliament* (1962); D.N. Chester in *The Commons Today* (S.A. Walkland and M. Ryle eds.), Chap. 8; S.O. No. 17.

answers are given at question time which lasts for 45 to 50 minutes every sitting day except Friday, and is attended by Ministers according to a published rota. Unless the Speaker gives special leave, written notice of intention to ask a question must be delivered beforehand to the Clerk of the House at the table. Where an oral answer is required, an asterisk is affixed to the notice. A member is limited to two oral questions a day and not more than eight during any period of ten sitting days. There is no limit to the number of questions for written answer which a member may ask on the same day. A member may not "preempt" time by giving more than ten sitting days' notice of an oral question. If there is no asterisk, or the member is not in the House, or the question is not reached by the time-limit, the Minister concerned has the answer printed in the Official Report. The member may, however, postpone or withdraw his question. A member who wishes to receive a written answer on a named day may indicate this by marking the question with the letter "W" and the specified date. Where a member considers a Minister's reply to an oral question is unsatisfactory supplementary questions may be asked. "Originally, questions were asked in order to secure an answer," says Jennings[68]; "Today they often serve as pegs on which to hand a more insidious 'supplementary.' "

Questions addressed to a Minister[69] must relate either to: (i) public affairs with which he is officially connected, (ii) proceedings pending in Parliament, or (iii) matters of administration for which he is *responsible,* that is, which come within the work of his department, or his official duties or powers.[70] An admissible question is one that asks for information or action, and not merely raises an interesting topic of the day. A question must relate to a matter within the Government's responsibility, or one that can be made so by legislation or administrative action.

The public corporations set up under various nationalisation Acts have given rise to a problem of considerable constitutional importance. How far are questions relating to them admissible and to what extent is a Minister, who has a general control over the policy of such a corporation, expected to answer questions arising out of its operations? This question, which is bound up with the entire constitutional framework of such corporations, has been much debated in Parliament, and it cannot be said that a satisfactory solution has yet been found.[71]

A problem also arises with regard to questions to the Prime Minister, who has few direct departmental responsibilities.[72] To circumvent this problem members have increasingly used "open" questions in which they ask for a list of the Prime Minister's official engagements for a certain day. The purpose of this type of question is to ask a topical or unex-

---

[68] Jennings, *op. cit.* p. 106.

[69] Questions may be asked of non-official members relating to Bills, motions or other matters concerned with the business of the House for which they are responsible, *e.g.* chairmen of certain Select Committees.

[70] H.C. Deb., Vol. 599, cols. 1181–1182 (1958–59); Select Committee on Parliamentary Questions 1971–72; (1972; H.C. 393). See *post,* p. 415 on questions to the Home Secretary in regard to police matters.

[71] See further *post,* Chap. 28.

[72] Select Committee on Procedure *Questions to the Prime Minister* (1976–77; H.C. 320).

pected question as a supplementary. Despite criticisms of this procedure, the House has decided that it should continue.[73]

The Speaker is the final authority on the admissibility of questions, and in his decisions he implements the rules of the House on the form and content of questions. For example, opinions must not be asked, and purely legal questions are not allowed, nor may a question refer to any debate that has occurred in either House in the current session. Questions may not be asked that bring the name of the Sovereign or the influence of the Crown directly before Parliament, or that cast reflections on the Sovereign or the Royal Family. Imputations on private character are not permitted, but imputations on official character may be made with certain reservations. Questions may not be put on matters pending in a committee till the report of that committee is issued. A question must be a question: argument or statements of fact are not permitted.

Since no Minister is obliged to answer a question a Minister may decline to answer a question on the ground of public policy, and the Foreign Secretary is on this account allowed great latitude. A Minister may also decline to answer a question or to supply information on security grounds.[74] The Prime Minister cannot be questioned on the date proposed for the dissolution of Parliament or on relations between herself and the Monarch.[75] Government supporters may ask "inspired questions" to enable a Minister to make an announcement.[76]

The work required to answer questions is done by the civil servants in the department concerned, and can take up a great deal of time. The cost of answering written questions in the session 1983–84 was £1,680,000.[77]

Debates[78]

There are a variety of occasions when private members may use the technique of debate to scrutinise government activities. The most frequent is the daily motion for adjournment of the House. This provides a half-hour at the end of the day in which almost any matter not involving legislation may be discussed. There is usually no division as adjournment is automatic when the time-limit is reached. A weekly ballot is held among those who wish to raise a matter on the daily adjournment. These debates are particularly valuable to private members who remain unsatisfied with answers to questions to Ministers. Adjournment debates also take place for a full day four times a year before the House adjourns for holidays, and these days are available to private members.

[73] H.C. Deb., Vol. 36 col. 423 (1982–83) February 3, 1983. The House has agreed to a report from the Select Committee on Procedure *Printing of Oral Questions to the Prime Minister* (1984–85) H.C. 298, whereby the cost of printing such questions could be reduced by £70,000 a year. H.C. Deb. Vol. 77, col. 20 (1984–85).

[74] As did Sir Anthony Eden in 1956 in connection with Commander Crabb, the "frogman." For a recent debate see H.C. Deb., Vol. 76, col. 1377–1384 (1985–86).

[75] H.C. Deb. Vol. 101, col. 1170 (1985–86).

[76] For example the question which led to the naming of Anthony Blunt H.C. Deb., Vol. 973, col. 679–681 (1979–80).

[77] H.C. Deb. Vol. 78, col. 15 (1984–85).

[78] For the rules of debate see *ante*, p. 204.

Under the supply procedure reforms introduced in 1982 there are two occasions which may be used by private members for scrutiny. First there are the 20 Opposition Days when the matters to be debated can be decided by the Opposition. Secondly, there is provision for the adjournment of the House at the conclusion of proceedings on the Consolidated Fund Bill and the Appropriation Bill. The debates which follow enable private members to raise matters of their choice, and the debate can continue all night.

Finally the Opposition may choose topics for debate during the Annual Address in reply to the Queen's speech. Debates may not be the best means of inquiring in depth into government administration, but they do enable topics to be aired in public and may result in further action elsewhere.

Select Committees

Parliament uses select committees[79] for a wide variety of purposes including scrutinising the administration. We have already considered one such committee, the Committee of Public Accounts. The other committees which chiefly fulfil this function are the 14 Select Committees established for the first time in 1979, after many years of discussion,[80] on the basis of a report from the Committee of Procedure.[81] Each of these committees, as its name indicates, is concerned with a different government department: Agriculture; Defence; Education; Science and Arts; Employment; Energy; Environment; Foreign Affairs; Home Affairs; Trade and Industry; Scottish Affairs; Social Services; Transport; Treasury and Civil Service.[82] The major omission is the Lord Chancellor's Department. This structure replaced the earlier ad hoc select committee arrangements whereby there were a variety of "subject" and "departmental" committees, but no permanent and comprehensive system of committees.[83] The system as introduced in 1979 marked a variety of other changes in the select committee system. The existence of the committees is regulated by standing order[84] and their continuation is therefore not dependent on the Government of the day. The selection of members of the committees is by the Selection Committee, which is composed of private members, and not by the party whips. This Committee has refused to appoint to the select committees anyone with an official position in the political parties. The staffing of the Committees

---

[79] *Ante* p. 208; S.O. No. 104–131.

[80] See, for example, R.S. Lankester, "Specialist Committees in the House of Commons" (1969) XXXVIII *The Table*, p. 64; *The Growth of Parliamentary Scrutiny by Committee*, a symposium by Alfred Morris M.P. and Others (1970); John Mackintosh M.P., *Specialist Committees in the House of Commons: Have they failed?* (University of Edinburgh, 1970); Ronald Butt, *The Power of Parliament* (1970); K. Bradshaw and D. Pring, *Parliament & Congress* (1972); M. Partington, "Parliamentary Committees: Recent Developments" (1969–70) 23 *Parliamentary Affairs* 366; D.R. Shell, "Specialist Select Committees" *ibid.* p. 380.

[81] First Report from the Select Committee on Procedure (1977–78; H.C. 588).

[82] With the exception of the Scottish Affairs Committee which has a maximum of 13 members, all the Committees have a maximum of 11 members. The Foreign Affairs Committee, the Home Affairs Committee and the Treasury and Civil Service Committee each have power to appoint one sub-committee.

[83] See O. Hood Phillips (6th ed.), p. 230–231.

[84] S.O. No. 130.

is much improved. In addition to a permanent staff of three or four, each Committee may recruit specialist advisers, such as professors and generals, who are paid on a *pro rata* daily basis. A further reform was the establishment of a Liaison Committee[85] made up of *all* the select committee chairmen. This Committee considers general matters relating to the work of Select Committees, for example it can help to prevent more than one Committee investigating the same subject. It can express the joint views of the various Select Committees and, since its inception, has produced two reports on the Select Committee System.[86]

Each Select Committee is empowered "to examine the expenditure, administration and policy"[87] of the department with which it is concerned, and also of "associated public bodies."[88] In common with all Select Committees, each Committee has power to send for "persons, papers and records."[89] The purpose of the departmental Select Committees is to assist the House of Commons to play an active role in the criticism and scrutiny of government and to help enforce the accountability of ministers to Parliament, a role which was highlighted by the "Westland Affair."[90] These committees have a wide discretion as to how they do their work, but broadly speaking they are concerned with monitoring departments by taking evidence, questioning witnesses and making reports upon matters which they think should be investigated. From their inception until April 1985 a total of 275 reports were made[91] and the House debated reports on substantive motions on four occasions. In addition reports have been useful in giving the House background facts for particular debates, and so enable members to be better informed. By convention the Government replies to Committee reports.

It is probably still too soon to decide whether the new departmental Select Committees have helped redress the balance of power between Parliament and the Executive.[92] The Government still has certain advantages in connection with the Committees. Ministers cannot be required to appear as witnesses,[93] and if they do attend may rely on the

---

[85] S.O. No. 131.

[86] (1982–83; H.C. 92), D. Pring "The New Select Committee System at Westminster" (1983) LXIV *The Parliamentarian*, p. 57, J. Sweetman "The New Select Committees At Westminster—An Interim Appraisal" (1983) 51 *The Table* 69; (1984–85; H.C. 363). These reports made several suggestions for reform.

[87] S.O. No. 130.

[88] This includes the boards of nationalised industries see *post*, p. 607, and other public corporations and advisory bodies such as the Equal Opportunities Commission.

[89] *Ante* p. 208.

[90] Fourth Report from the Defence Committee. *Westland* plc: The Governments' Decision-Making (1985–86; H.C. 519).

[91] (1984–85; H.C. 363). In the period October 1979—April 1985 a total of 19 reports were debated, while a further 45 were referred to as being relevant to a debate to take place in the House. Among the most notable reports have been: *The Future Defence of the Falkland Islands* (1982–83; H.C. 154); *Unions in G.C.H.Q.* (1983–84; H.C. 128); *The Special Branch of the Police Force* (1984–85; H.C. 71).

[92] A variety of assessments have been made. See, for example, A. Davies, *Reformed Select Committees: The First year* (1980); *Parliamentary Select Committees in Action: A symposium* ((D.M. Hill ed. 1984); *Commons Select Committees: Catalysts for Progress* (D. Englefield 1984), *The New Select Committees A study of the 1979 Reforms* (Gavin Drewry ed. 1985).

[93] This had been recommended by the Select Committee on Procedure (1977–78; H.C. 588), but rejected by the Government.

notion of collective responsibility so as not to answer certain questions. Civil servants, who are the most frequent witnesses before the Committees, are subject to the terms of a memorandum which was prepared by the Civil Service Department[94] and which enables them to withhold information in the interests of "good government" or national security. The definition of good government is wide and includes advice given to ministers by civil servants and exchanges between government departments on matters of policy.[95] Finally, it is for the Government to make time available to debate the reports of the Committees. Down to 1986 very little time was provided.

The new Select Committee system, together with the reforms in supply procedures, are important moves towards adapting the procedure of the House of Commons to the increasing power of government.[96]

---

[94] Select Committees—Memorandum of Guidance for Officials 80/83 See *The Times* May 30, 1983.

[95] (1982–83; H.C. 92). The "Westland Affair" gave rise to several reports which considered the position of civil servants and Ministers before select committees. See *e.g.* (1985–86; H.C. 92); (1985–86; H.C. 519); Cmnd. 9916; (1986–87; H.C. 62); (1986–87; H.C. 100).

[96] See Gavin Drewry "Select Committees and Back-bench Power," in *The Changing Constitution, op. cit.* Chap. 6.

CHAPTER 12

PARLIAMENTARY PRIVILEGE[1]

The nature of parliamentary privilege

Privilege, notably freedom from arrest, was originally part of the King's peace. It ensured the attendance of members of the Council, judicial and other public officers, and members of the royal household. From the reign of Henry VIII the Commons as well as the Lords have been left to enforce their own privileges.

Each House exercises certain powers and privileges which are regarded as essential to the dignity and proper functioning of Parliament. The members also have certain privileges, although these exist for the benefit of the House and not for the personal benefit of the members. "As every Court of justice hath laws and customs for its direction," says Coke, "so the High Court of Parliament *suis propriis legibus et consuetudinibus subsistit*. It is *lex et consuetudo parliamenti* that all weighty matters in any Parliament moved concerning the peers of the realm or commons in Parliament assembled, ought to be determined, adjudged and discussed by the course of the parliament, and not by the civil law, nor yet by the common laws of this realm used in more inferior Courts."[2] Erskine May defines parliamentary privilege as "the sum of the peculiar rights enjoyed by each House collectively as a constituent part of the High Court of Parliament,[3] and by members of each House individually without which they could not discharge their functions, and which exceed those possessed by other bodies or individuals."[4]

Parliamentary privilege is to some extent analogous to royal prerogative; both are exceptional, peculiar and discretionary; and both are part of the common law, not in the sense that they are judge-made, but in the sense that the courts recognise their existence and claim jurisdiction to keep the Crown or the Houses (as the case may be) within the limits so recognised. They differ, however, in that while the royal prerogative is part of the law enforced by the ordinary courts, parliamentary privilege is enforced by each House through its officers. Further, prerogative extends throughout Her Majesty's dominions, while privilege is limited to the United Kingdom.

Privilege is part of "the law and custom of Parliament"—to be collected, says Coke, "out of the rolls of Parliament and other records, and by precedents and continued experience." Some of it has the authority

---

[1] See Erskine May, *Parliamentary Practice* (20th ed., 1983). See also Anson, *Law and Custom of the Constitution*, Vol. I (5th ed., Gwyer), pp. 153–189, 242–247; Wittke, *Parliamentary Privilege*; Holdsworth, *History of English Law*, Vol. VI, pp. 92–100; Sir Ivor Jennings. *The Law and the Constitution* (5th ed.), pp. 112 *et seq.*; Viscount Kilmuir, *The Law of Parliamentary Privilege* (Athlone Press, 1959); R. F. V. Heuston, *Essays in Constitutional Law* (2nd ed. 1964), Chap. 4; O. Hood Phillips, *Reform of the Constitution* (1970), pp. 75–81.
[2] 4 Inst. 15.
[3] The House of Lords is a court of record, the House of Commons probably not.
[4] Erskine May, *op. cit.* p. 70. The power to commit for contempt, however, is not essential to the discharge of its functions; see *post*, p. 244.

of statute, notably the provision of the Bill of Rights 1688 relating to freedom of speech and debates or proceedings in Parliament. A Bill that concerns the privileges of either House should commence in the House to which it relates.

I. THE PRIVILEGES OF THE COMMONS

The privileges of the Commons have been described as "the sum of the fundamental rights of the House and of its individual Members as against the prerogatives of the Crown, the authority of the ordinary courts of law and the special rights of the House of Lords."[5] Some are available against the Crown, some against the House of Lords, and others against the citizen. They are much more important at the present day than the privileges of the Lords owing to the predominant position attained by the Commons, and there have been few disputes relating to the Lords' privileges (except in relation to the Commons) in modern times.

These privileges are commonly divided into two classes, namely, those specifically claimed by the Speaker at the opening of a new Parliament and those not so claimed, though the fact of a privilege being claimed by the Speaker carries with it no superior force. Indeed, some of those specifically claimed by the Speaker have been confirmed or limited by statute. The "ancient and undoubted" privileges formally claimed by the Speaker since the sixteenth century are: (i) freedom of speech in debate; (ii) freedom from arrest; (iii) access of the Commons to the Crown through the Speaker[6]; and (iv) that the Crown will place the best construction on the deliberations of the Commons. (This last is not now important.) The Lord Chancellor, on behalf of the Sovereign, declares that they are "most readily granted and confirmed." The privileges not specifically claimed by the Speaker are: (i) the right of the House to regulate its own composition; (ii) the right to take exclusive cognisance of matters arising within the House; (iii) the right to punish members and strangers for breach of privilege and contempt; (iv) the right of impeachment[7]; and (v) the right to control finance and initiate financial legislation.[8]

1. Freedom of speech and debate[9]

Freedom of speech and debate is the essential attribute of every free legislature, and may be regarded as inherent in the constitution of Parliament (*Haxey's Case*).[10] Strode's Act 1512 provided "that all suits, etc. against all persons of that particular or any other Parliament . . . for any

---

[5] Redlich and Ilbert, *Procedure of the House of Commons*, Vol. I, p. 46.
[6] Privy Councillors have a customary right of individual access, but modern convention requires that the Sovereign should take political advice from Ministers only.
[7] See Chap. 7.
[8] See Chap. 11.
[9] See David R. Mummery "The Privilege of Freedom of Speech in Parliament" [1978] 94 L.Q.R. 276; Patricia M. Leopold "Freedom of Speech in Parliament—its Misuse and Proposals for Reform," [1981] P.L. 30.
[10] (1397) Rot. Parl., iii, 434 (petition to Parliament for curtailment of King's household expenses). See Taswell-Langmead, *Constitutional History* (11th ed. Plucknett), pp. 174–175, 195.

Bill, or speaking . . . of any matter concerning the Parliament be of none effect." The Stuart lawyers regarded the Act as establishing freedom of debate, but *Strode's Case*,[11] out of which it arose, only concerned indictment in an inferior court for introducing a Bill into Parliament. Sir Thomas More, as Speaker, petitioned Henry VIII for freedom of speech in 1523, but did not consider it a matter of right. From the beginning of Elizabeth I's reign freedom of speech has been regularly claimed as a right,[12] although that monarch did not always respect it. In *R. v. Eliot, Hollis and Valentine*[13] three members were imprisoned and fined by the Court of King's Bench for "seditious words" spoken in the House, the Court holding that Strode's Act was not a public Act. The Houses in 1641 and 1667 passed resolutions against this judgment, and it was reversed by the Lords on a writ of error in 1668. After this case no legal proceedings were ever taken by the Crown for words spoken in the House. The Bill of Rights (1688) declares that "the freedom of speech and debates or proceedings in Parliament ought not to be impeached or questioned in any Court or place out of Parliament" (Art 9). The effect of this is that Members enjoy complete civil and criminal immunity in respect of things said by them in the course of proceedings in Parliament.[14] A citizen who regards himself as having been defamed will have no legal remedy, nor can a member who appears to say something which could be a contravention of the criminal law, be prosecuted.[15] However, members are subject to the Houses' own internal rules of conduct,[16] breach of which can be punished by the House itself.[17] Members are also under a duty to refrain from any course of action which could prejudice the privilege of freedom of speech, for example by entering into a contract which could limit a member's independence and freedom of action in Parliament.[18]

Proceedings in Parliament

What is said or done by a member is absolutely privileged provided it is part of a debate or "proceeding in Parliament." As Erskine May says " . . . it does not follow that everything that is said or done within the Chamber during the transaction of business forms part of proceedings in Parliament."[19] Yet, what amounts to a "proceeding in Parliament" has never been defined either by the courts or the Commons.[20] The

---

[11] Taswell-Langmead, *op. cit.* pp. 247–249, 377–378.

[12] J. E. Neale, "The Commons' Privilege of Free Speech in Parliament" *Tudor Studies* (ed. Selton-Watson, 1924).

[13] (1629) 3 St. Tr. 294; Taswell-Langmead, *op. cit.* pp. 377–378, 390. The members were also charged with an assault on the Speaker; see *post*, p. 237.

[14] *Wason v. Walter* (1868) L.R. 4 Q.B. 73; *Dillon v. Balfour* (1887) 20 L.R. Ir. 600.

[15] The *Duncan Sandys* case concerning the Official Secrets Act (1938–39; H.C. 101).

[16] For, *e.g.* the *sub judice* rule. Members may not use their freedom of speech to infringe the freedom of speech or action of other Members—See First Report from the Committee of Privileges (1983–84; H.C. 564); see P.M. Leopold [1984] P.L. 547.

[17] *Post*, p. 245.

[18] W.J. *Brown's* case (paid secretary of trade union) (1946–47; H.C. 118). See O. Hood Phillips (1947) 10 M.L.R. 420. Since 1975 there has been a compulsory (though unenforceable) register of Members' interests.

[19] *Op. cit.* p. 94.

[20] There have been several Reports in which suggestions for a statutory definition have been made *e.g.*: (1969–70; H.C. 261); Cmnd. 5909 (1975); (1976–77; H.C. 417).

opinion of the Committee of Privileges in the *Strauss* case (1958)[21] that it covers everything said or done by a Member of Parliament *in his capacity as a Member* is surely too wide. The expression obviously covers speaking in debate or on a question and voting in the House on parliamentary business; and it includes action taken by the officers of the House in pursuance of its orders.[22] There are dicta in *Burdett* v. *Abbot*[23] and *Bradlaugh* v. *Gossett*[24] to the effect that privilege does not cover crimes or breaches of the peace committed within the House. The answer may depend on whether the act would be regarded as part of the proceedings of the House.[25] It has been held to be contrary to Article 9 of the Bill of Rights to impugn the validity of the report of a Select Committee, especially when it has been accepted as valid by the House by being printed in its Journal.[26]

One of the particular problems which has arisen is whether a letter from a Member to a Minister is a proceeding in Parliament. This question arose in the *Strauss* case (1958) where H. G. Strauss M.P. wrote a letter to a Minister reflecting on the method of disposing of scrap cable by the London Electricity Board (a public corporation administering a nationalised industry). The Minister sent a copy to the chairman of the Board. The Board thereupon instructed their solicitors to commence a libel action against Mr. Strauss if he refused to withdraw his statements. Mr. Strauss raised a question of privilege. The House sought the opinion of the Privy Council on the question whether the House, if it treated the issue of the writ as a breach of privilege, would be acting contrary to the Parliamentary Privilege Act 1770 (which provides that any person may at any time bring any action in any court against any member of either House of Parliament, and that no such action shall be impeached on the ground of privilege). Their opinion was that the Act applies only to proceedings against members in their private capacity, *e.g.* actions for debt, and does not affect the privileges of Parliament. However their Lordships emphasised that by their answer they did not intend to pronounce on any other question connected with privilege, since they had not been asked to do so (*Re Parliamentary Privilege Act* 1770).[27] The House decided by a small majority that Strauss's letter was not a proceeding in Parliament, and that the Electricity Board and their solici-

---

[21] Fifth Report of the Committee of Privileges (1956–57; H.C. 305); And see *Att.-Gen. of Ceylon* v. *De Livera* [1963] A.C. 103 (P.C.); offer of bribe to member acting in that capacity; *Roman Corporation Ltd.* v. *Hudson's Bay Oil & Gas Co. Ltd.* (1971) 23 D.L.R. (3d) 292 (Ont. C.A.) statements made outside House by Ministers discharging their essential functions, and referring to an announcement made by them in the House, were "proceedings in Parliament."

[22] *Bradlaugh* v. *Gossett* (1884) 12 Q.B.D. 271.

[23] (1811) 14 East 1.

[24] *op. cit.*

[25] Stephen J. suggested in *Bradlaugh* v. *Gossett* that the accused in *R.* v. *Elliott, Hollis and Valentine* (1629) 3 St. Tr. 284, might have been properly charged in a separate indictment with assaulting the Speaker in the House.

[26] *Dingle* v. *Asssociated Newspapers Ltd.* [1960] 2 Q.B. 405.

[27] [1958] A.C. 331; (1958) Cmnd. 431; note by E. C. S. Wade in (1958) C.L.J. 134; Lord Denning, "The Strauss Case" [1985] P.L. 80.

tors had therefore not committed a breach of privilege.[28] The action for libel was not in fact brought, but the Minister held an independent inquiry which exonerated the Board.[29]

The Speaker later indicated that parliamentary privilege under the Bill of Rights would cover a letter written by a member to a Minister in response to his invitation made during a parliamentary debate, *e.g.* supplying information arising out of a question on the order paper.[30] On the other hand, it was held in *Rivlin* v. *Bilankin*[31] that a defamatory statement in a letter from B to a Member of Parliament concerning the conduct of B's former wife was not protected by parliamentary privilege, as it was not connected with any proceedings in Parliament.

Where a communication to a M.P. is not absolutely privileged, it may still have the common law defence of "qualified privilege" in tort, provided there is a common interest between the parties and an absence of malice.[32]

The Prevention of Corruption Acts 1889–1916 do not apply to members of Parliament in their capacity as such.[33] Although any action of a member that is not a proceeding in Parliament is subject to the ordinary law, it is doubtful whether a back-bench M.P. (as opposed to a Minister of the Crown) can be guilty of an offence under these Acts as he has no "employer or superior officer"; but there may be common law offences in the giving and taking of financial inducements by persons exercising public functions or occupying positions of trust. The Royal Commission on Standards of Conduct in Public Life[34] recommended that Parliament should consider bringing corruption, bribery and attempted bribery of a member acting in his parliamentary capacity within the ambit of the criminal law.

Right to exclude strangers

The Commons have always exercised the right to exclude strangers, that is, persons who are not members or officers of the House. This may be regarded both as a corollary to the principle of freedom of speech, and as necessary for the orderly conduct of business where there is a danger of disorderly interruption. If any member "spies strangers," the

---

[28] H.C.Deb., Vol. 430, col. 208 (1958); *cf.* Fifth Report of the Committee of Privileges, Session 1956–57. See S. A. de Smith "Parliamentary Privilege and the Bill of Rights" (1958) 21 M.L.R. 456; D. Thompson, "Letters to Ministers and Parliamentary Privilege" [1959] P.L. 10.

[29] (1958) Cmnd. 605. One difficulty in the *Strauss* case was that the matter concerned a public corporation in its day-to-day administration for which the Minister was not responsible; see *post*, Chap. 29.

[30] H.C.Deb. Vol. 591 col. 811.

[31] [1953] 1 Q.B. 485.

[32] *R.* v. *Rule* [1937] 2 K.B. 375 (letter from constituent to M.P. about conduct of police officer and magistrate); *Koolman-Darnley* v. *Gunter, The Times,* April 19, 1967 (C.A.) (letter from Minister to M.P.);. *Beach* v. *Freeson* [1972] 1 Q.B. 14 (letter from M.P. to Lord Chancellor and the Law Society); see Gatley, "Libel and Slander" (1981) Chap. 13.

[33] See Graham Zellick, "Bribery of Members of Parliament and the Criminal Law" [1979] P.L. 31.

[34] (1976) Cmnd. 6524; *cf.* note of dissent by Lord Salmon, the chairman. And see letter from Geoffrey Marshall to *The Times,* November 5, 1976, and from Sir John Foster to the *Observer,* October 24, 1976.

Speaker must put the question "that strangers do withdraw." The question is decided by vote, without debate. The resolution if carried operates for the rest of the day's sitting, but does not apply to members of the House of Lords. The Speaker also has the power of ordering strangers to withdraw.

The House may further resolve that the remainder of the day's sitting be a *secret session*, in which case it would be a contempt even for a member to disclose anything said or done unless the House resolves otherwise.[35]

Right to restrain publication of reports of proceedings

This was regarded as another corollary of the privilege of freedom of speech. The publication of parliamentary debates was forbidden by the House in the seventeenth century. Members at that time desired secrecy of debate to protect themselves from the Crown, and they later desired it to protect themselves from their constituents. The turning-point came with the case of *Miller* in 1771.[36] From then on the Commons ceased to enforce their standing orders against the publication of reports of debates and, after the Reform Act 1832, reporters' galleries were provided. However, it was, not until 1971 that the House of Commons resolved to renounce their claim to treat such publication as a breach of privilege. A further reform came in 1980, when the House resolved[37] that it would not regard as a breach of privilege the publication of reports of evidence given at public sittings of Select Committees, before the evidence had been reported to the House. However, the disclosure of the contents of a draft report is a contempt of Parliament, but one which has become increasingly difficult to enforce.[38]

The series of unofficial reports of parliamentary debates known as *Hansard*, from the name of the original publisher, began in 1803.[39] The "House of Commons Debates" have been an official publication of the House since 1909, and are still called "Hansard" although that family is no longer associated with them.[40]

Broadcasting of Proceedings[41]

In 1977 each House agreed to resolutions authorising the broadcasting the proceedings of the House and its committees, subject to the

---

[35] During the war this procedure was reinforced by Defence Regulations.

[36] May, *Constitutional History*, Vol. II, pp. 43–49. John Miller, a printer, was ordered to appear at the bar of the House for printing reports of debates, but he gave the messenger into custody for assault and false imprisonment. The City magistrates discharged Miller as not being guilty of any offence, and committed the messenger to prison for unlawful arrest. The Commons then committed the Lord Mayor and one of the magistrates to the Tower; but the citizens of London treated them as heroes until the prorogation of Parliament brought their release.

[37] See now S.O. No. 118.

[38] See Second Report from the Committee of Privileges, Premature Disclosure of Proceedings of Select Committee (1984–85; H.C. 417); First Report from the Committee of Privileges, Leak of Draft Report of Environment Committee (1985–86; H.C. 376) and see Leopold [1986] P.L. 368.

[39] J. C. Trewin and E. M. King, *Printer to the House: The Story of Hansard* (1952).

[40] *Cf.* The official report of proceedings contained in *Votes and Proceedings*.

[41] See First Report of the Select Committee on Sound Broadcasting (1981–82; H.C. 376).

directions of the House or a committee. A Select Committee on Sound Broadcasting was appointed by each House to give these directions. Since 1978 there has been regular sound broadcasting from both Houses, and since 1986 television broadcasting from the House of Lords on a permanent basis. Editorial control is the responsibility of the BBC and IBA and not with Parliament. Such broadcasts would appear not to be absolutely privileged, but only subject to qualified privilege at common law which probably only extends to defamation and not to criminal words.[42]

Parliamentary papers

It had long been established that immunity from judicial proceedings attached to a petition containing defamatory matter and circulated only among Members of Parliament (*Lake* v. *King*[43]); but it was held in *Stockdale* v. *Hansard*[44] that an order of either House authorising the publication of papers outside Parliament did not render the publisher immune from liability for libel. The latter decision was correct but inconvenient, and it was nullified by the Parliamentary Papers Act 1840. Section 1 provides that proceedings, criminal or civil, against persons for the publication of papers, reports, etc. printed *by order* of either House of Parliament are to be stayed. Section 2 provides that proceedings are to be stayed when commenced in respect of a correct *copy* of an authorised paper, report, etc. These provisions confer what in the law of tort is called "absolute privilege," *i.e.* immunity from judicial proceedings for libel. Section 3 provides that in proceedings for printing any *extract from or abstract of* an authorised paper, report, etc., it is a defence to show that such extract or abstract was published *bona fide* and without malice.[45] This is also the case for the broadcasting of extracts or abstracts of authorised papers, reports etc.[46] This in effect confers "qualified privilege," *i.e.* immunity from judicial proceedings if the publisher can show that the publication was in good faith and without malice, such as spite or improper motive.[47] The Act declares and enacts that nothing therein affects the privileges of Parliament (s.4). A member would not be liable if he *bona fide* published an extract from a parliamentary debate for the information of his constituents (*Davison* v. *Duncan*).[48]

However, the Parliamentary Papers Act does not provide any assistance for those who publish unauthorised accounts of parliamentary papers or proceedings, nor to those who broadcast live proceedings. In these cases reliance may be made on the common law defence of qualified privilege which exists with respect to defamation. It was held in

[42] See Leopold note 9 *op. cit* p. 43–47; Campbell [1984] P.L. 43.
[43] (1668) 1 Wms. Saund. 131.
[44] (1839) 9 A. & E. 1; *post*, p. 250.
[45] In *Dingle* v. *Associated Newspapers Ltd.* ([1960] 2 Q.B. 405) this defence was applied to an extract from the report of a Select Committee of the House of Commons.
[46] Defamation Act 1952, s.9.
[47] *Mangena* v. *Wright* [1909] 2 K.B. 958; *cf. Mangena* v. *Lloyd* (1908) 99 L.T. 824 (protection does not extend to headlines that are not part of the report).
[48] (1857) 7 E. & B. 229; *cf. R.* v. *Creevey* (1813) 1 M. & S. 273 (publication by a member in a newspaper of his own defamatory Parliament speech for the purpose of injuring an individual).

Wason v. *Walter*[49] to apply to an unauthorised report in *The Times* of a House of Lords debate, provided the report was fair and accurate and made without malice. This defence does not apply to garbled or partial reports, but can apply to a parliamentary sketch[50] in which a reporter gives his impression of a debate.[51]

The use of Reports of proceedings in Parliament in Court proceedings

Since 1980[52] it has not been necessary to seek leave of the House before referring to the official report of parliamentary proceedings in court. The use which can be made of reports is limited by the freedom of speech guaranteed to members by Article 9 of the Bill of Rights. In *Church of Scientology of California* v. *Johnson-Smith*[53] it was held that reports of parliamentary debates could not be read in court to prove malice in an action against a member for libel uttered in the course of a television interview.[54] Nor can a Report be used to cite something said in Parliament to support a ground for relief in proceedings for judicial review in respect of something which occurred outside Parliament.[55]

2. Freedom from arrest

Freedom from *civil* arrest was in former times an important privilege necessary for the proper functioning of Parliament, because arrest was often part of the process for commencing civil proceedings by compelling the appearance of the defendant before the court, and also of distress, that is, enforcing a money judgment. Owing to reforms in civil procedure in the nineteenth century, and the abolition of imprisonment for debt by the Debtors Act 1869, this privilege has lost most of its importance and only applies to a few cases, *e.g.* attachment for disobeying a court order for the payment of money.[56] The privilege lasted during a session of Parliament and forty days before and after; and it applied also where Parliament was dissolved or prorogued (*Goudy* v. *Dunscombe*).[57]

The privilege of freedom from arrest was never claimed by the Commons in cases of treason, felony (arrestable offence) or breach of the peace. In 1763 the Commons resolved that the privilege did not apply to seditious libel (a misdemeanour or non-arrestable offence), although the member concerned—the notorious John Wilkes—had been released

---

[49] (1868) L.R. 4 Q.B. 73, *per* Cockburn C.J.

[50] *Cook* v. *Alexander* [1974] Q.B. 279. See *per* Lord Denning M.R.

[51] It would appear that there is no comparable defence at common law for the publication of criminal words: see The Second Report from the Committee of Privileges (Col. "B" affair) (1978–79; H.C. 222), p. iv.

[52] When the House of Commons passed a resolution to implement a proposal made by the Committee of Privileges (1978–79; H.C. 102); H.C.Deb., Vol. 991, col. 916; (October 31, 1980).

[53] [1972] 1 Q.B. 522. The position in Australia is now governed by the Parliamentary Privileges Act 1987, passed to avoid the consequences of the interpretation of Art. 9 in *R.* v. *Murphy* (April 1986).

[54] See also *Dingle* v. *Associated Newspapers Ltd.* [1960] 2 Q.B. 405.

[55] *R.* v. *Secretary of State for Trade and others, ex p. Anderson Strathclyde p.l.c.* [1983] 2 All E.R. 233; See also David R. Mummery *op. cit.* note. 9.

[56] See *Stourton* v. *Stourton* [1963] P. 302; *post*, p. 249.

[57] (1847) 1 Exch. 430.

by the King's Bench on the ground of privilege. It does not cover acts prejudicial to the public safety or the defence of the realm under statutory Defence Regulations.[58]

When a Member of Parliament commits a crime he is arrested like anyone else,[59] and if he is convicted the court must notify the Speaker. The papers are then laid before the House at their request, and the member may be expelled. A member who is imprisoned by order of a court has no special privileges.[60]

3. Right of the House to regulate its own composition

This privilege covers: (i) the filling of casual vacancies, (ii) the determination of disputed election returns, (iii) the determination of legal disqualifications of persons returned to Parliament, and (iv) expulsion of members who are unfit to sit. These powers are exercised within the limits left by statute.

(i) *Filling casual vacancies.* The Speaker issues a warrant for the issue of a writ for an election to fill a casual vacancy.[61]

(ii) *Determination of disputed elections.* As has been seen, the right of the Commons to decide questions of disputed election returns was established as a result of the case of *Goodwin* v. *Fortescue,*[62] and was exercised until the Parliamentary Elections Act 1868. The Representation of the People Act 1983, s.144, which re-enacts with amendments the provisions of the Act of 1868 relating to election petitions, leaves nominally intact the privileges of the Commons, who in practice give effect to the findings of election courts.[63]

(iii) *Determination of legal disqualifications.* The House retains the right to determine of its own motion whether a person, who has otherwise been properly elected, is legally disqualified from sitting. If the House holds that the person is disqualified it will declare the seat vacant, and may refuse to admit him or may expel him if he has already been admitted.[64]

(iv) *Explusion of members who are unfit to serve.* The House may also expel a member who, although not subject to any legal disability, is in its opinion unfit to serve as a member. Until the Representation of the

---

[58] (1939–40; H.C. 164) (Re Captain Ramsey M.P.); it would have been otherwise if he had been detained for words spoken in the House. On the application of exclusion orders under the Prevention of Terrorism legislation see Clive P. Walker [1983] P.L. 537.

[59] But as to a crime committed in the House, see *ante,* p. 237.

[60] (1970–71; H.C. 185). This report of the Committee of Privileges arose out of the case of Miss Bernadette Devlin, M.P., who was sentenced to six months' imprisonment in 1970 by a court in Northern Ireland.

[61] *Cf. ante,* p. 184.

[62] (1604) 2 St. Tr. 91; *ante,* p. 199.

[63] *Ante,* p. 200.

[64] The House may seek the opinion of the Privy Council: *e.g. Re MacManaway* [1951] A.C. 161.

People Act 1981, which provides for the disqualification of any member who is detained for more than a year for any offence, this was commonly done when a court notified the Speaker that a member had been convicted of a serious criminal offence. The House cannot prevent an expelled member from being re-elected, as happened several times in the case of John Wilkes between 1769 and 1774, but it can refuse to allow him to take his seat.[65] Similar principles apply to expulsion for breach of privilege or contempt.

4. Exclusive right to regulate its own proceedings[66]

The courts must presume that so august an assembly as the House of Commons discharges its functions lawfully and properly. They will therefore not take cognisance of matters arising within the walls of the House, and they will accept the interpretation put by the Commons upon a statute affecting their internal proceedings. The case of *British Railways Board* v. *Pickin*[67] demonstrates that privilege is one of the main grounds on which the courts deny themselves jurisdiction to inquire into the legislative procedure in the House.

In *Bradlaugh* v. *Gossett*[68] Charles Bradlaugh, an atheist who had been elected as member for Northampton, brought an action in the High Court against the Serjeant-at-Arms for an injunction to restrain him from excluding him by force from the House of Commons, and a declaration that the order of the House preventing him from taking the oath was void. The Court gave judgment for the Serjeant-at-Arms on the ground that the privilege of the Commons to regulate its own *internal* proceedings—even where the application of the Parliamentary Oaths Act 1866 was involved—precluded the courts from inquiring into the question. The matter would have been different, said Stephen J., if the Commons had allowed Bradlaugh to sit, and had then purported by resolution to protect him against any statutory penalties at the instance of a common informer to which he might at that time have been liable *in the courts*.

A generous view of how far the House can regulate its own internal proceedings was taken in *R.* v. *Graham-Campbell, ex p. Herbert* (1935)[69] where the Divisional Court upheld the refusal of the Chief Metropolitan Magistrate for want of jurisdiction to try alleged breaches of a Licensing Act by the Kitchen Committee of the House. In any event the Court would probably have been prepared to hold that the Licensing Acts do not apply to the House of Commons, which is part of a royal palace. This case has been cited as an illustration of the right of the House "in a

---

[65] But under the R.P.A. 1981 the nomination of a person who is disqualified by virtue of this Act, is void.

[66] See G. F. Lock, "Labour Law Parliamentary Staff and Parliamentary Privilege" (1983) 12 I.L.J. 32.

[67] [1974] A.C. 765 (H.L.); *ante*, p. 52.

[68] (1884) 12 Q.B.D. 271. See also *Clarke* v. *Bradlaugh* (1881) 7 Q.B.D. 38; *Bradlaugh* v. *Clarke* (1883) App.Cas. 354; *Att.-Gen.* v. *Bradlaugh* (1885) 14 Q.B.D. 667. For the background, see W. L. Arnstein, *The Bradlaugh Case* (1965).

[69] [1935] 1 K.B. See R.F.V. Heuston *op. cit.* p. 94; *cf. Bear* v. *The State of South Australia.* 48(2) South Australian Industrial Reports 604; see G. F. Lock "Parliamentary Privilege and the Courts: The Avoidance of conflict" [1985] P.L. 64, 71.

proper case (to) claim exemption from Acts of Parliament which do not expressly apply to it."[70]

The House can always waive its privileges. For example, if one member killed or wounded another during a debate it would probably waive its privilege against arrest in the House.[71]

5. Power to punish for breach of privilege or contempt

Each House has power to enforce its *privileges* and to punish those—whether members or strangers—who infringe them. Each House also has power (this is one of its privileges) to punish members or strangers for *contempt.* Strickly speaking, "privileges"—and therefore breaches of them—are specific, whereas what constitutes "contempt," is not defined but is determinable by the House. *Contempts* generally are offences against the authority or dignity of the House, such as defamatory or disrespectful writings or statements about the House or its members as such, disobedience to orders of the House, or obstructions to the business or officers of the House. Offences against the authority or dignity of the House cannot be enumerated, the power to punish for contempt being discretionary. An act may be treated as a contempt even though there is no precedent of the offence. A breach of privilege is also a contempt, but a contempt is not necessarily a breach of privilege. Absence of wrongful intent, the truth of derogatory words, or ignorance of the facts does not exonerate, although it may affect the degree of punishment.[72]

The power to *punish* for contempt (as distinct from the ejection of persons who interrupt the proceedings), which has been exercised at least since the middle of the sixteenth century, is a judicial rather have a legislative power and not *necessary* to enable a legislature to function. The power is inherent in the Houses of the British Parliament for the historical reason that they are part of the High Court of Parliament and have been regarded as superior courts.[73] There is a strong argument for conferring the power of punishment on the courts, especially as regards the committal or other punishment of strangers for things said or done outside the House.

---

[70] Report from the Select Committee, on Parliamentary Privilege (1967–68; H.C. 34), p. xxvi. See also G. F. Lock, "The Application of the General Law to Parliament," [1985] P.L. 376.

[71] Spencer Perceval, the Prime Minister, was shot dead in the lobby of the House of Commons in 1812 by John Bellingham, who had a grievance against the government. Bellingham was tried within four days of the assassination, convicted (although probably insane) and executed two days later. During question time in January 1972 Miss Bernadette Devlin M.P. called the Home Secretary a "hypocritical liar" and assaulted him, pulling his hair and knocking off his spectacles. The Speaker called the Orders of the Day before members had the opportunity of raising a question of privilege, and no extra-parliamentary proceedings were taken.

[72] Cf. contempt of court: Administration of Justice Act 1960, ss.11, 12; reversing *R.* v. *Odhams Press, ex p. Att.-Gen.* [1967] 1 Q.B. 73.

[73] *R.* v. *Richards, ex p. Fitzpatrick and Browne* (1955) 92 C.L.R. 157 (Australian House of Representatives has the same privileges by statute). Cf. *Kielley* v. *Carson* (1842) 4 Moo.P.C. 63 (although colonial legislature can protect itself, *e.g.* by expelling those who disturb its proceedings, it cannot at common law punish for contempt); *Fenton* v. *Hampton* (1858) 11 Moo.P.C. 347.

Examples of breach of privilege and contempt

Without attempting to distinguish in the various instances between breach of privilege and contempt, we may give some further examples of these offences drawn from the parliamentary precedents. They include misconduct by strangers in the presence of either House, disobedience to the rules or wishes of either House; publication of false or perverted report of debates; summoning a member as witness or juror[74] (but the House usually allows a subpoena to be served outside the precincts); molesting a member of the House while he is going to or from it; bribery of a member (this would be contempt both by the member accepting and by the person giving the bribe); intimidation of members, or putting pressure on a member to execute his duties in a certain way (*W. J. Brown's* case, 1947)[75]; molesting or taking judicial proceedings against officers of either House in connection with their official conduct; obstructing or molesting witnesses summoned to either House or a committee thereof.

In *Allighan's* case (1947)[76] Allighan, a member, wrote a newspaper article stating that confidential information relating to parliamentary party meetings was conveyed by M.P.s to newspapers, partly for payment and partly under the influence of drink. The Committee of Privileges found the general statement untrue, but there were two exceptions—Allighan himself and another member who turned out to be Walkden. The House resolved that: (i) in writing the article Allighan was guilty of a "gross contempt" (it would still have been contempt even if the facts stated were true); (ii) he was guilty of "grave contempt" in the manner in which he answered the Committee for Privileges; and (iii) he was guilty of "dishonourable conduct" in accepting payment for disclosing the confidential information. Allighan was expelled from the House. The editor was summoned to the bar of the House: he apologised, was found guilty of "gross contempt" and reprimanded. The case is notable first, because it recognises private *party* meetings—at least in the Palace of Westminster, during the parliamentary session—held to discuss matters which are before, or to come before, Parliament; and, secondly, because the House claimed to punish "dishonourable conduct" that is neither breach of privilege nor contempt. In *Walkden's* case (1947),[77] which arose out of the above, Walkden was found guilty of "dishonourable conduct" and was reprimanded. Many members thought that the House had no power to punish for dishonourable conduct by itself. The House later passed a resolution that if any member was guilty of corruptly accepting payment for the disclosure of confidential information on matters to be proceeded with in Parliament, the person who *offered* such payment should incur the "grave displeasure" of the House, and the House would take such action as it might think fit.

There have been a number of instances in recent years of the House

---

[74] Juries Act 1974, s.9 and Pt. III of Sched. 1.
[75] *Ante*, p. 236 *note* 18.
[76] H.C. 138; 443 H.C.Deb., 5s., 1096–1200. See Hood Phillips (1948) 11 M.L.R. 214.
[77] 443 H.C.Deb., 5s., 1200–1231; 445 H.C.Deb., 1095–1159. Hood Phillips (1948) 11 M.L.R. 216.

complaining of contempt by journalists and others, although it is sometimes content with an apology at the bar of the House and often takes
no action at all. Many such affronts to its dignity partake more of the
nature of inaccurate and injudicious criticism than attempts to obstruct
the proper functioning of the House. A spate of complaints by members
against journalists for alleged breach of privilege or contempt because
of the publication of critical articles,[78] led the Committee of Privileges
in 1977 to recommend that the House should exercise its penal jurisdiction as sparingly as possible, and in particular " . . . only when the
House is satisfied that to exercise it is essential in order to provide
reasonable protection for the House, its members or its officers, from
such improper obstruction or attempt at or threat of obstruction as is
causing or is likely to cause substantial interference with the performance of their respective functions."[79] In a resolution in February 1978
the House approved this recommendation.[80]

A problem considered several times by the Committee of Privileges
in recent years[81] has been premature disclosure of draft reports from
Select Committees in breach of a resolution of 1837. The difficulty of
identifying the person who made the disclosure to the newspaper has
meant that although the committee has found a contempt of Parliament,
no further action has been taken.[82]

Procedure on complaint of a matter of privilege

The present procedure for raising complaints of breaches dates from
1978.[83] As soon as possible after the occurence of the alleged breach of
privilege or contempt a member must give written notice to the
Speaker, who will decide whether or not the matter should have precedence over other business of the House. The Speaker will inform the
member of his decision, and if it is in favour of giving the matter precedence, he will make an announcement in the House. This entitles the
member to table a motion the next day proposing that a reference
should be made to the committee of Privileges. The House will debate
the motion and decide whether or not to approve it.

The Committee of Privileges is a Select Committee of 17 members set
up for the duration of Parliament with the power to send for persons,
papers and records.[84] As with all committees with these powers, refusal
to appear or to answer, or knowingly to give false answers, is itself a
contempt. The Committee's recommendations are reported to the
House. The House's decision does not necessarily agree with the Committee's,[85] although it will often do so with modifications.

[78] See *e.g.* (1975–76; H.C. 43); (1976–77; H.C. 58).
[79] (1976–77; H.C. 417).
[80] H.C. Deb., Vol. 943, col. 1198 (February 6, 1978).
[81] For details see the Appendix to the First Report from the Committee of Privileges
(1984–85;. H.C. 308).
[82] *Ante*, p. 239 and *note* 38.
[83] Following the examination of the Report of the Select Committee on Parliamentary
Privilege (1966–67; H.C. 34) by the Committee of Privileges (1976–77; H.C. 417). For the
pre 1978 procedure see Erskine May *op. cit.* 19th ed., pp. 162 *et seq.*
[84] S.O. No. 121.
[85] *e.g.* the *Strauss* case *ante*, p. 237.

Methods of punishment

(a) *Expulsion*[86] of a member is regarded rather as a declaration of unfitness than a punishment. It causes a vacancy; but as we have said, the Commons cannot prevent his re-election, although they can refuse to let him take his seat if re-elected. The Commons admitted John Wilkes in 1774 after he had been expelled and re-elected several times. Allighan, who was expelled in 1947, did not seek re-election.

(b) *Suspension* of a member is available to assist the House to enforce discipline, as well as to punish particular offences laid down in Standing Orders.[87]

(c) *Imprisonment* of a member or stranger. The former is committed to the Clock Tower; the latter is handed over by the Serjeant-at-Arms to one of Her Majesty's prisons. The warrant is drawn up by the Speaker on the order of the House, and is executed by the Serjeant-at-Arms who may use necessary force and may call on the assistance of the Metropolitan Police. Imprisonment (or "committal") by the Commons is during the pleasure of the House, but cannot last beyond the end of the session, after which the prisoner would be entitled to release on habeas corpus. The Committee of Privileges has recommended that the power to imprison should be extinguished.[88]

(d) *Reprimand* and (e) *Admonition,* the mildest form. In both these forms the Speaker addresses the offender, who is at the bar of the House either in the custody of or attended by the Serjeant-at-Arms; except that a member (unless he is in the custody of the Serjeant) is reprimanded or admonished standing in his place.

Fine. The House of Commons has not imposed a fine since *White's Case* (1666), and it is doubtful whether it has the power to do so owing to the uncertainty whether it is a court of record. The power was denied by Lord Mansfield in *R. v. Pitt* and *R. v. Mead.*[89] There have been several reports in which it has been suggested that the House of Commons should be given the power to fine.[90] The House of Lords, as a court of record, has frequently imposed fines.

6. Proposals for reform

A Select Committee on Parliamentary Privilege was appointed in 1966 to review the law of parliamentary privilege as it affects the House of Commons and the procedure by which cases of privilege are raised and dealt with in the House, and to report whether any changes in the law or practice were desirable. The Committee reported in 1967,[91] recommending extensive changes which would meet some of the criticisms that have been made. Since this report there have been several reports from the Committee of Privileges suggesting reform. Some of the Select Committee and the Committee of Privileges proposals have

[86] See Enid Campbell, "Expulsion of Members of Parliament" (1971) 21 U.T.L.J. 15.
[87] S.O. No's 42, 43, 44.
[88] (1976–77; H.C. 417), para. 15.
[89] (1762) 3 Burr. 1335.
[90] (1967–68; H.C. 34), paras. 194–197; (1975–76; H.C. 22); (1976–77; H.C. 417), para. 18.
[91] (1967–68; H.C. 34). And see C. Seymour-Ure, "Proposed Reforms of Parliamentary Privilege: Assessment in the Light of Recent Cases" (1970) XXIII *Parliamentary Affairs,* 221.

been implemented, for example, the resolution that the publication of debates should not be regarded as a breach of privilege; the waiving of the privilege to forbid unlicensed references to Hansard in the course of judicial proceedings; a new procedure for raising questions of privilege. These and other reforms were implemented by Standing Order or resolution. The major reforms such as a definition of "proceedings in Parliament"; the provision of legal aid before the Committee of Privileges and the granting to the House of Commons of a power to fine, would require legislation, and parliamentary time has not been found for these purposes.

II. THE PRIVILEGES OF THE LORDS

Privileges of the House

The House of Lords has seldom come into conflict either with the Sovereign or with the courts in respect of its privileges. The juridical nature of the privileges of the House of Lords is similar to that of the privileges of the House of Commons, and strictly both are parts of the privileges of Parliament. The Lords passed a resolution in 1704 declaring that neither House has power to create for itself new privileges not warranted by the known laws and customs of Parliament, and the Commons assented.[92]

(1) The power to declare the law with regard to its own composition, and to determine the validity of the creation of new peerages (*Wensleydale Peerage Case*),[93] and the succession to existing peerages.[94]

(2) The exclusive right to regulate its own internal proceedings.

(3) The power to commit for breach of privilege or contempt for a definite period (*Lord Shaftesbury's Case*).[95] Where no period is fixed, the person committed is released when Parliament is either prorogued or dissolved.

(4) The power to summon the judges for advice on points of law.

(5) The power to issue a warrant for the release of a peer who is improperly arrested.

Until the Criminal Justice Act 1948 the House of Lords had the power to try peers and peeresses for treason and felony. In theory it still has power to try impeachments instituted by the Commons.

Personal privileges of Peers

These include:

(1) Freedom from civil arrest, that is, except in cases of treason, felony (arrestable offence) or refusal to give security to keep the peace[96] (*Earl of*

---

[92] 14 Commons Journals 555.

[93] (1856) 5 H.L.C. 958. The Lord Chancellor, Lord Cranworth, had advised the Prime Minister, Palmerston, that the creation of a life peerage was legal. "By an unfortunate, or as some will think, a fortunate, accident, Baron Parke was laid up with an attack of gout, and was unable to take his seat on the first day of the session, which otherwise he certainly would have done" (*Memoirs of Duke of Argyll*, ii, 11).

[94] *Annandale and Hartfell Peerage Claim* [1986] A.C. 319.

[95] (1673) 1 Mod.Rep. 144, *Cf. Stockdale* v. *Hansard* (1839) 9 A. & E. 1, *per* Lord Denman at p. 127.

[96] House of Lords S.O. No. 78.

Lonsdale v. *Littledale*[97]; *Duke of Newcastle* v. *Morris*[98]). The person of a peer (whether a Lord of Parliament or not) is by custom and statute[99] "for ever sacred and inviolable" during and for a period before and after a session. The privilege is not now of much importance since the abolition of arrest for debt and as a mesne process in civil cases; but it was held in *Stourton* v. *Stourton*[1] that a peer was privileged from attachment by a court for failing to comply with a court order in matrimonial proceedings. Scarman J. thought the privilege probably applied whether or not Parliament was sitting. It would appear to be uncertain whether or not the compulsory detention of a peer under the Mental Health Act 1983 would be a breach of the privileges of peerage or freedom from arrest or detention.[2]

(2) Freedom of speech in Parliament. This privilege is similar to that of the Commons.

III. CONFLICTS BETWEEN THE COMMONS AND THE COURTS CONCERNING PRIVILEGE[3]

The courts cannot interfere with the decision of either House where any of its undoubted privileges are infringed. On the other hand, neither House can create new privileges except by statute.[4] The controversial question is, whether the courts or the House has jurisdiction to decide whether an alleged privilege exists. The conflict between the Commons and the courts on this question has come to a head in two famous pairs of cases—*Ashby* v. *White* and *Paty's Case* at the beginning of the eighteenth century, and *Stockdale* v. *Hansard* and the *Case of the Sheriff of Middlesex* in the first half of the nineteenth century.

Ashby v. *White*[5] arose out of the refusal of White (the Tory mayor) and the other returning officers to accept the vote of Ashby (a Whig) in the election for Aylesbury. The Court of Queen's Bench by a majority (Holt C.J. *dissenting*), held that no action lay as the Commons had exclusive jurisdiction to determine claims to the franchise but the House of Lords reversed this decision. In doing so, it approved the principle stated by Holt C.J.[6] in his dissent that where there is a right there is a remedy (*ubi jus ibi remedium*). The Commons passed a resolution that this infringed

---

[97] (1793) 2 Anst. 356.
[98] (1870) L.R. 4 H.L. 661.
[99] Parliamentary Privilege Acts 1700 and 1703. The privilege extends, or extended, to the servants of peers.
[1] [1963] P. 302; *post*, p. 252.
[2] Report from the Committee of Privileges on Parliamentary Privilege and the Mental Health Legislation (1983–84; H.L. 254); see Leopold [1985] P.L. 9.
[3] See, G. F. Lock *op. cit.* note 69.
[4] See, *e.g.* Parliamentary Commissioner Act 1967, s.10(5); Public Order Act 1986, s.26.
[5] (1703–1704) 2 Ld.Raym. 938; 3 Ld.Raym. 320; 14 St.Tr. 695; Broom, *Constitutional Law* (2nd ed.), p. 846. And see Turberville, *The House of Lords in the Eighteenth Century*, pp. 58–71.
[6] "It is a vain thing to imagine there should be right without a remedy; for want of right and want of remedy are convertibles . . . and we are to exert and vindicate the Queen's jurisdiction, and not to be frightened because it may come in question in Parliament." Holt prepared a revised version of his judgment, probably for the House of Lords, in which he stressed the essential point that fraud and malice were alleged and proved.

their privilege of exclusively determining both the qualification of an elector and the right of any person elected. The Lords then passed counter-resolutions.

Paty's Case (*R.* v. *Paty*, or the *Case of the Men of Aylesbury*)[7] arose out of a similar action by Paty and four other electors of Aylesbury against the returning officers. The plaintiffs were committed to prison by order of the Commons for breach of privilege. Habeas corpus proceedings were brought. The Speaker's warrant of commitment stated that in bringing the action Paty had been guilty of "commencing an action at common law, in high contempt of jurisdiction, and in breach of the known privileges of this House." The Court of Queen's Bench held (Holt C.J. again dissenting) that the court had no jurisdiction. Holt C.J. held, however, that where—as here—the cause *shown* in the return to the writ was insufficient in law to constitute a breach of privilege or contempt, the plaintiffs ought to be released.[8] The Commons, hearing that plaintiffs' counsel intended to bring a writ of error in the House of Lords, committed the counsel also for "conspiring to make a difference between the Lords and the Commons"[9]; but Queen Anne resolved the deadlock by proroguing Parliament. This set the plaintiffs at liberty, and they went on to win their actions in the courts against the returning officers.[10]

In these two cases the question of the relation between parliamentary privilege and the courts was confused by the fact that the final court of appeal was the House of Lords, and each House was judge of its own privileges. In fact, it was the appeal to the House of Lords in the habeas corpus proceedings to which the Commons mainly objected.

In *Stockdale* v. *Hansard*[11] Stockdale sued Hansard, the parliamentary printers, for a libel contained in a report of prison inspectors that had been printed *by order* of the Commons and not only laid before the House but also *put on sale to the public*. The Commons instructed Hansard to plead that the report had been ordered by the Commons to be printed and published and was therefore covered by parliamentary privilege. The Queen's Bench gave judgment for Stockdale, holding that the courts had jurisdiction to determine whether an alleged privilege existed, although if a privilege did exist the House was the sole judge as to how it should be exercised. It found that parliamentary privilege extended to papers circulated among members by order of the House, but not to documents published outside the House, and that no resolution of either House could alter the law of the land. This was a reference to a resolution passed by the Commons in 1837[12] which provided that the publication of parliamentary reports and proceedings was essential

---

[7] (1704) 2 Ld.Raym. 1105, 1113; 14 St.Tr. 849, 857; Broom, *op. cit.* p. 862.

[8] In *Burdett* v. *Abbot* (1811) 14 East 1, Lord Ellenborough expressed an *obiter dictum* agreeing with the opinion of Holt C.J. in *Paty's Case*. Broom, *op. cit.* p. 968.

[9] One of them escaped arrest by climbing out of the window of his chambers in the Temple "by the help of his sheets and a rope."

[10] G. M. Trevelyan, *Ramillies and the Union with Scotland*, p. 25; K. Pickthorn, *Some Historical Principles of the Constitution* (1925), pp. 126–127.

[11] (1839) 9 Ad. & E. 1.

[12] Following the first action by Stockdale against Hansard for an earlier publication of the same libel, which the defendant won on a plea of justification, *i.e.* that the statement was true.

for the functions of Parliament; that the House had sole and exclusive jurisdiction to determine the existence and extent of its privileges; that to dispute those privileges by legal proceedings was a breach of privilege; and that for any court to decide on matters of privilege inconsistent with the determination of either House was contrary to the law of Parliament.

The Commons allowed the damages of £100 to be paid "under the special circumstances of the case," but declared that in future cases Hansard should not plead and the parties should suffer for their contempt. Stockdale nevertheless brought another action (the third) against Hansard for another publication of the same report. The defendants did not plead and judgment for £600 damages was given against them by default. The two Sheriffs of London, who jointly filled the office of Sheriff of Middlesex, levied the amount of the damages on Hansard's property, but cautiously refrained from paying the money over to Stockdale. The Commons desired them to refund the money to Hansard: they refused, and were committed for contempt. The *Case of the Sheriff of Middlesex*[13] was an application for habeas corpus on behalf of the two Sheriffs. The Speaker's warrant of committal produced by the Serjeant-at-Arms stated that the House had resolved that the Sheriff of Middlesex, having been guilty of a contempt and breach of privilege, be committed to custody; but it *did not set forth the facts* constituting the alleged breach of privilege or contempt. The court held that it could not go behind the warrant by inquiring into the facts: it must assume that the House of Commons was exercising its powers properly, and it therefore was not entitled to set the prisoners free.[14]

Stockdale, who had meanwhile been committed to prison by the Commons, commenced a fourth similar action through his solicitor, Howard. Hansard was again ordered not to plead, and judgment was once more entered against him by default. The Commons ordered Howard to attend the House, but he evaded service of the order. The Speaker, instead of having him brought before the House to be adjudged guilty of contempt, issued a warrant for his committal to Newgate, which the Serjeant-at-Arms (Gossett) executed. Howard sued Gossett for damages for unlawful arrest and imprisonment (*Howard v. Gossett*[15]), but the Court of Exchequer Chamber held that the Speaker's warrant was sufficient and the matter clearly within the Commons' privileges. As Stockdale, although in custody, could have instructed other attorneys to prosecute further actions, the Customs secured the passing of the Parliamentary Papers Act 1840, which settled the matter of privilege in relation to the courts so far as concerns the publication of parliamentary papers. This Act, as we have seen,[16] provides that actions shall be stayed on production of a certificate or affidavit that the paper complained of was published by order of either House.

The fact that an Act of Parliament was passed vindicates the judg-

---

[13] (1840) 11 Ad. & E. 273. The Court of Queen's Bench in this case included three of the four judges who had decided *Stockdale* v. *Hansard* in the previous year.

[14] One of them was in fact released on the ground of ill-health, and the other was released on the day on which the Parliamentary Papers Bill was introduced.

[15] (1845–1847) 10 Q.B. 359, 459; May, *op. cit.* p. 191.

[16] *Ante*, p. 240.

ment of the court in *Stockdale* v. *Hansard* that changes in the law can only be made by Act of Parliament and not by resolution of either House. A strong Judicial Committee in *Re Parliamentary Privilege Act 1770*[17] referred to "the inalienable right of Her Majesty's subjects to have recourse to her Courts of Law for the remedy of their wrongs"; and Scarman J. in *Stourton* v. *Stourton*[18] said that, where a matter of parliamentary privilege arises in court, the court looks to the common law as declared in judicial decisions rather than to parliamentary practice.

The Commons, however, have never formally admitted—indeed they have more than once denied—the jurisdiction of the courts to determine the existence of privilege. It looks at first sight as if the weapon of committal of parties and counsel for contempt (with no facts shown) would always be effective to prevent actions in the courts; but other counsel can be instructed to appear, and during a recess neither House could interfere with parties or counsel, so that judgment might be obtained and executed before the next meeting of Parliament. On the other hand, the House can recommit at the beginning of the next session. It is obviously unsatisfactory that there should be two sets of tribunals—the Houses of Parliament and the ordinary courts—with competing jurisdictions in a matter that may affect the liberty of the citizen. The anomaly could be removed if the Commons would allow an Act to be passed—as they did with the Parliamentary Elections Act 1868—transferring to the courts the exclusive jurisdiction to punish persons (or, at least, strangers) charged with contempt of Parliament. In this way the issue would be tried by an impartial tribunal that was not a party to the case; counsel and witnesses would be heard; the facts, perhaps, found by a jury; and there could be a right of appeal.[19] The scope for conflict would also be reduced if a statutory definition were given to the phrase "proceedings in Parliament," and greater thought were given as to whether legislation should be made expressly applicable in certain cases, such as labour laws to Parliamentary staff,[20] and the Mental Health Act 1983 to peers.

---

[17] [1958] A.C. 331; (1958) Cmnd. 431; *ante*, p. 237.
[18] [1963] P. 302.
[19] There is a right of appeal in cases of contempt of court under the Administration of Justice Act 1960.
[20] See G. F. Lock *op. cit.* note 69.

PART III

THE CENTRAL GOVERNMENT

CHAPTER 13

THE MONARCHY

Title to the Throne

The title to the Throne is both statutory and hereditary, while a trace of the Anglo-Saxon elective element is still found in the coronation ceremony. The Act of Settlement 1700[1] settled the Throne on Sophia, Electress of Hanover (granddaughter of James I), and the heirs of her body being Protestants. Sophia's son, George I (1714), succeeded Anne under this Act. Any person who is reconciled to or shall hold communion with the See or Church of Rome or shall profess the Popish Religion or shall marry a papist, is excluded from the succession. The successor to the Crown must take the Coronation Oath, in the manner and form prescribed by statute and must sign and repeat the declaration prescribed by the Bill of Rights. Any person who comes to the possession of the Crown must join in communion with the Church of England as by law established.

When in 1978 Prince Michael of Kent, a grandson of George V, obtained royal consent to his marriage to a Roman Catholic from the Austrian aristocracy he renounced the right of succession to the throne for himself, though not for his issue. Public discussion arose concerning the desirability of amending the Act of Settlement so far as it relates to the sovereign or heir to the throne marrying a Roman Catholic. Any such reform would require the members of the Commonwealth to be consulted, at least the "Realms," if not also the Republics.

The convention is recited in the preamble to the Statute of Westminster 1931 that, since the Crown is the symbol of the free association of the members of the Commonwealth, any alteration in the law touching the succession to the Throne requires the assent of the Parliaments of all the "Dominions" (*i.e.* now Canada, Australia and New Zealand).[2]

Accession

When a Sovereign dies his successor accedes to the Throne immediately. The automatic succession of the new monarch is sometimes expressed in the maxim "the King never dies."[3] At common law a person is never too young to succeed to the Throne.

As soon as conveniently possible after the death or abdication of a Sovereign, an Accession Council meets to acclaim the new Sovereign.

---

[1] The Act of Settlement was amended by the Union with Scotland and Ireland Acts, and by His Majesty's Declaration of Abdication Act 1936. The legitimacy of the succession based on the Act of Settlement cannot be questioned in court: *Hall* v. *Hall* (1944) 88 S.J. 383 (Hereford C.C.).

[2] Perhaps the assent is now required of all independent countries of the Commonwealth that recognise Her Majesty as Queen: *post,* p. 762.

[3] *Calvin's Case* (1608) 8 Co. Rep. 1a. 10b.

An Accession Council is composed of the Lords Spiritual and Temporal, assisted by members of the Privy Council, with the Lord Mayor and Aldermen of the City of London and the high commissioners of the Commonwealth countries. The new Sovereign takes the oath for the security of the Presbyterian Church in Scotland prescribed by the Union with Scotland Act 1706. Before the first meeting of Parliament or at his coronation he must declare that he is a faithful Protestant, and promise to uphold the enactments securing the Protestant succession to the Throne.[4]

Coronation

Coronation customarily takes place in Westminster Abbey some months after accession, and is conducted by the Archbishop of Canterbury, assisted by the Archbishop of York.[5] Coronation is not legally necessary. Indeed Edward VIII reigned for nearly a year before abdicating, and was never crowned. If a coronation is held, the following ceremonies are essential: (i) presentation by the Archbishop of Canterbury and recognition by the people in the presence of the hereditary officers of state; (ii) the Coronation Oath (post); (iii) anointing by the Primate; (iv) crowning by the Primate and enthroning; (v) homage by the bishops for the temporalities of their sees, and by peers.[6] These proceedings are organised by the Earl Marshal (Duke of Norfolk).

The Coronation Oath is based on the Coronation Oath Act 1688, and is obligatory by the Act of Settlement as amended by the Acts of Union. The Oath taken by Elizabeth II was to govern the peoples of the United Kingdom of Great Britain and Northern Ireland, Canada, Australia, New Zealand, the Union of South Africa, Pakistan and Ceylon,[7] and her possessions and the other territories to any of them belonging or pertaining, according to the statutes in Parliament agreed on and their respective laws and customs; to maintain in the United Kingdom the Protestant reformed religion established by law; and to maintain and preserve inviolably the settlement of the Church of England, and the doctrine, worship, discipline and government thereof in England.

Abdication

There is no precedent for a voluntary abdication[8] before 1936, when Edward VIII was given the choice of abdicating or giving up his proposed marriage with Mrs. Simpson, whom the Prime Minister (Mr. Baldwin) and the Dominion Prime Ministers regarded as unsuitable for

---

[4] Accession Declaration Act 1910.

[5] At the coronation of Elizabeth II in 1953 a minor part was played by the Moderator of the General Assembly of the Church of Scotland.

[6] For a description of the coronation ceremony, see A. B. Keith, The King and the Imperial Crown, pp. 20–29.

[7] These were the independent kingdoms or realms in the Commonwealth at that time. India was already a republic.

[8] Following the defeat of James II in battle and his flight from the country, the Declaration of Rights 1688, embodied in the Bill of Rights, asserted that the late King James II had "abdicated the Government" and the Throne was "thereby vacant."

a King's consort.[9] The King signed an Instrument of Abdication declaring his irrevocable determination to renounce the Throne for himself and his descendants. He then sent a message to Parliament asking that a Bill should be passed accordingly to alter the succession to the Throne, and issued a commission to signify his assent thereto. His Majesty's Declaration of Abdication Act 1936 accordingly provided that His Majesty should cease to be King and there should be a demise of the Crown, and the member of the Royal Family then next in succession to the Throne should succeed. It amended the Act of Settlement 1700 by excluding King Edward (thereafter Duke of Windsor) and his descendants from the succession to the Throne, and exempted them from the provisions of the Royal Marriages Act 1772.[10]

Royal Style and Titles

The Royal Style and Titles are altered from time to time by Act of Parliament, or by proclamation issued thereunder. Several changes have been made in the present century to take account of constitutional developments in the Commonwealth. The preamble to the Statute of Westminster 1931 recites the convention that any alteration of the Royal Style and Titles shall require the consent of the Parliaments of all the "Dominions."[11] On the accession of Elizabeth II, the Sovereign was for the first time proclaimed by different titles in the various independent countries of the Commonwealth. The Royal Titles Act 1953 empowers the Queen to use, in relation to the United Kingdom and all other territories for whose foreign relations the Government of the United Kingdom is responsible, such style and titles as she may think fit having regard to the agreement made between representatives of the member governments of the Commonwealth. The style and titles proclaimed under this Act are: "Elizabeth II by the Grace of God of the United Kingdom of Great Britain and Northern Ireland and of her other Realms

---

[9] For a background account, see H.R.H. The Duke of Windsor, *A King's Story* (1951), pp. 337–415; Frances Donaldson, *Edward VIII* (1974), Chaps. 20–23; G. M. Young, *Stanley Baldwin* (1952), pp. 232–244; J. W. Wheeler-Bennett, *King George VI*, pp. 275–289; Lord Birkenhead, *Walter Monckton* (1969) pt. III; Lord Beaverbrook, *The Abdication of King Edward VIII* (A. J. P. Taylor ed. 1966); J. Evelyn Wrench, *Geoffrey Dawson and our Times*, Chap. 29; K. Middlemas and J. Barnes, *Baldwin* (1969), Chap. 34; H. Montgomery Hyde *Baldwin, The Unexpected Prime Minister* (1973), Chap. 11. J. G. Lockhart, *Cosmo Gordon Lang*, Chap. 32; *Chips, The Diaries of Sir Henry Channon* (Robert Rhodes James ed. 1967), Chap. 2.

[10] For an account of the constitutional steps taken, see W. Ivor Jennings, "The Abdication of King Edward VIII" (1937) 2 *Politica* 287; K. H. Bailey, "The Abdication Legislation in the United Kingdom and in the Dominions" (1938) 3 *Politica* 1 and 147. Consultation with the Dominions is described in Lord Beaverbrook, *op. cit.* and Lord Birkenhead, *op. cit.* The Abdication Act was based on a draft prepared by Sir Frederick Pollock; see *The Pollock-Holmes Letters* (1942), Vol. I, pp. xiv–xv, 68–69. See also Sir Harold Kent, *In the Act: Mémoirs of a Lawmaker* (1980) pp. 69–72.

The Duke of Windsor retained his service ranks, and was Governor of the Bahamas from 1940 to 1945. He died in 1972 without issue. For the doubtful legality of withholding the title of "H.R.H." from the Duchess of Windsor, see Frances Donaldson, *op. cit.* pp. 339–340, and references there cited.

[11] *Cf. ante*, p. 128.

and Territories Queen, Head of the Commonwealth,[12] Defender of the Faith."[13]

The Royal family

The Sovereign.[14] The Queen Regnant has the same status and powers as a King. She is the Head of the State. The central government of the country is carried on in her name and on her behalf; she is an essential part of the legislature, and justice is administered in the royal courts in her name. But what were formerly the personal prerogatives of the Sovereign have now become largely the powers and privileges of the government.[15]

The official duties of the Queen in her capacity as Sovereign of the United Kingdom and of the other self-governing Commonwealth monarchies and the remaining colonial territories, Head of the Armed Services, and Supreme Governor of the Church of England and with her special responsibility to the Established Church of Scotland, include: (i) work arising out of the government such as approving and signing commissions, and reading ministerial, Cabinet, parliamentary and diplomatic papers for several hours a day; (ii) private audiences with ambassadors etc., receiving the Prime Minister and other Ministers, holding a Privy Council and investitures; (iii) attending at state occasions such as the opening of Parliament, Trooping the Colour and religious services; and (iv) exchanging state visits and visiting Commonwealth countries.[16]

The Sovereign's official expenditure is financed mainly out of the Civil List provided by Parliament.[17]

Husband of Queen Regnant. Prince Philip, Duke of Edinburgh, is granted precedence next to the Queen. He is a Privy Councillor. At common law he has the status of an ordinary subject, and is not protected by the law of treason.

The Prince of Wales. The life of the Sovereign's eldest son is protected by the Statute of Treason 1351. When the Sovereign's eldest son is born he immediately becomes by custom Duke of Cornwall.[18] When he succeeds to the Throne, the Duchy of Cornwall immediately vests in his eldest son. The Sovereign may create his of her eldest son Prince of Wales and Earl of Chester by letters patent. Prince Charles was created Prince of Wales and Earl of Chester in 1958, and his investiture as Prince of Wales took place at Caernarvon Castle in 1969.

---

[12] *Post,* Chap. 37.
[13] (1953) Cmd. 8748. See also S. A. de Smith, "The Royal Style and Titles" (1953) 2 I.C.L.Q. 263; and *post,* Chap. 37.
[14] See also *post,* Chap. 35.
[15] *Post,* Chap. 14.
[16] *Report from the Select Committee on the Civil List* (1971) H.C. 29, para. 17 and Appendix 13. See Christopher Hibbert, *The Court of St. James's: The Monarch at Work from Victoria to Elizabeth II* (1979).
[17] *Post,* p. 272. And for the Crown private estates, see *post,* p. 268.
[18] Duchy of Cornwall Management Acts 1863 to 1982.

Princes and princesses of the blood royal. Princes of the blood, till summoned by the House of Lords, are commoners. It is usual to give them dukedoms when they come of age. The chastity of the Sovereign's eldest daughter unmarried is protected by the law of treason. The style of "Royal Highness" is conferred by letters patent[19] on the children of Sovereigns, and on the wives and children of the sons of Sovereigns.

Royal marriages. By the Royal Marriages Act 1772 no descendant of the body of George II (other than the issue of princesses married into royal families[20]) may marry without the royal consent signified under the Great Seal and declared in Council, and marriages by these persons without such consent are void (*Sussex Peerage Case*[21]). Further, all persons solemnising such marriages, or who are privy and consenting thereto, commit an offence. If the royal consent is refused, a descendant of George II aged 25 or more may give notice to the Privy Council and may contract a valid marriage at the expiration of 12 months unless Parliament has objected in the interim.[22]

Regency Acts 1937–1953

The common law made no provision for a regency or the delegation of royal functions when the Sovereign was ill or absent from the realm. Great inconvenience was caused in 1811 by the fact that George III was already considered to be insane[23] and therefore could not in fact give his assent to the appointment of a Regent; and special provision for delegation of royal functions had to be made when George V was seriously ill in 1928. When George VI came to the Throne, his children consisting of two young princesses, it was decided to enact permanent legislation, and this was revised on the accession of Elizabeth II. These matters are now regulated by the Regency Acts 1937–1953.

(i) *Delegation of functions to Counsellors of State.* Before 1937 Counsellors of State were appointed under the Royal Prerogative and might include, in addition to members of the Royal Family, dignitaries such as the Archbishop of Canterbury, the Lord Chancellor and the Prime Minister. The Regency Act 1937 authorises the Sovereign to appoint Counsellors of State by letters patent, and to delegate to them such of the royal functions as may be specified in the letters patent, whenever he is absent or intends to be absent from the United Kingdom, or is suffering from infirmity of mind or body not amounting to incapacity such as would

[19] *London Gazette*, February 5, 1864.
[20] It is possible that this exception exempts from the provisions of the Act all, or nearly all, those who are in close succession to the Throne at the present day (see C. d'O. Farran, "The Royal Marriages Act 1772" (1951) 14 M.L.R. 53), but it continues to be the practice to ask for the royal consent.
[21] (1844) 11 Cl. & F. 85.
[22] It is suggested that the Act should be amended so as to be confined to descendants of George V; and also that a marriage without the royal consent should not be void or punishable, but should merely exclude the parties and their descendants from the succession to the Throne.
[23] Medical opinion now is that George III was not insane but suffered from an acute intermittent form of porphyria, a rare metabolic disorder: Ida MacAlpine and Richard Hunter, *George III and the Mad-Business* (1969).

warrant a regency under the Act. The persons to be appointed to be
Counsellors of State are the wife or husband of the Sovereign and the
four persons next in succession to the Throne, excluding any person
who would be disqualified from being Regent. The Regency Act 1953
includes Queen Elizabeth the Queen Mother among the persons who
may be appointed Counsellors of State. This modern practice that only
members of the Royal Family should be appointed to the exclusion of
United Kingdom Ministers,[24] reflects the significance of the Monarchy
to the Commonwealth. The Counsellors may not be given authority to
dissolve Parliament otherwise than at the express instructions of the
Sovereign—which may be given by telegraph—or to grant any rank,
title or dignity of the peerage.

(ii) *Regency.* (a) The Regency Act 1937 provides that if *the Sovereign is
under 18 years of age* the royal functions are to be performed until he is
18 by a Regent, who shall act in the name and on behalf of the Sovereign. The Sovereign is deemed to accede to the Throne when he attains
the age of 18 years for the purpose of taking statutory oaths and declarations. The Regent is to be the person of full age next in succession to
the Throne who is a British subject resident in the United Kingdom and
who is not disqualified on religious grounds. The Regency Act 1953,
however, provides that the Duke of Edinburgh shall be Regent if a child
of Queen Elizabeth and the Duke of Edinburgh succeeds to the Throne
under the age of 18, or if a regency is necessary in the lifetime of the
Queen. The Regent is to take oaths of allegiance, good government and
maintenance of the Protestant religion in England and Scotland. He is
empowered to exercise all royal functions, except that he may not assent
to a Bill altering the succession to the Throne or repealing the Acts for
securing the Scottish Protestant religion and Church.[25]

The Act of 1937 also provides for the *guardianship* of the person of a
Sovereign under eighteen years. Of an unmarried Sovereign his or her
mother is to be the guardian; of a married Sovereign the Sovereign's
spouse will be guardian. If in the first case the Sovereign has no mother
or in the second case the Consort is under age, then the Regent will be
guardian.

(b) The Regency Act 1937 further provides for the appointment of a
Regent if a declaration is made by certain persons that they are "satisfied by evidence which shall include the evidence of physicians that *the
Sovereign is by infirmity of mind or body incapable* for the time being of
performing the royal functions," or that they are "satisfied by evidence
that the Sovereign is for some definite cause *not available*" for the performance of those functions.[26] The regency will continue until a contrary declaration is made. The persons who may make such declaration
are the wife or husband of the Sovereign, the Lord Chancellor, the
Speaker, the Lord Chief Justice and the Master of the Rolls, or any three
or more of them. It will be noticed that the person who would be Regent

---

[24] See J. W. Wheeler-Bennett, *King George VI*, App. A.
[25] *Cf. ante*, p. 91.
[26] The Sovereign would not be available, *e.g.* if he were made a prisoner of war.

is not one of those who make this declaration. The declaration must be made in writing to the Privy Council, and is to be communicated to the governments of the "Dominions."

The Sovereign's Private Secretary[27]

The post of Private Secretary to the Monarch is comparatively modern. Before the reign of George III the theory was that the Home Secretary was the King's Private Secretary, and it was thought desirable that a person admitted to Cabinet secrets should be a Privy Councillor. George III for many years wrote his own letters, but in 1805, when he was almost blind, he appointed Sir Herbert Taylor his Private Secretary. William IV reappointed Taylor, who had by then become a Privy Councillor. Since the Prince Consort's death in 1861 the office has been regular and officially accepted, its prestige being built up by Sir Henry Ponsonby and Sir Arthur Bigge (Lord Stamfordham), who between them occupied that post from 1870 to 1931, except during Edward VII's reign.

The Sovereign's Private Secretary is always now sworn of the Privy Council. It appears that he informally seeks advice from various sources—governmental, opposition and official—and then briefs the Sovereign. His post is very important as he is concerned with the relations not only between the Sovereign and the British Cabinet, but also between the Sovereign and Governors-General and Commonwealth Prime Ministers

The publication of an article in *The Sunday Times* on July 20, 1986 which purported to describe the Queen's views on a wide range of political matters provoked, unusually, the Private Secretary to write a public letter denying the accuracy of the report.[28]

---

[27] Wheeler-Bennett, *King George VI*, App. B; Arthur Ponsonby, *Henry Ponsonby, Queen Victoria's Private Secretary*, Chap. 3; Sir Ivor Jennings, *Cabinet Government* (3rd ed.), pp. 343–351.

[28] Letter to *The Times*, July 28, 1986; *post*, p. 764.

CHAPTER 14

THE ROYAL PREROGATIVE[1]

I. General Nature of the Prerogative

THE term "royal prerogative" is not a technical one. It is sometimes used to cover all the powers of the Sovereign, or at least those which the Sovereign does not share with his subjects. Sometimes it refers to the powers of the Sovereign in relation to his subjects, as distinct from "acts of state" done in relation to foreign affairs. More often, and preferably, it is limited to those powers which the Sovereign has by the common law as distinct from statute—in other words, the common law powers of the Crown.[2]

So far as the executive powers of the Crown are concerned (and for practical purposes these are the most important) it should be pointed out at the beginning that in the last 100 years the government of the country has been carried on largely under statutory powers. Further we must remember that, in so far as the Crown does exercise prerogative powers, the exercise is governed mainly by constitutional conventions, especially the doctrine of ministerial responsibility.[3] Nevertheless, emphasis on the prerogative does illuminate the historical basis of the Constitution, and it helps to explain much of the theory underlying the forms taken by governmental action.

The laws of England (and Northern Ireland) may differ from the laws of Scotland on the extent of the royal prerogative.[4] Nonetheless, "As the Constitution of Scotland has been the same as that of England since 1707 there is a presumption that the same constitutional principles apply in both countries."[5]

Historical introduction

The distinction between the natural and politic capacities of the King appears in the sixteenth century.[6] Further subtlety of reasoning led to a distinction in the early seventeenth century between the "absolute" and the "ordinary" powers of the King (*Bate's Case*[7]). By ordinary powers was meant such powers as those involved in the administration of justice, which had long been exercised without discretion in accordance with definite principles and procedure. The absolute powers we

---

[1] J. Chitty, *A Treatise on the Law of the Prerogatives of the Crown* (1820); *Hale's Prerogatives of the King* (ed. D. E. C. Yale, 1976).

[2] For "the Crown," see *post*, p. 267.

[3] *Post*, p. 309–313.

[4] *Glasgow Corporation* v. *Central Land Board* 1956 S.C.(H.L.) 1; J. D. B. Mitchell, "The Royal Prerogative in Modern Scots Law," [1957] P.L. 304.

[5] *Macgregor* v. *Lord Advocate* 1921 S.C. 847, 848 *per* the Lord Ordinary (Lord Anderson). On appeal, Lord Salvesen said (at p. 853) "It would be anomalous if the liability of a Crown Department in Scotland differed from the liability of a Crown Department in England."

[6] *Case of the Duchy of Lancaster* (1562) Plowd. 212; *Calvin's Case* (1608) 7 Co.Rep. 1a.

[7] (1606) Lane 22; 2 St.Tr. 371; Broom, *Constitutional Law* (2nd ed.), pp. 245 *et seq.*

should now call discretionary, for example, the direction of foreign policy and the pardoning of criminals. There arose also a tendency to regard the absolute prerogatives as "inseparable," so that even Parliament could not detach them from the Crown (*Case of the King's Prerogative in Saltpetre*[8]). One certain principle was that the prerogative was limited by law: "the King hath no prerogative but that which the law of the land allows him" (*Case of Proclamations*[9]). Had not Bracton said in the thirteenth century that the King ought to be subject to God and the law, because the law makes him King?[10] Charles I might dispute the application of this principle in certain aspects of government, such as preventive detention (*Darnel's Case*[11]) and ship-money (*R. v. Hampden*[12]), but the Civil War and the Revolution of 1688 meant that henceforth the Sovereign would accept the limitation of the prerogative by law and its determination by the courts. It is now admitted, of course, that the Sovereign has no powers that are "inseparable"—none, that is, which cannot be taken away by Act of Parliament.[13]

Blackstone says: "By the word prerogative we usually understand that special pre-eminence which the King hath, over and above all other persons, and out of the ordinary course of the common law, in right of his regal dignity. It signifies, in its etymology (from *prae* and *rogo*) something that is required or demanded before, or in preference to, all others."[14] The essential characteristic of the royal prerogative, then, is that it is unique and pre-eminent. It is not "out of the ordinary course of the common law" in the sense of being above the law: it is part of the Common law, but an exception to the principles that apply to citizens generally. Dicey's description of the royal prerogative as "the residue of discretionary or arbitrary authority, which at any given time is legally left in the hands of the Crown" has been more than once judicially approved.[15] Dicey emphasises the discretionary nature of the prerogative—the word "arbitrary" is misleading—and confines it according to the best usage to common law as distinct from statutory powers.

Dicey went on to say "Every act which the executive government can lawfully do without the authority of the Act of Parliament is done in vir-

---

[8] (1607) 12 Co.Rep. 12. See Holdsworth, *op. cit.* Vol. IV, pp. 202–207.

[9] 12 Co.Rep. 74; 2 St.Tr. 723.

[10] (1610) *De Legibus et Consuetudinibus Angliae*, f. 5b.

[11] (1627) 3 St.Tr. 1; Broom, *op. cit.* pp. 158 *et seq.*

[12] (1637) 3 St.Tr. 825: And see Holdsworth, *op. cit.* Vol. VI, pp. 19–30; Broom, *op. cit.* pp. 303 *et seq.*

[13] *Att.-Gen.* v. *De Keyser's Royal Hotel Ltd.* [1920] A.C. 508; *post*, p. 271.

[14] Bl.Comm. I, 239. Blackstone in defining the Prerogative referred to Locke who in the *True End of Civil Government*, Chap. 14, wrote: "This power to act according to discretion for the public good, without the prescription of the law and sometimes even against it, is that which is called prerogative; for since in some governments the law-making power is not always in being and is usually too numerous and so too slow for the dispatch requisite to execution, and because, also, it is impossible to foresee and so by laws to provide for all accidents and necessities that may concern the public . . . therefore there is a latitude left to the executive power to do many things of choice which the laws do not prescribe." See *Laker Airways Ltd.* v. *Dept. of Trade* [1977] Q.B. 643, 705, *per* Lord Denning M.R.

[15] Dicey, *Law of the Constitution* (10th ed.), p. 424; approved, *e.g.* by Lord Dunedin in *Att.-Gen.* v. *De Keyser's Royal Hotel Ltd.* [1920] A.C. 508, 526; *Burmah Oil Co. Ltd.* v. *Lord Advocate* [1965] A.C. 75, 99, *per* Lord Reid; *C.C.S.U.* v. *Minister for the Civil Service* [1985] A.C. 374, 416, *per* Lord Roskill.

tue of this prerogative."[16] It has been pointed out that such a definition is much wider than that of Blackstone.[17] Whereas he confined the prerogative to "rights and capacities which the King enjoys alone, in contradistinction to others, and not to those which he enjoys in common with any of his subjects," Dicey's definition covers all the non-statutory power of the Crown, even those which it enjoys in common with its subjects, such as the power to enter into contracts. The correctness of Dicey's wide definition was assumed by the House of Lords in *Council of Civil Service Unions* v. *Minister for Civil Service*[18] where, however, there were also dicta that for the purposes of judicial review (which was the issue before the House), it was only of historical interest whether a power of the executive should be ascribed to the prerogative or not.[19]

The prerogative is a *residue* because Parliament can take away any prerogative and has frequently done so. It is seldom abolished expressly, however, but is impliedly abolished, curtailed or merely suspended (*Att.-Gen.* v. *De Keyser's Royal Hotel Ltd.*[20]). Since the prerogative is part of the common law, the Queen cannot claim that a new prerogative has come into existence.[21] In *British Broadcasting Corporation* v. *Johns*,[22] where the B.B.C. unsuccessfully claimed that the Crown had a monopoly of broadcasting exercised through the Corporation, and that the Corporation was entitled to Crown exemption from income tax, Diplock L.J. said: "It is 350 years and a civil war too late for the Queen's courts to broaden the prerogative." It can only be the residue at any given time of the rights and powers which the Sovereign had before the days of Parliament.

No new prerogative can be claimed, but to what extent can the prerogative be adapted to meet new situations? Being part of the common law, the prerogative is sufficiently adaptable, for example, to adjust itself to new dimensions and methods of warfare.[23] But the distinction between adapting a recognised prerogative and claiming a new power may be difficult to draw, as in *Malone* v. *Metropolitan Police Commissioner*[24] where Megarry V.-C. held that the Home Secretary had a limited power to authorise telephone tapping as an extension of the power to open articles sent through the post.[25]

There are dicta to the effect that a prerogative power in some circum-

---

[16] *op. cit.* p. 425.
[17] H. W. R. Wade, *Constitutional Fundamentals* (1980) p. 46; "Procedure and Prerogative in Public Law" (1985) 101 L.Q.R. 180.
[18] [1985] A.C. 374 (The Cheltenham G.C.H.Q. Case).
[19] *Post,* p. 265, Chap. 17 and Chap. 31.
[20] [1920] A.C. 508; *post,* p. 265.
[21] *Case of Monopolies* (1602) 11 Co. Rep. 84b.
[22] [1965] Ch. 32 (C.A.).
[23] See *e.g. Re A Petition of Right* [1915] 3 K.B. 649 (C.A.); *Att.-Gen.* v. *De Keyser's Royal Hotel Ltd.* [1920] A.C. 508, 565 *per* Lord Sumner.
[24] [1979] Ch. 344; *post,* p. 518.
[25] *Cf.* now, Interception of Telecommunications Act 1985; *post* p. 518. In *Att.-Gen. of the Duchy of Lancaster* v. *G. E. Overton (Farms) Ltd.* [1981] Ch. 333; [1982] Ch. 277 an attempt to extend the prerogative right to treasure trove so as to protect items of antiquarian value, whether or not gold or silver, failed: *post* p. 271. See generally, George Winterton, "The Prerogative in Novel Situations," (1983) 99 L.Q.R. 407.

stances may be lost by disuse.[26] The question may also arise whether a given prerogative survived the Bill of Rights 1688.[27] But generally we may say that a prerogative which has long fallen out of use, such as the sovereign's power to refuse the royal assent to Bills passed by both Houses of Parliament, is now bound by constitutional convention rather than by some legal doctrine of desuetude.

A prerogative power is *discretionary*, and, although its existence is determinable by the courts, the manner of the exercise was generally thought to be outside their jurisdiction. Dicta in the *G.C.H.Q.* Case,[28] however, suggest that prerogative powers, like discretionary powers of statutory origin, may be subject to judicial review.

The Prime Minister, as Minister for the Civil Service, gave instructions under an Order in Council made, as the House of Lords held, by virtue of the Royal Prerogative, forbidding staff at the Government Communications Headquarters from being members of trade unions. The House of Lords accepted the argument of the applicant unions and staff that past practice had created a legitimate expectation[29] that they would, in the normal course of events, be consulted before a decision affecting the terms of employment of civil servants at the headquarters was made. In so holding all the Law Lords agreed that the scope of judicial review of a Ministerial decision was the same whether it was made under statutory powers—whether Act of Parliament or delegated legislation made under an Act—or under an Order in Council deriving its authority from the prerogative. Lord Diplock, Lord Scarman and Lord Roskill were prepared to go further and were of the opinion that acts done directly under the royal prerogative were subject to judicial review, where the issues involved were *justiciable*.[30] Lord Fraser and Lord Brightman preferred to express no opinion on the point.[31] The House, however, accepted that the Minister had, on the facts, been entitled to issue the instruction without consultation because national security required such summary procedure.[32] (The issue of national

---

[26] *e.g. per* Lord Lyndhurst and Lord Campbell, C.J. in *Wensleydale Peerage Case* (1856) 5 H.L.C. 958; and *per* Lord Simon of Glaisdale in *M'Kendrick* v. *Sinclair* 1972 S.C. 25 (H.L.), a Scots case concerning the old action of assythment; see J. M. Thomson, "Desuetude and the Common Law" (1973) 89 L.Q.R. 27.

[27] See, *e.g. per* Lord Parmoor in *Att.-Gen.* v. *De Keyser's Royal Hotel Ltd.* [1920] A.C. 508, 570 and *per* Lord Reid in *Burmah Oil Co.* v. *Lord Advocate* [1965] A.C. 75, 99.

[28] [1985] A.C. 374. See the earlier dicta of Lord Denning, M.R. in *Laker Airways* v. *Department of Trade* [1977] Q.B. 643.

[29] As to "legitimate expectations," see post p. 674.

[30] at p. 407, *per* Lord Scarman; at p. 410, *per* Lord Diplock; at p. 417, *per* Lord Roskill.

[31] at p. 398 *per* Lord Fraser, who pointed out that to permit review would "run counter to the great weight of authority"; at p. 424 *per* Lord Brightman.

[32] The degree of control that the courts can exert over ministerial claims that a matter raises questions of national security is not clear. All the members of the House adverted to the need of evidence to justify such a claim by a minister. Lord Scarman envisaged, even in a case of national security, that the court might conclude that the opinion of a Minister that certain action was required was such that no reasonable minister could reasonably have held: [at p. 406]. Lord Diplock, on the other hand, having adverted to the need for evidence, went on to say that if a question of national security were established, the appropriate action was for the government: "It is par excellence a non-justiciable question. The judicial process is totally inept to deal with the sort of problems which it involves." (At p. 412) *Cf. Chandler* v. *D.P.P.* [1964] A.C. 763.

security had not been raised at all before Glidewell J. who found for the unions, and only briefly before the Court of Appeal which reversed the first instance judgment).

The Law Lords in the *G.C.H.Q.* Case who asserted the existence of a jurisdiction to review acts done under the Royal prerogative confined that jurisdiction to justiciable acts. As examples of non-justiciable acts Lord Roskill listed, "the making of treaties, the defence of the realm, the prerogative of mercy,[33] the grant of honours, the disolution of Parliament and the appointment of ministers as well as others . . . "[34] Thus there is no reason to doubt that the courts will continue to accept as conclusive Foreign Office certificates relating to the recognition of foreign states and governments,[35] the existence of a state of war[36] and whether individuals are entitled to claim sovereign[37] or diplomatic immunity[38] in the British courts.

Lastly, the prerogatives are *legally* vested in the Queen although this is now largely a matter of form. By custom and convention prerogative powers must be exercised through and on the advice of other persons. The necessity of knowing whether or not an executive act is an expression of the Sovereign's will and of making someone other than the Sovereign legally liable for its consequences has given rise to complex rules determining how the Sovereign's acts are to be authenticated. The forms in which the royal will is expressed are generally by: (i) proclamation, writ, letters patent, grant or other document under the Great Seal[39]; (ii) Order in Council; or (iii) warrant, commission, order or instructions[40] under the Sign Manual. The discretionary character of prerogative powers has also given rise to the doctrine of ministerial responsibility, the most important development in modern British constitutional history. There are very few occasions nowadays when the Queen can act without or against the advice of her Ministers; these exceptional cases may include the choice of Prime Minister[41] and the dissolution of Parliament or the dismissal of a ministry.[42]

Classification of the prerogative

(i) It is still possible to distinguish between *personal* and *political* prerogatives, that is, between those which the Queen has as a person and those which she has as Head of State. The personal, however, have tended to become absorbed by the political and in consequence they have lost most of their constitutional significance.

The political prerogatives are often spoken of as adhering to "*the*

[33] *Post* p. 373.
[34] At p. 418.
[35] *Duff Development Co.* v. *Government of Kelantan* [1924] A.C. 797 (H.L.); *Carl Zeiss Stiftung* v. *Rayner and Keeler Ltd.* (No. 2) [1967] A.C. 853 (H.L.) See also *R.* v. *S. of State for Foreign and Commonwealth Affairs, ex p. Trawnik, The Times,* April 18, 1985.
[36] *R.* v. *Bottrill, ex p. Kuechenmeister* [1947] K.B. 41 (C.A.).
[37] *Mighell* v. *Sultan of Johore* [1894] 1 Q.B. 149.
[38] *Engelke* v. *Musmann* [1928] A.C. 433. And *post* p. 288.
[39] *Ante,* p. 152n.
[40] *e.g.* to colonial Governors, *post,* Chap. 36.
[41] *Post,* Chap. 16.
[42] *Ante,* Chap. 7.

Crown." Thomas Paine called the Crown "a metaphor shown at the Tower for sixpence or a shilling a piece."[43] and Maitland said the expression was often used as a cover for ignorance.[44] In effect "the Crown" is equivalent to the executive or the central government.[45] Each organ of the Government is in law, part of the one, indivisible Crown of the United Kingdom.[46] More precisely it means the Queen in her public capacity, either: (a) in rare cases acting at her own discretion, *e.g.* choice of Prime Minister in exceptional circumstances; (b) acting on the advice of Ministers, *e.g.* opening Parliament; (c) acting through or by means of Ministers, *e.g.* negotiating treaties and pardoning criminals; or (d) Ministers acting on behalf of the Queen.[47] With regard to the last, in modern times many powers are conferred by statute directly on Ministers, *e.g.* to approve town-planning schemes or to acquire land compulsorily; in theory the Ministers act on behalf of the Queen.

(ii) So far we have spoken of the prerogatives as if they were composed entirely of powers. Another classification shows that this is not so. They can be analysed into: (a) *rights, e.g.* the Crown Estate and *bona vacantia* (but these are regulated largely by statute); (b) *powers, e.g.* to summon Parliament and to make treaties; (c) *privileges, e.g.* to ask for and to receive supply from Parliament; and (d) *immunities, e.g.* exemption from statutes imposing taxes or rates unless expressly mentioned, and from being sued or have property taken in execution (*cf.* Crown Proceedings Act 1947). This method of classification is one of analytical jurisprudence[48] rather than constitutional law, but it may sometimes help to a clearer understanding of the prerogative.

(iii) The most convenient classification for the present day is according to the branch of government to which the various prerogatives relate, *i.e. legislative, judicial* and *executive.* Those which relate to legislation and the administration of justice are mostly "ordinary" prerogatives in the sense used above, while those which relate to the executive are mainly "absolute"[49] or discretionary and regulated by convention.

Personal prerogatives

These consist mainly of immunities and property rights.

(i) *"The King never dies."* The Common law knows no interregnum. But this theory was of limited effect, because the death of the Sovereign entailed the dissolution of Parliament and the determination of the tenure of offices under the Crown (including judicial offices), until these inconveniences were remedied by various statutes.[50]

(ii) *"The King is never an infant."* The common law made no provision

---

[43] *Rights of Man* (1791).

[44] *Constitutional History*, p. 418.

[45] See further, Marshall, *Constitutional Theory* (1971), pp. 17–34.

[46] *Cmrs of Crown Lands* v. *Page* [1960] 2 Q.B. 274 (C.A.). The Crown is, however, divisible with reference to its liabilities and obligations in respect of its various territories and realms: *post* p. 730.

[47] *Post,* Chap. 35.

[48] See W.N. Hohfeld, *Fundamental Legal Conceptions.*

[49] *Ante,* p. 262.

[50] For Parliament and the demise of the Crown, see *ante,* p. 139; and for judicial tenure, *post,* Chap. 20. And see Crown Proceedings Act 1947, s.32.

for the Sovereign being a minor; but the contingency is now provided for by the Regency Acts.[51]

(iii) *"The King can do no wrong."* The Sovereign cannot be sued or prosecuted in the courts.[52] The significance of this immunity was greatly diminished by the Crown Proceedings Act 1947, which enables the citizen to sue government departments in contract or tort or for the recovery of property, while leaving unimpaired the Sovereign's personal immunity.[53]

(iv) *Crown private estates.*[54] At common law the general rule is that the same prerogatives attach to estates vested in the Sovereign in her natural capacity as apply to estates vested in the Sovereign in her political capacity in right of the Crown. The Crown Private Estates Acts 1800, 1862 and 1873 now regulate to some extent the disposition of such property. These Acts apply to property belonging to the Sovereign at the time of accession, property devised or bequeathed by any persons not being Kings or Queens of the realm, and property bought out of the privy purse. Sandringham and Balmoral are made subject to rates. Crown private estates may be disposed of by the Sovereign *inter vivos* or by will unless, like the Duchies of Lancaster and Cornwall (the incomes from which are not subject to income tax[55]), they are settled by charter having statutory effect. If undisposed of at the death of the Sovereign, they descend with the Crown and become lands held in right of the Crown.[56]

Effect of statute on the prerogative

A royal prerogative may be expressly abolished by Act of Parliament, as when the Crown Proceedings Act 1947 abolished the immunity of the Crown from being sued in contract and tort. An Act may be passed covering the same ground or part of the same ground as the prerogative, in which case the prerogative is to that extent by necessary implication abrogated, at least so long as the statute remains in force.

In *Attorney-General* v. *De Keyser's Royal Hotel Ltd.*[57] the respondent's hotel was required by the War Office in the First World War. Negotiations broke down over the amount of the rent, and possession was taken compulsorily by the Army Council under the Defence of the Realm Regulations on terms that compensation would be paid *ex gratia*. The respondents gave possession but claimed the right to full compensation under the Defence Regulations. The House of Lords unani-

---

[51] *Ante,* pp. 259 *et seq.*

[52] The legend perpetuated by Bracton, that writs lay against the King down to Edward I's time, is refuted by other authorities; see Holdsworth, *History of English Law,* Vol. IX, p. 12.

[53] It would seem that proceedings against the Queen in her private capacity can now be brought (if at all) only by way of the common law (pre-1860) petition of right; *post,* Chap. 35.

[54] (1971) H.C. 29.

[55] *Post.* p. 280.

[56] *Cf.* Crown Estate, *post,* p. 271.

[57] [1920] A.C. 508. There was argument about the effect (if any) of the Defence Act 1842, now amended by the Statute Law (Repeals) Act 1969. And see J. Golding, "The Impact of Statutes on the Royal Prerogative" (1974) 48 A.L.J. 434. See also *Walwin Ltd.* v. *West Sussex C.C.* [1975] 3 All E.R. 604; *Herbert Berry* v. *I.R.C.* [1977] 1 W.L.R. 1437 (H.L.); *Manitoba Fisheries Ltd* v. *The Queen* (1978) 88 D.L.R. (3d) 462 (Can. Sup. Ct.).

mously decided that the statutory Regulations specifying the manner in which compensation was to be assessed must be observed by the Crown. The Crown could not choose, said Lord Sumner, whether or not to act under the prerogative power (assuming that to exist) involving perhaps no compensation or only compensation *ex gratia*; it must act under the statutory power and in accordance with its terms for, as Lord Moulton said, that must be presumed to be the intention of Parliament in passing the statute. Their Lordships expressed various opinions on the question whether, where a statute impliedly covers the same ground as a prerogative power, the statute *pro tanto* abolishes the prerogative or merges it with the statute (Lord Parmoor); or whether, as Lord Atkinson preferred to say, the prerogative is merely in abeyance so long as the statute remains in force.

In *Laker Airways Ltd.* v. *Department of Trade*[58] consideration was given to the effect of the Civil Aviation Act 1971 on the powers of the Crown under the Bermuda Agreement 1946, a treaty between the United Kingdom and the United States covering the grant and revocation of permits for transatlantic air services. The Act set up a Civil Aviation Authority for the licensing of air transport, subject to "guidance" given by the Secretary of State. In furtherance of changed government policy the Secretary of State gave "guidance" to the authority to revoke the licence granted to Laker Airways to operate their "Skytrain" service between London and New York. The Court of Appeal held that the Secretary of State's action was *ultra vires* the Act, which impliedly fettered the use of the prerogative to cancel the designation of the plaintiffs under the treaty.

II. The Prerogative in Domestic Affairs

These consist largely of powers, and in theory of some duties.

1. Executive prerogatives[59]

The prerogatives that may be classed as executive, administrative or governmental are a relic of the powers which the King had when he really governed the country. The government at the present day is largely carried on under statutory powers—a subject too vast for discussion in a general book on constitutional law. Prerogative powers nowadays are mainly of importance in relation to the Civil Service, the armed forces, colonial administration, Commonwealth relations and foreign affairs. Moreover, they have to be read subject to the principle of ministerial responsibility. The government does not have to consult, or even to inform, Parliament before exercising prerogative powers. This is convenient, for many matters falling within the prerogative are not suitable for public discussion before the decision is made or the

---

[58] [1977] Q.B. 643, In *R.* v. *Secretary of State for the Home Department, ex p. Northumbria Police Authority,* [1987] 2 W.L.R. 998, the Divisional Court held that the Crown had not been deprived of its prerogative to take action to deal with actual or apprehended breaches of the peace by the terms of the Police Act 1964.

[59] *Cf.* J. B. D. Mitchell, "The Royal Prerogative in Modern Scots Law" [1957] P.L. 304.

action performed. On the other hand, the government must feel assured of parliamentary support afterwards, especially in a matter like war or where money will be required.

The Sovereign in theory also has duties, but these are not legally enforceable. "The principal duty of the King is, to govern his people according to law," says Blackstone, quoting Bracton and Fortescue to like effect. Blackstone cites the Coronation Oath, but adds that "doubtless the duty of protection is impliedly as much incumbent on the Sovereign before coronation as after."[60] The Sovereign is the general conservator of the peace of the Kingdom,[61] but although the preservation of the peace is a function of the Crown, police officers are not regarded as Crown servants.[62] In *China Navigation Co.* v. *Attorney-General.*[63] it was held that there is no duty enforceable by the Courts on the Crown to afford such protection as was asked for in that case, *viz.* armed protection against pirates in foreign waters, and the subject is not obliged to pay for such protection; but if the Crown agrees to provide special protection for payment, such payment can be recovered from the subject. And in *Tito* v. *Waddell (No. 2)*[64] it was held that any obligation by the Crown to pay royalties for the extraction of phosphates from the colony of Ocean Island was governmental, and not a fiduciary duty enforceable in the courts. In *Mutasa* v. *Attorney-General*[65] Boreham J. held that he had no jurisdiction to enforce the sovereign's duty to protect her subjects at the instance of the plaintiff who claimed that the Crown had failed to prevent his unlawful detention by the illegal Smith regime in Southern Rhodesia.

For our immediate purpose the following is probably the most convenient classification of the prerogatives relating to executive government:

(a) Appointment and dismissal of Ministers, other government officials; officers and men of the forces; the appointment and (subject to statute) dismissal of judicial officers and civil servants.

(b) Control of the services. The Queen is head of the Royal Navy, the Army and the Royal Air Force. The supreme command and government of all forces by sea, land and air, and of all forts and places of strength, is vested in the Crown both by common law and statute. The last Sovereign to exercise the command of the Army in person was George III in 1743 at the Battle of Dottingen. The raising of forces, their discipline and payment are now governed by statute,[66] but the movement and disposition of forces lawfully raised is entirely under the control of the

[60] Bl.Comm. I, Chap.6.
[61] Bl.Comm. I, 266. *R* v. *Secretary of State for the Home Department, ex p. Northumbria Police Authority*, [1987] 2 W.L.R. 998 (D.C.).
[62] *Post* p. 411.
[63] [1932] 2 K.B. 197 (C.A.).
[64] [1977] Ch. 106 (Megarry V.-C.).
[65] [1980] Q.B. 114. The learned judge quoted with approval the opening sentence of this paragraph from p. 272 of the 6th ed.
[66] *Post*, Chap. 18.

Crown.[67] The control of the Civil Service is similarly vested in the Crown.[68]

(c) Administration of dependencies. It is still a function of the Crown to provide for the government of British colonies and other dependencies; and also to make laws for colonies acquired by conquest or cession until Parliament takes over or the colony is granted representative institutions.[69]

(d) Revenue. The Norman and early Plantagenet Kings had "ordinary" and "extraordinary" revenues, and this terminology was still used at the beginning of the nineteenth century.[70] The "ordinary" revenues consisted of customary hereditary revenues such as feudal dues,[71] *bona vacantia*, income from Crown lands and other miscellaneous sources of income that are now exchanged for the Civil List (*infra*). "Extraordinary" revenues or "aids" were raised from time to time to meet the needs of war or other public emergency.

The Crown Estate consists of lands which have become vested in the Sovereign "in his body politic in right of the Crown," and include the ancient demesne lands of the Crown and lands subsequently acquired by prerogative right, *e.g.* by escheat or forfeiture, the foreshore and lands formed by alluvion. The Crown Estate is managed by the Crown Estate Commissioners, who are subject to the general directions of the Chancellor of the Exchequer and the Secretary of State for Scotland. Their annual reports are to be laid before Parliament.[72]

Bona vacantia include wreck,[73] treasure trove, waifs, estrays, royal mines and royal fish.[74] Land that formerly escheated[75] on failure of heirs goes to the Crown as *bona vacantia* under the Administration of Estates Act 1925. Treasure trove consists of gold or silver in coin, plate or bullion, hidden in the earth or other secret place, and subsequently found without trace of the owner.[76] It is hidden, and not abandoned, treasure. The finding of treasure trove is determined by a coroner[77] and a jury. Treasure trove goes by law to the Crown, and it is an offence at common

---

[67] *China Navigation Co.* v. *Att.-Gen.* [1932] 2 K.B. 197 (C.A.); *Chandler* v. *D.P.P.* [1964] A.C. 763 (H.L.); see *per* Viscount Radcliffe.

[68] *Rodwell* v. *Thomas* [1944] K.B. 596. *Post*, Chap. 17.

[69] *Post*, Chap. 36.

[70] Chitty, *Prerogatives of the Crown* (1820) p. 200.

[71] Most of these disappeared with the abolition of military tenure in 1660.

[72] Crown Estate Act 1961.

[73] Regulated by the Merchant Shipping Act 1894. See *Pierce* v. *Bemis* (*The Lusitania*) [1986] 2 W.L.R. 501.

[74] For these, see Bl.Comm. I, 290–299; Keith, *The King and the Imperial Crown*, p. 390.

[75] See *Re Lowe's Will Trusts* [1973] 1 W.L.R. 882 (Claim by Crown to the Phoenix Inn, Stratford-on-Avon, arising from death in 1851 of tenant in fee simple without heirs).

[76] *Att.-Gen of the Duchy of Lancaster* v. *G. E. Overton (Farms) Ltd.* [1981] Ch. 333; [1982] Ch. 277. See generally, Sir George Hill, *Treasure Trove In Law and Practice: from the earliest time to the present day* (1936).

[77] The chief duty of the coroner, whose court dates back to 1194, is to hold an inquest where a person has died in his district and there is reasonable cause to suspect that he died a violent or unnatural death, or where death was sudden and the cause unknown, or where the person died in prison: Coroners Courts Act 1887–1954; Criminal Law Act 1977.

law to conceal the discovery.[78] Nowadays the Crown as a matter of grace usually compensates the owner of the land and the finder.[79] As a prerogative right of the Sovereign it is exercisable over land of which the Sovereign is not the feudal lord.[80]

It is the privilege of the Crown to demand and receive supply from Parliament for the government of the country.[81] Since the Bill of Rights 1688 taxes can only be raised by authority of Parliament.

The Civil List. Since the accession of George III in 1760 it has been the custom for each Sovereign to surrender to the Exchequer for life the hereditary revenues held in right of the Crown, in exchange for an annual payment known as the Civil List. The revenues of the Duchies of Lancaster and Cornwall are excluded from the surrender. The surrendered revenues are paid into the Exchequer and form part of he Consolidated Fund. The main items of expenditure covered by the Civil List, which is charged on the Consolidated Fund, are the salaries and expenses of the official part of the royal household and royal bounty, and the Privy Purse (pensions for employees and the maintenance of Sandringham and Balmoral).[82] Provision is also made towards the expenses of performing public duties by certain other members of the Royal Family.[83] Various government departments meet other expenditure, *e.g.* for the Royal Yacht, the Queen's Flight and royal residences occupied by members of the Royal Family. The amounts fixed by Parliament on the accession of Queen Elizabeth II in 1952 were increased by the Civil List Act 1972 to offset inflation. Section 6 provides that the Treasury may increase from time to time the financial provision allocated for certain purposes by statutory instrument subject to annulment by resolution of the House of Commons; and the Civil List Act 1975 allows the Treasury to supplement such sums out of moneys provided by Parliament. It is doubtful whether the amounts paid by the Treasury and other Departments for the Monarchy exceed the hereditary revenues and income made over by the Queen to the Treasury.[84]

(e) Ecclesiastical prerogatives. Elizabeth I was described as the supreme ecclesiastical and temporal "Governor" of the realm by the Act of Supremacy 1558,[85] and the Book of Common Prayer refers to the Sovereign as "our Queen and Governor." The title suggests administrative rather than lawmaking powers; ecclesiastical but not spiritual. "Conceive it thus," says Selden, "there is in the Kingdom of England a

[78] *R.* v. *Toole* (1867) 11 Cox C.C. 75.
[79] *Att.-Gen.* v. *Moore* [1893] 1 Ch. 676; *Att.-Gen.* v. *Trustees of the British Museum* [1903] 2 Ch. 598. Notable finds that have been declared treasure trove and placed in the British Museum are a fine collection of Roman silver plate (Mildenhall, 1946), a hoard of 883 Anglo-Saxon coins (Norfolk, 1958), and a hoard of 1,326 medieval gold coins (Newstead Abbey, Notts., 1966).
[80] *Lord Advocate* v. *Aberdeen University,* 1963 S.C. 533; 1963 S.L.T. 361.
[81] *Ante,* Chap. 11.
[82] The Queen does not, in fact, draw the money allocated to her Privy Purse and her personal expenditure is paid from her own resources.
[83] *Report from the Select Committee on the Civil List* (1971) H.C. 29.
[84] The sum is complicated by the fact that the Sovereign does not pay direct taxes.
[85] Repealed, except section 8 by various Acts. The sidenote to that section reads "All Spiritual Jurisdiction United to the Crown." The Act of Supremacy 1534 (repealed in 1554) called Henry VIII the supreme "Head" on earth of the Church of England.

college of physicians; the King is supreme governor of those, but not the head of them, nor president of the college, nor the best physician." The Queen nominates bishops diocesan[86] of the Church of England on the advice of the Prime Minister. The Church has not been given the decisive voice in appointing its bishops,[87] mainly because its senior bishops sit in the House of Lords. The new practice is that the Church Commission on Crown Appointments[88] puts forward to the Prime Minister two names for a vacant bishopric, expressing a preference for one of them.[89]

Otherwise, the functions and powers of the Queen in relation to the Church of England are mainly regulated by statute, for example, the calling together and dissolving of the General Synod and the Convocations of Canterbury and York.[90] The Queen in person opened the Second General Synod in 1975. The Clergy Act 1533 requires the Queen's assent and licence for the making of Canon laws and also provides that no Canons may be made which are contrary or repugnant to the royal prerogative or the customs, laws or statutes of the realm. Since the Reformation new Canons, or changes in customary or Canon Law, can only bind the laity by authority of Act of Parliament (*Middleton* v. *Croft*[91]). Forms of service alternative to those prescribed by the Book of Common Prayer may now be authorised by the General Synod, without the need for an Act of Parliament.[92]

(f) The "fountain of honour." The Queen is the "fountain of honour."[93] The creation of peers is done on the advice of the Prime Minister.[94] Most honours in the United Kingdom are also conferred on the advice of the Prime Minister.[95]

Recommendations for *all* honours have, since 1979, been submitted for scrutiny to the Political Honours Scrutiny Committee, a body which

---

[86] Suffragan bishops are appointed on the nomination of diocesan bishops.

[87] The prerogative and procedure for confirming the election of bishops were preserved by the Ecclesiastical Jurisdiction Measure 1963, as amended.

[88] Consisting of the two Archbishops, six members elected by the General Synod, and two non-voting members (the Prime Minister's appointments secretary and the Archbishop's appointments secretary).

[89] A *congé d'elire* (permission to elect) is sent to the dean and chapter of the cathedral of the vacant bishopric (or to the cathedral chapter in the case of "a parish church cathedral" which does not have a dean), accompanied by a "letter missive" containing the name of the nominee. (In the case of the Bishopric of Sodor and Man where there is no chapter at all, nomination is effected by letters patent).

[90] Synodical Government Measure 1969, modifying the Church of England Assembly (Powers) Act 1919 and the Church of England Convocations Act 1966.

[91] (1743) Cas. T. Hard. 326 (Eccles. Ct.).

[92] Church of England (Worship and Doctrine) Measure 1974 (No. 3).

[93] *The Prince's Case* (1606) 8 Co.Rep. 1a, 18b; Bl.Com. I, 271.

[94] George V in 1924 personally offered Asquith, an ex-Prime Minister, a peerage on the day on which he lost his seat at a general election, when Baldwin was about to succeed MacDonald and the premiership was momentarily vacant; Roy Jenkins, *Asquith*, pp. 505–506.

[95] Some Orders are a matter for the Queen's personal choice; *viz*: awards to the Order of Merit, Orders of the Garter and the Thistle and the Royal Victorian Order. Thus the Queen made the Governor of Southern Rhodesia a K.C.V.O. at the time of U.D.I. in November 1965.

was established in the 1920s in the wake of disquiet about the sale of titles by Lloyd George. The Committee consists of three Privy Councillors. If the Prime Minister persists with a recommendation against the advice of the Committee, its adverse view is made known to the Queen which, it has been suggested, must imply that the monarch, in such circumstances, has a discretion to reject the recommendation.[96]

(g) **Miscellaneous prerogatives.** Other prerogatives or former prerogatives relating to coinage, mining of precious metals, administration of charities, guardianship of infants and mental patients, the use of patents and the creation of boroughs, are now largely regulated by statute.[97] The prerogative to issue the writ *ne exeat regno*[98] (to forbid a person to leave the realm) at the instance of a Secretary of State is obsolescent.[99] The right to publish the Bible and the New Testament does not extend to breach of copyright in modern translations.[1] It has been held that there is a prerogative to issue free information, *e.g.* a government pamphlet about the Common Market.[2]

(h) **Emergency and Defence.** The Crown may use such force as is reasonably necessary to put down riot or insurrection.[3]

The Crown is responsible for the defence of the realm by sea and land, and is the only judge of the existence of danger to the realm from external enemies (*R. v. Hampden*[4]), although it is not the sole judge of the means by which such danger is to be averted, *e.g.* the imposition of taxation or conscription (Bill of Rights 1688). In time of war the Crown may requisition ships, at least British ships in territorial waters, on pay-

---

[96] G. Marshall, *Constitutional Conventions* (1984), p. 23. Questions may not be asked of the Prime Minister relating to the grant of honours: Erskine May, *Parliamentary Practice* (20th ed.), p. 338.

[97] The Wild Creatures and Forest Laws Act 1971 abolished the prerogative right to wild creatures (except royal fish and swans), and any franchises of forest, free chase, park or free warren; abrogated the forest laws and repealed the statutes dating back to Edward I. On the coinage see now, Coinage Act 1971; Currency Act 1983. The determining of weights and measures was formerly done by the prerogative: A. Wharam, "The History of the Mile" [1979] N.L.J. 51.

[98] *Ne exeat regnum*: Bl.Comm. I. 265–266.

[99] *Felton v. Callis* [1969] 1 Q.B. 200 (Megarry J.); the writ *ne exeat regno* will now be issued at the instance of a private person only if the requirements of the Debtors Act 1869, s.6, are complied with. Followed, *Lipkin Gorman v. Cass The Times* May 29, 1985; *Al Nahkel for Contracting and Trading Ltd. v. Lowe* [1986] 2 W.L.R. 317. The writ was issued in 1893, but discharged: *Lewis v. Lewis* (1893) 68 L.T. 193 (Ch.D.); an an order was issued by Rowlatt J., vacation judge, sitting in his orchard in about 1912 (letter from D. N. Pritt Q.C. to *The Times*, August 15, 1968). And see J. W. Bridge, "The Case of the Rugby Football Team and the High Prerogative Writ" (1972) 88 L.Q.R. 83; F. M. Auburn, "Ne Exeat Regno" [1970] C.L.J. 183. A similar effect can be achieved by resort to the equitable jurisdiction of the High Court: *Bayer A.G. v. Winter* (No. 2) [1986] 1 W.L.R. 497 (C.A.).

[1] *Universities of Oxford and Cambridge v. Eyre and Spottiswoode* [1964] Ch. 736.

[2] *Jenkins v. Att.-Gen.* (1971) 115 S.J. 674. "Since all the Crown's subjects are at liberty to issue as much free information as they like . . . I offer you this as a choice example of a non-prerogative"; H. W. R. Wade, *Constitutional Fundamentals* (1980), p. 49. The Crown's subjects, however, would be using their own money. "Free" information from the government must be paid for by the taxpayer.

[3] See further, *post*, Chap. 19.

[4] (1637) 3 St.Tr. 825.

ment of compensation (*The Broadmayne*[5]), and may enter upon and use the lands of the citizen near the coast in order to repel invasion (*Case of the King's Prerogative in Saltpetre*[6]). After the danger is over the bulwarks ought to be removed: nothing otherwise was said about compensation in that case. But in modern times the Crown relies in time of war and other grave emergency on statutory powers, such as the Emergency Powers (Defence) Acts of the late war.[7]

Dicey goes so far as to say: "There are times of tumult or invasion when for the sake of legality itself the rules of law must be broken. The course which the Government must then take is clear. The Ministry must break the law and trust for protection to an Act of Indemnity."[8] If this is so, the duty of the Crown to protect the realm is paramount. Darling J. in *Re Shipton*[9] construing a Defence of the Realm Act approved *obiter* the old maxim, *salus populi suprema lex* (the safety of the people is the highest law).[10]

The question whether compensation is payable for loss or damage caused by (lawful) exercise of the prerogative was argued for the first time in the House of Lords as a preliminary question of law in *Burmah Oil Co.* v. *Lord Advocate*.[11] The company's oil installations had been destroyed by order of the British commander of the forces in Burmah (then a colony) in 1942, to prevent them from falling into the hands of the invading Japanese forces who would have found them of great strategic value. Their Lordships held by a majority of three to two that, although compensation had never been payable at common law for "battle" damage, whether accidental or deliberate, this was "denial" damage—really economic warfare—and there was no general rule that the royal prerogative can be exercised without compensation. Lord Reid in his majority speech said that there was no precedent of a claim for compensation in such cases not being paid, and it was therefore payable.[12] Lord Radcliffe in his dissenting speech said the prerogative was so vague and uncertain that he preferred to base his opinion on the idea of necessity: the Crown had as much a duty as a right to do what it did, and it was not a source of profit to the Crown. With logic equal to Lord Reid's he said there was no precedent of such a claim being paid, and therefore it was not payable.[13]

---

[5] [1916] P. 64; and see *The Sarpon* [1916] P. 306.

[6] (1606) 12 Co.Rep. 12.

[7] *Post*, Chap. 19.

[8] Dicey, *Law of the Constitution* (10th ed.), pp. 412–413.

[9] *Re Shipton, Anderson & Co. and Harrison Brothers & Co.* [1915] 3 K.B. 676, 684.

[10] The maxim was addressed by Cicero to a military commander. It is found in Bracton, Hobbes, Bacon, Coke, Hale and Hawkins. Sometimes, as in Selden's *Table Talk*, the verb is imperative (*esto*).

[11] [1965] A.C. 75. See A. L. Goodhart, "The Burmah Oil Case and the War Damage Act 1965" (1966) 82 L.Q.R. 97; and note by Paul Jackson in (1964) 27 M.L.R. 709.

[12] Cited as authority for this proposition in the Privy Council: *Société United Docks* v. *Government of Mauritius* [1985] A.C. 585, 600 *per* Lord Templeman.

[13] In *United States* v. *Caltex* (1952) 344 U.S. 149, a similar case relating to property in the Philippines, the majority of the United States Supreme Court held that no compensation was payable at common law, while the minority thought compensation was payable under the Fifth Amendment to the Constitution (private property not to be taken for public use without just compensation).

The War Damage Act 1965 abolished retrospectively[14] any right which the subject may have had at common law to compensation from the Crown in respect of lawful acts of damage to, or destruction of property done by, or under the authority of, the Crown during, or in contemplation of, a war in which he Sovereign was or is engaged. The Act thus nullified the decision of the House of Lords in the *Burmah Oil Company* case so far as war damage is concerned. It does not deal with unlawful acts by officers or servants of the Crown,[15] nor the mere taking possession of property (requisition or angary).[16] Any payment of compensation by the government for war damage, whether caused by the Crown in prosecution of a war or by enemy action, must therefore be authorised by Act of Parliament.

2. Judicial prerogatives
These are discussed later in Chapter 20 under "The Administration of Justice."

3. Legislative prerogatives
The prerogatives in relation to the legislature include the power to summon, prorogue and dissolve Parliament, and the giving of the Royal Assent to Bills. These have already been discussed in Chapter 7. It has also been seen that the Sovereign has no prerogative power to legislate within the realm (*Case of Proclamations*[17]). The Crown has a prerogative right to print and publish statutes.[18]

It is a parliamentary custom that legislation affecting the prerogatives or property of the Crown should be preceded by a message from the Crown; and the Speaker must not allow a Bill that affects the prerogative to be read a third time unless the royal consent has been signified by a Privy Councillor.

The Crown is not bound by an Act of Parliament—at any rate, to its detriment—except by express words or necessary implication. It was said in some earlier cases that the Sovereign is bound, even though not named therein, by statutes for the public good, for the preservation of public rights, suppression of public wrong, relief and maintenance of

[14] Lawyers in both Houses objected strongly to the retroactive effect of the Bill, but: (i) the company had been offered reasonable compensation by successive Chancellors of the Exchequer, and had been warned that if their claim were successful in the courts, legislation would be introduced to indemnify the Crown, *i.e.* the taxpayer; (ii) it is unlikely that the company destroyed the property acting in the belief that there was a common law right to compensation; *cf. Phillips* v. *Eyre* (1870) L.R. 6 Q.B. 1; (iii) the provision in the American Constitution against *ex post facto* laws is interpreted to refer to penal laws: *Calder* v. *Bull* (1798) 3 Dall. 386; (iv) by what method, and on what basis, would compensation be assessed? The Japanese captured the site on the day after the installations were destroyed, and the loss was estimated at anything from nil to £100,000,000; (v) by what common law procedure (*e.g.* petition of right) could compensation have been claimed before the Crown Proceedings Act 1947?

[15] *Cf.* Crown Proceedings Act 1947, s.2.

[16] Angary is the power of the Crown in time of war to requisition neutral chattels found within the realm on payment of compensation: *Commercial and Estates Co. of Egypt* v. *Board of Trade* [1925] 1 K.B. 271.

[17] (1610) 2 St.Tr. 723; *ante*, p. 42. For prerogative legislation by Order in Council for British dependencies, see *post*, Chap. 36.

[18] Paul Von Nessen, "Law Reporting: Another Case for Deregulation," (1985) 48 M.L.R. 412.

the poor, advancement of learning, religion and justice, the prevention of fraud, and by statutes tending to perform the will of a grantor, donor or founder.[19] In *Bombay Province* v. *Bombay Municipal Corporation*,[20] however, the Judicial Committee held that the inference that the Crown agreed to be bound by a statute could only be drawn if it was apparent from its terms at the time of its enactment that its beneficial purpose would be wholly frustrated if the Crown were not bound.

For the court to hold that Parliament intended an Act to bind the Crown there must be either express words to that effect, *e.g.* Crown Private Estates Acts; Crown Proceedings Act 1947; Law Reform (Limitation of Actions, etc.) Act 1954, s.5, Health and Safety At Work etc. Act 1974, s.48 and s.72, or words giving rise to such a strong implication that the court cannot reasonably help drawing it (*Attorney-General* v. *Donaldson*[21]). Thus it has been held that houses let by the Crown were not protected by Rent Restriction Acts,[22] royal palaces are not bound by the Licensing Acts,[23] vehicles driven by Crown servants were not subject to a statutory speed limit,[24] the Administrator of Austrian Property was not subject to statutes of limitation,[25] and land occupied by government departments does not require planning permission under Planning Acts.[26]

A corollary of that principle is the immunity of the Crown from income tax and rates, which can only be imposed by authority of Act of Parliament. The basis of the *prima facie* exclusion of the Crown from a taxing Act was discussed by the House of Lords in *Madras Electric Supply Corporation* v. *Boarland*.[27] While Lords Oaksey and Tucker thought it was not necessary to decide whether the Crown's immunity depended on the construction of the Act or arose from the prerogative, Lord MacDermott regarded it as a rule of construction, Lord Keith of Avonholm offered the questionable explanation that words in a statute capable of applying to the Crown might be overridden by the exercise of the prerogative, and Lord Reid expressed the preferable opinion that the presumption is a rule of construction taking account of the prerogative.

The question who represents the Crown for this purpose was

---

[19] *Case of Ecclesiastical Persons* (1601) 4 Co.Rep. 14b; *Magdalen College Case* (*Warren* v. *Smith*) (1615) 11 Co.Rep. 66b. In *Willion* v. *Berkley* ((1561) Plowd. 223) counsel argued that the presumption is that the Sovereign "does not mean to prejudice himself or to bar himself of his liberty and privilege."

[20] [1947] A.C. 58. See too *Department of Transport* v. *Egoroff, The Times* May 6, 1986.

[21] (1842) 10 M. & W. 117; *Gorton Local Board* v. *Prison Commissioners* (1887) reported in *Cooper* v. *Hawkins* [1904] 2 K.B. 165 (local byelaws); *Re Wi Matua's Will* [1908] A.C. 448.

[22] *Tamlin* v. *Hannaford* [1950] 1 K.B. 18; *cf.* Crown Lessees (Protection of Sub-Tenants) Act 1952. But tenants of the Crown Estates Commissioners, of the Duchy of Cornwall and the Duchy of Lancaster do enjoy statutory protection: Housing Act 1980, s.73; *Crown Estates Commissioners* v. *Wordsworth* (1982) 44 P. & C.R. 302 (C.A.).

[23] *R.* v. *Graham Campbell, ex p. Herbert* [1935] 1 K.B. 594.

[24] *Cooper* v. *Hawkins* [1904] 2 K.B. 164; for subsequent developments see (1983) 99 L.Q.R. 341 and *post* p. 703 n.5.

[25] *Administrator of Austrian Property* v. *Russian Bank for Foreign Trade* (1931) 48 T.L.R. 37 (C.A.). But see now, Limitation Act 1980, s.37.

[26] *Ministry of Agriculture, Fisheries and Food* v. *Jenkins* [1963] 2 Q.B. 317 (C.A.); *Campbell (A.G.) (Arcam)* v. *Worcestershire County Council* (1963) 61 L.G.R. 321. See now Town and Country Planning Act 1984.

[27] [1955] A.C. 667. The Crown is not bound by an admission made on its behalf that a statute applies to the Crown: *Att-Gen. for Ceylon* v. *A. D. Silva* [1953] A.C. 461 (P.C.).

reviewed in *Bank voor Handel en Scheepvaart N.V.* v. *Administrator of Hungarian Property*,[28] where the House of Lords by a majority held that the Custodian of Enemy Property was a servant of the Crown, and that the Crown had a sufficient interest in the disposal of property held by him in that capacity to entitle him to claim exemption from tax on the income. The majority of their Lordships approved of the classification made by Blackburn J. in *Mersey Docks and Harbour Board* v. *Cameron* (1864)[29] that the immunity extends to: (i) the Sovereign personally; (ii) Crown servants, *e.g.* government departments[30]; and land occupied or funds held for Crown purposes by persons in *consimili casu, e.g.* assize courts and judges' lodgings,[31] county courts,[32] police stations[33] and prisons.[34] The difficulty was to decide, first, whether the Custodian of Hungarian Property fell into any of the categories enumerated above, and (if so) whether the property held by him was entitled to Crown immunity. Their Lordships (except Lord Keith) were agreed that the Crown, through the Board of Trade and the Treasury, had sufficient control of him to make him a Crown servant, so that he fell into category (ii).

The general rule is subject to criticism. It has been suggested that the presumption ought to be reversed by legislation, so that the Crown would be bound by statute unless it was expressly declared not to be bound, or public policy required the exemption of the Crown in a particular case.[35]

III. THE PREROGATIVE IN FOREIGN AFFAIRS

Acts of state

There is no technical definition of "act of state" in British constitutional law,[36] but the expression is generally used for an act done by the Crown as a matter of policy in relation to another state, or in relation to an individual who is not within the allegiance to the Crown.[37] The

---

[28] [1954] A.C. 584.

[29] 11 H.L.C. 443, 465. See also *Mersey Docks and Harbour Board* v. *Gibbs* (1866) L.R. 1 H.L. 93; And see Holdsworth, *History of English Law*, Vol. X, pp. 295–299.

[30] *R.* v. *Stewart* (1857) 8 E. & B. 360. And see *Smith* v. *Birmingham Guardians* (1857) 7 E. & B. 483; *R.* v. *Kent Justices* (1890) 24 Q.B.D. 181; *Wirral Estates* v. *Shaw* [1932] 2 K.B. 247.

[31] *Hodgson* v. *Carlisle Board of Health* (1857) 8 E. & B. 116; and see *Coomber* v. *Berkshire Justices* (1883) 9 App.Cas. 61 (H.L.).

[32] *R.* v. *Manchester Overseers* (1854) 3 E. & B. 336.

[33] *Justices of Lancashire* v. *Stretford Overseers* (1858) E.B. & E. 225.

[34] *R.* v. *Shepherd* (1841) 1 Q.B. 170. And see *Territorial, etc. Forces Association* v. *Nichols* [1949] 1 K.B. 35.

[35] Glanville Williams, *Criminal Law*, I (1961). And see H. Street, *Governmental Liability* (1953) pp. 143–152; Peter W. Hogg, *Liability of the Crown* (1971), Chap. 7. In *Cain* v. *Doyle* (1946) 72 C.L.R. 409, the majority in the High Court of Australia speaking *obiter* did not reject the possibility of the Crown being convicted of a criminal offence, *e.g.* the State as employer. See W. Friedmann, "Public Welfare Offences, Statutory Duties, and the Legal Status of the Crown" (1950) 13 M.L.R. 24.

[36] See Harrison Moore, *Act of State in English Law* (1906); Holdsworth, "The History of Acts of State in English Law" (1941) 41 *Columbia Law Rev.* 1313; E. C. S. Wade, "Act of State in English Law" (1934) 15 B.Y.I.L. 98.

[37] "An act of the executive as a matter of policy performed in the course of its relations with another State, including its relations with the subjects of that State, unless they are temporarily within the allegiance of the Crown": Wade, *op. cit.* p. 103. *Cf. per* Lord Wilberforce in *Nissan* v. *Att.-Gen.* [1970] A.C. 179, *post*, p. 283.

two parts of this definition are best considered separately. Cases on acts in relation to foreign states usually arise out of attempts by private individuals to enforce contract or property rights *indirectly* accruing, while cases on acts in relation to individuals normally arise out of an attempt to obtain a remedy for a supposed wrong *directly* resulting; and, as will be seen, the class of individuals against whom acts of state may be done is not free from doubt. A distinct use of the term which Lord Wilberforce identified in *Buttes Gas and Oil Co.* v. *Hammer*[38] relates to cases which are concerned with the applicability of foreign municipal legislation within its own territory and with the recognition of such legislation in the British courts.

1. *Acts of state in relation to foreign states*

Acts of state in this class include the declaration of war and peace; the making of treaties[39]; the annexation and cession of territory; the sending and receiving of diplomatic representatives; and the recognition of foreign states and governments. A claimant whose property or contracts are indirectly affected will be unsuccessful in his attempt to use an act of state as a foundation of an action. Such acts are outside the jurisdiction of British courts in the sense that they cannot be questioned. They are non-justiciable. Nor can a citizen claim to enforce directly any rights to which he may be entitled under them.[40] One view is that they are not properly described as an exercise of the "prerogative" as they are not done in relation to British subjects.[41] (This was the term traditionally used. Its ambit in this context was never precisely defined as is shown by the discussion below of *Nissan* v. *Attorney-General*[42] In terms of the British Nationality Act 1981 it no doubt includes British citizens[43] and some, or all, categories of Commonwealth citizens[44] and, perhaps, those who under the Act are British subjects[45]). There seems to be no good reason why the term "prerogative" should be limited in this way; indeed, Lord Coleridge C.J. described the making of peace and war as "perhaps the highest acts of the prerogative of the Crown."[46]

In *Salaman* v. *Secretary of State for India*,[47] where a claim was brought to enforce an agreement between the Secretary of State for India and the Maharajah of the Punjab, Fletcher Moulton L.J. said: "An act of state is essentially an act of sovereign power, and hence cannot be challenged, controlled, or interfered with by municipal courts." He went on to say that the court must accept an act of state as it is without question; but the court may be called upon to decide whether or not there has been an

---

[38] [1982] A.C. 888 (As a general rule such matters are "non-justiciable": in exceptional cases the British courts may consider the effects of foreign legislation which is confiscatory or contrary to public policy).

[39] *Post,* pp. 285 *et seq.*

[40] Unless there is a special statutory provision to this effect, *e.g.* Foreign Compensation Act 1950.

[41] *Per* Warrington L.J. in *Re Ferdinand, Ex-Tsar of Bulgaria* [1921] 1 Ch. 107, 139.

[42] [1970] A.C. 179.

[43] S.1.

[44] S.37.

[45] S.30 and s.31.

[46] *Rustomjee* v. R. (1876) 2 Q.B.D. 69, 73.

[47] [1906] 1 K.B. 613 (C.A.). And see *Secretary of State for India* v. *Kamachee Boye Sahaba* (1859) 13 Moo.P.C. 22.

act of state, and (if so) its nature and extent.[48] Further, the court may have to consider the effect of an act of state on the rights of the government or of individuals. Thus, while the court will not enforce private rights arising under a treaty,[49] it may be concerned if the treaty creates or modifies rights between the Crown and individuals who are, or who thereby become, subjects. For example, the Crown may recover in the courts debts due to it as a result of annexation, and presumably debts can similarly be recovered from it. The Crown decides what rights and obligations it takes over from the government of a state which it has extinguished by conquest and annexation (*West Rand Central Gold Mining Co. v. The King*[50]); and so there was no redress where a colonial government declined to recognise concessions made to people who under the law then in force were British subjects[51] by the former ruler of territory that has been annexed (*Cook v. Sprigg*[52]). It will be noticed that in these cases the act of state was not done in relation to "British subjects," although it affected their interests.

A declaration of war affects the citizen's trading and contract rights with persons of enemy character, formerly prevented a British subject from becoming naturalised in the enemy state (*R. v. Lynch*[53]), and alters the status in this country of nationals of the enemy state. The court must accept the certificate of the Foreign Secretary as to whether the Crown is at war, or has ceased to be at war, with a foreign country (*R. v. Bottrill, ex p. Kuechenmeister*[54]). The recognition by the Crown of foreign states, Sovereigns and governments may affect the rights of private individuals because of the immunity,[55] from the jurisdiction of the courts which such recognition confers (*Duff Development Co. v. Government of Kelantan*[56]). The court must accept the certificate of the Crown as to recognition, although it will examine the declaration in order to see that the proper facts have been considered by the appropriate Ministers.[57]

---

[48] *Forester v. Secretary of State for India* (1872) L.R.Ind.App., supp. Vol., p. 10; *Musgrave v. Pulido* (1879) 5 App.Cas. 102 (P.C.).

[49] *Nabob of the Carnatic v. East India Co.* (1793) 2 Ves. 56; *Civilian War Claimants' Association v. The King* [1932] A.C. 14.

[50] [1905] 2 K.B. 391 (South African Republic).

[51] At that time "British subject" meant anyone born within the King's dominions who thereby owed allegiance to the King. Not until the British Nationality Act 1948 was the distinct category of citizen of the United Kingdom and Colonies recognised: *post* Chap. 23.

[52] [1899] A.C. 572 (annexation of Pondoland to Cape Colony).

[53] [1903] 1 K.B. 444. *Quaere* how far this prohibition extends.

[54] [1947] K.B. 41 (C.A.).

[55] Now limited by the State Immunity Act 1978; *post* p. 288.

[56] [1924] A.C. 797 (H.L.). And as to the Commonwealth, see *Mighell v. Sultan of Johore* [1894] 1 Q.B. 149; *Kahan v. Pakistan Federation* [1951] 2 K.B. 1003; *Mellenger v. New Brunswick Development Corporation* [1971] 1 W.L.R. 604 (C.A.). *Cf. Sultan of Johore v. Abubakar Tunku Aris Bendahar* [1952] A.C. 218 (P.C.). The practice of recognising *governments* which have come to power by unconstitutional means was abandoned by the British government in 1980. Future certificates will merely indicate what links exist between the regime in question and HM Government so, presumably, leaving the question of recognition to the courts: C. R. Symmons, "United Kingdom Abolition of the Doctrine of Recognition of Governments: A Rose by Another Name?" [1981] I.L. 249.

[57] *Sayce v. Ameer Ruler Sadig Mohammed Abbasi Bahawalpur State* [1952] 2 Q.B. 390 (C.A.).

Similar considerations apply to the recognition of diplomatic representatives, which confers diplomatic immunity (*Engelke* v. *Musmann*[58]).

The decisions of the British courts in such cases illustrate according to Lord Wilberforce, the undoubted judicial acceptance of the principle that, "In a matter affecting the sovereignty of the United Kingdom the courts are entitled to take account of the declared policy of Her Majesty's Government. . . . The courts should in such matters speak with the same voice as the executive."[59]

An act of state cannot alter the law administered by British courts. Thus in *The Zamora*[60] the Privy Council held that a prerogative Order in Council authorising reprisals could not increase the right of the Crown to requisition neutral ships and cargo. Although prize courts are said to administer "international law," it is such law—having its source in international law—as is recognised by English law. It may be modified by statute, but not by the prerogative.

2. Acts of state in relation to individuals

Acts done under the authority of the Crown in relation to individuals have been held to be acts of state, so as to prevent an aggrieved person from obtaining redress for damage done,[61] in the following classes of case. Where the plea "act of state" is successful, this means that the court declines jurisdiction. In such cases the Crown uses "act of state" as a shield in an action brought by a private individual.

(a) An alien outside British territory. In *Buron* v. *Denman*[62]) the captain of a British warship was held not liable for trespass for setting fire to the barracoon of a Spaniard on the west coast of Africa (not British territory) and releasing his slaves: the captain had general instructions to suppress the slave trade, and his conduct in this case was afterwards approved by the Admiralty and the Foreign and Colonial Secretaries. An act of state in relation to individuals, it was held, may be either previously authorised or subsequently ratified by the Crown. There is probably a prerogative power to exclude aliens from entering British territory, and at any rate aliens have no enforceable right at common law to enter (*Musgrove* v. *Chun Teeong Toy*[63]).

(b) An enemy alien within that country. In *R.* v. *Bottrill, ex p. Kuechenmeister*[64] a German national, who had lived in England since 1928 without being naturalised and was interned by the Home Secretary during the war, was unsuccessful in his application for a writ of habeas corpus,

---

[58] [1928] A.C. 433.

[59] *In re Westinghouse Electric Corporation Uranium Contract Litigation M.D.L. Docket No. 235* [1978] A.C. 547, *per* Lord Wilberforce. See too, *British Airways* v. *Laker Airways* [1985] A.C. 58, *per* Lord Diplock.

[60] [1916] 2 A.C. 77; "One of the most courageous of judicial decisions even in our long history"; *per* Lord Scarman, *C.C.S.U.* v. *Minister for Civil Service* [1985] A.C. 374, 404.

[61] Act of state may also be a defence to a criminal charge; see Stephen, *History of the Criminal Law*, II, pp. 61–65. And see *Carr* v. *Fracis Times & Co.* [1902] A.C. 176 (act of state by foreign ruler authorising British subjects to seize British-owned goods in British ships in foreign territorial waters).

[62] (1848) 2 Ex. 167. The case was settled on terms. Captain Denman, the successful defendant, was a son of Denman C.J.

[63] [1891] A.C. 491 (P.C.). The entry of aliens into this country is now regulated by the Immigration Act 1971 and Community Law.

[64] [1947] K.B. 41 (C.A.).

detention by the Crown of an enemy alien being an act of state. A similar principle applies to the deportation of an enemy alien (*Netz* v. *Chuter Ede*[65]).

(c) Formerly acts done by the Crown in British protectorates in relation to the local inhabitants were regarded as acts of state, protectorates being technically foreign countries.[66] This principle probably became untenable after the creation of the new status of British protected persons by the British Nationality Act 1948, but the question is no longer of practical importance.[67]

With regard to the defence of "act of state" against British citizens, Commonwealth citizens and British subjects outside British territory, there is no direct judicial authority.[68]

The Crown must claim "act of state" specifically.[69] But the mere plea "act of state" is not enough: the court can examine the facts in order to decide whether what has been done is an act of state. Thus in an action of trespass against the Governor of Jamaica for seizing and detaining the plaintiff's schooner, it was not enough for the defendant to plead that the acts were done by him in the exercise of his discretion as Governor and as acts of state; he had to show that the acts were done under and within the limits of his commission, or that they were really acts of state policy done under the authority of the Crown (*Musgrave* v. *Pulido*).[70]

On the other hand, if a wrong is committed by a servant of the Crown against a British citizen and, possibly Commonwealth citizens and British subjects or friendly aliens in British territory, it is no defence to plead "act of state." In *Walker* v. *Baird*,[71] where the commander of a British warship had taken possession of a lobster factory belonging to a British subject (under the law then in force) in Newfoundland, it was held no defence that the commander was acting under the orders of the Crown to implement a treaty with France. And in *Johnstone* v. *Pedlar*[72] the House of Lords held that a United States citizen in Dublin (at that time within the United Kingdom) was entitled to claim from the police commissioner money found on him at the time of his arrest for illegal drilling, "act of state" not being available as a defence to an action brought by the citizen of a friendly state for wrongful detention of property in this country.

---

[65] [1946] Ch. 224.
[66] *R.* v. *Earl of Crewe, ex p. Sekgome* [1910] 2 K.B. 576 (C.A.); *Sobhuza II* v. *Miller* [1926] A.C. 518 (P.C.); *Eshugbayi (Eleko)* v. *Government of Nigeria (Officer Administering)* [1931] A.C. 662 (P.C.); *R.* v. *Ketter* [1940] 1 K.B. 787. *Cf. Ex p. Mwenya* ([1960] 1 Q.B. 241 (C.A.)), where the petitioner was assumed to be a British subject by virtue of local citizenship laws (Federation of Rhodesia and Nyasaland). *Cf.* K. Polack, "The Defence of Act of State in Relation to Protectorates" (1963) 26 M.L.R. 138; L. L. Kato, "Act of State in a Protectorate—in Retrospect" [1969] P.L. 219.
[67] The status of British protected persons is preserved by the British Nationality Act 1981; s.38. It is believed that there are about 140,000 such persons, of whom 130,000 are in Brunei.
[68] See *Nissan* v. *Att.-Gen.* [1970] A.C. 179 (H.L.), *post.*
[69] *Nissan* v. *Att.-Gen.* [1970] A.C. 179, *post.*
[70] (1879) 5 App.Cas 102 (P.C.).
[71] [1892] A.C. 491 (P.C.). And see the *General Warrant Cases, post,* Chap. 25.
[72] [1921] 2 A.C. 262.

In *Nissan* v. *Attorney-General*.[73] Nissan, a citizen of the United Kingdom and Colonies, was lessee of an hotel in Cyprus, an independent republic in the Commonwealth.[74] The hotel was occupied by British troops for several months as part of a truce force under an agreement between the Governments of the United Kingdom and Cyprus for the purpose of restoring peace in the civil strife between the Greek and Turkish communities. The British forces then continued to occupy the hotel for a period as part of a United Nations peace-keeping force, on the recommendation of the Security Council of the United Nations and with the consent of the Cyprus Government. Nissan brought an action against the Crown in England, claiming declarations that he was entitled to compensation for damage to the contents of the hotel and the destruction of stores, on the ground that this was a lawful exercise of the prerogative[75]; and that the Crown was liable in damages for trespass to chattels by the British troops.[76] This case was fought on preliminary issues, in particular, whether the acts of the British forces were acts of state.[77] The House of Lords upheld the Court of Appeal in deciding that the acts of the British forces were not non-justiciable as acts of state. Although the agreement of the British Government with the Cyprus Government to send peace-keeping forces to Cyprus was no doubt an act of state, not all acts done incidentally in relation to individual persons or their property (such as occupying a particular hotel or damaging its contents) in the course of executing an act of state are themselves acts of state. All the Law Lords said it was unnecessary to discuss whether the acts of the Crown were an exercise of the prerogative, although Lord Denning M.R. in the Court of Appeal based the liability of the Crown to pay compensation on the exercise of the prerogative, referring to the *Burmah Oil Company* case.[78]

There are a number of dicta, which are not easily reconcilable, in the various judgments concerning "act of State" and its availability as a defence against British subjects. Their Lordships recognised that the latter term itself was open to various interpretations. Lord Morris wondered, without expressing a final opinion, whether the phrase was equivalent to "those owing allegiance to the Crown?" Lord Pearson was uncertain whether "British subject" extended only to a citizen of the United Kingdom and Colonies or to anyone within the wide definition of section 1 of the British Nationality Act 1948 or even whether, in the

---

[73] [1970] A.C. 179. See J. G. Collier, "Act of State as a Defence against a British Subject" (1968) C.L.J. 102, and note in (1969) C.L.J. 166; S. S. de Smith in (1969) 32 M.L.R. 427; *cf.* D. R. Gilmour, "British Forces Abroad and the Responsibility for their Actions" [1970] P.L. 120.

[74] But not one of Her Majesty's dominions.

[75] See *Burmah Oil Co.* v. *Lord Advocate* [1965] A.C. 75; *ante*, p. 275.

[76] Nissan also claimed that there was a contract by the High Commissioner on behalf of the Crown, with the consent of the Secretary of State, that he would receive compensation for occupation of the hotel.

[77] Also on the questions whether there was a contract, express or implied, that he would be compensated (a question of fact left to the trial court); and whether the British troops in the first period were agents of the Cyprus government, and whether in the second period they were agents of the United Nations, the decision as to both periods being "no."

[78] *Ante*, p. 275.

context, it had some other meaning. In the light of the British Nationality Act 1981 these doubts may be rephrased to ask: does "British Subject" for this purpose mean "British citizen" or does it include some or all of the following classes, Commonwealth citizens, British protected persons and British subjects (within the meaning of sections 30 and 31 of the 1981 Act)? If Commonwealth citizens *are* included, should a distinction be drawn between citizens of Commonwealth countries which are still realms and those which recognise the Queen merely as Head of the Commonwealth. (In view of the disintegration of the common law throughout the Commonwealth, also, the earlier cases may have to be reviewed on the questions: what is meant by "British territory," "abroad" and "foreign country?")

With regard to the question whether act of state might be pleaded against a British subject, in whatever sense that phrase is used in this context, Lord Reid stated the traditional doctrine that "act of state" is not available as a defence to interference with the rights of British subjects abroad, but Lord Morris, Lord Pearce and Lord Pearson were doubtful.[79] Lord Wilberforce thought that act of state *could* be pleaded; but in his speech he was concerned mainly not with acts *directly* causing harm which if done by a private individual would constitute a tort but non-justiciable acts of the Crown which *indirectly* cause harm. Lord Pearce thought there was an exercise of the prerogative, involving the obligation to pay, as the case was not covered by the War Damage Act 1965[80]; while Lords Reid and Wilberforce doubted whether the principle of the *Burmah Oil Company*[81] case applied to acts done on foreign soil.

Passports[82]

The Secretary of State has a discretion to grant, refuse, impound or revoke passports, which remain Crown property.[83] A passport was defined by Lord Alverstone C.J. in *R. v. Brailsford*[84] as "a document issued in the name of the Sovereign on the responsibility of a Minister of the Crown to a named individual, intended to be presented to the governments of foreign nations and to be used for that individual's protection as a British subject in foreign countries". It contains a request in the name of Her Majesty to allow the bearer pass freely, and to afford him such assistance and protection as may be necessary. The Crown has

---

[79] H. W. R. Wade suggests that the test whether "act of state" is a defence to an action for a tort against a British subject should be a matter of geography rather than nationality, *e.g.* British troops seizing Suez Canal damage house of British subject living in Egypt: *Administrative Law* (5th ed., 1982) pp. 718–719 citing *Cook v. Sprigg* [1899] A.C. 572.

[80] *Ante*, p. 275.

[81] [1965] A.C. 75.

[82] H. Street, *Freedom, the Individual and the Law* (5th ed., 1982), pp. 291–296; D. W. Williams, "British Passports and the Right to Travel" (1974) I, C.L.Q. 642; Justice, *Going Abroad: A Report on Passports* (1974); J. Jaconelli, (1975) 38 M.L.R. 314; D. C. Turack, "Selected Aspects of International and Municipal Law Concerning Passports" (1971) 12 *William & Mary Law Review*, 805.

[83] *Cf. Ghani v. Jones* [1970] 1 Q.B. 693 (C.A.), where the Pakistani passports taken by the police were not the property of the Crown.

[84] [1905] 2 K.B. 730, 745; approved *Joyce v. D.P.P.* [1946] A.C. 347, *per* Lord Jowitt, L.C.

a duty to protect its citizens abroad, although this is not legally enforceable.[85] A passport is not legally necessary at common law in order to go abroad, but it is universally used as a certificate of identity and nationality. Other countries may refuse entry without possession of one, and therefore transport companies may be expected to refuse to carry passengers abroad without passports.

The alleged prerogative power of the Crown to refuse or impound passports has been described as arbitrary, objectionable and of doubtful legality. Further, the right of establishment in Community Law means that nationals are entitled to identity cards or passports enabling them to leave and re-enter the country freely, subject to public policy, security and health.

Treaties

The treaty-making power is an executive power which in British constitutional law is vested in the Crown.[86] A treaty is analogous to a contract between states. Its binding force is a matter of international law. The negotiations are conducted by agents of the Crown, *e.g.* the Foreign Secretary or a diplomatic representative, and are usually made subject to ratification by the Crown under the Great Seal. Treaties are acts of state, and do not in general require parliamentary sanction.[87] Where treaties require ratification by the Crown (*i.e.* treaties between Heads of State, but not commercial or technical agreements at official level), it has been the practice since 1924 to lay them when signed before both Houses of Parliament for 21 days before they are ratified ("the Ponsonby Rule").[88] This practice may probably now be regarded as a constitutional convention. It has also been described as a "so-called rule . . . no more than a self denying ordinance on the part of the government; on occasions it has been waived or modified if expediency requires a treaty to be ratified more hurriedly."[89] On important treaties the government initiates a discussion; otherwise the Opposition may ask for a discussion.

There are, however, three classes of treaty which do require confirmation by Parliament[90]:

(i) *Treaties expressly made subject to confirmation by Parliament.* A treaty expressly made subject to confirmation by Parliament will not come into force, either by international law or by English law, unless an Act of Parliament is passed confirming it; for that is a condition in the treaty itself. Such parliamentary sanctions is sometimes spoken of as "ratification," but that word is properly used of the final authentication by the Crown.

---

[85] But the obtaining of a British passport, even by an alien, involves allegiance to the Crown: *Joyce* v. *D.P.P.* [1946] A.C. 347 (H.L.).
[86] *Att.-Gen. for Canada* v. *Att.-Gen. for Ontario* [1937] A.C. 326 (P.C.), *per* Lord Atkin.
[87] *Att.-Gen. for Canada* v. *Att.-Gen. for Ontario* [1937] A.C. 326 (P.C.).
[88] H.C.Deb., Vol. 171, ser. 53, col. 2001 (1924).
[89] K. Bradshaw and D. Pring, *Parliament and Congress* (1972), p. 401.
[90] Lord McNair, *The Law of Treaties*, Chap. 2; *Legal Effects of War* (3rd ed.), pp. 397–402; "When do British Treaties involve Legislation?" (1928) B.Y.I.L. 59.

(ii) *Treaties involving an alteration of English law or taxation.* Any alteration of English law involved in implementing a treaty, including the imposition of taxes or the expenditure of public money, needs to be authorised by Act of Parliament.[91] The most striking example is the European Communities Act 1972. The courts cannot have regard to the provisions of treaties until enacted by Parliament,[92] except to the extent that they relate to international relations within the "narrow field" where the courts are prepared to defer to the declared policy of Her Majesty's Government.[93] In other cases courts cannot take into account the terms of international agreements, as Lord Fraser emphasised in the *G.C.H.Q.* Case when criticising the Court of Appeal for taking into account I.L.O. Conventions which had not been enacted as part of United Kingdom law.[94] Dicta in some cases suggests that there is one exception to the general principle: the European Convention on Human Rights. In *Attorney-General* v. *B.B.C.*,[95] for example, Lord Fraser said that the courts should have regard to the provisions of the Convention "where our domestic law is not firmly settled. But the Convention does not form part of our law and the decision on what that law is for our domestic courts and for this House."

The courts must apply a statute whose terms are clear, irrespective of whether it is alleged to conflict with the terms of a treaty.[96] Where a statute incorporating a treaty into United Kingdom law is ambiguous the courts will interpret its provisions in the light of the treaty.[97]

(iii) *Treaties affecting private rights.* In *The Parliament Belge*[98] Sir Robert Phillimore said that treaties affecting the private rights of British subjects were inoperative without the confirmation of the legislature. The Crown, therefore, could not by a treaty with Belgium confer on a private ship engaged in trade the immunities of a public ship so as to deprive a British subject of the right to bring proceedings against the ship for damage sustained in a collision. This is really a particular aspect of (ii) above (treaties involving an alteration of English law). It is the reason why the European Communities Act 1972 was needed to cover enforceable Community rights and obligations, and also why Extradition Acts

---

[91] [1937] A.C. 326, 347 *per* Lord Atkin. This is the effect of the *Case of Proclamations* ((1610) 12 Co.Rep. 74) and the Bill of Rights.

[92] *Rustomjee* v. *The Queen* (1876) 2 Q.B.D. 69 *per* Lord Coleridge C.J. (treaty with China; subject could not claim against Crown share of compensation for loss of trading rights); *Blackburn* v. *Att.-Gen.* [1971] 1 W.L.R. 1037 (C.A.) *per* Lord Denning M.R. See D. G. T. Williams, "Prerogative and Parliamentary Control" [1971] C.L.J. 178.

[93] *British Airways* v. *Laker Airways* [1985] A.C. 58, 85–86, *per* Lord Diplock; *post* p. 429.

[94] *C.C.S.U.* v. *Minister for Civil Service* [1985] A.C. 374.

[95] [1981] A.C. 303. See *post* p. 429 for further discussion.

[96] *Cheney* v. *Conn* [1968] 1 W.L.R. 292.

[97] *Buchanan (James) & Co. Ltd.* v. *Babco Forwarding & Shipping (U.K.) Ltd.* [1978] A.C. 141; *Fothergill* v. *Monarch Airlines Ltd.* [1981] A.C. 251.

[98] (1879) 4 P.D. 129, 154. The Court of Appeal ((1880) 5 P.D. 197) reversed Sir Robert Phillimore's decision on the ground that the ship in that case was a public ship, but they carefully refrained from expressing disapproval of the principle stated by him, which is regarded as good law; applied by MacKenna J. in *Swiss-Israel Trade Bank* v. *Government of Malta* [1972] 1 Lloyd's Rep. 497. See also *British Airways* v. *Laker Airways* [1983] 3 W.L.R. 544, 580 *per* Sir John Donaldson, M.R.

are required to give legal effect to treaties made for surrendering persons accused of crimes committed abroad.[99]

In the exceptional case of treaties providing for any increase in the powers of the European Parliament the Crown cannot even *ratify* a treaty without Parliamentary approval: European Assembly Election Act 1978, s.6(1).

By the making of a treaty the Crown may morally bind Parliament to pass any legislation needed to give full effect to it. The negotiation of treaties, which must often be done in secret,[1] is less under parliamentary control than almost any other branch of the prerogative, and Parliament may be met with a *fait accompli*. But there is an increasing tendency to keep Parliament informed and to invite expressions of opinion before the Crown finally commits itself, as was done during the Common Market negotiations in 1962–1971. This is only expedient, as the government relies on the support of Parliament, and especially of the Commons. Where legislation will be required to supplement a treaty, there is probably a convention that Parliament should be consulted in principle before the treaty is concluded. Parliament will also be consulted in very important matters, such as the declaration of war or the conclusion of a peace treaty.

Treaties of cession and delimitation of maritime boundaries

Doubt has been expressed whether the Crown can by virtue of the prerogative cede territory, so as to deprive British subjects of their nationality and perhaps property and contract rights.[2] It may be that a distinction should be drawn between the United Kingdom, where the prerogative does not apply, and territories of the Crown overseas. The Crown was persuaded to seek parliamentary approval for the cession of Heligoland to Germany in 1890,[3] and since then it has been the practice to ask Parliament to confirm cessions.[4] Whatever the law may be, this seems to be now the convention. Indeed, convention probably demands that Parliament should be consulted beforehand, as in the case of the cession of Jubaland to Italy in 1927.

It has been asserted that the Crown possesses a prerogative to delimit the maritime boundaries of the United Kingdom and, in cases of doubt to provide conclusive certificates for the guidance of the courts.[5] The existence of such a prerogative is, however, open to doubt.[6]

---

[99] Maitland, *Constitutional History*, pp. 424–425.

[1] For example, negotiations with China *re* Hong Kong in 1984.

[2] See Anson, *Law and Custom of the Constitution*, II, ii (4th ed. Keith), pp. 137–142; Holdsworth, "The Treaty-making power of the Crown" (1942) 58 L.Q.R. 177, 183; Roberts-Wran, *Commonwealth and Colonial Law*, p. 118. *Cf. Damodhar Gordhan* v. *Deoram Kanji* (1876) 1 App.Cas. 352 (P.C.). And *cf.* Treaty of Paris 1783, recognising the independence of the former American colonies.

[3] Anglo-German Agreement Act 1890.

[4] *e.g.* Anglo-Italian (East African Territories) Act 1925; Dindings Agreement Approval Act 1934; Anglo-Venezuelan Treaty (Island of Patos) Act 1942.

[5] *The Fagernes* [1927] P.L. 311 (C.A.); *R.* v. *Kent Justices, ex p. Lye* [1967] 2 Q.B. 153; *Post Office* v. *Estuary Radio* [1968] 2 Q.B. 740.

[6] W. R. Edeson, "The Prerogative of the Crown to Delimit Britain's Maritime Boundary" (1973) 89 L.Q.R. 364.

Sovereign Immunity and Diplomatic representation

It is part of the royal prerogative in relation to foreign affairs to recognise, or to withhold recognition from, foreign states, their heads and, before 1980, governments.[7] Foreign states, their head, governments and diplomatic envoys recognised by the Crown enjoy certain immunities from the jurisdiction of English courts.

The privileges and immunities of the heads of foreign states have been placed on a statutory basis by the State Immunity Act 1978, s.20. The main purpose of that Act is to restrict the immunities of foreign governments and States by bringing the British rules on state immunity into line with the more restrictive rules adopted in other States. The Act lists various circumstances in which civil actions may be brought against foreign states in the British courts. Section 3, for example, gives jurisdiction over commercial transactions as opposed to those entered into by a State in the exercise of its sovereign authority. Section 4 deals with contracts of employment made in the United Kingdom or under which the work is to be performed in the United Kingdom. Other sections relate to personal injuries and damage to property arising from acts or omissions in the United Kingdom (s.5); the ownership and use of immovable property (s.6); patents (s.7) and ships used for commercial purposes (s.10). Important provisions in section 16 ensure that nothing in the Act curtails any privileges conferred by the Diplomatic Privileges Act 1964 or the Consular Relations Act 1968. The Act was successfully relied on by a landlord in an action against the French government to which property had been let to be used as a private dwelling.[8-9] In *Alconi Ltd.* v. *Republic of Colombia*[10] the House of Lords, reversing the Court of Appeal, interpreted complicated provisions relating to the enforcement of judgments (s.13) as generously as possible in favour of the respondent state to deny jurisdiction in the circumstances to the English courts.

The Diplomatic Privileges Act 1708 arose out of *Mattueof's Case*,[11] in which the Russian Ambassador had been arrested for debt and taken out of his coach in London. The Court of Queen's Bench was uncertain whether the Sheriff of Middlesex and his assistants were guilty of a criminal offence. Peter the Great demanded that they should be punished with instant death. Queen Anne replied that she could not punish any of her subjects except in accordance with law. The Act of 1708, which was largely declaratory, was therefore passed, providing that judicial proceedings brought against diplomatic envoys or their servants should be null and void, and that it should be a misdemeanour to commence such proceedings.[12]

---

[7] *Carl Zeiss Stiftung* v. *Rayner and Keeler Ltd (No. 2)* [1967] 1 A.C. 853 (H.L.). see *per* Lord Reid (German Democratic Republic).

[8-9] *Intro Properties (U.K.) Ltd.* v. *Sauvel* [1983] Q.B. 1019 (C.A.).

[10] [1984] A.C. 580; noted, S. Ghandhi (1984) 37 M.L.R. 597.

[11] (1709) 10 Mod.Rep. 4; Bl.Comm. I, 255–356; Martens, *Causes Célèbres du Droit des Gens* (1827), Vol. I, p. 47.

[12] The Queen sent an illuminated copy of the Act to Moscow, which appeased the Czar, and the offenders were discharged at his request. It is uncertain how far the 1708 Act covered the bringing of criminal proceedings. There is no record of a prosecution for contravening the Act.

The Diplomatic Privileges Act 1964, giving effect to most of the provisions of the Vienna Convention on Diplomatic Relations 1961, replaces the previous law on the privileges and immunities of diplomatic representatives in the United Kingdom. The Act distinguishes between members of the diplomatic staff, who have full personal immunity, civil and criminal, with certain exceptions; members of the administrative and technical staff, who enjoy full immunity for official acts, but are liable civilly (though not criminally) for acts performed outside the course of their duties[13]; and members of the service staff, who enjoy immunity only for official acts.

Privileges and immunities may be withdrawn by Order in Council from any state that grants less to British missions.

The certificate of the Foreign Secretary is conclusive as to whether a person falls into any (and, if so, which) of the above three classes. No question of diplomatic immunity can arise until a person has been notified to the Foreign and Commonwealth Office as a diplomat.[14]

Members of the diplomatic mission of a Commonwealth country or of Ireland and their private servants are entitled, if they are both citizens of that Commonwealth country or Ireland and also citizens of the United Kingdom and Colonies, to the privileges and immunities to which they would have been entitled if they had not been citizens of the United Kingdom and Colonies.

Diplomatic privilege may be waived in any particular case. Where an ambassador or other head of mission is concerned, waiver must be with the consent of his Sovereign (*Re Suarez*[15]); where a subordinate is concerned, waiver must be by head of the mission.[16] Unless the waiver extends to execution, which is unlikely, judgment in such a case cannot be enforced until a reasonable time after the envoy has been recalled.[17]

If a diplomatic envoy commits a breach of the law, the Foreign Secretary may request his government to recall him as *persona non grata*, as was done in the case of the Swedish Ambassador, Count Cyllenburg, in 1717.

Various incidents in the last few years, particularly the killing of a policewoman in April 1984 outside the Libyan People's Bureau in London, have led to calls for the revision of the Vienna Convention on Diplomatic Relations. It is believed that diplomatic premises may be used to harbour terrorists and that guns and explosives are smuggled into countries in diplomatic "bags," *i.e.* officially sealed packages which under the Convention are exempt from examination. Revision of such an international agreement is likely to prove difficult. In the meantime states could act more promptly to expel "diplomats" whose status is

[13] For applications of the Act see *Empson* v. *Smith* [1966] 1 Q.B. 426 (C.A.) noted (1965) 28 M.L.R. 710; *Shaw* v. *Shaw* [1979] Fam. 62. Whether an act is performed inside or outside the scope of a diplomat's duties is to be determined by the Courts.

[14] *R.* v. *Lambeth Justices ex p. Yusufu, The Times* February 20, 1985 (C.A.).

[15] *Re Suarez, Suarez* v. *Suarez* [1918] 1 Ch. 187.

[16] *Dickinson* v. *Del Solar* [1930] 1 K.B. 376; *Re Republic of Bolivia Exploration Syndicate Ltd.* [1914] 1 Ch. 139.

[17] *Re Suarez, ante.*

open to doubt while the subjection of suspect "bags" to X-Ray examination is possibly not in violation of the Convention.[18]

Under the International Organisations Acts 1968 and 1981 immunities and privileges may be accorded to international and Commonwealth organisations of which the United Kingdom is a member, and to persons connected with such organisations. Provision is also made for granting immunities and privileges to judges and suitors of the International Court of Justice, and to representatives of other states attending international conferences in the United Kingdom.

Diplomatic privileges and immunities have been extended to the high commissioners or ambassadors of the independent members of the Commonwealth, Associated States and the Republic of Ireland, their staff, families and servants; and to certain representatives of Commonwealth governments and of the Government of the Republic of Ireland attending conferences with the British Government.[19] Diplomatic immunity and privileges may also be extended by Order in Council to any international headquarters or defence organisations set up under an arrangement for common defence, e.g. NATO, and the Visiting Forces Act 1952 may be applied to them.[20]

The privileges and immunities of consuls are governed by the Consular Relation Act 1968, which gives effect to the Vienna Convention on Consular Relations; and (as to Commonwealth and Irish consuls) by section 4 of the Diplomatic and other Privileges Act 1971.

[18] S. Sutton, "Diplomatic Immunity and the Siege of the Libyan People's Bureau," [1985] P.L. 193.
[19] Diplomatic Immunities (Conferences with Commonwealth Countries and Republic of Ireland) Act 1961; Diplomatic Immunities (Commonwealth Countries and Republic of Ireland) Act 1952.
[20] International Headquarters and Defence Organisations Act 1964.

CHAPTER 15

THE PRIVY COUNCIL

I. THE COUNCIL AS AN INSTRUMENT OF GOVERNMENT

Historical introduction[1]

The *Curia Regis* exercised supreme legislative, executive and judicial powers, subject to general feudal customs. From the *Curia Regis* there developed in course of time the most important institutions of English central government, namely, the Exchequer and the Treasury (12th century), the courts of common law (13th–14th centuries) and Chancery (14th–15th centuries), and the House of Lords, *i.e.* the King's Council in Parliament[2] (14th century).

The Privy Council has been generally regarded as a continuation of the *Curia Regis* after these other bodies had separated, but it may be more precise to say that the *Curia Regis* ceased to exist, and that the Council which emerged as a distinct body in the thirteenth and fourteenth centuries was something new. The Council was used as a powerful instrument of government by the Tudors. In Henry VIII's reign the distinction was first drawn between "Ordinary Councillors," a fairly large number of lawyers and administrators, and "Privy Councillors," a select body of nobles who acted as the King's advisers. As the Tudor period progressed the tendency was for Privy Councillors to be drawn from humbler ranks of society.

Coke, in his treatment of the courts, deals after the High Court of Parliament with "the Councell Board or Table," and says: "This is a most noble, honourable, and reverend assembly of the King and his privy councell in the King's court or palace; with this councell the King himself doth sit at pleasure. These councellors like good centinels and watchmen, consult of and for the publique good, and the honour, defence, safety and profit of the realm."[3]

Committees composed of some only of the members of the Council were sometimes used by the Tudors for particular purposes or occasions, and temporary or permanent committees were used frequently in the seventeenth century. For various reasons Committees of the whole Council came to be employed in the eighteenth century, and, indeed, most of the Council's work was then carried on in Committee. Some of these committees in their turn became, or transferred their administrative functions to, separate government departments such as the Board of Trade and the former Boards of Agriculture and Education.

The eclipse of the Privy Council as a practical instrument of government came with the development in the eighteenth century of the Cabi-

---

[1] Holdsworth, *History of English Law*, Vol. I, Chap. 6; (1860) Baldwin, *The King's Council during the Middle Ages*; Turner, *The Privy Council, 1603–1784*; Dicey, *The Privy Council*; Williamson, *Studies in the Constitutional History of the Thirteenth and Fourteenth Centuries*.

[2] The House of Lords was not so called until Henry VII's reign.

[3] 4 Inst. 53. The official spelling now used is "Counsellor" although, according to the Clerk of the Council "Councillor" cannot be "called wrong." (*Observer*, August 1, 1982).

net as the policy-making organ and advisory body of the Crown, which is discussed in the next chapter.

The Privy Council at the present day: the composition of the Privy Council[4]

"The Lords, and others of Her Majesty's most Honourable Privy Council," now about three hundred in number, consist of persons who hold or have held high political or legal office, peers, Church dignitaries and persons distinguished in the services and professions. They are appointed by letters patent, and include the Lord President of the Council, all Cabinet Ministers by convention, the two Archbishops by prescription, and customarily some of the leading Commonwealth statesmen, British Ambassadors, the Speaker of the House of Commons, the Lords of Appeal in Ordinary, the Lord Chief Justice, the Master of the Rolls, the President of the Family Division, and the Lords Justices of Appeal.

A new member of the Privy Council must take the oath of allegiance and the special Privy Councillor's oath, which binds him to keep secret all matters committed or revealed to him or that are treated of secretly in council.[5] An affirmation may be made in lieu of oath.[6] The oath or affirmation probably does not add anything to the obligation later imposed by the Official Secrets Acts. The disclosure of such confidential information requires the consent of the Sovereign, which in practice means the Prime Minister of the day. Privy Councillors must be British subjects. They are addressed as "Right Honourable." Since the Demise of the Crown Act 1901 membership of the Privy Council is apparently not affected by a demise of the Crown.

Functions of the Privy Council[7]

The Privy Council became too unwieldy as an instrument of government. Owing to the development of the Cabinet and government departments, the Council lost most of its advisory and administrative functions and is today little more than an organ for giving formal effect to certain acts done under prerogative or statutory powers.

Proclamations and Orders in Council

The most important acts done by Her Majesty "by and with the advice of her Privy Council" take the form of proclamations or Orders in Council, the former normally being authorised by the latter. Proclamations are employed for such matters as proroguing, dissolving and summoning Parliament[8] and declaring war or peace—solemn occasions requiring the widest publicity. Orders in Council may be made under the Royal Prerogative or, more commonly, under statutory powers.[9] The

---

[4] The Union with Scotland (Amendment) Act 1707 provided that there should be one Privy Council for Great Britain.

[5] The oath dates back to the time of Edward I. For the modern form of Privy Councillor's oath, see Anson, *Law and Custom of the Constitution* (4th ed.) Vol. II, Pt. I, p. 153.

[6] Oaths Act 1978.

[7] For a descriptive account, see Sir Almeric Fitzroy, *The History of the Privy Council* (1928) pp. 294 *et seq.*

[8] For a specimen, see Anson, *op. cit.* (5th ed. Gwyer), Vol. I, pp. 55–56.

[9] For the form, see Anson, *op. cit.* (4th ed. Keith), Vol. II, Pt. I, p. 62.

nature of an Order in Council may be legislative, *e.g.* making laws for certain overseas territories and Statutory Instruments dealing with various aspects of the welfare state; executive, *e.g.* setting up a new government department, issuing regulations for the armed forces, determining the conditions of employment of civil servants[10] or declaring a state of emergency to exist or to be at an end; or judicial, *e.g.* giving effect to a judgment (technically advice) of the Judicial Committee of the Privy Council.

Miscellaneous functions

A Privy Council is also summoned for certain special occasions, such as the acceptance of office by newly appointed Ministers, and the annual "pricking" of sheriffs on Maundy Thursday.

Meetings of the Privy Council

Privy Councillors are summoned to attend at Buckingham Palace, or wherever else the Sovereign may be.[11] The quorum is three. Usually four are summoned, being Ministers concerned with the business in hand. The whole Council has not met (except at an Accession) since 1839, when Queen Victoria's forthcoming marriage was announced.[12]. The marriage of the Prince of Wales to Lady Diana Spencer was approved at a special meeting of the Privy Council in March 1981 where' those present, in addition to The Queen, the Prime Minister, the Lord Chancellor, the Lord President and other senior ministers, included the Prince of Wales, the Archbishop of Canterbury, the Speaker of the House of Commons, Leaders of the Opposition Parties and Privy Councillors from Australia, New Zealand and other Commonwealth Countries.

Lord Morrison of Lambeth, a former Lord President of the Council, gave this description of an ordinary meeting: "First of all, before the Council begins, the Lord President is received in Audience. The other Counsellors then enter and, having bowed and shaken hands with the King, take up their position. They stand in a line, headed by the Lord President, who has a List of Business, as the agenda is called. The items in this are already known to His Majesty, who, as they are read out by the Lord President, approves them or gives any other directions that may be needed. When the business is finished, the proceedings become rather less formal. There is some general conversation; then the Counsellors withdraw, leaving as they entered in accordance with their precedence."[13] According to Viscount Caldecote,[14] a former Lord

---

[10] The power to control the terms and conditions of employment of civil servants is exercised by the Prime Minister, acting as Minister for the Civil Service, by virtue of an order in Council made under the Royal Prerogative: *C.C.S.U.* v. *Minister for the Civil Service* [1985] A.C. 374.

[11] *e.g.* Balmoral or aboard the Royal Yacht.

[12] *Ante* p. 255 (Accession Council).

[13] Herbert Morrison, "The Privy Council today" (1948) 2 *Parliamentary Affairs* (Hansard Society), pp. 10, 12–13. See also Dermot Morrah, *The Queen at Work* (1958), pp. 142–144. R.H.S. Crossman, who resented having to travel to Balmoral for meetings of the Privy Council in his capacity as Lord President of the Council (particularly when there was no restaurant car on his train), described meetings as "the best example of pure mumbo jumbo you can find." (*Diaries of a Cabinet Minister*, Vol. 2, p. 44).

[14] Viscount Caldecote, "The King's prerogative" (1941) 7 C.L.J. 310, 320.

Chancellor, the Lord President reads out the titles of draft Orders in Council, and the Sovereign perfects the drafts by saying "Approved."

The Orders are authenticated by the signature of the Clerk to the Council and the seal of the Council. The Clerk also records the names of the Councillors present, who are legally responsible for what is transacted.

Committees of the Council

Any meeting of Privy Councillors at which the Sovereign or Counsellors of State are not present can only be a committee.[15] Apart from the Judicial Committee, which is discussed below, there are advisory or *ad hoc* committees concerned with such matters as scientific research, the older universities, and the grant of charters.

Provision would no doubt be made for dealing with such miscellaneous responsibilities as withdrawing recognition of a university medical school under the Medical Act 1983, s.9, when the need arose.

II. THE JUDICIAL FUNCTIONS OF THE PRIVY COUNCIL[16]

Historical introduction

Even after the separation of the courts of common law and the Court of Chancery, the King's Council retained some jurisdiction (i) in cases which in some way concerned the state, and (ii) in private cases where the ordinary courts could not provide a remedy. This jurisdiction, especially in the latter element, represented the residue of justice that always lay with the King. In the early Middle Ages the Council was not a court of record; it had no seal, and indeed it was not called a "court" at all.[17]

In the Tudor period most of the Council's jurisdiction relating to state offences and cases in which great men were involved was exercised by the Court of Star Chamber. In this period the Court of High Commission was set up to deal with important ecclesiastical causes, and the Court of Requests as a "minor Court of Equity" to hear the suits of poor persons. It was part of the struggle between Parliament and the King in the early seventeenth century that these courts of an "arbitrary" jurisdiction should be attacked as being closely associated with the royal prerogative. The Long Parliament, in the same year in which it abolished the Court of High Commission, also passed a statute commonly known as the Act for the abolition of the Star Chamber 1640. Certain other prerogative jurisdictions, such as those of the Councils of Wales and the Marches and of the North, were also expressly abolished. The Act further declared and enacted that neither His Majesty nor his Privy

---

[15] This idea dates from the middle of the eighteenth century.

[16] Holdsworth, *History of English Law*, Vol. I; N. Bentwich, *Privy Council Practice* (3rd ed. 1937), Chap. I; Viscount Haldane, "The Judicial Committee of the Privy Council" (1922) 1 C.L.J. 143; Sir George Rankin, "The Judicial Committee of the Privy Council" (1939) 7 C.L.J. 2; Lord Normand, "The Judicial Committee of the Privy Council—retrospect and prospect" (1950) C.L.P. 1; Robert Stevens, "The Final Appeal: Reform of the House of Lords and Privy Council 1867–1876" (1964) 80 L.Q.R. 343. Loren P. Beth, "The Judicial Committee: Its Development, Organisation and Procedure," [1975] P.L. 219.

[17] Leadam and Baldwin, Introduction to *Select Cases before the King's Council* (Selden Society Publications).

Council have or ought to have any jurisdiction over the land or chattels of English subjects. Although the Court of Requests was not mentioned, it ceased to function almost immediately afterwards.

The ancient judicial powers of the Privy Council survived only in the form of an appellate jurisdiction from the King's overseas dominions, namely, the Channel Islands, the Isle of Man, the colonies (or "foreign plantations," as they were at first called)[18] and, later, India. In the eighteenth century the Judicial Committees formed for this purpose acquired many of the characteristics of courts; they usually sat in public, and reports began to be published in 1829.

Appeals from the ecclesiastical courts, the Court of Admiralty and the vice-admiralty courts of the colonies were given to the Privy Council by statute in 1832. This statutory extension of the Privy Council's jurisdiction necessitated a reorganisation of its constitution.

The Judicial Committee—composition

The Judicial Committee Act 1833, passed "for the better administration of justice in His Majesty's Privy Council," constituted a Judicial Committee. The Judicial Committee Act 1844 authorised the Queen by Order in Council to admit any appeals to the Privy Council from any court within any British colony or possession abroad, even though such court might not be a court of error or of appeal. Hence appeals lay from the Australian states after federation. It has been questioned whether this Act put the prerogative power on a statutory basis, or merely regulated the manner of its exercise.

As a result of the Act of 1833 and various later statutes,[19] the Judicial Committee is composed of:

(a) the Lord Chancellor; the Lord President and ex-Lord Presidents of the Council (who do not sit)[20]; the Lords of Appeal in Ordinary; and the Lords Justices of Appeal (who seldom sit);

(b) ex-Lord Chancellors and retired Lords of Appeal;

(c) selected senior judges or ex-judges of Australia, New Zealand and other Commonwealth countries from which appeal lies.

The quorum is three.

It will be seen that the composition of the Judicial Committee is wider than that of the House of Lords sitting as a final court of appeal.

English, Scottish and Northern Irish barristers, and also certain Commonwealth and colonial practitioners, have the right of audience before the Committee. Privy Council agents consist of English solicitors, Scottish writers to the signet and Northern Irish solicitors, provided that their names are on the Privy Council roll.

Jurisdiction

The Judicial Committee was given the jurisdiction of the Privy Council set out above, namely, appeals from the courts of the Channel

---

[18] *Fryer* v. *Bernard* (1724) 2 P.W. 262.

[19] Appellate Jurisdiction Acts 1876, 1887, 1908; Judicial Committee Amendment Act 1895.

[20] The Lord President, Secretaries of State and other laymen often sat until the middle of the nineteenth century; for example, the Duke of Buccleuch, of whom the future Lord Kingsdown said: "Depend upon it, the natives of India would much rather have this case decided by a great Scottish Duke than by lawyers alone": Stevens, *op. cit.* p. 349.

Islands, the Isle of Man, the colonies and British India, and from the ecclesiastical courts and Admiralty Court, to which were later added appeals from prize courts.

Appeals in probate, divorce and admiralty causes (other than prize) were later transferred to the House of Lords. The Judicial Committee also has a limited appellate jurisdiction over the ecclesiastical courts of the Church of England.[21] A number of former colonies and protectorates, as well as India, have become independent members of the Commonwealth, and in most instances appeals from their courts to the Judicial Committee of the Privy Council have been abolished by local legislation.[22]

Modern statutes have given a right of appeal to the Judicial Committee from the tribunals of various professional organisations having power to strike a member off the register.[23]

It has been suggested that the judicial functions of the Privy Council should be merged with those of the House of Lords, and that the Judicial Committee should become a peripatetic Commonwealth Court.[24] The former idea was often discussed in the nineteenth century. The latter idea is not new, but seems to be no longer practicable in the present stage of Commonwealth development or disintegration.

Procedure

Rules of practice are made under the Act of 1833. Appeals, or requests for leave to appeal, are commenced by petition to the Crown. Usually only one "judgment" is given by the Board. This is in theory a report made to Her Majesty of the reasons why judgment should be given in favour of a particular party; but the Committee is regarded for practical purposes as a court, and the Queen is bound by convention to give effect to its advice, which is done by Order in Council.[25] Indeed, the report is made public before it is sent up to the Sovereign in Council.[26]

The advice was formerly required to be unanimous,[27] but an Order in Council in 1966[28] allowed dissenting opinions to be delivered.

Special reference

Section 4 of the Judicial Committee Act 1833[29] provides that the Crown may refer to the Committee for an advisory opinion any matter it may think fit. In practice, references under this section are confined to justiciable matters.[30] Thus in 1927 the Committee was asked to give an opinion on the Labrador boundary dispute between Canada and

[21] Ecclesiastical Jurisdiction Measure 1963, s.8.
[22] For appeals to the Privy Council from courts overseas, see *post*, Chap. 38.
[23] *e.g.* Medical Act 1983, Dentists Act 1984.
[24] Gerald Gardiner and Andrew Martin, *Law Reform Now* (1963), p. 16; *post*, Chap. 38.
[25] *British Coal Corp.* v. *The King* [1935] A.C. 500; *Ibralebbe* v. *R.* [1964] A.C. 900.
[26] *Hull* v. *M'Kenna* [1926] I.R. 402, *per* Viscount Haldane.
[27] *Cf. Cowie* v. *Remfrey* (1846) 5 Moo.P.C. 232.
[28] Judicial Committee (Dissenting Opinions) Order in Council, 1966. Lord Pearce, for example, delivered a dissenting opinion in *Madzimbamuto* v. *Lardner-Burke* [1969] 1 A.C. 645 (appeal from Southern Rhodesia). In *Riley* v. *Att.-Gen.* of Jamaica [1983] 1 A.C. 719 Lord Scarman and Lord Brightman delivered a joint dissenting opinion.
[29] 3 & 4 W.4. c. 41.
[30] See Sir Kenneth Roberts Wray, *Commonwealth and Colonial Law* (1966), p. 448 *et. seq.*

Newfoundland,[31] and in 1924 on the interpretation of the provisions of the Anglo-Irish Treaty of 1921 relating to the settlement of the boundary between Northern Ireland and the Irish Free State.[32] It was called on to advise on the elements of the international crime of piracy in *Re Piracy Iure Gentium*.[33] Its advice has also been sought by the Commons, through the Attorney-General, on whether a member was disqualified from sitting in the House[34] the law relating to Parliamentary privilege.[35] The opinion of the Committee might be required on the validity of legislation of the Northern Ireland Parliament under the Government of Ireland Act 1920.[36]

---

[31] (1927) 43 T.R. 289.
[32] (1924) Cmd. 2214.
[33] [1934] A.C. 584. See now the Tokyo Convention Act 1967, implementing the Geneva Convention on the High Seas 1958.
[34] *Re Sir Stuart Samuel* [1913] A.C. 514; *Re MacManaway, Re House of Commons (Clergy Disqualification) Act 1801* [1951] A.C. 161.
[35] *Re Parliamentary Privilege Act 1770* [1958] A.C. 352.
[36] Only one such reference was ever made: *Re a Reference under the Government of Ireland Act 1920* [1936] A.C. 352.

CHAPTER 16

THE CABINET AND THE PRIME MINISTER

I. DEVELOPMENT OF THE CABINET[1]

Origins in the Privy Council

The seventeenth and eighteenth centuries saw the growth of the practice of withdrawing the discussion and direction of government policy, as distinct from administration, into the hands of a few of the King's *confidential* advisers. The history of this subject is very obscure, owing to the secrecy of the proceedings and the lack of official and connected records, and the fact that during most of this period the practice was unpopular with Parliament and in the country, and was not openly avowed. The historian's difficulty is further increased by the confusing terminology employed by the writers of that time. The better opinion probably is that the body which we now know as the Cabinet should never at any stage in its history be identified with any particular committee of the Privy Council, such as the Committee for Foreign Affairs. No doubt the use of committees helped to crystallise the form that the Cabinet was to take. The process was further assisted by the appointment of regency councils, known as "the Lords Justices," during the frequent absence abroad of William III, George I and George II. In this case the absence of the King made it necessary to commit resolutions to writing, and even to frame rules of procedure.

In the eighteenth century the members of the Cabinet came to call themselves "His Majesty's servants" or "His Majesty's *confidential* servants." The names given to Charles II's group of confidential advisers were intended as terms of reproach. *Cabinet* was a French word then in vogue for a private room set apart for interviews, and the "Cabinet Council" or "Cabinet" was so called because it met literally or metaphorically in the King's cabinet or closet.

George I attended Cabinet meetings at the beginning of his reign, but is traditionally said to have ceased attending regularly after 1717, because he was little interested in English affairs, ignorant of the English language and institutions, and unable to influence policy owing to his dependence for support on the Whig leaders.[2] Both George II and George III seem occasionally to have been present at Cabinet meetings for some special reason. The absence of the Sovereign marks a definite epoch in the development of the power of the principal Ministers, although the decline of the royal power was gradual. Kings in the eighteenth century still exercised influence from their closet, and were "sometimes near, if not present."[3]

---

[1] Turner, *The Cabinet Council, 1622–1784*; A. B. Keith, *The British Cabinet System, 1830–1938* (2nd ed. Gibbs); D. L. Keir, *A Constitutional History of Modern Britain*; M. A. Thomson, *A Constitutional History of England, 1642–1801*; C. S. Emden, *The People and the Constitution*; Richard Pares, *King George III and the Politicians* (1953); Sir Lewis Namier, *Crossroads of Power* (1962), Chaps. 7 and 8.

[2] See, however, R. Hatton, *George I, Elector and King* (1979).

[3] Turner, *op. cit.* Vol. II, pp. 92–100.

A further process of division took place in the reign of George II, when a distinction was drawn between the "inner," "efficient," or "effective" Cabinet and the "outer" or "nominal" Cabinet. The former, also known as the "conciliabulum," had special access to important state papers, while the latter disclaimed responsibility for acts of the Ministry on which they had not been consulted. The inner Cabinet, which may be regarded as the direct ancestor of the modern Cabinet, was in existence at least as early as 1740.[4] The size of the Cabinet had increased from five to about twenty in George III's reign. Indeed, the Cabinet had become considerably larger than Elizabeth I's Privy Council, which numbered only twelve.

Opposition of Parliament

The practice of consulting confidentially a small group of Ministers, which had been intermittent in the reign of Charles I, was habitual in the reign of Charles II, and Parliament objected strongly to the secrecy of the deliberations, for it was difficult to know who were the responsible Ministers and how to enforce that responsibility. In order to put a stop to the practice, and to keep the House of Commons from being contaminated by the Sovereign's influence, Parliament inserted two clauses in the Act of Settlement 1700 to the effect that: (1) matters theretofore discussed in the Privy Council must be dealt with there and not elsewhere, and all resolutions must be signed by the members present, and (2) no person holding a place of profit under the Crown was to sit in the House of Commons. The operation of these provisions was postponed until the death of Queen Anne, by which time they had been repealed, although the second emerged in a modified form in the Succession to the Crown Act 1707.[5]

Growth of political ideas relating to the Cabinet

Political ideas grow gradually. The party system and the principle of the dependence of the government on the confidence of Parliament, and especially of the House of Commons, were developing in the eighteenth century.[6] The Cabinet often had political unity. Walpole, during his long period of office between 1721 and 1742, was skilful both in holding the favour of the King, partly through his friendship with Queen Caroline, and also in controlling the Commons, largely through bribery. At first the King chose as members of his Cabinet persons whom he liked and could trust. Eventually he had imposed upon him such advisers as Parliament, or the chief Ministers or the Prime Minister, wanted. There was an intermediate stage when the King no longer chose but could obstruct: when he was cajoled into accepting Ministers whom he did not like but to whom he did not profoundly object. This stage is illustrated by the long opposition of George II to the elder Pitt.

It was still possible for George III to hold a personal ascendancy during the earlier part of his reign by trading on the lack of political unity

---

[4] R. R. Sedgwick, "The Inner Cabinet from 1732 to 1741" 34 *English Historical Review* 290–302.

[5] *Ante*, Chap. 9.

[6] See Sir Ivor Jennings, *Party Politics*, Vol. II, "The Growth of Parties" (1961), for an account of the development of political parties since 1783.

among his Ministers, manipulating the two Houses, and making use of "honorary" members of the Cabinet. Some time during his reign, however, the Cabinet established the right to consider matters without reference from the King. The normal course had been for departmental matters to go from the Minister concerned to the King, and thence to the Cabinet if the King so willed. It now came to be recognised that, if the King had not actually a duty to consult the Cabinet, he was generally expected to do so. The King consulted Ministers individually in the closet, but they could agree beforehand in the ante-room what they would say. When the Cabinet were all of one party (which was not always so) they sometimes met, not as the King's advisers but as party leaders; and this paved the way for the Cabinet to become the general initiator of policy. The decline of the King's influence after the fall of the North Ministry in 1782 was accentuated by "the mental derangement which afflicted George III, the contemptible personal character of George IV, and the negligible qualities of William IV."[7] The younger Pitt asserted the necessity of having the King's confidence. In 1803 he insisted that it was essential that there should be "an avowed and real minister, possessing the chief weight in the Council and the principal place in the confidence of the King."[8]

The turning point came with the Reform Act 1832, which soon showed that henceforth a Ministry would depend on the support of a majority in the House of Commons, and ultimately on the electorate. Peel accepted responsibility for the King's action in forcing Melbourne to resign in 1834. The King granted Peel a dissolution, but he was returned with a minority and Melbourne displaced him in office until 1841. In the latter year the Whig Ministry was defeated in the Commons on the budget, but preferred to retain office. Peel moved a resolution that their continuance in office in such circumstances was at variance with the spirit of the Constitution; this was carried by one vote, and a dissolution followed. Nonetheless in 1851, when a Committee of the House of Commons proposed that some precedence be given to Cabinet Ministers at the opening and prorogation of Parliament the House rejected the proposal on the ground that the Cabinet was unknown to the Constitution.[9]

II. THE CABINET[10]

Functions of the Cabinet

The Cabinet system, or system of Cabinet government, was generally agreed to prevail between the wars. The main functions of the Cabinet at the end of the first war were summarised in the following way:

[7] Keir, op. cit. pp. 381–382.

[8] Quoted, Keith, op. cit. pp. 16–17.

[9] G. H. Le May The Victorian Constitution (1979), p. 96. The word "Cabinet" first appeared on the order paper of the House of Commons in 1900: Le May, loc. cit.

[10] J. P. Mackintosh, The British Cabinet (3rd ed., 1977); Sir Ivor Jennings, Cabinet Government (3rd ed., 1959); P. Gordon Walker, The Cabinet (revised ed., 1972); Harold Wilson, The Governance of Britain (1976); Herbert Morrison, Government and Parliament (1954); L. S. Amery, Thoughts on the Constitution (2nd ed., 1953); R. H. S. Crossman, Inside View (1972); Memoirs of a Cabinet Minister (3 Vols.); Ronald Butt, The Power of Parliament (2nd ed., 1969); Ian Colvin, The Chamberlain Cabinet (1971).

"(a) the final determination of the policy to be submitted to Parliament; (b) the supreme control of the national executive in accordance with the policy prescribed by Parliament; and (c) the continuous co-ordination and delimitation in the interests of the several Departments of State."[11] The Cabinet, giving collective "advice" to the Sovereign through the Prime Minister, was said to exercise under Parliament supreme control over all departments of state, and to be the body which co-ordinated the work on the one hand of the executive and the legislature, and on the other hand of the organs of the executive among themselves. The concept of the "Cabinet system" or "system of Cabinet government" may now need to be revised in the light of more recent developments, such as the predominance of the Prime Minister, the greater use of Cabinet committees and the growing influence of senior civil servants.[12] And the expression "policy prescribed by Parliament" must be read subject to the government's control of its party in the Commons, so that Parliament prescribes what the government wants.

Most important matters of policy are discussed at Cabinet meetings. For security reasons, however, specific Budget proposals (as distinct from the general Budget strategy) are disclosed orally to the Cabinet only a few days before the Chancellor of the Exchequer is to introduce them in the Commons, and for diplomatic reasons it is not always possible to consult the Cabinet before taking action in foreign affairs. Among matters not usually discussed by the Cabinet are the exercise by the Home Secretary of the prerogative of mercy (not of great importance since the abolition of the death penalty for murder),[13] the personnel of the Cabinet itself, the making of appointments and the conferment of honours, which are matters within the patronage of the Prime Minister.

The dissolution of Parliament after 1841 was formerly a matter for Cabinet decision; but in 1918 Lloyd George and Bonar Law, the party leaders in a Coalition Government, alone made the decision, the lapse of time since the last general election in 1910 having caused Ministers to forget what the practice was.[14] Lloyd George consulted a number of Cabinet colleagues about dissolution in 1922 because he had difficulty making up his mind.[15] Mr. Heath consulted his Cabinet before the ill-fated dissolution in February 1974, and they unanimously supported him.[16] A Prime Minister consults at least a few colleagues, of course, including the Chief Whip and the Chairman of the party. The principle may be discussed by members of the Cabinet, but the details are left to the Prime Minister.[17]

---

[11] Report of the Machinery of Government Committee Cd. 9230 (1918), p. 5.

[12] *Post*, pp. 323–325.

[13] But the decision not to exercise the prerogative of mercy in the case of Sir Roger Casement (1916) was made by the Cabinet for political reasons: Roy Jenkins, *Asquith*, pp. 403–404.

[14] Ivor Jennings, *Parliament must be Reformed* (1941); L. S. Amery, *op. cit.*, p. 23.

[15] Lord Beaverbrook, *The Decline and Fall of Lloyd George* (1963), Chaps. 7, 8, 11.

[16] Lord Hailsham, *The Door Wherein I Went* (1975), p. 298.

[17] B. E. Carter, *The Office of Prime Minister* (1956), pp. 289–291. For a discussion of the request for, timing of, and reasons for dissolutions in the present century, see B. S. Markesinis, *The theory and practice of Dissolution of Parliament* (1972) Pt. II and App. I. There may be an advantage in holding a general election a few months after rather than before the new electoral register comes into force on February 16.

Mr. Harold Wilson has called it "a lonely responsibility."[18]

It has been argued that this supposed convention lacks the essential quality that should mark a constitutional convention, namely the combination of consistent historical precedents and a convincing *raison d'être*.[19] It has been suggested that it is desirable to restore the balance of ministerial power by reverting to the convention that dissolution should be advised by, and granted to, the Cabinet.[20]

The Cabinet may meet anywhere, for example, in the Prime Minister's room in the House of Commons or at Chequers. Most often it meets at No. 10 Downing Street, usually once or twice a week. A summons to a Privy Council takes precedence. There is no quorum for a Cabinet. The agenda is determined by the Prime Minister. The regular items begin with parliamentary business and then foreign and Commonwealth affairs. These are followed by White Papers, which have been processed by committees; statistical reports on such subjects as unemployment and balance of payments. Finally there are current matters from committees, emergencies, etc. Elaborate precautions are taken to ensure secrecy: the Cabinet room has double doors, and a person waiting in attendance outside is brought in by a Cabinet Minister. Every attempt is made to promote unanimity by refraining where possible from formal voting, though Mr. Wilson is said to have "ticked off" the speakers. The Prime Minister "collects the voices" and announces the decision.[21]

Composition of the Cabinet

The Cabinet consists of a group of Ministers, normally about twenty in number, who are agreed to pursue a common policy and who are invited by the Prime Minister to attend Cabinet meetings. Most of them are heads of the chief government departments, for example, the Chancellor of the Exchequer, the Foreign Secretary and the Home Secretary, but a number of heads of departments will be outside the Cabinet, and the Cabinet will include some Ministers whose offices involve few or no departmental responsibilities. These last are free to carry out miscellaneous tasks, such as the co-ordination of policy and administration, responsibility for research, acting as chairmen of Cabinet committees and giving advice as elder statesmen. The "Ministry," "Government" or "Administration" is the name given to the whole body of about a hundred holders of ministerial office, all of whose offices are known to the law,[22] and who are appointed by the Sovereign on the advice of the Prime Minister. Under the standing orders adopted by the Parliamentary Labour Party in 1981 a Labour Prime Minister is required to appoint as Cabinet Ministers the individuals who had formerly been elected as members of the Shadow Cabinet.

The Cabinet itself has been mentioned a few times in statutes. The

---

[18] Harold Wilson, "Why I chose June," *Observer*, March 21, 1971.

[19] G. Marshall, *Constitutional Conventions* (1984), Chap. 3.

[20] O. Hood Phillips, *Reform of the Constitution* (1970), pp. 44–45, 51–52.

[21] For descriptions of a Cabinet meeting, see Morrison, *op. cit.* pp. 4–6; Gordon Walker, *op. cit.* Chap. 6.

[22] They (except the Lord Chancellor) are listed in the Second Schedule to the House of Commons Disqualification Act 1975, as amended.

Ministers of the Crown Act 1937 provided additional salaries to "Cabinet Ministers" who held offices at salaries less than a certain amount. The additional salary was made payable "if and so long as any Minister of the Crown to whom this section applies is a member of the Cabinet." The date on which any such Minister ceased to be a member of the Cabinet was to be published in the *London Gazette*, and such notification was to be "conclusive evidence" for the purposes of the Act.[23] The Parliamentary Commissioner Act 1967, s.8(4) provides that no person shall be required or authorised "by virtue of this Act" to furnish any information or documents or answer any question relating to proceedings of the Cabinet or any Cabinet Committee. For the purposes of the subsection any certificate issued by the Secretary of the Cabinet with the approval of the Prime Minister is conclusive.[24] The Data Protection Act 1984, s.27 entitles a Minister of the Crown to exempt certain information from the provisions of the Act if the Minister is a member of the Cabinet or the Attorney-General or the Lord Advocate. Cabinet meetings and the question of joint responsibility of the Cabinet were referred to by Lord Widgery C.J. in *Attorney-General* v. *Jonathan Cape Ltd.*[25]

The Cabinet is, then, the nucleus of the Ministry. In choosing the Cabinet the Prime Minister has a number of factors to consider, such as the importance of the various offices, the influence of members in the country, the authority of members in the Commons and their value in debate, the value of members as advisers in Committee, and the representation of the government in the House of Lords.[26] They are not generally experts in the subject-matter of their departments. By custom Cabinet Ministers are made Privy Councillors if they are not so already. Since 1951 the Chief Whip has been invited to attend, so that he may be asked what would be the probable attitude of the party.[27]

Cabinet Ministers in the House of Lords

Convention requires that all Ministers must sit in one or other of the Houses of Parliament, in order that their activities may be subject to parliamentary supervision.[28] The House of Commons Disqualification

---

[23] See now, Ministerial and other Salaries Act 1975, under which additional salaries are payable to the Lord President of the Council, the Lord Privy Seal, the Chancellor of the Duchy of Lancaster, the Paymaster General, the Chief Secretary to the Treasury, the Parliamentary Secretary to the Treasury, and Ministers of State so long as they are members of the Cabinet.

[24] It has been suggested, (G. Marshall, *Constitutional Conventions* (1984), p. 89) that a Minister may, if he wishes produce such documents or give such information.

[25] [1976] Q.B. 752; *post*, p. 313.

[26] See *The British Prime Minister* (Anthony King ed. 1969), pp. 60–79 (Attlee, "The Making of a Cabinet").

[27] The Chief Whip (Parliamentary Secretary to the Treasury) has recently been included as a member of the Cabinet. It appears that the Principal Private Secretary to the Prime Minister since Mr. Macmillan's time sits in at meetings of the full Cabinet and at most Cabinet committees.

[28] A temporary exception to this convention was the appointment of Mr. R. G. Casey, an Australian, as Minister of State in 1942, which was presumably made under the Re-election of Ministers Act 1919, s.2. And see as regards Asquith, *post*, p. 39; Mr. Gordon Walker and Mr. Frank Cousins (1964–65) *ante*, p. 124.

Act 1975 limits the number of Ministers who may sit in the House of Commons: the rest must therefore be peers. The Government in any case will want to be adequately represented in the House of Lords. As regards the House of Lords, the Lord Chancellor will be automatically included,[29] and in a Labour Government he may be the only Cabinet Minister there. It is inconceivable that the Chancellor of the Exchequer should be in the House of Lords, since the Commons have a monopoly of financial affairs. Another office that has raised controversy (apart from Prime Minister[30]) is that of Foreign Secretary. The appointment of Lord Halifax as Foreign Secretary in 1938 provoked some comment.[31] Considerable controversy arose in 1960 when the Earl of Home (now Lord Home of the Hirsel) was appointed Foreign Secretary. In 1979, however, Mrs. Thatcher appointed Lord Carrington to be Foreign Secretary, a post which he held until his resignation in 1982.[32] The Prime Minister in modern times is the overseer of foreign policy, and communicates personally with the heads of foreign governments or states and can answer for foreign affairs in the house of Commons if the Foreign Secretary is in the other House.[33]

More recently there was criticism of Mrs. Thatcher's decision in 1985 to appoint Lord Young of Graffham as Secretary of State for Employment. Lord Young had been created a life peer in the previous year and appointed a Minister without Portfolio. To meet the argument that employment was a matter of particular concern to the Commons, the Paymaster General was designated as chief Commons spokesman on employment.

Size of the Cabinet

The size of the Cabinet varies from time to time. Prime Ministers usually begin by hoping to cut the size of the Cabinet but find it impracticable. Between the wars there "full" Cabinets of over twenty members. After the last war there were "medium" Cabinets of sixteen to eighteen, but Sir Alex Douglas-Home and Mr. Wilson had Cabinets of 23. Mrs. Thatcher reduced the Cabinet to 22.[33a] During the two world wars there were "small" Cabinets of from six to ten members, although other Ministers were often present, and Chiefs of Staff, Dominion Prime Ministers and others were in attendance. It has been persuasively argued that the large volume of work assumed by the Cabinet is too great to be efficiently performed by a group of Ministers most of whom have heavy departmental responsibilities as well as the duty of constant attendance at the House. One suggestion is that there should be a small policy-making Cabinet of about six, whose members would

---

[29] It was wholly exceptional that in the "caretaker government" formed after the withdrawal of the Labour Party from the National Coalition in 1945, the Lord Chancellor—Viscount Simon, a National Liberal—was not a member of the Cabinet.

[30] *Post*, p. 323.

[31] He even remained a member of the Cabinet after being appointed Ambassador to the United States.   [32] *Post* p. 311.

[33] In 1923 Curzon inquired of King George V why, if in the circumstances of the times His Majesty thought that a peer ought not to be Prime Minister he had no objection to a peer being Foreign Secretary: "Because the Prime Minister is responsible for everything you do"; Kenneth Rose, *King George V* (1983), pp. 272–273.

[33a] And further in June 1987 to 21.

not be departmental heads.[34] Another is that more use should be made of Standing Committees of the Cabinet to co-ordinate the work of groups of departments whose interests overlap.[35] Attlee thought 16 the best number. There is difference of opinion on how many members of this supreme policy-making body should be free from departmental duties, the manner in which the work of the departmental (non-Cabinet) Ministers should be co-ordinated, and the way in which Parliament can call Ministers to account.

Churchill's experiment from 1951–1953 of having several Ministers as "Overlords," who without statutory authority supervised groups of other Ministers, was not successful as it degraded the Ministers who were supervised and confused ministerial responsibility. Since 1970, however, Cabinets have included several "super-Ministers" directly responsible for multiple departments formed by the merger of a number of previous departments—for example, the Secretary of State for the Environment embraced for a time the former Ministries of Housing and Local Government, Public Building and Works, and Transport, until a separate Department of Transport was established.

Ministers who are not members of the Cabinet may be called in if matters specially affecting their department are under discussion. Civil servants are rarely present, although the Permanent Secretary to the Treasury or the Permanent Under-Secretary of State of the Foreign Office may be summoned. Chiefs of Staff, on the other hand, may be present when military questions are being discussed.

Shadow Cabinet[36]

It has come to be an accepted part of the working of our Constitution that the Opposition should organise itself on parallel lines to the government. The idea emerged gradually, and the Shadow Cabinet in an inchoate form came into existence by the 1860s. It may be said to have become a convention that there should be a Shadow Cabinet. Statutory salaries are now provided for the Leader of the Opposition and the Chief Opposition Whip in each House. The Shadow Cabinet constitutes an alternative team from which the prospective Prime Minister can choose his senior colleagues, and which provides the electorate with an alternative choice of government.

The Conservative Party's Shadow Cabinet is technically its Consultative Committee, and the Labour Party's is its Parliamentary Committee.

---

[34] Amery, op. cit. pp. 87, 90–93. This would be something like the small war Cabinets in the two world wars, although these were reinforced from time to time by Commonwealth statesmen: Lord Hankey, Government Control in War (1945); Winston S. Churchill, The Second World War, Vol. II, Chap. 3; Vol. III, pp. 784–786; Vol. IV, Chap. 5 and App. G; Vol. V, App. G; Vol. VI, App. H; Jennings, op. cit. pp. 287–291; Keith, op. cit. pp. 136–141; Memoirs of Lord Chandos (1962), Chaps. 12–14. Several meetings were also held in the first war with Dominion Prime Ministers, and called the "Imperial War Cabinet"; D. Lloyd George, War Memoirs, Chaps. 38 and 55; Report of the Machinery of Government Committee Cd. 9230 (1918), pp. 4–6; The War Cabinet, Report for the Year 1917 Cd. 9005 (1918), pp. 1–10.

[35] Sir John Anderson, The Machinery of Government (Romanes Lecture, 1946). See also (1918) Cd. 9230 (ante): Lord Samuel, "A Cabinet of Ten." The Times, September 9, 1947.

[36] D. R. Turner, The Shadow Cabinet in British Politics (1969); Mackintosh, op. cit. pp. 259–261, 536–541, Jennings, Parliament (2nd ed.), pp. 81–83.

The Labour Shadow Cabinet since 1923 has been elected annually by the parliamentary Labour Party in the Commons. The Conservative Shadow Cabinet is chosen by the Leader of the Opposition.[37]

Like the Cabinet itself, the Shadow Cabinet observes the convention of collective responsibility—described by Mr. Foot, when Leader of the Opposition, in 1981 as a rule accepted by the Labour Party for generations.[38]

Cabinet Committees[39]

Committees of the Cabinet were set up ad hoc in the nineteenth century to expedite government business. An example was the War Committee (1855) at the time of the Crimean War. The first Standing Committee was the Committee of Imperial Defence set up by Balfour in 1903. This was not confined to Ministers, and it used the Privy Council secretariat. During the First World War a large number of committees were set up unsystematically by Asquith and Lloyd George. Between the wars committees came and went, there being on an average twenty ad hoc Committees at any one time. A system of Cabinet committees was developed in the last war. Attlee (Deputy Prime Minister) gave an account of these to the House of Commons in 1940, as did Churchill (Prime Minister) in 1941. Herbert Morrison has also given a full written account of the committees during the last war.[40] The most important of these was the Home Affairs Committee, which was responsible for a major part of domestic policy, such as the Education Bill. A new principle developed that a Cabinet committee had equal authority to the Cabinet, subject to possible reference to the Cabinet.

Attlee was the first Prime Minister to have a permanent committee structure in peace time. The pattern continued during the 1950s and 1960s, ad hoc committees continuing alongside Standing Committees. "The Prime Minister sets up and disbands committees, appoints the chairman and members and sets the terms of reference."[41] Some committees are chaired by the Prime Minister at No. 10; some by other Ministers in the Cabinet Office or at the House of Commons. Mr. Wilson raised the authority of Cabinet committees by ruling that a member could only appeal from a committee to the Cabinet with the agreement of the chairman. The recommendations of a committee can be turned down by the Cabinet.

The existence of a Cabinet committee, the name of its chairman and the terms of reference are not usually disclosed during the lifetime of a government, because of the principle of the unity and collective respon-

---

[37] *Quaere*, if a third party were the largest opposition party?

[38] *The Times*, November 14, 1981. For recognition of the principle by Mrs. Thatcher when in opposition see D. Ellis, "Collective Ministerial Responsibility and Solidarity" [1980] P.L. 367, 392.

[39] Walker, *op. cit.* pp. 38–47; App. (List of Standing Committees, 1914–64); Mackintosh, *op. cit.* pp. 521–529; Jennings, *Cabinet Government*, pp. 255–261; Wilson, *The Governance of Britain*; P. Hennessy and A. Arends, *Mr. Attlee's Engine Room: Cabinet Committee Structure and the Labour Government 1945–51* (1983) (Strathclyde Papers on Govt. & Politics, No. 26); M. Cockerell, P. Hennessy and D. Walker, *Sources Close to the Prime Minister* (1984).

[40] Herbert Morrison, *op. cit.* pp. 19–26.

[41] Walker, *op. cit.* p. 45.

sibility of the Cabinet. Despite the fact that their existence has been well known for many years Prime Ministers as recently as Mr. Callaghan in 1978 have urged the need for secrecy.[42] Paradoxically, we have been told most about the Defence Committee from White Papers on Defence.[43]

The committee system has increased the efficiency of the Cabinet, and enables a great deal more work to be done by Ministers. The Cabinet itself is left free to discuss controversial matters and to make more important decisions,[44] and its business is better prepared. The system also enables non-Cabinet Ministers to be brought into discussions.

Cabinet committees come and go, change their names and are impossible to enumerate. Modern Standing Committees include (or have included) Home Affairs (H.A.C.)[45]; Future Legislation (principles and provisional priority of government Bills); Legislation (drafting and settling priority of government Bills and important Statutory Instruments[46]); Defence[47]; Economic Policy; Incomes Policy; Public Expenditure Scrutiny (PESC); and Social Services. In May 1979 Mrs. Thatcher announced in the House of Commons the existence of four standing committees of the Cabinet: Defence and Overseas Policy, Economic Strategy, Home and Social Affairs, and Legislation. Many others are, none the less, reliably believed to exist.[48] There is also a long list of miscellaneous committees ("Miscs"). Recent *ad hoc* committees have included one on Rhodesia (1969). Mr. Wilson in 1968 announced the formation of a Parliamentary Committee to co-ordinate the work in Parliament, and to consider the broader aspects of the government's business. In his memoirs he speaks of a Management Committee to hold preliminary discussions on matters of policy, such as the Industrial Relations Bill, before putting the matter to the full Cabinet.[49] Commentators regarded both these as an Inner Cabinet.

The Committee on the South Atlantic which was established at the time of the Falklands crisis in 1982 has been described as a "War Cabinet" although, on the other hand, it has been argued that the need to secure Cabinet approval for major decisions throughout that undertaking helped to re-establish the importance of the Cabinet as a whole.[50]

"Inner Cabinet"

Prime Ministers in recent years are said to be in the habit of summoning an "Inner Cabinet."[51] The practice has been ascribed to Neville

---

[42] *New Statesman*, November 10, 1978.

[43] *Central Organisation for Defence* Cmd. 6923 (1946); Cmnd. 576 (1958); Cmnd. 2097 (1963).

[44] Mr. Wilson thought EEC affairs too important for a committee.

[45] The Attorney-General often attends: see Sir Jocelyn Simon in (1965) 81 L.Q.R. 292–293.

[46] The Attorney-General is a member. Civil servants may be present by permission of the Prime Minister or chairman of the committee.

[47] Chiefs of Staff are in attendance: Cmnd. 2097 (1963).

[48] On the Civil Contingencies Unit for dealing with emergencies of various kinds, see *post* p. 361.

[49] Harold Wilson, *The Labour Government, 1964–70: A Personal Record* (1971).

[50] P. Hennessy, "The Quality of Cabinet Government in Britain," (1985) 6 Pol. Stud. (Part 2), 15.

[51] Walker, *op. cit.* pp. 37–38; Anthony King, *op. cit.* pp. 64, 91, 174, 185–186. Attendance at an Inner Cabinet was referred to in evidence in *Churchill (Randolph)* v. *Nabarro, The Times*, October 25–29, 1960.

Chamberlain, Churchill, Attlee and Eden. Mr. Wilson's Parliamentary Committee and Management Committee (*supra*) were described as an Inner Cabinet. An Inner Cabinet is supposed to be the efficient part that directs the Cabinet's activities. Lord Gordon Walker, however, calls it a misnomer. According to him it is not a Cabinet or a Cabinet committee. It has no organic or set place in the Cabinet structure. It is merely an informal, small group of friends or confidants of the Prime Minister drawn from members of the Cabinet.[52] It is not formally set up; it has no papers or records; it is not served by the Cabinet secretariat. An Inner Cabinet has as such no power. It does not predigest Cabinet business, although it may among other things discuss questions that are to come before the Cabinet. The practice of different Prime Ministers in this respect varies. The Inner Cabinet, says Lord Walker, is "a loose and informal thing."[53] Similarly, Mackintosh describes an Inner Cabinet as a number of Cabinet Ministers who are regularly consulted by the Prime Minister, often singly; there is "no clearcut line which separates an inner from an outer ring."[54]

In contrast, Lord Walker talks of a *Partial Cabinet*, which can act for the Cabinet. This is a standing or ad hoc committee, presided over by the Prime Minister, but acting for a time as if they were the Cabinet. Examples are Attlee's group of Ministers who decided to make the atom bomb, and Eden's group who determined the Suez policy.[55]

The Cabinet Office[56]

Cabinet minutes were sometimes kept in the reigns of George II, III and IV, but the practice lapsed until the First World War. Ministers were expected to remember what was decided and to carry out those decisions in their departments. The Sovereign was kept informed by a letter from the Prime Minister after each meeting, retailing the topics considered and the decisions taken. It was a confidential letter written in the Prime Minister's own hand, and not shown to other members of the Cabinet.[57] Lloyd George, when Prime Minister, introduced a secretariat in 1916 by borrowing as Secretary of the War Cabinet Sir Maurice Hankey (later, Lord Hankey), at that time Secretary to the Committee of

---

[52] *Cf.* Churchill's "cronies" with whom he liked to talk late into the night: they were personal friends, not men of influence. The Prime Minister probably did most of the talking; *cf.* "Kitchen Cabinet," *post*, note 54.

[53] Mr. Gordon Walker, together with Mr. Goerge Brown and Mr. Callaghan, was a member of Mr. Wilson's Inner Cabinet that discussed such questions as devaluation and the Bank Rate.

[54] Mackintosh, *op. cit.* p. 542. *Cf.* "Kitchen Cabinet," a body of non-ministerial confidants "giving advice in a sympathetic manner"; *ibid.* p. 520.

[55] Walker, *op. cit.* pp. 87–91.

[56] R. K. Mosley, *The Story of Cabinet Office* (1969); Walker, *op. cit.* pp. 48–57; Jennings, *op. cit.* pp. 242–245; Mackintosh, *op. cit.* pp. 517 *et seq.* Stephen Roskill, *Hankey, Man of Secrets* (1972).

[57] The Public Record Office contains photographic copies of the 1,700 "Cabinet letters" written by Prime Ministers to the Sovereign from 1868 to 1916. The originals are at Windsor Castle. The letters constitute the only official record of decisions by the Cabinet in that period. There are also in the Public Record Office photographic copies of Cabinet memoranda from 1880 to 1914, and the Committee of Imperial Defence from 1902 to 1914.

Imperial Defence.[58] Since then minutes of Cabinet meetings have been sent to the Sovereign and circulated to members of the Cabinet.

The Secretariat, which has steadily grown in numbers and influence, serves all Cabinet committees as well as the full Cabinet. It organises the agenda, circulates reports, and records the Cabinet "Conclusions." This record contains not only the actual "Conclusions" or decisions, but also the subjects discussed and the relevant Papers, and a summary of the discussion. The arguments of individual Ministers are not usually recorded, in the interest of both of anonymity and secrecy. The Conclusions are circulated to the Cabinet, unless the matter is one of exceptional secrecy.

The Cabinet secretariat has always been on the Treasury vote: there is no Cabinet vote. The Secretary to the Cabinet also serves as Principal Private Secretary to the Prime Minister.

Mr. Heath in 1970 appointed a *Control Policy Review Staff* (CPRS or "Think-tank"), staffed partly by non-civil servants, to consider long-term and transdepartmental problems and to make recommendations for action.[59] It was located in the Cabinet Office, and a few years later became part of the civil service. The C.P.R.S. was abolished by Mrs. Thatcher in 1983. In 1974 Mr. Wilson introduced a *Policy Unit* of non-civil servants to help him in his political and administrative work.

A British Prime Minister has not been thought to need a department, as not only is he briefed by the Cabinet Secretary but also he can call on the Permanent Secretaries of any of the various departments. Since the last War, however, the Prime Minister has had a small *"No. 10 Office"* working as his and serving his personal needs. The staff includes his Principal Private Secretary, a press agent and experts on foreign affairs and parliamentary questions.

Ministerial responsibility

The responsibility of Ministers, as was indicated in Chapter 6, is both individual and collective. The individual responsibility of a Minister for the performance of his official duties is both legal and conventional: it is owed legally to the Sovereign, and also by convention to Parliament. "Responsible" here does not mean morally responsible or culpable, but accountable or answerable.[60] The responsible Minister is the one under whose authority an act was done, or who must take the constitutional consequences of what has been done either by himself or in his department.[61] The traditional method of expressing no confidence in an individual Minister has been to move that his salary be reduced by a nominal sum, though it was pointed out in February 1976 that as ministerial salaries are fixed by statute, legislation would be required to

[58] Lord Hankey, *Diplomacy by Conference*, Chaps. 2 and 3. See also John F. Naylor, A Man and an Institution: Sir Maurice Hankey, the Cabinet Secretariat and the custody of Cabinet secrecy, (1984).
[59] Cmnd. 4506.
[60] It also connotes a state of mind that acts as may be thought right after weighing the consequences: Amery, *op. cit.* p. 30.
[61] See G. K. Fry, "Thoughts on the Present State of the Convention of Ministerial Responsibility" (1969–70) XXIII *Parliamentary Affairs* 10.

reduce it.[62] A Minister must accept responsibility for the actions of the civil servants in his department, and he is expected to defend them from public criticism, unless they have done something reprehensible which he forbade, or of which he disapproved and of which he did not have and could not reasonably be expected to have had previous knowledge. In the latter case, which is unusual, he may dismiss them.[63] In normal circumstances, then, a Minister acts as a shield for his civil servants who are expected to be impartial and not able to answer public criticism for themselves; though this position is being eroded to some extent by the existence of the Parliamentary Commissioner[64] and Specialist Select Committees of the House.

It has been argued that an examination of ministerial resignations in the past century shows that the doctrine of individual responsibility in practice has no punitive effect, because either: (i) the erring Minister who resigns is appointed to another post; (ii) a timely reshuffle of ministerial posts renders resignation unnecessary; or (iii) a Minister who is unpopular with the Opposition is protected by the solidarity of his colleagues.[65] Often too the unearthing of incompetence and inefficiency is such a slow process that the minister responsible has long ceased to hold the position in question.[66] The number of resignations in the last 50 years is small. Those that involve personal misbehaviour or alleged immorality do not help establish a principle of accountability for the proper working of a minister's department. Mr. Ian Harvey in 1958, Mr. Galbraith in 1962, Lord Jellicoe in 1973 and Mr. Cecil Parkinson in 1983 resigned as a result of publicity about their private lives. Mr. Profumo resigned in 1963 but in his case, in addition to private immorality which was said to involve risks to the national security, there was the added factor of misleading Parliament.[67] Other ministers had been guilty of disclosing Budget proposals prematurely— J.H. Thomas in 1936 and Hugh Dalton in 1947. More remarkable is the list of ministers who have not resigned despite serious errors in areas within their responsibility: Mr. Lennox Boyd, the Colonial Secretary, despite the atrocities at Hola Prison Camp in Kenya[68]; Mr. Whitelaw, when Home Secretary, despite the defects in police security which allowed an intruder to make his way into the Queen's bedroom[69]; Mr. Prior, when Secretary of State for Northern Ireland, despite the escape

---

[62] A motion to reduce the salary of the Secretary of State for Industry by £1,000 was carried as the result of a muddled vote, but the cut was restored after another motion a few days later.

[63] 520 H.C. Deb. cols. 1287 et seq.: following the Report of the Crichel Down Enquiry Cmd. 9176 (1954).

[64] Post, Chap. 30.

[65] S. E. Finer, "The Individual Responsibility of Ministers" (1956) Public Administration 377. Cf. R. K. Alderman and J. A. Cross, The Tactics of Resignation (1967); K. C. Wheare, Maladministration and its remedies (1973), Chap. 3; G. Marshall, Constitutional Conventions (1984), pp. 61 et seq.; A. Barker, "Spreading the Blame", The Listener September 13, 1984.

[66] See G. Ganz "Parliamentary Accountability of the Crown Agents" [1980] P.L 454.

[67] Cmnd. 2152 (1963) (Lord Denning's Report); P. J. Madgwick, "Resignations" (1966–67) XX Parliamentary Affairs 59.

[68] 607 H.C. Deb. col 248 and 610 H.C. Deb. col. 182.

[69] Mr. Michael Fagan, on July 9, 1982.

of terrorists from the Maze Prison.[70] Two examples may seem to support the convention that ministers are ultimately responsible for misjudgment in the performance of their duties or errors of policy in their departments. First, the resignation of Sir Thomas Dugdale in 1954 over the Crichel Down affair where he admitted maladministration in his department although he defended its policy.[71] Secondly, the resignation in 1982 of Lord Carrington the Foreign Secretary, Mr. Luce and Mr. Atkins who accepted personal responsibility for what in retrospect was found to be the miscalculation by the Foreign Office of the threat posed to the Falkland Islands by Argentina. A possible third example is the resignation of Mr. Brittan, Secretary of State for Trade and Industry in January, 1986, following the "leaking" of parts of a confidential letter from the Solicitor General by a civil servant in Mr. Brittan's Department. That resignation formed part of the remarkable Westland Affair.[72] Apparently Mr. Brittan resigned because he accepted responsibility for having authorised an action by a member of his Department which was improper and, as it turned out, inexpedient. At the other extreme the resignation of Ministers as in the case of Sir Samuel Hoare, over the Hoare-Laval Pact concerning Abyssinia in 1935, may be cases of ministers being "thrown to the wolves."

The conclusion must be that while there is no doubt that a minister is responsible in the sense that he is answerable for his department it is not clear in what circumstances convention requires that he resign when his department errs. So long as he retains the support of the Prime Minister he is safe in effect unless his own party is willing to risk bringing down the Government.

The doctrine of the individual responsibility of ministers is frequently cited as an important feature of the British Constitution. "The enduring effect of the doctrine of ministerial responsibility has been over the past century or so that powers have been vested in ministers and on a relentlessly increasing scale."[73] The Courts have referred to the doctrine in seeking the intention of Parliament when interpreting statutes.[74] The existence of the doctrine has been invoked to disprove the need for proposed new remedies against abuse of power or maladministration.[75] There is, it may be thought, something unsatisfactory in putting so much weight on such an uncertain foundation.

It should be borne in mind that the Prime Minister may always

---

[70] H.C. Deb., cols. 1041–1047 (February 9, 1984).

[71] Farmland had been compulsorily purchased during the Second World War. The owners from whom it was acquired were given an assurance that they would be given an opportunity to buy it back if the Crown subsequently had no use for the land. In due course the previous owners sought, unsuccessfully, to re-acquire the land. Various allegations were made of inefficiency and shortcomings of various kinds on the part of the civil servants concerned. Sir Andrew Clark Q.C. was appointed to hold an inquiry: he found evidence of muddle, bias and bad faith; Cmd. 9176 (1954). See J. A. G. Griffith, "The Crichel Down Affair" (1955) 18 M.L.R. 557.

[72] For a chronology and comment see G. Marshall, "Cabinet Government and the Westland Affair," [1986] P.L. 184. See further The Defence Implications of the Future of Westland plc., Third Report from the Defence Committee, July 1986.

[73] N. Johnson, In Search of the Constitution (1977), p. 84.

[74] e.g. Liversidge v. Anderson [1942] A.C. 206; Raymond v. Att.-Gen. [1982] 2 W.L.R. 849.

[75] e.g. the need for, and appropriateness of, the Parliamentary Commissioner for Administration: post, p. 654.

advise the Sovereign to dismiss a Minister, as in the case of Mr. Heffer, a Minister of State who spoke in the House in April, 1975, against continued membership of the EEC, but it is seldom necessary to resort to this expedient, for it is usually sufficient if the Prime Minister invites a Minister to resign.

The collective responsibility is owed by convention both to the Sovereign and to Parliament. As we have seen in connection with the dissolution of Parliament the Ministry as a whole (including the Cabinet) must retain the confidence of the House of Commons. To the Sovereign Ministers must tender unanimous advice: to Parliament and the nation they should show a united front by vote and speech. Cabinets in the late nineteenth and early twentieth centuries sometimes agreed that certain topics should be treated as "Open Questions" where collective responsibility did not apply and each minister might speak and voted as he pleased.[76] The convention is illustrated by the resignations of dissenting Ministers—Eden in 1938 over the policy of appeasement, Aneurin Bevan in 1951 over National Health Service charges, and Lord Salisbury in 1957 over the release of Archbishop Makarios. Mr. Frank Cousins resigned from his post of Minister of Science and Technology in 1966 because he disagreed with the Government's Prices and Incomes Bill: being a trade union leader he could not keep quiet about it. Mr. Heseltine resigned as Secretary of State for Defence in January 1986, the first of the two ministers to do so in the course of the Westland affair. To the extent that he resigned because he felt unable to accept the view of the rest of the Cabinet on the matters in issue his resignation illustrates the continued working of the traditional convention. Mr. Heseltine himself, however, gave different reasons at different times for his resignation and on one occasion denied that it was required by the doctrine of collective responsibility.[77] Custom allows a dissenting Minister who resigns to make a personal statement in the House.

The principle of collective responsibility is not applied in its full rigour to non-Cabinet Ministers, for they are often not consulted in matters that do not affect their department. In their case the responsibility is passive rather than active. Sir Edward Boyle, one of the two junior Ministers who resigned from Sir Anthony Eden's Government in 1956 because they disagreed with the Government's intervention in the Suez Canal Crisis, joined the Government formed by Mr. Harold Macmillan early in 1957 although the new Ministry confirmed its support for Eden's Suez policy. Technically they were different Ministries, but the policy disapproved of was the same, although it was no longer possible to pursue it.

The convention of the collective responsibility of Ministers, as we have seen,[78] has been weakening in recent years.[79] Mr. Wilson in the period 1974–76 had to remind his colleagues several times of this principle, and Mr. Callaghan in April, 1976 rebuked the Secretary of State for Energy (Mr. Benn) in the House of Commons for abstaining at a meet-

[76] e.g. Catholic emancipation 1812–1829; Women's Suffrage 1884 and 1906–1914; tariff reform 1903–1905.
[77] See Marshall, op. cit. supra n. 73.
[78] Ante, p. 125.
[79] Unless Mr. Heseltine's resignation can be seen as a strengthening of the convention.

ing of the Labour Party National Executive in a vote concerning proposed cuts in public expenditure. In March—April, 1975 Mr. Wilson allowed Ministers as well as Labour back-benchers "in the unique circumstances of a referendum" to advocate, outside Parliament, opposition to continued membership of the EEC, although continued membership was Government policy. Later in a broadcast he said "after June 6 there will be one Cabinet and one Cabinet view."[80] Another episode was that of the European Assembly Elections Bill 1977 to provide for direct elections to the European Assembly, an item of Government policy contained in the Queen's Speech and implementing a Treaty obligation. Mr. Callaghan, the Prime Minister, stated that Ministers as well as Labour back-benchers would be free to vote against the Bill on second reading. When questioned by Mrs. Thatcher, Leader of the Opposition, Mr. Callaghan replied: "I certainly think that doctrine [collective responsibility] should apply except in cases where I announce that it does not."[81] In the event 31 Ministers, including six Cabinet Ministers, voted against the Bill, but it was easily carried with the help of Opposition parties.[82] So long as a Government can keep its majority in the House of Commons, its main concern nowadays appears to be its image amongst the electorate. Dissent in public is allowed if it is thought it will do the party less harm than resignations and press reports of "splits."[83]

Confidentiality

Access to, and use of Cabinet papers is governed by convention.[84] Cabinet and other government papers are, in law, Crown property. In deciding who may have access to such papers the Crown by convention acts on the advice of the Government. It is accepted that, as a general rule, Cabinet ministers may not see Cabinet papers of former ministers of a different party. Nor may they see other papers (with certain exceptions) which contain unpublished views or comments of those predecessors on advice submitted to them. Ministers may normally see papers of their predecessors of their own party in the course of their duties, with the agreement, where appropriate, of any former Prime Minister. Former ministers may have access to but not retain, any documents which they saw when in office.[85]

A highly unusual exception to the general principle was supplied when a Committee of Privy Councillors was established in 1982 under

---

[80] *The Times*, May 12, 1975. *Cf.* the "agreement to differ" in 1932, when there was a coalition Government, no referendum or general election was involved, and the dissentients in fact soon resigned office: *ante*, p. 125.

[81] *The Times*, June 15, 16 and 17, 1977.

[82] Not so basic was the defeat at the Committee stage of the Prime Minister's recommendation of the regional list system of proportional representation for the first direct elections to the European Assembly, in favour of the first-past-the-post system.

[83] Mackintosh, *op. cit.* p. 533. And see R. Brazier, "The Constitution in the New Politics" [1978] P.L. 117.

[84] Lord Hunt of Tanworth, "Disclosure of Government Papers" [1982] P.L. 514; *ante* p. 116.

[85] In 1980 Mrs. Thatcher, while recognising the convention that Mr. Alfred Morris, former Minister for the Disabled, could consult papers prepared by officials while he was minister, refused to agree to allow the photocopying of the papers: *The Times*, February 7, 1980.

the Chairmanship of Lord Franks to review the way in which government departments had discharged their responsibilities to the Falkland Islands in the period before the Argentinian invasion.[86] The Committee was given access to departmental papers, Cabinet and Cabinet committee memoranda and minutes, and intelligence assessments which had been prepared for previous governments of both major parties. On a matter of less grave political controversy, in 1986 Mr. Callaghan agreed to allow Conservative ministers to examine papers prepared when he was Prime Minister relating to the controversy whether to equip the Royal Air Force with the Nimrod early warning system or the American Awacs system.[87] The decision to adopt the Nimrod system had been taken in 1977, with the support of both the Labour and Conservative parties but the subsequent delay in producing the equipment and the increase in cost had called in question the wisdom of the original decision.

Cabinet or ex-Cabinet ministers who wished to refer in their memoirs to Cabinet discussions or papers during the period when official documents are protected by statute,[88] were formerly required by convention to obtain the consent of the Sovereign expressed through the Prime Minister, who delegated the vetting to the Secretary of the Cabinet.[89] Convention also required the disclosure of confidential State or official papers or information by Ministers or ex-Ministers to have the approval of the Government of the day, application being made to the Secretary of the Cabinet. Ex-civil servants were expected to apply for such permission to their Department. The legal effect of these requirements was tested in *Attorney-General* v. *Jonathan Cape Ltd.*[90] where the Attorney-General sought to restrain the posthumous publication of volume I of Richard Crossman's *Diaries of a Cabinet Minister*, covering events of about ten years before. Lord Widgery C.J., declined to grant the injunction. It was conceded by the Attorney-General that there was no breach of the Official Secrets Acts.[91] Lord Widgery held that the court has power on the ground of public policy to restrain publication of information in breach of confidence,[92] but this volume disclosed no details that should still remain confidential.

A Committee of Privy Councillors on Ministerial Memoirs under the chairmanship of Lord Radcliffe, whose report[93] came out after the decision in *Attorney-General* v. *Jonathan Cape*, recommended that ministerial authors should be precluded for fifteen years from publish-

---

[86] *Falkland Islands Review* Cmnd. 8787 (1983).

[87] *Ante.* p. 116.

[88] The Public Records Acts 1958 and 1967 provide that public records in the Public Record Office (including Cabinet minutes) shall not be available for public inspection until they are 30 years old. The period may be extended by the Lord Chancellor if they include information received in confidence or liable to prejudice national security or trade.

[89] Because it is difficult for the Prime Minister to deal with comments about his colleagues or predecessors, and he does not know about the activities of members of opposite parties when they were in office.

[90] [1976] Q.B. 752.

[91] Nor does the Privy Councillor's oath add to the Cabinet Minister's legal obligation.

[92] In its equitable jurisdiction: see, *e.g.* Argyll *(Duchess)* v. Argyll *(Duke)* [1967] Ch. 302.

[93] Cmnd. 6386 (1976).

ing information falling within three categories: (i) the requirements of national security operative at the time of publication; (ii) injury to foreign relations; and (iii) destructive of the confidential relationships on which the system of government is based, *i.e.* relations between Ministers and colleagues or their advisers in the civil service or outside. "Government is not to be conducted," said the report, "in the interests of history." The report was accepted by the Prime Minister, Mr. Wilson, who said manuscripts should still be submitted for inspection and these working rules of reticence should be accepted as an obligation of honour.[94]

Influence of the Sovereign

Since the Sovereign acts on the advice of the Cabinet, tendered through the Prime Minister, and the government is carried on in the name of the Sovereign, the Cabinet is expected to keep the Sovereign informed of any departure in policy, of the general march of political events, and in particular of the deliberations of the Cabinet. The *power* of the Monarch in modern times is confined—in Bagehot's well-known words[95]—to "the right to be consulted, the right to encourage, the right to warn." The *influence* of a Sovereign who has been on the Throne for some years, however, is far from negligible, for his experience will be wider and more continuous than that of most or all of his Ministers.

Queen Victoria cannot perhaps be taken as a model for the twentieth century, but George V's reign of a quarter of a century shows a number of examples of the influence exerted by the Throne. By his advice, warnings and encouragement the King helped to bring the parties together in negotiating the Anglo-Irish Treaty of 1921; but he left the conduct of the negotiations entirely to the Prime Minister, Lloyd George, and refrained from any comment or intervention while the conference lasted.[96] In 1923 the King tried unsuccessfully to dissuade Baldwin from a dissolution,[97] and later in the same year he persuaded Baldwin not to resign before meeting Parliament when the Conservatives at a general election had lost their absolute majority but were still the largest party in the Commons.[98] George V took the initiative in the formation of the National (coalition) Government under Ramsay MacDonald in 1931 when the "economic crisis" caused the latter's minority Labour Government to break up. The King consulted the Conservative and Liberal leaders, each of whom had a considerable following in the House, and then entrusted MacDonald with the task of resuming office as the head of a coalition and in spite of the defection of his own Labour Party.[99]

As the Sovereign's influence may be underestimated, so on the other

---

[94] On the security of Cabinet documents, see Report of Houghton Committee Cmnd. 6677 (1976).

[95] Bagehot, *The English Constitution* (World's Classics ed.), p. 67.

[96] Harold Nicolson, *King George the Fifth*, p. 360.

[97] *Ibid.* pp. 379–380.

[98] *Ibid.* pp. 382–384.

[99] *Ibid.* pp. 460–469; G. M. Young, *Stanley Baldwin*, Chap. 16; K. Middlemas and J. Barnes, *Baldwin* (1969), Chap. 23; D. Macquand, *Ramsay MacDonald* (1977), Chaps. 25 and 26. The importance of the King's role is described in Kenneth Rose, *King George V* (1983), pp. 371–379.

hand it may be exaggerated. Thus Lord Attlee discounts certain incidents given in the official biography of George VI[1] as examples of interference by that King, notably the choice of Ernest Bevin as Foreign
Secretary and the holding of a general election in 1951. Attlee later said
that the reason for the first was that he, as Prime Minister, wanted to
keep Ernest Bevin away from Herbert Morrison; and the reason for the
second was that he did not want the King to worry about the precarious
position of the Government (majority 6) while he was abroad.[2] It is too
early to say what influence, if any, the present monarch has exercised.

The exchange of views between Sovereign and Prime Minister on any
matter is strictly confidential between them. It would be improper for
the Sovereign herself or for any member of the Royal Household to give
public expression to her opinions on political matters.[3] (Conversely the
Prime Minister does not answer questions in the House of Commons
relating to her relations with the monarch[4]).

III. THE PRIME MINISTER[5]

Formal position
The emergence of the position of Prime Minister in the modern sense
begins with the Ministries of Sir Robert Walpole (1721–42) and the
younger Pitt (1783–1801; 1804–1806), although the former disclaimed the
title. It was brought about by a combination of a number of factors,
including royal confidence, pre-eminence among Ministers, patronage
as First Lord of the Treasury, and especially control of the Commons
(not necessarily as leader of the largest party). The authority of the
Prime Minister was firmly established during the latter part of the nineteenth century by the outstanding personalities of Disraeli and Gladstone, making use of the effects brought about by the Representation of
the People Acts and the development of the party system. As we have
seen, the Prime Minister was until recently hardly known to the law:
like the Cabinet, he was the creature of convention. He is mentioned in
the Treaty of Berlin 1878; a royal warrant of 1905 which gives him precedence next after the Archbishop of York; the Schedule to the Chequers
Estate Act 1917, in which Parliament gave effect to the gift of the
Chequers estate as a country residence for the Prime Minister of the
day[6]; the Physical Training and Recreation Act 1937; the Parliamentary
and other Pensions Act 1972; the House of Commons Disqualification
Act 1975 ("Prime Minister and First Lord of the Treasury") and the
Chevening Estate Act 1959, under which this Kent estate was given on

---

[1] Wheeler-Bennett, *King George VI.*
[2] "The Role of the Monarchy" *The Observer,* August 23, 1959.
[3] Letter from the Private Secretary to The Queen (Sir William Heseltine) *The Times* July
28, 1986. *Post* p. 763.
[4] *Ante* p. 230.
[5] B. E. Carter, *The Office of Prime Minister* (1956); Anthony King (ed.), *The British Prime
Minister* (1969); Lord Blake. "The Office of Prime Minister" (British Academy Lecture),
1975; Mackintosh, *op. cit.;* Humphry Berkeley, *The Power of the Prime Minister* (1968); P.
Gordon Walker, *op. cit.* Chap. 5; Jennings, *op. cit.;* Thomson, *Constitutional History of
England,* 1642–1801.
[6] *Robertson v. Secretary of State for Environment* [1976] 1 W.L.R. 371 (Q.B.D.).

certain trusts as regards occupation, including "any Minister of the Crown nominated by the Prime Minister."

The Prime Minister now invariably takes the office of First Lord of the Treasury,[7] and occasionally some other office as well, such as that of Chancellor of the Exchequer (Gladstone), War Office (Asquith),[8] Foreign Secretary (Ramsay MacDonald) or Minister of Defence (Winston Churchill). The Prime Minister has no legal powers except as First Lord of the Treasury and (since 1968) Minister for the Civil Service. The office of First Lord of the Treasury down to 1937 provided him with his salary. It places him technically at the head of the most important government department (the Treasury), yet with departmental duties which (apart from patronage) are only nominal, as the working head of that department is the Chancellor of the Exchequer. In the eighteenth and early nineteenth centuries, before the reform of the Civil Service and the parliamentary franchise, the fact that the First Lord of the Treasury exercised a very extensive patronage over many kinds of official appointments meant that the Prime Minister could control departmental appointments, and this helped him to obtain a parliamentary majority for his party. The Ministers of the Crown Act 1937 first provided for a salary to be paid to "the person who is Prime Minister and First Lord of the Treasury." The Ministerial and other Salaries Act 1975 now provides a salary to the "Prime Minister and First Lord of the Treasury," so it is unlikely that these positions will be held separately in future, although the Act does not require them to be held together. The Act of 1937 also provided former Prime Ministers with a pension. The Parliamentary and other Pensions Act 1972, s.26, now provides that any person who has been Prime Minister and First Lord of the Treasury shall be entitled to a pension charged on the Consolidated Fund.

Functions of the Prime Minister[9]

The primary functions of the Prime Minister are to form a government, and to choose and preside over the Cabinet. He gives advice to his ministerial colleagues on matters before they come to the Cabinet, and he is the main channel of communication between the Cabinet and the Sovereign, with whom he has a weekly audience.[10] He advises the Sovereign on a dissolution.[11]

The Prime Minister is normally the leader of his party, having either been chosen as Prime Minister because he is the leader of the largest party or elected leader because he is Prime Minister.[12] He is primarily

[7] They were last separated when Balfour was First Lord of the Treasury in Lord Salisbury's administrations (1891–92, 1895–1902).

[8] At that time (1914) a member accepting this office had to seek re-election, so that for a time Asquith was Prime Minister without a seat in the House.

[9] For first-hand accounts see Harold Macmillan, *Pointing the Way, 1959–61* (1972); Harold Wilson, *The Governance of Britain* (1976).

[10] Other Ministers may communicate with the Sovereign on matters concerning their department.

[11] Lord Beaverbrook recounts that the decision of Lloyd George and his colleagues in January, 1922 not to hold a general election was induced by the intervention of a parrot: *Men and Power* (1956), pp. 340–341. And see *ante*, p. 301.

[12] Lloyd George (1916), MacDonald (1931) and Churchill (1940) were not leaders of their party when appointed Prime Minister, though Churchill soon accepted the leadership.

responsible for the organisation of the business of the House, even if (as is now usual) this work is delegated to the Leader of the House.[13] In the House he is expected to speak in debates, and to answer questions on general government policy, the future business of the House and any residual matters. A Prime Minister is willing to give confidential information to the Leader of the Opposition on such matters as defence, security, the EEC and Northern Ireland.

The Prime Minister has special responsibilities in the areas of Security and Intelligence. A Cabinet Committee of Ministers, chaired by the Prime Minister, supervises MI5, MI6 and G.C.H.Q. A Joint Intelligence Committee (J.I.C.) chaired by a Cabinet Office official, collates intelligence reports and prepares assessments for ministers. Since 1952 the Director General of the Security Service has been responsible to the Home Secretary and not, as formerly, to the Prime Minister. The Director General has, however, the right of direct access to the Prime Minister, as has the Chairman of J.I.C.[14] The decision to refer any matter relating to security to the Security Commission[15] for investigation is taken by the Prime Minister.

The Prime Minister sees that Cabinet decisions are carried out by the departments, although, as we have said, the extent to which he supervises the administration varies with different holders of the office. His contact with the affairs of the Foreign Office is often especially close. The Cabinet secretariat is under his control, and consults him in preparing the agenda. He communicates directly with the other Commonwealth Prime Ministers, and presides when they meet in this country.

Many Crown appointments, in addition to ministerial offices, are made on his advice. These include the Lords of Appeal in Ordinary, the Lords Justices of Appeal, bishops and deans of the Church of England, peerages, Privy Councillors and most honours.[16] As First Lord of the Treasury and Minister for the Civil Service,[17] the Prime Minister approves the senior appointments in the Civil Service.

Choice of Prime Minister

The Sovereign chooses the Prime Minister. Conventions ensure that in most cases the "choice" is formal, for the Sovereign is expected to send for the leader of the party or group of parties that has, or can control, a majority in the House of Commons. The choice became formal owing to the development of the party system. Thus in 1855 Queen Victoria, who preferred Derby, was constrained to appoint Palmerston;

[13] The Leader of the House is responsible for steering the Government's legislative programme through the House of Commons and must also pay regard to the interests of the House as a whole.

[14] See G. Marshall, *Constitutional Conventions* (1984) pp. 122 *et seq.*; G. Drewry, "The House of Commons and the Security Services" [1984] P.L. 370; G. Zellick, "Government Beyond the Law" [1985] P.L. 283, 299.

[15] A non-statutory body, established in 1964, consisting of distinguished public figures, chaired by a senior judge. The present chairman is Lord Griffiths.

[16] Recommendations for some honours and decorations are also made by the Foreign Secretary, the Defence Minister, Commonwealth Prime Ministers, and on the Queen's personal initiative.

[17] *Post,* p. 330.

and in 1880 she reluctantly appointed Gladstone when she would have preferred Hartington, though Rosebery was Victoria's choice after Gladstone's resignation. If the government is defeated at a general election the Prime Minister resigns[18] (and with him the other Ministers), and the Sovereign on the advice of the resigning Prime Minister sends for the Leader of the Opposition. The Leader of the Opposition is known, because both the Labour Party and (since 1964) the Conservative Party in opposition select a leader by ballot, and he has a statutory salary. The Leader of the Opposition will accept office if his party commands a majority in the Commons, which it usually will if the Government was defeated at a general election.[19]

If the Prime Minister dies in office or retires on *personal* grounds, such as ill health or old age, the Sovereign has really no discretion in the common case where the government has an absolute majority and one other Cabinet Minister in the Commons is obviously regarded as ranking next to the Prime Minister. In this way Neville Chamberlain succeeded Baldwin in 1937 and Mr. Eden succeeded Sir Winston Churchill in 1955.[20] A *retiring* Prime Minister is probably not entitled to proffer advice as to his successor,[21] but he can make his views known beforehand, and anyway the Sovereign is free to consult him and other members of the government party.

There are exceptional circumstances when the Sovereign really has to exercise a personal discretion within limits; and this is perhaps the most important function of the Sovereign at the present day. There may

---

[18] See G. H. Le May, *The Victorian Constitution* (1979), pp. 57–58; "Disraeli created a constitutional precedent after the general election of 1868, when he chose to accept defeat at the hands of the constituencies instead of those of the new House of Commons, and resigned without meeting Parliament. This was a clear example of precedent crystallising about accident. Disraeli had no wish to consolidate the Liberal Party by presenting himself as a common target for its various elements. The party had disintegrated in the previous Parliament, it might do so again, and the chances of that happening would be better if it was not allowed to bind itself together in a vote of censure. In spite of its peculiar origin, the precedent was found to be convenient; it was followed by Gladstone in 1874 and by Disraeli (then Earl of Beaconsfield) in 1880. [Queen Victoria] did not think that immediate resignation ought to become a general rule, 'because it might be a means for a Government, who had committed some grievous fault, to escape condemnation by Parliament, as the adverse party was seldom inclined to attack a fallen Government.' But become a general rule it did, whenever the result of a general election was sufficiently clear to make the carrying of a vote of no confidence a certainty; its adoption may be taken as a measure of the development of party cohesion and solidarity. Gladstone resigned at once after the election of 1886. Salisbury chose to meet Parliament after the election of 1885, as Baldwin did after that of 1923; both were turned out almost at once. In 1929, in conditions roughly similar to those of 1923, Baldwin resigned at once: however obscure the result might be, he said, it showed that the electorate did not want him."

[19] The Leader of the Opposition is not bound to accept office. Disraeli in 1873, when the parties were very even, thought it would be more advantageous if Gladstone carried on for a while.

[20] Partly at least through the influential advice of Lord Kemsley, proprietor of the *Sunday Times* and Lord Woolton, Chairman of the Conservative Party: J. Margach, *The Abuse of Power* (1978), pp. 104–105.

[21] In March, 1955 Churchill said to Mr. Eden and Mr. Butler: "I am going and Anthony will succeed me. We can discuss details later": Lord Butler, *The Art of the Possible* (1971), p. 176; but he refrained from mentioning to the Queen the question of his successor: J. Wheeler-Bennett (ed.) *Action This Day* (1968), p. 234.

be more than two parties in the House of Commons with no one party having an absolute majority, either as a result of a general election or on a defeat in the Commons of a government that has already been granted one dissolution; and the question arises whether one of the minority parties, and if so which, will be able to carry on the government with the support of one of the other parties, or whether a coalition shall be formed; or the government may break up owing to internal dissension. The Sovereign then may consult all interested parties with a view to the formation of a Ministry that can hold a majority in the House. When Baldwin's minority Conservative Government was defeated in the House in 1924 not long after a general election, the King did not seek any advice before sending for Ramsay MacDonald, the leader of the second largest party.[22]

Neville Chamberlain, the Conservative Prime Minister, resigned in 1940 because, although he had not been defeated in the House (his normal majority of about 200 was reduced to 81, a number of Conservatives voting against him or abstaining) he realised that he had lost the confidence of his own party as well as of the Labour Party, which was supporting the Government in the conduct of the war. A coalition government was needed, and Labour members intimated that they would not serve under Chamberlain. The possible choice of a successor lay between Winston Churchill, First Lord of the Admiralty, and Lord Halifax, Foreign Secretary. The Labour Party were willing to serve under Churchill. Lord Halifax expressed the view, in a conference between the three statesmen, that it would be impracticable to try to lead the government from the Lords in wartime.[23] Chamberlain then tendered his resignation to George VI, who accepted it. In an informal discussion as to his successor the King suggested Lord Halifax, but Chamberlain told the King what Lord Halifax had said. "I asked Chamberlain his advice," the King recorded, "and he told me Winston was the man to send for . . . . I sent for Winston and asked him to form a Government."[24]

The most difficult case is where a Prime Minister dies in office or resigns on personal grounds, such as health or age, leaving no obvious successor. There may be no obvious successor because it has not been the practice for a Conservative Party in office to elect a deputy leader. The first time the Conservative Party in opposition has appointed a deputy leader was the appointment of Mr. Maudling in 1965. When the parliamentary Labour Party are in opposition they elect both a leader and a deputy leader annually.[25] It was wholly exceptional that twice during the last war George VI asked Churchill to advise him on his successor if the Prime Minister should die as a result of enemy action while abroad. George VI objected to Mr. Eden being described as Deputy

---

[22] Nicolson, op. cit. pp. 382–386; cf. Sidney Webb, "The First Labour Government" (1961) 32 Political Quarterly 6.

[23] Winston S. Churchill, Second World War, Vol. I, pp. 523–526; K. Feiling, The Life of Neville Chamberlain, pp. 439–441; Earl of Halifax, Fulness of Days, pp. 218–220; Earl of Birkenhead, Halifax (1965), pp. 453–455.

[24] Wheeler-Bennett, King George VI, pp. 438–445.

[25] See A. Howard and R. West, The Making of the Prime Minister (1965) for the election of Mr. Harold Wilson as party leader after the death of Gaitskell in 1963.

Prime Minister in 1951, as it would imply a line of succession and so restrict the royal prerogative.[26] There have been appointments by both the main parties of Deputy Prime Minister, notably Attlee (Leader of the Labour Party) in the coalition Government during the last war.[27] The title generally is not known to our Constitution, and it does not imply any right of succession to the Prime Minister.[28]

In 1923 Bonar Law, the Conservative Prime Minister, was so ill that he sent his resignation to George V. The choice of successor lay between Lord Curzon, Foreign Secretary and former Viceroy of India, a statesman of brilliant gifts and vast experience; and Mr. Baldwin who, although recently appointed Chancellor of the Exchequer, had little political experience and was not well known either inside or outside the House. After the King or his Private Secretary had consulted Lord Balfour (former Prime Minister) and Lord Salisbury (Lord President of the Council) and members of the government party, the King chose Baldwin both on personal grounds and because he was in the Commons, although the latter reason was emphasised in breaking the news to Curzon.[29]

When Sir Anthony Eden, Conservative Prime Minister, resigned in 1957 because of serious ill-health, the succession lay by common consent between Mr. R. A. Butler (Lord Privy Seal and Leader of the House of Commons) and Mr. Harold Macmillan (Chancellor of the Exchequer). All that was publicly known was that the Queen consulted two elder statesmen of the Conservative Party—Lord Salisbury (Lord President of the Council and son of the adviser of 1923) and Sir Winston Churchill, the former Prime Minister—and selected Mr. Macmillan. We now know that they both recommended Mr. Macmillan, and that only one member of the Cabinet supported Mr. Butler.[30] Eden was neither asked for his advice nor did he volunteer it.[31]

In 1963 (after the Peerage Act had been passed) Mr. Macmillan became ill, entered hospital for an operation and announced his intention to resign. In accordance with the practice of the Conservatives at that time "soundings" were taken in the party. The result of these soundings was communicated by the Lord Chancellor to the Prime Minister, who then sent a letter of resignation to the Queen, presumably intimating that he had advice to give if requested. The Queen (who is not known to have sought any other advice) visited Mr. Macmillan in hospital, and immediately afterwards sent for the Earl of Home and

---

[26] Wheeler-Bennett, op. cit. p. 797.
[27] See K. Harris, Attlee (1982), pp. 192–254.
[28] Butler, op. cit. p. 234.
[29] Robert Blake, The Unknown Prime Minister (1955), pp. 514–527; Winston S. Churchill, Great Contemporaries, pp. 215–220; L. S. Amery, op. cit. pp. 21–22; Harold Nicolson, King George the Fifth, pp. 375–379; Curzon, The Last Phase, pp. 353–355; G. M. Young, Stanley Baldwin, pp. 48–49; Keith Middlemas and John Barnes, Baldwin, Chap. 8. K. Rose, King George V (1983), pp. 266–273.
[30] Mackintosh, op. cit. pp. 522–523. Lord Salisbury and Lord Kilmuir (Lord Chancellor) sounded the Cabinet Ministers. "What they wanted was a straight answer to the question: 'Who's best—Rab or Harold?' They got it": Lord Egremont, Wyndham and Children First (1968), pp. 158–159.
[31] Harold Macmillan, Riding the Storm 1956–1959 (1971), Vol. 4, Chap. 5.

invited him to form an Administration.[32] (She might have invested him with office straight away, as was done with Eden and Macmillan.) A day or two later Lord Home informed the Queen that he was able to form an Administration.[33]

In 1964 the Conservatives adopted a new method of selecting their party leader. A ballot was taken of the party in the Commons, and the candidate so selected was then presented for election at a party meeting.[34] On Sir Alec Douglas-Home's resignation (after the defeat of his party general election) this led to the election of Mr. Heath. A more elaborate procedure was introduced after defeat in a general election in 1974 for filling a vacancy in the leadership, involving consultation with Conservative peers and constituency associations and holding (if necessary) three secret ballots among the party's M.P.s. The candidate elected by the latter is presented for confirmation as leader to a party meeting consisting of M.P.s, peers and parliamentary candidates. The first election by ballot resulted in the defeat of Mr. Heath by Mrs. Thatcher.

The leadership of the Labour Party until 1976 had never changed while the party was in office.[35] The party expressed the view in 1957 that they would not expect anyone to accept office as Prime Minister until he had been elected leader of the parliamentary party. There is much to be said for this practice, which is adopted in Australia and New Zealand.[36] In March, 1976 Mr. Wilson, Labour Prime Minister, announced his intention to retire from office and to return to the back-benches when the parliamentary Labour Party had had the opportunity to elect a new leader. A ballot led to the election of Mr. Callaghan, and the Queen appointed him Prime Minister. Mr. Wilson in the previous December had informed the Queen of his intention, and presumably Her Majesty approved of this course.

It is probable that in future the Conservatives in office would follow the Labour practice of filling a vacancy by electing a new leader, who would then be appointed Prime Minister. In view of the Conservative Party's new system of electing a leader, it would appear that the Sovereign in practice no longer has a discretion in the choice of Prime Minister, at least when the normal two-party system is operating.[37]

---

[32] "What is certain is that Macmillan . . . acted . . . with utter determination and dispatch, making a definite recommendation of Home": Lord Butler, *The Art of the Possible* (1971) pp. 247–248. Lord Hailsham says that Macmillan in 1963 favoured him as a leader of the Conservative Party and Prime Minister. Viscount Hailsham (as he then was) did not disclaim his hereditary title until after Home had been appointed Prime Minister: *The Door Wherein I Went* (1975), Chap. 32.

[33] He forthwith renounced his peerage under the new Act, and (being a Knight of the Thistle) became known as Sir Alec Douglas-Home. He had then, of course, to fight a by-election to get into the House of Commons.
    See A. Howard and R. West, *op. cit.* Chap. 4.

[34] See Humphry Berkeley, *Across the Floor* (1972).

[35] Since 1981 the Leader is elected by a process in which the members of the Parliamentary Labour Party have 30 per cent. of the votes, the constituencies 30 per cent. and the Trades Unions 40 per cent.

[36] E. M. McWhinney, "Constitutional Conventions" (1957) 35 Can. Bar Rev. 92, 242, 368, 369.

[37] See also R. Brazier, "Choosing a Prime Minister," [1982] P.L. 395.

Should a Prime Minister be a peer?

The question whether it is constitutionally proper for a Prime Minister to be in the House of Lords in modern times has often been discussed, especially in connection with the resignation of Bonar Law in 1923. No peer has been Prime Minister[38] since Lord Salisbury (1895–1902). Even in the nineteenth century Prime Ministers who were peers found it difficult to control the Commons; but as late as 1921 Cabinet colleagues seriously considered Lord Birkenhead (Lord Chancellor) as Prime Minister to succeed Lloyd George, and in 1922 they offered the position to Lord Derby.[39] Lord Halifax saw the difficulty in 1940, but neither he nor Neville Chamberlain acknowledged a convention. George VI suggested to Chamberlain that Lord Halifax's peerage could be "placed in abeyance for the time being," apparently meaning that legislation should be passed allowing Lord Halifax to speak in the House of Commons.[40] In 1957 Lords Salisbury and Kilmuir considered themselves excluded by virtue of their peerage.[41]

The weight of opinion is in favour of the view that it is undesirable and impracticable for the Prime Minister to have a seat in the Lords. The House of Commons is the centre of interest and influence; it has exclusive control over national finance and, although the office of First Lord of the Treasury is only nominally concerned with financial matters, it would be absurd for the holder of that office to sit in the upper House; it is in the elected Second Chamber that governments are made and defeated; and the Labour Party is under-represented in the Lords, so that the real opposition to a Conservative Government is in the lower House. The question has lost much of its importance since the Peerage Act 1963 allowed existing hereditary peers, and persons who later succeed to hereditary peerages, to renounce their peerages within a time limit.

Prime Ministerial government?[42]

Some writers say we no longer have Cabinet government as we used to know it, but that since the last war—if not before—we have had "Prime Ministerial government." Policy is not usually initiated by the Cabinet. Decisions tend to be taken either by the Prime Minister alone or by him after consulting one or two Ministers, or else by Cabinet committees or informal meetings of the Ministers concerned. To these factors may be added the unification and centralisation of an expanding

---

[38] Apart from the Earl of Home in 1963 for a period of four days before the renunciation of his hereditary title took effect.

[39] Lord Beaverbrook, *The Decline and Fall of Lloyd George* (1963), pp. 68 *et seq.*; pp. 181.

[40] Wheeler-Bennett, *op. cit.* p. 444.

[41] Mackintosh, *op. cit.* p. 425. *Cf.* Lord Moran, *Churchill: The Struggle for Survival, 1940–65,* where Lord Salisbury is said to have suggested in 1953 that Churchill, who had had a stroke, ought to go the Lords while remaining Prime Minister—an idea that commended itself to the Queen's Private Secretary but not to Churchill, who was 77.

[42] Richard Crossman, *The Diaries of a Cabinet Minister;* G. W. Jones, "Prime Ministers and Cabinets" (1972) 20 Pol. Stud. 213; A. H. Brown, "Prime Ministerial Power" [1968] P.L. 28, 96; Harold Wilson, "Where the Power Lies," *Listener,* February 9, 1967. And see: Mackintosh, *op. cit.*; Gordon Walker, *op. cit.*; King, *op. cit.*; Hood Phillips, *Reform of the Constitution,* pp. 42–47, 51–54.

Civil Service under the Prime Minister, who is the only political master of the powerful trinity consisting of the Permanent Secretary of the Treasury, the head of the Civil Service, and the Secretary to the Cabinet.

Crossman attached great importance to committees of officials or inter-departmental meetings of civil servants, which he described as "the key to the control of the civil service over the politicians."[43] Mr. George Brown (later Lord George Brown), Deputy Prime Minister and Foreign Secretary, resigned over an emergency decision for a bank holiday because it seemed to him that the Prime Minister (Mr. Wilson) was introducing a presidential system.[44]

In considering the relative positions of the Prime Minister and the Cabinet we have to take note of such factors as the moral authority of his office as Leader in the eyes of the public and his standing in his party; the power of the Prime Minister to appoint and reshuffle Ministers, to determine the scope of the various offices, to control the Cabinet agenda and to advise a dissolution. The Prime Minister has the advantage of knowing more than his colleagues what is going on. It is difficult to overthrow a Prime Minister, because the Cabinet must not only be united against him but agreed on his successor, and backbenchers are not likely to want to precipitate a general election in which many of them may lose their seats. On the other hand, if the Cabinet does not often initiate policy, it co-ordinates. The Cabinet "reconciles, records and authorises."[45] The Cabinet is not the only decision-making body in the central government, but all important matters must go before the Cabinet at some stage. Also, the Cabinet have greater *legal* powers than the Prime Minister.

The relative positions of the Prime Minister and the Cabinet are variable, depending on personalities, not only that of the Prime Minister but also those of his colleagues. A Prime Minister cannot ride roughshod over his Cabinet—even Churchill gave way on occasion. Their positions may also vary in different aspects of policy and administration. The main influence of the Prime Minister tends to lie in foreign policy, defence and national security, and in emergencies, like a general strike, abdication, the Rhodesian U.D.I. and the Falkland Islands crisis. His influence fluctuates in economic policy, and he does not usually intervene in person in such matters as education and housing. Thus the Prime Minister is more powerful than any other Minister, and than most combinations of Ministers, but less powerful than the Cabinet collectively.

Mr. Harold Wilson sees the role of the Prime Minister as "if not that of a managing director, as that of an executive chairman." According to Mr. Wilson power still lies in the Cabinet, but as the Cabinet must keep the confidence of the House, it is the Cabinet in Parliament. The power-base lies in his party in Parliament. A similar conclusion is reached by

---

[43] *The Diaries of a Cabinet Minister*, Vol. I, p. 616.

[44] George Brown, *In My Way* (1971), p. 169.

[45] Mackintosh, *op. cit.* p. 630. Mackintosh pictures the form of government as a cone with the Prime Minister at the apex. Beneath him is a widening series of rings of senior Ministers, the Cabinet, its committees, non-Cabinet Ministers and departments. The only one above the level of the civil service that has formal existence is the Cabinet, *op. cit.* p. 543.

Lord Gordon-Walker, who finds "the Cabinet in Parliament" to be the central feature of the British Constitution.

If we cannot say we have Prime Ministerial government, still less can we say we have "Presidential government."[46] The American Presidential or Congress system is so different from ours that comparison is difficult. The American party system is looser, the President has a fixed term of office and he is not immediately dependent on Congress.

[46] See Berkeley, *The Power of the Prime Minister; cf.* Max Beloff, "Prime Minister and President" (Hugh Gaitskell Memorial Lecture, University of Nottingham, 1966), who admits, however, that the pull of the American pattern is very strong.

CHAPTER 17

CENTRAL GOVERNMENT DEPARTMENTS AND CIVIL-SERVICE

I. CENTRAL GOVERNMENT DEPARTMENTS

Offices of state

The origin of the great offices of state is to be found in the royal household of the Saxon and Norman Kings. The Saxon King had his chamberlain, steward, marshal and cupbearer, and the Norman King his Lord High Steward, Lord Great Chamberlain, Constable and Marshal. In the process of time these offices became hereditary and honorary. Their public, as distinct from purely personal, services came to be performed by others who duplicated the offices and were appointed from time to time on merit and received a salary.[1] Two of the original offices survive as non-political appointments, namely, the hereditary Earl Marshal (Duke of Norfolk) in charge of styles and precedence, and the Lord Great Chamberlain.[2] Their "doubles," Master of the Horse and Lord Chamberlain (former censor of plays), and the Lord Steward of the Household (who was the "double" of the Lord High Steward who presided over the trial of peers and the Court of Claims which determined the validity of claims to perform honorary services at coronations)[3] used to be political officers. The offices of Treasurer, Comptroller and Vice-Chamberlain of the Household are still often given to members of the House of Commons who, together with the Joint Parliamentary Secretaries and the Junior Lords of the Treasury, act as Government Whips.

As the work of government grew, it became necessary for the King to employ secretaries and other officers to transact state business as distinct from the administration of the affairs of the royal household. The earliest and most important of these was the Lord Chancellor, who, as the King's chaplain, was both an educated "clerk" and the Keeper of the King's Conscience. His name is derived, says Holdsworth,[4] from "the *cancelli* or screen behind which the secretarial work of the royal household was carried on." To him was entrusted the custody of the Great Seal, under which the most important state documents were issued. For more than 400 years the use of the Privy Seal, held by the Lord Privy Seal, was a necessary prerequisite before letters patent under the Great

---

[1] Maitland, *Constitutional History*, pp. 390–394; S. B. Chrimes, *Introduction to the Administrative History of Medieval England* (1952), describes the origins and early history of the royal household; Randolph S. Churchill, *They Serve the Queen* (1953) is a popular account.

[2] This office descends in tail general, daughters, in the absence of a male heir, taking as co-heirs. Since 1779, the office has been vested in co-heirs who nominate a deputy to perform the duties of the office.

[3] Such claims are now dealt with by a Committee of Claims, the office of Lord High Steward having become merged in the Crown in the reign of Henry IV. Trials in the House of Lords were, thereafter, presided over by a peer appointed Lord High Steward, *pro hac vice*.

[4] Holdsworth, *History of English Law* (5th ed.), Vol. I, p. 37.

Seal could be passed. Other secretaries were appointed in Plantagenet times, and they also held royal seals for affixing to appropriate documents. There is strictly only one office of Secretary of State, although it may be held by several persons whose powers are, with certain statutory exceptions,[5] equal and interchangeable. They are appointed by the delivery of three seals, namely, the signet, a lesser seal and a small seal called the *cachet*.[6]

For the functions of finance and defence the great officers of state were the Lord High Treasurer, the Lord High Admiral, the Lord High Constable and the Earl Marshal. The first office has for a long time been in commission, the work being carried on by the First Lord of the Treasury and the Chancellor of the Exchequer, the two most important members of the Treasury Board. Queen Elizabeth II assumed the title of Lord High Admiral in 1964 in order to perpetuate the name of an office dating back 600 years, which would otherwise have been lost on the abolition of the Lords Commissioners of the Admiralty. The Constable and the Earl Marshal issued regulations for the army. A Lord High Constable is still appointed for the coronation ceremony. The courts in which the Constable and Earl Marshal enforced military discipline disappeared soon after the Bill of Rights, giving way to the courts martial which now function under statutory authority. The only vestige is the High Court of Chivalry presided over by the Earl Marshal to try complaints of usurpation of arms. The English law of arms is a civilian jurisdiction.[7] This court was revived in 1954 after a lapse of 223 years.[8]

The Lord President of the Council is in charge of the Privy Council Office, but his departmental duties are light. He is usually a member of the Cabinet entrusted by the Prime Minister with special duties.

The office of Lord Privy Seal was considered important in the Middle Ages, but under modern statutes the use of the Privy Seal is no longer necessary. The Lord Privy Seal has now no departmental duties. He is generally used by the Prime Minister for special duties, although he is not always in the Cabinet. The same applies to the Chancellor of the Duchy of Lancaster, whose department administers the estates of the Duchy of Lancaster, and who appoints and removes justices of the peace within the Duchy.[9]

Until recent times some of our government departments were boards that were once committees of the Privy Council.[10] The last survival was the Board of Trade, dating from the seventeenth century. The post of

---

[5] A recent example is provided by the Somerset House Act 1984 which confers powers of leasing part of Somerset House on the Secretary of the State for the Environment.

[6] For an account of these seals and their use, see Anson, *Law and Custom of the Constitution*, (4th ed. Keith) Vol. II, Pt. I, pp. 182–184. See also, F. M. G. Evans, *The Principal Secretary of State* (1923).

[7] See G. D. Squibb Q.C., *The High Court of Chivalry*.

[8] *Manchester Corporation* v. *Manchester Palace of Varieties* [1955] P. 133; verbatim report, The Heraldry Society, 1955. The Earl Marshal (Duke of Norfolk) was assisted by his surrogate (Lord Goddard D.C.L.), who delivered judgment, and the officers of arms. Lord Goddard was Lord Chief Justice, but he sat as a Doctor of Civil Law, his robes including a scarlet D.C.L. (Oxon.) gown, white bow tie and bob wig. The comparable Scottish Court of the Lord Lyon has always retained—and retains—an active jurisdiction.

[9] Justices of the Peace Act 1979, s.68.

[10] Anson, *op. cit.* p. 160.

President of the Board of Trade is now held by the Secretary of State for Trade and Industry.

The Sovereign can create Ministers by virtue of the prerogative; but statutory authority is requisite in most cases, first, because it will usually be necessary for the Minister and his staff to be paid out of money voted by Parliament, and, secondly, because of the statutory restrictions on the number of Ministers who may sit in the House of Commons. The transfer of functions from one department to another, the dissolution of departments and the change of titles of Ministers are effected by Order in Council made under the Ministers of the Crown Act 1975.

The Ministry

As has been seen in connection with a discussion of the disqualification for membership of the House of Commons,[11] the number of holders of ministerial posts is now about one hundred, including Cabinet Ministers, Ministers not in the Cabinet and Junior Ministers. The Ministerial and other Salaries Act 1975 provides a salary to the Chancellor of the Exchequer, the Secretaries of State and the holders of the senior ministerial posts mentioned in Schedule 1. Ministers of State are to be paid such an amount (within the statutory limits) "as the First Lord of the Treasury may determine." The same applies to the Lord President of the Council, the Lord Privy Seal, the Chancellor of the Duchy of Lancaster or the Paymaster-General "when not a member of the Cabinet." Parliamentary Secretaries are also provided with a salary.

Part V of Schedule 1 to the Act fixes a maximum number of paid Ministers in various classes, namely: holders of the office of Secretary of State; Ministers of State; Treasury Secretaries; Junior Lords of the Treasury; Assistant Government Whips in the House of Commons; Lords in Waiting; and Parliamentary Secretaries.

Organisation of Government Departments

Ministers

At the head of each political department or Ministry is the Secretary of State or Minister. He is, of course, a member of the government and changes with the Ministry of the day; he may also be a member of the Cabinet.

Parliamentary Secretaries[12]

Under the Secretary of State or Minister will be one or more Parliamentary Under-Secretaries of State or Parliamentary Secretaries. As their name implies, they are members of one or other of the Houses of Parliament; they are Junior Ministers[13] who change with the government of the day. They assist their chief in the parliamentary or political side of his work, as well as the administration of his department. In the

---

[11] *Ante*, Chap. 9.

[12] These are to be distinguished from Parliamentary Private Secretaries, whose office is unofficial and unpaid: See N. Henderson, *The Private Office* (1984).

[13] Junior Ministers include the Parliamentary Secretaries, Treasury Commissioners (Government Whips) and H.M. Household.

past they were usually chosen from the House in which the Minister did not sit,[14] but since 1945 Junior Ministers, as well as the heads of departments, have been recruited mainly from the lower House.

The Treasury[15]

The Treasury is the department entrusted by the Crown and by Parliament with the supervision and control of national finance. It is regarded as the senior government department. The Treasury was an offshoot of the Exchequer, which in the twelfth century was the *Curia Regis* sitting for revenue purposes. The Upper Exchequer, which audited and managed the King's accounts, developed into the Court of Exchequer; while the Lower Exchequer, from which the Treasury emerged, was concerned with the receipt of the royal revenue. The office of Treasurer, which is described in the *Dialogus de Scaccario* (1177), has been in commission since 1714.[16]

The Treasury Board consists of the First Lord of the Treasury (nowadays invariably the Prime Minister), the Chancellor of the Exchequer (whose office dates from Henry III) and five Junior Lords. Meetings of the full Board became less frequent by the beginning of the nineteenth century, and were discontinued altogether in 1856. The Junior Lords (who act mainly as Government Whips) still have certain formal functions, such as signing Treasury warrants.[17] The management of the department is in the hands of the Chancellor of the Exchequer, who is also Under-Treasurer. In addition to his traditional duties with regard to national finance, the Chancellor in recent times has acquired responsibilities relating to economic policy.[18] Under him are the Chief Secretary, the Economic Secretary, the Minister of State and the Parliamentary Secretary (and Government Chief Whip in the Commons).

The Treasury Solicitor's Office, which is staffed by barristers and solicitors, is available to the departments for legal advice and conveyancing. The senior official of this department is H.M. Procurator-General and Treasury Solicitor,[19] who in the latter capacity acts as solicitor to government departments in litigation. He is also appointed *Queen's Proctor* in connection with proceedings for Admiralty droits and matrimonial causes. The general practice is that departments whose work is primarily the administration of detailed legal rules have their own solicitor's department, while departments whose legal problems are likely to be involved with policy rely on the Treasury Solicitor, whose position is independent of department policy.

[14] A Minister has not the right—as he has in some constitutions—to address both Houses of the legislature.
[15] Lord Bridges, *The Treasury* (2nd ed., 1966) H. Roseveare, *The Treasury* (1969); J. Barnett, *Inside the Treasury* (1982).
[16] Holdsworth *History of English Law* (5th ed.), Vol. I, pp. 42–44.
[17] Treasury Instruments (Signature) Act 1849.
[18] *Control of Public Expenditure* Cmnd. 1432, (1961). And see *Report of the Machinery of Government Committee* Cmd. 9230 (1918), pp. 18–19; S. H. Beer, *Treasury Control: The Co-Ordination of Financial and Economic Policy in Great Britain* (1956); Sir Ivor Jennings, *Cabinet Government* (3rd ed.), Chap. 7.
[19] G. Drewry, "The Office of Treasury Solicitor" (1980) 130 N.L.J. 753. The Solicitor to the Secretary of State performs similar functions in relation to Scotland.

Parliamentary Counsel to the Treasury. The First Parliamentary Counsel and his staff, whose office was established in 1869, acting under instructions from the sponsoring Departments are responsible for drafting Government Bills and much subordinate legislation; also for statute law revision and consolidation Bills.[20]

Management and Personnel Office

A Civil Service Department was established in 1968 to take over from the Treasury responsibility for the management of the Home Civil Service. In 1981 responsibility for pay and allied matters was restored to the Treasury while the remaining functions of the Department were transferred to a newly established Management and Personnel Office. The Prime Minister is Minister for the Civil Service, and approves the appointment of the two senior posts in each department. In Mrs. Thatcher's administration at the beginning of the 1985–1986 Session of Parliament the Chancellor of the Duchy of Lancaster was also attached to the Management and Personnel Office. The Permanent Secretary is the Secretary to the Cabinet who is also Head of the Home Civil Service. The selection of civil servants continues to be done by the Civil Service Commission set up in 1855.

Proposals were made in the summer of 1986 for the creation of a single minister for the Civil Service to take over the responsibilities at present shared between the Prime Minister's Office, the Management and Personnel office and the Treasury. It was also argued that the Head of the Home Civil Service should be a full Permanent Secretary under the new Minister and one person should no longer combine the positions of Head of the Home Civil Service and Secretary to the Cabinet.[20a]

Lord Chancellor's Department

The Lord Chancellor's Department is usually classified under the Supreme Court rather than as a government department. The civil service staff includes the Clerk of the Crown in Chancery and Permanent Secretary to the Lord Chancellor; the Deputy Clerk of the Crown in Chancery; the Secretary for Ecclesiastical Patronage (who is also the Prime Minister's Appointments Secretary); the Secretary of Commissions of the Peace; and solicitors and legal assistants.

Law Officers' department[21]

The Law Officers are legal advisers to the Crown and the Houses of Parliament. They hold ministerial posts and therefore change with the government. The Law Officers consist of the Attorney-General[22] and Solicitor-General for England and Wales, and the Lord Advocate and

---

[20] Sir Harold S. Kent, *In on the Act* (1979). Legislation relating to Scotland is drafted in the Lord Advocate's Department.

[20a] *Civil Servants and Ministers: Duties and Responsibilities,* Seventh Report from the Treasury and Civil Service Committee.

[21] J. Ll. J. Edwards, *The Law Officers of the Crown* (1964); and review by Sir Jocelyn Simon in (1965) 81 L.Q.R. 289; Sir Elwyn Jones, "Office of Attorney-General" (1969) 27 C.L.J. 43. J. Ll. J. Edwards, *The Attorney-General, Politics and the Public Interest* (1984).

[22] Under the Northern Ireland Constitution Act 1973, s.10 the Attorney-General for England and Wales is also Attorney-General for Northern Ireland.

Solicitor-General for Scotland.[23] The Attorney-General is the leader of the Bars in England and Northern Ireland.[24] They are consulted by the various departments on legal problems. Although they are responsible to Parliament, they should not be questioned on particular criminal cases until after the proceedings are ended.

The Attorney-General was so called in 1461. The Solicitor-General dates from 1515. Formerly the Law Officers were summoned to advise the House of Lords,[25] and there was some doubt whether the Attorney-General was entitled to sit in the Commons; but his attendance in the Lords is dispensed with except in peerage cases, and his right to sit in the Commons has not been seriously questioned since Bacon's time.[26] The Solicitor-General also became entitled to sit in the Commons during the seventeenth century, although strictly he need not be a member.

The Attorney-General represents the Crown in civil proceedings in which it is specially concerned. His consent is necessary for the prosecution of certain offences, e.g. under the Official Secrets Acts. In criminal proceedings he or the Solicitor-General, or their deputies, prosecute in important cases.[27] It is the practice for the Attorney-General to lead in treason and important constitutional cases. He may intervene in a private law suit whenever it may affect the prerogatives of the Crown. He may at the invitation or with the permission of the court intervene whenever a suit raises any question of public policy on which the executive has a view which it wishes to bring to the notice of the court.[28] The Attorney-General can sue on behalf of the public to enforce public rights. He may lend his name to such an action at the instance of a private citizen—a proceedings known as a relator action. If he refuses to consent to the bringing of a relator action, his refusal cannot be questioned in the courts.[29] Owing to the increase in their ministerial work, the Law Officers appear less frequently in criminal cases nowadays. The Attorney-General advises the House of Lords Committee for Privileges in peerage claims, and is a member of the House of Commons Committee of Privileges.[30] The Director of Public Prosecutions[31] is responsible to him for the exercise of his duties. Actions may be brought against the Attorney-General under the Crown Proceedings Act 1947 if there is no appropriate department in respect of matters relating to the

---

[23] Other Officers are the Attorney-General of the Duchy of Lancaster, the Attorney-General and Solicitor-General of the County Palatine of Durham, and the Attorney-General to the Prince of Wales in respect of the Duchy of Cornwall.

[24] The leader of the Scottish Bar is the Dean of the Faculty of Advocates.

[25] They still are, but they attend for ceremonial purposes only.

[26] Lord Campbell, Lives of the Chancellors, III, Chap. 54.

[27] R. v. Wilkes (1768) Wilson 322; (1678) 4 Burr. 2829.

[28] Adams v. Adams [1971] P. 188, 197, per Sir Jocelyn Simon P.

[29] Gouriet v. U.P.W. [1978] A.C. 435 post p. 700. On the right of local authorities to bring actions to protect public rights see post, p. 599. On the Attorney-General's right to stop a trial by entering a nolle prosequi see post, p. 372.

[30] The Attorney-General may also demand a trial at Bar (i.e. now, before a divisional court); he has the right to choose the venue for any civil or criminal proceedings in which the Crown is concerned; and he may file an ex officio criminal information. This procedure was last used in the case of a criminal libel against King George V: R. v. Mylius, The Times, February 2, 1911. See further Attorney-General's Written Answer to Parliamentary Question: November 12, 1984.

[31] See post, Chap. 19.

Crown in England, Wales and Northern Ireland only; he cannot be sued in relation to matters concerning acts of the Crown in its other dominions.[32] The Law Officers are forbidden by Treasury Minute to engage in private practice, but they receive a salary which takes some account of the loss entailed by being unable to practice. Fees which are paid when they appear in contentious business on behalf of the Crown are set-off against their salaries.

The better opinion is that the Attorney-General should not be in the Cabinet because of his quasi-judicial functions with regard to prosecutions, and also because it is desirable to separate the giving of advice from those who decide whether to act on the advice.[33] Indeed it must be open to question in view of his unfettered discretion to refuse to initiate proceedings[34] and his power to terminate criminal proceedings[35] whether the appointment should not be non-political. The Attorney-General (and sometimes the Solicitor-General) is a member of the Legislative Committee of the Cabinet, and he is sometimes a member of (and in any case frequently attends) the Home Affairs Committee.[36] As regards the decision whether or not to institute public prosecutions, the Attorney-General acts in a quasi-judicial capacity, and does not take orders from the government that he should or should not prosecute in particular cases.[37] In political cases, such as sedition, he may seek the views of the appropriate Ministers, but he should not receive instructions. He may consider broad questions of public policy, but he should not be influenced by party political factors. Ministers may not be questioned in the House as to what advice the Law Officers have given, although they may be asked whether they have sought such advice. The fact that the Attorney-General consults informally and selectively, emphasises that both the decision whether or not to prosecute and the responsibility are his alone.[38] This makes his position anomalous in relation to the doctrine of collective ministerial responsibility.

The Solicitor-General is a subordinate of the Attorney-General, and often gives a joint opinion with him on legal matters. His duties are in general similar to those of the Attorney-General, and he usually succeeds to that post if it becomes vacant. He may deputise for the

---

[32] *Trawnik* v. *Gordon Lennox* [1985] 2 All E.R. 368 (C.A.).

[33] Lord Silkin, a former Attorney-General, has expressed the view that it is desirable that the Attorney-General should normally be in attendance at Cabinet meetings: [1984] P.L. 179, 183. Sir Michael Havers thinks it is better that the Attorney-General attend only on the occasions when his advice is specifically required so that he will be listened to as an impartial adviser: *The Times*, December 6, 1984.

[34] *Ante*, p. 331.

[35] *Post*, p. 372.

[36] The Attorney-General is in the Cabinet in some Commonwealth countries, *e.g.* Australia. In other Commonwealth countries the corresponding office is not regarded as a political one.

[37] H.C.Deb., Vol. 600, col. 58 (1959). And see Lord MacDermott, *Protection from Power under English Law*, pp. 25–40; Sir Patrick Devlin, *The Criminal Prosecution in England*, p. 18; Marshall and Moodie, *Some Problems of the Constitution*, pp. 172–180; Jennings, *op. cit.* pp. 236–257. J. Ll. J. Edwards, *The Attorney-General, Politics and the Public Interest*, (1984) Chap. 11.

[38] Sir Jocelyn Simon, *loc. cit.*

Attorney-General if the office becomes vacant, or if the latter is absent or ill or authorises him to do so.[39]

The Scottish Law Officers have analogous functions with regard to Scotland.

Home Office[40]

The work of the two Secretaries of State then existing was divided in 1782 into home affairs and foreign affairs. The Home Secretary collaborates with the Secretary of State for Scotland in certain matters affecting that country. He is the medium of communication between the British Government, the Channel Islands and the Isle of Man.[41] Formerly, this arrangement extended to Northern Ireland.

The Home Secretary exercises the prerogative of the Queen's pleasure in many ways. He is the channel of communication between the subject and the Queen for addresses and petitions, and he authorises many of the royal commissions set up from time to time to examine various matters. He is also the medium of communication between the Church of England and the Queen, its Governor.

Matters connected with the administration of justice which are not dealt with by the Lord Chancellor or the Attorney-General come within the sphere of the Home Secretary. He is ultimately responsible for the maintenance of the Queen's peace, and in this capacity he is in direct control of the Metropolitan Police and indirectly supervises the local police forces, and provides for co-operation between magistrates, the police, special constables and the armed forces. He exercises the prerogative of mercy.[42] He is also responsible for prisons[43] and other penal institutions; the treatment of offenders; the probation and aftercare services and legislation on criminal justice.

The Home Secretary administers the law relating to naturalisation, supervision of aliens, immigration, deportation and extradition.[44]

The Home Office, being the residuary department of state, is concerned with many other miscellaneous matters under various statutes, including the supervision of the fire service; civil defence; community relations; the law relating to parliamentary and local government elections; explosives; fire-arms; dangerous drugs; liquor licensing; betting and gaming; and such other internal affairs of England and Wales as are not assigned to other departments.

Foreign and Commonwealth Office[45]

The Foreign Office is concerned with the formulation and conduct of foreign policy, and controls the Foreign Service. The Foreign Office combined in 1968 with the Commonwealth Office which (as the Com-

[39] Law Officers Act 1944.
[40] Sir Frank Newsam, The Home Office (1954); Report of the Committee on the Machinery of Government Cd. 9230 (1918), pp. 63–78.
[41] See, now, post, Chap. 36.
[42] See post, p. 373.
[43] See R. v. Home Secretary, ex p. McAvoy [1984] 1 W.L.R. 1408.
[44] Post, Chap. 23.
[45] Lord Strang, The Foreign Office (1955); Sir Charles Jeffries, The Colonial Office (1956); Sir George Fiddes, The Dominions and Colonial Offices (1926); J. A. Cross, Whitehall and the Commonwealth (1967).

monwealth Relations Office) had merged with the Colonial Office in 1966. The Secretary of State maintains direct contact with the diplomatic representatives of foreign and Commonwealth states, with foreign and Commonwealth governments, and with the British diplomatic representatives overseas. He is in constant communication with the Queen, the Prime Minister and the Cabinet on all important matters relating to foreign and Commonwealth affairs. The Passport Office is a subordinate directorate. The Permanent Under-Secretary is head of the Diplomatic Service.

The Secretary of State is ultimately responsible for the government of British dependent territories.

Privy Council Office

The Lord President is, at present, also Leader of the House of Lords. The Lord Privy Seal is also the Leader of the House of Commons.

Scottish Office[46]

Scottish affairs were formerly conducted by the Home Secretary and various other departments. In 1885 a Secretary for Scotland, with a Scottish Office, was created by statute, and in 1926 he was made a Secretary of State. The office also includes a Minister of State and three Under-Secretaries. The department has offices in London and Edinburgh.

The Secretary of State for Scotland is the keeper of the Great Seal of Scotland, which the Union with Scotland Act requires to be used for Scottish matters. He exercises in Scotland the powers of a Secretary of State (especially the Home Secretary), except in certain matters such as aliens.[47]

Welsh Office[48]

A Minister for Welsh Affairs was appointed in 1951, but for some years this office was held by the Minister of another department, usually of Cabinet rank. Since 1964 there has been a Secretary of State for Wales, and, at present two Under-Secretaries. The department has offices in London and Cardiff.

Ministry of Defence

Churchill assumed the title of Minister of Defence on becoming Prime Minister in 1940. The Ministry was constituted in 1946 to co-ordinate the policy of the three services and to allocate funds between them. Later its responsibility was extended to the defence programme and the administration and efficiency of the armed forces as a whole. The Ministry of Defence was reconstituted in 1964 as a unified department, absorbing the Admiralty, War Office and Air Ministry.[49] There is a Sec-

---

[46] *The Thistle and the Crown: A History of the Scottish Office* (H.M.S.O. 1985). See also *post*, Appendix on Devolution.

[47] See *e.g.* the unsuccessful attempt by the applicant in *R. v. Secretary of State for the Home Dept. ex. p. Hosenball* [1977] 1 W.L.R. 766 to raise in the Scottish courts the validity of the deportation order made by the Home Secretary. [*The Times*, February 24, 1977.]

[48] See *post*, Appendix on Devolution.

[49] *Central Organisation for Defence* Cmnd. 2097 (1963); Defence (Transfer of Functions) Act 1964.

retary of State for Defence, who is a Cabinet Minister, two Ministers of
State and two Parliamentary Under-Secretaries.

Departments of the Environment and Transport

The Department of the Environment was formed in 1970 by the merg-
ing of the Ministries of Housing and Local Government, Public Building and Works, and Transport. Its head is the Secretary of State for the
Environment. The Department also includes the Minister for Environment, Countryside and Local Government, the Minister for Housing
and Construction, Urban Affairs and three Under-Secretaries of State.
In 1976 the responsibilities of the Department for Transport were transferred to a newly established Department of Transport under a Secretary of State for Transport.

Other government departments

The other government departments not specifically dealt with here
are mainly the creation of twentieth-century statutes. Their powers are
almost entirely statutory, and their functions are sufficiently indicated
by their names. They are subject to frequent transformation, amalgamation, division or mere change of name.[50] Some of the more important
at the time of writing are: the Department of Health and Social Security
(formed out of the Ministry of Health and Social Security) under the
Secretary of State for Social Services; the Department of Employment;
the Department of Education and Science; the Department of Energy;
the Ministry of Agriculture, Fisheries and Food; and the Department of
Trade and Industry.

Advisory Committees

There are about 250 permanent bodies outside the Civil Service set up
to give advice direct to senior Ministers.[51]

II. THE CIVIL SERVICE

The detailed administration of the work of a government department is
carried out by civil servants. Although, like Ministers, they are servants
of the Crown, civil servants are called "permanent" since their appointment is non-political and in practice lasts during good behaviour, as
opposed to Ministers and Parliamentary Secretaries who are responsible to Parliament and change office with the government.

The backbone of the department or Ministry is the secretariat under
the Permanent Under-Secretary of State or Permanent Secretary. There
used to be a hierarchy of administrative, executive and clerical classes;
but following the recommendation of the Fulton Report,[52] these classes
(up to and including the level of assistant secretary) have been merged
in one administrative group. Departments with technical functions will
also require a number of inspectors, accountants, contract officers, pro-

---

[50] *The Organisation of British Central Government 1914–1969* (ed. F. M. G. Willson, 2nd ed.,
1968).
[51] *Advisory Committees in British Government* (P.E.P. 1965).
[52] Cmnd. 3638, (1971).

duction officers, scientific officers and others with professional or technical qualifications.[53]

Who is a civil servant?

A civil servant is one kind of Crown servant, and whether or not a person is a Crown servant depends on the facts of the case.[54] There is no formal definition of "Crown servant," although we may say that generally he is appointed by or on behalf of the Crown to perform public duties which are ascribable to the Crown; usually, but not necessarily, he is paid by the Crown out of the Consolidated Fund or out of moneys voted by Parliament. Modifications must be made for servants of the Crown in overseas territories.[55]

All civil servants are Crown servants, but not all Crown servants are civil servants, for the term is not applied to Ministers, their Parliamentary Secretaries and Parliamentary Private Secretaries, or other holders of political offices, nor to members of the armed forces.[56] Local government officers and the employees of public corporations are not civil servants, although the nature of their work and their conditions of employment bear many similarities.[57] A subordinate engaged by, or working under, a civil servant is himself a servant of the Crown and not of his superior.[58]

Civil servants may be established (*i.e.* entitled to statutory superannuation), non-established or temporary. In *Mulvenna* v. *The Admiralty*[59] it was held by a Scottish court that a civilian telephone attendant employed at a naval dockyard had the same immunity from the arrestment of wages as a Crown servant. Civil servants who may render the Crown liable in actions of tort by third parties are those appointed directly or indirectly by the Crown and paid wholly out of the Consolidated Fund or moneys provided by Parliament, or holding an office which would normally be so paid: Crown Proceedings Act 1947, s.2(6).[60]

Appointment and conditions of service

Recruitment and examination of entrants to the Civil Service is conducted by the Civil Service Commission, established by Order in Council in 1855. Negotiations and consultation about pay[61] and conditions of employment take place through the Civil Service National Whitley

---

[53] The personnel of the royal household and the government departments in the United Kingdom is given in *The British Imperial Calendar and Civil Services List*, published annually by H.M.S.O.

[54] *Post*, Chap. 35.

[55] H. H. Marshall, "The Legal Relationship between the State and its Servants in the Commonwealth" (1966) 15 I.C.L.Q. 150.

[56] N. E. Mustoe, *Law and Organisation of the British Civil Service*, p. 26.

[57] See *The British Civil Servant*, and *Public Enterprise* (ed. Robson); *The Civil Service in Britain and France* (ed. Robson).

[58] *Lane* v. *Cotton* (1701) 1 Ld.Raym. 646; *Bainbridge* v. *Postmaster-General* [1906] 1 K.B. 178; *Town Investments* v. *Department of the Environment* [1978] A.C. 359.

[59] 1926 S.C. 824.

[60] *Post*, Chap. 35.

[61] See *Dudfield* v. *Ministry of Works* (1964) 108 S.J. 118; *The Times*, Jan. 24, 1964, *Kendall* v. *Morgan*, *The Times*, December 3, 1980.

Council which consists of an official side (senior officials representing the Crown as employer) and the staff side (which consists of representatives of the recognised civil service staff associations and unions).

At common law civil servants hold office, as do other Crown servants, at the pleasure of the Crown, but in practice established civil servants are not dismissed except for misconduct. Although there has been controversy about the status of the civil servant and the nature of the relationship between the Crown and civil servants,[62] the House of Lords has recently indicated very clearly its view that the employment of civil servants is governed by the royal prerogative; *Council of Civil Service Unions* v. *Minister for the Civil Service*[63]; *Hughes* v. *D.H.S.S.*[64]

The detailed legal and other rules regulating the Civil Service are contained in statutes, law reports (*e.g.* common law relating to liability), prerogative Orders in Council and Regulations made thereunder, Treasury Minutes and Circulars. The Civil Service is governed mainly under prerogative powers through the Management and Personnel Department,[65] although maximum salaries and superannuation benefits are prescribed by statute.

At common law a civil servant was dismissible at pleasure,[66] even if he was engaged for a definite period that had not yet expired.[67] There was an implied term to this effect, resting on public policy and not on the incapacity of the Crown to bind itself.[68] In such cases no action for damages lay against a superior Crown servant[69]; nor, apparently, did an action lie for breach of warranty of authority.[70] The Employment Protection ((Consolidation) Act 1978, s.138 provides that the provisions of that Act shall apply, with certain modifications, to Crown employment and Crown employees. Thus the rights not to be unfairly dismissed and to membership of a trades unions apply to civil servants. A Minister may issue a certificate that certain employment, or the employment of a cer-

---

[62] It has been argued that the civil servant, like the soldier, has a status and is subject to a special kind of law contained in Royal Warrants, Treasury Minutes, etc.; and on the other hand that civil servants (unlike the armed forces) are not governed by prerogative; *cf.* L. Blair, "The Civil Servant—A Status Relationship?" (1958) 21 M.L.R. 265; "The Civil Servant—Political Reality and Legal Myth" [1958] P.L. 32; J. D. B. Mitchell, *The Contracts of Public Authorities*, pp. 32 *et seq.*; H. Street, *Governmental Liability*, pp. 111 *et seq.*; Margaret Cowan, "Contracts with the Crown" (1965) C.L.P. 153.

[63] [1985] A.C. 374.

[64] [1985] A.C. 716, 782 *per* Lord Diplock.

[65] *Ante*, p. 330.

[66] *Shenton* v. *Smith* [1895] A.C. 229 (P.C.); *Gould* v. *Stuart* [1896] A.C. 575; *Nobrega* v. *Att.-Gen.* (1966) 10 W.I.R. 187; *Kodeeswaran Chelliah* v. *Att.-Gen. of Ceylon* [1970] A.C. 1111 (P.C.).

[67] *De Dohsè* v. *R.* (1886) 3 T.L.R. 114 (H.L.); *Dunn* v. *The Queen* [1896] 1 Q.B. 116 (C.A.); *Hales* v. *R.* (1918) 34 T.L.R. 589 (C.A.); *Denning* v. *Secretary of State for India* (1920) 37 T.L.R. 138 (Bailhache J.); *Terrell* v. *Secretary of State for the Colonies* [1953] 2 Q.B. 482; Nettheim, "*Dunn* v. *The Queen* Revisited" (1975) 35 C.L.J. 253.

[68] *Inland Revenue Commission* v. *Hambrook* [1956] 2 Q.B. 640; *Att.-Gen. for New South Wales* v. *Perpetual Trustee Co. Ltd.* [1955] A.C. 457 (P.C.); *Riordan* v. *War Office* [1961] 1 W.L.R. 210 (C.A.); *Denning* v. *Secretary of State for India* (1920) 37 T.L.R. 138; *Rodwell* v. *Thomas* [1944] K.B. 596; *Thomas* v. *Att.-Gen. of Trinidad and Tobago* [1982] A.C. 113.

[69] *Gidley* v. *Lord Palmerston* (1822) 3 Brod. & B. 275; *Worthington* v. *Robinson* (1897) 75 L.T. 446.

[70] *Dunn* v. *MacDonald* [1896] 1 Q.B. 555; see also *Kenny* v. *Cosgrave* [1926] I.R. 517; *Riach* v. *Lord Advocate*, 1932 S.C. 138; *The Prometheus* (1949) 182 Ll.L.Rep. 859 (C.A.).

tain person, requires to be excepted from the provisions of the Act for the purpose of safeguarding national security.

The right of Civil Servants to be members of unions was considered by the House of Lords in *Council of Civil Service Unions* v. *Minister for the Civil Service*[71] (the *G.C.H.Q.* Case). The statutory protection accorded to the right had been withdrawn by certificates issued by the Secretary of State for Foreign and Commonwealth Affairs, on the ground of national security, under the Employment Protection Act 1975, s.121(4) and the Employment Protection (Consolidation) Act 1978, s.138(4). The validity of those certificates was not pursued by the Unions before the House of Lords, where the issue was the legality of an instruction given by the Minister for the Civil Service that the terms and conditions of service of civil servants serving at the G.C.H.Q. should be revised to exclude membership of any trade union other than a departmental staff association approved by the Director of the G.C.H.Q. The instruction was given under an Order in Council made in 1982, which authorised the Minister for the Civil Service to "make regulations or give instructions . . . for controlling the conduct of the Service and providing for . . . the conditions of service of all such persons . . . " The House of Lords held that the Order in Council had been made under Royal Prerogative. The House then considered whether the Unions were entitled, in principle, to be consulted before an instruction changing the terms of employment was made and, secondly, if such a right were held to exist, whether national security justified the Minister in refusing to consult. The staff had been encouraged to join unions since G.C.H.Q. was established in 1947. They had, in the words of Lord Diplock, prima facie . . . :

> "a legitimate expectation that they would continue to enjoy the benefits of such membership and of representation by those trade unions in any consultations and negotiations with representatives of the management of that government department as to changes in any term of their employment. So, but again prima facie only, they were entitled, as a matter of public law under the head of 'procedural propriety,' before administrative action was taken on a decision to withdraw that benefit, to have communicated to the national trade unions by which they had therefore been represented the reason for such withdrawal, and for such unions to be given an opportunity to comment on it."

The Minister, however, argued that events leading up to the decision to issue the instruction justified the belief that national security required action without consultation. In his account of those events Lord Fraser referred to industrial action on seven occasions between 1979 and 1981 which took various forms: one-day strikes, work to rule and overtime bans. The most serious disruption occurred on March 9, 1981, when about 25 per cent. of the staff went on one-day strike and, according to Sir Robert Armstrong, the Secretary to the Cabinet, who made an affidavit in the proceedings, parts of the operations at

---

[71] [1985] A.C. 374.

G.C.H.Q. were virtually shut down. The industrial action was taken mainly in support of national trade unions, when they were in dispute with the government about conditions of service of civil servants generally, and not about local problems at G.C.H.Q. In 1981 especially it was part of a campaign by the national trade unions, designed to do as much damage as possible to government agencies including G.C.H.Q. The seriousness of the intended challenge to the security system of this country could be gauged from the literature issued at the time by the C.C.S.U. The House of Lords held that, although the courts cannot decide what national security requires in a particular case, they can require evidence that a ministerial decision was in fact taken on that ground. The evidence before them established that the Minister's decision had been based on considerations of national security and that she was, therefore, justified in issuing her instruction without consultation. Lord Fraser and Lord Roskill both referred to another argument—that consultations were not required because they would have been futile since the statements of union leaders showed that they would not have been willing to come to a "no-strike agreement" with the minister. Lord Fraser thought, without expressing a final view, that consultations would have been futile; Lord Roskill abstained from expressing any opinion.

Can a civil servant recover arrears of pay for services rendered, either during the subsistence of his employment or after his employment has been terminated? It was held in an early case that no action lay against the East India Company to recover a non-statutory pension.[72] In *Mulvenna* v. *Admiralty*[73] it was held that the rule that members of the forces may only claim on the bounty of the Crown and not for a contractual debt applies also to civilians as an implied condition in the terms of their contract. The latter case was followed in *Lucas* v. *Lucas and High Commissioner for India*,[74] where Pilcher J. held that the salary due to a civil servant was not a debt for the purpose of garnishee proceedings. The decision was much criticised, and in any case it could have been based on another ground.[75] In *Sutton* v. *Att.-Gen.*,[76] on the other hand, the House of Lords assumed that a civil servant's pay was recoverable, and the only question in that case was, how much was due. The question was regarded as one of the interpretation of an enlistment circular for Post Office[77] telegraphists in the first war. None of the judgments

---

[72] *Gibson* v. *East India Co.* (1839) 5 Bing.N.C. 262.

[73] 1926 S.C. 842.

[74] [1943] P. 68.

[75] D. W. Logan, "A Civil Servant and his Pay" (1945) 61 L.Q.R. 240. *Cf.* Crown Proceedings Act 1947, s.27(1). *Cf. Considine* v. *McInerney* [1916] 2 A.C. 162 (H.L.); *ex gratia* pension paid to civil servant should be taken into account in fixing the amount of compensation under Workmen's Compensation Acts.

[76] (1923) 39 T.L.R. 294. Considered by the Privy Council in *Kodeeswaran Chelliah* v. *Att.-Gen. of Ceylon* [1970] A.C. 1111, where dicta of Lord Blackburn in *Mulvenna* v. *The Admiralty, ante* were strongly criticised as being a *non sequitur* from the Crown's right to terminate a contract of service at will. It was not necessary in *Dudfield* v. *Ministry of Works* and *Faithful* v. *Admiralty* (1964) 108 S.J. 118, to decide whether industrial civil servants could have sued their departments for arrears of pay, because there was no contractual right to receive the negotiated increases that were postponed by a "pay pause."

[77] The Post Office was at that time a government department.

raised the question whether the pay was legally recoverable at all, and counsel for the Crown do not seem to have argued the point. Lord Goddard C.J. expressed the opinion *obiter* in *Terrell* v. *Secretary of State for the Colonies*[78] that a civil servant who had been dismissed could recover arrears of salary up to the time of dismissal, and in *Inland Revenue Commissioners* v. *Hambrook*[79] that civil servant (although perhaps not a soldier) could recover for services rendered on a *quantum meruit*.

On the question whether at common law there subsists between the Crown and a civil servant a contractual relationship, a contract of service the terms of which are enforceable, the decisions and dicta are conflicting. In *Sutton* v. *Att.-Gen.* (*ante*) all the judgments in the Court of Appeal and the House of Lords assumed that there was a contract of employment and that the terms as regards pay were enforceable. On the other hand, Pilcher J. in *Lucas* v. *Lucas* (*ante*) based his judgment on the ground that there was no contract the terms of which could be enforced by the civil servant. Further support for the latter view is to be found in the G.C.H.Q. Case where "It was common ground before your Lordships, although it was not common ground below, that there was no contractual relationship between the Crown and the staff at the G.C.H.Q."[80]

As far as third parties are concerned, a contractual relationship may be said to exist between the Crown and a civil servant. The House of Lords in *Owners of S.S. Raphael* v. *Brandy*,[81] where a stoker on board a merchant ship was injured in an accident, held that the retainer he was paid as a member of the Royal Naval Reserve must be taken into account as earnings under a concurrent contract of service in assessing compensation under the Workmen's Compensation Act 1906. In *Picton* v. *Cullen*[82] the Irish Court of Appeal held that, where a judgment debt had been entered against a school teacher employed by the Board of National Education, the court could appoint a receiver over an instalment of salary that had actually become due, although there could be no attachment of such future income.

In *Reilly* v. *The King*[83] the appellant had been appointed a member of a statutory board in Canada for a term of five years, but after two years the board was abolished by a Canadian statute. His office was therefore terminated, and he brought a petition of right for breach of contract. It was held that further performance of the contract had become impossible by legislation, and the contract was therefore discharged. The case is notable for Lord Atkin's dicta[84] because, although they were *obiter*, he was delivering the opinion of a strong Judicial Committee. He said that "in some offices at least it is difficult to negative some contractual rela-

---

[78] [1953] 2 Q.B. 482, 499.

[79] [1956] 2 Q.B. 641, 654. See further *Nobrega* v. *Att.-Gen.* (1966) 10 W.I.R. 187; *Kodeeswaran Chelliah* v. *Att.-Gen. of Ceylon ante*.

[80] *C.C.S.U.* v. *Minister for the Civil Service* [1985] A.C. 374, 419, *per* Lord Roskill.

[81] [1911] A.C. 413. The Crown itself would have been expressly not liable under the Workmen's Compensation Act.

[82] [1900] 2 I.R. 612.

[83] [1934] A.C. 176 (P.C.).

[84] *Ibid.* at pp. 179–180. And see *per* Denning J. in *Robertson* v. *Minister of Pensions* [1949] 1 K.B. 227, 231.

tions, whether it be as to salary or terms of employment on the one hand, and duty to serve faithfully and with reasonable care and skill on the other." Lord Atkin also said: "If the terms of the appointment definitely prescribe a term and expressly provide for a power to determine 'for cause' it appears necessarily to follow that any implication of a power to dismiss at pleasure is excluded." This statement is difficult to reconcile with Lord Goddard's statement in *Terrell's* case[85] that, where the Crown has the right to dismiss at pleasure, it cannot be taken away by any contractual arrangement made by a Secretary of State or an executive officer or department of state.

The answer seems to be that statute or letters patent creating an office may prescribe a definite term with power to determine "for cause" within that period, excluding the implication of a power to dismiss at will, but no such binding arrangement can be made *ad hoc* between an officer on behalf of the Crown and a prospective Crown servant. In *Riordan* v. *War Office*[86] Diplock J. gave reason for saying that the Crown might be held bound by other terms in the regulations than length of service or dismissal, and that the civil servant for his part would be bound by the express terms; but this also was *obiter*.

Security and confidentiality

In the *G.C.H.Q.* case, *supra*, the House of Lords was concerned with the activities of unions which, in the view of the responsible ministers, constituted a threat to national security. A different type of threat may be posed by the activities of individual civil servants, whether motivated by political ideals or not.

Security measures have been taken since the war in respect of civil servants engaged on work that is vital to the national security who are suspected of being sympathetic to Communism or Fascism. If after inquiry the Minister finds that a civil servant engaged on such work is politically unreliable he may (subject to an appeal to three advisers) either post him to non-secret work or dismiss him.[87] Where a breach of security is known to have occurred in the public service, the Prime Minister may ask the Security Commission[88] to investigate and make recommendations.

The interests of national security may clearly require civil servants to refrain from communicating to third parties what they learn in the course of their official duties, although the obligation of confidentiality imposed on civil servants goes far beyond matters of national security. On taking up their appointment civil servants are required to sign a declaration that they have read extracts from, and will observe, the Official Secrets Acts. The scope of these Acts and proposals for reform will be considered later.[89] The Civil Service Pay and Conditions of Ser-

[85] *Terrell* v. *Secretary of State for the Colonies* [1953] 2 Q.B. 482, 497–500.
[86] [1959] 1 W.L.R. 1046; [1959] 3 All E.R. 552. And see note by C. Grunfeld in (1960) 23 M.L.R. 194.
[87] *Statement on the findings of the Conference of Privy Councillors on Security* Cmd. 9715 (1955).
[88] *Ante*, p. 318.
[89] *Post*, p. 483.

vice Code sets out the obligations of civil servants with regard to refraining from disclosure of official information. Disclosure of information in return for reward may constitute a criminal offence under the Prevention of Corruption Acts 1906 and 1916 and the Public Bodies Corrupt Practices Act 1889.

It has been argued that civil servants should be able to justify the disclosure of official information where to do so is "in the public interest."[90] The prosecution of Mr. Clive Ponting in 1985 for sending departmental papers to an M.P.[91] directed attention to the possibility of conflict between the duty of the civil servant to his department or minister and his duty as a citizen to reveal wrong-doing. As a result of that case a "note of guidance"[92] was circulated by Sir Robert Armstrong, Secretary to the Cabinet and head of the Home Civil Service. The note emphasised that the Civil Service as such has no constitutional personality or responsibility separate from the duly elected government. The determination of policy is the responsibility of the minister, and in the determination of policy the civil servant has no constitutional responsibility or role distinct from that of the minister. Civil servants are in breach of their duty, and damage their integrity, if they deliberately withhold relevant information or give ministers other advice than the best, or seek to obstruct or delay a decision simply because they do not agree with it.

That there may be circumstances in which a citizen finds himself faced with a moral imperative which is inconsistent with the law of the land was recognised judicially by Sir John Donaldson M.R. in *Francome* v. *Mirror Group Newspapers Ltd.*[93] But, the Master of the Rolls added, such circumstances must be "very rare." He might have added that they also require the courage to defy the law openly and accept the consequences. The anonymous informer hardly shows the courage of his moral conviction and by his conduct may well involve others in suspicion.

In a rather different position is the unfortunate civil servant who "leaks" information with the authorisation and approval of his or her minister, as happened during the Westland affair when the Director of Information at the Department of Trade and Industry "leaked" parts of a confidential letter from the Solicitor General with the approval of Mr. Brittan, then Secretary of State for Trade and Industry. In theory—and in this case, in practice—the minister is responsible for such wrongdoing and should accept responsibility by resigning. Normally the circumstances of such a leak would not come to light since the minister most closely concerned would have no interest in pursuing the matter. In this instance, however, a full inquiry was undertaken by Sir Robert Armstrong, Secretary to the Cabinet and Head of the Home Civil Service at the request of the Prime Minister. The extent to which pressure from the Attorney-General resulted in the setting-up of the inquiry is

---

[90] Y. Cripps, "Disclosure in the Public Interest: The Predicament of the Public Sector Employee" [1983] P.L. 600.
[91] *Post*, p. 485.
[92] *The Times*, Feburary 26, 1985.
[93] [1984] 1 W.L.R. 892, 897.

unlikely ever to be known fully.[94] Newspaper reports spoke of threats to "have the police into No. 10," if an inquiry were not established.

Political activities of civil servants

In determining the extent to which civil servants shall be free to take part in political activities, the government has to effect a compromise between two conflicting principles. On the one hand it is desirable in a democratic society "for all citizens to have a voice in the affairs of the state and for as many as possible to play an active part in public life"; on the other hand "the public interest demands the maintenance of political impartiality in the Civil Service and confidence in that impartiality as an essential part of the structure of government in this country."[95]

(i) As we have seen, civil servants are disqualified by statute from sitting in the House of Commons, and by the Servants of the Crown (Parliamentary Candidature) Order 1960 a civil servant must resign his office before standing as a candidate for a parliamentary election.

(ii) With regard to other political activities, civil service regulations issued in 1953 distinguished, first, between three classes of civil servants and, secondly, between national and local politics.[96]

(a) The administrative and professional grades, and those members of the executive and clerical grades who work with them and come into contact with the public, are restricted from taking an active part in national politics. They may be permitted where possible to take part in local government, but most would probably not have time to do so.

(b) The remaining members of the executive and clerical grades may be permitted to take part in national as well as local politics (except parliamentary candidature), subject to a code of "discretion" with regard to the expression of views on governmental policy and national political issues.

(c) The minor, manipulative and industrial grades are free to engage in both national and local politics (other than parliamentary candidature), except when on duty or on official premises or while wearing uniform. They remain subject, of course, to the Official Secrets Acts.

A Committee to review the rules governing the participation in political activities of Civil Servants was set up in May 1976, under the Chairmanship of Sir Arthur Armitage and reported in 1978,[97] recommending the relaxation of the rules then in force. In 1984 the Government agreed that the numbers in the most severely restricted class should be substantially reduced. All but a small part of the restricted class are now subject to the rules governing class (b).

---

[94] For references to the Westland affair, see, *ante*, p. 311. To ensure her full co-operation with the inquiry the Director of Information was offered immunity from prosecution by the Attorney-General for any criminal offences which her evidence might show her to have committed: *post*, p. 373.

[95] *Report of the Committee on the Political Activities of Civil Servants* (Masterman), Cmd. 7718 (1949).

[96] *Political Activities of Civil Servants* Cmd. 8783 (1953). The merger of the administrative and executive classes following the Fulton report (*ante*, p. 000) has not affected these regulations.

[97] (1978) Cmnd. 7057.

CHAPTER 18

THE ARMED FORCES

I. THE ARMED FORCES AND THE CONSTITUTION

History of the armed forces[1]

After the Norman Conquest came the feudal levy, which could be called upon to serve within England for 40 days in the year. All military tenants served at their own expense. Henry I is reported to have invented scutage (shield money) whereby personal service was dispensed with, and the military tenant, instead of serving himself, had to equip and maintain a knight. Scutage was a subject of grievance in Magna Carta, and after 1215 it was supposed not to be levied without the consent of the Great Council and afterwards of Parliament. At the Restoration military tenures were abolished,[2] and with them scutage. The militia was retained by the Militia Act 1661.[3] James II raised an army by voluntary enlistment, which caused such apprehension that a standing army in time of peace was forbidden by the Bills of Rights 1688, which declared that "the raising or keeping of a standing army within the Kingdom in time of peace, unless it be with the consent of Parliament, is against law."

It was soon realised, however, that a standing army was necessary for the national safety. The solution was found in the Mutiny Act 1688, which authorised the keeping of an army for one year, and provided that the Act should not exempt any officer or soldier from the ordinary process of law. This force was maintained (except for short intervals) by annual Mutiny Acts down to 1879 and continued by the Army Act 1881, which formed to a large extent a military code. The Act of 1881 was annually renewed with amendments by short Army (Annual) Acts down to 1956. Meanwhile the Royal Air Force was established as a separate force by Parliament in 1917. Authority for this was renewed by Army and Air Force (Annual) Acts down to 1956.

From 1955 Parliament, instead of passing annual Acts, gave the Army and Air Force Acts a maximum life of five years, subject to annual renewal by Order in Council. Such Orders in Council must be laid in draft before Parliament and are subject to an affirmative resolution by each House. The current legislation is to be found in the Armed Forces Act 1986.

Legislation was necessary to legalise not only the raising of a standing army but also the enforcement of military discipline, which would infringe the common law, as well to provide the money for its upkeep. The practice of authorising the keeping of an army for one year at a time was devised to ensure the observance of the convention that Parliament

---

[1] Clode, *Military Forces of the Crown* (1869); Bl.Comm. I, Chap. 13; Anson, *Law and Custom of the Constitution*, II, ii (4th ed. Keith), pp. 199–222; *Manual of Military Law, Part II, Section 1*; Maitland, *Constitutional History*, pp. 275–280.

[2] Tenure Abolition Act 1660.

[3] Repealed by the Statute Law (Repeals) Act 1969, except sections 4 and 9.

should be summoned at least once a year. The money is now provided by annual Appropriation Acts, which might be taken to imply the lawfulness of maintaining the forces for which funds are appropriated.

Public opinion has never feared the existence of a standing navy, so that the history of the Royal Navy has been free from constitutional problems.[4] It was the customary duty of the coastal towns, and especially the Cinque Ports, to provide ships and men in an emergency. The maintenance of the Navy has always been, and still is, within the royal prerogative; but terms of enlistment and naval discipline are now regulated by the Naval Discipline Act, and of course in modern times the money has come from Parliament. The Naval Discipline Act is now subject to continuance in the same manner as the Army and Air Force Acts.[5]

Conscription, or compulsory military service, was introduced by statute in both world wars.[6]

The law relating to the various Reserve forces, the Territorial Army and the Ulster Defence Regiment is now to be found in the Reserve Forces Act 1980 and the Reserve Forces Act 1982.

Legal position of members of the armed forces

The control of the armed forces is part of the royal prerogative: *Chandler* v. *D.P.P.*[7] Despite the power of judicial review claimed in the G.C.H.Q.[8] case over acts done by virtue of the royal prerogative it is probable that the direction and disposition of the forces of the Crown will continue to be regarded as non-justiciable. The prerogative powers in relation to such matters as the training of the forces are preserved by the Crown Proceedings Act 1947. The provisions of the Employment Protection (Consolidation) Act 1978 relating to such matters as unfair dismissal, do not apply to members of the armed forces.[9]

Contract of service

Officers are commissioned by the Crown. They may be dismissed at the pleasure of the Crown, but may not resign their commission without leave.[10]

Other ranks are recruited—apart from statutory conscription or compulsory national service—by voluntary enlistment by attestation before a recruiting officer. Enlistment being a civil contract, its terms cannot be varied without the consent of the soldier, but he can be discharged at the pleasure of the Crown.

---

[4] But *cf. The Case of Ship Money* (R. v. *Hampden*) (1637) 3 St.Tr. 825.

[5] Armed Forces Act 1976.

[6] The prerogative of "impressment" or "pressing" mariners into the Navy whenever the public safety requires, has never been abolished by statute although in practice it is obsolete: *R.* v. *Broadfoot* (1743) 18 St.Tr. 1323; Foster, *Crown Law,* p. 154; *R.* v. *Tubbs* (1776) Cowp. 512, *per* Lord Mansfield; *Ex p. Fox* (1793) 5 St.Tr. 276, *per* Lord Kenyon; *Barrow's Case* (1811) 14 East 346; Foster, 158.

[7] [1964] A.C. 763 (H.L.). *Ante* p. 270; *Post,* p. 484.

[8] *C.C.S.U.* v. *Minister for Civil Service* [1985] A.C. 374; *ante,* p. 265 and p. 338.

[9] s.138(3).

[10] *Vertue* v. *Lord Clive* (1769) 6 Burr. 2472; *R.* v. *Cuming, ex p. Hall* (1887) 19 Q.B.D. 13; *Hearson* v. *Churchill* [1892] 2 Q.B. 144; *Marks* v. *Commonwealth of Australia* (1964) 111 C.L.R. 548.

No action lies against the Crown to enforce the terms of service for damages for wrongful dismissal or to recover arrears of pay.[11]

Subject to ordinary law

A soldier becomes subject to military law, but he also remains bound by the ordinary civil and criminal law.[12] It is hardly correct to say that he is governed by two systems of law, for military law is part of the law of the land.[13] Statutory exceptions include the right to make an informal will on actual military service[14] or at sea, exemption from jury service, and the right to a "service qualification" under the Representation of the People Act 1983, ss.14–17.[15]

Superior orders as a defence

A member of the armed forces is primarily bound to obey the civil (*i.e.* non-military) law, even though such obedience may render him liable to be tried by court-martial. "A soldier for the purpose of establishing civil order," it has been said,[16] "is only a citizen armed in a particular manner." Although military regulations forbid the firing on rioters except under an order from a magistrate who is present, the existence or absence of a magistrate's order neither justifies what is done nor excuses what is not done in the eyes of the civil law. The soldier may therefore sometimes find himself in a dilemma if he is ordered by a superior officer to do something which is unlawful; and the question has arisen how far, if at all, he can plead obedience to superior orders—one of the first duties of a soldier—as a defence. In *R. v. Smith*,[17] a case heard by a special tribunal of three civilian judges set up in the Cape of Good Hope during the Boer War, Solomon J. said: "I think it is a safe rule to lay down that if a soldier honestly believes he is doing his duty in obeying the commands of his superior, and if the orders are not so manifestly illegal that he must or ought to have known that they were unlawful, the private soldier would be protected by the orders of his superior officer." In that case it was held that the order to shoot an African if he did not fetch a bridle was not so plainly illegal that the accused would have been justified in the circumstances in refusing to obey it, and it was therefore not necessary to decide whether in the circumstances the order was unreasonable or unnecessary. The accused was therefore not guilty of murder.

In *Keighley v. Bell*,[18] Willes J., a great authority on the common law, said *obiter*: "I hope I may never have to determine that difficult ques-

---

[11] *Grant* v. *Secretary of State for India* (1877) 2 C.P.D. 445; *Mitchell* v. *R.* [1896] 1 Q.B. 121; *Leaman* v. *R.* [1920] 3 K.B. 663. See Z. Cowen, "The Armed Forces of the Crown (1950) 66 L.Q.R. 478.

[12] The subjection of the soldier to English law is indeed wider than that of a civilian in that the soldier takes English law with him wherever he goes; *post*, p. 349.

[13] *Burdett* v. *Abbot* (1812) 4 Taunt. 401, *per* Mansfield C.J.; *Grant* v *Gould* (1792) 2 H.Bl. 98, *per* Lord Loughborough.

[14] *Re Wingham* [1949] P. 187. *Re Jones decd.* [1981] Fam. 7. (Privilege extends to service in N. Ireland: actual military service not confined to war between sovereign states).

[15] *Ante* p. 189 and see Crown Proceedings Act 1947, s.10; *post*, Chap. 35.

[16] *Report of the Commission on the Featherstone Riots* (1893) C. 7234. See also *Att.-Gen. of Northern Ireland's Reference (No. 1 of 1975)* [1977] A.C. 105; *post*, Chap. 19.

[17] [1900] Cape of Good Hope S.C. 561.

[18] (1866) 4. F. & F. 763, 790.

tion, how far the orders of a superior officer are a justification. Were I compelled to determine that question, I should probably hold that the orders are an absolute justification in time of actual war—at all events, as regards enemies or foreigners—and I should think, even with regard to English-born subjects of the Crown, unless the orders were such as could not legally be given. I believe that the better opinion is, that an officer or soldier acting under the orders of his superior—not being necessarily or manifestly illegal—would be justified by his orders." If modified to the extent that the soldier's belief in the lawfulness of the order must be reasonable. Willes J.'s opinion would probably be accepted by the legal profession.

The soldier's obligation is to obey any *lawful* command. "Lawful command" is described in the *Manual of Military Law*[19] as a command which is not contrary to English or international law and is justified by military law. "A superior has the right," says the *Manual*, "to give a command for the purpose of maintaining good order or suppressing a disturbance or for the execution of a military duty or regulation or for a purpose connected with the welfare of troops . . . . If a command is manifestly illegal the person to whom it is given would be justified in questioning and even refusing to execute it." With regard to a soldier's responsibility for carrying out an order which is not manifestly illegal, on the other hand, the *Manual* disagrees with the dictum in *Keighley* v. *Bell (ante)*, but says that "It may give rise to a defence on other grounds, *e.g.* by establishing a claim of right made in good faith in answer to a charge of larceny, or by negativing a particular intent which may be a complete defence or reduce the crime to one of a less serious nature, or by excusing what appears to be culpable negligence.[20]

Whichever view is accepted it is obvious that a soldier may be placed in a serious dilemma, with the prospect of being proceeded against in the ordinary courts if he commits a crime or tort and of being court-martialled if he refuses to obey the command. So far as criminal liability is concerned, the soldier's position is somewhat mitigated by the power of the Crown to enter a *nolle prosequi* or to pardon after conviction, and the jurisdiction of the Courts-Martial Appeal Court to hear appeals from courts-martial which provides a forum for resolving any conflict of jurisdictions. Ultimately, the House of Lords could dispose of the problems as regards liability in tort as well.

With regard to liability for war crimes, *i.e.* violations of the principles of international law relating to warfare, the edition of the *Manual of Military Law* still issued at the beginning of the Second World War allowed superior orders as a valid defence. An amendment drafted by the Law Officers of the Crown was made in 1944 so as to read: "Obedience to the orders of a government or of a superior, whether military or civil, or to a national law or regulation, affords no defence to a charge of committing a war crime but may be considered in mitigation of punishment."[21] The Nuremberg Charter similarly provided that:

---

[19] Part I (12th ed., 1972). The *Manual* is not authoritative: *R.* v. *Tucker* [1952] 2 All E.R. 1074; 36 Cr.App.R. 192.

[20] Citing *R.* v. *James* (1839) 8 C. & P. 131; *R.* v. *Trainer* (1864) 4 F. & F. 105.

[21] Part III, p. 176. *Cf.* Shakespeare, *Henry V*, Act IV, sc. 1, 11. 138–140.

"The fact that the defendant acted pursuant to orders of his government or of a superior shall not free him from responsibility, but may be considered in mitigation of punishment" (Art. 8). The true test, said the International Military Tribunal, is not the existence of the order, but whether moral choice is in fact possible.[22]

II. MILITARY LAW AND COURTS-MARTIAL

Military law[23]

When a person joins the armed forces he becomes subject to the special code of military law in addition to the ordinary law. The objects of military law are disciplinary and administrative. It provides in the first place for the maintenance of discipline and good order among the troops, and secondly, for administrative matters such as terms of service, enlistment, discharge and billeting.

The sources of military law are statutes supplemented by the Queen's Regulations and royal warrants. The laws and customs of war established by international conventions (*i.e.* multilateral treaties) are also required to be observed by members of the forces. It was argued in *R. v. Durkin*[24] that there is also a "common law of the army," and the Courts-Martial Appeal Court did not reject it, but the existence of such a common law is doubtful. In addition to legally binding rules, there is "the custom of the service and military usage."

Employed civilians and followers with the Regular forces anywhere when on active service are subject (with modifications) to Part II of the Army Act, which deals with discipline and the trial and punishment of military offences. All civilians listed in Schedule 5 to the Army Act are subject to the "civil offences" and certain specific offences within the jurisdiction of the Act, when in the command area of any part of the Regular forces abroad at any time. These include employed persons, persons attached to the forces for the purposes of their profession, and resident families. Civilians may be awarded a fine or any punishment less than imprisonment by court-martial, or fined if dealt with summarily by "the appropriate superior authority."[25] The Armed Forces Act 1976 provides for the creation of Standing Civilian Courts to deal with civilians who would otherwise be liable to be tried by courts-martial.[26]

The civil courts have jurisdiction to determine in proceedings brought before them, *i.e.* in the exercise of their supervisory jurisdiction by way of judicial review and in actions for damages in tort, whether a person is subject to military law.

Courts-martial

The King's troops in medieval times were governed by regulations or articles of war issued by the King and administered in the Court of the

---

[22] See Viscount Kilmuir, *Nuremberg in Retrospect* (Holdsworth Club, University of Birmingham, 1956), pp. 14–17.

[23] It is convenient here to speak of "military law," which is the law of the Army; but similar considerations apply to Air Force law and Naval discipline.

[24] [1953] 2 Q.B. 364 (C.-M.A.C.).

[25] See G.J. Borrie, "Courts-martial, civilians, and civil liberties" (1969) 32 M.L.R. 350.

[26] ss.6–8.

Constable and the Marshal, two hereditary officers of state.[27] The office of Constable became extinct in the reign of Henry VIII, but the Court of the Constable and the Marshal continued to exist. During the early eighteenth century the Court ceased to function although it was never formally abolished.[28] From that time articles of war governing Army discipline were issued under parliamentary authority. The modern system of courts-martial for the trial of persons subject to *military law* was established by the Mutiny Act 1688, and the Army Act 1881 combined it with the statutory articles of war.

The courts-martial that exist today enforce military law, Air Force law and Naval discipline, but do not administer martial law, although there has inevitably been some confusion on the point. "As a matter of etymology," says Maitland,[29] "*marshall* has nothing whatever to do with *martial*—the marshall is the master of the horse—he is marescallus, mareschalk, a stable servant—while of course Martial has to do with Mars, the God of war. Still, when first we hear of martial law in England, it is spelt indifferently *marshall* and *martial*, and it is quite clear that the two words were confused in the popular mind . . . ." Courts-martial have jurisdiction to try and to punish persons subject to military law for two classes of offences: first, military offences created by Part II of the Army Act, as to which their jurisdiction is exclusive; and secondly, under certain conditions, civil offences (*i.e.* criminal offences under non-military law), as to which their jurisdiction in this country is concurrent with the civil (*i.e.* non-military) courts.[30] Civil offences are acts or omissions punishable by the law of *England*, even where the accused is a Scottish soldier in a Scottish regiment stationed in Scotland.[31] Courts-martial have no jurisdiction, however, to try cases of treason, murder, manslaughter, treason-felony or rape committed in the United Kingdom.

The members of a court-martial are judges of both fact and law. Counsel may appear for either side. Courts-martial must observe the rules of English criminal law relating to the admissibility of evidence, although these were largely designed for use in jury trial. Witnesses and other persons whose duty it is to attend a court-martial are entitled to the same immunities and privileges as in the High Court, in particular, immunity from being sued for defamation.

The Army Act does not restrict the offences for which persons may be tried in the civil courts, or the jurisdiction of the civil courts to try a per-

---

[27] For the history of this Court, see Holdsworth, *History of English Law* (5th ed.), Vol. I, pp. 573–580. See also Clode, *Military Forces of the Crown*, Vol. I, pp. 76–77; Richard O'Sullivan, *Military Law and the Supremacy of the Civil Courts* (1921), pp. 1–12.

[28] The last case tried by the Court of the Marshal appears to be *Sir H. Blount's Case* (1737) 1 Atk. 296. *Cf.* Court of Chivalry, *ante*, p. 327.

[29] *Constitutional History*, p. 266. For martial law, see *post*, Chap. 19.

[30] See, *e.g.* R. v. *Gordon-Finlayson* [1941] 1 K.B. 171; *Cox* v. *Army Council* [1963] A.C. 48 (H.L., on appeal from C.-M.A.C.). With regard to murder committed abroad, see R. v. *Page* [1954] 1 Q.B. 170 (C.-M.A.C.); *cf.* M.J. Prichard, "The Army Act and Murder Abroad" (1954) C.L.J. 232.

[31] Army Act 1955, s.70(2); Air Force Act 1955, s.70(2); Naval Discipline Act 1957, s.42(1). For comments on this anomalous position see Sir T.B. Smith, *British Justice: The Scottish Contribution* (1961), pp. 30–33; *Studies Critical and Comparative* (1962), p. 20.

son subject to military law for any offence; but where a person is tried by a civil court the fact that he has been punished by a court-martial must be taken into consideration in awarding punishment. On the other hand, a person subject to military law who has been tried by a civil court may not subsequently be tried by court-martial for the same offence.

A judge-advocate must be appointed to sit on a general court-martial, and may be appointed to sit on a field general court-martial or a district court-martial. The prosecutor and the accused are entitled to the opinion of the judge-advocate on any question of law or procedure, and during the trial he must advise the court on any questions of law or procedure. The judge-advocate advises the court on the law before the court deliberates on its findings. The Judge-Advocate-General advises on the confirmation of the findings and sentences of all court-martial proceedings which are referred to him. His advice is given on the legal aspects, not on the merits of the case.

Courts-Martial may impose the death sentence for a number of offences including treason (outside the United Kingdom), mutiny, serious misconduct in action, and assisting the enemy. No sentence of death has been passed under the Army Act or other Service Discipline Acts since 1953.[32]

Since 1951[33] it has been possible to appeal against conviction by a court-martial to a Courts-Martial Appeal Court, composed of judges of the Court of Appeal and Queen's Bench Division, nominated by the Lord Chief Justice; Lords Commissioners of Justiciary nominated by the Lord Justice General; judges of the Supreme Court of Northern Ireland, nominated by the Lord Chief Justice of Northern Ireland, and other persons of legal experience, nominated by the Lord Chancellor. Appeal lies to the House of Lords with leave of the Appeal Court or the House where the Appeal Court has certified that a point of law of general public importance is involved in the decision and the Court or the House of Lords thinks that the point is one which ought to be considered by the House.[34]

Visiting forces

The Visiting Forces Act 1952 provides that visiting forces belonging to the member states of the Commonwealth and other countries specified by Order in Council under arrangements for common defence (e.g. NATO),[35] may be tried in the United Kingdom by the service courts of their own country according to their own service law; but a death sentence may not be carried out in the United Kingdom unless the law of the United Kingdom provides for the death sentence in such a case. In

---

[32] Army Act 1955 and Air Force Act 1955, ss.24–31 and s.70; Naval Discipline Act 1957, ss.2–4, 9–10 and s.42.

[33] Courts-Martial (Appeals) Act 1951. See now the Courts-Martial (Appeals) Act 1968. See, e.g. R. v. Tucker [1952] 2 All E.R. 1074; 36 Cr.App.R. 192; R. v. Bisset [1980] 1 W.L.R. 335 (unsuccessful attempt to rely on defence of "condonation" by superior officer under Army Act 1955, s.134; for comment on this "most unusual" provision see per Lawton L.J. at p. 339.

[34] E.g. R. v. Garth [1986] A.C. 268 (H.L.).

[35] See G.I.A.D. Draper, Civilians and the Nato Status of Forces Agreement (1966).

R. v. *Thames Justices, ex p. Brindle*,[36] the Court of Appeal held that although the jurisdiction of the relevant military courts under Part I of the Act extended only to members of visiting forces stationed in the United Kingdom, the provisions in Part II of the Act dealing with deserters were not so limited. Hence a deserter from an American army unit stationed in Germany who was arrested in England could properly be handed over to the American army authorities under the Act.

This jurisdiction does not oust the jurisdiction of British criminal courts over such visiting forces except in relation to offences arising in the course of service duty, offences against the person of a member of the same or another visiting force, and offences against the property of the visiting force or of a member of such force; and in these cases the appropriate authority may waive its jurisdiction. British courts may not try a member of a visiting force for an offence for which he has already been tried by his service court.

Civil actions may be brought in the ordinary courts against members of visiting forces; but the Secretary of State for Defence may arrange, under regulations issued by the Lord Chancellor's department, for the settlement of claims in tort.

Supervisory jurisdiction of the High Court

Courts-martial are inferior courts over which the High Court exercises a supervisory jurisdiction, distinct from the system of appeals to the Courts-Martial Appeal Court. This supervisory jurisdiction is exercisable by means of the prerogative writ of habeas corpus and application for judicial review by way of certiorari, prohibition or mandamus.[37] Civil actions may be brought against individual officers for damages for false imprisonment, assault, malicious prosecution, defamation, etc. Criminal proceedings against officers may take the form of a prosecution for *e.g.* murder, manslaughter or assault.

Actions for damages

As regards actions in tort the true principles are probably those stated by McCardie J. in *Heddon* v. *Evans*,[38] an action brought by a private soldier against his commanding officer for false imprisonment and malicious prosecution in confining him to barracks on charges of making a frivolous complaint and conduct to the prejudice of good order and military discipline. His Lordship stated that: (1) an action lies if the court-martial or officer commits what would be a wrong at common law while acting without or in excess of jurisdiction[39]; but (2) no action lies

---

[36] [1975] 1 W.L.R. 1400. See also R. v. *Tottenham Magistrates' Court ex p. Williams* [1982] 2 All E.R. 705 (D.C.) (Magistrate must be satisfied beyond reasonable doubt that prisoner is subject to foreign military law and that there is evidence to justify the bringing of proceedings against him).

[37] See also *post*, Chap. 34.

[38] (1919) 35 T.L.R. 642. McCardie J. went on to hold (although he did not consider it necessary for the decision) that the plaintiff had not established that the defendant did act maliciously or without reasonable and probable cause. A verbatim report is given in R. O'Sullivan, *Military Law and the Supremacy of the Civil Courts* (1921), pp. 43 *et seq*. See P. Hogg, *Liability of the Crown* (1971), pp. 96–98.

[39] *Grant* v. *Gould* (1792) 2 H.Bl. 100.

if the court-martial or officer commits what would be a common law wrong while acting within its or his jurisdiction, even if the act was done maliciously[40] or without reasonable and probable cause.[41] The first proposition His Lordship thought was clear from the authorities as well as on principle. The second proposition he based on five cases, two of them in the Court of Appeal.[42] Only the House of Lords is free to hold that an action will lie for malicious abuse of military authority (within jurisdiction) without reasonable and probable cause.

In *Dawkins* v. *Lord F. Paulet*[43] an officer sued a superior officer for libels contained in letters written by the superior to the Adjutant-General in the course of his duty. The majority of the Court of Queen's Bench (Cockburn C.J. dissenting) held that the civil courts would not interfere in such cases even if the superior officer acted maliciously,[44] first, because the alleged wrong was done in the course of duty, and motive is therefore irrelevant; secondly, on grounds of convenience and public policy, as otherwise a superior officer would be unduly hampered in the performance of his duty; and, thirdly, because the party complaining of injustice has his remedy under military law.

In *Johnstone* v. *Sutton*[45] Lord Mansfield and Lord Loughborough in the Court of Exchequer Chambers gave it as their opinion that even if malice were proved, an action would not lie by a person subject to naval or military law against someone who had used his authority under that law to injure him; but the question was admittedly left undecided. Johnstone, an admiral, had Sutton, a naval captain, put under arrest for disobedience to orders and sent to England to be tried by a court martial. He was honourably acquitted and then brought an action for malicious prosecution against Johnstone. The jury found for Sutton. Johnstone moved for arrest of judgment and was successful in the Court of Exchequer Chamber and the House of Lords, not, however, on the broad ground that an action did not lie against a superior officer but because there had been reasonable and probable cause for the prosecution.

A court-martial would act without jurisdiction if it proceeded against a person who was not subject to military law,[46] or if it was not properly convened or properly constituted in accordance with the relevant Act, or if it convicted a man of an offence which is not an offence under the Act. It would exceed its jurisdiction if it awarded a heavier punishment than it had authority to award.

Habeas Corpus: Judicial Review

As regards the issue of habeas corpus and orders of certiorari and prohibition against courts-martial, post-war cases such as *Martyn's*

---

[40] *Dawkins* v. *Lord F. Paulet* (1869) L.R. 5 Q.B. 94.

[41] *Johnstone* v. *Sutton* (1786) 1 T.R. 493, 510, 784.

[42] *Dawkins* v. *Lord F. Paulet* (*ante*); *Dawkins* v. *Lord Rokeby* (1866) 4 F. & F. 806; *Marks* v. *Frogley* [1898] 1 Q.B. 888; *Fraser* v. *Hamilton* (1917) 33 T.L.R. 431; *Fraser* v. *Balfour* (1918) 34 T.L.R. 502.

[43] (1869) L.R. 5 Q.B. 94.

[44] The occasion was privileged; see *Dawkins* v. *Lord Rokeby* (1875) L.R. 7 H.L. 744.

[45] (1786) 1 T.L.R. 493, 510, 784.

[46] *R.* v. *Wormwood Scrubs Prison (Governor), ex p. Boydell* [1948] 2 K.B. 193.

case[47] and *Elliott's* case[48] indicate that the High Court has gone a long way towards relinquishing its control, by ascribing jurisdiction to a court-martial merely because the applicant was a soldier, by requiring the infringement of some ill-defined "civil right" instead of some right (whether of life, liberty or property) recognised by the law, by refusing relief if there is a remedy provided by military law, and by declining to deal with matters of "military procedure." It has been persuasively argued[49] that in this respect the same general rule should apply to courts-martial as to other inferior courts, namely, that prerogative writs and orders may be issued to prevent a court-martial from exceeding its jurisdiction (see *per* Lord Loughborough in *Grant* v. *Gould*[50]), with the proviso that some right recognised by the civil law is involved and not merely dismissal from the service of the Crown (see *per* Cockburn C.J. in *Re Mansergh*[51]).

Since the courts will not interfere with the administration of military law by the properly constituted tribunals acting within their jurisdiction, the cases in which a soldier has applied to the civil courts successfully have been very rare. It does not appear that mandamus has ever been issued.[52] Prohibition[53] and certiorari[54] have generally been refused.

Habeas corpus, on the other hand, has occasionally been granted.[55] Habeas corpus may be issued, even though the court-martial would be acting within its jurisdiction, if it oppressively delays the trial, but this would not prevent the court-martial from subsequently trying the case.[56]

---

[47] R. v. *Secretary of State for War, ex p. Martyn* [1949] 1 All E.R. 242.

[48] R. v. *O.C. Depot Battalion, R.A.S.C. Colchester, ex p. Elliott* [1949] 1 All E.R. 373.

[49] D.C. Holland "The Law of Courts-Martial" (1950) C.L.P. 173, 174–192.

[50] (1792) 2 H.Bl. 69, 100.

[51] (1861) 1 B. & S. 400.

[52] Mandamus was refused in R. v. *Secretary of State for War* (1891) 2 Q.B. 326; R. v. *Army Council, ex p. Ravencroft* [1917] 2 K.B. 504; and R. v. *Army Council ex p. Sandford* [1940] 1 K.B. 719.

[53] Prohibition was refused in *Grant* v. *Gould* (1792) 2 H.Bl. 69; R. v. *Gordon-Finlayson* [1941] 1 K.B. 171.

[54] *Re Mansergh* (1861) 1 B. & S. 400.

[55] *e.g. Re Porrett* (1844) Perry's *Oriental Cases* 414.

[56] R. v. *O.C. Depot Battalion, R.A.S.C. Colchester, ex p. Elliott* [1949] 1 All E.R. 373, *per* Lord Goddard C.J.

Chapter 19

EMERGENCY POWERS OF THE EXECUTIVE

I. Common Law Powers to Deal with an Emergency

Use of force to maintain public order[1]

Before the development of statutory professional police forces during the nineteenth century, the duty of maintaining internal order rested mainly on the sheriffs, mayors of boroughs and county magistrates, who were charged with the duty of suppressing riots and dispersing unlawful assemblies. This duty has never been expressly abrogated, but in practice the function of maintaining order is now the responsibility of the local chief constable.[2] Force must not be used unless necessary, and then only in a degree proportionate to the necessity. Those who adopt excessive or cruel measures will be criminally liable (*Wright* v. *Fitzgerald*[3]), but if the right amount of force is applied, incidental assaults or trepasses will be justified. It is only as a last expedient that the civil authority should invoke the assistance of the military.

At the time of the Gordon Riots in 1780 Wedderburn, the Attorney-General, advised that as soldiers are also citizens they may lawfully be used to prevent felony, even without the Riot Act proclamation being read. The military, if invoked, should act under the direction of the civil authority (usually a magistrate): they should not, in ordinary cases, fire without his orders, nor fail to fire when ordered by him. Exceptional circumstances may exist which make it the duty of the troops to ignore or act in independence of the orders of the magistrate. In *R.* v. *Kennett*[4] Lord Mansfield laid it down that magistrates who neglected their duty of "reading the Riot Act" were guilty of misdemeanour. Alderman Kennett, Lord Mayor of London, was convicted of neglect of duty in failing to act during the Riots and releasing some prisoners, but he died before sentence was passed.

In *R.* v. *Pinney*[5] the Mayor of Bristol was charged with neglect of duty

---

[1] G. Marshall, *Constitutional Conventions* (1984) Ch. 9; D. Bonner, *Emergency Powers in Peacetime* (1985); C.J. Whelan, "Military Intervention in Industrial Disputes," (1979) 8 Ind. L.J. 222; S. L. Greer, "Military Intervention in Civil Disturbances: The Legal Basis Reconsidered," [1983] P.L. 573; K. Jeffery and P. Hennessy, *States of Emergency: British Governments and Strikebreaking since 1919* (1983).

[2] *Post* Chap. 21.

[3] (1799) 27 St.Tr. 759; Forsyth, *Cases and Opinions on Constitutional Law, p. 557; and cf. Wolfe Tone's Case* (1798) 27 St.Tr. 613, 624–625.

[4] (1781) 5 C. & P. 282. The Riot Act 1714 was repealed by the Criminal Law Act 1967; *post* Chap. 27.

[5] (1832) B. & Ad. 947. See also *Case of Armes* (1597) Pop. 121. Mayors were formerly *ex officio* magistrates. And see the charge of Tindal C.J. to the Bristol Grand Jury, as reported in 3 St.Tr.(N.S.) 11, approved by Willes J. in *Phillips* v. *Eyre* (1870) L.R. 6 Q.B. 1, 15. (Ct.Exch.Ch.). The plaintiff, in the latter case brought a civil action for damages against the defendant, the former Governor of Jamaica, for assault and false imprisonment in the course of suppressing rebellion. The defendant successfully pleaded an Act of Indemnity passed by the legislature of Jamaica; *post*, p. 740.

in failing to suppress a serious riot, directed in the first instance against the Recorder who had expressed unpopular views in Parliament about parliamentary reform. "A person, whether a magistrate or peace officer, who has the duty of suppressing a riot," Littledale J. told the jury, "is placed in a very difficult situation; for if, by his acts, he causes death, he is liable to be indicted for murder, or manslaughter, and if he does not act he is liable to an indictment on an information for neglect. He is, therefore, bound to hit the exact line between excess and failure of duty." The jury found that the Mayor had acted "according to the best of his judgment, with zeal and personal courage," and acquitted him. A prosecution for such neglect of duty is in fact extremely rare.

The common law principles, particularly in relation to the use of military force, were explained in the report of the commission appointed to report on the disturbances at Featherstone Colliery, near Wakefield, during a coal strike in 1893. All the available Yorkshire constables were concentrated at Doncaster, and the Home Secretary (Asquith) at the request of the local magistrates approved the sending of an infantry platoon. A magistrate, who was present with the troops, appealed repeatedly to the crowd to cease destroying property; the proclamation in the Riot Act was read; a bayonet charge proved unavailing; and as the defensive position held by the soldiers was becoming untenable and the complete destruction of the colliery was imminent, the magistrate gave orders to the commander to fire. Two men on the fringe of the crowd were killed. The coroners' juries disagreed on whether there had been sufficient reason for the troops to fire. Asquith appointed a Special Commission consisting of Lord Justice Bowen (afterwards Lord Bowen), Haldane (later Lord Chancellor), and Sir Albert Rollitt, M.P., a solicitor.[6] "Officers and soldiers," said the Commissioners in their Report,[7] "are under no special privileges and subject to no special responsibilities as regards this principle of the law. A soldier for the purpose of establishing civil order is only a citizen armed in a particular manner. . . . One salutary practice is that a magistrate should accompany the troops. The presence of a magistrate on such occasions, although not a legal obligation, is a matter of the highest importance. . . . The question whether, on any occasion, the moment has come for firing on a mob of rioters, depends, as we have said, on the necessities of the case. . . . An order from the magistrate who is present is required by military regulations . . . but the order of the magistrate has at law no legal effect. Its presence does not justify the firing of the magistrate is wrong. Its absence does not excuse the officer to fire when the necessity exists. . . . The justification of Captain Barber and his men must stand or fall entirely by the common law [i.e. it was not affected by the Riot Act]. Was what they did necessary, and no more than was necessary, to put a stop or to prevent felonious crime? In doing so, did they exercise all ordinary skill and caution, so as to do no more harm than could reasonably be avoided?" The Commission exonerated the magistrates, officers and troops from blame.

---

[6] H. H. Asquith, Memories and Reflections, Vol. I, p. 130.
[7] (1893) C. 7234. See also Lynch v. Fitzgerald [1938] I.R. 382, per Hanna J.

In *Attorney-General for Northern Ireland's Reference (No. 1 of 1975)*,[8] which concerned the use of force by soldiers to effect an arrest under the Northern Ireland (Emergency Provisions) Act 1973, Lord Diplock, speaking of the position at common law, said[9]:

> "There is little authority in English law concerning the rights and duties of a member of the armed forces of the Crown when acting in aid of the civil power; and what little authority there is relates almost entirely to the duties of soldiers when troops are called on to assist in controlling a riotous assembly. Where used for such temporary purposes it may not be inaccurate to describe the legal rights and duties of a soldier as being no more than those of an ordinary citizen in uniform. But such a description is in my view misleading in the circumstances in which the army is currently employed in aid of the civil power in Northern Ireland. In some parts of the province there has existed for some years now a state of armed and clandestinely organised insurrection against the lawful government of Her Majesty by persons seeking to gain political ends by violent means, that is by committing murder and other crimes of violence against persons and property. . . . In theory it may be the duty of every citizen when an arrestable offence is about to be committed in his presence to take whatever reasonable measures are available to him to prevent the commission of the crime; but the duty is one of imperfect obligation and does not place him under any obligation to do anything by which he would expose himself to the risk of personal injury, nor is he under any duty to search for criminals or seek out crime. In contrast to this a soldier who is employed in aid of the civil power in Northern Ireland is under a duty, enforceable under military law, to search for criminals if so ordered by his superior officer and to risk his own life should this be necessary in preventing terrorist acts. For the performance of this duty he is armed with a firearm, a self-loading rifle, from which a bullet, if it hits the human body, is almost certain to cause serious injury if not death."

Although the duty on a private citizen may be described as one of imperfect obligation, it was held in *R. v. Brown*[10] to be an indictable misdemeanour for a bystander to refuse to aid a police officer in suppressing a riot, if reasonably called upon by him to do so. Alderson B. said that liability for this offence requires three conditions: (i) the constable must actually see a breach of the peace committed by two or more persons; (ii) there must be a reasonable necessity for the constable to call on other persons for assistance; and (iii) the defendant must have refused to render assistance without any physical impossibility or lawful excuse. It is immaterial whether the help the defendant could have

---

[8] [1977] A.C. 105. The common law rule had been replaced by the Criminal Law (Northern Ireland) Act 1967, s.3 which, like the English Act, refers to force "reasonable in the circumstances."

[9] At p. 136.

[10] (1841) C. & Mar. 314. See also *R. v.Pinney*, 1832 3 S.T. (N.S.) 4; H.E.L., viii, 350. *Cf. Miller v.Knox* (1838) 4 Bing N.C. 574.

given would have proved sufficient or useful. Prosecutions for failing to assist the police are very rare.

The degree of force that may properly be exercised in the preservation of the Queen's peace is unclear. Section 3 of the Criminal Law Act 1967, which replaces the common law rule, refers to "such force as is reasonable in the circumstances." It is thought that the destruction of life or property might well be reasonable in circumstances of grave disorder.[11] The question, what degree of force is reasonable, is one of fact for the jury.[12]

In circumstances where a chief constable felt unable to cope with serious civil disturbance, even with the help of men from other police forces,[13] the decision to use troops would be taken by the Home Secretary and not, as in earlier times, by the local magistrates.[14] In such circumstances he would, no doubt, consult colleagues including the Prime Minister and the Secretary of State for Defence, if, indeed, the decision were not regarded as one to be taken by the Cabinet.

Martial Law

Uses of the term "martial law"

The question is often raised, whether the Crown has a prerogative power to declare martial law. The term "martial law" is sometimes incorrectly used to cover any one or more of the following:

(i) Military law, *i.e.* the codes governing the armed forces at home and abroad, in war and in peace. In former times, what we now call military law was sometimes referred to as martial law.

(ii) The law administered by a military commander in occupied enemy territory in time of war. This is sometimes called martial law by international lawyers. It is unnecessary to say more than that the law so administered amounts to arbitrary government by the military, tempered by international custom (*e.g.* the Hague Convention), and such disciplinary control as the British Government think fit to exercise.

(iii) The common law right and duty to maintain public order by the exercise of any degree of necessary force in time of invasion, rebellion, insurrection or riot (*ante.*)

Martial law in the strict sense means the suspension of the ordinary law, and the substitution therefor of discretionary government by the

---

[11] Lord Diplock in *Att.-Gen. for Northern Ireland's Reference (No. 1 of 1975)* [1977] A.C. 105, quoted *ante*, seems so to have assumed. See also Report of the Widgery Tribunal of Inquiry (H.C. 200 1971–72)). *Farrell* v. *Secretary of State for Defence* [1980] 1 W.L.R. 172. Possibly a private citizen acting on his own initiative may not be justified in using as much force as the Crown itself may be entitled to use; *cf. Burmah Oil* v. *Lord Advocate* [1965] A.C. 75.

[12] *Att.-Gen. for Northern Ireland's Reference (No. 1 of 1975).*

[13] Police Act 1964, s.14. Mutual help is now co-ordinated through the National Reporting Centre. The effectiveness of the Centre was demonstrated during the Miners' Strike of 1984–1985; *post* p. 415.

[14] Mr. Jenkins, replying as Home Secretary, to a question in the House of Commons on April 8, 1976; H.C.Deb., Vol. 909, col. 617. See further Wilcox, "Military aid to the civil power" (1976) 126 New L.J. 404.

executive exercised through the military.[15] In France a state of siege (*état de siège*) may be decreed in the Council of Ministers, but only Parliament may authorise its extension beyond 12 days.[16] It involves the temporary and partial transfer of powers from the civil to the military authorities. The purpose of a state of siege in France is merely to maintain public order: for the conduct of a war it is necessary, as in England, for emergency powers to be conferred on the executive by legislation.[17]

Is martial law known to English law?[18]

Dicey asserted that martial law in this last sense is unknown to our Constitution.[19] Other writers have drawn a distinction between martial law in time of peace and in time of war, and contend that while the Petition of Right (1628) declared it illegal in the former case, it may still validly be proclaimed in the latter. The Petition of Right complained that commissions had been issued to certain persons giving them power to proceed "within the land" against such soldiers or mariners or other dissolute persons joining with them as should commit crimes, and to try them by such summary course "as is agreeable to martial law and as is used in armies in time of war"; and it prayed that no such commissions should thereafter issue. Cockburn C.J. in his charge to the grand jury in *R. v. Nelson and Brand*[20] pointed out that no distinction was made until after the time of Blackstone between "martial law" in the modern sense and what is now called "military law." In Great Britain, at any rate, the Crown cannot proclaim martial law by prerogative in time of peace. Nor has the Crown purported to proclaim it in time of war since the reign of Charles I, and it makes no difference whether or not a state of war has been proclaimed.

What on rare occasions has been called "martial law" since 1628 by British constitutional writers has been a state of affairs outside Great Britain in which, owing to civil commotion, the ordinary courts were unable to function, and it was therefore necessary to establish military tribunals. It is merely an extended application of the principle, discussed above, that the executive has such powers as are necessary for the preservation of public order. Even then specific powers have usually been obtained from Parliament, as in Ireland in 1799 and Jamaica in 1865.

Some authorities hold, nevertheless, that martial law may validly be called into operation in time of war both in Great Britain and outside, and that when this has been done the civil courts have no authority to call in question the actions of the military authorities. They rely on the

---

[15] The principles generally recognised for the imposition of martial law are: (i) necessity, *i.e.* the ordinary courts are unable to function; (ii) proportionality *i.e.* acts done should be proportional to the need; (iii) limitations of area *i.e.* only in areas (which might include the whole country) where the ordinary courts are unable to function; (iv) limitation of time, *i.e.* martial law should continue only so long as the necessity lasts.

[16] *Constitution of the Fifth French Republic*, Art. 36.

[17] *Constitution of the Fifth French Republic*, Art. 16.

[18] On the position before the Petition of Right see J. V. Capua, "The early history of Martial Law in England from the fourteenth century to the Petition of Right" (1977) 36 C.L.J. 152.

[19] Dicey, *Law of the Constitution* (10th ed.), p. 293.

[20] (1867) *Special Report*, pp. 99–100.

preamble to certain Irish Acts of Parliament, *e.g.* (1799) 39 Geo. 3, c.11, which referred to "the wise and salutary exercise of His Majesty's undoubted prerogative in executing martial law." They also pray in aid language used by Lord Halsbury in *Ex p. D. F. Marais*[21]: "The framers of the Petition of the Right well knew what they meant when they made a condition of peace the ground of the illegality of unconstitutional procedure." One answer to this line of reasoning was anticipated by Lord Blackburn when he said in his charge in *R. v. Eyre*[22]: "It would be an exceedingly wrong presumption to say that the Petition of Right, in not condemning martial law in time of war, sanctioned it." Another answer is afforded by the fact that when martial law has been proclaimed, the Crown has almost invariably protected its servants after the event by obtaining the passing of Acts of Indemnity.[23]

It is sometimes difficult to determine when a state of war exists in a particular district. Coke, Rolle and Hale were of the opinion that time of peace is when the civil courts are open, and that when they are closed it is time of war. The decision of the Privy Council in *Ex p. D. F. Marais*,[24] however, shows that this test is not conclusive and that the existence of a state of war in a given district is compatible with the continued functioning for some purposes of the civil courts within that district. To exclude the legality of martial law, says Holdsworth,[25] "the courts must be sitting in their own right and not merely as licensees of the military authorities."

The judicial decisions are few and inconclusive and mostly Irish, but the following seem to be the general principles:

(i) The ordinary courts have jurisdiction to determine as a question of fact whether a state of war exists, or did exist at the relevant time, in a given area so as to justify the setting up of a military tribunal (*R. v. Allen*[26]; *R. (Garde) v. Strickland*[27]).

(ii) If it is held that a state of war does or does not exist, then the military tribunal—not being a court but merely a body of military officers to advise the military commander—would not be bound by the ordinary law or procedure. In *Re Clifford and O'Sullivan*[28] the appellants had been sentenced to death for being in possession of firearms by a military tribunal constituted under the authority of the Commander-in-Chief in Ireland, and they applied for a writ of prohibition. The House of Lords held that if in fact a state of war exists or existed at the time of question, a military tribunal is not a court in the ordinary sense, but merely a body of military officers advising their commander; such a tribunal is not bound by the ordinary law of procedure, and therefore prohibition

---

[21] [1902] A.C. 109. This decision gave rise to four articles on martial law in (1902) 18 L.Q.R. 117, 133, 143 and 152.

[22] (1868) Finlayson, 73.

[23] See *R. v. Nelson and Brand* (1867) F. Cockburn's Reports, 59, 79; Forsyth, *Cases and Opinions on Constitutional Law*, pp. 198, 199, 553, 556–557; Holdsworth, *History of English Law*, Vol. X, pp. 705–713.

[24] [1902] A.C. 109, and see *Elphinstone v. Bedreechund* (1830) 1 Knapp 316.

[25] Holdsworth, *History of English Law*, Vol. I, p. 576.

[26] [1921] 2 I.R. 241.

[27] [1921] 2 I.R. 313. And see *R. (O'Brien) v. Military Governor, N.D.U. Interment Camp* [1924] 1 I.R. 32.

[28] [1921] 2 A.C. 570.

would not lie. Further, in this case the military "court" had concluded its business, so that prohibition was too late anyway: relief might be sought by habeas corpus when order was restored if the appellants were still alive. There is no remedy during the state of war (*Ex p. D. F. Marais, ante*). During the disturbances in Ireland that followed the passing of the Irish Free State Constitution Act 1922, many persons were sentenced to death by courts-martial, among them Erskine Childers. He applied for a writ of habeas corpus, which was refused on the ground that a state of war existed in Ireland at the time, and that the civil courts were unable to discharge their duties (*R. v. Portobello Barracks Commanding Officer, ex p. Erskine Childers*[29]). Nor is there any remedy after the war is over, if what was done was done in good faith or at least was dictated by necessity (*Wright v. Fitzgerald*[30]).

(iii) If on the other hand it is held that a state of war does not or did not exist at the relevant time, the person injured has his remedy by habeas corpus (*Wolfe Tone's Case*[31]) or otherwise for injury done to him, subject to the terms of an Act of Indemnity which will probably have been passed in the meanwhile (*Tilonko v. Att.-Gen. for Natal*[32]).

II. Statutory Powers to Deal with an Emergency: In Time of Peace

The Emergency Powers Act 1920

This is a *permanent* statute, and was designed to meet emergencies such as the coal strike of 1921 or the General Strike of 1926. The Act, as amended in 1964,[33] provides that Her Majesty may by proclamation declare a state of emergency if at any time it appears that there have occurred, or are about to occur, events of such a nature as to be calculated, by interfering with the supply and distribution of food, water, fuel or light, or with the means of locomotion, to deprive the community, or any substantial portion of the community, of the essentials of life. No such proclamation remains in force for more than a month, without prejudice to the issue of a fresh proclamation during that period. (s.1(1)). Where a proclamation of emergency has been made Parliament is to be informed thereof forthwith, and if the Houses be then adjourned or prorogued they are to be summoned to meet within five days (s.1(2)).

Where a proclamation of emergency has been made, and so long as it is in force, Her Majesty in Council may make regulations for securing the essentials of life of the community; and those regulations may confer on a Secretary of State or other government department, or any other person in Her Majesty's service or acting on Her Majesty's behalf, such powers and duties as Her Majesty may deem necessary for preserving the peace, securing to the public the necessaries of life, the means of

[29] [1923] I.R. 5.

[30] (1799) 27 St.Tr. 759; P. O'Higgins, "*Wright v. Fitzgerald* Revisited" (1962) 25 M.L.R. 413.

[31] (1798) 27 St.Tr. 613. "No more splendid assertion of the supremacy of the law can be found than the protection of Wolfe Tone by the Irish Bench"; Dicey, *Law of the Constitution* (10th ed.), p. 294. See further, R. F. V. Heuston, *Essays in Constitutional Law* (2nd ed., 1969, pp. 36 *et seq*). Before the dispute between the Courts and the military could be settled, Wolfe Tone had cut his throat.

[32] [1907] A.C. 93.

[33] Emergency Powers Act 1964.

locomotion and the general safety. Nothing in the Act authorises the making of regulations imposing military or industrial conscription, the alteration of the rules of criminal procedure, or making it an offence to take part in a strike or peacefully to persuade other persons to take part in a strike (s.2(1)).

All regulations so made must be laid before Parliament as soon as may be after they are made, and cease to remain in force after the expiration of seven days from the time they were laid before Parliament unless a resolution is passed by both Houses providing for their continuance (s.2(2)). Regulations may provide for the trial by courts of summary jurisdiction of persons offending against the regulations. The maximum penalty for breach of the regulations is imprisonment for three months or a fine of £100 or both, together with the forfeiture of any goods or money in respect of which the offence has been committed. Regulations may not alter criminal procedure or confer any right to punish without trial (s.2(3)).

The Act was fully invoked during the General Strike of 1926. Proclamations of a state of emergency have been issued during strikes a number of times since. On some occasions regulations have been laid before Parliament, but they are usually dormant until put into force by orders, and they have not often needed to come into operation as most strikes are not sufficiently serious or are settled before the need arises. A proclamation of emergency was issued at the time of the seamen's strike in 1966. Regulations were then laid before Parliament making provision for control over maximum prices for such foods as might be specified; control of ports and dock labour; direction of the supply of fuel, food and animal foodstuffs, restriction of postal services, and control of home trade, shipping and cargoes; and the requisitioning of land, including houses and buildings. At the time of a miners' strike in February 1972, which cut off supplies of coal to power stations, emergency regulations come into force authorising electric power cuts and restricting the use of electricity in advertising and display-lighting. In 1973, emergency regulations were made to deal with the consequences of industrial action taken by miners and electricity workers.

The Emergency Powers Act 1964

Section 1 of the 1964 Act merely amended the Emergency Powers Act 1920. Section 2, however, is an important and separate provision which gives permanent effect to a regulation made under wartime legislation which permits the Defence Council to authorise the temporary employment of members of the Armed Forces in agricultural work or other urgent work of national importance. Under this section troops may be employed without any need for Parliamentary approval or the proclamation of a state of emergency. The section has been relied on in a number of cases; troops, for example, in 1975 went into action to remove refuse when Glasgow dustmen went on strike and in 1977–1978 when there was a national strike of firemen.

Civil Contingencies Unit

The co-ordination of measures to deal with emergencies is the responsibility of the Civil Contingencies Unit, a standing Cabinet

Committee of ministers and civil servants which was set up in 1972 to replace the Emergencies Committee.

Emergency Legislation in Northern Ireland

Members of the Armed Forces have not, since the General Strike, been employed in England, Scotland or Wales for the purposes of maintaining law and order. In Northern Ireland, however, the Army has been involved in preventing civil disorder since 1969. To rely on vague common law powers would have been impossible. At first legislation was passed by the Northern Ireland Parliament. When that was successfully challenged in the Courts,[34] legislation was passed by the Westminster Parliament. The Northern Ireland Act 1972, in one short section provided that

> "The limitations imposed on the powers of the Parliament of Northern Ireland to make laws shall not have effect, and shall be deemed never to have had effect, to preclude the inclusion in laws made by that Parliament for the peace, order or good government of Northern Ireland of all provisions relating to members of Her Majesty's forces as such or to things done by them when on duty, and in particular shall not preclude, and shall be deemed never to have precluded, the conferment on them by, under or in pursuance of any such law of powers, authorities, privileges or immunities in relation to the preservation of the peace or maintenance of order in Northern Ireland."

In 1972 direct rule was introduced[35] and subsequently various statutes have been passed by the United Kingdom Parliament conferring emergency powers on the civil authorities and armed forces in Northern Ireland.[36] The legislation gives wide powers of arrest, search and entry to troops, as well as police constables. It creates new offences and provides for the proscribing of organisations. It provides for detention without trial and for trial without jury. Without considering the details of such provisions it is necessary to emphasise the width of the powers conferred. Apart, for example, from specific provisions relating to entering and searching premises, section 19(1) of the 1978 Act allows any member of the forces or any constable to enter any premises if he considers it necessary to do so in the course of operations for the preservation of peace or the maintenance of order; or if authorised to do so by or on behalf of the Secretary of State. Powers of detention—which have not been used since 1975—allow persons to be detained

> "where it appears to the Secretary of State that there are grounds for suspecting that a person has been concerned in the commission or attempted commission of any act of terrorism or in directing, organising or training persons for the purpose of terrorism,"

---

[34] R. (Hume) v. Londonderry Justices [1972] N.I. 91.

[35] Ante, p. 19.

[36] Much of the legislation, which began with the Northern Ireland (Emergency Provisions) Act 1973, has been consolidated in the Northern Ireland (Emergency Provisions) Act 1978.

(defined as the use of violence for political ends and includes any use of violence for the purpose of putting the public or any section of the public in fear). The continued detention of such persons depends on reports made to the Secretary of State by "Advisers".[37-38]

Fears of widespread intimidation of juries led to the introduction of trials of "Scheduled Offences" by a judge sitting alone.[39] The judge must, however, give reasons for a conviction and there is an unlimited right of appeal.[40]

Prevention of terrorism legislation

The Prevention of Terrorism (Temporary Provisions) Act 1984 and other legislation dealing with terrorism and allied crimes in the United Kingdom generally and in Northern Ireland in particular will be considered later in connection with Offences against the State.[41]

III. STATUTORY POWERS TO DEAL WITH AN EMERGENCY: IN TIME OF WAR

Defence of the Realm Act 1914–15

The experience of the two great wars of the present century shows that the executive rely in time of war almost exclusively on statutory powers. Shortly after the outbreak of war in 1914, the United Kingdom was in effect placed under military law by the Defence of the Realm Act 1914, and British subjects and aliens were triable by court-martial in connection with certain offences for some months. Subsequent Defence of the Realm Acts allowed British subjects to claim a civil trial on taking the prescribed steps, and gave to the King in Council such powers as were necessary for the efficient prosecution of the war. The doctrine of *ultra vires*, of course, still applied (*Chester* v. *Bateson*[42]; *Att.-Gen.* v. *Wilts. United Dairies.*[43] But as Scrutton L.J. is reported to have said in *Ronnfeldt* v. *Phillips*[44]; "It has been said that a war could not be conducted on the principles of the Sermon on the Mount. It might also be said that a war could not be carried on according to the principles of Magna Carta. Very wide powers had been given to the Executive to act on suspicion on matters affecting the interests of the State."

The Indemnity Act 1920

The liability of the executive for action taken to put down grave civil disturbances, and acts done in the prosecution of a war, may be greatly limited by Acts of Indemnity. These may be quite narrow in scope, or they may be framed in general terms as in the Indemnity Act 1920. This provided that no civil or criminal proceedings should be instituted for anything done in or outside British territory during the war before the passing of the Act, if done in good faith, and done or purported to be

---

[37-38] s.12, s.31 and Sched. 1.
[39] s.7, s.30 and Sched. 4.
[40] The working of the 1978 Act was reviewed by Sir George Baker; Cmnd. 9222 (1984). For comment, see D. Bonner, [1984] P.L. 348.
[41] *Post*, Chap. 24.
[42] [1920] 1 K.B. 829.
[43] (1922) 91 L.J.K.B. 897. *Cf. Yoxford and Darsham Farmers' Association Ltd.* v. *Llewellin* (1946) 62 T.L.R. 347.
[44] (1918) 35 T.L.R. 46, 47 (confirming Darling J. at (1917) 34 T.L.R. 556).

be done in the execution of duty or for the defence of the realm or the public safety, or for the enforcement of discipline or otherwise in the public interest, by any servant of the Crown, military or civil, or any person acting under his authority.

The Emergency Powers (Defence) Acts 1939 and 1940

The main provisions of the Emergency Powers (Defence) Act 1939, which was passed a week before the outbreak of war with Germany, were as follows: section 1 gave a special power to His Majesty by Order in Council to make such Regulations "as appear to him to be necessary or expedient for securing the public safety, the defence of the realm, the maintenance of public order and the efficient prosecution of any war in which His Majesty may be engaged, and for maintaining supplies and services essential to the life of the community." Without prejudice to the generality of the preceding powers, it specified certain particular matters which might be the subject of Defence Regulations, *viz..*: the apprehension, trial and punishment of persons offending against the Regulations; the detention of persons whose detention appeared to the Secretary of State to be expedient in the interests of public safety or the defence of the realm; the taking of possession or control of any property or undertaking; the acquisition of any property other than land; the entering and searching of any premises; and the amendment, suspension or modification of any enactment.[45]

Section 2 of the Act of 1939 authorised the Treasury to impose charges in connection with any scheme of control authorised by Defence Regulations, *e.g.* the grant of licences or permits (*cf. Att.-Gen.* v.*Wilts. United Dairies, ante*); but any such order had to be laid before the Commons and would cease to have effect unless approval within 28 days by a resolution of the House.

Every Order in Council containing Defence Regulations had to be laid before Parliament, subject to annulment by either House within 28 days.

The Emergency Powers (Defence) Act 1940, passed at a time when invasion seemed to be imminent, allowed Defence Regulations, issued for the purposes prescribed by the Act of 1939, to make provision *"for requiring persons to place themselves, their services, and their property at the disposal of His Majesty."* This very remarkable piece of legislation, which was passed through all its stages in both Houses and received the Royal Assent in one day, described itself as an extension of powers, but it is doubtful whether it did extend the powers already contained in the earlier Act.[46] The Emergency Powers (Defence) (No. 2) Act 1940, which was passed a few months later in order to remove doubts, declared that provision might be made by Defence Regulations "for securing that, where by reason of recent or immediately apprehended enemy action the military situation is such as to require that criminal justice should be administered more speedily than would be practicable

---

[45] This meant any enactment passed before the Emergency Powers (Defence) Act 1940.

[46] Sir Ivor Jennings suggested that it was rather an act of defiance to the all-conquering Germans which "put into a legal formula the 'blood and tears and sweat' that Mr. Churchill had promised as the British contribution to the war effort": *Law and the Constitution* (3rd ed.) pp. xxv–xxvi.

by the ordinary Courts, persons, whether or not subject to the Naval Discipline Act, to military law, or to the Air Force Act, may . . . be tried by such special courts, not being courts-martial, as may be so provided."

The Emergency Powers Act 1964, s.2, as we have seen, made permanent the Defence (Armed Forces) Regulations 1939, which authorise the temporary employment of members of the armed forces in agricultural work or other urgent work of national importance. Otherwise the Emergency Laws (Re-enactments and Repeals) Act 1964 repealed the remaining Defence Regulations, re-enacting some of them with modifications.

Emergency powers and personal freedom

Judicial review of the legality of ministers' acts under legislation conferring emergency powers and of the validity of delegated legislation made under such legislation is subject to the same principles as apply to other cases involving statutory interpretation.[47] Nonetheless cases dealing with this particular type of legislation cannot safely be taken as authorities in other spheres because of the courts' reluctance to interfere with ministerial decisions when the safety of the state may be at risk.

In *Liversidge* v. *Anderson*[48] Regulation 18B(1) of the Defence (General) Regulations issued under the Emergency Powers (Defence) Act 1939 provided that: "If the Secretary of State *has reasonable cause to believe* any person to be of hostile origin or associations . . . and that by reason thereof it is necessary to exercise control over him, he may make an order against that person directing that he be detained." Persons aggrieved by a detention order might make objections to an advisory committee, and it was the duty of the chairman to inform the objector of the grounds on which the order had been made against him. A detention order was made by the Home Secretary against Liversidge (alias Perlzweig) on the ground that he had reasonable cause to believe that Liversidge was a person of hostile associations, and that by reason thereof it was necessary to exercise control over him. Liversidge was accordingly detained in Brixton Prison, and next year he issued a writ against the Home Secretary claiming a declaration that his detention was unlawful and damages for false imprisonment. The Home Secretary did not make any affidavit showing why, or on what information, he had reached his decision, but merely produced the order purporting to be made under Regulation 18B(1).[49] The action proceeded on a claim for particulars of defence: there was no suggestion that the Home Secretary had not acted in good faith; and the House of Lords (Lord Maugham L.C. and Lords Macmillan, Wright and Romer, with Lord Atkin dissenting) held that the order was valid and the Home Secretary's answer sufficient.

Lord Maugham L.C. emphasised the points that this was a matter for executive discretion; the Home Secretary was not acting judicially, his decision must necessarily be based on confidential information, and he

[47] *Post* p. 663.
[48] [1942] A.C. 206. See R. F. V. Heuston, "*Liversidge* v. *Anderson* in retrospect" (1970) 86 L.Q.R. 331, and note in (1971) 87 L.Q.R. 161.
[49] *Cf. R.* v.*Home Secretary, ex p. Lees* [1941] 1 K.B. 72 (application for habeas corpus; Court of Appeal held Home Secretary's affidavit sufficient answer).

was responsible to Parliament. It may be noticed that this last point was not merely a constitutional convention, for the Regulation required the Home Secretary to make a monthly report to Parliament of his exercise of this power. His Lordship further said that the words "if he has reasonable cause to believe" drew the attention of the Home Secretary to the fact that he should personally consider the matter himself: the only requirement was that he must have acted in good faith. The other majority opinions emphasised the facts that these were emergency executive powers, conferred at a time of great national danger on a responsible Minister who was answerable to Parliament, and whose sources of information were confidential on security grounds.

Lord Atkin, in his spirited dissenting judgment,[50] contended that the words "if he has reasonable cause" to believe did not mean "if he *thinks* he has reasonable cause": they have an objective meaning and give rise to justiciable issue. He supported his argument by references to the common law and statutory power of arrest, statutes dealing with other criminal matters, and actions at common law for malicious prosecution. His Lordship did not consider that the case of *R. v. Halliday* (*ante*) was relevant, as in that case (on which he had sat as a member of the Divisional Court) the appellant's contention was that the Regulation was *ultra vires*. Nor was he suggesting that the courts should substitute their opinion for that of the Home Secretary as to whether, for example, a person is of hostile origin; the question was, whether the Home Secretary had reasonable cause to believe that he was of hostile origin.

In *Greene* v. *Home Secretary*[51] the House of Lords dismissed an appeal on an application for habeas corpus arising out of the same regulation. Lord Atkin in this case agreed with his colleagues, as the Home Secretary had filed an affidavit setting out a number of particulars and stating that he had acted on information from responsible and experienced persons.

Both Liversidge and Greene were, in fact, released shortly after these decisions.

Liversidge v. *Anderson* and *Greene* v.*Home Secretary* were applied by Asquith J. in *Budd* v. *Anderson*,[52] a case arising out of Regulation 18B(1A). The decision in *Liversidge* v. *Anderson*, however, met with a mixed reception outside the courts,[53] and we cannot do better than

---

[50] *Ibid.* at pp. 225–247. A similar stand had been taken in his dissenting speech by Lord Shaw in *R. v. Halliday, Ex p. Zadig* [1917] A.C. 260.

[51] [1962] A.C. 284. See R. F. V. Heuston in (1971) 87 L.Q.R. 163. The Court of Appeal refused habeas corpus in *R. v. Home Secretary, ex p. Lees* [1941] 1 K.B. 72, in a case arising under Regulation 18B(1A).

[52] [1943] K.B. 642. *Cf. R. v. Home Secretary, ex p. Budd* [1942] 2 K.B. 14, where the Court of Appeal held that the Home Secretary must apply himself to each case under the Regulation, and sign the detention order, otherwise the person detained was entitled to release under habeas corpus; but if the procedure is regularised after release, the person may be detained again for the same cause.

Liversidge v. *Anderson* has also been followed in the courts of India and Pakistan in cases for preventive detention. See also *Ross-Clunis* v. *Papadopoullos* [1958] 1 W.L.R. 546 (P.C.).

[53] For: Keith, *Journal of Comparative Legislation* (1942) 3rd Ser., Vol. XXIV, Pt. I, pp. 63–64; Holdsworth (1942) 58 L.Q.R. 1–3; Goodhart, *ibid.* pp. 3–8 and 243–246. Against: Allen, *ibid.* pp. 232–242; Keeton (1942) 5 M.L.R. 162–173; Allen, *Law and Orders* (2nd ed.), App. 1. Neutral: Jennings, *The Law and the Constitution* (3rd ed.), pp. xxx–xxxi.

adopt the conclusion of the late Professor Berriedale Keith: "The question is one of great difficulty, but the concurrent view of so many judges leaves little doubt that the decision has been rightly taken on the wording of the regulation."[54]

In *Nakkuda Ali* v. *Jayaratne*[55] a strong Privy Council held that *Liversidge* v. *Anderson* must not be taken to lay down any general rule on the construction of the expression "has reasonable cause to believe." Subsequently *Liversidge* v. *Anderson* was described by Lord Reid in *Ridge* v. *Baldwin*[56] as a "very peculiar decision." Lord Diplock in *I.R.C.* v. *Rossminster Ltd.*[57] thought that "the time has come to acknowledge openly that the majority of this House in *Liversidge* v. *Anderson* were expediently and, at that time, perhaps, excusably, wrong and the dissenting speech of Lord Atkin was right." Lord Scarman, in the same case, said that the ghost of *Liversidge* v. *Anderson* had been laid to rest by Lord Radcliffe in *Nakkuda Ali* v. *Jayaratne*.[58] It should not, however, be forgotten that the House of Lords, as evidenced by *McEldowney* v. *Forde*[59] in construing powers for dealing with emergencies may still give greater scope to ministerial discretion than subsequent judicial criticisms of *Liversidge* v. *Anderson* might suggest.

Other war legislation

Legislation for the purposes of the last war was mostly carried out by means of Defence Regulations, but Acts of Parliament were necessary where: (i) what was wanted to be done was outside the scope of the Emergency Powers (Defence) Acts 1939 and 1940, or (ii) the provisions were not to be limited to the war period, or (iii) it was necessary to raise money. The practice with regard to the last was for the Government to ask Parliament periodically for votes of £1,000,000,000, while for security reasons the estimates for each of the service and supply departments were put at the nominal figure of £100.

Many of the Emergency Acts[60] passed on account of the war contained a provision to the effect that they were to continue in force until such date as His Majesty might by Order in Council declare to be the date on which the emergency which was the occasion of the passing of the Act should have ended. In *Willcock* v. *Muckle*[61] it was held that there must be an order in Council declaring the end of the emergency in relation to the particular Act.

The dearth of judicial decisions after 1939 on the nature and extent of the prerogative in time of war is due to the fact that the Emergency

---

[54] *The Constitution under Strain* (1942), p. 51.
[55] [1951] A.C. 66. The application for certiorari failed on the ground that the Controller's function was executive and not judicial.
[56] [1964] A.C. 40.
[57] [1981] A.C. 952, 1011.
[58] At p. 1025. See also *Att.-Gen of St. Christopher* v. *Reynolds* [1980] A.C. 637 (P.C.).
[59] [1971] A.C. 632, Lord Diplock and Lord Pearce dissenting; *post* p. 663n. Further evidence is to be found in *McKee* v. *Chief Constable for Northern Ireland* [1984] 1 W.L.R. 1358. (H.L.) (Power of arrest under anti-terrorist legislation: question is state of mind of constable, not reasonableness of his belief).
[60] See Carr, *Concerning English Administrative Law*, Chap. 3, for the spate of legislative activity in the first week of the war.
[61] [1951] 2 K.B. 844.

Powers (Defence) Acts and the other emergency statutes mentioned covered practically everything that the Government would want to do, except for taxation and the acquisition (as distinct from the taking possession) of land.[62]

---

[62] Cf. Requisitioned Land and War Works Acts 1945 and 1948; Land Powers (Defence) Act 1958. And cf. Burmah Oil Co. case, ante, p. 275.

PART IV

JUSTICE AND POLICE

CHAPTER 20

THE ADMINISTRATION OF JUSTICE

In much of the earlier part of this book it has been convenient, and often correct, to refer to the British Constitution or to the United Kingdom without adverting to the existence of separate legal systems in England, Scotland and Northern Ireland. In this chapter, however, it is impossible to ignore the fact that the legal systems of England and Scotland developed separately in the centuries before 1707 and have remained largely distinct since them, if only because of Article XIX of the Union with Scotland Act which provided for the continued existence of the Court of Session and the High Court of Justiciary and Article XVIII which, as was mentioned earlier, provided that "no alteration be made in the laws which concern private right, except for evident utility of the subjects within Scotland."[1] The differences between the legal systems of England and Northern Ireland are less marked. Ireland it has been said, was the scene of "The First Adventure of the Common Law"[2] and over eight hundred years the law developed along similar lines in both countries.

The main emphasis of this chapter will be on the English legal system and while important distinctions between the systems will be referred to, it must not be assumed that any statement is equally true of the three parts of the United Kingdom unless such is said to be the case.

I. Prerogative and Administration of Justice

The administration of justice is one of the prerogatives of the Crown, but it is a prerogative that has long been exercisable only through duly appointed courts and judges.[3] The various courts and their jurisdictions are now almost entirely on a statutory basis.[4] The Sovereign is "the fountain of justice" and general conservator of the peace. "By the fountain of justice," Blackstone explains,[5] "the law does not mean the *author* or *original*, but only the *distributor* .... He is not the spring, but the reservoir; from whence right and equity are conducted, by a thousand channels, to every individual." In the contemplation of the law the Sovereign is always present in court and therefore cannot be non-suited. Instances are recorded of Plantagenet Kings personally dealing with criminal cases, and Edward IV sat with his judges for three days to see how they did their work; but the personal interference of the Sovereign with the judges was infrequent, and Coke told James I that although he might be present in court he could not give an opinion

---

[1] *Ante*, p. 64.
[2] W. J. Johnston, "The First Adventure of the Common Law" (1920) 36 L.Q.R. 9; A. G. Donaldson, *Some Comparative Aspects of Irish Law* (1957) Chap. 1. and *passim*; F. E. Moran, "The Migration of the Common Law: The Republic of Ireland" (1960) 76 L.Q.R. 69.
[3] *Prohibitions del Roy* (1607) 12 Co.Rep. 63.
[4] *e.g.* See *post*, p. 375.
[5] Bl.Comm. I, 266.

(*Prohibitions del Roy*,[6]). Criminal proceedings, whether initiated by the Crown or a private individual, are conducted on behalf of the Crown and indictments are in the Queen's name. Writs commencing civil actions used to be issued in the Queen's name,[7] and in her name judgment is executed, but the Crown has no control over the conduct of civil cases. The prerogative power to create courts is now virtually useless, because, first (if Coke was right), such courts could not administer equity or any other system except the common law; and secondly, the expense of maintaining such courts would require parliamentary authority.[8] For practical purposes, then, the following may be regarded as the most significant of the existing prerogatives relating to the administration of justice.

The maxim "the King can do no wrong" extended to the Sovereign in his public capacity and in effect to the government generally. The common law rule that no civil action might be brought against the Crown must now be read subject to the important exceptions contained in the Crown Proceedings Act 1947; although even then there are savings with regard to prerogative powers, such as defence and the training of the forces. The Crown still has procedural privileges with regard to discovery and interrogatories, and no execution may be levied against the Crown.[9]

Time does not run against the Crown at common law. *Nullum tempus occurrit regi.*[10] But there are numerous statutes providing that specified criminal proceedings must be taken within a limited period; and the Crown Proceedings Act 1947 expressly makes the Crown bound by statutes limiting the time within which civil proceedings must be commenced, *e.g.* Limitation Acts.

The Attorney-General has a discretion by his fiat (*nolle prosequi*) to discontinue any criminal proceedings on indictment, whether the proceedings were initiated by the Crown or a private prosecutor.[11] He is answerable *ex post facto* to Parliament for the exercise of this power, although it is seldom questioned. This power does not extend to summary proceedings in a magistrates' court, where the leave of the court for the withdrawal of a prosecution is required. A *nolle prosequi* does not have the effect of an acquittal, although if further proceedings were brought the Attorney-General could enter a *nolle prosequi* again. An alternative course in appropriate cases, therefore, is for the Crown to offer no evidence, so that the jury can formally acquit the accused.

---

[6] (1607) 12 Co.Rep. 63, 64. And see Holdsworth, *History of English Law* (5th ed.), Vol. 1, pp. 194, 207.

[7] Writs ceased to be issued in the name of the Crown after June 3, 1980: R.S.C. (Writ and Appearance) 1979, (S.I. 1716). The reform was said to make writs less obscure and to ensure that they presented no obstacle to national susceptibilities when served outside the jurisdiction.

[8] Whether there is a surviving prerogative to entrust the trial of criminal charges to a body other than a court of law (for example, a Royal Commission) has been a matter of recent controversy: *Re Winneke* (1982) 56 A.L.J.R. 506; D. R. Mummery, "Due Process and Inquisitions" (1981) 97 L.Q.R. 287.

[9] *Post*, Chap. 35.

[10] *Magdalen College Case* (1615) 11 Co.Rep. 66b.

[11] R. v. *Allen* (1862) 1 B. & S. 850. See J. Ll. J. Edwards, *The Law Officers of the Crown* (1964), pp. 227–237.

The power of the Attorney-General to discontinue criminal proceedings enables him effectively to promise immunity from the risk of subsequent prosecution to persons who might not otherwise be prepared to assist in investigations, for example, into alleged cases of espionage or the leaking of government papers.[12]

The prerogative of mercy[13]

The Sovereign, acting in England and Wales by the Home Secretary,[14] may pardon offences of a public nature, which are prosecuted by the Crown.[15] The exercise of the prerogative is not subject to judicial review; "Mercy is not the subject of legal rights. It begins where legal rights end."[16] A pardon is generally granted after a conviction. Pardons also used to be granted before conviction in order to guarantee immunity from prosecution to Crown witnesses. There is no reason to believe that such a prerogative no longer exists.[17] No pardon may be pleaded as a bar to impeachment (Act of Settlement 1700),[18] nor may the Crown remit the penalties prescribed by the Habeas Corpus Act 1679 for sending a prisoner out of the realm. The Crown cannot by a pardon deprive a third party of his rights.[19]

A pardon removes all "pains penalties and punishments whatsoever" ensuing from a conviction but does not eliminate the conviction itself which can only be quashed by a court.[20]

---

[12] *e.g.* Anthony Blunt (the art historian and self-confessed Russian spy) and Colette Bowe (the civil servant in the *Westland* affair; *supra* p. 311). See A. T. H. Smith, "Immunity from Prosecution" (1983) 42 C.L.J. 299. Similarly in the case of the Director of Public Prosecutions: *post* p. 380.

[13] *Thomas* v. *The Queen* [1980] A.C. 125 (P.C.) (Statutory power to seek "assistance" of Court by Governor-General exercising prerogative of mercy: no appeal from opinion of Court which was not a judicial determination) Sixth Report, Home Affairs Committee of the House of Commons *Miscarriages of Justice* (1981–82; H.C. 421): *Government Reply* Cmnd. 8856 (1983); C. H. Rolph, *The Queen's Pardon* (1979). A. T. H. Smith, "The Prerogative of Mercy, The Power of Pardon and Criminal Justice" [1983] P.L. 398; C. H. W. Gane, "The Effect of a Pardon in Scots Law" [1980] J.R. 18.

[14] In Scotland and Northern Ireland, pardons are granted on the advice of the respective secretaries of State.

[15] Although this is the traditional formulation of the extent of the prerogative it has been suggested that there are no legal obstacles to the pardoning power being exercised after a private prosecution: A. T. H. Smith, *op. cit.*, *supra*, p. 409.

[16] *De Freitas* v. *Benny* [1976] A.C. 239, 247, *per* Lord Diplock. (Convicted murderer has no right to know on what information the appropriate Minister decides on how to advise on the exercise of the Royal Prerogative to commute a sentence of death.) See also *Hanratty* v. *Lord Butler of Saffron Walden* (1971) 115 S.J. 386 (C.A.). (It is outside the competence of the courts to inquire whether a former Home Secretary was negligent in the exercise of this prerogative).

[17] Prerogative powers are not lost by disuse: *ante*, p. 264. Immunity from the risk of prosecution for treason was granted to Bishop Muzorewa and Mr. Ian Smith when they attended the constitutional conference on Rhodesia in London in 1979 by the making of the Southern Rhodesia (Immunity for Persons attending Meetings and Consultations) Order 1979 (S.I. No. 820), p. 2, under powers conferred by the Southern Rhodesia Act 1965: see J. Ll. J. Edwards, *The Attorney General, Politics and the Public Interest* (1984), p. 475.

[18] *Cf. Danby's Case* (1679) 11 St.Tr. 599.

[19] *Thomas* v. *Sorrell* (1674) Vaughan 330.

[20] *R.* v. *Foster* [1985] Q.B. 115 (C.A.). See also *Royal Commission on Thomas* [1980] 1 N.Z.L.R. 602.

In addition to a "full" or "free" pardon the Crown may grant a reprieve, which temporarily suspends the execution of sentence; or (within statutory limits) may remit the whole or part of a penalty.

The prerogative power of pardon exists to remedy the miscarriages of justice which must occur from time to time in any legal system. Such occasions should be exceptional. The first safeguards against the conviction of the innocent are to be found in the rules of evidence and procedure to be applied in criminal trials. Further protection is given by statutory rights of appeal to higher courts. In addition to the general rules relating to appeals, the Home Secretary has a power, under section 17 of the Criminal Appeal Act 1968, wherever a person has been convicted on indictment or tried on indictment and found not guilty by reason of insanity, to refer the case to the Court of Appeal, which will treat the reference as an appeal by the person concerned.[21-22] The Home Secretary may, under the same section, seek the assistance of the Court of Appeal by referring any point in a case to the Court which must consider the point and furnish him with their opinion thereon.

Dissatisfaction with the present system of dealing with alleged cases of wrongful convictions has led to the suggestion[23] that all such cases be dealt with by an independent review body which would recommend to the Home Secretary whether it was appropriate to grant a pardon, remit sentence or take no further action. The term "pardon" itself is thought to be inappropriate in cases where the convicted person is subsequently found to be innocent and the present position, under which a conviction is not removed by a pardon, unsatisfactory.

Appointment of judges

The appointment of judges by the sovereign is now largely governed by statute, supplemented by convention.

The sovereign appoints the Lords of Appeal in Ordinary,[24] the Master of the Rolls, the President of the Family Division, the Vice-Chancellor and the Lords Justices of Appeal,[25] by convention on the advice of the Prime Minister, who consults the Lord Chancellor. The Queen appoints the puisne judges of the High Court[26] by convention on the advice of the Lord Chancellor,[27] who no doubt consults the Prime Minister. The Queen on the recommendation of the Lord Chancellor also appoints Circuit judges to serve in the Crown Court and county courts, and Recorders to act as part-time judges of the Crown Court.[28] Stipendiary magistrates are appointed by the Crown on the advice of the Lord

---

[21-22] For the extent of the Court's jurisdiction see R. v. Chard [1984] A.C. 279.

[23] See Report of House of Commons Committee, supra.

[24] Appellate Jurisdiction Act 1876, s.2.

[25] Supreme Court Act 1981, s.10. See too Judicature (Northern Ireland) Act 1978, s.12.

[26] The Lord Chancellor advises on the appointment of the Scottish as well as the English Lords of Appeal but plays no role in other Scottish judicial appointments.

[27] The procedures followed by the Lord Chancellor in advising on and making judicial appointments are described in a booklet issued by the Lord Chancellor's Department in 1986, Judicial Appointments.

[28] Courts Act 1971, ss.16, 21.

Chancellor.[29] Lay justices are appointed to the Commission of the Peace in the name of the Queen, but on the nomination of the Lord Chancellor or the Chancellor of the Duchy of Lancaster.[30] The Lord Mayor and aldermen of the City of London are *ex officio* justices of the peace.[31]

In Scotland the judges of the Court of Session and the High Court of Justiciary are appointed by the Sovereign on the advice of the Secretary of State for Scotland who, in turn, is advised by the Lord Advocate. There is no convention that the Lord Advocate should not nominate himself for judicial preferment.

Judges and magistrates on appointment take the judicial oath, by which they promise "to do right to all manner of people after the laws and usages of this realm, without fear or favour, affection or ill-will."[32]

II. THE COURTS

In states with written constitutions it may be a matter of great moment whether a particular body which has power to deal with certain matters or disputes is a "court" exercising "judicial powers." It is common for written constitutions to provide that only courts established under the constitution or by a special legislative procedure can exercise judicial power. In the United Kingdom the question whether a body is a court or not is most likely to arise when there is a doubt about whether its activities are protected by the law of contempt, whether its members are entitled to absolute privilege under the law of defamation and whether they are immune from liabilities for errors they have committed in performing their duties.[33] The difficulties in answering such questions are illustrated by *Attorney-General* v. *B.B.C.*[34] where the House of Lords considered whether a local valuation court, which determined appeals from the rating assessments of valuation officers, was a court to which the law of contempt applied. The House of Lords held that it was not such a body but their Lordships gave various reasons for their conclusions. Viscount Dilhorne, Lord Fraser and Lord Scarman thought that it was a court, but one discharging administrative functions, not a court of law and only the latter type of court was within the law of contempt. Lord Salmon was prepared to hold that it was an "inferior court" but the law of contempt did not extend to "the host of modern inferior courts and tribunals." Lord Edmund-Davies concluded that the valuation court was not, despite its name, a court at all. There is, as Lord Edmund-Davies said, no sure guide, no unmistakable hall-mark by which a court may unerringly be identified. (The problem will be dis-

---

[29] Justices of the Peace Act 1979, s.13 (Stipendiary Magistrates other than Metropolitan: role of Lord Chancellor expressly mentioned). s.31 which deals with Metropolitan Stipendiaries makes no reference to the Lord Chancellor except in connection with removal from office.

[30] Justices of the Peace Act 1979, s.6 and s.68.

[31] Justices of the Peace Act 1979, s.39 retains this anomaly. Other instances of *ex officio* appointment were abolished by the Justices of the Peace Act 1968, s.1(1).

[32] Promissory Oaths Act 1868.

[33] See *post*, pp. 394–397. Whether a body is exercising "judicial functions" was formerly important in deciding whether the rules of natural justice applied: see *post*, p. 670.

[34] [1981] A.C. 303. See also *R.* v. *Cripps, ex p. Muldoon* [1984] Q.B. 68 (C.A.). (Is local election court an "inferior court"?)

cussed later in Chapter 31.) Various features have been suggested as the means of distinguishing courts from other bodies. While, as we have seen, there is no unmistakable hall-mark, the more of these features possessed by a particular institution the less likelihood there is of its not being regarded a court. For our present purposes some of the more important features, all of which are possessed by the courts considered in the following pages, are that

(1) the tribunal is established by the State, as opposed, for example, to an arbitral tribunal established by the parties.
(2) It usually decides a dispute between two parties.
(3) Its decision is on the basis of evidence given to it by the parties.
(4) The hearing of a dispute takes place in public unless the law specifically allows otherwise, for example, in the interest of national security or public decency.
(5) Its decision is on the basis of law and legal rights.
(6) Its decision is final, subject only to an appeal to a higher court.

The name of a tribunal does not necessarily settle whether it is a court: the Employment Appeal Tribunal, for instance, is a superior court of record.[35] Nor must the members of a court be legally qualified, as evidenced in England by the magistrates' courts.

The United Kingdom

Within the United Kingdom there are three separate systems of courts.

The House of Lords has appellate jurisdiction over the three systems although in the case of Scotland, appeal lies only on civil matters.[36]

In many matters the Courts, in whatever part of the United Kingdom they sit, administer the same statutory provisions and the English Court of Appeal may, for example, follow a decision of the Court of Session on the interpretation of an Act which both Courts have to apply.[37] Scottish Courts, faced with the words "charity" and "charitable" in taxing legislation have to apply the English law of charitable trusts.[38] In two instances Parliament has entrusted the application of legislation to a specially created court whose jurisdiction extends throughout the United Kingdom. The Restrictive Practices Act 1956 created a Restrictive Practices Court whose judges are chosen from the English, Scottish and Northern Irish courts. The Industrial Relations Act 1971 created the National Industrial Relations Court which also drew its members from existing courts and administered the same law wherever it sat. Proof of the unitary nature of the court was that appeals from industrial tribunals which sat in the North of England could be heard

---

[35] Employment Protection Act (Consolidation) Act 1978, s.135 and Sched. 11. The Iron and Steel Arbitration Tribunal is, despite its name, a court of record: Iron and Steel Act 1982, s.26. It is also, however, subject to the supervision of the Council on Tribunals.
[36] *Ante*, p. 66.
[37] *Prasad* v. *Wolverhampton B.C.* [1983] Ch. 333.
[38] *I.R.C.* v. *Glasgow Police Athletic Association* [1953] A.C. 530. See W. A. Wilson, *Introductory Essays on Scots Law* (1978), pp. 43–50.

by a Scottish judge sitting in Edinburgh. A similar system now prevails in the case of the Employment Appeal Tribunal.[39] In one instance, that of the Courts Martial Appeal Court, there is one court, composed of judges drawn from all three court systems, which administers English law.[40]

England

Since the Judicature Act of 1873 the superior English courts have formed part of one Supreme Court of Judicature which is divided into a Court of Appeal and a High Court.[41] The latter, for convenience of business, is divided into three divisions but each judge of each division possesses unlimited jurisdiction. Two judges of a particular division may sit together in a Divisional Court which has powers not possessed by a single High Court Judge.[42] The Divisional Court through its supervisory jurisdiction[43] plays a particularly important role in the field of constitutional and administrative law.

The Courts Act 1971 which reformed the administration of criminal justice created the Crown Court which also forms part of the Supreme Court. County Courts were created by statute in the mid-nineteenth century to provide a cheaper and more expeditious trial of civil matters, falling within certain limits, than could the superior courts of law sitting at Westminster.[44]

One of the most remarkable features of the English system of the administration of justice is the large part played by laymen, either as lay magistrates or as jurymen.[45] The appointment of lay justices dates from the earliest days of English law. Statutes of Edward I (Statute of Winchester 1285) and Edward III confirmed and extended the practice of commissioning conservators, custodians or guardians of the peace. In 1344 the custodians of the peace were given judicial powers to hear and determine felonies and trespasses. They were first called justices of the peace in the Justices of the Peace Act 1361 which remains in force, despite later consolidating legislation,[46] and is the source of the useful and sometimes controversial power of justices to "bind over."[47] Justices formerly sat in Courts of Petty Sessions and Quarter Sessions. The former became the magistrates courts and the latter were absorbed in the Crown Court system. Lay magistrates are supplemented in London and

---

[39] J. M. Thomson, "Contempt of NIRC—Some Constitutional Reflections" (1984) 90 L.Q.R. 164. See now, Employment Protection Act 1975, s.87.

[40] *Ante*, p. 349.

[41] See now Supreme Court Act 1981. On the long history of the many ancient courts swept away by the Judicature Act 1873, see *Radcliffe and Cross The English Legal System* (6th ed., 1977) (ed. by G. J. Hand and D. J. Bentley).

[42] Paul Jackson, "The Divisional Court, Precedent and Jurisdiction" (1985) 101 L.Q.R. 157.

[43] *Post*, p. 661.

[44] See now County Courts Act 1984.

[45] Sir Carleton Allen, *The Queen's Peace* (1953) Chap. 5; R. M. Jackson, *The Machinery of Justice in England* (7th ed. 1977). Chap. 4, para. 8; Glanville Williams, *The Proof of Guilt*, Chap. 11; Maitland, *Justice and Police* (1885), Chaps. 8 and 9; Leo Page, *Justice of the Peace* (3rd ed.); B. Osborne, *Justices of the Peace, 1361–1848* (1960); "Magistrates 1361–1961; [1961] Crim.L.R. 653–736.

[46] Justices of the Peace Act 1979, Magistrates' Courts Act 1980.

[47] *Post*, p. 502.

some other cities by stipendiary magistrates who are legally qualified[48]; but the system they represent—involving the trial of 95 per cent. of all criminal cases, and the preliminary examination of the rest—is perhaps an even more remarkable feature of our judicial system than the jury system as it now survives. In addition to their criminal jurisdiction magistrates also have an important civil jurisdiction in the field of matrimonial proceedings.

Northern Ireland

The structure of the superior courts in Northern Ireland is similar to that in England.[49] Justice in the Magistrates' Courts is administered by legally qualified Resident Magistrates. Lay Justices of the Peace perform such tasks as signing warrants and issuing summonses.

Scotland[50]

The Court of Session, which dates from 1532, is the superior court of civil jurisdiction in Scotland. The Outer House corresponds to the High Court in that its jurisdiction is first instance and an appeal from a judge of the Outer House (Lord Ordinary) lies to the Inner House which sits in two Divisions. Criminal jurisdiction is exercised by the High Court of Justiciary which consists of the same judges as the Court of Session. The senior judge of the Court of Session is the Lord President who, as Lord Justice—General, presides in the High Court of Justice.

Limited but important civil and criminal jurisdiction is exercised by Sheriffs, legally qualified judges. The role of stipendiary magistrates and lay justices of the peace who, since 1975, sit in District Courts, is far less significant than in England.[51]

Initiation of proceedings

Civil litigation

The right of access to the courts is in itself an important constitutional right, and for that reason, the courts have been unwilling, for example, to accept that Parliament meant to authorise a minister to remove the right of access by delegated legislation.[52] Anyone may commence a civil action, subject to the risk of losing money if he is unsuccessful. The Courts also possess jurisdiction to strike out actions which are frivolous, vexatious or an abuse of process[53] and under section 42 of the Supreme Court Act 1981 any person who has habitually instituted vexatious legal proceedings may, on the application of the Attorney-

---

[48] Justices of the Peace Act 1979, ss.13–16 and ss.31–34. Unlike lay justices, stipendiary magistrates may sit alone.

[49] See the Judicature (Northern Ireland) Act 1978, as amended by the Administration of Justice Act 1982, s.70 and Sched. 8.

[50] D. M. Walker, *The Scottish Legal System* (5th ed., 1981).

[51] District Courts (Scotland) Act 1975.

[52] *Chester v. Bateson* [1920] 1 K.B. 829 (D.C.); *R. v. Secretary of State for the Home Dept., ex p. Anderson* [1984] Q.B. 778 (D.C.); *post*, p. 663. See too in relation to the scope of the applications for judicial review, discussed later in Chapter 34, *Wandsworth L.B.C. v. Winder* [1985] A.C. 461.

[53] R.S.C. Ord. 18, r. 19.

General, be restrained from instituting further proceedings without the leave of the High Court.[54]

For many people, a right of access to the courts is meaningless unless they can claim assistance from the State with the costs of litigation. Legal aid in civil proceedings was first introduced on a statutory basis by the Legal Aid Act 1949.[55] The current law provides for the giving of legal aid and assistance otherwise than in the course of litigation (the "green form scheme") and in connection with legal proceedings, in both cases subject to an inquiry as to the applicant's means. A committee appointed by the Lord Chancellor has recommended the abolition of the green form scheme and the transfer of the responsibility for giving advice in civil matters to agencies such as the Citizens Advice Bureau.

Criminal proceedings

In general, anyone may commence criminal proceedings subject to the risk of paying the costs of an unsuccessful action and, in some cases, of being sued for malicious prosecution.[56] Certain statutes, however, require the consent of the Attorney-General[57] or the Director of Public Prosecutions[58] to the bringing of prosecutions. Exceptionally, the order of the Commissioners of Customs and Excise is required to the bringing of proceedings for certain offences relating to breach of customs and excise legislation.[59] The Attorney-General may also end any criminal proceedings brought on indictment by entering a *nolle prosequi*.[60]

Most criminal prosecutions were brought by the police[61]; in theory they were private prosecutions. There were various objections to the same persons investigating an offence and deciding whether or not to prosecute. The investigator might be too closely involved with the crime to make a dispassionate judgment about the wisdom of beginning a prosecution. There might be risks—real or imagined—that a combination of the two functions may imperil the impartiality of the investigator in collecting and assembling evidence. The enforcement of the law might be seriously inconsistent from one part of the country to another depending on the view different police forces takes about the desirability of prosecuting cases known to them of particular types of crime.

In Scotland the decision to prosecute is taken by procurators fiscal who, under the Lord Advocate, are entirely independent of the police.

---

[54] See, for example, *Re Fletcher*, *The Times*, June 12, 1984 (C.A.).

[55] See now Legal Aid Act 1974; Legal Advice and Assistance Act 1972; Legal Aid Act 1979. H.M.S.O. publishes an annual guide to the current law, *Legal Aid Handbook*.

[56] In any court other than a magistrates' court a private prosecutor cannot conduct the case himself but must instruct solicitor and counsel: *R. v. Maxwell* [1980] 2 All E.R. 99 (Crown Ct.).

[57] *e.g.* Explosive Substances Act 1883; Official Secrets Act 1911; Public Order Act 1986.

[58] *e.g.* Sexual Offences Act 1967, s.8.

[59] Customs and Excise Management Act 1979, s.145.

[60] *Ante*, p. 372.

[61] In 1981 it was estimated that about 87 per cent. of prosecutions were brought by the police; about 10 per cent. by Government Departments, Local Authorities and Retail Traders, and less than 3 per cent. by private individuals. Other prosecutors included charities such as the R.S.P.C.A.: (1981) N.L.J. 160.

General policy can be laid down by the Lord Advocate which reduces the likelihood of inconsistent enforcement of the law from area to area. On the other hand such a system can amount to a power to issue a general dispensation from a provision of the criminal law.[62]

The Royal Commission on Criminal Procedure[63] recommended reform of the English system and, following a Government White Paper,[64] that has been effected by the Prosecution of Offences Act 1985. The Act does not take away the right of private prosecution, nor does it deprive the police of the power to decide whether to initiate proceedings. But it entrusts the conduct of prosecutions begun at the instance of the police to a Crown Prosecution Service and gives to that Service the power to discontinue proceedings. Thus indirectly, there is a control over the police discretion to prosecute in individual cases and presumably the police in future situations where the facts are similar will be influenced by their knowledge of the fate of earlier proceedings.

The Director of Public Prosecutions is the head of the Crown Prosecution Service. The office of Director of Public Prosecutions was established in 1879.[65] He was formerly appointed by the Home Secretary although responsible to the Attorney-General for the exercise of his powers. Section 2 of the 1985 Act, however, provides that for the future he will be appointed by the Attorney-General. Before 1985 the Director of Public Prosecutions could be required to take over certain prosecutions and could take over the conduct of any prosecution. The latter power might be used to continue a prosecution to a successful conclusion, but it could also be used to ensure that a prosecution failed by offering no evidence: *Raymond* v. *Attorney-General.*[66]

The powers and duties of the Director of Public Prosecutions are now to be found largely in section 2 of the 1985 Act. He is under a duty to take over the conduct of all criminal proceedings (other than those excluded from the section by the Attorney-General) which have been instituted by a police force; to institute and conduct proceedings where the importance or the difficulty of a case makes it appropriate that he should do so, or where it is otherwise appropriate; to take over binding-over proceedings begun by a police force; to appear for the prosecution when directed by the Court to do so in certain categories of criminal appeals. He may give advice to police forces on all matters relating to criminal offences and must discharge such other functions as may be assigned to him by the Attorney-General.

The conduct of proceedings will be the responsibility of members of the Service designated Crown Prosecutors. In each area into which the

---

[62] For a recent study of the Scottish system see S. R. Moody and J. Tombs, *Prosecution in the Public Interest* (1982).

[63] Cmnd. 8092 (1981). See J. Ll. J. Edwards, *The Attorney General, Politics and the Public Interest* (1984), Chap. 4.

[64] *An Independent Prosecution Service for England and Wales* Cmnd. 9074 (1983).

[65] Prosecution of Offences Act 1879. See J. Ll. J. Edwards, *Law Officers of the Crown* (1964), Chaps. 16 and 17; *The Attorney General, Politics and the Public Interest* (1984), Chap. 2. Sir Theobald Mathew, *The Office and Duties of the Director of Public Prosecutions* (1950); Sir Norman Skelhorn, *Public Prosecutor* (1981).

[66] [1982] Q.B. 839 (C.A.) See also *In re Thorpe, The Times,* November 17, 1978 (Div. Ct.) (Promise of immunity to witness in Crown prosecution and further promise to take over and discontinue any private prosecution.)

Director divides England and Wales for the purpose of the Act a Chief Crown Prosecutor will be appointed. Section 10 of the Act requires the Director to issue a code to Crown Prosecutors giving guidance on the general principles to be followed by them in deciding whether to institute proceedings, and what charges should be preferred. The terms of the code is contained in the report which the Director must make each year to the Attorney-General who then lays it before Parliament (section 9). Crown Prosecutors have all the powers of the Director as to the institution and conduct of proceedings but they must exercise their powers under his direction. The most important power is that contained in section 23 which authorises the Director to discontinue proceedings at the preliminary stage. The accused may, however, give notice that he requires the proceedings to continue. (He may wish to establish his innocence clearly in open court). If the Director does not discontinue or the accused wishes the proceedings to proceed, there is nothing to stop the Director (or Crown Prosecutor) from deciding to offer no evidence, with the inevitable result of an acquittal: *Raymond* v. *Attorney-General*, *supra*.

The right of private prosecution is preserved by section 6 which is of importance not merely to the individual but to government departments, local authorities and other public bodies, apart from the police. Section 24 extends the law relating to vexatious litigation[67] to criminal proceedings.

In criminal cases, at least as much as in civil, legal aid may be required if a prisoner is to defend himself effectively. Legal aid in criminal proceedings was introduced in 1903.[68] In addition to assistance with the cost of legal representation the Legal Aid Act 1982 introduced a Duty Solicitor Scheme under which solicitors are available at magistrates' courts to advise accused persons. The Police and Criminal Evidence Act 1984, s.59 also provides for legal advice and assistance to be available to persons detained at police stations.[69] The Administration of Justice Act 1985 empowers the Lord Chancellor to make provision for the payment of work done prior to the grant of a legal aid order in criminal proceedings.

Trial by jury[70]

The belief was strongly held in the eighteenth century, and it has since become an accepted tradition, that trial by jury is one of the chief protections of the rights of the citizen and a bulwark of the Constitution. Thus Blackstone, after discoursing upon the "antiquity and excellence of this trial" in civil cases,[71] says that his remarks "will hold much stronger in criminal cases; since, in times of difficulty and danger, more is to be apprehended from the violence and partiality of judges

---

[67] *Ante*, p. 378.
[68] Poor Prisoners' Defence Act 1903. The current statutes are the Legal Aid Act 1974 and Legal Aid Act 1982.
[69] *Post*, p. 495.
[70] See Sir Patrick Devlin, *Trial by Jury* (revised ed. 1966); R. M. Jackson, *The Machinery of Justice in England* (7th ed.), Chap. 6, para. 7; Glanville Williams *The Proof of Guilt* (3rd ed.), Chap. 10; W. R. Cornish, *The Jury* (1968); J. Baldwin and M. McConville, *Jury Trials* (1979).
[71] Bl.Comm. III, 379.

appointed by the Crown, in suits between the King and the subject, than in disputes between one individual and another . . . . Our law has therefore wisely placed this strong and twofold barrier, of a present- ment[72] and a trial by jury, between the liberties of the people and the prerogative of the Crown . . . . So that the liberties of England cannot but subsist so long as this *palladium* remains sacred and inviolate."[73] So Lord Camden said: "Trial by jury is indeed the foundation of our free constitution; take that away, and the whole fabric will soon moulder into dust"; and Lord Eldon is stated when Solicitor-General to have professed "a most religious regard" for the institution of juries. The right of trial by jury was enshrined in the Constitution of the United States, where much greater use is made of juries (both civil and crimi- nal) than here, by the Sixth and Seventh Amendments.

A prisoner who is indicted is tried by a petty jury, except that some indictable offences may be dealt with summarily by the magistrates with the consent of the accused or, in some instances, without his con- sent.[74] Summary offences are triable on information by magistrates' courts without formal indictment or jury. At the present day about 85 per cent. of *indictable* offences are in fact tried summarily. Of the 15 per cent. sent for trial by jury, about two-thirds plead "guilty." Thus only about 5 per cent. even of indictable offences are actually tried by jury. A majority verdict may be accepted in criminal proceedings where not fewer than ten out of twelve (or nine out of eleven) jurors agree, pro- vided that the jury have had at least two hours for deliberation.[75] (In Scotland the jury in a criminal trial numbers 15 and it has always been possible for a verdict of guilty to be returned by eight jurors.)

A coroner must summon a jury (of seven to eleven jurors) in certain cases, and may accept a majority verdict if the dissentients are not more than two.[76]

The use of the jury in civil cases has declined greatly since the first war. The Supreme Court Act 1981, s.69 provides that where a party to an action in the Queen's Bench Division so requests the action will be tried by a jury if the Court is satisfied (i) that there is in issue a charge of fraud; a claim in respect of libel, slander, malicious prosecution or false imprisonment or any other issue added to the list by a Rule of Court; and (ii) that the trial will not involve any prolonged examination of documents or accounts or any scientific or local investigation which cannot conveniently be made with a jury. In other cases the court may in its discretion order a trial with a jury. The number of jury trials in

---

[72] The jury of presentment, or grand jury, was abolished by the Administration of Justice (Miscellaneous Provisions) Act 1933 and the Criminal Justice Act 1948.

[73] Bl.Comm. IV, 349. The jury which Blackstone praised was not the modern jury; his was "chosen by lot from among those of the middle rank" (III. 379) as distinct from the mul- titude whose decisions would be "wild and capricious" and the aristocracy whose rule produced "the most oppressive of absolute governments."

[74] Criminal Law Act 1977, ss.15, 16 and 23.

[75] Juries Act 1974, s.17; *R.* v. *Pigg* [1983] 1 W.L.R. 6 (H.L.). A verdict of "not guilty" simi- larly requires unanimity or not more than two dissentients. For a criticism of this rule see G. Maher, "Jury Verdicts and the Presumption of Innocence," (1983) 3 Leg.Stnd. 146.

[76] Coroners Acts 1887–1954; Criminal Law Act 1977, s.56(2) and Administration of Justice Act 1982, s.62. See *R.* v. *H.M. Coroner, ex p. Peach* [1980] Q.B. 211 (C.A.).

civil cases in the Queen's Bench Division is now minimal. The power to summon juries in the Chancery Division introduced by the Chancery Amendment Act 1858, has been practically neglected. The right to apply for a jury (of eight) in the county courts is very rarely exercised.[77] Majority verdicts may now be accepted in civil proceedings in the High Court if ten out of 12 (or nine out of 11) jurors agree, and in a county court if seven (out of eight) jurors agree; provided that it appears to the court that the jury have had a reasonable time for their deliberations having regard to the nature and complexity of the case.[78]

Jury service

Persons between the ages of 18 and 65 are liable to jury service if they have been resident for five years in the United Kingdom.[79] The reduction in the minimum age for jury service and the abolition of a property qualification renders out-dated the description of the typical jury as "middle-aged, middle minded and middle class." Jurors are entitled to travelling and subsistence allowances, and compensation for loss of earnings. The jury list is based on the Electoral Register. There is an opportunity to claim exemption while the electoral lists are on view. Various classes of person are exempt, or may claim exemption from jury service, including peers, Members of Parliament, councillors, clergymen, practising barristers, solicitors, police and prison officers, medical practitioners, members of the armed forces, and justices of the peace.[80]

The Juries Act 1974 and the Juries (Disqualification) Act 1984[81] disqualify from jury service anyone who at any time has been sentenced within the United Kingdom, the Channel Islands or the Isle of Man to imprisonment for life, for a term of five years or more or to be detained during Her Majesty's pleasure. No one may serve on a jury who within the preceding ten years has served any sentence of imprisonment, youth custody or detention, been detained in a Borstal or been the subject of a suspended sentence of imprisonment or detention or of a community service order. An order of probation disqualifies a person from serving on a jury for the following five years.

Any prospective juror may be questioned by the appropriate officer to establish whether he is disqualified from jury service.[82]

The Lord Chancellor undertakes the responsibility for summoning and preparing panels of jurors, and making arrangements for payments in respect of jury service. A person may be excused if he can show that he has served on a jury within the previous two years. Failure to attend without excuse, or serving on a jury while disqualified, is punishable by fine.

The Impartiality of the jury: challenge and vetting

The right to a jury chosen at random from among those qualified to serve is recognised by "the right of challenge to the array" that is the

---

[77] But see *Harmsworth* v. *London Transport Executive* (1979) 123 S.J. 825 (C.A.). The current statutory provision is County Courts Act 1984, s.66(3).

[78] Juries Act 1974, s.17.

[79] Juries Act 1974, s.1.

[80] Juries Act 1974, Sched. 1.

[81] Similar provisions apply to Coroners' Juries by virtue of the Coroners' Juries Act 1983.

[82] Juries Act 1974, s.2(5); Administration of Justice Act 1982, s.61.

right of challenge on the ground that the official responsible for summoning the jurors was biased or acted improperly. (Juries Act 1974, s.12(6)).[83]

The Crown or the Defendant may, however, be concerned not at bias in the process of selection but bias on the part of individual jurors. The alleged bias may be said to arise from a general prejudice likely to exist, for example, on the part of white jurors against black defendants. Or it may be thought to arise from some particular circumstances such as the relationship of a juror to someone involved in the proceedings.[84]

In the absence of any evidence of specific bias the defendant may nonetheless challenge without cause (*i.e.* without giving any reason) not more than three potential jurors.[85] In trials where there are a number of defendants it is possible, by each exercising his right, for a large number of potential jurors to be successfully challenged. Corresponding to the defendant's right is that of the Crown to "stand-by," again without cause, potential jurors. There is no limit to the exercise of this right and an entire panel of potential jurors may be stood-by.[86]

Subject to the right of challenge without cause and the Crown's right to stand-by, a juror is not disqualified from serving by reason of some possible general prejudice based on racial or religious or sexual[87] grounds and a judge should not excuse a juror on such general ground.[88] In R. v. Pennington[89] the Court of Appeal held that a miner who had not been on strike was not thereby disqualified from serving on a jury which was trying miners on various charges arising out of the strike in which the accused had been involved.

In the absence of prima facie evidence a juror cannot be questioned in an attempt to discover a disqualifying bias.[90]

Since the late 1970s it has become known that the Attorney-General

---

[83] For an unsuccessful challenge see R. v. Danvers [1982] Crim.L.R. 680.

[84] R. v. Spencer [1986] 3 W.L.R. 348 (H.L.). Trial of nurses at Rampton Hospital accused of ill-treating patients: Juror discharged when it became known that his wife worked at another mental hospital which had been mentioned in evidence; risk of bias arising from remaining jurors having discussed case with him.

[85] Formerly seven: Juries Act 1974, s.12(1)(a); reduced to three by Criminal Law Act 1977, s.43.

[86] R. v. Burns [1982] Crim.L.R. 522.

[87] The Sex Disqualification (Removal) Act 1919, s.1 had allowed a judge to order that a jury should be composed exclusively of men or women: see R. v. Sutton (1969) 53 Cr.App.R. 128. That provision was repealed, however, by the Courts Act 1971, s.35(7).

[88] Practice Note (Jurors: Excusal from Service) [1973] 1 W.L.R. 134. See also Lord Hailsham L.C., H.L.Deb. 5th Series, Vol. 338, col. 584. On the other hand a judge has a discretion to "stand by" jurors to try to produce a balanced jury: R. v. Binns [1982] Crim.L.R. 522.

[89] The Times, April 3, 1985. In R. v. Marlowe, The Times, March 23, 1973 M was a postman, charged in the Crown Court on seven counts of stealing postal packets. Two members of the jury were discovered to be postmen and the prosecution successfully applied for the discharge of the jury and the empanelling of a new one. M sought mandamus to quash the order of the judge and also purported to appeal. Both applications were heard by the same judges sitting first as a Divisional Court to deal with the application for mandamus and then as the Court of Appeal (Criminal Division) to hear the appeal. Both applications had failed on jurisdictional grounds so the question whether the judge had been right to discharge the jury did not arise—although Lord Widgery L.C.J. did say that the judge's discretion might "possibly have been, he would not say, 'wrongly' but 'unwisely' exercised."

[90] R. v. Chandler (No. 2) [1964] 2 Q.B. 322; M. v. H.M. Advocate 1974 S.L.T. (Notes) 25; [1975] Crim.L.R. 108.

from time to time issues guidance on the "vetting" of prospective jurors, that is the investigation of their past criminal records, if any, and checks on their political affiliations. The prosecution can then stand-by jurors on the basis of the information discovered, whether or not the jurors are disqualified under the Juries Act 1974 or because of the likelihood of bias. In *R. v. Crown Court at Sheffield, ex p. Brownlow*,[91] Lord Denning M.R., in an obiter dictum, described the practice of vetting as "unconstitutional." In *R. v. Mason*,[92] however, the Court of Appeal upheld the legality of the practice. Following that case the Attorney-General issued a revised set of guidelines on vetting.[93] These envisage two types of case where vetting is required, (a) cases in which national security is involved and part of the evidence is likely to be heard in camera, and (b) terrorist cases. In security cases there is a danger that a juror, either voluntarily or under pressure, may make an improper use of evidence which has been given in camera. In both security and terrorist cases there is a danger that a juror's political beliefs may be biased as to go beyond normally reflecting the broad spectrum of views and interests in the community to reflect the extreme views of sectarian interest or pressure group to a degree which might interfere with his fair assessment of the facts of the case or lead him to exert improper pressure on his fellow jurors.

In order to ascertain whether in such cases either of these factors might seriously influence a potential juror's impartial performance of his duties, further investigation beyond one on criminal records made for disqualifications may only be made on the records of police Special Branches. No checks other than on these sources and no general inquiries are to be made save to the limited extent that they may be needed to confirm the identity of a juror about whom the initial check has raised serious doubts. No investigation of the records of police Special Branches should be made save with the personal authority of the Attorney-General on the application of the Director of Public Prosecutions. When a chief officer of police has reason to believe that it is likely that an authorised check may be desirable and proper in accordance with the guidelines he should refer the matter to the Director of Public Prosecutions with a view to his having the conduct of the prosecution from an early stage.

The result of any authorised check is sent to the Director of Public Prosecutions who decides what information ought to be brought to the attention of prosecuting counsel.

No right of stand-by should be exercised by counsel for the Crown on the basis of information obtained as a result of an authorised check unless the information is such as, having regard to the facts of the case and the offences charged, to afford strong reason for believing that a particular juror might be a security risk, be susceptible to improper approaches or be influenced in arriving at a verdict.

Where a potential juror is asked to stand by for the Crown, there is no duty to disclose to the defence the information on which it was

[91] [1980] Q.B. 530.
[92] [1981] Q.B. 881.
[93] [1980] 3 All E.R. 785; (1981) 72 Cr.App.R. 15.

founded; but counsel may use his discretion to disclose it if its nature and source permit it.

When information revealed in the course of an authorised check is not such as to cause counsel for the Crown to ask for a juror to stand by but does give reason to believe that he may be biased against the accused, the defence should be given, at least, an indication of why that potential juror may be inimical to their interests. There is, no doubt, great force in the Attorney-General's arguments but it is difficult to see the justification for introducing such checks in the way in which it has been done, as opposed to the introduction of legislation.

In 1986 the Attorney-General admitted to the House of Commons that the guidelines which he issued in 1980 had inadvertently failed to point out that in cases involving national security a second vetting of jurors has, since 1974, been carried out by the Security Service.[94]

Reform

Proposals for the reform of the jury may be based on the premise that the greater willingness of jurors to acquit than magistrates demonstrates that something is wrong[95] or on the need to reduce delays in the hearing of criminal cases. The right of peremptory challenge is particularly seen by some politicians as contributory to unreasonable acquittals and the Government is committed to abolition or restriction of the right.[96] The reduction in delays in the hearing of cases lay behind the recommendation of the James Committee in 1975[97] that the right to trial by jury should be removed in cases of theft and related offences where the value of the property concerned was less than £20. That proposal was not acted upon at the time but has recently been revised with the recognition that in some circumstances an offence may be of exceptional gravity and so justify trials by jury, even if the value of the property involved is small.[97a]

The report of a committee chaired by Lord Roskill on Fraud Trials recommended the abolition of jury trials and the introduction of specially constituted tribunals to deal with cases of fraud where the complexity of the facts involved rendered them unsuitable for trial by jury. Here again the Government has promised reform.

III. THE JUDICIARY

Judicial independence[98]

The Independence of the judiciary from interference by the executive has been mentioned in Chapter 2 as one of the most important principles of British constitutional law. Here we will say something more about the means by which this independence is secured. The main

[94] *The Times,* June 2, 1986.
[95] A Home Office Research and Planning Unit Report (Managing Criminal Justice) found that juries are twice as likely to acquit as magistrates.
[96] White Paper on Criminal Justice, *Cmnd. 9658,* March 1986.
[97] Cmnd. 6323, 1975.
[97a] Consultative Paper published with White Paper on Criminal Justice, *supra,* note 97.
[98] See generally, S. Shetreet, *Judges on Trial* (1976).

topics under this heading are the tenure of the judicial office and the manner in which judges may be removed.

Judges of superior British courts

Down to the reigns of James I and Charles I, judges in England (other than the Barons of the Exchequer) usually held office *durante bene placito nostro* (during the King's pleasure). Like other Crown servants, they could be dismissed by the King at will, although they seldom were. The fact that office was held during pleasure had a certain effect on some of the decisions of the courts in those reigns. Coke was dismissed by writ of *supersedeas* in 1616 for the attitude he adopted in the *Case of Commendams* concerning the staying of suits *Rege inconsulto*.[99] In the Commonwealth period judges were appointed to hold office *quamdiu se bene gesserint* (during good behaviour), but Charles II and James II in many cases revived the former practice.[1] William III's judges held office during good behaviour, but when Parliament in 1691 wanted to put the matter on a statutory basis owing to the doubt whether at common law "good behaviour" meant only good behaviour in relation to the Crown, William refused his consent because the Bill charged their salaries on the hereditary revenues.[2] At last the Act of Settlement (1700), which was to come into force when the Hanoverians ascended the throne, provided "that . . . judges' commissions be made *quamdiu se bene gesserint*, and their salaries ascertained and established, but upon the address of both Houses of Parliament it may be lawful to remove them."

The statutory provisions now in force are the Supreme Court Act 1981, s.11 under which all the Judges of the High Court and the Court of Appeal, with the exception of the Lord Chancellor, hold their offices during good behaviour subject to a power of removal by His Majesty on an address presented to His Majesty by both Houses of Parliament,[3] and the Appellate Jurisdiction Act 1876, s.6: "Every Lord of Appeal in Ordinary shall hold his office during good behaviour . . . but he may be removed from such office on the address of both Houses of Parliament." Such an address must be introduced in the House of Commons. Most Commonwealth countries prescribe a more judicial procedure for the removal of judges, in some cases involving a reference to the Judicial Committee of the Privy Council.

It is commonly but erroneously stated that since the Act of Settlement judges can be dismissed by the Crown *only* on an address from both Houses of Parliament.[4] The true position, however, is stated by Anson: "the words mean simply that if, in consequence of misbehaviour in

---

[99] *Colt and Glover v. Bishop of Coventry* (1616) Hob. 140; see Maitland, *Constitutional History*, pp. 270–271. It was admitted that a charge of misconduct was required for the removal of a judge: *Earl of Shrewsbury's Case* (1611) 9 Co.Rep. 42a, 50. In the case of Coke this was difficult. The charge eventually brought was that he had introduced into his Reports statements in derogation of the royal prerogative. Coke was ordered to correct his Reports, and he declared that in the eleven volumes, containing 500 cases, there were only four errors.

[1] Holdsworth, *History of English Law* (5th ed.), Vol. I, p. 195.

[2] Holdsworth, *op. cit.* Vol. VI, p. 234.

[3] Re-enacting Judicature Act 1875, s.5; Supreme Court of Judicature (Consolidation) Act 1925, s.12(1). For Northern Ireland, see Judicature (Northern Ireland) Act 1978, s.13(1).

[4] This is the position in some Commonwealth countries.

respect of his office or from any other cause, an officer of state holding
on this tenure has forfeited the confidence of the two Houses, he may be
removed, although the Crown would not otherwise have been disposed
or entitled to remove him. Such officers hold, as regards the Crown, *during good behaviour*; as regards Parliament, also during good behaviour,
though the two Houses may extend the term so as to cover any form of
misconduct which would destroy public confidence in the holder of the
office."[5] The Crown could remove without an address for official misconduct, neglect of official duties, or (probably) conviction for a serious
offence (*Earl of Shrewsbury's Case*[6]). The Queen would be bound by convention to act on an address from both Houses.[7] The first case in which
Parliament initiated proceedings for the removal of a judge under the
Act of Settlement was that of Mr. Justice Fox, of the Irish Bench, in 1805;
but it was abandoned on the ground that the proceedings should have
commenced in the Commons instead of in the Lords. The only case
which has resulted in removal under the Act of Settlement procedure
was that of Sir Jonah Barrington, another Irish judge, in 1830. Most of
the cases—and they are few—have concerned colonial judges, or judges
accused of partiality in hearing election petitions.[8]

Judges of the Supreme Court are appointed by letters patent, and the
writ of *scire facias* appears to have been the method of enforcing forfeiture of an office held by letters patent for breach of a condition of tenure.
Scire facias in civil proceedings was abolished by the Crown Proceedings Act 1947; this would include *scire facias* on the Revenue side of the
Queen's Bench Division but not on Crown side.[9] Criminal information
at the suit of the Attorney-General could perhaps be used, and it has
been suggested that the Crown would take proceedings by way of
motion in the Queen's Bench Division for the cancellation of the letters
patent on the ground of misbehaviour.[10]

There is now a compulsory retiring age of seventy-five for Lords of
Appeal in Ordinary and judges of the Supreme Court appointed after

---

[5] Anson, *Law and Custom of the Constitution* (4th ed. Keith). Vol. II, Part I, pp. 234–235.

[6] (1611) 9 Co.Rep. 42a, 50.

[7] As to what amounts to misbehaviour in a public office, and the methods by which an
office in which a person has a life interest may be forfeited, see Todd, *Parliamentary
Government in England* (2nd ed.), Vol. II, pp. 857–859; Anson, *ibid.* at pp. 235–236. But all
judges (except the Lord Chancellor) are now subject to a statutory age of retirement.

[8] For an account of a number of cases, and the principles and proceedings established,
see Todd, *ibid.* at pp. 86 *et seq.*; Hearn, *The Government of England* (2nd ed.), pp. 82–89;
Keith, *Responsible Government in the Dominions*, II, pp. 1073–1074. The last address in
the Houses in relation to an English judge seems to have been the case of Wright C.J.,
the predecessor of Holt C.J.; see Veeder, *Select Essays in Anglo-American Legal History*,
Vol. II, p. 141.

[9] *Att.-Gen.* v. *Colchester Corporation* [1955] 2 All E.R. 124, 127, *per* Lord Goddard C.J. And
see Bickford Smith, *The Crown Proceedings Act 1947*, p. 108; Glanville L. Williams,
Crown Proceedings, p. 114.

[10] R. M. Jackson, *op. cit.* p. 461n. Sir Kenneth Roberts-Wray, *Commonwealth and Colonial
Law* (1966) pp. 489–490, mentions impeachment, but this is a parliamentary and not a
royal method, and does not appear to have any advantage over an Address under the
statute; and also "the exercise of the inquisitorial and judicial jurisdiction of the House
of Lords." The latter expression is obscure, unless it refers to the trial of peers, which
has been abolished. The House of Lords might have some privilege jurisdiction over
Lords of Appeal.

1959.[11] Beyond that age retired judges may, however, be asked to sit from time to time under the Supreme Court Act 1981, s.9. It is hardly necessary to add that judges could be removed by Act of Parliament, although there seems to be no point in adopting that form except to circumvent the House of Lords under the provisions of the Parliament Acts 1911 and 1949 in a case where the Crown was not justified in dismissing by itself.[12]

Judges of the superior courts in Scotland were traditionally appointed *ad vitam aut culpam* and it is generally assumed that this represents the present law.[13] In view, however, of the fact that the Act of Settlement does not extend to Scotland there is doubt about the procedure by which the removal of a judge might be effected.[14] Appointments are no longer for life. As in England judges of the superior courts must retire at the age of 75.[15] A judge who retires before that age may be called upon to sit as a judge from time to time so long as he has not reached 75.[16]

Judges' salaries are charged by statute on the Consolidated Fund, so that they do not come up for review by the Commons every year as do most estimates of national expenditure. They may now be increased, though not reduced, by Order in Council.[17]

Circuit judges

Circuit judges are judges of the superior courts in so far as they sit in the crown court which is a superior court of record.[18] They also sit in the county court which is not a superior court. They may be removed by the Lord Chancellor "on the ground of incapacity or misbehaviour."[19] They are subject to a retiring age of 72, except that the Lord Chancellor may in the public interest continue them in office up to the age of 75.[20] The Lord Chancellor may terminate the appointment of a Recorder on the ground of incapacity or misbehaviour or of failure to comply with the terms of his appointment.[21] The Lord Chancellor has indicated that

---

[11] Judicial Pensions Act 1959; Supreme Court Act 1981, s.11(2). See Supreme Court Act 1981, s.11(8) for the compulsory retirement of judges incapacitated by ill health from resigning.

[12] The tenure of judicial office is no longer affected by the demise of the Crown: Commissions and Salaries of Judges Act 1760; Demise of the Crown Act 1901.

[13] Claim of Right, 1689, art. 13. P. G. B. McNeill, "The Independence of the Scottish Judiciary" [1958] J.R. 132. See dictum in *Mackay* v. *Lord Advocate* 1937 S.C. 860, 864.

[14] Dicta in cases concerned with the immunity of judges from liability for judicial acts assume that removal would be a Parliamentary matter: *Cruickshank* v. *Gordon* (1843) 5 D. 963; *M'Murchy* v. *Campbell* (1887) 14 R. 725; *M'Creadie* v. *Thomson* 1907 S.C. 1176, 1182.

[15] Judicial Pensions Act 1959.

[16] Law Reform (Miscellaneous Provisions) (Scotland) Act 1985, s.22. Compare the position in England where there is no age limit.

[17] Administration of Justice Act 1973; Supreme Court Act 1981, s.12. On judicial pensions see Judicial Pensions Act 1981; Supreme Court Act 1981, s.12(7).

[18] Courts Act 1971, s.4.

[19] Courts Act 1971, s.17(4). A circuit judge who was convicted on a charge of smuggling was removed from office by the Lord Chancellor in 1983: *The Times*, December 6, 1983.

[20] Courts Act 1971, s.17.

[21] Courts Act 1971, s.21(6). Section 21(3) provides that a Recorder's appointment shall specify the frequency and duration of the occasions on which he must be available to perform his duties.

he supports the proposal that in exercising his powers of removal he should be advised by an advisory board.

In Scotland a Sheriff may be removed from office by the Secretary of State but only after an investigation by the Lord President and the Lord Justice Clerk into his fitness and an order for removal must be laid before both Houses of Parliament, subject to annulment by either House.[22]

Other judicial officers

Justices of the peace may be removed from the Commission of the Peace by the Lord Chancellor[23] if he thinks fit, although by convention he does not remove them except for good cause, such as refusal to administer the law because the justice does not agree with it.[24] The Justices of the Peace Act 1979 also requires the Lord Chancellor to keep a Supplemental List of justices who are no longer entitled to exercise judicial functions. The Lord Chancellor may direct that the name of a justice be put on the Supplemental List on the ground of "age or infirmity or other like cause," or if he "declines or neglects" his judicial functions, and his name must be put on this List when he reaches the age of seventy.[25] A justice of the peace whose name has been put on the Supplemental List may authenticate signatures, e.g. on passport applications, but he may not sign any information, complaint, summons or warrant.

The Act of Settlement does not apply to judges of colonial courts, who therefore—subject to the colonial constitution or any local statute—hold office at the pleasure of the Crown (Terrell v. Secretary of State for the Colonies[26]).

Are judges "Crown servants"?

In 1931 the Commissioners of Inland Revenue reduced the salaries of the judges of the Supreme Court, purporting to act under the authority of an Order in Council made under the National Economy Act of that year. The Act provided that, in order to effect economies at a time of economic crisis, the remuneration "of persons in His Majesty's Service" might be reduced, even though the amount of the remuneration "in respect of certain officers in the service of His Majesty" was specified in statutes. It was widely thought that the Inland Revenue were not justified in making the deductions, as judges are not properly regarded as servants of the Crown. There was no tribunal which could determine

---

[22] Sheriff Courts (Scotland) Act 1971, s.12. An example of the exercise of the statutory power is provided by the dismissal by the Secretary of State of a Sheriff for alleged improper political activities. See H.C.Deb., Vol. 940, col. 1288 (December 6, 1977), for the controversy caused thereby.

[23] Or the Chancellor of the Duchy of Lancaster; Ex p. Ramshay (1852) 18 Q.B. 173; Justices of the Peace Act 1979, s.68.

[24] In 1984, 13 magistrates were removed by the Lord Chancellor. They included one magistrate who refused to pay a fine imposed for obstruction; one who made a false claim for court expenses and was convicted; another for fraud not connected with the Bench; and another for "misconduct of a sexual nature": The Times, November 27, 1985.

[25] Justices of the Peace Act 1979, s.8(2).

[26] [1953] 2 A.C. 482; post, Chap. 36. Service regulations now give greater security of tenure.

the question, because a judge cannot be judge in his own cause.[27] It should be added that the judges themselves were willing to make the same sacrifices as many other members of the community, but it was considered that if Parliament had intended the Act to apply to them they should have been specifically mentioned. Holdsworth[28] argued that the judges are not properly called "servants" of the Crown because they are not subject to the orders of the Crown as to the manner in which they shall discharge their duties. On the contrary, such eminent authorities as Bracton, Fortescue and Coke could be cited—against Bacon—to the effect that the Sovereign is subject to the law, and the judges enforce the law even against the Sovereign. It was not relevant to the question to consider whether judges were paid or dismissed by the Crown. "It is a nice problem," Holdsworth added, "but the difficulty is to find out who is to solve it."

As theory, the question was not solved; but it was solved in practice soon afterwards by the Inland Revenue restoring the cuts in deference to public opinion.

No general duty to advise the executive

It is often said that one of the hallmarks of the independence of the English judiciary is that they have no duty to advise the executive on cases that do not come before the courts in the ordinary course of litigation. In 1925 a great outcry was raised in the House of Lords when it was proposed in the Rating and Valuation Bill that advisory judgments should be allowed on rating questions.[29] That such a duty does not necessarily impair the independence of the courts is shown by the fact that it exists in many constitutions, including some in the Commonwealth, and also in our judicial system in the case of the Judicial Committee[30] and the Courts-Martial Appeal Court. Further, where a person has been convicted on indictment, or been tried on indictment and found not guilty by reason of insanity, the Home Secretary may at any time either refer the whole case to the Court of Appeal, and the case is then to be treated as an appeal to the court by that person; or refer any point to the court for their opinion.[31] A similar power exists following an acquittal.[32]

Such advisory functions should be distinguished from the ancient duty of the judges to advise the House of Lords in its judicial capacity, and from the binding declaratory judgments that may be given in certain cases.[33]

Concern was voiced in both Houses of Parliament in 1983 when it

---

[27] But see *O'Byrne* v. *Minister for Finance and Attorney General* [1959] I.R. 1 where the judges of the Irish Supreme Court discussed their liability to pay income tax.

[28] The story is now more fully told, with the Memorandum of Lord Sankey, the Lord Chancellor, in R. F. V. Heuston, *Lives of the Lord Chancellors 1885–1940* (1964), pp. 513–519.

[29] See E. C. S. Wade, "Consultation of the Judiciary by the Executive" (1930) 46 L.Q.R. 169.

[30] *Ante*, p. 296.

[31] Criminal Appeal Act 1968, s.17.

[32] Criminal Justice Act 1972, s.36. This section has not, however, "created a system for referring mere 'moots' to appellate courts"; *Att.-Gen. for Northern Ireland's Reference No. 1 of 1975* [1977] A.C. 105, 156 *per* Lord Edmund Davies.

[33] *Dyson* v. *Att.-Gen.* [1911] 1 K.B. 410.

became known that in 1982 the Permanent Secretary at the Department of the Environment had sought the advice of Sir John Donaldson M.R. on matters relating to the law on industrial relations. Fears were expressed that such private consultations were inconsistent with the separate roles of the executive and judiciary. There is nothing improper or unusual in consulting the judges to seek their expert views but, as the discussion concerning the Master of the Rolls shows, in areas of the law which are politically controversial there is a risk that the judges might themselves be the object of political criticism if they seem to be giving private advice to the executive.

Apart from their strictly judicial duties judges of the superior courts are, from time to time, called upon to conduct inquiries of one kind and another.[34] 28 High Court judges carried out non-judicial duties such as conducting inquiries, chairing commissions and producing reports in the year 1983–84.[35] Whether such a practice is desirable is a question on which different views have been expressed. The danger of relying on judges to examine contentious issues is that they become themselves controversial figures.

Judicial impartiality

The impartiality of the judiciary is recognised as an important, if not the most important element, in the administration of justice. To define what is meant by the concept is not, however, easy nor is there general agreement on the extent to which judges are—or can be—"impartial" in the exercise of their duties. Without attempting to discuss the theoretical and jurisprudential issues involved[36] certain legal rules and conventions are clearly intended to facilitate the impartial administration of justice so far as that is possible.

Thus in modern times there is a doctrine or convention that judges—except, perhaps, the Lord Chancellor—should not take part in political and party controversy. To avoid this risk rules have been adopted by successive Lord Chancellors governing the activities of judges outside their courts. In reliance on these rules judges have, for example, been told (or advised) not to participate in radio or television programmes dealing with legal matters. Whether such blanket prohibitions are wise or necessary may be open to doubt.[37]

---

[34] *e.g.* Lord Denning's Report on the Profumo Affair; Roskill J.'s Commission on the siting of a third London Airport; inquiries into events in Northern Ireland by Lord Widgery C.J., Scarman L.J. and Lord Cameron; inquiry into the Grunwick dispute by Scarman L.J. See further S. Shetreet, *Judges on Trial* (1976), pp. 354–363; Zellick [1972] P.L. 1. For the views of judges themselves see *Sunday Telegraph*, November 13, 1977.

[35] H.C.Deb., Vol. 63, col. 628; July 12, 1984.

[36] See for example, Benjamin N. Cardozo, *The Nature of the Judicial Process* (1921), especially Lecture 4; W. A. Robson, *Justice and Administrative Law* (3rd ed., 1951), Chaps. 2 and 5. Critical accounts of judicial law making are to be found in J. A. G. Griffith, *The Politics of the Judiciary* (3rd ed., 1985) and J. P. W. B. McAuslan, "Administrative Law, Collective Consumption and Judicial Policy" (1983) 46 M.L.R. 1. For a different approach see D. N. MacCormick, *Legal Reasoning and Legal Theory* (1978). See also *post*, p. 671.

[37] In controversies relating to judicial participation in such programmes the relevant rules were referred to as Kilmuir Rules although in one form or another restrictions on judicial utterances ante-date that Lord Chancellor. See also [1986] P.L. 383.

Exclusion from the House of Commons

The exclusion by law of the holders of judicial office (other than lay magistrates) from sitting in the House of Commons[38] is now based on the doctrine that judges should not take part in political controversy. Formerly, the exclusion of judges from the House of Commons was based on different principles. When the Commons asserted their right to exclude James I's judges they did so on the ground of parliamentary privilege, because the judges of the common law courts were advisers of the House of Lords. For the same reason the Law Officers of the Crown should have been disqualified, but in this case the disqualification was eventually waived.[39]

Natural justice

The principles of natural justice which are discussed in Chapter 33 in relation to the judicial control of public authorities, apply *a fortiori* to the conduct of the courts. The right of each side to a dispute to be heard (*audi alteram partem*) and the requirement that a judge should be free from personal interest or bias in the case before him (*nemo iudex in re sua*)[40] both help to insure the impartial discharge of judicial duties.

Publicity of proceedings

One of the chief safeguards of the impartial administration of justice lies in the common law right of the public, including the Press, to be present and to publish accurate reports and fair comments on the proceedings. This is embodied, too, in the maxim that it is not sufficient that justice be done, but it must be seen to be done: *Scott v. Scott*.[41] "Proceedings in open court ensure that justice is done and is seen to be done and that the public may be able to ponder whether justice has been done": *Home Office v. Harman*.[42]

The courts have a discretion, which must be carefully exercised, to hear proceedings *in camera* on grounds of public policy, *e.g.* where secret information that might endanger the safety of the state is to be divulged, or to clear the court for the suppression of disorder.[43]

In *R. v. Chief Registrar of Friendly Societies ex p. New Cross Building Society*,[44] the Court of Appeal pointed out that in exceptional circumstances the paramount object of the courts—to do justice in accordance

---

[38] House of Commons Disqualification Act 1975.

[39] *Report and Minutes of Evidence on the Select Committee on Offices or Places of Profit under the Crown* (1941; H.C. 120, 147).

[40] In *Bridgman v. Holt* (1693) Shower P.C. 111, when the puisne judges of the King's Bench were determining the question whether the valuable sinecure office of Chief Clerk of the King's Bench was in the gift of the Chief Justice, the latter took no part in the decision but sat "near the defendant's counsel upon a chair uncovered." And see *Dimes v. Grand Junction Canal* (1852) H.L.C. 759, *post*, Chap. 33. The Lord Chancellor, however, formerly sat in the House of Lords or the Judicial Committee in cases involving political questions in which the government of which he was a member was interested. See *e.g. Marais v. G.O.C. ex p. Marais* [1902] A.C. 109. There is probably now a convention that the Lord Chancellor and ex-Lord Chancellors do not participate in appeals involving controversial political issues with which they have been concerned. *e.g. Heaton's Transport Co. v. T.G.W.U.* [1973] A.C. 15.

[41] [1913] A.C. 417.

[42] [1981] Q.B. 534, *per* Templeman L.J.

[43] See *R. v. Denbigh J.J. ex p. Williams* [1974] Q.B. 759.

[44] [1984] 2 Q.B. 227.

with the law—could only be achieved by proceedings in camera. In the instant case the Chief Registrar had made orders requiring the Building Society, in effect, to cease trading. A public hearing of the action by the Society to quash the orders would have inevitably so affected public confidence in the Society that whatever the outcome, it would have been forced to close. The application was heard in camera and only after judgment had been given, against the Society, were details of the proceedings made public. Statutory limitations on grounds of public morality are imposed in certain cases on the details that may be published, *e.g.* under the Judicial Proceedings (Regulation of Reports) Act 1926 and various statutes relating to children and young persons, divorce, nullity, and domestic proceedings.[45]

Fair reports of contemporary judicial proceedings are privileged (*Kimber* v. *The Press Association*[46]). Restrictions on reporting may be imposed to prevent the risk of prejudicing proceedings under the Contempt of Court Act 1981.[47]

Judicial immunity[48]

The absolute privilege accorded by the law of defamation to those taking part in judicial proceedings extends to magistrates as well as judges (*Law* v. *Llewellyn*[49]). With regard to torts other than defamation the law is not altogether clear. The distinction usually taken is that between superior courts and inferior courts,[50] other than magistrates who are in a special position.

Judges are exempt from civil or criminal liability for things done or said while acting within their jurisdiction, even if done maliciously and without reasonable or probable cause (*Anderson* v. *Gorrie*[51]). Judges of *superior* courts are apparently not liable for judicial acts done outside their jurisdiction[52] (*Hammond* v. *Howell*,[53] *Anderson* v. *Gorrie, ante*), and the acts of a superior court are presumed to be within their jurisdiction (*Peacock* v. *Bell*[54]). Anyway, there is no tribunal to enforce such liability. Judges of *inferior* courts, including county courts,[55] courts-martial[56]

---

[45] *e.g.* Domestic and Appellate Proceedings (Restriction of Publicity) Act 1968; *Barritt* v. *Att.-Gen.* [1971] 1 W.L.R. 1713; Magistrates' Courts Act 1980, s.71.

[46] (1893) 62 L.J.Q.B. 152.

[47] *Post*, p. 406.

[48] Winfield, *The Present Law of Abuse of Legal Procedure* (1921), Chap. 7; *cf.* D. Thompson, "Judicial Immunity and the Protection of Justices" (1958) 21 M.L.R. 517; L. A. Sheridan, "The Protection of Justices" (1951) 14 M.L.R. 267; A. Rubinstein, "Liability in Tort of Judicial Officers" (1963) 15 U.T.L.R. 317.

[49] [1906] 1 K.B. 487.

[50] Thompson, *op. cit.*, however, argues that the distinction in English law between courts of record and courts not of record ought also to be taken into account. This distinction is admittedly not applicable to Scottish or Colonial courts.

[51] [1895] 1 Q.B. 668 (colonial court); see also *Scott* v. *Stansfield* (1868) L.R. 3 Ex. 220 (county court).

[52] *Cf.* ministerial acts; *Ferguson* v. *Earl of Kinnoull* (1842) 9 Cl. & F. 251, 311 (H.L.).

[53] (1677) 2 Mod. 219.

[54] (1666) 1 Wms.Saund. 74. See also *Taffe* v. *Downes* (1813) 3 Moo.P.C.

[55] *Houlden* v. *Smith* (1850) 14 Q.B. 841.

[56] *Dawkins* v. *Lord F. Paulet* (1869) 5 Q.B. 94; *Dawkins* v. *Lord Rokeby* (1873) L.R. 8 Q.B. 255; *Heddon* v. *Evans* (1919) 35 T.L.R. 642.

and consular courts,[57] have been traditionally regarded as liable for judicial acts done without, or in excess of, their jurisdiction (*Peacock* v. *Bell*, *ante*). The judge of an inferior court will not be deemed to have acted without jurisdiction if he was induced to act by some false allegation of fact which, if true, would have given him jurisdiction (*Houlden* v. *Smith*[58]; *Calder* v. *Halket*[59]). The distinction between superior and inferior courts began to develop in the seventeenth century, and was the product of two principles: first, the jurisdiction of inferior courts is limited by subject-matter, persons or place, while superior courts are not so limited; and, secondly, inferior courts are answerable to the superior courts if they exceed their jurisdiction, while superior courts are answerable only to God and the King.[60]

In *Sirros* v. *Moore*,[61] the Court of Appeal, in refusing to hold a judge of the Crown Court liable for a wrongful order of imprisonment, expressed the view that the immunity of judges of inferior courts should be assimilated to that of judges of superior courts. The House of Lords, however, in *Re McC*[62] thought that the distinction between the immunity of superior and inferior courts was so deeply rooted in the law that it could not be eradicated by the Court of Appeal and probably not even by the House of Lords itself.[63]

Limits to the liability of justices of the peace, apart from defamation (*Law* v. *Llewellyn*, *ante*), were considered by the House of Lords in *Re McC*,[64] an appeal from Northern Ireland. Their Lordships held that magistrates are liable for acts committed outside their jurisdiction. Whatever doubts had formerly existed as a result of the obscurely worded provisions of the Justices Protection Acts 1848 (England) and 1849 (Ireland), the Justices of the Peace Act 1979, s.45, and the Magistrates Courts (N.I.) Act 1964, s.16, clearly gave statutory force to the old common law rule of liability for actionable wrongs suffered by persons pursuant to orders made by justices outside their jurisdiction. (In such cases the justices are entitled to be indemnified, if they acted reasonably and in good faith, from local authority funds in England and by the Lord Chancellor in Northern Ireland: Justices of the Peace Act 1979, s.53; Magistrates' Courts (N.I.) Act 1964, s.20; Magistrates' Courts (Northern Ireland) Order 1981, Art. 10). Although no question of malice had been raised and the act complained of had been done outside the jurisdiction, the members of the House all considered the possible liability of justices for malicious acts within their jurisdiction. Lord Bridge, with whom Lord Templeman fully agreed, thought the old common law action for such acts no longer lies. Lord Brandon agreed that such was the case in Northern Ireland, but was doubtful about the position in

---

[57] *Haggard* v. *Pelisier Frères* [1892] A.C. 61.
[58] *Ante.*
[59] (1839) Moo.P.C. 28.
[60] Holdsworth, *op. cit.* Vol. VI, pp. 234–240.
[61] [1975] Q.B. 118.
[62] [1985] A.C. 528.
[63] *Sirros* v. *Moore* was described as "a very unusual case" which could be supported on its own peculiar facts.
[64] [1985] A.C. 528.

England. Lord Keith preferred to leave the question until it arose for decision.

Section 52 of the Justices of the Peace Act 1979 may operate to limit the liability of a justice for acts done in excess of jurisdiction where they were done by him "in the execution of his office." In such a case, where a plaintiff is (apart from the section) entitled to recover damages in respect of a conviction or order, and . . . proves that he was imprisoned under the conviction or order but it is also proved (a) that he was actually guilty of the offence of which he was so convicted . . . and (b) where he was imprisoned, that he had undergone no greater punishment than that assigned by law for the offence of which he was so convicted or for non-payment of the sum which he was so ordered to pay, he shall not be entitled to recover . . . any sum beyond the sum of one penny as damages for imprisonment and shall not be entitled to any costs. The section was applied in *R. v. Waltham Forest Justices, ex p. Solanke*[65-66] where justices purported to commit a man to prison for failure to pay money due to his wife under a High Court order. The order had never been registered in the magistrates' court and hence they had no jurisdiction to commit in the circumstances; nonetheless they had been acting in execution of their office.

In order to protect the administration of justice, immunity from suit also attaches to words spoken in the course of judicial proceedings by the parties,[67] witnesses[68] and counsel[69] and to the verdicts of juries.[70] In *Rondel v. Worsley*[71] the House of Lords held that the barristers are immune—for reasons of public policy, and not inability to sue for fees—from actions for negligence in respect of their professional work in conducting litigation.

The extent of the immunity is not fully settled. In *Saif Ali v. Sidney Mitchell & Co.*[72] the House of Lords held that it extended only to the work of barristers intimately connected with the course of a case in court. Thus advising parties and settling pleadings before litigation has begun fall outside the scope of immunity. *Dicta* in *Rondel v. Worsley* support the application of the immunity to solicitors appearing as advocates in court.

Immunity from suit for things done in a judicial capacity extends not only to the ordinary courts but also to other persons and bodies exercising judicial functions whether, for example, the eighteenth century Censors of the College of Physicians exercising control over doctors[73] or their nineteenth century equivalent.[74] The position where a tribunal

---

[65-66] [1986] Q.B. 479 (C.A.).

[67] *Astley* v. *Younge* (1759) 2 Burr. 807. See also *Re Hunt* [1959] 2 Q.B. 69 (C.A.).

[68] *Seaman* v. *Netherclift* (1876) 2 C.P.D. 53. See also *Evans* v. *London Hospital Medical College* [1981] 1 W.L.R. 184.

[69] *Munster* v. *Lamb* (1883) 11 Q.B.D. 588.

[70] *Bushell's Case* (1670) 6 St.Tr. 999; (1677) Vaughan 135. The practice of punishing jurors for finding against the evidence of direction of the judge was finally stopped by this case.

[71] [1969] 1 A.C. 191.

[72] [1980] A.C. 198. See *Biggar* v. *McLeod* [1978] 2 N.Z.L.R. 9 (Immunity extends to settling action by compromise in court).

[73] *Groenvelt* v. *Burwell* (1700) 1 Salk 396.

[74] *Partridge* v. *G.M.C.* (1890) 25 Q.B.D. 90.

has acted in excess of jurisdiction is obscure in the absence of express statutory provisions.[75]

Immunity for words spoken is absolute in the case of the courts in the strict sense and tribunals which have similar attributes to a court. The extent of absolute immunity was considered by the House of Lords in *Trapp* v. *Mackie*.[76] Lord Diplock emphasised that the first requirement was that the tribunal had been established by law, although not necessarily by statute[77] so that absolute immunity does not extend to domestic tribunals. A tribunal may be entitled to absolute immunity even although its decision may be subject to confirmation by another body as in the case of a military court of inquiry; *Dawkins* v. *Lord Rokeby*.[78] It is important, although not an essential requirement,[79] that the tribunal's proceedings are held in public. Other characteristics listed by Lord Diplock included the right to legal representation, the calling of witnesses by each party; the compellability of the witnesses and the right to cross-examine witnesses. *Trapp* v. *Mackie* concerned the status of an inquiry which was ordered to be held by the Secretary of State under statutory powers into the reasons for the dismissal of Dr. Trapp from his post as Headmaster. The inquiry was conducted by a leading Scottish advocate and the procedure possessed all the characteristics referred to by Lord Diplock. The Secretary of State was not bound in law by the inquiry but in practice he was likely to accept the report. Whether he did or not, the report of the inquiry and the Secretary of State's action would finally determine the dispute. The House of Lords held that absolute privilege attached to the proceedings of the inquiry. On the other hand a meeting of a local authority to grant licences for music and dancing was held to be entitled to qualified privilege in *Royal Aquarium Society* v. *Parkinson*.[80]

IV. Contempt of Court[81]

Courts, if they are to serve their purpose of administering justice, must have the power to secure obedience to their judgments, to prevent interference with their proceedings and to ensure a fair trial to parties who resort to them to vindicate their rights. It is the public interest in seeing these ends achieved that is served by the law relating to Con-

---

[75] Members of Mental Health Review Tribunals, for example, can rely on the Mental Health Act 1983, s.139, which provides that there is no liability for acts done in excess of jurisdiction unless done in bad faith or without reasonable care. See further, A. Rubinstein, *Jurisdiction and Illegality* (1965) 127 *et seq.*; *de Smith's Judicial Review of Administrative Action* (4th ed., J. M. Evans, 1980) 121 *et seq.*

[76] [1979] 1 W.L.R. 177. (A Scottish appeal, the House declaring that on this point English and Scottish law are the same).

[77] *e.g. Lincoln* v. *Daniels* [1962] 1 Q.B. 237 (C.A.): (disciplinary proceedings in Inns of Court); *Marrinan* v. *Vibart* [1963] 1 Q.B. 528.

[78] (1873) L.R. 8 Q.B. 255; (1875) L.R. 7 H.L. 744.

[79] *Addis* v. *Crocker* [1961] 1 Q.B. 11 (C.A.) (Disciplinary Committee constituted under Solicitors Act 1957).

[80] [1892] 1 Q.B. 431.

[81] Sir John C. Fox, *The History of Contempt of Court* (1927); Sir Gordon Borrie and N. V. Lowe, *The Law of Contempt* (2nd ed., 1983).

tempt of Court.[82] The latter phrase is misleading and inaccurate, particularly because it suggests that the purpose of the law is to protect the dignity of the Court. "It is justice itself that is flouted by contempt of court, not the individual court or judge who is attempting to administer it."[83] Lord Scarman has expressed the view that "It is high time . . . that we re-arranged our law so that the ancient but misleading term 'contempt of court' disappeared from the law's vocabulary."[84] Similar views have been expressed by other judges and in the Phillimore Committee Report but an acceptable alternative has not yet been suggested.

The law relating to contempt covers a variety of very different situations, from the disgruntled litigant who throws a tomato at a judge to the publication of an article on a matter of public interest by a newspaper before litigation on some aspect of that matter has even begun. Thus, in varying degrees the law of contempt will be in conflict with the right of free speech. In all cases judges will be judging in matters in which they may be thought to have a personal interest.[85] It is not, then, surprising that the law of contempt is an area of controversy. The generally accepted unsatisfactory nature of the law led to the establishment in 1971 of a committee under Phillimore L.J. Its *Report* was published in 1974.[86] Legislation did not follow until 1981—the Contempt of Court Act—and then largely because of the decision of the European Court of Human Rights in *Sunday Times* v. *U.K.*[87] The 1981 Act reforms but does not entirely replace the common law on contempt. Although the law of contempt in Scotland differs from the common law, the Act applies to both jurisdictions.

The common law distinguishes between civil and criminal contempt. Scots law draws no such distinction but recognises all forms of contempt as *sui generis*.[88] That is more logical because, on the one hand civil contempt at common law is, like a criminal offence, punishable with imprisonment and the standard of proof required is the standard in criminal law, proof beyond reasonable doubt.[88a] On the other hand criminal contempt is usually tried summarily,[89] a form of procedure otherwise confined to minor offences dealt with by magistrates. The importance of the distinction in English law formerly lay in the fact that no appeal was possible in the case of criminal contempt.[90] The Administration of Justice Act 1960, s.13, now, however, provides a right of

---

[82] The difficulty of determining what constitutes a court is discussed *ante*, p. 375. See also N. V. Lowe and H. F. Rawlings, "Tribunals and the Laws Protecting the Administration of Justice" [1982] P.L. 418.

[83] *Att.-Gen.* v. *Leveller Magazine* [1979] A.C. 440, 449, *per* Lord Diplock.

[84] *Att.-Gen.* v. *BBC* [1981] A.C. 303, 362.

[85] See Willes J.'s answer to such a charge in *ex p. Fernandez* (1862) 19 C.B. (N.S.) 3, 56.

[86] Cmnd. 5794 (1974).

[87] [1979] 2 E.H.R.R. 245. (*The Thalidomide Case*).

[88] G. H. Gordon, *The Criminal Law of Scotland* (2nd ed., 1978), Chap. 51.

[88a] *Dean* v. *Dean, The Times,* November 13, 1986 (C.A.)

[89] Trial on indictment, where the facts permit, was recommended by the Court of Appeal in *Balogh* v. *Crown Court of St. Albans* [1975] Q.B. 73. Stephenson L.J. said that the jurisdiction to deal summarily with a case in which the judge himself was interested should "never be invoked unless the ends of justice really require such drastic means: it appears to be rough justice, it is contrary to natural justice, and it can only be justified if nothing else will do." (*ibid.,* p. 90).

[90] *Scott* v. *Scott* [1913] A.C. 417.

appeal in all cases of contempt, so that the distinction is of little practical importance.[91] One remaining difference is that in cases of criminal contempt enforcement of the law is a matter for the Attorney-General or the Court itself; in civil contempt the choice of whether to pursue the matter of disobedience to the order of the court is usually a matter for the private litigant in whose favour the order has been made.[92]

Civil contempt

Civil contempt of court consists of disobedience to an order of the court made in civil proceedings. Formerly a contemnor was liable to punishment for an indefinite period until he was prepared to "purge" his contempt by apologising and complying with the order of the court. Section 14 of the Contempt of Court Act 1981 now provides a maximum sentence "on any occasion" of two years for any contempt in the case of a superior court and one month in the case of an inferior court.[93] In *Lee* v. *Walker*[94] the Court of Appeal held that the High Court retained an inherent jurisdiction to impose consecutive sentences of imprisonment where there are a number of separate acts of contempt.

Because of the gravity of the consequences of breach of an order made in contempt proceedings the Court of Appeal has emphasised in several decisions the need for certainty and clarity in the order with which the alleged contemnor must comply if he is to avoid imprisonment[95] and "meticulous adherence to the required formalities."[96] Although there is authority for the view that a person in contempt cannot subsequently bring proceedings in the same cause until he has purged his contempt, "It is a strong thing for a court to refuse to hear a party . . . and it is only to be justified by grave considerations of public policy."[97] In all cases the court, probably, has a discretion whether or not to hear the party.

The Official Solicitor has a responsibility to keep under review the cases of all persons imprisoned for contempt and to bring to the notice of the court any circumstances which might lead to a prisoner's release. He may act irrespective of the prisoner's own wishes.[98]

Disobedience to a court order may take many forms, from the obvious

---

[91] At least in the absence of a constitutional right to trial by jury in criminal proceedings: see *The State (D.P.P.)* v. *Walsh* [1981] I.R. 412 where the Irish Supreme Court managed to reconcile the traditional common law rule of summary procedure in contempt cases with the right to trial by jury under Article 38 of the Irish Constitution.

[92] *Home Office* v. *Harman* [1983] 1 A.C. 280, 310 *per* Lord Scarman.

[93] For penalties in Scotland, see s.15. Where a judge erroneously commits to prison for an indefinite period the Court of Appeal can substitute a lawful penal order: *Linnett* v. *Coles*, [1986] 3 All E.R. 652.

[94] [1985] 1 All E.R. 781. A similar power is possessed by the County Court by virtue of the Supreme Court Act 1981, s.14(4A), see the County Courts (Penalties for Contempt) Act 1983.

[95] *Chiltern D.C.* v. *Keane* [1981] 1 W.L.R. 619. See also *Lee* v. *Walker* [1985] Q.B. 1191.

[96] *Re C. (a Minor)*, The Times, November 15, 1985.

[97] *Hadkinson* v. *Hadkinson* [1952] P. 285, 298. See also *Yager* v. *Musa* [1961] 2 Q.B. 214.

[98] See *Churchman* v. *Joint Shop Stewards' Committee* [1974] 1 W.L.R. 1094 (C.A.) (Release of three dockers imprisoned for contempt by N.I.R.C.); *Midland Cold Storage Ltd.* v. *Turner* [1972] I.C.R. 230; *Enfield L.B.C.* v. *Mahoney* [1983] 1 W.L.R. 749 (C.A.) (Refusal to deliver up the "Glastonbury Cross": inherent power of Court to release before termination of fixed period of imprisonment).

case of defiance of an injunction[99] to more controversial cases such as breach of the implied undertaking which a party gives to the court not to use for a collateral or improper purpose documents which are disclosed in the course of litigation under an order for discovery. The importance and effect of this implied undertaking were revealed in *Home Office* v. *Harman*.[1] H, who was the legal officer of the National Council for Civil Liberties, had, in her capacity as a solicitor, obtained discovery of a large quantity of documents from the Home Office. At the hearing several hundred pages of the documents were read out in open court. H later allowed a journalist to inspect the pages in question and make notes on their contents in order that he could write an article based on them. The House of Lords held, by a majority that such conduct amounted to contempt because it was a breach of H's implied undertaking to use the documents only in the course of the litigation. Lord Diplock said that the case was not about freedom of speech, freedom of the press or any of the human rights and fundamental freedoms enshrined in the European Convention on Human Rights. It was about the law of discovery. The law of England, unlike civil systems, required parties to give documents in their possession. The law had, therefore, to ensure that these documents were used only for the purposes for which discovery was compelled. The weakness of the majority view is that it had to concede that a reporter present in court could have properly reported the contents of the documents which were read out to the extent that his memory or his skill at shorthand allowed him to do. It was for that reason—that the documents were no longer confidential—that Lord Simon of Glaisdale and Lord Scarman dissented.

Criminal contempt
Criminal contempt of court takes various forms.

(i) *Scandalising the court*[2]
This form of contempt, picturesquely also known in Scotland as "murmuring judges"[3] is intended to preserve public confidence in the administration of justice by punishing words and conduct which are scurrilously abusive or impugn the impartiality of the courts. O'Higgins C.J. in *The State (D.P.P.)* v. *Walsh*[4] said "Such contempt occurs where wild and baseless allegations of corruption or malpractice are made against a court" and went on to quote Gavan Duffy P. in *Attorney-General* v. *Connolly*[5] who spoke of holding up judges "to the odium of the people as actors playing a sinister part in a caricature of justice." In *R.* v. *Gray*[6] it was held to be contempt to say, in a newspaper, of Darling J., that he was an "impudent little man in horsehair . . . a microcosm of conceit and empty headedness." The article

[99] *e.g. Clarke* v. *Chadburn* [1985] 1 W.L.R. 78. (Contempt by N.U.M.).
[1] [1983] 1 A.C. 280.
[2] C. Walker, "Scandalising in the Eighties" (1985) 101 L.Q.R. 359.
[3] The Judges Act 1540 (no longer in force) provided that if "ony maner of persoun murmuris ony Juge temporale or spirituale als weill lordis of the sessioune as vtheris and previs nocht the samin sufficientlie he salbe pvnist".
[4] [1981] I.R. 412, 421.
[5] [1947] I.R. 213, 220.
[6] [1900] 2 Q.B. 36.

went on to say, "No newspaper can exist except upon its merits, a condition from which the Bench, happily for Mr. Justice Darling, is exempt." In *R. v. Editor of New Statesman, ex p. D.P.P.*[7] it was held to be contempt to say that it was impossible for certain people to hope for a fair trial from Avery J.

The risk of judges confusing their own self esteem with the interests of justice is more serious here than in other areas of the law of contempt. It is necessary to bear in mind Lord Atkin's words, "Justice is not a cloistered virtue, she must be allowed to suffer the scrutiny and respectful, though outspoken comments of ordinary men."[8] In *R. v. Commissioner of Police of the Metropolis, ex p. Blackburn (No. 2),*[9] for example, where Mr. Quintin Hogg Q.C., M.P., as he then was, had published an article in *Punch* criticising the decisions of Court of Appeal on the Gaming Acts, the court held that criticisms of a court's decisions do not amount to contempt of court, even though they are in bad taste and contain inaccuracies of fact, provided they are in good faith and do not impute improper motives to those taking part in the administration of justice.

In *Badry* v. *D.P.P.*[10] the appellant had made various comments about a judge of the Supreme Court of Mauritius who had been appointed to conduct an inquiry into allegations of fraud. Translated into English from Creole they amounted to a charge of bias and a threat "when the children of the coolies take their revenge" to tear off the judge's trousers. The Privy Council held that, however vulgar and abusive the language, the words were not directed at the judge in his judicial capacity and the law of contempt was not applicable because it was confined to courts of justice properly so called and to judges of such courts.

The English Law Commission has proposed reform of the law relating to scandalising the court by the creation of an offence of making false statements alleging corruption in the performance of judicial duties. The intention of the proposed reform is to restrict the ambit of the law and lessen the restraints on the publication of comments on judicial proceedings.[11]

(ii) *Interference with justice as a continuing process*

Here again, the concern of the law is not to protect the conduct of particular proceedings but the administration of justice in general and public confidence in the courts. At common law this category of contempt probably prohibited in certain cases the publication of details of the deliberations of the jury before it reached its verdict: *Attorney-General* v. *New Statesman National Publishing Co.*[12] Whatever the uncertainties of the common law the Contempt of Court Act 1981, s.8, now provides that it is contempt of court to obtain, disclose or solicit any information about the details of the deliberations of a jury in any legal

---

[7] (1928) 44 T.L.R. 301.
[8] *Ambard* v. *Att.-Gen. for Trinidad and Tobago* [1936] A.C. 323, 335.
[9] [1968] 2 Q.B. 150 (C.A.).
[10] [1983] 2 A.C. 297.
[11] *Offences Relating to Interference With the Course of Justice.* (Law Com.No. 96, 1979).
[12] [1981] Q.B. 1.

proceedings. Proceedings under the section may only be instituted by or with the consent of the Attorney-General or on the motion of a court having jurisdiction to deal with the alleged contempt. The publication of the names of blackmail victims has been held to be a contempt because it interferes with the administration of justice by deterring future victims of such crimes from resorting to the courts: *R.* v. *Socialist Worker Printers and Publishers Ltd., ex p. Attorney-General.*[13] The House of Lords, however, in *Attorney-General* v. *Leveller Magazine Ltd.*[14] emphasised that at common law there is no general right to anonymity on the part of witnesses and parties. In proceedings before examining magistrates under the Official Secrets Acts 1911 to 1939 a witness had been referred to as "Colonel B." From information which he gave about himself reporters were able to discover his identity and his name was published in a magazine. The House of Lords held that the publication of his name did not interfere with the due administration of justice. Differing views were expressed on whether courts possessed a power specifically to order the press refrain from revealing the identity of a witness and whether, if such a power existed, the magistrates had purported to make such a ruling. Section 11 of the Contempt of Court Act 1981 provides for the future that where a court (having power to do so) allows a name or other matter to be withheld from the public in judicial proceedings the court may give such directions prohibiting the publication of that name or matter as appear to the court to be necessary for the purpose for which it was ordered to be withheld.[15] The section does little to clarify the common law position. It refers to courts which have the power to make directions without conferring those powers or making clear which courts possessed them under the common law. It does not make clear the effect of a breach of a direction and it does not deal with the publication of information in the absence of an express direction.

"Victimising" witnesses after the conclusion of legal proceedings provides another example of conduct which generally undermines public willingness to participate in legal proceedings and confidence in the ability of courts to protect those who appear before them.

> "The administration of justice is, after all, a continuing thing. It is not bounded by the day's cases. It has a future as well as a present. And, if somebody pollutes the stream today so that tomorrow's litigant will find it poisoned, will he appeal to the court in vain?"[16]

In *Attorney-General* v. *Royal Society for the Prevention of Cruelty to Animals*[17] the society had brought disciplinary proceedings against one of its officers for giving evidence for the defence at the hearing of a private prosecution brought by the society. The Divisional Court described

---

[13] [1975] Q.B. 637.
[14] [1979] A.C. 440.
[15] A court which has not allowed a name to be withheld during proceedings cannot later attempt to prohibit publication of the name under s.11: *R.* v. *Arundel Justices ex p. Westminster Press Ltd.* [1985] 1 W.L.R. 708.
[16] *Re Att.-Gen.'s Reference, Att.-Gen.* v. *Butterworth* [1963] 1 Q.B. 696, 725, *per* Donovan L.J.
[17] *The Times,* June 22, 1985.

such conduct as "a serious and unmitigated contempt" and fined the society the sum of £19,000.

(iii) *Contempt in the face of the court*

Conduct in a court designed to interrupt the administration of justice or expose the court to ridicule falls within this category. It covers assaults, threats, insults or disturbing proceedings, for example by shouting slogans and singing songs: *Morris* v. *Crown Office*.[18] The alleged contempt does not have to be committed in the court room itself so long as it is closely connected with the case in progress, for example, threatening a witness outside the court room or putting a cylinder of laughing gas on the roof of the court building with the object of introducing gas into a particular court: *Balogh* v. *St. Albans Crown Court*.[19]

Whatever the position at common law the taking of photographs and the making of sketches in court is forbidden by the Criminal Justice Act 1925, s.41. The use of tape recorders or other instruments for recording sound, without the consent of the court, is made contempt by section 9 of the Contempt of Court Act 1981.

(iv) *Deliberate interference with particular proceedings*

Any act interfering with the outcome of particular proceedings, such as attempts to bribe or intimidate judges, jurors or witnesses may constitute contempt. This type of contempt extends also to attempting to deter litigants from exercising their legal rights or impeding their access to the courts. To hold a litigant up to public obloquy, for example, with the object of coercing him into compromising an action is a contempt of court: *Attorney-General* v. *Times Newspapers*.[20] In *Raymond* v. *Honey*[21] the interception by a prison governor of an application by a prisoner to the High Court for leave to commit the governor for contempt of court as a result of his action in opening a letter, addressed to the prisoner's solicitor, and refusing to forward it because of its contents, was held by the House of Lords to be a contempt of court because it interfered with the prisoner's right of unimpeded access to a court.

(v) *Unintentional interference by prejudicial publications*

At common law a person might be guilty of contempt by publishing material which might prejudicially affect legal proceedings whether or not he intended to do so. Such a rule, based on strict liability, is a particularly serious threat to the right of free speech, especially in the light of the uncertainty of the rule, as evidenced by the speeches in *Attorney-General* v. *Times Newspapers Ltd*.[22] It was because the European Court of Human Rights[23] concluded that the granting of an injunction in that case to restrain the publication by the *Sunday Times* of a proposed article dealing with the Thalidomide tragedy constituted a violation of Article

---

[18] [1970] 2 Q.B. 114 (C.A.).
[19] [1975] Q.B. 73 (C.A.).
[20] [1974] A.C. 273. *Re Martin (Peter) The Times*, April 23, 1986 (D.C.); contempt to attempt to deter barrister from bringing private prosecution by threatening to report him to the Benchers of his Inn.
[21] [1983] 1 A.C. 1.
[22] [1974] A.C. 273.
[23] *Sunday Times* v. *U.K.* [1979] 2 E.H.R.R. 245.

10 of the European Convention on Human Rights[24] that the British Government finally introduced the Bill which became the Contempt of Court Act 1981. The *Sunday Times* case involved the publication of an article at a time when writs had been issued and the parties were attempting to reach a settlement. The House of Lords unanimously agreed that publication would constitute contempt because it amounted to a prejudgment of the dispute ("trial by newspaper"). In the light of an earlier article, which had been published but not made the subject matter of proceedings, the House expressed various views on the extent to which it is permissible to try to persuade parties not to insist on their legal rights. To some extent the differences may reflect different interpretations of the article. Lord Reid and Lord Cross thought public comment, if fair and temperate, directed to a litigant, was permissible and the article fell within acceptable limits. Could it be contrary to public policy, Lord Reid asked, to seek by fair comment to dissuade Shylock from proceeding with his action? Lord Morris seemed to adopt a similar view but Lord Diplock and Lord Simon thought the article held up Distillers (the manufacturers of the drug) to "public obloquy" or "execration." Their speeches suggest that any public comment directed to a litigant would constitute a contempt. The Contempt of Court Act 1981 attempts in a number of sections to clarify and limit the rule of strict liability exemplified in the *Sunday Times* case, so far as that rule relates to "particular legal proceedings" (section 1). The rule is to apply only to a publication which creates a substantial risk that the course of justice will be seriously impeded or prejudiced (section 2) and at the time of the publication proceedings are "active," a term which is defined with particularity in Schedule 1. Substantial has been explained by the Court of Appeal as meaning "not insubstantial" or "not minimal"; it does not mean "weighty."[25] Section 3 provides a defence where the publisher, having taken all reasonable care, did not know proceedings were active. Section 5 exempts from the strict liability rule a publication which discusses or is part of a discussion in good faith of public affairs or other matters of general interest if the risk of prejudice to particular legal proceedings is merely incidental. Section 7 requires the consent of the Attorney-General or the motion of a court having the appropriate jurisdiction for the institution of proceedings under the strict liability rule.

[24] Article 10.

(1) Everyone has the right to freedom of expression. This right shall include freedom to hold opinions and to receive and impart information and ideas without interference by public authority and regardless of frontiers. This Article shall not prevent States from requiring the licensing of broadcasting, television or cinema enterprises.

(2) The exercise of these freedoms, since it carries with it duties and responsibilities, may be subject to such formalities, conditions, restrictions or penalties as are prescribed by law and are necessary in a democratic society, in the interests of national security, territorial integrity or public safety, for the prevention of disorder or crime, for the protection of health or morals, for the protection of the reputation or rights of others, for preventing the disclosure of information received in confidence, or for maintaining the authority and impartiality of the judiciary.

[25] *Att.-Gen.* v. *News Group Newspapers Ltd.,* [1986] 3 W.L.R. 365 (C.A.). Publication repeating materials the subject of pending libel proceedings which were unlikely to come to trial for a further ten months: risk of prejudice not sufficiently serious to oust rule that injunction not normally available to restrain publication of libellous material before trial where defendant intends to plead justification.

In *Peacock* v. *London Weekend Television Ltd.*[26] the Court of Appeal held that section 7 did not prevent interested parties from applying for an interlocutory injunction to restrain a *threatened* contempt. Section 7 merely relates to the punishment of a contempt which has been committed.

The effect of section 2 and section 5 were considered by the House of Lords in *Attorney-General* v. *English.*[27] A doctor had been charged with murdering a handicapped baby, by directing a course of treatment which inevitably resulted in the baby's death. After the trial had begun a newspaper published an article in support of a "pro-life" candidate in a Parliamentary by-election. The article discussed in general terms the sanctity of life and the morality of attempting to ensure that only healthy babies survived birth. The House of Lords took the view that the article did create a substantial risk of seriously prejudicing the criminal trial within section 2(2) but was not a contempt of court because it clearly fell within section 5 as a comment in good faith on a matter of public interest.[28]

Contempt and related crimes

In many instances conduct which is punishable as a contempt may equally constitute a distinct common law or statutory crime. In addition to a variety of specific (and, in some instances, largely obsolescent) offences,[29] there exist the extremely wide offences of perverting (or attempting or conspiring to pervert) the course of justice.[30]

Contempt and refusal to reveal sources of information

A particular problem which has arisen in connection with legal proceedings has been the right—if any—of a journalist or other person to refuse to reveal the source of information when required to do so by the court. Both the English and the Scottish courts refused to recognise any such privilege.[31] Section 10 of the 1981 Act, however, provides that no court may require a person to disclose the source of information contained in a publication for which he is responsible unless it is established to the satisfaction of the court that disclosure is necessary in the interests of justice or national security or for the prevention of disorder or crime. The meaning of the section was discussed by the House of Lords in *Secretary of State for Defence* v. *Guardian Newspapers.*[32] The Secretary of State sought the delivery up by *The Guardian* newspaper of a copy of a Crown document which had been anonymously sent to the newspaper. The purpose of obtaining the copy was to be able to ident-

---

[26] *The Times*, November 27, 1985.

[27] [1983] 1 A.C. 116.

[28] See also *Att.-Gen.* v. *Times Newspapers Ltd.*, *The Times*, February 12, 1983 (Div.Ct.) (Newspaper articles relating to Fagan, the intruder in the Queen's bedroom).

[29] *See Offences Relating to Interference With the Course of Justice*, (Law Com. No. 96, 1979).

[30] *R.* v. *Machin* [1980] 1 W.L.R. 763 (C.A.); *R.* v. *Selvage* [1982] Q.B. 372 (C.A.).

[31] See *Att.-Gen.* v. *Clough* [1963] 1 Q.B. 773; *Att.-Gen.* v. *Mullholland* [1963] 2 Q.B. 477; *British Steel Corp.* v. *Granada Television Ltd.* [1981] A.C. 1096; *H.M. Advocate* v. *Airs* 1975 S.C. 64 (J.C.).

[32] [1985] A.C. 339; followed, *Maxwell* v. *Pressdram Ltd. The Times*, November 12, 1986 (C.A.). For the Public Interest Privilege against revealing the sources of information see *post* p. 718.

ify the civil servant who had copied the original. By the time the case reached the House *The Guardian* had already complied with the order made at first instance and the person responsible had been identified, so lifting suspicion from other innocent civil servants. The House unanimously took the view that "necessary" imposed a strict test; "necessary" was not to be equated with convenient or expedient. A majority of the House held that the affidavit sworn by the responsible civil servant was sufficient to establish that it was necessary in the interest of national security to identify the person concerned: the possibility of copies of documents relating to defence matters finding their way into the hands of newspapers constituted a threat to the United Kingdom's defence and to its relations with foreign governments. Contrary to views expressed in the courts below, the House of Lords indicated that the protection given by section 10 existed even where delivery was sought of a document which was the property of the plaintiff.

Jurisdiction to punish contempts

Although the law of contempt applies to protect proceedings in all courts, inferior courts have limited jurisdiction to enforce the law of criminal contempt. At common law an inferior court of record such as a coroner's court has jurisdiction to punish contempts in the face of the court: *R. v. West Yorkshire Coroner, ex p. Smith.*[33] Inferior courts, not of record, have no jurisdiction except where there is statutory authority; for example, magistrates' courts under the Contempt of Court Act, 1981, s.12[34] and county courts under the County Courts Act 1984, s.118.[35] In other cases provision is made for enforcement of the law by the Divisional Court.[36]

Reporting of judicial proceedings

Section 4 of the Contempt of Court Act provides that a person is not guilty of contempt of court under the strict liability rule in respect of a fair and accurate report of legal proceedings held in public[37] published contemporaneously and in good faith To avoid a substantial risk of prejudice to the administration of justice in proceedings before it or other proceedings, pending or imminent, the Court may restrain the publication of any report of the proceedings or of any part of them for such period as it thinks necessary for that purpose.[38]

---

[33] [1985] 1 All E.R. 100.

[34] See *R. v. Newbury Justices, ex p. du Pont* (1983) 78 Cr.App.R. 255 (D.C.). For the purposes of civil contempt County Courts are superior courts: County Courts (Penalties for Contempt) Act 1983.

[35] *Bush v. Green* [1985] 1 W.L.R. 1143 (C.A.).

[36] R.S.C., Ord. 52.

[37] *R. v. Rhuddlan Justices ex p. H.T.V. Ltd., The Times,* December 21, 1985 (D.C.). (Arrest not within "legal proceedings held in public" and justices could not prohibit the publication of a film of a prisoner's arrest until the completion of his trial. Appropriate remedy for prisoner, if he objected to the film being shown was to apply to the High Court for an injunction.)

[38] *Practice Direction (Contempt: Reporting Restrictions)* [1982] 1 W.L.R. 1475 (C.A.).

CHAPTER 21

THE POLICE[1]

ALTHOUGH the preservation of the peace, which is a royal prerogative, is one of the primary functions of any state, the administration of the police has always been on a local basis in this country. That there is still no national police force today is partly a historical accident. In the sixteenth and seventeenth centuries constables were controlled both administratively and judicially by the justices of the peace, and they in their turn were controlled by the Council. The Long Parliament put an end to conciliar government by abolishing in 1642 the Star Chamber, through which this control was exercised. The Revolution Parliament had an equally strong fear of government by means of a standing army, as is witnessed by the famous declaration in the Bill of Rights 1688, and this traditional fear has since then been sufficient to prevent the formation of a national police force.

History of the police[2]

In early English law the duty of seeing that the peace was preserved and of apprehending malefactors lay on the local communities of township and hundred. These duties—represented by such terms as frankpledge, hue and cry and sheriff's tourn—were reinforced by the Assize of Arms 1181, an ordinance of 1252 which first mentions constables, and the Statute of Westminster 1285. Under this legislation a high constable was appointed for each hundred,[3] and one or more petty constables in each township. The office of constable was an annual duty and unpaid. The constables gradually came under the control of the justices of the peace, who were introduced in the fourteenth century. In the latter part of the seventeenth century the petty constables, appointed and dismissed by the local justices, came to be identified with the parish.[4] Towns had also an inefficient system of watch by night and ward by day.

No one did more to rouse public opinion in the eighteenth century on the necessity for efficient organisation for the prevention of crime than Henry Fielding, both as author and magistrate. Sir Robert Peel, when Home Secretary, laid the foundation of a permanent professional police force for the metropolis. Nineteenth-century legislation made away

---

[1] G. Marshall, *Police and Government* (1965); G. Marshall, *Constitutional Conventions* (1984) Ch. VIII; T. Jefferson and R. Grimshaw, *Controlling the Constable* (1984); L. H. Leigh, *Police Powers in England and Wales* (2nd ed. 1985); L. Lustgarten, *The Governance of Police* (1986).

[2] L. Radzinowicz, *History of English Criminal Law and its Administration* (1956), Vol. III, (1968), Vol. IV, Chap. 7; Sir Carleton Allen, *The Queen's Peace* (1953) Chap. 4; Sir Frank Newsam, *The Home Office* (1954), Chap. 4; Sir Harold Scott, *Scotland Yard* (1954); Holdsworth, *History of English Law*, Vol. IV, pp. 122–126; W. L. M. Lee, *History of the Police in England* (1905); Maitland, *Constitutional History*, pp. 235–236, 486–489; *Justice and Police* (1885), Chap. 10; T. A. Critchley, *A History of the Police in England and Wales* (1967).

[3] High constables were abolished by the High Constables Act 1869.

[4] Parish constables were abolished by the Police Act 1964.

with the ancient arrangements for trying to preserve the peace. Following on Peel's Metropolitan Police Act 1829,[5] the Municipal Corporations Act 1835 required boroughs to maintain a paid police force. Every borough at one time maintained its own police force, but many of these were too small for efficiency and a series of statutes pursued a general policy of reducing their number. The borough police were administered by a Watch Committee of the Council, consisting of not more than one-third of the councillors. Meanwhile the City of London had obtained similar powers under a local Act, the City of London Police Act 1829. Optional powers were conferred on county Quarter Sessions by the Rural Police Act 1839. Not all counties availed themselves of these powers, and eventually the County and Borough Police Act 1856 extended the metropolitan scheme with modifications to all counties in England and Wales.[6] When county councils were created by the Local Government Act 1888, the control of county police was transferred by way of compromise to a Joint Standing Committee of county councillors and justices.

By 1964, then, there were in London the Metropolitan Police Force under the direct control of the Home Secretary, and the City of London Police, the appointment of whose Commissioner requires the approval of the Home Secretary; and in the rest of England and Wales there were three groups of police forces, all under the indirect supervision of the Home Secretary—county, county borough, and combined (county and county borough). In Scotland similarly the nineteenth century saw a succession of statutes from 1833 onwards dealing with police matters and, as in England, a distinction between town and country forces.[7]

Main functions of the police

The Royal Commission on the Police (1962) outlined the main functions of the police at the present day as follows[8]:

  (i) The duty to maintain law and order, and to protect persons and property.
 (ii) The duty to prevent crime.[9]
(iii) Responsibility for the detection of criminals. Particularly in the case of terrorists and other politically motivated criminals this may involve infiltration by the police of suspect groups. The gathering of intelligence is the particular responsibility of Special Branch officers who are in close contact with the Security Service. They should not, however, procure the commission of crimes through agents provocateurs in order to secure the evidence required for conviction. Nonetheless, English law does not have a defence of "entrapment"; allegations of police encouragement

---

[5] See D. Ascoli, *The Queen's Peace: the Origins and Development of the Metropolitan Police 1829–1979* (1979). Modern statutory police forces may be traced back to the Dublin Police Act passed by the Irish Parliament in 1786, which established the Royal Irish Constabulary.

[6] H. Parris, "The Home Office and the Provincial Police in England and Wales: 1856–1870" [1961] P.L. 230.

[7] *e.g.* Police (Scotland) Act 1857 and Burgh Police (Scotland) Act 1892.

[8] Cmnd. 1728, pp. 157 *et seq.*

[9] This duty extends to the suppression of crime in other parts of the world through co-operation with Interpol: *X* v. *Metropolitan Police Commissioner* [1985] 1 W.L.R. 420.

in the committing of a crime would only go to the question of sentence.[10] In the course of interrogating suspected persons, they have a part to play in the early stages of the judicial process, acting within the limits now provided by the Police and Criminal Evidence Act 1984.[11]

(iv) Responsibility in England and Wales (though not in Scotland) of deciding whether to prosecute suspected criminals.[12]

(v) The duty of controlling road traffic, and advising local authorities on traffic questions.[13]

Duty and discretion

Detailed consideration of what is implied in these duties and of the powers and privileges that the police also possess in connection with them will be found in later chapters.[14] Some general points may be made here. First, the police have no privilege in carrying out their work to break the law: *Morris* v. *Beardmore.*[15] Secondly, they may (and must), as will be seen later, possess powers not possessed by ordinary citizens, for example, to question, search, detain and arrest. Thirdly, although the police are described as being under a duty to maintain law and order and to prevent crime, in most cases that duty involves a large element of discretion and judgment. In some, unusual cases, the duty may allow of little or no discretion; the police constable who takes no action when an assault occurs before his eyes may be guilty of the common law offence of misconduct in a public office.[16] But usually even the ordinary constable is possessed of a wide discretion; should he arrest wrongdoers or merely warn them; arrest all or some of the participants in a brawl? Superior officers, too, must exercise a discretion whether to charge offenders and, if so, with what offence or offences. In the case of a Chief Constable the element of discretion extends to general questions of policy: should he concentrate his resources on suppressing illegal trafficking in drugs, on catching burglars or enforcing the laws against pornography. During a strike should he take steps to enable non-strikers to work if they wish, and, if so, what steps?

In exercising their discretionary powers the police, like other public

---

[10] *R.* v. *Mealey*; *R.* v. *Sheridan* (1974) 60 Cr.App.R. 59 (C.A.); *R.* v. *Sang* [1980] A.C. 402.

[11] In particular, the Code of Practice for the Detention, Treatment and Questioning of Persons by the Police, made under ss.66 and 67 of the 1984 Act: *post*, p. 495.

[12] The importance of this power has been diminished by the Prosecution of Offences Act 1985.

[13] In 1960 traffic wardens were introduced to assist the police in the control and regulation of road traffic. They are appointed by the police authority, and act under the direction of the chief officer of police. They perform such functions as may be prescribed including the control of parking meters and the operation of the "ticket" system of fixed penalties, payable on the spot. See now Road Traffic Regulation Act 1984, ss.95–97. Whether "traffic warden" is included within the term "constable" in a particular statutory provision is a question of construction in each case: *Rumbles* v. *Poole* [1980] R.T.R. 449 (D.C.).

[14] E.g., Chap. 25 and Chap. 27.

[15] [1981] A.C. 446.

[16] *R.* v. *Dytham* [1979] Q.B. 722 (C.A.).

authorities, are ultimately subject to judicial review. A constable's decision to arrest, for example, is open to challenge on the ground that it was unreasonable (in the sense given to that term in the law of judicial review[17]): *Mohammed-Holgate* v. *Duke*.[18] The exercise by a Chief Constable of his wider discretionary powers has been considered by the Court of Appeal in four decisions in which the Court has claimed a right of review, while at the same time asserting the independence of the Chief Constable from control by his Police Authority. The earliest three cases concerned the Metropolitan Police Force whose Commissioner is not in law a constable,[19] although the Court of Appeal equated his position with what they asserted to be that of a constable. A private citizen challenged the legality of directions issued by the Commissioner which, he alleged, meant in effect that the Metropolitan Police were not enforcing the laws against gaming[20] and pornography.[21] In all three cases the citizen failed in his applications; in the gaming case the Commissioner withdrew the offending instructions in the course of the litigation in the light of a decision of the House of Lords relating to the legality of certain forms of gambling. In the cases relating to pornography, however, he lost because the Court of Appeal emphasised that it could not tell the Commissioner how to exercise his discretion; it could only interfere if he did not exercise his discretion at all.

The extent of the Court's control over Chief Constables came before the Court of Appeal again in the very different circumstances of *R.* v. *Chief Constable of Devon and Cornwall*[22] where the Central Electricity Generating Board sought the assistance of the police to remove demonstrators who for some months had been occupying land in order to prevent the Board beginning the construction of a nuclear power station. The Court of Appeal held that the Board were entitled to the help of the police but refused to issue an order of mandamus. Templeman L.J. said that the police are not bound in all circumstances to act every time there is a breach of the law. On the other hand there came a time when they should act; but even then it was not for the court to tell the police how and when their powers should be exercised.[23] It remains to be seen whether, following the decision of the House of Lords in *Mohammed-Holgate (supra)* the Courts may begin to apply to decisions of chief officers the general law of judicial review.

A final point to be made at this stage is that the execution by the police of their powers and the carrying out of their duties may interfere with the rights and powers of law abiding citizens. A citizen who obstructs a constable in the execution of his duty is guilty of an offence under the Police Act 1964, s.51.[24] It may, however, be a matter of contro-

---

[17] *Post,* p. 669.
[18] [1984] A.C. 437.
[19] Metropolitan Police Act 1829.
[20] *R.* v. *Commissioner of Police of the Metropolis ex p. Blackburn* [1968] 2 Q.B. 118.
[21] *R.* v. *Commissioner of Police of the Metropolis (No. 3)* [1973] Q.B. 241; *R.* v. *Commissioner of Police of the Metropolis, The Times,* March 7, 1980. (C.A.).
[22] [1982] 2 Q.B. 458 (C.A.).
[23] See also *R.* v. *Oxford, ex p. Levey, The Times,* December 18, 1985 (D.C.) (Alleged "no-go" areas in Toxteth: the applicant failed because he lacked *locus standi;* chief constable in any case using his judgment in a difficult predicament).
[24] Similarly in Scotland, Police (Scotland) Act 1967, s.41.

versy whether a constable has a particular power or is acting within the scope of his duty. To what extent must the citizen in a particular instance accept the constable's view of his powers or his judgment on what is necessary in certain circumstances to prevent a breach of law? This problem will be discussed later.[25]

Legal status of police officers

The Queen's peace is part of the prerogative.[26] Police officers are not, however, Crown servants. The Home Secretary on behalf of the police in the course of litigation may claim privilege in the public interest in respect of documents that may be used in a criminal *prosecution*[27]; and a letter written by a police officer may be protected by Crown privilege, although it does not emanate from a government department and is not in the possession of a civil servant.[28]

A constable is an officer of the peace, and as such has common law powers and duties.[29] The office is very ancient, older than that of justice of the peace, and was originally associated with the village.[30] These powers are exercised by a constable by virtue of his office, and not on the responsibility of anyone else, nor as a delegate or agent.[31] Although a constable exercised original, not delegated, discretionary powers, this was not incompatible with his being a member of a disciplined body subject to the lawful orders of his superior officers.[32] The Royal Commission on Police Powers and Procedure 1929[33] said that a policeman in the view of the common law is only "a person paid to perform, as a matter of duty, acts which if he were so minded he might have done voluntarily." "Indeed," they added, "a policeman possesses few powers not enjoyed by the ordinary citizen." This statement may have been true at common law but it gives a dangerously misleading picture of the position at the present day, when the policeman has many statutory powers and duties. A constable also exercises statutory powers and duties on behalf of his police authority. One may imagine the "ordinary citizen" trying to identify the finger-prints of a gang of train robbers, or to control the traffic in Piccadilly Circus.[34] The constable's main power is the power of arrest and search, and his main duty the execution of the justices' warrants.[35] Apart from earlier legislation a police constable has

---

[25] *Post*, p. 497.

[26] *Coomber* v. *Berks. Justices* (1883) 9 App.Cas. 61, 67 *et seq.*, *per* Lord Blackburn.

[27] *Conway* v. *Rimmer* [1968] A.C. 910 (H.L.); see *per* Lord Reid.

[28] *R.* v. *Lewes Justices, ex p. Home Secretary* [1973] A.C. 388 (H.L.); *post*, Chap. 35.

[29] *Lewis* v. *Cattle* [1938] 2 K.B. 454 (D.C.). Before the establishment of a professional police force petty constables were equated with servants of the Crown, such as sheriffs and justices of the peace, in *Mackalley's Case* (1612) 9 Co.Rep. 68a–b.

[30] H. B. Simpson, "The Office of Constable" (1895) *English Historical Review* 625.

[31] *Enever* v. *The King* (1906) 3 C.L.R. 969, *per* Griffiths C.J. at p. 977; approved in *Fisher* v. *Oldham Corporation* [1930] 2 K.B. 364, and *Att.-Gen. for New South Wales* v. *Perpetual Trustee Co.* [1955] A.C. 457 (P.C.).

[32] See now Police Act 1964, s.5(1) and, more explicitly, Police (Scotland) Act 1967, s.17(2).

[33] Cmd. 3297.

[34] *Cf.* Dr. A. L. Goodhart: "To say that a constable is a citizen in uniform is no more accurate than it would be to say that all citizens are constables in plain clothes" Cmnd. 1728 (1962), p. 162.

[35] Warrants are mostly applied for by the police themselves.

powers under the Police and Criminal Evidence Act 1984 to stop and search people in the street, to arrest without warrant, to enter premises, to detain people at police stations. Further, he is protected if he acts on a justice's warrant which is beyond the latter's jurisdiction (Constables Protection Act 1750). In *Sirros* v. *Moore*[36] the Court of Appeal held that a constable who obeyed an order of a judge was not liable even if the order was wrongful, provided he did not know that the judge was acting beyond his jurisdiction. He also has certain statutory powers of entry and inspection,[37] and extensive duties in connection with traffic control.

The Police and Criminal Evidence Act 1984 in conferring certain powers, distinguishes between different ranks of police officers. Under section 55, for example, what are euphemistically described as "intimate searches" can only be authorised by an officer holding at least the rank of superintendent.[38]

Nineteenth-century legislation preserved the traditional obligation of a constable to obey the legal orders of a justice of the peace. The Royal Commission on the Police in 1962 found no evidence that justices of the peace nowadays ever exercise their powers over the police except in the normal course of their judicial business, *e.g.* in issuing warrants for the arrest of suspected criminals[39] and the Police Act 1964 repealed the statutory provisions in question.[40] In times of riot or serious civil disturbance, however, there may still be some ultimate responsibility laid on justices to see that order is restored,[41] or, more likely, on the police authority which now consists as to one-third of justices.[42]

A police officer who exceeds or abuses his powers to the injury of another may make himself personally liable in tort. Thus in *Christie* v. *Leachinsky*[42a] two police officers were held liable by the House of Lords for damages for false imprisonment because in arresting the plaintiff without a warrant and detaining him overnight they misinformed him of the nature of the charge.[43]

Vicarious liability

The Police Act 1964, s.48 provides for the vicarious liability of a Chief Constable for torts committed by constables under his direction and

---

[36] [1975] Q.B. 118; *ante*, p. 395.

[37] *Post*, Chap. 24.

[38] See too s.36 (Custody Officers); s.42 (authorisation of continued detention by superintendent).

[39] *Report of the Royal Commission of the Police 1962*, Cmnd. 1728, paras. 82–84.

[40] County and Borough Police Act 1856, s.6 and the Municipal Corporations Act 1882, s.191(2).

[41] See *O'Kelly* v. *Harvey* (1883) 14 L.R.Ir. 105. In *R.* v. *Pinney* (1832) 5 C. & P. 254; (1832) 3 St.Tr.(N.S.) 11, this duty was held to be that of the mayor, but mayors are no longer *ex officio* magistrates. The Lord Mayor of Birmingham until recently had a consultative committee of three J.P.s to confer with him in time of public tumult or riot or other exceptional circumstances, and there was a rota of five J.P.s to act in times of tumult or riot.

[42] Police Act 1964, ss.2(2) and 3(2); Local Government Act 1985, ss.24 and 29.

[42a] [1947] A.C. 573.

[43] But see *Glinski* v. *McIver* [1962] A.C. 762 (H.L.) for the difficulty of establishing the tort of malicious prosecution against a police officer. See Lustgarten, *op. cit.*, 132 *et seq.*

control in the performance or purported performance of their functions in the same way as a master is liable for the torts of his servants.[44]

Reform

The organisation of police administration and the legal status of the police officer grew up piecemeal.[45] A Royal Commission was set up in 1960 to consider the constitutions and functions of local police authorities; the status and accountability of members of police forces, including chief officers of police; the relationship of the police with the public, and the means of ensuring that complaints by the public against the police are effectively dealt with. In their Report published in 1962,[46] the Royal Commission rejected the case for creating a national police system, although many of the members thought a national police service would be more effective in fighting crime and handling road traffic, and the Commission did not think it would be constitutionally objectionable or politically dangerous. While recommending the continuance of the system of separate local police forces, they advocated better liaison between them, and also greater responsibilities being transferred to the Secretaries of State. Although the Police Act 1964 accepted in general the majority recommendations of the Royal Commission, and did confer greater responsibility on the Home Secretary, the primary duty of ensuring the efficient policing of an area rests not (as the Commission appear to have intended) on the Home Secretary, but on the Chief Constable.

The Royal Commission also recommended that there should be further amalgamations of small police forces, the optimum size being over 500 men; that the appointment and continuance in office of all Chief Constables should require the approval of the Secretary of State; that a Chief Inspector of Constabulary for Great Britain should be appointed, who would be responsible for research and planning; and that justices of the peace should compose a third of the members of the Police Committees in boroughs as well as counties. The Commission would clarify relations between Chief Constables and police authorities, but they did not favour a separate corps of traffic police.

The Police Act 1964[47] re-enacted certain previous statutes, with modifications which implement to a greater or less degree the recommendations of the Royal Commission. The main provisions are dealt with in the following paragraphs.

Organisation of police forces

In England and Wales police areas outside London after the Police Act 1964 came into force were counties, county boroughs and combined

---

[44] The comparable provision in the Police (Scotland) Act 1967 is section 39. The need for a statutory provision is to be found in *Fisher* v. *Oldham Corporation* [1930] 2 K.B. 364; *post*, p. 417. *Cf. Adamson* v. *Martin* 1916 S.C. 319. For a successful attempt to rely on s.48 see *Rigby* v. *Chief Constable of Northamptonshire* [1985] 1 W.L.R. 1242. See further *post*, Chap. 33.

[45] *Post*, p. 413 *et seq.*

[46] *Final Report* (1962) Cmnd. 1728. *Cf.* Dr. A. L. Goodhart's *Memorandum of Dissent*, pp. 157 *et seq.*

[47] The relevant Scottish legislation is to be found in the Police (Scotland) Act 1967.

areas. The police authority for a county was the Police Committee, for a county borough the Watch Committee. In each case the Committee consisted of two-thirds councillors and one-third magistrates. The police authority for a combined area was similarly composed of two-thirds members of the constituent councils and one-third magistrates for the constituent areas. Under the Local Government Act 1972 the police authorities outside London were metropolitan counties and the other counties or amalgamated counties. The abolition of metropolitan county councils by the Local Government Act 1985 has lead to the creation of a new type of police authority: the joint authority whose councillor members will be drawn from the councils which were formerly district councils in each metropolitan county. Similarly the magistrates will represent the magistrates in the former districts comprised in the county.[48]

In Scotland, following the Police (Scotland) Act 1967, police areas were counties, burghs or combined areas. The police authorities in counties were the county councils, in burghs the town councils and in combined areas a joint police committee. Under the Local Government (Scotland) Act 1973 the police areas are regions and combined areas. In the former case the police authority is the regional council and in combined areas a joint police committee. In contrast to the position in England and Wales Scottish police authorities are not required to include a proportion of non-elected members of the judiciary.

A number of public bodies have statutory powers to maintain bodies of constables not subject to the Police Act 1964 and the Police (Scotland) Act 1967. These include, for example, the Atomic Energy Authority,[49] the British Railways Board and the British Airports Authority.[50] Legislation is at present before Parliament to consolidate various earlier Acts under which special constables can be appointed with jurisdiction in and within a defined vicinity of naval, military and airforce premises.[51]

Prison officers while acting as such have all the powers of a constable.[52]

Functions of police authorities

In England and Wales it is the duty of every police authority to secure the maintenance of an adequate and efficient police force for the area (Police Act 1964, s.4(1)). No such general duty is mentioned in the Police (Scotland) Act 1967 which merely requires the authority to provide such vehicles, buildings and other equipment as may be required (s.2(3)).

---

[48] Local Government Act 1985, s.24. (Greater Manchester, Merseyside, South Yorkshire, West Midlands and West Yorkshire). In the exceptional case of the Northumbria Joint Authority, the members represent the districts of Tyne and Wear and the county of Northumberland—which have shared a common police force since 1973.

[49] Atomic Energy Act 1954, s.6(4); Atomic Energy Authority (Special Constables) Act 1976.

[50] British Transport Commission Act 1949, s.53; Transport Act 1962, ss.69–71. Airports Authority Act 1975, s.10. But see also Aviation Security Act 1982, s.25 which empowers the Secretary of State to provide that the policing of an airport should be the responsibility of the appropriate local force. On the growth of private "police forces" see D. G. T. Williams, "Crime Prevention and Private Security" (1974) 48 A.L.J. 380.

[51] See now, Ministry of Defence Police Act 1987.

[52] Prison Act 1952, s.8; *Home Office* v. *Robinson* [1982] I.C.R. 31.

The police authority, subject to the approval of the Home Secretary,[53] appoints the Chief Constable and determines the number of members of the force; after consulting the Chief Constable and with the approval of the Home Secretary, it appoints the Deputy Chief Constable and Assistant Chief Constable; with the consent of the Home Secretary it provides buildings, and subject to any regulations it provides vehicles and equipment.

The Chief Constable has direction and control of his force (Police Act 1964, s.5).[54] The police authority, with the approval of the Home Secretary, may call on the Chief Constable, Deputy Chief Constable or Assistant Chief Constable to retire in the interests of efficiency. (This does not necessarily imply the inefficiency of the officer himself.) Before seeking the approval of the Home Secretary, the police authority is required to give the Chief Constable or other officer an opportunity to make representations, and to consider any representations so made (Police Act 1964, s.5(5); s.6(5); Police (Scotland) Act 1967, s.4(4) and (5); s.5(6)). By contrast the Commissioner of the Metropolitan Police is appointed by the sovereign under the sign manual and holds office during Her Majesty's pleasure. (Metropolitan Police Act 1829, s.1).

Appointments and promotions below the rank of Assistant Chief Constable are made by the Chief Constable, subject to regulations made by the Home Secretary (s.7 of the 1964 Act; s.6 of the 1967 Act).

The Chief Constable must submit an annual report to the police authority, and the latter may require him to report on specific matters from time to time (s.12 of the 1964 Act; s.15 of the 1967 Act).

Provision is made in the Police Acts for collaboration and mutual aid between police forces, to be arranged by Chief Constables with the approval of their police authorities (ss.13 and 14 of the 1964 Act; ss.11 and 12 of the 1967 Act). These provisions have assumed a new importance and effectiveness as a result of the establishment at New Scotland Yard of the National Reporting Centre which co-ordinates the requirements and needs of police forces during, for example, strikes such as the miners' in 1984–1985 and large scale disorders. The Chief Constable may agree to provide special police services at any premises in his area, *e.g.* at demonstrations on private premises: charges are payable to the police authority on such a scale as may be determined by that authority (s.15 of the 1964 Act; ss.13 and 14 of the 1967 Act).

The Home Secretary may order the amalgamation of police forces if he considers it expedient in the interests of efficiency (s.21). Police authorities may propose amalgamation, in which case the proposals must be submitted to the Home Secretary for his approval.[55]

Functions of the Secretary of State

The Home Secretary has a general duty to exercise his powers under the Act in such manner and to such extent as appears to him to be best

---

[53] In Scotland these powers are exercised by the Secretary of State for Scotland.

[54] The Police (Scotland) Act 1967, s.17(2) explicitly makes the performance by a constable of his functions "subject to the direction of the appropriate chief constable."

[55] The comparable provisions in the Scottish Act of 1967 are ss.19 and 20. The number of police forces in England and Wales is now 43; in May, 1966 there were 117. A similar process in Scotland has reduced the number of forces to 8.

calculated to promote the efficiency of the police (s.28).[56] This gives the Home Secretary a wider responsibility outside London than he had before, and so extends the range of questions he may be asked in Parliament. He may be asked, for example, whether he intends to call for a report from, or to require the removal of, a Chief Constable. The Home Secretary may require a police authority to exercise its power to call on a Chief Constable to retire in the interests of efficiency, after hearing his representations and holding an inquiry (s.29). He may require a Chief Constable to submit a report on specific matters, and a copy of the Chief Constable's annual report to the police authority must be sent to him (s.30).[57]

The Home Secretary may make grants to police authorities of such amounts, and subject to such conditions, as he may with the approval of the Treasury determine (s.31). The police grant has for some years amounted to 50 per cent. of police expenditure. The Home Secretary may withhold, or threaten to withhold, the whole or part of this grant if, for example, a police authority tries to appoint or declines to dismiss a Chief Constable contrary to his wishes.[58]

The Home Secretary and the Secretary of State for Scotland may cause local inquiries to be held into local police matters, either in public or in private (s.32 and s.29). They have power to make regulations concerning the government, administration and conditions of service generally. In particular they may make regulations concerning discipline.[59] The police authority is the disciplinary authority with regard to the Chief Constable, any Deputy and any Assistant. The Chief Constable is the disciplinary authority for other ranks. Appeal lies ultimately to the Secretary of State in disciplinary cases.

The Home Secretary determines the number of Inspectors of Constabulary who are appointed to the Crown to inspect and report on the efficiency of police forces (s.38). He may appoint a Chief Inspector of Constabulary. The latter, who is concerned with research and planning, must report annually to the Home Secretary, and his report is laid before Parliament.[60]

The Chief Constable: police accountability

The historical background and statutory framework outlined in the preceding pages provide the context in which must be answered a question to which increasing attention has been given in the last few years, to what extent is the Chief Constable subject to political control? This has at least two aspects; his relationship with his police authority and the responsibility in Parliament of the appropriate Secretary of State for police matters. There are various reasons for the prominence this question has assumed. The reduction in the number of police forces

---

[56] The Scottish Act again prefers to avoid generality and lists the powers and duties of the Secretary of State in s.26 and subsequent sections.

[57] See similarly Police (Scotland) Act 1967, ss.15(2) and 31.

[58] See too Police (Scotland) Act 1967, s.32.

[59] Police Act 1964, s.33, as amended by Police and Criminal Evidence Act 1984, s.101; Police (Scotland) Act 1967, s.26, as amended by Police and Criminal Evidence Act 1984, s.111.

[60] See too Police (Scotland) Act 1967, s.33.

has made individual Chief Constables more important and powerful. The willingness of individual chief officers to express views on controversial issues in public has also helped to increase an awareness of their powers and their unique position. More important, however, have been controversies arising from the activities of the police in dealing with both the riots and large scale disorders which have, since 1981, taken place in London, Birmingham, Bristol and Liverpool, and industrial disputes such as the miners' strike in 1984–1985, the Grunwick affair in 1977 and currently the Wapping Controversy. Police measures to deal with these events—and their effectiveness in doing so—have drawn attention to the degree of co-operation between forces achieved through the National Reporting Centre,[61] so that it has seemed that the United Kingdom had acquired a *de facto* national police force. Armed police, to deal with terrorists and the threat of terrorism; visored police equipped with shields and staves to deal with rioters and looters, and to uphold the law against violent masses of striking workers have become almost common place.

As we saw earlier, the Court of Appeal in the *Blackburn* litigation,[62] while asserting a degree of judicial control over chief officers of Police denied that they were subject to political control. That may have been the assumption behind the drafting of the Police Acts 1964 and 1967, although it cannot be said to be explicitly stated in those statutes. Even if such an assumption had become the orthodox view by some earlier stage in this century the correctness of that view is open to doubt.[63] It can hardly find an adequate foundation in *Fisher* v. *Oldham Corporation*,[64] where the corporation was held not liable through its Watch Committee for false imprisonment on account of the arrest and detention of the plaintiff by one of its police inspectors through mistaken identity. A police officer, said McCardie J., was not a servant or agent of the police authority in exercising his powers of arrest and detention. A decision on the vicarious liability for the wrongful act of an individual constable on the part of a police authority is not necessarily relevant to the position of the chief constable in relation to his authority with regard to general matters of policy.

The *Blackburn* thesis has the advantage from the point of view of the Secretaries of State that they are, by and large, not liable to be questioned on police matters. An exception to this general evasion of responsibility is to be found in the case of the Metropolitan Police Force. The terms of the Metropolitan Police Act 1829 itself and the precedents of over a century would prevent any attempt by a Home Secretary to deny a large degree of control over and therefore responsibility for the metropolitan police.[65]

In principle the lack of political accountability is hard to justify, particularly when it is impossible to believe that Chief Constables decide

[61] The Centre was apparently first extensively used to cope with the problems of crowd control caused by the visit to the United Kingdom of Pope John Paul II in 1982.
[62] *Supra*, p. 410.
[63] See works cited p. 407, n. 1.
[64] [1930] 2 K.B. 364.
[65] See further R. Plehwe, "Police and Government: The Commissioner of the Police for the Metropolis" [1974] P.L. 316.

whether or not to prevent pickets from barring access to mines, for example, across the country without paying some attention to the views of the government. In the light of the traditional British dislike of a national police force it is difficult to envisage legislation vesting political control in the central government. On the other hand, "democratic accountability" to local authorities might result, in very different patterns of law enforcement from area to area.[66] There may be room for a community interest in policing, as is recognised in the Police and Criminal Evidence Act 1984, s.106 which requires arrangements in each area to be made for obtaining the views of people in that area about matters concerning the policing of the area and for obtaining their co-operation with the police in preventing crime in the area.[67] The maintenance of essential services and of law and order are, on the other hand, matters of national interest.

Complaints against police officers[68]

An important aspect of genuine accountability of the police to the public, as opposed to the members of a police authority, is the existence of a satisfactory system to deal with complaints against the police. To say that the citizen has the right of recourse to the courts is unrealistic on various accounts. He may not be able to obtain the necessary evidence by his own efforts; the conduct he complains of may not constitute a crime or tort but still fall below the standard properly expected of a public servant. The Police Act 1964, s.49 required the Chief Officer of each force to record any complaint made against a police officer and (unless the complaint alleged an offence with which the officer has already been charged) to investigate it. In view of concern in some quarters that complaints against police officers were investigated by fellow officers the Police Act 1976 introduced outsiders into the investigatory process. The Act established a Police Complaints Board. No one was eligible to be a member of the Board who was or had been a police officer. The procedure laid down in 1976 involved the investigation of a complaint by the police, followed by a report to the Board. Where an investigation revealed the likelihood of a criminal offence a report was to be made to the Director of Public Prosecutions. Where a disciplinary offence, not amounting to a crime, seemed to have been committed further proceedings were to take place either before the Chief Constable or in some cases, a tribunal consisting of the Chief Constable and two members of the Board.[69]

The system introduced by the 1976 Act was criticised on the grounds that the investigation of a complaint remained in the hands of the police at the initial stage; it made no distinction between minor and serious complaints and the requirement that cases involving the likelihood of the commission of a crime be referred to the Director of Public Prosecu-

---

[66] And for some might be open to the criticisms trenchantly made by G. Marshall, *Constitutional Conventions*, p. 143.

[67] The importance of this issue was stressed by Lord Scarman in his report on the Brixton Disorders: Cmnd. 8427 (1981).

[68] This section has no application to Scotland.

[69] A separate procedure applied to officers above the rank of superintendent.

tions resulted in a large number of cases being sent to him which, for one reason or another, were unlikely to end in criminal proceedings.

The Police and Criminal Evidence Act 1984 has introduced a new scheme[70] for dealing with complaints which it is hoped will meet the criticisms levelled at the 1976 scheme. The Complaints Board has been replaced by a Police Complaints Authority whose independence is emphasised by the provision that its chairman shall be appointed by the Queen. The other members, none of whom may be, or have been, police constables, shall be appointed by the Secretary of State (s.83 and Sched. 4). Complaints may be made by a member of the public or by anyone on behalf of a member of the public—for example, the M.P. of a person aggrieved. The chief officer in whose area a complaint is made must take steps to obtain or preserve evidence relating to the complaint although he may subsequently refer the complaint to the Chief Officer of another force if it appears that it is appropriate to do so (s.84). Complaints relating to officers above the rank of chief superintendent (senior officers) cannot be dealt with by a chief officer of a force but must be referred to the relevant police authority (s.86).[70a] In the case of other ranks the procedure subsequent to the making of a complaint is the responsibility of a chief officer. Unlike the earlier system for dealing with complaints, provision is made for the informal resolution of complaints where that is appropriate (s.85). Chief constables or police authorities *must* refer to the Police Complaints Authority any complaint alleging that conduct complained of resulted in death or serious injury (s.87). Any matter *may* be referred to the Complaints Authority where it appears that a police officer has committed a criminal offence or an offence against discipline and the matter has not been made the subject of a complaint and (2) the matter ought to be referred by reason of its gravity or exceptional circumstances (s.88). In the light of the discussion earlier of the accountability of chief officers it should be noted that it is expressly provided by section 84 that the new procedure does not apply to any complaint "in so far as it relates to the direction or control of a police force by the chief officer or the person performing the functions of the chief officer."

A new feature of the procedure laid down by the 1984 Act is that the investigation stage of complaints is to be subject to the supervision of the Complaints Authority in all cases involving death or serious injury and in other cases if they consider it desirable in the public interest (s.89). Supervision may take the form of approving a particular officer to carry out the investigation and imposing specific requirements as to the carrying out of the investigation (s.89).

Once the investigation is complete the procedure depends on whether the complaint relates to senior officers or not. In the case of senior officers the report must be sent to the Director of Public Prosecutions unless the police authority (of the relevant force) is satisfied that

---

[70] See further M. Zander, *The Police and Criminal Evidence Act* (1985), p. 122 *et seq.*

[70a] See, for example, the investigation into allegations against the deputy chief constable of the Greater Manchester force, Mr. John Stalker. The Police Authority appointed the Chief Constable of another force to examine the allegations. He produced a 1,500 page report at an estimated cost of £250,000. Mr. Stalker was ultimately cleared of all charges against him.

no criminal offence has been committed (s.90(1)). In the case of other officers the chief officer of the force must decide whether the report indicates that a criminal offence has been committed and that the offence is such that the officer ought to be charged: if he does so decide he must forward the report to the Director of Public Prosecutions. He must, after the Director has dealt with the question of criminal proceedings, inform the Complaints Authority whether he intends to prefer disciplinary charges.[71] If the chief officer decides that the officer ought not to be charged with a criminal offence he must inform the Complaints Authority and again indicate whether he intends to prefer disciplinary proceedings. Finally if the chief officer concludes that the report does not indicate the commission of a criminal offence he must relay his conclusion to the Complaints Authority and indicate whether he intends to prefer disciplinary proceedings (s.90(3)–(7)). The Authority may, if it thinks an officer below the rank of chief superintendent should have been charged, direct a chief officer to send a report to the Director of Public Prosecutions (s.92). Similarly they may require disciplinary charges to be laid (s.93). Charges laid under s.93, or in other cases where the Complaints Authority direct, are to be heard by a disciplinary tribunal, consisting of the chief officer and two members of the Authority.[72]

Police authorities and Inspectors of Constabulary are required to keep themselves informed about the way in which complaints are dealt with (s.95). The Complaints Authority is required to make an annual report to the Secretary of State and may make other reports on any matter coming to their notice in connection with their responsibility (s.97).

---

[71] The standard of proof required in disciplinary proceedings is that required in criminal cases before the courts, *i.e.* beyond reasonable doubt: Police (Discipline) Regulations 1985, S.I. 1985 No. 518, reg. 23(2)(*b*). This restores the position to what had formerly believed to be the law: R. v. *Police Complaints Board, ex p. Madden* [1983] 1 W.L.R. 447, 467. In R. v. *Hampshire C.C., ex p. Ellerton* [1985] 1 W.L.R. 749, the Court of Appeal refused to hold that the criminal standard applied to the disciplinary code of the Fire Service (although it thought the graver the offence the higher the degree of probability required) and doubted the correctness of McNeill J.'s dictum in *ex p. Madden*.
[72] s.96 provides for the application of the complaints procedure to constables maintained by bodies other than local government police authorities, *e.g.* British Transport Police: *supra*, p. 414.

PART V

RIGHTS AND DUTIES OF THE INDIVIDUAL

CHAPTER 22

RIGHTS AND DUTIES GENERALLY

In this Part we discuss the civil rights which have been traditionally recognised as the hall marks of a free society. We discuss also some areas of the criminal law which are designed to preserve a society in which these rights can be exercised and to protect individuals against undue invasion of their rights by the actions of others. Dicey was concerned in his discussion of basic civil rights to demonstrate that they had been deduced as principles from judicial decisions determining the rights of private persons in particular cases brought before the Courts "whereas under many foreign constitutions the security (such as it is) given to the rights of individuals results, or appears to result, from the general principles of the constitution."[1] At this stage of the twentieth century it may be difficult to feel as sanguine as Dicey did about the role of the Courts in guaranteeing freedom. In many important areas rights depend on practices and understandings outside the ambit of case law or statute "so that legal and political accountability is for some purposes only minimal."[2] On the other hand in some areas rights are now to be found defined in statutes and, increasingly, international agreements are invoked, whether as having legal effect in the United Kingdom or as setting a standard for our domestic laws.

I. RIGHTS OF THE INDIVIDUAL

Rights of the individual under the United Kingdom Constitution[3]
As has been seen in Chapter 2, there are under the constitution of the United Kingdom no rights strictly fundamental, in the sense of entrenched (basic, inalienable), because of the supremacy of Parliament and the absence of a written constitution with entrenched provisions and judicial review of Acts of Parliament.[4] Yet no country in history has made a greater contribution than Britain to the recognition of the rights of the individual and their protection by an independent judiciary against government authorities. The idea that men have, or are entitled to, certain natural rights which are inherent in the nature of man, derived from the natural law of Greek philosophers, was disseminated

---

[1] *The Law of the Constitution* (10th ed.), p. 195.
[2] D. G. T. Williams, "Civil Liberties and the Protection of Statute" [1981] Cur.Leg Prob. 25.
[3] For rights generally, see Maurice Cranston, *What are Human Rights?* (1973); Bernard Schwartz, *The Great Rights of Mankind* (1977). For rights in English law, see Harry Street, *Freedom, the Individual and the Law* (5th ed., 1982); I. N. Stevens and D. C. M. Yardley, *The Protection of Liberty* (1982); S. H. Bailey, D. J. Harris and B. L. Jones, *Civil Liberties, Cases and Materials* (2nd ed., 1985).
[4] *Ante*, p. 40. This general principle is true although the detailed laws on individual rights and duties differ in England and Scotland.

in the eighteenth century. In the political context such rights are often called civil, as they are regarded as belonging to men as citizens; and they may be contrasted with social, economic or cultural rights, such as the right to work, holidays with pay, medical services and social security, which are ideals of State policy as many countries cannot afford them and they cannot be guaranteed merely by legislation. In the international sphere the rights of the individual have been elaborated in the twentieth century under the name of human rights, regarded as belonging to men as human beings, universal in place as well as time, and imposing an international obligation on States to protect them.

Jurists might classify most of the constitutionally important "rights" of the individual as liberties (freedoms) and immunities.[5] In the United Kingdom the liberties of the individual, such as freedom of expression and association, are residual; they represent the freedom of action left over when the limitations imposed by statute and common law have been subtracted. No legal system can allow absolute rights. There must be a balance or compromise between the interests of one individual and the interests of other individuals and of society (public order and security).

International Covenants[6]

Popularisation of the concept of human rights in the western world began in 1941[7] during the Second World War with the Atlantic Charter, a joint declaration by the United States President (Franklin Roosevelt) and the United Kingdom Prime Minister (Churchill), and Roosevelt's message to Congress proclaiming the Four Freedoms—freedom of speech and expression, freedom of religion, freedom from fear and freedom from want; followed by a declaration of United Nations war aims in 1942 that victory was essential to defend life, liberty, independence and religious freedom, and to preserve human rights and justice. These rights were elaborated in the Universal Declaration of Human Rights adopted and proclaimed in 1949 by the General Assembly of the United Nations, including the United Kingdom.[8] No attempt was made at the time to specify limitations on those rights; to distinguish political, economic and social rights; or to provide machinery for enforcement. The United Nations drew up more elaborate formulations in 1966—in some respects improving on the European Convention—in the International Covenant on Economic, Social and Cultural Rights and the International Covenant on Civil and Political Rights, which were ratified by the United Kingdom in 1976 with certain reservations in relation to education and dependent territories.

---

[5] The best analysis is still W. N. Hohfeld, *Fundamental Legal Conceptions as Applied in Judicial Reasoning* (ed. W. W. Cook, Yale Univ. Press, 1923).

[6] Ian Brownlie (ed.), *Basic Documents on Human Rights* (1971); H. Lauterpacht, "The Universal Declaration of Human Rights" (1948) B.Y.L.L. 354; *International Law and Human Rights* (1950).

[7] Important work has been done (and continues to be done) in its own field by the International Labour Organisation which was established after the First World War.

[8] *Ante*, p. 16.

The European Convention[9]

The Member States of the Council of Europe,[10] being a number of democratic European countries including the United Kingdom, drew up the European Convention for the Protection of Human Rights and Fundamental Freedoms in 1950 as a first step in the collective enforcement of certain of the rights stated in the Universal Declaration. The United Kingdom ratified the Convention in 1951,[11] and although it is not part of English or Scots law[12] the Convention has begun to exert so strong an influence on the way civil rights are regarded in this country that it is appropriate to include here some account of the contents of the Convention and the machinery for its enforcement.

Article 1 binds the State parties to secure to everyone within their jurisdiction the rights and freedoms defined in the Convention, and Article 13 provides that everyone whose rights and freedoms are violated shall have an effective remedy, even though the violation has been committed by persons acting in an official capacity. Typical limitations on the rights are those necessary in a democratic society in the interests of national security or public safety, for the prevention of disorder or crime, for the protection of health or morals, or for the protection of the rights and freedoms of others. Article 14 forbids discrimination on any ground such as sex, race, colour, language, religion, political or other opinion, national or social origin, association with a national minority, property, birth or other status. No state, group or person has any right to perform any act aimed at the destruction of any of the rights set forth in the Convention (Art. 17); nor may the rights be abused by being applied for any purpose other than those for which they have been prescribed (Art. 18). A State party may take measures, within limits, to derogate from the rights in time of war or serious emergency (Art. 15).

[9] Cmd. 8969 (1953), *European Convention;* (1954) Cmd. 9221, Ian Brownlie (ed.) *Basic Documents on Human Rights* (1971); F. G. Jacobs, *The European Convention on Human Rights* (1975); A. H. Robertson, *Human Rights in Europe* (2nd ed., 1977); J. E. S. Fawcett, *The Application of the European Convention on Human Rights* (1969); R. Beddard, *Human Rights and Europe* (2nd ed. 1980); A. Drzemczewski, *European Human Rights Convention in Domestic Law* (1983).

[10] The Council of Europe was established in 1949: the aim of the Council was declared by its founding Statute to be "to achieve a greater unity between its Members for the purpose of safeguarding and realising the ideals and principles which are their common heritage and facilitating their economic and social progress." The Council now has twenty-one members (Austria, Belgium, Cyprus, Denmark, France, West Germany, Greece, Iceland, Ireland, Italy, Liechtenstein, Luxembourg, Malta, Netherlands, Norway, Portugal, Spain, Sweden, Switzerland, Turkey and the United Kingdom).

[11] Lord Jowett, then Lord Chancellor, thought that accepting the Convention would "jeopardise our whole system of law, which we have laboriously built up over the centuries, in favour of some half baked scheme to be administered by some unknown court": see Anthony Lester, "Fundamental Rights, The United Kingdom Isolated" [1984] P.L. 46, 51.

[12] An unarguable proposition, strengthened by judicial authority: *R. v. Secretary of State for the Home Dept. ex p. Fernandes, The Times,* November 21, 1980 (C.A.); *Taylor v. Co-operative Retail Society* [1982] I.C.R. 600 (C.A.); *R. v. Secretary of State for the Home Department, ex p. Kirkwood* [1984] 1 W.L.R. 913; *R. v. Secretary of State for the Home Department, ex p. McAvoy* [1984] 1 W.L.R. 1408; *Kaur v. Lord Advocate* [1980] 3 C.M.L.R. 79; 1981 S.L.T. 322; *post,* p. 429.

Enforcement of the European Convention

A State party may refer to the *European Commission of Human Rights* any alleged breach of the provisions of the Convention by another State party. The Commission may also receive petitions from any person or group of individuals claiming to be the victim of a violation by a State party of the rights set forth in the Convention, if the State party against which complaint is made has recognised the competence of the Commission to receive individual petitions, as the United Kingdom has done.[13] The European Commission consists of one national of each State party,[14] though they serve as individuals and not as national representatives, elected by the Committee of Ministers (*post*) from a list drawn up by the Consultative Assembly consisting of parliamentarians of the member States. The Commission may only deal with a matter after all domestic remedies have been exhausted. Over ninety per cent. of individual petitions fall at the first hurdle, that of admissibility. The Commission investigates the case *in camera* together with the representatives of the parties, and if it thinks there is a prima facie breach it tries to secure a friendly settlement. If a settlement is not reached, the Commission reports to the Committee of Ministers and to the States concerned its opinion as to whether a breach of the Convention has been committed.

The Committee of Ministers, composed of the Foreign Ministers of the State parties or their deputies, is the executive organ of the Council of Europe. The Committee considers the Commission's report. If the question is not referred to the Court (*post*), the Committee of Ministers decides whether there has been a violation of the Convention. If so, the State concerned has a certain time in which to take the required measures. If satisfactory measures are not taken, the Committee of Ministers decides what effect shall be given to its decision.

The European Court of Human Rights, which sits at Strasbourg, consists of a number of judges equal to that of the members of the Council of Europe, not more than one national from the same State. The judges, who are part-time, are elected by the Consultative Assembly from a list of qualified persons nominated by the Council of Europe. The Court elects its own President. Each case is heard by seven judges, a judge who is a national of any State party concerned sitting *ex officio*. The Court's jurisdiction extends to the interpretation and application of the Convention. Cases may be brought before the Court only by State parties[15] or the Commission, and not by individuals. The Court may only deal with a case after the Commission has failed to secure a friendly settlement. In accordance with the general principle of international law as well as the Convention itself, a State party is not subject to the jurisdiction of the Court unless it has accepted its jurisdiction as compulsory. The United Kingdom has accepted the compulsory jurisdiction of the Court for five-yearly periods. The Court cannot annul acts and has no power to enforce its decisions, though State parties undertake to

---

[13] Most recently for a further five year period from Jan. 1st. 1986: H.C.Deb. vol. 84, col. 213, Oct 24, 1985.

[14] Strictly the Commission consists of a number of members equal to that of the State parties.

[15] *i.e.* a State party whose national is alleged to be a victim, or which referred the case to the Commission or against which the complaint has been lodged.

abide by its decisions in cases to which they are parties. Its judgment is sent to the Committee of Ministers, which supervises its execution. Decisions of the Committee of Ministers on reports of the Commission, and its directives on decisions of the Court, are binding on State parties, that is, binding in international law by treaty though not in British constitutional law. The Convention may be renounced after five years.

Cases against the United Kingdom in the European Court of Human Rights

The first case brought to the Court by a State was *Republic of Ireland* v. *United Kingdom*[16] concerning the treatment by security forces of internees in Northern Ireland in 1971. The United Kingdom admitted that certain sensory deprivation techniques constituted inhuman and degrading treatment (Art. 3), and the Court found the United Kingdom guilty on this ground; but all these methods had been stopped after a few months in 1971 and their victims compensated. The Court, delivering its judgment in January, 1978, held that there was no torture (Art. 3) or discrimination against Roman Catholic internees (Art. 14), and that internment of suspects was justified by the emergency in Northern Ireland (Art. 15). The first case against the United Kingdom to reach the Court arising from an individual application to the Commission was *Golder* v. *United Kingdom*[17] where a former prisoner had been refused access to his solicitor and so denied the opportunity to bring an action against a police officer. The Court held the British prison rules to be in breach of the Convention (Art. 6, access to the courts; Art. 8, respect for correspondence), and the Home Secretary later announced a change of rules. In *Handyside* v. *United Kingdom*[18] the Court held that the order of an English court to seize and destroy copies of the *Little Red Schoolbook* under the Obscene Publications Acts was not a violation of Article 20 (freedom of expression) or Article 1 of the First Protocol (peaceful enjoyment of possessions), the State having a discretion whether measures are "necessary in a democratic society." In 1978 the Court decided in the case of *Tyrer* v. *United Kingdom*[19] that the use of birching as a judicial punishment in the Isle of Man was a degrading punishment (under Art. 3). The United Kingdom, although it disapproves of birching, had to defend the Isle of Man because it is responsible for the Island's external affairs. For the future the difficulty has been solved by abrogating the right of individual petition in the case of the Isle of Man. The law of contempt of court as interpreted by the House of Lords in *Attorney-General* v. *Times Newspapers Ltd.*[20] was found to be in breach of the Convention by a majority of the members of the Court in the case of the *Sunday Times* v. *United Kingdom*.[21] In *Dudgeon* v. *United Kingdom*[22] the

---

[16] (1978) 2 E.H.R.R. 25.

[17] (1975) 1 E.H.R.R. 524; a decision described as "almost grotesque": F. A. Mann, "Britain's Bill of Rights" (1978) 94 L.Q.R. 512, 524. See also *Silver* v. *U.K.* (1983) 5 E.H.R.R. 347.

[18] (1976) 1 E.H.R.R. 737.

[19] (1978) 2 E.H.R.R. 1. See further *Teare* v. *O'Callaghan* (1981) 4 E.H.R.R. 232; S. Ghandhi, (1983) 46 M.L.R. 513.

[20] [1974] A.C. 273; *ante*, p. 403.

[21] (1979) 2 E.H.R.R. 245.

[22] (1981) 4 E.H.R.R. 149.

Court held that Northern Irish legislation which forbade homosexual acts between consenting male adults was in violation of Article 8 (respect for private life). The procedure for recalling to mental hospitals patients released on conditions by the Secretary of State under section 66(3) of the Mental Health Act 1959 was held to be in breach of Article 5 in X v. *United Kingdom*.[23] The Court has held that the use of corporal punishment in schools, contrary to the wishes of parents, violates the right of parents under Article 2 of the First Protocol, to have their philosophical convictions respected by the State in the education of children: *Campbell and Cosans* v. *United Kingdom*.[24] In *Young, James and Webster* v. *United Kingdom*[25] the Court found that provisions of the Trade Union and Labour Relations Act 1974 violated the right of workers not to join a union (Article 11). The distinction drawn by the United Kingdom's immigration laws between the rights of wives and husbands to join spouses lawfully settled in the United Kingdom was held to be discrimination in violation of Article 14 and Article 13 (no effective remedy under domestic law) *Abdulaziz, Cabales and Balkandali* v. *United Kingdom*.[26] *Malone* v. *United Kingdom*[27] held that the law on telephone tapping, in force at the time of the acts complained of, violated Article 8 (right to private life). The rights of prisoners were again before the Court in *Campbell and Fell* v. *United Kingdom*[28] where the procedure for dealing with charges against prisoners by prison Boards of Visitors was found to be in breach of Article 6. On the other hand in *James* v. *United Kingdom*[29] the Court rejected the argument that the right given to leaseholders to buy their freeholds in certain circumstances at a price calculated by a statutory formula was a taking of property in violation of Article 1 of the First Protocol.

In some of the cases before the Court the law of the United Kingdom had been changed before the hearing took place. In the others the United Kingdom has later attempted to comply with the decision of the Court, whether by legislation, delegated legislation or ministerial circular.

Applications against the United Kingdom to the European Commission of Human Rights

A large number of applications to the Commission against the United Kingdom have been concerned with immigration and internment in Northern Ireland.[30] The Commission reported to the Council of Ministers against the United Kingdom on the grounds of degrading treatment (Art. 3), discrimination (Art. 14) and interference with family life (Art. 8) in the East African Cases, which were settled by admission of the applicants to the United Kingdom.[31] The application of Amakrane, a

---

[23] (1981) 4 E.H.R.R. 188.
[24] (1982) 4 E.H.R.R. 293.
[25] (1981) 4 E.H.R.R. 38.
[26] (1985) 7 E.H.R.R. 471.
[27] (1985) 7 E.H.R.R. 14.
[28] (1985) 7 E.H.R.R. 165.
[29] (1986) 8 E.H.R.R. 123. There had been a similar lack of success in *Lithgow* v. *U.K.* (1986) 8 E.H.R.R. 329.
[30] For the following Court proceedings, see *ante*, p. 427.
[31] (1981) 3 E.H.R.R. 76.

rebel Moroccan officer extradited from Gibraltar for a political offence, was held admissible by the Commission (1973), but the United Kingdom made him an *ex gratia* payment and the application was withdrawn. The Commission upheld a complaint by a prisoner of Broadmoor about the conditions of his detention and a settlement was agreed with the government: *A* v. *United Kingdom* (1980).

Proceedings were brought before the Commission following the decision of the House of Lords in *Home Office* v. *Harman*[32] (contempt of court) but compromised when the Government undertook to introduce legislation to amend the law. Applications which have been ruled inadmissible by the Commission include those relating to the status of boy servicemen (1968) (Art. 4, servitude, etc.); the conviction of Bernadette Devlin M.P. (1971) for riotous behaviour during street fighting in Northern Ireland (Art. 6, fair trial); the deportation of Philip Agee, an American journalist, on security grounds (Art. 6, public hearing: discretion of Home Secretary)[33]; religious discrimination in the case of a Muslim teacher (*Ahmad*)[34] and the right to join a trade union (*Cheall*).[35]

The European Convention in the courts of the United Kingdom

Treaties cannot affect rights and duties of persons in the United Kingdom unless their provisions have been incorporated into domestic law by legislation. That fundamental principle, was illustrated in the *G.C.H.Q.* Case[36] when Lord Fraser in the part of his speech headed "Minor matters" declined to consider the interpretation of certain international labour conventions because they were "not part of the law in this country." In *British Airways Board* v. *Laker Airways Ltd.*[37] Lord Diplock said, "The interpretation of treaties to which the United Kingdom is a party but the terms of which have not either expressly or by reference been incorporated in English domestic law by legislation is not a matter that falls within the interpretative jurisdiction of an English court of law." Nonetheless the Convention is frequently cited in the courts and judges on various occasions have referred to its provisions although no decision can be said to have been based on the Convention. In *Kynaston* v. *Secretary of State for the Home Department*[38] the Court of Appeal held that the clear words of the United Kingdom mental health legislation prevailed over the provisions of Article 5 (right to liberty of the person). Article 6 (right to a hearing) was involved in *Trawnik* v. *Lennox.*[39] Sir Robert Megarry V.-C. said "The [European] Convention [of Human Rights] is not, of course, law though it is legitimate to consider its provisions in interpreting the law; and naturally I give it full weight for this purpose."[40] Nonetheless, he (and subsequently the Court of Appeal) applied the letter of the Crown Proceed-

---

[32] [1983] A.C. 280.
[33] See *R.* v. *Secretary of State for the Home Department, ex p. Hosenball* [1977] 1 W.L.R. 766 (C.A.).
[34] A sequel to *Ahmad* v. *Inner London Education Authority* [1978] Q.B. 36 (C.A.); *post*, p. 430.
[35] A sequel to *Cheall* v. *APEX* [1983] A.C. 180 (H.L.); *post*, p. 430.
[36] *Council of Civil Service Unions* v. *Minister for the Civil Service* [1985] A.C. 374.
[37] [1985] A.C. 58.
[38] (1981) 73 Cr.App.R. 281.
[39] [1985] 1 W.L.R. 532.
[40] At p. 541.

ings Act 1947. Article 8 (respect for private and family life) was similarly invoked in vain in an attempt to challenge the legality of telephone tapping in *Malone* v. *Commissioner of Police of the Metropolis*.[41] Article 8 and Article 14 (enjoyment of rights without discrimination) have failed to aid immigrants in the light of the provisions of the Immigration Act 1971 and the Immigration Rules: "The Convention is not part of the law of this country. If it happens to be in accord with the law so much the better. But on the other hand if it does not accord with the law . . . then it is a matter of which we cannot take any account: *R.* v. *Immigration Appeal Tribunal ex p. Ali Ajmal*,[42] per Lord Lane C.J.

Article 9 (freedom of religious expression) was unsuccessfully relied on in *Ahmad* v. *Inner London Education Authority*.[43] Lord Denning M.R. described the convention as "drawn in such vague terms that it can be used for all sorts of unreasonable claims and provoke all sorts of litigation." Article 9 was invoked by Lord Scarman in *R.* v. *Lemon*[44] to justify limitations on free speech. Article 10 (freedom of speech) was cited by Lord Simon and Lord Scarman in their dissenting speech in *Home Office* v. *Harman*[45] (as well as Milton and the Constitution of the United States). In *R.* v. *Wells Street Stipendiary Magistrate ex p. Deakin*[46] the House of Lords indicated the need for a reform of the law of criminal libel and Lord Diplock described the present English law as being contrary to Article 10. In *Schering Chemicals* v. *Falkman*[47] a majority in the Court of Appeal upheld the granting of injunction to prevent the showing of a television programme which had been sought on various grounds. Lord Denning M.R. (dissenting) referred to the importance of freedom of expression and quoted both Blackstone and Article 10. He said, "I take it that our law should conform as far as possible with the provisions of the European Convention of Human Rights." In a number of cases relating to trades unions references have been made to Article 11 (right to join and form unions)[48] but judges have differed sharply about the correct significance to draw from the Article when applied to particular facts. In *Cheall* v. *APEX*,[49] for example, Donaldson L.J. agreed with Lord Denning M.R. that "in matters of legal policy regard should be had to this country's international obligations to observe the treaty as interpreted by the European Court of Human Rights." Nonetheless, he found the conclusion drawn by the Master of the Rolls from Article 11 a "somewhat surprising proposition."

A provision of the Convention does not acquire any greater authority from having been interpreted by the European Court of Human Rights.

---

[41] [1979] Ch. 344; *post*, p. 518.
[42] [1982] Imm.A.R. 102 (C.A.).
[43] [1978] Q.B. 36 (C.A.); Scarman L.J. dissenting. See also *Panesar* v. *Nestlé Co.* [1980] I.C.R. 144 (C.A.).
[44] [1979] A.C. 617.
[45] [1983] 1 A.C. 280.
[46] [1980] A.C. 477.
[47] [1982] Q.B. 1.
[48] *e.g. R.* v. *G.L.C., ex p. Burgess* [1978] I.C.R. 991 (D.C.); *U.K.A.P.E.* v. *A.C.A.S.* [1979] 1 W.L.R. 570; [1981] A.C. 424; *Taylor* v. *Co-operative Retail Services Ltd.* [1982] I.C.R. 600 (C.A.).
[49] [1982] I.C.R. 231. Article 11 was also referred to in the House of Lords which reversed the decision of the Court of Appeal: [1983] 2 A.C. 180.

It is no defence to a criminal charge to plead a judgment of that Court; for example, a parent accused of refusing to send a child to a school where corporal punishment is administered to children cannot rely on *Campbell and Cosans (supra)*: *Jarman* v. *Mid-Glamorgan Education Authority.*[50]

At most, therefore, it can be said that the courts *may* look at the Convention when faced, as Donaldson L.J. suggested in *Cheall* v. *APEX (supra)*,[51] with a question of legal policy (or public policy), or where the substantive law is unclear as Lord Fraser suggested in *Attorney-General* v. *B.B.C.*,[52] "This House, and other courts in the United Kingdom should have regard to the provisions of the Convention [on Human Rights] and to the decisions of the Court of Human Rights in cases . . . where our domestic law is not firmly settled. But the Convention does not form part of our law and the decision on what that law is is for our domestic courts and for this House."

The Construction of Statutes

A particular example of the use of the Convention to aid in resolving uncertainty in the law may be said to be found in having recourse to its provisions as an aid to statutory interpretation.

The justification for doing so is that Parliament must know that the United Kingdom has ratified the Convention and so must be taken to intend not to legislate contrary to it. Thus in *R.* v. *Miah*,[53] where the question was whether penal provisions of the Immigration Act 1971 were retrospective, Lord Reid referred to Article 11 of the Universal Declaration and Article 7 of the European Convention (no *ex post facto* criminal laws) and said: "It is hardly credible that any government department would promote or that any Parliament would pass retrospective criminal legislation." In *Birdi* v. *Secretary of State for Home Affairs*,[54] where a detained illegal immigrant applied unsuccessfully for habeas corpus alleging violations of Article 5 (liberty of person), Article 6 (fair trial) and Article 13 (effective remedies), Lord Denning M.R. stated *obiter* that the courts could and should take the Convention into account when construing statutes, since all concerned with framing legislation after the Convention came into force must be assumed to have borne the Convention in mind. His Lordship even went so far as to suggest that an Act which did not conform might be held invalid (*cf. post*). Lord Denning in *Ex p. Bhajan Singh*,[55] where an illegal immigrant

---

[50] *The Times*, February 2, 1985.
[51] See similarly F. A. Mann, "Britain's Bill of Rights" (1978) 94 L.Q.R. 512. *Cf. R.* v. *Secretary of State for the Home Dept., ex p. Fernandes, The Times*, November 21, 1980; [1981] Imm.A.R. 1; *R.* v. *Secretary of State for the Home Dept., ex p. Kirkwood* [1984] 1 W.L.R. 913 (Secretary of State under no duty to consider Convention before deporting).
[52] [1981] A.C. 303.
[53] [1974] 1 W.L.R. 683 (H.L.). On the first reference to the Convention in an English court, see note by Stephenson L.J., (1979) 85 L.Q.R. 35.
[54] February 11, 1975 (C.A. unreported). *Cf. Minister of Home Affairs* v. *Fisher* [1980] A.C. 319 (P.C.). (Interpretation of Constitution of Bermuda in light of United Nation Conventions).
[55] *R.* v. *Secretary of State for Home Department, ex p. Bhajan Singh* [1976] Q.B. 198 (C.A.).

applied unsuccessfully for mandamus against the Home Office to permit him to marry while in custody and relied on Article 12 (marriage
and family), stated *obiter* that the courts should take account of the Convention when interpreting statutes affecting the rights and liberties of
the citizen; and that it was hardly credible that Parliament or any
government department would act contrary to the provisions of the
Convention, and regard must be had to them by Ministers and government officials. But His Lordship admitted he went too far in *Birdi*
(*supra*): if an Act did not conform to the Convention the Act would prevail. And Scarman L.J. in *Ex p. Phansopkar*,[56] where a Commonwealth
immigrant wife of a patrial was refused entry under the Immigration
Act 1971 on the ground that she had not obtained a certificate of patriality, referring to Article 8 (respect for family life) said it was the duty of
the courts to have regard to the Convention and to construe statutes so
as to promote those rights, so long as they do not disregard clear and
unequivocal provisions of the statute.

Subsequent English dicta have been somewhat more moderate. Thus
in *Ex p. Salamat Bibi*[57] where the wife and children of a Pakistani resident who sought to join him here after Pakistan had left the Commonwealth, were treated as foreign nationals and the wife cited Article 8 of
the Convention (family life), Lord Denning, after stating that the courts
can look to the Convention as an aid to clear up ambiguity in our statutes or uncertainty in our law,[58] added: "But I would dispute altogether
that the Convention is part of our law. Treaties and declarations do not
become part of our law until they are made law by Parliament. I desire,
however, to amend one of the statements I made in the *Bhajan Singh*
case [*ante*] . . . that the immigration officers ought to bear in mind the
principles stated in the Convention . . . . They must go simply by the
immigration rules laid down by the Secretary of State, and not by
the Convention." A Muslim teacher was held in *Ahmad* v. *I.L.E.A.*[59] not
to be entitled, either by the Education Act 1944 or by the European Convention, to preferential treatment to enable him to attend a Mosque in
school hours; Lord Denning saying that, although the Convention is
not part of our law the courts do their best to see that their decisions are
in conformity with it, but Article 9 (freedom of religion) was too vague
to be relied on here. Scarman L.J. in his dissenting judgment, however,
thought the Education Act 1944 had to be construed today in accordance
with that Article.[60]

---

[56] *R. v. Secretary of State for Home Department, ex p. Phansopkar* [1976] Q.B. 606 (C.A.).
[57] *R. v. Chief Immigration Officer, Heathrow Airport, ex p. Salamat Bibi* [1976] 1 W.L.R. 979
(C.A.).
[58] If this means common law, the statement is questionable.
[59] *Ahmad* v. *Inner London Education Authority* [1978] Q.B. 36 (C.A.). A subsequent application to the Commission was ruled inadmissible: (1982) 4 E.H.R.R. 126.
[60] See also *Broome* v. *Cassell & Co.* [1972] A.C. 1027, 1133 (H.L.), *per* Lord Kilbrandon (free
speech); *Blathwayte* v. *Baron Cawley* (1976) A.C. 397, 426, *per* Lord Wilberforce (public
policy); *R.* v. *Deevey* [1977] Crim.L.R. 550, *per* Sir Robert Lowry C.J.N.I. (Firearms Act);
R. v. *Secretary of State for Home Department, ex p. Hosenball* [1977] 1 W.L.R. 766 (C.A.)
(deportation on security grounds). *Cf. per* Scarman L.J. in *Pan-American World Airways
Inc.* v. *Department of Trade* [1976] 1 Lloyd's Rep. 257 (C.A.) (whether Bermuda Agreement on air travel part of English municipal law).

Even this moderate approach has been criticised in Scotland. Lord Ross in *Kaur* v. *Lord Advocate*[61] said "With all respect to the distinguished judges in England who have said that the courts should look to an international convention such as the European Convention of Human Rights for the purposes of interpreting a United Kingdom statute, I find such a concept extremely difficult to comprehend. If the Convention does not form part of the municipal law, I do not see why the court should have regard to it at all. It was His Majesty's government in 1950 which was a High Contracting Party to the Convention. The Convention has been ratified by the United Kingdom but . . . its provisions cannot be regarded as having the force of law . . . . Under our constitution it is the Queen in Parliament who legislates and not Her Majesty's government, and the court does not require to have regard to acts of Her Majesty's government when interpreting the law."

No decision of the British courts has actually been based on the European Convention. These dicta on the construction of statutes not purporting to implement a treaty do not follow from precedents concerned with construing statutes consistently with the general principles of international law[62] or statutes designed to implement particular treaties on such matters as diplomatic privilege. It is submitted, further, that their approach is potentially dangerous.[63] The judges wish to keep government officers to their international obligations, but in fact they are challenging the cardinal principle laid down in the *Case of Proclamations*[64] and our own Bill of Rights of 1688, that the Executive by itself cannot make law for this realm. Indeed, one might argue that the fact that Parliament has hitherto refrained from incorporating the European Convention into our law indicates an intention that its provisions should not be taken into account by the courts, so that the Convention ought not to be cited by counsel or looked at by judges.[65] In any event it is not clear whether the presumption that Acts of Parliament conform to the Convention applies only to statutes passed before the Convention was ratified, nor whether it applies only in proceedings against public authorities (however they may be defined).

Community Law

We saw in Chapter 5 that the law of the European Communities does have legal effect inside the United Kingdom. Unlike the European Convention, the Treaties establishing the Communities have been adopted by legislation of the United Kingdom Parliament. In some areas, particularly that of discrimination on the grounds of sex, British citizens have successfully claimed rights under EEC law. (Ironically, in the light

---

[61] [1980] 3 C.M.L.R. 79; 1981 S.L.T. 322.

[62] *Ante*, p. 57. The dicta may claim support of a dictum of Diplock L.J. in *Salamon* v. *Commissioners of Customs and Excise* [1967] 2 Q.B. 116, for which, however, he cited no authority.

[63] This sentence was quoted with approval from the 6th ed. (p. 446) by Lord Ross in *Kaur* v. *Lord Advocate (supra)*.

[64] (1610) 12 Co.Rep. 74.

[65] The fact that the treaty was presumably laid before both Houses of Parliament before being ratified by the Crown (*ante*, p. 285) does not affect the argument.

of their historical position, aliens too have established rights in the field of immigration and deportation.)

The European Court has recognised respect for fundamental human rights as one of the general principles of law which form part of Community law[66] and the Commission has accepted the desirability of the EEC becoming a signatory to the Convention on Human Rights.[67] Nonetheless, for the moment, it cannot be said that the Convention creates enforceable rights in the United Kingdom indirectly through our membership of the EEC: *Allgemeine Gold und Silberscheideanstalt* v. *Customs and Excise Commissioners.*[68]

Should the United Kingdom enact a new Bill of Rights?

Many modern constitutions contain a declaration of guaranteed rights, such as personal freedom, freedom of expression and of association.[69] In the Commonwealth the Indian Constitution (1950 as amended)[70] possesses probably the fullest formulation of fundamental rights based on English and American experience; several African members of the Commonwealth adopted formulations in the 1960s taking account of the European Convention; and later Malta and some Caribbean members followed suit, taking account also of other international covenants. Such expressions as a "Bill of Rights" or "Declaration of Rights" or "fundamental" or "guaranteed" rights in most democratic countries imply that the rights concerned are entrenched or legally protected against repeal or amendment by ordinary legislative process. This country has no codified constitution into which an enacted declaration of fundamental rights could be fitted; and the inability of Parliament to bind itself or its successors, and the incompetence of the courts to examine or question the procedure by which an Act of Parliament came to be enacted,[71] would apply to an Act for the repeal or amendment of an enacted Bill of Rights. As we have suggested[72] nothing short of a revolution in the basis of our constitutional system would enable this country to entrench a Bill of Rights so as to preserve it from repeal or abridgment by an ordinary Act of Parliament and to provide for judicial review of Acts of Parliament. An attempt to bring about such a drastic constitutional transformation would scarcely be worth undertaking except as part of a general reform of our constitution, including such matters as a reformed Second Chamber, a revision of the exercise of the prerogative of dissolution, the formulation of cer-

---

[66] For references, see *ante*, p. 111.

[67] See too the reference to the European Convention on the Preamble to the Single European Act (1986).

[68] [1978] 2 C.M.L.R. 292; affirmed [1980] Q.B. 390. The point made by Donaldson J. was not expressly discussed in the Court of Appeal but its correctness was accepted, as shown by the dictum of Lord Denning M.R., "[the Convention] is not part of our English law yet. But we do pay attention to the Convention as it stands." The legality of the seizure of the coins was upheld by the European Court of Human Rights; *The Times*, October 25, 1986.

[69] *Ante*, p. 14.

[70] H. M. Seervai, *Constitutional Law of India* Vol. i (Bombay & London, 3rd ed., 1983) contains a comparative discussion.

[71] *Ante*, p. 84.

[72] *Ante*, p. 91.

tain conventions relating to the Prime Minister and the Cabinet, and the procedure for constitutional amendment.[73]

However, there has been much discussion in the last few years among distinguished judges, political leaders, academics and others of the question whether the United Kingdom should enact a new (unentrenched) Bill of Rights, taking account especially of the European Convention, and (if so) what form it should take.[74] The arguments in favour of such a Bill of Rights include the desire to restrain excess or abuse of power on the part of public authorities and officials, to provide a national minimum standard of protection for the rights of citizens throughout the United Kingdom, to bring the United Kingdom into line with its international obligations, notably the European Convention; to provide a forum for the judicial enforcement in this country of the rights contained in the European Convention, rather than that so many complaints should be brought by individuals against this country before European institutions[75]; and to provide an influential moral and educational force in the moulding of public opinion.

On the other hand it may be said that a declaration of rights is contrary to our national traditions[76]; individual rights are already adequately protected by our law, or (in so far as they are not) piecemeal reforms can easily be made by ad hoc legislation, such as recent statutes against race or sex discrimination[77]; it would lead to excessive litigation; it would produce great uncertainty if applied to existing statute and common law as well as future legislation; it would require the judges to decide policy questions for which they are unsuited by training and functions and its enactment might well delay preparations for much-needed wider constitutional reforms.

Membership of the European Community may be thought to reinforce the argument in favour of a Bill of Rights. The attitude of the European Court of Justice and of the other Community institutions to human rights suggest that it would be of advantage for the United Kingdom to formulate its own statement of fundamental or human

---

[73] O. Hood Phillips, *Reform of the Constitution* (1970) especially Chaps. 6 and 7; "Self-limitation by the United Kingdom Parliament" (1975) 2 *Hastings Constitutional Law Quarterly* 443, 474.

[74] The growing literature includes: *Legislation on Human Rights: A Discussion Document* (Home Office, 1976); (1977) Cmnd. 7009; *The protection of human rights by law in Northern Ireland*; Report of Standing Commission on Human Rights in Northern Ireland; Sir Cyril Salmon, *The Law and Individual Liberty* (Haldane Memorial Lecture 1970, Birkbeck College); Sir Leslie Scarman, *English Law—The New Dimension* (Hamlyn Lectures, 1974); Lord Hailsham, *Elective Dictatorship* (Richard Dimbleby Lecture, BBC, 1976); Richard O'Sullivan Memorial Lecture, 1977); Michael Zander, *A Bill of Rights?* (1985); Lord Lloyd of Hampstead, "Do We Need a Bill of Rights?" (1976) 39 M.L.R. 121; J. Jaconelli, *Enacting a Bill of Rights: The Legal Problems* (1980).

[75] The number of individual complaints against the United Kingdom has been exaggerated, because at one period many were concerned with the two matters of East African Indian immigration and internment in Northern Ireland. Further, it should be remembered when considering the enactment of the European Convention that the United Kingdom also recognises the right of individuals to bring complaints against it for a period of five years at a time.

[76] The classic exposition is A. V. Dicey, *Law of the Constitution* (10th ed., E. C. S. Wade, 1959), pp. 197–202.

[77] *Post*, pp. 438 *et seq.*

rights, otherwise this country's approach towards this matter may be overlooked on the European scene.

What form should a new Bill of Rights take?

Advocates of a new Bill of Rights tends to evade the problem of entrenchment and rest content with some device to make it more difficult in practice for a Government to introduce, and Parliament to pass, statutes infringing an enacted Bill of Rights, and so most of the discussion has centred on the question of whether we should draw up our own indigenous declaration or merely incorporate the relevant provisions of the European Convention into our domestic law. The latter would be the easiest method and Bills for this purpose were introduced in 1975–77 by Liberals in each House. The Bill of Rights Bill introduced by Lord Wade in 1977 was referred to a Select Committee of the House of Lords to report whether a Bill of Rights was desirable and, if so, what form it should take. The Committee agreed unanimously that if there were to be a Bill of Rights it should be a Bill based on the European Convention. On the question whether there should be a Bill at all the Committee were divided, six for and five against.[78-79] The Bill received a Third Reading in the Lords but, as a private member's bill made no progress in the House of Commons in face of Government Opposition. A further unsuccessful attempt to secure the enactment of a similar bill, introduced by Lord Scarman, occurred in 1985.[80] Since the United Kingdom is already bound by the Convention in international law and therefore morally, this method would command the readiest general assent. However, the European Convention is nearly thirty years old and is defective, first, in the selection of rights—for example, it does not mention property and succession, or compensation for compulsory acquisition except for "peaceful enjoyment of possessions" in the First Protocol, or freedom *not* to join a trade union[81]; (a shortcoming made good by judicial interpretation: *Young, James and Webster* v. *United Kingdom*[82]) and, secondly, in their formulation, especially their wide limitations and exceptions such as "necessary in a democratic society," which is hardly justiciable. Further, its jurisprudence is not static, so account would need to be taken of decisions of the Strasbourg Court and opinions of the Human Rights Commission.[83] The Convention applies only to State parties, who are responsible for ensuring that their law prohibits infringements and provides remedies; and so it would be

---

[78-79] *Report of the Select Committee on a Bill of Rights* (1978) H.L. 176; *Minutes of Evidence*, (1977) H.L. 276 and (1977) H.L. 81.

[80] Lord Denning, opposing the idea of incorporating the Convention into an Act of Parliament, expressed the view that to do so "would result in a myriad of cases brought by crackpots."

[81] The Universal Declaration, Art. 20(1), provides that "No one may be compelled to belong to an association": and the International Covenant on Economic, Social and Cultural Rights, Art. 8(1), ensures the right of everyone to "join the trade union *of his choice*" (emphasis supplied).

[82] (1981) 4 E.H.R.R. 38; (1982) 5 E.H.R.R. 201.

[83] A difficulty met by the ingenious suggestion that the Convention be amended to allow domestic courts to request preliminary rulings by the Court of Human Rights: A. Arnill, "Making the European Convention Work" [1985] P.L. 378.

for consideration whether the new Bill of Rights would provide remedies against public authorities only, or also against other persons and bodies (corporations, trade unions, private individuals). If an enacted Bill of Rights applied only against public authorities it would cover delegated legislation, including prison rules, immigration regulations and rules of court; executive action by public officers, including police; and the proceedings of courts and statutory tribunals.

To draw up our own indigenous Bill of Rights appears ideally to be the preferable method; but considerable difficulty and delay would no doubt be experienced in obtaining general consensus, within Parliament and outside, on the selection of rights to be included as well as on the formulation of the necessary limitations and exceptions. Rights affecting private medicine, independent schools, the closed shop and picketing are controversial issues. A problem would also arise that, if such a Bill of Rights were enacted, we should have three competing superior laws—our own Bill of Rights, the European Convention and (within its field) Community law.

Lastly, what attempt should be made to protect the Bill of Rights from infringement by subsequent Parliaments at the instigation of the Government of the day? One device would be for the Bill of Rights to provide that a special majority (say 66 per cent. in one or both Houses) shall be required for repeal or amendment of any of the provisions of this enactment.[84] This would impose a moral obligation on any Government[85] and on the Houses themselves, and the longer the Bill of Rights remained in force the stronger would be the convention against infringement by simple majority. Another method would be similar to that adopted by the former Canadian Bill of Rights, providing that in case of conflict the Bill of Rights should override previous enactments and imposing on the courts a presumption of interpretation excluding implied derogation by subsequent enactments, by requiring for intended amendment a self-styled "Bill of Rights Amendment Bill" containing a clause to the effect that "This Act shall operate notwithstanding the Bill of Rights." A general presumption for the construction of statutes could also be imposed by inserting a simpler version of section 2(4) of the European Communities Act 1972[86]: "Any enactment passed or to be passed shall be construed and have effect subject to this Bill of Rights." It would be desirable also to insert a clause rebutting the presumption there would otherwise be that this declaration is exclusive of any other rights that may already exist in our domestic law, for English law may be more generous to the individual in some respects than the European Convention. Some Minister, probably the Attorney-General, would be given the responsibility of examining in the light of the enacted Bill of Rights, all Bills introduced into Parliament and of advising the Government or the House as to their compatibility with the Bill of Rights at an early stage, perhaps after second reading.

---

[84] See *ante*, p. 87 for the New Zealand Electoral Act 1956.
[85] "[But] things that do not bind may satisfy for the time"; Bacon, *History of Henry VII* (1622), p. 133.
[86] *Ante*, p. 74.

II. DISCRIMINATION[87]

In the following Chapters particular rights are discussed, which have traditionally been recognised as important and for the exercise of which nothing is required except that the law does not interfere.

In those areas of the law and life where it is necessary to enter into legal relationships with other citizens—housing, employment, schooling, for example—it has increasingly been recognised that the law must intervene to ensure that the possibility of entering into such relationships is not adversely affected by such factors as an individual's sex, race or religion. Legislation on such matters may be seen as creating a right not to be discriminated against, or a duty not to discriminate.

Against the recognition of such a right the rules of a legal system themselves may be open to criticism (or legal challenge) as being discriminatory, for example in relation to the acquisition of nationality or the right of abode in a country.[88]

An International Convention on the Elimination of All Forms of Racial Discrimination was agreed in 1966; a Convention on the Elimination of All Forms of Discrimination against Women in 1979. The International Labour Organisation adopted a Convention on Equal Remuneration for Men and Women Workers for Work of Equal Value in 1951. Article 14 of the European Convention provides that "The enjoyment of the rights and freedoms set forth in this Convention shall be secured without discrimination on any ground such as sex, race, colour, language, religion, political or other opinion, national or social origin, association with a national minority, property, birth or other status."

Following these international precedents the United Kingdom Parliament has, in recent legislation (The Equal Pay Act 1970, the Sex Discrimination Act 1975,[89] the Race Relations Act 1976,[90]) prohibited, in certain circumstances, discrimination against the members of groups identifiable by sex, colour, race, nationality or ethnic or national origins.[91] In the area of employment discrimination is also prohibited against married persons.[92] In Northern Ireland alone, discrimination is prohibited on the grounds of religious belief or political opinion by the Fair Employment (Northern Ireland) Act 1976. None of these basic concepts is explained in the legislation, an omission which has already led to litigation, for example, on the question, what is a woman.[93]

More difficulty has been caused and no doubt will in future be caused

---

[87] I. A. Macdonald, *Race Relations, the New Law* (1977); L. Lustgarten, *Legal Control of Racial Discrimination* (1980).

[88] *Ante*, p. 428, *post*, p. 439.

[89] For a commentary on this Act see Michael Beloff, *Sex Discrimination* (1976).

[90] See also section 44(1) of the British Nationality Act 1981 which requires that any discretion vested by the Act in the Secretary of State shall be exercised without regard to race, colour or religion. Earlier Acts on race relations were the Race Relations Acts 1965 and 1968. See generally, G. Bindman and A. Lester, *Race and Law* (1972).

[91] Race Relations Act 1976, s.1(1)(b)(ii) by referring to nationality, is intended to extend the ambit of the Race Relations Act 1968, on which see *Ealing L.B.C.* v. *Race Relations Board* [1972] A.C. 342. The size of the group concerned is immaterial; the Act does not protect "minorities" as such.

[92] Sex Discrimination Act 1975, s.3.

[93] *White* v. *British Sugar Corporation* [1977] I.R.L.R. 121.

by the failure of the Race Relations Act to explain what is meant by "ethnic origins." The question was considered by the House of Lords in *Mandla* v. *Dowell Lee*.[94] Their Lordships concluded that Sikhs constituted an ethnic group for the purposes of the Act. Lord Fraser defined an ethnic group by reference to the possession of a number of features.

"For a group to constitute an ethnic group . . . it must . . . regard itself, and be regarded by others, as a distinct community by virtue of certain characteristics. Some of these characteristics are essential; others are not essential but one or more of them will commonly be found and will help to distinguish the group from the surrounding community. The conditions which . . . [are] essential are . . . : (1) a long shared history, of which the group is conscious as distinguishing it from other groups, and the memory of which keeps it alive; (2) a cultural tradition of its own, including family and social customs and manners, often but not necessarily associated with religious observance. In addition . . . the following characteristics are . . . relevant; (3) either a common geographical origin, or descent from a small number of common ancestors; (4) a common language, not necessarily peculiar to the group; (5) a common literature peculiar to the group; (6) a common religion different from that of neighbouring groups or from the general community surrounding it; (7) being a minority or being an oppressed or a dominant group within a larger community, for example, a conquered group (say, the inhabitants of England shortly after the Norman conquest) and their conquerors might both be ethnic groups."[95]

Lord Templeman said more succinctly[96]:

" . . . a group of persons defined by reference to ethnic origins must possess some of the characteristics of race, namely, group descent, a group of geographical origin and a group history."

While the decision is said to accord with the intention of Parliament, it is nonetheless unfortunate that it should be thought appropriate to legislate in vague terms, the meaning of which is said to be found in statements by government ministers in the course of debates. Nor has the decision removed all difficulties; Lord Templeman's definition does not entirely accord with Lord Fraser's and questions may arise in the future with regard, for example, to gypsies, tinkers or Yorkshiremen. Are Highland or Gaelic speakers distinct ethnic groups from Lowland Scots? Jews clearly, from references to them in *Mandla*, do constitute an ethnic group for the purposes of the Act.

Discrimination is not made illegal *per se* but only in the circumstances set out in the Acts: thus it is not open to an immigrant to challenge the Immigration Rules that in laying down different rules for husbands and wives they are discriminatory: *R.* v. *Immigration Appeal Tribunal, ex p. Kassam*.[97]

The statutory provisions prohibit both direct and indirect discrimination. *Direct* discrimination occurs whenever in any circumstances covered by the legislation a person treats another on the grounds of that

[94] [1983] 2 A.C. 548. For a critical comment, see H. Benyon and N. Love, "*Mandla* and the Meaning of Racial Group" (1984) 100 L.Q.R. 120.
[95] At p. 562.
[96] At p. 569.
[97] [1980] 1 W.L.R. 1037 (C.A.).

other's sex, colour, race, nationality or ethnic or national origins less favourably than he treats or would treat other persons. The Race Relations Act 1976 specifically provides that, for the purposes of that Act, segregating a person from other persons on racial ground is treating him less favourably than those other persons are treated. *Indirect* discrimination occurs when a requirement or condition (*e.g.* of height or educational attainment) is applied to a person which is also applied or would be applied to persons not of the same colour, race, etc., or sex but which is such that the proportion of persons of the group to which the person alleging discrimination belongs who can comply with it is considerably smaller than the proportion of persons not of that group who can comply with it. The requirement or condition must also be to the detriment of the person complaining because of his (or her) inability to comply with it and not "justifiable" irrespective of sex or colour or race, etc., of the person to whom it is applied. In *Price* v. *Civil Service Commission*[98] the Employment Appeal Tribunal held that a maximum age limit on candidates applying for posts in the Civil Service amounted to indirect discrimination since the proportion of women who could comply with the age limit was considerably smaller than that of men since many women in their 20s (and 30s) would be giving birth to, and bringing up, children. The fact that in the abstract women could comply with the rule as easily as men was said to be irrelevant; the test is whether, in practice, in the light of normal female behaviour by the current standards of society, the rule is one with which a substantially lower percentage of women, than of men, can comply. Similarly in *Mandla* v. *Dowell Lee*[99] the House of Lords, having concluded that Sikhs constituted an ethnic group, held that a prohibition at a school on the wearing of turbans was discriminatory because the proportion of Sikhs who "can in practice" or "can consistently with the customs and cultural conditions of [their] racial group" comply with such a rule is lower than that of persons not belonging to the group.

Rules which would otherwise be indirectly discriminatory may be justifiable within section (1)(1)(*b*)(ii) on grounds of public health and hygiene, for example, a prohibition on beards, even although Sikhs "can not" comply with such a rule: *Singh* v. *Rowntree Mackintosh*[1]; *Panesar* v. *Nestlé Co. Ltd.*[2] Justifiable does not mean strictly necessary, but on the other hand it is not enough that the rule merely has practical convenience.[3]

Both Acts specifically make victimisation of a person for bringing proceedings under the Acts or giving evidence in connection with proceedings discrimination for the purposes of the legislation[4] if the per-

---

[98] [1977] I.R.L.R. 291. The Civil Service Commission did not argue that, even if discriminatory, the age limit might be justifiable under s.1(1)(*b*)(ii).

[99] [1983] 2 A.C. 548.

[1] [1979] I.R.L.R. 199.

[2] [1980] I.C.R. 144 (C.A.).

[3] A defence may also be available under s.51(1) of the 1975 Act: (acts necessary to comply with the provisions of earlier legislation): *Greater London Council* v. *Farrar* [1980] 1 W.L.R. 608 (E.A.T.) (female wrestlers); *Page* v. *Freight Hire (Tank Haulage) Ltd.* [1981] I.C.R. 299 (E.A.T.) (female lorry drivers).

[4] Sex Discrimination Act 1975, s.4; Race Relations Act 1976, s.2. See *Kirby* v. *Manpower Services* [1980] 1 W.L.R. 725.

son concerned is treated less favourably than other persons would be treated. Arguably the sections are apt to cover cases where employees are dismissed for refusing to obey discriminatory instructions from employers.[5] There is no doubt that such dismissals *are* discriminatory in the eyes of the Courts which have with some difficulty managed to bring them within section 1(1)(a) in two reported cases under the Race Relations Act.[6]

The meaning of discrimination, in the context of the legislation has not been free from doubt. In *Peake* v. *Automotive Products,*[7] a male employee objected that his employer discriminated against him and other male employees by allowing female employees to leave work five minutes before men. The Court held that there had been no discrimination. Although five minutes a day over a working year amounted to the equivalent of two and a half days the Court thought the claim could be dismissed on the ground *de minimis non curat lex.* Lord Denning also said that the Act had not obliterated the differences between men and women or done away with the chivalry and courtesy which mankind gives to womankind while Shaw L.J. referred to "chivalry" and the need "to cling to common sense."[8] With respect to the Court of Appeal, it is difficult to see what purpose the Act has, other than to obliterate the differences between men and women in those circumstances—such as employment—which fall within its terms.[9] *Peake's* case has suffered the indignity of being explained. In *Ministry of Defence* v. *Jeremiah*[10] Lord Denning M.R. said that the Court had been at a disadvantage because the litigant had appeared in person and relevant sections of the Act had not been drawn to the attention of the Court. In *Jeremiah* the Court of Appeal upheld a decision of the Employment Appeal Tribunal that an Industrial Tribunal was entitled to hold that male employees had suffered a detriment under the Act by being required to undertake dirty work in an ordnance factory which, it was said, women employees disliked doing because of the effect on their hair. In *Gill* v. *El Vino Co. Ltd.*[11] the Court of Appeal held that to forbid women customers to stand at a bar when men customers were allowed to do so was to subject the women to a detriment within the Act. It was, said Eveleigh L.J. "treating a woman less favourably than a man. It is as stark as all that . . . . I find it very difficult to evoke the maxim *de minimis non curat lex* in a situation where that which has been denied to the plaintiff is the very thing

---

[5] s.4(1)(c) and s.2(1)(c) include among the acts which can involve victimisation "otherwise done anything under or by reference to [the relevant legislation] in relation to the discriminator or any other person."

[6] *Zarczynska* v. *Levy* [1979] 1 W.L.R. 125 (E.A.T.) (Dismissal of white barmaid who disobeyed instruction not to serve black customers); *Showboat Entertainment Centre Ltd.* v. *Owens* [1984] 1 W.L.R. 384 (E.A.T.). (White manager dismissed for disobeying instructions not to allow black youths into amusement arcade).

[7] [1977] Q.B. 780.

[8] Shaw L.J.'s fear that any other decision would lead to allegations of discrimination where separate provisions are made for hygiene and sanitation seems unreal in the light of s.7(2) and s.35.

[9] The Equal Opportunities Commission decided to assist the complainant in an appeal but the House of Lords refused leave to appeal; [1978] Q.B. 233.

[10] [1980] Q.B. 87 (C.A.).

[11] [1983] Q.B. 425 (C.A.).

that Parliament seeks to provide, namely facilities and services on an equal basis."[12]

The Sex Discrimination Act 1975 and the Race Relations Act 1976 are drafted on broadly similar lines. Both forbid discrimination in employment subject to exceptions, for example, where sex is a genuine occupational qualification "for reasons of physiology (excluding physical strength or stamina) or, in dramatic performances or other entertainment, for reasons of authenticity."[13] The same section recognises exceptions because of the need to preserve decency. The Race Relations Act 1976, recognises that race may be a genuine occupational quality for "reasons of authenticity" in dramatic performance or when working in a restaurant.[14] British shipowners are exempt from the provisions of the same Act in the case of persons applying for, or engaged for, employment outside Great Britain.[15]

The rights of women in the field of employment are further protected by the Equal Pay Act 1970 as amended by the Sex Discrimination Act 1975. Under these provisions women are entitled to be paid at the same rate as men employed for work which is "rated as equivalent" or "like."[16]

The meaning of "like work" was considered by the Employment Appeal Tribunal in *Dugdale* v. *Kraft Foods Ltd.*[17] where female workers were paid less than their male counterparts who, unlike the women, worked nightshifts. The Tribunal concluded that the time at which the work is performed must be disregarded in considering claims under the Act. Otherwise "the Act could never apply in cases where it must obviously have been intended to apply." In *Shields* v. *Coomes (Holdings) Ltd.*[18] the Court of Appeal held that men employed in a betting shop were not entitled to be paid more than a woman doing a comparable clerical job on the ground that they had the extra responsibility of dealing with trouble, if any broke out. There was no evidence that the men were recruited with such a responsibility in mind. The company did not look for "fierce and formidable" men; they might happily have employed "small nervous [men] who could not say 'boo to a goose'."[19]

Discrimination is forbidden in the field of education. Exceptions are recognised for single sex education establishments[20] and educational

---

[12] Distinguish from "discrimination" as used in s.1 of both Acts, "detriment" used in Sex Discrimination Act 1975, s.6 and Race Relations Act 1976, s.4. See, *e.g. De Souza* v. *Automobile Association*, [1986] I.C.R. 514 (C.A.) (E.A.T.).

[13] Sex Discrimination Act 1975, s.7(2)(*a*).

[14] s.5.

[15] Race Relations Act 1976, s.9. See also s.8. *Deria* v. *General Council of British Shipping* [1985] I.C.R. 847 (E.A.T.) (A sequel to the Falkland War).

[16] Equal Pay Act 1970, s.1.

[17] [1976] 1 W.L.R. 1288.

[18] [1978] I.C.R. 1159 (C.A.).

[19] For the problems connected with determining whether pensions and other benefits constitute pay and the amendment of the Equal Pay Act 1970 to comply with EEC law, see *ante* p. 110. See further I. T. Smith and J. C. Wood, *Industrial Law* (3rd ed., 1986), p. 69 *et seq.* and p. 362 *et seq.* See also *Marshall* v. *Southampton and South West Hampshire Area Health Authority (Teaching)* [1986] Q.B. 401 (E.C.J.) (Retiring ages and sex equality).

[20] Sex Discrimination Act 1975, s.26. There is no prohibition on the establishment of new single sex educational institutions after the coming into effect of the Act.

institution offering facilities to meet the special needs of particular racial groups.[21] Discrimination is also forbidden in the provision of goods, facilities or services and the sale or letting of property to the public or a section of the public,[22] again subject to exceptions, for example, the fostering of children.[23] The Race Relations Act 1976 extends the prohibition on discrimination to membership of "any association of persons however described" which is so conducted that the members do not constitute a section of the public, if in fact the association has 25 or more members.[24] Such associations may, however, discriminate, otherwise than on the grounds of colour, if their main object is to enable the benefits of membership to be enjoyed by persons of a particular racial group defined otherwise than by colour.[25] The Sex Discrimination Act 1975, however, far from extending to private clubs and associations exempts from its provisions voluntary bodies not carried on for a profit even if membership is open to the public or a section of the public.[26] Both Acts provide certain exceptions in the case of sporting activities.[27] Both statutes also render unlawful a variety of acts connected with discrimination, for example, the publication of advertisements whether they indicate an intention to commit an unlawful discriminatory act or even, in certain cases, to commit a lawful act of discrimination.[28] Thus although discrimination in the case of employment in private households is not forbidden by section 4(3) of the Race Relations Act 1976, advertising for a Scottish cook for a private household is forbidden by section 29. On the other hand, advertising for Scottish cooks for a restaurant offering Scottish food is lawful because section 5(2) allows discrimination where race is a genuine occupational qualification and section 29(2) exempts advertisements dealing with situations falling within section 5 from the statutory prohibition on discriminatory advertisements.

The Sex Discrimination Act 1975 exempted from its provisions relat-

---

[21] Race Relations Act 1976, s.35.

[22] The Inland Revenue offers services to the public for the purposes of the legislation: *Savjani* v. *I.R.C.* [1981] Q.B. 458. The Secretary of State, in making decisions under the Immigration Act 1971, does not: *R.* v. *Immigration Appeal Tribunal ex p. Kassam* [1980] 1 W.L.R. 1037 (C.A.); *R.* v. *Entry Clearance Officer ex p. Amin* [1983] 2 A.C. 818 (H.L.). On the difficulty of defining for this purpose a "section of the public" see Colin Munro, *Race Relations—The Discriminating Distinction* (1975) 38 M.L.R. 210.

[23] Race Relations Act 1976, s.23(2). This provision reverses the law under the Race Relations Act 1968 as interpreted by the House of Lords in *Race Relations Board* v. *Applin* [1975] A.C. 259.

[24] s.25 thus reversing the law as laid down in *Race Relations Board* v. *Charter* [1973] A.C. 868 (H.L.); *Race Relations Board* v. *Dockers' Labour Club* [1976] A.C. 285 (H.L.).

[25] s.26.

[26] s.34.

[27] Sex Discrimination Act 1975, s.44; in *Greater London Council* v. *Farrar* [1980] 1 W.L.R. 608, the E.A.T. found the section difficult to construe; Race Relations Act 1976, s.39.

[28] Sex Discrimination Act 1975, s.38; Race Relations Act 1976, s.29. For an unsuccessful attempt to rely on the similar provisions of s.6 of the Race Relations Act 1968 see *Commission for Racial Equality* v. *Associated Newspapers Group* [1978] 1 W.L.R. 905 (C.A.) (reference in advertisement, inviting nurses to apply for jobs in South Africa, to all "white patients" not caught by the Act; advertisement was informing nurses about their likely patients, not indicating an intention to recruit white nurses).

ing to employment private households and businesses . . . employing not more than five workers: section 6(3). These provisions were held to be contrary to Community law by the European Court in *E.C. Commission* v. *United Kingdom.*[29] The Sex Discrimination Act 1986 section 1 has repealed the earlier provision and exempts employment where work is to be done in a private house which involves a degree of contact with the employer which might reasonably involve objection to a worker of a particular sex.

The only remedies available to a victim of an unlawful act of discrimination are those provided by statute.[30] In claims relating to employment resort may be had to an industrial tribunal which has power to declare the rights of the complainant, award damages and recommend appropriate steps to be taken by the defendant to obviate or reduce the adverse effect of his wrongful act.[31] Claims relating to discrimination in the fields of education, goods, facilities or services and the sale or letting of property, must be brought in specially designated county courts, or Sheriff Courts in Scotland. Proceedings in relation to discriminatory advertisements and certain other types of unlawful acts may only be brought by the Commissions established by the two Acts.[32]

The Equal Opportunities Commission and *the Commission for Racial Equality,*[33] established by the Acts, are given power to enforce certain parts of those Acts in the Courts and to assist private complainants. More importantly, however, they are given general duties and powers in connection with furthering the objectives of the legislation by working towards the elimination of discrimination, promoting equality of opportunity and keeping under review the working of the legislation. They may issue Codes of Practice containing guidance on the elimination of discrimination. They may conduct investigations into alleged instances of discrimination, in the course of which they have power to compel parties to give written information and produce documents. Following investigations—or in the course of them—the Commissions may make recommendations.

Both Commissions may carry out general formal inquiries or "named persons" inquiries, that is an inquiry into discrimination into, for example, a particular company. In the second type of case, the House of Lords has held in two cases concerning the Commission for Racial Equality that it must have a belief that the person to be investigated is in breach of the statute before it begins an inquiry. It cannot conduct an inquiry in order to discover if discrimination is being practised.[34]

---

[29] [1984] 1 All E.R. 353. The Court was prepared to accept, for the time being, the exemption of midwifery from the Act (s.20).

[30] Sex Discrimination Act 1975, s.62; Race Relations Act 1976, s.53.

[31] Sex Discrimination Act 1975, ss.63–65; Race Relations Act 1976, ss.54–56.

[32] Sex Discrimination Act 1975, s.72; Race Relations Act 1976, s.63.

[33] Sex Discrimination Act 1975, ss.53–61 and ss.67–75; Race Relations Act 1976, ss.43–52 and ss.58–66. Neither body is an emanation of the Crown or acts as a servant or agent of the Crown; Sched. 3 to the 1975 Act; Sched. 1 to the 1976 Act. See *post,* p. 551.

[34] R. v. *Commission for Racial Equality, ex p. London Borough of Hillingdon* [1982] A.C. 779 (H.L.); *Re Prestige Group plc* [1984] 1 W.L.R. 335 (H.L.); noted G. Applebey and E. Ellis, (1984) 100 L.Q.R. 349.

On the completion of an investigation a report is to be prepared which may be published. The Commissions also have power to issue non-discrimination notices and to apply for enforcement of them, if necessary, to a designated county court or to a sheriff court.[35]

---

[35] The work of the two Commissions is considered by George Applebey and Evelyn Ellis, "Formal Investigations: The Commission for Racial Equality and the Equal Opprtunities Commission as Law Enforcement Agencies" [1984] P.L. 236.

CHAPTER 23

NATIONALITY, CITIZENSHIP, IMMIGRATION AND EXTRADITION

I. INTRODUCTION

Nationality and allegiance

Nationality is a nineteenth-century concept. It is important in international law as well as constitutional law in connection with such matters as diplomatic protection abroad, immigration, deportation and the negotiations of treaties. In constitutional law the distinction between nationals and aliens is also important because the latter are subject to certain disabilities, especially as regards public or political rights.

Until 1948, British nationality law, which had been put on a statutory basis in 1914, was founded on the common law doctrine of allegiance. Allegiance was defined by Blackstone as "the tie, or *ligamen*, which binds the subject to the King, in return for that protection which the King affords the subject."[1] A natural or permanent allegiance was owed by subjects, who at common law were persons born within the King's dominions: while aliens within the King's dominions owed the Sovereign a local or temporary allegiance. No one could relinquish his nationality ("*nemo potest exuere patriam*"). Conversely, a special Act of Parliament was necessary to give an alien English or British nationality.

The distinction between natural-born subjects and others (including naturalised aliens) was in earlier times more important than that between subjects and aliens.[2] General provision was made by the Naturalisation Act 1870 to enable aliens to acquire British nationality by executive grant of the Home Secretary instead of by private Act of Parliament.

The common law doctrine of allegiance plays no part in the new concept of nationality. Allegiance is no longer a source of British nationality, although it may be a consequence of it. It must be regarded henceforth as relevant to the law of treason rather than nationality, and perhaps also to "acts of state."[3]

The Act of 1914

The British Nationality and Status of Aliens Act 1914 repealed the Naturalisation Act 1870 (except as regards persons born before 1915)

---

[1] Bl.Comm. I, 366. See also *Calvin's Case* (1608) Co.Rep. 1a, where it was decided that "*postnati*," *i.e.* persons born in Scotland after the accession of James VI of Scotland to the English throne as James I, were not aliens in England. *Cf. Isaacson* v. *Durant* (1886) 17 Q.B.D. 54 (Hanoverian born before accession of Queen Victoria).

[2] An Act of 1705 provided that the lineal descendants of Princess Sophia should be deemed to be natural-born British subjects: see *Att.-Gen.* v. *Prince Ernest Augustus of Hanover* [1957] A.C. 436; Clive Parry, "Further Considerations upon the Prince of Hanover's Case" (1956) 5 I.C.L.Q. 61; note by C. d'O. Farran in (1956) 19 M.L.R. 289. And see *Duke of Brunswick* v. *King of Hanover* (1844) 6 Beav. 1, 19, 34.

[3] *Ante*, Chap. 14; *post*, Chap. 24.

and provided a comprehensive code for the acquisition and loss of British nationality. Part I, relating to natural-born British subjects, applied throughout the British Empire. The general principles governing the status of natural-born British subjects were: (a) birth in British territory; or (b) birth abroad of a father who was a British subject; and (c) a married woman acquired British nationality if she married a British subject, and she lost British nationality if she married an alien. Part II related to naturalisation.

Further Acts were passed dealing notably with the status of married women, and this legislation was known as the British Nationality and Status of Aliens Act 1914–1943. These Acts were almost entirely repealed by the British Nationality Act 1948, but they are still of practical importance for they determine whether any person born before 1949 was a British subject, so as to retain British nationality under the transitional provisions of the Act of 1948.

British Nationality Act 1948[4]

Before 1948 British nationality was based on the common law doctrine that (with certain exceptions) every person born in British territory was a natural-born British subject. The pre-1948 statutes embodied this doctrine, but also laid down conditions on which persons born outside British territory might become natural-born British subjects, and made rules regarding naturalisation, the status of married women and children, and loss of British nationality. The combination of United Kingdom legislation and Dominion legislation along similar lines would constitute, it was hoped, a common code of British nationality for the British Commonwealth.

In the course of time divergencies began to appear between the laws of various members of the Commonwealth, in particular in relation to married women. In 1946 Canada enacted a Citizenship Act which defined Canadian *citizens*, provided that all Canadian citizens were British subjects, and further provided that all persons who were British subjects under the law of any other Commonwealth country would be recognised by Canada as British subjects. The Act thus retained the common status of British subjects, but abandoned the common code of nationality. A Commonwealth legal conference was held in London in 1947, and it was decided to accept the principles of the Canadian Citizenship Act 1946 for general application throughout the Commonwealth. The British Nationality Act 1948, as amended from time to time, gave effect to these principles so far as the United Kingdom and British colonies are concerned. It provided a new method of giving effect to the principle that people of each of the self-governing countries within the Commonwealth have both a particular status as citizens of their own country and a common status as members of the wider association of peoples comprising the Commonwealth. The Act was divided into two main parts: Part I dealt with British nationality, Part II with citizenship of the United Kingdom and colonies.

---

[4] See E. C. S. Wade, "British Nationality Act, 1948" (1948) xxx *Journ. Comp. Leg.* 67; Clive Parry, *Nationality and Citizenship Laws of the Commonwealth* (2 vols. 1957–60).

Section I of the British Nationality Act 1948 provided that:

"(1) Every person who under this Act is a citizen of the United Kingdom and Colonies,[5] or who under any enactment for the time being in force in any country mentioned in subsection (3) of this section is a citizen of that country, shall by virtue of that citizenship have the status of a British subject.

(2) Any person having the status aforesaid may be known either as a British subject or as a Commonwealth citizen: and accordingly in this Act and in any other enactment or instrument whatever, whether passed or made before or after the commencement of this Act, the expression 'British subject' and the expression 'Commonwealth citizen' shall have the same meaning."

Subsection (3), specifying the Commonwealth countries concerned, was amended from time to time so as to include all independent members of the Commonwealth, Southern Rhodesia, as it then was, and any other Commonwealth country that had been granted power to enact its own citizenship laws. Each of the countries mentioned in subsection (3), as amended, was a legislative unit for nationality or citizenship purposes. It was intended that each of them should enact a citizenship law containing the principle of section 1(1), *ante*, by which mutual recognition as British subjects would be given to the citizens of other Commonwealth countries. The result would be that "British subjects," instead of being ascertained by a common code, would simply comprise the citizens of all Commonwealth countries, as is shown by the alternative title "Commonwealth citizens."

The 1948 Act provided for the acquisition of citizenship by *birth* in the United Kingdom and Colonies on or after January 1, 1948 (s.4)[6]; and by *descent* if a child's father was a citizen of the United Kingdom and Colonies at the time of the birth (s.5).[7]

Any person who was a British subject immediately before January 1, 1949[8] became a citizen of the United Kingdom and Colonies if: (a) he was born in the United Kingdom and Colonies; or (b) he was naturalised in the United Kingdom and Colonies; or (c) he became a British subject by annexation of territory to the United Kingdom and Colonies; or (d) his father was a British subject and fulfilled any of the above conditions: or (e) he was born in a British protectorate, protected state or trust territory (s.12).[9]

Provision was also made for the acquisition of citizenship by *naturalisation* (in the case of aliens and British protected persons) and by *regis-*

---

[5] *Post*, pp. 452 *et seq.*

[6] Unless (a) the father of the child enjoyed diplomatic immunity and was not a citizen of the United Kingdom and Colonies, or (b) the father was an enemy alien and the birth occurred in a place then under enemy occupation.

[7] Subject to the proviso that if the father were a citizen by descent one of a number of other conditions had to be satisfied.

[8] Under the British Nationality and Status of Aliens Act 1914–1943 the following persons born after 1914 were natural-born British subjects:

(a) Any person born within His Majesty's dominions and allegiance; and

(b) Any person born out of His Majesty's dominions whose father was, at the time of that person's birth, a British subject and fulfilled one of a number of conditions; and

(c) Any person born on board a British ship.

[9] See *post*, p. 732 for protectorates, protected states and trust territories.

tration in the case of Commonwealth citizens and the wives of citizens of the United Kingdom and colonies.

Aliens

Under the medieval common law aliens had practically no public or private rights. The rules were gradually relaxed by statute and a more liberal attitude on the part of the common law courts. By the end of the sixteenth century it was recognised that aliens in the King's dominions owed a temporary and local allegiance. Friendly aliens could bring personal actions such as trespass and debt, and could own personal property, including leaseholds.

At common law an alien had no right to enter this country.[10] The Crown probably had no prerogative power to send an alien (other than an enemy alien) compulsorily out of the realm,[11] but since the eighteenth century[12] the government has sought statutory powers to do so.

Friendly aliens, i.e. citizens of countries with which the Crown is not at war,[13] have long had the right to contract, to own and dispose of personal property, and to bring and defend actions. They may now own and dispose of real property. Resident aliens owe allegiance to the Crown, and are subject to the general civil and criminal law.[14] They do not enjoy the parliamentary or local government franchise, they may not sit in either House of Parliament[15] or hold any public office; but they may be employed in any civil capacity under the Crown (a) outside the United Kingdom, or (b) under a certificate issued by a Minister with Treasury approval. Aliens are subject to restrictions with regard to employment in the armed forces, the Civil Service in this country, and the merchant navy; jury service; the ownership of British ships; holding a pilot's certificate; change of name; and taking part in certain industrial activities.[16]

---

[10] *Musgrove* v. *Chun Teeong Toy* [1891] A.C. 272; criticised, Thornberry (1963) 12 I.C.L.Q. 422. But see *Schmidt* v. *Secretary of State for Home Affairs* [1969] 2 Ch. 149, 168, *per* Lord Denning M.R. Nothing in the Immigration Act 1971 impairs any prerogative powers possessed by the Crown in relation to aliens (s.33(5)).

[11] Forsyth, *Cases and Opinions on Constitutional Law* (1869) p. 181; Holdsworth, *History of English Law*, Vol. X, pp. 393–400. *Cf.* dictum of Lord Atkinson in *Johnstone* v. *Pedlar* [1921] A.C. 262, 283.

[12] Aliens Act 1793.

[13] "Friendly" aliens may in some context include nationals of countries with which the Crown is at war, but who have come to reside or are allowed to remain here by the Sovereign's licence: *Wells* v. *Williams* (1697) 1 Ld.Raym. 282. The Sovereign's licence, express or implied, gives the protection of the law and the courts: *Sylvester's Case* (1702) 7 Mod. 150. A licence is commonly implied by the fact that an alien has registered and has been allowed to remain: *Thurn and Taxis (Princess)* v. *Moffitt* [1915] 1 Ch. 58; *Schaffenius* v. *Goldberg* [1916] 1 K.B. 284. See further, W. E. Davies, *The English Law relating to Aliens* (1931), Chap. 1.

[14] See also the Aliens Restriction (Amendment) Act 1919, s.3 which makes it an offence punishable by 10 years imprisonment for an alien to attempt or do any act calculated to cause sedition or disaffection among the civilian population; and by 3 months imprisonment if he promotes or attempts to promote industrial unrest in any industry in which he has not been bona fide engaged in the United Kingdom for the previous two years.

[15] Act of Settlement 1700.

[16] See generally British Nationality and Status of Aliens Act 1914; Aliens Restriction (Amendment) Act 1919; Aliens Employment Act 1955.

Enemy aliens,[17] *i.e.* nationals of countries with which the Crown is at war, were at one time virtually rightless, unless exceptionally they were here with the licence of the King. In course of time it came to be seen that what mattered so far as commerce was concerned was to prevent any trade with the enemy country, regardless of what persons were carrying it on. And so an "enemy" came to mean any person (whether a British subject or not) who voluntarily resided or carried on business in an enemy country.[18] An enemy alien in this sense cannot enter into contracts by English law, and contracts entered into with him before the war are suspended for the duration of the war. "Enemy character" is largely of importance in relation to corporations, and in relation to offences under the Trading with the Enemy Acts.

An enemy alien cannot bring an action in the British courts; nor, if he was plaintiff in an action begun before the war, can he appeal during the war; for the enemy cannot be given the advantage of enforcing his rights by the assistance of the Sovereign with whom he is at war. On the other hand an enemy alien can be sued during the war, as that permits British subjects or friendly aliens to enforce their rights with the assistance of the Sovereign against the enemy; and if he is sued justice demands that he be allowed to appear and defend. Further, if he is unsuccessful as defendant he may appeal, for he is entitled to have the case decided according to law and therefore to have the error of a court of first instance rectified (*Porter* v. *Freudenberg*[19]). The Crown has the prerogative of confiscating enemy property, but if it is taken it is usually handed over to a Custodian during the war.[20]

With regard to the control of aliens for the security of the realm in time of war, the original distinction between enemy and friendly aliens is commonly used. Wartime legislation and emergency powers during both the two world wars gave the Crown very extensive powers of control over enemy aliens in this sense. The legislation expressly preserved the Crown's prerogative in relation to enemy aliens. At common law their licence to remain at large may be revoked at any time at the complete discretion of the Crown, and they can be interned[21] or deported.[22] The internment of an enemy alien is an act of state, and he has no right to apply for a writ of habeas corpus against the executive to challenge the Crown's power to intern or deport (*R.* v. *Bottrill, ex p. Kuechenmeister*[23]). In the last case it was discussed, but not decided, whether an

---

[17] See McNair, *Legal Effects of War* (3rd ed.).

[18] *Wells* v. *Williams* (1697) 1 Ld.Raym. 282; *The Hoop* (1799) 1 C.Rob. 196; *Janson* v. *Driefontein Consolidated Mines* [1902] A.C. 484. For the position of corporations, see *Daimler Co.* v. *Continental Tyre and Rubber Co.* [1916] 1 A.C. 307; as to firms, see *Rodriguez* v. *Speyer Bros.* [1919] A.C. 59. Territory occupied by the enemy is regarded as enemy territory: *Sovfracht (V.O.)* v. *Van Udens Scheepvaart en Agentur Maatschappij (N.V.Babr.)* [1943] A.C. 203.

[19] [1915] 1 K.B. 857 (C.A.) *per* Lord Reading C.J. See also *Eichengruen* v. *Mond* [1940] 1 Ch. 785; *cf. Weber's Trustees* v. *Riemer*, 1947 S.L.T. 295 (counterclaim not permissible).

[20] See *e.g. Administrator of Austrian Property* v. *Russian Bank for Foreign Trade* (1931) 48 T.L.R. 37; *Bank voor Handel en Scheepvaart N.V.* v. *Administrator of Hungarian Property* (1954) A.C. 584.

[21] *R.* v. *Commandant of Knockaloe Camp* (1917) 117 L.T. 627; *Ex p. Liebmann* [1916] 1 K.B. 268; *Ex p. Weber* [1916] A.C. 421.

[22] *Netz* v. *Chuter Ede* [1946] Ch. 224; *Att.-Gen. for Canada* v. *Cain* [1906] A.C. 542 (P.C.).

[23] [1947] K.B. 41 (C.A.).

interned enemy alien is in the position of a prisoner of war. Internment, however, does not revoke the licence to bring civil actions in the courts, or, probably, to commence habeas corpus proceedings against private persons.[24]

EEC nationals constitute, as will be seen, a special class of aliens so far as immigration, deportation and employment are concerned.

Irish citizens
The Ireland Act 1949, section 2 provided that citizens of the Republic of Ireland were not to be regarded as aliens.[25]

II. THE BRITISH NATIONALITY ACT 1981

Introduction
British subjects were free at common law to come into or leave the "mother country." The British Nationality Act 1948, which created citizenship of the United Kingdom and Colonies, retained the old term "British subject" as an alternative to the new term "Commonwealth citizen" for the citizens of other independent Commonwealth countries. In 1962 Parliament passed the Commonwealth Immigrants Act 1962 to give some power to control immigration into the United Kingdom by citizens of Commonwealth countries. All other Commonwealth countries had power to control such immigration.[26] The power of control conferred in 1962 applied to all Commonwealth citizens except those born in the United Kingdom and those holding United Kingdom passports, and also to British protected persons and Irish citizens.

The Home Secretary was also given for the first time a limited power to deport from the United Kingdom Commonwealth citizens,[27] British protected persons and Irish citizens on the recommendation of a court that had sentenced them to imprisonment. The power to deport in such cases was possessed by practically every other territory in the Commonwealth.

The Commonwealth Immigrants Act 1968 amended the Act of 1962 with regard to (*inter alia*) exemption from control enjoyed by citizens of the United Kingdom and Colonies holding United Kingdom passports, and made it an offence to land otherwise than in accordance with immigration regulations. The Acts of 1962 and 1968 were repealed and replaced by the Immigration Act 1971.

The result of the introduction of immigration controls was that there were two categories of citizens in the United Kingdom and Colonies: those entitled to enter and reside in the United Kingdom (called by the Immigration Act "patrials") and those not entitled ("non-patrials"). The

---

[24] *Ibid. per* Asquith L.J.

[25] The Ireland Act, s.5(1), provided for the retention of British nationality (with certain exceptions) by persons born in Eire, or the Irish Free State, before 1922 (the date of the Anglo-Irish Treaty) who were British subjects immediately before 1949.

[26] Colonies can also restrict immigration: see *Thornton* v. *The Police* [1962] A.C. 339 (P.C.).

[27] *Cf. R.* v. *Sabri, The Times,* November 10, 1964 (C.C.A.). Before 1962 a deportation order against a British subject would be quashed: *R.* v. *Home Secretary ex p. Château Thierry (Duke)* [1917] 1 K.B. 922, 930 *per* Swinfen Eady L.J.

object of the British Nationality Act 1981[28] is to distinguish clearly a category of citizenship which carries with it the right of entry and residence from other categories. The old law which was outlined in the previous section remains of importance because (i) it defines the nationality or citizenship of people born before the 1981 Act came into effect (January 1, 1983) and (ii) the terminology of the old law is to be found in the case law and confusion can be caused unless it is realised that, for example, British subject is used in the new law in an entirely different sense from that in which it was formerly used.

Categories of citizenship

The 1981 Act recognises three categories of citizenship:
  (i) British;
  (ii) British Dependent Territories;
  (iii) British Overseas.
It also recognises the special status of
  (i) British protected persons; and
  (ii) British subjects without citizenship (British subjects).
The term Commonwealth citizen embraces all categories (apart from that of British Protected Persons) and citizens of independent Commonwealth countries.[29]

Citizens of Eire continue to enjoy their own unique status; they are not aliens and possess the right to vote when resident in the United Kingdom.[30]

British citizenship

British citizenship is the only type of citizenship under the 1981 Act which confers a legal right to live in, and to come and go into and from, the United Kingdom by right.

British citizenship is acquired, as a general rule, in the case of persons born before January 1, 1983 if they were patrials, that is citizens of the United Kingdom and Colonies who under the Immigration Act 1971, were entitled to enter the United Kingdom by right.[31]

Patrials were (a) citizens of the United Kingdom and Colonies and (b) Commonwealth citizens who possessed one of the special links with the United Kingdom defined in the Immigration Act. That status largely corresponds to British citizenship as defined in the 1981 Act in the case of persons born after January 1, 1983.[32]

In the case of persons born after the commencement of the Act, British citizenship may be acquired by
  (i) *Birth* in the United Kingdom provided that one parent was at the time of birth a British citizen or was settled in the United King-

---

[28] See commentaries by C. Blake, "Citizenship, Law and the State" (1982) 45 M.L.R. 179 and R. White and F. J. Hampson, "The British Nationality Act 1981" [1982] P.L. 6.

[29] s.37.

[30] s.50(1); Representation of the People Act 1983, s.1. Citizens of Eire can continue to claim to be British subjects under s.31.

[31] The term patrial was given legal significance and currency but not invented by the Immigration Act 1971. It has been removed from the 1971 Act by s.39 of the 1981 Act and replaced by British citizen.

[32] Some patrials do not become British citizens; and lose their right of abode: s.11(2). Some patrials do not become British citizens but retain a right of abode: s.39(2).

dom.[33] This provision marks the abandonment of the former principle that, subject to minor exceptions, birth in the United Kingdom conferred British nationality.[34] A person who does not acquire citizenship by birth in the United Kingdom may, however, be subsequently entitled to citizenship, for example, if one of his parents later acquires citizenship or he spends the first ten years of his life in the United Kingdom.[35]

(ii) *Descent*: when birth occurs abroad but one parent is a British citizen other than by descent.[36] This represents an extension of the rule in the 1948 Act which allowed the acquisition of citizenship by descent only through the father. The new rule, however, is more restrictive than the old in that, subject to exceptions, it allows acquisition by descent for one generation only. Formerly United Kingdom citizenship could be transmitted indefinitely by registration at a British consulate in a foreign country. Persons born abroad whilst a parent possessing British citizenship is in the service of the Crown are treated as acquiring citizenship by birth and can transmit that citizenship even if the relevant parent was a citizen by descent.[37] In some cases British citizenship may be claimed following birth abroad where one of the parents was a British citizen by descent but had resided in the United Kingdom for the three years preceding the birth.[38]

Citizenship by naturalisation

Naturalisation is now governed by section 6 of and Schedule 1 to the British Nationality Act 1981. Naturalisation is a matter within the discretion of the Secretary of State. Section 44 provides that in exercising any discretion under the Act the Secretary of State must pay no regard to "race, colour or religion."[39] Section 6 distinguishes between applications by persons of full age and capacity (subs. 1) and applications by persons of full age and capacity who at the date of the application are married to a British citizen (subs. 2). In the case of naturalisation under subs. 1 the applicant must first satisfy a residence requirement which involves within the five years before the application presence in the United Kingdom, subject to absences not exceeding 450 days, and in the twelve months before application presence except for a maximum absence of 90 days.[40] In the alternative an application can show that at the date of application he is serving outside the United Kingdom in Crown service under the United Kingdom government. Secondly he

[33] s.1. "Settled" has a technical meaning: s.50(1)–(4); *post*, p. 460.
[34] *Supra*, p. 447.
[35] s.1(3); s.1(4).
[36] s.2.
[37] s.2.
[38] s.3(3).
[39] *Sed quaere* whether his decision is open to judicial review on the ground that he has failed to follow s.44(1); subs. (2) seems to exclude judicial review while subs. (3) preserves it: see *post*, p. 697.
[40] Furthermore the applicant must not at any time in the five year period have been in breach of the immigration laws and in the final twelve months must not at any time have been subject to any restriction on the period for which he might remain in the United Kingdom.

must establish that he is of good character; thirdly that he has sufficient knowledge of the English, Welsh or Scottish Gaelic language, and fourthly that he intends (i) to reside in the United Kingdom, or (ii) to enter into or continue in Crown service under the United Kingdom Government, or service under an international organisation of which the United Kingdom Government is a member, or service in the employment of a society or company established in the United Kingdom. The Home Secretary is expressly given a wide discretion to waive the requirements relating to residence and language proficiency.

The requirements to be satisfied by the spouse of a British citizen who seeks naturalisation under subsection 2 are less onerous. The period of five years is reduced to three (subject to absences not exceeding 270 days) and there is no need to show "sufficient knowledge" of the three listed languages.

Citizenship by registration

The Home Secretary is given a discretion to register minors as British citizens by Section 3 which spells out particular requirements to be satisfied in specific types of application.

Registration by right is available to British Dependent Territories citizens, British Overseas citizens, British subjects and British protected persons who satisfy the residence requirements of section 4.

Registration is available by right to British Dependent Territories citizens who are nationals of the United Kingdom for the purpose of the Community Treaties, that is people having a link with Gibraltar (section 5).[41]

Transitional provisions preserve for five years after the commencement of the 1981 Act the rights of individuals to register as British citizens who could formerly have registered as citizens of the United Kingdom (i) by virtue of residence (section 7); (ii) in the case of women, by marriage to a citizen of the United Kingdom (section 8) and (iii) by registration at a United Kingdom consulate (section 9).

British Nationality (Falkland Islands) Act 1983

This Act which is deemed to have come into effect on the same day as the British Nationality Act confers British citizenship on inhabitants of the Falkland Islands born before January 1, 1983 who would otherwise be British Dependent Territories citizens by virtue of a link with the Falkland Islands—for example, birth, naturalisation or registration there. In the case of persons born after January 1, 1983 British citizenship is conferred on persons born in the Islands who satisfy *mutatis mutandis* the requirements of the 1981 Act. Provision is also made for acquisition of British citizenship by registration and descent.

Loss of citizenship

In the case of naturalised citizens and citizens by registration, citizenship may be lost by *deprivation* under section 40 of the British Nationality Act 1981. The Home Secretary may deprive any person to whom the section applies of citizenship if satisfied that the registration or cer-

---

[41] K. Simmonds, "The British Nationality Act 1981 and the definition of the term 'national' for Community purposes" (1984) C.M.L. Rev. 675.

tificate of naturalisation was obtained by fraud, false representation or concealment of any material fact; or if he is satisfied that the person has shown himself disloyal to Her Majesty, or has traded with the enemy during any war, or (unless the effect of deprivation would be to render that person stateless) has been sentenced to not less than twelve months' imprisonment within five years of naturalisation. A person is not to be deprived of citizenship under the section unless the Home Secretary is satisfied that it is not conducive to the public good that that person should continue to be a British citizen; and except in the case of continuous residence abroad, a person against whom an order is proposed to be made may require that the case be referred to a committee of inquiry called the Deprivation of Citizenship Committee.[42]

A British citizen of full age and capacity may under section 12 of the 1981 Act *renounce* his British nationality.[43] A declaration must be made in a prescribed form and registered by the Home Secretary if he is satisfied that after registration the person concerned will acquire some citizenship or nationality other than British citizenship. If another citizenship or nationality is not acquired within six months of registration the person shall be deemed to be and have remained a British citizen. It is provided, however, that the Home Secretary may withhold registration of any such declaration if made during any war in which Her Majesty may be engaged in right of Her Majesty's government in the United Kingdom.[44]

Resumption of citizenship

Provision is made for resumption of citizenship by persons who have earlier renounced citizenship, for example a wife might have to renounce British citizenship under the law of her husband's state and wish to return to the United Kingdom on divorce or following his death.[45]

British Dependent Territories Citizenship

This, in effect, is a colonial citizenship, acquired by a connection with a colony analogous to that needed with the United Kingdom to establish the status of British citizenship.[46] The status does not confer a right of entry to the United Kingdom or to any particular colony, immigration being a matter left to each colony to determine for itself. As we have seen, Gibraltarians and Falkland Islanders have, within this category,

[42] There is no right to an inquiry where the registration or naturalisation has been procured by fraud as to identity: R. v. *Secretary of State for the Home Department ex p. Akhtar* [1981] Q.B. 46.

[43] For the purposes of s.40 any person who has been married is deemed to be of full age.

[44] At common law a British subject could not become naturalised in a foreign country (*ante*, p. 446). The Naturalisation Act 1870 provided that if he did so he should be deemed to have ceased to be a British subject and be regarded as an alien. The 1948 Act in order to prevent statelessness provided that the acquisition of a foreign nationality or of another Commonwealth citizenship, instead of involving automatic forfeiture, should entitle a person to renounce his citizenship of the United Kingdom and Colonies if he so desired. In R. v. *Lynch* [1903] 1 K.B. 444, it was held that naturalisation in a country with which Britain was at war not only amounted to treason, but was probably null and void: *post*, p. 474.

[45] s.13. See also s. 10.

[46] British Nationality Act 1981, Part II. For dependent territories, see *post*, Chap. 36.

special rights to British citizenship; on the other hand the Hong Kong Act 1985 makes provision for converting this type of citizenship arising from a connection with Hong Kong into "a new form of British nationality the holders of which shall be known as British Nationals (Overseas)".[47]

British Overseas Citizenship[48]

This status was conferred on citizens of the United Kingdom and Colonies who did not, when the 1981 Act came into effect, acquire British citizenship or British Dependent Territories Citizenship. It is a transitional and residual status. They may at the same time hold another citizenship.

British subjects[49]

Unlike British Overseas Citizens, British subjects cannot possess any other citizenship. They are persons who were British subjects under the 1948 Act who failed to acquire citizenship when the country in which they lived adopted its own nationality laws.

British Overseas Citizens and British Subjects are entitled to British passports but, as will be seen, have no right of entry to the United Kingdom. If admitted to the United Kingdom they may under section 4 acquire British citizenship by registration.

British Protected Persons

British Protected Persons are defined by Order in Council made under section 38 of the 1981 Act and the Solomon Islands Act 1978. They are connected with territories which were protectorates, protected states or United Kingdom trust territories.[50] They may hold citizenship of a non-Commonwealth country. Like the two preceding categories, the significance of this one is the right to a British passport and, if admitted to the United Kingdom, the chance of registration as a British citizen.

III. IMMIGRATION AND DEPORTATION[51]

Introduction

Since 1962 Parliament has, as we saw above, extended controls over entry into and residence in the United Kingdom so that they now apply not merely to aliens but to all categories (subject to minor exceptions) of

---

[47] See further, *post*, Chap. 36.

[48] Part III. This category includes East African Asians in India and East Africa and certain classes of inhabitants of Malaysia.

[49] Part IV. British subjects are believed to number about 50,000 and reside mainly in Sri Lanka, India and Pakistan.

[50] *Post*, Chap. 36. The vast majority of this category reside in Brunei. Before 1949 they were regarded as aliens while in this country: *R. v. Ketter* [1940] 1 K.B. 787. See further, *post*, p. 664.

[51] J. M. Evans, *Immigration Law* (2nd ed., 1983); I. A. Macdonald, *Immigration Law and Practice in the United Kingdom* (1983); L. Grant and I. Martin, *Immigration Law and Practice* (1982) (with *Supplement*, 1985).

citizens and subjects recognised by United Kingdom law other than British citizens. The detailed rules governing immigration and deportation are to be found in the Immigration Act 1971 and the Immigration Rules made under section 3(2) of that Act. The content of the Act and the Rules, the application of the law and the role of the courts in reviewing the decisions of immigration officials and the Home Secretary have all been matters of controversy. To the individuals involved hardly any matter could be of greater moment than whether they are to be allowed entry to a particular country where, for one reason or another, they wish to live or whether, having settled in the United Kingdom they are to be required to leave. The legislation is couched in the widest terms, conferring extensive discretionary powers. The reluctance of Parliament to fetter the executive (or of the executive to be fettered) can hardly be better shown than by the fact that the Immigration Rules are not in the strict sense, delegated legislation which clarify and restrict the wider provisions of a statute. Section 3(2) speaks of "statements of the rules . . . laid down by [the Secretary of State] as to the practice to be followed in the administration of this Act."[52] A typical judicial comment on the status of the Rules is that of Lord Bridge in *R. v. Immigration Appeal Tribunal ex p. Singh*.[53]

"The rules do not purport to enact a precise code having statutory force. They are discursive in style, in part merely explanatory and, on their face, frequently offer no more than broad guidance as to how discretion is to be exercised in different typical situations. In so far as they lay down principles to be applied, they generally do so in loose and imprecise terms."

They nonetheless have legal status to the extent that section 19 requires an adjudicator to allow an appeal against a decision that was "not in accordance with the law or with any immigration rules applicable." (Appeals under the Act are discussed below at p. 462.)

In addition to immigration controls and powers of deportation the Secretary of State possesses statutory powers to exclude certain persons from Great Britain, from Northern Ireland or from the United Kingdom under the Prevention of Terrorism (Temporary Provisions) Act 1984 which is discussed in Chapter 24.

EEC Nationals

In the case of EEC nationals the powers of the Home Secretary may be subject to restrictions under Community Law.

Article 48, for example, of the EEC Treaties protects the free right of movement of workers and their dependants.[54] Persons entitled to claim

---

[52] The rules must be laid before Parliament and, if disapproved by either House the Home Secretary shall make such changes as seem required. Four sets of rules were made initially, dealing with Commonwealth citizens (H.C. 79 and H.C. 80), and EEC and non-Commonwealth nationals (H.C. 81 and H.C. 82) (the 1973 Rules). A revised version was produced in 1980: H.C. (1979–1980) No. 394 (Statement of Change in Immigration Rules). The current rules are H.C. (1982–83) No. 169, as amended, H.C. (1984–5) No. 503.

[53] [1986] 1 W.L.R. 910, 917. See further, *post*, p. 624.

[54] *Supra*, p. 108. See further R. O. Plender, "The Right to Free Movement in the European Communities," in *Fundamental Rights* (1973) (ed. Bridge. Lasok, Perrott and Plender).

the protection of Article 48 may only be refused entry to, or deported from, a state on the grounds of public policy, public security or public health. In *Van Duyn* v. *Home Office*,[55] which arose from a refusal by the Home Office to allow a Dutch national to enter the United Kingdom to work as a secretary for the Church of Scientology, the European Court held that "public policy" justified such a refusal where the organisation for which the national wished to work was regarded as socially harmful even although its activities had not been forbidden by law. In *R.* v. *Bouchereau*[56] the Court considered a number of matters arising from the power to recommend deportation conferred by the Immigration Act 1971. The Court emphasised that "public policy" should be strictly construed. As a justification for deportation on the ground of a criminal conviction it required a genuine and serious threat to a fundamental interest of society going beyond the disturbance of the social order which every crime inevitably involves. The Court also expressed the view that a past conviction may justify deportation even without the proof of the likelihood of the commission of further crimes in the future.

EEC law also regulates the procedure which must be followed before deportation may be ordered: *R.* v. *Secretary of State for the Home Department ex p. Santillo*[57]; *R.* v. *Secretary of State for the Home Department ex p. Dannenberg.*[58]

Immigration Act 1971

General principles

The Immigration Act 1971, which came into effect on January 1, 1973, deals with the regulation of entry and stay in the United Kingdom, of Commonwealth citizens, British Protected Persons, Irish citizens and aliens. Section 1 sets out the general principles. All persons who have the "right of abode" under section 2 are free to live in, and to come and go into and from, the United Kingdom. Persons not having that right may live, work and settle in the United Kingdom by permission and subject to regulation and control; and those who were settled here when the Act came into force are treated as if they had been given definite leave to enter or remain. The Act does not control local journeys between the United Kingdom, the Isle of Man, the Channel Islands and the Republic of Ireland ("the common travel area"), subject to section 10 (*infra*).

Section 2, as amended by the British Nationality Act 1981, s.39 provides that a person has the right of abode in the United Kingdom if he is

(i) a British citizen; or

(ii) a Commonwealth citizen who satisfies certain requirements set out in the Section which in effect preserve for their lifetimes the right of

---

[55] Case 41/74 [1974] E.C.R. 1337; [1975] 1 C.M.L.R. 1; *supra*, p. 108.
[56] [1978] Q.B. 732. See too *Re a Belgian Prostitute* [1976] 2 C.M.L.R. 527; *Adoui* v. *Belgian State* [1982] 3 C.M.L.R. 631.
[57] [1981] Q.B. 778.
[58] [1984] Q.B. 766.

abode possessed by certain Commonwealth citizens before the enactment of the 1981 Act.[59]

British citizen is used under the Act to include both categories of persons (s.2(2) as amended).

The burden of proving a right of abode rests on the person claiming the status (s.3(8)). Various methods of proof are set out in section 3(9), as amended by the 1981 Act. These include a certificate of entitlement which replaces the former certificate of patriality.

Regulation and control

Section 3 makes general provisions for regulation and control. Persons who are not British citizens require leave to enter, which may be given for a limited or indefinite period, and may be subject to conditions restricting employment and occupation or requiring registration with the police.

Crews of ships or aircraft may enter for limited periods without leave. Diplomats and their families and members of home, Commonwealth and visiting forces are exempt from control (s.8). Provision may be made by Order in Council with regard to persons entering otherwise than by ship or aircraft[60] e.g. by land from the Republic of Ireland. Such provisions may exclude the Republic of Ireland from the common travel area (s.10).

Refusal of leave

Persons who fail to satisfy immigration officials that they fulfil the requirements of the Immigration Rules will normally be refused leave to enter the United Kingdom. Even compliance with the requirements does not guarantee leave to enter.[61] Applicants who prima facie satisfy the requirements may be refused entry if already subject to a deportation order or if they have been convicted of an extraditable offence or on medical grounds.[62] Leave may also be refused because in the view of the Home Secretary an individual's exclusion is conducive to the public good.[63] This last reason for refusal confers a very wide discretion on the Home Secretary.[64]

---

[59] s.2(1)(d). He is a Commonwealth citizen born to or legally adopted by a parent who at the time of the birth or adoption had citizenship of the United Kingdom and Colonies by his birth in the United Kingdom or in any of the Islands.

(2) A woman is under this Act also to have the right of abode in the United Kingdom if she is a Commonwealth citizen and either—

(a) is the wife of any such citizen of the United Kingdom and Colonies as is mentioned in subsection (1)(a), (b) or (c) above or any such Commonwealth citizen as is mentioned in subsection (1)(d); or

(b) has at any time been the wife—

(i) of a person then being such a citizen of the United Kingdom and Colonies or Commonwealth citizen; or

(ii) of a British subject who but for his death would on the date of commencement of the British Nationality Act 1948 have been such a citizen of the United Kingdom and Colonies as is mentioned in subsection (1)(a) or (b).

[60] By swimming the Channel?

[61] H.C. 169 para. 76.

[62] H.C. 169 paras. 80 and 83.

[63] H.C. 169 para. 85.

[64] Cf. Schmidt v. Secretary of State for the Home Affairs [1969] 2 Ch. 149.

Illegal entrants

An illegal entrant is defined by section 33(1) of the Immigration Act 1971 as meaning "a person unlawfully entering or seeking to enter in breach of a deportation order or of the immigration laws, and includes also a person who has so entered."

Before examining the meaning given to that definition by the Courts the consequences of being held to be an illegal immigrant need to be considered. First, a criminal offence is committed under section 24 if an immigrant enters the country illegally. Secondly, an illegal entrant can be removed from the United Kingdom before he is entitled to appeal against the order. If he wishes to appeal he must do so from outside the United Kingdom (section 16 and Schedule 2). (In some circumstances the decision to remove an individual on the ground that he is an illegal entrant may be open to judicial review, as we shall see). Thirdly, for the purposes of the British Nationality Act 1981, an illegal entrant cannot claim to be "settled" in the United Kingdom for the purposes of that Act.

The meaning of "in breach of a deportation order" is clear but the Courts have found great uncertainty in the meaning of "in breach of the immigration laws." The law seems now to be settled that an immigrant is an illegal entrant not merely if he has evaded the immigration authorities in his entry but if he has obtained leave to enter by fraud or deception. There is no general duty of candour on an applicant to draw every fact to the attention of the immigration authorities which they might, had they known, have regarded as material; *R. v. Secretary of State for the Home Department ex p. Khawaja.*[65] The definition of section 33(1) has retrospective effect and applies to immigrants who had unlawfully entered the United Kingdom before the 1971 Act came into effect: *R. v. Governor of Pentonville Prison ex p. Azam.*[66]

The House of Lords in *Khawaja* (*supra*) not merely restricted the previously wide definition of illegal entrant but also extended judicial control over the removal of illegal entrants by holding that whether a person is an illegal entrant is a fact to be established to the satisfaction of the court: it is not sufficient that the immigration authorities regard him as such.[67]

Deportation

Section 3(5) and (6) provides that anyone who is not a British citizen is liable to deportation if: (i) he does not observe a condition or remains beyond the time limit: or (ii) the Home Secretary deems his deportation to be conducive to the public good[68]; or (iii) another person to whose

---

[65] [1984] A.C. 74 (H.L.); reversing *R. v. Secretary of State for the Home Department ex p. Zamir* [1980] A.C. 930.

[66] [1974] A.C. 18.

[67] *i.e.* the question of status is a jurisdictional fact which must exist before the power of removal can be validly exercised, not a matter within the judgment or discretion of the relevant official or minister: see *post*, Chap. 33.

[68] Those deported on this ground include Rudi Dutschke, the German political activist, in 1970, and Mark Hosenball and Philip Agee in 1977: see *R. v. Secretary of State for the Home Department ex p. Hosenball* [1977] 1 W.L.R. 766 (C.A.).

family he belongs is deported[69]; or (iv) being seventeen or over he is convicted of an offence punishable with imprisonment and the court recommends him for deportation.[70] A deportation order is an order requiring a person to leave and prohibiting him from entering the United Kingdom (s.5). The Home Secretary has a discretionary executive power to make such an order,[71] and is not bound to afford the deportee a hearing.[72] The Home Secretary may order the deportation of an illegal entrant whom he is entitled to be ordered to be removed from the United Kingdom (supra). If he chooses the former course statutory appeals and judicial remedies may be available which would not be in the latter case.

The Home Secretary may give directions for the deportation of a person to a country of which he is a national or citizen, or to which there is reason to believe that he will be admitted.[73] Such directions may be given to the captain or owners of a ship or aircraft,[74] or arrangements may be made by the Home Secretary. A bona fide order of deportation for the public good may be made to send an alien back to his own country, even though that country has requested his surrender for a criminal offence that is not extraditable (Ex p. Soblen[75]). Where a court has recommended deportation and the person is neither detained under sentence or order of the court nor released on bail, he may be either detained or released by order of the Home Secretary pending the making of a deportation order.

Section 6 deals with recommendations by a court for deportation. A court may not make such recommendation unless the person has been given seven days' notice of his rights and liability. The validity of a recommendation by a court may only be questioned in an appeal against the recommendation or against conviction.[76] Commonwealth citizens or citizens of the Republic of Ireland who, when the Act came into force, were ordinarily resident in the United Kingdom, are not liable to be deported if they had been ordinarily resident for five years at the time of the Home Secretary's decision or at the time of conviction; and such a person is not liable to deportation on the ground that the Home Secretary deems his deportation to be conducive to the public

---

[69] *Quaere* the compatibility of this provision with EEC law which requires that deportation should be on account of the individual's personal conduct.

[70] Guidelines to be followed by courts in exercising this power were laid down in *R. v. Nazari* [1980] 1 W.L.R. 1366 (C.A.).

[71] *Ex p. Venicoff* [1920] 3 K.B. 72. Cf. *R. v. Chiswick Police Superintendent, ex p. Sacksteder* [1918] 1 K.B. 578.

[72] *R. v. Governor of Brixton Prison, ex p. Soblen* [1963] 2 Q.B. 243 (C.A.), *per* Lord Denning M.R. There is nothing in the 1971 Act to change the law on this point. In certain cases a statutory right of appeal is provided, see *post.*

[73] Cf. *R. v. Home Secretary, ex p. Duke of Château Thierry* [1917] 1 K.B. 922; *R. v. Governor of Brixton Prison, ex p. Sliwa* [1952] 1 K.B. 169 (C.A.).

[74] Cf. *R. v. Governor of Richmond Remand Centre, ex p. Ashgar* [1971] 1 W.L.R. 129 (D.C.).

[75] *R. v. Governor of Brixton Prison, ex p. Soblen* [1963] 2 Q.B. 243 (C.A.). The action of the Home Secretary was criticised as "disguised extradition"; P. O'Higgins, "Disguised Extradition: the Soblen case" (1964) 27 M.L.R. 521; and see C. H. R. Thornberry, "Dr. Soblen and the Alien Law of the United Kingdom" (1963) 12 I.C.L.Q. 414.

[76] For this purpose such recommendation is treated in England as a sentence and in Scotland in the same manner as a conviction.

good if at the time of the Home Secretary's decision he had at all times since the Act came into force been ordinarily resident (s.7).

Appeals

Part II of the Immigration Act creates a system of statutory appeals. The possibility of judicial review is considered in the following section. Section 12 continues the Immigration Appeal Tribunal and adjudicators provided for by the Immigration Appeals Act 1969. Members of the Tribunal are appointed by the Lord Chancellor, the President and some of the other members being legally qualified. Adjudicators are appointed by the Home Secretary. There is a right of appeal to an adjudicator (or direct to the Tribunal in respect of a deportation order otherwise than on the recommendation of a court) against refusal of leave to enter and refusal of certificate of entitlement, entry certificate or visa, against certain conditions of entry, a deportation order made otherwise than on the recommendation of a court, or the destination to which it is proposed to remove him (ss.13–17). Regulations governing the giving of notice of a right of appeal against a decision taken under the Act may be made under section 18.

There is no appeal against a decision of a Home Secretary that refusal of entry is conducive to the public good (s.13(5)), or that deportation is conducive to the public good as being in the interests of national security or foreign relations or for other reasons of a political nature (s.15(3)). In these cases, however, a non-statutory three man panel of advisers will hear representations and report to the Home Secretary who is not bound by the advice which he receives.[77]

An appeal is to be allowed by an adjudicator (or the Tribunal where appeal is to the Tribunal in the first instance) if the adjudicator or Tribunal considers that the decision was contrary to law or to the immigration rules, or that a discretion should have been exercised differently.

Appeal lies to the Immigration Appeal Tribunal from the determination of an adjudicator, subject to any requirement about leave to appeal. The Home Secretary, after an appeal has been dismissed, may refer a case back to an adjudicator or the Tribunal for an opinion of any matter that was not before them in the earlier proceedings.

It may be argued that natural justice applies to proceedings before adjudicators and the Immigration Appeal Tribunal as a general principle although it does not apply to proceedings before the advisers to the Home Secretary, in cases of deportation orders made in the interests of national security.

Judicial Review

Although the Immigration Act 1971 does not provide for *appeal* to the High Court, decisions of immigration officials and tribunals, and of the Home Secretary may be open to *review* on the grounds discussed later in Chapter 33. Thus a decision can be examined to see if the facts precedent to the valid exercise of a statutory power exist: is the applicant

---

[77] H.C.Deb., Vol. 819, col. 375.

an illegal entrant?[78] A decision can be quashed if it is based on an error of law.[79] In R. v. *Immigration Appeal Tribunal ex p. Begum*[80] Simon Brown J. quashed a decision on this ground, holding that the tribunal ought not to have applied a Rule in the Immigration Rules which was so unreasonable that it was invalid. Immigration officials must act fairly[81] and the Home Secretary must not, having created a "legitimate expectation" that he would reach a decision on the basis of certain grounds, take into account other considerations.[82]

Judicial review is, however, a discretionary procedure and the Court of Appeal has recently indicated that it should not be used as a means to avoid recourse to statutory procedures which are available under the Act. Normally the appropriate way to challenge a decision by an immigration officer is by the appellate process laid down in the 1971 Act: *R. v. Secretary of State for the Home Department ex p. Swati*.[83]

On the other hand the Courts may refuse to interfere because the dispute does not involve a justiciable issue. For example, the special voucher scheme under which British Overseas citizens may be admitted to the United Kingdom has been held by the House of Lords to operate outside the Immigration Act 1971 and not to give rise to enforceable legal rights.[84] Whether an applicant was a refugee and therefore entitled to asylum was similarly regarded as non-justiciable by the Court of Appeal.[85]

In the area of immigration law the remedy which is particularly important is that of habeas corpus; the writ by which an immigrant can challenge the legality of his detention before he is returned to the country from which he came or is deported to a third state which is prepared to accept him. The origins of the writ is discussed later in Chapter 26. It is in the sphere of immigration law that it has been most invoked in recent times. Dicta and decisions before the decision of the House of Lords in *R. v. Secretary of State for the Home Department ex p. Khawaja*[86] had cast doubt on the efficacy of habeas corpus in immigration cases. In *Khawaja*, however, the House of Lords emphasised that once the applicant has established a prima facie case the burden of justifying the legality of any restraint of liberty lies on the executive. Lord Bridge said that the House should "regard with extreme jealousy any claim by the executive to imprison a citizen without trial and allow it only if it is clearly justified by the statutory language relied on. The fact that, in the

---

[78] R. v. *Secretary of State for the Home Department ex p. Khawaja* [1984] A.C. 74.

[79] R. v. *Chief Immigration Officer, Gatwick Airport ex p. Kharrazi* [1980] 1 W.L.R. 1396 (C.A.). R. v. *Immigration Appeal Tribunal ex p. Singh* [1986] 1 W.L.R. 910 (H.L.).

[80] *The Times*, July 24, 1986; applying to the Rules the test applicable to by-laws (*Kruse* v. *Johnson* [1898] 2 Q.B. 91), on the basis that the Rules were not delegated legislation in the normal sense; *post*, pp. 623–624.

[81] *Re H.K.* [1967] 2 Q.B. 617.

[82] R. v. *Secretary of State for the Home Department ex p. Asif Khan* [1984] 1 W.L.R. 537.

[83] [1986] 1 W.L.R. 477 (C.A.).

[84] R. v. *Entry Clearance Officer ex p. Amin* [1983] 2 A.C. 818.

[85] R. v. *Secretary of State for the Home Department ex p. Bugdaycay* [1986] 1 W.L.R. 155 (C.A.). The House of Lords held that the question of refugee status was for the Home Secretary to determine but the Courts could intervene if in so doing he had acted unreasonably within the *Wednesbury* principles: [1987] 2 W.L.R. 606; *post*, p. 669.

[86] [1984] A.C. 74.

case we are considering detention is preliminary and incidental to expulsion from the country . . . strengthens rather than weakens the case for a robust exercise of the judicial function in safeguarding the citizen's rights" (p. 122).[87]

Habeas corpus, although not available as of right may not be refused *merely* because of the existence of an alternative remedy.[88]

IV. EXTRADITION AND FUGITIVE OFFENDERS

Introduction

Extradition may be used in a wide sense to refer to any surrender of a criminal—suspected or convicted—from one jurisdiction to another. In a narrow sense it may be used to refer to surrender under the Extradition Acts 1870 to 1935, as opposed to surrender under the Fugitive Offenders Act 1967 or under the Backing of Warrants (Republic of Ireland) Act 1965. (Inside the United Kingdom a warrant issued in any part of the Kingdom may be executed in any other: Criminal Law Act 1977, s.38.) The increased ease of travel between countries, and more recently the growth of violent terrorist crimes, have emphasised the importance of effective arrangements for the extradition of criminals (and have cast doubt on the sanctity of the asylum formerly given to the perpetrators of political offences). Some reforms have, as we shall see, already taken place; others are promised.[88a]

Extradition is not, unlike deportation, a punishment or sanction but part of the procedure of enforcing the criminal law and on that ground the English courts have rejected the argument that in the case of EEC nationals the process may be a violation of Article 48.[89]

Extradition Acts[90]

The Extradition Acts 1870 to 1935, as amended, provide that the Crown may, subject to certain restrictions and formalities, hand over to any state with which a reciprocal treaty has been made any persons (whether British subjects or aliens) who have been found guilty of committing in that state any offence covered by the Extradition Acts.[91] The offences are listed in Schedule 1 to the 1870 Act, as amended. Genocide and hijacking, for example, have been added[92] and offences under the Internationally Protected Persons Act 1978 and the Suppression of Ter-

---

[87] See C. Vincenzi, "Aliens and the Judicial Review of Immigration Law" [1985] P.L. 93.

[88] *R.* v. *Governor of Pentonville Prison, ex p. Azam* [1974] A.C. 18, 32; *Quigley* v. *Chief Constable, Royal Ulster Constabulary* [1983] N.I. 238, 239; *post* p. 508.

[88a] A Green Paper on Extradition was published in 1985 (Cmnd. 9421) and subsequently the Government made proposals in its White Paper on Criminal Justice.

[89] *R.* v. *Governor of Pentonville Prison, ex p. Budlong* [1980] 1 W.L.R. 1110 (D.C.); *R.* v. *Governor of Pentonville Prison, ex p. Healy,* The Times, May 11, 1984 (D.C.) (Proceedings under Backing of Warrants (Republic of Ireland) 1965 Act).

[90] There is no prerogative power to seize an alien in this country and hand him over to a foreign state: Forsyth, *Cases and Opinions on Constitutional Law,* pp. 369–370; *cf. East India Co.* v. *Campbell* (1749) Ves.Sen. 246; *Mure* v. *Kaye* (1811) 4 Taunt. 43.

[91] See I. and C. Stanbrook, *The Law and Practice of Extradition* (1980); I. A. Shearer, *Extradition in International Law* (1971).

[92] Genocide Act 1969; Aviation Security Act 1982. The Suppression of Terrorism Act 1978 adds various offences connected with the use of firearms and explosives.

rorism Act 1978. In determining the validity of extradition proceedings the Extradition Acts must be read in conjunction with the relevant treaty which may, under section 2 of the 1871 Act, provide for conditions, exceptions and qualifications subject to which the Act is to operate.[93] The foreign state in return undertakes to surrender to the United Kingdom persons who have committed extraditable crimes in British territory. The Act of 1870 enables the Crown to make an Order in Council directing that the Extradition Acts shall apply to any given state.

When extradition is requested through diplomatic channels, the accused can be arrested either by warrant of the Chief Metropolitan Magistrate at Bow Street issued on order of the Home Secretary, or by warrant of a justice of the peace issued on information, which warrant may be cancelled by the Home Secretary. The Chief Magistrate or another metropolitan magistrate at Bow Street receives the extradition order and documents from the Home Office, and decides whether there is a prima facie case that would *according to the law of England* justify the committal for trial of the accused for an offence described in the Schedule to the 1870 Act, (as amended by later Acts) and that such offence is also included in the extraditable crimes listed in the English language version of the extradition treaty. The English magistrate is concerned with English law alone: *In re Nielsen*.[94] The requirement of sufficient evidence to justify a committal is generally thought to be one of the unsatisfactory features of the United Kingdom law of extradition because it makes difficult the return of fugitive criminals and shows a lack of trust in the grounds on which foreign legal systems are prepared to issue warrants for arrest.

There must also be sufficient evidence of the identity of the accused.[95] If the magistrate does not commit him he is discharged. Since the Extradition Acts apply to Scotland as well as England a criminal arrested in Stornaway must normally be taken to Bow Street. Although in two cases[96] proceedings may take place in Scotland they still involve the absurdity of a Scottish sheriff applying English law.[97] The Home Sec-

---

[93] *Beese* v. *Governor of Ashford Remand Centre* [1973] 1 W.L.R. 1426 (H.L.).

[94] [1984] A.C. 606 (H.L.). See also *U.S. Government* v. *McCaffery* [1984] 1 W.L.R. 867. In these two cases the House of Lords rejected the view that an English court must examine the law of the requesting state to establish whether there was substantial similarity between the requirements of the two legal systems as to the crime whose name appeared in the Extradition Act and the relevant treaty: the principle of "double criminality" which found favour after *R.* v. *Governor of Pentonville Prison ex p. Budlong* [1980] 1 W.L.R. 1110 (D.C.). Exceptionally a particular treaty may import some requirement of similarity between the two systems. In *re Nielsen* has been applied by the Court of Appeal in *R.* v. *Governor of Pentonville Prison ex p. Herbage, The Times,* August 6, 1986.

[95] The magistrate may consider evidence—for example police photographs—to establish identity which would be excluded at a trial by a judge because of prejudicial effect: *R.* v. *Governor of Pentonville Prison, ex p. Voets* [1986] 1 W.L.R. 470 (D.C.). See also on the width of admissible evidence *In re Rees* [1986] A.C. 937 (H.L.).

[96] (1) Under s.16 of the Extradition Act 1870 where the crime for which extradition is sought was committed on board a ship which docks at a Scottish port; (2) under the Extradition Act 1985 if the removal to London of a prisoner arrested under the 1870 Act would be prejudicial to his life or health.

[97] W. Finnie, "The Procedure of Extradition from Scotland" [1983] S.L.T. News 25 and 41.

retary has a discretion not to surrender a fugitive criminal if he thinks it would be unjust or oppressive to do so.[98]

Section 3 of the Act of 1870 provides that a person is not to be surrendered for "an offence of a political character." Thus in *Re Castioni*,[99] where a native of the Swiss canton of Ticino had committed murder during an insurrection and escaped to England, he was not surrendered. An offence is normally political only when there are two parties in the state each trying to impose its own government on the other. The mere fact that the prisoner is accused of murder in a political disturbance does not in itself justify the refusal of an order for his extradition, and an explosion caused by an anarchist is not a political offence within the Act.[1] In *Schtraks* v. *Government of Israel*,[2] where the charges involved were perjury and child-stealing, the case had become a political issue in Israel but that did not make it an offence of a political character. The idea behind the latter phrase, said Viscount Radcliffe, is that the fugitive is at odds with the state that applies for his extradition on some issue connected with the political control or government of the country. On the other hand in *Ex p. Kolczynski*,[3] where the members of a Polish trawler had taken charge of a ship, putting the master under restraint, and steered her into an English port because they feared they would be punished for their political opinions if they returned to Poland, they were successful in their application for habeas corpus, the Divisional Court holding that the offences were committed in order to escape from political tyranny. In *R.* v. *Governor of Winson Green, ex p. Littlejohn*[4] Lord Widgery C.J., after reviewing the earlier authorities, said, "An offence may be of a political character either because the wrongdoer had some direct ulterior motive of a political kind when he committed the offence, or because the requesting state is anxious to obtain possession of the wrongdoer's person in order to punish him for his politics rather than for the simple criminal offence referred to in the extradition proceedings." An offence which might otherwise be of a political character will fall outside section 3 if it is committed not in the state against whose government it is directed but in the territory of a third state which is the state requesting extradition.[5]

The concern which was earlier felt for offering asylum to political refugees has in recent years been replaced by a desire to ensure that terrorists cannot escape justice by claiming that status for themselves. We shall see in Chapter 24 that modern statutes have indirectly dealt with the problem by conferring power on United Kingdom courts to deal

---

[98] *Atkinson v. United States Government* [1971] A.C. 197 (H.L.); *Royal Government of Greece v. Brixton Prison Governor* [1971] A.C. 250 (H.L.).

[99] [1891] 1 Q.B. 149.

[1] *Re Meunier* [1894] 2 Q.B. 415.

[2] [1964] A.C. 556 (H.L.). See C. F. Amerasinghe, "The *Schtraks* Case, defining Political Offences and Extradition" (1965) 28 M.L.R. 27.

[3] *R.* v. *Brixton Prison Governor, ex p. Kolczynski* [1955] 1 Q.B. 540.

[4] [1975] 1 W.L.R. 893 (D.C.).

[5] *Cheng* v. *Governor of Pentonville Prison* [1973] A.C. 931. (Appellant convicted in New York of an attempted murder there of visiting member of the ruling Taiwan regime; appellant, member of organisation dedicated to the overthrow of the regime; alleged crime not "of a political character.")

with violent crimes committed abroad which are in many cases likely to be the work of terrorists. In order to facilitate the surrender of wanted criminals steps have also been taken to limit the availability of reliance on the plea that a crime was a political offence. The Suppression of Terrorism Act 1978 prevents the plea being raised by a criminal accused of a crime listed in Schedule 1 (which includes most crimes against the person, certain offences against property and hijacking) where extradition is requested by a state to which the Secretary of State has by order extended the provisions of the Act. The defence which has been lost is replaced by an amendment to section 3 of the Extradition Act 1870 which allows a defendant to show that an extradition request has been made with a view to try or punish him on account of his race, religion, nationality, or political opinions, or that he might, if surrendered, be prejudiced at his trial or punished, detained or restricted in his personal liberty by reason of his race, religion, nationality or political opinions.

(This amendment brings the Extradition Act 1870 into line with the Fugitive Offenders Act 1967; *infra*).

If the magistrate commits a prisoner for surrender, he must be informed of his rights to apply for habeas corpus. Again, Parliament overlooked, in applying the Extradition Acts to Scotland, the difference between the two legal systems. Scots law does not know of habeas corpus.[6] In view of the general rule that fresh evidence cannot be admitted on an application for habeas corpus, a prisoner cannot raise before the court the political character of his alleged offence if he did not raise that defence initially before the magistrate.[7] On an application for habeas corpus the question for the Court is not whether there was sufficient evidence to justify committal but whether there was any evidence upon which the magistrate could have reached his finding: *R. v. United States Government, ex p. Blair.*[8] He may not be surrendered within fifteen days of the committal order, nor until a final decision on habeas corpus proceedings had been made (Extradition Act 1870, s.11). If he is not conveyed out of the Kingdom within two months after committal, or if a writ of habeas corpus is issued after the decision thereon, any judge of a superior court may, on the prisoner's application and on proof that the Home Secretary has had reasonable notice of such application, order the discharge of the prisoner unless sufficient cause is shown to the contrary (s.12). If the prisoner is not discharged, he is surrendered under the warrant of the Home Secretary.

Where a prisoner has been extradited to the United Kingdom from a foreign state the British courts, in determining the offence with which he may properly be charged under the Extradition Act 1870, will interpret that Act for themselves, unfettered by the view of the foreign court as to the prisoner's liability under its provisions.[9]

---

[6] *Wan Ping Nam* v. *West German Federal Minister of Justice, Secretary of State for Scotland and Lord Advocate* 1972 S.C. 43 (J.C.). (Absence of Habeas Corpus made good by exercise of nobile officium of the High Court).

[7] *R. v. Farringdon Police Station, Officer in Charge ex p. Nobbs* [1977] Crim.L.R. 422 (case arising under the Backing of Warrants (Republic of Ireland) Act 1965).

[8] *The Times*, June 21, 1985 (D.C.).

[9] *R. v. Davidson* (1976) 64 Cr.App.R. 209 (C.A.).

A prisoner cannot, on his return to the United Kingdom, be proceeded against for any offence other than that for which he was extradited if such a proceeding is contrary to the terms of the relevant Order in Council made under the Act.[9a]

Fugitive Offenders Acts

The Fugitive Offenders Act 1881[10] made provision for the arrest and surrender of persons of any nationality accused of crimes to which the Act applied, when they fled from one part of Her Majesty's dominions to another part. The Act was a relic of the time when the Crown was indivisible throughout the Empire. It continued to apply not only between the United Kingdom (which for this purpose includes the Channel Islands and the Isle of Man) and colonies and other British dependencies,[11] but also between them and independent Commonwealth countries. The Act did not exclude political offences (*Ex p. Enahoro*[12]), but a superior court might discharge a fugitive for various reasons.[13]

The Fugitive Offenders Act 1967,[14] based on an agreement among the Law Ministers of 20 Commonwealth countries that reciprocal and uniform arrangements should be made for offenders who flee from one part of the Commonwealth to another, replaces the Act of 1881. The new Act applies to the United Kingdom, the Channel Islands, the Isle of Man and (with modifications) to British dependencies. With regard to arrest, proceedings before the Bow Street Magistrate and applications to the High Court for habeas corpus, the Act is similar to the Extradition Act, but in other respects it is an improvement.[15]

A person is not liable to be returned to another Commonwealth country unless the offence not only falls within the list of offences in Schedule 1 to the Act, but is punishable by the law of that country with imprisonment for 12 months, and also would be an offence against the

---

[9a] R. v. *Uxbridge Justices ex p. Davies* [1981] 1 W.L.R. 1080. *Cf.* the principle known in International Law as speciality.

[10] Sir Kenneth Roberts-Wray, *Commonwealth and Colonial Law*, pp. 604–611; Paul O'Higgins, "Extradition within the Commonwealth" (1960) 9 I.C.L.Q. 486; Note on "The Enahoro Case" (1963) 12 I.C.L.Q. 1364; "Recent Practice under the Fugitive Offenders Acts" [1965] Crim.L.R. 133; S. A. de Smith, "Political Asylum and the Commonwealth" (1963) 16 *Parliamentary Affairs* 396.

[11] The Act might be extended to protectorates and protected states by Order in Council under the Foreign Jurisdiction Act 1890; R. v. *Secretary of State for Home Affairs, ex p. Demetrious* [1966] 2 Q.B. 194.

[12] R. v. *Brixton Prison Governor, ex p. Enahoro (No. 2)* [1963] 2 Q.B. 455 (D.C.).

[13] R. v. *Brixton Prison Governor, ex p. Naranjan Sing* [1962] 1 Q.B. 211; *cf. Zacharia* v. *Republic of Cyprus* [1963] A.C. 634 (H.L.), where the Home Secretary exercised his discretion not to hand the appellant over to Cyprus. And see *Armah* v. *Government of Ghana* [1968] A.C. 192 (H.L.).

[14] See *Scheme Relating to the Rendition of Fugitive Offenders within the Commonwealth* (1966) Cmnd. 3008; Paul O'Higgins, "The Reform of Intra-Commonwealth Extradition" [1966] Crim.L.R. 361; Alex Samuels, "English Fugitive Offenders Act 1967" (1968) 18 U.T.L.R. 198.

[15] It recognises more clearly that Scotland has its own legal system. Proceedings may begin in Scotland before a Sheriff of Lothian and Borders (s.6) and committals may be challenged by an application to the High Court for review under s.8.

law of the United Kingdom if it took place here (s.3).[16] The Fugitive Offenders Act 1967 excludes offences of a political character, though not offences against the life or person of the Head of the Commonwealth. Further, a person may not be returned if the request for his return is in fact made in order to try him on account of his race, religion, nationality or political opinions; or he might be prejudiced at his trial on account of his race, etc.[17-18] or unless arrangements secure that he is not tried for a different (and not lesser) offence (s.4). Once a magistrate is satisfied that the requirements of the 1967 Act have been complied with he is not required to consider, before making a committal order, what defences, if any, might be open to the alleged offender under the law of the requesting state.[19]

The appropriate High Court in each jurisdiction may discharge a person from custody if it appears that it would be unjust or oppressive to return him, because: (a) the offence is trivial; or (b) of the length of time since the offence is alleged to have been committed[20]; or (c) the accusation is not made in good faith in the interests of justice[21] (s.8(3)). Despite the use of the word "may" in section 8 the court has no real discretion, once it has decided that it would be unjust or oppressive to return the applicant.[22] Its decision is one of fact as to the correct inference to be drawn from the primary facts proved to it.

The Home Secretary may not make an order for return if it appears to him that it would be unjust or oppressive to do so, on the same grounds as section 8(3) above; and he has a discretion not to order a person's return if he would be liable to the death penalty (s.9).

Backing of warrants

The surrender of wanted criminals between the Republic of Ireland and the United Kingdom is governed by the Backing of Warrants (Republic of Ireland) Act 1965[23] and the Criminal Jurisdiction Act 1975. By Section 1(1) of the 1965 Act a warrant issued in the Republic of Ireland by a judicial authority shall, subject to the provisions of the Act, be indorsed by a justice of the peace upon police application. Subsection (2) provides that an Irish warrant for the arrest of an accused person cannot be indorsed unless it is issued (a) in respect of an indictable offence, or (b) in respect of an offence punishable on summary convic-

---

[16] R. v. Brixton Prison Governor, ex p. Gardner [1968] 2 Q.B. 399 (D.C.); cf. R. v. Brixton Prison Governor, ex p. Rush [1969] 1 W.L.R. (D.C.); Tarling v. Govt. of Singapore (1980) 70 Cr.App.R. 77 (H.L.). It is not necessary, however, that the name or the precise details of the offence under the two systems of law should exactly correspond: R. v. Pentonville Prison Governor, ex p. Teja [1971] 2 Q.B. 274 (D.C.). Leave to appeal to the House of Lords was refused; [1971] 1 W.L.R. 678.

[17-18] Fernandez v. Singapore Government [1971] 1 W.L.R. 987 (H.L.).

[19] Government of Australia v. Harrod [1975] 1 W.L.R. 745 (H.L.).

[20] R. v. Brixton Prison Governor, ex p. Cook (1970) 114 S.J. 827 (D.C.) (eighteen months).

[21] R. v. Pentonville Prison Governor, ex p. Teja, ante.

[22] R. v. Governor of Pentonville Prison, ex p. Narang [1978] A.C. 247 (H.L.). The House of Lords also held that the court can only take into account the facts relevant to the particular ground under s.8 on which the applicant relies. Kakis v. Government of Republic of Cyprus [1978] 1 W.L.R. 779 (H.L.) (witness no longer available; Cyprus government originally willing that K. should settle in England).

[23] See "Anglo-Irish Extradition," (1967) 2 Irish Jurist 43; (1966) 29 M.L.R. 186.

tion with imprisonment for six months and the requirements of the subsection relating to service or failure to appear before the Irish court is satisfied. The endorsement is a formal process, the English (or Scottish) judge is not concerned with the existence of evidence to support the warrant.[24] Subsection (3) provides that an Irish warrant for the arrest of a person convicted of any offence against the laws of the Republic shall not be endorsed unless the purpose of the arrest is to enable him to be brought before a court of the Republic for sentence in respect of the conviction. In *Re Lawlor*[25] habeas corpus was granted to release a prisoner arrested on an Irish warrant where the Divisional Court was satisfied that it had been issued not to secure the return of the applicant to sentence him for an offence of which he had been earlier convicted but to ensure his availability as a witness at a murder trial.

Section 2 provides that after being brought before a magistrates' court on an endorsed warrant the court shall order his delivery to the Republican authorities unless (a) the offence specified does not correspond to any offence under the law of the relevant part of the United Kingdom which his an indictable offence, or is punishable on summary conviction with imprisonment for six months, or (b) is of a political character[26] or an offence under military law which is not also an offence under the general criminal law, or (c) an offence under an enactment relating to taxes, duties or exchange control, or (d) there are *substantial grounds* for believing that if returned to the Republic the prisoner will be prosecuted or detained for another offence within category (b). The Suppression of Terrorism Act 1978 has added to section 2 of the 1965 Act similar words to those quoted earlier in relation to section 3 of the Extradition Act. Until the 1978 Act is extended to the Republic of Ireland criminals sought under the Backing of Warrants Act will still, in addition, be able to rely on the traditional "political offence" plea.

A defendant who cannot bring himself within section 3 cannot resist extradition proceedings on the ground that he is liable on his return to be prosecuted for a non-political crime but a different crime from that for which his return has been sought: the Act leaves no room for the application of the international law rule of speciality: *In re McFadden*.[27]

The Criminal Jurisdiction Act 1975[28] sought to avoid the difficulties inherent in the surrender of wanted criminals from one jurisdiction in Ireland to the other by conferring extra territorial jurisdiction on the courts of Northern Ireland in the case of certain crimes. Any act committed in the Republic of Ireland which, if committed in Northern Ireland, would constitute one of the crimes listed in Schedule 1 (serious crimes

---

[24] *Keane* v. *Governor of Brixton Prison* [1972] A.C. 204; *R.* v. *Governor of Risley Remand Centre ex p. Marks* [1984] Crim.L.R. 238 (D.C.) (Similar rule applicable to return of convicted prisoner).

[25] (1977) 66 Cr.App.R. 75 (D.C.).

[26] For an unsuccessful attempt to rely on this provision see *R.* v. *Governor of Durham Prison ex p. Carlisle* [1979] Crim.L.R. 175 (D.C.) (Detention in England under Prevention of Terrorism (Temporary Provisions) Act 1974 which defined terrorism as use of violence for political ends: Irish warrant issued for offences relating to explosions).

[27] *The Times*, March 13, 1982.

[28] See Report of the Law Enforcement Commission (Cmnd. 5627). There is corresponding legislation in the Republic of Ireland.

EXTRADITION AND FUGITIVE OFFENDERS 471

of violence against the person, damage to property by fire, offences involving explosives and fire arms) will constitute a crime by the law of Northern Ireland. The Act also creates a new offence of hijacking a vehicle or ship anywhere in Northern Ireland or the Republic of Ireland which is triable in Northern Ireland. Consequential amendments are made to the Backing of Warrants (Republic of Ireland) Act 1965 to prevent the enforcement of warrants issued in the Republic against offenders who are or have been convicted or acquitted of an extraterritorial offence in Northern Ireland.

CHAPTER 24

OFFENCES AGAINST THE STATE

Classification of offences against the state

IN a wide sense, all crimes are offences against the State. The object of this chapter is to consider the more important of those criminal offences that have a political aspect and overlap the field of constitutional law, in so far as they are not dealt with in later chapters.

Offences of a public nature are usually classified in the following manner:

(i) *Offences against the Crown and government.* These have traditionally included treason, misprision of treason, treason-felony, incitement to mutiny, sedition and disclosure of official secrets, as well as illegal training and drilling, illegal wearing of uniforms, associating with military organisations and incitement to disaffection. In modern times terrorist offences of various kinds must be added.

(ii) *Offences against public peace and morals.* These include blasphemy, obscene and defamatory libels, violent disorder, riot and public nuisance.

(iii) *Offences against public justice.* These include perjury, bribery, embracery and interference with witnesses, contempt of court, obstructing or resisting the police, and corrupt or illegal practices at elections.

(iv) *Offences connected with trade and commerce.* These include trading with the enemy, coinage offences and smuggling.

Some of these offences have been discussed in earlier chapters; others will be discussed later. The arrangement of topics in this chapter is to be justified by convenience, not logic.

Treason

The law of treason is a reminder of the antiquity of much of the Constitution. It dates from a time when an attack on the monarch was likely to be the most effective way to undermine the government of the State. It is worthy of note that even in the case of the most serious terrorist outrages of the last few years prosecutions have not been brought under the law of treason. No doubt that is explicable partly by the wish to avoid the uncertainties of an ancient part of the law but also, perhaps, because it is felt that the execution of persons convicted in peace time would cause undesirable controversy, and, it is arguable, provoke further crimes of violence.

Treason is a betrayal (*trahison*) or breach of the faith and allegiance due to the Sovereign. Allegiance is correlative to protection. It is owed to the Crown by British citizens wherever they may be; by citizens of other Commonwealth countries and Irish citizens while they are in the United Kingdom[1]; and by aliens[2] while they are in British territory by

---

[1] Citizens of other Commonwealth countries which owe allegiance to the Queen as Queen also owe allegiance by the law of their respective countries.

[2] *Semble,* including civilian enemy aliens who remain at large within the realm by licence, and internees; *cf.* prisoners of war.

the Sovereign's licence, express or tacit. It has been held that aliens resident in the Sovereign's dominions may continue to owe allegiance even after protection is withdrawn.[3] Foreign diplomatic representatives and members of foreign invading or occupying forces, however, do not owe allegiance.

The earliest statute on the subject is the Treason Act 1351, which was supposed to be declaratory of the common law.[4] The statute is still in force, with amendments, and constitutes the following offences high treason[5]: (i) compassing or imagining the death of the King (or Queen Regnant) Queen Consort,[6] or the sovereign's eldest son and heir; or (ii) violating the King's consort or the King's eldest daughter unmarried or the wife of the king's eldest son and heir; or (iii) levying war against the King in his realm; or (iv) adhering to the King's enemies in his realm, giving them aid or comfort in the realm or elsewhere; or (v) slaying the Chancellor, Treasurer[7] or the King's justices assigned to hear and determine, being in their places doing their offices.

Compassing or imagining the death of the Sovereign

The words "compass or imagine" import design, which must be manifested by an overt act.[8] The following are overt acts according to Blackstone[9]: providing weapons, conspiring to imprison the King though not intending his death, or assembling and consulting to kill the King.

Levying of war in the realm

This has been held to include not only levying of war to dethrone the King, but also levying war to reform religion, remove councillors or redress grievances. Resistance to the royal forces by defending a castle against them is levying War, and so is an insurrection with an avowed design to pull down all chapels and the like. In *Damaree's Case* (1709)[10] Damaree and Purchas were convicted of treason for burning Nonconformist meeting-houses, the court being of opinion that the design was a general one against the state, and therefore a levying of war. Blackstone says that merely conspiring to levy war is not a treasonable levying of war, but that it constitutes compassing the King's death where it is pointed at the royal person or government. To enlist men in the realm to go to the aid of the King's enemies abroad is not levying war in the

---

[3] *De Jager* v. *Att.-Gen. of Natal* [1907] A.C. 326.
[4] See J. G. Bellamy, *The Law of Treason in England in the Later Middle Ages* (1970); G. P. Bodet, "Sir Edward Coke's *Third Institute*: a primer for treason defendants" (1971) 20 U.T.L.J. 469.
[5] Petit treason under this statute consisted of: (a) the killing of a master by his servant, (b) the killing of a husband by his wife, and (c) the killing of a prelate by his ecclesiastical inferior. Since 1828 these offences have been regarded as ordinary murder.
[6] The consort of a Queen Regnant is not protected by the law of treason.
[7] There has been no Treasurer since 1714; *ante*, p. 329.
[8] *R.* v. *Thistlewood* (1820) 33 St.Tr. 681.
[9] Bl.Comm. IV, 74 *et seq.*
[10] *R.* v. *Damaree* (1709) 15 St.Tr. 521.

realm, but it may be brought under compassing the King's death and adhering to the King's enemies.

Adhering to the King's enemies

It is an offence under (iv) above either to give the King's enemies in his realm aid and comfort in his realm, or to give aid and comfort elsewhere to the King's enemies elsewhere. "Enemies" here means public belligerents as understood in international law, and not mere pirates or British rebels; but to aid the latter in the realm would constitute levying of war. Persons acting under duress as regards life or person cannot be convicted as traitors, provided that they leave the King's enemies at the first opportunity.

In *R. v. Lynch*,[11] where a British subject during the Boer War commanded an Irish brigade on the side of the Boers against the British forces, the court held that the words "adhering to the King's enemies in his realm" did not mean that the "accused person *being in the realm* has been adherent to the King's enemies *wherever they were*," to the exclusion of such a case as that before the court. So narrow a construction not only would enable an Englishman to engage with a foreign hostile power against his own country, so long as he took care to remain abroad, but also ignores the words "or elsewhere" in the same sentence of the section. *R. v. Lynch* also decided that section 6 of the Naturalisation Act 1870 did not enable a British subject to become naturalised in an enemy state in time of war, and, further, that the very act of purporting to become naturalised in those circumstances constituted an overt act of treason.[12]

In *R. v. Casement*[13] it was decided that a subject may "adhere to the King's enemies in his realm" and so be found guilty of treason under the statute of 1351, whether the act complained of was committed within or outside the realm. In that case Sir Roger Casement, a British subject,[14] was found guilty on the ground that he went to Germany when the United Kingdom was at war with that country, and while there endeavoured to persuade Irish prisoners of war (who were British subjects) to join the enemy's forces and thus to assist the liberation of Ireland. The Court of Criminal Appeal had to interpret the statute of Edward III, which was written without punctuation, according to its meaning when it was passed.

It was resolved by the judges in 1707[15] that a resident alien, who during a war with his native country returned there and adhered to the King's enemies, leaving his family and effects here, might be dealt with as a traitor: "For he came and settled here under the protection of the Crown; and though his person was removed for a time, his effects and family continued still under the same protection." The principle of this rule was extended by the House of Lords in *Joyce v. Director of Public*

---

[11] [1903] 1 K.B. 444.

[12] *Quaere* extent of application of this rule to the British Nationality Act 1981 in the light of s.12(4); s.24; s.29; s.30.

[13] [1917] 1 K.B. 98. A. Wharam, "Casement and Joyce" (1978) 41 M.L.R. 681.

[14] An Irishman by birth: at that time the whole of Ireland was part of the United Kingdom.

[15] Foster's *Crown Cases* (3rd ed.), p. 185.

Prosecutions[16] to an alien who departed entirely from this country, but who was held in the particular circumstances to have remained under the protection of the Crown.

Mens rea is required for treason as for other crimes. In *R. v. Ahlers*[17] the accused was German Consul at Sunderland, and it was therefore part of his ordinary duty to give his compatriots assistance, monetary and otherwise. He took steps on the outbreak of war in 1914 to assist German subjects of military age to return home to fight in the German army. A statutory Order in Council limited the time for the departure of alien enemies: of this the accused knew nothing, but he believed he was acting in accordance with international law. His conviction for treason by adhering to the King's enemies was quashed for lack of proof that he was aware that he was assisting the King's enemies.

Slaying the Chancellor, etc.

As the Lord Chancellor and judges represent the Sovereign in court, Blackstone considered them entitled to equal protection and justified this section of the statute accordingly. However, attempted murder of the Chancellor and judges in court is, according to the same authority, not treason.

Treason Acts subsequent to 1351

The Treason Act 1495 provided that a subject who obeyed a usurper while he was occupying the throne would not later be charged with treason after the lawful King had regained the throne, but no protection was given to any person who thereafter declined from his allegiance.[18]

Under the Treason Act 1702, endeavouring to deprive or hinder any person next in succession to the Throne under the Act of Settlement from succeeding thereto, and maliciously and directly attempting the same by any overt act, is treason. The Succession to the Crown Act 1707 made it treason maliciously and directly by writing or print to maintain and affirm that any other person has any right to the Crown other than in accordance with the Act of Settlement, or that Parliament has not power to make laws to bind the Crown and the descent thereof. The Treason Act 1708 applied the English law of treason to Scotland.[19]

---

[16] [1946] A.C. 347. William Joyce (popularly known as "Lord Haw-Haw") was brought back from Germany at the end of the last war and charged with high treason in that he, while owing allegiance to the Crown, adhered to the King's enemies elsewhere than in the realm by broadcasting Nazi propaganda. He had obtained a British passport by falsely declaring himself to be a British subject, when he was in fact a citizen of the United States. For criticisms of the decision, see Cobbett's *Cases on International Law* (6th ed. W. L. Walker), i, p. 199; Glanville L. Williams, "The Correlation of Allegiance and Protection" (1948) 10 C.L.J. 54; S. C. Briggs, "Treason and the Trial of William Joyce" (1947) 7 U.T.L.J. 162.

[17] [1915] 1 K.B. 616 (C.A.).

[18] *Madzimbamuto* v. *Lardner-Burke* [1969] 1 A.C. 645 (P.C.); A. M. Honoré, "Allegiance and the Usurper" (1967) C.L.J. 214; *cf.* Taswell-Langmead, *English Constitutional History* (11th ed. Plucknett), pp. 224–225, 446–447.

[19] 7 Anne c. 21. "Such crimes and offences which are high treason or misprision of high treason within England shall be construed adjudged and be taken to be high treason within Scotland."

Judicial interpretation of the statute of 1351 relating to compassing the King's death led to a number of "constructive treasons."[20] Some of these were enacted as treasons by the Treason Act 1795[21] which covered compassing, imagining, devising or intending the death, wounding or imprisonment of the King, whether within the realm or without, provided such compassing, etc. was expressed in writing or by any overt act.

Trial and punishment

The punishment prescribed for treason is now death by hanging or, under royal warrant, by beheading.[22] Formerly a male traitor was hanged and quartered, after being drawn on a hurdle to the place of execution[23]; a female traitor was burnt. Until the Forfeiture Act 1870 conviction was followed by forfeiture and corruption of blood.

Treason or misprision of treason committed abroad is triable in England.[24]

Treason committed within the realm must be prosecuted within three years after its commission, except in the case of designing or attempting the assassination of the Sovereign.[25] Bail cannot be granted by magistrates, but only by the Secretary of State or a judge of the Queen's Bench Division.

Misprision of treason

The Treason Act 1554 created a statutory offence of misprision of treason, punishable by imprisonment for life. Although that statute was repealed by the Criminal Law Act 1967, the common law offence of misprision of treason remains in existence[26] and is an offence punishable by fine or imprisonment at the discretion of the court. It is committed whenever a person knows that another has committed treason and fails to bring this information, or any material part of it, to the attention of the public authorities within a reasonable time.

Treason-felony

By the Treason Felony Act 1848 a person is guilty of felony if, by writing or overt act within or without the United Kingdom, he compasses, imagines, devises or intends to deprive or depose the Queen from the style, honour or royal name of the imperial crown of the United Kingdom, or of any other of Her Majesty's dominions and countries; or to levy war against Her Majesty within any part of the United Kingdom, in order to compel her to change her measures or counsels, or in order to intimidate or overcome both Houses or either House of Parliament; or

---

[20] e.g. R. v. Hardy (1794) 24 St.Tr. 199; R. v. Horne Took (1794) 25 St.Tr. 1. See further, Stephen, History of the Criminal Law, Vol. II; Holdsworth, History of English Law, Vol. III, pp. 309–322. For criticism of the use of the term "constructive treason" see A. Wharam, "Treason in Rhodesia" [1967] C.L.J. 189.

[21] A temporary Act made permanent by the Treason Act 1817.

[22] Treason Act 1814. Beheading is in practice obsolete.

[23] These barbarous practices were gradually discarded and were finally abolished by the Forfeiture Act 1870.

[24] Treason Act 1543.

[25] Treason Act 1695.

[26] See the Law Commission Working Paper No. 72, para. 41 (1977).

to move any foreigner with force to invade the United Kingdom or any other of Her Majesty's dominions. Some of these offences had been enacted as treason by the Treason Act 1795 (*ante*). The Treason Felony Act does not affect the Act of 1795, but provides an alternative remedy in some cases. Its object was partly to cover Ireland, and partly to encourage juries to convict, which they had been loath to do in recent treason trials.

The maximum punishment under the Act of 1848 is imprisonment for life. If a person is indicted for treason-felony and the offence turns out to be treason, he may be convicted of treason-felony.

Attempt to alarm or injure the Sovereign

An attempt to alarm or injure the Sovereign by discharging or aiming or producing a gun, whether loaded or not, at or near the person of Her Majesty was made an offence punishable by imprisonment for seven years by the Treason Act 1842, after an incident involving Queen Victoria.

Proposals for reforming the law of treason

The present law of treason is clearly in need of reform. It is based on the concept of allegiance which has little connection with the modern concept of nationality. It covers a wide range of crimes, of varying degrees of gravity, some of which can appropriately be dealt with by the ordinary criminal law. Proposals for reform were made by the Law Commission in 1977 but they have not been acted upon.[27]

Sedition

The law of sedition, too, is largely an historic survival, except in its more precise, statutory forms.

The word "sedition" covers three indictable but non-arrestable common law offences: the publication of a seditious libel, the uttering of seditious words, and conspiracy to do an act in furtherance of a seditious intention.[28] A seditious intention is necessary for all three offences. It is an intention to bring into hatred or contempt, or to excite disaffection against, the person of the Sovereign, or the government and Constitution of the United Kingdom as by law established, or either House of Parliament or the administration of justice, or to excite Her Majesty's subjects or attempt, otherwise than by lawful means, the alteration of any matter in Church or state by law established, or to raise discontent or disaffection among Her Majesty's subjects, or to promote feelings of ill will or hostility between different classes of her subjects (*R.* v. *Burns,* per Cave J.[29]). On the other hand, it is not seditious to show the government has been mistaken, or to point out defects in the Con-

---

[27] Working Paper No. 72, *supra* n.26. See L. H. Leigh, "Law Reform and the Law of Treason and Sedition" [1977] P.L. 128.

[28] Stephen, *History of the Criminal Law*, Vol. II, Chap. 24. For the law in Scotland see G. H. Gordon, *Criminal Law* (2nd ed., 1978), Chap. 39.

[29] 16 Cox. 355; approving Stephen, *Digest of the Criminal Law* (see 8th ed. art. 114).

stitution, or to excite people to attempt by lawful means the alteration of the law relating to Church or state, or to point out (with a view to their removal) matters which produce feelings of hatred or ill will between classes of Her Majesty's subjects (ibid.).

Seditious libel is the publication in permanent form of matter which is of a seditious nature. The truth of a statement is no defence to a criminal charge if it is seditious.[30]

At common law conspiracy was formed when two or more persons combined to do an unlawful act, or to do a lawful act by unlawful means. A seditious conspiracy was a conspiracy having a seditious object.[31] The Criminal Law Act 1977 provided that, subject to exceptions,[32] a conspiracy must involve an agreement to commit a crime. Thus an agreement to effect an act which if committed by one person would constitute the crime of sedition will still amount to a seditious conspiracy.

It is doubtful if any useful purpose is served by the retention of a crime of sedition, for few if any acts which might be regarded as constituting sedition do not also fall within the scope of other common law or statutory offences.[33]

Incitement to mutiny or disaffection. By the Incitement to Mutiny Act 1797, passed after the naval mutiny at the Nore, persons maliciously endeavouring to seduce British soldiers or sailors from their duty *and* allegiance, or to commit an act of mutiny or traitorous practice, are to be guilty of an offence, and may receive a maximum punishment of imprisonment for life.

The Aliens Restriction (Amendment) Act 1919, s.3 creates an offence of causing or attempting to cause sedition or disaffection.[34]

The Incitement to Disaffection Act 1934 makes it an offence for any person maliciously and advisedly to endeavour to seduce any member of Her Majesty's forces from his duty *or* allegiance[35] to Her Majesty (s.1); or to be in possession, with intent to commit, abet, counsel or procure the commission of an offence under section 1, of any document such that dissemination of copies among members of the forces would be an offence against section 1 (s.2). The Act enables a Judge of the High Court, if satisfied by sworn information that an offence has been committed, and that evidence thereof is to be found on premises named in the information, to grant a search warrant to the police on their application therefor. A prosecution under this Act requires the consent of the Director of Public Prosecutions.

It is a misdemeanour under the Police Act 1964, s.53, to cause, or attempt to cause, disaffection amongst the members of any police force, or to induce, or attempt to induce, any member of a police force to withhold his services or to commit breaches of discipline.

---

[30] *R. v. Burdett* (1821) 4 B. & Ald. 314. See *post*, p. 535.
[31] *R. v. Hunt* (1820) 3 B. & Ald. 566; *O'Connell v. R.* (1844) 11 Cl. & Fin. 155.
[32] See J. C. Smith and B. Hogan, *Criminal Law* (5th ed., 1983) pp. 240 *et seq.*
[33] *Supra*, n.27.
[34] *Ante*, p. 449.
[35] *R. v. Arrowsmith* [1975] Q.B. 678.

Incitement to racial hatred[36]

Common law offences, such as sedition, were unable to deal adequately with the increasing problem of incitement to racial hatred. To fill this gap, a new offence of incitement to racial hatred was included in the Race Relations Act 1965. This law was generally regarded as ineffective[37] and was altered by the 1970 Race Relations Act, which also moved the offence into the Public Order Act 1936 as section 5A. The Public Order Act 1986 has further reformed and extended the offence of incitement to racial hatred which is now contained in Part III of that Act which applies to Scotland, as well as to England and Wales. Section 17 defines "racial hatred" as hatred against a group of persons in Great Britain defined by reference to colour, race, nationality (including citizenship) or ethnic or national origin. Section 18 makes it an offence to use threatening, abusive or insulting words or behaviour, or to display written material possessing those characteristics with intent to stir up racial hatred or in circumstances where racial hatred is likely to be stirred up. An offence under the section can be committed in public or private but in the latter case there is no offence where the words were used or the material displayed in a dwelling house and were not heard or seen by anyone outside the dwelling. It is a defence to show that the accused was inside a dwelling at the time of an alleged offence and that he had no reason to believe that persons outside the dwelling would hear or see the words or material. A person who is not shown to have intended to stir up racial hatred is not guilty of an offence under the section if he did not intend his words or behaviour to be, and was not aware that it might be, threatening, abusive or insulting (subs. 5). Section 19 creates an offence of publishing and distributing written material which is threatening, abusive or insulting. Sections 20, 21 and 22 make similar provisions in the case of the public performance of plays, the distributing or showing or playing of recordings of visual images or sounds and the broadcasting of threatening, abusive or insulting visual images or sounds. The possession of threatening, abusive or insulting written material or records with a view to distribution is made an offence by section 23. Nothing in Part III of the Act applies to fair and accurate reports of proceedings in Parliament (s.26(1)) or to fair and accurate reports of judicial proceedings, if published contemporaneously or as soon as reasonably practicable and lawful (subs. 2).

As with the previous law, prosecutions in England and Wales may only be instituted by or with the consent of the Attorney-General (s.27(1)). Additional new provisions found in the 1986 Act are offences by corporations (s.28); entry and search powers in respect of a contravention of section 23 (s.24) and a power to order forfeiture of written matter after a conviction (s.25).

---

[36] D. G. T. Williams, "Racial Incitement and Public Order" [1966] Crim.L.R. 320; A. Dickey, "Prosecution under the Race Relations Act 1965, s.6" [1968] Crim.L.R. 489, 186; Patricia M. Leopold "Incitement to Hatred, The History of a Controversial Criminal Offence" [1977] P.L. 389; G. Bindman, "Incitement to Racial Hatred" [1982] N.L.J. 299; R. Cotterell, "Prosecuting Incitement to Racial Hatred" [1982] P.L. 378.

[37] In the report on the Red Lion Square disorders (Cmnd. 5919, 1974), Scarman L.J. (as he then was) described it as an embarrassment to the police (para. 125).

Terrorism

If treason and sedition reflect the earlier centuries of constitutional law, terrorism is a phenomenon of recent years.[38] In the Prevention of Terrorism (Temporary Provisions) Act 1984 terrorism is defined as "the use of violence for political ends, and includes any use of violence for the purpose of putting the public or any section of the public in fear." It is difficult to envisage an act falling within that definition which is not a crime under existing criminal law. To a large extent that fact is reflected in the United Kingdom legislation which devotes little effort to defining terrorism and creating new offences but concentrates largely on extending the jurisdiction of courts to deal with serious crimes which indirectly should ensure that terrorists, if caught, are more likely to be tried and sentenced. Jurisdiction is extended by giving courts power to convict persons for acts committed outside the territory in which they function and by restricting the grounds on which a fugitive offender can resist a request for his surrender to the state where he is alleged to have committed a crime. Provision is also made for conferring increased powers on the executive and police which are intended to facilitate the discovery of crime and to prevent its commission.

Apart from the international problem of terrorism, the United Kingdom has had to deal with the particular problem presented by the situation in Northern Ireland. In addition to the legislation applicable to that part of the United Kingdom,[39] a series of Acts have been passed since 1974[40] containing provisions which apply throughout the United Kingdom: the current one being the Prevention of Terrorism (Temporary Provisions) Act 1984.[41] Part I of the Act (which does not apply in Northern Ireland[42]) makes it an offence to belong to a proscribed organisation; to solicit money or make financial contribution to such a body or to participate in a meeting of three or more persons, knowing that the meeting is to support, or further the activities, or be addressed by a member of, such an organisation. An organisation is proscribed if its name appears in Schedule 1.[43] The Secretary of State may add to that list the name of any organisation "that appears to him to be concerned in terrorism occurring in the United Kingdom and connected with Northern Irish affairs or in promoting or encouraging it." Section 2 makes it an offence to wear in a public place any item of dress or to wear or carry any article in such a way or such circumstances as to arouse reasonable apprehension that the person is a member or supporter of a proscribed

---

[38] But not unknown in earlier times, as shown by cases such as *Re Meunier* [1894] 2 Q.B. 415 or novels such as Joseph Conrad's *The Secret Agent*. See George Woodcock, *Anarchism* (2nd ed. 1986).

[39] *Ante*, p. 362.

[40] Acts which find an earlier model in the Prevention of Violence (Temporary Provisions) Act 1939—an Act which had a "temporary" life of 15 years.

[41] The working of earlier Acts were examined by Lord Shackleton in 1978 (Cmnd. 7324) and by Lord Jellicoe in 1983 (Cmnd. 8803). See D. Bonner, *Emergency Powers in Peacetime* (1985) Chap. 4; C. Walker, "Prevention of Terrorism (Temporary Provisions) Act 1984" (1984) 47 M.L.R. 704.

[42] Where the notion of proscribed organisations is no novelty: *McEldowney* v. *Forde* [1971] A.C. 632 (H.L.).

[43] The Schedule lists the Irish Republican Army and the Irish National Liberation Army.

organisation.[44] Prosecutions can only be brought in England and Wales
with the consent of the Attorney-General. It is difficult to believe that
either section has any significance in reducing terrorism. On the other
hand in practical terms neither constitutes a serious interference with
individual rights. To prohibit two organisations leaves many more to
be joined. Indeed, what is an organisation? Why should a group of
people meet regularly without being an organisation or without having
a name?

Part II of the Act, however, confers powers on the Secretary of State
which, when exercised, do constitute a serious infringement of individual liberty and the question of the justification for such powers is therefore a serious one. The Secretary of State is given power to make
exclusion orders by which he may exclude a person (i) from Great
Britain; or (ii) Northern Ireland; or (iii) the United Kingdom. Section
3(1) provides that the Secretary of State shall exercise the powers conferred on him "in such way as appears to him expedient to prevent acts
of terrorism to which this Part of this Act applies." These acts are
defined as acts of terrorism designed to influence public opinion or
Government policy with respect to affairs in Northern Ireland (s.3(3)). It
is unlikely that the courts would be willing to review the exercise by the
Secretary of State of these powers because of the element of national
security and the subjective terms in which the duty is couched.[45] The
limitations on the power to make exclusion orders vary in each section.
A British citizen, for example, cannot be excluded from the United
Kingdom; a British citizen can not be excluded from Great Britain if
ordinarily resident[46] for three years or already subject to an order
excluding him from Northern Ireland.[47] In making an exclusion order
the Secretary of State must consider whether the person's connection
with any country or territory outside the area of exclusion is such as to
make it appropriate that an order should be made. An exclusion order
lasts for three years, unless revoked earlier. It may be renewed. Section
7 provides a procedure for the making of representations against an
Order. The grounds of objection must be set out in writing, within 7
days of receiving notice of the making of the order[48] and an interview
may be requested with one of the Secretary of State's advisers. The Secretary of State will then reconsider the matter; the final decision is his.[49]

Part III creates a number of criminal offences connected with terrorism in relation to Northern Irish affairs. Section 10 prohibits the raising
of funds for terrorist activities by solicitation or invitation and the giving of property to any person knowing or suspecting that it may be
used to assist in the commission of terrorist activities. Section 11 makes
it an offence to fail to disclose as soon as reasonably practicable infor-

[44] Presumably a less demanding requirement than that of the Public Order Act 1936, s.1
(Uniform). But see *O'Moran* v. *D.P.P.* [1975] Q.B. 864 (Black beret a uniform).

[45] *Post*, p. 698.

[46] s.4. The meaning of resident is defined in Sched. 2.

[47] Similar provisions apply *mutatis mutandis* to exclusion from Northern Ireland: a power
which seems largely cosmetic: s.5.

[48] Fourteen days, if the applicant has agreed to leave in accordance with the order and
appeal from outside the area from which excluded (s.7(5)).

[49] *Cf.* non-statutory procedure in cases of deportation on grounds of national security:
ante, p. 462.

mation which might be of material assistance in preventing terrorist activities or securing the apprehension of terrorists. (This is a modern version of the old law of misprision of felony which in England and Wales was abolished by the Criminal Law Act 1967). Prosecutions for alleged offences under both sections cannot be brought without the consent of the Attorney-General.

Part IV confers powers of arrest and detention (section 12) and of control of entry over persons arriving in or leaving Great Britain or Northern Ireland. Section 12 empowers a police constable to arrest without warrant anyone whom he has reasonable grounds for suspecting to be guilty of an offence under section 1 (membership of a proscribed organisation), section 9 (offences in connection with an exclusion order) and section 10 (financial support). A similar power of arrest is also conferred in the case of a person concerned in the commission, preparation or instigation of acts of terrorism whether connected with the affairs of Northern Ireland or of any other description except acts connected solely with the affairs of the United Kingdom or any part of the United Kingdom other than Northern Ireland (subss. (1)(b) and (2)(b)).[50] A person arrested under section 12 may initially be detained for 48 hours, subject to extensions by the Secretary of State, such extensions not to exceed five days in all. Section 13 entitles the Secretary of State to make regulations[51] to provide for the examination of persons entering or leaving Great Britain with a view to determine whether they are concerned with terrorism, in the wider sense adopted in Part IV, or are subject to an exclusion order or have committed offences under Section 9. The section also confers powers of detention and arrest for carrying out examinations and powers of searching persons, ships and aircraft.

The provisions of the foregoing sections are supplemented by powers contained in Schedule 3. A justice of the peace may issue search warrants (para. 4). A constable may stop and search a person whom he has power to arrest under section 12 to ascertain whether he has in his possession any documents which constitute evidence that he is a person liable to arrest (para. 6).

As we have seen certain powers in the Prevention of Terrorism (Temporary Provisions) Act 1984 relate to the detection and suppression of terrorist activities where ever they may occur. Other statutes, in response to international agreements, aim at suppressing terrorism by extending the jurisdiction of the courts of the United Kingdom over acts committed abroad which from their nature are likely in most cases to have been committed by terrorists. The Internationally Protected Persons Act 1978[52] gives jurisdiction over acts committed abroad, whether the perpetrators are British citizens or not, (i) where those acts consti-

---

[50] Cf. *McKee* v. *Chief Constable for Northern Ireland* [1984] 1 W.L.R. 1358 (H.L.). (No requirement of reasonableness in Northern Ireland (Emergency Provisions) Act 1978 s.11(1)).

[51] Prevention of Terrorism (Supplemental Temporary Provisions) Order 1984 (S.I. No. 418); Prevention of Terrorism (Supplemental Temporary Provisions) (N.I.) Order 1984 (S.I. No. 417).

[52] Which gives effect to the Convention on the Prevention and Punishment of Crimes against Internationally Protected Persons, adopted by the United Nations General Assembly in 1973. (Cmnd. 6176).

tute attacks or threats of attacks against Heads of States, Heads of Government or Foreign Ministers, outside the territories of the States in which they hold office, or members of their families; and (ii) if committed in the United Kingdom would constitute one of the crimes listed in section 1 of the Act. The Suppression of Terrorism Act 1978[53] similarly extends the jurisdiction of the courts, in this instance to the territories of states designated by the Secretary of State, over a wide range of acts which if committed in a part of the United Kingdom would have constituted one of the crimes listed in Schedule 1 (s.4). These range from murder to offences under the Firearms Act 1968. Under section 1 of the Aviation Security Act 1982[54] the crime of hijacking is committed when a person on board an aircraft in flight[55] unlawfully seizes the aircraft or exercises control over it by the use of force or by threats of any kind. Subject to exceptions, the jurisdiction of the United Kingdom courts extends to an act of hijacking, wherever it occurs and whatever the nationality of the hijacker. The Taking of Hostages Act 1982[56] provides that it is an offence (punishable with imprisonment for life) for anyone, whatever his nationality, whether in the United Kingdom or elsewhere, to detain any person and in order to compel a State, international organisation or person to do or abstain from doing an act, to threaten to kill, injure or continue to detain that person.

Public order

Many of the offences already discussed could be argued to relate to public order, but there are other offences which are perhaps more immediately thought of when that phrase is used. In particular there are a number of crimes relating to the holding of meetings of every kind which are clearly the subject matter of public order; these, however, are more conveniently discussed in Chapter 27 (Freedom of Assembly and Association). Another important group of offences relevant to public order regulate the ownership, use and control of explosives, firearms and offensive weapons generally. The details of such offences are out of place in a general work on Constitutional law.[57]

Official secrets[58]

The Bill that became the Official Secrets Act 1911 was introduced into the House of Lords after the Agadir crisis.[59] The Bill had been carefully considered for some time in the Department but passed through Parliament with scarcely any debate. Section 1(1) makes it an offence if any person "for any purpose prejudicial to the safety or interests of the

---

[53] Which gives effect to the Convention on the Suppression of Terrorism, adopted by the Council of Europe in 1977: See Cmnd. 7031. By the end of 1986 the Convention had not been ratified by France, Greece, Malta and the Republic of Ireland.

[54] Originally s.1 of the Hijacking Act 1971 which gave effect to the Convention for the Suppression of Unlawful Seizure of Aircraft.

[55] An aircraft is in flight from when all its external doors are closed following embarkation until any such door is opened for disembarkation: s.38(3).

[56] Which gives effect to the International Convention against the taking of Hostages.

[57] See J. C. Smith and B. Hogan, *Criminal Law* (5th ed., 1983) Chap. 6.

[58] See D. G. T. Williams, *Not in the Public Interest* (1965); K. Robertson, *Public Secrets: A Study in the Development of Governmental Secrecy* (1982).

[59] Germany's action in sending a gunboat to the port of Agadir, with a promise to assist the Moroccans against France, nearly precipitated a European war.

State" (a) approaches or enters a prohibited place; or (b) makes a sketch or plan, etc. calculated or intended to be, or which might be useful to an enemy; or (c) obtains, publishes or communicates to any other person any sketch, etc., document or information which is calculated to be or might be or is intended to be useful to an enemy.[60] Purpose prejudicial to the safety or interests of the State may be inferred from the circumstances; and if the accused acted without lawful authority in communicating information relating to a prohibited place he is presumed to have acted for a prejudicial purpose (s.1(2)). The prejudicial purpose refers to the intention of the accused, not the actual or potential effect of his conduct. Section 1 is not limited to time of war: an enemy may be actual or potential.

The Official Secrets Act 1939[61] provides that a chief officer of police may, with the permission of the Secretary of State, authorise a police officer not below the rank of inspector to require a suspect to give information in connection with offences under section 1 of the 1911 Act.

In *Chandler* v. *Director of Public Prosecutions*[62] members of the Committee of 100 were convicted under section 1 for entering an RAF station, which was a prohibited place. Their intention was to sit in front of aircraft so as to prevent them from taking off; their ultimate object being to bring about nuclear disarmament, which they considered would be beneficial to this country. The House of Lords, unanimously upholding their convictions, held: first, that the section (in spite of the marginal note: ("Penalties for spying") covered sabotage; secondly, that the question whether the purpose of the accused was "prejudicial to the safety or interests of the State" was a question for the jury. "Purpose" meant direct purpose or object, not indirect purpose or motive, and the accused might not give evidence as to the latter. Ministers could not assert their opinion as to what was or was not prejudicial to the interests of the State, though an officer of the Crown could give evidence about what were the interests of the Crown and as to the airfield being part of the defence system maintained for the protection of the realm.

Their Lordships had difficulty with the meaning of "the State," an unusual expression in English law in relation to internal affairs.[63] Lord

---

[60] *R.* v. *Britten* [1969] 1 W.L.R. 151 (C.A.); deterrent sentences may be appropriate.

[61] Section 6 of the Official Secrets Act 1920 had given power to require information to be given in connection with offences under the Official Secrets Acts generally. The 1939 Act, amending this provision, was passed following a question of privilege raised by Mr. Duncan Sandys M.P., who complained of his being questioned by the Attorney-General about certain defence information Mr. Sandys had sent to the Secretary of State for War.

[62] [1964] A.C. 763. The decision was clearly right according to the method of interpretation used by the courts; but it had been pointed out that this interpretation of s.1 is inconsistent with statements made by Lord Chancellors and Attorneys-General in parliamentary debates on Official Secrets Bills to the effect that s.1 of the 1911 Act was intended to be restricted to espionage: Donald Thompson, "The Committee of 100 and the Official Secrets Act 1911" [1963] P.L. 201.

[63] The 1911 Act replaced with alterations the Official Secrets Act 1889, in which s.1 on disclosure of information referred to "the interests of the State," and s.2 on breach of official trust referred to "the interest of the State, or otherwise in the public interest." No further light has been cast on the meaning of "State" by the use of the term by Lord Templeman in *Ross* v. *Lord Advocate* [1986] 1 W.L.R. 1078 (ownership of assets of Trustee Savings Bank: Trustee Savings Banks Act 1981; Trustee Savings Banks Act 1985).

Reid said "the State" did not mean the Government or the Executive, but meant perhaps the country, the realm or the organised community. Viscount Radcliffe in the context of this case spoke of the defence of the realm. According to Lord Hodson the organised State comprised those persons who dwelt therein and whose safety was to be considered. For Lord Devlin the State meant the organs of government of a national community, which in respect of the armed forces meant the Crown. It is suggested that the difficulty lies largely in the fact that the Government as the only agent legally capable of speaking for the Crown is liable to be confused, by itself and others, with the Government as a group of party politicians.

Under section 2(1) of the Act it is also an offence if a person having in his possession or control any document or information which has been entrusted in confidence to him by any person holding office under Her Majesty, or which he has obtained or to which he has had access owing to his position as a person who holds or has held office under Her Majesty: (a) communicates the document or information to any person, other than a person to whom he is authorised to communicate it, or a person to whom it is in the interest of the State his duty to communicate it; or (b) retains the document when he has no right, or it is contrary to his duty, to retain it. If a person receives a document or information knowing, or having reasonable ground to believe, that it is communicated to him in contravention of the Act, he is guilty of an offence, unless he proves that the communication to him was contrary to his desire (s.2(2)). The authorisation under paragraph (1)(*a*) may be express or implied.[64]

Two recent prosecutions have kept alight public controversy over section 2. Sarah Tisdall, a civil service clerk, was convicted under section 2(1) and sentenced to 6 months' imprisonment in 1984 for leaking to a newspaper a memorandum setting out the Minister's plans for maintaining public order at the imminent arrival of cruise missiles at Greenham Common. Early next year Clive Ponting, an assistant secretary in the Department of Defence, was charged under the same section with communicating to Mr Tam Dalyell confidential documents relating to the sinking of the Argentine warship *General Belgrano* during the Falkland Islands war. McCowan J. summed up along the lines of the House of Lords decision in *Chandler* v. *Director of Public Prosecutions* (*supra*), but to the general surprise Ponting, who admitted the communication, was acquitted by the jury. The documents were shown to the jury *in camera*, but it is difficult to account for their verdict. Ponting was certainly not *authorised*, nor can it be said to have been his *duty*, to communicate the documents to an opposition MP notoriously hostile to the Government about the sinking of the *Belgrano*. It is true that the documents were not classified and the communication was not made for gain,[65] but these would be matters for the judge to consider in sentencing. One can only suppose that the jury—like some of the juries in prosecutions for seditious libel in the late eighteenth and early nine-

---

[64] It is not certain whether *mens rea* is required under s.2, nor whether "the interest of the State" necessarily has the same meaning here as in s.1.
[65] See *R.* v. *Ponting* [1985] Crim.L.R. 318.

teenth centuries[66]—were expressing their disapproval of the law, or thought the prosecution ought not to have been brought.

A "prohibited place" includes any defence works, arsenal, naval or air force station, camp, ship or aircraft belonging to or occupied by the Crown (s.3). Section 6 gives power to arrest any person found committing or who is suspected of having committed or of being about to commit an offence under the Act. It is also an offence to harbour spies (s.7). Prosecution under the Acts is by or with the concent of the Attorney-General or Lord Advocate (s.8). Search warrants may be granted where an offence under the Act is suspected (s.9). The Acts apply to offences committed in any part of Her Majesty's dominions, and to offences committed anywhere by British officers or subjects (s.10).

The Official Secrets Act 1920 was passed after experience of security problems during the First World War and was designed to enact for peace time the content of certain Defence of the Realm Regulations. s.1(1) provides that it is an offence to wear an unauthorised uniform, make a false declaration, forge a permit or impersonate a government official for the purpose of gaining admission to a prohibited place, or for any other purpose prejudicial to the safety or interests of the State. It is also an offence for a person to retain an official document for a purpose prejudicial to the safety or interests of the State, or to allow any other person to have possession of an official document issued for his use alone (s.1(2)). Section 2 provides that communication with a foreign agent is evidence of obtaining, or attempting to obtain, information calculated or intended to be useful to an enemy contrary to section 1 of the Act of 1911.[67] Section 3 provides that no person "in the vicinity of" a prohibited place shall obstruct or interfere with a military or police guard. In *Adler* v. *George*[68] it was held that such obstruction *in* a prohibited place, *viz.* an RAF airfield was an offence. Section 7 provides that it is an offence to attempt to commit any offence under the 1911 Act or the 1920 Act or[69] to do any act preparatory to the commission of an offence under either Act. Thus preparatory acts which are not even attempts may be punishable. It suffices for a conviction, to show merely that the accused realised that a substantive offence might possibly follow the preparatory act, not that it must or probably would follow.[70]

Section 2 of the Official Secrets Act 1911 has long been widely criticised as being a "catch-all" provision making a large number of relatively unimportant acts subject to criminal sanctions. The Franks Committee (1972)[71] recommended that this section should be repealed and replaced by an Official Information Act, which would apply only to official information which: (i) is classified information relating to defence or internal security, or to foreign relations, or to the currency,

---

[66] See *post*, pp. 535–536.

[67] The archives of a foreign embassy in London can be the subject-matter of a charge under the Acts: *R.* v. *A.B.* [1941] 1 K.B. 455.

[68] [1964] 2 Q.B. 7 (D.C.).

[69] *R.* v. *Oakes* [1959] 2 Q.B. 350.

[70] *R.* v. *Bingham* [1973] Q.B. 870 (C.A.).

[71] *Departmental Committee on Section 2 of the Official Secrets Act 1911* (1972) Cmnd. 5104. See G. Ganz, *Administrative Procedures* (1974), pp. 86–91; W. Birtles, "Big Brother Knows Best" [1973] P.L. 100; J. Jaconelli (1973) 36 M.L.R. 68.

the unauthorised disclosure of which would cause serious injury to the interests of the nation; or (ii) is likely to assist criminal activities or to impede law enforcement; or (iii) is a Cabinet document; or (iv) has been entrusted to the Government by a private individual or concern. It would be an offence: (a) for a Crown servant to communicate information to which the Act applies, contrary to his official duty; (b) for a person entrusted with official information in confidence to communicate information of one of the kinds in (i), (ii) and (iii) otherwise than for the purposes for which it was entrusted; (c) for any person to communicate information of one of the kinds in (i), (ii) and (iii) which he knows, or has reasonable ground to believe, has reached him as the result of a contravention of the Act; (d) to communicate or use official information of any kind for purposes of private gain. Prosecutions would require the consent of the Attorney-General or, in the case of information likely to assist criminal activities or to impede law enforcement or communicated for the purposes of private gain, that of the Director of Public Prosecutions.

Several abortive attempts have since been made by Governments of both main parties to deal with this matter,[72] but so far none has succeeded in drafting a satisfactory provision to secure the confidentiality of civil servants, which has been a problem for the last hundred years.[73]

"D" Notices

Closely connected with the topic of the scope of the Official Secrets Acts is that of "D" Notices, which may, according to taste, be represented as a further form of control over the publication of information which government departments do not wish to be publicised, as guidelines for self-censorship or as a safety valve against the rigours of the Official Secrets Acts. Since 1912 there has been an official Defence, Press and Broadcasting Committee consisting of civil servants in defence departments and representatives of the press and broadcasting, whose purpose is to indicate to the press and broadcasting authorities when they may safely commit an offence against the Official Secrets Acts without risk of being prosecuted. A "D" notice asks editors and publishers not to publish certain specified items of defence information, the publication of which would be prejudicial to the national interest. It is true that some of these items might not be covered by the Acts, but on the other hand much defence information that is strictly speaking secret is communicated to the Press for background knowledge, and no prosecution follows if it was not in a "D" notice.

The operation of the "D" Notice system was considered by the Commons Select Committee on Defence in 1980[74] which concluded that it should continue in a modified form, at least until a reform of the Official Secrets Acts. In particular the Committee felt that even under the present law the Government should give assurance that no prosecution would follow the publication of material which was in accordance with

---

[72] *Reform of Section 2 of the Official Secrets Act 1911*, (1978), Cmnd. 7285; (1979) Cmnd. 7520, Green Paper on Open Government.

[73] *e.g.* Viscount Radcliffe, *Not in Feather Beds* (1968), Chap. 2; Lord Scarman, *The Right to Know* (Granada Guildhall Lectures 1984), pp. 70 *et seq.*

[74] (1979–80) H.C. 773; J. Jaconelli, "The D Notice System" [1982] P.L. 37.

a "D" notice. Following the report of the Select Committee's reports the Defence Press and Broadcasting Committee produced a short general introduction to the working of the system and reduced the number of categories of Notice.

The aftermath of the Falkland Islands War led to further consideration of the publication of "sensitive" information.[75] When the nation is engaged (or about to engage) in military activities some form of censorship is inevitable but equally it must be clear that the publication of information approved by censors does not run the risk of subsequent prosecution.

---

[75] Commons Select Committee on Defence, First Report 1982–3 H.C. 17; *The Protection of Military Information,* Cmnd. 9112 (1983). (Study Group appointed by Secretary of State for Defence.)

CHAPTER 25

FREEDOM OF PERSON AND PROPERTY

I. FREEDOM OF THE PERSON[1]

General principles

"The right to personal liberty as understood in England," says Dicey,[2] "means in substance a person's right not to be subjected to imprisonment, arrest, or other physical coercion in any manner that does not admit of legal justification." It is "one of the pillars of liberty," said Lord Atkin in *Liversidge* v. *Anderson*,[3] that "in English law every imprisonment is prima facie unlawful, and that it is for a person directing imprisonment to justify his act." The justification is usually that the person is arrested and detained pending trial in court on a charge of crime, or after trial by a court of competent jurisdiction he has been convicted and sentenced to imprisonment or some other kind of detention provided by statute. Other kinds of lawful detention are committal for contempt of court or Parliament, custody pending deportation or extradition, children in need of care and protection, patients under Mental Health and Public Health Acts, and imprisonment for failing to make certain payments in spite of having had the means to do so.[4] Preventive detention may take place under statutory war time regulations and anti-terrorist legislation. Detention for limited periods is also now permitted under the Police and Criminal Evidence Act 1984.

The European Convention provides for "the right to liberty and security of person" (Art. 5), "right to life" (Art. 2), and "a fair and public hearing" in the determination of civil rights and criminal charges (Art. 6); and forbids torture (Art. 3), forced labour (Art. 4) *ex post facto* penal laws (Art. 7) and imprisonment for debt (Protocol 4, Art. 1). Exceptions to Article 5 (personal liberty) are: (a) lawful detention after conviction by a court; (b) lawful arrest for non-compliance with the lawful order of a court; (c) lawful arrest on reasonable suspicion of having committed an offence, or where reasonably necessary to prevent an offence or an escape from justice; (d) education of a minor; (e) public health (infectious diseases, etc.); (f) unlawful entry or deportation or extradition. Conditions applying to these exceptions are that a person should be brought promptly before a court, speedy proceedings to test legality of detention and compensation for wrongful arrest or detention.

---

[1] Dicey, *Law of the Constitution* (10th ed. E. C. S. Wade) Chap. 5; H. Street, *Freedom, the Individual and the Law* (5th ed., 1982), Chap. 1; R. F. V. Heuston, *Essays in Constitutional Law* (2nd ed. 1964), Chaps. 5 and 6.

[2] Dicey, *op. cit.* pp. 207–208.

[3] [1942] A.C. 206 (H.L.).

[4] The Debtors Act 1869 abolished imprisonment for debt with certain exceptions, *e.g.* non-contractual penalties, sums recoverable summarily before magistrates, and certain defaults by trustees, solicitors and bankrupts, provided that the debtor has had the means to pay. The Administration of Justice Act 1970, attempted to do away with such "imprisonment for debt" by extending the use of attachment of earnings orders, but many judgment debtors have no settled jobs.

For wrongful deprivation of liberty the following remedies are available in English law; (i) civil proceedings for damages in respect of malicious prosecution, false imprisonment or assault; (ii) criminal prosecution for assault, battery, or in respect of false imprisonment itself; (iii) application for a writ of habeas corpus[5] to obtain release; (iv) appeal against conviction or sentence to a higher court; (v) in appropriate cases an order of certiorari or prohibition.[6]

Personal liberty is, however, increasingly seen as not being confined to freedom from physical restraint. Modern methods of surveillance enable telephone calls to be intercepted or private conversations to be overheard. The use of computers has led to concern about the storing of information about individuals and the use of that information by government agencies, the police or private commercial organisations. These and similar matters are discussed later under the heading Privacy.

Police powers

The powers of the police derived from the common law and statute. The former were open to criticism for their uncertainty, the latter for varying in many cases from force to force, depending on the existence of local Acts of Parliament. The police were unhappy with the law on the ground that it did not give them sufficient powers to fight crime—and were inclined to behave as if the law were what they wished it to be, rather than as what it was: *R. v. Holmes ex p. Sherman.*[7] A wider dissatisfaction with the whole criminal process had found expression in the introduction into England of majority jury verdicts by the Criminal Justice Act 1967, s.13[8] and subsequently in the 11th Report of the Criminal Law Revision Committee in 1972[9] which achieved little because of the controversy occasioned by its recommendations. Police methods used in investigating crimes had come under critical scrutiny in the report on the *Confait* Case.[10] In 1977 the then Labour Government set up a Royal Commission on Criminal Procedure which reported in 1981.[11] The Report has been followed by two Acts, the Prosecution of Offences Act 1985[12] and the Police and Criminal Evidence Act 1984.[13] The latter Act attempts to strike a balance between the freedom of the citizen and the powers of the police. The powers of the police are increased but their exercise is subject to the restrictions contained in the Act. Unfortunately although the Act replaces much re-existing law it is not an exhaustive code of police powers.

---

[5] *Post*, p. 506. In Scots Law an application may be made to the nobile officium of the High Court. Protection is also given by the Criminal Justice (Scotland) Act 1980, s.14.
[6] *Post*, Chap. 34 *cf.* comparable Scots remedies, *e.g.* order for reduction; interdict.
[7] [1981] 2 All E.R. 612.
[8] *Ante*, p. 382.
[9] Cmnd. 4991.
[10] Fisher Report on the Confait Case (1977–78) H.C. 338.
[11] Cmnd. 8092, 8092–1.
[12] *Ante*, p. 380.
[13] Michael Zander, *The Police and Criminal Evidence Act 1984* (1985); V. Bevan and K. Lidstone, *A Guide to the Police and Criminal Evidence Act 1984* (1985); L. H. Leigh, *Police Powers in England and Wales* (2nd ed., 1985).

Stop and Search

The introduction of a generalised right to stop persons and vehicles was a particularly controversial provision of the 1984 Act. Powers existed under the earlier law to stop and search for stolen goods in the case of the Metropolitan Police by virtue of the Metropolitan Police Act 1839, s.66, and in the case of other forces by virtue of local Acts of Parliament. All forces possessed (and continue to possess) a power to stop and search for the possession of drugs under the Misuse of Drugs Act 1971, s.23(2). The value of stopping and searching as a crime prevention measure has been doubted and it is argued to have an adverse effect on public—police relations.

Section 1 confers a power to detain and search on a constable in a place to which the public has access or in any other place "to which people have ready access at the time when he proposes to exercise the power but which is not a dwelling" (s.1(1)). The power extends to (i) persons and vehicles, (ii) to search for stolen or prohibited articles, (iii) which he has reasonable grounds to suspect that he will find. Prohibited articles are offensive weapons[14] or articles made or adapted for use in burglary theft and other defined crimes. The main guarantee that the power conferred by section 1 will not be abused is the requirement of reasonable grounds that a prohibited article will be found. Annex B to the Code of Practice on Powers of Stop and Search emphasises that reasonable grounds require a foundation in fact, as opposed to mere suspicion, a hunch which cannot be explained or justified.[15] Procedural safeguards are contained in section 2 which, for instance, requires that a constable not in uniform should produce documentary evidence that he is a constable. In any case the constable must give his name and that of the station to which he is attached and the object of the search. Section 3 requires the making of a written record of searches carried out unless it is not practicable to do so.

A power to stop vehicles in a particular locality is conferred by section 4 for the purposes set out in the section, for example to ascertain whether a vehicle is carrying a person who has committed an offence other than a road traffic offence or a vehicles excise offence; or a person who is unlawfully at large. Such checks must, except as a matter of urgency, be authorised by an officer of at least the rank of superintendent. Again there must be reasonable grounds to believe that one of the requirements of the section has been satisfied.

Section 5 requires the inclusion in the annual reports of chief officers' statistics relating to the exercise of search powers under section 1 and section 4. This is intended to facilitate supervision over the exercise of these powers by police authorities and the Inspectors of Constabulary.

---

[14] s.1(9)(a) "Offensive Weapon" means any article—
    (a) made or adapted for use for causing injury to persons; or
    (b) intended by the person having it with him for such use by him or some other person.
Presumably the courts will follow the existing case law decided under the Prevention of Crime Act 1953.

[15] See S. H. Bailey and D. J. Birch, "Recent Developments in the Law of Police Powers," [1982] Crim. L.R. 475; Leigh, *op. cit.* p. 160.

Arrest

Arrest is the restraint of a man's person or liberty, obliging him to be obedient to the law. Arrest commonly involves actual physical seizure (apprehension) of a person, using no more force than reasonably necessary, or a token restraint of a person's liberty indicating its compulsory nature.[16] The common law allows a person to use a reasonable amount of force to resist unlawful arrest without warrant, whether by a police officer or private citizen; but it is inadvisable to resist arrest by a police constable as the arrest may turn out to be lawful and resistance therefore an offence. A person is normally entitled to have someone of his choice informed when he is arrested and held in custody by the police.[17]

(a) *By warrant*

No man may be arrested or imprisoned except under due process of law (Petition of Right 1627[18]). Where a person is suspected of having committed a serious indictable offence, the usual course is for the police to apply to a magistrate for a warrant for his arrest. That warrant can only be granted on sworn information. Sufficient particulars of the charge must be specified in the warrant in non-technical language. A "general warrant," *i.e.* one which does not name the person to be arrested, is illegal. In *Leach* v. *Money*[19] a Secretary of State (Lord Halifax) had issued a warrant to search for the authors, printers and publishers of No. 45 of the *North Briton*, alleged to contain seditious libels, and to apprehend them together with their papers. Leach, who was arrested but released as he was not the printer, obtained damages against the King's messenger for trespass and false imprisonment. "There is no case for these uncertain warrants," said Lord Mansfield C.J.; " . . . The magistrates ought to judge and give definite directions to the officer as to the person to be arrested." In *Wilkes* v. *Lord Halifax*[20] John Wilkes, a Member of Parliament and the author of No. 45 of the *North Briton* which strongly criticised the King's speech on the prorogation of Parliament and the recent Peace of Paris, eventually obtained £4,000 damages against Lord Halifax, the Secretary of State under whose general warrant he was arrested and his papers seized.

In minor cases a summons is usually applied for.[21]

(b) *Without warrant*

The Criminal Law Act 1967, was passed to give effect to a report of the Criminal Law Revision Committee which recommended the abolition

---

[16] Not every deprivation of liberty (detention) constitutes an arrest, which can only be effected in exercise of an asserted authority: *R.* v. *Brown* [1977] R.T.R. 160 (C.A.).

[17] Police and Criminal Evidence Act 1984, s.56. For a maximum of 36 hours a superintendent, in the case of a person arrested for a serious arrestable offence, (see *infra*) may prevent exercise of this right.

[18] Relying on Magna Carta (9 Hen. III, c. 29.).

[19] (1765) 3 Burr. 1962, 1974; 19 St.Tr. 1001; Holdsworth, *History of English Law*, Vol. X. pp. 659 *et seq.*

[20] (1769) 19 St.Tr. 1407, summing-up by Wilmot C.J.

[21] Magistrates' Courts Act 1980, s.1(4). See further Leigh, *op. cit.* p. 91 *et seq.*

of the distinction between felonies and misdemeanours.[22] The Act introduced a new terminology: non-arrestable offences were those for which a warrant was required before an arrest could be effected; in the case of arrestable offences a warrant was not required. The Police and Criminal Evidence Act 1984 retains that terminology but redefines it so that arrestable offence now has a wider meaning than it did under the 1967 Act.

An arrestable offence[23] under section 24 of the Police and Criminal Evidence Act 1984 is

(i) any offence for which the sentence is fixed by law: that is murder and treason;

(ii) offences carrying a penalty of five years or more imprisonment;

(iii) various listed statutory offences.

Any person may arrest without warrant any person who is in the act of committing such an offence or whom he has reasonable grounds for suspecting to be committing such offence; or anyone who has committed such an offence or whom he has reasonable grounds for suspecting to have committed such an offence. In addition a constable may, if he has reasonable grounds for suspecting an offence has been committed, arrest any person whom he has reasonable grounds for suspecting to be guilty of the offence.[24] He may also arrest anyone about to commit an arrestable offence or anyone whom he has reasonable grounds for suspecting to be about to commit an arrestable offence.[25] The powers conferred by the section extend also to conspiring to commit an arrestable offence, to attempting to commit and to inciting, aiding, abetting, counselling or procuring the commission of such an offence.

Section 25, however, provides a further power of arrest without warrant in the case of non-arrestable offences where one of the "general arrest conditions" in the section exists. A constable has the power under the section if he has reasonable ground for suspecting the commission of a non-arrestable offence and it appears to him that the service of a summons is impracticable for one of the reasons stated: for example that the name of the person concerned cannot be ascertained; that arrest is necessary to prevent the person causing himself or other physical harm, or to prevent the commission of an offence against public decency.

Section 26 rather confusingly repeals earlier statutory provisions authorising arrest without warrant but, by sub-section (2), preserves a total of forty two such provisions. Nor does section 26 affect common law powers, for example, to arrest for breach of the peace without warrant, another vague offence which can be invoked as the justification for

---

[22] *Felonies and Misdemeanours*, 7th Report, (1965) Cmnd. 2659.

[23] Arrestable Offence is to be distinguished from serious arrestable offence, defined in s.116. Under the 1984 Act the police have additional powers in this type of offence: *infra*.

[24] He may properly arrest in order to facilitate questioning: *Mohammed-Holgate* v. *Duke* [1984] A.C. 437 (H.L.). M. Dockray, "Arrest for Questioning" (1984) 47 M.L.R. 727.

[25] The extended statutory powers of the constable reflect the old common law—and are a reminder of the danger of the citizen taking upon himself the right of arrest: *Walters* v. *W. H. Smith & Son Ltd.* [1914] 1 K.B. 595 (C.A.).

arresting without warrant a person charged with obstructing a constable under section 51 of the Police Act 1964.[26]

In the effecting of an arrest section 3 of the Criminal Law Act 1967 provides that any person may use such force as is reasonable in the circumstances in the prevention of crime, or in effecting or assisting in the lawful arrest of offenders or suspected offenders[27] and section 117 of the Police and Criminal Evidence Act 1984 provides that a constable may use reasonable force in the exercise of any power conferred by the Act.

The requirements of a valid arrest are defined in section 28. When a person is arrested otherwise than by being informed that he is under arrest, the arrest is not lawful unless the person arrested is informed as soon as practicable that he is under arrest. Where the arrest is by a constable the person arrested must be informed of his arrest even if the fact must be obvious. Whether a person has been told is a matter of fact: polite words of request, inviting a person to go to a police station, may fail to convey that he is being arrested.[28] The ground for the arrest must also be made clear at the time of the arrest or as soon as practicable after the arrest.[29] Again, in the case of arrest by a constable, this requirement must be complied with, even if the ground for arrest is obvious.

If an arrest takes place other than at a police station then the constable who makes the arrest or to whom another person[30] transfers the custody of the arrested person must take the arrested person to a designated police station as soon as practicable (section 30). (A designated station is defined by section 35(1); *infra*.)

Where an arrest takes place other than at a police station a constable may search an arrested person if he has reasonable grounds for believing that the arrested person may present a danger to himself or others. The arrested person may also be searched for anything which might be used by the person to assist him to escape or which might be evidence relating to an offence. Premises in which a person was arrested may similarly be searched. Again reasonable grounds for believing evidence may be found are required and in the case of a search of premises, a search is permitted only to the extent that it is reasonably required for the purpose of discovering the evidence.[31]

---

[26] *Post*, p. 497. See *R.* v. *Howell (Errol)* [1982] Q.B. 416 (C.A.). (Swearing in public street at 4.00 a.m.; P.C. entitled to arrest for likely breach of the peace.) See too *G.* v. *Chief Superintendant of Police, Stroud, The Times*, November 29, 1986. (Use by 15-year-old of abusive language in vicinity of playground for young children: crude gesture to constable summoned by frightened mothers.)

[27] *Swales* v. *Cox* [1981] Q.B. 849 (D.C.); *Allen* v. *Metropolitan Police Commissioner, The Times*, March 25, 1980; *Farrell* v. *Secretary of State for Defence* [1980] 1 W.L.R. 172 (H.L.).

[28] *Alderson* v. *Booth* [1969] 2 Q.B. 216 (D.C.): *R.* v. *Inwood* [1973] 1 W.L.R. 647: question of fact whether he is aware that he has been arrested.

[29] Similarly, at common law, *Christie* v. *Leachinsky* [1947] A.C. 573 (H.L.).

[30] See *John Lewis & Co. Ltd.* v. *Tims* [1952] A.C. 676 (H.L.). (Appellant company's private detectives took the respondent to its office in order that the circumstances of her arrest might be explained to the managing director and to obtain authority to prosecute for theft: not an unreasonable delay before handing her over to the police: appellants therefore not liable for false imprisonment.)

[31] For the common law position see *Dillon* v. *O'Brien and Davis* (1887) 16 Cox C.C. 245; *R.* v. *O'Donnell* (1835) 7 C. & P. 138.

Detention

Police have no power to detain (apart from exceptional anti-terrorist and emergency legislation) for questioning a person whom they have not arrested.[32] Section 29 of the 1984 Act recognises this common law principle.[33]

Difficult questions formerly rose, however, about the power, if any, of police to detain persons after arresting them in order to pursue their inquiries.[34] The elaborate provisions of Part IV of the 1984 Act recognise a power of detention but attempt to regulate its use.

Persons may not be detained for longer than six hours at a police station which is not a designated police station (ss.30 and 35). At each designated station there must be one or more custody officers whose duty is to ensure that the requirements of Part IV of the Act are complied with. It is the duty of the custody officer to decide whether there is sufficient evidence to charge an arrested person or, if not, whether to detain or release him. Detention must be reviewed at regular intervals by a custody officer, if the person has been arrested and charged, or by a review officer (who must be at least the rank of inspector) if the person has been arrested but not charged (s.40). A general maximum period of detention without charge of 24 hours is established by section 41. An officer of the rank of superintendent or above may authorise a further period of detention up to 36 hours in the case of a serious arrestable offence (s.42). An extension can be granted by magistrates for a maximum of 36 hours; and further extensions to a maximum of 96 hours (s.43).

The treatment and questioning of persons during detention is regulated by Part V of the Act. A power of search is conferred by section 54 and a right to retain any object which might be used by the person in custody to injure himself or aid his escape. Items may also be retained if the officer has reasonable grounds for believing that they may be evidence relating to an offence. In theory the decision to search must be made in each instance in the light of the facts: the invariable searching of persons or removal of items of clothing will be, as formerly, illegal: *Lindley* v. *Rutter*[35]; *Brazil* v. *Chief Constable of Surrey*.[36]

If section 54 might be thought to clarify a power which arguably existed formerly at common law, section 55 creates an entirely new power under which a superintendent can authorise an "intimate search," that is a physical examination of a person's bodily orifices (s.118(1)). He must have reasonable grounds for believing that the person arrested and detained has concealed about him (i) anything which he might use to cause physical injury to himself or others and which he might so use while in police detention or the custody of a court; or (ii) a Class "A" drug which he was in possession of, with criminal intent, before arrest.[37] Normally such a search must be conducted by a medi-

[32] *R.* v. *Lemsatef* [1977] 1 W.L.R. 812 (C.A.); *R.* v. *Houghton and Francoisy* (1978) 68 Cr.App.R. 197 (C.A.). *Cf. Collins* v. *Wilcock* [1984] 1 W.L.R. 1172; 79 Cr.App.R. 299 (D.C.).
[33] Contrast the Criminal Justice (Scotland) Act 1980, s.2 which allows detention for six hours before arrest.
[34] C. Munro, "Detention after Arrest" [1981] Crim. L.R. 802.
[35] [1981] Q.B. 128 (D.C.).
[36] [1983] 1 W.L.R. 1155 (C.A.).
[37] Over eighty Class "A" drugs are listed in Schedule 2 of the Misuse of Drugs Act 1971.

cally qualified person but a constable (of the appropriate sex) may carry out a search for an object within (i) if the superintendent does not think an examination by a medically qualified person is practicable.[38] Constables carrying out searches under the section are entitled to use reasonable force (s.117).

When a person is being detained in connection with an investigation into a serious arrestable offence[39] two sections provide detailed rules for the taking of bodily samples to aid in the investigation. Where a superintendent believes a detained person is involved in the commission of a serious arrestable offence he may authorise the taking of an intimate bodily sample (*i.e.* a sample of blood, semen or any other tissue fluid, urine, saliva or pubic hair, or a swab taken from a person's body orifice: s.65). An intimate sample cannot be taken without the consent of the person detained. A court may, however, draw such inference from a refusal as appears proper and a refusal may be treated as constituting corroboration: (s.62). Non-intimate samples (hair other than pubic hair, a sample taken from a nail or from under a nail, a swab taken from any part of a person's body other than a body orifice, a footprint or a similar impression of any part of a person's body other than a part of his hand: s.65) may be taken with the consent of the person detained or without his consent if a superintendent so authorises where he has reasonable grounds for suspecting the involvement of the person detained in a serious arrestable offence and believes that the sample will tend to prove or disprove his involvement.

A detained person's fingerprints may, under section 61, be taken without his consent if (i) a superintendent so authorises and he has reasonable grounds for suspecting the person's involvement in a criminal offence and that his fingerprints will tend to confirm or disprove his involvement or (ii) he has been charged with a recordable offence[40] or he has been warned that he may be so charged.

In the case of the three preceding sections, where the person detained is under the age of 14 the consent required is that of the parent or guardian; between 14 and 17 both the person detained and his parent or guardian must consent.

Other sections provide additional safeguards for children and young persons (s.57), and a right of access to legal advice (s.58). Codes of Practice are required to be made to regulate the tape-recording of interviews (s.60) and the exercise of powers under the Act generally (ss.66 and 67). Breach of a provision of a Code does not of itself give rise to criminal or civil liability but a Court may take into account any provision of a Code which is relevant to proceedings before it. Section 78 also gives Courts a discretion to refuse to admit evidence if it appears that "having regard

---

[38] Are such searches "degrading treatment" within Article 3 of the European Convention on Human Rights?

[39] Section 116 creates two categories of serious offences; (i) those listed in Schedule 5 (ranging from treason, murder and rape to indecent assault which constitutes an act of indecency) and (ii) any other arrestable offence if it has led to or is intended to lead to any of the consequences listed in sub-section (b) which include serious harm to the security of the state or to public order, serious interference with the administration of justice, the death of any person or serious injury and substantial financial gain or serious loss to any person.

[40] *i.e.* offences recordable in national police records: s.27(4).

to all the circumstances, including the circumstances in which the evidence was obtained, the admission of the evidence would have such an adverse effect on the fairness of the proceedings that the court ought not to admit it."

Assaulting and obstructing a constable

Section 51(1) of the Police Act 1964, as amended, provides that it is an offence to assault a constable (or a person assisting him) in the execution of his duty, punishable on summary conviction with a term of imprisonment not exceeding six months or a fine not exceeding level 5 (at present £2,000) or both.[41]

Section 51(3) provides that it is an offence to resist or wilfully obstruct a constable (or a person assisting him) in the execution of his duty, punishable with a term of imprisonment not exceeding one month or a fine not exceeding level 3 (at present £400) or both.

The importance of these provisions in a chapter on the Freedom of the Individual is that it is often through litigation arising under section 51 that the scope of the powers and duties of the police are elucidated. A policeman, as we have seen, cannot normally detain without arresting: if he does so he is acting outside his powers. But is it an unlawful detention to tap a person on his shoulder and request him to stop and answer a question?[42] The limits of a statutory power to detain may well arise in proceedings under section 51.[43] The meaning of such phrases as "reasonable grounds"[44] and "reasonable force"[45] when used in the Police and Criminal Evidence Act 1984 and the distinction, if any, between "believing" and "suspecting "[46] are likely to be raised in this indirect way by prosecutions and appeals under section 51. The freedom of the individual may be affected by the extent to which the courts are willing to recognise a discretion in constables to take decisions which they regard as necessary to prevent disorder,[47] or to keep traffic moving.[48] Equally important is the meaning the courts give to "obstruction," a word which could properly be confined to physical opposition but, on the other hand, has, in English courts, been extended to, for

---

[41] The Section re-enacts and partially replaces earlier legislation. Assault on a person other than a constable (or some one assisting him) in the effecting of a lawful arrest is an offence under the Offences Against the Person Act 1861, s.38.

[42] *Donnelly* v. *Jackman* [1970] 1 W.L.R. 562 (D.C.) (Action of constable within execution of duty). Distinguished subsequently: courts are careful to distinguish between a touch to draw someone's attention and to apprehend or detain: *Collins* v. *Wilcock* [1984] 1 W.L.R. 1172 (D.C.); *Bentley* v. *Brudzinski* (1982) 75 Cr.App.R. 217 (D.C.); *Ludlow* v. *Burgess* (1982) 75 Cr.App.R. 227 (D.C.).

[43] *e.g. Pedro* v. *Diss* [1981] 2 All E.R. 59 (D.C.) (Prisoner entitled to resist detention because P.C. had not told him, as the Court held he was bound to, that he was detaining him under statutory powers: Metropolitan Police Act 1839, s.66).

[44] *e.g.* s.1(3); s.25(1); s.32(1); s.54(4); s.55. *Cf. Brazil* v. *Chief Constable of Surrey* [1983] 1 W.L.R. 1155 (C.A.) ("reasonable cause": Misuse of Drugs Act 1971 s.23(2): issue raised but not necessary to be determined by Court); *R.* v. *Forde* [1985] Crim. L.R. (D.C.).

[45] s.117.

[46] Contrast s.1(3) and s.1(4); s.25(1) and s.32(1); s.61(4)(a) and (b).

[47] *e.g. Duncan* v.*Jones* [1931] 1 K.B. 218; *post* Chap. 27.

[48] *Johnson* v. *Phillips* [1976] 1 W.L.R. 65 (obstruction to refuse to drive wrong way down a one way street when directed to do so by a constable). See U. Ross, "Two Cases on Obstructing a Constable," (1977) Crim.L.R. 187.

example, taking action which ensures that the criminal law is not broken so that the police find themselves, on arriving at what they expected to be the scene of a crime, unable to arrest anyone—other than the person who gave the warning of their coming.[49]

Assaulting

The elements of assault are those required normally under the criminal law.[50] It is no defence that the person accused was unaware that he was assaulting a constable.[51]

Obstructing[52]

In *Hinchliffe* v. *Sheldon*,[53] Lord Goddard L.C.J., defined obstructing as "making it more difficult for the police to carry out their duties." Such a wide definition would require citizens to carry out willingly police constables' instructions (unless they had, correctly, determined that they fell outside the execution of the constables' duties) and to co-operate fully in the investigation of crimes (so that much of the Police and Criminal Evidence Act 1984 would be unnecessary). It cannot be the criminal offence of obstructing a constable to do what one is entitled to do, namely refuse to answer questions. In *Rice* v. *Connolly*[54] the Divisional Court reached that conclusion by reliance on the wording of section 51(3), "to . . . *wilfully* obstruct." It could not, according to Lord Parker L.C.J. be wilful to do that which one had a legal excuse to do, refuse to answer questions. In *Ashton* v. *Merseyside Police*[55] it was similarly held that to remind a person being questioned by a constable of her right to remain silent was not an obstruction within section 51(3). A positive act, such as drinking a quantity of alcohol to prevent the effective administration of a breathalyser test, may be more likely to be regarded as an obstruction than a mere refusal to act: *Dibble* v. *Ingleton*.[56] On the other hand a refusal to obey a constable's instruction which is given with a view to avoiding a breach of the peace[57] or to protect life[58] may constitute an obstruction.

A number of cases have considered the intention required before the offence of obstruction is committed. In *Willmott* v. *Atack*[59] it was held that physically obstructing a constable who was attempting to arrest

---

[49] *Green* v. *Moore* [1982] Q.B. 1044 (D.C.); *Moore* v. *Green* [1983] 1 All E.R. 663 (After-hours drinking at Castle Hotel, Chepstow).

[50] J. C. Smith and B. Hogan, *Criminal Law* (5th ed., 1983) Chap. 12.

[51] *R.* v. *Forbes* (1865) 10 Cox C.C. 362.

[52] R. C. Austin, "Obstruction—the policeman's best friend" (1982) 35 Cur. Leg. Prob. 558; P. M. Leopold, "Obstructing the Police" [1982] P.L. 558; T. Gibbons, "The Offence of Obstruction" [1983] Crim.L.R. 21; M. Duggan, "Muzzling the Concientious (sic) Citizen" (1983) 46 M.L.R. 662.

[53] [1955] 1 W.L.R. 1207.

[54] [1966] 2 Q.B. 414 (D.C.) It is difficult to see how, as a matter of law, liability can be affected by whether the refusal to answer questions is politely worded or accompanied by obscenities: *quaere Ricketts* v. *Cox* (1981) 74 Cr.App.R. 298 (D.C.).

[55] [1984] C.L. 2096 (Crown Ct.).

[56] [1972] 1 Q.B. 480 (D.C.).

[57] *Duncan* v. *Jones* [1931] 1 K.B. 218; *ante* p. 497; *post* Chap. 27. See also *Tynan* v. *Bulmer* [1967] 1 Q.B. 91 (obstructing the highway; refusal to move).

[58] *Johnson* v. *Phillips* [1976] 1 W.L.R. 65; *ante* p. 497.

[59] [1977] Q.B. 498 (D.C.).

someone did not constitute an offence under section 51(3) when the intention had been to help the police. Croom Johnson J. paraphrased "wilfully" as meaning "done with the idea of some form of hostility to the police." But interference with a policeman who is attempting to arrest someone on the ground that the wrong person is being arrested, constitutes wilfully obstructing: *Hill* v. *Ellis*.[60] Both decisions were considered in *Lewis* v. *Cox*[61] where the Divisional Court held that justices had erred in refusing to convict an accused who had opened the door of a police vehicle to ask a drunk who had been put inside the vehicle where he was being taken. A constable closed the door and warned the accused not to interfere. The latter, however, again opened the door and so prevented the vehicle from being driven away. The court held that the offence of wilful obstruction was committed by doing an act which interfered with the execution by the police of their duty, knowing or intending that it would interfere. Motive was irrelevant and the court found the use of such phrases as "hostility to the police" or "aimed at the police" unhelpful.[62]

Execution of duty

A constable is not acting within the execution of his duty when he does something which he has no right to do at law, for example, to attempt to detain someone whom he has not arrested,[63] to search someone whom he has no right to search,[64] to use force to take a person's fingerprints when not entitled to do so,[65] to attempt to enter premises with an invalid search warrant,[66] or to trespass on property.[67] In all these circumstances the citizen is entitled to refuse to co-operate with the instructions of a constable and, if necessary, to use reasonable force to resist unlawful demands.

Where, however, a constable is doing what he is legally entitled to do then he is acting within the execution of his duty, although a jurist might prefer to say that he was acting within the scope of his lawful powers. To resist arrest where a constable is entitled to arrest, for

---

[60] [1983] Q.B. 680 (D.C.).

[61] [1985] Q.B. 509 (D.C.).

[62] The Court did not attempt to cast doubt on *Willmott* v. *Atack supra* which may perhaps be explained as being correctly decided on the ground that the accused did not intend to obstruct or realise that he was obstructing whereas in *Hill* v. *Ellis*, whatever his motive, the accused did intend to prevent the effecting of an arrest. On precedent in the Divisional Court see (1985) 101 L.Q.R. 157 and 484.

[63] *Collins* v. *Wilcock* [1984] 1 W.L.R. 1172; *Bentley* v. *Brudzinski* (1982) 75 Cr.App.R. 217; *Pedro* v. *Diss* [1981] 2 All E.R. 59. See also *Hickman* v. *O'Dwyer* [1979] Crim.L.R. 309 (D.C.) (No reason to apprehend breach of peace; youth lying on park bench entitled to resist P.C.'s attempt "to move him on").

[64] *Lindley* v. *Rutter* [1981] Q.B. 128 (D.C.); *Brazil* v. *Chief Constable of Surrey* [1983] 1 W.L.R. 1155 (C.A.); *R.* v. *Eeet* [1983] Crim.L.R. 806 (Crown Ct.). *Cf. McBean* v. *Parker, The Times*, February 8, 1983 (D.C.).

[65] *R.* v. *Jones (Yvonne)* (1978) 67 Cr.App.R. 166 (C.A.).

[66] *Syce* v. *Harrison* [1980] Crim.L.R. 649 (D.C.).

[67] *McLorie* v. *Oxford* [1982] Q.B. 1290 (D.C.); *R.* v. *McKenzie and Davis* [1979] Crim.L.R. 174 (Crown Ct.). Whether a P.C. is trespassing or not may be a difficult question: *Robson* v. *Hallett* [1967] 2 Q.B. 939.

example for an apprehended breach of the peace,[68] or to refuse to keep a vehicle stationary as required under legislation to enable a constable to make inquiries under the relevant Act[69] are examples of assaulting or obstructing a constable in the execution of his duty. In *Coffin* v. *Smith*[70] police officers had been called to a youth club to ensure that no disorder occurred during a social function. They were assaulted by two people and magistrates dismissed charges brought under section 51(1) on the ground that the police officers were not acting in the execution of their duty. In the Divisional Court, however, Donaldson L.J. held that "a police officer's duty is to be a keeper of the peace and to take all necessary steps with that in view." To attend at the club was, in effect, to stand there "on their beat in the execution of their duty." It is also part of the duty of the police to take steps to apprehend the perpetrators of crimes which they have reason are likely to be committed. In *Green* v. *Moore*[71] the warning of a licensee that police officers were keeping watch on his premises with a view to securing evidence that he and his customers were breaking the licensing laws was held to be an obstruction of police officers in the execution of their duty.

It should finally be noted that there is no power to arrest without warrant for an offence under section 51 unless a breach of peace has occurred or is reasonably apprehended: *Wershof* v. *Commissioner of the Police for the Metropolis.*[72] In the case of assaulting or resisting a constable a breach of the peace is almost inevitably involved. In many cases of obstruction it is difficult to believe that there can be any real risk of a breach of the peace.

Bail

In many cases a person who has been arrested may be released on bail pending trial. Initially a justice of the peace on issuing a warrant for arrest may grant bail by endorsing a direction to that effect and subject to the terms of section 117 of the Magistrates' Courts Act 1980, as amended by the Police and Criminal Evidence Act 1984, s.47(8). Section 37 of the Police and Criminal Evidence Act 1984 regulates the granting of bail by the custody officer where (a) a person is arrested without a warrant or under a warrant not endorsed for bail or (b) a person returns to a police station to answer to bail. If the custody officer decides that he has sufficient evidence he may charge the person in which case section 38 provides for release from detention, either on bail or without bail, unless one of the conditions in that section is not complied with, for example the name and address of the person charged cannot be ascertained or the custody officer has reasonable grounds for believing that the detention of the person arrested is necessary for his own protection

---

[68] R. v. *Howell (Errol)* [1982] Q.B. 416. See too *Moses* v. *McLachlan* [1985] I.R.L.R. 77 (D.C.).
[69] *Lodwick* v. *Sanders* [1985] 1 W.L.R. 382 (D.C.) (Assault in the execution of duty).
[70] [1980] 71 Cr.App.R. 221 (D.C.).
[71] [1982] Q.B. 1044 (D.C.) See too *Moore* v. *Green* [1983] 1 All E.R. 663 (D.C.). Contrast *Bastable* v. *Little* [1907] 1 K.B. 59 described by Donaldson L.J. in *Green* v. *Moore* as "a very curious decision based upon a highly eccentric view of the facts."
[72] (1978) 68 Cr.App.R. 82. See also *Hickman* v. *O'Dwyer* [1979] Crim.L.R. 309 (D.C.). *Cf.* "general arrest conditions," Police and Criminal Evidence Act 1984, s.25.

or to prevent him causing physical injury to any other person. If the custody officer decides that he does not have sufficient evidence to charge the person arrested he must release him, on bail or without bail, unless he is entitled within the terms of the Act to detain him to secure the necessary evidence. If an arrested person is detained the provisions described earlier operate and at the end of each period defined in the Act either the person must be released on bail unless a further period of detention can be justified. Where a person charged appears before magistrates or the Crown Court in connection with criminal proceedings the Bail Act 1976 confers a general right to bail. The main exceptions to the right of bail of a person accused or convicted of an imprisonable offence are if the court is satisfied that the defendant if released on bail would: (a) fail to surrender to custody; (b) commit an offence while on bail, or (c) interfere with witnesses. A person charged with treason can only be granted bail by order of a judge of the High Court or the Secretary of State.[73] A Magistrates' Court or Crown Court must give reasons for refusing bail or imposing conditions on bail (s.5(3)). A person refused bail may apply to the High Court,[74] and he must be informed of his right. Bail may also be granted by the higher courts in the course of their proceedings or pending an appeal. It is a criminal offence to fail without reasonable cause to surrender to custody at the time and place appointed (s.6).[75]

Bail can be fixed at any amount, but the Bill of Rights provides that the bail shall not be "excessive." In such cases as theft, fraud or smuggling, the amount of money involved may be very large, with a corresponding danger that the accused may leave the country. If the accused objects to the amount of bail he may appeal to a judge, or in appropriate cases may apply for a writ of habeas corpus.[76]

The exercise by justices of their power to grant bail is subject to judicial review by the High Court on the grounds discussed in Chapter 33. In particular they must consider each application on its merits and not in the light of a pre-determined policy. In *R. v. Nottingham Justices, ex p. Davies*[77] the applicant sought mandamus to require justices to hear his application for bail. On two previous occasions in the preceding weeks he had applied for and been refused bail. On the third occasion the justices, having satisfied themselves that circumstances had not changed since the earlier applications, refused the application without hearing further argument. The Divisional Court held that the magistrates were entitled to conclude that after two applications the full facts had been established and to adhere to their previous decisions in the

---

[73] Magistrates Court Act 1980, s.41.

[74] The application is to the High Court and cannot be made to successive judges in the hope of obtaining a favourable decision: *R. v. Crown Court at Reading, ex p. Malik* [1981] Q.B. 451 (D.C.).

[75] *R. v. Harbax Singh* [1979] Q.B. 319 (C.A.). (Drunkenness not a reasonable cause: punished under s.6(5) as a criminal contempt of court.)

[76] *Ex p. Thomas* [1956] Crim.L.R. 119 (D.C.). *Cf. R. v. Governor of Brixton Prison, ex p. Goswami, The Times*, December 22, 1966; *Ex p. Goswami* (1966) 111 S.J. 17 (D.C.): bail of £50,000 not too high, although the defendant could not find sureties.

[77] [1981] Q.B. 38 (D.C.).

absence of new circumstances. Their policy was not an improper abandonment of their discretion. In *R. v. Mansfield Justices, ex p. Sharkey*[78] certiorari was sought to quash grants of bail, made subject to the condition that the applicants, who had been charged with offences under the Public Order Act 1936, section 5 and obstructing police officers under the Police Act 1964, section 51(3), did not visit any premises for the purposes of picketing or demonstrating in connection with the miners' strike, other than peacefully to picket at their own places of work. It was argued that the condition had been imposed as a general rule, without a proper consideration of each individual case. The Divisional Court held that justices are entitled to impose conditions on bail if they perceive a real and not a fanciful risk of an offence being committed.[79] In the light of their knowledge of local conditions, outlined graphically in Lord Lane L.C.J.'s judgment, they were justified in concluding that there was such a real risk.[80]

Binding over[81]

The power of magistrates to make a binding over order is a form of preventive justice, that is a power to subject to restriction someone who has not necessarily committed a criminal offence. Such a jurisdiction clearly impinges on individual freedom and unless kept within the narrowest confines may constitute a threat to it. A binding-over order requires that a person should enter into a recognisance (a bond whereby he binds himself under a penalty) with or without sureties (other persons who will vouch for him under penalty) to keep the peace or to be of good behaviour or both for a certain period. If that person commits a breach of the order, he and his sureties are liable to forfeit the whole or part of the sums in which they are bound. There is no legal limit to the amount of the recognisances or of the sureties, or to the period of the order (which is commonly twelve months). If the person concerned refuses to enter into a recognisance, or if he is unwilling or unable to find satisfactory sureties, the magistrates may commit him to prison for not more than six months or until he sooner complies with the order. In *Lansbury v. Riley*[82] George Lansbury M.P., who incited suffragettes to militant action, was bound over to be of good behaviour in the sum of £1,000 with two sureties of £500 each; as he was unable or unwilling to find the sureties he was committed to prison for three months. The power to bind over to keep the peace is probably of common law origin, and may have been exercised by the Conservators of

---

[78] [1985] Q.B. 613 (D.C.).

[79] s.3(b) gives the power to attach conditions to a grant of bail imposes a lower standard of proof than Sched. 1, para. 2 which only allows a *refusal* of bail if there are substantial grounds for believing that the defendant, if released would commit an offence. Lord Lane L.C.J. admitted that while this distinction was "logical," other provisions of Sched. 1 caused some difficulty "due to indifferent drafting."

[80] For a critical note see A. L. Newbold, "Picketing Miners and the Courts" [1985] P.L. 30.

[81] See Asher D. Grunis "Binding Over to Keep the Peace and Be of Good Behaviour in England and Canada" [1976] P.L. 16. The Law Commission is reviewing the power of magistrates to make a binding-over order.

[82] [1914] 3 K.B. 229 (D.C.); *Everett v. Ribbands* [1952] 2 Q.B. 198.

the Peace. The power to bind over to be of good behaviour towards the Queen and her people is ascribed to the Justices of the Peace Act 1361.[83]

Under the Magistrates' Courts Act 1980, s.115, the power on the complaint of any person to bind over another person to keep the peace or to be of good behaviour towards the complainant, must be exercised on complaint. It was said in *R. v. Aubrey-Fletcher, ex p. Thompson*,[84] that for making a binding-over order under the Magistrates' Courts Act there has to be a complaint adjudged to be true; whereas an order under the Justices of the Peace Act 1361 can be made at any time during proceedings if it emerges that there might be a breach of the peace. In that case, however, where the charge was one of insulting words whereby a breach of the peace might be occasioned under the Metropolitan Police Act 1839, that stage had not yet been reached.

The question when the magistrates can make a binding-over order is not free from doubt. It appears that they may make such an order: (i) where a breach of the peace has been committed, or is threatened, or is reasonably apprehended[85]; or (ii) where an offence against public order has been committed and is likely to be repeated.[86] The Court has a duty to warn a complainant or witness before binding him over, giving him an opportunity to say why he should not be bound over.[87] A binding-over order is not a conviction and therefore at common law there was no appeal, but a right of appeal to Quarter Sessions (now the Crown Court) was given in 1956.[88]

Detention on Medical Grounds

Various statutes authorise the detention of individuals on medical grounds whether in their own interests or those of the community at large. The National Assistance Act 1948, s.47 empowers a court to order, on the report of a designated medical officer, the compulsory removal to hospital or other place of persons who (a) are suffering from grave chronic disease or being aged, infirm or physically incapacitated are living

---

[83] *Lansbury v. Riley, ante; R. v. County of London Quarter Sessions, ex p. Commissioner of Metropolitan Police* [1948] 1 All E.R. 72, *per* Lord Goddard C.J. The Act was amended by the Criminal Law Act 1967, Sched. 3, Pt. II. And see C. K. Allen, *The Queen's Peace*, pp. 61–66; Glanville Williams, "Preventive Justice and the Rule of Law" (1953) 16 M.L.R. 417. The Act of 1361 may in fact have been intended to empower justices to require sureties from persons who *are* of good fame, as distinct from the power to punish rioters and other offenders against the peace. Superior courts may bind over convicted persons to come up for sentence if called upon, *e.g.* Morris v. *Crown Office* [1970] 2 Q.B. 114 (C.A.), and are not limited to six months' imprisonment.

[84] [1969] 1 W.L.R. 872 (D.C.).

[85] *Wilson v. Skeock* (1949) 65 T.L.R. 418 (D.C.) *per* Lord Goddard C.J., is authority for saying a breach of the peace need not actually have been committed.

[86] See David Williams, *op. cit.* p. 94.

[87] *R. v. Hendon Justices, ex p. Gorchein* [1973] 1 W.L.R. 1502 (D.C.); *R. v. Keighley Justices ex p. Stoyles* [1976] Crim.L.R. 573 (D.C.); *R. v. Ilminster Justices ex p. Hamilton, The Times,* June 23, 1983 (D.C.); *R. v. Swindon Crown Court ex p. Pawittar Singh* [1984] 1 W.L.R. 449 (D.C.); *R. v. Central Criminal Court ex p. Boulding* [1984] Q.B. 813 (D.C.).

[88] Magistrates' Courts (Appeals from Binding-Over Orders) Act 1956: *R. v. Preston Crown Court, ex p. Pamplin* [1981] Crim.L.R. 338 (D.C.); *Shaw v. Hamilton* [1982] 1 W.L.R. 1308 (D.C.).

in insanitary conditions and (b) are unable to devote to themselves and are not receiving from other persons proper care and attention.

The Public Health (Control of Disease) Act 1984 provides for the compulsory removal to, and detention in, hospital of any person suffering from a notifiable disease (that is cholera, plague, relapsing fever, smallpox and typhus—section 10) by order of a justice of the peace (ss.37 and 38). The Secretary of State (by s.13) and local authorities (by s.16) have power to extend the compulsory detention provisions of the Act to other diseases.

The provisions which occasion most controversy, however, are those relating to the detention and treatment of people suffering from mental ill-health currently to be found in the Mental Health Act 1983.[89] These affect large numbers of individuals; involve, in many cases, prolonged periods of incarceration and the administration of treatments, to which the recipients may not have consented, which in some cases may have the most far reaching and irreversible mental and physical effects, without any guarantee of achieving their desired aims. The patient may, moreover, dispute that he or she is mentally ill or that compulsory detention or treatment is necessary. The Mental Health Act 1983 authorises admission for assessment and detention for treatment, in a mental hospital, against the wishes of a patient, where two registered medical practitioners so recommend (ss.2 and 3). The legality of detention under these sections is open to challenge by an application for a writ of habeas corpus (*infra*) or by an application for judicial review.

An accused person may be remanded to a hospital by order of the Crown Court or a magistrates' court for a report on his mental condition (s.35). The Crown Court, on the evidence of two registered medical practitioners, may remand an accused person to hospital for treatment (s.36). On conviction the Crown Court and magistrates' courts have power to commit the prisoner to a hospital (s.38) and in the case of the Crown Court to make a restriction order which prevents the prisoner (or patient) from being released except after an order of a Mental Health Review Tribunal or the Secretary of State (s.41). A restriction order can only be made where it appears to the Court that it is necessary for the protection of the public from serious harm in the light of the nature of the offence, the antecedents of the offender and the risk of his committing further offences if set at large. In the case of a prisoner serving a sentence of imprisonment the Secretary of State may on the advice of two registered medical practitioners direct that he be removed to a hospital (s.47).

A patient who believes that he is entitled to be discharged from a hospital where he is being detained may apply to a Mental Health Review Tribunal which has powers to order conditional or unconditional discharges of patients (ss.73 and 74 (restricted patients)). The Chairman of a Tribunal must be legally qualified; of the other two members one must be a registered medical practitioner and the other have such experience in administration or such knowledge of social services or such other qualifications as the Lord Chancellor considers suitable. Restrictions are imposed on the occasions when a patient may apply to

---

[89] Brenda M. Hoggett, *Mental Health Law* (2nd ed. 1984).

a Tribunal (s.66). The managers of a hospital are under a duty to refer to a Tribunal, according to the times laid down, the cases of patients who do not themselves apply for a review of their cases (s.68). A residual power to refer cases to a Tribunal is possessed by the Secretary of State.

Part IV of the Act deals with the difficult question of consent to treatment by mentally ill patients. The Act recognises three types of treatment. The first and most serious, for example surgery to destroy brain tissue, can only be administered with the consent of the patient and the approval of a registered medical practitioner appointed for the purposes of Part IV and two other persons, not being medical practitioners, appointed by the Secretary of State for the purposes of the section. Furthermore the medical practitioner must consult two persons professionally concerned with the patient's medical treatment, one of whom must be a nurse; the other must be neither a nurse nor a registered medical practitioner; presumably a psychologist or a social worker would qualify for this purpose (s.57). The safeguards contained in this section are applicable to voluntary patients as well as to those detained against their wishes (s.56(2)). Section 58 applies to less serious types of treatment which it leaves to be specified from time to time by the Secretary of State. A typical example is E.C.T. Treatments within the section may be given (i) where the patient has consented and a medical practitioner, appointed for the purposes of Part IV, has certified that he is capable of giving informed consent, or (ii) such a practitioner has certified that the patient is incapable of giving consent but the treatment should be given having regard to the likelihood of its alleviating or preventing a deterioration of his condition. In the second case the medical practitioner must as under section 57, consult two other persons, as there defined (s.58). Neither section applies where treatment is immediately necessary to save a patient's life or in other types of emergencies, subject to the provisions of section 62. Types of treatment not falling within sections 57 and 58 may be administered without the patient's consent on the authority of the responsible medical authority (s.63). The provisions of Part IV do not apply to patients detained under the emergency provisions of the Act (s.56) but it is unlikely that such patients would be subjected to the forms of treatment falling within section 57.

The right of persons detained under the Mental Health Act 1983 to bring proceedings in relation to acts done under the legislation is curtailed by section 139. Subsection (1) provides that no one shall be liable for acts done under the Act on the ground of want of jurisdiction or any other ground unless the act was done in bad faith or without reasonable care.[90] Any civil proceedings in relation to acts done under the mental health legislation require to be brought with the leave of the High Court and criminal proceedings require the consent of the Director of Public Prosecutions except in the case of proceedings against the Secretary of State or a health authority.

The prohibition on the bringing of proceedings except in cases of bad faith or lack of reasonable care does not prevent a challenge by way of

---

[90] *Kynaston* v. *Secretary of State for Home Affairs* (1981) 73 Cr.App.R. 281 (C.A.) (Unsuccessful attempt to sue Home Secretary).

an application for judicial review to the validity of an order committing a patient to hospital: *ex p. Waldron.*[91]

Writ of habeas corpus[92]

In origin this writ, which is found in Edward I's reign, was merely a command by the court to someone to bring before itself persons whose presence was necessary to some judicial proceedings. In other words, it was "originally intended not to get people out of prison but to put them in it."[93] Habeas corpus[94] was a "prerogative" writ, that is, one issued by the King against his officers to compel them to exercise their functions properly. In the form *habeas corpus ad subjiciendum* (the form now commonly used)[95] it came to be available, under certain conditions, to private individuals. In the seventeenth century members of the parliamentary opposition imprisoned by command of the King availed themselves of the writ to seek release (*e.g. Darnel's Case*),[96] and it is from this application that originated its constitutional importance as the classic common law guarantee of personal liberty. The Petition of Right 1627 declared that the orders of the Sovereign were not to be sufficient justification for the imprisonment of his subjects.

Habeas corpus is available against any person who is suspected of detaining another unlawfully, and not merely against prison governors, the police or other public officers whose duties normally include arrest and detention. It is applicable where a tribunal has no jurisdiction to detain the petitioner, but not where the detention is the result of a wrong decision made in exercise of jurisdiction: in the latter case there may be an appeal to a higher court.[97] Habeas corpus was used in the eighteenth and early nineteenth centuries to set free slaves brought into this country by their owners, or who had escaped for protection to British warships, during the period when slavery was still lawful in parts of the British Empire and in other countries.[98]

Habeas corpus has been used to test the validity of detention by orders of a court-martial.[99] Since the seventeenth century, and before a system of criminal appeals was established, habeas corpus was the normal method of applying for bail.[1] The writ is available to question

---

[91] [1986] Q.B. 824 (C.A.).

[92] See R. J. Sharpe, *The Law of Habeas Corpus* (Oxford, 1976). William F. Duker, *A Constitutional History of Habeas Corpus* (1982); de Smith, *Judicial Review of Administrative Action* (4th ed., 1980) App. 2.

[93] Jenks, "The Story of Habeas Corpus," (1902) 18 L.Q.R. 64, 65.

[94] Habeas corpus = have (*i.e.* bring) the body [of X before the court].

[95] For a recent decision on the form *ad respondendum* see *R. v. Governor of Brixton Prison, ex p. Walsh* [1985] A.C. 154 (H.L.).

[96] (1627) *The Five Knights' Case*, 3 St.Tr. 1; Holdsworth, *History of English Law*, Vol. VI, pp. 32–37.

[97] *Cf.* A. Rubinstein, "Habeas Corpus as a means of Review" (1964) 27 M.L.R. 322.

[98] *Somersett* v. *Steuart* (1772) 20 St.Tr. 1 (Lord Mansfield C.J.): Somersett was later appointed wharf-master of the new settlement of Sierra Leone (E. Fiddes in (1934) 50 L.Q.R. 1, 459); *Forbes* v. *Cochrane* (1824) 2 B. & C. 448; *The Slave Grace* (1827) 2 Hag.Adm. 94 (Lord Stowell); *cf. Hottentot Venus' Case* (1810) 13 East 195. For Scots law, to similar effect, see *Knight* v. *Wedderburn* (1778) Mor. 14545.

[99] *Re Porrett* (1844) Perry's *Oriental Cases* 414, *Cf. Re Clifford and O'Sullivan* [1921] A.C. 570 (no prohibition to military tribunal administering martial law; *quaere* habeas corpus).

[1] *Re Kray* [1965] Ch. 736 (Lord Gardiner L.C.).

detention by the police,[2] detention pending deportation[3] and for breach of immigration regulations,[4] and also during proceedings under the Extradition Acts[5] and Fugitive Offenders Acts.[6] It is also available to challenge the legality of detention under Mental Health legislation.[7] For detention by order of the House of Commons reference should be made to the *Case of the Sheriff of Middlesex*.[8]

For constitutional purposes the special significance of this remedy is that it is available against Crown servants acting in the name of the Crown.[9] Thus in *Home Secretary* v. *O'Brien*[10] the writ was issued against the Home Secretary, who had ordered the detention of an Irishman in England during the Irish "troubles." On the other hand it was held in *Re Ning Yi-Ching*[11] that habeas corpus would not lie for Chinese subjects on foreign territory, and that in any event the writ would not issue against the Foreign Secretary acting merely in an advisory capacity.

Habeas Corpus Act 1679

The passing of this Act followed the case of *Jenkes*[12] who, after being arrested for delivering a speech urging the summoning of Parliament, was kept in prison for several months without bail. The Act applied only to persons imprisoned (not after conviction by a court) for "criminal or supposed criminal matters." If the applicant showed that there was any ground for supposing that the prisoner was wrongfully imprisoned, the writ would be issued requiring the person detaining the prisoner to bring him before the court and to inform it of the grounds of his detention. If it is appeared that the prisoner was confined without lawful authority, the court would release him; otherwise it would release him on bail, or make provision for his speedy trial.

Habeas corpus cannot be granted to a person who is serving a sentence passed by a court of competent jurisdiction,[13] unless, probably,

---

[2] *R.* v. *Holmes, ex p. Sherman* [1981] 2 All E.R. 612.

[3] *R.* v. *Home Secretary, ex p. Soblen* [1963] 1 Q.B. 829 (C.A.); *R.* v. *Durham Prison Governor, ex p. Singh*, [1984] 1 W.L.R. 704. See also *R.* v. *Governor of Holloway Prison, ex p. Giambi* [1982] 1 W.L.R. 535 (D.C.) (Unsuccessful application based on "absurd construction" of Act.)

[4] *R.* v. *Governor of Brixton Prison, ex p. Ahsan* [1969] 2 Q.B. 222 (D.C.); *R.* v. *Governor of Richmond Remand Centre, ex p. Ashgar* [1971] 1 W.L.R. 129 (D.C.); *R.* v. *Governor of Risley Remand Centre, ex p. Hassan* [1976] 1 W.L.R. 971 (D.C.).

[5] *Re Castioni* [1891] 1 Q.B. 149; *R.* v. *Governor of Brixton Prison, ex p. Cabon-Waterfield* [1960] 2 Q.B. 498 (D.C.).

[6] *R.* v. *Brixton Prison Governor, ex p. Naranjan Singh* [1962] 1 Q.B. 211 (D.C.); *R.* v. *Brixton Prison Governor, ex p. Sadri* [1962] 1 W.L.R. 1304 (D.C.); *Zacharia* v. *Republic of Cyprus* [1963] A.C. 634 (H.L.).

[7] *R.* v. *Board of Control, ex p. Rutty* [1956] 2 Q.B. 109.

[8] (1840) 11 Ad. & E. 273; *ante*, Chap. 12.

[9] *Cf.* Mandamus which is not available against the Crown or a servant of the Crown to enforce a duty owed to the Crown: *post* p. 689: injunction and specific performance not available; Crown Proceedings Act 1947, s.21(1); *post*, p. 715.

[10] [1923] A.C. 603 (H.L.).

[11] (1939) 56 T.L.R. 3.

[12] (1676) 6 St.Tr. 1190. For an account of the passing of this Act, see Holdsworth, *History of English Law*, Vol. IX, pp. 112–117. The Bill is said by Bishop Burnett to have been saved at one stage by a teller counting one fat peer as ten.

[13] *Re Wring, Re Cook (Practice Note)* [1960] 1 W.L.R. 138 (D.C.). For the practice where a prisoner persists in his desire to apply for habeas corpus, see *Re Greene* (1941) 57 T.L.R. 533.

the Divisional Court is satisfied that the prisoner is being detained after the term of his sentence has expired.[14] The Divisional Court does not sit as a court of appeal on an application for habeas corpus, and it will not rehear matters decided by the judicial authority,[15] but it may consider whether that judicial authority had any evidence which would justify its assumption of jurisdiction.[16]

The Habeas Corpus Act 1679 imposed heavy penalties for not making due returns to the writ, not delivering to the prisoner promptly a true copy of the warrant of commitment, or shifting the custody of the pris- oner from one place to another, or sending prisoners out of England. The obligation to hear applications for habeas corpus was laid on the Lord Chancellor and judges of the King's Bench, Common Pleas, Exche- quer and Chancery. It appears that under section 9, judges of the Supreme Court are still liable to a penalty of £500 for wrongfully refus- ing to issue a writ of habeas corpus in the case of a person in custody on a criminal charge, but it is uncertain whether this applies only in vacation.

Habeas Corpus Act 1816

This Act provided that the Act of 1679 (with certain improvements) should extend to detention otherwise than on a charge of crime.[17] The judges were required, on complaint made to them by or on behalf of the person in custody showing a prima facie ground for the complaint, to issue a writ of *habeas corpus ad subjiciendum*; and in cases to which the Act applied they might inquire into the truth of the return to the writ. Any person disobeying a writ sued out under this Act is guilty of con- tempt of court and becomes liable to imprisonment.

Lord Scarman, in *R. v. Home Secretary, ex p. Khawaja*[18] referred to "The great statute of 1816" which, he said, was "the beginning of the modern jurisprudence the effect of which" is that the courts will deter- mine for themselves the existence of the facts which the executive cites as justifying its decision, for example that a person detained is an illegal immigrant.

Modern procedure on habeas corpus

Habeas corpus is a writ of right, but not of course, that is a prima facie case must be shown before it will issue. Otherwise as Lord Goddard C.J. said, all the prisoners of England could delay or even defeat jus- tice.[19] It will not be refused *merely* become another remedy is avail-

---

[14] *Re Featherstone* (1953) 37 Cr.App.R. 146, *per* Lord Goddard C.J.

[15] *Ex p. Hinds* [1961] 1 W.L.R. 325 (D.C.); afirmed by the House of Lords in *Re Hinds, The Times*, February 15, 1961.

[16] *R. v. Board of Control, ex p. Rutty* [1956] 2 Q.B. 109.

[17] Except in the case of persons imprisoned for debt or on process in a civil action. These kinds of imprisonment (except for certain debts due to the Crown and judgment debts where the debtor has had the money to pay) were abolished by the Debtors Act 1869; *ante*, p. 489.

[18] [1984] A.C. 74 (H.L.). See *R. v. Brixton Prison Governor, ex p. Ahsan* [1969] 2 Q.B. 222 (D.C.); *Re Shahid Iqbal* [1979] Q.B. 264 (D.C.); [1979] 1 W.L.R. 425 (C.A.); *Re Quigley* [1983] N.I. 245.

[19] *Re Corke* [1954] 1 W.L.R. 899.

able.[20] No application will be heard in person save for some exceptional reason.[21] The present procedure is governed by Rules of the Supreme Court, especially Order 54.

Proceedings are generally to be heard by a Divisional Court of the Queen's Bench Division. Exceptionally, application may be made to a single judge of any division in court. In vacation, or at any time when no judge is sitting in court (*e.g.* at weekends or at night), application may be made to a judge sitting otherwise than in court, *e.g.* in vacation to a judge in chambers; at other times in an emergency, anywhere.[22] Application is to be *ex parte* in the first instance, and on affidavit. The affidavit is made by the person restrained, or by someone on his behalf if he is incapable, setting out the nature of the restraint. The application is usually adjourned in order that notice may be given to the respondent. On the hearing of the application the court or judge may order that the person restrained be released. Such order is a sufficient warrant for his release, so that there is no need to issue the actual writ.

There is still power to order the immediate issue of the writ,[23] though this is rarely done. Where the writ is issued it is accompanied by a notice that in default of obedience proceedings for contempt of court against the party disobeying will be taken. The return to the writ must contain a copy of all the causes of the prisoner's detention. Argument then takes place on the return to the writ.

The Administration of Justice Act 1960, s.14, provides that on a criminal application for habeas corpus an order for release may be *refused* only by a Divisional Court of the Queen's Bench Division, even where the original application is made to a single judge, *e.g.* in vacation.

Habeas corpus is a remedy designed to facilitate the release of persons detained unlawfully, not to punish the person detaining and it is not therefore, issued after the detention complained of has come to an end: *Barnardo* v. *Ford*.[24]

Usually the question at issue is the legality of an admitted detention but the writ is available where it is the fact of detention that is in dispute: *Quigley* v. *Chief Constable, Royal Ulster Constabulary*.[25]

Successive applications

Before 1876 an application for habeas corpus could be made to each of the Courts of Queen's Bench, Common Pleas, Exchequer and Chancery. The judges of the common law courts available in London sat together

---

[20] *Quigley* v. *Chief Constable, Royal Ulster Constabulary* [1983] N.I. 238, 239, *per* Lord Lowrie, L.C.J. Dicta suggesting a discretion on the court to refuse the writ are to be found in *Re Keenan* [1972] 1 Q.B. 533 (C.A.).

[21] *Re Greene* (1941) 57 T.L.R. 533. For informal applications by prisoners, see *Re Wring, Re Cook* [1960] 1 All E.R. 536 *per* Lord Parker C.J. C. Drewry, S. Hughes and A. Shaw "Informal Applications for the Writ of Habeas Corpus" [1977] P.L. 149.

[22] In the *Soblen* case, *ante*, p. 461, application was made to the chambers judge at his home in the middle of the night, and the order signed on the dining-room table: *R.* v. *Home Secretary, ex p. Soblen, The Times*, July 27, 1962.

[23] Even on an *ex parte* application.

[24] [1892] A.C. 326 (H.L.); *Re Nicola Raine, The Times*, May 5, 1982 (D.C.).

[25] [1983] N.I. 238. See subsequently, *In re Quigley* [1983] N.I. 245. (Was Mrs. Quigley detained at a secret address against her will by the R.U.C., or was she willingly living under police protection to avoid intimidation by terrorists).

in banc, and each court was bound to hear the case *de novo* on its merits, because the refusal of the writ was not regarded as a judgment and therefore the matter was not *res judicata.*[26] After the Judicature Acts 1873–75 had amalgamated these courts into one High Court, there were dicta in the House of Lords and the Privy Council to the effect that Parliament could not have intended impliedly to restrict the rights of the subject in the vital matter of personal liberty, and that there was therefore a right to apply not only to each Division of the High Court but to each High Court judge individually.[27] In *Re Hastings,*[28] however, a series of decisions showed that two differently constituted Queen's Bench Divisional Courts, as well as the Chancery Division, were all parts of the same High Court for this as for other purposes, and therefore the decision of any one Division was the decision of the whole court. Further, Rules of Court did not permit application to be made to a single judge in term time.[29]

The Administration of Justice Act 1960, s.14, provided that no *second* criminal or civil application may be made on the same grounds, whether to the same or any other court or judge, unless fresh evidence is adduced; and no such application may be made in any case to the Lord Chancellor.[30] Whether successive applications may be made in vacation is still not certain.[31]

Appeal

An incidental effect of the Judicature Acts 1873–75 was that in non-criminal matters the persons detained might appeal to the Court of Appeal and thence to the House of Lords against a refusal to issue the writ or to discharge him under the writ.[32] On the other hand, a prisoner had no appeal against refusal to issue the writ in a criminal cause or matter, *i.e.* a matter of which the direct outcome might be his trial and possible punishment for an illegal act by a court claiming jurisdiction in that regard (*Amand* v. *Home Secretary and Minister of Defence of the Royal Netherlands Government*[33]). The person detaining had no appeal against an order of the High Court discharging a prisoner from custody under the writ of habeas corpus (*Cox* v. *Hakes*[34]).

The Administration of Justice Act 1960, s.15, provides that an appeal

---

[26] Lord Goddard. "A Note on Habeas Corpus" (1949) 65 L.Q.R. 30 *Cf.* D. M. Gordon, "The Unruly Writ of Habeas Corpus" (1963) 26 M.L.R. 520.

[27] *Cox* v. *Hakes* (1890) 15 App.Cas. 506 (H.L.), *per* Lord Halsbury L.C.; *Eshugbayi (Eleko)* v. *Government of Nigeria (Officer Administering)* [1928] A.C. 459 (P.C.), *per* Lord Hailsham L.C.; and see [1931] A.C. 662; *Home Secretary* v. *O'Brien* [1923] A.C. 603 (H.L.), *per* Lord Birkenhead L.C. These dicta were disapproved *obiter* by the Irish Supreme Court in *The State (Dowling)* v. *Kingston (No. 2)* [1937] I.R. 699; see R. F. V. Heuston, "Habeas Corpus Procedure" (1950) 66 L.Q.R. 79.

[28] *Re Hastings (No. 1)* [1958] 1 W.L.R. 372 (D.C.); *(No. 2)* [1959] 1 Q.B. 358 (D.C.); *(No. 3)* [1959] 1 All E.R. 698 (D.C.); [1959] Ch. 368 (C.A.).

[29] See *Ex p. Le Gros* (1914) 30 T.L.R. 249 for an unsuccessful attempt to apply to the Lord Chief Justice alone.

[30] In effect, application for habeas corpus can no longer be made to the Lord Chancellor as he is not liable to serve as vacation judge: *Re Kray* [1965] Ch. 736 (Lord Gardiner L.C.).

[31] Heuston, *Essays in Constitutional Law* (2nd ed.), p. 127.

[32] *Ex p. Woodhall* (1888) 20 Q.B.D. 832 (C.A.); see *per* Lindley L.J. at p. 838.

[33] [1943] A.C. 147 (H.L.), *per* Viscount Simon L.C.

[34] (1890) 15 App.Cas. 506 (H.L.).

shall lie in criminal as well as civil applications for habeas corpus, and that the appeal may be brought against an order for release as well as against the refusal of such an order.[35] In civil cases appeal lies through the Court of Appeal to the House of Lords. In criminal cases the appeal lies direct from the Divisional Court to the House of Lords.[36] It is not necessary to obtain a certificate that a point of law of general public importance is involved. Proceedings under Extradition Acts and Fugitive Offenders Acts, and for breaches of regulations under Immigration Acts, are classed as criminal.[37] Deportation cases generally are classed as civil.

A Divisional Court which has granted an application for habeas corpus in a criminal case can order the applicant's detention or release on bail pending an appeal; but if no such order is made (*i.e.* if he has been released without bail) he may not be detained again if the appeal in the House of Lords goes against him. Where an application for habeas corpus has been granted in a civil case, the applicant may not in any event be detained again if the appeal goes against him, the right of appeal in such cases being to enable questions of law to be settled by the House of Lords.

Habeas Corpus to places overseas

The old rule, as stated by Lord Mansfield, was that a writ of habeas corpus could be issued out of England to any part of the dominions of the King of England. The writ did not lie to Scotland or the Electorate of Hanover.[38] It did, however, lie to the Isle of Man[39] and the Channel Islands.[40]

The Habeas Corpus Act 1862,[41] now provides that no writ of habeas corpus shall issue out of England into any "colony or foreign dominion of the Crown" where a court has been established with authority to issue the writ and to ensure due execution thereof. The expression "foreign dominion of the Crown" is obscure. It cannot have been meant to apply to protectorates because there were none at that time. Cockburn C.J.[42] suggested that it meant a country which had once formed part of the dominions of a foreign state, but which had been acquired by the Crown by conquest or cession.

---

[35] See *e.g. R.* v. *Metropolitan Police Commissioner, ex p. Hammond* [1965] A.C. 810 (H.L.).
[36] Administration of Justice Act 1960, s.1.
[37] *Ex p. Woodhall; Amand* v. *Home Secretary and Minister of Defence of the Royal Netherlands Government, ante.*
[38] *R.* v. *Cowle* (1759) 2 Burr., 834, 855–856.
[39] *Re Crawford* (1849) 13 Q.B. 613.
[40] *Carus Wilson's Case* (1845) 7 Q.B. 984.
[41] The Act was passed as a result of the case of *ex p. Anderson* (1861) 3 El & El 487 in which the British and Foreign Anti-Slavery Committee successfully applied to the Court of Queen's Bench for habeas corpus on behalf of Anderson, a negro slave who, after killing Seneca T. P. Diggs in defence of his freedom, had escaped from the United States into the colony of Upper Canada where he was arrested. The court, however, indicated that it thought the issue of the writ to a self-governing colony was inconvenient, unnecessary and *infra dignitatem.* (In subsequent proceedings in Canada it was held that there was no evidence for a charge of murder according to the law of Canada: hence the attempt to extradite him to the United States failed.) For a full account of the facts see *Annual Register,* 1861, pp. 520–528.
[42] *Ex p. Brown* (1864) 5 B. & S. 280.

In *Ex p. Mwenya*[43] the applicant, who was assumed to be a British subject by virtue of citizenship of Rhodesia and Nyasaland applied to a Divisional Court in England for a writ of habeas corpus against the Secretary of State for the Colonies,[44] the Governor and the District Commissioner on the ground that he was unlawfully confined to the Mporokoso district in Northern Rhodesia, then a British protectorate. His contentions that the Order in Council setting up a High Court in Northern Rhodesia was invalid and that his confinement was sufficient for the application, were accepted for the sake of argument. The Court of Appeal held that the jurisdiction of the English court to issue the writ of habeas corpus to territories outside England was not limited to "colonies or foreign dominions" strictly so called, but extended to territories which, having regard to the extent of the dominion in fact exercised, could be said to be "under the subjection of the Crown" and in which the issue of the writ would be regarded as "proper and efficient." This did not necessarily mean that the writ would run in *any* protectorate. The case was inconclusive, because Mwenya was in fact released.

English Courts have no jurisdiction to issue habeas corpus on behalf of persons detained in Northern Ireland. In *Re Keenan*[45] the Court of Appeal held that the effect of the Habeas Corpus Act (Ireland) 1782 was to confer exclusive jurisdiction on the Irish Courts and nothing in the subsequent constitutional history of Ireland had affected that position.

It is doubtful whether habeas corpus can be issued to bring before the Queen's Bench Division an alien in a British ship on the high seas.[46]

Prisoner's rights

"A convicted prisoner . . . retains all civil rights which are not taken away expressly or by necessary implication": *Raymond* v. *Honey*.[47] Examples of rights being taken away expressly are provided by the Representation of the People Act 1983, s.3(1) ("A convicted person during the time that he is detained in a penal institution in pursuance of his sentence is legally incapable of voting at any parliamentary or local government election"); the Representation of the People Act 1981, s.1 ("A person found guilty of one or more offences . . . and sentenced or ordered to be imprisoned indefinitely or for more than one year, shall be disqualified for membership of the House of Commons while detained anywhere in the British Islands or the Republic of Ireland in pursuance of the sentence or order or while unlawfully at large at a time when he would otherwise be so detained") and the Juries Act 1974, s.1, Sched. 1, Part II which disqualifies from jury service any person (i) who has been sentenced in the United Kingdom, the Channel Islands or the

---

[43] [1960] 1 Q.B. 214. See notes by E. C. S. Wade in [1960] C.L.J. 1; L. J. Blom-Cooper in (1960) 23 M.L.R. 73; R. F. V. Heuston in (1960) 75 L.Q.R. 25; and G. I. A. D. Draper in (1960) 76 L.Q.R. 211. And *cf. R.* v. *Earl of Crewe, ex p. Sekgome* [1910] 2 K.B. 576 (C.A.).

[44] The Court of Appeal did not decide whether the Secretary of State had "control" over Mwenya.

[45] [1972] 1 Q.B. 533. *Cf.* D. E. C. Yale, "Habeas Corpus—Ireland—jurisdiction," (1972) 30 C.L.J. 4.

[46] *R.* v. *Secretary of State for Foreign Affairs, ex p. Greenberg* [1947] 2 All E.R. 550.

[47] [1983] A.C. 1, 10, *per* Lord Wilberforce.

Isle of Man to imprisonment for life or for a period of five years or more or to be detained during Her Majesty's pleasure, or (ii) within the previous ten years has served any part of a sentence of imprisonment or detention of three years or more or has been detained in a borstal institution.

The right of which a prisoner is most obviously deprived is that of freedom of movement. Once sentenced he is liable to be detained in prison until the expiration of his sentence, subject to the control of the Secretary of State within the limits laid down by the Prison Act 1952 and the Prison Rules made under that Act. Attempts to question the Home Secretary's wide powers of control with regard to the conditions and place of detention (s.47, *infra* and s.12) have met with little success. An action claiming that the conditions of detention constituted false imprisonment failed in *Williams* v. *Home Office (No. 2)*[48] where Tudor Evans J. and, on appeal, Brightman L.J. expressed the view that, even if the detention were in breach of Prison Rules that would not in itself give rise to a cause of action. In *R.* v. *Secretary of State for the Home Department, ex p. McAvoy*,[49] Webster J. refused to interfere with a decision of the Home Secretary to remove the applicant, who was detained in custody pending trial, from one prison to another. The power granted under section 12 was very wide and the court could not examine a decision made under the section for "operational and security reasons." The learned judge nonetheless asserted that decisions under section 12 were "reviewable in principle" and the court could interfere if the Secretary of State could be shown to have misdirected himself in law.

A prisoner may be released before the end of the sentence laid down by the court which convicted him either because he has earned remission for good conduct[50] or because he has been granted parole by the Secretary of State.[51] In *O'Reilly* v. *Mackman*[52] the House of Lords emphasised that a prisoner has no *right* to remission; he does, however, have a *legitimate expectation*, recognised by public law, that the procedures followed in determining questions relating to remission will be fair. In *Re Findlay*[53] the House of Lords held, similarly, that a prisoner seeking parole had no more than a legitimate expectation that his application would be examined individually in the light of the policy adopted at any time by the Secretary of State. He had no right (or even legitimate expectation) that the policy would not be changed from time to time.

The Prison Act 1952, s.47 authorises the Secretary of State to make rules for "the classification, treatment, employment, discipline and control of" prisoners. The validity of such rules is open to challenge on the ground that they are *ultra vires, i.e.* beyond the limits of the power delegated to the minister by Parliament.[54] In *R.* v. *Secretary of State for the*

---

[48] [1981] 1 All E.R. 1211; [1982] 2 All E.R. 564 (C.A.).
[49] [1984] 1 W.L.R. 1408.
[50] Prison Act 1952, s.25.
[51] Criminal Justice Act 1967, s.59. See also Criminal Justice Act 1972, s.35.
[52] [1983] 2 A.C. 237 (H.L.); *post*, Part VI, Introduction and Chap. 34.
[53] [1985] A.C. 318; *post*, Part VI, Introduction and Chap. 34.
[54] *Post*, Chap. 33.

Home Department, ex p. Anderson[55] a restriction on visits by a legal adviser to a prisoner contemplating legal proceedings in respect of complaints about treatment in prison which he had not also made through the internal prison procedure was held to be *ultra vires* because it conflicted with the right of unimpeded access to the courts, a right so fundamental that it could only be taken away by express language.

The enforcement of discipline is the responsibility of the Governor and of the Board of Visitors. The Governor is empowered under the Prison Rules to punish offences against discipline with various sentences including the loss of not more than 28 days remission. The Board of Visitors is intended to be an independent, supervisory body which oversees conditions in the prison for which it is responsible. The Board also has a disciplinary function, with more extensive powers than the governor. They may, among other punishments, order the loss of not more than 180 days remission.

The Courts are unwilling to interfere with decisions taken by a prison governor. He is performing, on behalf of the Home Secretary, a "management function" and a dissatisfied prisoner should exercise his right of complaint to the Board of Visitors and, subsequently, if necessary, petition the Home Secretary: *R. v. Deputy Governor of Camphill Prison, ex p. King*.[56] The Court of Appeal was, however, prepared to allow judicial review where a governor's conduct was alleged to amount to the infliction of cruel and unusual punishment under the Bill of Rights: *R. v. Secretary of State for the Home Department ex. p.* Herbage (No. 2).[56a] The Board of Visitors has on the other hand, been recognised since *R. v. Board of Visitors of Hull Prison, ex p. St. Germain*[57] as exercising a judicial function and its procedure is subject to judicial review.

With the passing of the Crown Proceedings Act 1947 there has no longer been any bar to a prisoner suing the Home Secretary for injuries which he has suffered in prison. Prison staff have been held to be under a duty to take reasonable care for the safety of their prisoners which extends to protecting them from attacks by fellow inmates[58] and to providing appropriate equipment to prisoners undertaking dangerous work.[59] In *Freeman* v. *Home Office* (No. 2)[60] a prisoner brought an action in trespass, alleging that medical treatment had been given to him without his consent. The Court of Appeal upheld the conclusions of the trial judge that, on the facts, consent had been given and, on the law, that a prisoner could give a genuine consent to treatment, despite the pressures which the court recognised that he might be under in the setting of a prison. Whether in any circumstances treatment can be given against

---

[55] [1984] Q.B. 778 (D.C.).

[56] [1985] Q.B. 735 (C.A.).

[56a] [1987] 2 W.L.R. 226.

[57] [1979] Q.B. 425 (C.A.). See also *R.* v. *Blunderston Prison Board of Visitors, ex p. Fox-Taylor* [1982] 1 All E.R. 646; *R.* v. *Secretary of State for the Home Department, ex p. Tarrant* [1985] Q.B. 251 (D.C.); *R.* v. *Board of Visitors of Pentonville Prison, ex p. Rutherford, The Times,* June 17, 1985.

[58] *Ellis* v. *Home Office* [1953] 2 Q.B. 135 (C.A.).

[59] *Morgan* v. *Att.-Gen.* [1965] N.Z.L.R., 134; *Ferguson* v. *Home Office, The Times,* October 8, 1977.

[60] [1984] Q.B. 524.

a prisoner's consent remains unclear. In *Freeman* McCowan J. quoted from the *Report on the Work of the Prison Department* for 1979 which disclaimed any statutory authority to treat prisoners against their consent but went on to claim a right to treat without consent where, without treatment, "his life would be endangered, serious harm to the prisoner or others would be likely, or there would be irreversible deterioration in his condition." A duty to treat a prisoner even against his wishes was asserted by Lord Alverstone L.C.J. in his direction to the jury in *Leigh* v. *Gladstone*[61] when a suffragette who had been forcibly fed while in prison sought damages for assault and an injunction against the Home Secretary, the prison governor and the prison doctor. The Lord Chief Justice said that "It was the duty, both under the rules and apart from the rules, of the officials to preserve the health and lives of the prisoners, who were in the custody of the Crown." If the Lord Chief Justice's direction correctly represents the law a prison doctor must, for example, order the forcible feeding of a prisoner who refuses to eat if, in the doctor's medical judgment, such treatment is necessary to save life. Thus the announcement by Mr. Jenkins, then Home Secretary, in 1974, of the ending of forcible feeding in British prisons would mean no more than that the decision was in the future a purely medical one. Doctors need no longer act, if they formerly had done, on the basis that forcible feeding was required by the Home Secretary.[62] A limited statutory recognition of a right to submit prisoners to medical examination against their consent is to be found in section 17 of the Prison Act 1952 which forbids a medical officer of a prison to apply any "painful tests" to a prisoner for the purpose of detecting malingering or for any other purpose except with the permission of the Secretary of State or the visiting committee or the board of visitors.

During their detention prisoners are subjected to restrictions on their rights to communicate with legal advisers and bring actions against prison staff, for obvious reasons.[63] The legality of these restrictions have been the subject matter of litigation before the European Court of Human Rights[64] and the English Courts.[65] As a result of these decisions restrictions on correspondence with legal advisers has been considerably modified.

Further reform is foreshadowed by the report of a Home Office Departmental Committee on the Prison Disciplinary System which recommends the establishment of independent tribunals to take over the disciplinary functions of the Boards of Visitors and the removal of the two offences of mutiny and assault on prison officers from the internal disciplinary code to be dealt with as criminal offences by the Crown

---

[61] (1909) 26 T.L.R. 139.

[62] See further G. Zellick, "The Forcible Feeding of Prisoners: An Examination of the Legality of Enforced Therapy" [1976] P.L. 152.

[63] "If the courts were to entertain actions by disgruntled prisoners, the governor's life would be made intolerable"; *Becker* v. *Home Office* [1972] 2 Q.B. 407, 418 *per* Lord Denning M.R.

[64] *Golder* v. *U.K.* (1975) 1 E.H.R.R. 524; *Silver* v. *U.K.* (1980) 3 E.H.R.R. 475; *Campbell and Fell* v. *U.K.* (1985) 7 E.H.R.R. 165; [1984] P.L. 341.

[65] *Raymond* v. *Honey* [1983] A.C. 1; *R.* v. *Secretary of State for the Home Department, ex p. Anderson* [1984] Q.B. 778.

Court.[66] A report from a committee of Justice,[67] chaired by Sir Brian McKenna, calls for a recognition of prisoners' rights to adequate accommodation and, as far as possible, a full and normal life. It recommends the appointment of a Prisoners' Ombudsman[68] and the transfer of disciplinary functions from the Boards of Visitors to magistrates sitting at prisons.

Privacy

Privacy is a vague term[69] and it may be for that reason that English judges regularly affirm that no such general right is known to English law.[70] Nonetheless, many specific rules of the common law clearly protect individuals from intrusion on their private lives and to some extent give them control over public use of what they (and the law) regard as private information. (It might be said to be the absence of legal rules that protects the privacy of religious belief.)

The law of trespass prohibits physical intrusion but embarrassing or distressing surveillance which does not constitute trespass will not be tortious unless possibly it constitutes a nuisance.[71] There is no right not to be photographed and no right to prevent a photograph being used, for example, in an advertising campaign unless the law of copyright is infringed or the law of libel can be invoked.[72] The civil law of defamation does not give a remedy for distress or financial loss caused by telling the truth about someone although protection may be afforded by the criminal law of libel because in the latter case truth is no defence to a charge unless the accused can establish that publication was in the public interest.[73] The Rehabilitation of Offenders Act 1974 also restricts the telling of the truth, forbidding the publication of details of "spent" convictions and entitling convicted persons to deny, in certain circumstances, their criminal records. The law of confidential information affords a remedy against the misuse of business secrets or the publication of the intimacies of the marriage bed.[74]

Concern about possible invasions of privacy arising from the increasing use of computers and the ease with which people can be kept under surveillance by modern electronic devices has led to the publication of

---

[66] (1985), Cmnd. 9641–1; Clive Lewis, the Prior Report on the Prison Disciplinary System [1986] P.L. 213.

[67] *Justice in Prison* (1983).

[68] Such an office was created in Canada in 1973: see the Annual Reports of the Correctional Investigator. *Post*, 653 *et seq.*

[69] R. Wacks, "Privacy" *of* 'Privacy' " (1980) 96 L.Q.R. 73; *The Protection of Privacy* (1980). The earlier literature begins with the article of S. Warren and L. Brandeis, "The Right to Privacy," (1890) 4 Harv.L.R. 193. See too P. H. Winfield, "Privacy" (1931) 47 L.Q.R. 23.

[70] *Bernstein v. Skyviews and General Ltd.* [1978] Q.B. 479; *Malone v. Metropolitan Police Commissioner* [1979] Ch. 344.

[71] *Bernstein v. Skyviews and General Ltd., supra.* See too *Victoria Park Racing and Recreation Grounds Co. Ltd. v. Taylor* (1938) 58 C.L.R. 479. (No remedy where broadcasting from adjoining property deprived owner of race course of chance of selling broadcasting rights).

[72] T. Fraser, "Appropriation of Personality" (1983) 99 L.Q.R. 281.

[73] *Post*, p. 534.

[74] *Seager v. Copydex* [1967] 2 All E.R. 415 (C.A.); *Schering Chemicals Ltd. v. Falkman Ltd.* [1982] Q.B. 1 (C.A.); *Argyll (Duchess) v. Argyll (Duke)* [1967] Ch. 302; *post,* Chap. 26.

two reports, a Government White Paper[75] and the two statutes to be considered on the following pages.

Data Protection Act 1984[76]

In addition to providing protection against any threat to privacy posed by the rapid growth in the use of computers the Act was passed to give effect to the Council of Europe Data Protection Convention.

"Data" is defined to mean information recorded in a form in which it can be processed by equipment operating automatically in response to instructions given for that purpose (s.1(2)). The Act, therefore, has no application to information recorded on conventional files, cards and medical case-sheets. "Personal data" means information as defined in the section which relates to a living individual who can be identified from that information, or from that information and other information in the possession of the data user, that is the person who controls the contents and use of a collection of data (subss.(3) and (5)). Section 2 and Sched. 1 set out data protection principles which apply to personal data and are meant to protect individuals against the misuse of data information and the recording of inaccurate information. The seventh principle entitles an individual to be informed by any data user whether he holds personal data of which that individual is the subject, to access to any such data and, where appropriate, to have such data corrected or erased. The principles also include an obligation to take appropriate security measures against unauthorised access to personal data.

Data users and computer bureaux (that is persons who provide services for others in connection with the arranging and holding of data) are required by section 4 to obtain registration on a public register which is maintained by the Data Protection Registrar (s.3). The Registrar is responsible for ensuring that registered data users observe the data protection principles. Where he is satisfied that a data user is not observing the principles he may serve an "enforcement notice" and ultimately take steps to remove his name from the register. A data user may appeal against the issuing of a notice and a threat to remove to the Data Protection Tribunal, established by section 3.

Any person who holds personal data while not registered shall be guilty of an offence under section 5(1). Any registered person who knowingly or recklessly holds personal data of any description other than that specified in his entry in the public register shall be guilty of an offence under section 5(2). Other offences relate to improper disclosure of data and breaches of section 5 by servants or agents of data users. Prosecutions in England and Wales for offences under the Act must be brought by the Registrar or with the consent of the Director of Public Prosecutions.

The Act creates a right of access to personal data on the part of data subjects (s.21) and a right to compensation for loss caused by the recording of inaccurate information and for distress suffered by reason

---

[75] *Report of the Committee on Privacy* (1972, Cmnd. 5012) (the Younger Committee); *Computers and Privacy* (1975, Cmnd. 6353); *Report of the Committee on Data Protection* (1978, Cmnd. 7341) (the Lindop Committee).

[76] R. C. Austin, "The Data Protection Act 1984: The Public Law Implications" [1984] P.L. 618; B. Niblett, *Data Protection Act 1984*.

of the inaccuracy (s.22). Damage caused by the loss, destruction or improper disclosure of personal data also gives rise to a right to compensation (s.23). Jurisdiction is given to the courts to order the rectification of inaccurate data or, where appropriate, its erasure (s.24).

Various categories of data are exempt from the right of access conferred by section 21 and to differing degrees from control by the Registrar. There is, for example, no right of access to data which a Cabinet Minister, the Attorney General or the Lord Advocate certifies to require exemption in the interests of national security. Such data is also exempt from all the other provisions of the Act. Data relating to the prevention and detection of crime are exempt from the right of access and from the first data protection principle requiring data to be obtained and processed fairly and lawfully (s.28(4)). Complete exemption from the Act is given to data held by an individual and concerned only with the management of his personal, family or household affairs and to other categories such as personal data held by unincorporated members' clubs (s.33). Data relating to the making of judicial appointments or protected by the law relating to legal professional privilege are exempt from the right of access (s.31). Data consisting of information on the physical or mental health of the data subject may be withheld by order of the Secretary of State (s.29) as may information held for the purpose of discharging statutory functions in connection with the protection of the public from loss caused by fraud or incompetence in the provision of banking, insurance and other financial services (s.30).

The Act applies to government departments and, for the purposes of the Act each department shall be treated as a separate entity from any other department and a person in the public service of the Crown shall be treated as a servant of the department to which his duties relate. Government departments are not, however, liable to prosecution under the Act although civil servants who infringe its terms are (s.38).

Interception of Communications Act 1985

The immediate occasion of the Interception of Communications Act 1985 was the decision of Sir Robert Megarry V.-C. in *Malone* v. *Metropolitan Police Commissioner*[77] that English law did not prevent the tapping of telephones by public authorities on the authority of a warrant from the Home Secretary. The subject was, however, in the view of the judge one "which cries out for legislation." Subsequently the European Court of Human Rights held that the absence of legal controls over the circumstances in which warrants could be issued was incompatible with the recognition given by Article 8 of the Convention to the right to respect for private and family life, home and correspondence subject only to interference in accordance with law and necessary in a democratic society in the interests of national security, public safety, the economic well being of the country, for the prevention of disorder or crime, the protection of health or morals, or for the protection of the rights and freedoms of others.[78]

The legality of telephone tapping and the interception of items sent

[77] [1979] Ch. 344.
[78] (1985) 7 E.H.R.R. 14.

through the post had been a matter of controversy for some years before *Malone*. In 1957 a report of a Committee of Privy Councillors, chaired by Lord Birkett,[79] recommended that communications should only be intercepted either to detect serious crime or to safeguard the security of the state, and that material obtained by interception should not be made available to anyone outside the public service. The Committee also recommended certain other safeguards which were accepted by the Government, namely, that such warrants should be individual, specific and temporary, that a regular review should be made and that full records should be kept at the Home Office.

The legal basis for the right to intercept communications, whether with or without warrant, could be found, if at all, in the royal prerogative. The Post Office had originated as a part of the Crown which explained, and explains, its unusual legal position.[80] Statutes which created offences relating to the interception of postal packets and interference with telephones recognised that persons prosecuted could plead a warrant issued by the Secretary of State as a defence but the legality of issuing such warrants was not expressly authorised.[81]

Following the decision of the Vice-Chancellor in the *Malone* case the Government announced that it did not intend to introduce legislation but would designate a judge to monitor the system.[82] The sequel, however, to the decision of the European Court's decision was the Interception of Communications Act 1985.[83]

Section 1 of the Act creates an offence of unlawfully intercepting a communication sent by post or by means of a public telecommunication system, being punishable by fine or a maximum of two years imprisonment or both. It is a defence to a charge under section 1 that the interception was authorised by a warrant issued under section 2. Such a warrant shall only be issued if the Secretary of State considers it necessary in the interests of national security, for the purpose of preventing or detecting serious crime[84] or for the purpose of safeguarding the economic well-being of the United Kingdom.[85] A warrant must be issued under the hand of the Secretary of State or, in an urgent case where the Secretary of State has expressly authorised its issue and a statement of

---

[79] *Report of the Committee of Privy Councillors appointed to enquire into the interception of Communications* (1957) Cmnd. 283.

   The Committee criticised the conduct of the Home Secretary in disclosing intercepted information to the Bar Council and the Benchers of Lincoln's Inn in connection with the case of *Re Marrinan, The Times*, June 28, 29; July 2, 4; October 3, 1957.

[80] *Post*, p. 000.

[81] Post Office Act 1953, s.58; Post Office Act 1969, Sched. 5, para. 1(1).

[82] Cmnd. 7873 (1980); H.C.Deb. April 1, 1980 col. 205.

[83] *The Interception of Communications in the United Kingdom* (1985, Cmnd. 9438); I. Lloyd, "The Interception of Communications Act 1985" (1986) 49 M.L.R. 86; I. Leigh, "A Tapper's Charter?" [1986] P.L. 8.

[84] Serious crime is defined by s.11(3) as
   (a) involving the use of violence or resulting in substantial gain or conduct by a large number of persons in pursuit of a common purpose; or
   (b) an offence for which a person who has attained the age of 21 and has no previous convictions could reasonably be expected to be sentenced to imprisonment for a term of three years or more.

[85] In this category the warrant is likely to be granted by the Foreign Secretary and not the Home Secretary.

that fact is endorsed thereon, under the hand of an official of his department of or above the rank of Assistant Under Secretary of State.[86] (Such a warrant is valid for a period of two days only.) A warrant under the hand of the Secretary of State is valid for two months and may be renewed for a maximum period of six months in cases involving national security and economic well-being and for a period of one month on the case of criminal investigations (s.4). The Secretary of State is directed by section 6 to take steps to ensure that intercepted material not covered by a warrant is not seen or heard by any person, that the number of people who have access to material is kept to a minimum and that material intercepted is destroyed as soon as its detention is no longer required for the purpose for which a warrant had been issued.

Any person who believes that communications sent to him or by him have been unlawfully intercepted may apply to the Tribunal established by section 7. The Tribunal will investigate whether a warrant has been issued and, if so, the relevant terms of the Act have been observed. If there has been a breach the Tribunal shall inform the complainant, report to the Prime Minister and it may quash the warrant, direct the destruction of intercepted material and the payment of compensation. If the Tribunal concludes that no warrant has been issued they shall inform the complainant that there has been no breach of the provisions of the Act regulating interception by warrant. A complainant in such circumstances must rely on the police to establish unlawful interception under section 1.

The Tribunal is given exclusive jurisdiction in the domain of the Act by a remarkable provision which forbids the adducing of evidence or the asking of questions before any court or tribunal (other than that established by the Act) which tends to suggest that any interception of communications has taken place by any person holding office under the Crown, by the Post Office and any person engaged in the business of the Post Office and any public telecommunications operator and any person engaged in running a public telecommunications operator (s.9).

A general supervisory role in relation to the working of the Act is assigned by section 8 to a Commissioner (who must be a judge), appointed by the Prime Minister.

The Act does not apply to electronic surveillance[87] by means, for example, of long range microphones or infra red cameras. The inability of the Tribunal to deal with interceptions effected without warrant is open to criticism. The decisions of the Tribunal, including any as to its own jurisdiction, are not subject to appeal or liable to be questioned in any court.[88] Information supplied to the Tribunal in its investigations is not to be revealed to the complainant without the consent of the person supplying it and no reasons shall be given for their conclusions (Sched. 1(4)).

Freedom of Religion

An aspect of privacy of interest to all citizens, not merely the few suspected criminals and terrorists whose telephones may be tapped, is the

---

[86] Such an express provision is unusual in statutes: *post*, p. 675.

[87] C. P. Walker, "Police Surveillance by Technical Devices" [1980] P.L. 184.

[88] Another remarkable provision: *post*, p. 695.

freedom of religious belief: a freedom which has been bitterly disputed in this country as in others in earlier centuries.

The law no longer concerns itself with citizens' religious beliefs. The monarch, however, is still prohibited by the Act of Settlement 1701 from being reconciled to or holding communion with the See or Church of Rome or professing the Popish religion or marrying a Papist.[89] On accession the monarch "shall joyn in Communion with the Church of England as by Law established" and swear to maintain both the Church of England and the Church of Scotland.[90] Any doubts about restrictions on the religious beliefs of the Lord Chancellor were removed by the Lord Chancellor (Tenure of Office and Discharge of Ecclesiastical Functions) Act 1974.[91]

Freedom of belief does not, however, give a right to disregard the law of the land. To withhold medical treatment from a child may be manslaughter whatever the religious views of the parents: R. v. Senior.[92] Religious belief would not constitute a defence to a charge under the Prohibition of Female Circumcision Act 1985. Indeed that Act while recognising a defence based on medical grounds expressly provides that no account is to be taken of any belief "that the operation is required as a matter of custom or ritual" (s.2(2)). Only exceptionally does Parliament take account of religious beliefs in framing legislation. Sikhs, for example, are exempt from the necessity of wearing crash helmets when riding motor cycles[93] and the general rules regulating the slaughter of animals and poultry do not apply to slaughter in accordance with Jewish and Moslem religious beliefs.[94] The Abortion Act 1967, s.4, recognises a right not to participate in treatment authorised by that Act on the ground of "conscientious objection," a plea which may extend beyond religious belief.[95]

---

[89] Any right of succession to the throne is subject to a similar restriction; ante, p. 255.

[90] On the legal position of the Church of England see ante, p. 158 and p. 272; post, p. 536. On the Church of Scotland see T. B. Smith, A Short Commentary on the Law of Scotland (1962) p. 72 et seq.

[91] Where the Lord Chancellor is an "adherent of the Roman Catholic faith" Her Majesty may provide for his religious functions and powers of patronage to be performed by the Prime Minister or any other Minister.

[92] [1899] 1 Q.B. 283.

[93] Motor-Cycle Crash-Helmets (Religious Exemption) Act 1976. The Act exempts "any follower of the Sikh religion while he is wearing a turban." Who can claim to be a follower of the Sikh religion? Quaere Sikhs wearing turbans on cultural (ethnic?) but not religious grounds?

[94] Slaughter of Poultry Act 1967, s.1(2). Slaughterhouses Act 1974, s.36(3). The Shops Act 1950, s.53 allows a shopkeeper "of the Jewish religion" to apply for permission to local authorities to open a shop on Sundays in lieu of Saturdays if he can establish that he "conscientiously objects on religious grounds" to trading on Saturdays. See R. v. London Committee of Deputies of British Jews, ex p. Helmcourt Ltd., The Times, July 16, 1981 (C.A.).

[95] In the United Kingdom legislation on military service has usually exempted anyone who "conscientiously objects": e.g. National Service Act 1948, s.17. See Sir Carleton Kemp Allen, Administrative Jurisdiction (1956) p. 27 ("This branch of judicature . . . is perhaps of more interest to the psychologist and the theologian than to the lawyer.") The right to refuse to join a union, if on the grounds of "conscience or other deeply held conviction," receives statutory recognition and protection by the Employment Protection (Consolidation) Act 1978, s.58, as amended by the Employment Act 1982, s.3.

Except in Northern Ireland[96] the law does not forbid religious discrimination in the fields of employment, education, and the provision of services to the public.[97] The British Nationality Act 1981, s.44 requires that powers rested by the Act in the Secretary of State shall be exercised with regard to race, colour or religion. The Courts continue to accept that interests under trusts may be made conditional on adherence to a particular religious faith.[98]

II. FREEDOM OF PROPERTY

The Englishman's castle

"The house of every one is to him as is his castle and fortress, as well for his defence against injury and violence, as for his repose," it was said in *Seymayne's Case*[99]: "if thieves come to a man's house to rob him, or murder him, and the owner or his servants kill any of the thieves in defence of himself and his house, it is not felony, and he shall lose nothing. So it is held every one may assemble his friends and neighbours to defend his house against violence . . . because *domus sua cuique est tutissimum refugium.*" "By the laws of England," said Lord Camden C.J. in *Entick* v. *Carrington,*[1] "every invasion of private property, be it ever so minute, is a trespass. No man can set his foot upon my ground without my licence. . . . If he admits the fact, he is bound to show by way of justification, that some positive law has empowered or excused him." More recently Donaldson L.J. has said, "That 'An Englishman's home is his castle' is one of the few principles of law known to every citizen and was affirmed as early as 1604 in *Seymayne's Case* . . . and reaffirmed as recently as 1980 in *Morris* v. *Beardmore* [1981] A.C. 446. The rule is, of course, subject to exceptions, but they are few and it is for the police to justify a forcible entry."[2]

Trespass, even to a dwelling house, is not a crime at common law; a rule to which public attention was drawn in 1982 when an intruder was found in the Queen's bedroom at Buckingham Palace. In practice, of course, juries are unlikely to believe that a trespasser found in a dwelling did not possess the intent required by section 9 of the Theft Act 1968 to turn his entry into the offence of burglary.

Forcible entry, as by violence or breaking open doors or windows and forcible retainer, which had probably been common law offences, were made indictable by the Forcible Entry Acts 1381 to 1623. All these Acts

---

[96] Fair Employment (Northern Ireland) Act 1976.
[97] Unless a particular prohibition might be regarded as constituting indirect racial discrimination: *ante*, p. 440.
[98] *Blathwayt* v. *Baron Cawley* [1976] A.C. 397; *Re Tuck's Settlement Trusts* [1978] Ch. 49 (C.A.). In the case of charitable trusts religious restrictions may be removed under the cy près jurisdiction where, for example, an educational institution to which funds have been bequeathed feels that such restrictions would hamper the efficacy of the gift: *Re Lysaght* [1966] Ch. 191 (Royal College of Surgeons unwilling to accept scholarships which were not to be available to men of the Jewish or Roman Catholic Faith).
[99] (1603) 5 Co.Rep. 91, 91b. The maximum was anticipated by Staunford, *Plees del Coron* (1567) "*ma meason est a moy come mon castel.*" Cf. D.2.4.21: *de domo sua nemo extrahi debet.* "A man's home is looked upon as his castle"; Hawkins, *Pleas of the Crown*, Bk 1. C. 28, s.10; quoted by Cave J. in *Beatty* v. *Gillbanks* (1882) 15 Cox C.C. 138.
[1] (1765) 19 St.Tr. 1029, 1066.
[2] *McLorie* v. *Oxford* [1982] Q.B. 1290.

were repealed by the Criminal Law Act 1977 which makes it an offence for a person (not being a displaced residential occupier) without lawful authority to use or threaten violence for the purpose of securing entry into premises on which to his knowledge someone is present who is opposed to the entry (s.6). Section 7, dealing with adverse occupation of residential premises, affects squatters. A person who is on premises as a trespasser, after having entered as a trespasser, is guilty of an offence if he fails to leave the premises on being required to do so by or on behalf of a displaced residential occupier or a protected intending occupier.[3] It is also an offence to trespass on premises with a weapon of offence (s.8) and to enter or to be on premises of a diplomatic or consular mission as a trespasser (s.9).[4]

Concern in the summer of 1986 about "hippy-convoys" trespassing on farm land in the South West of England has led to the inclusion of a new offence in the Public Order Act 1986.[5]

Police Powers of entry and search[6]

The powers of police officers to enter premises to arrest or search are now governed by statute. The Police and Criminal Evidence Act 1984 Part II lays down general rules while various statutes confer specific powers in particular circumstances.

Common law powers to enter premises without a warrant are abolished with the exception of any power of entry to deal with or prevent a breach of peace (s.17(5) and (6)). The modern authority for such a power is *Thomas* v. *Sawkins*[7] where the Divisional Court held that the police may, without warrant or licence, enter private premises—at least if a public meeting is being held there—in which they have reasonable grounds for believing that an offence (or, at least, a breach of the peace) is likely to be committed. The case is unsatisfactory because the police attended in plain clothes as members of the public, after the licence to the police had been withdrawn. In *Davis* v. *Lisle*[8] a Divisional Court held that the police have no right without a warrant, in connection with a summary offence not involving breach of the peace (in this case, a car obstructing the highway), to enter private premises, or to remain against the owner's wishes on premises into which they are invited to enter.

Section 17 of the Police and Criminal Evidence Act authorises a constable to enter and search any premises for the purpose of (i) executing a

---

[3] An owner or tenant who requires the premises for his own residential occupation, *e.g.* a recent purchaser, a person who has been authorised to occupy a council house, or a returning holiday-maker.

[4] Trespass may also be a criminal offence by virtue of byelaws made, for example, by the British Railways Board: Transport Act 1962, s.67 (as amended).

[5] *Post*, p. 554. It is difficult to see why the police could not have acted on the basis of an apprehended breach of the peace, *infra*. For similar reluctance to act see *R.* v. *Chief Constable of Devon and Cornwall, ex p. C.E.G.B.* [1982] Q.B. 458 (C.A.).

[6] R. Stone, *Entry, Search and Seizure* (1985).

[7] [1935] 2 K.B. 249.

[8] [1936] 2 K.B. 434; approving *Great Central Ry.* v. *Bates* [1921] 3 K.B. 578, *per* Atkin L.J. at p. 582: "nobody has a right to enter premises except strictly in accordance with authority" (L.R. headnote to *Great Central Ry.* v. *Bates* corrected by du Parcq J. at [1936] 2 K.B. 439–440). *Cf. Robson* v. *Hallett* [1967] 2 Q.B. 939 (D.C.).

warrant of arrest issued in connection with or arising out of criminal proceedings; (ii) arresting a person for an arrestable offence; (iii) arresting a person for an offence under the Public Order Act 1986 Section 4 or sections 6 to 8 or 10 of the Criminal Law Act; (iv) recapturing a person unlawfully at large whom he is pursuing; or (v) saving life or limb or preventing serious damage to property. Except in the case of (v) the constable must have reasonable grounds for believing that the person he is seeking is on the premises. The power of search conferred by the section is only a power to the extent that is reasonably required for the purpose for which the power of entry is exercised.

The powers conferred by the section are without prejudice to any existing under other statutes. Various Acts confer specific powers of entry to ensure that their terms are being complied with. The Misuse of Drugs Act 1971, s.23(1) for example empowers police to enter the premises of producers and suppliers of controlled drugs and examine books and documents relating to dealings in such drugs and inspect stocks of such drugs.[9]

Entry and search after arrest

In *McLorie* v. *Oxford*[10] it had been held that there was no common law power to enter premises to search for evidence after a person had been arrested. A power to enter premises to search for evidence has, however been conferred by section 18 where a person has been arrested for an arrestable offence. The constable must have reasonable grounds for suspecting that there is on the premises evidence other than items subject to legal privilege[11] that relates to the offence for which the person has been arrested or to some other arrestable offence connected with or similar to that offence. Anything which the constable is entitled to search for may, if found, be seized and retained. The power (as in s.17) is exercisable only to the extent reasonably required for the purpose of the section. As a general rule a search under section 18 must be authorised in writing by an officer of the rank of inspector or above. A constable may, however, search without authorisation before taking a person to a police station "if the presence of that person at a place other than a police station is necessary for the effective investigation of the offence." Whatever the exact meaning of these words they seem to confer a power to search if the constable thinks it *necessary* (subs.(5)).

Seizure of articles

Section 19 confers a wide power to seize articles found by a constable who is lawfully on premises.[12] It is not necessary that they relate to the offences for which the owner or occupier has been arrested, or other or

---

[9] See also Theatres Act 1968, s.15(3); Gaming Act 1968, s.43(2); Wildlife and Countryside Act 1981, s.19; Cinematograph (Amendment) Act 1982, s.5(1).

[10] [1982] Q.B. 1290. There was a power, of uncertain extent, to seize material if the police were lawfully on premises at the time of the arrest: *Ghani* v. *Jones* [1970] 1 Q.B. 693.

[11] Defined in s.10 to mean communications between a professional legal adviser and his client and items enclosed with or referred to in such communications when in the possession of a person entitled to possession of them but not including items held with the intention of furthering a criminal purpose.

[12] *Foster* v. *Attard*, *The Times*, January 4, 1986. (Entry under particular statute made presence on premises lawful for all purposes.)

similar offences committed by the owner or occupier or that they implicate third parties in the offence for which the search was being conducted.[13] Any article (other than one protected by legal privilege) may be seized if the constable has reasonable grounds for believing that it has been obtained in consequence of the commission of an offence or that it is evidence in relation to an offence which he is investigating or *any other offence*. In both cases the right to seize is conditional on a belief that seizure is necessary to prevent the item being concealed, lost, altered or destroyed or (in the case of articles in the first category) damaged.

Section 21 provides in the case of articles seized under any of the provisions of the 1984 Act or any other enactment rights to be furnished with details of articles seized and subsequent access to them, under police supervision.

Section 22 recognises and regulates the right of police to retain for as long as necessary articles which they have seized.

Search Warrants

It is a principle of the common law that a *general warrant* to search premises, *i.e.* one in which either the person or the property is not specified is illegal. Thus in *Wilkes* v. *Wood* (1763)[14] John Wilkes recovered £1,000 damages for trespass against Wood, an Under-Secretary of State, for entering his house and seizing his papers under a warrant to arrest the (unnamed) authors, printers and publishers of No. 45 of the *North Briton*. In *Entick* v. *Carrington* (1765)[15] Entick, suspected to be the author of the *Monitor, or British Freeholder*, obtained £300 damages for trespass against Carrington and other King's messengers for breaking and entering his house and seizing his books and papers under a general search warrant from the Secretary of State. Lord Camden L.J. delivered a powerful judgment against the legality of such general warrants.

A number of statutes authorise the issue by magistrates of search warrants on sworn information, concerning *e.g.* stolen goods,[16] forged documents,[17] coinage,[18] official secrets,[19] criminal damage,[20] obscene publications[21] and dangerous drugs.[22] Section 24 of the Public Order Act 1986 confers a power on justices to issue warrants to search for "racially inflammatory material," as defined by section 23 of the Act. In certain cases, for example, under the Incitement to Disaffection Act 1934

---

[13] On the previous common law position: *Chic Fashions (West Wales) Ltd.* v. *Jones* [1968] 2 Q.B. 299 (C.A.); *Ghani* v. *Jones* [1969] 3 All E.R. 1700 (C.A.); *Garfinkel* v. *Metropolitan Police Commissioner* [1972] Crim.L.R. 44; *Frank Truman Export Ltd.* v. *Metropolitan Police Commissioner* [1977] Q.B. 952; *Reynolds* v. *Metropolitan Police Commissioner* [1985] Q.B. 811 (C.A.).

[14] 19 St.Tr. 1153.

[15] 19 St.Tr. 1029. See *Dillon* v. *O'Brien and Davis* (1887) 16 Cox C.I. 245, 250 *per* Palles C.B.

[16] Theft Act 1968, s.26.

[17] Forgery and Counterfeiting Act 1981, s.7.

[18] Forgery and Counterfeiting Act 1981, s.24.

[19] Official Secrets Act 1911, s.9; Official Secrets Act 1920, s.1.

[20] Criminal Damage Act 1971, s.6.

[21] Obscene Publications Act 1959 ss.2 and 3; *R.* v. *Adams* [1980] Q.B. 575 (C.A.).

[22] Misuse of Drugs Act 1971, s.23.

a High Court judge may issue a warrant to enter and seize documents, etc. The Finance Act 1976 s.57 empowers a Crown Court judge to issue a search warrant to obtain documents in connection with a suspected tax fraud.

Before the Police and Criminal Evidence Act 1984 there were, however, no general statutory provisions governing the granting of search warrants and there were some remarkable gaps in the array of specific statutory provisions, for example, in the case of murder.[23] Part II of the 1984 Act introduces general provisions in a number of sections which were the subject of acute controversy during their passage through Parliament. Section 8 entitles a justice of the peace to grant a search warrant on the application of a constable when the justice is satisfied that there are reasonable grounds for believing that a serious arrestable offence[24] has been committed and that there is material on the premises described in the application which is likely to be of substantial value to the investigation of the offence. The material must be likely to be relevant evidence (*i.e.* legally admissible) and not consist of items subject to legal privilege, excluded materials or special procedure material. The justice must also be satisfied that it is not practicable to communicate with any person entitled to grant entry to the premises; or that, if practicable it is not practicable to communicate with any person entitled to grant access to evidence; or that entry to the premises will not be granted unless a warrant is produced; or that the purpose of a search may be frustrated or seriously prejudiced unless a constable arriving at the premises can secure immediate entry. A constable may seize and retain anything for which a search has been authorised under the section. The power to issue a warrant is in addition to any other specific statutory provisions. A circuit judge may authorise a search which extends to excluded material and special procedure material under section 9 and Schedule 1.[25]

The scope of items subject to legal privilege is defined in section 10.[26] Excluded material is defined in section 11. It includes personal records acquired in the course of any business or occupation which are held in confidence, medical samples taken for medical purposes held in confidence and journalistic materials held in confidence. Special procedure material is, in effect, confidential papers which fall outside the scope of excluded materials because they are not personal records as defined in section 12 and journalistic material not held in confidence. Into the latter category would fall, for example, photographs taken by newspaper photographers during riots.[27]

General provisions, applicable to the enforcement of search warrants under any enactment are contained in sections 15 and 16. Section 15

---

[23] *Ghani* v. *Jones* [1969] 3 All E.R. 1700, 1702, *per* Lord Denning M.R.

[24] s.116; *ante*, p. 496.

[25] *R.* v. *Central Criminal Court, ex p. Adegbesan,* [1986] 1 W.L.R. 1292. (D.C.). (Order under s.9 quashed because it did not set out in sufficient detail the special procedure material to which access was sought.)

[26] *Ante*, p. 524n.

[27] The *Western Daily Press* and the *Bristol Evening Post* were ordered to hand over such evidence to aid Avon and Somerset Police in their inquiries into serious crimes committed in Bristol: *The Times*, October 24, 1986.

requires a degree of particularity in specifying the grounds on which an application is made, the premises to be entered and the articles or persons to be sought. A warrant shall authorise entry on one occasion only.[28] Section 16 requires entry and search to be made within one month from the date of issue of the warrant. Entry must be at a reasonable hour, unless it appears to the constable executing the warrant that the purpose of the search would be frustrated by an entry at a reasonable hour.

Customs, revenue and other officials

In addition to police powers of law enforcement, important powers are possessed by the Commissioners of Customs and Excise, the Inland Revenue and a wide range of inspectors and officers employed by local authorities or public corporations.

The Customs and Excise Management Act 1979 confers power to board ships, aircraft and vehicles to "rummage and search" in connection with the preventing of smuggling (s.27). Officers may require information about goods being imported or exported and inspect documents relating to such goods (s.77). A right of entry on premises concerned with trading in alcohol is conferred by section 112 and a power to break open any part of such premises in order to look for any "secret pipe or other means of conveyance, cock vessel or utensil" (s.113). Without prejudice to specific powers section 161 confers a general power to search in connection with offences against the law relating to Customs and Excise on any customs officer having with him a writ of assistance. Such a writ which is issued by the High Court, has been described as, in effect, a general search warrant. Writs of assistance are made out at the beginning of each reign and are effective throughout the reign and for six months thereafter.[29]

Under Schedule 7 of the Value Added Tax Act 1983 the Commissioners have further powers to enter premises, seize documents or other articles and search persons.

The powers of the Inland Revenue to enter and search premises were highlighted in the case of R. v. Inland Revenue Commissioners, ex p. Rossminster Ltd.[30] Inland Revenue officials, accompanied by police constables carries out, in the words of Lord Denning M.R., a military style operation. The search was organised by a team of sixty officials of the revenue. It began at seven o'clock in the morning at four different premises and involved the removal of van loads of documents. The authority for the search and seizure of the documents was a warrant issued by a circuit court judge under section 20C of the Taxes Management Act 1970. That section requires reasonable grounds for suspecting the commission of an offence involving fraud relating to tax matters and that evidence of the offence is to be found on premises specified. On entering premises with a warrant the officer may seize and remove anything

---

[28] Cf. R. v. Adams [1980] Q.B. 575 (C.A.).

[29] G.J.Z. [1983] P.L. 1 and 345.

[30] [1980] A.C. 952 (H.L.). The substantive point of law is complicated by the form the proceedings took—interlocutory applications for the immediate return of the documents—and the question of the availability of an interim declaration against the Crown: post, p. 715. No criminal proceedings have taken place as a result of the search.

whatsoever which he has reasonable cause to believe may be required as evidence for the purpose of proceedings in connection with the suspected offence of fraud. The tax payer challenged the validity of the warrant on the ground that it referred to "an offence involving fraud in connection with or in relation to tax" but gave no specific details. Nor, it was argued, could the officials have reasonable cause for believing that the papers which they removed could furnish evidence of fraud because they did not read them before removing them but simply emptied the contents of filing cabinets into sacks and loaded them into vans. The Court of Appeal quashed the warrants, holding that they were too general and granted a declaration that the papers had been unlawfully seized. In the House of Lords, however, the Inland Revenue was successful. Their Lordships (Lord Salmon dissenting) held that the general allegation in the warrant was all that was required by the Act. So far as the second point was concerned the House held that the appropriate procedure to challenge the legality of the seizure of the documents was by means of an action for damages for trespass when the Revenue would have to establish reasonable cause for believing that the documents which they removed constituted evidence of fraud. Concern was expressed at the width of the statutory powers and pious hopes uttered that Parliament would take a fresh look at the matter.[31]

Many statutes confer powers of entry and search on public officials, attached to various departments, public corporations, regulatory bodies and local authorities.[32] There is no consistency with regard to the persons authorised, the nature of the authorising document, length of notice, or whether notice is to be given to the owner or the occupier.[33] The statute usually prescribed that the official must produce his written authority to any person who reasonably requires to see it.[34] If the conditions of entry prescribed by statute are not strictly fulfilled the owner is entitled to oppose entry. "When the sanitary inspector of the council arrived," said Lord Goddard C.J. in *Stroud* v. *Bradbury*,[35] "the appellant obstructed him with all the rights of a free-born Englishman whose premises are being invaded and defied him with a clothes prop and a spade. He was entitled to do that unless the sanitary inspector had a right to enter."

Examples of statutory powers of entry are afforded by the Building Act 1984, s.95 (authorised officer of local authority entitled to enter any premises at all reasonable hours to ascertain whether there has been any breach of building regulations: access to premises other than factories or workplaces requires 24 hours' notice); the Health and Safety at Work etc. Act 1974, s.20 (inspectors entitled to enter premises to ensure compliance with the provisions of the Act); the Milk (Cessation of Pro-

---

[31] The Committee on Enforcement Powers of the Revenue Departments, chaired by Lord Keith of Kinkel was established in 1980 and has produced four volumes of reports: (1983) Cmnd. 8822 (2 vols.); (1984) Cmnd. 9120; (1985) Cmnd. 9440.

[32] *An Inspector At the Door* (1979, Adam Smith Institute) attempts to list exhaustively statutory provisions conferring powers of entry on inspectors of various kinds.

[33] See D. Waters, "Public Right of Entry" [1958] C.L.P. 132.

[34] *Grove* v. *Eastern Gas Board* [1952] 1 K.B. 77 (C.A.), re Gas Act 1948. Rights of entry enjoyed by employees of the Gas and Electricity Boards are now consolidated in the Rights of Entry (Gas and Electricity Boards) Act 1954, as amended by the Gas Act 1972.

[35] [1952] W.N. 306; [1952] 2 All E.R. 76 (D.C.) (Public Health Act 1936).

duction) Act 1985, s.2 (authorised official of Ministry of Agriculture, Fisheries and Food entitled to enter land to establish whether a person has ceased to produce milk after receipt of a cessation payment under the Act) and the Local Government (Miscellaneous Provisions) Act 1982, s.17 (authorised officer of local authority entitled to enter premises if he has reason to suspect that unregistered person is engaging in acupuncture, tattooing, ear-piercing or electrolysis) and s.27 (power to enter to repair drains).

Anton Piller orders

The Courts themselves have added to the number of persons entitled to enter premises and search for and seize items by the introduction of the *Anton Piller* order, named after the leading case of *Anton Piller K.G. v. Manufacturing Process Ltd.*[36] Further decisions have refined the principle which in that case received the approval of the Court of Appeal.[37] In theory a defendant is requested to consent to admit the plaintiff to his premises to conduct a search: to refuse consent would, however, be contempt of court. The order is made *ex parte*, that is without warning to the defendant, where the plaintiff can satisfy the court that he has a strong prima facie case, that there is a risk of serious damage to him from the alleged wrongdoing, that the defendants have possession of incriminating documents or other items of evidential value and there is a real possibility that they may be destroyed before proceedings *inter partes* can take place. The jurisdiction originated in the field of intellectual property law but is not confined to that area of the law. Statutory recognition of the new order is to be found in section 72 of the Supreme Court Act 1981 which provides that in proceedings relating to intellectual property as defined in the section the danger of self incrimination is not a justification for refusing to comply with an order of the court.[38]

Liability to taxation

Since the Bill of Rights (1688) it has been firmly established that taxation may only be imposed by authority of an Act of Parliament (*Att.-Gen. v. Wilts United Dairies*).[39] This is done by Parliament either directly, as in the case of income tax, customs and excise duties, capital gains and transfer taxes, or indirectly through the delegation of power to local authorities to levy rates. Inland Revenue officials have an extensive power to "discover" what is not there and to assess taxpayers on that, in order to induce the latter to disclose what *is* there. The illegal conduct of

---

[36] [1976] Ch. 55. For a consideration of the constitutional implications see M. Dockray, "Liberty to Rummage—A Search Warrant in Civil Proceedings?" [1977] P.L. 369. See also A. Staines, "Protection of Intellectual Property Rights" (1983) 46 M.L.R. 274.

[37] *Cook Industries* v. *Galliher* [1979] Ch. 439; *Emanual* v. *Emanual* [1982] 1 W.L.R. 669; *Yousif* v. *Salama* [1980] 1 W.L.R. 1540; *Distributori Automatici Italia S.p.A.* v. *Holford General Trading Co. Ltd.* [1985] 1 W.L.R. 1066; *Altertext Inc.* v. *Advanced Data* [1985] 1 W.L.R. 457; *Randolph M. Fields* v. *Watts, The Times,* November 22, 1984; *EMI Records Ltd.* v. *Kudhail, The Times,* June 28, 1983 (C.A.); *I.T.C. Film Distributors Ltd.* v. *Video Exchange Ltd., The Times,* November 18, 1981; (Subsequent proceedings are reported at [1982] Ch. 431) *Universal City Studios Inc.* v. *Hubbard* [1983] Ch. 241; [1984] Ch. 225 (C.A.); *Bayer A.G.* v. *Winter (No. 2)* [1986] 2 All E.R. 43.

[38] Overruling *Rank Film Distributors Ltd.* v. *Video Information Centre* [1982] A.C. 380.

[39] (1921) 91 L.J.K.B. 897; (1921) 37 T.L.R. 844.

the Postmaster-General in charging fees for wireless licences without complying with the requirements of the Wireless Telegraphy Act 1904 was pointed out in the case of *Davey Paxman & Co. Ltd.* v. *Post Office*[40] and the position was regularised retrospectively by the Wireless Telegraphy (Validation of Charges) Act 1954.

Statutory restrictions on freedom of property

Parliament authorises and controls the compulsory acquisition of land by the Crown for defence purposes[41]; and by various Ministers, local authorities and public corporations under a great variety of statutes. A compulsory purchase by a local authority or public corporation must be confirmed by a Minister. Statutes prescribe both the procedure of compulsory acquisition and the method of assessing compensation.

The process of compulsory acquisition, with compensation, underwent a rapid expansion into the field of movable property with the passing of the nationalisation Acts, which since 1945 took a considerable part of the industrial resources of the country out of private ownership. There is no right to compensation except by statute[42]; but there is a strong presumption that if a statute authorises the compulsory acquisition of property, the owner is entitled to reasonable compensation (*Newcastle Breweries* v. *The King*[43]).

Article 1 of the First Protocol to the European Convention on Human Rights recognises the right to peaceful enjoyment of property and the right not to be deprived of it except in the public interest and subject to the conditions provided for by law and by the general principles of international law. In reliance on that Article the adequacy of compensation paid on the nationalisation of shipbuilding companies by the Aircraft and Shipbuilding Industries Act 1977 was unsuccessfully challenged before the European Court[44] while in later litigation a challenge to the compensation provisions of the Leasehold Reform Act 1967 similarly failed.[45]

From these decisions it can be assumed that the European Court on Human Rights is not anxious to interfere with political decisions of signatory governments, a reluctance which removes one obstacle at least to any future attempt by a Labour government to renationalise industries privatised[46] in the last few years on terms that ensure that compensation to shareholders does not allow for any speculative gain.

---

[40] *The Times,* November 16, 1954.
[41] *Cf. Att.-Gen.* v. *De Keyser's Royal Hotel Ltd.* [1920] A.C. 508 (H.L.).
[42] *Sisters of Charity of Rockingham* v. *The King* [1922] 2 A.C. 315, 322 (P.C.). *per* Lord Parmoor.
[43] [1920] 1 K.B. 584; *Att.-Gen.* v. *De Keyser's Royal Hotel Ltd.* [1920] A.C. 508 (H.L.R.); *Manitoba Fisheries Ltd.* v. *The Queen* (1978) 88 D.L.R. (3d) 462.
[44] *Lithgow* v. *U.K.,* (1986) 8 E.H.R.R. 329, *ante* p. 428.
[45] *James* v. *U.K.* (1986) 8 E.H.R.R. 123.
[46] *Post,* p. 619.

CHAPTER 26

FREEDOM OF EXPRESSION[1]

Introduction

The First Amendment to the Constitution of the United States provides that no law shall be made "abridging the freedom of speech or of the press."[2] In the United Kingdom, however, freedom of speech (or expression) is, like other freedoms, residual and subject to limitation by common law and statute.

Even where freedom of expression is constitutionally guaranteed the question may arise, what is meant by such freedom. It must no doubt include writings and words meant to influence political views, for example, the desirability of proportional representation as a method of electing members of the House of Commons. But does freedom of expression include symbolic gestures intended to convey a political message: the wearing of a particular coloured shirt to indicate support for a political party; the vulgar sign in the presence of royalty intended to indicate a profound conviction of the need for a republican form of government? There may be doubts too about whether the right is confined to communicating political ideas, and what is meant by communication? Does the freedom to publish books criticising Marxism extend to the freedom to publish books criticising conventional views on matrimony or sexual mores in general? Are collections of pornographic photographs (assuming agreement could be reached on the meaning of pornographic) also expressions of views about morality which are therefore entitled to claim the protection of the law?

While agreeing on the importance of the freedom of expression there may be doubts about the propriety of limiting that freedom to achieve other ends, for example to protect the young from corruption or to prevent public disorder. The extent to which such limitations are thought appropriate is likely to depend on why freedom of expression is believed to be important. Some may wish to argue that restrictions on free expression may prevent society from ascertaining the truth on mat-

---

[1] Dicey, *Law of the Constitution* (10th ed.), Chap. 6; E. Barendt, *Freedom of Speech* (1985); H. Street, *Freedom, the Individual and the Law* (5th ed., 1982); D. G. T. Williams, *Not in the Public Interest*; A. Boyle, "Freedom of Expresson as a Public Interest in English Law" [1982] P.L. 574. See also Holdsworth, *History of English Law*, Vol. X, pp. 672 *et seq.*
[2] The European Convention on Human Rights is more cautious. Article 10 (1) recognises the right to freedom of expression but goes on to state:
"This Article shall not prevent States from requiring the licensing of broadcasting, television or cinema enterprises.
(2) The exercise of these freedoms since it carries with it duties and responsibilities, may be subject to such formalities, conditions, restrictions or penalties as are prescribed by law and are necessary in a democratic society, in the interests of national security, territorial integrity or public safety, for the prevention of disorder or crime, for the protection of the reputation or rights of others, for preventing the disclosure of information received in confidence, or for maintaining the authority and impartiality of the judiciary."

ters of debate.[3] Others may see freedom to speak, write and read as an aspect of each individual's right to moral independence.[4]

The United Kingdom Parliament and the English and Scottish courts have, however, no entrenched constitutional rights to concern them when dealing with issues of freedom of expression. Parliament, as will be obvious in this and the succeeding chapters places no particular value on free speech in competition with the claims, real or alleged, of public order. In the area of censorship on grounds of obscenity it is willing to legislate hastily and with little thought, at the instigation of the latest pressure groups. The importance of freedom of speech, particularly in the political sphere, may be recognised by the courts as in *Verrall* v. *Great Yarmouth B.C.*[5] But the wide meaning which they give, or allow magistrates to give, to "insulting" and their willingness to foresee the likelihood of words leading to a breach of the peace reflect a different attitude.[6] The decision that a local authority has a reputation which it can protect by suing its critics in defamation, as a trading company can sue to protect its reputation, (*Bognor Regis D.C.* v. *Campion*[7]) may also be thought to show little respect for the right to criticise freely political institutions.

Limitations on the freedom of expression which have been considered in earlier chapters include treason, sedition, incitement to racial hatred, official secrets, contempt of court or Parliament and incitement to mutiny or disaffection among the armed forces and police. In this chapter we will consider defamation, civil and criminal, seditious libel, blasphemy, obscenity and the application of the restrictions imposed by these areas of law on newspapers, wireless, television and theatres.

Defamation

Defamatory matter is matter which exposes the person about whom it is published to hatred, ridicule or contempt, or which causes him to be shunned or avoided.[8] Such matter if in writing, printing or some other permanent medium,[9] is a libel, if in spoken words or significant ges-

---

[3] "The ultimate good desired is better reached by free trade in ideas . . . the best test of truth is the power of the thought to get itself accepted in the competition of the market"; *per* Mr. Justice Holmes (dissenting) *Abrams* v. *U.S.*, 250 U.S. 616, 630 (1919); J.S. Mill, *On Liberty*, Chap. 2.

[4] "Our society—unlike most in the world—presupposes that freedom and liberty are in a frame of reference that makes the individual, not government the keeper of his tastes beliefs and ideas"; *per* Mr. Justice Douglas (dissenting) *Paris Adult Theatre* v. *Slaton* 413 U.S. 49, 73 (1973). R. Dworkin, "Is there a right to pornography," (1981) O.J.L.S. 177.

[5] [1981] Q.B. 202.

[6] *Williams* v. *D.P.P.* (1968) 112 Sol.J. 599. (D.C.) (To hand leaflets to people entering U.S. Servicemen's clubs, criticising Vietnam war and inviting servicemen to desert was "insulting" and likely to lead to a breach of the peace: *per* Melford Stevenson J). But *cf R.* v. *Arrowsmith* [1975] Q.B. 678 (C.A.).

[7] [1972] 2 Q.B. 169; "a quite extraordinary case"; Barendt, *op. cit.* 174. Criticised by J. A. Weir [1972] C.L.J. 238.

[8] *Capital and Counties Bank* v. *Henty* (1882) 7 App.Cas. 741, 771, *per* Lord Blackburn; *cf. Sim* v. *Stretch* (1936) 53 T.L.R. 669.

[9] A defamatory talking film is libel; *Youssoupoff* v. *Metro-Goldwyn-Mayer Pictures Ltd.* (1934) 50 T.L.R. 581; so is a defamatory radio or television broadcast; Defamation Act 1952, ss.1 and 16. Similarly public theatrical performances: Theatres Act 1968, s.4.

tures, a slander. Where the defendant had no intention of referring to the plaintiff, he may make an offer of amends involving the publication of a correction and apology, which (if accepted) stays the action.[10]

Communications made on certain occasions enjoy *absolute privilege*, either at common law or by statute, that is to say, no proceedings can be brought in respect of them. These occasions include: judicial proceedings and statements made in the course of litigation by judges, counsel and witnesses[11]; words uttered in either House of Parliament by members[12]; state communications, which include communications about state business made by persons in government service[13]; proceedings at a court-martial, and reports made in pursuance of military duty[14]; fair and accurate reports in *newspapers* or *broadcasts* from the United Kingdom of proceedings publicly heard before a court in the United Kingdom exercising judicial authority,[15] if published contemporaneously[16] and neither blasphemous nor indecent[17]; reports and other documents published *by order* of either House of Parliament,[18] the Parliamentary Commissioner's report to Parliament, communications by the Commissioner and M.P.s, and communications by the Commissioner or M.P.s to complainants.[19]

Communications on certain other occasions enjoy *qualified privilege*, that is to say, they are protected in the absence of actual malice or "malice in fact," *i.e.* spite, fraud or some other indirect motive of which the law disapproves. These occasions include the following: fair and accurate reports (whether in newspapers or not)[20] of judicial proceedings not covered by section 3 of the Law of Libel amendment Act 1888[21] published in good faith and not blasphemous or indecent, and not prohibited by order of the court[22] or by statute[23]; the printing or broadcasting of (unauthorised) extracts from, or abstracts of, parliamentary papers[24]; fair and accurate (unauthorised) reports of parliamentary debates[25]; fair and accurate reports in any *newspaper* of the proceedings of a public meeting, or (except where neither the public nor newspaper reporters are admitted) of a meeting of any public body specified in the

---

[10] Defamation Act, 1952, s.4.
[11] *Royal Aquarium Society* v. *Parkinson* [1892] 1 Q.B. 431. The exception extends to certain tribunals possessing similar attributes to a court: *Trapp* v. *Mackie* [1979] 1 W.L.R. 177 (H.L.). *Ante*, p. 397. *Cf. Hasselblad (G.B.) Ltd.* v. *Orbinson* [1985] Q.B. 475 (C.A.).
[12] *Cf. R.* v. *Creevey* (1813) 1 M. & S. 273.
[13] *Isaacs & Sons* v. *Cook* [1952] 2 K.B. 391; but see *Szalatnay-Stacho* v. *Fink* [1947] K.B. 1.
[14] *Dawkins* v. *Lord Rokeby* (1875) L.R. 7 H.L. 744.
[15] *Cf.* an administrative tribunal, *Collins* v. *H. Whiteway & Co.* [1927] 2 K.B. 378.
[16] Contempt of Court Act 1981 s.4(3).
[17] Law of Libel Amendment Act 1888, s.3; Defamation Act 1952, ss.8, 9; *Kimber* v. *Press Association* (1893) 62 L.J.Q.B. 152; *Ponsford* v. *Financial Times* (1900) 16 T.L.R. 248; *McCarey* v. *Associated Newspapers Ltd.* [1964] 1 W.L.R. 855.
[18] Parliamentary Papers Act 1840, ss.1, 2.
[19] Parliamentary Commissioner Act 1967, s.10.
[20] *Steele* v. *Brannan* (1872) L.R. 7 C.P. 261.
[21] Note 17, *ante*.
[22] *R.* v. *Clement* (1821) 4 B. & Ald. 218.
[23] *e.g.* the Judicial Proceedings (Regulation of Reports) Act 1926; Contempt of Court Act 1981, s.4.
[24] Parliamentary Papers Act 1840, s.3; Defamation Act 1952, s.9.
[25] *Wason* v. *Walter* (1868) L.R. 4 Q.B. 73.

Public Bodies (Admission to Meetings) Act 1960 and Local Government (Access to Information) Act 1985, and the agenda of meetings of local authorities and other bodies specified in both Acts except meetings from which the public and the Press are excluded. A copy or fair and accurate report or summary of any notice other matter issued for the information of the public by or on behalf of any government department, officer of state, local authority or chief officer of police, if published in a newspaper enjoys qualified privilege under the Defamation Act, (s.7).[26]

An election address does not enjoy qualified privilege.[27]

Criminal libel

Defamation is usually treated as a civil wrong, and as such it belongs to the law of tort. *Slander* is not a crime merely as defamation, but is only a crime if the words are also treasonable or seditious, etc. *Libel* may be a crime if it is likely to cause a breach of the peace or would seriously affect the reputation of the person defamed.[28] No prosecution for criminal libel against the proprietor, publisher or editor of a newspaper may be brought without the leave of a judge in chambers.[29] Leave was given by Wien J. in *Goldsmith* v. *Pressdram Ltd.*[30] where a magazine had, in the view of the judge, engaged in a campaign of vilification for month after month against a person occupying a position of considerable public importance. On the other hand, in *Desmond* v. *Thorne*,[31] leave was refused by Taylor J. to an applicant who wished to commence proceedings over an article which appeared in a newspaper and described his alleged activities under a headline, "Bully Boasts 'I Beat Up Tragic Deb.' " In the light of the facts to which the applicant admitted, the judge held that a prosecution would not be in the public interest.

In *R.* v. *Wells St. Stipendiary Magistrate ex. p. Deakin*[32] the House of Lords expressed concern at the involvement of judges in granting leave to bring proceedings in cases involving newspapers and the absence of control over the commencement of proceedings in other cases. In the view of the House the bringing of proceedings should in all cases require the leave of the Attorney General or the Director of Public Prosecutions.

Truth is normally a defence to a *civil* action for libel, for a person cannot lose a reputation which he has not got or does not deserve. However, the Rehabilitation of Offenders Act 1974, s.8, prevents a defendant who has acted with malice from relying on the truth of statements he made about previous convictions of the plaintiff, if those convictions are, under the Act, "spent." In *criminal* libel truth is not a defence at

---

[26] *Blackshaw* v. *Lord* [1984] Q.B. 1 (C.A.).

[27] Defamation Act 1952, s.10; *cf. Plummer* v. *Charman* [1962] 1 W.L.R. 1469 (C.A.).

[28] *R.* v. *Wicks* [1936] 1 All E.R. 384, 386, *per* du Parcq. J.; *Goldsmith* v. *Pressdram Ltd.* [1977] Q.B. 83; *R.* v. *Wells St. Stipendiary Magistrate ex p. Deakin* [1980] A.C. 477 (H.L.); *Desmond* v. *Thorne* [1983] 1 W.L.R. 163.

[29] Law of Libel Amendment Act 1888, s.8.

[30] [1977] Q.B. 83. The action was subsequently settled.

[31] [1983] 1 W.L.R. 163.

[32] [1980] A.C. 477 (H.L.) (Private prosecutor alleged that he had been criminally libelled by book linking him with a bizarre and gruesome murder.)

common law.[33] By section 6 of the Libel Act 1843 ("Lord Campbell's Act"), however, it is a defence to a prosecution for criminal libel if the accused can prove not only that the matter published was true in substance but also that the publication was for the public good. Truth, of course, is no defence if the matter is also seditious, etc.

The Law Commission has recommended the abolition of criminal libel and its replacement by a new statutory offence of publishing defamatory material knowing it to be seriously defamatory of another. Proceedings would require the leave of the Attorney General.[34]

Seditious libel[35]

Prosecutions for seditious libel were frequent during the reign of George III, at the instance either of the government or the House of Commons. The growth of political parties, the development of periodical publications, and fear of the consequences of the French Revolution all contributed at various periods to this result. The prosecution of Wilkes in 1765 for his criticism of the Government in No. 45 of the *North Briton*[36] gave rise to the cases of *Wilkes* v. *Wood*[37] and *Leach* v. *Money*[38]; and it was the seizure in the same year of the books and papers of Entick, who was suspected of being the author of the *Monitor or British Freeholder*, that led to the case of *Entick* v. *Carrington*.[39]

Fox's Libel Act 1792

At common law a jury in a prosecution for criminal libel could not give a verdict on the general issue (*i.e.* "guilty" or "not guilty"). In *R.* v. *Almon*,[40] where a bookseller was charged with selling a reprint of Junius's "Letter to the King" from the *Morning Advertiser*, Lord Mansfield C.J. said it was for the judge to decide whether the libel was seditious: the jury could only determine the fact of publication and whether the libel had the meaning alleged in the indictment. After further celebrated and controversial cases,[41] the law was changed by the Libel Act 1792 ("Fox's Libel Act").

"This celebrated Act, and the discussions which led to it," said Stephen,[42] "are perhaps the most interesting and characteristic passages in the whole history of the criminal law." The Act provides that

---

[33] A rule explicable in cases where a breach of the peace is feared; the greater the truth the greater the risk of a breach of the peace. The rule is not, perhaps, so easily explained where, as modern cases emphasise may happen, proceedings are founded on the gravity of the libel alone.

[34] (1985) Law Com. No. 149; Cmnd. 9618.

[35] See also *ante*, pp. 477–478. For Scots law, see G. H. Gordon, *The Criminal Law in Scotland* (2nd ed., 1978) Chap. 39.

[36] *R.* v. *Wilkes* (1770) 4 Burr, 2527, 2574.

[37] (1763) 19 St.Tr. 1153; and see *ante*, p. 492.

[38] (1765) 3 Burr. 1692, 1742; 19 St.Tr. 1001; *ante*, p. 492.

[39] (1765) 19 St.Tr. 1030; *ante*, p. 522.

[40] (1770) 20 St.Tr. 803.

[41] *R.* v. *Woodfall* (1770) 20 St.Tr. 870; *R.* v. *Miller* (1770) 20 St.Tr. 895; *R.* v. (*Shipley Dean of St. Asaph's Case*) (1783) 4 Doug. 73, 162; 21 St.Tr. 847, 1033; *IR.* v. *Stockdale* (1789) 22 St.Tr. 237.

[42] *History of the Criminal Law*, II, p. 347. For historical accounts see *ibid.* Chap. 24; Holdsworth, *History of English Law*, Vol. X, pp. 673–695; Z. Chafee, *Free Speech in the United States* (Harvard, 1941), Chap. 13. And see *R.* v. *Burdett* (1820) 4 B. & Ald. 95.

the jury may give a general verdict of "guilty" or "not guilty" on the whole matter in issue, and may not be directed by the court to find the defendant guilty merely on proof of the publication by him of the paper charged to be libel and of the sense ascribed to it in the indictment. In Stephen's view, whereas before the Act it was only necessary that there should be intention to publish matter that was seditious, since the Act the intention must be seditious. In *R. v. Lemon*[43] Viscount Dilhorne denied that Fox's Libel Act had had any such effect but the requirement of a seditious intention may have been introduced by subsequent cases.

Charges of seditious libel continued to be brought, although not always so successfully for the prosecution. One of the latest cases of the old type—though here the accused was ultra conservative—was that of John Reeves,[44] the author of a well-known *History of English Law*.

After the Reform Act 1832 prosecution for seditious libel ceased to be a political weapon. The mid-nineteenth-century conception of seditious intent formulated by Stephen[45] is still regarded as good law. Prosecutions nowadays for seditious libel are rare, and in practice they are not instituted unless there is incitement to violence.[46] In *R. v. Caunt*[47] a newspaper proprietor was unsuccessfully prosecuted for seditious libel for writing an avowedly anti-Semitic article, in terms which could scarcely fail to "promote feelings of ill will and hostility between different classes." Birkett J. in his summing-up said it must be proved that the accused published the libel "with the intention of promoting violence."

Blasphemy[48]

"Every publication is said to be blasphemous which contains any contemptuous, reviling, scurrilous or ludicrous matter relating to God, Jesus Christ or the Bible, or the formularies of the Church of England as by law established. It is not blasphemous to speak or publish opinions hostile to the Christian religion or to deny the existence of God, if the publication is couched in decent and temperate language. The test to be applied is as to the manner in which the doctrines are advocated and not as to the substance of the doctrines themselves."[49] The common law misdemeanour of blasphemous words or writing seems to have been

---

[43] [1979] A.C. 617 (H.L.) (Lord Diplock and Lord Edmund-Davies dissenting).

[44] (1796) 29 St.Tr. 530. The Commons put pressure on the Government to prosecute him for seditious libel for expressing opinions in a pamphlet based on his reading of legal history—exalting the prerogative of the Crown in relation to the authority of the Commons. He had likened the Crown, the source of all legal power, to the timber of a tree, and the other parts of the Constitution to the branches and leaves. Found, "not guilty": pamphlet showed no seditious intent. Holdsworth describes his predecessor's *History of English Law* as uninteresting, but not unreadable: *H.E.L.* Vol. XII, pp. 412–415.

[45] *Ante*, p. 463.

[46] *The King* v. *Aldred* (1909) 22 Cox C.C. 1, *per* Coleridge J.

[47] *The Times*, November 18, 1947. An account of the trial is given in H. Montgomery Hyde, *Norman Birkett* (1964) pp. 532–535. See note by E. C. S. Wade in (1948) 64 L.Q.R. 203; and see *Boucher* v. *R.* [1951] 2 D.L.R. 369. *Cf. R.* v. *Leese*, *The Times*, September 19 and 20, 1936.

[48] For the law in Scotland (where the last case was in 1843) see G. H. Gordon, *The Criminal Law of Scotland* (2nd ed., 1978) p. 997.

[49] Sir J. F. Stephen, *Digest of Criminal Law* (9th ed.), p. 163.

first recognised by the King's Bench in *R. v. Attwood.*[50] In the earlier cases blasphemy was virtually equivalent to a kind of seditious libel.[51]

After the decision of the House of Lords in *Bowman* v. *Secular Society*[52] that an attack on or denial of the truth of Christianity, unaccompanied by vilification, ridicule or irrelevance, was not contrary to the law it came to be assumed that the gist of the offence of blasphemy lay in a tendency to cause a breach of the peace and prosecutions were rare.[53] In *R. v. Lemon*[54] the matter came before the House of Lords as the result of a private prosecution brought against the editor and publishers of a magazine *Gay News* for blasphemous libel contained in a poem entitled "The Love that Dares to Speak its Name" and a drawing illustrating the poem which were said to "vilify Christ in His life and in His Crucifixion." The question directly before the House was the mens rea requisite to establish liability for blasphemy. A majority of the House held that it was sufficient for the prosecution to prove that publication was intended and that the matter published was blasphemous, that is calculated to shock or outrage the feelings of ordinary Christians. Lord Scarman, one of the majority, and Lord Edmund-Davies, one of the dissentients, expressly said that they did not regard the likelihood of a breach of the peace as being of the essence of the offence. The true test was the likelihood of outrage and insult. Lord Scarman alone went on to say that far from regarding the law of blasphemy as a dead letter he would criticise it on the ground that, shackled by the chains of history, it is not sufficiently wide in scope. It ought, in his view, to be extended to protect all religious beliefs.

The Law Commission, on the other hand, came to the conclusion that the crime of blasphemy should be abolished.[55] To extend the existing law would inevitably involve difficult questions about what is a religion. Ought the criminal law in any case, to be used to protect outraged feelings? There are many existing crimes which cover much of the ground of blasphemy and the Law Commission proposed the creation of two new offences of using offensive or disorderly behaviour or words to disrupt services of religious worship and offensive behaviour in a place of worship.

Obscene publications

In early times jurisdiction over obscenity was exercised by the ecclesiastical courts as a matter of morals; but this jurisdiction was taken over by the common law courts in *Curl's Case,*[56] where the misde-

---

[50] (1617) Cro.Jac. 421. See G. D. Nokes, *History of the Crime of Blasphemy* (1928), pp. 21 *et seq.*

[51] "Sedition and blasphemy were in origin twin types of criminal libel"; *per* Lord Edmund-Davies, *R. v. Lemon* [1979] A.C. 617.

[52] [1917] A.C. 406 (H.L.).

[53] *R. v. Gott* (1922) 16 Cr.App.R. 87 (C.A.).

[54] [1979] A.C. 617. An application to the European Commission of Human Rights was rejected as manifestly ill-founded: (1983) 5 E.H.R.R. 123.

[55] *Offences against Religion and Public Worship,* (1985) Law Com. No. 145.

[56] (1727) Stra. 788.

meanour of obscene libel was recognised. The Obscene Publications Act 1857 also empowered magistrates to authorise the seizure and destruction of obscene articles kept for sale or other purpose of gain. The test of obscenity for the purpose of both the misdemeanour and a destruction order was that laid down by Cockburn C.J. in *R. v. Hicklin.*[57]

"... I think the test of obscenity is this, whether the tendency of the matter charged as obscenity is to deprave and corrupt those whose minds are open to such immoral influences, and into whose hands a publication of this sort may fall."

The Obscene Publications Act 1959

This Act created the statutory offence of publishing obscene matter, which superseded the common law misdemeanour, and repealed and replaced the Act of 1857 as regards the seizure and forfeiture of obscene matter. The test of obscenity for the purposes of the Act is whether the effect "is, if taken as a whole, such as to tend to deprave and corrupt persons who are likely, having regard to all relevant circumstances, to read, see or hear the matter contained or embodied in it." The tendency to deprave and corrupt, instead of being a presumed consequence of obscenity, has become the test of obscenity and what has to be proved.[58] The question is not whether an item can be described by terms regarded as synonyms of obscene, for example, filthy, shocking, repulsive, lewd, but whether it has a tendency to deprave and corrupt: *R. v. Anderson; R. v. Oz Publications Ltd.*[59] Thus it could be argued that the very degree of lewdness of a book might be such that, far from depraving it would produce feelings of horror and revulsion and so morally improve the reader: *R. v. Calder and Boyars Ltd.*[60] The depraving and corruption to which the statute refers has been held to extend beyond the sexual sphere to, for example, corrupting by advocating the illicit use of drugs: *Calder (John) Publications Ltd. v. Powell.*[61] Whether an item is obscene is a question of fact for the jury on which expert evidence is inadmissible except in the case of material aimed at young children where the jury may require the help of psychiatric experts.[62]

An item is not obscene for the purposes of the 1959 Act if it is likely to corrupt only a minute number of people exposed to its influence, a "lunatic fringe of readers." On the other hand an item likely to corrupt a significant proportion of people exposed to it would be obscene.[63] Where it can be established that the particular persons to whom an item has been published (for example by sale) are not capable of being

---

[57] (1868) L.R. 3 Q.B. 360, 371.
[58] *D.P.P. v. Whyte* [1972] A.C. 849, in which the House of Lords held that middle-aged men who are already addicts of pornography are capable of being further depraved and corrupted.
[59] [1972] 1 Q.B. 304 (C.A.).
[60] [1969] 1 Q.B. 151 (C.A.).
[61] [1965] 1 Q.B. 509.
[62] *D.P.P. v. A. and B.C. Chewing Gum Ltd.* [1968] 1 Q.B. 159 (D.C.). Similarly in cases of obscenity involving drug use: jury not qualified to assess effect of drugs and of methods of using them recommended in book: *R. v. Skirving: R. v. Grossman* [1985] Q.B. 819 (C.A.).
[63] *R. v. Calders and Boyars Ltd., supra.*

depraved by the item, it cannot be obscene under the 1959 Act.[64] That absurdity in the earlier legislation was remedied by creating a new offence of having an obscene article for publication for gain; Obscene Publications Act 1964, section 1 which provides that the question whether the article is obscene shall be determined by reference to such publication for gain of the article as in the circumstances it may reasonably be inferred the person charged had in contemplation and to any further publication that could reasonably be expected to follow from it.

It is a defence under Section 4 of the 1959 Act[65] to prove that publication "is justified as being for the public good on the ground that it is in the interests of science, literature, art or learning,[66] or of other objects of general concern." The Act of 1959 also declares that, contrary to the former practice, the opinion of experts may be admitted either to establish or to negative this defence.[67]

For the purposes of the Act an "article" includes matter to be read or looked at, a sound record or film,[68] or thing intended to be used for the reproduction or manufacture of obscene articles, *e.g.* a photographic negative, or cinematograph exhibition.

As will be seen later in this chapter, films are to some extent treated differently from items such as books and magazines.

Forfeiture

Where a person has been convicted of publishing (or having for gain for publication) obscene articles, the court shall order the forfeiture of these articles.

Under the Obscene Publications Act 1959 a justice of the peace may issue a warrant empowering a constable to enter and search any premises, stall or vehicle, and to seize and remove any articles which he has reason to believe to be obscene articles kept for publication for gain. When the owner of the premises or user of the stall or vehicle has been summoned to appear to show cause why the articles should not be forfeited, the magistrates' court may order the articles to be forfeited if it is satisfied that they were obscene articles kept for publication for gain. The owner, author or maker may also appear to show cause against forfeiture. The defence of "public good" may be set up, and the opinion of experts may be admitted on either side. Appeal against a forfeiture order lies to the Crown Court or by case stated to the High Court.[69]

---

[64] R. v. *Clayton and Halsey* [1963] 1 Q.B. 163 (the case of the incorruptible police officers).

[65] As amended by the Criminal Law Act 1977, s.53.

[66] "Learning" is a noun, meaning "product of scholarship"; it is not a verb meaning teaching or educating: Att.-Gen.'s *Reference (No. 3 of 1977)* [1978] 1 W.L.R. 1123 (C.A.).

[67] But evidence of supposed therapeutic benefit is inadmissible: R. v. *Staniforth; R.* v. *Jordan* [1977] A.C. 699 (H.L.).

[68] A video-cassette is within the Act: Att.-Gen.'s *Reference (No. 5 of 1980)* [1981] 1 W.L.R. 88 (C.A.).

[69] The Obscene Publications Act 1959 does not apply to Scotland which enables Gordon (*op. cit.*, pp. 992) to comment, "That the Scots have not had to engage in discussion of such elevating topics as the susceptibility to corruption of police officers or dirty old men, or whether material which revolts can also corrupt, or to attempt the appalling task of reading mountains of pornography in order to define the limits of obscenity may be attributed to the poverty of Scots pornographers or the sense of proportion of Scots legal practitioners. Be that as it may, it is now fairly clear that the 'deprave and corrupt' test is unworkable."

Obscene Libel

The Obscene Publications Act 1959 does not expressly abolish the common law misdemeanour of obscene libel but provides in section 2(4) that a person publishing an article shall not be proceeded against for an offence at common law consisting of the publication of any matter contained or embodied in the article where it is of the essence of the offence that the matter is obscene. In *Shaw* v. *Director of Public Prosecutions*[70] the House of Lords held that the section did not prevent the bringing of proceedings for a common law conspiracy to corrupt public morals or outrage public decency by the publication of an obscene article since the essence of the offence was the agreement not the publication.

Indecency

A number of statutes refer to "indecency" by which is meant a lower degree of moral depravity than connoted by obscenity. From the point of view of the prosecutor this renders his task easier, particularly because the evidence of experts is not relevant. The Post Office Act 1953 section 11 makes it an offence to " . . . send or attempt to send or procure to be sent a postal packet which: (b) encloses any indecent or obscene print, painting, photograph, lithograph, engraving, cinematograph film, book, card or written communication, or any indecent or obscene article whether similar to the above or not . . . ."[71]

In *R.* v. *Anderson; R.* v. *Oz Publications Ltd.*[72] the defendants, although acquitted under the 1959 Act were convicted under the Post Office Act. Articles imported into the country are liable to be forfeited if they are "indecent or obscene." Thus books which, if published in England and prosecuted under the 1959 Act, might be shown to be works of art or literature by expert evidence, are liable if published abroad to be seized by zealous customs officers.[73]

The public display of indecent matter is prohibited by the Indecent Displays (Control) Act 1981,[74] an Act which, is designed to prevent people from being brought into unwelcome proximity with indecent matter. The Act does not attempt to define indecent. Matter is defined as "anything capable of being displayed, except that it does not include an actual human body or any part thereof" (s.1(5)). The Act does not apply to television broadcasts, displays inside art galleries or museums, displays inside buildings owned by the Crown or local authorities, theatrical performances or cinematograph exhibitions. The effect of the exemption in the cases other than that of television broadcasts, is that

---

[70] [1962] A.C. 220. See too *Knuller Publishing Printing and Promotions* v. *D.P.P.* [1973] A.C. 435. The conspiracies recognised by the House of Lords in these decisions are preserved in existence by the Criminal Law Act 1977, s.5(3).

[71] Telecommunications Act 1984, s.43(1)(*a*) (grossly offensive, indecent or obscene telephone calls).

[72] [1972] 1 Q.B. 304 (C.A.).

[73] Customs Consolidation Act 1876 s.42; Customs and Excise Management Act 1979, s.49; C. Manchester, "Customs Control of Obscene Literature" [1981] Crim.L.Rev. 531. Such control in the case of books is not contrary to EEC law: *ante*, p. 108.

[74] This Act extends to Scotland. The principle behind it is not new: see the Indecent Advertisements Act 1889, repealed by the 1981 Act.

the buildings concerned do not have to carry a statutory warning that indecent matter may be exhibited inside—as would a shop displaying such matter.

The taking or possessing for the purpose of showing to others of indecent photographs of children under the age of 16 is prohibited by the Protection of Children Act 1978.[75] Apart from the undesirable vagueness of this statute and the probability that it adds nothing by way of protection to children that the law did not already offer, this is not aimed, as is much of the law considered in this section, at censorship because of the supposed deleterious effect on the users of obscene materials but at the easily identifiable harm to children who are involved in the taking of indecent photographs.

Reform

Attempts to reform the law relating to obscene publications raise difficult questions about what the purpose of the law is and what the justifications are for the criminal law interfering with the freedom of rational adults.

At present the law is explicable only on the basis that censorship is aimed at the minds of the people reading the books or viewing the films. There may be an argument that pornography ultimately leads to criminal acts against others but that is not the justification for the law at present.[76] Should the law concern itself with whether someone wishes to read Shakespeare or pornography.[77] To some extent it seems that the law (or some law) against obscenity is justified on the ground that people are disgusted at the thought that other members of the community are reading pornography. But to base criminal laws on disgust alone is at best dangerous and at worst a denial of individuals' rights.

Comprehensive proposals for reform in this area of the law were made by the Committee on Obscenity and Film Censorship under the Chairmanship of Bernard Williams in 1979.[78] The Committee suggested the abandonment of such terms as "obscene," "indecent" and "deprave and corrupt." They argued that material should be banned only where an identifiable harm could be said to be involved. In other cases restrictions on the availability of material were justifiable to recognise the public's legitimate interest in not being offended by the display of such material. The Committee also distinguished between the printed word and other forms of communication—films and theatre, for example— because of their differing impacts.[79] The printed word, in the view of the Committee should neither be restricted nor prohibited because its nature prevents it being immediately offensive nor is it capable of involving "harm" in the sense in which the Committee uses that term and because of its importance in conveying ideas. Prohibited materials

[75] In Scotland similar provisions are to be found in the Civic Government (Scotland) Act 1982, s.52.
[76] As shown by *D.P.P.* v. *Whyte* [1972] A.C. 849.
[77] Assuming pornography can be identified. Are the novels of Genet works of genius or the obscene products of a perverted mind, or both?
[78] Cmnd. 7772. There is no reason to expect any action will be taken on these proposals in the near future.
[79] Whatever the good sense of the Committee's proposals, their attempts to justify them are open to challenge: R. Dworkin, *Ante*, p. 532, n. 4.

are narrowly defined to include films (and photographs) whose production appears to have involved the exploitation for sexual purposes of persons under sixteen or live performances involving actual sexual activity. Restricted materials would be those whose unrestricted availability would be offensive to reasonable people by reason of the way they deal with or portray violence, cruelty or horror or sexual or other bodily functions or genital organs. In both categories it would not be a defence to rely on the intrinsic merit of the material. The committee also recommended that the right to bring a private prosecution for an obscenity offence should be abolished. In the case of restricted materials they suggested that the police or the Director of Public Prosecutions should be entitled to bring proceedings; in the case of prohibited materials, only the Director of Public Prosecutions.

Liberty of the Press

"The Press" generally covers printed matter of all kinds, and not merely newspapers and periodicals. "The liberty of the press," says Blackstone,[80] "consists in laying no *previous* restraints upon publications, and not in freedom from censure for criminal matter when published." This liberty, said Lord Mansfield in *Dean of St. Asaph's Case*,[81] consists in "printing without any previous licence, subject to the consequences of law." "The liberty of the press," said Alexander Hamilton,[82] "is the right to publish with impunity, truth, with good motives, for justifiable ends though reflecting on government, magistracy, or individuals." It has existed in this country since the end of the seventeenth century.

Soon after the introduction of the art of printing in the fifteenth century, a series of proclamations began to be issued to restrict and control printing, in addition to the law of treason, sedition, heresy and blasphemy. In England the printing of books in the early period was confined to the members of the Stationers' Company in London and to the Universities of Oxford and Cambridge.[83] Throughout most of the sixteenth and seventeenth centuries all printing required a licence. By an assumption of the prerogative of the Crown as *custos morum*[84] in the late Tudor and early Stuart periods, secular printing was controlled by the Star Chamber and theological printing by the High Commission. Soon after the abolition of these bodies in 1641, a licence to print was required by the Licensing Act 1662. Several Licensing Acts followed, but the last expired in 1695. The Commons refused to renew it, not so much out of respect for freedom of expression but rather because experience showed that licensing did not succeed in its object. Since

---

[80] Bl.Comm. IV, 151. He adds that "to censure the licentiousness, is to maintain the liberty, of the press": *ibid.* p. 153. And see *R. v. Burdett* (1820) 4 B. & Ald. 95, *per* Best J.: "Where vituperation begins, the liberty of the press ends."

[81] *R. v. Shipley* (1783) 21 St.Tr. 847, 1040; *ante*, p. 535. *Cf. British Steel Corporation v. Granada Television* [1981] A.C. 1096, 1168 *per* Lord Wilberforce.

[82] In *People v. Croswell* (1804) 3 Johns (N.Y.) 337.

[83] For the history of the law of the Press, see Holdsworth, *History of English Law*, Vol. VI, pp. 360–378.

[84] For a modern exercise of jurisdiction by the court as *custos morum* see *Shaw v. Director of Public Prosecutions* [1962] A.C. 220 (H.L.), conspiracy to corrupt public morals; *ante*, p. 540.

1695, then, the press has been governed by the ordinary law of sedition and libel. No prosecution for criminal libel against the proprietor, publisher or editor of a newspaper may be brought without the order of a judge in chambers.[85] A curious survival from the time of the Napoleonic Wars is the requirement that every newspaper (and other printed object) shall bear the name and address on it of the printer concerned.[86] The Newspaper Libel and Registration Act 1881 establishes a register of proprietors of newspapers (s.8) and requires printers to make annual returns of the titles and proprietors of newspapers which they have printed.

Censorship is no less censorship when approved by bodies or persons other than the government or public officers. Censorship of the press in recent years has come from those who in former times were most concerned to establish the freedom of the press; *e.g.* the National Union of Journalists and printers unions.[87] The Trade Unions and Labour Relations (Amendment) Act 1976, s.2, inserted a section 1A into the Trade Unions and Labour Relations Act 1974 which made provision for a quasi-legal "Charter on matters relating to freedom of the press" containing practical guidance to be drawn up by employers' associations, editors and trade unions, or in default by the Secretary for Employment. No progress was made in talks under the chairmanship of Lord Pearce and Section 1A was repealed by the Employment Act 1980, section 19. That Act in turn provided for the issuing of Codes of Practice by the Secretary of State (s.3). That on the Closed Shop contains provisions intended to protect press freedom which is recognised as an essential part of our democratic society. Among other specific points the Code recognises the right of an editor to decide whether or not to publish any material submitted to him from any source.[88]

Confidentiality and public interest

In the previous chapter we saw that the development of the law of confidential information provided a protection for aspects of family life and for commercial secrets. It applies also to protect government secrets. The principle was recognised, although held not to be applicable on the facts, in relation to the confidentiality of cabinet discussions in *Attorney-General* v. *Jonathan Cape Ltd.*[89] In *Attorney-General* v. *The Observer Ltd.*[90] the Court of Appeal granted an interlocutory injunction to restrain a newspaper publishing information about the secret services which had been obtained from a former secret service agent in

---

[85] Law of Libel Amendment Act 1888, s.8; *ante*, p. 534.
[86] Newspapers, Printers and Reading Rooms Repeal Act 1869 is the current legislation: see C. Manchester, (1982) 2 Leg.Stud. 180.
[87] See *The Times*, January 14, 1977; article by David Astor on Censorship itself censored for 24 hours by the printers: *The Times*, July 9, 1977, Press Council Report concerning advertisements and editorial matter connected with the Grunwick dispute. An article by Woodrow-Wyatt in *News of the World* was censored by N.G.A. members on December 4, 1983. See further Woodrow Wyatt in *The Times*, May 12, 1984. The Press Council criticised the editor of the *The Observer* for refusing to permit a review to which the printworkers objected because of its author's association with *The Times*, with which their unions were in dispute; October, 1986.
[88] *Code of Practice*: *The Closed Shop*; issued May 18, 1983.
[89] [1976] Q.B. 752; *ante*, p. 116 and p. 314.
[90] *The Times*, July 26, 1986 (C.A.).

breach of his duty of confidentiality. In October 1986 the Foreign Secretary obtained an injunction to prevent *The New Statesman* publishing
the text of the valedictory dispatch of the British Ambassador to Saudi
Arabia on the ground of breach of confidence.[91] (The Foreign office was
concerned that the dispatch, with its references to the incompetence
and arrogance of the Saudis would give offence to them.)

The Courts have, however, recognised that the public interest may
sometimes justify the publication of information obtained in breach of
confidence. In *Lion Laboratories Ltd.* v. *Evans*[92] disclosure of a confidential memorandum relating to the efficiency of a computerised instrument for measuring the level of alcohol in blood was held to be justified
because of the public's entitlement to information which raised doubts
about a device which was providing the evidence on which people
were being convicted. The Court of Appeal, therefore, discharged the
injunction granted at first instance against The Daily Express. In *Francome* v. *Mirror Group Newspapers*[93] unidentified persons had tapped the
telephone of the plaintiff, the champion National Hunt jockey, and sold
the recordings of his conversations to the Daily Mirror which wished to
publish extracts from them on the ground that they disclosed breaches
by the jockey of the rules of racing. The Court of Appeal upheld the
award of an injunction to restrain publication. Sir John Donaldson said
it was impossible to see what public interest would be served by publishing the contents of the tapes which would not equally be served by
giving them to the police or the Jockey Club. "Any wider publication
could only serve the interests of the 'Daily Mirror'."

Disclosure of sources of information

The common law relating to the obligation of the press to reveal the
sources of their information when ordered to do so by a court and the
effect of section 10 of the Contempt of Court Act 1981 are discussed in
Chapter 20, Part IV.[94]

Protection is given by the provisions of the Police and Criminal Evidence Act 1984 to journalistic material in relation to police powers to
search premises and seize evidence found there. This is discussed in
Chapter 25 Part II.

The Press Council

It might be argued that at present it is not censorship of the press
which is a cause of concern but the behaviour of the press itself; in particular its triviality, vulgarity and offensive intrusion into peoples' pri-

---

[91] *The Glasgow Herald,* not subject to the injunction, went ahead with plans to publish the
dispatch. The government's application for an interdict was heard before Lord Davidson at his home at 4.00am. An interdict was granted but the first edition had by then
been printed: The *Glasgow Herald,* October 9 and 10, 1986.
[92] [1985] Q.B. 526 (C.A.). See also *Woodward* v. *Hutchins* [1977] 1 W.L.R. 760 (C.A.). (Unsuccessful application by Tom Jones, Engelbert Humperdinck and others to prevent publication of "the most explosive showbusiness story of the decade."); *Cork* v. *McVicar, The
Times* October 31, 1984. (Injunction refused to prevent publication of conversation
showing corruption in Metropolitan Police.)
[93] [1984] 1 W.L.R. 892 (C.A.).
[94] An order for disclosure of sources was refused in *Francome* v. *Mirror Group Newspapers,
supra,* because disclosure was not required at the stage proceedings had reached. Thus
the Court did not have to decide whether s.10 has any application *before* publication.

vate lives. As was seen in the previous chapter English law recognises no right of privacy—and vulgarity and triviality are hardly justiciable issues.

In an attempt to provide a mechanism for dealing with complaints about the standards of newspapers the Press Council was established in 1953.[95] It consists of an equal number of lay members and press members. It has no power to do other than censure. For some years its Chairman has been a lawyer which no doubt gives it both the appearance and reality of independence of the press. It has produced general statements, for example, on the undesirability of "cheque-book journalism" as well as adjudicating on specific matters referred to it. No one (except perhaps members of the council) regard it as performing a particularly useful function.[96]

Broadcasting

It is, perhaps, not surprising that the content of programmes broadcast by wireless and television can generate particularly heated controversies about freedom of expression. A visit to a theatre is a deliberate choice; wireless and television are already in the house. To the person who objects to a film it can be said that it is not necessary to go to the cinema to see it. The person who objects to a television programme is entitled on the contrary, to argue that he has to pay a licence to have a set; his views on what is suitable for showing have therefore, some weight.

The legal restrictions relating to the content of programmes are broadly similar in the case of the BBC and the I.B.A.[97] which has responsibility for commercial television programmes. In the case of the BBC they are to be found in the Royal Charter which establishes it and in the case of the I.B.A. in the Broadcasting Act 1981. Programmes must not offend against good taste or decency or be likely to encourage or incite to crime or to lead to disorder or to be offensive to public feeling. Codes must regulate the showing of violence. The use of subliminal images (those shown for so brief a period of time that the brain is influenced without the person concerned realising the fact) is specifically forbidden by section 4(3) of the 1981 Act.[98] Other requirements relate to the provision of accurate and impartial news features and due impartiality on the part of persons providing programmes on matters of political or industrial controversy or current public policy.[99]

The Broadcasting Act 1980 established a Broadcasting Complaints Commission which was continued in existence by the 1981 Act (ss.53–60). The Commission can hear any complaint relating to unjust or

[95] Some years after the report of a Royal Commission on the Press (1949, Cmnd. 7700). A later Royal Commission reported critically on the work of the Press Council in 1977 (Cmnd. 6810).

[96] Geoffrey Robertson, *People against the Press, An Enquiry into the Press Council* (1983).

[97] The structure and legal powers of the B.B.C. and the I.B.A. are discussed in Chapter 29.

[98] Breach of the prohibition is not a criminal offence; *R. v. Horseferry Road Justices ex p. I.B.A.* [1986] 3 W.L.R. 132 (D.C.); *post*, 681.

[99] The requirement of impartiality gave rise to controversy in the autumn of 1986 in connection with the BBC's coverage of the American bombing of Libya and a successful libel action brought by two conservative M.P.'s accused of associations with extreme right wing groups.

unfair treatment in programmes broadcast by a broadcasting body or to unwarranted infringement of privacy in or in connection with the obtaining of material included in broadcast programmes. The Commission is directed to make an annual report to the Secretary of State who shall, after considering it, lay it before both Houses of Parliament. In *R. v. Broadcasting Complaints Commission ex. p. Owen.*[1] The Court of Appeal held that the jurisdiction of the Commission was not confined to dealing with complaints by individuals relating to particular programmes but extended to more general complaints by groups such as political parties relating to unfairness over a period of time.

The courts regard the duty relating to the type of programmes which may not be broadcast as ultimately, enforceable by judicial action but they have also made it equally clear that they would not attempt to substitute their aesthetic judgments for those of the properly constituted broadcasting authorities: *Attorney-General ex rel. McWhirter* v. *I.B.A.*[2]; *R.* v. *I.B.A. ex p. Whitehouse.*[3]

Possible future developments in broadcasting are provided for by the Cable and Broadcasting Act 1984 which establishes a Cable Authority to licence the provision of programmes supplied by cable systems and a Satellite Broadcasting Board (consisting of equal numbers of representatives of the BBC and I.B.A.) to take responsibility for the provision of programmes by direct satellite broadcasting. The only explicit restriction on the contents of cable programmes is that they shall not be obscene (ss.25 and 26) although other requirements could be included in the terms of licences granted by the Authority. Programmes broadcast by direct satellite must be of "high quality" both in the method of transmission and content (s.42) and are, in effect, subject to the standards and controls laid down in the Broadcasting Act 1981 (s.44). It remains to be seen whether the early enthusiasm for these methods of broadcasting can be sustained.[4]

The theatre

Under the Theatres Act 1843 there was a censorship by the Lord Chamberlain of the public performance of stage plays written after 1843. The Theatres Act 1968 abolished this censorship and repealed the Act of 1843. The 1968 Act, in effect, applies to theatrical performances (other than those given on a domestic occasion in a private dwelling: s.7(1)) the provisions of the Obscene Publications Act 1959.[5] It is an offence to present or direct the performance of a play which is obscene, that is if taken as a whole its effect was such as to tend to deprave and corrupt persons who were likely, having regard to all relevant circumstances, to attend it.

Like the 1959 Act, a defence of justification on the ground of public

---

[1] [1985] Q.B. 1153.

[2] [1973] Q.B. 269 (C.A.).

[3] *The Times*, April 14, 1984 (D.C.).

[4] *Cable Expansion and Broadcasting Policy* (1982, Cmnd. 8679) (Committee of Enquiry under Lord Hunt); White Paper, *The Development of Cable Systems and service* (1983, Cmnd. 8866); *Direct Broadcasting by Satellite* (1982, Cmnd. 8751).

[5] The Theatres Act 1968, unlike the 1959 Act, applies to Scotland which may result in that jurisdiction having to concern itself with the English case law on the earlier Act.

good is recognised (s.3). Again, following the earlier precedent, section 1(4) provides that prosecutions cannot be brought in respect of a performance within the Act for any common law offence of indecency or for various statutory offences under English and Scots law. The 1968 Act goes further than its predecessor and provides that no person shall be proceeded against for an offence at common law of conspiring to corrupt public morals, or to do any act contrary to public morals or decency, in respect of an agreement to present or give a performance of a play, or to cause anything to be said or done in the course of such a performance.

By section 8 proceedings in England may not be commenced under the Act without the leave of the Attorney General.

A way round what seems to be the obvious intention of the Act was found by Mrs Whitehouse, after the Attorney General had refused leave to bring proceedings against the director of a play at the National Theatre, *The Romans in Britain*. In *Whitehouse* v. *Bogdanov*[6] she began proceedings alleging that the director, in staging a scene involving a sexual assault by actors portraying Roman soldiers on another purporting to be a druid priest, had been guilty of procuring the commission of an act of gross indecency between males contrary to section 13 of the Sexual Offences Act 1956. Staughton J. held that the prosecution could be brought because it was outside the prohibition contained in section 1(4); it related neither to a common law offence nor to one of the listed statutory offences. The law having been decided in her favour Mrs. Whitehouse cleverly abandoned the proceedings.

Theatrical performances are subject to the law against incitement to racial hatred (formerly by virtue of the Theatres Act 1968, s.5) and now by virtue of the Public Order Act 1986, s.20).

The cinema

The Cinematograph Act 1909 required a licence from the county council or the county borough council for the exhibition of inflammable films.[7] This was a safety measure, but local authorities soon began to refuse to license films which they thought offended public morals, a practice that was declared to be lawful.[8] The film industry thereupon set up its own unofficial British Board of Film Censors, to certify and classifies films intended for public exhibition.

Local authorities have no duty to censor films, except in the case of children (Cinemas Act 1985, s.1(3)). They may, however, be liable if the terms of a licence allows the showing of films which are contrary to the law. They cannot delegate their responsibilities to the Board of Film Censors[9] but they may properly rely on its advice and require cinemas to which they grant licences not to show films which have not been approved by the Board.[10]

---

[6] *The Times*, March 19, 1982.
[7] Extended to non-inflammable films by the Cinematograph Act 1952. Exemption from licensing requirements on the part of private cinema clubs, run for profit, was removed by the Cinematograph (Amendment) Act 1982.
[8] *London County Council* v. *Bermondsey Bioscope Ltd.* [1911] 1 K.B. 445.
[9] *Ellis* v. *Dubowski* [1921] 3 K.B. 621.
[10] *R.* v. *Greater London Council ex p. Blackburn* [1976] 1 W.L.R. 550.

The Obscene Publications Act 1959 did not originally apply to public exhibitions of films, which were thus left subject to common law offences relating to indecency.[11] The Criminal Law Act 1977 amended the 1959 Act to bring the showing of films within the protection of that Act and further provided that no prosecution can be brought without the consent of the Director of Public Prosecutions, where the article is a moving picture film not less than 16mm. wide and publication of it took place or could reasonably be expected to take place only in the course of a cinematograph exhibition. (Obscene Publications Act 1959, s.3A.) Nor can any prosecution be brought for any common law offence or any conspiracy to corrupt public morals.

It is clearly illogical that a system of censorship should evolve out of legislation concerned with public safety. Decisions of the Board of Censors in earlier years showed British prudery at its worst. If there is to be censorship it is arguable that the responsibility must be that of a state organisation. The Williams' Committee recommended the replacement of the present arrangements with a statutory system with a five fold classification of films from those suitable for all ages to a restricted exhibition category to be shown to adults only in cinemas designated by local authorities.

Video recordings

Video recordings are subject to a scheme of statutory censorship, introduced by the Video Recordings Act 1984[12] which creates an offence of supplying an uncensored video unless the video or the supply fall within the exempting provisions of the Act. The offence is triable only summarily but the maximum fine is £20,000 (ss.9 and 15).

Classification certificates indicate whether a video is suitable for general viewing or only by persons over the age (not being over 18) specified on the certificate. In the latter case a further restriction may require that supplies of the video may only take place in licensed sex shops (s.7).

Elaborate provisions deal with the definitions of "exempted works" and "exempted supplies." Section 2(1) exempts from the necessity to be classified (i) videos which are designed to inform educate or instruct; concerned with sport, religion or music; and (ii) video games. But no video in these categories is exempt if to a significant extent it depicts human sexual activities, torture, human genital organs and other listed activities and functions. The definition of exempted supply is even longer and, for example, includes supplying videos for medical training; thus non-exempt videos under section 2(2) may be the subject of exempt supplies.

---

[11] R. v. Greater London Council ex p. Blackburn, supra.

[12] "The Video Recordings Act 1984 is an example of British legislative procedure at its worst. Its passage was a caricature of parliamentary democracy. Its drafting showed most of the defects of which British statutory style is accused. It raises serious questions about private members' Bills. And it confirms once again that public bodies devote time to an issue in inverse proportion to its importance. Above all, it displayed an unusual degree of intellectual and political dishonesty." Neville March Hunnings, "Video Censorship" [1985] P.L. 214. The Act applies to Scotland.

The designation of the authority to carry out the task of censoring the thousands of videos already in existence is left to the Secretary of State who has appointed an enlarged British Board of Film Censors to discharge the duty (s.4).

CHAPTER 27

FREEDOM OF ASSEMBLY AND ASSOCIATION[1]

Introduction

These freedoms include: (a) taking part in public meetings, processions and demonstrations; and (b) forming and belonging to political parties, trade unions, societies and other organisations. They are
liberties rather than rights in the strict sense, and (like the other liberties of the individual in English law) they are residual.

Freedom to assemble means that there is no law forbidding people to
assemble. If a number of people choose to go to the same place at the
same time this is not unlawful, provided that they keep within the
limits of the law, individually and collectively. An assembly convened
for the purpose of effecting a breach of the peace is unlawful at common
law, and there are various statutory offences, notably under Public
Order Acts, Highways Acts, the Police Act 1964 and local by-laws.

Similarly there is liberty to join an association, provided that it does
not involve a criminal conspiracy[2] or a civil conspiracy (which is a tort);
and provided that the association is not organised to usurp the functions of the police or armed forces, or for the purpose of using force for a
political object. It is important to notice that "force" does not necessarily mean armed force. As an exceptional and temporary measure the
Prevention of Terrorism (Temporary Provisions) Act 1984, Schedule 1[3]
proscribes the Irish Republican Army, and the Irish National Liberation
Army and section 2 makes public support of such organisations illegal.

Conversely, no one is obliged by law to join any association against
his will, although in practice it may be impracticable for a person to get
a certain kind of employment or to engage in a particular occupation or
trade unless he joins a trade union or professional association. However, where a "closed shop agreement," or more accurately a "union
membership agreement,"[4] is in operation, it will, in certain circumstances,[5] amount to unfair dismissal to dismiss an employee who
refuses to join a specified union in a closed shop.

The European Convention (Art. 11) provides that everyone has the
right to freedom of peaceful assembly and to freedom of association

---

[1] Dicey, *Law of the Constitution* (10th ed.) Chap. 7; David Williams, *Keeping the Peace: The
Police and Public Order* (1967); H. Street, *Freedom, the Individual and the law* (5th ed.,
1982); R. F. V. Heuston, *Essays in Constitutional Law* (2nd ed., 1964); L. Radzinowicz,
History of English Criminal Law, Vol. 4 (1968) especially Chap. 4; Brownlie, (M. Supper-
stone ed.), *Law of Public Order and National Security* (1981); A. T. H. Smith, *The Offences
Against Public Order* (1987); D. G. T. Williams, "Protest and Public Order" [1970] C.L.J.
96; "Offences against the State 1964–73" [1974] Crim.L.R. 635; A. T. H. Smith "Public
Order 1974–1983: Developments and Proposals" [1984] Crim.L.R. 643.
[2] Criminal Law Act 1977, s.1.
[3] Replacing the Act of 1976 see *ante*, p. 480 which replaced the Act of 1974.
[4] See s.30(1) of the Trade Union and Labour Relations Act 1974.
[5] See Employment Protection (Consolidation) Act 1978, s.58, as amended by the Employment Act 1980.

with others, including the right to form and to join trade unions for the protection of his interests,[6] with the usual restrictions as prescribed by law and necessary in a democratic society. Members of the armed forces, the police and public officials and civil servants[7] may be subject to special restrictions. The United Kingdom has also ratified the International Labour Office Convention on Freedom of Association.

Some statutory offences

There are a wide variety of statutory offences available in connection with the preservation of public order.

Highways Act 1980

Wilful obstruction of the highway without lawful authority or excuse is a summary offence under the Highways Act 1980, s.137. There is now only a power of arrest without warrant under the general arrest conditions provided by the Police and Criminal Evidence Act 1984, s.25. It is not necessary on a prosecution to prove that anyone was actually obstructed,[8] nor is it a good defence that there was a way round the obstruction,[9] or that there was no intention to obstruct,[10] although these facts may go to mitigation.

In *Hurst* v. *Chief Constable of Yorkshire*[11] the Divisional Court considered this section and suggested that in deciding whether there was an obstruction it should be asked whether what was being done was incidental to the right of passing and repassing. If not, than there was an obstruction, but it would not amount to an offence if it was a reasonable obstruction. In considering this question Otton J. suggested that account should be taken of the fact that the defendants were exercising rights of assembly and demonstration.

The Public Meeting Act 1908

Under this Act, as amended by the Public Order Act 1936, disorderly conduct designed to break up a lawful public meeting is a summary offence.[12] However, the fact that a meeting is held on the highway is not enough in itself to make the meeting unlawful for the purposes of the Public Meeting Act 1908, in the absence of some other element such as obstruction. Thus in *Burden* v. *Rigler*[13] a political meeting was held on the highway, after being advertised in advance; the police were present and did not object. B tried to make a speech in favour of tariff reform,

---

[6] *Cf. ante*, p. 429.
[7] See R. v. *Secretary of State for Foreign and Commonwealth Affairs, ex p. Council of Civil Service Unions and another* [1984] I.R.L.R. 309 (H.L.). See Gillian S. Morris "The Ban on Trade Unions at Government Communications Headquarters" [1985] P.L. 177.
[8] *Gill* v. *Carson and Nield* [1917] 2 K.B. 674.
[9] *Homer* v. *Cadman* (1888) Cox C.C. 51.
[10] *Arrowsmith* v. *Jenkins* [1963] 2 Q.B. 561 (D.C.). This was in fact under the similar provision in the 1959 Highways Act.
[11] (1987) 151 J.P. 304; *Cf. Waite* v. *Taylor* (1985) 149 J.P. 551.
[12] In the case of a political meeting held between the issue of a writ for the return of an M.P. and the return, the offence is an illegal practice under s.97 of the Representation of the People Act 1983.
[13] [1911] 1 K.B. 337 (D.C.).

but R and others created a disturbance. B charged R and others under the Public Meeting Act, and it was held that the defendants could be convicted of disorderly conduct at a lawful public meeting. Under the Act of 1908, as amended, if a constable reasonably suspects any person of committing an offence under that Act he may, if requested by the chairman of the meeting, require the person to give his name and address. If the person refuses to give his name and address, or gives a false name and address, he is guilty of an offence. The constable may arrest without warrant if the person refuses to give his name and address, or if the constable reasonably suspects him of giving a false name and address.[14]

Miscellaneous Statutory Offences

There are also offences of wilfully obstructing or assaulting a police officer in the execution of his duty,[15] incitement to racial hatred,[16] and prohibiting the possession of an offensive weapon in any public place.[17] In addition there are general laws governing criminal damage, the possession of firearms and explosives, and offences against the person.

In addition, local authorities have power to make by-laws for the good order and government of their areas, and these may create minor offences triable summarily in the magistrates' courts. By-laws usually require the written permission of the council for holding a meeting on ground, such as a square or park, belonging to the local authority as the highway authority or otherwise; and permission may be refused if a breach of the peace is apprehended.

Public Order Acts 1936, 1986

The most important statutes are the Public Order Acts 1936 and 1986. In June 1976 the Home Secretary announced a review of the statute law in Great Britain connected with public order.[18] Following the publication of a report by the Law Commission[19] on the common law offences relating to public order, the review was extended to cover riot, unlawful assembly and affray. During the period of the review outbreaks of violence in a variety of different circumstances—public demonstrations, football matches, industrial disputes, inner-city rioting, demonstrated[20] the need for the reform of public order law. The Public Order Act 1986 creates several new offences, both to replace common law offences, which are repealed, and to cover new ground; it also

---

[14] See Police and Criminal Evidence Act 1984, s.25, s.26 and Sched. 7.

[15] Police Act 1964, *ante*, p. 497.

[16] *Ante*, p. 479.

[17] Prevention of Crime Act 1953 as amended by the Public Order Act 1986, Sched. 2.

[18] See the Green Paper, *Review of the Public Order Act 1936 and Related Legislation* (Cmnd. 7891); Select Committee on Home Affairs Report *The Law Relating to Public Order* (1980) H.C. 756 I and II.

[19] (1983) H.C. 85, Law Com. No. 23 see D. G. T. Williams "Public Order and Common Law" [1984] P.L. 12. Before publishing this Report the Law Commission produced a Working Paper entitled *Offences Against Public Order* (No. 82); see A. T. H. Smith [1982] Crim.L.R. 485.

[20] Scarman Report on the Brixton riots (1981) Cmnd. 8427.

extensively amends and repeals several important sections of the Public Order Act 1936.

Public Order Act 1936[21]

It is an offence under section 1 to wear in any public place or at any public meeting a *uniform* signifying association with any *political* organisation or with the promotion of any political object. The Home Secretary may give permission for the wearing of such uniform on a ceremonial or other special occasion. The consent of the Attorney-General is necessary for the continuance of a prosecution after a person has been charged in court. In *O'Moran* v. *D.P.P.*[22] men wearing dark glasses, black or blue berets and dark clothing when escorting the coffin of a fellow supporter of the I.R.A. in a funeral procession in London, were held to be wearing a uniform for this purpose. The corresponding offence under the Prevention of Terrorism (Temporary Provisions) Act 1984, is the wearing of "any item of dress" or the display of "any article signifying such association,"(s.2[23]).

The statutes against liveries and maintenance passed in Tudor times were repealed in the nineteenth century as being no longer necessary. In the years between the wars, however, the growth of militant fascist, communist and other extreme organisations led, or threatened to lead, to serious public disorder. Section 2 of the Public Order Act 1936 therefore enacted that if members or adherents of any association of persons are: "(a) organised or trained or equipped for the purpose of enabling them to be employed in usurping the functions of the police or of the armed forces of the Crown: or (b) organised and trained or organised and equipped either for the purpose of enabling them to be employed for the use or display of physical force in promoting any political object or in such manner as to arouse reasonable apprehension that they are organised and either trained or equipped for that purpose," then any person who takes part in the control or management of the association or in so organising or training its members or adherents, is guilty of an offence punishable by fine and imprisonment. The consent of the Attorney-General is necessary before initiating a prosecution under this section. A person charged with taking part in the control or management of such an association may plead that he neither consented to nor connived at the unlawful organisation, training or equipment. The first conviction under section 2 was *R.* v. *Jordan and Tyndall*[24] for organising and equipping an association called "Spearhead" in such a manner as to arouse reasonable apprehension that they would be used for the use or display of physical force in promoting a political object. The Court of Criminal Appeal, upholding sentences of nine months' and six months' imprisonment as being appropriate deterrents, held that it was not necessary that there should be evidence of actual attacks or plans for attacks on opponents.

---

[21] Which applies to Scotland.
[22] [1975] Q.B. 864 (D.C.).
[23] Replacing the Act of 1976: see *ante*, p. 480.
[24] *The Times*, November 10, 1962; [1963] Crim.L.R. 124. For the case of *Father Fell and Stagg* (Birmingham Crown Court), see *The Times*, October 9, 1973.

Public Order Act 1986[25]

Part I of this Act abolishes the common law offences of riot, rout, unlawful assembly and affray (s.9) and several statutory offences,[26] the most significant of which was the offence of conduct conducive to breach of the peace (Public Order Act 1936, s.5). It introduces a variety of new offences to replace those repealed.[27] Part II contains new provisions in connection with processions and assemblies.[28] A much extended offence of racial hatred is contained in Part III,[29] while Part IV[30] provides for the making of exclusion orders in respect of those convicted of certain offences in connection with football matches. Part V contains miscellaneous and general provisions. Of particular significance in this Part is the introduction of the schedules which extensively amend the Sporting Events (Control of Alcohol etc.) Act 1985 and Part V of the Criminal Justice (Scotland) Act 1980 (which is also concerned with the control of alcohol at sporting events). Part V also contains two new offences. First that of the contamination of, or interference with, goods with the intention of causing public alarm or anxiety or personal injury or economic loss (s.38). Secondly, a provision whereby, in certain circumstances, a senior police officer may direct trespassers to leave land, and creating an offence of failing to leave the land or re-entering the land within three months of the direction to leave (s.39).

Riot (s.1)

The miners' dispute in 1984–85 was notable not only for the record number of charges brought for the common law offences of riot and unlawful assembly,[31] but also for subsequent decisions by the police to offer "no evidence" in many of the trials, and for the high number of acquittals.[32] Both can be explained, in part, by certain technical difficulties with the offences.[33] Riot, one of the most serious of the common law offences was triable only on indictment and punishable by imprisonment and/or a fine at the discretion of the court. The five essential elements for riot, or riotous assembly, were said to be: (i) three or more persons, (ii) a common purpose, whether lawful or unlawful of a private nature, (iii) execution or inception of the common purpose causing alarm or terror, (iv) intent to help one another by unlawful force if necessary, against anyone who may oppose them, (v) force or violence displayed

---

[25] See Richard Card, *Public Order The New Law* (1987); March [1987] Crim L.R. p.153–193.

[26] s.1 of the Tumultuous Petitioning Act 1661 (presentation of petition to the monarch or Parliament accompanied by excessive number of persons); s.1 of the Shipping Offences Act 1793; s.23 of the Seditious Meetings Act 1817 (prohibition of certain meetings within one mile of Westminster Hall when Parliament is sitting). Only the repeal provisions of Part I apply to Scotland, since it retains its own common law offences.

[27] *Post*, pp. 555–560. The offence of rout has not been replaced.

[28] *Post*, pp. 560–570.

[29] *Ante*, p. 479.

[30] *Post*, p. 573.

[31] A total of 137 charges of riot and 509 of unlawful assembly were brought. *The Times*, March 20, 1985.

[32] See *e.g.*, *The Times*, July 19, 24 1985; August 5, 6, 8, 1985.

[33] Lord Scarman in his report on the Brixton Disorders (1981) Cmnd. 8427, referred to the "forensic confusion . . . which now prevails when a jury has the complex task of deciding whether the necessary elements of riot (or unlawful assembly) have been proved." Para 7.39.

in such a manner as to alarm at least one person of reasonable firmness (*Field* v. *Metropolitan Police Receiver*).[34] Problems with the offence included the requirement of a common purpose; the intent to help one another, by force if necessary, in the execution of the common purpose; and the borderline between riot and unlawful assembly.[35] Until the miners' dispute most of the cases on riot arose out of the Riot (Damage) Act 1886, which replaced the old law whereby the inhabitants of the hundred had to compensate persons who lost property owing to the conduct of rioters.[36] This Act provides that where premises are injured or the property therein is destroyed or stolen by any persons *riotously and tumultuously* assembled, compensation to the persons aggrieved is to be paid out of the local police fund. Thus in *Ford* v. *Metropolitan Police District Receiver*[37] it was held that when a good-humoured crowd entered an empty house on a peace night in 1919, and took away the woodwork and flooring to make a bonfire, to the alarm of the next-door neighbour, their conduct embraced all the ingredients of a riot.

The offence of riot, in section 1 of the Public Order Act 1986, is the most serious of the new public order offences. It is triable only on indictment and punishable by imprisonment for up to 10 years or a fine or both. A new provision is the requirement of the consent of the Director of Public Prosecutions before a prosecution for riot, or incitement to riot, can be instituted (s.7(1)). The definition of riot is in some ways narrower than at common law. The minimum number required for riot is 12 persons present together who use or threaten unlawful violence for a common purpose. Those involved do not have to use or threaten violence simultaneously (s.1(2)). Only those who *use* unlawful violence in the prescribed circumstances are guilty of riot. Provided at least one person is so liable, the other members of the group may be guilty of aiding and abetting riot or of a lesser offence, such as violent disorder. Violence for this offence, and for the offences of violent disorder (s.2) and using threatening abusive or insulting words or behaviour (s.4), means any violent conduct towards property or persons, whether or not damage or injury is caused or intended (s.8). For this offence, and for the offences of violent disorder, affray and threatening, abusive or insulting behaviour, the definition of the offence is in terms of *unlawful* violence. The definition of violence concentrates on the conduct rather than the consequences of the violence and provides that "it is not restricted to conduct causing or intended to cause injury or damage but includes any other violent conduct" (s.8). To assist in overcoming some of the previous problems with proving a common purpose, it is provided that "the common purpose may be inferred from conduct" (s.1(3)). The conduct of the "persons who are present together" must be such as could cause a person of reasonable fitness present at the scene to fear for his personal safety. For this offence, as with those of violent disorder (s.2) and affray (s.3) no person of reasonable firmness need

---

[34] [1907] 2 K.B. 853.
[35] See generally *R.* v. *Caird and Others* (1970) 54 Cr.App.R.499 (C.A.); O. Hood Phillips, "Limits of the Freedom to Demonstrate" (1970) 86 L.Q.R. 453.
[36] See A. Samuels, "Compensation for Riot Damage" [1970] Crim.L.R. 336.
[37] [1921] 2 K.B. 344. And see *Pitchers* v. *Surrey County Council* [1923] 2 K.B. 415; *Jarvis* v. *Surrey County Council* [1925] 1 K.B. 554.

actually be, or be likely to be, present at the scene. In common with all the offences in Part I, riot may be committed in private as well as in public places (s.1(5)).[38] It must be proved that a person accused of riot either intended to use violence or was aware that his conduct may be violent (s.6(1)).[39] For the purpose of the Riot (Damages) Act 1886,[40] "riotous" and "riotously" are to be construed in accordance with section 1 (s.10(1)).[41] Riot is an arrestable offence by virtue of section 24 of the Police and Criminal Evidence Act 1984.

Violent disorder (s.2)[42]

A new offence of violent disorder (s.2) is designed to replace the common law offence of unlawful assembly.[43] At common law unlawful assembly was triable and punishable in the same way as riot. The definition of unlawful assembly, as developed by the courts, was uncertain.[44] In effect it arose where three or more persons either assembled to commit, or when assembled did commit, a breach of the peace; *or* assembled with intent to commit a crime by open force; *or* assembled for any common purpose, whether lawful or unlawful, in such manner as to give firm and courageous persons in the neighbourhood reasonable cause to fear that a breach of the peace would occur.[45] The new offence of violent disorder has little in common with the old offence of unlawful assembly. It is a wide offence since it covers both the actual use of violence *and* the threat of violence. The offence requires that three or more persons present together use or threaten unlawful violence and that their conduct, taken together, would cause a (hypothetical) person of reasonable fitness present at the scene to fear for his personal safety. There is no longer a need for a common purpose on the part of the three or more persons, which marks an important distinction between the new offences of riot and unlawful assembly compared to the common law offences, and may make violent disorder a more frequent charge than that of riot. Nor is it necessary for violent disorder that the persons

---

[38] Since the offences in Part I can be committed in a public or a private place (subject to certain exceptions for private dwellings), there is no need for a definition of public place in this Part.

[39] For all offences in Part I of the Act a provision is made with regard to those who are intoxicated. A person whose awareness is impaired by intoxication, whether by drink, drugs or other means, shall be taken to be aware of "that of which he would be aware if not intoxicated, unless he shows either that his intoxication was not self-induced or that it was caused solely by the taking . . . of a substance in the course of medical treatment," (s.6(5)).

[40] Also the Merchant Shipping Act 1894, s.515.

[41] Any enactment in force before s.10 came into effect, which contained the word "riot" or cognate expressions, which would have been construed in accordance with the common law offence of riot, is to be construed in accordance with s.1 (s.10(3)).

[42] For elements which this offence has in common with riot, see earlier section.

[43] The Law Commission had recommended two offences to replace unlawful assembly *viz.* violent disorder and conduct intended or likely to cause fear or provoke violence. The Government did not accept that a separate offence of "conduct intended etc." was necessary, and instead amended the offence of violent disorder to include those who threatened unlawful violence: Cmnd. 9510 (1985) *paras.* 3.4, 3.13, 3.14.

[44] For a summary of the various views see Law Com. Working Paper No. 82 pp. 38–43; also *R. v. Chief Constable of Devon and Cornwall, ex p. Central Electricity Generating Board* [1982] Q.B. 458 *cf.* Lord Denning M.R. at p. 471 with Lawton L.J. at pp. 473–474.

[45] *R. v. Vincent* (1839) 3 St.Tr. (N.S.) 1037; *R. v. Billingham* (1825) 2 C. & P. 234.

concerned used or threatened unlawful violence simultaneously (s.2(2)). This *mens rea* is an intent to use or threaten violence or an awareness that conduct may be violent or threaten violence (s.6(2)). The offence of violent disorder is triable either way, and is an arrestable offence by virtue of section 24 of the Police and Criminal Evidence Act 1984.[46]

Affray (s.3)[47]

The common law offence of affray fell into disuse from 1847 until 1957[48] when it was revived to deal with gangs who fight and disturb the peace, including football hooligans. At common law an affray was an unlawful fight or display of force[49] by one[50] or more persons to the terror of bystanders. Affray could be in a private[51] or a public place, and when in a public place there was no need to produce a witness to provide evidence that he was put in terror.[52] The new offence of affray, although broadly based on the common law offence as developed by the courts, is in fact more extensive than at common law. By section 3 a person is guilty of affray if he uses or threatens unlawful violence towards another and his conduct is such as would cause a (hypothetical) person of reasonable firmness present at the scene to fear for his personal safety (s.3(1)). Where two or more persons use or threaten the unlawful violence, it is the conduct of them taken together that must be considered for the purpose of section 3(1) (s.3(2)). The threat of unlawful violence must be a physical threat and cannot be made by the use of words alone (.3(3)). In this section, unlike sections 1 and 2, violence does not include violent conduct towards property (s.8). The provision that affray may be committed in private as well as public (s.3(5)), and that no person of reasonable firmness need actually be, or be likely to be, present at the scene, means that a fight in a private house could amount to the public order offence of affray. The *mens rea* is the same as for the offence of violent disorder (s.6(2)), and a constable may arrest without warrant anyone he reasonably suspects *is committing* affray (s.3(6)).[53] This is a more limited power of arrest than that which applies to sections 1 and 2 by virtue of section 24 of the Police and Criminal Evidence Act 1984. It is likely that the common law power to arrest without warrant for an actual or threatened breach of the peace will be available in circumstances which would amount to an offence under sections 1, 2, or 3.

---

[46] The penalties on conviction on indictment are up to five years imprisonment, or a fine or both; on summary conviction up to six months imprisonment or a fine not exceeding the statutory maximum (at present £2,000, see Criminal Justice Act 1982, s.74 which can be varied by statutory instrument by the Home Secretary acting under s.143 Magistrates' Court Act 1980).

[47] See A. T. H. Smith "The Metamorphosis of Affray" [1986] N.L.J. 521. For elements which this offence has in common with riot, see earlier section.

[48] *R. v. Sharp* [1957] 1 Q.B. 552 (C.C.A.).

[49] It was held in *R. v. Summers* (1972) 56 Cr.App.R. 604 (C.A.) that a fight or actual violence was not necessary.

[50] One man unlawfully fighting can be convicted of affray: *R. v. Taylor (Vincent)* [1973] A.C. 964 (H.L.).

[51] *R. v. Button and Swain* [1966] A.C. 591.

[52] *R. v. Taylor (Vincent) ante; Att.-Gen.'s Reference (No. 3 of 1983)* [1985] 1 Q.B. 242.

[53] The mode of trial and punishment is the same as for violent disorder, except that on conviction on indictment the maximum term of imprisonment is three years (s.3(7)).

Threatening, abusive or insulting words or behaviour (s.4)[54]

This offence replaces section 5 of the Public Order Act 1936,[55] one of the most common public order offences, and used in a wide variety of situations, for example, political meetings,[56] football hooliganism,[57] and disputes between neighbours on the highway.[58] Section 5 had been subject to extensive judicial interpretation, and the new offence is aimed at avoiding some of these decisions. The new offence in section 4 is a mixture of aspects of section 5 of the 1936 Act and the Law Commission's proposed offence of conduct intended or likely to cause fear or provoke violence.[59]

There are two alternative limbs to section 4. The accused must either (a) use towards another person threatening, abusive or insulting words or behaviour, or (b) distribute or display to another person any writing, sign or other visible representation which is threatening, abusive or insulting. In either case, the accused must do so with an "intent to cause that person to believe that immediate unlawful violence will be used against him or another by any person, or to provoke the immediate use of unlawful violence by that person or another, or whereby that person is likely to believe that such violence will be used or it is likely that such violence will be provoked" (s.4(1)). This list of possible consequences of the accused's words or behaviour covers a wide spectrum, and makes section 4 potentially much more far reaching than its predecessor.

The words "threatening, abusive or insulting" appeared in section 5 of the 1936 Act, and the cases interpreting them presumably will apply to the new offence.[60] In *Cozens* v. *Brutus*[61] it was held that "insulting" must be given its ordinary meaning: "it is a question of fact in each case and not a question of law." The section differs from recent interpretations of section 5 of the 1936 Act[62] in that it requires an offender to either intend, or be aware that his words, behaviour, writing, sign or other visible representation, is threatening, abusive or insulting (s.6(3)). A further change is that the threatening, abusive or insulting words or behaviour must be used *towards another person*, or distributed or displayed *to another*. One of the main differences in section 4 is with regard to the consequences of the threatening, abusive or insulting words, behaviour, writing etc. Section 5 of the 1936 Act had been in terms of either an intended or likely breach of the peace. Judicial interpretation of this part of section 5 had suggested that where the victim of

---

[54] For elements which this offence has in common with riot, see earlier section.

[55] As substituted by s.7 of the Race Relations Act 1965. Section 5 of the Public Order Act 1936 had applied to Scotland, but was little used because of the alternative common law offence of breach of the peace. It was decided therefore that s.4 should not apply to Scotland.

[56] *Jordan* v. *Burgoyne* [1963] 2 Q.B. 744 (D.C.)

[57] *Allen and others* v. *Ireland* [1984] 1 W.L.R. 903 (D.C.).

[58] *Ward* v. *Holman* [1964] 2 Q.B. 580 (D.C.).

[59] Report *op. cit.*, Part V.

[60] For example *Simcock* v. *Rhodes* (1977) Cr.App.Rep.192 (D.C.); *Jordan* v. *Burgoyne, ante.*

[61] [1973] A.C. 854 (H.L.) (anti-apartheid demonstration on Wimbledon tennis court; spectators angered, but not insulted). *Cf. Masterson* v. *Holden* [1986] 1 W.L.R. 1017 (D.C.). (Overt homosexual conduct in Oxford St. at 1.55 a.m. Justices "most likely to know what is insulting behaviour" at that hour in that place)

[62] *Parkin* v. *Norman* [1983] Q.B. 92 (D.C.); *cf.* Viscount Dilhorne in *Cozens* v. *Brutus ante,* at pp. 865–866.

intimidatory conduct was, for example, a policeman or an elderly lady, who was unlikely to be provoked into a breach of the peace, there was no offence.[63] Two aspects of section 4 are designed to avoid this problem. First there is the expanded list of possible consequences of the accused's words or behaviour,[64] and secondly the phrase "breach of the peace" has been replaced by "immediate unlawful violence." The latter change had been suggested by the Law Commission as preferable to a statutory definition of breach of the peace, since breach of the peace was a concept which had been subject to differing judicial interpretations,[65] and which was of importance to remaining common law police powers.[66] The meaning of "immediate unlawful violence" is certainly as wide as that of breach of peace suggested in *R. v. Howell.*[67] Where an accused cannot be shown to have intended to cause another person to believe that immediate unlawful violence will be used against him or another by any person etc., the alternative is to show that another person was "likely to believe that such violence will be used or it is likely that such violence will be provoked" (s.4(1)). In considering the "likely" effect of the accused's conduct, it is probable that the existing law, whereby the accused must "take his audience as he finds them," will continue to apply.[68]

Unlike section 5 of the 1936 Act, an offence under section 4 can be committed in a private as well as in a public place, but excluding, in effect, domestic disputes (s.5(2)). A constable may arrest without warrant anyone he reasonably suspects *is* committing an offence under section 4 (s.4(3)). For this offence, and the offence under section 5, the police could also, in certain circumstances, rely on their common law powers of arrest without warrant in connection with a breach of the peace; and their powers under section 25 of the Police and Criminal Evidence Act 1984. Offences under this section are triable summarily only.[69]

Offensive conduct (s.5)[70]

This is a new offence designed to cover minor acts of hooliganism which would not amount to offences under section 4. An offence is

---

[63] *Parkin* v. *Norman ante; Marsh* v. *Arscott* (1982) 75 Cr.App.Rep. 211. In both cases the only people present were the respective defendant and the police officers; *Read* v. *Jones* (1983) 77 Cr.App.Rep. 246 and *Nicholson* v. *Gage* (1985) 80 Cr.App.Rep. 40.

[64] s.4(1).

[65] *R.* v. *Chief Constable of Devon and Cornwall ex p. Central Electricity Generating Board, ante,* Lord Denning M.R. at p. 471 and *R.* v. *Howell* [1982] Q.B. 416 (D.C.), *per* Watkins L.J. at p. 426, "We cannot accept that there can be a breach of the peace unless there has been an act done or threatened to be done which either actually harms a person, or in his presence his property, or is likely to cause such harm, or which puts someone in fear of such harm being done."

[66] For example the common law powers to deal with or prevent a breach of the peace.

[67] *Ibid.* p. 426.

[68] *Jordan* v. *Burgoyne, ante, Parkin* v. *Norman, ante.* For an argument to the contrary, see A.T.H. Smith [1987] Crim. L.R. 156 at p. 164.

[69] The penalties for this offence are imprisonment for up to six months or a fine not exceeding level 5 on the standard scale (at present £2,000) or both. Where a person has been tried on indictment for violent disorder or affray, and found not guilty, the jury may, as an alternative, find him guilty of an offence under s.4 (s.7(3)).

[70] For elements which this offence has in common with riot, see *ante,* p. 555.

committed where a person either "a) uses threatening, abusive or insulting words or behaviour, or disorderly behaviour or b) displays any writing, sign or other visible representation which is threatening, abusive or insulting." In either case it must be "within the hearing or sight of a person likely to be caused harassment, alarm or distress thereby" (s.5(1)). There is no need for *actual* harassment, alarm or distress, it is sufficient that the words or behaviour are *likely* to cause harassment, alarm or distress. The accused must either intend or be aware that his words, behaviour, writing etc. is threatening, abusive or insulting or he intends or is aware that his behaviour is or may be disorderly (s.6(4)). The exception with regard to private dwellings found in section 4 also applies to this offence (s.5(2)). Three additional defences are provided for section 5, in each case the onus of proof is on the accused. These are that he had no reason to believe that there was anyone with hearing in sight who was likely to be caused harassment, alarm or distress; that he was inside a dwelling and had no reason to believe that his words, behaviour, writing etc. would be heard or seen by a person outside that or any other dwelling; that his conduct was reasonable (s.5(3)). If a person engages in "offensive conduct", which means conduct which a police officer reasonably suspects to constitute an offence under s.5 (s.5(5)), and the police officer's warning to stop such conduct is ignored, then the police officer may arrest that person without warrant. An offence under section 5 is triable summarily only.[71] This is potentially a very wide offence and its use, application and interpretation is likely to be controversial.

Public meetings, assemblies and demonstrations

The common practice of holding public meetings dates from the habit of promoting meetings to discuss and present petitions to Parliament in the late eighteenth and early nineteenth centuries, the popular interest in parliamentary affairs being no doubt stimulated, first, by a more widespread dissemination of newspapers, and then by the extension of the franchise. The restrictive legislation of that period shows that the executive was concerned with criticism of the government, whereas the later statutes are intended mainly to prevent outbreaks of disorder (although the Public Order Act 1986 goes beyond this). Public meetings and processions have engaged the attention of Parliament and the courts a good deal in the past; and although the old election meeting, or meeting held to advocate or criticise some projected legislation or government action, has largely given way to the radio or television talk, this topic has received a revived importance in the last few years as a result of the modern "demonstration" against nuclear armament, apartheid and other objects of popular protest, and the use of mass picketing at the scenes of industrial disputes. There has also been an increase in counter-demonstrations by those opposed to meetings held by certain groups. It should be noted that demonstrations do not form a special legal category, and those who take part are subject to the same laws and are liable for the same range of public order and other offences as is any

---

[71] On conviction, a fine not exceeding level 3 on the standard scale (at present £400) may be imposed.

participant at a public meeting.[72] Would it make any practical difference if what has hitherto been regarded as a residual liberty becomes a right to demonstrate or protest in a public place?[73] Lord Denning M.R. in his dissenting judgement in *Hubbard* v. *Pitt*,[74] a case of picketing in the highway not in connection with an industrial dispute and where there was no evidence of obstruction, breach of the peace or nuisance, said that "so long as good order is maintained, the right to demonstrate must be preserved"; but the question in issue was whether an interlocutory injunction should be granted, largely on the ground of alleged defamation. And Scarman L.J (as he then was) in a report on a disorderly demonstration,[75] pointed out the conflict of interest between those who seek to use the streets for the purpose of passage and those who seek to use them for the purpose of demonstration. There is a right to demonstrate he said, subject only to limits required by the need for good order and the passage of traffic.

A "public meeting" may be defined as a meeting held for the purpose of discussing or expressing views on matters of public interest, and which the public or any section thereof is invited to attend. A public meeting may be held either on private premises or in a public place. "Private premises" are premises to which the public have access only by permission of the owner or occupier. A "public place" includes any highway[76] or any other premises or place (such as a public park, sea beach or public road) to which the public have or are permitted to have access, whether on payment or otherwise,[77] or by virtue of express or implied permission. The Public Order Act 1986, s.14[78] enables, for the first time, conditions to be imposed in certain circumstances, on a "public assembly" which is defined in section 16.

There is a general liberty to promote or take part in a public meeting on private premises, subject to infringement of particular legal rules. It is doubtful whether there is such a general liberty to promote or take part in a public meeting in a public place without the licence of the owners (often the local authority), since this will almost invariably involve trespass to land as well as in many cases an obstruction or a public nuisance, although a public meeting in a public place is not necessarily unlawful.[79] There are special provisions[80] whereby candi-

---

[72] See *e.g. Cozens* v. *Brutus* [1973] A.C. 854 (H.L.), *ante*, p. 558, (Public Order Act); *Chandler* v. *D.P.P.* [1964] A.C. 763 (H.L.), *ante*, p. 484 (Official Secrets Acts); *Arrowsmith* v. *Jenkins* [1963] 2 Q.B. 561 (D.C.), *ante*, p. 551 (obstruction of highway).

[73] K. J. Keith, "The Right to Protest" in *Essays on Human Rights* (ed. Keith, N.Z., 1968), p. 49; O. Hood Phillips, "A Right to Demonstrate?" (1970) 86 L.Q.R. 1; "Limits of the Freedom to Demonstrate," *ibid.* p. 453; V. T. Bevan "Public Protest and Public Order" [1979] P.L. 163.

[74] [1976] Q.B. 142 (C.A.). And see P. Wallington, "Injunctions and the 'Right to Demonstrate'" [1976] C.L.J. 82; Hazel Carty "The Legality of Peaceful Picketing on the Highway" [1984] P.L. 600.

[75] (1975) Cmnd. 5919: *The Red Lion Square Disorders of June 15, 1974.*

[76] In Scotland, any road within the meaning of the Roads (Scotland) Act 1984.

[77] Definitions adapted from Public Order Acts and Criminal Justice Act 1972.

[78] *Post*, p. 566.

[79] *Cf.* A. L. Goodhart, "Public Meetings and Processions" (1937) 6 C.L.J. 161. See also E. C. S. Wade, "The Law of Public Meetings" (1938) 2 M.L.R. 177; E. R. Ivamy, "The Right of Public Meeting" (1949) C.L.P. 183.

[80] Representation of the People Act 1983, ss.95, 96.

dates at local and parliamentary elections are entitled to the use of schools and other public rooms for the purpose of holding election meetings.

Among the common law rules that may be infringed by the holding of a public meeting or demonstration are those relating to sedition[81]; public nuisance;[82] assault, and trespass to land, which by itself in English law is a tort.[83] There may, in addition, be a species of the tort of private nuisance where there is unreasonable interference with the rights of others to use the highway,[84] which may give rise to an action for damages or the granting of an injunction. A meeting that would otherwise be lawful will not be so if there is intention or provocation or incitement of others to cause a disturbance or to commit other unlawful acts.

Public meetings in private premises

The owner or occupier of private premises, for example, the hirer of a hall, may hold a public meeting there or licence others to do so. The organiser of the meeting may exclude or eject trespassers, after first asking them to leave; if they refuse he may use reasonable force, although he may not arrest or detain them. The exercise of this right by the occupier or licensee may be embarrassed by the decision in *Thomas* v. *Sawkins*[85] that the police may enter the premises if they have reasonable grounds for believing that, if they were not present, seditious speeches would be made or breaches of the peace would occur.[86] In that case the meeting was held to protest against the Incitement to Disaffection Bill, and to demand the dismissal of the Chief Constable of Glamorgan. The scope of the decision is uncertain. Lord Hewart L.C.J. said the police had a right to enter if they had reasonable grounds for believing that "an offence is imminent or is likely to be committed," while Avory J. said they had this right if "seditious speeches would be made and/ or . . . a breach of the peace would take place." Lawrence J. did not express an opinion on this point. Emphasis was laid in the judgments on the fact that, as the public were invited, the police could attend as members of the public; but the conveners can withdraw an invitation from particular persons of sections of the public, and in this case they did in fact ask the police to leave. The police may have been trespassers, but Avory J. seems to have thought that the revocation of the licence to the police was ineffective. If the licence to the police as members of the

---

[81] *Ante*, Chap. 24.

[82] *Post*, p. 567.

[83] *Cf.* Trespass (Scotland) Act 1865, under which lodging in premises or camping on land without the owner's permission is a criminal offence. And *cf.* trespassing with firearms. See also Public Order Act 1986, s.39.

[84] *Thomas* v. *N.U.M.* [1985] I.R.L.R. 136, at p. 149. See also Hazel Carty, *loc. cit.* and also [1985] P.L. 542. *News Group Newspapers Ltd. and others* v. *S.O.G.A.T. '82* [1986] I.R.L.R. 336.

[85] [1935] 2 K.B. 434.

[86] s.17(2) Police and Criminal Evidence Act 1984 abolishes all common law powers to enter premises without a warrant, except for the power of entry to deal with or prevent a breach of the peace (s.17(6)).

public was effectively revoked, the decision in *Thomas* v. *Sawkins* may apply also to private meetings. Shortly after that case it was held in *Davis* v. *Lisle*[87] that the police have no right to enter private premises without a warrant in connection with a summary offence not involving a breach of the peace. Section 14 of the Public Order Act 1986 is not applicable to indoor meetings.

Public meetings in public places

The highway is in a special category, because members of the public have a right to pass and repass on their lawful occasions, with such reasonable extensions as looking at shop windows, talking to one's friends and parking cars.[88] To exceed this right is technically the tort of trespass against the owner of the surface of the highway, which is usually the local highway authority.[89] If repeated, such abuse might amount to nuisance, public or private.[90] There is also the possibility of an offence under section 137 of the Highways Act 1980[91] or section 14 of the Public Order Act 1986[92] Special regulations may apply to meetings and processions in the vicinity of Parliament. At the commencement of the session each House, by order, gives directions that the Commissioner of Metropolitan Police shall keep, during the session, the streets leading to the Houses of Parliament free and open, and that no obstruction shall be permitted to hinder the passage of the Lords or Members. To effect enforcement of this order the Metropolitan Police Commissioner issues a direction specifying the streets concerned by virtue of his powers under the Metropolitan Police Act 1839, s.52 which is enforceable by a fine under section 54.[93]

Rather more latitude is allowed in public parks and gardens, which are intended for recreation and exercise rather than merely passing up and down. Yet there is no common law right in the strict sense to hold public meetings on a common,[94] on the foreshore,[95] in Hyde Park[96] or Trafalgar Square.[97] Public meetings may take place in Trafalgar Square, and perhaps Hyde Park, only with the permission of the Secretary of State for the Environment, under regulations made by the Minister of the Environment. The general regulations restrict the holding of public meetings in Trafalgar Square to daylight on Saturday afternoons, Sundays and bank holidays, and require previous notice to be given to the

---

[87] [19361 2 K.B. 434 (D.C.).
[88] Parking is a liberty only where there are no parking regulations. House-owners adjacent to the highway have no *right* to park in the highway, but they may in some areas obtain a licence from the local authority.
[89] *Tunbridge Wells Corporation* v. *Baird* [1896] A.C. 434; *Llandudno U.D.C.* v. *Woods* [1899] 2 Ch. 705.
[90] *Post*, p. 567.
[91] *Ante*, p. 551.
[92] *Post*, p. 566.
[93] See *Papworth* v. *Coventry* [1967] 1 W.L.R. 663 (D.C.), and Brownlie *loc. cit.* pp. 349–351.
[94] *De Morgan* v. *Metropolitan Board of Works* (1880) 5 Q.B.D. 155.
[95] *Brighton Corporation* v. *Packham* (1908) 72 J.P. 318.
[96] *Bailey* v. *Williamson* (1873) L.R. 8 Q.B. 118.
[97] *R.* v. *Cunninghame Graham and Burns* (1888) 16 Cox C.C. 420. And see *Ex p. Lewis* (1888) 21 Q.B.D. 191.

police and their directions as to the approach route of any procession to be accepted.[98]

Prevention and dispersal of meetings, assemblies and demonstrations

The executive have no power to prohibit a meeting beforehand, unless it is to be on government property. The police, however, have a primary duty to preserve the peace.[99] They may therefore prevent people from reaching a meeting or demonstration where they have reasonable grounds to fear there may be an imminent breach of the peace.[1] They may also prevent a meeting from starting, or may order it to disperse at any time after it has stated, if they reasonably believe that it is necessary to do so for the purpose of preserving or restoring public order. These powers are backed up by the power to arrest without warrant for breach of the peace[2]; the possibility of a later charge of obstructing a police officer in the execution of his duty,[3] if the police order is disregarded; and the use of the power to seek a binding over order.[4] The question whether there has been a reasonable apprehension of a breach of the peace is an objective one, and the court must be satisfied that there existed "proved facts from which a constable could reasonably have anticipated such a breach."[5] However the courts have been reluctant to interfere with a police officer's assessment of a situation.

In *Beatty* v. *Gillbanks*[6] an appeal was made to a Divisional Court against a binding-over order made by magistrates. The magistrates had no jurisdiction to try Beatty and two other officers of the Salvation Army for the offence of unlawful assembly, but, as a preliminary to binding them over, found the allegations of unlawful assembly proved. The Divisional Court held that Beatty and the other Salvation Army officers had been wrongly adjudged to have committed an unlawful assembly merely because they had persisted, in spite of a justices' notice and a police direction, in holding their processions and meetings in Weston-super-Mare knowing that a rival organisation called the "Skeleton Army" systematically opposed them, with the result that considerable disturbance occurred. They were therefore wrongly bound over. The Salvation Army did not incite or intentionally provoke a breach of the peace, nor did they intend to meet force by force if opposed. "The finding of the justices comes to this," said Field J., "that a man may be indicted for doing a lawful act, if he knows that his doing it will cause another to do an unlawful act. There is no authority for such a proposi-

---

[98] These regulations were first issued in 1892 by Asquith (Home Secretary), who had defended Cunninghame Graham when at the Bar: Roy Jenkins, *Asquith*, pp. 64–65. See S.I. 1952 No. 776.

[99] See *Coffin* v. *Smith* (1980) 71 Cr.App.Rep. 221 " . . . a police officer's duty is to be a keeper of the peace and to take all necessary steps with that in view" per Donaldson L.J. See L. H. Leigh *Police Powers in England and Wales* (1985) Chap. 9.

[1] See *Moss and others* v. *McLachlan* [1985] I.R.L.R. 77 (D.C.); and *post*, p. 571.

[2] This is not affected by the Police and Criminal Evidence Act 1984.

[3] Police Act 1964, s.51(3). There is no general power to arrest without warrant for this offence: *Wershof* v. *Metropolitan Police Commissioner* [1978] 3 All E.R. 540, but there is such power if the "general arrest conditions" set out in s.25(3) of the Police and Criminal Evidence Act 1984 apply. *Ante*, p. 493 and 500.

[4] *Post*, p. 502.

[5] *Piddington* v. *Bates* [1961] 1 W.L.R. 162 at p. 169.

[6] (1882) 15 Cox C.C. 138.

tion." It should be mentioned that the magistrates' notice prohibiting the processions and meetings, issued on the advice of the Home Secretary, was of no legal effect: it was merely a warning of the fact that disorder was likely to follow. The principle of *Beatty* v. *Gillbanks*, that the unlawful must yield to the lawful,[7] must be considered in the light of subsequent cases, and the statutory powers to regulate meetings and processions.[8]

In the Irish case of *O'Kelly* v. *Harvey*[9] it was held that a police officer may disperse a public meeting if he believes that there will be a breach of the peace and that there is no other way of preventing it. And in another Irish case, *Humphries* v. *Connor*,[10] where a disturbance was caused by the fact that a Protestant woman, without intending to disturb the peace, wore an orange lily while walking through a crowd of Roman Catholics, a constable was held justified in removing the lily on the ground that it was necessary for the preservation of the peace. Similarly, the procession in *Beatty* v. *Gillbanks*, *ante* could properly have been dispersed if the rival factions had come to blows.

Provocation is a different matter. In *Wise* v. *Dunning*,[11] Wise, a Protestant pastor who led a Protestant "Crusade" in Liverpool and held street meetings in Catholic districts, was held to have been properly bound over for deliberately using insulting words and gestures, intended or likely to result in a breach of the peace. Darling J. emphasised the provocation, although there was a local Act under which Wise might have been charged. Channell J. pointed out that although "the law does not as a rule regard an illegal act as being the natural consequence of a temptation which may be held out to commit it . . . the law does regard the infirmity of human temper to the extent of considering that a breach of the peace, although an illegal act, may be the natural consequence of insulting or abusive language or conduct." Wise's conduct would now be covered by the Public Order Act 1986.

Since the case of *Duncan* v. *Jones*,[12] the offence of obstructing a police officer in the execution of his duty has been used to enforce the public order powers of the police. In this case Mrs. Duncan, a Communist, was about to make a speech in a street opposite a training centre for the unemployed. On a former occasion when she had done so, there had been a disturbance among sympathisers in the training centre. Jones, a police inspector, told her she must not hold a meeting there, but might do so a couple of hundred yards round the corner. Mrs. Duncan persisted in her attempt to hold a meeting, and she was arrested and charged with wilfully obstructing a police officer in the execution of his duty. Her conviction was upheld by Quarter Sessions on the grounds that: (i) she must have known that a disturbance was probable; (ii) Jones reasonably apprehended a breach of the peace; (iii) Jones

---

[7] See *Howard E. Perry Ltd.* v. *B.R.B.* [1980] 1 W.L.R. 1375 at p. 1385.

[8] *Post* pp. 567–570.

[9] (1883) 14 L.R.Ir. 105, 109.

[10] (1864) 17 Ir.C.L.R. 1.

[11] [1902] 1 K.B. 167.

[12] [1936] 1 K.B. 218. See E. C. S. Wade, "Police Powers and Public Meetings" (1937) 6 C.L.J. 175; T. C. Daintith, "Disobeying a Policeman—A Fresh Look at *Duncan* v. *Jones*" [1966] P.L. 248.

therefore had a duty to prevent the meeting; and (iv) Mrs. Duncan obstructed Jones in the execution of his duty.

What is the effect of the decision in *Duncan* v. *Jones*, emphasising the maintenance of public order, on the principle laid down in *Beatty* v. *Gillbanks* emphasising freedom of assembly? The audience in *Duncan* v. *Jones* was not hostile, but there was an atmosphere of excitement. Mrs. Duncan was not charged with obstructing the highway. The Divisional Court in *Duncan* v. *Jones* denied that the case raised any constitutional issue, and did not give the police any guidance as to how they should exercise their discretion in such cases. It has been pointed out that a charge which was intended to be a defensive or preventive weapon (obstructing a police officer) has come to be used by the police as an offensive or punitive weapon. It appears that persons in Mrs. Duncan's position should obey the police, and then pursue any remedy in the courts afterwards.

Restrictions on Public Assemblies under Public Order Act 1986, s.14

The Public Order Act 1936 which enabled conditions to be imposed on processions and marches (s.3(1)), and provided a power to ban processions and marches in certain circumstances (s.3(2), (3)), did not apply to static demonstrations, assemblies or meetings. Serious public order problems at static demonstrations led to the enactment of section 14 which enables conditions to be imposed on a public assembly of 20 or more people held in a public place which is wholly or partly open to the air (s.16). However there is no power to ban such assemblies. Before conditions may be imposed on such an assembly, the senior officer of police,[13] having regard to the time, place and circumstances of either an existing or proposed assembly, must reasonably believe that either "(a) it may result in serious public disorder, serious damage to property or serious disruption to the life of the community, or (b) the purpose of the persons organising it is the intimidation of others with a view to compelling them not to do an act they have a right to do, or to do an act they have a right not to do."[14] (s.14(1)). If the senior police officer has a reasonable belief as outlined above, he may then give such directions[15] "as appear to him necessary to prevent such disorder, damage, disruption or intimidation." The directions which may be imposed on the organiser of the assembly, or those taking part, are with regard to the place of the assembly, its maximum duration, or the maximum number of persons who may take part (s.14(1)). Anyone who organises or takes part in a public assembly and knowingly fails to comply with a condition imposed commits a summary offence.[16] In both cases it is a

---

[13] Defined in s.14(2). In relation to an assembly being held it means the most senior in rank of the police officers present at the scene; in relation to an assembly intended to be held, it means the chief officer of police who can delegate his functions to a deputy or assistant chief constable (s.15(1)).

[14] For a discussion of these criteria and the possibility of judicial review see the section on public processions, *post*, p. 569.

[15] Directions in respect of a proposed assembly must be in writing (s.14(3)).

[16] It is also an offence to incite another not to comply with a condition imposed on an assembly (s.14(6)).

defence for the accused to prove that his failure to comply with the condition arose from circumstances beyond his control (s.14(4)(5)). A constable in uniform may arrest without warrant anyone he reasonably suspects is committing an offence under section 14. The decision by the senior officer of police that conditions should be imposed on an assembly, or on a procession, can be subject to judicial review.

Public Processions

A public procession is defined by section 16 of the Public Order Act 1986 as a procession in a public place. Many of the general common law principles mentioned in connection with public meetings are applicable also to public processions. Indeed, a procession has been described as a meeting on the move, and many processions are in fact preliminary to the holding of a meeting. Since the right to use the highway is for passing and repassing, it was possible, prior to section 11 of the Public Order Act 1986 which requires advance notice for many public processions, to say that a procession on the highway was prima facie lawful.[17] In addition to many of the offences outlined earlier, and specific offence provided in the Public Order Act 1986 in connection with processions[18] a public procession may easily involve a public nuisance.

A public nuisance will be caused if the user of the highway, although reasonable from the point of view of those taking part in the procession, is not reasonable from the point of view of the public. This question depends on the circumstances of the case, and may be affected by the numbers taking part.[19] The occasion, duration, place and hour must be considered, and also whether the obstruction is trivial, casual, temporary and without wrongful intent (*Lowdens* v. *Keaveney*[20]). Thus in *R.* v. *Clark*[21] a conviction for inciting persons to commit a nuisance by obstructing the highway, after taking part in a demonstration during a visit of Greek royalty, was quashed on the ground that a procession is lawful[22] if there was a reasonable use of the highway, even though the highway is temporarily obstructed, and the jury had not been directed to consider whether or not there was a reasonable use of the highway.

The same principles apply whether the obstruction is caused by the procession itself or by onlookers.[23] Thus in *Lowdens* v. *Keaveney* (*supra*) it was held that a band which marched through Belfast playing party airs, with the result that a crowd of several hundreds collected, was not liable for causing a material obstruction.

Notice, conditions and prohibition of processions

Since the enactment of section 3 of the Public Order Act 1936 there has been a national power to impose restrictions on processions or, in certain circumstances, to prohibit them. This power has been revised and expanded in sections 11–13 of the Public Order Act 1986.

[17] Goodhart, "Public Meetings and Processions," *loc. cit.* pp. 169–174.
[18] *Post*, p. 568.
[19] *Att.-Gen.* v. *Brighton and Hove Co-operative Supply Association* [1900] 1 Ch. 276.
[20] [1903] Ir.R. 82.
[21] [1964] 2 Q.B. 315 (C.C.A.).
[22] Subject now to s.11 of the Public Order Act 1986.
[23] *Bellamy* v. *Wells* (1890) 7 T.L.R. 135.

Notice (s.11)

Written advance notice of a procession intended to demonstrate support for or opposition to the views or actions of any person or body of persons; to publicise a cause or campaign; or to commemorate an event must be delivered to the relevant police station, not less than 6 clear days before the date of the intended procession. Where this is not "reasonably practicable," then delivery should be as soon as delivery is reasonably practicable. The notice must specify the date, time and route of the proposed procession, and the name and address of the organiser (s.11(3)). Each of the persons organising a procession for which proper notice has not been given, or in respect of which the date, time or route differs from that given in the notice, is guilty of an offence. To allow for processions in response to an unexpected event, the above provisions will not apply if it is "not reasonably practicable to give advance notice of the procession" (s.11(1)). The requirement of notice does not apply to processions commonly or customarily held in an area, and funeral processions organised by a funeral director acting in the normal course of his business (s.11(2)).

Section 11 does not apply to Scotland, since the position there is already regulated by the Civic Government (Scotland) Act 1982, ss.62 and 65.

Conditions (s.12)

Before the senior police officer[24] can impose conditions on an actual or proposed procession he must have regard to the time, place, circumstance and route or proposed route of the procession. In the light of these if he reasonably believes that either "(a) it may result in serious public disorder, serious damage to property or serious disruption to the life of the community, or (b) the purpose of the persons organising it is the intimidation of others with a view to compelling them not to do an act they have a right to do, or to do an act they have a right not to do," then he may give directions[25] to the organisers or participants imposing conditions on the procession. These criteria are much wider than those found in the Public Order Act 1936 section 3(1) (which was limited to the risk of serious public disorder), and could prove controversial. For example, the requirement of serious disruption to the life of the community is capable of wide interpretation, while the intimidation provision does not necessarily require any connection with public disorder. A wide discretion is given to the police as to the conditions which are imposed since the section provides that he may impose "such conditions as appear to him necessary to prevent such disorder, damage, disruption or intimidation, including conditions as to the route of the procession or prohibiting it from entering any public place specified in the directions" (s.12(1)). To organise or take part in a procession and knowingly to fail to comply with a condition is an offence.

[24] Defined in s.12(2). In relation to a procession being held or a procession intended to be held where persons are assembling with a view to taking part in it, it means the most senior in rank of the police officers present at the scene. In the case of a proposed procession, it means the chief officer of police, who may delegate his functions to a deputy or assistant chief constable (s.15).

[25] Directions in respect of a proposed procession must be in writing (s.12(3)).

However it is a defence to prove that the failure arose from circumstances beyond the control of the accused (s.12(4)(5)). It is also an offence to incite another not to comply with a condition imposed on a procession (s.12(6)). A constable in uniform may arrest without warrant anyone he reasonably suspects is committing any of the above offences.

In Scotland, conditions may be imposed in advance on proposed processions by virtue of section 63 of the Civil Government (Scotland) Act 1982, which differs in several respects from section 12. However, section 12 does apply to Scotland in relation to a procession being held and to a procession intended to be held where persons are assembling with a view to taking part in the procession. (s.12(11)).

The police decision to impose conditions on a procession will be, as before, subject to judicial review. This could be on one of two grounds. First that there was no basis for the police officer's reasonable belief that the procession would result in serious public disorder, serious damage to property or serious disruption to the life of the community. This could include a challenge to the meaning of, for example, "serious disruption to the life of the community." Secondly, that even if there was a basis for the police officer's beliefs, the conditions imposed were not necessary to prevent disorder, damage, disruption or intimidation. Given that section 12(1) provides that the police officer may give such directions *as appear to him necessary*, it may prove difficult to challenge the legality of directions given, except on the ground that they are totally unreasonable.

Prohibition (s.13)

The power to prohibit public processions is virtually the same as that found in section 3(2) and (3) of the Public Order Act 1936. Where the senior police officer reasonably believes that, because of particular circumstances existing in any district or part of a district, the powers under section 12 will be insufficient to prevent the holding of a public procession from resulting in "serious public disorder," then he shall apply to the council of the district for an order prohibiting for up to three months, the holding of all public processions or of any class of public processions so specified in the district or part of the district (s.13(1)). On receiving such an application, the council may, with the consent of the Secretary of State, make an order either in the terms of the application or with such modifications as may be approved by the Secretary of State (s.13(2)). Where the area concerned is the City of London, or the metropolitan police district, then the power to seek an order is given to the Commissioner of Police for the City of London or the Commissioner of Police of the Metropolis, who may, with the consent of the Secretary of State, make a similar order to that outlined above. It is an offence to organise, take part, or incite another to take part in a prohibited procession (s.13(7)(8)(9)), and all three offences are arrestable without warrant by a constable in uniform (s.13(10)).

Orders prohibiting processions will also be subject to judicial review. It should be noted that the section is worded in terms of the "reasonable belief" of the senior police officer, as compared with section 3 of the 1936 Act which required the senior police officer to be of the "opinion" that the imposition of conditions would be insufficient to prevent serious public disorder, which may provide a greater possibility for successful judicial review than previously.[26]

Picketing[27]

The word picket is used to describe those who gather outside a particular place with the aim of persuading others not to enter. Although usually connected with industrial disputes, this is not necessarily the case.[28] There is no legal right to picket as such, but "peaceful picketing" in industrial disputes has long been recognised as being lawful. There is therefore a statutory freedom or liberty to picket peacefully in certain circumstance. The present law is contained in the Trade Union and Labour Relations Act 1974, section 15 as substituted by the Employment Act 1980. This provides that "It shall be lawful for a person in contemplation or furtherance of a trade dispute to attend—(a) at or near his own place of work, or (b) if he is an official of a trade union, at or near the place of work of a member of that union whom he is accompanying and whom he represents, for the purpose only of peacefully obtaining or communicating information, or peacefully persuading any person to work or abstain from working." The immunity given by this section is to attend at or near certain places for particular purposes, so that such attendance does not of itself constitute the torts of trespass or nuisance, or the criminal offences of obstructing the highway or "watching or besetting."[29] However this may not be the case where mass picketing (*infra*) is involved. The immunity given to those covered by section 15 is in respect only of peaceful picketing, which means without causing a breach of the peace.[30] It is also only in respect of the attendance of pickets for the purposes set out in the section, and if the attendance of the pickets is for any other purpose the immunity is lost.[31] The section was described in *Broome* v. *D.P.P.*[32] as giving a narrow but real immunity, which gives "no protection in relation to anything the pickets may say or do whilst they are attending if what they say or do is itself unlawful."[33] Any pickets who are not covered by the terms of section 15, run the risk of committing the same range of criminal offences and torts as any other demonstrators. In addition they can be sued for certain industrial torts, such as inducement to breach of contract or prosecuted for an offence under section 7 of the Conspiracy and Protection of Property Act 1875.[34] This section creates a variety of offences, and was used in England for the first time in many years during the 1984/85 miners' dispute. The most significant of the offences found in section 7 are: intimidating any other person with a view to compelling him to abstain from doing any act which such other person has a legal right to do; and watching and besetting the place where another person works, with the same view.

---

[26] See *Kent* v. *Metropolitan Police Commissioner, The Times,* May 15, 1981.

[27] See Bryn Perrins *Trade Union Law* (1985) Chap. 20; Brownlie *loc. cit.* Chap. 3.

[28] For *e.g.* Consumer picketing and see *Hubbard* v. *Pitt ante,* p. 561.

[29] An offence under s.7 of the Conspiracy and Protection of Property Act 1875 *infra*.

[30] *e.g. Piddington* v. *Bates* [1961] 1 W.L.R. 162 (D.C.).

[31] *e.g. Tynan* v. *Balmer* [1967] 1 Q.B. 91 (D.C.).

[32] [1974] A.C. 587.

[33] *Ibid., per* Lord Salmon at p. 603.

[34] See Francis Bennion "Mass Picketing and the 1875 Act" [1985] Crim.L.Rev. 64.

Mass picketing

Although mass picketing is not unlawful under section 15, the greater the number of pickets involved, the easier it will be to infer a purpose other than that of peacefully obtaining or communicating information. In *Broome* v. *D.P.P.* Lord Reid said that in a case of mass picketing "it would not be difficult to infer as matter of fact that pickets who assemble in unreasonably large numbers do have the purpose of preventing free passage"[35]—in other words a purpose outside the limits of section 15. In *Thomas* v. *N.U.M.* (*South Wales Area*) *and others*[36] Scott J. suggested that "mass picketing—by which I understand to be meant picketing so as by sheer weight of numbers to block the entrance to premises or to prevent the entry thereto of vehicles or people— . . . is clearly both common law nuisance and an offence under section 7 of the (Conspiracy and Protection of Property Act)".[37] Although there is no statutory limit to the number of pickets, the Code of Practice on Picketing,[38] while recognising this,[39] goes on to suggest that "pickets and their organisers should ensure that in general the number of pickets does not exceed six at any entrance to a workplace; frequently a smaller number will be appropriate."[40] Scott J. in *Thomas* v. *N.U.M.* was clearly influenced by this guidance since the injunction granted was to restrain the organisation of picketing at colliery gates by more than six persons.[41]

Breach of the peace

The most important powers relied on by the police in connection with the maintenance of public order at picket lines are those connected with breach of the peace. These powers, backed up by the offences of obstructing and assaulting a police officer in the execution of his duty,[42] and obstructing the highway, have enabled the police to limit both the number of pickets,[43] and their activities.[44] Relying on their powers to prevent a reasonably apprehended breach of the peace, during the miners strike 1984/85 the police used road blocks to prevent pickets reaching proposed picket sites.[45] In *Moss* v. *McLachlan*[46] four would-be picketers ignored police requests to turn back and attempted to force their way though a police cordon which was on a road between one and a half and four miles from likely picket sites. Their subsequent conviction for obstruction of the police was upheld by the Divisional Court, on the ground that there was ample evidence to justify the police view

---

[35] *Ante*, at p. 598.
[36] [1985] I.R.L.R. 1365.
[37] *Ibid.*, at p. 153.
[38] Published in 1980 by the Secretary of State for Employment as authorised by s.3 of the Employment Act 1980.
[39] Para. 28.
[40] Para. 31.
[41] See also *News Group Newspapers Ltd.* v. *S.O.G.A.T. '82* [1986] I.R.L.R. 337.
[42] *Ante*, p. 497.
[43] *Piddington* v. *Bates* [1960] 1 W.L.R. (D.C.).
[44] *Tynan* v. *Balmer* [1967] 1 Q.B. 91 (D.C.).
[45] The setting up of road blocks is now governed by s.4 of the Police and Criminal Evidence Act 1984.
[46] [1985] I.R.L.R. 77 (D.C.).

that there was a real possibility of a breach of the peace at the sites of the proposed picketing. The Court held that in deciding whether or not there was a reasonable apprehension of a breach of the peace, the police were entitled to take into account their knowledge of the course of the dispute.

Public Order Act 1986

Various aspects of this Act have significance for the legality of picketing and associated activities. All the offences in Part I[47] could be used in respect of non peaceful picketing. Of particular significance will be the new offences of violent disorder (s.2), and threatening behaviour (s.4). This latter offence is wider than its predecessor, section 5 of the Public Order Act 1936 in respect of the consequences which it prohibits and because it can be committed in a private as well as a public place.[48] The most important section so far as picketing is concerned is section 14,[49] which enables the police to impose conditions on an open air assembly of more than 20 persons in a public place. This will allow the police to limit the location, duration or size of a picket. Although the extensive common law powers of the police did in effect enable them to impose such restrictions on pickets, it was only where it was necessary to do so to keep the peace. Section 14 extends the grounds upon which the police may impose conditions on assemblies to include a reasonable belief that the assembly will result in "serious disruption to the life of the community" or where there is a reasonable belief that "the purpose of the persons organising (the assembly) is the intimidation of others with a view to compelling them not to do an act they have a right to do, or to do an act they have a right not to do." Knowingly to fail to comply with conditions is an offence for which there is a power of arrest without a warrant. This will give the police additional powers to limit pickets.

The general requirement to give advance notice of public processions (s.11) is likely to limit the possibility of mobile demonstrations in the course of industrial disputes. Finally the offence under section 7 of the Conspiracy and Protection of Property Act 1875, which was used during the miners' strike, becomes arrestable without warrant, and penalties for this offence are increased.[50]

Sporting events

The levels of violence and general public order problems at sporting events, and in particular at football matches, led to the enactment of specific legislation. The Criminal Justice (Scotland) Act 1980 and the Sporting Events (Control of Alcohol etc.) Act 1985 both aim to reduce the perceived cause of the problems by creating offences in connection with the carrying of alcohol on coaches and trains, with drunkeness at designated sports grounds, and regulating the sale and supply of alcohol within sports grounds. These provisions have been further amended by Part IV of the Public Order Act 1986. Part IV of the Public Order Act

[47] *Ante*, pp. 554–560.
[48] See Cmnd. 9510, para. 3.8.
[49] *Ante*, p. 566.
[50] See Sched. 2.

introduces a new procedure whereby a person who appears before a court for an offence of actual or threatened violence to person or property committed in connection with a prescribed football match, may be subjected to an exclusion order (s.30). Such an order would preclude the person concerned from attending football matches for a specified period. There is provision in section 37 for the Secretary of State, by order, to extend the exclusion order provisions to other sporting events.

Various aspects of the Public Order Act will be of use in connection with disorder at sporting events. Section 11, requiring written notice for most processions, will give the police extra powers to deal with marches by supporters.[51] The extension of the meaning of violence to cover violence towards property as well as violence towards person and the specific provision that violent conduct includes "throwing at or towards a person a missile of a kind capable of causing injury which does not hit or falls short" (s.8), will make the offences in Part I particularly useful in the context of the type of disorder which occurs, in particular, at football matches.

---

[51] See also *Allen and others* v. *Ireland* [1984] 1 W.L.R. 903 which suggests that a court is entitled to conclude that the voluntary presence of a defendant as part of a crowd (here of football supporters) engaged in threatening behaviour raised a prima facie case of participation against that defendant. This case was concerned with Public Order Act 1936, s.5, but the principle would also apply to a charge under Public Order Act 1986, s.4.

PART VI

ADMINISTRATIVE LAW

The preceding chapters, with the exception of that on the European Communities, have all been concerned with areas of law that would have been known to Blackstone. The centre of political power may have shifted over the centuries but in legal theory the legislature (Parliament) and the executive (the Crown) are the bodies known to the common law from time immemorial. The armed forces and the police nowadays derive their existence and powers from statute but both discharge the primary duty of any state, to protect the lives and property of its citizens from attack whether from enemies abroad or criminals at home. The acquisition of nationality and the control of aliens are equally areas of law as old as the constitution even if they are nowadays based on statute. In the nineteenth century, however, the State began to recognise new obligations. To carry them out it created organisations of a kind unknown in earlier times and gave to them powers which were similarly unknown formerly. It is with these new developments that the following chapters are concerned. At first sight the chapters on Local Government and Crown Proceedings may seem to be out of place in such a discussion. Local Government, however, properly falls within this Part because, although there were local authorities before the nineteenth century, modern local government bodies are the creatures of statute; the duties they perform are those which the state began to undertake in the nineteenth century and the controls over the way the local authorities exercise their powers are typical, too, of the developments of the nineteenth and twentieth centuries. Crown Proceedings is a subject which has its origins in the beginnings of the Constitution but its modern importance is not in connection with the position of the monarch in her private capacity but with the position of the government and the many public bodies which can claim, in the eyes of the law, to form part of "the Crown." Moreover, despite the long history of the law relating to the unique legal position of the Crown, the current law is explicable only in the light of the Crown Proceedings Act 1947.

It is the law relating to these new developments that can conveniently be described as Administrative Law, to which must be added the law relating to the control of the exercise of these statutory powers by the courts, Judicial Review. Here also, the origins of the law stretch back into history but the link between the control exercised by the Court of King's Bench over justices of the peace in the eighteenth century and the review of the legality of decisions of local authorities and other public bodies is little more than a formal one.

In a book dealing with both constitutional and administrative law it is not necessary to attempt to define with any particularity where the line between the two should be drawn. For practical purposes the foregoing general description of the contents of the following chapters could be said to suffice. It may seem strange that writers and judges[2]

---

[1] H. W. R. Wade, *Administrative Law* (5th ed, 1982); P. P. Craig, *Administrative Law* (1983); J. F. Garner and B. L. Jones, *Administrative Law* (6th ed, 1985); D. Foulkes, *Administrative Law* (6th ed, 1986); D. C. M. Yardley, *Principles of Administrative Law* (2nd ed, 1986).
[2] *Supra* p. 32.

had disputed with vigour the very existence of administrative law and the desirability of the adoption of administrative law (if such a subject does exist) into the law of the United Kingdom. To a large extent the dispute is, or was, one of words. If, by administrative law, is meant a system of rules applicable to public bodies which are enforced in special courts, the United Kingdom did not recognise administrative law in 1885[3] and it does not do so now. If by administrative law is meant that the ordinary courts possess a power of review over the legality of administrative acts then clearly the United Kingdom does recognise administrative law and presumably in that sense Dicey would approve.[4] The dispute may also be a political one, disguised as a question about law. The statement that a country does not, or should not, have a body of administrative law may conceal the writer's political view that the State ought not to have the types of organisation and undertake the types of activities which typically are regarded as falling within the scope of administrative law.

Since the decision of the House of Lords in *O'Reilly* v. *Mackman*[5] the courts have begun to use a new terminology in which they distinguish between private law and public law. The latter, vague phrase is sufficiently wide to cover both constitutional and administrative law. Indeed in those jurisdictions where the distinction, borrowed from Roman law,[6] has long been followed public law includes criminal law— although it may be doubted whether the House of Lords had that area of law in mind. Lord Wilberforce has warned of the danger of using, except as convenient shorthand, terms taken from other legal systems where they belong and applying them out of context.[7] Certainly the discovery of public law and, even more, of public law rights, unknown to private law, as a consequence of procedural reforms,[8] designed to rationalise the remedies available where public bodies have acted unlawfully, was somewhat surprising. The availability of remedies to litigants in cases where formerly the courts could not interfere may, at least to the litigants concerned, seem to be proof of the merits of the new distinction between private and public law.[9] On the other hand, it can be argued that by the adoption of the terminology the courts have, in effect, given themselves an almost unlimited power to decide when to strike down decisions of public bodies, untrammelled by earlier rules

---

[3] The date of the first edition of Dicey's *The Law of the Constitution*.

[4] It is in this sense that the judges have congratulated themselves on creating a body of administrative law: *Breen* v. *A.E.U.* [1971] 2 Q.B. 175, *per* Lord Denning M.R., *Mahon* v. *Air New Zealand* [1984] A.C. 808, 816 *per* Lord Diplock.

[5] [1983] 2 A.C. 237.

[6] In the Institutes public law is defined as *"quod ad statum rei Romanae spectat"* while private law is *"quod ad singulorum utilitatem pertinet"*: I.1.1.4. In the Digest Ulpian describes public law as that which *"in sacris, in sacerdotibus, in magistratibus consistat"*: D.1.1.1.2.

[7] *Davy* v. *Spelthorne B.C.* [1984] A.C. 262. See too Parker L.J. in *Wandsworth L.B.C.* v. *Winder* [1983] 3 W.L.R. 563 (C.A.); affirmed H.L. [1985] A.C. 461.

[8] *Post* p. 682.

[9] In practice the individual litigant may be more impressed by the risk of an action failing because it was begun by what turned out to be the wrong procedure: see the criticisms of H.W.R.W. "Public Law, Private Law and Judicial Review," (1983) 99 L.Q.R. 166, and the rebuttal of those criticisms by Woolf L.J., "Public Law-Private Law: Why the Divide? A Personal View," [1986] P.L. 220; *post* p. 691.

and precedents. Despite the general terms in which the House of Lords has in the last few years referred to public law it is difficult to believe that in effect it can mean more than administrative law. It can hardly be thought, for example, that by reference to public law, the courts would claim the right (which they have carefully denied themselves in the past) to scrutinise the proceedings of Parliament or to set limits to the legislative competence of Parliament.[10] Nor is it likely that the actions of the government in the sphere of foreign affairs are now susceptible to judicial review.[11]

The growth of administrative law[12]

Almost 100 years ago Maitland pointed out that, at first sight, Parliament in the eighteenth century got through more work than it did in the nineteenth. But, on inspection, a volume of statutes from that earlier period contained little that in subsequent ages would be regarded as legislation. Many Acts, public as well as private, dealt with individual cases rather than attempted to lay down general rules. The public acts for 1786, for example, included

> "an act for establishing a workhouse at Havering, an act to enable the king to license a playhouse at Margate, an act for erecting a house of correction in Middlesex, an act for incorporating the Clyde Marine Society, an act for paving the town of Cheltenham, an act for widening the roads in the borough of Bodmin. Fully half of the public acts are of this petty local character. Then as to the private acts, these deal with particular persons: an act for naturalizing Andreas Emmerich, an act for enabling Cornelius Salvidge to take the surname of Tutton, an act for rectifying mistakes in the marriage settlement of Lord and Lady Camelford, an act to enable the guardians of William Frye to grant leases, an act to dissolve the marriage between Jonathan Twiss and Francis Dorrill. Then there are almost countless acts for enclosing this, that and the other common. One is inclined to call the last century the century of *privilegia*. It seems afraid to rise to the dignity of a general proposition; it will not say, 'All commons may be enclosed according to these general rules,' 'All aliens may become naturalized if they fulfil these or those conditions,' 'All boroughs shall have these powers for widening their roads,' 'All marriages may be dissolved if the wife's adultery be proved.' No, it deals with this common and that marriage."[13]

In the nineteenth century, however, soon after the Reform Act of 1832 Parliament began, in Maitland's words again:

> "to legislate with remarkable vigour, to overhaul the whole law of the country—criminal law, property law, the law of procedure, every department of the law—but about the same time it gives up

---

[10] *Ante* p. 49.

[11] *Cf. Ex p. Molyneaux* [1986] 1 W.L.R. 332 *ante* p. 20 and p. 265.

[12] A. V. Dicey, *Law and Public Opinion During the Nineteenth Century* (2nd ed. 1914, reprinted 1962); H. W. Arthurs, *Without the Law* (1985).

[13] F. W. Maitland, *Constitutional History of England* (1908) p. 383.

the attempt to govern the country, to say what commons shall be enclosed, what roads shall be widened, what boroughs shall have paid constables and so forth. It begins to lay down general rules about these matters and to entrust their working partly to officials, to secretaries of state, to boards of commissioners, who for this purpose are endowed with new statutory powers, partly to the law courts."[14]

In this outburst of legislative activity is to be found the origins of that area of law now generally regarded as administrative law.

Maitland attributed Parliament's anxiety in the eighteenth century *to govern* the country by deciding individual cases itself to jealousy of the Crown. Memories of the power of the monarch were too recent; by the nineteenth century that fear had receded. But, at least equally important, was the transformation wrought by the Industrial Revolution. Without that Bentham, Brougham and others might have called for reform in vain or, if it came, it would have taken a different form; "Watt and Stephenson were much more responsible for undermining the dominantly feudal legal system expounded by Blackstone, than Bentham and Brougham."[15] The concentration of people in large cities presented new problems in sanitation, public health and housing. Working conditions in mines and factories produced calls for legal regulation. The construction of canals and railways was possible only because Parliament was prepared to grant to the companies powers to acquire land compulsorily where the owners refused to sell. Education came to be seen as a concern of the government in the public interest as well as for the benefit of individual citizens. In this century the State has further concerned itself with making provision for a wide range of financial payments to the elderly, the unemployed and others in need. From compulsory purchase the legislature has progressed to attempting generally to control the use to which land is put through various Town and Country Planning Acts. From detailed legislation restricting and regulating the activities of money-lenders and hire purchase companies the legislature has proceeded to make general provision for the protection of consumers when obtaining credit in one form or another.[16]

The consequences of these legislative developments from 1832 onwards largely form the subject matter of the succeeding chapters of this Part. Parliament has entrusted the carrying out of legislation to bodies of various kinds, whether elected local authorities (Chapter 28) or non-elected public corporations of widely differing composition and constitution (Chapter 29). These bodies may be under duties to provide services or have powers to ensure compliance with statutory standards. Duties and powers, too, may be conferred on individual ministers. Legislation cast in wide, general terms and often dealing with highly technical subject matter requires more detailed implementation by

---

[14] *Op. cit.* p. 384.

[15] Mr. Justice Frankfurter, "Foreword to a Discussion of Current Developments in Administrative Law," (1937–8) 47 Yale L.J. 515, quoted H. W. Arthurs, *op. cit.* p. 34.

[16] Consumer Credit Act 1974: a statute of 193 sections and 5 Schedules which nonetheless can be described as "merely a blueprint for the system of regulation and licensing which it establishes"; Guest and LLoyd, *Current Law Statutes Annotated.*

rules and regulations, usually but not always made by ministers (Chapter 30). Disputes relating to the provision of services and the regulation of activities may be best dealt with by particular tribunals established outside the structure of the civil and criminal courts (Chapter 31). The increase in the powers of ministers and the proliferation of bodies with the legal ability to affect the rights and duties of citizens (and public bodies) has led to the recognition of the need for procedures to deal with grievances of various kinds relating to the working of the administration (Chapter 32). Where it is alleged that the administration has acted in such a way that it has exceeded its legal powers the appropriate remedy is recourse to the Courts (Chapters 33 and 34). Finally something must be said about the cases and circumstances in which the rights and duties of public officials and bodies under the general law may differ from those of the private citizen (Chapter 35).

CHAPTER 28

LOCAL GOVERNMENT

THIS account of local government authorities is confined to England and Wales. Local government in Scotland at the present day bears some resemblance to the English system, but it has quite a different history and is under the supervision of the Secretary of State for Scotland.[1] The organisation of local government in Northern Ireland is based on different legislation, its main peculiarities being that the county councils are rating authorities and there are no civil parishes. Supervision is exercised by the Secretary of State for Northern Ireland.

It is only possible in the space available to give an outline of the structure of the various local authorities, their relations with one another and with the central government, and to say something about local government elections and finance and the source of their powers. It is not practicable to describe the detailed powers which the various local authorities possess in relation to specific services.[2]

I. INTRODUCTION

Development of local government[3]

The present structure of local government authorities in England and Wales is based on recent legislation, and most of their powers are based on nineteenth- and twentieth-century statutes, although counties, boroughs and parishes as units for various purposes are ancient. In the shire, hundred and vill is found the key to the present organisation of rural areas for local government purposes—the county, the district and the civil parish. An antithesis between centralisation and decentralisation runs through the history of the organisation of English government. In the early Middle Ages, both before and after the Norman Conquest, the chief royal officer for the control of local government was the sheriff of the county or shire, subject to the supervision of the King's Council. The general administration was carried on in the county court, the assembly of the freeholders of the county over which the sheriff presided.

Over a period of centuries the sheriff gradually lost nearly all his functions, so that Maitland could say in 1885 that the whole history of English justice and police might be described as "the decline and fall of the sheriff."[4] After various experiments, the local administration of jus-

---

[1] For the current legislation see Local Government (Scotland) Act 1973.
[2] See further C. Cross and S. Bailey, *Cross on Local Government* (7th ed, 1986). M. Loughlin *Local Government in the Modern State* (1986).
[3] Redlich and Hirst, *History of Local Government in England* (ed. B. Keith-Lucas. 2nd ed., 1970); W. A. Robson, *The Development of Local Government* (3rd ed. 1954); S. Webb, *The Evolution of Local Government* (ed. 1951); Holdsworth, *History of English Law*, Vol. X, pp. 126–339; *A Century of Municipal Progress 1835–1935* (ed. Laski, Jennings and Robson, 1935); K. B. S. Smellie, *A Hundred Years of Local Government* (2nd ed., 1950).
[4] *Justice and Police* (1885), p. 69. For the modern sheriff, see *The High Sheriff* (*The Times*, 1961).

tice was given in the middle of the fourteenth century to justices of the peace. For nearly 500 years, that is, until the year 1834, the control of local government outside the boroughs was mainly in the hands of these justices of the peace, for besides the judicial functions in which they displaced the sheriffs and the county and hundred courts, a long series of statutes cast on them numerous administrative duties concerning such matters as highways, poor relief, wages and licensing.[5] The justices themselves were controlled by the King's Council until the Star Chamber was abolished in 1640. For the next 200 years local government was, subject to the legislative power of Parliament, almost autonomous: practically the only control was exercised by the courts in applying the doctrine of *ultra vires* and issuing prerogative writs.

The period from the Middle Ages down to the early nineteenth century also saw a great growth in the size and number of towns, and to the justices of the peace as local government authorities we must add the boroughs. Further, the statutory institution of ad hoc bodies for specific purposes, which began with the Statute of Sewers 1531, was increasingly adopted in the eighteenth century for such purposes as the poor law, turnpike roads and urban sanitation.

Modern local government, characterised by *locally elected councils*, was inaugurated by the Poor Law Amendment Act 1834 and the Municipal Corporations Act 1835. The former Act reorganised the administration of the poor law which, apart from police, had hitherto been the most important function of local government. The Municipal Corporations Act provided for an elected borough council in place of an oligarchy of co-opted burgesses. The process of creating elected councils was continued by the introduction, first, of county councils and county borough councils in 1888,[6] and then of urban district councils, rural district councils and parish councils in 1894.[7] Ad hoc authorities continued to be created during the nineteenth century for highways, schools and sanitation, but they gradually disappeared. The general principle in modern times was to have one local authority for all services in its area, and this was largely brought about by 1930.[8] The Local Government Act 1933 consolidated the legislation relating to the structure of local government outside London, and remained the basis of the law until the coming into effect of the Local Government Act 1972.

The government of London has always stood apart from the general system, owing to the maintenance of the ancient privileges of the City of London and the great size and population of Greater London. The organisation outside the City was greatly simplified by the creation of the London County Council and the metropolitan borough councils in 1899,[9] and this was replaced by the reforms contained in the London Government Act 1963, which created the Greater London Council.

Since the last war there has also been consolidation, as well as reform, of the statute law relating to particular services such as town and

---

[5] Sir Carleton Allen, *The Queen's Peace*, Chap. 5.
[6] Local Government Act 1888.
[7] Local Government Act 1894.
[8] Local Government Act 1929; Poor Law Act 1930.
[9] Local Government Act 1899.

country planning, housing, education, highways, and the national health service.

Areas and authorities (excluding London)

The Local Government Act 1972[10] reorganised local government structure in England and Wales on a two-tier basis throughout the country. The Act retains important responsibilities at local level, and greatly reduces the number of authorities. Local authorities are given more discretion in certain fields, and greater freedom to arrange their committee structure, to delegate the exercise of their functions and to appoint officers. The Act consolidates most of the existing Local Government Acts, the Act of 1933 being largely repealed.

The country (outside London) is divided into counties, and the counties into districts. The Act also created six *metropolitan counties* of Tyne and Wear, Merseyside, Greater Manchester, West Yorkshire, South Yorkshire and the West Midlands. The *non-metropolitan counties* corresponded roughly with the pre-existing counties; but there were many boundary changes, some counties, (*e.g.* Worcestershire and Herefordshire, Cumberland and Westmorland, and some Welsh counties) were merged, Avon (Bristol and Bath) was created, Glamorgan was divided into three, and Rutland disappeared. Both metropolitan and non-metropolitan counties were divided into *districts*, the number of districts in the latter being reduced. Rural *parishes* continued in England, (which for the purposes of the Act excludes Monmouthshire and the county borough of Newport).[11]

The metropolitan counties were abolished by the Local Government Act 1985[12] which provided for the creation of Joint Authorities, consisting of representatives of the relevant district councils to take responsibility for such services as police.[13]

The principal councils in England are the *county councils* and *district councils*, consisting of a chairman and councillors elected by the local government electors. Each council is a body corporate. Existing boroughs lost that status, but a district council may petition for a charter conferring the status of a borough (section 245). The chairman is elected annually by the council from among the councillors or persons qualified to be councillors.

In rural areas in England there is a *parish meeting* of the local government electors for the purpose of discussing parish affairs and exercising the functions conferred on parish meetings. A larger parish or group of parishes may have a *parish council*, consisting of a chairman and elected councillors. Parish councils have powers rather than duties.

In Wales (which includes Monmouthshire) every district is to consist of one or more *communities*. Communities in the first instance will cover the existing boroughs, urban districts and parishes. In place of parish

---

[10] Based on *Local Government in England: Proposals for Reorganisation* (1971) Cmnd. 4584, and *The Reform of Local Government in Wales: Consultative Government in England* (Maud), (1969) Cmnd. 4040, and *Reform of Local Government in England* (1970) Cmnd. 4276. See now, *English Local Government Reformed* (1974).

[11] S.1(12).

[12] See *Streamlining the Cities*, Cmnd. 9063.

[13] ss.23–42.

meetings and councils, therefore, there will be *community meetings or councils* with similar executive powers, but greater ability to express local wishes and needs.

Changes in local government areas

Separate permanent *local government boundary commissions* for England and Wales were set up by Part IV of the 1972 Act to review local government boundaries and local electoral arrangements. Both commissions are advisory and report to the Secretary of State, who may give effect by order to their recommendations.[14] No local authority may promote a Bill for forming, altering or abolishing any local government area, or for changing its status or electoral arrangements (section 70).

London

In the earlier part of the nineteenth century the government of London outside the City was somewhat chaotic owing to the way in which the town had grown outwards from what we should now regard as a small nucleus. Its government was mainly in the hands of the justices and parish vestries.[15] There were also the Metropolitan Police under the Home Secretary, and the poor law guardians. The London County Council was created in 1888.[16] In 1899[17] the metropolitan borough councils, incorporated into the administrative county of London outside the City, displaced the vestries and district boards. There were also *ad hoc* authorities such as the Metropolitan Water Board (1902), the Thames Conservancy Board (1854), the Port of London Authority (1908) and the London Passenger Transport Board (1933).

The London Government Act 1963[18] reorganised the local government of London. Greater London was constituted as a local government area, the counties of London and Middlesex ceasing to exist.

The Local Government Act 1972 did not alter the structure of local government in London, but it applies its provisions relating to the working machinery of local authorities to those in Greater London, and it incorporates in a schedule the provisions of the London Government Act affecting the constitution of the Greater London authorities.

1. *Greater London and the Greater London Council*

Greater London is the administrative area comprising the London boroughs, the City and the Temples.

The Greater London Council was established by the 1963 Act as the successor to the London County Council. The G.L.C. was itself abolished by the Local Government Act 1985 which makes provision for the

---

[14] For an unsuccessful challenge to a recommendation of the English Commission see *Enfield L.B.C.* v. *Local Government Boundary Commission for England* [1979] 3 All E.R. 747 (H.L.).
[15] A vestry was originally a meeting of the parishioners, and later of the ratepayers of the parish.
[16] Local Government Act 1888.
[17] London Government Act 1899.
[18] Based on *Report of Royal Commission on Local Government in Greater London* (1960) Cmnd. 1164; *London Government: Government Proposals for Reorganisation* (1961) Cmnd. 1562.

transfer of its functions to the London Boroughs, to Joint Authorities and the newly established Inner London Education Authority.

2. London boroughs

Thirty-two London boroughs were created. The 12 Inner London boroughs cover the areas of the former metropolitan boroughs, and the remaining 20 Outer London boroughs cover the areas formerly contained in neighbouring counties or county boroughs.

The Local Government Act 1985 established the Inner London Education Authority as a corporate body whose members are to be elected in the manner of existing local authorities. The jurisdiction of the Authority is confined to the areas covered by the twelve Inner London Boroughs.[19-20]

3. City of London Corporation

The City of London Corporation is a body corporate by prescription, its full style according to a statute of 1690 being "The Mayor and Commonalty and Citizens of the City of London." The Corporation was not affected by the Municipal Corporations Acts 1835–1882, but it is governed—mostly in accordance with royal charters granted from time to time—by three courts. The City of London is a common law corporation with some financial resources that are not subject to statutory control.

(i) *The Court of Common Council* consists of the Lord Mayor, aldermen and common council men.[21] The Court of Common Council is in some respects the sole authority within its area. It controls the property of the Corporation; elects the City Solicitor and the Town Clerk; is responsible for housing and for certain Thames bridges; and is the market authority within a seven-mile radius. It also controls the City of London police force.

(ii) *The Court of Common Hall* consists of the Lord Mayor, Sheriff, not less than four aldermen, and those liverymen of the City companies who are freemen of the City. This is the body that annually nominates two aldermen for the office of Lord Mayor. It also elects the Chamberlain (treasurer) and the City auditors.

(iii) *The Court of Aldermen* consists of the Lord Mayor and aldermen. Some time before November 9 it elects the Lord Mayor for the coming year from among the two aldermen nominated by the Court of Common Hall. It also elects the Clerk to the Lord Mayor, the Clerk to the Guildhall Magistrates and the district surveyors.

The Temple

The Temple has always claimed to be outside the jurisdiction of the City of London, mainly on the ground that it was so excluded when it was ecclesiastical property belonging to the Knights Templar, and was

---

[19-20] s.18. The Secretary of State may, before 31st March 1991 review the exercise by the Authority of its functions relating to education: s.22.

[21] The franchise is restricted and in fact there is seldom a contest; Robson, *Government and Misgovernment of London*, p. 30.

not among the formerly monastic properties over which the City was given jurisdiction by charter.[22] The Inner Temple and Middle Temple are within the City of London for judicial purposes.

The London Government Act 1985, section 94[23] provides that any functions exercisable by a London borough council may by Order in Council be made exercisable by the Sub-Treasurer of Inner Temple or the Under-Treasurer of Middle Temple, or (as respects both the Temples) by the Common Council of the City of London.[24] Expenses incurred by the Sub-Treasurer and the Under-Treasurer under the Act may be defrayed out of a general rate levied in their respective Inns.

The structure of local authorities

Despite the increasing grip on local authorities of the national political parties councils are organised quite differently from the House of Commons. Whatever the *de facto* power of the caucus of the largest party, council affairs are conducted through Committees where elected members work closely with appointed officers. Section 101 of the Local Government Act 1972 empowers a local authority to discharge any of its functions through a committee, sub-committee, or officer of the authority. An authority cannot, acting under this section, purport to discharge its functions through a committee consisting of one member: *R. v. Secretary of State for the Environment, ex parte Hillingdon London Borough Council.*[25]

Local authorities have a discretion to appoint such officers as they think necessary for the discharge of their functions (London Government Act, 1972, s.112). Specific statutory provisions relate to the appointment, for example, of a Chief Education Officer and a Director of Social Services.

Local councillors are not paid a salary but are entitled to allowances in respect of attendance, financial loss, travelling and subsistence under sections 173–178 of the 1972 Act, as subsequently amended.

Access to information and meetings

Councillors

At common law a councillor is entitled to have access to all written material in the possession of the local authority of which he is a member to the extent that is necessary for the proper performance of his duty: *R. v. Birmingham City Council, ex parte. O*[26] He has, however, "no right to a roving commission to go and examine books or documents . . . because he is a councillor. Mere curiosity or desire to see and inspect documents is not sufficient."[27] In the case of a councillor wishing to see papers of a committee or sub-committee of which he is not a member he will have to establish a "need to know" and, in cases of dis-

---

[22] Other curious arguments put forward in 1668 by Sir Heneage Finch, Treasurer of the Inner Temple, are summarised in Williamson, *The History of the Temple, London*, p. 480.

[23] Re-enacting s.82 of the Local Government Act 1963.

[24] Responsibility for public health matters is vested in the two Temples by the London Government Act 1972, s.180.

[25] [1986] 1 W.L.R. 192; affirmed [1986] 1 W.L.R. 807 (C.A.).

[26] [1983] 1 A.C. 578 (H.L.).

[27] *R. v. Southwold Corporation ex p. Wrightson* (1908) 97 L.T. 431.

pute, that committee or sub-committee or, ultimately the full council will have to determine whether he has a good reason for seeing the documents. The fact that the documents are confidential is not a good reason for refusing disclosure[28] but their contents may justify a decision to release only an abridged version.[29]

The Local Government (Access to Information) Act 1985 creates a right of access to documents which is stated to be in addition to any other rights apart from the Act.[30] The new statutory right is subject to a power to withhold documents containing exempt information, as defined in the Act.

In *R. v. Hackney L.B.C., Ex p. Gamper*[31] Lloyd L.J. held that the right of access to meetings on the part of councillors was subject to the same limitations as their right to see documents.

Members of the Public

The Public Bodies (Admission to Meetings) Act 1960 provided that meetings of local authorities and certain other bodies, such as education committees should be open to the public. The scope of the Act was extended to committees generally by the Local Government Act 1972, section 100. The Act now applies only to parish and community councils and certain other public bodies. A public body within the Act my exclude the public whenever publicity would be prejudicial to the public interest by reason of the confidential nature of the business or for other special reasons arising from the nature of the business or of the proceedings.[32] Public notice must be given of meetings to which the public are entitled to be admitted, and copies of the agenda must be supplied on request to any newspaper. These provisions extend where any body to which the Act applies resolves itself into a committee. The power remains to exclude persons in order to suppress or prevent disorderly conduct at a meeting. (*Infra.*)

The Local Government (Access to Information) Act 1985 applies to principal councils, that is councils other than parish and community councils, and a number of bodies listed in the Act, including the Inner London Education Authority, joint authorities and combined police authorities with corporate status. The Act also applies to committees and sub-committees of these bodies. Its provisions have been further extended by the Health Service Joint Consultative Committees (Access to Information) Act 1986.

Meetings of bodies within the Act must normally be open to the public except when there is a risk of the likelihood of the disclosure of confidential information which is defined as information furnished by a

---

[28] *R. v. Hackney L.B.C. ex p. Gamper* [1985] 1 W.L.R. 1229.

[29] *R. v. Lancashire County Council Police Authority ex p. Hook*, [1980] Q.B. 603. (C.A.).

[30] The Act applies to England, Wales and Scotland. It takes effect by inserting new sections (numbered 100A–100K) in the Local Government Act 1972 and in the Local Government (Scotland) Act 1973 (numbered 50A–50K).

[31] *Supra* n. 28.

[32] *Quaere*, whether the public may be excluded for a special reason (*e.g.* lack of seating) which does not relate to the nature of the business or of the proceedings. See *R. v. Brent Health Authority ex p. Francis* [1985] Q.B. 869 where Forbes J. doubted dicta that the grounds for exclusion were not so limited in *R. v. Liverpool City Council ex p. Liverpool Taxi Fleet Operators Association* [1975] 1 W.L.R. 701.

Government department upon terms which forbid its disclosure to the public or information the disclosure of which is prohibited by any enactment or any order of a court (section 100A(3). A principal council may exclude the public when there is a risk of disclosure of exempt information which is defined in schedule 12A and consists largely of information relating to the private affairs of individuals.

The right of admission on the part of the public and the press[33] is without prejudice to any power of exclusion to suppress or prevent disorderly conduct. In *R. v. Brent Health Authority, ex parte Francis*[34] the Health Authority was held to be entitled to arrange to meet privately after previous meetings were disrupted by members of the public exercising their statutory right of attendance. In a number of cases, particularly at meetings in some London Boroughs, there have been interruptions and attempts at intimidation by members of the public. The Widdicombe Committee referred in its report to a suspicion of connivance between trouble-makers and the Chairmen of some meetings.[35]

Notice must be given of the holding of meetings to which the public has access and copies of the agenda and any reports for a meeting must be available for public inspection.

After a meeting minutes or a copy of the minutes, a copy of the agenda and a copy of reports must be retained and kept available for public inspection for six years (section 100C). A person inspecting a document is entitled to make a copy or an extract or to require a photographic copy to be supplied, on the payment of such reasonable fee as may be required (section 100H(2)).[36]

II. Local Government Elections

1. Local government franchise

The franchise has been uniform for all local government elections since 1918. Until 1948 the local franchise was based on occupation as owner or tenant of premises in the area for a qualifying period of three months. The assimilation of the parliamentary and local franchise was effected by the Representation of the People Act 1948. Remaining differences were that in local elections there was an alternative occupation qualification, removed in 1969,[37] and that peers have the right to vote.

The local government franchise under the Representation of the People Act 1983, as amended by the Representation of the People Act 1985, is enjoyed by:

  (i) Commonwealth citizens or citizens of the Republic of Ireland, who are

  (ii) not subject to any legal incapacity, and who are

  (iii) eighteen years of age or over on the date of the poll; and

---

[33] S.100(*a*)(*b*)(*c*) requires, as far as practicable, the provision of reasonable facilities for members of the press to make reports and the use of a telephone (if there is a telephone).

[34] [1985] Q.B. 869.

[35] *The Conduct of Local Authority Business* (HMSO, 1986).

[36] Cf. *Russell Walker* v. *Gimblett, The Times,* March 14, 1985 (D.C.).

[37] Representation of the People Act 1969.

(iv) resident[38] in the area on the qualifying date, or qualified as members of the services or as merchant seamen.

The law governing the conduct of local elections was adapted by the Local Government Act 1972. Electoral areas are coterminous as far as practicable with parliamentary electoral areas. The areas in counties are electoral divisions, and in districts they are wards. Local elections are held under rules made by the Secretary of State. The qualifying date is October 10, and the registers come into force on the February 16 following.[39] Registration officers are appointed by the council of the district, or London borough or the Common Council. Returning officers for county elections are appointed by the county council; for district, parish or community elections they are appointed by the district council; and for London boroughs elections they are the "proper officer" of the borough. The names of electors on the register who are qualified to vote in that area at local but not parliamentary elections (*i.e.* peers) are marked to indicate that fact (section 9).

2. Qualifications and disqualifications for election[40]

The qualification for election as councillor are narrower than those sufficient for a Member of Parliament. A councillor must have some connection with the area for which he seeks election, while a Member of Parliament need not.

A person is *qualified* for election as a councillor if on the day of nomination and the day of election he has attained the age of 21 years and is a Commonwealth citizen or citizen of the Republic of Ireland and: (a) he is a local government elector for the area; or (b) he has during the whole of the preceding 12 months occupied as owner or tenant any land or premises in that area; or (c) his principal place of work during that 12 months has been in that area; or (d) he has during the whole of those 12 months resided in that area; or (e) in the case of a parish community council, he has during the whole of those 12 months resided within three miles of the parish or community.

A person is *disqualified* for election as a councillor if he: (a) holds any paid office under the local authority concerned, including local government officers and teachers in schools established or maintained by it[41]; or (b) he is an undischarged bankrupt or has made a composition with his creditors; or (c) he has within the preceding five years been sentenced to imprisonment for not less than three months whether suspended or not; or (d) he has been convicted in certain cases for corrupt or illegal practices under the Representation of the People Act 1983[42]; or (e) a Court has made an order disqualifying him from membership of a

---

[38] *Fox* v. *Stirk; Ricketts* v. *Cambridge City Electoral Registration Office* [1970] 2 Q.B. 463 (C.A.); *Hipperson* v. *Electoral Registration Officer for the District of Newbury* [1985] Q.B. 1060; *ante,* Chap. 9.

[39] Representation of the People Act 1983, s.4.

[40] Local Government Act 1972, ss.79–81, as amended by Local Government Act 1985, Sched. 14, paras. 2 and 3, and Sched. 17.

[41] There is nothing to prevent a councillor from holding paid office under another local authority. It has been proposed that local authority employees at the rank of principal officer and above should be barred from standing for election in adjacent council areas: *The Conduct of Local Authority Business* (H.M.S.O. 1986).

[42] Local Government Act 1972, s.80.

local authority for a specified period because of involvement in expenditure contrary to law; or (f) the auditor has certified that he is responsible by wilful misconduct for any loss or deficiency while serving as a member of a local authority.[43]

Elections

Local authorities, unlike Parliament, are elected for fixed terms. In the case of County Councils,[44] and London Borough Councils[45] elections are held every four years and all members retire together.

District Councils may be elected once every three years, with all councillors retiring simultaneously or by annual elections in which one third of the members retire each year.[46]

Parish Councils are elected every four years, all councillors returning together. Community Councils are similarly elected every four years.[47]

The validity of a local election may be questioned before a local election court which is constituted by a barrister appointed for that function under the procedure laid down by the Representation of the People Act 1983, sections 127–131.[48]

III. Local Government Finance

Income of local authorities

Local authorities derive their income mainly from rates and grants-in-aid from the central government. A part of the income of the principal local authorities is derived from rents, profits on trading undertakings, and charges for licences and fees; but profits derived from these sources are generally applied towards the expenses and improvement of these services and to reduction of rates. The proportion of local authorities' income derived from rates and fees has declined steadily during the last century. At present rates represent something like a quarter of authorities' income, fees a similar proportion while government grants contribute almost half.

(a) Rates

Rates are taxes which Parliament empowers local authorities to levy.[49] Under the Local Government Act 1972 section 49 the "rating authorities" are the London borough councils, the district councils, the Common Council of the City of London, the Sub-Treasurer of the Inner Temple and the Under Treasurer of the Middle Temple. County councils, parish and community councils have power to issue "precepts" (i.e. demands to meet their needs) on the rating authorities. Other bodies with powers to issue precepts include the Inner London Education

---

[43] Local Government Finance Act 1982, ss.19 and 20.
[44] Local Government Act 1972, s.7(1).
[45] Local Government Act 1972 s.8; Sched. 2, para. 6(3) as amended by the London Councillors Order 1976 (S.I. 1976, No. 213).
[46] Local Government Act 1972 s.7(4).
[47] Local Government Act 1972, s.16 and s.35.
[48] On the status of the court, see R. v. Cripps ex p. Muldoon [1984] Q.B. 686 (C.A.).
[49] Re a Reference under the Government of Ireland Act 1920 [1936] A.C. 352.

Authority and the Joint Authorities established by the Local Government Act 1985 (section 68), the Receiver for the Metropolitan Police[50] and the Water Authorities.[51] Each rating authority, after considering the annual estimates of its various departments, "makes" a rate sufficient to meet its own needs and also the precepts it receives. To avoid any doubt, the Local Government Act 1986, section 1, imposes a legal duty on each authority to make a rate for a financial year on or before April 1st of that year.[52] Rates may be made only for the period of one year and no supplementary rates may be made during that year.[53]

Rates are levied on the *occupiers* of "hereditaments" (land and buildings) in the area, according to their "rateable value." The rateable value of property is assessed with reference to the "gross annual value" of the property which is, in theory, the rent which a hypothetical yearly tenant might reasonably be expected to pay. Deductions for the estimated cost of insurance and repairs give the "net annual value," and this is equivalent to the rateable value. The valuation of dwelling-houses is carried out by district valuers of the Inland Revenue Department, on the principles laid down by the consolidating General Rate Act 1967. Appeals against assessment lie to local valuation courts, and thence to the Lands Tribunal, and on a point of law to the Court of Appeal and then to the House of Lords.[54] Crown property is immune,[55] and places of public worship and agricultural hereditaments are exempted from rates. Relief may be granted to charities, and to domestic ratepayers with low incomes (section 49).

Ever since the Poor Relief Act 1601 the sanction for non-payment of rates has been distress and sale of chattels. A defaulter was formerly regarded as an "offender," but the obligation may now be said to be quasi-contractual, although there is no right of action to recover rates.[56] The modern process, which was consolidated in the General Rates Act 1967, is for the rating authority to bring a summons before the magistrates' court, and (if there is no good defence) to apply for a warrant for distraint on goods. If the distrainable goods are insufficient, and the failure to pay is due to wilful refusal or culpable neglect, the debtor may be committed to prison for three months.

Recent legislation has given the government power to control the making of rates and issuing of precepts. The Rates Act 1984[57] includes a selective scheme applicable to authorities which the Secretary of State has designated (Part I). Part II of the Act introduces a general scheme of control which will not come into effect unless the Secretary of State makes an order bringing it into force. Part I is directed at large local

---

[50] Local Government Act 1948, s.121.

[51] Land Drainage Act 1976, ss.45–47.

[52] Even in the absence of such a provision the Court of Appeal held that councillors who caused, without good reason, the deferring of the making of a rate were guilty of wilful misconduct and disqualified from continuing as councillors: *Lloyd* v. *McMahon* [1987] 2 W.L.R. 821; affirmed, H.L.

[53] Local Government Finance Act 1982, ss.1 and 2.

[54] See, for example, *K Shoe Shops Ltd.* v. *Hardy* [1983] 1 W.L.R. 1273 (H.L.).

[55] *Ante*, Chap. 14.

[56] *Liverpool Corporation* v. *Hope* [1938] 1 K.B. 751.

[57] The Act gave effect to proposals in a White Paper entitled "Rates" (Cmnd. 9008).

authorities[58] whose expenditure exceeds their "grant related expenditure" (that is the notional figure arrived at by the provisions of the Local Government, Planning and Land Act 1980)[59] and is excessive having regard to general economic conditions. If the Secretary of State exercises his power to designate he must report his decision to the House of Commons, giving the names of the authorities affected. The report must contain a statement of the principles in accordance with which the authorities have been designated. The Act lays down the procedure by which the Secretary of State shall determine the permissible maximum rate or precept in the case of a designated authority and by section 6 provides that a rate or precept in excess of the maximum figure will be invalid.[60]

The Rates Act 1984 also imposes on authorities to which Part I applies a duty to consult persons or bodies appearing to them to be representative of industrial and commercial ratepayers in their area about its proposals for expenditure and finance in the next financial year before they determine their estimated expenditures. In deciding whom to consult, and when and how, the authorities shall have regard to any guidance issued by the Secretary of State.

Dissatisfaction with rating as a system for helping to finance local government has been widely expressed for many years.[61] In England (but not in Scotland) the periodic revaluation of property has been abandoned.[62] The system's survival is largely explicable by the absence of a generally acceptable alternative. The Government has indicated that it does not intend to attempt to amend the system in England before the next election. In the case of Scotland, however, legislation has been introduced which is intended to replace rates with a community charge, that is a charge levied on persons not property.[63]

(b) *Government grants*

The government makes annual grants to local authorities under the authority of Parliament. The reasons for making government grants are to relieve the rates, especially where a service is imposed on local authorities by government policy; to encourage the provision of new services; to compensate for loss due to government activity, *e.g.* de-rating; and to equalise the resources of local authorities. Since the election of the Conservative Government in 1979 the system of government grants has been modified in an attempt to control and curtail expenditure by local authorities.

Certain services provided by local authorities receive specific grants from the Exchequer. There is, for example, a grant to meet 50 per cent of

---

[58] *i.e.* those whose expenditure exceeds £10.5 million in the case of Welsh authorities and £10.6 million in the case of English authorities: Rate Limitation (Designation of Authorities) (Exemption) (Wales) Order 1985 (S.I. 1985 No. 823) and the Rate Limitation (Designation of Authorities) (Exemption) Order 1985 (S.I. 1985 No. 863).

[59] *Post*, p. 594.

[60] Maximum rates and precepts were prescribed for the year 1985–1986.

[61] See, *e.g. Report of the Committee of Inquiry on Local Government Finance* (The Layfield Committee) (1976, Cmnd. 6453).

[62] The current Valuation List in England came into effect on 1st April 1973.

[63] Green Paper 1986, "Paying for Local Government."

the cost of maintaining a police force.[64] A wide range of grants are made under Housing legislation towards the cost of improvement grants and slum clearances. Other legislation provides grants for a variety of purposes including student grants,[65] Welsh language training[66] the provision of caravan sites for gypsies[67] and special social needs.[68]

By far the major share of grants from central funds takes the form of the rate support grant, introduced by the Local Government Act 1966 and now governed by the Local Government, Planning and Land Act 1980, Part VI, as amended by the Local Government Finance Act 1982, Part II. The rate support grant consists of two parts; (i) *the domestic rate relief*, a sum calculated to cover the cost to each authority of the rate rebate scheme; (ii) *the block grant*, a sum calculated by a formula designed to penalise local authorities whose planned expenditure exceeds their notional expenditure (grant related expenditure) as determined according to the statutory scheme. Before applying the formula to each individual authority the Secretary of State is required by section 54 to determine the aggregate amount of the rate support grants available for the year. He is required to consult with such associations of local authorities as appear to him to be concerned and with any local authority with whom consultation appears to him to be desirable and to take into account various financial and economic factors listed in the section. In the light of the overall figure the Secretary of State then applies the principles laid down in the following sections to determine the individual block grants.[69] He must lay a Rate Support Grant Report before the House of Commons each year and no grants may be paid unless the Report is approved by a resolution of the House. In *R. v. Secretary of State for the Environment ex parte Nottinghamshire County Council*[70] the House of Lords held that in view of that procedure it would be wrong for the courts to intervene, except in the most exceptional circumstances, by way of judicial review with decisions taken by the Secretary of State. The matter was one of "political judgment" for the Secretary of State and the House of Commons. The *Nottinghamshire* Case, however, concerned the principles by which the aggregate amount was to be divided among individual authorities. It does not necessarily preclude, judicial review of the original decision under section 54 if it could be shown that the Secretary of State had failed to consult or had ignored the factors expressly listed in the section.[71] The complicated state of the current law is evidenced by the need to pass the Rate Support Grants Act 1986 which retrospectively validated certain block grant determinations which had been found to have been made without complying with the terms of the 1980 Act and amended that Act for the future.

[64] Police Act 1964, s.31.
[65] Local Government Act 1974, s.8.
[66] Education Act 1980, s.21.
[67] Local Government, Planning and Land Act 1980, s.70.
[68] Local Government Grants (Social Needs) Act 1969.
[69] Local Government, Planning and Land Act 1980, ss.56–62, as amended by the Local Government Finance Act 1982, s.8. and the Rate Support Grants Act 1986.
[70] [1986] 2 W.L.R. 1.
[71] For cases on failure to consult see *post*, p. 664 and, generally, on judicial review, Chap. 33.

(c) *Fees and charges*

Fees and charges represent about a quarter of local authorities' income, less than was the case a century ago. There are various reasons for this including the loss by local authorities of commercial services which they provided in the past—for example, gas and electricity supplies—and an unwillingness on political or social grounds to charge an "economic" price. The possibility of increasing the contribution made to local authorities' income by fees and charges was noted by the Layfield Committee (*supra*) in 1976 and the proposal accepted by the then (Labour) Government. Subsequently legislation has included provision for charging for various services.[72]

(d) *Loans*

The sources of income discussed above are available to meet the revenue expenditure of local authorities, that is their current costs and outgoings. Loans are the means by which capital expenditure is financed. A general power to raise money by borrowing is contained in the Local Government Act 1972 section 172 and Schedule 13. Loans may not be used for revenue purposes except to meet expenses pending the receipt of revenues in respect of the period of account in which the expenses occur (Sched. 13). Capital Expenditure is governed by the terms of the Local Government, Planning and Land Act 1980, Part VIII.

Audit[73]

An important aspect of control by the central government and of the Courts of the legality of actions of local authorities is to be found in the statutory provisions relating to the auditing of local governments accounts. A finding that expenditure is contrary to law may result in the disqualification of councillors and involve personal liability for large sums of money on the part of those deemed responsible.[74]

The audit of local government accounts is now governed by Part III of the Local Government Finance Act 1982 which establishes an Audit Commission to take responsibility for supervising the auditing of accounts within the scope of the Act. The members of the Commission are appointed by the Secretary of State after consultations with associations of local authorities and bodies representing accountants and local authority employees (section 11). The Commission appoints auditors to audit accounts falling within the Act, after consulting the authority concerned. Auditors may be employees of the Commission or employed in private practice as accountants. Formerly, under the Local Government Act 1972, local authorities could choose whether to have their accounts audited by an "approved auditor" from a list approved by the Secretary of State or by a district auditor appointed by the Secretary of State.[75]

---

[72] Education Act 1980, ss.22 and 23; Health and Social Services and Social Adjudications Act 1983, Part VII.

[73] R. Jones, *Local Government Audit Law* (2nd ed., 1985).

[74] Local Government Finance Act 1982, ss.19 and 20.

[75] District auditors were first appointed by the Poor Law Amendment Act 1844 which endowed them with the powers of disallowing accounts and charging disallowed sums against the persons responsible. The 1982 Act marks the end of the office.

The district auditor alone possessed statutory sanctions: an approved auditor could only make a report to the Secretary of State who could then direct the holding of an extraordinary audit by a district auditor. All auditors now possess the same statutory powers.

The Commission, in addition to responsibility for auditing local authority accounts is given other duties by the 1982 Act. Section 26 directs the Commission to undertake or promote comparative and other studies designed to enable it to make recommendations for improving economy, efficiency and effectiveness in the provision of local authority services. Section 27 enables the Commission to undertake or promote studies to enable it to prepare reports on the effect of any statutory provisions or directions or guidance given by a minister on the economy, efficiency and effectiveness in the provision of local authority services. The Commission at the request of a local authority, may undertake studies to promote economy, efficiency and effectiveness in the management or operations of that authority. In reliance on these sections the Commission has undertaken a number of studies. A report in 1984 criticised the effectiveness of the steps taken by the government to restrict local government spending and drew attention to the increasing unreliability of the current valuation list as a guide to the value of property in each local authority area.[76] In 1986 the Commission began an investigation into the economy efficiency and effectiveness with which the Inner London Boroughs provide services.

The auditor is required to satisfy himself that the accounts which he examines have been properly compiled in accordance with statutory regulations and that the body concerned has made proper arrangements for securing economy efficiency and effectiveness in its use of resources. The auditor must comply with the code of audit practice laid down by the Commission under section 14.[77] He must also consider whether, in the public interest, to make a public report on any matter coming to his notice (Section 15). The auditor has a statutory right of access to documents and may seek further information or explanation from any officer or member of a body (section 16). At an audit any person interested[78] may inspect the accounts and bills, vouchers and receipts relating to them. A local government elector for the area to which the accounts relate may question the auditor about the accounts and may personally, or by a repesentative, appear before the auditor to make objections to any item in the accounts (section 17).

Where it appears to the auditor that any item of account is *contrary to law* he may apply to the court for a declaration to that effect (section 19(1)).[79] The court may order the person responsible for incurring or authorising any unlawful expenditure to repay the sum in whole or part. If the sum exceeds £2,000 and the person responsible was at the

---

[76] *The Impact on Local Authorities' Economy, Efficiency and Effectiveness of the Block Grant System* (1984, H.M.S.O.).

[77] The Code must be laid before both Houses of Parliament and does not come into force until approved by resolutions of each House. On Codes of Practice see *post*, p. 623.

[78] Interested must mean "having a legal interest," not "curious."

[79] Until the Local Government Act 1972 the district auditor himself disallowed items contrary to law and surcharged the person responsible. For an example of an (unsuccessful) application to the court see *Pickwell* v. *Camden L.B.C.* [1983] 1 Q.B. 962 (D.C.).

relevant time a member of a local authority the court may disqualify him from such membership for a specified period, (section 19(2)). Any local government elector who has objected to an item may, if the auditor decided not to seek a declaration, apply to the court (section 19(4)). Expenditure is contrary to law where it is outside the powers of the local authority (*ultra vires*) or otherwise open to challenge on one of the grounds considered in Chapter 33. A power, for example, to pay such wages as a council thinks fit does not authorise it to reach a decision without considering the factors legally relevant to the decision or to take into account legally irrelevant considerations such as "eccentric principles of socialistic philanthropy": *Roberts* v. *Hopwood*.[80] The auditor may not seek a declaration under section where any item of account has been sanctioned by the Secretary of State. Although such a sanction would prevent proceedings by the auditor it would remain open to a ratepayer to challenge the legality of the item by judicial review, if not under section 19.

Where it appears to the auditor that any person has *failed to account* for a sum or that a loss or deficiency has been caused by *wilful misconduct* he may certify that that sum is due from the person responsible (unless in the case of failure to account the Secretary of State has sanctioned the failure). Any person aggrieved by his decision may appeal to the court, as may any local government elector against the auditor's refusal to certify failure to account or misconduct (section 20(1)–(3)). Where the sum exceeds £2,000, if the person responsible was at the time a member of a local authority he will be disqualified from further membership for a period of five years (section 20(4)).

Failure to account involves liability in, for example, the case of a local government officer who fails to collect fees which he was legally obliged to collect,[81] even if his council had decided not to charge the fee or of the official who fails to prevent money being misappropriated by someone for whose actions he is responsible.[82] Wilful misconduct has been held to cover delaying making a rate so that an authority loses interest which it would otherwise have earned on money collected: *Lloyd* v. *McMahon*.[83]

IV. POWERS AND FUNCTIONS

Acquisition of powers by local authorities

Local authorities acquire their powers, which are all statutory, in various ways. The exercise of their powers is subject to judicial control by virtue of the doctrine of *ultra vires*.[84]

---

[80] [1925] A.C. 578 *per* Lord Atkinson. (For the background: B. Keith-Lucas, "Poplarism" [1962] P.L. 52; G. W. Jones, "Herbert Morrison and Poplarism" [1975] P.L. 11). The earlier case law is considered in *Pickwell* v. *Camden L.B.C.* (*supra*).

[81] *R.* v. *Roberts* [1901] 2 K.B. 117.

[82] *R.* (*O'Carroll*) v. *King* (1910) (1916) 50 I.L.T.R. 193.

[83] [1987] 2 W.L.R. 821 (C.A. and H.L.). See too *Graham* v. *Teesdale* (1981) 81 L.G.R. 117. On the slightly different wording of the earlier legislation see *Asher* v. *Lacey* [1973] 1 W.L.R. 1412 (the Clay Cross Case).

[84] *Post*, p. 662 and Chap. 33.

Public general Acts may confer general powers such as the making of contracts, the bringing or defending of legal proceedings and the making of by-laws, on all local authorities or all authorities of a certain kind, *e.g.* Local Government Acts and London Government Acts. Powers relating to specific services are also granted by such statutes as Public Health Acts, Housing Acts, Town and Country Planning Acts, Education Acts and Social Services Acts; some are obligatory and others permissive. The Local Government (Miscellaneous Provisions) Act 1976 and the Local Government (Miscellaneous Provisions) Act 1982 confer on local authorities a variety of miscellaneous powers of the kind which, formerly, were commonly acquired by local Acts of Parliament.[85]

Adoptive Acts are public general Acts that come into force for a particular authority only if and when the latter adopts it, either by formal resolution or by order of the Minister. Examples are certain provisions of the Public Health Acts.

Local Acts

A particular local authority may acquire powers by procuring the passing of a private Act, known in this case as a local Act.[86] The Local Government Act 1972 provides that county councils and district councils may promote or oppose local or personal Bills. The resolution must be passed by a majority of the total number of members of the council after a meeting held after 10 days' notice in the local Press; and, in the case of the promotion of a Bill, must be confirmed by a like majority at a further meeting held as soon as may be after 14 days after the Bill has been deposited in Parliament.

The promotion of local Bills is in any event an expensive procedure, and its place has largely been taken in recent years (except in the larger county boroughs) by the method of Provisional Order or Special Procedure Orders where they are applicable (*post*).

A local Bill may set out *standard clauses* contained in "model Bills" which have been found acceptable to the House of Commons, and have been printed with the sanction of the Speaker to act as a guide to parliamentary agents.

A local Bill may incorporate by reference certain clauses contained in *Clauses Acts, i.e.* public general Acts which set out clauses for this purpose. A number of Clauses Acts were passed 1845–1847 and later relating to such matters as water, gas, electricity, markets and fairs, harbours and docks, and cemeteries. Some of these have now been incorporated by general legislation, in some cases by reference.

Provisional Order confirmation Acts[87]

Many of the particular powers of local authorities are—or were until recently—conferred by these Acts, which confirm *Provisional Orders* made under statutory powers by the Minister concerned.

---

[85] For a comparable Scottish mélange, see Civic Government (Scotland) Act 1982.
[86] For the procedure in Parliament, see *ante*, Chap. 10.
[87] *Ante*, Chap. 10. Procedure modified by the Local Government Act 1972, s.240.

Orders subject to special parliamentary procedure[88]

Since 1945, statutory powers which are expressed to be subject to "special parliamentary procedure" are acquired in accordance with the requirements of the Statutory Orders (Special Procedure) Act 1945.

Ministerial (or Special) Orders

Local authorities may put forward schemes (*e.g.* clearance schemes under the Housing Acts) for confirmation after public inquiry, by the appropriate Minister. A ministerial order, unless rejected by parliamentary resolution (which has no power to amend it), gives the local authority statutory powers.

Power to make byelaws

An important power possessed by local authorities is that of making byelaws, that is legislation having effect within a defined locality. Section 235 of the Local Government Act 1972 confers a power on district and London borough councils to make byelaws for "good rule and government of the whole or any part of the district or borough" and for "the prevention and suppression of nuisances." Section 236 lays down a general procedure which applies to the making of byelaws under any Act in the absence of specific provisions. Byelaws must be confirmed by a Minister (depending on the relevant Act). The confirming authority for the 1972 Act is the Secretary of State for the Home Department. Other statutes conferring the power to make byelaws include the Housing Act 1985, the Water Resources Act 1963, various Public Health Acts, the Countryside Act 1968, the Weights and Measures Act 1985, the Food Act 1984 and the Children and Young Persons Act 1933. Offences against byelaws are punishable on summary conviction by a fine, the maximum level of which depends on the terms of the relevant statute.

The validity of byelaws is open to challenge on various grounds which are discussed in Part V of this Chapter and later in Chapter 30.

Power to bring legal proceedings

Section 222 of the local Government Act 1972 allows a local authority where it considers it expedient for the promotion or protection of the interests of the inhabitants of their area to prosecute, defend or appear in any legal proceedings and, in the case of civil proceedings, to institute them in their own name. This section has been interpreted to mean that local authorities, unlike private citizens, can bring proceedings for injunctions to protect public rights without obtaining the consent of the Attorney-General to use his name in a relator action.[89] In *Gravesham Borough Council* v. *British Railways Board*[90] the Council successfully claimed a right to seek an injunction to prevent a public nuisance arising from the wrongful withdrawal of a ferry service. Despite the views expressed by the House of Lords in *Gouriet* v. *Union of Post Office Workers*[91] about the care with which injunctions should be used to

---

[88] *Ante*, Chap. 10 and *post*, Chap. 30. Procedure modified by the Local Government Act 1972, s.240.

[89] *Ante*, p. 331 and *post*, p. 700.

[90] [1978] Ch. 379. See also *Solihull M.B.C.* v. *Maxfern* [1977] 1 W.L.R. 127.

[91] [1978] A.C. 435.

enforce the criminal law, local authorities may obtain injunctions under section 222 where there is not merely an infringement of the criminal law but a deliberate and fragrant flouting of the law: *Stoke-on-Trent City Council* v. *B. & Q. (Retail) Ltd.*[92]

The power conferred by section 222 is available only to "local authorities' as defined by section 270(1) of the Local Government Act 1972 so that a body such as the London Docklands Development Corporation cannot seek an injunction to enforce public rights without the consent of the Attorney-General: *London Docklands Development Corporation* v. *Rank Hovis McDougall Ltd.*[93]

Miscellaneous powers and ultra vires

Local authorities, like other bodies created by statute, may only exercise powers which have been vested in them, whether expressly or by implication. A power, for example, to establish wash houses does not entitle a local authority to operate a laundry, run by employees of the corporation, with provision for clothing to be collected and delivered after laundering: *Att.-Gen.* v. *Fulham Corporation.*[94]

The common law on the scope of implied powers is given statutory expression in section 111 of the Local Government Act 1972 which provides that a local authority shall have power to do anything (whether or not involving the expenditure, borrowing or lending of money or the acquisition or disposal of any property or rights) which is calculated to facilitate or is conducive or incidental[95] to, the discharge of any of their functions.

A relaxation of the ultra vires rules was introduced by the Local Government (Financial Provisions) Act 1963 and re-enacted by section 137 of the Local Government Act 1972[96] under which a local authority may spend up to the product of a 2p rate on expenditure which in the opinion of the authority is in the interests of their area or any part of it or all or some of their inhabitants. Such expenditure may include contributing to expenditure by other local authorities and to the funds of charitable bodies or other bodies providing public services otherwise than for gain.

The use of section 137 as a basis for spending funds on party political campaigns by local authorities gave rise to some concern[97] and led to a prohibition on the publication by local authorities of material which "appears to be designed to affect public support for a political party" (Local Government Act 1986, section 2).[98]

---

[92] [1984] A.C. 754; followed *Runnymede B.C.* v. *Ball* [1986] 1 W.L.R. 353 (C.A.). *Cf. Bradford M.C.C.* v. *Brown* (1986) 84 L.G.R. 731 (C.A.). (Unsuccessful claim to right to seek injunction under Public Health Act 1936, s.100).

[93] (1985) 84 L.G.R. 101 (C.A.).

[94] [1921] 1 Ch. 440.

[95] *Att.-Gen.* v. *Crayford U.D.C.* [1962] Ch. 575.

[96] Local Government (Scotland) Act 1973, s.83. Both sections were amended by the Local Authorities (Expenditure Powers) Act 1983.

[97] The government referred the matter to the Committee of Inquiry into the Conduct of Local Authority Business (The Widdicombe Committee) which produced an interim report on political campaigning by local authorities in July 1985.

[98] Section 3 amends s.142 of the Local Government Act 1972 (s.88 of the Local Government (Scotland) Act 1973) which confers a power to make information available to prevent a similar abuse: see *post* p. 604.

Power to enter into contracts

Local authorities may make contracts in accordance with their standing orders.[99] A person entering into a contract with a local authority is not bound to inquire whether standing orders have been complied with, and non-compliance with such orders does not invalidate contract which would otherwise be valid.[1]

Functions

Elected local authorities acquired towards the end of the last century and in the early years of this century a wide range of functions, replacing in the process a variety of bodies which had formerly been responsible for particular services.

At present local authorities are responsible for many matters concerned with the environment, for example, public health, planning and highways. Other areas of responsibility include police, fire services, education, housing and social services. They are given powers to licence almost anything or anyone which Parliament thinks from time to time should be controlled by licensing: tattooing, common lodging houses, food hawkers, peddlars, pleasure boats, places of entertainment, sex shops, wild animals and performing animals.

The nationalisation legislation of the Labour government, passed in the years following the end of the Second World War, removed their responsibility for electricity and gas supplies and for hospitals. Water and sewerage became the responsibility of non-elected regional water authorities by the Water Act 1973. After three hundred years the administration of the poor law (national assistance and, currently, supplementary benefits) was finally taken over by the central government by the National Assistance Act 1948. Most recently the Transport Act 1985 has "deregulated" the provision of bus-services. Even in the field of education the government announced in 1986 plans to build and fund directly from central funds Technical Colleges in selected cities throughout the country.

Allocation of Functions

Non-metropolitan county councils and metropolitan district councils are the authorities for education, personal social services and libraries.

The functions of county councils include: co-ordination of transport policies; highways generally; traffic; transport generally; police (subject to amalgamation); reserve powers of housing (*e.g.* overspill); refuse disposal (in England); environmental health; and fire (subject to amalgamation).

The functions of district councils include: local planning; municipal transport; urban roads and footpaths; housing (house-building, house management, slum clearance, house and area improvement, building regulations); refuse collection (in England); refuse disposal and collection (in Wales).

---

[99] Local Government Act 1972, s.135. A council *may* make standing orders to regulate the making of contracts in general and *shall* make standing orders with respect to contracts for the supply of goods or materials or for the execution of works.

[1] *North West Leicestershire D.C.* v. *East Midlands Housing Association Ltd.* [1981] 1 W.L.R. 1396 (C.A.).

County councils and district councils have concurrent functions in relation to museums and art galleries; parks and open spaces; playing fields and swimming baths; and coast protection.

In the area of Greater London the Outer London Boroughs are the authorities for education while responsibility in Inner London rests in the elected Inner London Education Authority.

V. CONTROL BY CENTRAL GOVERNMENT AND COURTS

Central government control[2]

Central authority

The experiment made in 1834 of appointing poor law commissioners who were neither in Parliament nor responsible to Parliament was not successful, and was superseded by other methods of central control. A Local Government Board with a President in Parliament displaced the existing Poor Law Board. The Local Government Board was the central department responsible for the general supervision, from 1871 until the Ministry of Health was created in 1919. Since 1951 the general supervision of the work of local government (other than personal health services) has been entrusted to various Ministries, and now comes under the Department of the Environment.

The central government exercises a considerable degree of administrative control over local authorities in the interests of the community as a whole; for what is administered locally is often a national policy. This supervision is closer in respect of some services than of others. The most effective single agency is the control over finance exercised by the Secretary of State, and by the Home Secretary in the case of the police. The various methods are only mentioned here very briefly and by way of illustration.

The main significance of these supervisory powers lies in their cumulative effect. Their mere existence is generally enough to ensure that local authorities exercise their functions, not only as laid down by law but in consultation with, and in accordance with the policy of, the appropriate central government department.

Orders and regulations

Extensive powers to issue orders and regulations are given to Ministers in relation to food and drugs, public health, housing social security and water supply. Under the Education Act 1944, s.99, the Secretary of State for Education and Science, if satisfied that a local education authority has failed to discharge any duty imposed on it by the Act, may make an order and give directions for its execution, and may enforce such directions by mandamus. Section 68 of the same Act confers similar powers in cases where the Secretary of State is satisfied that a local authority is proposing to exercise its powers unreasonably.[3]

---

[2] See J. A. G. Griffith, *Central Departments and Local Authorities* (1966).

[3] For the meaning of "unreasonably" in this context see *Secretary of State for Education and Science* v. *Tameside Metropolitan B.C.* [1977] A.C. 1014, *post*, p. 601. See subsequently the Education Act 1976 and the Education Act 1979.

Sanctioning of schemes

Often it is the duty of a local authority to prepare schemes for the administration of a particular service within its area, *e.g.* planning and schools, and to submit such schemes to the appropriate Minister for approval.

Control over officials is exemplified by the power given to the Minister to regulate the qualifications for appointment and promotion of all ranks in the fire service under the Fire Services Act 1947, s. 18. The Home Secretary issues regulations concerning the salaries, duties and uniforms of local police forces, and may veto the appointment of a chief constable or children's officer. The Secretary of State for Education and Science may veto the appointment of a chief education officer.

Inspection

The Minister may provide for inspection of local welfare services in the regulations which he is empowered to issue by the Social Security Acts. Inspection by Home Office and Department of Education inspectors is also the chief means for securing that local police and education authorities are performing their duties and complying with regulations.

Inquiry

A Minister who is authorised to act by the Local Government Act 1972, and the Secretary of State concerned with local government, may cause a local inquiry to be held.

Confirmation of byelaws is required by the Home Secretary, the Secretary of State for the Environment or other appointed Minister. This check on the lawmaking powers of local authorities is in addition to the limits imposed by Parliament and enforced under the doctrine of *ultra vires* by the courts.

Default Powers[4]

The Minister may take over functions relating e.g. to education or civil defence, if it appears after a local inquiry that the authority has failed to discharge such functions. In practice, this power is very seldom exercised, as the knowledge of its existence—let alone the mere threat of using the power—is generally sufficient to induce the local authority to discharge its functions.[5]

Control over loans

The consent of the Secretary of State to the raising of loans by local authorities is required in most cases.

Control over grants

This is the most important kind of financial control exercised by the central government over local authorities. The events of the last few

---

[4] For a list of default powers see [1984] P.L. 485.

[5] But see *R. v. Secretary of State for the Environment, ex p. Norwich C.C.* [1982] Q.B. 808 (C.A.); noted, S. H. Bailey, "Central and Local Government and the Courts," [1983] P.L. 8.

years have shown, however, the difficulty of controlling local authorities which are determined to engage in controversy with the government. The attempts to deal with such bodies in the Local Government, Planning and Land Act 1980 and subsequent legislation are discussed, *supra*, in connection with Rates.

The Home Secretary may withhold any portion of the grant for police from any authority whose administration falls below the minimum standard required, or is not in accordance with statutory duties or ministerial regulations. Similarly other ministers may withhold or reduce earmarked grants.

Judicial control

The general principles of judicial control over public bodies and the remedies available will be discussed in detail in Chapters 33 and 34. Nonetheless something must be said here of the role of the courts in reviewing the legality of local authorities' actions if only because of the number of important decisions in this area of the law as a result of an increasing willingness on the part of local authorities to resort to litigation rather than to settle disputes with the Secretary of State or between themselves by political means.

As we have seen above a local authority cannot act *ultra vires*, that is beyond the limits of its statutory powers. The importance of this principle could be said to lie in its extension to cases where public bodies are regarded by the courts as having acted so unreasonably that they have exceeded the limits of the powers conferred on them by Parliament. Modern case law on unreasonableness in this sense traces its origins to a local authority case: *Associated Picture Houses Ltd.* v. *Wednesbury Corporation.*[6] A local authority acts unreasonably if it fails to take into account relevant considerations or, on the other hand, is swayed by irrelevant considerations. In cases such as *Bromley London Borough Council* v. *Greater London Council*[7] issues of unreasonableness and of *ultra vires* in the strict sense may be hard to disentangle. A local authority will also act *ultra vires* if it exercises a statutory power for a purpose for which it was not intended. For example, section 142 of the Local Government Act 1972 allows a local authority to arrange for the publication of information on matters relating to local government. In *R. v. I.L.E.A. ex parte Westminster City Council*[8] Glidewell J. held that the section did not authorise expenditure on publications which were intended to persuade the public, on a matter of controversy, to adopt the view held by I.L.E.A.

A recent example of a local authority's decision being held to be *ultra vires* is *In Re Westminster City Council,*[9] where the House of Lords held

---

[6] [1948] 1 K.B. 223 (C.A.). (Not *ultra vires* on grounds of unreasonableness to attach to a licence permitting Sunday opening of a cinema a condition that no child under 15 be admitted on that day.)

[7] [1983] 1 A.C. 768.

[8] [1986] 1 W.L.R. 28.

[9] [1986] A.C. 668 (H.L.). The main difficulty in the way of the House was its own previous decision in *Manchester City Council* v. *Greater Manchester County Council* (1980) 78 L.G.R. 560 (H.L.). See also *R. v. Liverpool City Council, ex p. Ferguson, The Times* November 20, 1985 (D.C.). (Acts, such as dismissal of teachers, taken in consequence of making illegal rate must themselves be *ultra vires.*)

that the Greater London Council had no power to make grants to fund for the future a number of voluntary bodies because in principle local authority finance is conducted on an annual basis.

The wide scope capable of being given to unreasonableness is illustrated by *Wheeler* v. *Leicester City Council*[10] where the House of Lords held that a local authority acted unreasonably in withdrawing permission from a rugby club to use municipally owned facilities because the club was not prepared to answer questions relating to a rugby tour of South Africa in the only way that the Council was prepared to accept.

The question of who has the right (locus standi) to challenge local authority decisions is discussed later in Chapter 34.

[10] [1985] A.C. 1954.

CHAPTER 29

PUBLIC CORPORATIONS AND REGULATORY BODIES[1]

I. Nature and Purpose of Public Corporations[2]

In addition to the central government departments under the direct control of Ministers of the Crown, and the local government authorities elected by the local electors, public affairs in Great Britain are administered by or with the aid of various public bodies.

Once Parliament had begun in the nineteenth century, in Maitland's words to legislate instead of trying to govern,[3] it became necessary to establish bodies to carry out the purposes of legislation themselves or to supervise and regulate other bodies. Particularly since the end of the Second World War, Parliament has established public bodies to provide commercial services which had formerly been provided by private companies and local authorities. The increasing acceptance of responsibility by the State for matters cultural, environmental and artistic is shown by the establishment of Councils and Commissions. Racial harmony and sexual equality are seen to be best fostered by establishing Commissions. Tourism, the interests of Consumers, the supervision of Gaming, the encouragement of Design are all appropriate matters for a board or committee. The more important of these bodies are created by statute or royal charter.[4] They all possess a considerable, although varying, degree of independence from ministerial and therefore parliamentary control. To the extent that they are all directly responsible neither to Parliament nor to local authorities they can be said to belong to the class of Quangos, an acronym which can be translated either to mean quasi autonomous non-governmental organisation or quasi autonomous national government organisations.[5] Whether such a classification, which can include at one extreme Boards of nationalised industries and at the other the National Association of Youth Clubs, is of great value

[1] *Government Enterprise* (ed. W. Friedmann and J. F. Garner, 1970); J. A. G. Griffith and H. Street, *Principles of Administrative Law* (5th ed., 1973), Chap. 7; W. A. Robson, *Nationalised Industry and Public Ownership* (2nd ed., 1962); Herbert Morrison, *Government and Parliament* (1954), Chap. 12; Sir Arthur Street, "Quasi-Government Bodies since 1981," in *British Government since 1918* (by Sir G. Campion and Others); *Public Enterprise* (ed. Robson); D. N. Chester, *The Nationalised Industries: A Statutory Analysis* (Institute of Public Administration, 2nd ed., 1951); *The Nationalised Industries* (Cmnd. 7131, 1978); T. Prosser, *Nationalised Industries and Public Control* (1986).
[2] The term was first used in the Report of the Crawford Committee on Broadcasting in 1926 (Cmnd. 2599).
[3] *Ante*, p. 579. The Poor Law Commissioners had been followed by the Inclosure Commissioners (1844), the Railway Commission (1846) and the General Board of Health (1848). This century saw, *inter alia*, the Port of London Authority (1908) and the London Passenger Transport Board (1933).
[4] Other methods include, royal warrant, treasury minute, registration under the Companies Act or as a charitable trust.
[5] P. Holland, *Quango, Quango, Quango* (1978). *What's Wrong With Quangos?* (Outer Circle Policy Unit 1979). The vagueness of the term "quango" is obvious from the differences in the lists of such organisations in these two publications. See also *Report on Non Departmental Public Bodies* (1980, Cmnd. 7797).

may be doubted. In this chapter the main attention will be devoted to public authorities or public corporations[6] in a rather narrower sense, with particular emphasis on nationalised industries and bodies of constitutional significance, whether, strictly speaking, corporations or not.

It is difficult to generalise about these public corporations. A possible classification is as follows:

(i) Managerial—industrial or commercial

Executive bodies set up to manage nationalised industries or branches of commerce, *e.g.* National Coal Board; British Railways Board; British Steel Corporation; Central Electricity Generating Board, Electricity Council and area electricity boards; South of Scotland Electricity Board, North of Scotland Hydro-electricity Board; Post Office; Bank of England; United Kingdom Atomic Energy Authority.

After the Second World War nationalisation usually took the form of the compulsory acquisition of the assets of existing private undertakings and the vesting of them in a public corporation.[7] From the time of Disraeli's purchase of shares in the Suez Canal Company the government had been aware of the possibility of establishing public control of a private undertaking through ownership of its shares. A similar procedure ensured government control of the Cable and Wireless Co. In 1938 a small government holding was established and in 1946 all the shares of the company were transferred into the ownership of named civil servants.[8] The Bank of England, established by statute and Royal Charter in 1694 was similarly brought into public control by the transfer of its stock to Treasury ownership.[9] In 1971 Rolls Royce was rescued from financial collapse by the purchase of its shares by a new company created by statute[10] and in 1975 legislation enabled the government to buy the shares of British Leyland when it, too, faced financial disaster.[11]

Among the public corporations providing commercial services the Post Office occupies a unique position. Historically, it originated as a department of State providing an essential service to the Crown. The opening of its services to the public was a device to raise money. Blackstone discussed "the post office or duty for the carriage of letters" in that part of the Commentaries devoted to the King's Revenue. "There cannot," he said, "be devised a more eligible method . . . of raising money upon the subject [than by a duty on letters]; for therein both the government and the people find a mutual benefit. The government

---

[6] There is no consistency of usage in statutes; the Post Office, for example, is "a public authority"; Post Office Act 1969. The British Telecommunications Act 1981, however, creates "a public corporation."

[7] Coal Industry Nationalisation Act 1946; Transport Act 1947; Electricity Act 1947; Gas Act 1948, as amended by the Gas Act 1972; Airways Corporations Act 1949 (see now Civil Aviation Act 1980). A late example of this type of nationalisation is provided by the Aircraft and Shipbuilding Industries Act 1977 (British Aerospace and British Shipbuilders).

[8] Cable and Wireless Act 1946. Similarly in 1914 the government acquired a majority shareholding in Anglo Persian Oil Co. (now BP, in which the government at present holds 32% of the shares).

[9] Bank of England Act 1946.

[10] Rolls-Royce (Purchase) Act 1971.

[11] British Leyland Act 1975.

acquires a large revenue; and the people do their business with greater ease, expedition, and cheapness, than they would be able to do if no such tax (and of course no such office) existed."[12] In the nineteenth century telegraphs and telephones were added to its monopoly. In 1967 a government White Paper recommended turning the Post Office into a public corporation in order that it could be run on commercial lines, bringing to its business a structure and method drawing on the best modern practice.[13] The legislation which followed that report preserved for the Post Office its remarkable immunity from actions in tort which had been explicable when it was part of the Crown in earlier centuries and had even survived the passing of the Crown Proceedings Act 1947.[14] Nor has it ever been suggested that the new status of the Post Office affects the long established rule that there is no contractual relationship between the Post Office and the sender of a letter or parcel.[15] As will be seen below the Post Office not merely has the longest history of modern commercial public corporations but has also been directly involved in the latest stage in the history of such bodies, privatisation.

(ii) Managerial—social services

Executive bodies set up to manage social services, e.g. development corporations for the various new towns,[16] the New Towns Commission[17] and the Urban Development Corporations[18]; Regional and Area Health Authorities[19–20]; British Broadcasting Corporation; Water Authorities; Manpower Services Commission.

The British Broadcasting Corporation is unusual in having been created by royal charter and in deriving its income from a licence fee levied on the holders of (formerly) wireless and (now) television sets. Its first charter was granted in 1926; the current charter was granted in 1981 to last until 1996. Because of the way the B.B.C. has operated since its foundation it is thought of as providing a social service but broadcasting can be regarded as a commercial undertaking, which is the case with the services falling under the control of the Independent Broadcasting Authority.

The Water Authorities similarly tend to be thought of as providing a public service although they charge for their services and there is no reason why, by means of meters in each house or other building, their charges should not be directly related to the individual customer's consumption. The present Authorities were constituted by the Water Act 1973 which removed responsibility for the supply of

---

[12] Bl. Comm. i. 323. "A branch of the revenue"; Whitfield v. Le Despencer (1778) 2 Cowp. 754, 764 per Lord Mansfield.

[13] Reorganisation of the Post Office (Cmnd. 3233, 1967).

[14] Crown Proceedings Act 1947, s.9; Post Office Act 1969, s.29; American Express v. British Airways Board [1983] 1 W.L.R. 701.

[15] Triefus Co. Ltd. v. Post Office [1957] 2 Q.B. 352 (C.A.). See [1972] P.L. 97. See too its statutory privileges, e.g. the Telegraph Act 1878; Post Office v. Mears Construction [1979] 2 All E.R. 814.

[16] New Towns Act 1946; New Towns Act 1965.

[17] New Towns Act 1981; New Towns and Urban Development Corporations Act 1985.

[18] Local Government, Planning and Land Act 1980.

[19–20] National Health Service Reorganisation Act 1973.

water from local authorities and statutory undertakers and transferred it to the new regional authorities which were also to be responsible for water resources generally—conservation, sewage disposal, pollution and drainage.[21]

The Manpower Services Commission is a body corporate created by statute with the duty of making arrangements for assisting persons to train for and obtain employment.[22]

(iii) *Regulatory and advisory*

(a) Bodies set up to regulate private enterprise in certain fields, *e.g.* agricultural marketing boards[23]; the Wheat Commission[24]; Food from Britain[25]; the British Hall Marking Council[26]; the Civil Aviation Authority[27]; the Director General of Fair Trading, and the Health and Safety at Work Commission and Executive; the Securities and Investment Board.

The Independent Broadcasting Authority is a statutory corporation which was established by the Independent Broadcasting Act 1973. Its powers and duties are currently regulated by the Broadcasting Act 1981. Section 2 requires the IBA to provide programmes of "high quality," while recognising that the actual production of programmes may be entrusted to "programme contractors." Section 4, which was cited earlier in Chapter 26, imposes the duty on the I.B.A. of ensuring that nothing included in any programme for which it is responsible shall offend against good taste or decency or be likely to encourage or incite to crime or to lead to disorder or to be offensive to public feeling.

The office of Director General of Fair Trading was created by the Fair Trading Act 1973. The Consumer Credit Act 1974 confers on the Director General a wide range of duties and powers which exemplify strikingly the devices to which Parliament has recourse to ensure the effective operation of much modern legislation. It is the duty of the Director General:

   (*a*) to administer the licensing system set up by the Consumer Credit Act;

   (*b*) to exercise the adjudicating functions conferred on him by the Act in relation to the issue, renewal, variation, suspension and revocation of licences, and other matters;

   (*c*) generally to superintend the working and enforcement of the Act, and regulations made under it; and

   (*d*) where necessary or expedient, himself to take steps to enforce the Act, and regulations so made.

---

[21] H. M. Purdue, "The Implications of the Constitution and Functions of Regional Water Authorities" [1979] P.L. 119. The Act which applies only to England and Wales was amended by the Water Act 1983. For Scotland, see the Water (Scotland) Act 1980.

[22] Employment and Training Act 1973, as amended by the Employment and Training Act 1981.

[23] Agricultural Marketing Act 1958.

[24] Wheat Act 1932.

[25] Agricultural Marketing Act 1983.

[26] Hallmarking Act 1973.

[27] Civil Aviation Act 1982.

The Director is also required to keep under review and from time to time advise the Secretary of State about—

(a) social and commercial developments in the United Kingdom and elsewhere relating to the provision of credit or bailment or (in Scotland) hiring of goods to individuals, and related activities; and

(b) the working and enforcement of this Act and orders and regulations made under it (section 1).

In addition, he is to arrange for the dissemination of such information and advice as it may appear to him expedient to give to the public about the operation of the Act, the credit facilities available and other matters within the scope of his functions (section 4). The Director is also a tribunal, for the purposes of the Tribunal and Inquiries Act 1971, with regard to the exercise of his licensing functions (section 3).

The Health and Safety Commission and the Health and Safety Executive are bodies corporate established by the Health and Safety at Work etc. Act 1974 to further the purposes of the Act (sections 10 and 11). In addition to very general statements of their responsibilities for advising, monitoring and overseeing various sections deal with specific matters; for example, section 16 provides for the approval by the Commission of Codes of Practice issued under the Act. Section 18 imposes on the Executive the duty of making adequate arrangements for the enforcement of the provisions of the Act, except to the extent that other authorities have specific responsibilities.

The Securities and Investment Board is an unusual form of regulatory body. The Financial Services Act 1986 provides for the regulation of financial and investment services but it does not establish a statutory regulatory body. It provides that a "self regulating organisation"[28] (such as the S.I.B.) may apply to the Secretary of State for recognition.

(b) Bodies set up to advise Ministers and other authorities with regard to the exercise of their powers and responsibilities, e.g. Police Council[29]; Nature Conservancy Council[30]; Pilotage Commission[31]; Employment Medical Advisory Service.[32] The Audit Commission, established by the Government Finance Act 1982 is an advisory body in so far as it is required to make recommendations for improving economy, efficiency and effectiveness in the provision of local government services and to report on the impact of such services of statutory provisions and directions given by ministers (sections 26 and 27). As the body responsible for organising the auditing of local government accounts it can perhaps be regarded as a regulatory or managerial body (section 12).

(c) Miscellaneous Bodies. Two important bodies with powers of advising, monitoring and enforcing legislation are the Commission for Racial Equality and the Equal Opportunities Commission, both of

---

[28] Defined by s.8 as a body which regulates the carrying on of investment business of any kind by enforcing rules which are binding on persons carrying on business of that kind either because they are members of that body or otherwise subject to its control.

[29] Police Act 1964, s.45(4).

[30] Wildlife and Countryside Act 1981, s.24.

[31] Pilotage Act 1983.

[32] Health and Safety At Work etc. Act 1974, s.55.

which were established by statute to operate in areas formerly falling outside the direct concern of the law.[33] The Commonwealth Development Corporation was established "to assist overseas countries . . . in the development of their economies."[34] The National Biological Standards Board is a body corporate which is responsible for the establishment of standards for, the provision of standard preparations of, and the testing of biological substances.[35] The English Industrial Estates Corporation provides, facilitates the provision of, and manages sites and premises in England for occupation by industrial or commercial undertakings and may provide advisory services in relation to the building of factories or the development of industrial estates in England and outside Great Britain.[36] The Crown Agents were constituted as a body corporate by the Crown Agents Act 1979 and their full title (Crown Agents for Overseas Governments and Administrations) explains their role: to act as agents on behalf of governments and public authorities specified in Schedule 3 of the Act. The range of functions they may undertake are defined in sections 4 and 5 and Schedule 4.

II. LEGAL POSITION OF PUBLIC CORPORATIONS[37-38]

The main constitutional problems relate to the legal status of those public corporations that manage some nationalised industry or branch of commerce or public service, especially their liability in contract and tort, and the question of parliamentary supervision. The latter is discussed in section III below.

Appointment and powers

To ascertain the legal position of any public corporation it is necessary first of all to look at the particular Act of Parliament that created it, for no two of them are alike. It is generally provided that they are bodies corporate, with perpetual succession and a common seal and power to hold land. The chairmen and other members of the boards are appointed and may be removed by the competent Minister or by the Crown. Their members do not have to be representative of any particular interests. Their salaries are generally fixed by the Minister with the approval of the Treasury. The large number of appointments to be made, subject to no effective form of control, has placed in the hands of ministers a power of patronage undreamed of even in the eighteenth century. As there are no shareholders to exercise any control over the board, the Acts provide that the Minister may set up advisory committees or councils to advise him.

The powers of a public corporation are set out in the constituent Act.

---

[33] Race Relations Act 1976; Sex Discrimination Act 1975; *ante*, p. 438.
[34] Commonwealth Development Corporation Act 1978.
[35] Biological Standards Act 1975.
[36] English Industrial Estates Corporation Act 1981.
[37-38] Glanville Williams, *Crown Proceedings* (1948), pp. 4–8, 21–28, 30–37, 85; J. A. G. Griffith, "Public Corporations as Crown Servants" 9 U.T.L.J. 169; H. Street, *Government Liability* (1953), pp. 28–36; W. Friedmann, "The New Public Corporations and the Law" (1947) 10 M.L.R. 233–254, 377–395; W. A. Robson, "The Public Corporations in Britain Today" (1959) 63 Harv. Law Rev. 1321–1348.

They are subject to judicial determination by the doctrine of *ultra vires* (*Smith* v. *London Transport Executive*[39]), but their powers in some cases are very wide. There is generally no legal means by which these bodies may be compelled by private citizens to exercise their functions. The Minister might be able to apply for mandamus or a declaration in some cases, unless this is expressly excluded by statute. The Transport Act 1962, s.3(1), provided that it should be the "duty" of the Railways Board to provide railway services, and in connection therewith such other services and facilities as might appear to the Board to be expedient; but section 3(4) went on to say that no such duty or liability should be enforceable by judicial proceedings. A similar provision is contained in the Post Office Act 1969, s.9(4).[40] Exceptionally, the Transport Act 1968, s.106(1), allows any person to apply to the court for an order requiring the Waterways Board to maintain commercial and cruising waterways for public use. Usually statutes provide that the Minister may give directions "of a general character" in the public interest.[41] In some cases he has power to give specific directions, *e.g.* to the National Enterprise Board.[42] In the cases of the B.B.C. and the I.B.A. the Home Secretary has powers to give directions requiring that an announcement be broadcast, or requiring that those bodies refrain from broadcasting particular items.[43] The Minister has power to control capital expenditure and borrowing, and also to direct the use of surplus revenues.

The industrial and commercial corporations are independent in the day-to-day conduct of their business, and subject only to indirect ministerial control. The Minister's powers—notably that of giving general directions—are kept in the background; but their existence enables him to exert a fair amount of unofficial pressure which may take the form of "requests."[44] A Minister cannot give a direction which contradicts the provisions of the Act of Parliament under which he is purporting to act.[45]

Public corporations must keep proper accounts, as far as possible[46] on commercial lines, and submit them to audit. The Public Accounts Committee may examine accounts presented to Parliament.

A public corporation must make an annual report to the Minister, who must lay it before Parliament together with a report of any action taken, or declined to be taken, by him. Any directions given by the Minister must be published in the board's report, unless he directs that publication would be contrary to the national interest.[47] The Minister is responsible to Parliament for the exercise of his powers, such as they are, and also for failing to exercise them.

The degree of financial control of nationalised industries depends on the extent to which corporations are financially independent and the

---

[39] [1951] A.C. 555 (H.L.); and see *post*, Chap. 33.
[40] See *Harold Stephen & Co.* v. *The Post Office* [1977] 1 W.L.R. 1172 (C.A.).
[41] *e.g.* Coal Industry Nationalisation Act 1946, s.3(1).
[42] Industry Act 1975, s.7(1); *Booth & Co.* v. *N.E.B.* [1978] 3 All E.R. 624. See now the Industry Act 1980. For another example see Petroleum and Submarine Pipelines Act 1975, s.4.
[43] Broadcasting Act 1981, s.29.
[44] See Coombes [1965] P.L. 9; Wade (1965) 81 L.Q.R. 357, 361–363.
[45] *Laker Airways Ltd.* v. *Department of Trade* [1977] Q.B. 643 (C.A.).
[46] *e.g.* Iron and Steel Act 1982, s.24.
[47] *e.g.* Iron and Steel Act 1982, s.6.

particular political views of different governments.[48] Initially the nationalisation statutes set a duty on the industries concerned to balance their books, from one year to the next. In the nineteen sixties, however, concern about inefficiency and inadequate returns on their assets led to the government introducing financial targets, requiring a rate of return on capital assets. Subsequently further controls over pricing and planning were introduced. The most controversial current element of control is the application to nationalised industries of cash limits, under the name of External Financing Limits. In the case of profitable industries these limits have been set as negative figures which results in those industries in fact contributing funds to the Treasury, a procedure which has been attacked as taxation unauthorised by Parliament.[49]

Liability to judicial proceedings

The question whether a public corporation is a servant or agent of the Crown is of considerable legal importance. If it is a servant or agent of the Crown, civil proceedings would be governed by the Crown Proceedings Act 1947 (unless it was set up by a later statute expressly or impliedly inconsistent with the Act), and the action (if available) would have to be brought by or against the authorised department or the Attorney-General. The corporation would also have the advantage of the Crown privileges relating to injunction, execution and interrogatories,[50] and would not be bound by Acts of Parliament (including rates and taxes) unless expressly or by necessary implication.[51] And this might well affect the position of individual members of the board and its employees.

If the corporation is not a servant or agent of the Crown, the Crown Proceedings Act does not apply: it would be liable in the ordinary way in contract and tort; its staff would be employees of the corporation and not Crown servants; and proceedings by or against it (in so far as not expressly excluded or limited by the statute) would be in the name of the corporation (*Mersey Docks and Harbour Board* v. *Gibbs*[52]).

Where the statute is not explicit

Most of the earlier Acts creating public corporations were not explicit on the question whether the corporation was a servant or agent of the Crown. In so far as such Acts have not been replaced by later legislation, if the matter should come before the court it would be a question of interpretation.

In *Tamlin* v. *Hannaford*[53] the Court of Appeal held that the British Transport Commission[54] was not a servant or agent of the Crown. The

---

[48] White Paper, 1978, Cmnd. 7131; First Report, Energy Committee H.C. 276, 1983–4; T. Prosser, "Nationalised Industries as Instruments of Financial Policy" [1986] P.L. 18.

[49] Prosser, *op. cit.*, note 1 and *supra*, note 48.

[50] *Post*, Chap. 35.

[51] *Ante*, Chap. 14.

[52] (1866) L.R. 1 H.L. 93; *Gallagher* v. *Post Office* [1970] 1 All E.R. 712; *Westwood* v. *Post Office, The Times*, November 24, 1972 (C.A.).

[53] [1951] 1 K.B. 18. And see *British Broadcasting Corporation* v. *Johns* [1965] Ch. 32; *Mellinger* v. *New Brunswick Development Corporation* [1971] 1 W.L.R. 604; *Trendtex Trading Corporation* v. *Central Bank of Nigeria* [1977] Q.B. 529.

[54] Predecessor of the British Railways Board.

question in issue was whether a house which had been leased from the Great Western Railway was withdrawn from the protection of the Rent Restriction Acts by reason of its being vested in the British Transport Commission under the Transport Act 1947.[55] In considering whether any subordinate body is entitled to the Crown privilege of not being bound by a statute unless Parliament shows an intention that it should be bound, said Denning L.J. in delivering the judgment of the Court, the question is not so much whether it is an "emanation of the Crown"[56] but whether it is properly to be regarded as a servant or agent of the Crown.[57] This depended on the true construction of the Transport Act 1947, especially the powers of the Minister in relation to the Commission.[58] When Parliament intends that a new corporation should act on behalf of the Crown, it usually says so expressly.[59] In the absence of express provision the proper inference, in the case (at any rate) of a commercial corporation, is that it acts on its own behalf.

It is probable that none of the recently created industrial or commercial corporations is a servant or agent of the Crown. None of them is in the list of "authorised departments" issued by the Treasury under the Crown Proceedings Act 1947, s.17, although this is not conclusive as proceedings may be taken under that Act against the Attorney-General. Many proceedings have been brought by and against industrial corporations in their own names without the question being raised in court.[60]

Where the statute is explicit

The National Health Service Act 1946, s.13, expressly stated that a regional hospital board, notwithstanding that it exercised functions on behalf of the Minister, should be entitled to enforce rights and be liable for liabilities (including liability in tort) as if it were acting as a principal: proceedings were to be brought by or against the board in its own name, and it was not entitled to the privileges of the Crown in respect of discovery or production of documents. Similar principles applied to a hospital management committee, although it exercised its functions on behalf of the regional hospital board.[61] On the other hand, the Crown might claim privilege in respect of its documents; and it was held in *Nottingham Area No. 1 Hospital Management Committee* v. *Owen*[62] that a hospital vested in the Minister of Health under the Act of 1946 was "premises occupied for the public service of the Crown" under the Public Health Act 1936, and that the justices had therefore no jurisdiction to make an order under that Act to abate a nuisance constituted by a smoking chimney.

---

[55] *Cf.* Crown Lessees (Protection of Sub-Tenants) Act 1952, which extended to sub-tenants of Crown lands the benefit of the Rent Restriction Acts.

[56] *Cf. Gilbert* v. *Trinity House Corporation* (1886) 17 Q.B.D. 795.

[57] *International Ry.* v. *Niagara Parks Commission* [1941] A.C. 328 (P.C.).

[58] See *Central Control Board (Liquor Traffic)* v. *Cannon Brewery Co.* [1918] 2 Ch. 123; [1919] A.C. 757.

[59] *e.g.* Central Land Board (now dissolved); Town and Country Planning Act 1947; *Glasgow Corporation* v. *Central Land Board*, 1956 S.L.T. 41. Also the former National Assistance Board and Land Commission.

[60] *e.g. National Coal Board* v. *Galley* [1958] 1 W.L.R. 16.

[61] *Bullard* v. *Croyden Hospital Group Management Committee* [1953] 1 Q.B. 511.

[62] [1958] 1 Q.B. 50 (D.C.). And see *Pfizer* v. *Ministry of Health* [1965] A.C. 512.

Subsequent Acts which have re-organised the National Health Service has dealt explicitly with the status of the various authorities which they have created.[63] The immunity of hospital premises from public health and other legislation has been removed by the National Health Service (Amendment) Act 1986.

Later Acts constituting public corporations have been explicit on the point, at least in cases where there might be doubt, as in the case of corporations that own or occupy land or have taken over functions formerly exercised by a Minister. Thus the Atomic Energy Authority Act 1954 provided that land occupied by the Authority was deemed for rating purposes to be occupied by the Crown for public purposes; otherwise the Authority was not to enjoy Crown privileges. The Electricity Act 1957, s.38, stated: "It is hereby declared for the avoidance of doubt that neither the Electricity Council nor the Generating Board nor any of the Area Boards are to be treated as the servant or agent of the Crown or as enjoying any status, immunity or privilege of the Crown, and no property of the Council or any of those Boards is to be regarded as property of, or held on behalf of, the Crown." Similar provision was made by the New Towns Act 1965, s.35(3), with regard to the Commission for the New Towns.[64]

The Crown Agents Act 1979, section 1(5) provides that the Crown Agents, "despite their name" are not to be regarded as servants of the Crown nor as agents except to the extent that they so act by virtue of any provision in the Act authorising them to do so.

Post office

The purpose of the Post Office Act 1969 was that the Post Office should cease to be a government department and should become an independent corporation, and the Act is, of course, quite explicit on this point. The functions and powers formerly exercised by the Postmaster-General as a Minister of the Crown are transferred to the new corporation. The postal service as we saw above is a public service derived from a prerogative monopoly of the Crown.[65] Although it is now a public corporation it retains immunity from actions in tort which even other government departments lost under the Crown Proceedings Act 1947.[66] Section 29 of the Post Office Act provides that, subject to section 30, no proceedings in tort lie against the Post Office for any loss or damage arising out of the postal or telecommunication service. The Post Office is exempt, for example, from liability for loss of or damage to unregistered postal packets, and for defamation published by telegram, telephone or postmark.[67] The section further provides that (contrary to common law) no individual—whether officer, servant, agent or inde-

---

[63] National Health Service Reorganisation Act 1973, Sched. 1, Part III, para. 15; National Health Service Act 1977, Sched. 5, Part III, para. 15.

[64] New Towns Act 1981, s.35.

[65] In *Malins* v. *Post Office* [1975] I.C.R. 60. Thesiger J. held that, at least in the case of employees engaged prior to the 1969 Act, the Post Office had inherited the right of the Crown to dismiss at will or upon reasonable notice, whatever the terms of the servant's contract.

[66] *Post*, Chap. 35.

[67] *Boakes* v. *Postmaster-General, The Times*, October 27, 1962 (C.A.): postmark, "Remember that Road Accidents are Caused by People Like You.."

pendent contractor of the Post Office—is subject, except at the suit of
the Post Office, to any civil liability for any loss or damage from which
the Post Office is exempt. The question whether, despite this wide
measure of immunity, the Post Office might, in some circumstances, be
liable as a bailee was raised but not answered in *Stephen & Co.* v. *The
Post Office.*[68] Section 30 of the Post Office Act provides that the Post
Office is liable for the loss of, or damage to, a *registered inland*[69] *postal
packet* due to the wrongful act, neglect or default of an officer, servant or
agent of the Post Office while dealing with the packet; proceedings
must be brought within *twelve months* instead of the usual six years.
The amount recoverable is not to exceed (a) the market value of the postal packet, or (b) the compensation appropriate to the registration fee
paid.[70]

Public Bodies
   Public corporations which carry out public or statutory duties for the
benefit of the public and not for private profit are "public bodies"
within the meaning of the Public Bodies Corrupt Practices Act 1889 and
the Prevention of Corruption Act 1916.[71]

III. PARLIAMENTARY SUPERVISION OF PUBLIC CORPORATIONS[72]

An important constitutional problem that has not yet been completely
solved is how to secure adequate parliamentary supervision of public
corporations in the interests of the consumer and taxpayer, while pursuing the policy of decentralisation and freedom from detailed control.
As far as the industrial corporations are concerned, experience shows
that it is extremely difficult to draw the line between general policy and
day-to-day administration. The powers of the board and of the Minister
need to be more clearly defined, and the Minister's intervention should
more often take the form of a definite, published direction. Parliament
needs more information, and better opportunities to make constructive
use of its supervisory powers. A possible solution is to abolish the
theoretical distinction between general policy and day-to-day administration, and to make the board entirely responsible to the Minister.
Conventions would then be developed whereby it was left to the Minister to decide in what matters he should intervene, and he would have to
be prepared to defend his non-intervention.[73] We shall see below that

---

[68] [1977] 1 W.L.R. 1172 (C.A.). (Mandatory injunction to order Post Office to deliver up
   postal packets in its possession, detained as a result of industrial action, refused.)
[69] *i.e.* posted in the United Kingdom, the Isle of Man or the Channel Islands for delivery
   therein.
[70] See *Building and Civil Engineering Holidays Scheme Management* v. *Post Office* [1966] 1
   Q.B. 247.
[71] *R.* v. *Hirst and McNamee* (1975) 64 Cr.App.R. 151 (C.A.); *R.* v. *Manners* [1977] 2 W.L.R.
   178; *R.* v. *Braithwaite* [1983] 1 W.L.R. 385 (C.A.).
[72] See Sir Ivor Jennings, *Parliament* (2nd ed., 1957), Chap. 10; Herbert Morrison, *Government and Parliament* (1954), Chap. 12; W. A. Robson, *Nationalised Industry and Public
   Ownership*, Chaps. 7, 8, 10; *Report from the Select Committee on Nationalised Industries*
   (1952) H.C. No. 332, I, pp. 130–133; A. H. Hanson, *Parliament and Public Ownership*
   (Hansard Society, 1961).
[73] Hanson, *op. cit.* Chap. 8.

questions of ministerial control remain even where nationalised industries are privatised.

1. Debate

Members may criticise the working of nationalised industries in any debate on which the matter is relevant:

(a) *Debate on motions*, including motions specifically concerning one or more of the industries, "ballot motions" in private members' time, debates on the Address in reply to the Queen's Speech, the daily half-hour adjournment, and adjournment motions moved by a Minister. In the last two, ministerial responsibility is required, and matters involving legislation are not permitted. In a debate on the Queen's Speech any topic is relevant, and on a Consolidated Fund Bill or adjournment motion any topic is relevant except a proposal for legislation.

(b) *Opposition days* when the subject of debate is initiated by the Opposition.

(c) *Estimate days.* The external financing of a nationalised industry by way of government grant or by borrowing will be included in the public expenditure planning total, and most of it will be supply expenditure, which can be made subject to the new Estimates procedure.[74]

(d) *Debate on Bills* dealing with one or more of the industries.

(e) *Debate on motions to approve or annul orders* or other statutory instruments made by Ministers under the various nationalisation Acts.

(f) *Debate on annual report and accounts.* The annual reports and accounts of the various public corporations are required by statute to be laid before Parliament by the Minister concerned, together with the Minister's report on the exercise of his own functions. They are then the subject of debate, but these facilities also are strictly limited. The debate on each corporation comes only once a year, usually a considerable time after the events reported; and the range open for debate is then so wide that there is little opportunity of discussing details.

2. Questions to Ministers

The other chief opportunity for members to acquire information about the nationalised industries is by putting questions to Ministers in the House. As has been seen, the rules of the House and parliamentary practice place on the putting of questions to Ministers limits which in relation to public corporations are stringent. Questions addressed to the Minister must relate to the public affairs with which he is *officially connected*, to proceedings pending in Parliament, or to matters of administration for which he is responsible.

Matters for which a Minister is responsible include matters which the nationalised industries are required by statute to lay before Parliament; and appointments, finance, and matters on which he himself has statu-

[74] *Ante*, p. 220.

tory powers or duties. A question may be asked concerning the exercise by a Minister of his power to give a general direction in the national interest to the board of a public corporation. Questions are also admissible concerning specific responsibilities set out in statutes relating to certain nationalised industries, for example, research and training schemes. Ministers have power to require information from the boards, and therefore questions whose purpose is purely to seek information are prima facie admissible; but Ministers are not bound to answer, and they often refuse on the ground that the matter falls within the day-to-day administration of the boards. Further questions dealing with the class of matters concerning which an answer has been refused may be ruled out of order, unless the Speaker rules that they raise a matter of "urgent public importance." But it was announced by the Leader of the House in 1960 that Ministers would consider sympathetically the extent to which they could properly reply to "questions of general policy relating to Ministers' responsibilities." In any case, if a member really seeks information he can ask the board direct, and they will often supply it.

3. Select Committees

From 1956 to 1979 there was a Select Committee on Nationalised Industries which had power: "to examine the Reports and Accounts of the nationalised industries established by Statute whose controlling Boards are appointed by Ministers of the Crown and whose annual receipts are not wholly or mainly derived from moneys provided by Parliament or advanced from the Exchequer." This Committee was very active and issued a number of reports, several of which were critical of the role Ministers played in the running of nationalised industries.[75] The reform of the select committee system in 1979 resulted in the abolition of this committee.[76]

The departmental select committees established in 1979 are empowered to examine "the expenditure, administration and policy of the principle government departments . . . and associated public bodies,"[77] which includes the nationalised industries. The effect of this is that the scrutiny of a nationalised industry is performed by the relevant departmental committee, for example the Transport Committee can investigate British Rail and the Energy Committee the National Coal Board. Several Committees have made investigations and reports. These have been either directly concerned with a nationalised industry[78] which is within the powers of the Committee or have dealt in passing with a nationalised industry as an aspect of a more general report.[79] Provision was made[80] for the setting up, from time to time, of joint sub-committees to consider matters affecting two or more nation-

---

[75] See, e.g. Second Report from the Select Committee on Nationalised Industries, *The British Steel Corporation*, H.C. 26 (1977–78) and Fourth Report from the Select Committee, *British Waterways Board*, H.C. 239 (1977–78).

[76] *Ante,* p. 231.

[77] S.O. No. 130.

[78] For example First Report from the Energy Committee, *Gas and Electricity Prices*, H.C. 276 (1983–84).

[79] For example Sixth Report from the Treasury and Civil Service Committee, *Government Expenditure Plans 1985–86, 1987–88*, H.C. 213 (1984–85), paras. 41–47.

[80] S.O. No. 130(4).

alised industries. However this power has never been used,[81] and instead several committees have made reports which are of concern to more than just the nationalised industry over which it has jurisdiction. For example the Transport Committee considered the form of the nationalised industries' reports and accounts.[82]

Select Committees other than those related to government departments can, and do, investigate and report on matters concerning the nationalised industries. In particular the Committee of Public Accounts has undertaken several wide ranging and critical reviews in response to reports from the Comptroller and Auditor General.[83] However such reviews are limited in that the National Audit Act 1983,[84] which extended the powers of the Comptroller, expressly provided that the new powers did not extend to the nationalised industries.

IV. Privatisation

Since 1979 the Government has pursued a policy of divesting itself of control of nationalised industries by turning them into companies in which the shares are owned by members of the public or, in some cases selling to the public shares which the government owned in a company.

The first method of privatisation is exemplified by the case of British Telecommunications. The British Telecommunications Act 1981 established a public corporation whose duty was to provide throughout the British Islands such telephone services as satisfy all reasonable demands for them except to the extent that provision was, in the corporations' opinion, impracticable or not reasonably practicable (section 3). The Telecommunications Act 1984 abolished British Telecommunications' monopoly in the field of telecommunications and provided that on a date nominated by the Secretary of State all the assets of the corporation should vest in a company nominated by the minister (section 60). Subsequently shares in the company were offered for public sale. Similar arrangements were made in relation to British Airways by the Civil Aviation Act 1980, in relation to British Aerospace by the British Aerospace Act 1980 and in relation to British Gas by the Gas Act 1986. The Ordnance Factories and Military Services Act 1984 empowers the Secretary of State to make a scheme or schemes for transferring the assets of Royal Ordnance Factories to a company or companies so that the shares in that company or those companies can be sold. Privatisation of the British Airports Authority is provided for by the Airports Act 1986.

Where the government owns shares in a pre-existing company privatisation can be achieved by statutory authorisation for the sale of the shares as in the case of Cable and Wireless Ltd.[85]

In other instances privatisation can take the form of authorising the

---

[81] The Liaison Committee has suggested that this provision should be scrapped, H.C. 92 (1982–83), para. 42.

[82] H.C. 390 (1981–82). See too the Eighth Report from the Treasury and Civil Service Committee, *Financing of the Nationalised Industries*, H.C. 348 (1980–81).

[83] See H.C. 115 (1980–81); H.C. 139 (1983–84) in response to a report from the Comptroller and Auditor-General, H.C. 553 (1983–84); H.C. 58 (1984–85).

[84] Section 7(4) and Sched. 4, p. 226 *ante*.

[85] British Telecommunications Act 1981, s.79.

disposal of part or parts of a public corporation as was done for example in the cases of the British National Oil Corporation and the British Gas Corporation by the Oil and Gas (Enterprise) Act 1982. British Rail was empowered to dispose of its subsidiary undertakings by the Transport Act 1981, section 1 and the Secretary of State was empowered to direct them to exercise their power by section 3 of the Act.

Privatisation of a publicly owned corporation does not necessarily mean that the government ceases to retain some control over its activities. Thus the Telecommunications Act 1984 establishes a licensing system under the supervision of a Director General of Telecommunications. Conditions imposed by the Director General as part of the licence required by any company providing a public telecommunications system can regulate the prices which may be charged and ensure the provision of a system which extends to the less populous parts of the country.[86] The licensing system is also meant to ensure that British Telecommunications cannot operate a monopoly. If, however, some or all of the Water Authorities are privatised it will obviously be impossible to arrange competition in each authority's former area and the need for continuing government control in such a case is unarguable, quite apart from the unique importance of a water supply.

The importance of telecommunications in relation to national security is recognised by section 94 of the Act which authorises the Secretary of State to give to persons operating telecommunications systems "such directions of a general character" as appear to him to be requisite in the interests of national security or relations with a foreign government. He may also give a direction requiring such persons "to do, or not to do, a particular thing specified in the direction." Any direction given under the section will be laid before each House of Parliament unless the Secretary of State is of opinion that disclosure of the direction is against the interests of national security or relations with a foreign government or the commercial interests of any person. On those grounds the Secretary of State may also forbid any person to reveal that he has received a direction.

---

[86] Similarly, the Gas Act 1986 which creates the office of Director General of Gas Supply (s.1) and empowers the Secretary of State, after consultation with the Director General, to authorise persons to supply gas in defined areas (s.7).

CHAPTER 30

DELEGATED LEGISLATION[1]

In this chapter it is proposed to discuss delegated legislation in the sense in which that phrase is commonly used to refer to regulations and rules made under powers delegated by Parliament to Ministers, local authorities and other bodies.

I. NATURE AND PURPOSE OF DELEGATED LEGISLATION

The delegation of lawmaking power by Parliament to other persons or bodies is no new practice, although it has greatly increased in frequency and importance in the nineteenth and twentieth centuries.[2] In the period between the Wars the growth of delegated legislative powers was a matter of controversy among writers on the newly emerging subject of administrative law. There has been no diminution in resort to such powers since 1945 but widespread use of them has come to be accepted. Since 1974, the government of Northern Ireland has, exceptionally, been conducted through the form of delegated legislation under the Northern Ireland Act 1974.

The judicial control of delegated legislation, exercised mainly under the doctrine of *ultra vires*, is discussed later in Chapter 33.

The executive has no inherent power, as it has in France, to issue ordinances or decrees filling out the details of statutes. The authority of an Act of Parliament is necessary: *Case of Proclamations*.[3] When the government commands a majority in Parliament it can procure from Parliament any powers it thinks it needs.

We consider in this section the nature and purpose of delegated legislation, and in the next section the parliamentary safeguards that have been provided.

---

[1] *Report of the Committee on Ministers' Powers ("Donoughmore Committee")* (1932) Cmd. 4060, s.II; *Select Committee on Procedure, First Report* (1977–1978, H.C. 588–I) Chap. 3; Sir Carleton Allen, *Law and Orders* (3rd ed., 1965); H. W. R. Wade, *Administrative Law* (5th ed., 1982), Chap. 22; J. E. Kersell, *Parliamentary Supervision of Delegated Legislation* (1960); Sir Cecil Carr, *Concerning English Administrative Law* (1941), Chaps. 2, 3 and 5; "Parliamentary Control of Delegated Legislation" [1956] P.L. 200; Sieghart, *Government by Decree*, pp. 98–148; J. A. G. Griffith, "The Constitutional Significance of Delegated Legislation in England" (1950) 48 *Michigan Law Review* 1079; "The Place of Parliament in the Legislative Process" (1951) 14 M.L.R. 279, 425; B. Schwartz, *Law and the Executive in Britain*, Chaps. 2, 4, 6 and 9.

[2] *The First Report of the Select Committee on Procedure* showed that while the number of statutory instruments made each year had fallen in the interval between the end of the Second World War and the mid–1960s (in 1948, for example, the figure was 1508; in 1966, 790) it had subsequently risen to reach a plateau of between 1,100 and 1,300 per year. Even more remarkable was the increase in length of individual instruments. In 1955 the total length of all statutory instruments was 3240 pages; in 1965, 6435 pages and in 1974, 8,667 pages.

[3] (1610) 32 Co.Rep. 74; (1610) 2 St.Tr. 723. The exception is the prerogative of the Crown to legislate by Order in Council; *ante*, Chap. 17 and *post*, Chap. 37.

Forms of delegated legislation

Delegated legislation takes various forms and assumes a variety of names. The primary classification is according to the person or body which has the legislative power, of which for present purposes the chief are:

(i) *The Queen in Council*—power to issue Statutory Orders in Council, *e.g.* under the Emergency Powers Act 1920. This kind of delegated legislation has the most dignified and "national" character.

(ii) *Ministers and other heads of government departments*—power to issue departmental or ministerial regulations, rules, orders, etc. These are extremely numerous, and legislation made under them is now much greater in bulk year by year than Acts of Parliament.

(iii) *Local authorities*—power to make byelaws for their areas under the Local Government Act 1972, and many other Acts.

(iv) *Public bodies*—power conferred by their constituent Acts to make byelaws and other regulations for the purposes for which they were created.[4]

(v) *Rule committees*—power to make rules for procedure in court, *e.g.* Supreme Court Rule Committee (Supreme Court Act 1981, s.85[5]); Crown Court Rule Committee (Supreme Court Act 1981, s.86[6]); County Court Rule Committee (County Courts Act 1984, s.75[7]); and judges or committees with power to make rules of procedure relating to matrimonial causes, bankruptcy, legal aid, etc.

(vi) *Measures*: Under the Church of England (Assembly) Powers Act 1919 delegated legislation relating to the Church of England is framed by the General Synod of the Church and presented for Royal Assent after approval by both Houses of Parliament. A Measure may amend or repeal the whole or any part of any Act of Parliament, including the 1919 Act.[8]

---

[4] *E.g.* Drainage Authorities (Land Drainage Act 1976, s.34); Nature Conservancy Councils (Wildlife and Countryside Act 1981, s.37); British Railways Board (Transport Act 1962, s.67); British Airways Authority (Airport Authorities Act 1975, s.9); Pilotage Authorities (Pilotage Act 1983).

[5] The Committee consists of the Lord Chancellor and four or more of the following persons: Lord Chief Justice, Master of the Rolls, President of the Family Division, the Vice-Chancellor, three other judges of the Supreme Court, two practising barristers and two practising solicitors. These Rules must be laid before Parliament. See *Hume* v. *Somerton* (1890) 25 Q.B.D. 239.

[6] The Committee consists of the Lord Chief Justice, two other judges of the Supreme Court, two circuit judges, the registrar of criminal appeals, a justice of the peace, two practising barristers and two practising solicitors.

[7] The Committee consists of five County Court judges appointed by the Lord Chancellor, two barristers, two registrars and two solicitors.

[8] *E.g.* Synodical Government Measure 1969 which amended the 1919 Act. A Measure to amend the procedure for the appointment of Bishops was rejected by the House of Commons in July 1984.

(vii) *Special Procedure Orders* under the Statutory Orders (Special Procedure) Act 1945.[9] The Act of 1945 itself applied to Orders made under Water, Planning and certain other Acts. The "special parliamentary procedure" also applies where any subsequent Act so specifies. This has been done in a number of statutes.[10] The "special parliamentary procedure" provides for an opportunity to objectors to a proposed order to be heard at a local inquiry. If the Minister then lays the order before Parliament it goes to a Joint Committee of both Houses which consider any petitions. If a Special Procedure Order gives rise to no objections, or if, after a petition has been heard, the Joint Committee reports the Order without amendments or with amendments to which the Minister agrees, the Order becomes law after the prescribed period without the necessity of a Bill to confirm it. On the other hand, if the Joint Committee report that the Order be not approved or report the Order with amendments to which the Minister does not agree, he may introduce a Bill to confirm it: such Bill is treated as a public Bill, and is deemed to have passed through all its stages up to and including the committee stage.[11]

As has been seen, Schedule 1 to the House of Commons Disqualification Act 1975 may be revised by resolution of the House,[12] and certain taxes may be collected for a limited period by resolution of the Commons under the Provisional Collection of Taxes Act 1968.[13] Legislation by the Queen and Commons under the Parliament Acts 1911 and 1949 may arguably be regarded as a special kind of delegated legislation.[14]

In addition to delegated legislation, of various kinds, statutes increasingly provide for the making of "Codes of Practice" which have legal effect to the extent that their terms are usually laid before Parliament and must be taken into account by tribunals and courts where they are relevant to proceedings. Breach of their provisions is not in itself unlawful but may be evidence of failure to behave according to a requisite standard, whether that of the careful driver or the reasonable employer.[15] Differing views were initially expressed about the legal

---

[9] As amended by the Statutory Orders (Special Procedure) Act 1965.

[10] *E.g.* Public Health Act 1936, ss.6, 9 and 315; Local Government Act 1972, s.181(7), s.240; Acquisition of Land Act 1981, ss.17, 18, 19, 20.

[11] A controversial recent example is provided by the Okehampton Bypass (Confirmation of Orders) Act 1985. Opponents of the Bill objected that where a minister is determined to introduce a confirming Bill even if the Joint Committee should reject an Order, he ought, in fairness to the Petitioners, save them the expense of a hearing before such a Committee: Lord Molson, letter to *The Times*, December 2, 1985 and reply from Lord Ardwick, *The Times*, December 4, 1985.

[12] *Ante*, Chap. 9.

[13] *Ante*, Chap. 11.

[14] *Ante*, Chap. 7.

[15] Road Traffic Act 1972, s.37 (The Highway Code); Employment Protection Act 1975, s.6; Police and Criminal Evidence Act 1984, ss.66–67. The same Act provides that the Secretary of State may issue "guidance" relating to the conduct of disciplinary hearings. Failure to observe such guidance "shall be admissible in evidence on any appeal." (s.105). Under the Health and Safety at Work etc. Act 1974 the Health and Safety Commission may approve and issue Codes of Practice with the consent of the Secretary of State under ss.16 and 17. There is no requirement of laying before Parliament.

status of the immigration rules made under the Immigration Act 1971[16] but there can now be no doubt that they form a kind of "quasi-law," to be interpreted in a less technical way than statutes and delegated legislation.[17] The growing resort to informal legislation of various kinds is open to question on grounds of inadequate Parliamentary control and a large degree of immunity from judicial control.[18] Indirectly, however, informal legislation may be challenged in the courts. For example, a minister entrusted with a discretion by statute cannot fetter that discretion[19] but must in each case consider the relevant merits before reaching a decision. Hence if a minister issues a circular declaring how he is going to deal with individual cases in advance, a particular decision may be attacked on the ground that the minister had prejudged the issue.[20] Moreover, in *Gillick* v. *West Norfolk Area Health Authority*[21] the House of Lords recognised that its own earlier decision in *Royal College of Nursing* v. *Department of Health and Social Security*[22] involved the existence of a jurisdiction in the courts to declare that advice contained in a public document, even if non-statutory in form, was erroneous in law. Such a jurisdiction, according to Lord Bridge, was no doubt "salutary and indeed a necessary one in certain circumstances" but it should be exercised sparingly. The number of cases, his Lordship thought, where a non-statutory publication by a department raised "a clearly defined issue of law, unclouded by political, social or moral overtones, [would] be rare."

Sub-delegation

The power of delegated legislation vested in one authority is itself sometimes delegated to another authority, and this sub-delegation may go through several stages in a hierarchy of lawmaking authorities. Thus section 1(3) of the Emergency Powers (Defence) Act 1939, which gave power to issue Defence Regulations by Order in Council, stated that Defence Regulations might empower any authorities or persons to make orders, rules and by-laws for any of the purposes for which Defence Regulations might themselves be made. Ministerial orders

---

[16] In R. v. *Chief Immigration Officer, Heathrow Airport ex p. Salamat Bibi* [1976] 1 W.L.R. 979, Roskill L.J. thought the rules had the force of delegated legislation. In R. v. *Secretary of State for the Home Department ex p. Hosenball* [1977] 1 W.L.R. 766, Lord Denning M.R. described the rules as "rules of practice laid down for the guidance of immigration officers and tribunals." Geoffrey Lane L.J. said, "These rules are very difficult to categorise or classify. They are in a class of their own."

[17] R. v. *Immigration Appeal Tribunal ex p. Alexander* [1982] 1 W.L.R. 1076, 1080 *per* Lord Roskill; R. v. *Immigration Appeal Tribunal ex p. Bakhtaur Singh* [1986] 1 W.L.R. 910, 917, *per* Lord Bridge who cited with approval the dictum of Geoffrey Lane L.J. in *ex p. Hosenball, supra,* n. 16. See similarly R. v. *Secretary of State for the Home Department ex p. Swati* [1986] 1 All E.R. 717, 719, *per* Sir John Donaldson, M.R.; "documents called House of Commons Statements." See also R. v. *Immigration Appeal Tribunal ex p. Begum The Times,* July 24, 1986; *post,* p. 670.

[18] R. Baldwin and J. Houghton, "Circular Arguments: The Status and Legitimacy of Administrative Rules" [1986] P.L. 239.

[19] *Post,* p. 668.

[20] R. v. *Secretary of State for the Home Department, ex p. Bennett, The Times,* August 18, 1986 (C.A.).

[21] [1981] A.C. 800.

[22] [1986] A.C. 112.

were issued under the Regulations, directions under these orders, and licences under these directions.

Sub-delegation is only lawful if expressly or impliedly authorised by the enabling Act, for the prima facie principle is *delegatus non potest delegare*,[23] which is discussed more fully later. The requirement of authorisation applies throughout the hierarchy of rules, as does the doctrine of *ultra vires* below the enabling Act itself. Sub-delegation should not usually be required except in emergencies.

"Statutory Instruments"

The Statutory Instruments Act 1946, which is mainly concerned with the publication[24] of the more important kinds of delegated legislation, provides in section 1 that where by that Act or any subsequent Act power to make, confirm or approve orders, rules, regulations or other subordinate legislation is conferred on the Crown in Council or any Minister or government department, then *if the power is expressed to be exercisable by Order in Council or by Statutory Instrument*, as the case may be, any document by which that power is exercised shall be known as a "Statutory Instrument." The expression is also important in connection with laying before Parliament[25] and the work of the Scrutiny Committees.[26] The term "Statutory Instrument" also extends to any legislative instrument made after January 1, 1948, in exercise of a power conferred before that date to make "Statutory Rules" within the meaning of the (repealed) Rules Publication Act 1893.[27]

The reasons for delegated legislation

In spite of much criticism it has been generally accepted since the report of the Committee on Ministers' Powers in 1932 that delegated legislation has come to stay in our legal system, and that there are the following legitimate reasons for its use:

(i) *Pressure on parliamentary time*

Parliament in its legislative work—especially in the House of Commons—barely has time to discuss essential principles. Much time can be saved, and amendments to Acts of Parliament obviated, by delegating the consideration of procedure and subordinate matters to Ministers and their departments.

(ii) *Technicality of subject-matter*

The subject-matter of modern legislation is often highly technical. Technical matters, as distinct from broad policy, are not susceptible to discussion in Parliament and therefore cannot readily be included in a Bill. Delegation to Ministers enables them to consult expert advisers and interested parties while the regulations are still in the draft stage.

---

[23] *Post*, p. 675.
[24] *Post*, p. 633.
[25] *Post*, p. 628.
[26] *Post*, p. 631.
[27] See Statutory Instruments Regulations 1947 (S.I. 1949 No. 1) which, broadly provide, *inter alia*, that every instrument of a *legislative* character made by a rule-making authority (which includes Her Majesty in Council and any Government Department) shall be a Statutory Instrument if made after January 1, 1948.

Under the Building Act 1984, for example, the Secretary of State is given wide powers to make regulations relating to the design and construction of buildings in order to secure the health safety and welfare of persons, to conserve energy and to prevent waste and contamination of water (s.1.). In making such regulations he is to take the advice of the Buildings Regulations Advisory Committee and to consult other bodies representative of the interests concerned (s.14).

(iii) *Flexibility*

In large and complex measures it is not possible to foresee all the contingencies and local conditions for which provision will have to be made, and it would be difficult to settle all the administrative machinery in time for insertion in the Bill. Delegated legislation provides a degree of flexibility, as changes can be made from time to time in the light of experience without the necessity for a series of amending Acts, *e.g.* under Road Traffic and Social Security legislation. Further, it allows for experimentation, as in Town and Country Planning Acts.

(iv) *Emergency powers*

In emergencies, such as war, serious strikes and economic crises, there would often not be time to pass Acts of Parliament, even if (as may not be the case) Parliament is sitting. Within limits unlawful acts can be done bona fide on the authority of the government in the expectation of later being legalised by an Act of Indemnity, but this is clearly not a desirable proceeding. Hence the emergency powers delegated by the Defence of the Realm Acts 1914–15 and the Emergency Powers (Defence) Act 1939–40 in two world wars, and the permanent peacetime provisions of the Emergency Powers Act 1920.

Exceptional types of delegated legislation

(i) *Power to impose taxation*[28]

Section 2 of the Emergency Powers (Defence) Act 1939 provided that the Treasury might by order impose, in connection with any scheme of control authorised by Defence Regulations (themselves delegated legislation), such charges as might be specified in the order. A "new economic regulator" introduced by the Finance Act 1961 empowered the Chancellor of the Exchequer at any time of the year to vary by order the main customs and excise revenue duties and purchase tax. The maximum change was to be 10 per cent. in either direction, and the power was given on a yearly basis only. The Chancellor of the Exchequer forthwith increased these duties by 10 per cent.

(ii) *Power to modify or adapt the enabling Act or other Acts of Parliament*

Parliament sometimes delegates to a Minister the power of modifying the enabling Act so far as may appear to him to be necessary for the purpose of bringing the Act into operation. Such provisions are usually transitional.[29]

---

[28] See *Att.-Gen.* v. *Wilts United Dairies* (1922) 91 L.J.K.B. 897; (1921) 37 T.L.R. 884.

[29] By a far-fetched analogy to the Statute of Proclamations 1539 (repealed in 1547), which gave the king a limited power to legislate by proclamation, this kind of provision became known as "the Henry VIII clause."

Power to modify or adapt other Acts of Parliament is given, for example, by the Local Government Act 1972, section 254(2) which allows the Secretary of State or appropriate Minister to amend, repeal or revoke any provision of any Act passed before 1st April 1974[30] and more recently by the Housing (Homeless Persons) Act 1977 section 2(3). The alternative would often involve the drafting and passing of large numbers of amending Acts. The power may be innocuous so long as Parliament is aware of what it is doing, and imposes a short time limit. None the less, such a power, allied to wide ranging powers of making delegated legislation subject to few, if any, limits, may be a cause for concern.[31]

(iii) Powers excluded from the jurisdiction of the courts

The right of the citizen to ask the court to declare delegated legislation *ultra vires* may be expressly excluded by Parliament,[32] although it is not clear precisely what words in an Act will be held to have this effect.[33] The Committee on Ministers' Powers regarded such a clause as generally objectionable, and only justifiable in very exceptional cases, *viz.* in emergency legislation and in cases where finality is desirable, *e.g.* Regulations under the Foreign Marriage Act 1892, on which the validity of marriages may depend. In these non-emergency cases, where property or status may be affected, the Committee suggested that the regulations should be open to challenge for a short initial period.

II. Parliamentary Safeguards for Delegated Legislation[34]

Apart from the common law jurisdiction of the courts to prevent a power of delegated legislation from being exceeded by declaring its exercise void as *ultra vires* in cases that may be brought before them,[35] Parliament provides a number of safeguards—of varying degrees of efficacy—to secure the proper use of the power. No attempt has been made in this country to establish a uniform code of procedure for the making and testing of delegated legislation, such as has been provided in somewhat different circumstances[36] by the American Administrative Procedure Act 1946. A Joint Select Committee of both Houses on Delegated Legislation reported in 1972.[37]

---

[30] This wide power may extend to Acts passed after April 1, 1974 by a provision that for this purpose a later Act is to be treated as if passed before that date; *e.g.* Salmon and Freshwater Fisheries Act 1975, s.42(6).

[31] See V. Korah "Counter Inflation Legislation. Whither Parliamentary Sovereignty?" (1976) 92 L.Q.R. 42.

[32] *Cf. Chester* v. *Bateson* [1920] 1 K.B. 829.

[33] See *post*, Chap. 33.

[34] Report of Committee on Ministers' Powers (1932) Cmd. 4060, pp. 41–48, 64–70; J. E. Kersell, *Parliamentary Supervision of Delegated Legislation*; Erskine May, *Parliamentary Practice* Chap. 23 Report from the Select Committee on Procedure (1977–1978) H.C. 588.

[35] *Post*, Chap. 31.

[36] See B. Schwartz and H. W. R. Wade Q.C., *Legal Control of Government* (1972) App. I; J. F. Garner, *Administrative Law* (6th ed., 1985), App.; K. C. Davis, *Administrative Law* (1951), Chaps. 5 and 6; L. Jaffe, *Administrative Cases and Materials* (1953), pp. 110–111, 280–282; "The American Administrative Procedure Act" [1956] P.L. 218.

[37] See *Report from Joint Committee on Delegated Legislation* (1971–1972) H.L. 184 and H.C. 475.

1. Laying before Parliament

There is no general Act which requires delegated legislation to be laid before Parliament. Even the Statutory Instruments Act 1946 does not require all Statutory Instruments to be so laid. The enabling Act has to be examined in each case. Enabling Acts now usually, but not invariably, require Statutory Instruments to be laid. Laying is usually before both Houses, except as regards financial matters when it is before the Commons only.[38] Conversely, statutes may require the laying before Parliament of delegated legislation which does not fall within the Statutory Instruments Act; for example, Immigration Rules made under section 3 of the Immigration Act 1971 or Recommendations for the Welfare of Livestock under section 3 of the Agriculture (Miscellaneous Provisions) Act 1968.[39]

There is no uniformity in the requirements, which may take any of the following forms:

(a) *"Negative parliamentary procedure"*

(i) To be laid before Parliament with immediate effect, but *subject to annulment* (by Order in Council) following a resolution of either House *("negative resolution")*, usually without prejudice to the validity of anything done thereunder before annulment. This is the commonest form. Before 1948 there was no uniform period for the passing of negative resolutions, but section 5 of the Statutory Instruments Act 1946 prescribes a period of 40 days after laying excluding any time during which Parliament is dissolved or prorogued or both Houses are adjourned (s.7). Where an instrument is subject to negative resolution, a member of the Commons may move a "prayer" for its annulment at the end of the ordinary public business and a division can be taken.

In practice instruments have seldom been annulled,[40] because the Minister could count on the government's majority. Even if the government were "caught napping," the Minister could introduce another instrument in identical terms. The procedure by negative resolution was seldom used before 1943. There has not been enough time in recent years for members to debate prayers for annulment. No amendment of the instrument is possible, although as a result of criticism the Minister may withdraw it and submit another in a modified form. A better procedure might be to allow motions that a Statutory Instrument be referred to the government for consideration. The Select Committee on

---

[38] See Local Government, Planning and Land Act 1980, s.60. "Parliament" in s.4 of the Rates Act 1984 was held to mean the House of Commons alone for the purpose of laying in *R. v. Secretary of State for the Environment ex p. Greenwich L.B.C., The Times,* December 19, 1985 (C.A.).

[39] See also directions under s.7 of the Industry Act 1975. In *Booth & Co. Ltd. v. National Enterprise Board* [1978] 3 All E.R. 624, Forbes J. was faced with "a novel form of statutory provision." The Secretary of State directed the NEB to comply with the parts of a document printed in heavy type set out as a schedule to the direction. "What of the light type? . . . Because the heavy type is often embedded in a surrounding area of light type I think one is entitled to look at the light type for assistance at any rate . . . if assistance is required in any case where the meaning of the heavy type is possibly equivocal or not immediately apparent" (at p. 629).

[40] *Cf. ante,* p. 192.

Procedure (1970–71)[41] recommended that "negative" instruments adversely reported on by the Scrutiny Committee (*post*) should automatically become subject to affirmative procedure.

(ii) To be laid *in draft* before Parliament, but subject to a resolution that no further proceedings be taken. An adverse resolution may be passed by either House within forty days (Statutory Instruments Act 1946, s.6), which stops further progress on that draft but does not prevent fresh drafts being laid. Prison Rules are made in this way.

(b) "Affirmative parliamentary procedure"

(i) To be laid before Parliament, either in draft or when made, but not to take effect until approved by *affirmative resolution* in each House. This is the second most common method. A Minister must present the instrument for approval, and for this the government has to find time in each House. No amendment is usually possible.

The Minister who introduces the enabling Act decides what method of laying (if any) shall be prescribed. There are no rules, but the practice is for the positive (affirmative) procedure to apply to the more important kinds of delegated legislation, *e.g.*: where the exercise of the power of delegated legislation would substantially affect Acts of Parliament, except merely consequential adaptations; the imposition of financial charges; skeleton powers, *i.e.* powers to make schemes where only the purpose is fixed by the enabling Act and the substance is left to delegated legislation; and other powers of an exceptional or politically important nature.

(ii) Sometimes an instrument is to be laid before Parliament with immediate effect, but will cease to have effect unless approved by resolution within the prescribed period. This method combines prompt operation with parliamentary control, *e.g.* regulations made under the Emergency Powers Act 1920; and also a method of imposing taxation, *e.g.* import duties, where prior notice is undesirable.

(c) *To be laid without further provision for control*

This method is now very uncommon. It is used where Parliament contemplates that a Minister should take some action, and merely demands to be kept informed of the action taken, *e.g.* the postponing order under the New Valuation Lists (Postponement) Act 1952. No resolution is necessary for the instrument to take effect. Where an instrument is merely laid before the House, it is usually impracticable to find time during the ordinary business of the Commons to move an address for its annulment, and if it is raised on the motion for adjournment no division is allowed. Questions may be asked about regulations lying on the table of the House.

The procedure of the two Houses and the time available—especially in the Commons—are not adequate to take full advantage of the opportunity for control offered by the laying of regulations before Parliament. The procedure in the House of Lords is similar, but rather more serviceable. A peer can call attention to a regulation lying on the table by moving for papers, or can move a resolution to annul any regulation which

---

[41] *The Process of Legislation* (1970–1971) H.C. 538.

is subject to annulment, and in either case a division can be taken. Neither House can propose an amendment to a regulation laid before it.

Local instruments, dealing with such matters as local authorities' powers, are far more numerous than general instruments. They are registered, but Parliament is usually not concerned with control or even information, and they are seldom required to be laid before Parliament.

Legal effect of the requirement of laying

The legal effect of the requirement that instruments are to be laid before Parliament is uncertain. Is it "mandatory" (imperative), so that the instrument is invalid if the requirement is not fulfilled; or merely "directory," imposing on a public officer a duty of imperfect obligation, but not affecting validity?[42] It seems that so far as concerns instruments subject to negative resolution, and probably also those subject to affirmative resolution, the requirement is directory.[43] There is no penalty specified if the requirement is not observed. In 1944 it was discovered that the Home Secretary had for three years overlooked the requirement that National Fire Service Regulations should be laid before Parliament "as soon as may be" after they were made.[44] An indemnity Act[45] was therefore passed indemnifying the Home Secretary against "all consequences whatsoever, if any" incurred by this failure. The Turks and Caicos Islands Order 1962[46] was inadvertently not laid before Parliament, and was replaced retrospectively by another Order issued in 1965.[47]

Section 4(1) of the Statutory Instruments Act 1946 provides that where any Statutory Instrument is required to be laid before Parliament after being made, a copy of the instrument shall be laid before each House before the instrument comes into operation, except in cases of urgency notified to the Lord Chancellor and the Speaker of the Commons.[48]

What constitutes "laying before the House" is for each House to decide. The Laying of Documents before Parliament (Interpretation) Act 1948 defined statutory references to "laying" as taking such action as is directed by virtue of any Standing Order or Sessional Order or other direction or practice of either House to constitute laying, even though it involves action taken when the House is not sitting.[49]

---

[42] *Post*, p. 664.

[43] It was so held by the West Indian Court of Appeal in *Springer* v. *Doorly* (1950) L.R.B.G. 10; (1950) 66 L.Q.R. 299. The regulations in that case were to be laid "as soon as possible." And see *Bailey* v. *Williamson* (1873) L.R. 8 Q.B. 118, *Starey* v. *Graham* [1899] 1 Q.B. 406, 412; A. I. L. Campbell, "Laying and Delegated Legislation," [1983] P.L. 43.

[44] Fire Services (Emergency Provisions) Act 1941.

[45] National Fire Service Regulations (Indemnity) Act 1944. See also Price Control and other Orders (Indemnity) Act 1951 and the Town and Country Planning Regulations (London) Indemnity Act 1971. *Cf.* Documentary Evidence Act 1868. Sir Carleton Allen, *op. cit.* p. 146, remarked that the Home Secretary in 1944 "lost a unique opportunity of studying the prison system from the inside."

[46] No. 1649.

[47] No. 1861.

[48] Sections 4 and 5 do not apply to orders which are subject to special parliamentary procedure or to any other instrument which is required to be laid before Parliament before it comes into operation (s.7(3)). And see s.4(2), *post*, p. 573.

[49] Rules presented to Parliament in a command paper are "laid before Parliament": *R.* v. *Immigration Appeal Tribunal, ex p. Joyles* [1972] 1 W.L.R. 1390 (D.C.).

2. Scrutinising committees

Select Committee on Statutory Instruments

Following a debate in the Commons after the incident of the National Fire Service Regulations in 1944, a Select Committee on Statutory Rules and Orders was set up by the Commons, with terms of reference based on the recommendations of the Committee on Ministers' Powers. As a consequence of the Statutory Instruments Act 1946, the Committee was renamed the Select Committee on Statutory Instruments (commonly known as "the Scrutiny Committee"), and its terms of reference were extended from time to time. The Committee did not consider it necessary to draw the attention of the House to more than a very small proportion of the instruments which it considered; but the very existence of the Committee has had an indirect effect in bringing about some improvement in the form and nomenclature of ministerial regulations, and in encouraging the practice of providing explanatory notes. Reports of the Scrutiny Committee were sometimes debated.

House of Lords Special Orders Committee

The House of Lords had, from 1925 to 1973 a Committee to consider any instruments laid before the House requiring an affirmative resolution ("Special Orders"), with certain exceptions such as regulations issued under the Emergency Powers Act 1920 and measures passed in accordance with the Church of England Assembly (Powers) Act 1919.[50] In the case of Special Orders of a public character, the Committee considered, and reported whether they had any doubt that the order was *intra vires*, or whether there was any other matter in the order or in the parent Act to which they thought it expedient to call the attention of the House. No motion for an affirmative resolution might be moved before the report of the Committee had been laid before the House.

Joint Select Committee on Statutory Instruments

Since 1973, a Joint Committee of both Houses has scrutinised statutory instruments (including draft statutory instruments and those implementing European Communities Directives) which are required to be laid before both Houses of Parliament[51]—and, in the case of general statutory instruments, whether or not they are required to be laid.

Its terms of reference are to consider whether the special attention of the House should be drawn to any instrument on any of the following grounds, that:

   (i) it imposes a charge on the public revenues, or requires the payment of a fee to a public authority for services or a licence;

   (ii) it is made in pursuance of an Act specifically excluding it from challenge in the courts;

   (iii) it purports to have retrospective effect, where the parent Act confers no such authority;

---

[50] As modified by the Synodical Government Measure 1969.

[51] A House of Commons Select Committee considers statutory instruments which are required to be laid only before that House.

  (iv) there appears to have been unjustifiable delay in its publication, or in laying it before Parliament;

  (v) there appears to have been unjustifiable delay in notifying the Speaker where, on the ground of urgency, the instrument came into operation before being laid before Parliament;

  (vi) there appears to be a doubt whether it is *intra vires* or it appears to make some unusual or unexpected use of the powers conferred by the statute under which it is made[52];

  (vii) for any special reason its form or purport calls for elucidation;

  (viii) the drafting appears to be defective;

or on any other ground which does not impinge on its merits or on the policy behind it.

The Scrutiny Committee has the assistance of Counsel to the Speaker and of Counsel to the Lord Chairman of Committees. It may require the government department concerned to explain, either by memorandum or witness, any instrument under consideration; and the Committee is instructed, before drawing the special attention of the House to any instrument, to afford the department concerned an opportunity of furnishing an explanation. The Committee is concerned with matters of *form*, as set out in its terms of reference. It is not concerned with policy, which is a matter for Parliament. The practice has developed of electing a member of the Opposition as chairman of the Scrutiny Committee, who would not be embarrassed by conflicting loyalties if the Committee criticises departmental action.

Since 1973 it has been possible for statutory instruments to be referred to Standing Committees to consider their *merits*. References may, however, only be made by Ministers and the Committee cannot make any kind of reference to the House.

The Select Committee on Procedure considered the adequacy of Parliamentary controls over delegated legislation in its *First Report*[53] and made a number of proposals, none of which has yet been given effect to. The Committee recommended the adoption by the House of Commons of a new standing order, similar to the existing order of the House of Lords, which would provide that a statutory instrument should not be brought before the House or a standing committee until the Joint Committee on Statutory Instruments (or the Select Committee) had completed consideration of the instrument. The Committee also recommended that, where necessary, the 40 day period under the Statutory Instruments Act be extended to give 10 days from the date of the report of the Joint Committee (or Select Committee) in the case of instruments drawn to the particular attention of the House by either Committee. Various detailed suggestions were made to strengthen the control of the House over the merits of delegated legislation; for example, to increase the time available for examination by a standing committee and to allow it to recommend, or not, by a substantive motion.

---

[52] *e.g.* Dutch Elm Disease (Local Authorities) Order 1971, No. 1708, made by the Forestry Commission under the Plant Health Act 1967, authorising local authorities to cut down diseased elms if the owner failed to do so, and to recover the cost from the owner.

[53] (1977–1978, H.C. 588–I) Chap. 3.

The Select Committee did not conclude that the present system under which the House must approve or reject delegation legislation should be replaced by one in which the House might amend statutory instruments laid before it. The Committee, however, drew attention to the practice under which Orders are put before the Northern Ireland Committee in a preliminary form as "Proposals" and recommended its wider adoption.

3. Other controls in Parliament
  (a) Motions of censure on the Minister responsible for the instrument.
  (b) Debate and possibly motion.
  (c) Questions to Ministers. In either House questions may be asked about instruments lying on the table, but no debate is allowed on a question.

4. Publication
The Rules Publication Act 1893, s.1 requires antecedent publicity for limited classes of statutory rules. Subsequent publication was provided for by section 3, which required all statutory rules made after 1893 to be sent forthwith after they were made to the Queen's printer.

The Statutory Instruments Act 1946 repealed the Rules Publication Act 1893 and generalised the procedure for subsequent publication; but it made no provision for antecedent publicity, the reason given being that the practice of informal consultation with outside interests had become general. Immediately after the making of any "Statutory Instrument" as defined in section 1,[54] it is to be sent to the Queen's printer and numbered, and copies shall "as soon as possible" be printed and sold (s.2). The Stationery Office is to publish lists showing the date on which every Statutory Instrument printed and sold by the Queen's printer was first *issued* by that office; and in any legal proceedings a copy of any list so published purporting to bear the imprint of the Queen's printer shall be received in evidence as a true copy, and an entry therein shall be conclusive evidence of the date on which any Statutory Instrument was first issued by the Stationery Office (s.3(1)).

Delegated legislation generally comes into operation when it is made, unless some other date is specified therein. Failure to comply with any requirement for publication will not normally affect the validity of the instrument concerned.[55] The Statutory Instruments Act 1946, s.3(2), however, provides that where any person is charged with an offence under a Statutory Instrument, it shall be a defence to prove that the instrument had not been "issued" by the Stationery Office at the date of the alleged contravention, unless it is proved that at that date reason-

---

[54] *Ante*, p. 625.
[55] *Jones* v. *Robson* [1901] 1 Q.B. 680; but *cf. Johnson* v. *Sargant* [1918] 1 K.B. 101; Lanham, (1974) 37 M.L.R. 510 [1983] P.L. 395. Publication may be a prerequisite of validity in a case such as that of the immigration rules, which are defined by the Immigration Appeals Act 1969, s.24(2) as "rules . . . which have been published and laid before Parliament." An Act of Parliament comes into operation on the date on which it receives the Royal Assent (printed beneath the title), unless some other date is specified: Acts of Parliament (Commencement) Act 1793; *R.* v. *Smith* [1910] 1 K.B. 17.

able steps had been taken for the purpose of bringing the purport of the instrument to the notice of the public, or of persons likely to be affected by it, or of the person charged.

Where any Statutory Instrument is required to be laid before Parliament after being made, copies sold by the Queen's printer must show the date on which it came or will come into operation; and either the date on which copies were laid before Parliament or a statement that such copies are to be laid before Parliament (s.4(2)).

The Treasury, with the concurrence of the Lord Chancellor and the Speaker of the Commons, is empowered to make regulations for the purposes of the Act, including the numbering, printing and publication of Statutory Instruments, and the exemption of any classes of Statutory Instrument from the requirement of being printed and sold (s.8). The Statutory Instruments Regulation 1947 made thereunder are contained in S.I. 1948 No. 1, which begins the printed series of *Statutory Instruments* that replaces the previous *Statutory Rules and Orders*.

The Regulations exempt from the printing requirement Statutory Instruments which are local, or are otherwise regularly printed as a series (Reg. 5); or temporary (Reg. 6); contain bulky Schedules (Reg. 7); or where it would be contrary to the public interest that they should be printed before coming into operation (Reg. 8). Such exemption requires the certificate of the "responsible authority," *i.e.* the authority that makes the instrument. In *Simmonds* v. *Newell*[56] a conviction for the offence of selling in contravention of an Iron and Steel Prices Order was quashed by the Divisional Court, because the Schedules had not been printed and no certificate had been issued under Regulation 7 exempting from printing, and presumably reasonable steps had not been taken under section 3(2). Parker J. said it was not necessary to decide whether a Statutory Instrument is wholly invalid if it is required by section 2 to be printed and it is not printed, or whether section 3(2) provides a defence whether the Statutory Instrument is required to be printed or not. In *R.* v. *Sheer Metalcraft*,[57] a prosecution for buying in contravention of an Iron and Steel Price Order, the Schedules had not been printed and no certificate of exemption had been issued; but the jury found the accused guilty, because sufficient steps had been taken to bring the Schedules to their notice. Streatfeild J. told the jury that a Statutory Instrument is "made" (*i.e.* effective) when it is made by the Minister and (presumably, where laying is required) laid before Parliament: whether a Statutory Instrument has been "issued" (*i.e.* printed) is a different question, which can be raised as a defence under section 3(2). The neglect to print or to certify exemption from printing did not make the order invalid, and it was admissible in evidence.

5. Prior consultation[58]

Acts of Parliament delegating legislative power sometimes provide that the Minister may, or shall, consult interested bodies or an advisory

---

[56] [1953] 1 W.L.R. 846; *sub nom. Defiant Cycle Co.* v. *Newell* [1953] 2 All E.R. 38.
[57] [1954] 1 Q.B. 586.
[58] See J. F. Garner, "Consultation in Subordinate Legislation" [1964] P.L. 105; A. D. Jergesen, "The Legal Requirements of Consultation," [1978] P.L. 290.

committee before issuing regulations.[59] The interested bodies may be specified in the Act or left to the Minister's discretion. The Minister is not usually bound to accept such advice. Thus the Minister must consult the Council on Tribunals before making procedural rules for tribunals that come under its supervision; and the Lord Chancellor must consult the Council before making procedural rules for statutory inquiries.[60] In some cases a draft scheme is to be prepared by the interested body (*e.g.* a local authority), and confirmed or approved by the Minister. Exceptionally, the Minister is required to submit draft regulations to an advisory committee, without being bound to accept their suggested amendments. Apart from such statutory provisions, the practice of consultation has become generally established.

---

[59] *e.g.* Building Act 1984, s.14, *ante*, p. 626. The Health and Safety Commission is required similarly to consult before drafting Codes of Practice under the Health and Safety at Work etc. Act 1984: see s.16.

[60] Tribunals and Inquiries Act 1971, ss.10 and 11.

CHAPTER 31

ADMINISTRATIVE JURISDICTION[1]

Introduction

"Administrative jurisdiction" or "administrative justice" is a name given to various ways of deciding disputes outside the ordinary courts. It is not possible to define precisely what bodies constitute the "ordinary courts," although that expression was used in the Tribunals and Inquiries Acts 1958 and 1971. There are some bodies that might be placed under the heading either of ordinary courts or of special tribunals. Guidance cannot be found in the name of a body; the Employment Appeal Tribunal, for example, is a superior court of record[2] while it has been doubted whether a local valuation court is really a court.[3] Certain matters involving calculations of figures or scientific problems, such as the assessment of rates and taxes, local audit, patents, inventions and performing rights, have been considered by Parliament unsuitable for the ordinary courts. Then there has been a great increase of governmental activity, both central and local, under statutory powers in the late nineteenth and twentieth centuries, and a number of social services are provided in the Welfare State. Under both these heads there are complex systems of regulation and control, such as national insurance, pensions, the health service, education, public transport, the regulation of agriculture, rent control, housing and redevelopment, town and country planning and the consequent compulsory acquisition of land. It is inevitable that disputes should arise, or conflicts of rights and interests between the individual citizen and the central or local government authority. The ordinary courts are appropriate for the decision of purely legal rights; but in many[4] of the kinds of cases of which we are speaking, the question in issue is not one of purely legal rights but a conflict between private and public interests, bound up in a greater or lesser degree with ministerial policy as outlined by statute.

Where Parliament does not consider the ordinary courts suitable for the decision of such disputes, especially at first instance, it prescribes one of three other methods of deciding them:

    (i) administrative tribunals;

---

[1] *Report of Committee on Administrative Tribunals and Enquiries* ("Franks Committee") (1957) Cmnd. 218; *Memoranda submitted by Government Departments* (6 vols., H.M.S.O. 1956); *Minutes of Evidence* (H.M.S.O. 1956–1957); *Report of the Committee on Ministers' Powers* (1932) Cmd. 4060, s.III.

J. F. Garner, *Administrative Law* (6th ed., 1986); Sir Carleton Allen, *Administrative Jurisdiction* (reprinted from [1956] P.L. 13–109); Griffith and Street, *Principles of Administrative Law* (5th ed., 1973); W. A. Robson, *Justice and Administrative Law* (3rd ed., 1951); H. W. R. Wade. *Administrative Law* (5th ed., 1982); *Towards Administrative Justice* (Michigan, 1963); Harry Street, *Justice in the Welfare State* (2nd ed., 1975); G. Ganz, *Administrative Procedures* (1974).

[2] Employment Protection (Consolidation) Act 1978, s.135.

[3] *Att.-Gen.* v. *B.B.C.* [1981] A.C. 303; *ante*, Chap. 20, Part II.

[4] But not all: Industrial Tribunals deal with disputes between private employers and employees. Similarly Agricultural Land Tribunals.

(ii) ministerial decision after statutory inquiry[5];
(iii) ministerial decision, in which the Minister uses his discretion without any prescribed procedure.[6]

The Franks Committee (1957)[7] regarded both tribunals and other administrative procedures as essential to our society. Preference should be given, however, to entrusting adjudication to the ordinary courts rather than to tribunals, unless there are clearly special reasons which make a tribunal more appropriate. Similarly, a tribunal is to be preferred to a Minister, but it is not always possible to express policy in the form of regulations capable of being administered by an independent tribunal. The Franks Committee examined the working of administrative law in other countries, notably the United States and France; but concluded that, although there are advantages in comparative study, each country must work out for itself, within the framework of its own institutions and way of life, the proper balance between public and private interest.

I. TRIBUNALS[8]

These are independent statutory tribunals whose function is judicial. The tribunals are so varied in composition, method of appointment, functions and procedure, and in their relation to Ministers on the one hand and the ordinary courts on the other, that a satisfactory formal classification is impossible.

Reasons for creating special tribunals

The reasons why Parliament increasingly confers powers of adjudication on special tribunals rather than on the ordinary courts may be stated positively as showing the greater suitability of such tribunals, or negatively as showing the inadequacy of the ordinary courts for the particular kind of work that has to be done. In the following summary we choose mainly the former method.

(i) *Expert knowledge*

Many of the questions that have to be decided under modern social legislation call for an expert knowledge of matters falling outside the training of the lawyer; also an understanding of the policy of the legislature and experience of administration. They are not primarily legal questions, although at some stage a judicial habit of mind may be required. Members of the Lands Tribunal, for example, may be lawyers or persons experienced in questions relating to valuation of land.[9] Men-

---

[5] *Post*, p. 646.
[6] *Post*, p. 647.
[7] (1957) Cmnd. 218, paras. 406–408; see *post*, p. 583. *Cf. Report of the Committee on Ministers' Powers* (1932) Cmd. 4060, pp. 115–118.
[8] Exhaustive information down to 1957 is contained in the *Memoranda submitted by Government Departments* to the Franks Committee. For the current position see *Tribunals, Practice and Procedure* (1985, ed. J. Bowers). See also R. E. Wraith and D. G. Hutchesson, *Administrative Tribunals* (1973); J. A. Farmer, *Tribunals and Government* (1974); H. Street, *Justice in the Welfare State* (2nd ed., 1975); J. Fulbrook, *Administrative Justice and the Unemployed* (1978).
[9] Lands Tribunal Act 1949.

tal Health Review Tribunals include legal, medical and lay members.[10] Industrial Tribunals include one member representing associations of workers and one representing employers' associations.[11]

(ii) *Cheapness*

The vast number of questions that arise from day to day, affecting the interests of thousands of people, must be disposed of much more cheaply than can be done in the stately and costly courts of law. The speed and informality mentioned below contribute to the relative cheapness of administrative justice.

(iii) *Speed*

Again, if these multitudinous questions are to be disposed of without the delay that would clog the administrative machine and work great hardship on interested parties, institutions must be devised and procedure adopted that will dispatch the business much more speedily than the ordinary courts can do. Indeed, the courts would not have time to take over this work, in addition to what they already have, without being entirely reconstituted and so losing their present identity.

(iv) *Flexibility*

Although every body of men that has to make decisions evolves in course of time general working principles, and government departments tend to follow their own precedents, the new tribunals are not hampered by the rigid doctrine of binding precedent adhered to by the courts.[12] They thus have greater freedom to develop new branches of law on the basis of modern social legislation and suitable to the needs of the Welfare State, as in times past the Court of Chancery developed Equity.[13] This does not mean that the decisions of tribunals are entirely capricious and unpredictable: there is a growing practice for some of them to publish selected decisions.

(v) *Informality*

Tribunals are not bound by such complex rules of procedure or such stringent rules of evidence as prevail in the ordinary courts.[14] They may admit hearsay evidence[15]; they must observe the rules of natural justice but there is not necessarily a right in all cases to cross examine witnesses.[16] Unlike the judges of the ordinary courts, members of tribunals are entitled to rely in deciding cases not merely on the evidence before them but on their professional or industrial knowledge relating to the subject matter of the dispute before them. To hold otherwise would, of

---

[10] Mental Health Act 1983.
[11] Employment Protection (Consolidation) Act 1978.
[12] *Merchandise Transport* v. *B.T.C.* [1962] 2 Q.B. 173.
[13] *Cf. James* v. *Minister of Pensions* [1947] K.B. 867 (Denning J.).
[14] *R.* v. *Deputy Industrial Injuries Commissioner, ex p. Moore* [1965] 1 Q.B. 456.
[15] *Miller (T. A.)* v. *Ministry of Housing and Local Government* [1968] 1 W.L.R. 992 (C.A.).
[16] *R.* v. *Newmarket Assessment Committee, ex p. Allen Newport Ltd.* [1945] 2 All E.R. 371, 373; *R.* v. *Deputy Industrial Injuries Commissioner, ex p. Moore (supra); Nicholson* v. *Secretary of State for Energy* (1977) 76 L.G.R. 693; decisions recognising in the circumstances a right to cross examine. *Contra, Kavanagh* v. *Chief Constable of Devon and Cornwall* [1974] Q.B. 624.

course, reduce if not completely destroy the value of choosing members of tribunals by reference to their special knowledge. They may rely on "their cumulative knowledge and experience of the matter in hand."[17] A doctor, for example, may advise other members of a tribunal from his personal experience of the weight to be given to evidence relating to medical matters.[18]

Examples of statutory tribunals

In many important areas of everyday life matters affecting a large part of the population are subject to the jurisdiction of statutory tribunals— for example social security benefits of all kinds, employment law, questions of discrimination, immigration, rents, rating, mental health. In other areas, of concern perhaps to smaller numbers, tribunals are also to be found—for example the Plant Varieties and Seeds Tribunal, the Wireless Telegraphy Appeal Tribunal,[19] the Tribunal established under the Interception of Communications Act 1985 or the Iron and Steel Arbitration Tribunal.[20] Most tribunals are of recent origin but some have a long history. The General Commissioners of Income Tax date back to 1798.

A common structure, particularly in the case of tribunals of modern origin which deal with large numbers of cases and sit throughout the United Kingdom, is a tribunal of three; a legally qualified Chairman and two members chosen because of their expertise in the relevant field and representing "both sides" where that can be said to be applicable, for example in industrial tribunals. In other cases, for example the Lands Tribunal, there is a small number of members from whom a tribunal is constituted when required. In the particular instance of the Lands Tribunal one member of the panel sitting alone constitutes the Tribunal.

Social security

There is an elaborate arrangement of tribunals in this wide and important area which covers entitlement to benefits and payments of various kinds.[21] At first instance applications are heard by Adjudication Officers who are officials of the Department of Health and Social Security. Appeals lie to a Social Security Appeals Tribunal. Each tribunal consists of a legally qualified Chairman and two members chosen from a panel of persons having knowledge or experience of conditions in the area and being representative of persons working and living in the area. The system of tribunals as a whole is under the control of a President

---

[17] *Metropolitan Properties* v. *Lannon* [1969] 1 Q.B. 577, 603 *per* Edmund-Davies L.J. (Rent Assessment Committee).

[18] *R.* v. *Medical Appeal Tribunal, ex p. Hubble* [1958] 2 Q.B. 228, 240 *per* Diplock J., affirmed [1959] 2 Q.B. 408. See also *Dugdale* v. *Kraft Foods Ltd.* [1977] I.C.R. 48 (E.A.T.).

[19] Established under the Wireless Telegraphy Act 1949, it is said never to have heard an appeal.

[20] This body, which according to the Iron and Steel Act 1982 is also a court of record, has never been convened since its establishment in 1949.

[21] Social Security Act 1975; Child Benefit Act 1975; Supplementary Benefit (Amendments) Act 1976; Family Income Supplements Act 1970. On the structure of tribunals see Health and Social Services and Social Security Adjudication Act 1983.

who is responsible for superintending the general working of the tribunals.

Appeal lies, subject in some cases to leave, to the Social Security Commissioners, of whom at present there are 13, in addition to the Chief Social Security Commissioner. An appeal is normally heard by one Commissioner. The Chief Commissioner decides which decisions shall be reported.

Industrial tribunals

This is another important body of tribunals, sitting throughout the United Kingdom, with a wide and varied jurisdiction. Established in 1965 to deal with claims relating to redundancy payments[22] they subsequently acquired jurisdiction over unfair dismissals,[23] discrimination claims under the Sex Discrimination Act 1975 and the Race Relations Act 1976 and appeals against improvement and prohibition notices served under the Health and Safety at Work etc. Act 1974. The tribunals are under the supervision of a President. Each tribunal consists of a legally qualified chairman and two laymen, one chosen from a list prepared in consultation with employers' representatives, the other from a list prepared in consultation with trades unions.

A special feature of Industrial Tribunals is that appeal lies to the Employment Appeal Tribunal which consists of a High Court Judge and two lay members.[24]

Immigration

The provision for hearing appeals relating to immigration by Immigration Adjudicators and the Immigration Appeal Tribunal has been outlined earlier in Chapter 23.

Mental health review tribunals

These important bodies and the difficult jurisdiction which they have to exercise have been discussed in Chapter 25.

Rent control

Rent Assessment Committees have jurisdiction to determine fair rents for unfurnished houses[25] and also now exercise the power formerly exercised by rent tribunals to determine rents for furnished premises.[26] Here again a tribunal consists of a legally qualified Chairman and two lay members.

Rating

Appeals against rating are heard in the first instance by a local valuation court which normally consists of three members chosen from a local valuation panel. Appeal lies to the Lands Tribunal.

---

[22] Redundancy Payments Act 1965.
[23] Industrial Relations Act 1971.
[24] On the unusual status of this Court as a United Kingdom court see *ante* p. 376.
[25] Rent Act 1965; Rent Act 1977.
[26] Furnished Houses (Rent Control) Act 1946 was the source of this jurisdiction. The amalgamation of the two bodies was effected by the Housing Act 1980.

Taxation

Appeals against assessments to income tax lie in some cases to General Commissioners, in some to Special Commissioners. The former are appointed by the Lord Chancellor and are residents with knowledge of the area in which they sit.[27] Usually two Commissioners hear an appeal which is conducted informally. Special Commissioners[28] are appointed by the Treasury. They are senior civil servants; hearings are in London, sometimes before two, sometimes one Commissioner.

Value Added Tax is collected by the Customs and Excise. Appeals are heard by Value Added Tax Tribunals which are under the supervision of a President. Each tribunal consists of a Chairman, appointed by the Lord Chancellor, and one or two laymen chosen from a panel nominated by the Treasury. (The Chairman may sit alone).[29]

Further examples which illustrate the width of matters referred to administrative tribunals of various kinds might include Commons Commissioners,[30] the Foreign Compensation Commission,[31] the Independent Schools Tribunal,[32] the Comptroller General of Patents, Designs and Trademarks,[33] the Performing Rights Tribunal,[34] the Plant Varieties and Seeds Tribunal[35] and the Vaccine Damage Tribunal.[36]

Tribunals of Inquiry, established under the Tribunals of Inquiry (Evidence) Act 1921 belong in a class of their own and are discussed earlier in Part I of Chapter 7.

Domestic tribunals

Some disciplinary bodies set up for professional or other associations are established by statute, often with appeal to the courts, and therefore find a place here since bodies exercising statutory powers against individuals will normally be regarded as operating in the area of public law.[37]

The supervisory jurisdiction of the High Court[38] is exercised over statutory domestic tribunals in a similar way to that over administrative tribunals, in that they must observe the principles of natural justice; and this supervisory jurisdiction over them provides useful precedents for administrative law.[39] However, whereas excess of jurisdiction ren-

---

[27] Taxes Management Act 1970, s.2.
[28] Taxes Management Act 1970, s.4.
[29] Value Added Tax Act 1983, s.40 and Sched. 8.
[30] Commons Registration Act 1965.
[31] Foreign Compensation Acts 1950 and 1969.
[32] Education Act 1944, s.71.
[33] Patents Act 1977; Registered Designs Act 1949; Trade Marks Act 1938.
[34] Copyright Act 1956.
[35] Plant Varieties and Seeds Act 1964; Plant Varieties Act 1983.
[36] Vaccine Damage Payments Act 1979.
[37] R. v. General Medical Council ex p. Gee [1986] 1 W.L.R. 226; affirmed [1986] 1 W.L.R. 1247 (C.A.).
[38] Post, Chap. 33.
[39] Lord Justice Morris, "The Courts and Domestic Tribunals" (1953) 69 L.Q.R. 318; D. Lloyd, "The Disciplinary Powers of Professional Bodies" (1950) 13 M.L.R. 281 and (1952) 15 M.L.R. 413; J. D. B. Mitchell, "Domestic Tribunals and the Courts" (1956) 2 British Journal of Administrative Law 80; J. Gareth Miller, "The Disciplinary Jurisdiction of Professional Tribunals" (1962) 25 M.L.R. 531; Report of Departmental Committee on Powers of Subpoena of Disciplinary Tribunals (1960) Cmnd. 1033.

ders a statutory tribunal liable to damages, excess of jurisdiction by a non-statutory tribunal does not, unless there is a breach of contract or malice.[40] Proceedings against non-statutory domestic tribunals may be commenced in the normal way by writ. In addition to damages, where appropriate, declarations and injunctions are available but not certiorari and prohibition.[41]

Disciplinary committees have been created by statute for a large number of professions to hear complaints of misconduct and with power to strike members off the register. The Medical Act 1983, for example, establishes a Professional Conduct Committee with power to remove a doctor's name from the register of medical practitioners, either for a fixed period or indefinitely, on proof of conviction of a criminal offence or of serious professional misconduct. Appeal lies to the Privy Council.[42] Architects, Farriers and Pharmacists, on the other hand, may appeal from professional bodies to the High Court.[43]

The legal professions for historical reasons have unusual domestic disciplinary arrangements which reflect their close connections with the Courts.

The Masters of the Bench of each of the four Inns of Court have a customary jurisdiction, said to have been delegated by the judges, to disbar members of their Inn for professional misconduct.[44] Appeal by a barrister from debarring or suspension lies to the Lord Chancellor and the judges of the High Court. The Solicitors' Disciplinary Tribunal owes its jurisdiction to statute, currently the Solicitors Act 1974. Appeal lies from the tribunal in certain cases to the Master of the Rolls, in others to the High Court.

Universities in this country are mostly created by royal charter, although some are governed by private Acts of Parliament. The former (chartered corporations) ought to be classed as non-statutory bodies, their "statutes" being prerogative Orders in Council. Disciplinary powers of university authorities have been judicially described as "judicial"[45] or "quasi-judicial"[46]; and university disciplinary bodies or committees must observe the principles of natural justice as a matter of

---

[40] *Byrne* v. *Kinematograph Renters Association* [1958] 1 W.L.R. 762.

[41] *R.* v. *National Joint Council for the Craft of Dental Technicians ex p. Neate* [1953] 1 Q.B. 704 (D.C.). *Post*, p. 687.

[42] Medical Act 1983, s.36 and s.40. Similarly, Dentists Act 1984 s.27 and s.29. Appeal also lies to the Privy Council under the Veterinary Surgeons Act 1966 and the Professions Supplementary to Medicine Act 1960.

[43] Architects (Registration) Act 1931; Farriers (Registration) Act 1975; Pharmacy Act 1954; Medicines Act 1968. Appeals by doctors, dentists and veterinary surgeons and practitioners from decisions of the tribunal established under the Misuse of Drugs Act 1971 lie to the High Court.

[44] From time to time the Inns have vested this disciplinary power in other bodies exercising control over the Bar generally. See *Re S (A Barrister)* [1981] Q.B. 683.

[45] *Ceylon University* v. *Fernando* [1960] 1 W.L.R. 223 (P.C.), declaration refused because natural justice observed. See also *De Verteuil* v. *Kraggs* [1918] A.C. 551, 560; *cf. Ex p. Death* (1852) 18 Q.B. 647.

[46] *Glynn* v. *University of Keele* [1971] 1 W.L.R. 487 (Pennycuick V.C.), principles of natural justice not complied with, but court exercised discretion to refuse injunction; see H. W. R. Wade, "Nudism and Natural Justice" (1971) 87 L.Q.R. 320.

implied contract.[47] It has been stated or presumed in several cases that—apart from the ordinary remedies of damages, declaration and injunction—certiorari would lie against university disciplinary authorities,[48] but in so far as they are not statutory bodies this is contrary to the principles of administrative law. Domestic disputes among members of a university concerning the conduct of examinations, the classification of candidates and the conferment of degrees are within the exclusive jurisdiction of the Visitor, commonly the Queen in Council; *Thorne* v. *University of London*.[49] The High Court, said Diplock L.J. in that case, fortunately does not act as a court of appeal from university examiners.[50]

In *Thomas* v. *Bradford University*[51] the House of Lords upheld the exclusive jurisdiction of the visitor over members of universities, subject only to the supervisory jurisdiction of the High Court and specific statutory incursions on that jurisdiction.

An important group of domestic tribunals are those set up by trades unions. Their decisions can be of great importance to individuals, particularly where expulsion from a union can mean the loss of a person's livelihood. The courts will intervene to ensure that their hearings are in accordance with the principles of natural justice[52] and that the tribunals correctly interpret the rules of their unions.[53] (Parliament, too, has intervened to give protection to anyone whose application for membership of a union is unreasonably refused or who has been unreasonably expelled from a trade union.[54])

---

[47] *Herring* v. *Templeman* [1973] 3 All E.R. 569.
[48] *R.* v. *Aston University Senate, ex p. Roffrey* [1969] 2 Q.B. 538 (D.C.); principles of natural justice not complied with, but court in its discretion refused certiorari and mandamus because of delay in making application; *R.* v. *Oxford University, ex p. Bolchover, The Times,* October 7, 1970 (D.C.), expulsion not unfair, leave to apply for certiorari refused; cf. *Vidyodaya University Council* v. *Silva* [1965] 1 W.L.R. 77 (P.C.), certiorari not available for dismissal of professor: see H. W. R. Wade, "Judicial Control of Universities" (1969) 85 L.Q.R. 468; J. F. Garner, "Students—Contract or Status?" (1974) 90 L.Q.R. 6. Doubts have been cast on *Ex p. Roffey* in *Herring* v. *Templeman, supra, Patel* v. *University of Bradford Senate* [1978] 1 W.L.R. 1488; [1979] 1 W.L.R. 1066 and *Law* v. *National Greyhound Racing Club* [1983] 1 W.L.R. 1302 (C.A.).
[49] [1966] 2 Q.B. 237 (C.A.), following *R.* v. *Dunsheath, ex p. Meredith* [1951] 1 K.B. 127 (D.C.). Similarly *Patel* v. *University of Bradford Senate* [1978] 1 W.L.R. 1488; [1979] 1 W.L.R. 1066 (C.A.) (right to re-sit examination).
[50] So in *Sammy* v. *Birkbeck College, The Times,* May 20, 1965 (C.A.), a student who failed to obtain the first-class degree he thought he deserved, lost his action against his former college for breach of contract, fraud and negligence.
See J. W. Bridge, "Keeping Peace in the Universities: the Role of the Visitor" (1970) 86 L.Q.R. 531; P. M. Smith, "The Exclusive Jurisdiction of the University Visitor," (1981) 97 L.Q.R. 610.
[51] *The Times,* February 27, 1987, approving *Hines* v. *Birkbeck College* [1986] 2 W.L.R. 97 and doubting *Casson* v. *University of Aston in Birmingham* [1983] 1 All E.R. 88 (Lord Hailsham L.C., on behalf of the Visitor).
[52] *Hiles* v. *Amalgamated Society of Woodworkers* [1968] Ch. 440; *Breen* v. *A.E.U.* [1971] 2 Q.B. 175; *Roebuck* v. *N.U.M. (Yorkshire Area)* (No. 2) [1978] I.C.R. 676.
[53] *Bonsor* v. *Musicians' Union* [1956] A.C. 104 (H.L.); *Edwards* v. *SOGAT* [1971] Ch. 534 (C.A.).
[54] Employment Act 1980, s.4. (The section applies to employment by an employer with respect to which it is the practice, in accordance with a union membership agreement, for the employee to belong to a specified trade union or one of a number of specific trade unions: subs.(1).)

Tribunals and Inquiries Act 1971

A Committee on Administrative Tribunals and Inquiries under the chairmanship of Sir Oliver Franks (later Lord Franks) was appointed by the Lord Chancellor: "To consider and make recommendations on: (a) The constitution and working of tribunals other than the ordinary courts of law, constituted under any Act of Parliament by a Minister of the Crown or for the purposes of a Minister's functions. (b) The working of such administrative procedures as include the holding of an inquiry or hearing by or on behalf of a Minister on an appeal or as the result of objections or representations, and in particular the procedure for the compulsory purchase of land." The Committee reported in 1957.[55]

The purpose of Parliament in providing that certain decisions should not be left to the ordinary courts but should be subject to special procedures, said the Committee, must have been to promote good administration; and the general characteristics that should mark these special procedures are "openness, fairness and impartiality." It was not possible to define the principles on which it had been decided that some adjudications should be made by tribunals and others by Ministers: the distinction was a fact that had to be accepted. Tribunals should be regarded as machinery provided by Parliament for adjudication, rather than (as the Committee on Ministers' Powers had suggested in 1932) as part of the machinery of administration.

The Government accepted most of the recommendations of the Franks Committee in the Tribunals and Inquiries Act 1958. Certain reforms could be introduced by administrative directions to government departments or local authorities. The most important innovation made by the Act was the creation of a Council on Tribunals.[56] (The composition and work of the Council is considered in Chapter 32.) The Act also made further provision as to the appointment, qualifications and removal of the chairman and members, and as to the procedure, of certain tribunals; it provided for appeals to the courts from certain tribunals; it required the giving of reasons for certain decisions of tribunals and Ministers; and it extended the supervisory powers of the High Court. The Act was amended in 1959[57] and 1966,[58] and the law was consolidated by the Tribunals and Inquiries Act 1971.

Appointment of members of tribunals

The chairmen of some tribunals are appointed by the Lord Chancellor, and the chairmen of certain other tribunals are selected by the

---

[55] (1957) Cmnd. 218.

[56] The idea appears to have originated with Professor W. A. Robson, who proposed a "Standing Council on Administrative Tribunals" (see Franks Report, *Minutes of Evidence*, p. 496), in addition to an Administrative Appeal Tribunal. It was reinforced by H. W. R. Wade's proposal for an "Administrative Court" (*ibid.* pp. 551–555).

[57] Town and Country Planning Act 1959, s.33 (provision of rules of procedure for statutory inquiries).

[58] Tribunals and Inquiries Act 1966 (provision of rules of procedure for discretionary inquiries).

appropriate Minister from a panel of persons appointed by the Lord Chancellor[59] (s.7).

The Council on Tribunals may make to the appropriate Minister general recommendations as to the appointment of members of the tribunals specified in Schedule 1 (*i.e.* those under the supervision of the Council), and also of the relevant panels, and the Minister "shall have regard" to such recommendations.

A Minister may not, with certain exceptions, terminate the appointment of a member of a tribunal specified in Schedule 1, or of a relevant panel, without the consent of the Lord Chancellor[59] (s.8).

Procedure

The Minister must consult the Council on Tribunals before making or approving procedural rules for the tribunals that come under its supervision. There are now no restrictions on legal representation before most statutory tribunals.[60] Legal aid is not available except before the Lands Tribunal and the Commons Commissioners, two formal tribunals which closely resemble courts. In the case of other tribunals, however, legal advice is available.[61] In many cases litigants will in fact have the help of their unions or similar bodies. Presumably, too, the right which the Court of Appeal recognised in *McKenzie* v. *McKenzie*[62] for a litigant to be accompanied by a friend to assist by taking notes and giving advice applies to tribunals as much as to the ordinary courts.

Appeals from tribunals

A party to proceedings before most statutory tribunals, who is dissatisfied with the tribunal's decision on a point of law, may either appeal to the High Court or require the tribunal to state a case for the opinion of the High Court. Appeal lies by leave of the High Court or of the Court of Appeal to the Court of Appeal,[63] and thence to the House of Lords (s.13).

The scope of this right depends on the view of the courts on what constitutes a point of law as opposed to a question of fact. Whether or not the facts were as alleged by an applicant is a matter for the tribunal. Whether those facts in the light of the appropriate rules of law give rise, for example, to a contract of employment is a matter of applying the law to the facts. If a court does not wish to interfere it can call that second stage too a question of fact. If it does wish to interfere it can conclude that it raised a point of law because no reasonable tribunal could have reached such a conclusion unless it had made an error in understanding or applying the law.[64]

---

[59] Or the Lord President of the Court of Session or the Lord Chief Justice of Northern Ireland.

[60] An exception is provided by tribunals which deal with complaints against National Health Service practitioners: Health and Social Security Act 1984, s.5 and Sched. 3.

[61] Assistance with representation is available in the case of Mental Health Review tribunals: S.I. 1982/1592.

[62] [1971] p. 33.

[63] The Court of Session takes the place of the High Court and the Court of Appeal in relation to proceedings in Scotland.

[64] *Post* p. 695.

Extension of supervisory powers of superior courts

Any provision in an Act passed *before* August 1, 1958, that any order or determination shall not be called into question in any court, or any similar provision which excludes any of the powers of the High Court, shall not prevent the removal of the proceedings into the High Court by order of certiorari or prejudice the powers of the High Court to make orders of mandamus (s.14).[65] Despite the terms of the side note this preserves, rather than "extends" the supervisory jurisdiction of the High Court over tribunals.[66] It does not, however, affect statutory provisions prescribing a special time limit within which applications to the High Court must be made.

Reasons to be given for decisions

Where a tribunal which comes under the supervision of the Council gives a decision, it is the duty of the tribunal to furnish a written or oral statement of the reasons for the decision *if requested to do so* by persons concerned. The statement may be refused, or the specification of the reasons restricted, on the grounds of national security. Such a statement forms part of the decision and must be incorporated in the record, so that the order will be a "speaking order" for the purposes of certiorari.[67]

The courts have subsequently held that the reasons given must be "proper, adequate reasons" which are intelligible and deal with the substantial points which had been raised.[68]

II. MINISTERIAL DECISIONS AND INQUIRIES

Parliament often provides that, before a decision is made by a Minister or other public authority which affects the rights of citizens, an inquiry must be held at which those whose interests are concerned may state their objections to the action proposed before a final decision is made. Inquiries are usually prescribed by statute before land is compulsorily acquired for such purposes as town development, slum clearance, the building of housing estates, schools and hospitals, and road improvement; and also before town and country planning schemes are confirmed. Inquiries may also be prescribed in relation to the provision of social services, and for other schemes of control. Most inquiries are arranged by the Ministry for the purposes of its own housing and planning cases and those of local authorities. The procedure provides a framework for a fair hearing in the weighing of the proposals of a public authority against the interests of persons affected by them. The Minister is not bound by the recommendations of the Inspector who holds the inquiry: he must, on the contrary form his own independent decision.[69]

[65] There is a corresponding provision in relation to Scotland.

[66] *Post*, Chap. 34.

[67] *Post*, Chap. 34.

[68] *Re Poser and Mills' Arbitration* [1964] 2 Q.B. 467. For other statutory provisions requiring the giving of reasons for decisions see *Iveagh (Earl)* v. *Minister of Housing and Local Government* [1964] 1 Q.B. 395; *Givaudan & Co.* v. *Minister of Housing and Local Government* [1967] 1 W.L.R. 250; *Elliott* v. *Southwark L.B.C.* [1976] 1 W.L.R. 499; *French Kier Developments* v. *Secretary of State for the Environment* [1977] 1 All E.R. 296.

[69] *Nelsovil Ltd.* v. *Minister of Housing and Local Government* [1962] 1 W.L.R. 404.

Some Ministers have the power—often without appeal—to make decisions directly affecting the rights of individuals or other public authorities. This power of decision may be either original or appellate. In either case it may involve a dispute between a public authority and an individual or between two public (often local) authorities. The power is in a greater or less degree discretionary, usually there is no kind of appeal from it, and in the cases we are now considering no public inquiry or other form of procedure is prescribed by statute. Normally, therefore, citizens can only complain about these decisions through such political means as letters to Members of Parliament, questions in the House and motions in debates on the adjournment.

Examples are the Home Secretary's power to hear appeals from police officers against dismissal or reduction in pay, and his powers relating to prison administration; and the judicial functions of various Ministers in relation to such matters as bankruptcy, weights and measures, registration of business names and trademarks, licensing of road transport, and appeals from district auditors.

The Minister *may* hold an inquiry in many of these cases but in such cases the parties concerned will lack the rights which they have where an inquiry must be held.[70]

Inquiries[71]

A typical provision requiring the holding of an Inquiry is to be found in the Acquisition of Land Act 1981. The Act lays down general procedural rules to be observed before compulsory purchase powers conferred by various statutes can be exercised. Section 13 of the 1981 Act provides that if any objection has been made to a proposed compulsory purchase order the Minister shall before confirming the order either cause a public local inquiry to be held or afford to any objector a hearing. Little can be learned from the Act of any rules relating to the holding of such an inquiry or who might hold it. Section 9 of the Town and Country Planning Act 1971 similarly requires the minister, before confirming a structure plan proposed for a planning authority for the development of its area, to afford to any objectors "an opportunity of appearing before and being heard by a person appointed by him for the purpose." Sections 16 and 106 of the Highways Act 1980 require the holding of inquiries and, in some instances, section 16 requires an inquiry under the Statutory Orders (Special Procedure) Act 1945.[72]

Procedure

The Franks Committee made a number of recommendations relating to procedure at inquiries and, in particular, advocated the adoption of statutory rules to regulate procedure.

The Lord Chancellor was given statutory power to make rules for procedure, after consultation with the Council of Tribunals, by the Town and Country Planning Act 1959, s.33: see now the Tribunals and Inquiries Act 1971, s.11. In due course rules were made for many of the more

---

[70] *Essex County Council* v. *Ministry of Housing and Local Government* (1967) 18 P. & C.R. 531 (Stansted Airport Inquiry).
[71] R. E. Wraith and G. B. Lamb, *Public Inquiries as an Instrument of Government* (1971).
[72] *Ante*, p. 623.

important types of inquiry[73] and are usually followed by analogy in cases where strictly they do not apply. The rules relate to the notice to be given to persons entitled to appear before the inquiry; the right to representation and the right to call evidence and cross examine. The rules define the right to appear by reference to people whose legal rights are effected by the scheme or proposal. Within limits Inspectors allow parties to appear who may not be within the terms of the rules and there is judicial support for the view that a local inquiry is open to anyone living in the locality.[74]

Apart from express procedural rules an inspector must observe the rules of natural justice (or act fairly or not behave with procedural impropriety[75]). Hence he must not receive evidence from one party in the absence of another[76] or base his report on considerations which the objectors had not known were in his mind so that they had had no chance to deal with them.[77]

Fairness and the general nature of local inquiries were considered by the House of Lords in *Bushell* v. *Secretary of State for the Environment*,[78] an inquiry held under the Highways Act 1959, before the Highways Inquiries Rules had come into force. The House of Lords, Lord Edmund-Davies dissenting, upheld the refusal of the inspector to allow cross-examination of the department's expert witnesses on the reliability and statistical validity of the methods of traffic prediction used by the department to produce its estimates of future traffic needs. Lord Diplock, whose speech contains the lengthiest analysis of the role of the inspector, preferred to use the word "fair" to describe the procedure required to be followed by the inspector; natural justice was too liable to connote "the procedure followed by English courts of law." What is fair is to be determined in the light of the nature of the subject matter of the inquiry and of the practical realities as to the way in which administrative decisions forming judgments based on technical considerations are reached. A refusal to permit cross-examination is not *per se* unfair. In *Bushell* the method of computing traffic flow was not a topic suitable for investigation by individual inspectors at individual inquiries, unlike the route of a particular stretch of motorway. It was more akin to a question of policy—should motorways be built at all?—which is a matter for Parliament, not local inquiries.[79]

---

[73] Compulsory Purchase by Public Authorities (Inquiries Procedure) Rules 1976, S.I. No. 746. Town and Country Planning (Inquiries Procedure) Rules 1974, S.I. No. 419; Highways (Inquiries Procedure) Rules 1976, S.I. No. 721.

[74] *Wednesbury Corporation* v. *Ministry of Housing and Local Government* (No. 2) [1966] 2 Q.B. 275, 302 *per* Diplock L.J.

[75] *Post,* p. 670.

[76] *Hibernian Property Co. Ltd.* v. *Secretary of State for the Environment* (1973) 27 P. & C.R. 197.

[77] *Fairmount Investments* v. *Secretary of State for the Environment* [1976] 1 W.L.R. 1255 (H.L.).

[78] [1981] A.C. 75. See too *R.* v. *Secretary of State for Transport, ex p. Gwent County Council,* [1987] 1 All E.R. 161.

[79] The extent to which policy is a proper issue to be raised at an inquiry may depend on whether it is a "local inquiry" or a more far ranging inquiry, in which policy questions are inevitably involved, such as that into proposals to build an airport at Stansted or a nuclear reactor at Sizewell: M. Purdue, R. Kemp and T. O'Riordan, "The Government at the Sizewell B Inquiry," [1985] P.L. 475.

The Inspector's Report

Inspectors are, largely, full time members of the departments for which they hold inquiries. Although this could give rise to some doubt about their independence and impartiality the Franks Committee emphasised that it had received "virtually no criticism of the qualifications of inspectors or of the manner in which they conduct enquiries." Nonetheless the Committee finally decided to recommend that inspectors should be put under the control of the Lord Chancellor rather than being employed as full-time members of particular departments or being appointed from time to time by a department to conduct a particular inquiry. That recommendation was not accepted by the Government. However, the Departments of the Environment and Transport did agree that highway inquiries should in future be conducted by inspectors nominated by the Lord Chancellor.[80]

Another important aspect of public confidence in the operation of inquiries is the right to know the contents of the inspector's report. There is likely to be suspicion about a system which grants a hearing and requires ministers in some cases to reopen inquiries or allow further representations, if the report at the centre of the procedure is withheld from the parties. The courts gave no right to see the report but the Franks Committee recommended publication on the ground that "fair play for the citizen" required that he should know what the inspector said to the minister. This recommendation has been accepted and is specifically included in the statutory rules of procedure governing various classes of inquiries. The report is not, however, made available until the minister has made his decision.

The role of the Minister

Once the inspector has concluded his hearing and produced his report the rights of the ministers and objectors are now largely governed by statutory rules. The Franks Committee had been concerned about the extent to which a minister might take into account new evidence received after an inquiry had concluded. The committee suggested a distinction between new factual evidence and advice on policy, which the Government accepted. A minister is, in many cases, now required to notify all the parties concerned if (i) he intends to differ from an inspector on a finding of fact or (ii) he is likely to disagree with the inspector's recommendations because he has taken into consideration new evidence (which includes expert evidence on a matter of fact) or any new issue of fact (which does not include questions of government policy). Where the minister is differing on a finding of fact the parties have 21 days in which to make written representations. In the other cases the parties have 21 days within which to ask for the reopening of the inquiry. An example of the rules being successfully invoked to invalidate a ministerial decision is to be found in *French Kier Developments Ltd.* v. *Secretary of State for the Environment*.[81] In making his report, an inspector disregarded a document put before him but the minister relied on that document to justify a refusal to accept the

---

[80] Report on the Review of Highway Inquiry Procedures, Cmnd. 7133 (1978).
[81] [1977] 1 All E.R. 296.

inspector's recommendations. Willis J. held that to attach any weight to the contents of the document in the circumstances amounted to the taking into consideration of new evidence and the parties should therefore have had the opportunity to reopen the inquiry. The difficulty which may arise in interpreting the new rules is illustrated by *Murphy (J.) and Sons Ltd.* v. *Secretary of State for the Environment.*[82] An inspector had recommended against allowing a site to be developed for residential use because of the amount of noise coming from the plaintiff company's adjoining premises. The minister, however, granted permission for the development and the plaintiff's company claimed that, in doing so, he had differed from the inspector on a finding of fact. Ackner J. held that the minister had not differed from the inspector on a finding of fact but from the inspector's expression of opinion on the planning merits, which did not give the plaintiff the right to make further representations.[83] In the case of inquiries governed by these or similar rules the right to make further representations or to reopen the inquiry only arises if the minister differs from his inspector.

In *Bushell* v. *Secretary of State for the Environment*[84] the House of Lords emphasised that, whatever the restrictions on the minister in reaching his decision, he is perfectly entitled to consult his departmental officials and obtain from them the best advice that he can: "Once he has reached his decision he must be prepared to disclose his reasons for it, because the Tribunals and Inquiries Act 1971 so requires; but he is, in my view, under no obligation to disclose to objectors and give them an opportunity of commenting on advice, expert or otherwise, which he receives from his department in the course of making up his mind. If he thinks that to do so will be helpful to him in reaching the right decision in the public interest he may, of course, do so; but if he does not think it will be helpful—and this is for him to decide—failure to do so cannot in my view be treated as a denial of natural justice to the objectors."[85]

---

[82] 1973 1 W.L.R. 560.
[83] See *Lord Luke of Pavenham* v. *Minister of Housing and Local Government* [1968] 1 Q.B. 172.
[84] [1981] A.C. 75.
[85] At p. 102 *per* Lord Diplock.

CHAPTER 32

NON-JUDICIAL REMEDIES

Introduction

People may wish to resort to non-judicial remedies where they have a grievance to complain of, or a wrong to be righted, for various reasons and in many different circumstances. Where there is a dispute about the law the courts may ultimately provide the only effective remedy. But in many cases complainants may be unhappy about the way a decision was reached, delays and rudeness on the parts of public officials, for example. There may be no doubt about what the law is: it may, however, be thought that the law should be changed. In some cases people may simply want information; why, for example, did a patient fail to recover after an operation. A decision may be thought to have been reached on a mistaken view of the facts; a complainant may want to be able to produce new evidence or to have an opportunity to rebut conclusions reached by a public official.

In the following Parts of this chapter we shall examine the Council on Tribunals and the Parliamentary Commissioner for Administration and other Commissioners with specialised jurisdictions. Other statutory non-judicial remedies which have been discussed in earlier chapters include the Police Complaints Authority[1] and the Broadcasting Complaints Commission.[2] The current concern with providing procedures for dealing with complaints of every kind is illustrated by the Hospital Complaints Procedure Act 1985 which requires the provision in each hospital of arrangements for dealing with complaints by patients and former patients or persons on their behalf. The Law Society has established a Solicitors' Complaints Bureau to investigate complaints against solicitors as a possible first step to proceedings before the Solicitors Disciplinary Tribunal.

Apart from procedures and bodies established to deal with complaints relating to specific types of problems, Members of Parliament discharge an important role in offering a means of redress for grievances of every kind.[3] Constituents may, and do, write to their M.P.'s about grievances for which they have found no remedy elsewhere. In some cases it may be appropriate to pass the complaint to the Parliamentary Commissioner for Administration (*infra*, Part II). In others the appropriate action may be a letter to a minister or some public body or a question in the House. The importance of this aspect of the work of M.P.'s has grown steadily in the last thirty years.

---

[1] Chapter 21.
[2] Chapter 26.
[3] Alan C. Page, "M.P.s and the Redress of Grievances" [1985] P.L. 1.

I. The Council on Tribunals[4]

The Franks Report[5] recommended the creation of a Council on Tribunals to exercise various functions in relation to Statutory Tribunals. The Council was established by the Tribunals and Inquiries Act 1958 and continued in existence by section 1 of the Tribunals and Inquiries Act 1971. The functions of the Council are

(a) to keep under review the constitution and working of the tribunals specified in Schedule 1,[6] and from time to time to report on their constitution and working;

(b) to consider and report on such particular matters as may be referred to the Council with respect to "tribunals other than the ordinary courts of law," whether or not specified in Schedule 1; and

(c) to consider and report on such matters as may be referred, or as the Council may determine to be of special importance, with respect to administrative procedures involving the holding by a Minister of a statutory inquiry.

The Council consists of 10 to 15 members appointed by the Lord Chancellor and the Lord Advocate. There is a Scottish Committee of the Council, consisting of two or three members of the Council and three or four other persons appointed by the Secretary of State. The chairmen of the Council and of the Scottish Committee are paid a salary, and the other members may be paid fees.

The Council reports to, and receives references from, the Lord Chancellor and the Secretary of State. The Council is required to make an annual report on its proceedings, and the Lord Chancellor and the Secretary of State are to lay the annual report before Parliament, with such comments (if any) as they think fit.

Work of the Council on Tribunals

There are more than 2,000 tribunals under the supervision of the Council. The Council not only acts as a "watchdog" but also as a focus of information. It keeps under review the constitution and working of tribunals. With regard to statutory inquiries its function is to consider and report on such matters as may be referred to it by the Lord Chancellor or the Secretary of State, or as the Council may determine to be of special importance. It does not recommend the kinds of person who should be appointed to conduct inquiries. Complaints are digested by a complaints committee. The Council's powers are not executive but advisory, and it does not act as a court of appeal from tribunals. Nor does it seek to impose uniformity on all tribunals.

Although the work of the Council is mainly of a routine nature it has, on two occasions at least, become involved in controversial cases of notoriety which illustrate the Council's strengths and weaknesses.

The *Chalk Pit* case[7] was the subject of a special report to the Lord

---

[4] *Council on Tribunals: Special Report on Functions* (1980) Cmnd. 7805; D. C. M. Yardley, "The Functions of the Council on Tribunals," [1980] Jo. Soc. Wel. Law 265; D. G. T. Williams, "The Council on Tribunals: The First Twenty Five Years" [1984] P.L. 73.

[5] (1967) Cmnd. 218.

[6] Other tribunals may be added by Statutory Instrument.

[7] See Griffith and Street, *A Casebook of Administrative Law* (1964) pp. 142–174.

Chancellor. Major Buxton, a landowner, complained to the Council[8] about the decision of a Minister to allow a firm to use a gravel pit adjoining his piggeries for the production of chalk. The inspector who conducted the inquiry reported that the production of chalk would result in dust being blown onto adjoining land, with serious detriment to animals and crops. Major Buxton alleged that the Minister consulted the Minister of Agriculture privately between the end of the inquiry and the announcement of his decision, thus stultifying the inquiry. The Council made a report to the Lord Chancellor on the problem of handling new factual evidence noted by Ministers after statutory inquiries; with the result that a Statutory Instrument was later issued directing a Minister to re-open an inquiry on request if he disagrees with the inspector on receiving new evidence (including expert opinion) or has considered a new issue of fact not raised at the inquiry.

The *Packington Estate* case, on which the Council also produced a special report, was interesting not only for the light it threw on the way the Minister of Housing and Local Government (Richard Crossman) dealt with an application by a local authority for planning permission but also for what it revealed of the importance one Minister, at least, attached to the work of the Council. Although the Ministry had agreed to meet members of the Council to discuss the complaints of local landowners about the procedure being followed, the Minister sent a letter to the local authority granting planning permission two days before the date arranged for the meeting with the Council—a procedure which might fairly be described as "a deliberate and blatant attempt to stultify the activities of an independent statutory body established to act as a watchdog. . . ."[9]

Annual reports show that the Council is consulted on rules of procedure for a number of tribunals and for Inquiries. It has made representations about accommodation, public hearings and legal aid. The Council is also consulted on Bills affecting existing or creating new tribunals. Where, however, its views are rejected there is no procedure for making this publicly known.

II. PARLIAMENTARY COMMISSIONER FOR ADMINISTRATION[10] AND OTHERS

Maladministration

Neither courts nor tribunals can offer a remedy when private citizens complain that public authorities, although they have acted within the law, have failed to observe the proper standards of administrative con-

---

[8] He had been unsuccessful in the courts as he was not a "person aggrieved": *Buxton v. Minister of Housing and Local Government* [1961] 1 Q.B. 278; *post* p. 694.

[9] [1966] P.L. 1, 6.

[10] *The Parliamentary Commissioner for Administration* (1965), Cmnd. 2767; *The Citizen and the Administration*, Part III, A report by *Justice* (Whyatt Report, 1961); *The Ombudsman: Citizen's Defender*, ed. D. C. Rowat (2nd ed., 1968); *Our Fettered Ombudsman*, A report by *Justice* (1977); Sir Edmund Compton, "Parliamentary Commissioner for Administration" (1969) 10 J.S.P.T.L. 106; Paul Jackson, "The Work of the Parliamentary Commissioner for Administration" [1971] P.L. 39; Sir Alan Marre, "Some Thoughts on the Role of the Parliamentary Commissioner for Administration" (1972) 3 *Cambrian Law Rev.* 54; Sir Cecil Clothier, "The Value of an Ombudsman," [1986] P.L. 204; G. Marshall, *Constitutional Conventions* (1984) Chap. V; F. Stacey, *Ombudsmen Compared* (1978); R. Gregory and P. G. Hutchesson, *The Parliamentary Ombudsman* (1975).

duct. It is faults of this kind which are often described as *maladministration*. Mr. Crossman, in the debate on the Parliamentary Commissioner Bill, gave as examples of such conduct "bias, neglect, inattention, delay, incompetence, ineptitude, perversity, turpitude, arbitrariness and so on."[11] An example is the *Crichel Down* case,[12] where a landowner complained that the Ministry of Agriculture had refused to hand back to him after the war part of his land which had been requisitioned during the war and was no longer required by the Ministry for the purposes for which it had been requisitioned. In this particular case the Minister was induced by the outcry to hold a departmental inquiry, which criticised the conduct of certain officials in the Ministry, with the result that the officials were moved to different work and the Minister (although not personally involved) resigned his office. The citizen's only remedies at that time were for his Member of Parliament to ask a question in the House, to raise the matter in the debate on the adjournment or in debates on supply, to correspond with the Minister or to persuade the Minister to hold an *ad hoc* inquiry.

Parliamentary Commissioner for Administration

For some years there had been discussion on the suggestion[13] that a Parliamentary Commissioner, with an independent status like that of the Comptroller and Auditor-General, should be appointed for this country, whose functions would be similar to those of the Ombudsman known to Scandinavian countries and then recently introduced into New Zealand. Hesitation in the past was due largely to the fear that the appointment of such an independent official would interfere with ministerial responsibility, which is stronger here than in Scandanavia; and to a less extent to the fact that it was difficult to foresee how much work would fall to a Commissioner in a country with a population much greater than that of any of the Scandinavian countries or New Zealand. In 1967 the Parliamentary Commissioner Act was passed.[14]

Appointment

The Parliamentary Commissioner Act 1967 provides for a Parliamentary Commissioner of Administration to be appointed by letters patent. In 1977 the Government agreed that in future before an appointment was made it would consult the Chairman of the Select Committee on the Parliamentary Commissioner of Administration (see *infra*). His salary is charged on the Consolidated Fund.[15] He may be removed on an address

---

[11] 734 H.C. Deb., col. 51.

[12] (1954) Cmd. 9176; C. J. Hamson, "The Real Lesson of Crichel Down" (1954) 32 *Public Administration* 383. *Cf.* R. M. Jackson, "Judicial Review of Legislative Policy" (1955) 18 M.L.R. 571.

[13] The suggestion for an Inspector-General of Administration was originally made by Professor F. H. Lawson in [1957] P.L. 92–95. The Government turned down the suggestion for a Parliamentary Commissioner in 1961: 640 H.C.Deb., cols. 1693–1756.

[14] For the geographical spread of the institution in the last few years see *Our Fettered Ombudsman*, A report by *Justice* (1977), App. A. For a comparison of the Parliamentary Commissioner and the French médiateur see L. Neville Brown and P. Lavirotte, (1974) 90 L.Q.R. 211; L. Neville Brown and J. F. Garner, *French Administrative Law* (3rd ed., 1983). See too Colin T. Reid, "The Ombudsman's Cousin: The Procuracy in Socialist States" [1986] P.L. 311.

[15] See further, Parliamentary and other Pensions and Salaries Act 1976, s.6.

from both Houses, and he is excluded from membership of the Commons. He is an *ex officio* member of the Council on Tribunals, whose functions (as in cases like the *Chalk Pit* case) overlap his own, and in some cases the citizen may choose whether to complain to the Commissioner or the Council. He is also a member of the Commissions for Local Administration (*infra*).

Investigation of complaints

A person who thinks he has suffered injustice as a result of maladministration by a department or authority of the central government may complain to a member of the House of Commons in writing within twelve months from first having notice of the matter. The Commissioner has a discretion whether or not to conduct an investigation.[16] An investigation is conducted in private. The principal officer of the department or authority concerned must be given an opportunity to comment on the allegation. The complainant has no right to appear, but the Commissioner may see him if he thinks fit. The Commissioner has the same powers as the High Court to require a Minister, civil servant or other persons to furnish information or produce documents, excluding proceedings or papers of the Cabinet or a Cabinet committee. There is no Crown privilege[17] at the investigation stage; but a Minister may claim Crown privilege in respect of the *publication* or passing on of documents or information if their disclosure would in his opinion be prejudicial to the safety of the state or otherwise contrary to the public interest. The Official Secrets Act would prevent the Commissioner from including such information in his reports.

Departments and authorities covered

The departments and authorities in respect of whom the Commissioner may investigate complaints are set out in Schedule 2. They include most of the central government departments, but do not cover local authorities, public corporations, the police or the National Health Service. The list may be added to or reduced by Order in Council, the instrument being subject to annulment by resolution of either House.

Matters excluded from investigation are set out in Schedule 3. The excluded matters are within the functions of the departments listed in Schedule 2, *viz.*: foreign relations; action taken outside the United Kingdom (except by consular officials)[18]; the government of Her Majesty's overseas dominions; extradition, fugitive offenders, investigation of crime,[19] and security of the state (including passports); civil or criminal proceedings in any court, court-martial or international tribunal; the prerogative of mercy; medical matters; commercial contracts; personnel matters of the armed forces, civil service, teachers or police; the grant of honours, and royal charters. This list may be reduced by Order in Council.

---

[16] *Re Fletcher's Application* [1970] 2 All E.R. 527n. (C.A.); mandamus does not lie.
[17] *Post*, Chap. 35. For the position of the Local Commissioners, see *post*, p. 658.
[18] Parliamentary Commissioner (Consular Complaints) Act 1981.
[19] *i.e.* by or on behalf of the Home Office.

Reports by Commissioner

Where the Commissioner conducts or decides not to conduct an investigation he must send a report to the member concerned; and when he conducts an investigation he must send a report to the principal officer of the department concerned. If he thinks injustice has been caused, and that it has not been or will not be remedied, he may lay a special report before each House.

The Commissioner must lay a general report annually before each House on the performance of his functions, and he may lay special reports from time to time.

The Commissioner's reports show annually a large percentage—often over 50—of complaints that fall outside his jurisdiction. The proportion of cases investigated in which maladministration is found has risen year by year which suggests more thorough investigations as his staff have become more experienced and, perhaps, a widening view of what constitutes maladministration. One of the most controversial findings of maladministration was made in his Third Report on the *Sachsenhausen* Case.[20] The Commissioner concluded that the Foreign Office had, in determining whether a number of applicants were entitled to be compensated as inmates of German concentration camps as opposed to ordinary prison camps failed to attach due weight to various pieces of evidence. The Foreign Secretary finally accepted the Commissioner's report, while commenting,

> "When the Ombudsman has made enough decisions perhaps we shall have an Ombudsman to look at the Ombudsman's decisions and if he gets 100 per cent. right I shall be surprised."[21]

Select Committee on the Parliamentary Commissioner for Administration[22]

A Select Committee of the Commons was set up to deal with complaints by Members of Parliament who think the Commissioner has failed to deal properly with complaints forwarded by them, to consider what remedial action has been taken by the departments, and to recommend changes in the law. The Select Committee does not act as a court of appeal from the Commissioner's findings. In its first two annual reports the Committee criticised the narrow way in which the Commissioner was interpreting his jurisdiction.[23] It recommended an extension of the Commissioner's powers to cases where the departmental procedure for reviewing a rule, or the grounds for maintaining it, could be shown to be defective. The Committee has more than once recommended that the Commissioner should have power to investigate personnel matters and staffing within the Civil Service. In 1984 the

---

[20] (1967–68) H.C. 54. See G. F. Fry, "The Sachsenhausen Concentration Camp Case and the Convention of Ministerial Responsibility" [1970] P.L. 336.

[21] Hansard, H.C.Deb, 5 Feb. 1968.

[22] R. Gregory, "The Select Committee on the Parliamentary Commissioner for Administration" [1982] P.L. 49.

[23] (1967–68) H.C. 258; (1967–68) H.C. 350. See Geoffrey Marshall in *The Commons in Transition* (ed. A. H. Hanson and B. Crick, 1970), Chap. 6.

Committee recommended that the Commissioner's jurisdiction should be extended to a number of Quangos, a proposal which, for once the government was prepared to accept.[24]

Reform

To the extent that, in many cases, the Parliamentary Commissioner has achieved redress for individuals where otherwise they would have been left without a remedy, his office must be regarded as fulfilling a useful function. In a number of ways, however, that usefulness might, it is thought, be increased. To allow complaints to be made directly to the Commissioner rather than through Members of Parliament, and to give greater publicity to his activities might help to raise the public standing of the office.

The rule that complaints can only be made through a member has to some extent been circumvented by the practice of forwarding complaints sent to the Commissioner to the complainant's member and seeking his agreement to the Commissioner dealing with it. The exclusion from his jurisdiction of personnel matters in the civil service and the commercial and contractual dealings of the Government has been regularly criticised by the Commissioner and the Select Committee and by Justice.[25] The Government, however, so far remains unmoved.[26]

Justice has recommended the extension of the Ombudsman system to Nationalised Industries[27] and Prisons.[28]

Health Service Commissioners

The solution adopted in the Parliamentary Commissioner Act 1967 for dealing with complaints against the administration has been extended by subsequent legislation to the National Health Service. Three Health Service Commissioners for England, Wales and Scotland were established in 1972 and 1973.[29] Since their inception all three posts have been held by the Parliamentary Commissioner for Administration. With some slight variation between the 1972 and 1973 Acts, the Health Service Commissioners may investigate alleged instances of maladministration arising out of the provision of medical services under the National Health Services by a wide range of boards and authorities. General practitioners, dentists, chemists and opticians are excluded from the Commissioner's jurisdiction. Nor may any action taken solely as a result of a clinical judgment be investigated. Com-

---

[24] A list of fifty bodies, including the Commission for Racial Equality, the Equal Opportunities Commission, the Arts Council, the Research Councils, Developments Corporations and such other less well known bodies as the Red Deer Commission and The Commissioners of Northern Lighthouses.

[25] *Our Fettered Ombudsman* (1977).

[26] Cmnd. 8274 (1981).

[27] *The Citizen and the Public Agencies* (1976).

[28] *Ante*, p. 516. The Parliamentary Commissioner has a limited jurisdiction in relation to prisons by virtue of his jurisdiction over the Home Office.

[29] National Health Service (Scotland) Act 1972; National Health Service Re-organisation Act 1973. See now National Health Service Act 1977, Part V and National Health Service (Scotland) Act 1978, Part VI. See also the Parliamentary and other Pensions and Salaries Act 1976, s.7.

plaints may be made directly by a person aggrieved and need not be forwarded by a Member of Parliament.

Reports on maladministration within the Health Services have dealt with individual complaints relating to delays in admission to hospital, failure to indicate to patients that they may refuse to be examined in the presence of medical students and allegations of operations carried out without consent, as well as more general matters such as the failure of health departments to issue adequate warnings to doctors and parents on the dangers of whooping cough vaccine.[30]

Northern Ireland

The jurisdiction of the Parliamentary Commissioner extends to Northern Ireland in the case of complaints relating to actions of the United Kingdom Government. Legislation by the then Northern Ireland Parliament introduced a Parliamentary Commissioner for Northern Ireland and a Commissioner for Complaints to whom the public had a right of direct access.[31] The latter Commissioner has jurisdiction over personnel matters, which reflects one of the reasons for the creation of the office, a wish to provide a remedy for allegations of discrimination in employment. A person whom the Commissioner finds to have suffered injustice as the result of maladministration may apply to court for damages and the Commissioner may request the Attorney-General to apply for an injunction or other relief where he concludes that a public body is likely to continue in a course of maladministration. The Northern Ireland Act 1974 provides that the reports of the Northern Irish Parliamentary Commissioner and of the Commissioner for Complaints shall for the future be laid before Parliament at Westminster and complaints shall be made through members of the House of Commons.[32]

Commissions for local administration[33]

The Ombudsman system was extended to local government by the Local Government Act 1974 which established two Commissions for Local Administration, one for England and one for Wales.[34] The Parliamentary Commissioner is a member of each of the Commissions. The jurisdiction of the Commissions extends to local authorities, police authorities, other than the Secretary of State, and water authorities. Complaints of maladministration must be referred to the commissioner responsible for the area in question through a member of the authority against which the complaint is made. If, however, a member refuses to refer a complaint the local commissioner may proceed to investigate it—

---

[30] Parliamentary Commissioner for Administration, 6th report, *Whooping Cough Vaccine* (1977).

[31] Parliamentary Commissioner (Northern Ireland) Act 1969; Commissioner for Complaints (Northern Ireland) Act 1969; K. P. Poole, "The Northern Ireland Commissioner for Complaints" [1972] P.L. 131.

[32] Sched. 1, para. 4.

[33] D. Foulkes, "The Work of the Local Commissioner for Wales" [1978] P.L. 264; D. C. M. Yardley, "Local Ombudsmen in England" [1983] P.L. 522; *The Local Ombudsman—a review of the first five years* (Justice Report, 1980).

[34] The Local Government (Scotland) Act 1975 similarly established a Commissioner for Local Administration in Scotland. In Northern Ireland local government is within the jurisdiction of the Commissioner for Complaints.

as happened, for example, in *R. v. Local Commissioner for Administration for the North and East Area of England ex p. Bradford Metropolitan City Council*.[35] The requirement of an initial reference to a member of a local authority is justified on the ground that it affords the authority an initial opportunity to remedy an alleged wrong before a commissioner becomes involved. It is also said to protect the commissioners from being overwhelmed by unsubstantial complaints. The Act expressly provides that a local commissioner cannot question the merits of a decision taken without maladministration (s.34(3)). In the *Bradford* Case (*supra*) Lord Denning M.R. said, "Parliament did not define 'maladministration.' It deliberately left it to the ombudsman himself to interpret the word as best he could: and to do it by building up a body of case law on the subject." His Lordship then quoted the list of examples given by Mr. Crossman. It was, he added, "a long and interesting list, clearly open-ended, covering the *manner* in which a decision is reached or discretion is exercised: but excluding the merits of the decision itself or of the discretion itself." A Commissioner cannot deal with a complaint relating to any action in respect of which the person aggrieved has a right of appeal or review, whether to the Courts or to a Minister, or any other remedy by way of legal proceedings unless the commissioner is satisfied that it would be unreasonable to expect resort to be had to that right or remedy.

Initially the effectiveness of local commissioners was limited by the interpretation put by the Courts on section 32(3) of the 1974 Act which allowed local authorities to withhold documents on the ground of public interest.[36] That shortcoming has been remedied by amending legislation.[37] A second weakness (shared by other Commissioners, with the exception of the Commissioner for Complaints in Northern Ireland) is that they have no power to remedy injustices caused by maladministration. Local authorities are merely required to consider any reports submitted to them and notify the appropriate commissioner what action, if any, they propose to take. In a number of cases where commissioners found maladministration local authorities have refused to take any action.[38]

Conclusion

There can be no doubt of the continuing popularity of the Ombudsman concept. It is offered as a solution to every problem. The banks and insurance companies have, for instance, introduced their own voluntary systems of dealing with complaints by an Ombudsman. In the case of building societies, an Ombudsman with statutory powers has been created by the Building Societies Act 1986, ss. 83–85. But it should not be overlooked how firmly governments resist attempts to extend the jurisdiction of the Parliamentary Commissioner into the vary areas where it might be thought that he could be effective. It is difficult to avoid the feeling that the "filtering" or "screening" of complaints by

[35] [1979] Q.B. 287 (C.A.).
[36] *Re a Complaint against Liverpool City Council* [1977] 1 W.L.R. 995 (D.C.).
[37] Local Government Planning and Land Act 1980, s.184.
[38] 92 cases (out of 1,500) over ten years.

members of Parliament and councillors has little to do with concern for the best interests of the complainants. Nor should it be forgotten that the provision of a remedy may be a poor substitute for the elimination of a problem.

CHAPTER 33

JUDICIAL CONTROL OF PUBLIC AUTHORITIES: I. LIABILITY[1]

We consider in this chapter the general principles in accordance with which the courts control the exercise of powers by public authorities. The remedies available for this purpose are dealt with in the next chapter, and civil proceedings by and against the Crown in Chapter 35. In the terminology of Lord Diplock in *O'Reilly* v. *Mackman*[2] Part I of this chapter deals with judicial control through Public Law while Part II deals with control through the mechanism of Private Law.

I. PUBLIC LAW: EXCESS OR ABUSE OF POWERS

Judicial control of powers

The exercise by public bodies of powers conferred on them by statute or by the common law[3] may be open to review in the courts on a number of grounds. As a general principle it can be said that the courts do not concern themselves with the wisdom of a particular decision; they cannot, as it is said, examine the merits. They can, however, examine whether a public body has exceeded the powers given to it so that its decision is *ultra vires,* or whether the procedure followed in reaching a decision was flawed by a failure to observe the principles of natural justice. A decision may also be open to review because it is one that no reasonable body could have reached: the *Wednesbury*[4] principle. For present purposes it is unnecessary to consider whether all these grounds should be regarded as aspects of the *ultra vires* doctrine.[5] In the following pages the various bases for judicial review will be examined by reference to the traditional terminology which formerly was to be found in the case law. Reference must, however, be made to Lord Diplock's new terminology which has begun to appear in judgments and which, as will be seen, may be of importance if it extends the scope of judicial review. In the *G.C.H.Q.* Case Lord Diplock said:

> "Judicial review has I think developed to a stage today when . . . one can conveniently classify under three heads the grounds upon which administrative action is subject to control by judicial review. The first ground I would call *"illegality,"* the second *"irrationality,"* and the third *"procedural impropriety."* That is not to say that

---

[1] See S. A. de Smith, *Judicial Review of Administrative Action* (4th ed., 1980); C. T. Emery and B. Smythe, *Judicial Review* [1986]. For the position in Scotland see the title, Administrative Law, The Laws of Scotland (1987), Vol. i.

[2] [1983] 2 A.C. 237.

[3] *Council of Civil Service Unions* v. *Minister for the Civil Service* [1985] A.C. 374.

[4] *Associated Provincial Picture Houses* v. *Wednesbury Corporation* [1948] 1 K.B. 223; *post,* p. 669.

[5] Lord Diplock described review on the *Wednesbury* grounds of unreasonableness as involving a type of *ultra vires: British Airways* v. *Laker Airways* [1985] A.C. 58.

further development on a case by case basis may not in course of time add further grounds."[6]

Within a year that classification had been described as "a valuable and already 'classical' but certainly not exhaustive analysis of the grounds upon which courts will embark on the judicial review of an administrative power exercised by a public officer."[7]

Ultra Vires rule

A Minister, a local authority and any public body may only validly exercise powers within the limits conferred on them by common law or statute. A decision may fall outside those powers and so be *ultra vires* because the body concerned has attempted to deal with a matter outside the range of the power conferred on it—substantive *ultra vires*—or because it has failed, in reaching its decision, to follow a prescribed procedure—procedural *ultra vires*.

In so far as the common law powers of public authorities are part of the royal prerogative the jurisdiction of the courts over them was asserted in such cases as the *Case of Monopolies*[8] the *Case of Proclamations*[9] and *The Zamora*.[10] In the G.C.H.Q. Case the House of Lords clearly affirmed that the exercise of prerogative powers is subject to judicial review, although that case was concerned with natural justice (or procedural impropriety), where the powers relate to matters which are "justiciable."[11]

As regards the innumerable statutory powers, the question is one of interpretation of the statute concerned. The acts of a competent authority must fall within the four corners of the powers given by the legislature.[12] The court must examine the nature, objects and scheme of the legislation, and in the light of that examination must consider what is the exact area over which powers are given by the section under which the competent authority purports to act.[13]

In *Attorney-General* v. *Fulham Corporation*,[14] for example it was held that a local authority which had power under the Baths and Wash-houses Acts 1846 to 1878 to establish baths, wash-houses and open

---

[6] *Council of Civil Service Unions* v. *Minister for the Civil Service* [1985] A.C. 374, 410. One development to which Lord Diplock referred specifically was the possible recognition of the principle known to the European Court of Justice as proportionality: see, for example, *R.* v. *Intervention Board for Agricultural Produce ex p. E. D. & F. Man (Sugar) Ltd.* [1986] 2 All E.R. 115. The decision of the Court of Appeal in *R.* v. *Barnsley Metropolitan Borough Council ex p. Hook* [1976] 1 W.L.R. 1052 has been cited as an application of the principle by an English court: L. Neville Brown, "General Principles of Law and the English Legal System," *New Perspectives for a Common Law of Europe* (1978) 171, 183.

[7] *R.* v. *Secretary of State for the Environment ex p. Nottinghamshire C.C.* [1986] A.C. 240, *per* Lord Simon.

[8] (1602) 11 Co.Rep. 84b.

[9] (1610) 12 Co.Rep. 74.

[10] [1916] 2 A.C. 77.

[11] *C.C.S.U.* v. *Minister for the Civil Service* [1985] A.C. 374; *ante*, p. 265.

[12] *Per* Lord Greene M.R. in *Carltona Ltd.* v. *Commissioners of Works* [1943] 2 All E.R. 560, 564.

[13] *Per* Sachs J., in *Commissioners of Customs and Excise* v. *Cure and Deeley Ltd.* [1962] 1 Q.B. 340.

[14] [1921] 1 Ch. 440.

bathing places was not entitled to carry on the business of a laundry, and was acting *ultra vires* in washing or partly washing customers' clothes as distinct from providing facilities for persons to wash their own clothes.

A more controversial and difficult example is provided by *Bromley L.B.C.* v. *G.L.C.*[15] where the legality of a grant by the G.L.C. to the London Transport Executive was challenged on a number of grounds. The House of Lords held, *inter alia*, that the grant was *ultra vires* because the authority did not have the power to make grants to the Transport Executive merely for the purpose of reducing fares. In *Re Westminster City Council*[16] the House of Lords held that attempts by the G.L.C. in the last months of its existence to provide funding for future years for the Inner London Education Authority and an array of voluntary bodies was *ultra vires*.

Delay in exercising a statutory power, if contrary to express or implied requirements in the relevant Act, may invalidate the decision on the ground of *ultra vires*.[17]

Legislative Powers

Delegated legislation has been held void on the ground of *ultra vires* in a number of cases. In *Chester* v. *Bateson*,[18] it was held that a regulation made by the Minister under the Defence of the Realm Act 1914 was *ultra vires* in that it made it an offence to take, without the consent of the

---

[15] [1983] A.C. 768; "An ultra vires case which involved difficult questions of construction of some obscurely worded statutory provisions"; *Pickwell* v. *Camden L.B.C.* [1983] 1 All E.R. 602, 628 *per* Ormrod L.J. See further: PVB, (1982) 98 L.Q.R. 177; J. Dignan, "Policy-Making, Local Authorities and the Courts," (1983) 99 L.Q.R. 605. A subsequent scheme for reducing fares was approved by the Divisional Court in *R.* v. *London Transport Executive ex p. G.L.C.* [1983] Q.B. 484. Overall control of the LTE was transferred to the Secretary of State for Transport by the London Regional Transport Act 1984. The Secretary of State was no more successful than the G.L.C. in attempting to exercise his powers: *R.* v. *Secretary of State for Transport, ex p. G.L.C.*. [1985] 3 All E.R. 300. The sequel was further legislation: the London Regional Transport (Amendment) Act 1985.

[16] [1983] 1 A.C 768. In the case of the voluntary bodies the House, in reaching its conclusion, had to distinguish its own previous decision in *Manchester C.C.* v. *Greater Manchester C.C.* (1980) 78 L.G.R. 560; something which Lord Bridge found himself unable to do.

[17] *Simpsons Motor Sales (London) Ltd.* v. *Hendon Corporation* [1963] Ch. 57, 82–83 *per* Upjohn L.J.; cited and approved [1964] A.C. 1088, 1117; *Collector of Land Revenue South West District Penang* v. *Kam Giu Paik* [1986] 1 W.L.R. 412 (P.C.).

[18] [1920] 1 K.B. 829 (D.C.). Applied to invalidate a Home Office standing order restricting access to solicitors by prisoners in *R.* v. *Secretary of State for the Home Dept. ex p. Anderson* [1984] Q.B. 778 (D.C.). And see *Att.-Gen.* v. *Wilts United Dairies* (1921) 91 L.J.K.B. 897; (1921) 37 T.L.R. 884 (H.L.), no authority to impose charges; *Utah Construction & Engineering Pty Ltd.* v. *Pataky* [1966] A.C. 629 (P.C.), power to make regulations relating to "the manner of carrying out excavation work" did not extend to imposing an absolute duty of care on employers; *Hotel and Catering Industry Training Board* v. *Automobile Proprietary* [1969] 1 W.L.R. 697; [1969] 2 All E.R. 582 (H.L.), power to establish training boards for persons "in any activities of industry or commerce" did not extend to persons employed by private clubs. For an unsuccessful attempt to claim that regulations were *ultra vires* because of vagueness and arbitrariness see *McEldowney* v. *Forde* [1971] A.C. 632 (H.L.); discussed, D. N. MacCormick, "Delegated Legislation and Civil Liberty" (1970) 86 L.Q.R. 171.

Minister, any proceedings in the courts for the recovery of possession of houses occupied by workmen employed on war production in special areas so long as they continued to pay their rent and to observe the other conditions of the tenancy. In *Commissioners of Customs and Excise v. Cure and Deeley*[19] a purchase tax regulation which provided that if any person furnished an incomplete return the Commissioners might determine the amount of tax appearing to them to be due and demand payment thereof, which amount should be deemed to be proper tax due unless within seven days it was shown *to the satisfaction of the Commissioners* that some other amount was due, was held *ultra vires* the Finance (No. 2) Act 1940. In *Daymond v. Plymouth C.C.*[20] the House of Lords held that a power to fix such charges as a water authority might "think fit" did not authorise the making of an Order levying charges for sewage services on the occupiers of properties which were not connected to public sewers.

The fact that a rule has been laid before the Houses and not been annulled does not bar review by the courts,[21] and it is immaterial that a Statutory Instrument has been affirmed by a resolution of both Houses.

Where the enabling Act prescribes a particular *procedure* for the exercise of a power, the exercise of the power may be void if that procedure is not followed.[22] In *Agricultural Horticultural and Forestry Industry Training Board v. Aylesbury Mushrooms Ltd.*[23] the Minister purported to make an industrial training order under the Industrial Training Act 1964, s.1(4) which required him, before making an order to "consult any organisation," appearing to him to be representative of substantial numbers of employers engaged in the activities concerned. . . . " Donaldson J. held that failure to consult the body representing mushroom growers rendered the order in question invalid as against mushroom growers.

In considering the effect of procedural irregularities the Courts distinguish between mandatory requirements, breach of which results in

---

[19] [1962] 1 Q.B. 340. The Purchase Tax Act 1963, s.27(2), later provided that where a person did not keep proper accounts and the Commissioners estimated the amount of tax due, the amount should be recoverable unless *in any action relating thereto* the person liable proved the amount properly due and that amount was less than the amount estimated. For a more recent example see *R. v. Customs and Excise Commissioners ex p. Hedges & Butler Ltd.* [1986] 2 All E.R. 164.

[20] [1976] A.C. 609. See now Water Charges Act 1976; *South West Water Authority v. Rumbles* [1984] 1 W.L.R. 800 (C.A.).

[21] *Mackay v. Marks* [1916] 2 I.R. 241; *Institute of Patents Agents v. Lockwood* [1894] A.C. 347, 366; *Hoffman La Roche v. Secretary of State for Trade and Industry* [1975] A.C. 295; *Laker Airways Ltd. v. Department of Trade* [1977] Q.B. 643 (C.A.); cf. *Bowles v. Bank of England* [1913] 1 Ch. 57.

[22] See *R. v. Minister of Health ex p. Yaffe* [1930] 2 K.B. 98 (failure to follow appropriate procedure at local inquiry invalidated subsequent Ministerial order). Cf. *Minister of Health v. The King (on the prosecution of Yaffe)* [1931] A.C. 494, where the House of Lords approved the principle laid down by the Court of Appeal but upheld the scheme.

[23] [1972] 1 W.L.R. 190. See too *R. v. Secretary of State for Transport ex p. Philippine Airlines, The Times* Oct. 17 (1984) (C.A.). For an unsuccessful attempt to invoke procedural *ultra vires* see *Port Louis Corporation v. Att.-Gen. of Mauritius* [1965] A.C. 1111 (P.C.). See too *R. v. Post Office ex p. Association of Scientific, Technical and Managerial Staffs* [1981] I.C.R. 76 (C.A.); *R v. Secretary of State for Trade and Industry, ex p. Ian Kynaston Ford* (1985) 4 Tr. L. 150.

invalidity, and directory requirements, breach of which does not result in invalidity. The more important the requirement, the more likely it is that it will be held to be mandatory. To attempt to deduce clear principles from the case law is, however, impossible.[24] Moreover, even where the court holds that a mandatory requirement has not been complied with, relief may be withheld.[25]

Byelaws are *ultra vires* if they are repugnant to the general law; but it is not easy to decide in what circumstances a byelaw will be held invalid on that ground. It obviously must not be contrary to statute, although it can, of course, forbid what would otherwise be lawful at common law. In *Powell* v. *May*[26] a byelaw made by a county council forbidding generally any person to frequent or use any street or other public place for the purpose of bookmaking or betting or wagering, was held invalid as being repugnant to the Street Betting Act 1906 and the Betting and Lotteries Act 1934, which would have allowed the appellant bookmaker certain defences.

Where a statutory instrument or byelaw contains *ultra vires* provisions it may be possible to sever the offending portions and preserve other parts of the instrument or byelaw which fall within the powers conferred by Parliament.[27]

Judicial Powers

A tribunal or other body with a limited jurisdiction acts *ultra vires* if it purports to decide a case falling outside its jurisdiction. Thus a rent tribunal which is given power to fix the rent of a dwelling house cannot make an order relating to premises which are let for business purposes.[28] If such a tribunal erroneously concludes that the facts of a case fall within its jurisdiction its decision is *ultra vires* and can be set aside by the courts. Facts which must exist if a tribunal is to exercise its jurisdiction validly are known as *jurisdictional facts*. On matters which do not go to jurisdiction the tribunal may err without exceeding its jurisdiction. No satisfactory test has ever been suggested to distinguish jur-

---

[24] "The law relating to the effect of failure to comply with procedural requirements resembles an inextricable tangle of loose ends"; de Smith, *Judicial Review of Administrative Action* p. 142. For recent discussions of the distinction see *Coney* v. *Choyce* [1975] 1 All E.R. 979; *London & Clydeside Estates Ltd.* v. *Aberdeen D.C.* [1980] 1 W.L.R. 182 (H.L.); *R.* v. *St. Edmundsbury B.C. ex p. Investors Ltd.* [1985] 1 W.L.R. 1168; *Steeples* v. *Derbyshire C.C.* [1984] 3 All E.R. 468; *Walsh* v. *Barlow* [1985] 1 W.L.R. 90.

[25] *R.* v. *Secretary of State for Social Services ex p. Association of Metropolitan Authorities* [1986] 1 W.L.R. 1.

[26] [1946] K.B. 330. And see *Thomas* v. *Sutters* [1900] 1 Ch. 10; *White* v. *Morley* [1899] 2 Q.B. 30; *Gentel* v. *Rapps* [1902] 1 K.B. 160, 166; *R. and W. Paul Ltd.* v. *Wheat Commission* [1917] A.C. 139.

[27] *Dunkley* v. *Evans* [1981] 1 W.L.R. 1522 (D.C.). For severance of *ultra vires* condition attached to grant of planning permission see *R.* v. *North Hertfordshire D.C. ex p. Cobbold* [1985] 3 All E.R. 486. The Court cannot, however, rewrite a decision to render it *intra vires*: there must be a clearly divisible part of an order or instrument which is invalid and a separable valid part: *R.* v. *Secretary of State for the Environment ex p. G.L.C.* [1985] 3 All E.R. 300.

[28] *R.* v. *Hackney, Islington and Stoke Newington Rent Tribunal ex p. Keats* [1951] 2 K.B. 15n. See too *White and Collins* v. *Minister of Health* [1939] 2 K.B. 838; *supra*, p. 462 for immigration cases.

isdictional from non-jurisdictional facts but there is no doubt that the courts use the distinction as the basis for exercising their supervisory control.[29]

Since *Anisminic Ltd.* v. *Foreign Compensation Commission*[30] it has also been the law that a tribunal acting within its jurisdictional limits may act *ultra vires* if it errs in applying the relevant law to the facts. Prior to that case it had been believed that errors of law made after embarking on consideration of a matter within a tribunal's jurisdiction could not deprive it of jurisdiction.[31] Such errors were only open to review if they were apparent from the formal statement of the tribunal's decision: error of law on the fact of the record.[32] It is not yet clear whether *Anisminic* has established that every error of law amounts to an excess of jurisdiction, in which case error of law on the face of the record no longer has any significance. In the case of tribunals, as distinguished from courts of limited jurisdiction (such as county courts) there is support for the wide view of *Anisminic* in *Re A Company*.[33] On the other hand the Privy Council in *South East Asia Fire Bricks Sdn. Bhd.* v. *Non-Metallic Mineral Products Manufacturing Employees Union*[34] has affirmed the continued distinction between jurisdictional and non-jurisdictional errors.

Abuse of power

Statutes often confer upon ministers, local authorities and other public bodies discretionary powers, for example in the area of planning law or when a trade or occupation is subject to a system of licensing. The courts, in the absence of a statutory right of appeal, cannot review the correctness of a decision made in the exercise of such a discretionary power. They may, however, interfere where the power has been improperly exercised so that the person exercising the power has acted in a way not intended by Parliament. Abuse of power, in this sense, includes exercising a power for an unauthorised purpose,[35] disregard-

---

[29] See de Smith, *Judicial Review of Administrative Action* (4th ed.) 114; Rubinstein, *Jurisdiction and Illegality* (1965) pp. 212–218; D. M. Gordon, (1929) 45 L.Q.R. 459; (1944) 60 L.Q.R. 250; (1960) 76 L.Q.R. 506; (1966) 82 L.Q.R. 263 and 515. The distinction is defended by Bentley, [1962] P.L. 7.

[30] [1969] 2 A.C. 147.

[31] A view often expressed in the words of Lord Sumner in *R. v. Nat Bell Liquors Ltd.* [1922] A.C. 128, 151. (P.C.)

[32] This head of review raises the difficult matter of distinguishing between questions of law and questions of fact. C. T. Emery and B. Smythe, "Error of Law in Administrative Law" (1984) 100 L.Q.R. 612; J. Beatson, "The Scope of Judicial Review for Error of Law" (1984) 4 O.J.L.S. 22; G. Pitt, "Law, Fact and Casual Workers" (1985) 101 L.Q.R. 217; *post*, p. 695.

[33] [1981] A.C. 374.

[34] [1981] A.C. 363. The Privy Council preferred the dissent of Geoffrey Lane L.J. in *Pearlman* v. *Harrow School Governors* [1979] Q.B. 56 to the view expressed in that case by Lord Denning M.R.

[35] E.g. *R. v. Leigh* [1897] 1 Q.B. 132; power to require pensioner to present himself for medical examination was used to attempt to secure L's return to the United Kingdom to subject him to the jurisdiction of the Bankruptcy Court. See too *Webb* v. *Minister of Housing and Local Government* [1965] 1 W.L.R. 755; *Westminster Bank* v. *Minister of Housing and Local Government* [1971] A.C. 508; H. W. R. Wade (1970) 86 L.Q.R. 165; *R. v. Hillingdon L.B.C. ex p. Royco Homes* [1974] Q.B. 720.

ing relevant considerations in reaching a decision[36] or taking into account irrelevant considerations.[37]

Even where a discretion seems unfettered the courts will interfere where it has been exercised in a way which thwarts or frustrates the objects of the Act conferring the power: *Padfield* v. *Minister of Agriculture, Fisheries and Food.*[38] A Minister possessing an apparently unlimited power to revoke licences has been held not to be entitled to use that power to revoke licences bought before the date of an announced increase in licence fees.[39]

It cannot be assumed merely from a Minister's refusal to give reasons for the way he has exercised a discretionary power that he has reached his decision by taking into account factors which he ought to have ignored or that he has disregarded factors which he ought to have regarded as relevant.[40]

Abuse of power may be either in good faith or in bad faith. An authority acts in bad faith if it acts dishonestly, in order to achieve an object other than that for which it believes the power has been given; or maliciously, if it acts out of personal animosity. Thus a local authority which has the power of compulsory acquisition of land for civic extensions or improvements would not be entitled to acquire compulsorily if its purpose were merely to reap the benefit of enhanced values (*Municipal Council of Sydney* v. *Campbell*[41]); nor may an education authority which has power to dismiss teachers on educational grounds dismiss them in order to effect economy (*Hanson* v. *Radcliffe Urban District Council*[42]). The court may infer the purpose for which the enabling Act granted the power, and hold that the power has been abused, *e.g.* where a local authority referred tenancies in bulk to a rent tribunal so as in effect to turn the tribunal into a general rent-fixing agency (*R.* v. *Paddington Rent Tribunal ex p. Bell Properties Ltd.*[43]). The High Court can control the exercise of statutory powers if they are being exercised otherwise than in accordance with the purpose for which they were conferred. Thus a compulsory purchase order made in 1951 in order to provide a car park was set aside as it was based on a notice to treat served in 1939 for the purpose of widening the street and creating a market hall (*Grice* v. *Dudley Corporation*[44]).

The question is complicated where a power is exercised both for an

---

[36] *R.* v. *Greater Birmingham Appeal Tribunal ex p. Simper* [1974] Q.B. 543; *Grunwick Processing Laboratories* v. *A.C.A.S.* [1978] A.C. 655.

[37] *Short* v. *Poole Corporation* [1926] Ch. 66; the red hair of a teacher clearly irrelevant to consideration of exercise by a local authority of its powers and duties in connection with maintaining "efficient" schools. *Bromley L.B.C.* v. *G.L.C.* [1983] A.C. 768. (G.L.C. improperly influenced by terms of policital manifesto).

[38] [1968] A.C. 997, *post*, p. 689.

[39] *Congreve* v. *Home Office* [1976] Q.B. 629. For a critical comment see G. Ganz, [1976] P.L. 14.

[40] *Gouriet* v. *Union of Post Office Workers* [1978] A.C. 435; *British Airways* v. *Laker Airways* [1985] A.C. 58.

[41] [1925] A.C. 338.

[42] [1922] 2 Ch. 490.

[43] [1949] 1 K.B. 606.

[44] [1958] Ch. 339. And see *Webb* v. *Minister of Housing and Local Government* [1965] 1 W.L.R. 755; [1965] 2 All E.R. 195 (C.A.), *supra*.

authorised and an unauthorised purpose.[45] The courts on the whole have tried to find the true purpose for which the power was exercised. Thus in *Westminster Corporation* v. *L. & N. W. Ry.*,[46] where the local authority had power to construct underground public conveniences, the court considered whether this was the true purpose which the Corporation sought to affect in acquiring land compulsorily, or whether it was merely a colourable device to enable it to make a subway for pedestrians. Where a public body has exercised a power to achieve a legitimate purpose, the fact that incidentally it achieves another purpose of its own which is not a relevant objective in the eyes of the law does not invalidate the decision. But where the purpose of the exercise is improper it is irrelevant that a legitimate purpose is also served. In *R.* v. *I.L.E.A. ex p. Westminster C.C.*[47] Glidewell J. had to consider the legality of the expenditure of funds by I.L.E.A. under the Local Government Act 1972, s.142 which authorises expenditure on the publication of "information on matters relating to local government." The learned judge concluded that the publication of certain facts by ILEA was intended not merely to inform but to persuade the public to accept ILEA's views about the wisdom of the Government's education policies. The expenditure was held to be unlawful; persuasion not information had been the true purpose of the authority; its decision had been materially affected by its wish to pursue an unauthorised objective. The courts tend to avoid the question of motive, which seems to be immaterial if the purpose is within the statute (*Robins & Son Ltd.* v. *Minister of Health*[48]), for they must not usurp the discretion given to administrative authorities.

A difficulty which has arisen in a number of cases is the extent to which a body exercising a discretionary power has the right in reaching decisions in individual cases to have regard to a general policy which it has formulated. Clearly, licensing justices who refuse all applications for licences because they have a policy of attempting to stop the sale of alcohol are not exercising the discretion vested in them.[49] But concern about drunkenness and hooliganism in the late evening may justify a general policy of not granting late licences provided that each application is genuinely considered on its merits.[50] In the words of Ackner L.J. in *R.* v. *Secretary of State for the Environment, ex p. Brent L.B.C.*[51] it is not necessary that each case must be approached with an open mind

---

[45] See *e.g. Earl Fitzwilliam's Wentworth Estate Co.* v. *Minister of Town and Country Planning* [1951] 2 K.B. 284 (C.A.); [1952] A.C. 362 (H.L.).

[46] [1905] A.C. 426.

[47] [1986] 1 W.L.R. 28. See also *R.* v. *Broadcasting Complaints Commission ex p. Owen* [1985] Q.B. 1153, 1177 *per* May L.J.; decision lawful even although reached in reliance on a reason bad in law if Commission would have reached the same decision in reliance on other valid reasons.

[48] [1939] 1 K.B. 537.

[49] *R.* v. *L.C.C. ex p. Corrie* [1918] 1 K.B. 68. See too *Sagnata Investments* v. *Norwich Corporation* [1971] 2 Q.B. 614.

[50] *R.* v. *Torbay Licensing Justices ex p. White* [1980] 2 All E.R. 25. See too *Docherty* v. *South Tyneside Borough, The Times* July 3, 1982; *R.* v. *Secretary of State for the Home Dept., ex p. Bennett, The Times*, August 18, 1986 (C.A.). The leading authority for the legality of the adoption in principle of a policy is *British Oxygen* v. *Board of Trade* [1971] A.C. 616. For a survey of the problem see D. J. Galligan, "The Nature and Function of Policy Within Discretionary Power," [1976] P.L. 332.

[51] [1982] Q.B. 593 (D.C.).

in the sense of an empty mind but the mind of the person exercising the discretion "must be kept 'ajar.' "

Unreasonableness

The requirement that public bodies vested with statutory powers must exercise them reasonably was asserted by Lord Macnaghten in *Westminster Corporation* v. *London and North Western Railway.*[52] Modern discussions of unreasonableness in the field of judicial review almost inevitably, however, start from the judgment of Lord Greene, M.R. in *Associated Provincial Picture Houses Ltd.* v. *Wednesbury Corporation.*[53] The Master of the Rolls cited various defects which might render a decision "unreasonable," of the kind discussed in the previous pages. He went on, however, to envisage the possibility of a decision being open to challenge on the ground that it is unreasonable in the sense that, in the view of the court, it was a decision which no reasonable body could reach. Lord Greene's judgment has been frequently quoted in subsequent cases and is so well known that later judges often refer to "the *Wednesbury* principle" without any further explanation. In *Secretary of State for Education and Science* v. *Tameside Metropolitan Borough Council*[54] the House of Lords referred to Lord Greene's judgment in the *Wednesbury* case and Lord Diplock said,

> "In public law 'unreasonable' as descriptive of the way in which a public authority has purported to exercise a discretion vested in it by statute has become a term of legal art. To fall within this expression it must be conduct which no sensible authority acting with due appreciation of its responsibilities would have decided to adopt."

Because of the frequent citation of Lord Greene's words it is important, as judges have emphasised, not to treat them as a legislative text, not to take them out of context and to read the whole of the judgment since at different places the principle of unreasonableness is defined (or described) in different terms.[55]

Usually where an administrative decision has been quashed on the ground of unreasonableness at least one of the specific vitiating factors already discussed has been held to have been present. Is, however, unreasonableness merely a short hand way of referring to those factors or does it go beyond them? While there is no clear judicial authority the current tendency of the courts to widen the scope of judicial review suggests that it would be unsafe to assert that unreasonableness must be confined to the former of the two meanings, *i.e.* a synonym for the various specific issues discussed earlier. The argument for the widest possible meaning is strengthened—or at least not weakened—by Lord Diplock's choice in the *G.C.H.Q.* case of the term irrationality to refer to

---

[52] [1905] A.C. 426.
[53] [1948] 1 K.B. 223. (Condition attached to licence for opening of cinema on Sunday that no child under the age of 15 should be admitted not unreasonable).
[54] [1977] A.C. 1014. See *post*, p. 698.
[55] *Pickwell* v. *Camden L.B.C.* [1983] Q.B. 962, *per* Ormrod L.J.; *R.* v. *Chief Registrar of Friendly Societies ex p. New Cross Bldg. Society* [1984] 2 W.L.R. 370, *per* Griffiths L.J.; *R.* v. *Home Secretary ex p. Benwell* [1984] 3 W.L.R. 843, 855 *per* Hodgson J.

cases falling within the *Wednesbury* principle.[56] He went on to explain that head of review as applying to "a decision which is so outrageous in its defiance of logic or of accepted moral standards that no sensible person who had applied his mind to the question to be decided could have arrived at it."

Byelaws may be held void for unreasonableness. In *Kruse* v. *Johnson*[57] Lord Russell of Killowen C.J. said that local byelaws are not unreasonable merely because particular judges may think that they go farther than is necessary or convenient; but a court might hold them unreasonable if they were found to be partial or unequal in their operation between classes, or if they were manifestly unjust, disclosed bad faith, or involved such oppressive or gratuitous interference with the rights of those subject to them as could find no justification in the minds of reasonable men. Applying this test, the court held that the byelaw in question, which authorised a householder or police constable to request a person to desist from playing a musical instrument within fifty yards of any dwelling house, was not unreasonable.

In subsequent cases the courts have emphasised the heavy burden lying on anyone who challenges the reasonableness of a byelaw.[58]

It is doubtful whether the principle laid down in *Kruse* v. *Johnson* applies to delegated legislation[59] although it might be open to argument that a particular rule or regulation is so unreasonable that it must be beyond the limits envisaged by Parliament. The special status of Immigration Rules made under the Immigration Act 1971[60] has been held to justify the courts applying to them the test of reasonableness as laid down in *Kruse* v. *Johnson*.[61]

Natural justice: procedural impropriety[62]

Natural justice, at least as that phrase is normally used by lawyers, refers principally to two fundamental principles of procedure: that whoever takes a decision should be impartial, having no personal interest in the outcome of the case (*nemo judex in re sua*) and that a decision

---

[56] *Ante*, p. 669.
[57] [1898] 2 Q.B. 91. "The judgment in *Kruse* v. *Johnson* has been quoted so frequently in subsequent cases that it has almost been erected into a sacred text"; *Belfast Corporation* v. *Daly* [1963] N.I. 78, 88, *per* Black L.J. For byelaws made by non-elected bodies see *Cinnamond* v. *British Airports Authority* [1980] 1 W.L.R. 582; *British Airways Authority* v. *Ashton* [1983] 3 All E.R. 6; *R.* v. *British Airways Authority ex p. Wheatley* [1983] R.T.R. 466 (C.A.).
[58] *Burnley B.C.* v. *England* (1978) 76 L.G.R. 393; 77 L.G.R. 227; *Startin* v. *Solihull M.B.C.* [1979] R.T.R. 228.
[59] *Sparks* v. *Edward Ash Ltd.* [1943] 1 K.B. 222 (C.A.); *Taylor* v. *Brighton B.C.* [1947] K.B. 737 (C.A.). In *Maynard* v. *Osmond* [1977] Q.B. 240 the Court of Appeal rejected a claim that a ministerial regulation was unreasonable; hence the question of invalidity on that ground did not arise. See further A Wharam, "Judicial Control of Delegated Legislation: the Test of Reasonableness" (1973) 36 M.L.R. 611; J. P. Casey, "Ministerial Orders and Review for Unreasonableness" [1978] P.L. 130.
[60] *Ante*, p. 457.
[61] *R.* v. *Immigration Appeal Tribunal ex p. Begum, The Times*, July 24, 1986.
[62] D. J. Hewitt, *Natural Justice* (1972); Paul Jackson, *Natural Justice* (2nd ed., 1979); H. H. Marshall, *Natural Justice* (1959); G. P. Flick, *Natural Justice: Principles and Practical Application* (2nd ed., 1984).

should not be taken until the person affected by it has had an opportunity to state his case (*audi alteram partem*). Natural justice may sometimes be used in a wider sense to refer to a number of fundamental principles which are said to underlie the common law[63] but in these pages attention will be directed to natural justice in its narrower sense.

The principles of natural justice were originally applied to the process by which courts themselves made their decisions. A breach of natural justice was one of the grounds on which the decision of a lower court could be upset by a higher court. In the course of time these principles came to be applied to administrative authorities.

There is authority for regarding the requirements of "natural justice" as a special part of the *ultra vires* rule, on the ground that a decision made contrary to the principles of natural justice, when the rights of particular individuals are adversely affected, is no decision within the terms of the enabling Act.[64]

1. A man may not be a judge in his own cause

This, said the Committee on Ministers' Powers, is "the first and most fundamental principle of natural justice."[65] Thus in *Dimes* v. *Grand Junction Canal*[66] a decree of Lord Chancellor Cottenham, granting an injunction to a company and confirming its title, was held voidable and set aside by the House of Lords on the ground that he was a shareholder in the company, although it was not suggested that Lord Cottenham was influenced by the interest he had in the company. The interest need not be pecuniary or proprietary. Lord Evershed M.R. once directed that an appeal should be heard by another division of the Court of Appeal on the ground that as Master of the Rolls he was an *ex officio* member of the Church Commissioners for England who were parties to the action.[67] Acquaintance with one of the parties to litigation, preconceived notions on the merits of a dispute or strongly held beliefs may all constitute disqualifying bias.[68] It is contrary to natural justice for the judge to be, in substance, accuser or prosecutor as well.[69]

Any financial interest is sufficient to disqualify a judge on the ground of bias.[70] In other cases, however, a judge is only disqualified if there is

---

[63] *Ong Ah Chuan* v. *Public Prosecutor* [1981] A.C. 648.

[64] *Spackman* v. *Plumstead District Board of Works* (1885) 10 App.Cas. 229, per Lord Selbourne L.C.; *Errington* v. *Minister of Health* [1935] 1 K.B. 249, 268, per Greer L.J., and p. 279, per Maugham L.J. *Cf. General Medical Council* v. *Spackman* [1943] A.C. 627, 640, per Lord Wright; *White* v. *Kuzych* [1951] A.C. 585 (P.C.) per Viscount Simon at p. 600.

[65] (1943) Cmd. 4060, p. 76. See D. E. C. Yale, "*Iudex propria causa*, an historical excursus" (1974) 33 C.L.J. 80.

[66] (1852) 3 H.L.C. 759.

[67] *The Times*, October 30, 1956. *Cf. Hanson* v. *Church Commissioners for England* [1978] Q.B. 823 (C.A.).

[68] But see *R.* v. *Board of Visitors of Frankland Prison ex p. Lewis* [1986] 1 W.L.R. 130: member of Board not disqualified from hearing charge against prisoner despite knowledge of earlier convictions for similar offences arising from considering parole application; duties of Boards such that members must often have prior knowledge of records of prisoners appearing before them.

[69] *Leeson* v. *G.M.C.* (1889) 43 Ch.D. 366; *Law* v. *Chartered Institute of Patent Agents* [1919] 2 Ch. 276.

[70] *R.* v. *Rand* (1866) L.R. 1 Q.B. 230; *Sergeant* v. *Dale* (1877) 2 Q.B.D. 558.

"a real likelihood of bias" or "a reasonable suspicion of bias."[71] It is not necessary to establish that a judge or other person making a decision was in fact biased.[72]

The Courts will not hold a judge (or other person) disqualified from hearing a case because of a general allegation of bias, for example that all judges are prejudiced against laymen who sue solicitors.[73] In hearings before the domestic tribunal of a trades union it might be argued that all the members of the tribunal would favour the union as against the member in dispute with it. Such a general "bias," however, is not disqualifying. But a member of the tribunal who had been involved, for example, in the expulsion of the member against which an appeal was being made would have such a personal interest that he would be disqualified.[74]

In some cases a decision may be quashed not because of the likelihood or reasonable suspicion of bias but on the principle enunciated by Lord Hewart C.J. in *The King* v. *Sussex Justices ex p. McCarthy*.[75] The conviction of McCarthy for a motoring offence was quashed because the clerk to the justices, a member of a firm of solicitors who were to represent the plaintiff in civil proceedings arising out of the collision in connection with which McCarthy was charged, retired with the justices, although in fact he did not give them any advice on the conviction. Lord Hewart L.C.J. said in that case: "A long line of cases shows that it is not merely of some importance, but is of fundamental importance that justice should not only be done but should manifestly and undoubtedly be seen to be done." Where a social worker involved in adoption proceedings retired with the justices their determination was quashed because justice had not been seen to be done.[76]

2. *"Audi alteram partem"*

Each party must have reasonable notice of the case he has to meet; and he must be given an opportunity of stating his case, and answering (if he can) any arguments put forward against it. In criminal cases this elementary principle of justice is expressed in the saying that "no one ought to be condemned unheard." As was quaintly stated in *Dr. Bentley's Case* (1723)[77]: "Even God himself did not pass sentence upon Adam before he was called upon to make his defence."

The maxim *audi alteram partem*, where it applies, does not mean that a

---

[71] It is doubtful if there is any distinction between these two tests: R. v. St. Edmondsbury B.C. [1985] 1 W.L.R. 1168.

[72] Metropolitan Properties v. Lannon [1969] 1 Q.B. 577.

[73] Williams v. Beesley [1973] 1 W.L.R. 1295. See also Rothermere v. The Times [1973] 1 W.L.R. 448.

[74] Roebuck v. N.U.M. (Yorkshire Area) (No. 2) [1978] I.C.R. 676.

[75] [1924] 1 K.B. 256, 259. R. v. Lower Munslow Justices ex p. Pudge [1950] 2 All E.R. 756. See also R. v. East Kerrier Justices ex p. Mundy [1952] 2 Q.B. 719; Practice Note (Justices' Clerks) [1953] 1 W.L.R. 1416; [1953] 2 All E.R. 1306; Metropolitan Properties v. Lannon [1969] 1 Q.B. 577; R. v. Altrincham Justices ex p. Pennington [1975] Q.B. 549.

[76] Re B (Adoption by Parents) [1975] Fam. 127.

[77] R. v. Chancellor of Cambridge University (1716) 1 Str. 557. R. F. V. Heuston has pointed out that divine punishment may be administered without a preliminary hearing: Belshazzar's Feast, Dan v: Essays in Constitutional Law (2nd ed., 1964) p. 185.

person is entitled to be heard orally.[78] Nor does the maxim necessarily mean that a person has the right to have his case determined by the person who heard the evidence at first instance. Thus in *Local Government Board* v. *Arlidge*[79] the House of Lords refused a house owner's application to quash a decision of the Local Government Board confirming a closing order made by a borough council, although he had not been told which members of the Board gave the decision, and had not been given an oral hearing by the Board or allowed to see the report of the inspector. It would, in the view of the House of Lords, be unrealistic and impracticable to expect a large department of state to deal with each case before it in the way in which a court might be expected to.[80] Natural justice requires adequate warning of a hearing and details of the charges to be met in order to allow a party to prepare his case properly.[81] Legal representation is not necessarily essential to a fair hearing.[82] None the less the gravity of a charge, or the consequences of an adverse decision, may require a tribunal to allow legal representation. Lord Denning has suggested that the question must turn, in each case, on the exercise by the tribunal concerned of a genuine discretion as opposed to the application of an inflexible rule.[83] Nor does natural justice require that reasons for decisions should be given.[84]

The importance of natural justice in administrative law lies in the wide range of administrative powers which must be exercised in accordance with the two principles discussed in the previous pages. In *Board of Education* v. *Rice*[85] Lord Loreburn said that to "act in good faith and fairly listen to both sides . . . is a duty lying upon everyone who decides anything." Throughout succeeding years in this century, however, the courts took a more cautious view and only required public bodies to observe the rules of natural justice when they were acting "judicially," a concept which was interpreted restrictively. A decisive change in judicial attitude occurred in *Ridge* v. *Baldwin*.[86] Under the Municipal Corporations Act 1882, s.191(4) a Watch Committee was empowered at any time to suspend or dismiss any borough constable whom the Committee thought to have been negligent in the discharge of his duty or otherwise unfit to carry out his duty. The Chief Constable of Brighton had been acquitted at the Old Bailey on charges of corruption, but the judge in the trial of two of his subordinates cast aspersions on his leadership of the force, and remarked that a new chief constable was needed. The Watch Committee then dismissed him for neglect of

---

[78] *Board of Education* v. *Rice* [1911] A.C. 179 (H.L.), *per* Lord Loreburn L.C. And see *Lloyd* v. *McMahon* [1987] 2 W.L.R. 821 (H.L.).
[79] [1915] A.C. 120.
[80] But see *post* on sub-delegation. The question, in the case of statutory bodies, is one of statutory interpretation.
[81] *Sloan* v. *General Medical Council* [1970] 1 W.L.R. 1130; *R.* v. *Thames Magistrates' Court ex p. Polemis* [1974] 1 W.L.R. 1371.
[82] *Pett* v. *Greyhound Racing Association (No. 2)* [1970] 1 Q.B. 46; *Fraser* v. *Mudge* [1975] 1 W.L.R. 1132 (C.A.); *Maynard* v. *Osmond* [1977] Q.B. 240 (C.A.).
[83] *Enderby Town Football Club* v. *The Football Association* [1971] Ch. 591; J. Alder, "Representation before Tribunals" [1972] P.L. 278.
[84] *R.* v. *Gaming Board for Great Britain ex p. Benaim* [1970] 2 Q.B. 417 (C.A.).
[85] [1911] A.C. 179, 182.
[86] [1964] A.C. 40.

duty, but without formulating any specific charge or giving him an opportunity to be heard except that his solicitor addressed the Committee at one of two meetings. The House of Lords, reversing a unanimous Court of Appeal, gave judgment for the Chief Constable. Their Lordships held that the rules of natural justice applied, so that the Watch Committee ought to have informed him of the charges and given him an opportunity to be heard. Merely to describe a statutory function as "administrative," "judicial," "quasi-judicial," said Lord Reid, is not in itself enough to settle the requirements of natural justice. Where officials and others have power to make decisions affecting the rights of individuals, the rules of natural justice must be observed.

In *Schmidt* v. *Secretary of State for Home Affairs*[87] Lord Denning M.R. extended the scope of natural justice to decisions involving *legitimate expectations*. In subsequent cases the House of Lords has contrasted legitimate expectations in the sphere of public law with rights in the private sphere.[88] A legitimate expectation can arise from past conduct, *e.g.* regularly granting a hearing before issuing licences,[89] or an assurance, *e.g.* that any illegal immigrant who gives himself up to the authorities will not be deported without being given a hearing.[90] There seems no reason why a legitimate expectation cannot exist in the private sphere. A non-statutory body which governs a sport may be bound to grant a hearing to an applicant for a licence if it has done so in the past: *McInnes* v. *Onslow Fane*.[91] Whether a legitimate expectation exists is a question for the court to determine. The hope of a prisoner that the existing rules for granting parole will not be altered does not amount to a legitimate expectation that the Secretary of State will not change them in the exercise of his statutory powers: In *Re Findlay*.[92] An expectation created by an assurance can be terminated by notice.[92a]

Particularly in the context of legitimate expectations the courts, following the lead of Lord Diplock in the *G.C.H.Q.* case,[93] increasingly refer to *procedural impropriety* rather than breach of natural justice. It

[87] [1969] 2 Ch. 149, 170. In *Kioa* v. *West* (1985) 62 A.L.R. 321 Brennan J. said the seed planted by Lord Denning in *Schmidt* had subsequently grown luxuriantly. (The judgments in *Kioa* v. *West* offer exhaustive analyses of the concept of legitimate expectation.) See further, P. Cane, "Natural Justice and Legitimate Expectation" (1980) 54 A.L.J. 546; S. Churches, "Justice and Executive Discretion in Australia" [1980] P.L. 397; K. Mackie, "Expectations and Natural Justice" (1985) 59 A.L.J. 33.

[88] *O'Reilly* v. *Mackman* [1983] 2 A.C. 237; *Council of Civil Service Unions* v. *Minister for the Civil Service* [1985] A.C. 374.

[89] *O'Reilly* v. *Mackman, supra.* (Hearings normally granted to prisoners before revoking remission—to which there is no right—for misconduct); *Council of Civil Service Unions* v. *Minister for Civil Service supra*, per Lord Diplock; *R.* v. *Wear Valley D.C. ex p. Binks* [1985] 2 All E.R. 699; noted (1986) 102 L.Q.R. 24.

[90] *Att.-Gen. of Hong Kong* v. *Ng Yuen Shiu* (1983) 2 A.C. 629 (P.C.); noted (1983) 99 L.Q.R. 499; *R.* v. *Liverpool Corporation ex p. Liverpool Taxi Fleet Operations' Association* [1972] 2 Q.B. 299.

[91] [1978] 1 W.L.R. 1520.

[92] [1985] A.C. 319. Nor can landowners rely on the more generous terms of treaty when land is compulsorily acquired under the less generous terms of legislation: an "elementary fallacy" that treaties give rise to rights enforceable in British courts: *Winfat Enterprise (H.K.) Co. Ltd.* v. *Att.-Gen. of Hong Kong* [1985] A.C. 733. (The full background is to be found in [1983] H.K.L.R. 211; [1984] H.K.L.R. 32.)

[92a] *Hughes* v. *D.H.S.S.* [1985] A.C. 776.

[93] *Council of Civil Service Unions* v. *Minister for the Civil Service, supra.*

has been objected that it is "hard on that old faithful friend [Natural Justice] which has rendered such signal service, if it is now to be cast aside."[94] The new phrase, however, seems to provide grounds of review going beyond what traditionally had been regarded as constituting breaches of natural justice. Lord Diplock in the *G.C.H.Q.* case included within procedural impropriety breach of statutory rules of procedure which did not necessarily amount to a breach of natural justice. Later cases suggest the phrase can cover various forms of "unfairness," such as going back on an assurance,[95] giving misleading advice on the grounds on which a minister exercises his discretion[96] or the unreasonable manner in which a decision is reached.[97]

Sub-delegation of powers[98]

The prima facie rule is that a person or body to whom powers are entrusted may not delegate them to another, *delegatus non potest delegare*[99]—unless expressly or impliedly authorised to do so.[1] Thus in *Allingham* v. *Minister of Agriculture*[2] a Divisional Court held that the Bedfordshire War Agricultural Committee, to which the Minister of Agriculture had validly delegated his power under Defence Regulations to give directions with respect to the cultivation of land, and which had decided that sugar beet should be grown on eight acres of the appellant's land, had no power to delegate to their executive officer the power to specify the particular field to be cultivated. On the other hand, in *Smith* v. *London Transport Executive*[3] the Executive was validly acting as delegate of the British Transport Commission in operating a bus service. Certain powers, such as that conferred by Defence Regulations on the Home Secretary to intern persons of hostile origin or association,[4] must be exercised by the Minister personally; but generally it is contemplated that a Minister may authorise civil servants in his department to perform routine administrative functions on his behalf.[5] This is not delegation in the strict sense, for the act of the official is really the act of the Minister, who retains control and responsibility. In *Woollett* v. *Minister of Agriculture and Fisheries*,[6] where members of an agricultural land tribunal were to be appointed by the Minister, it was held that they could be appointed by X on behalf of the Minister, but not by X in

94 H.W.R. Wade, (1985) 101 L.Q.R. 153, 155.
95 *R.* v. *I.R.C. ex p. Preston* [1985] A.C. 835; *post* p. 676.
96 *R.* v. *Home Secretary ex p. Asif Khan* [1984] 1 W.L.R. 1337. ("Bad and grossly unfair administration . . . positively cruel"; *per* Parker L.J. at p. 1348).
97 *Wheeler* v. *Leicester City Council* [1985] A.C. 1054.
98 See D. Lanham, "Delegation and the Alter Ego Principle," (1984) 100 L.Q.R. 587.
99 *Delegata potestas non potest delegari*: 2 Co.Inst. 597.
1 Building Act 1984, s.13, for example, expressly provides that the Secretary of State may delegate to "a person or body" his powers under s.12 to approve particular building materials as satisfying statutory requirements.
2 [1948] 1 All E.R. 780 (D.C.). And see *Ellis* v. *Dubowski* [1921] 3 K.B. 621.
3 [1951] A.C. 555 (H.L.).
4 See *Liversidge* v. *Anderson* [1942] A.C. 206 (H.L.).
5 *Carltona Ltd.* v. *Commissioners of Works* [1943] 2 All E.R. 560 (requisitioning of land); *R.* v. *Skinner* [1968] 2 Q.B. 700 (C.A.) (approval of breathalyser); *Re Golden Chemical Products Ltd.* [1976] Ch. 300 (presentation of winding-up petition under s.35 of the Companies Act 1967).
6 [1955] 1 Q.B. 103.

his capacity as the secretary of the tribunal. In *Vine* v. *National Dock Labour Board*,[7] where the Board had purported to delegate its disciplinary powers to a committee, the House of Lords said that both the nature of the duty and the character of the person to whom it is entrusted have to be considered. Judicial authority cannot normally be sub-delegated; administrative powers sometimes may but often may not be sub-delegated; as regards the disciplinary powers in this case, whether called judicial or quasi-judicial, their Lordships held that they could not be sub-delegated.[8]

When a power has been validly delegated by one authority to another, the exercise of the power by the latter must be within the power delegated by the former,[9] and any conditions attached to the delegation must be complied with.[10]

Estoppel

The converse of the problem discussed in the preceding sections is that which arises where an individual maintains that a public body's exercise of a statutory power is valid while the authority concerned seeks to challenge its validity. A dispute of this nature raises the question of the extent to which the doctrine of estoppel is applicable to public authorities.[11] It might seem unjust that a citizen who has erected a building in the belief, induced by an official of a planning authority, that everything was in order should have to demolish that building because the authority alleges that the official had no power to grant permission.[12] On the other hand, to apply the doctrine of estoppel to public bodies might be thought to destroy the *ultra vires* doctrine by allowing them to extend their powers by making representations which would bind them by estoppel.[13] Recent developments in judicial review have suggested a solution to the dilemma. For a public body to attempt to go back on a decision which it has made might be "unfair" and judicial review would be available where the action in question would have been equivalent to a breach of a representation giving rise to an estoppel in the case of a private individual: *R.* v. *Inland Revenue Com-*

---

[7] [1957] A.C. 488; approving *Barnard* v. *National Dock Labour Board* [1953] 2 Q.B. 18 (C.A.).

[8] See also *Re S (A Barrister)* [1970] 1 Q.B. 160; *R.* v. *Race Relations Board ex p. Selvarajan* [1975] 1 W.L.R. 1686; Paul Jackson (1974) 90 L.Q.R. 158; (1975) 91 L.Q.R. 469. For valid subdelegation of an administrative power see *Meaden* v. *Wood, The Times*, April 30, 1985 (D.C.) (Home Secretary as police authority, entitled to delegate regulation of street collections under statutory powers to Commissioner of Metropolitan Police.)

[9] *Smith* v. *London Transport Executive, ante.*

[10] *Blackpool Corporation* v. *Locker* [1948] 1 K.B. 349 (C.A.): Minister delegated to local authorities power to requisition houses, subject to making provision for disposal of furniture; requisition *ultra vires* because conditions not complied with.

[11] For the position of the Crown, see *post*, p. 714.

[12] *Wells* v. *Minister of Housing and Local Government* [1967] 1 W.L.R. 1000; *Lever Finance* v. *Westminster L.B.C.* [1971] 1 Q.B. 222. See also *H.T.V.* v. *Price Commission* [1976] I.C.R. 170; *Re Liverpool Taxi Owners Association* [1972] 2 Q.B. 299.

[13] *Minister of Agriculture and Fisheries* v. *Mathews* [1950] 1 K.B. 148; *Rhyl U.D.C.* v. *Rhyl Amusements* [1959] 1 W.L.R. 465; *Southend-on-Sea Corporation* v. *Hodgson (Wickford)* [1962] 1 Q.B. 416 (D.C.) *Western Fish Products Ltd.* v. *Penwith D.C.* [1981] 2 All E.R. 204; (1978) 77 L.G.R. 185, (C.A.); *Rootkin* v. *Kent C.C.* [1981] 1 W.L.R. 1186 (C.A.) See further P. P. Craig, "Representations by Public Bodies" (1977) 93 L.Q.R. 398; G. Ganz, "Estoppel and *Res Judicata* in Administrative Law" [1965] P.L. 237; M. A. Fazal, "Reliability of Official Acts and Advice" [1972] P.L. 43.

missioners ex p. Preston.[14] Another way of reaching a similar result is to say that the re-opening of a decision is "unreasonable" or "irrational": *R. v. West Glamorgan C.C. ex p. Gherssary.*[15] The limits to this new approach are, at present, unclear. It could hardly be applied where a public body had attempted to do what it had no power to do at all.[16] In some cases it might be reasonable (or rational or fair) for a public body to go back on its previous decision after informing the person affected of its wish to do so and affording a full hearing before reaching a new conclusion.

II. Private Law: Ordinary Judicial Control

Where a tort or breach of contract has been committed by a public authority, its liability may be said to be prima facie the same as that of a private individual. The authority is moreover responsible for the torts and contracts of its employees and agents in the same way as an ordinary individual or corporation. This presumption, however, is subject to certain important qualifications. The great difference between public authorities and private individuals is that the former have so many and various *powers* conferred on them which ordinary individuals or corporations do not have, and which may cause harm to private citizens but the proper exercise of which does not entitle an injured person to a right of action. Local authorities, for example, have power to order houses to be demolished, to acquire land compulsorily, and to do works—such as the making of sewage farms—which would ordinarily constitute nuisances. These powers are given because the authority is acting on behalf of the public, and where public and private interests conflict, policy generally requires that the former must prevail.

On the other hand, public authorities are mostly the creations of statute, and have only such powers as are expressly conferred by statute. The citizen may therefore find that a contract which he thought he had entered into is void as being beyond the power of the authority to make.

Further, when the citizen has a remedy he may find that it does not lie against the public authority, but only against the person who appeared to be (but who in law was not) the servant of that authority.

Lastly, the fact that a public authority has failed to perform some duty does not necessarily mean that a citizen can take proceedings against it either to compel it to perform the duty or for damages for failing to do so.

Liability in contract

Statutory public authorities, such as local authorities and public corporations, have a general power to make contracts in the discharge of their functions. They may have specific contractual powers as well. If a public authority enters into a contract in relation to some matter that is beyond its powers—a question of statutory interpretation—the contract

---

[14] [1985] A.C. 835 (H.L.).

[15] *The Times,* December 18, 1985.

[16] *e.g.* purporting to create a lease when the authority concerned had no power to do so: *Minister of Agriculture and Fisheries* v. *Mathews, supra.*

is *ultra vires* and void.[17] For *intra vires* contracts, public authorities are generally liable in the ordinary way, *e.g.* a contract by a local authority to sell coke (*Bradford Corporation* v. *Myers*[18]).

Some countries, such as France, have a theory of "administrative contracts," whereby many of the contracts made by public authorities are governed by different rules from private-law contracts.[19] English law has no theory of "administrative" or "public" contracts, but a public authority cannot by contract bind itself not to exercise powers conferred on it by statute (*Ayr Harbour Trustees* v. *Oswald*[20]). The exact scope of this principle is not clear. It has been suggested that the underlying principle is that of governmental effectiveness, so that "no contract would be enforced in any case where some essential governmental activity would be thereby rendered impossible or seriously impeded."[21] Such a contract, it is suggested, is not void if it is the kind of contract that the authority has power to make, but it is not specifically enforceable. This leaves open the question of compensation to the other contracting party, which is due in justice but for which the common law does not seem to make provision. If this suggestion is sound, it applies to public authorities generally the principle of Crown contracts stated in the *Amphitrite* case.[22]

The old theory of freedom of contract is giving way in public law to standard forms of contract with large monopolies like the public corporations that provide electricity, gas and railway transport. Here the terms and conditions and the charges are regulated, and the consumer's only choice is to accept the terms *in toto* or reject the service altogether.

Liability for nuisance

There is a presumption that statutory powers are not intended to be exercised in such a way as to cause a nuisance, *e.g.* that the power of a local authority to build hospitals does not authorise the erection of a small-pox hospital in a residential area. If the power is *imperative, i.e.* imposes a duty to perform some act in a certain manner, so that it appears expressly or by necessary implication that it cannot be performed without causing a nuisance, then a nuisance may be commit-

---

[17] *Rhyl U.D.C.* v. *Rhyl Amusements* [1959] 1 W.L.R. 465; [1959] 1 All E.R. 257. But see *ante*, p. 676 as to the effect of estoppel.

[18] [1916] 1 A.C. 242.

[19] H. Street, *Governmental Liability*, pp. 81–84; L. N. Brown and J. F. Garner, *French Administrative Law* (3rd ed., 1983) p. 125 *et seq.* French public authorities may also enter into private-law contracts, *e.g.* a commercial lease.

[20] (1883) 8 App.Cas. 623 (H.L.), *per* Lord Blackburn at p. 634. And see *York Corporation* v. *Henry Leetham & Son* [1924] 1 Ch. 557; *Birkdale District Electricity Supply Co.* v. *Southport Corporation* [1926] A.C. 355, *per* Lord Birkenhead at p. 364; *William Cory & Son Ltd.* v. *City of London Corporation* [1951] 1 K.B. 8.; *Dowty Boulton Paul* v. *Wolverhampton Corporation* [1971] 1 W.L.R. 204; *Triggs* v. *Staines U.D.C.* [1969] 1 Ch. 10; *Leicester (Earl of)* v. *Wells-next-the-Sea U.D.C.* [1973] Ch. 110; *Cudgen Rutile (No. 2) Ltd.* v. *Chalk* [1975] A.C. 520; *Royal Borough of Windsor and Maidenhead* v. *Brandrose Investments* [1983] 1 W.L.R. 509.

[21] J. D. B. Mitchell, *The Contracts of Public Authorities* (1954), p. 7. And see Mitchell, "Limitations on the Contractual Liability of Public Authorities" (1950) 13 M.L.R. 318, 455; "Theory of Public Contract Law" (1951) 63 Jur.Rev. 60.

[22] *Rederiaktiebolaget Amphitrite* v. *The King* [1921] 2 K.B. 500; *post*, Chap. 35.

ted[23] but if the power is expressly or impliedly *permissive*, *i.e.* the performance of the act is merely rendered not illegal in itself, then ways and means must be found to prevent its causing a nuisance. The burden of proving that the power is imperative rests on the party purporting to act thereunder (*Metropolitan Asylum District* v. *Hill*[24]). Similar considerations arise where fumes from a power station injure neighbouring property (*Corporation of Manchester* v. *Farnworth*[25]).

A nuisance may be caused either by an act or an omission, so that where this tort is committed the distinction between misfeasance and non-feasance, is irrelevant (*Pride of Derby Angling Association Ltd.* v. *British Celanese Ltd.*[26]).

Liability for negligence

Even where a statutory power is bound to interfere with private rights to some extent, the power must be exercised with due care towards those likely to be affected. Parliament never authorises the commission of negligence. The leading case is the decision of the House of Lords concerning one of the first large public corporations, *Mersey Docks and Harbour Board* v. *Gibbs*,[27] where the Board was held liable to the owners of a ship and her cargo for damage caused by its negligence in leaving a mud bank at the entrance to the docks.[28]

So local authorities have been held liable for damage caused by negligence due to leaving a heap of stones unlighted on the highway (*Foreman* v. *Corporation of Canterbury*[29]), due to failing to detect a leak in the water supply system (*Corporation of Manchester* v. *Markland*[30]), and to carelessly inserting or failing to maintain a traffic stud (*Skilton* v. *Epsom and Ewell Urban District Council*[31]). In *Fisher* v. *Ruislip and Northwood Urban District Council*,[32] where the local authority was held liable for failing to give reasonable notice of the existence of a surface air-raid shelter with which the plaintiff collided in the blackout, the Court of Appeal reviewed a number of "blackout" and similar cases arising out of the two world wars, and distinguished negligent misfeasance, where the authority has itself created the danger by the exercise of its power, from mere failure, by not exercising its powers, to prevent damage arising independently.[33]

Before the decision of the House of Lords in *Anns* v. *Merton London*

---

[23] See *Department of Transport* v. *N. W. Water Authority* [1984] A.C. 336 (H.L.); *Allen* v. *Gulf Oil Refining Ltd.* [1981] A.C. 1001.

[24] (1881) 6 App.Cas. 193 (H.L.). *Cf. Hammersmith and City Ry.* v. *Brand* (1869) L.R. 4 H.L. 171; *Edgington* v. *Swindon Corporation* [1939] 1 K.B. 86; *Marriage* v. *East Norfolk Rivers Catchment Board* [1950] 1 K.B. 284.

[25] [1930] A.C. 171 (H.L.). See also *R.* v. *Epping (Waltham Abbey), ex p. Burlinson* [1947] 2 All E.R. 537 (D.C.).

[26] [1953] Ch. 149 (C.A.).

[27] (1866) L.R. 1 H.L. 93. And see *Geddis* v. *Proprietors of the Bann Reservoir* (1878) 3 App. Cas. 430.

[28] *Post*,. p. 699.

[29] (1871) L.R. 6 Q.B. 214.

[30] [1934] 2 K.B. 101.

[31] [1937] 1 K.B. 112.

[32] [1945] K.B. 584. *Cf. Baxter* v. *Stockton-on-Tees Corporation* [1959] 1 Q.B. 441 (C.A.).

[33] But *quaere* the possible effect of *Anns* v. *Merton L.B.C.* [1978] A.C. 728, *post*.

Borough Council[34] it was thought that if a public authority exercised a statutory power, it could not be liable in negligence if the damage complained of would have occurred even if the authority had decided not to act at all. Thus, in *East Suffolk Rivers Catchment Board* v. *Kent*[35] a farmer's land had been flooded when high tides burst a dyke. The Board's inadequate attempts to repair the dyke resulted in the land being flooded for longer than it would have been if they had used proper equipment and sufficient labour but for a shorter period than if it had taken no action at all. The House of Lords held that the Board was not liable. In *Anns* v. *Merton London Borough Council* Lord Wilberforce thought that the *East Suffolk* case had been decided before the full impact of *Donoghue* v. *Stevenson*[36] had been recognised, while Lord Salmon described the earlier decision as "not very satisfactory." The House of Lords held that a public authority may be under a common law duty to exercise a particular power with reasonable care. A local authority which could be shown to have negligently exercised its powers under the Public Health Act 1936 to examine the foundations of a building could, for instance, be liable in damages for loss arising from defects in building caused by its having been erected on inadequate foundations.[37]

Nonetheless, negligence in exercising a statutory discretion or power may be difficult to establish. At the initial (discretionary or policy) stage a public body must be allowed to reach a decision *bona fide*. At the second (executive or operational) stage liability may be more easily shown. The distinction is illustrated by *Rigby* v. *Chief Constable of Northamptonshire*.[38] The plaintiff's premises had been destroyed by fire when police threw a tear-gas cylinder into them in an attempt to dislodge a criminal who had taken refuge there. The plaintiff argued that it was negligent of the Chief Constable to have recommended to the police authority the purchase of that particular type of cylinder. Taylor J. rejected the claims on the ground that the statutory discretion had been properly exercised. But to use that cylinder, knowing that its use involved a risk of fire, in the absence of fire fighting equipment was negligent.

Failure to perform statutory duties

Whether a public authority is liable for damages to a private individual for injury caused by the failure to perform a statutory duty, depends on the facts of the case and the interpretation of the statute imposing the duty. The plaintiff has to show that the duty was owed to himself and not merely to the public generally, that the damage he suffered was caused directly by the breach of duty, and that the damage was of the kind contemplated by the statute.[39] The provision of some other rem-

---

[34] [1978] A.C. 728.

[35] [1941] A.C. 74.

[36] [1932] A.C. 562 (H.L.).

[37] See further *Fellowes* v. *Rother D.C.* [1983] 1 All E.R. 513; *Peabody Fund* v. *Sir L. Parkinson & Co.* [1985] A.C. 210; P. P. Craig, "Negligence in the Exercise of a Statutory Power" (1978) 94 L.Q.R. 428; M. J. Bowman and S. H. Bailey, "Negligence in the Realms of Public Law—A Positive Obligation to Rescue?" [1984] P.L. 277.

[38] [1985] 1 W.L.R. 1242.

[39] *Groves* v. *Lord Wimborne* [1898] 2 Q.B. 402, 415, per Vaughan Williams L.J.; *Cutler* v. *Wandsworth Stadium Ltd.* [1949] A.C. 398. Cf. *Gorris* v. *Scott* (1874) L.R. 9 Exch. 125.

edy, such as complaint to the Minister, will often be held to exclude an action for damages.[40]

Authorities such as Coke, Hawkins and Blackstone asserted that failure to perform a statutory duty constituted an indictable misdemeanour. Disobedience to the words of a statute constituted a form of contempt, punishable by the King's justices. This doctrine of contempt of statute was held by the Divisional Court in *R. v. Horseferry Road Justices ex p. Independent Broadcasting Authority*[41] to be no more than a rule of statutory construction. In modern statutes, at any rate, very clear words would be required before the court would hold that a breach of statutory duty constituted a crime.

On an application for judicial review the court may order the carrying out of a statutory duty by granting mandamus.[42]

---

[40] See further *Thornton* v. *Kirklees M.B.C.* [1979] Q.B. 626 (C.A.). For a useful survey see R. A. Buckley, "Liability in Tort for Breach of Statutory Duty" (1984) 100 L.Q.R. 204. See further, K. M. Stanton, *Breach of Statutory Duty in Tort* (1986).

[41] [1986] 3 W.L.R. 132; claim that I.B.A. had failed to carry out its duty under Broadcasting Act 1981, s.4(3) to prevent transmission of images for such a short duration that they could influence television viewers without their realising what had been done. The complainant alleged that during a programme called "Spitting Image" an image of his face had been briefly transmitted superimposed on the body of a naked woman.

[42] *Post*, Chap. 34.

CHAPTER 34

JUDICIAL CONTROL OF PUBLIC AUTHORITIES: II. REMEDIES

THE legality of acts and decisions of public bodies may be challenged directly by recourse to the supervisory jurisdiction of the High Court, that is by seeking to show that a decision has been vitiated by one or more of the factors considered in the previous chapter such as unreasonableness or breach of natural justice. The challenge may, however, arise in the course of an action in tort or contract or criminal proceedings. The owner of property may, for example, after it has been demolished by a local authority bring an action in trespass which, if he is to be successful, involves establishing that the decision to demolish lacked legal authority because it had been reached without giving him a hearing.[1] A tenant who believes that his local authority has unlawfully increased his rent may refuse to pay the increase and when, sued for possession, raise the invalidity of the decision as a defence.[2] Yet another possibility is to seek an injunction to restrain a public body from acting unlawfully[3] or a declaration that it has so acted.[4] Until recent reforms in the law of remedies the choice of the remedy was in the hands of the individual claiming to be aggrieved. In 1977, however, a new procedure—application for judicial review—was introduced by adding a new Order 53 to the Rules of the Supreme Court and subsequently given statutory recognition by the Supreme Court Act 1981, section 31. Judicial interpretation of the new procedure has established a distinction, as we have seen earlier, between public and private law rights and duties. In the former case a plaintiff must proceed by way of an application for judicial review; he can no longer choose to challenge the act of a public body in the course of litigation begun in the normal way by writ. In certain cases, discussed later in Part III of this chapter, decisions of ministers and tribunals are subject to statutory rights of appeal.

I. SUPERVISORY JURISDICTION OF THE HIGH COURT:

"Prerogative writs" were writs brought by the King against the officers to compel them to exercise their functions properly or to prevent them from abusing their powers. They could be issued at various periods of their history either out of the Court of King's Bench or the Court of Chancery, or both. The term "prerogative writ" was applied to habeas corpus in the reign of James I; but it is not until Lord Mansfield[5] and Blackstone that we find it grouped with certiorari, prohibition and mandamus as "prerogative writs" because they were not directed immediately to the tribunal or person concerned but were supposed to

---

[1] *Cooper* v. *Wandsworth Board of Works* (1863) 14 C.B.(N.S.) 180.
[2] *Wandsworth London Borough Council* v. *Winder* [1985] A.C. 461.
[3] *E.g. Boyce* v. *Paddington Corporation* [1903] 1 Ch. 109 (C.A.).
[4] *E.g. Vine* v. *National Dock Labour Board* [1957] A.C. 488 (H.L.).
[5] *R.* v. *Cowle* (1759) 2 Burr. 834, 855.

issue from the King to a royal officer, such as the sheriff.[6] The chief prerogative writs were habeas corpus, prohibition, certiorari, mandamus and *quo warranto*; but of these only the first remains as a writ,[7] the last has been abolished, and the others are now orders.[8]

Before the reforms of 1977 litigants who resorted to the supervisory jurisdiction of the High Court had to choose which order they wished to seek. A prerogative order could not be sought together with or as an alternative to other remedies such as damages or an injunction. The ambit of certiorari and prohibition was limited to bodies performing judicial functions, a concept of uncertain width. Other characteristics (and defects) of the orders led litigants increasingly to prefer the remedies of the injunction and the declaration.[9] Following various proposals for reform,[10] the Rules of the Supreme Court were amended in 1977 to provide a procedure known as the application for judicial review which enables a litigant to seek relief while leaving to the court the decision as to which particular remedy is appropriate.[11]

A litigant may proceed by way of an application for judicial review where the remedy sought is (i) an order of certiorari, prohibition or mandamus or (b) a declaration or injunction. The latter remedies may be granted on an application for judicial relief if the court considers it just and convenient to do so having regard (a) to the nature of the matters in respect of which relief may be granted by way of certiorari, prohibition or mandamus, and (ii) the nature of the persons and bodies against which relief may be granted by such orders. An application for judicial review cannot be made without the leave of the Court. The first request for leave can be dealt with by a judge on the basis of the written application and he need not sit in open court. If leave is refused a second application may be made to a judge sitting in open court (or in certain cases to a Divisional Court of the Queen's Bench). A claim for damages may be included in an application for judicial review. Where the court considers that the proceedings should have been commenced by writ it may order them to continue as if so commenced.[12] To be entitled to seek judicial review the applicant must have what the court considers to be a "sufficient interest" in the matter to which the application relates.

---

[6] For an account of their origin and development, see S. A. de Smith, "The Prerogative Writs" (1951) 11 C.L.J. 40; D. C. M. Yardley, "The Scope of the Prerogative Orders in Administrative Law" (1957–1958) 12 N.I.L.Q. 78; de Smith, *Judicial Review of Administrative Action*, Appendix 1.

[7] For habeas corpus, see *ante*, Chap. 25.

[8] Administration of Justice (Miscellaneous Provisions) Acts 1933 and 1938.

[9] See G. J. Borrie, "The Advantages of the Declaratory Judgment in Administrative Law," (1955) 18 M.L.R. 138.

[10] *Remedies in Administrative Law: Law Com. Report No. 73.* Cmnd. 6407 (1976). See H. W. R. Wade, "Remedies in Administrative Law," (1976) 92 L.Q.R. 334.

[11] See now also Supreme Court Act 1981, s.31. For details of the new procedure see R. J. E. Gordon, *Judicial Review: Law and Procedure* (1985).

[12] There is no provision for the converse situation but Woolf L.J. has said that there is no obstacle in an appropriate case for the court to give leave then and there in an action before it begun by writ: "Public Law—Private Law: Why the Divide" [1986] P.L. 220, 232.

A. The Remedies

Order 53 and Section 31 of the Supreme Court Act 1981 do not introduce new remedies but a new, general procedure for applying for a group of remedies. Hence the old law relating to the scope of the individual remedies remains relevant, except where changed by the reforms.[13]

1. Certiorari[14]

This is an order issued to an "inferior court" or a person or body exercising what the High Court regards as a "judicial" or "quasi-judicial" function, to have the record of the proceedings removed into the High Court for review, and (if bad) to be quashed.

What is an "inferior court" for this purpose, or whether a person or body exercises powers of a "judicial" or "quasi-judicial" nature, is a question for the High Court to decide. The former *locus classicus* was the dictum of Atkin L.J. in *R. v. Electricity Commissioners*[15]: "Whenever any body of persons having legal authority to determine questions affecting the rights of subjects, and having the duty to act judicially, act in excess of their legal authority, they are subject to the controlling jurisdiction of the King's Bench Division, exercised in these writs" (*i.e.* certiorari and prohibition). It was made clear in *Ridge v. Baldwin*[16] (a declaratory action) that authority to determine questions affecting the rights of subjects and the duty to act judicially are not two separate requirements: the latter is not additional to the former. Certiorari has been held to lie against a county court judge, a coroner, the Patents Appeal Tribunal, the Medical Appeal Tribunal, a local valuation court, rent tribunals, a Minister holding a public inquiry and a local election court.[17] By statute, certiorari lies to the Crown Court except in relation to that Court's jurisdiction in matters relating to trials on indictment.[18] In *Board of Education v. Rice*[19] certiorari and mandamus were granted against the Board of Education because, in a dispute between the managers of a school

---

[13] For example a generalised test of "sufficient interest" has replaced the former rules relating to *locus standi; post* p. 690.

[14] The former writ of certiorari appears first to have been used against the Commissioners of Sewers charged by a statute of 1531 to see to the repair of sea walls, but most of the earlier cases were against justices. For the history, see Holdsworth, *History of English Law*, Vol. X, pp. 199–206; D. C. M. Yardley, "The Grounds for Certiorari and Prohibition" (1959) 37 Can.Bar Rev. 294; and *R. v. Northumberland Compensation Appeal Tribunal ex p. Shaw* [1951] 1 K.B. 711, *per* Lord Goddard L.C.J.; [1952] 1 K.B. 338 *per* Denning L.J.

[15] [1924] 1 K.B. 171.

[16] [1964] A.C. 40, *per* Lord Reid; *cf. per* Lord Hewart C.J. in *R. v. Legislative Committee of the Church Assembly ex p. Haynes-Smith* [1928] 1 K.B. 411. Atkin L.J.'s dictum is too wide as regards certiorari and ecclesiastical law; *post*, p. 625.

[17] *R. v. Worthington-Evans ex p. Madan* [1959] 2 Q.B. 145 (D.C.); *R. v. Hurst (Judge), ex p. Smith* [1960] 2 Q.B. 133 (D.C.); *Pearlman v. Keepers and Governors of Harrow School* [1979] Q.B. 56; *R. v. Greater Manchester Coroner ex p. Tal* [1985] Q.B. 67 (D.C.); *Baldwin and Francis Ltd. v. Patents Appeal Tribunal* [1959] A.C. 663 (H.L.); *R. v. Medical Appeal Tribunal ex p. Gilmore* [1957] 1 Q.B. 574 (C.A.); *R. v. East Norfolk Local Valuation Court* [1951] 1 All E.R. 743; *R. v. Fulham Rent Tribunal* [1951] 2 K.B. 1; *R. v. Paddington Rent Tribunal ex p. Bell Properties* [1949] 1 K.B. 666; *Errington v. Minister of Health* [1935] 1 K.B. 249; *R. v. Cripps ex p. Muldoon* [1984] Q.B. 686 (C.A.).

[18] Supreme Court Act 1981, s.29(3); *In re Smalley* [1985] A.C. 622 (H.L.); *R. v. Central Criminal Court ex p. Raymond* [1986] 1 W.L.R. 710 (D.C.).

[19] [1911] A.C. 179 (H.L.).

and the local education authority, they had not decided the question which the statute directed them to decide. In *R. v. Manchester Legal Aid Committee ex p. Brand*[20] Parker J. concluded that a legal aid committee, being unconcerned with questions of policy and having to decide wholly on the facts of a particular case solely on the evidence before them, "must act judicially, not judiciously," and was therefore subject to certiorari.

Scope of certiorari
The grounds on which certiorari lies are:

(i) *Want or excess of jurisdiction.* For this reason certiorari was granted against a licensing authority which had given permission to open a cinema on Sunday, whereas this was prohibited by statute[21]; and against a legal aid committee which had granted a legal aid certificate to a trustee in bankruptcy on the basis of the means of the bankrupt instead of the means of the trustee (*R. v. Manchester Legal Aid Committee, ante*[22]).

(ii) *Denial of natural justice.*[23] Certiorari has been issued at the instance of a ratepayer to quash the decision of a rural district council permitting a certain development of land, since one of the councillors who voted on the resolution was interested in thhe use of the land[24]; and to quash a decision of the General Medical Council removing a doctor's name from the medical register, because the Council had refused to hear certain evidence which it ought to have heard (*General Medical Council v. Spackman*[25]). In *R. v. Barnsley M.B.C. ex p. Hook*[26] the Court of Appeal granted certiorari to quash a decision of a committee of the defendant corporation on the ground of bias.

(iii) *Error on the face of the record.* It was commonly thought at one time that certiorari was limited to cases of jurisdiction and natural justice, but the Court of Appeal held in *R. v. Northumberland Compensation Appeal Tribunal ex p. Shaw*[27] that this remedy is also available where an inferior tribunal has issued a "speaking order" (*i.e.* an order showing

---

[20] [1952] 2 Q.B. 413 (D.C.).
[21] *The King v. London County Council ex p. Entertainments Protection Association* [1931] 2 K.B. 215.
[22] [1952] 2 Q.B. 413. See also *R. v. Fulham Rent Tribunal* [1951] 2 K.B. 1, on review of jurisdictional facts.
[23] For the principles of natural justice, see *ante*, pp. 602 *et seq.*
[24] *The King v. Hendon Rural District Council, ex p. Chorley* [1933] 2 K.B. 696.
[25] [1943] A.C. 627 (H.L.).
[26] [1976] 1 W.L.R. 1052.
[27] [1952] 1 K.B. 338; confirming Divisional Court at [1951] 1 K.B. 711; following *Walsall Overseers v. London and North Western Ry.* (1879) 4 App.Cas. 30 (H.L.) and *R. v. Nat Bell Liquors Ltd.* [1922] 2 A.C. 128 (P.C.).
  And see *R. v. Patents Appeal Tribunal ex p. Swift & Co.* [1962] 2 Q.B. 647 (D.C.); *R. v. Medical Appeal Tribunal ex p. Gilmore* [1957] 1 Q.B. 574 (D.C.) *per* Denning L.J.

the reasons on which it is based), and an error of law appears on its face. In that case the applicant complained that the tribunal had made an error in computing the compensation to which he was entitled by statute for loss of employment on the nationalisation of the health service. The award set out the manner in which the sum was computed, and this enabled the court to hold that the computation was not in accordance with the statutory regulations and that the decision must be quashed. Error on the face of the record renders a decision voidable. There was usually no obligation on a tribunal to make a "speaking" or reasoned order before the Tribunals and Inquiries Act 1958, replaced by section 12 of the 1971 Act.[28]

"Record" was defined by Denning L.J. (as he then was) in *Ex p. Shaw* as including the document initiating the proceedings, the pleadings, if any, and the adjudication but not the evidence and not the reasons for the decision unless incorporated into adjudication by the tribunal. In *Baldwin & Francis* v. *Patents Appeal Tribunal*[29] Lord Denning said the record also included all documents which appear from the formal order of the tribunal to constitute the basis of its decision. In *R.* v. *Southampton Justices ex p. Green*[30] the Court of Appeal held that affidavits from justices as to their reasons for a decision constituted part of the record and revealed an error of law on the face of the record.

A record may be written or oral under section 12 of the Tribunal and Inquiries Act 1971. The courts have cited that section to justify a liberal approach to the meaning of "record" in cases outside the scope of the Act: *R.* v. *Knightsbridge Crown Court ex p. International Sporting Club (London) Ltd.*[31] Following Order 53 and *O'Reilly* v. *Mackman* the court should not, according to Woolf J. "be shackled and prevented from doing justice by restrictive historical decisions."[32]

Errors of law, falling short of excess jurisdiction,[33] arise for example when a tribunal takes into account extraneous considerations which it ought to have ignored in reaching its decision; fails to consider relevant considerations, or in any way fails to apply correctly the relevant law.[34]

Certiorari does not lie to review subordinate legislation.[35] It does not lie against ecclesiastical courts, because ecclesiastical law is a different system of law from that administered in the High Court,[36] or against

---

[28] *Ante*, p. 646

[29] [1959] A.C. 663; the other members of the House expressly refused to consider what documents, if any, other than the actual order of the tribunal, constituted the record. Lord Denning's definition was followed in *Ex p. Swift, ante. Cf. Belsfield Court Construction Co.* v. *Pywell* [1970] 2 Q.B. 47; pleadings not part of arbitrator's award.

[30] [1976] 1 Q.B. 11.

[31] [1982] Q.B. 304 (D.C.) (Quashing of oral judgment).

[32] *R.* v. *Knightsbridge Crown Court ex p. The Aspinall Curzon Ltd., The Times*, December 16, 1982. (Affidavit evidence could be treated as part of the record.)

[33] On the assumption that the distinction survives *Anisminic; ante* p. 666.

[34] In addition to cases cited *ante*, see *R.* v. *West London Supplementary Benefits Appeal Tribunal ex p. Clarke* [1975] 1 W.L.R. 1396; *R.* v. *Greater Birmingham Appeal Tribunal ex p. Simper* [1974] Q.B. 543.

[35] *R.* v. *Legislative Committee of the Church Assembly ex p. Haynes-Smith* [1928] 1 K.B. 411.

[36] *The King* v. *Chancellor of St. Edmundsbury and Ipswich Diocese* [1948] 1 K.B. 195. *Cf.* prohibition.

voluntary (*i.e.* non-statutory) domestic tribunals,[37] nor does it lie for dismissal of a person under an ordinary contract of employment.[38] In the case of statutory tribunals it is not every error of law on the face of the record which will result in interference by the courts. Certiorari is not to be used as a means of appeal from decisions of tribunals, and the courts will therefore only deal with points of law of general application.[39]

2. Prohibition

The former writ of prohibition issued out of the King's Bench or other superior court directing the judge and parties to a suit in any inferior court to cease from the prosecution thereof on the ground that the cause did not belong to that jurisdiction.[40] The penalty for disobedience is committal for contempt. It was mainly by this writ that the common law courts in earlier days contested the jurisdiction of the Admiralty and ecclesiastical courts.

The order of prohibition issues to *prevent* an inferior court or tribunal from exceeding or continuing to exceed its jurisdiction or infringing the rules of natural justice. Prohibition is governed by similar principles to certiorari, except that it does not lie when once a final decision has been given. It will issue to prevent magistrates exceeding their jurisdiction[41] and to prevent a Board of Prison Visitors from hearing a charge which they were not entitled to deal with.[42] In *R.* v. *Liverpool Corporation ex p. Liverpool Taxi Fleet Operators' Association*[43] it was granted to prohibit a local authority from acting on a resolution with regard to the number of taxicab licences to be issued, without first hearing representations on behalf of interested persons.

Prohibition has been granted against Electricity Commissioners to prevent them from holding an inquiry with a view to bringing into force an *ultra vires* scheme for the supply of electricity (*R.* v. *Electricity Commissioners*[44]); and against Income Tax Commissioners, an assess-

---

[37] *R.* v. *National Joint Council for the Craft of Dental Technicians ex p. Neate* [1953] 1 Q.B. 704 (D.C.); *R.* v. *Post Office ex p. Byrne* [1975] I.C.R. 221. This limit on the availability of certiorari was overlooked by the Divisional Court in *R.* v. *Aston University Senate ex p. Roffrey* [1969] 2 Q.B. 538; criticised on that ground, *Herring* v. *Templeman* [1973] 3 All E.R. 569, 585 *per* Russell L.J. *Cf. R.* v. *Criminal Injuries Compensation Board, ex p. Lain* [1967] 2 Q.B. 864 (C.A.): certiorari may be issued against a public body set up by prerogative as part of an administrative scheme approved by both Houses and financed by parliamentary funds. See also *R.* v. *Takeover Panel* [1987] 2 W.L.R. 699 (C.A.).

[38] *Vidyodaya University of Ceylon* v. *Silva* [1965] 1 W.L.R. 77; [1964] 3 All E.R. 865 (P.C.): dismissal of university professor. The remedy is an action for damages if the dismissal was in breach of contract.

[39] *R.* v. *Preston Supplementary Benefits Appeal Tribunal ex p. Moore* [1975] 1 W.L.R. 624; *R.* v. *Barnsley Supplementary Benefits Appeal Tribunal ex p. Atkinson* [1976] 1 W.L.R. 1047: [1976] 2 All E.R. 686; *R.* v. *National Insurance Commissioner ex p. Michael* [1977] 1 W.L.R. 109; [1977] 2 All E.R. 420 (C.A.); see too the cases cited *ante*, n. 34.

[40] Bl.Comm. iii, 105. See D. C. M. Yardley, "The Grounds for Certiorari and Prohibition" (1959) 37 Can.Bar Rev. 294.

[41] *E.g. R.* v. *Horseferry Road Justices ex p. I.B.A.* [1986] 3 W.L.R. 132.

[42] *R.* v. *Board of Visitors of Dartmoor Prison ex p. Smith* [1986] 3 W.L.R. 61 (C.A.).

[43] [1972] 2 Q.B. 299 (C.A.).

[44] [1929] 1 K.B. 171, *per* Atkin L.J. Certiorari was refused in that case.

ment committee and rent tribunals.[45] But it was decided in *The King* v. *Legislative Committee of the Church Assembly ex p. Haynes-Smith*,[46] where application was made for an order to prohibit the Church Assembly from proceeding further with the Prayer Book Measure 1927, that it would not issue against a legislative or deliberative body. Nor will prohibition be issued to a military tribunal administering martial law (*Re Clifford and O'Sullivan*[47]).

Where a final decision has been made by the inferior court prohibition is obviously useless, but certiorari is available to enable the High Court to review and, if necessary, to quash the decision. Thus prohibition was the appropriate remedy to prevent the Minister of Health from proceeding to confirm an *ultra vires* housing scheme (*R. v. Minister of Health ex p. Davis*[48]), but certiorari was appropriate when an *ultra vires* scheme had already been approved by the Minister (*Minister of Health v. R. ex p. Yaffe*[49]). Certiorari and prohibition may be granted together, for example, to quash a decision already made by a rent tribunal and to prevent it continuing to exceed or abuse its jurisdiction (*R. v. Paddington Rent Tribunal, ex p. Bell Properties Ltd.*[50]).

Prohibition and mandamus were issued together in *R. v. Kent Police Authority ex p. Godden*[51] where, on the compulsory retirement of a police chief inspector on the ground that he was permanently disabled, it was held that the chief inspector's medical advisers were entitled to see all the material placed before the medical practitioner appointed to make the decision about disablement.

3. Mandamus

The order of mandamus may be issued to any person or body (not necessarily an inferior court) commanding him or them to carry out some public duty.

Mandamus has been issued to compel the hearing of an appeal by a statutory tribunal,[52] the determination of a dispute between a local education authority and school managers (*Board of Education* v. *Rice*[53]), to procure the production of a local authority's accounts for inspection,[54] against a returning officer to declare a councillor elected,[55] against an electoral registration officer to correct the register of electors[56] against a county court judge to make a legal aid order,[57] and against the Board of Trade requiring them to investigate the affairs of the applicant company

---

[45] *Kensington Income Tax Commissioners* v. *Aramayo* [1916] 1 A.C. 215; *R. v. North Worcestershire Assessment Committee ex p. Hadley* [1929] 2 K.B. 397; *R. v. Tottenham and District Rent Tribunal ex p. Northfield* [1957] 1 Q.B. 103.

[46] [1928] 1 K.B. 411. The House of Commons rejected the Prayer Book Measure.

[47] [1921] 2 A.C. 570 (H.L.).

[48] [1929] 1 K.B. 619.

[49] [1931] A.C. 494.

[50] [1939] 1 K.B. 666.

[51] [1951] 2 Q.B. 662 (C.A.).

[52] *The King* v. *Housing Tribunal* [1920] 2 K.B. 334.

[53] [1911] A.C. 179.

[54] *R. v. Bedwellty U.D.C., ex p. Price* [1934] 1 K.B. 333.

[55] *R. v. Soothill ex p. Ashdown, The Times*, April 2, 1955.

[56] *R. v. Calderwood ex p. Manchester Corporation, The Times*, February 27, 1974.

[57] *R. v. Judge Fraser Harris ex p. The Law Society* [1955] 1 Q.B. 287.

under the Companies Act.[58] Mandamus was not granted to compel the College of Physicians to admit an applicant (*R.* v. *Askew*[59]), to order a magistrate to hear a case covered by parliamentary privilege,[60] or to compel the Chairman of Convocation of London University to call a meeting, as the matter could have been put to the Visitor (*R.* v. *Dunsheath ex p. Meredith*[61]).

Mandamus is not available against the Crown itself, nor against a servant of the Crown to enforce a duty owed exclusively to the Crown (*R.* v. *Secretary of State for War;*[62] *The Queen* v. *Lords of the Treasury*[63]), because a third party cannot require an agent to perform a duty which he owes solely to his principal. But mandamus may be issued against Ministers or other Crown servants to enforce a statutory duty owed to the applicant as well as to the Crown (*The Queen* v. *Special Commissioners for Income Tax*[64]). In *Padfield* v. *Minister of Agriculture, Fisheries and Food*[65] the House of Lords held that where a minister had by statute an unfettered discretion whether or not to refer a complaint to a committee, he must consider only relevant matters and exclude irrelevant ones, and that even where he gave no reasons for not referring the matter to the committee he should be required by mandamus to consider the complaint lawfully.

4. Injunction and Declaration

Where the right claimed by a litigant is a public law right these remedies must be sought by means of an application for judicial review.[66] The substantive rules relating to these remedies are discussed later in Part V which deals with private law remedies.

An injunction is a court order requiring the defendant to do or refrain from doing an act while a declaration (or declaratory judgment) declares what the law is. Although, as will be seen in Part V, the declaratory judgment is not available to answer hypothetical questions, recent developments in the public law sphere establish that it is not confined to disputes relating to decisions of public bodies. In appropriate cases the court has jurisdiction to declare that a ministerial circular is based on a mistaken view of the law[67] or that an intended payment by a local authority, if made, would be *intra vires*.[68] The prospect of obtaining a

---

[58] *R.* v. *Board of Trade ex p. St. Martin's Preserving Co.* [1965] 1 Q.B. 603 (D.C.).

[59] (1768) 4 Burr. 2186.

[60] *R.* v. *Graham-Campbell, ex p. Herbert* [1935] 1 K.B. 594; *cf. R.* v. *Ogden ex p. Long Ashton R.D.C.* [1963] 1 W.L.R. 274; [1963] 1 All E.R. 574 (D.C.).

[61] [1951] 1 K.B. 127. And see *Sammy* v. *Birkbeck College, The Times,* November 3, 1964, and May 20, 1965 (C.A.) (mandamus refused).

[62] [1891] 2 Q.B. 326.

[63] (1872) L.R. 7 Q.B. 387. See E. C. S. Wade, "The Courts and the Administrative Process" (1947) 63 L.Q.R. 164.

[64] (1889) 21 Q.B.D. 313. And see *R.* v. *Board of Trade ex p. St. Martin's Preserving Co., supra.*

[65] [1968] A.C. 997.

[66] *O'Reilly* v. *Mackman* [1983] 2 A.C. 237 was an unsuccessful attempt to obtain a declaration without using the procedure of judicial review; *Cocks* v. *Thanet D.C.* [1983] 2 A.C. 286, an unsuccessful attempt to obtain an injunction.

[67] *Gillick* v. *West Norfolk and Wisbech Area Health Authority* [1986] A.C. 112.

[68] *R.* v. *Bromley L.B.C. ex p. Lambeth L.B.C., The Times,* June 16, 1984.

declaration that an intended course of action would or would not be criminal is extremely remote.[69]

B. Sufficient Interest

An applicant for judicial review must satisfy the court that he has a sufficient interest in the matter to which the application relates.[70] This general requirement replaces the rules relating to locus standi which formerly applied to each individual remedy. Then, as now, a member of the public had no right to impugn the legality of a decision taken by a public body unless he could establish an individual right or claim of some kind. The test to be satisfied was defined (or described) in varying terms in relation to particular remedies. It was possible for an applicant to satisfy the requirement of locus standi in relation to one remedy but not to another.[71]

The meaning of "sufficient interest" was considered by the House of Lords in *R.* v. *Inland Revenue Commissioners ex p. National Federation of Self Employed and Small Businesses Ltd.*[72] In line with the current judicial approach to judicial review sufficient interest was given the widest possible meaning while reserving to the court a discretion in particular cases to refuse a hearing or deny a remedy. The House of Lords was reluctant to separate locus standi from the facts and merits of an application. The requirement of standing should, it seems, be looked at twice: first when the applicant applies for leave to seek judicial review. At that stage the court is concerned to do no more than "prevent abuse by busybodies, cranks, and other mischief-makers."[73] If leave is granted, the court may, when the merits of the case are clear to it, revise its initial judgment and conclude that the applicant lacks the necessary interest. The application before the House had been made by an association of taxpayers who wished to challenge the legality of a compromise which the Inland Revenue had made with a group of print-workers who had been defrauding the revenue. The House of Lords held that while it had been correct to grant leave to apply for review, the applicants, on the facts, lacked sufficient interest to challenge the legality of the compromise. The assessment of one taxpayer is no concern of another; indeed, each individual's tax liability is a confidential matter. The Inland Revenue was reasonably trying to carry out its duty to collect taxes. Dicta did envisage the possibility of cases of sufficient gravity where taxpayers might have locus standi.[74] The House distinguished the position of the taxpayer from that of the ratepayer. In the latter case assessments of property are a public matter and there is a common fund so that each ratepayer's contribution is affected by the assessment of his

---

[69] *Imperial Tobacco Ltd.* v. *Att.-Gen.* [1980] 1 W.L.R. 322 (H.L.).
[70] Supreme Court Act 1981, s.31(3); R.S.C. Ord. 53(7).
[71] *E.g. Gregory* v. *Camden L.B.C.* [1966] 1 W.L.R. 899. But see now *Steeples* v. *Derbyshire C.C.* [1985] 1 W.L.R. 256.
[72] [1982] A.C. 617.
[73] At p. 653, *per* Lord Scarman.
[74] *E.g.* Allegations of large scale fraud and corruption on the part of the revenue.

neighbour.[75] An individual taxpayer, by contrast, seeking to challenge decisions of the revenue authorities in relation to his own affairs has, without doubt, sufficient interest.[76] In *R. v. H.M. Treasury ex p. Smedley*[77] a taxpayer challenged the legality of a draft Order in Council laid by the Treasury before Parliament.[78] The Court of Appeal decided the substantive question against Smedley and therefore did not have to express a concluded view on whether he has a sufficient interest to apply for judicial review. Slade L.J. emphasised the width of the test laid down in the *Inland Revenue* case, *supra* and indicated that the court would hear an application provided it was satisfied that it was not "of a frivolous nature."

C. THE SCOPE OF JUDICIAL REVIEW

Judicial review is a procedure available only in disputes raising questions of public law. The court must before an application can succeed be satisfied that the respondent is a public authority and that the right at issue is a public right.

Although the courts have not attempted to define what is meant by public authority guidance can be gained from the cases cited in the preceding pages in relation to the particular remedies. Generally it might be said that judicial review is available against any minister or body exercising common law or statutory powers which affects the rights of individuals unless there is a reason to the contrary.[79] Thus it will be available not merely against departments of central and local government but also against the General Medical Council because of its statutory powers of control over the medical profession,[80] and against Boards of Prison Visitors.[81] The new procedure does not, however, give the High Court a jurisdiction which it formerly lacked. Decisions of superior courts are not, therefore, subject to review.[82] Nor is an organisation necessarily a public authority because it has been created by statute. The question is whether the powers it is exercising are of a public law or governmental kind. A commercial decision, for example, by a nationalised industry is unlikely to be subject to judicial review: *R. v. National Coal Board ex p. National Union of Mineworkers*.[83]

---

[75] So ultimately is each taxpayer's liability affected by his neighbour's contribution. In *Arsenal Football Club Ltd.* v. *Ende* [1979] A.C. 1. (the correctness of which the House was concerned to uphold) the plaintiff was not applying under o.53 but as a "person aggrieved" under the General Rate Act 1967, s.69; see *post* p. 694.

[76] E.g. *R.* v. *Special Commissioners ex p. Stipplechoice Ltd.* [1985] 2 All E.R. 465 (C.A.).

[77] [1985] Q.B. 657.

[78] *Ante* p. 97.

[79] *R.* v. *Secretary of State for the Home Department ex p. McAvoy* [1984] 1 W.L.R. 1408; no judicial review of decision taken for "operational and security reasons."

[80] *R.* v. *G.M.C. ex p. Gee* [1986] 1 W.L.R. 226. Domestic Tribunals exercising a jurisdiction based on contract are outside o.53: *Law* v. *National Greyhound Racing Club Ltd.* [1983] 1 W.L.R. 1302 (C.A.).

[81] E.g. *R.* v. *Board of Visitors of Dartmoor Prison ex p. Smith* [1986] 3 W.L.R. 61 (C.A.).

[82] The Crown Court is subject to review except with regard to "matters relating to trial on indictment"; Supreme Court Act 1981 s.29(3); In re *Smalley* [1985] A.C. 622 (H.L.); *R.* v. *Central Criminal Court ex p. Raymond* [1986] 1 W.L.R. 710 (D.C.).

[83] *The Times*, March 8, 1986.

Judicial review is not available unless the right involved is a public law right. This requirement has been discussed in the Introduction to this Part. The converse is that an action relating to a private law right can be commenced by writ even against a public body.

D. THE AVAILABILITY OF OTHER REMEDIES

The availability of another remedy may be relevant in one of two ways to an application for judicial review.

First, the court may decide that the alternative remedy is the exclusive remedy provided by law and there is no jurisdiction to grant review.[84] A recent, unsuccessful, attempt on this ground to deny jurisdiction to the court is to be found in *R. v. Secretary of State for the Environment ex p. Ward.*[85] Section 9 of the Caravan Sites Act 1968 entitled the minister to give directions to local authorities requiring them to provide caravan sites in accordance with their statutory duties: "any such directions shall be enforceable, on the application of the Minister, by mandamus." A local authority was unwilling to carry out its duty and the Secretary of State was unwilling to seek mandamus against them. The applicant, a gypsy, sought judicial review against the local authority and the Secretary of State. Woolf J. held that section 9 did not preclude an application for judicial review although it would have precluded any private law application by an individual litigant.

Secondly, more commonly the existence of an alternative remedy is a factor to be taken into account by the court in deciding whether, in its discretion, to grant relief.

"Judicial review should not be granted where an alternative remedy is available."[86] The courts are particularly reluctant to intervene where Parliament has provided a comprehensive appellate system, for example, in the field of social services: *R. v. Secretary of State for Social Services ex p. Connolly.*[87] Similarly in relation to immigration the Court of Appeal emphasised the undesirability of granting leave to seek judicial review before applicants had exhausted their statutory rights under the Immigration Act 1971: *R. v. Secretary of State for the Home Department ex p. Swati.*[88] On the other hand, an application may be granted if there are special circumstances such as the inordinate delay in the domestic disciplinary process in *R. v. Chief Constable of the Merseyside Police ex p. Calveley.*[89]

---

[84] *Barraclough v. Brown* [1897] A.C. 615; *Pasmore v. Oswaldtwistle Urban District Council* [1898] A.C. 387.

[85] [1984] 1 W.L.R. 834; distinguishing *Kensington and Chelsea L.B.C. v. Wells* (1973) 72 L.G.R. 289 (C.A.). See generally, *Pyx Granite Co. v. Ministry of Housing* [1960] A.C. 260.

[86] *R. v. Inland Revenue Commissioners ex p. Preston* [1985] A.C. 835, 852 *per* Lord Templeman.

[87] [1986] 1 W.L.R. 421.

[88] [1986] 1 W.L.R. 477; See too *R. v. Chief Adjudication Officer ex p. Bland, The Times,* February 6, 1985 (D.C.).

[89] [1986] 2 W.L.R. 144 (C.A.). The judgments contain a useful survey of earlier authorities. For judicial review of revenue decisions see *R. v. Commissioner for the Special Purposes of the Income Tax Acts ex p. Stipplechoice Ltd.* [1985] 2 All E.R. 465; *R. v. Inspector of Taxes ex p. Kissane* [1986] 2 All E.R. 37.

E. DISCRETIONARY

Judicial review is a procedure in which the court has a discretion whether to grant relief at two stages. First, the applicant must obtain leave to apply. At that stage he must, as we have seen, demonstrate *prima facie* a sufficient interest to be allowed to proceed. He must also give some reason for believing that there is ground for challenging the decision of which he complains and, if there is an alternative remedy available, suggest why that should not prevent leave being granted. It was because the applicant failed to satisfy both these preliminary hurdles that the Court of Appeal refused leave to apply for judicial review of an immigration officer's decision in *R.* v. *Secretary of State for the Home Department ex p. Swati.*[90] The House of Lords has emphasised the need to have some ground to believe that a decision is subsequently open to challenge before granting leave in *R.* v. *Secretary of State for the Environment ex p. Puhlhofer.*[91] The applicants had been granted leave to challenge a decision of the Hillingdon Council under the Housing (Homeless Persons) Act 1977.[92] The House held that the Council had correctly decided that the applicants were not homeless. It also indicated, however, concern that leave to apply should not be given too easily in future cases. Lord Brightman said that he was

> "troubled at the prolific use of judicial review for the purpose of challenging the performance by local authorities of their functions under the 1977 Act. Parliament intended the local authority to be the judge of fact. The Act abounds with the formula when, or if, the housing authority are satisfied as to this, or that, or have reason to believe this, or that. Although the action or inaction of a local authority is clearly susceptible to judicial review where they have misconstrued the Act, or abused their powers or otherwise acted perversely, I think that great restraint should be exercised in giving leave to proceed by judicial review. The plight of the homeless is a desperate one, and the plight of the applicants in the present case commands the deepest sympathy. But it is not, in my opinion, appropriate that the remedy of judicial review, which is a discretionary remedy, should be made use of to monitor the actions of local authorities under the Act save in the exceptional case. . . . Where the existence or non-existence of a fact is left to the judgment and discretion of a public body and that fact involves a broad spectrum ranging from the obvious to the debatable to the just conceivable, it is the duty of the court to leave the decision of that fact to the public body to whom Parliament has entrusted the decision-making power save in a case where it is obvious that the public body, consciously or unconsciously, are acting perversely."

In *R.* v. *Monopolies and Mergers Commission ex p. Argyll Group plc*[93] the

[90] [1986] 1 W.L.R. 477.
[91] [1986] A.C. 484.
[92] See now Housing Act 1985, ss.58–78. *Cocks* v. *Thanet D.C.* [1983] 2 A.C. 286, *supra* p. 689 had established that decisions under the Act required to be challenged by judicial review.
[93] [1986] 1 W.L.R. 763.

Court of Appeal held that a judge had been right to refuse leave to seek judicial review of a decision taken by the Chairman of the Commission. The decision, in the view of the Court, was outside his statutory powers but equally the Court had no doubt that the Commission itself, which did have the power to decide, would have come to the same conclusion.

Secondly, where leave has been granted and the application for relief has been successful the court still has a discretion with regard to the granting of remedies. The nude sunbathers in *Glynn* v. *Keele University*,[94] for example, failed to obtain an injunction because of their own behaviour and because, even after a hearing, a similar decision would have been reached. The Court may be concerned about the inconvenience and upheaval that would be caused if it quashed a statutory instrument in reliance on which parties had been acting.[95] In *R.* v. *Secretary of State for the Environment ex p. Ward*,[96] Woolf J. refused to grant mandamus against the Secretary of State because it could not be said that he had acted improperly or irrationally in reaching the decision which he had and interference would, in the light of the complicated situation, be premature. The learned judge quashed the decisions of the council which had been challenged (by certiorari) but refused to issue injunctions ordering them what to do next.

III. STATUTORY RIGHTS OF APPEAL

A right of appeal on a question of law may lie to the High Court from the decision of a tribunal or Minister. The Tribunal and Inquiries Act 1958, s.9 (now s.13 of the 1971 Act) introduced a general right of appeal from a wide range of tribunals listed in Schedule 1 to the Act.[97] In addition rights of appeal are contained in many other statutes. The Acquisition of Land Act 1981 for example provides that any person who wishes to challenge the validity of a compulsory purchase order on the ground that it is *ultra vires* the Act may apply to the High Court.[98] The Town and Country Planning Act 1971 provides for appeals to the High Court against decisions of the Secretary of State (ss.246, 247).

Appeals to the ordinary courts may be by an indirect route as for example, in the case of objections to decisions of valuation officers where the General Rate Act 1967 provides ultimately for an appeal to the Lands Tribunal, from which an appeal on a point of law lies to the Court of Appeal.

As in the cases discussed in the preceding section an applicant must show that he has the necessary *locus standi* or, in the commonly used statutory words, is a person aggrieved. In *Ex p. Sidebotham*[99] James L.J. said: "A 'person aggrieved' must be a man who has suffered a legal grievance, a man against whom a decision has been pronounced which has wrongfully deprived him of something or wrongfully refused him

---

[94] [1971] 1 W.L.R. 487.
[95] *R.* v. *Secretary of State for Social Services ex p. Association of Metropolitan Authorities* [1986] 1 W.L.R. 1.
[96] [1984] 1 W.L.R. 834.
[97] *Ante*, p. 585.
[98] See *Smith* v. *East Elloe Rural District Council* [1956] A.C. 736; discussed *post*, p. 696.
[99] (1880) 14 Ch.D. 458, 465.

something, or wrongfully affected his title to something." In line with that narrow approach it was held that a landowner had no *locus standi* to appeal against planning permission granted to a neighbouring land-owner.[1] In *Arsenal Football Club* v. *Ende*[2] the House of Lords adopted a more generous approach and held that a ratepayer was entitled to challenge the valuation of any property in his rating area whether or not he could show that the decision challenged had a demonstrable effect on his pocket, rights or interests.

An applicant must also show that his appeal relates to a question of law as opposed to a question of fact, a distinction which it is not always easy to draw.[3] Whether A threw soup over B is clearly a question of fact. A tribunal may, however, in the light of a number of facts relating to the terms and conditions of A's work, have to decide whether A is an employee of B or an independent contractor or whether indeed there is any form of legal relationship between the two at all. If the courts wish to extend their appellate jurisdiction over a particular type of tribunal they can categorise problems involving the classification of facts—was A an employee—as questions of law.[4] If they wish to avoid interfering with a tribunal's exercise of its jurisdiction they can treat such questions as matters of fact.[5] Or, as a compromise they can say that a question of law arises only when a decision on the application of the law to the facts is such that no tribunal properly instructed could have reached that conclusion.[6]

IV. EXCLUSION OR RESTRICTION OF THE JURISDICTION OF THE COURTS

Statutes have purported or appeared to exclude judicial review by the courts by the use of various drafting formulae, though with scant success. The Tribunals and Inquiries Act 1971, s.14 (replacing the Act of 1958, s.11) now provides that any provision in an Act *passed before August 1, 1958*, that any order or determination shall not be called in question in any event, or any provision in such an Act which by similar words excludes any of the powers of the High Court, shall not prevent the use of the remedies of certiorari or mandamus except in the case of Acts making special provision for applications to the High Court within a limited time.

It was held by the Court of Appeal in *R.* v. *Medical Appeal Tribunal ex p. Gilmore*[7] that a formula like "any such order or decision shall be final" does not bar certiorari: it makes the decision final on the facts, but not final on the law. The formula that an order or rules made "shall have

---

[1] *Buxton* v. *Minister of Housing and Local Government* [1961] 1 Q.B. 278.

[2] [1979] A.C. 1. In *Steeples* v. *Derbyshire C.C.* [1985] 1 W.L.R. 256 Webster J. said that it would "make an ass of the law" to require in other contexts a stricter test of *locus standi*; than that now required by Order 53.

[3] See articles cited *ante* p. 666, n. 32.

[4] *Davies* v. *Presbyterian Church of Wales* [1986] 1 W.L.R. 323 (H.L.) (Question whether minister was employee of his church a question of law.)

[5] *O'Kelly* v. *Trust House Forte plc* [1984] Q.B. 90.

[6] *Edward* v. *Bairstow* [1956] A.C. 14.

[7] [1957] 1 Q.B. 575 (C.A.). See also *South East Anglia Fire Bricks* v. *Non-Metallic Mineral Products Manufacturing Employees Union* [1981] A.C. 363.

effect as if enacted in this Act" has dicta of the House of Lords both for and against the exclusion of judicial control.[8]

A different kind of provision is that found in some Acts concerning planning and the compulsory acquisition of land, which set a *time limit* (commonly six weeks) in which the validity of the order may be challenged in the High Court, and specifying the permitted grounds of complaint as (a) *ultra vires* or (b) non-compliance with the statutory procedure, and stating that subject to these provisions the order may not be questioned in any legal proceedings. The main purpose of such provision is to limit the time within which an order or decision may be questioned in the courts, so as to ensure that the *title* to land acquired by a public authority for building, etc. should not remain uncertain after a short time. In *Smith* v. *East Elloe Rural District Council*[9] the House of Lords held, by a majority of three to two, that after the six weeks' period a compulsory purchase order could not be challenged even on the ground that it had been procured by bad faith. It was not necessary to decide whether the order could be challenged for bad faith within six weeks. Of the minority who thought the order could be challenged for bad faith after six weeks, Lord Reid thought this was not excluded by the statute and Lord Somervell thought such remedy lay under general principle. The majority decision was much criticised as offending against the principles of natural justice; but although justice may require compensation for loss brought about by fraud, that does not necessarily mean that an order on which title to land is based should be upset.

The question was considered by the House of Lords in *Anisminic* v. *Foreign Compensation Commission*.[10] The Foreign Compensation Act 1950, s.4, provided that "the determination by the Commission of any application made to them under this Act shall not be called in question in any court of law"; but the House of Lords (reversing the Court of Appeal) held by four to one that this provision did not prevent the court from making a declaration that the Commission's determination was a nullity. Lord Reid said: "It is one thing to question a determination which does exist: it is quite another thing to say that there is nothing to

---

[8] *Institute of Patent Agents* v. *Lockwood* [1894] A.C. 347, *obiter dicta* that judicial review was excluded; *Minister of Health* v. *R. ex p. Yaffe* [1931] A.C. 494, *obiter dicta* that judicial review was not excluded; see *R.* v. *Minister of Health ex p. Yaffe* [1930] 2 K.B. 98 (C.A.).

[9] [1956] A.C. 736. The plaintiff had previously obtained damages against the council and contractors for trespass, as the continuance of wartime requisition was done in bad faith; *Smith* v. *East Elloe R.D.C.* [1952] *Current Property Law*. In subsequent proceedings by the plaintiff against the clerk and a representative of the Ministry for damages for conspiracy to injure, Diplock J. held that there was no conspiracy, that damages had already been recovered for trespass, and his Lordship was not satisfied that the clerk had in fact acted in bad faith: *Smith* v. *Pyewell*, *The Times*, April 29, 1959.

[10] [1969] 2 A.C. 147. Browne J.'s judgment at first instance, which was upheld by the House of Lords, is reported at [1969] 2 A.C. 223. See H. W. R. Wade, "Constitutional and Administrative Aspects of the *Anisminic* Case" (1969) 85 L.Q.R. 198; B. C. Gould, "Anisminic and Jurisdictional Review" [1970] P.L. 258; D. M. Gordon, "What did the Anisminic Case decide?" (1971) 34 M.L.R. 1; note by S. A. de Smith in [1969] C.L.J. 161.

Cf. Foreign Compensation Act 1969, s.3: No determination by the Commission may be called in question in any court of law, except (a) case stated on question of law to Court of Appeal concerning jurisdiction or interpretation of Order in Council and (b) proceedings on ground that determination is contrary to natural justice.

be questioned. . . . It is a well established principle that a provision ousting the ordinary jurisdiction of the court must be construed strictly. . . . No case has been cited in which any other form of words limiting the jurisdiction of the court has been held to protect a nullity. . . . Undoubtedly such a provision protects every determination which is not a nullity." Cases where the decision of a tribunal may be a nullity are: where it had no jurisdiction to enter into the inquiry; where it gave its decision in bad faith; where it made a decision which it had no power to make; where it failed to comply with the requirements of natural justice; where in good faith it decided the wrong question; and where it failed to take account of something of which it was required to take account, or based its decision on a matter which it ought not to have taken into account. Something much more specific than this Act would be required if it is to be held that Parliament intended to exclude the court's jurisdiction on any of these grounds.

The *East Elloe* case (*ante*) was distinguished in the *Anisminic* case. Lord Reid did not regard the former case (in which he had dissented) as very satisfactory. It is not certain, he said, whether the plaintiff was claiming that the authority which made the order had itself acted in bad faith, in which case the order would be a nullity; or whether she was alleging that the clerk had fraudulently misled the council and the Ministry, in which case the result would be quite different.

In *R. v. Secretary of State for the Environment ex p. Ostler*[11] the Court of Appeal held, for a variety of reasons, that *East Elloe* had not been overruled by *Anisminic* and was applicable to a case involving a six week time limit under the Highways Act 1959. *Anisminic* was distinguished as applying only where there is a complete ouster of the courts' jurisdiction as opposed to an ouster after a time limit[12]; that it dealt with a determination by a judicial body whereas *East Elloe* dealt with an order of an administrative character; that it dealt with an actual decision whereas *East Elloe* dealt with the validity of the process by which the decision was reached; that it dealt with the ultimate question of jurisdiction as opposed to an attack on the validity of an order made within jurisdiction; and, finally that it dealt with the ultimate question of the payment of compensation as opposed to the validity of a compulsory purchase order.[13]

An exclusion clause which seems to have been drafted with the intention of defeating the reasoning in *Anisminic* is to be found in the Interception of Communications Act 1985. Section 7 establishes a tribunal to investigate complaints relating to the interception of communications under the Act." Subsection (8) provides that "the decisions of the Tribunal (*including any decisions as to their jurisdiction*) shall not be subject to appeal or liable to be questioned in any court." (Italics added.) An exclusion clause of rather doubtful effect is to be found in the British

---

[11] [1977] Q.B. 122.

[12] *per* Lord Denning, citing H. W. R. Wade, *Administrative Law* (3rd ed.), pp. 151–153. See (4th ed.) pp. 579–582.

[13] See J. Alder, "Time Limit Clauses and Judicial Review—*Smith* v. *East Elloe* Revisited" (1975) 38 M.L.R. 274; J. Alder, "Time Limit Clauses and Conceptualism, A Reply," (1980) 43 M.L.R. 670; L. H. Leigh, "Time Limit Clauses and Jurisdictional Error," [1980] P.L. 34.

Nationality Act 1981 s.44. Subsection (1) directs that any discretion vested by or under the Act in the Secretary of State shall be exercised without regard to the race, colour or religion of any person who may be affected by its exercise. Subsection (2) then provides that the Secretary of State shall not be required to give any reason for any decision made under his discretionary powers and any such decision "shall not be subject to appeal to, or review in, any court." Then subsection (3), apparently inconsistently provides that "Nothing in this section affects the jurisdiction of any court to entertain proceedings of any description concerning the rights of any person under any provision of this Act". Has subsection (1) given applicants a right not to be discriminated against?

In various contexts statutes[14] may provide that the issuing of a certificate is conclusive evidence that the requirements of an Act have been complied with[15] or that certain facts have occurred. In an earlier chapter reference was made to the conclusive effect of the Speaker's certificate issued under the Parliament Act 1911.[16] In the following chapter it will be seen that a Secretary of State may issue conclusive certificates under sections 10 and 40 of the Crown Proceedings Act 1947.[17] Such a form of ouster clause leaves little scope for judicial review, unless the validity of the certificate itself is attacked, for example on the ground of forgery. In R. v. Registrar of Companies, ex. p. Central Bank of India[18] the Court of Appeal refused to inquire into whether the requirements of the Companies Act 1948 had been complied with in the light of a certificate that they had, such certificate being "conclusive evidence" under the Act. Lawton L.J. said that Parliament, by making the certificate conclusive evidence had excluded not the jurisdiction of the court but the admission of evidence.

Apart from directly excluding judicial review statutes may restrict the jurisdiction of the courts by conferring powers on ministers in subjective terms: the minister may act "if satisfied." In such cases the courts may accept that they can only enquire if the minister was satisfied, not if he had reasonable grounds to be so.[19] Lord Salmon accurately, if unhelpfully, summarised the case law when he said, "[Those words] may confer an absolute discretion on the Executive. Sometimes they do, but sometimes they do not."[20] The courts have had to consider the scope of its jurisdiction where statutes use subjective language in two cases in the controversial area of relations between central and local government. The Education Act 1944, section 68 provides that the Secretary of State may give directions to a local education authority if he is satisfied that it had acted or was proposing to act "unreasonably." In

---

[14] The courts themselves have recognised the conclusive effect of certificates in the sphere of foreign affairs: ante p. 280.
[15] e.g. Ex p. Ringer (1909) 25 T.L.R. 718 (D.C.).
[16] Ante p. 145.
[17] Post p. 704 and p. 712.
[18] [1986] Q.B. 1114 The current legislative provision is s. 401 of the Companies Act 1985.
[19] See ante Chap. 19, p. 365.
[20] Att.-Gen of St. Christopher, Nevis and Anguilla v. Reynolds [1980] A.C. 637 (P.C.).

Secretary of State for Education and Science v. *Tameside Metropolitan Borough Council*[21] the House of Lords held that the section required the existence of certain facts, *i.e.* those from which a properly directed minister could conclude the existence of unreasonableness in the *Wednesbury* sense. The evaluation of the facts was a matter for the subjective judgment of the minister; their existence was a matter for the court. (The House held that no facts existed from which an inference of unreasonableness could be drawn.) In *R.* v. *Secretary of State for the Environment ex p. Norwich County Council*[22] the Council challenged the legality of the Secretary of State using his default powers under the Housing Act 1980 s.23(1) which provided that the Secretary of State could give notice of his intention to exercise his statutory powers "where it appears . . . that tenants . . . have or may have difficulty in exercising the right to buy effectively and expeditiously."[23] The Court of Appeal held that no question of unreasonableness on the part of the Council was involved: unlike the *Tameside* case that word had not been used in the statute. Thus the power of the Minister was wider in the *Norwich* case. The Court held that in exercising his power he must act fairly and reasonably. On the facts he had done so since there was overwhelming evidence that tenants were having difficulty in exercising their rights.

The widest ministerial discretion of all, and the most complete exclusion of judicial control, occurs where the courts conclude that a particular issue is "non-justiciable." We have seen earlier that the courts are willing to recognise that Acts of State may be acts over which they have no jurisdiction[24] and in the GCHQ case, while asserting the right of review over powers derived from the Royal Prerogative, the House of Lords admitted that the exercise of certain prerogative powers would continue to fall outside the scope of judicial review.[25]

V. PRIVATE LAW REMEDIES AGAINST PUBLIC AUTHORITIES

1. Action for damages

When an injury is done to a citizen's person or property by a public authority acting *ultra vires* or in abuse of power, an action for damages may be brought in circumstances where an action would lie against a private individual. The actions most commonly brought are for trespass,[26] false imprisonment,[27] negligence,[28] and nuisance.[29] It has been suggested that in cases not following within the limits of established

---

[21] [1977] A.C. 1014. See too *Secretary of State for Employment* v. *ASLEF* (No. 2) [1972] 2 Q.B. 455.

[22] [1982] Q.B. 808.

[23] See now Housing Act 1985, s.164.

[24] *Nissan* v. *Att.-Gen.* [1970] A.C. 179.

[25] *Council of Civil Service Unions* v. *Minister for the Civil Service* [1985] A.C. 374.

[26] *Cooper* v. *Wandsworth Board of Works* (1863) 14 C.B. (N.S.) 180; *ante* p. 682.

[27] *Percy* v. *Glasgow Corporation* [1922] A.C. 299.

[28] *Mersey Docks and Harbour Board* v. *Gibbs* (1866) L.R. 1 H.L. 93, *ante*, p. 612; *Davy* v. *Spelthorne B.C.* [1984] A.C. 262 (H.L.); private law action for damages available even though negligence alleged occurred in connection with exercise of statutory powers.

[29] *Metropolitan Asylum District* v. *Hill* (1881) 6 App.Cas. 193.

torts there may be a liability in damages for malicious use of statutory powers.[30]

If a public authority commits a breach of contract which it was within the powers of the authority to make, an action for damages will lie.[31]

2. Injunction and specific performance

Where a public authority threatens to do or to continue to do some unlawful act, such as a nuisance, an action may be brought for an injunction to restrain the authority from doing or continuing to do so. The breach of an injunction amounts to contempt of court. An injunction was originally an equitable remedy. It may be sought in addition to or instead of damages, but will only be granted at the discretion of the court exercised judicially and in the type of cases in which it would lie against a private individual. In *Pride of Derby Angling Association* v. *British Celanese Ltd.*[32] an injunction was granted against the Derby Corporation and the British Electricity Authority to restrain them from continuing a nuisance by polluting a river. Although injunction is discretionary and will not be granted if, for example, damages would be a sufficient remedy, yet there is a prima facie right to an injunction if the defendant threatens to continue the nuisance.

Injunction is the appropriate method for questioning the right of a person to hold a particular office.[33] Proceedings in such a case must be brought by an application for judicial review.[34]

Where an act done by a public authority affects the public generally, the Attorney-General may sue for an injunction on behalf of the public. In some cases he may allow his name to be used at the request ("on the relation") of some individual ("the relator") who is substantially the party affected. This is called a "relator action."[35] A citizen may claim an injunction against a public authority in his own name only where, in addition to the threatened breach of a public right, either some private right of his is affected or he will suffer some damage peculiar to himself (*Boyce* v. *Paddington Borough Council*[36]; *Gouriet* v. *Union of Post Office Workers*[37]).

An action for specific performance of a contract may be brought against a public authority in similar circumstances to those in which specific performance would be granted against an ordinary corporation

---

[30] P. P. Craig, "Compensation in Public Law," (1980) 96 L.Q.R. 412, 426 *et seq.* See also *Dunlop* v. *Woollahra Municipal Council* [1982] A.C. 158 (P.C.). The possibility of such an action was recognised by Parker L.J. in *Bourgoin S.A.* v. *Minister of Agriculture, Fisheries and Food,* [1986] Q.B. 716.

[31] *Armour* v. *Liverpool Corporation* [1939] Ch. 422.

[32] [1953] Ch. 149 (C.A.).

[33] Supreme Court Act 1981, s.30. Until its abolition by the Administration of Justice Act (Miscellaneous Provisions) 1938 the procedure in such cases had been by way of *Quo Warranto*.

[34] Supreme Court Act 1981, s.31(1)(c).

[35] *Att.-Gen.* v. *Wimbledon House Estate Co.* [1904] 2 Ch. 34; *Att.-Gen.* v. *Bastow* [1957] 1 Q.B. 514; *Att.-Gen* v. *Smith* [1958] 2 Q.B. 173.

[36] [1903] 1 Ch. 109.

[37] [1978] A.C. 435.

or private individual.[38] The contract must, of course, be one of the kind that is on principle enforceable against government authorities.[39]

3. Action for a declaration[40]

An action for a declaration asks for a "declaration of right." It may be brought in the High Court even though no damages or other relief is claimed. The claim is often brought together with a claim for an injunction, and similar rules apply with regard to suing in the plaintiff's own name or at his relation by the Attorney-General.[41] There must be a justiciable issue,[42] and this remedy cannot be brought in order to ask hypothetical questions.[43] The Court, in its discretion, will not grant a declaration unless the remedy would be of real value to the plaintiff.[44] The Court will not grant declarations "which are academic and of no practical value."[45] A declaratory judgment cannot be directly enforced, but it may be assumed that a public authority will observe the law when the High Court declares what it is.

The action for a declaration has been used to test the validity of delegated legislation, and the *vires* of decisions of tribunals whether statutory or voluntary.[46] But a declaratory judgment cannot quash a decision, and the remedy may not be appropriate where the decision was within jurisdiction but there is error on the face of the record.[47] Since the adoption of the application for judicial review it will not, of course, be possible to apply for a declaration by writ if the issue is one of public law.[48]

---

[38] *Crook* v. *Corporation of Seaford* (1871) L.R. 6 Ch. 551; *cf. Crampton* v. *Varna Ry.* (1872) 7 Ch.App. 562.

[39] See *ante*, p. 677.

[40] I. Zamir, *The Declaratory Judgment* (1962); E. Borchard, *Declaratory Judgments* (2nd ed., 1941), especially pp. 875–926.

[41] *Ante*, p. 331.

[42] *Cox* v. *Green* [1966] Ch. 216; a question of professional etiquette is not justiciable. But *cf. Pharmaceutical Society of Great Britain* v. *Dickson* [1970] A.C. 403.

[43] *Re Barnato, Joel* v. *Sanger* [1949] Ch. 258. *Mellstrom* v. *Garner* [1970] 1 W.L.R. 603. *Cf. Hampshire County Council* v. *Shonleigh Nominees* [1970] 1 W.L.R. 865.

[44] *Bennett* v. *Chappell* [1966] Ch. 391 (C.A.).

[45] *Williams* v. *Home Office* (No. 2) [1981] 1 All E.R. 1211, 1248 *per* Tudor Evans J. (Appeal dismissed on procedural grounds: [1982] 2 All E.R. 564 (C.A.).)

[46] *Davis* v. *Carew-Pole* [1956] 1 W.L.R. 833; [1956] 2 All E.R. 524; *Ceylon University* v. *Fernando* [1960] 1 All E.R. 631 (P.C.).

[47] *Punton* v. *Ministry of Pensions and National Insurance* (No. 2) [1964] 1 W.L.R. 226; (C.A.) decision of National Insurance Commissioner. But see P. Cane, "A Fresh Look at Punton's Case," (1980) 43 M.L.R. 266.

[48] Even before the decision in *O'Reilly* v. *Mackman* [1983] 2 A.C. 237 the courts could, and did, refuse to hear applications for declarations where they thought that the procedure under Order 53 would be more appropriate: *e.g. Bousfield* v. *North Yorkshire C.C.* [1982] 44 P. & C.R. 203; *sub nom Re Tillmire Common*, [1982] 2 All E.R. 615. (Dillon J. refused to hear a summons for a declaration that a decision of a Commissioner under the Commons Registration Act 1965 was voidable for error of law on the face: proceedings in the Chancery Division were "misconceived and an abuse of process.")

CHAPTER 35

CROWN PROCEEDINGS

I. LIABILITY OF THE CROWN

Introduction[1]

Two ancient and fundamental rules of English constitutional law were abolished by the Crown Proceedings Act 1947. The first, that proceedings against the Crown for breach of contract or restitution of property could only be taken after obtaining a *fiat* by the inconvenient procedure of petition of right, was due to the principle that the King could not be impleaded in his own courts.[2] The second, that the Crown could not be proceeded against at all in tort, was due to the same principle coupled with the doctrine that "the King could do no wrong." No action lay at common law against the Sovereign personally, whether for public or private acts. Also—contrary to the law of agency and of master and servant—no action lay against the Sovereign for breach of contract or torts committed by Ministers, other officers or departments acting as servants or agents of the Crown. In certain cases, however, a petition of right would lie. The maxim "the King can do no wrong" meant not only that the King could not be made liable by action, but also that wrong could not be imputed to the King, and therefore he could not be said to have authorised another to commit a wrong. This ruled out the maxim *qui facit per alium facit per se* where the Crown was the employer. As there is no concept of the state in English law, and as government departments are merely groups of Crown servants, this meant that the citizen could not claim satisfaction out of public funds for torts committed by the Crown.

The immunity of the Crown at common law, subject to the limited and inconvenient procedure by petition of right, became increasingly serious in modern times owing to the growth of state activity, for the Crown had become the largest employer, contractor and occupier of property in the country. The grievance that it was necessary to apply to the Home Secretary for a *fiat* before bringing a petition of right was more a matter of form than of substance, for in practice the Attorney-General always recommended that the *fiat* should be granted where there was any sort of prima facie case against the Crown. On the other hand, the personal liability incurred by Crown servants for torts committed in their official capacity often failed to satisfy injured parties, who might not even know which individual was responsible; while the

---

[1] Gleeson E. Robinson, *Public Authorities and Legal Liability* (1925); G. S. Robertson, *Civil Proceedings by and against the Crown* (1908). For the history, see Holdsworth, *History of English Law*, Vol. IX, pp. 7–45; "The History of Remedies against the Crown" (1922) 38 L.Q.R. 141, 280.

[2] A privilege probably peculiar to the Sovereign and not an incident of feudal lordship. The immunity of the ordinary lord from actions in his own courts is anyway doubtful: Paul Jackson, "Sovereign Immunity: A Feudal Privilege?" (1975) 91 L.Q.R. 171; S. F. C. Milsom, *The Legal Framework of English Feudalism* (1976), pp. 80 *et seq.*

702

practice whereby the Treasury, in what it considered appropriate cases, paid ex gratia compensation where Crown servants were unsuccessful defendants was illogical, arbitrary and probably unlawful.

Matters came to a head at the end of the Second World War in two cases of persons injured by the condition of premises occupied by the Crown. In *Adams* v. *Naylor*[3] two boys were injured by a minefield which was negligently marked and fenced. An action was brought against an officer of the Royal Engineers, whose name had been supplied by the War Department as the responsible officer. It was not known who was personally responsible for the state of affairs at the time of the accident, and the House of Lords criticised *obiter*[4] the practice of government departments putting up "nominated" or "nominal" defendants as whipping-boys. Soon afterwards the Court of Appeal in *Royster* v. *Cavey*[5] felt constrained to follow the considered dicta of the House of Lords, where an employee in a Ministry of Supply ordnance factory, who had received personal injuries while so employed, wished to bring an action for negligence at common law and for breach of statutory duty under the Factories Act 1937. The plaintiff was supplied by the Treasury Solicitor with the name of the superintendent of the factory, but the latter had no connection with the factory at the time of the accident. The court held that it had no jurisdiction to try an action against him, as he was neither the occupier of the factory nor the plaintiff's employer.[6]

A comprehensive Crown Proceedings Bill[7] was then introduced by the Lord Chancellor, Viscount Jowitt. The Bill was privately examined by an informal committee of Law Lords and others, presided over by Viscount Simon, while the Lord Chancellor consulted all the other available judges. Lord Jowitt could therefore fairly claim that the Bill received "the unanimous approval of the entire Bench of Judges."

Crown Proceedings Act 1947[8]

The main objects of the Act were, as far as practicable, to make the Crown liable in tort in the same way as a private person, and to reform the rules of procedure governing civil litigation by and against the

---

[3] [1946] A.C. 543.

[4] The case was decided on the Personal Injuries (Emergency Provisions) Act 1939.

[5] [1947] 1 K.B. 204. For a more recent attempt to resurrect John Doe as a defendant in an action against a government department see *Barnett* v. *French* [1981] 1 W.L.R. 848; "On the Demise of John Doe," (1983) 99 L.Q.R. 341. For the statutory solution to the problem see Road Traffic Regulation Act 1984, s.130.

[6] *Lane* v. *Cotton* (1701) 1 Ld.Raym. 646.

[7] Based partly on a draft Bill of 1927 (Cmd. 2842) prepared by a committee under two earlier Lord Chancellors, Birkenhead and Haldane. The delay was due largely to the misgivings of the Service Departments and the Post Office (then a government department).

[8] R. McM. Bell, *Crown Proceedings* (1948); J. R. Bickford Smith, *The Crown Proceedings Act, 1947* (1948); Glanville L. Williams, *Crown Proceedings* (1948); Sir Carleton Allen, *Law and Orders* (3rd ed., 1965), Chap. 10; H. Street, "Crown Proceedings Act, 1947" (1948) 11 M.L.R. 129–142; Sir Thomas Barnes, "The Crown Proceedings Act, 1947" (1948) 26 Can.-Bar Rev. 387; G. H. Treitel, "Crown Proceedings: Some Recent Developments" [1957] P.L. 321.

For comparative surveys, see H. Street, *Governmental Liability* (1953); B. Schwartz and H. W. R. Wade, *Legal Control of Government* (1972); L. Neville Brown and J. F. Garner, *French Administrative Law* (2nd ed., 1973); P. W. Hogg, *Liability of the Crown in Australia, New Zealand and the United Kingdom* (1971).

Crown, especially by allowing an action without a *fiat* where the petition of right previously lay. The Act adopts the Anglo-American principle of treating the state (or "the Crown") for the purpose of litigation
as nearly as possible in the same way as a private citizen, instead of borrowing the Continental idea of a separate system of administrative law.
The effect is to bring English constitutional law nearer in one way to the
conception of "the rule of law" than it was when Dicey wrote.

Part V applies the Act with appropriate modifications to Scotland,[9]
and section 53 provided for the extension of the Act by Order in Council
to Northern Ireland with any necessary modifications.

The Act is only concerned with the liability of the Crown in respect of
the government in the United Kingdom (section 40 (2)). A certificate of a
Secretary of State to the effect that any alleged liability of the Crown
arises otherwise than in respect of Her Majesty's Government in the
United Kingdom shall, for the purposes of the Act be conclusive as to
the matter certified (section 40(3)).[10] As a result of such a certificate
being issued, Sir Robert Megarry V.-C. held that he had no jurisdiction
under the Act to hear a case relating to alleged tortious acts committed
by British forces in Berlin.[11] (Apart from the Act no proceedings lay
because the Crown is not otherwise liable in tort and the Attorney-
General could not be sued because he has no responsibilities or functions outside England, Wales and Northern Ireland.)[12]

Right to sue the Crown in contract, etc.

"Section 1. *Where any person has a claim against the Crown after the
commencement of this Act, and, if this Act had not been passed, the claim
might have been enforced, subject to the grant of His Majesty's fiat, by petition of right, or might have been enforced by a proceeding provided by any
statutory provision repealed by this Act, then, subject to the provisions of
this Act, the claim may be enforced as of right, and without the fiat of His
Majesty, by proceedings taken against the Crown for that purpose in accordance with the provisions of this Act."*

This section gives the individual a right to sue the Crown without
any *fiat* in cases where, if the Act had not been passed, he could (i) bring
a petition of right or (ii) take any proceedings under special statutory
provisions repealed by the Act, *e.g.* War Department Stores Act 1867.
Proceedings by way of petition of right were abolished by section 13.

Most of the actions in contract brought against the Crown since the
Act came into force have been settled out of court. Disputes over building contracts with the government usually go to arbitration.

Section 1 did not create a new cause of action, and so the limitations

---

[9] J. R. Bickford Smith, *The Crown Proceedings Act, 1947* (1948), pp. 49–58 (by K. W. B. Middleton); Fraser, *Outline of Constitutional Law* (2nd ed.), Chap. 11; J. D. B. Mitchell, *Constitutional Law* (2nd ed. 1968), Chap. 17.

[10] *R. v. Secretary of State for Foreign and Commonwealth Affairs ex p. Trawnik, The Times,*
April 18, 1985 (D.C.) (Certificate not reviewable unless a nullity, *i.e.* not a genuine certificate, or on its face it had been issued outside the statutory power. The Court "would
not use the *Anisminic* principle to trespass on the royal prerogative.")

[11] *Trawnik* v. *Lennox* [1985] 1 W.L.R. 532.

[12] So held by the Court of Appeal, reversing the Vice Chancellor on this second point:
[1985] 1 W.L.R. 544.

on the scope of the former petition of right continue to apply to this right of action.

Scope of petition of right[13]

The theory of the petition of right was that as the King was the fountain of justice, he would cause justice to be done as soon as the matter was brought to his notice. Petition of right lay first for the recovery of land of which the Crown had wrongly taken or retained possession, and for the recovery of chattels real and probably chattels personal. It also apparently lay for certain cases of damage caused by undue user of Crown property, such as the wrongful assertion of an easement causing damage.[14] When the law of contract developed, a petition of right came to be granted for breach of contract, at first for debt or liquidated damages (e.g. on a contract for goods supplied), and later for unliquidated damages.[15] In *Thomas* v. *The Queen*[16] it was held that Thomas, an engineer, was entitled to bring a petition of right claiming a reward and his expenses in respect of an artillery invention in accordance with an agreement with the Secretary of State for War. The remedy was also available to recover liquidated or unliquidated sums due under a statute where no other remedy was provided (*Attorney-General* v. *De Keyser's Royal Hotel Ltd.*[17]) and was probably available in quasi-contract.[18]

There were four limitations or exceptions to the availability of a petition of right:

(i) Owing to the prerogative immunity in tort, a petition of right did not lie for a pure tort, that is, a tort unconnected with the wrongful taking of property, such as negligence or trespass. Thus in *Viscount Canterbury* v. *Attorney-General*.[19] an ex-Speaker failed in his claim for compensation from the Crown for damage done to his furniture by the negligence of certain Crown servants who, by burning an excessive quantity of old Exchequer tallies, caused a fire which destroyed the Houses of Parliament in 1834. Similarly, in *Tobin* v. *The Queen*[20] the owners of a ship trading in palm oil off the coast of Africa failed in their claim for compensation from the Crown for the destruction of the ship and cargo by the captain of *H.M.S. Espoir*, who had falsely assumed that she was engaged in the slave trade which he had statutory authority to suppress. The same rule would apply to false imprisonment, conversion and libel.

(ii) Contracts of service with members of the armed forces are con-

---

[13] Clode, *Petition of Right* (1887); Holdsworth, *History of English Law*, Vol. IX, 7–45.

[14] *Tobin* v. *The Queen* (1864) 16 C.B.(N.S.) 310, *per* Erle C.J. at pp. 363–365.

[15] *The Bankers' Case* (1700) 14 St.Tr. 1.

[16] (1875) L.R. 10 Q.B. 31.

[17] [1920] A.C. 508 (H.L.). And see *Commercial and Estates Co. of Egypt* v. *Board of Trade* [1925] 1 K.B. 271 (angary; compensation payable by international law).

[18] Cf. *Brocklebank Ltd.* v. *R.* [1925] 1 K.B. 52. Since the Crown Proceedings Act, if not before, the question of waiver of tort is irrelevant. See further, Street, *Governmental Liability*, pp. 125–127; A. W. Mewett, "The Quasi-Contractual Liability of Governments" (1959–60) 13 U.T.L.J. 56.

[19] (1843) 1 Phillips 306; (1843) 12 L.J.Ch. 281.

[20] (1864) C.B.(N.S.) 310; *ante*. The judgment of Erle C.J. suggests that an action would have lain against the captain.

trolled by the prerogative.[21] The position of civilian officers and civil servants is in some respects not free from doubt.[22]

(iii) Contracts that fetter future executive action. During the First World War the Swedish (neutral) owners of *S.S. Amphitrite* were induced to send the ship to a British port by a letter from the British Legation at Stockholm stating that she would be released if she proceeded to the United Kingdom with a cargo of approved goods. The ship did so but was nevertheless refused a clearance, and the owners brought a petition of right for damages for breach of contract: *Rederiaktiebolaget Amphitrite* v. *The King*.[23] Rowlatt J. gave judgment for the Crown, on the ground that there was no enforceable contract. "It is not competent for the Government," said his Lordship, "by enforceable contract to fetter its future executive action, which must necessarily be determined by the needs of the community when the question arises. It cannot by contract hamper its freedom of action in matters which concern the welfare of the State." The judgment was an unconsidered one and no authorities were cited, but it is generally taken as an authority for the principle stated above. On the facts of the case it would have been sufficient to hold that the letter from the British Legation was merely an expression of present intention of what the government would do, and that the Crown did not intend to enter into contractual relations.[24] Rowlatt J. distinguished "commercial" contracts, on which the Crown can be made liable. Otherwise the limits of the supposed rule are uncertain,[25] and in fact no subsequent English decision has been based on it.[26] The common law makes no provision for compensation in such cases.

(iv) Contracts dependent on grant from Parliament. In *Churchward* v. *R.*[27] Churchward contracted with the Admiralty Commissioners to

---

[21] *Ante*, Chap. 18. And see Z. Cowen, "The Armed Forces of the Crown" (1950) 66 L.Q.R. 478.

[22] *Ante*, Chap. 17.

[23] [1921] 3 K.B. 500.

[24] This reasoning was approved by Denning J. in *Robertson* v. *Minister of Pensions* [1949] 1 K.B. 227, 231. And see *Australian Woollen Mills Ltd.* v. *Commonwealth of Australia* [1956] 1 W.L.R. 11; [1955] 3 All E.R. 711 (P.C.).

[25] See Holdsworth in (1929) 45 L.Q.R. 166 for a strong criticism of the rule. According to one view, the *Amphitrite* case, if kept within due limits, supports the general principle of "governmental effectiveness": J. D. B. Mitchell, *The Contracts of Public Authorities*, pp. 27, 52. *Cf.* Street, *op. cit.* p. 98.

[26] *Cf. The Steaua Romana* [1944] p. 43. The *Amphitrite* case was followed by the High Court of Southern Rhodesia in *Waterfalls Town Management Board* v. *Minister of Housing* [1956] Rhod. and Ny. L.R. 691. It was not referred to in *Board of Trade* v. *Temperley Steam Shipping Co.* (1927) 27 Ll.L.R. 230 where the Court of Appeal held that the implied obligation of a party to a contract not to interfere with the performance of the contract did not apply to prevent a Crown servant exercising his statutory powers so as to interfere with a contract to which the Crown was a party. It was referred to by Devlin L.J. in *Crown Land Commissioners* v. *Page* [1960] 2 Q.B. 274, where it was held that the Crown as lessor was not prevented by implied covenant for quiet enjoyment from exercising a statutory power to requisition from one of its tenants, and in *Dowty Boulton Paul Ltd.* v. *Wolverhampton Corporation* [1971] 1 W.L.R. 204 where, however, Pennycuick V.-C., in interlocutory proceedings, thought that it would not avail to release the Corporation from contractual liabilities. See further *Cudgen Rutile (No. 2) Ltd.* v. *Chalk* [1975] A.C. 520 (P.C.); C. Turpin, *Government Contracts* (1972), pp. 19–25; Rogerson, "On the Fettering of Public Powers" (1971) P.L. 288; *ante*, p. 677.

[27] (1865) L.R. 1 Q.B. 173; 6 B. & S. 807.

maintain a mail service between Dover and the Continent for eleven years, expressly in consideration of an annual sum to be provided by Parliament. The Admiralty terminated the contract in the fourth year, and the Appropriation Act of that year provided that no part of the sum appropriated towards the post office packet service should be paid to Churchward after a certain date. Churchward naturally failed in his petition of right for breach of contract, but dicta in that case have led to the view that the provision of funds by Parliament is an implied precedent condition for the liability of the Crown on its contracts, and even for the validity of Crown contracts.[28] There is no good reason, however, why funds should be antecedently or specifically appropriated by Parliament in order that the Crown may make contracts through responsible Crown servants in the course of their official duties. Enforceability, on the other hand, is a different matter from validity, and the other party cannot obtain satisfaction from the Crown if parliamentary funds are not available when the time arrives for payment.[29]

The Petitions of Right Act 1860 provided a simpler procedure than that which existed at common law, following complaints by Army contractors during the Crimean War about the difficulty of recovering debts from the War Department.

A Crown servant is not personally liable at common law for the breach of a contract entered into by him in his official capacity. Thus in *Macbeath* v. *Haldimand*[30] the King's Bench held General Haldimand, Governor of Quebec, not liable for stores ordered by him from Macbeath for the Fort of Michilimakinac. The plaintiff knew that the goods were for government use, and that the defendant was not contracting personally. Thus stated, it is merely an application of the general law of agency. It is now clear that a petition of right would have lain before 1948 in the circumstances of this case.[31]

There were some statutory exceptions. Parliament occasionally used language referring to the bringing of actions by or against a government department or Minister in his official capacity, with or without incorporating that department or Minister. The effect of such language and the extent (if any) of liability to be sued depended on the interpretation of the words used in the particular statute. The matter was reviewed by the Court of Appeal in *Minister of Supply* v. *British Thomson-Houston Co.*,[32] where it was held that the War Department Stores Act 1867 rendered the Minister of Supply liable to be sued on official contracts concerning military stores. The Ministry of Transport Act 1919 expressly made the Minister officially liable in tort as well as contract.

---

[28] (1865) L.R. 1 Q.B. 173, 209, *per* Shee J.; *Cf. per* Cockburn C.J. at pp. 200–201.

[29] *Commercial Cable Co.* v. *Government of Newfoundland* [1916] 2 A.C. 610, 617 (P.C.) *per* Viscount Haldane; *Mackay* v. *Att.-Gen. for British Columbia* [1922] 1 A.C. 457, 461, *per* Viscount Haldane; *Commonwealth of Australia* v. *Kidman* (1926) 32 A.L.R. 1, 2–3 (P.C.) *per* Viscount Haldane; *New South Wales* v. *Bardolph* (1934) 52 C.L.R. 455, 474, *per* Evatt J.: and see *per* Dixon J. *Cf. Att.-Gen.* v. *Great Southern and Western Ry. of Ireland* [1925] A.C. 754, 773, 779 (H.L). See further, Colin Turpin, *op. cit.*

[30] (1786) 1 T.R. 172.

[31] *Thomas* v. *R.* (1875) L.R. 10 Q.B. 31. Few petitions of right on contracts were brought from the time of the Restoration, when the Sovereign came to rely almost entirely on parliamentary grants to finance the government of the country, until the Crimean War.

[32] [1943] K.B. 478.

Liability of the Crown in tort

"Section 2(1). *Subject to the provisions of this Act, the Crown shall be subject to all those liabilities in tort to which, if it were a private person of full age and capacity, it would be subject:*

   (a) *in respect of torts committed by its servants or agents;*

   (b) *in respect of any breach of those duties which a person owes to his servants or agents at common law by reason of being their employer; and*

   (c) *in respect of any breach of the duties attaching at common law to the ownership, occupation, possession or control of property . . . "*

This is the most important section, which provided the *raison d'être* of the Act. The marginal note reads: "Liability of the Crown in tort," but the Act does not make the Crown liable generally in tort: subsection (1) makes the Crown liable in three classes of case:

(a) *Vicarious liability to third parties for torts,* such as negligence or trespass committed by servants in the course of their employment, and for the authorised or ratified torts of independent contractors.

At common law actions in tort could not be brought against government departments, for they are not legal entities but consist of a number of individual Crown servants. Nor could the injured party sue the head of the department or other superior officer of the Crown servant who committed the tort, because they are fellow servants of the Crown and do not stand to each other in the relation of master and servant[33]; unless the superior officer actually ordered or directed the commission of the tort, in which case it would also be his act.[34] The general rule was therefore that the action had to be brought against the actual wrongdoer or wrongdoers, and it had to be brought against them personally and not as servants or agents of the Crown or of the department, nor as a department. Thus in *Raleigh* v. *Goschen*[35] an action for trespass to land brought against Goschen (First Lord of the Admiralty), the Lords Commissioners of the Admiralty and the Director-General of Naval Works was dismissed on the ground that it should have been brought against the engineer employed by the Admiralty and/or the two marines who actually committed the trespass with him, and/or against such (if any) of the defendants personally as had actually ordered or directed the trespass.

A proviso to section 2(1) adds that the Crown shall not be liable unless, apart from the Act, an action in tort would have lain against the servant or agent. This may be intended to preserve such defences as act of state or acting under prerogative or statutory powers (which in any case is provided for by section 11); but is has the effect of exempting the Crown in any exceptional cases which might arise where an ordinary

---

[33] *Bainbridge* v. *Postmaster-General* [1906] 1 K.B. 178; *Town Investments* v. *Department of the Environment* [1977] 2 W.L.R. 450 (H.L.).

[34] *Lane* v. *Cotton* (1701) Ld.Raym. 646.

[35] [1898] 1 Ch. 73: the Admiralty wanted the land at Dartmouth in order to build a naval college. See also *Madrazo* v. *Willes* (1820) 3 B. & Ald. 353, and *Walker* v. *Baird* [1892] A.C. 491 (naval captains liable for wrongful damage to property inflicted in the supposed course of duty).

employer might be held liable even though the servant who actually committed the tort could not for some reason be sued.[36]

In *Dorset Yacht Co. Ltd.* v. *Home Office*,[37] where the plaintiff's yacht was damaged by Borstal trainees who had escaped from a nearby camp where they were under the control of Borstal officers, the House of Lords held as a preliminary issue that the Home Office owed a duty of care to the plaintiffs capable of giving rise to liability in damages if negligence could be proved. Lord Denning M.R. in the Court of Appeal said that the Crown would be similarly liable if it negligently permitted prisoners to escape and they commit foreseeable damage.[38]

The tortious acts of prison staff *to* prisoners may also give rise to cases of vicarious liability.[39]

(b) *Breach of common law duties owed by an employer to his employees, viz.* to supply proper plant, to provide a safe system of working and to select fit and competent fellow-servants.[40]

(c) *Common law liability attaching to the ownership, occupation, possession or control of property.* This would include liability for nuisance; the rule in *Rylands* v. *Fletcher*[41]; liability for dangerous chattels, etc. The right to sue under section 2 is implied, for *ubi jus ibi remedium.*[42]

Section 2(2) provides that, in those cases where the crown is bound by *statutory duties* which are also binding on persons other than the Crown and its officers, the Crown shall be liable in tort for breach of such statutory duties if private persons are so liable.[43] In order to make the Crown liable under this subsection it must be shown, first, that the Crown is *bound* by the statute (*e.g.* Factories Act 1961; Occupiers' Liability Act 1957; the Health and Safety at Work etc. Act 1974),[44] the presumption against this[45] being preserved by section 40(2); secondly, that other persons (including local authorities or public corporations) are also bound by the statute; and thirdly, that other persons can be made

---

[36] *e.g. Smith* v. *Moss* [1940] 1 K.B. 424. And see *Twine* v. *Bean's Express Ltd.* [1946] 1 All E.R. 202, 204.

[37] [1970] A.C. 1004. In *Greenwell* v. *Prison Commissioners* (1951) 101 L.J. 486; (1952) 68 L.Q.R. 18 the plaintiffs obtained damages in a county court for damage to their vehicle caused by boys who had escaped from an "open" Borstal. See C. J. Hamson, "Escaping Borstal Boys and the Immunity of Office" (1969) 27 C.L.J. 273. See too *Writtle (Vicar of)* v. *Essex C.C.* (1979) 77 L.G.R. 656 (The case of the infant arsonist). The limitations to *Dorset Yacht* in the context of general principles of tortious liability are discussed in *King* v. *Liverpool C.C.* [1986] 1 W.L.R. 890 (C.A.).

[38] See *Greenwell* v. *Prison Commissioners, ante.*

[39] *Morgan* v. *Att.-Gen.* [1965] N.Z.L.R. 134; *Ferguson* v. *Home Office, The Times,* October 8, 1977. A claim in negligence failed in *Ellis* v. *Home Office* [1953] 2 Q.B. 135 where the Home Secretary successfully claimed that Crown Privilege entitled the withholding of documents vital to the plaintiff's case. A claim alleging assault and trespass against a prison doctor failed in *Freeman* v. *Home Office (No. 2)* [1984] Q.B. 524; *ante.* p. 514.

[40] *Joseph* v. *Ministry of Defence, The Times,* March 4, 1980 (C.A.). (Unsuccessful claim by employee of Ministry of Defence for illness allegedly caused by breach of employer's duty.)

[41] (1866) L.R. 1 Ex. 265; (1868) L.R. 3 H.L. 330.

[42] *Ashby* v. *White* (1703) 1 Smith L.C. (13th ed.), p. 251; 2 Ld.Raym. 320, 938.

[43] *Cf. Royster* v. *Cavey* [1947] K.B. 204; *Cooper* v. *Hawkins* [1904] 2 K.B. 164.

[44] *Pisicani* v. *Post Office, The Times,* May 11, 1967 (C.A.).

[45] *Ante,* p. 276.

liable in tort for such breach. Thus the Ministry of Transport owes a duty to take reasonable care when siting large road signs.[46]

Where functions are conferred by law directly on an officer of the Crown, he is regarded for the purpose of this section as if he were acting as an agent under instructions from the Crown (subs.(3)). The Crown has the benefit of any statute regulating or limiting the liability of a government department or Crown officer (subs.(4)).

Subsection 5 excludes proceedings against the Crown for acts done by any person "while discharging or purporting to discharge any responsibilities of a judicial nature vested in him, or any responsibilities which he has in connection with the execution of judicial process".[47-48] Thus if judges, magistrates or constables exceed the limits of their immunity, they do not—even if they are regarded as Crown servants or agents[49]—render the Crown liable for torts committed while discharging or purporting to discharge their judicial functions.

Officers (i.e Ministers and other servants: section 38(2)) who may render the Crown liable under section 2 are limited to those appointed directly or indirectly by the Crown and paid wholly out of the Consolidated Fund or moneys provided by Parliament, or holding an office which would normally be so paid (subs.(6)). This provision, which is narrower than the vague common law definition of a Crown servant,[50] covers unpaid temporary civil servants, but not police or other public officers forming part of the government of the country who are appointed or paid by local or other public authorities.[51]

Many actions against the Crown in tort have been commenced in the High Court and county court, but most have been settled.[52] A number of writs have been in running-down cases, involving the negligence of drivers of government-owned vehicles.[53]

Where the Crown is liable under Part I of the Act, section 4 applies to the Crown the law relating to indemnity and contribution between tortfeasors and contributory negligence.[54] It is presumed that the Crown is bound by certain statutes reforming the law of tort, whether passed

---

[46] *Levine* v. *Morris* [1970] 1 W.L.R. 71 (C.A.).

[47-48] See A. Rubinstein, "Liability in Tort of Judicial Officers" (1963) 15 U.T.L.J. 317.

[49] *Cf.* Holdsworth, "The Constitutional Position of the Judges" (1932) 48 L.Q.R. 25–26; *Lewis* v. *Cattle* [1938] 2 K.B. 454 (police constable).

[50] *Bank voor Handel en Scheepvaart N.V.* v. *Administrator of Hungarian Property* [1954] A.C. 584 (H.L.). See also *Ranaweera* v. *Ramachandran* [1970] A.C. 962 (P.C.) at 972–973, *per* Lord Diplock.

[51] See now Police Act 1964, s.48 for vicarious liability of Chief Constables; *ante* p. 412. For a successful claim in negligence see *Rigby* v. *Chief Constable of Northamptonshire* [1985] 1 W.L.R. 1242. *Stanbury* v. *Exeter Corporation* [1905] 2 K.B. 838 (agricultural inspector); *Tamlin* v. *Hannaford* [1950] 1 K.B. 18 (British Transport Commission).

[52] See, *e.g. Churchill* v. *Foot, The Times,* January 28, 1968; *Freshwater Biological Association* v. *Ministry of Defence, The Times,* December 14, 1970.

[53] In *Browning* v. *War Office* [1963] 1 Q.B. 750 (C.A.), where a member of the United States Air Force was injured through the negligence of a driver of a British army lorry, the question in issue was the measure of damages. See also *Brazier* v. *Ministry of Defence* [1965] 1 Lloyds Rep. 26; *The Tramontana II* v. *Ministry of Defence and Martin* [1969] 2 Lloyds Rep. 94; *Bright* v. *Att.-Gen.* [1971] 2 Lloyds Rep. 68 (C.A.).

[54] In particular, the Law Reform (Married Women and Tortfeasors) Act 1935 and the Law Reform (Contributory Negligence) Act 1945.

before or after the Crown Proceedings Act, even though the intention to bind the Crown does not appear either in the Crown Proceedings Act or expressly or by necessary implication in such statutes themselves. Section 10 of the Crown Proceedings Act (*infra*) seems to imply that the Fatal Accidents Act 1846 (compensation for dependants of deceased) and the Law Reform (Miscellaneous Provisions) Act 1934, s.1 (survival of causes of action on death) apply to the Crown.[55] But nothing is said about the Crown, for instance, in the Defamation Act 1952, which Act put the defendant in a better position than he was at common law.[56]

Section 3 makes the Crown liable if it authorises a servant or agent to infringe a patent, trademark or design or copyright.[57] The statutory right of the Crown is preserved to use patents on paying compensation assessed by the Treasury,[58] as are rights of the Crown under the Atomic Energy Act 1946.

There are certain matters where the analogy between the Crown and the subject breaks down, for in these spheres the functions of the Crown involve responsibility of a kind which no subject undertakes. Examples are the defence of the realm and the maintenance of the armed forces.[59]

Provisions relating to the armed forces
Section 10 provides that

"(1) *Nothing done or omitted to be done by a member of the armed forces*[60] *or the Crown while on duty as such*[61] *shall subject either him or the Crown to liability in tort for causing the death of another person, or for causing personal injury to another person, in as far as the death or personal injury is due to anything suffered by that other person while he is a member of the armed forces of the Crown if—(a) at the time when that thing is suffered by that other person, he is either on duty as a member of the armed forces of the Crown or is, though not on duty as such, on any land, premises, ship, aircraft or vehicle for the time being used for the purposes of the armed forces of the Crown; and (b) [the Secretary of State] certifies that his suffering that thing has been or will be treated as attributable to service for the purposes of entitlement to an award under the Royal Warrant, Order in Council or Order of His Majesty relating to the disablement or death of members of the force of which he is a member: Provided that this subsection shall not exempt a mem-*

---

[55] In *Levine* v. *Morris* [1970] 1 W.L.R. 71 (C.A.) the personal representatives of a man killed in a motor accident successfully sued the Ministry of Transport as well as a private driver for negligence.

[56] See G. H. Treitel, "Crown Proceedings: Some Recent Developments" [1957] P.L. 321, 322–326; Hogg, *op. cit.* p. 100, note 6 and p. 232, note 3.

[57] The infringement of a patent copyright is not properly classified as a tort, but it was held in *Feather* v. *Reg.* (1865) 6 B. & S. 257 that a petition of right was not appropriate.

[58] Since the Patent Act 1907 patents are effective against the Crown, but the Crown has a right to use patents on paying compensation. See *Pfizer Corporation* v. *Ministry of Health* [1965] A.C. 512 (H.L.), use of patented drugs by hospital under National Health Service. See now, Patents and Design Act 1977, ss.55–59.

[59] Also formerly the Post Office, *ante*, Chap. 29.

[60] Including pensionable members of any organisation established under the control of the Admiralty, the Army Council or the Air Council; s.38(5).

[61] Including civil defence duty; Civil Defence (Armed Forces) Act 1954.

ber of the said forces from liability in tort in any case in which the court is
satisfied that the act or omission was not connected with the execution of his
duties as a member of those forces."

The meaning of subsection (1) was considered by the Court of Appeal
in *Bell* v. *Secretary of State for Defence.*[62] A soldier had been injured in
the course of a fight in a British army camp in Germany. He was sent to
a German civilian hospital for treatment where he died. His death was
alleged to be the result of the negligent failure of the army doctor to supply the hospital with adequate medical information about the injuries
sustained in the camp. In the view of the majority of the Court the
'thing suffered" by the soldier was the continuing, allegedly, negligent
omission of the doctor which operated to cause his death at the hospital
so that it occurred outside the limits of section 10. Sir John Donaldson
M.R. (dissenting) held that the "thing suffered" was the act of sending
him from the camp without adequate medical records. Once that thing
had occurred within the camp section 10 operated to bar an action if the
Secretary of State issues a certificate under subsection 1(b).

The immunity conferred on the Crown by section 10(1) operates if a
certificate is issued, even if a pension is not subsequently paid.

In *Adams* v. *War Office*[63] A, a reservist, was killed while on duty by
the bursting of a shell fired by other members of the armed forces on
duty. The minister certified that A's death was attributable to service for
the purposes of entitlement to an award, but later decided that no
award should be made as A's father did not satisfy the conditions of the
royal warrant under which parents may claim a pension. A's father then
claimed damages against the War Office for negligence, arguing that the
Minister's certificate was void and therefore the exemption of the
Crown under section 10 did not apply; but it was held that as the Minister's certificate had been issued, the Crown was exempt under section
10.

If any question arises as to whether a soldier was on duty, whether
the premises were being used for the purposes of the armed forces, etc.,
the Secretary of State may, "if satisfied" of the facts issue a certificate
which, for the purposes of the section is conclusive as to the fact which
it certifies (section 10(3)).[64]

The result of section 10(1) is that as regards the Crown, the doctrine of
common employment—which has been abolished for civilians[65]—is
applied in an extended form to members of the armed forces. The section answers the question (raised by Lord Jowitt, not Tennyson)

---

[62] [1986] Q.B. 322; followed by Caulfield J., *Pearce* v. *Secretary of State for Defence* [1987] 2
W.L.R. 782. (Allegation of illness following participation in tests of nuclear weapons
conducted by the Atomic Energy Authority. Illness not something suffered as result of
nature of the premises, etc. Judge was concerned with s. 10(2); subs. 1 not applicable
because A.E.A. not member of the forces.)

[63] [1955] 1 W.L.R. 1116; approved *Bell* v. *Secretary of State for the Defence, supra.*

[64] In *Smith* v. *Ministry of Defence* [1985] C.L. 912 Woolf J. is recorded as having held that he
had jurisdiction to review the exercise of the minister's discretion under s.10 but on the
facts before him there was no ground to interfere.

[65] Law Reform (Personal Injuries) Act 1948. One soldier could sue another at common law
for wrongful injury done to him when both were on duty: *Weaver* v. *Ward* (1616) Hob.
134.

whether a trooper whose leg was shattered by a cannonball in the charge of the Light Brigade could recover damages on the ground that Raglan had blundered.

Subsection (2) confers a similar immunity on the Crown from actions for death or injury suffered in consequence of the nature or condition of land, premises, ship, vehicle or aircraft which are being used for the purposes of the armed forces of the Crown provided that the Secretary of State certifies as in subsection 1(b). Nor will any action lie against any officer of the Crown whose act has caused death or injury if the Secretary of State certifies in the terms of subsection 1.

An attempt to circumvent section 10 was made in *Brown* v. *Lord Advocate*.[66] The pursuer had been injured while taking part in a Territorial Army exercise in West Germany. A certificate had been issued under section 10 which, it was conceded, barred an action against the officer whose negligence was said to have caused the accident on the autobahn in which Brown was injured. He claimed, however, that a duty was owed by the Ministry of Defence to ensure that such exercises were carried out safely. The Lord Ordinary (Mayfield) held that the action was incompetent; the allegations against the Ministry were simply a device to evade section 10. Nor, apart from the section, did the learned judge believe that any duty of care had been shown to be owed to the pursuer by the Ministry.

There is nothing in section 10 to exclude the possibility of a civilian injured by the negligent act of a member of the armed forces suing the Crown in reliance on section 2(1)(a).[67]

Towards the end of 1986 the Government announced that it was willing to see the repeal of section 10 because it accepted that the compensation payable to members of the armed forces whose claims for injuries fell within the section was often lower than would have been obtained by way of damages in actions in the courts.

Acts done under prerogative or statutory powers

Section 11 states that nothing in the above provisions shall extinguish or abridge the prerogative or statutory powers of the Crown: in particular, the powers exercisable by the Crown, whether in peace or war, for the defence of the realm or the training or maintenance of the armed forces. Among prerogative powers not mentioned are those relating to the treatment of aliens, the employment of Crown servants and the principle of the *Amphitrite* case.[68] Statutory powers would include the billeting of soldiers.

A Secretary of State, "if satisfied" as to the facts, may issue a conclusive certificate that the act was necessarily done in the exercise of the prerogative, for example that it was necessary for the sake of practice to fire guns that have broken windows or kept people awake at night. It

---

[66] 1984 S.L.T. 146.
[67] See Hogg, *op. cit.* pp. 93 *et seq.* An unsuccessful attempt at such an action is to be found in *Farrell* v. *Secretary of State for Defence* [1980] 1 W.L.R. 172 (H.L.). See also *Lynch* v. *Ministry of Defence* [1983] N.I. 216.
[68] *Rederiaktiebolaget Amphitrite* v. *The King* [1921] 3 K.B. 500; *ante*, 706.

remains the function of the court to decide whether, and to what extent, the alleged prerogative exists.[69] This section is of fundamental importance for the word "prerogative" has a very wide range.

No such certificate may be made in the case of statutory powers, and indeed their express preservation was not necessary.

The Queen in her private capacity

The Act does not apply to proceedings by or against, nor does it authorise proceedings in tort to be brought against, the Queen in her private capacity (section 40(1)), or in right of the Duchy of Lancaster or Cornwall (section 38(3)). This preserves the Queen's personal immunity in tort; but it is uncertain whether for breach of contract (*e.g.* sale of groceries to Buckingham Palace) or wrongful detention of property by the Queen personally the subject can still proceed under the Petitions of Right Act 1860, or whether he is thrown back on the ancient common law petition of right.[70] There are in fact no reported instances of petitions of right against a Sovereign in his private capacity, but the doubt as to procedure is inconvenient as Her Majesty might legitimately wish to deny liability or dispute the amount.

Estoppel

The arguments for and against applying the doctrine of estoppel to public bodies generally have been discussed earlier.[71] The same arguments apply to the Crown in its public capacity and there is judicial authority for the view that the same answer applies to the Crown.[72] In *Laker Airways Ltd.* v. *Department of Trade*[73] Lord Denning M.R. said, "The underlying principle is that the Crown cannot be estopped from exercising its powers, whether given in a statute or by common law, when it is doing so in the proper exercise of its duty to act for the public good, even though this may work some injustice or unfairness to a private individual. . . . It can, however, be estopped when it is not properly exercising its powers, but is misusing them; and it does misuse them if it exercises them in circumstances which work injustice or unfairness to the individual without any countervailing benefit for the public.[74]

---

[69] *Case of Monopolies* (1602) 11 Co.Rep. 84b; *Case of Proclamations* (1610) 12 Co.Rep. 74; *Att.-Gen.* v. *De Keyser's Royal Hotel Ltd.* [1920] A.C. 506 (H.L.); *Burmah Oil Co.* v. *Lord Advocate* [1965] A.C. 75 (H.L.).

[70] See post, p. 717.

[71] *Ante*, p. 676.

[72] *e.g. Robertson* v. *Minister of Pensions* [1949] 1 K.B. 227; In *Re 56 Denton Road Twickenham* [1953] Ch. 51. But see *Howell* v. *Falmouth Boat Construction Co. Ltd.* [1951] A.C. 837, 845 per Lord Simonds. The application of estoppel by representation was discussed, but not decided, in *Territorial and Auxiliary Forces Association* v. *Nichols* [1944] 1 K.B. 35 (C.A.).

[73] [1977] Q.B. 643.

[74] See further, H. Street, *Governmental Liability* (1953), p. 156; P. W. Hogg, *Liability of the Crown* (1971), p. 146. There seems to be no doubt that the Crown is bound by equitable proprietary estoppel: *Plimmer* v. *Mayor of Wellington* (1884) 9 App.Cas. 699; *Att.-Gen. to Prince of Wales* v. *Collom* [1916] 2 K.B. 193.

II. Civil Proceedings by and Against the Crown[75]

Jurisdiction and procedure

The Crown Proceedings Act 1947 provides that the civil proceedings[76] by and against the Crown which are allowed by Part I of the Act shall be heard in the High Court (section 13) or the county court (section 15) as in actions between subjects and in accordance with rules of court, and similar principles apply to appeals (section 22).

The Treasury is required to publish a list of authorised government departments, and proceedings are to be instituted by or against the appropriate department, or—if there is, or appears to be, no appropriate department—the Attorney-General (section 17). It will be noticed that proceedings under the Act are not taken by or against either the Queen or the ministerial head of the department.

Section 21 of the Crown Proceedings Act prohibits the granting of an injunction or specific performance against the Crown or against an officer of the Crown if the effect of the order would be to give any relief against the Crown which could not have been obtained directly in proceedings against the Crown. The Court may, however, grant an order declaratory of the rights of the parties, *e.g. R. v. Secretary of State for the Home Department ex p. McAvoy*.[77] Nor will the Court order a stay of proceedings against the Crown when to do so is equivalent to granting an injunction against the Crown; *R. v. Secretary of State for the Home Department ex p. Kirkwood*.[78] According to a recent High Court decision, however, an injunction may be granted against the Crown or a Crown officer in proceedings brought by way of application for judicial review under Order 53; *R. v. Governor of Pentonville Prison ex p. Herbage*.[79]

The House of Lords considered section 21 in *R. v. Inland Revenue Commissioners, ex p. Rossminster*.[80] The applicants challenged the legality of warrants under which the Inland Revenue entered their premises and removed quantities of documents. On the day of the search they obtained an injunction ordering the Revenue to leave their premises. In later proceedings they sought a declaration that the warrants were invalid. In the Court of Appeal it was accepted that the injunction ought not to have been issued; the officials of the Inland Revenue were entitled to the protection of section 21 of the 1947 Act. The Court of Appeal, however, held that it had jurisdiction to grant a declaration that

---

[75] R. M. Bell, *Crown Proceedings* (1948); J. R. Bickford Smith, *The Crown Proceedings Act 1947* (1948); Glanville L. Williams, *Crown Proceedings* (1948); Carleton Allen, *Law and Orders* (3rd ed.), Chap. 10; S. A. de Smith, *Judicial Review of Administrative Action* (2nd ed., 1968); H. Street, *Governmental Liability* (1953); B. Schwartz and H. W. R. Wade Q.C., *Legal Control of Government* (1972). The procedure in Scotland is governed by Part V of the Crown Proceedings Act; see J. D. B. Mitchell, *Constitutional Law* (2nd ed., 1968) Chap. 17; Bickford Smith, *op. cit*.pp. 53–58, 100–106 (by J. W. B. Middleton); Fraser, *Outline of Constitutional Law* (2nd ed.), pp. 157–169.

[76] The Act does not apply to criminal or Prize proceedings; nor does it affect proceedings on the Crown side of the Queen's Bench Division, *e.g.* habeas corpus, certiorari, prohibition and mandamus (s.38(2)).

[77] [1984] 1 W.L.R. 1408.

[78] [1984] 1 W.L.R. 913. *R. v. Secretary of State for the Home Department ex p. Mohammed Yaqood* [1984] 1 W.L.R. 920 (C.A.).

[79] [1986] 3 W.L.R. 504. Hodgson J. refused relief on the facts.

[80] [1980] A.C. 952; *ante* p. 527.

the warrants were invalid although the proceedings were, in fact, interlocutory. The House of Lords upheld the validity of the warrants and expressed grave doubts about whether in the absence of a power to grant an interim declaration,[81] the Court of Appeal ought to have granted a final declaration in interlocutory proceedings.[82] Lord Diplock thought that a serious procedural defect in administrative law had been revealed; the absence of any means of obtaining interlocutory relief against the Crown and its officers.[83] Lord Wilberforce, Viscount Dilhorne and Lord Scarman all expressed doubt about the wisdom of interim remedies being available against the Crown; "The State's decisions must be respected unless and until they are shown to be wrong."[84]

If the Crown seeks an injunction it may, since 1947, be required to give an undertaking in damages as a condition of its being granted, as in the case of a private litigant, except where the injunction is sought, not to enforce a proprietary or contractual right of the Crown, but to restrain a breach of the law in the public interest.[85]

The remedies provided by the Act do not limit the discretion of the Court to grant mandamus in cases where that might have been granted before the commencement of the Act, i.e. (semble) where a duty is owed to a citizen.[86]

An action may be brought against the Attorney-General or (since the Crown Proceedings Act) against the appropriate authorised department, asking the court to declare what the law is on a given point where the Crown or servants of the Crown threaten to do something which is thought to be illegal. This remedy against the Crown originated in the Court of Exchequer.[87] In *Dyson* v. *Attorney-General*[88] the Court of Appeal held that this was a proper procedure where the plaintiff contended that a threat by the Inland Revenue Commissioners to impose a pecuniary penalty for neglecting to make certain returns within a specified time was illegal and *ultra vires* the Finance Act 1910.[89] The action cannot be brought where a petition of right was formerly appropriate, e.g. for a money claim against the Treasury.[90]

---

[81] *International General Electric Co. of New York Ltd.* v. *Customs & Excise Cmrs.* [1962] Ch. 784.

[82] But see *Clarke* v. *Chadburn* [1985] 1 W.L.R. 78 where Sir Robert Megarry V.-C. held that the special circumstances (wilful contempt of a court order and the rights of a large number of people) justified a final declaration in interlocutory proceedings.

[83] See similarly the Law Commission, *Remedies in Administrative Law* (1976) Law Com. 73, Cmnd. 6407.

[84] [1980] A.C. 952, 1027 *per* Lord Scarman. Compare the attitude of the House of Lords to challenges to the validity of delegated legislation: *Hoffman La Roche & Co.* v. *Secretary of State for Trade and Insustry* [1975] A.C. 295.

[85] *Hoffman La Roche & Co.* v. *Secretary of State for Trade and Industry* [1975] A.C. 295.

[86] See *Padfield* v. *Minister of Agriculture, Fisheries and Food* [1968] A.C. 997; *ante*, p. 689.

[87] *Pawlett* v. *Att.-Gen.* (1668) Hardr. 465. See *Tito* v. *Waddell (No. 2)* [1977] Ch. 106, 256.

[88] [1911] 1 K.B. 410; discussed by the House of Lords in *Gouriet* v. *Union of Post Office Workers* [1978] A.C. 435. See also *Hodge* v. *Att.-Gen.* (1839) 3 Y. & Co.Ex. 342; *Esquimalt and Nanaimo Ry.* v. *Wilson* [1920] A.C. 358 (P.C.).

[89] See also *Gillick* v. *West Norfolk and Wisbech Area Health Authority* [1986] A.C. 112; *ante* p. 689.

[90] *Bombay and Persia Steam Navigation Co.* v. *Maclay* [1920] 3 K.B. 402, 408. Nor can the court make an interim (interlocutory) declaration against the Crown in such cases: *Underhill* v. *Ministry of Food* [1950] 1 All E.R. 591.

Certain existing procedures which were already working satisfactorily were retained, *e.g.* relator actions, and proceedings by or against the Public Trustee, Charity Commissioners and Registrar of the Land Registry (section 23). Proceedings against the Crown by petition of right and *monstrans de droit* were abolished, and the Petitions of Right Act 1860 was wholly repealed.[91]

Statutes relating to the limitation of actions now generally bind the Crown.[92]

Proceedings against the Sovereign in her private capacity

The Petitions of Right Act 1860 contemplated that petitions of right could be brought against the Sovereign in her private capacity, for section 14 distinguished these from petitions relating to any public matter. In the case of public matters the Treasury were authorised to pay out of moneys legally applicable thereto or voted by Parliament for that purpose, while in the case of private matters the amount to which the suppliant was entitled was to be found out of such moneys as Her Majesty should be graciously pleased to direct. At first sight section 29(1) and the Second Schedule to the Crown Proceedings Act appear to repeal the Petitions of Right Act completely; and as section 40(1) of all the Crown Proceedings Act provides that "nothing in this Act shall apply to proceedings by or against, or authorise proceedings in tort to be brought against, His Majesty in His private capacity," it would seem that a citizen in proceeding against the Queen in her private capacity (*e.g.* for groceries supplied to her at Buckingham Palace), is thrown back on the old common law procedure by petition of right—for it cannot be contemplated that the Act intended to render the subject altogether remediless in such cases. On the other hand, the saving clause in section 40(1) above and the expression "subject to the provisions of this Act" in sections 1 and 13 could be held to mean that neither the abolition of petitions of right nor the repeal of the petitions of Right Act applies to proceedings against Her Majesty in her private capacity. The latter is probably the better interpretation, although the draftsman has gone a clumsy way about it.[93]

Judgments and execution

The Crown is put in the same position as subjects with regard to interest on debts, damages and costs (s.24). The Act requires the appropriate department to pay any damages and costs certified in the order of the court; but no execution can be levied against the Crown,[94] and no

---

[91] *Cf. Franklin* v. *Att.-Gen.* [1974] Q.B. 185 where claims to interest on Rhodesian government stock under the Colonial Stock Act 1877 were brought under the old common law procedure governing petitions of right. See also *Franklin* v. *Att.-Gen. (No. 2)* [1974] Q.B. 205 (C.A.); *Barclays Bank* v. *The Queen* [1974] Q.B. 823.

The following proceedings by the Crown were also abolished: Latin and English informations; writs of *capias ad respondendum, subpoena ad respondendum,* and appraisement; writs of *scire facias;* writs of extent and of *diem clausit extremum;* and writs of summons under Part V of the Crown Suits Act 1865.

[92] Limitation Act 1980, s.37. But special periods may apply to claims by the Crown, *e.g.* to recover land or foreshore: Limitation Act 1980, Sched. 1, Part II.

[93] See further D. B. Murray, "When is a repeal not a repeal?" (1953) 16 M.L.R. 50.

[94] *Wick and Dennis' Case* (1589) 1 Leo. 190.

person is individually liable under any order for payment by the Crown (s.25).[95] On the other hand, the Crown relinquished its former prerogative modes of execution; and it lost its special rights to imprison for debt, except in two cases where the person would already have had the money, *viz.* failure to pay death duties or purchase tax (s.26).[96] The procedure for enforcing payment of fines, *e.g.* for smuggling, is retained.

Creditors are entitled to attach moneys owing to their debtors by the Crown in the same way as if the Crown were a subject, except for (a) wages and salaries payable by any officer of the Crown and (b) any money which by law is exempted from being taken in execution or assigned (section 27)[97]

Discovery and interrogatories

The Crown Proceedings Act allowed the court for the first time to require the Crown, *in civil proceedings to which the Crown is a party,* to make discovery of documents and to answer interrogatories (s.28(1)).[98] Discovery is the disclosure which one party to an action commenced by writ is generally required to make to the other party of relevant documents which are, or have been, in his possession, custody or power. In exceptional cases a court order for discovery is necessary. Certain documents are privileged from production.[99] Interrogatories are written questions relevant to the action which a party may administer to his opponent to be answered on affidavit. Leave of the Master is required, and privilege may be claimed on the same grounds as in discovery of documents.

Crown Privilege and Public Interest Immunity

The proviso to section 28(1) preserves the rule—*applying also to actions to which the Crown is not a party,* and covering the trial as well as interlocutory proceedings—which authorises or requires the withholding of any document or the refusal to answer any question on the ground that the disclosure of the document or the answering of the question would be *injurious to the public interest.* The objection to such disclosure or answer is usually made by the head of the department concerned.

Subsection (2) goes further by providing that any rules of court made for the purpose of section 28 shall secure that the *existence* of a document will not be disclosed if, in the opinion of a Minister of the Crown,

---

[95] It is still possible, however, to sue a Crown servant personally for damages in a case like *Raleigh* v. *Goschen* [1898] 1 Ch. 73 (*ante*, p. 708) although there does not seem to be much point in doing so.

[96] The provision relating to purchase tax was repealed by the Finance Act 1972, s. 54(8) and Sched. 28, Pt. II.

[97] Formerly this section (and section 46 which applied to Scotland) also exempted the National Savings Bank from its provisions. In England this exemption was removed by the Supreme Court Act 1981 s.139. See *Brooks Associates Inc.* v. *Basu* [1983] Q.B. 220 where Woolf J. applied English law although the head office of the Bank is in Scotland. Scots Law was amended by the Law Reform (Miscellaneous Provisions) (Scotland) Act 1985 s.49.

[98] And see Administration of Justice Act 1970, s.35, applying Part III of the Act (Discovery and Related Procedures) to the Crown, including inspection of property before certain proceedings.

[99] See further Rules of the Supreme Court, Order 24.

it would be injurious to the public interest[1] to disclose the existence thereof. This exception was necessary because the general rules of court require that the documents which the party objects to producing should be set out in the affidavit of documents, and the Crown may wish to claim privilege for the fact that a document exists.

At the time of the passing of the 1947 Act, and for many years afterwards, it was believed to be the law in England, as the result of dicta in *Duncan* v. *Cammell, Laird*, that the Crown possessed a right to withhold documents on the grounds of public interest in a wide range of cases without such right being, in any real sense, subject to judicial control.[2] However, after criticism of this wide view of "Crown Privilege" in a number of decisions in the Court of Appeal,[3] the House of Lords restated the Law in *Conway* v. *Rimmer*.[4] In that case C, a former probationary police constable, brought an action for malicious prosecution against R, his former superintendent. The Home Secretary, on behalf of the police, objected to the production of reports made concerning the plaintiff during his probation—one of which was made for transmission to the Director of Public Prosecutions concerning the prosecution which was the subject-matter of these proceedings—on the ground that they belonged to classes of documents the production of any of which would be contrary to the public interest. The House of Lords held unanimously that: (i) the classes were not such that their production would obviously be contrary to the public interest; (ii) the Home Secretary's claim was therefore not conclusive; and (iii) the court might call for the documents, and decide after inspecting them whether an order for their production to the other party ought to be made. *Duncan* v. *Cammell, Laird* was not followed, and may be said to have been overruled so far as concerns the inspection by the court of documents in a civil case for which the Crown claims privilege. Otherwise the main effect of *Conway* v. *Rimmer* was to narrow the ratio of *Duncan* v. *Cammell, Laird* by holding that Viscount Simon's dicta were too wide, although the actual decision was, on the facts, undoubtedly right.

Lord Reid later in *Conway* v. *Rimmer* announced that he had examined the documents, and could find nothing in any of them the dis-

---

[1] The Memorandum accompanying the Crown Proceedings Bill specified "defence, foreign affairs, and related matters." On the second reading, suggestions that "public security," "public safety" or "defence of the realm" should be substituted for "public interest" were not accepted by the government.

For the appalling case of *Odlum* v. *Stratton* (1946), see Allen, *Law and Orders* (3rd ed.), App. 2.

[2] [1942] A.C. 624. The dependants of sailors who were drowned in a new British submarine, *Thetis*, which sank on her trials just before the beginning of the Second World War had brought an action against the builders of *Thetis*. War had begun when the litigation commenced and the House of Lords upheld the First Lord of the Admiralty's objection to the production of plans of the submarine which were in the possession of the contractors. Captain H. P. K. Oram, one of the four survivors of the disaster, died in June 1986, aged 92.

[3] *Merricks* v. *Nott-Bower* [1965] 1 Q.B. 57; *Re Grosvenor Hotel, London (No. 2)* [1965] Ch. 1210; *Wednesbury Borough Council* v. *Ministry of Housing and Local Government* [1965] 1 W.L.R. 261; [1965] 1 All E.R. 186.

[4] [1968] A.C. 910, citing Scottish, Australian and American cases. In *Glasgow Corporation* v. *Central Land Board*, 1956 S.C.(H.L.) 1 the House of Lords had held that *Duncan* v. *Cammell, Laird* did not represent Scots Law.

closure of which would be prejudicial to the proper administration of the local constabulary or to the general public interest. He was therefore of the opinion that they must be made available in the litigation. Their Lordships accordingly voted "that the defendant do produce for inspection at the solicitor's office to the plaintiff and his advisers on reasonable notice the five documents."[5]

Subsequent decisions of the House of Lords have established that the phrase "Crown Privilege," used to describe the withholding of documents on the ground of public interest, is a misnomer for two reasons. First, because the Crown does not have the choice whether or not to withhold the documents in question. Non-production is *required* by the public interest and is a matter which may be raised by any party to the litigation or by the court itself.[6] Second, public interest as a ground for non-disclosure of documents is not confined to the functioning of departments or organs of the central government. In so holding, the House of Lords, in *D. v. N.S.P.C.C.*,[7] allowed the respondent society to withhold the sources of information which it received of an alleged instance of cruelty to children.

The right (or duty) to withhold documents in the public interest is now generally described as *Public Interest Immunity*. Lord Scarman, however, sounded a warning note in *Science Research Council v. Nassé*[8] when he said,

> "I regret the passing of the currently rejected term 'Crown Privilege'. It at least emphasised the very restricted area of public interest immunity . . . [which] exists to protect from disclosure only information the secrecy of which is essential to the proper working of the government of the state. Defence, foreign relations, the inner workings of government at the highest level . . . and the prosecution process in its pre-trial stage are the sensitive areas where the Crown must have the immunity of the government of the nation is to be effectually carried on. We are in the realm of public law, not private right."

Lord Scarman regarded the *N.S.P.C.C.* case as exceptional, turning on the special position of the Society in enforcing the provisions of the Children and Young Persons Act 1969 which was comparable with that of a prosecuting authority in criminal proceedings.

In deciding whether to allow documents to be withheld the courts now try to weigh in the balance the public interest of the nation or the public service in non-disclosure against the public interest of justice in the production of the documents. The balancing of the conflicting

---

[5] *Conway v. Rimmer* (Note) [1968] A.C. 996; [1968] 2 All E.R. 304n. (Nevertheless, the plaintiff eventually lost his action for malicious prosecution because he failed to prove want of reasonable cause: *The Times*, December 17, 1969.) See also *Norwich Pharmacal Co. v. Customs and Excise Commissioners* [1974] A.C. 133; Tapper (1974) 37 M.L.R. 92.

[6] *Rogers v. Home Secretary* [1973] A.C. 388; applied, *R. v. Cheltenham Justices* [1977] 1 W.L.R. 95; *Crompton (Alfred) Amusement Machines v. Customs and Excise Commissioners (No. 2)* [1974] A.C. 405; *Air Canada v. Secretary of State (No. 2)* [1983] 2 A.C. 394; *Cf. Medway v. Doublelock Ltd.* [1978] 1 W.L.R. 710.

[7] [1978] A.C. 171.

[8] [1980] A.C. 1028, 1088.

claims involved in a claim of privilege will inevitably lead to different conclusions in different cases depending on the weight particular judges give, for example, to the need to protect confidential information or facilitate inquiries into allegations of misconduct. Thus the House of Lords upheld the refusal of an order of discovery in *Lonrho Ltd.* v. *Shell Petroleum*[9] on the ground of the need to guarantee to informants complete confidentiality if a government inquiry were to have any likelihood of success in discovering the truth. The need to protect informants has also been held to outweigh a claim to discovery in two cases relating to material gathered in the course of investigations under section 49 of the Police Act 1964.[10] But in *Peach* v. *Commissioner of the Police of the Metropolis*[11] the Court of Appeal distinguished those earlier cases where documents were sought in connection with a civil action in which it was alleged that the deceased had been unlawfully killed by a police constable. The public interest in establishing the cause of a violent death outweighed the claim to confidentiality. In *Conerney* v. *Jacklin*[12] the Court of Appeal again distinguished the two earlier authorities and held that public interest immunity did not attach to the complaint, as opposed to statements made in the course of investigations, when the constable against whom the complaint had been laid sought to sue the complainant in libel.

Following the *N.S.P.C.C.* case the confidential nature of information has been recognised as justifying a claim to public interest immunity in *Gaskin* v. *Liverpool C.C.*[13] but not in *R.* v. *Bournemouth Justices ex p. Grey*[14] where information obtained by an adoption society in relation to the child of an unmarried couple was held admissible in affiliation proceedings between the same couple. Hodgson J. pointed out that in the *N.S.P.C.C.* case and *Gaskin* the objections to production had not been taken, as here, by a private person, the social worker employed by the agency, but by a public body with statutory duties. In *Campbell* v. *Thameside M.B.C.*[15] the Court of Appeal held that a teacher who had been attacked by a pupil was entitled, in an action in negligence against the local authority, to see reports made to the authority by psychologists which, she alleged, showed that the pupil was known to be violent. The importance of the documents to the teacher's case and the nature of the

---

[9] [1980] 1 W.L.R. 627. ("The circumstances which have given rise to the disputes about discovery are quite exceptional; they are unlikely to recur in any other case and, for that reason, they do not in my view provide a suitable occasion for any general disquisition by this House upon the principles of law applicable to the discovery of documents"; *per* Lord Diplock at p. 632.)

[10] *Neilson* v. *Laugharne* [1981] 1 Q.B. 736 (C.A.) criticised (1981) 97 L.Q.R. 525 (Jeffrey Price); *Hehir* v. *Commissioner of Police of the Metropolis* [1981] 1 W.L.R. 715 (C.A.). See also *Buckley* v. *The Law Society* (No. 2) [1984] 1 W.L.R. 1101 (Law Society entitled to protect names of informants when beginning statutory proceedings against solicitor accused of dishonesty). See on the other hand *London & County Securities Ltd.* v. *Nicholson* [1980] 1 W.L.R. 948 (Inquiry under Companies Act 1948 s.165).

[11] [1986] Q.B. 1064 (C.A.).

[12] [1985] Crim.L.R. 234 (C.A.).

[13] [1980] 1 W.L.R. 1549 (Child care service records) Lord Denning M.R. described the plaintiff as "a psychiatric case, mentally-disturbed and quite useless to society." For the plaintiff's side of the story, see James MacVeigh, *Gaskin* (1982).

[14] *The Times*, May 31, 1986.

[15] [1982] Q.B. 1065.

action justified distinguishing cases involving issues of wardship, child care and adoption where discovery had been refused. In *Williams* v. *Home Office*[16] McNeill J. ordered production of Home Office documents relating to the establishment of "control units" in prisons to deal with difficult prisoners because of the importance of the issues involved.

The Courts will not order discovery where it is sought by a plaintiff who is engaged on a "fishing expedition," hoping to find in documents in the defendant's possession information which might support a case against them for which he has no other evidence.[17] In *Air Canada* v. *Secretary of State for Trade (No. 2)*[18] the House of Lords refused to inspect documents for which public interest immunity had been claimed when the plaintiff had failed to show that there were reasonable grounds for believing that they contained information likely to help their case or damage their adversary's.

A claim to discovery will also fail if the action to which it is incidental must for some reason be struck out. In the context of the law relating to the Crown this is illustrated by *Buttes Gas and Oil Co.* v. *Hammer (No. 3)*[19] where the House of Lords granted an order staying all proceedings between the parties because they amounted to an attempt to require the courts to adjudicate on transactions between foreign sovereign states. Such matters fall outside the jurisdiction of the English courts.

It now seems that there are no classes of document, for example Cabinet minutes or papers, which are always immune from production. In *Burmah Oil Co. Ltd.* v. *Bank of England*[20] the appellant company sought discovery of various documents despite a detailed affidavit by the Chief Secretary to the Treasury objecting to their production on the ground of public interest. The documents included memoranda of meetings attended by Ministers but did not include Cabinet papers. The House of Lords ultimately agreed, after inspecting the documents, that production should not be ordered because disclosure of their contents was not necessary for disposing fairly of the company's case. The importance of the case lies, however, in dicta which suggest that there is no *class* of document which is, in all circumstances, immune from discovery.[21]

The claim of "Public Interest Immunity" is the personal responsibility of the ministerial head of the department, although if it does not appear that he has himself considered the documents he may be given an opportunity to swear a further affidavit.[22] Where the documents are those of a former government the affidavit may properly be sworn by a

---

[16] [1981] 1 All E.R. 1151.

[17] *Gaskin* v. *Liverpool Corporation* [1980] 1 W.L.R. 1549.

[18] [1983] 2 A.C. 394; T. S. R. Allen, "Abuse of Power and Public Interest Immunity: Justice, Rights and Truth" (1985) 101 L.Q.R. 200.

[19] [1982] A.C. 888.

[20] [1980] A.C. 1090.

[21] Lord Wilberforce at p. 1113; Lord Edmund-Davies at p. 1127; Lord Keith of Kinkel at p. 1134; Lord Scarman at p. 1144. The opposite view is expressed by Lord Salmon at p. 1121: J. Hannan, "Inspection of Cabinet Documents—To Yield or Not to Yield" (1982) 45 M.L.R. 471. See also Lord Fraser in *Air Canada* v. *Secretary of State for Trade (No. 2), supra.*

[22] *Re Grosvenor Hotel (No. 1)* [1964] Ch. 464 (C.A.).

senior civil servant because "a powerful convention prevents ministers have access to papers of their predecessors."[23]

Normally, protection can only be claimed because of the contents of a particular document and not because it belongs to a class some members of which may be justifiably withheld.[24] The courts are no longer impressed by the argument that a document must be withheld in order to ensure candour in the functioning of the public service.[25] Nor does the fact that information was communicated in confidence of itself protect that information from discovery although it may be an important factor in making the decision.[26] Oral evidence of the contents of a privileged document cannot be admitted, nor may a document which the court has ruled shall be withheld from production in the public interest be used by a witness to refresh his memory.[27]

[23] *Air Canada* v. *Secretary of State for Trade, supra, per* Lord Wilberforce.
[24] *Conway* v. *Rimmer, ante.*
[25] *e.g. Norwich Pharmacal Co.* v. *Customs and Excise Commissioners, ante.*
[26] *D.* v. *N.S.P.C.C. ante.* See also *United States* v. *Nixon* (1974) 418 U.S. 683.
[27] *Gain* v. *Gain* [1961] 1 W.L.R. 1467; *sub nom. Gane* v. *Gane* [1962] 1 All E.R. 63.

Part VII

THE COMMONWEALTH

Chapter 36

DEPENDENT TERRITORIES

I. The British Islands

The British Islands consist of the United Kingdom, the Isle of Man and the Channel Islands.[1] The Isle of Man and the Channel Islands are neither part of the United Kingdom nor are they colonies; but they are part of Her Majesty's dominions, and persons born in them are British citizens by birth. For the purposes of the British Nationality Act 1981 they are treated as part of the United Kingdom.

The inclusion of the Channel Islands and the Isle of Man in the EEC presented constitutional, administrative and economic difficulties. Accordingly, after consultation with them, the United Kingdom sought for the islands arrangements short of full membership, and proposed a form of association under Article 238 of the Treaty of Rome.[2]

Isle of Man[3]

The Isle of Man was formerly under the suzerainty of the Kings of Norway and Scotland, but Kings of England exercised some degree of control over the island after 1290 (Edward I), and the island finally came into the allegiance of the English Crown in 1399 (Henry IV). It was held more or less independently[4] by the Stanley family (Earls of Derby) as Lords of Man under letters patent until 1736, when it passed to the Duke of Atholl. The Crown bought out the Duke's regalities and customs rights in 1765.[5] To these were added the ecclesiastical patronage and other general manorial rights in 1825.[6] The island has retained its ancient internal constitution as modified by statute,[7] and has legislative autonomy in most respects. The island is, however, in strict theory subject to the authority of the United Kingdom Parliament, although Westminster legislation extending to the Isle of Man is, in practice, restricted to such matters as defence, postal services, wireless telegraphy, copyright, merchant shipping and civil aviation.[8] Not being part of the

---

[1] Interpretation Act 1978, s.5 and Sched. 1.

[2] *The United Kingdom and European Communities* (1971) Cmnd. 4715; K. R. Simmonds, "The British Islands and the Community": I Jersey (1969) 6 C.M.L.Rev. 156; II Isle of Man (1970) 7 C.M.L.Rev. 454; III Guernsey (1971) 8 C.M.L.Rev. 475.

[3] See *The British Commonwealth: Development of its Laws and Constitutions: I The United Kingdom*, pp. 485 *et seq.* (by D. C. Holland); *Report of the Commission on the Isle of Man Constitution* (1959) (Chairman, Lord MacDermott); *Report of the Joint Working Party on the Constitutional Relationship between the Isle of Man and the United Kingdom* (1969); *Royal Commission on the Constitution 1969–1973* (Kilbrandon) (1973) Cmnd. 5460, I. Part XI; G. Kinley, "The Isle of Man," *Guardian Gazette*, January 25, 1978.

[4] Although appeal lay to the Privy Council: *Christian v. Corrin* (1716) 1 P.Wms. 329.

[5] Isle of Man Purchase Act 1765.

[6] Duke of Atholl's Rights, Isle of Man, Act 1825.

[7] *e.g.* Isle of Man Constitution Acts 1961 to 1971, passed by the Manx legislature largely to implement recommendations of the MacDermott Commission (1959).

[8] For a recent example see the Isle of Man Act 1979 which deals *inter alia* with law relating to customs and excise.

United Kingdom[9] it is not bound by Acts of Parliament except where it is included either expressly or by necessary implication.[10] Statutes, such as the Prevention of Terrorism (Temporary Provisions) Act 1984, may be extended to the Island by Order in Council.

The legislature is known as the Court of Tynwald.[11] Legislation may be initiated in either branch of the legislature (Legislative Council and House of Keys,[12] and is debated in each branch separately, although there are provisions for conferences. Bills are signed in Tynwald at joint sittings of the branches: they require the confirmation of the Sovereign in Council and a declaration of the Royal Assent in Tynwald.[13]

The Queen's representative is the Lieutenant-Governor. A confidential Executive Council was set up in 1961 to advise the Lieutenant-Governor on matters of principle, policy and legislation. The Home Secretary is the main channel of communication between the United Kingdom and the Isle of Man, and advises the Lieutenant-Governor.

The island has its own system of courts. Manx land law is largely Norse in origin and is unique. Appeal lies to the Judicial Committee of the Privy Council from the Staff of Government Division.[14]

The Channel Islands[15]

The Channel Islands formed part of the Duchy of Normandy, and remained to the King of England when the rest of Normandy reverted to France in the thirteenth century. They are not part of the United Kingdom.[16] The common law of the Channel Islands is still the ancient custom of the Duchy, the principal authority being *Le Grand Coustumier du Pays et Duché de Normandie* which was compiled in the thirteenth century.

The islanders, though loyal to the Crown, affect to recognise the Sovereign only in right of the Duchy of Normandy, and they deny the

[9] *Davison* v. *Farmer* (1851) 6 Ex. 242.

[10] *Sodor and Man (Bishop)* v. *Derby (Earl)* 1751) 2 Ves.Sen. 337.

[11] Probably derived from Norse *Thing-vollr* or *Thing-Wald* = Parliament field or meeting-place of the assembly.

[12] The original of the term "Keys" is obscure: it is perhaps a corruption of a Manx Gaelic expression meaning "the twenty-four." The earliest use of the word "Keys" seems to have been in 1585.

[13] Before the Acts of Tynwald (Emergency Promulgation) Act 1916, Acts had to be promulgated in English and Manx at Tynwald Hill, St. John's, before they became law. Since the Act (s.3) they cease to have force if they are not promulgated in the customary manner within twelve months. The Royal assent was signified in 1982 by the Lieutenant Governor instead of the Queen in Council as previously.

[14] For the history of appeals, see J. H. Smith, *Appeals to the Privy Council from the American Plantations*, pp. 171–174.

[15] See *The British Commonwealth: Development of its Laws and Constitutions: I The United Kingdom*, pp. 1141 *et seq.* (by L. A. Sheridan); *Royal Commission on the Constitution 1969–1973* (Kilbrandon), (1973) Cmnd. 5460, I. Pt. XI; *Report of Committee of Privy Council on Proposed Reforms in the Channel Islands* (1947) Cmd. 7074; F. De L. Bois, "Parliamentary Supremacy in the Channel Islands" [1983] P.L. 385. J.H. Le Patourel, *The Medieval Administration of the Channel Islands, 1199–1399: Minquiers and Ecrehos Case*, I.C.J. Reports (1953) p. 47.

[16] *Navigators and General Insurance Co.* v. *Ringrose* [1962] 1 W.L.R. 173; [1962] 1 All E.R. 97 (C.A.): (commercial document). In *Re a Debtor ex p. Viscount of the Royal Court of Jersey* [1981] Ch. 384, Goulding J. held that the Royal Court of Jersey is a "British Court elsewhere" for the purpose of the Bankruptcy Act 1914, s.122.

right of the United Kingdom Parliament or the Queen in Council to legislate for them without the consent of the States (the legislatures) confirmed by registration in the local Royal Court.[17] There is no real doubt of the legislative competence of Parliament, which legislates for the islands in such matters as customs and excise, the armed forces, extradition, fisheries, telegraphs, Post Office, copyright, merchant shipping and civil aviation; but the efficacy of legislation by prerogative Orders in Council is uncertain. In practice, the consent of the States (legislatures) is obtained and the Act or Order is registered, the islanders asserting—contrary to the British view—that it is the local registration which gives it legal effect. Statutes such as the Prevention of Terrorism (Temporary Provisions) Act 1984, may be extended to the Islands by Order in Council.

The Crown appoints a Lieutenant-Governor for each of the Bailiwicks of Jersey and Guernsey,[18] who summon the States and have powers, subject to the Home Secretary and the Secretary of State for Defence, in relation to the preservation of peace and defence. The Home Secretary is the channel of communication between the Channel Islands and the Crown.

Appeal lies as of right in civil cases from the courts of Jersey and Guernsey to the Judicial Committee of the Privy Council.[19] There is no appeal to the Judicial Committee as of right in criminal cases; but it was held in *Renouf* v. *Attorney-General for Jersey*[20] that the prerogative power to grant special leave to appeal had never been relinquished, although special leave would only be granted where there was a grave miscarriage of justice.

II. Territories of the Commonwealth[21]

The British Empire

This name has now fallen into disuse. For a long time it was employed to mean all territories over which the Crown exercised or claimed some degree of control, *viz.* the British Islands (including the United Kingdom), British India, British colonies, protectorates, and those self-governing colonies which in the early part of this century came to be known as the Dominions. The expression probably included protected states but not mandated (later trust) territories.

The sixteenth and seventeenth centuries saw some colonial expansion, mainly for the purpose of trade. English colonial expansion was the result of private enterprise and not government policy. If British

---

[17] See further R.E.M. *"The Jersey Incident of 1889 : Re Daniel"* (1984) 100 L.Q.R. 41.

[18] Alderney and Sark are dependencies of Guernsey. See A. R. de Carteret, *The Story of Sark* (1956).

[19] For the early history of appeals, see J. H. Smith, *op. cit.* pp. 4 *et seq.*, 63 *et seq.*

[20] [1936] A.C. 445. For later cases, see *Quin* v. *The King, The Times,* November 8, 1951; *Manley-Casimir* v. *Att.-Gen. for Jersey, The Times,* February 12, 1965 (Jersey law and practice apply); *Vaudin* v. *Hamon* [1974] A.C. 569 (application of *La Charte aux Normans* 1314 to law of property in Sark).

[21] See further on general matters, Sir William Dale *The Modern Commonwealth* (1983), Sir Kenneth Roberts-Wray, *Commonwealth and Colonial Law* (1966) Chaps. 1 and 2; S. A. de Smith, *The Vocabulary of Commonwealth Relations* (1954). There are statutory definitions for particular purposes of some of the expressions used in this section.

subjects took possession of territory by settlement, the authority of the
Crown extended to them; if they took by conquest, they acquired for
the Crown.[22] The earliest colonial constitutions were letters patent to a
proprietor or company, authorising him or it to trade and exercise jurisdiction within the area. "Royal" colonies, in which the direct governmental authority was the Crown, came later, the first being Virginia in
1624. It was clear that Parliament had jurisdiction in settled colonies,
and the common law extended to settlers all the constitutional rights of
Englishmen. The prerogative was more extensive in conquered colonies, which in the first instance the King could govern as he pleased,
but the King could not without Parliament take away constitutional
rights that he had granted.[23] Central political control over the colonies
was vested in the Privy Council, which formed committees for trade
and plantations. Parliament interfered chiefly in revenue matters and
the passing of Acts of trade and navigation.

With the American declaration of independence in 1776 Britain lost
thirteen North American colonies. She learned by this experience, and
retained and developed "the second British empire," which expression
covers the period from the loss of the American colonies to the development of colonial self-government in the middle of the nineteenth century. The main common law principles relating to colonial government
were established by the middle of the eighteenth century in such cases
as *Campbell v. Hall.*[24]

The expression "the third British Empire" is sometimes used to describe the period of the development of self-government in certain colonies, *e.g.* in Canada, Australia and New Zealand, from the middle of
the nineteenth century to the formal recognition of Dominion status by
the Statute of Westminster 1931; and the name "fourth British Empire"
has been given to the looser association of the Commonwealth since the
end of the Second World War.[25]

Her Majesty's dominions

These are all territories under the sovereignty of the Crown. A synonym sometimes used is "British territory." The expression would not
ordinarily include protectorates[26] or trust territories, although it might
do so for the purposes of particular statutes.[27]

At common law it was said that the Crown was one and indivisible
throughout the Sovereign's dominions, and the King was everywhere
present in his dominions.[28] Thus in *Williams v. Howarth*[29] the Privy

---

[22] *Campbell v. Hall* (1774) 1 Cowp. 204; (1774) 20 St.Tr. 287, 322–323.

[23] *Calvin's Case* (1609) 7 Co.Rep. 1 at f. 17b. Later this was taken to mean, when representative institutions had been granted.

[24] (1774) 1 Cowp. 204.

[25] *Post,* Chap. 37.

[26] *Cf.* Roberts-Wray, *op. cit.* p. 23, where sovereignty in the sense of ownership is distinguished from sovereignty in the sense of governmental power. In the latter sense,
the Crown may be said to have sovereignty in protectorates.

[27] *e.g.* reciprocal enforcement of foreign judgments.

[28] See *Amalgamated Society of Engineers v. Adelaide Steamship Co.* (1920) 28 C.L.R. 129; *Re
Bateman's Trusts* (1873) L.R. 15 Eq. 355; *Re Oriental Bank Corpn. ex p. The Crown* (1884) 28
Ch.D. 643. Cf. *post,* p. 764.

[29] [1905] A.C. 551.

Council held that the debt due from the Government of New South Wales in respect of the pay of a soldier who had fought in the Boer War (when New South Wales was a colony) was discharged by the payment of a smaller amount from the Imperial Government. But in *R. v. Secretary of State for Foreign and Commonwealth Affairs ex p. Indian Association of Alberta*,[30] the Court of Appeal held that the doctrine of the indivisibility of the Crown no longer represented the law, and hence an English Court could not grant to the Indian peoples of Canada a declaration relating to the treaty obligations entered into by the Crown. In each of its realms the Crown is now answerable only for obligations relating to that realm. Lord Denning M.R. thought that while it had been "a settled doctrine of constitutional law that the Crown was one and indivisible" in the eighteenth and nineteenth centuries,[31] a change had occurred in "the first half of this century—not by statute—but by constitutional usage and practice."[32] The Master of the Rolls referred in particular to the definition of the status of the relationship of the United Kingdom and the Dominions adopted in 1926 at the Imperial Conference. Kerr and May L.JJ. traced the recognition of the divisibility of the Crown to the nineteenth century. In support of their view they relied on the decision of Page-Wood V.-C. in *Re Holmes*[33] that a petition of right relating to land in Canada could not be heard in an English court.

British possessions

They are any parts of Her Majesty's dominions exclusive of the United Kingdom.[34]

British colonies

These are any parts of Her Majesty's dominions excluding the British Islands, and excluding independent members of the Commonwealth, their provinces and states.[35] Formerly persons born in a British colony were citizens of the United Kingdom and Colonies by birth. After the coming into effect of the British Nationality Act 1981 such persons become British Dependent Territories citizens or British Overseas citizens.[36] Acquisition of British Dependent Territories citizenship by birth after the commencement of the 1981 Act is limited to the children of a parent already possessing that citizenship or being settled in a dependent territory.[37] Inhabitants of Gibraltar[38] and the Falkland Islands[39] are, exceptionally, entitled to British citizenship.

---

[30] [1982] Q.B. 892 (C.A.); pet. dis. 937 [not for] "any technical or procedural grounds [but because of] the accumulated reasons given in the judgment of the Court of Appeal": *per* Lord Diplock. See further, Paul Jackson, "The Crown: Some Recent Proceedings" (1982) 7 *Holdsworth Law Rev.* 91.

[31] At p. 911 and p. 917.

[32] At p. 916.

[33] (1861) 2 John & H. 527. See also *Att.-Gen.* v. *Great Southern and Western Ry. Co. of Ireland* [1925] A.C. 754; *R.* v. *Secretary of State for the Home Department ex p. Bhurosah* [1968] 1 Q.B. 266; *Mellenger* v. *New Brunswick Corpn.* [1971] 1 W.L.R. 604.

[34] Interpretation Act 1978, s.5 and Sched. 1.

[35] *Ibid.*

[36] ss.23 and 26.

[37] s.15. See similar restrictions on acquisition of British citizenship: *ante* p. 452.

[38] British Nationality Act 1981 s.5.

[39] British Nationality (Falkland Islands) Act 1983.

British protectorates

These were territories under the protection of the Crown. They were not British territory, and did not form part of Her Majesty's dominions. The Crown was responsible for their defence and external affairs. Internally some were administered in a similar way to colonies ("protectorates" in the strict sense).[40] These are now all independent. Others were administered, with varying degrees of British supervision, by their native rulers ("protected states").[41] They are specified in the British Protectorates, Protected States and Protected Persons Order 1982.[42] Their inhabitants, if they have not acquired the citizenship of an independent Commonwealth country have the status of British Protected Persons.[43]

British trust territories

These were former mandated territories whose administration was entrusted to the Crown by the allied and associated powers in 1919 to be executed on behalf of the League of Nations. After the last war they were administered under the name of trust territories by the United Kingdom or other Commonwealth governments on behalf of the Crown in accordance with the Charter of the United Nations. Trust territories were not British territory, and did not form part of Her Majesty's dominions.[44] All have now acquired independence. Their inhabitants, unless they have acquired the citizenship of an independent Commonwealth country may have the status of British Protected Persons.[45]

Dependent territories

This was a non-technical term which came into use to refer to all territories in the Commonwealth which were not independent. It is a convenient way of referring to colonies, protectorates, protected states and trust territories. It has received statutory recognition in the British Nationality Act 1981, s.50(1).[46]

---

[40] Where the Crown had acquired jurisdiction in a foreign country by treaty, grant or other lawful means, this jurisdiction was exercised under the Foreign Jurisdiction Act 1890 (replacing the Foreign Jurisdiction Act 1843): see *R. v. Ketter* [1940] 1 K.B. 787; *Nyali Ltd. v. Att.-Gen.* [1956] 1 Q.B. 1 (C.A.); *Ex p. Mwenya* [1960] 1 Q.B. 241 (C.A.). See further Hall, *Foreign Jurisdiction of the British Crown*; Jenkyns, *British Rule and Jurisdiction beyond the Seas.*

[41] *Mighell v. Sultan of Johore* [1894] 1 Q.B. 149; *Duff Development Co. v. Kelantan Government* [1924] A.C. 797 (H.L.); *Sultan of Johore v. Abubakar Tunku Aris Bendahar* [1952] A.C. 318.

[42] No. 1070, made under the British Nationality Act 1981; amended by British Nationality (Brunei) Order 1983, No. 1699.

[43] British Nationality Act 1981, s.38 and s.50(1).

[44] H. Duncan Hall, *Mandates, Dependencies and Trusteeship*; Clive Parry, "The Legal Nature of Trusteeship Agreements" (1950) B.Y.I.L. 164.

[45] Note 43, *ante.*

[46] Sched. 6 lists as British Dependent Territories: Anguilla, Bermuda, British Antarctic Territory, British Indian Ocean Territory, Cayman Islands, Falkland Islands and Dependencies, Gibraltar, Hong Kong, Montserrat, Pitcairn, Henderson, Ducie and Oeno Islands, St Helena and Dependencies, The Sovereign Base Areas of Akrotiri and Dhekelia (as defined in the Cyprus Act 1960, s.2(1)), Turks and Caicos Islands and Virgin Islands.

Dependencies

This too was not a technical term.[47] It was sometimes used in the same sense as "dependent territories" (*ante*), but was not popular there. It is better applied to miscellaneous territories, such as a territory dependent placed under the authority of another (*e.g.* Ascension Island and Tristan da Cunha as dependencies of St. Helena); British possessions which are so small as to be virtually unadministered (*e.g.* the Great and Little Basses and Minicoy); and similar outposts under the jurisdiction of independent members of the Commonwealth. It has received formal recognition by its use in the British Nationality Act 1981.

The Commonwealth

In 1884 Lord Rosebery said in a speech in Australia that "the Empire is a Commonwealth of Nations."[48] The name "British Empire" began to fall into disfavour between the Wars in those countries that were acquiring independence, and "the British Commonwealth of Nations"[49] or "British Commonwealth"[50] came into use, either as synonymous with the whole British Empire, or as referring to the independent parts as in "the British Empire and Commonwealth." The "British Commonwealth" then ousted "the British Empire" almost completely in popular usage. The Asian and African members, however, preferred "the Commonwealth"[51] simply and this last name on account of its shortness has come into general favour, except perhaps in the Commonwealth of Australia where it is ambiguous. The term now usually includes dependent territories as well as independent members.

Independent members of the Commonwealth[52]

This expression covers—in addition to the United Kingdom—those countries still in the Commonwealth whose "Dominion status" was recognised by the Statute of Westminster 1931 (now Canada,[53] the Commonwealth of Australia[53] and New Zealand); and those former dependent territories that have since been granted independence by special statutes, *e.g.* India, Sri Lanka (Ceylon), Ghana (Gold Coast) and Nigeria, and whose membership has been agreed by the other members of the Commonwealth. Sometimes they are called "members of the Commonwealth" or "Commonwealth countries." Citizens of these

---

[47] *Re Maryon-Wilson's Estate* [1912] 1 Ch. 55, 66, *per* Farwell L.J.; *Re Brassey's Settlement* [1955] 1 W.L.R. 192; [1955] 1 All E.R. 577.

[48] "I say that these are no longer colonies in the ordinary sense of the term, but I claim that this is a nation. . . . There is no need for any nation, however great, leaving the Empire, because the Empire is a Commonwealth of Nations": Robert Rhodes James, *Rosebery* (1963), p. 196. Lloyd George also used this expression at the Imperial War Cabinet in 1917.

[49] Anglo-Irish Treaty 1921.

[50] J. X. Merriman (Prime Minister of Cape Colony) in the 1880s: General Smuts at the Imperial War Conference 1917.

[51] Nehru, 1948.

[52] See *post*, Chap. 37.

[53] The provinces of Canada and the states of Australia are *sui generis*: see *Mellenger* v. *New Brunswick Development Corporation* [1971] 1 W.L.R. 604 (C.A.); *cf.* Canada Act 1982 and Australia Act 1986.

countries are Commonwealth citizens under the British Nationality Act 1981, section 3.

III. British Colonies[54]

Introduction

The Crown is immediately related to a colony[55] as Sovereign. Colonies are under the sovereignty of the Crown both in the sense of governmental power and in the sense of ownership or belonging.[56] The duty of the Crown to afford protection to citizens of colonies is one of imperfect obligation and is unenforceable in the courts.[57]

The constitution of a colony is contained in several documents. The basic instrument is usually an Order in Council or letters patent, but sometimes an Act of Parliament. This provides for the government of the colony, and generally includes provisions relating to the composition and powers of the legislative and executive councils and the superior courts. Letters patent constitute the office of Governor and define his duties and powers. Royal instructions, issued from time to time by the Secretary of State, prescribe the manner in which the Governor is to exercise his functions. A Royal Commission appoints the Governor for the time being.

The central purpose of British colonial policy at the end of the last war was stated to be to guide the colonial territories to responsible self-government within the Commonwealth in conditions that ensure to the people both a fair standard of living and freedom from oppression from any quarter. The Secretary of State is ultimately responsible for their government, but this is discharged by a Governor or Administrator working through the civil service. The remaining dependent territories are now few. They include the colonies of Hong Kong,[58] Gibraltar,[59] the

[54] Dale, *op. cit.* pp. 305 *et seq.* Sir Kenneth Roberts-Wray, *Commonwealth and Colonial Law* (1966); *Changing Law in Developing Countries* (ed. J. N. D. Anderson, 1963); Sir Hilary Blood, *The Smaller Territories* (1958); Sir Ivor Jennings, *The Approach to Self-Government* (1956); Sir Keith Hancock, *Colonial Self-Government* (1956); O. Hood Phillips, "The Making of a Colonial Constitution" (1955) 71 L.Q.R. 51.

For the history, see Holdsworth, *History of English Law*, Vol. XI pp. 35–139, 229–267; A. B. Keith, *Responsible Government in the Dominions* (2nd ed., 1928); C. E. Carrington, *The British Overseas* (1950); Sir Alan Burns, *In Defence of Colonies*; John Bowle, *The Imperial Achievement* (1974); W. D. McIntyre, *The Commonwealth of Nations: Origin and Impact* (1977). See also *Forsyth's Cases and Opinions on Constitutional Law* (1869); *Opinions on Imperial Constitutional Law*, ed., D. P. O'Connell and A. Riordan (Melbourne, 1971).

[55] *Ante,* p. 731.

[56] See, *e.g. Tito v. Waddell (No. 2)* [1977] Ch. 106 (Megarry V.-C.); obligation of Crown in respect of extraction of phosphates in Ocean Island was governmental, not fiduciary; *Buck v. Att.-Gen.* [1965] Ch. 745 (C.A.): if Crown were a trustee of certain lands in Sierra Leone, such trust could not be enforced in English courts.

[57] *Mutasa v. Att.-Gen.* [1980] Q.B. 114.

[58] Parts ceded by China in 1842 and 1860, and part leased by China in 1898 for 99 years. The Hong Kong Act 1985, based on an agreement with China, makes provision for the ending of British sovereignty and jurisdiction over the whole of Hong Kong from July 1, 1997. Persons who by virtue of a connection with Hong Kong were British Dependent Territories citizens may after July 1, 1997 acquire a new form of British nationality and be known as British Nationals (Overseas).

[59] Ceded by Spain under the Treaty of Utrecht in 1713. Spain for some years has been agitating for its return.

Falkland Islands,[60] St. Helena[61] in the South Atlantic, Pitcairn[62] in the Pacific, and several Caribbean islands acquired in various ways.

In pursuance of the dual policy of political advancement and economic development, the United Kingdom parliament has provided large sums of capital for economic development and social welfare in the colonies and other dependent territories. Political changes in the direction of self-government or independence have indeed been so rapid in recent years that they have outstripped economic and social development; and the constitutions of particular territories are nowadays so transitory that it is impracticable to describe them here individually.

Colonies may be classified according to the manner in which they were acquired, which may have been : (i) by *settlement* in territory where there was no population or primitive tribes, or (ii) by *conquest or cession* of territory having an organised society. (The terms of any treaty of cession do not give the inhabitants of a colony rights which are enforceable in the local courts or by the Privy Council.[63]) This distinction, which came to be recognised in the seventeenth century,[64] affects the constitutional position of the colony, especially the legislative power. It also determines the system of private law that prevails in a given colony. But both the private and the public law are subject to legislative changes, so that this distinction is now largely of historical interest.

A more modern classification is that into (i) colonies *possessing responsible government* (commonly called "self-governing colonies"), and (ii) colonies *not possessing responsible government* ("non-self-governing colonies," formerly known as "Crown colonies"). This distinction rests on whether or not the executive is responsible for most purposes to the colonial legislature (to the lower House if that legislature is bicameral). Any remaining non-self-governing territories would be those with very small populations.

Settled colonies[65]

Settlement might be by: (i) occupation by British settlers under the authorisation of the Crown, *e.g.* Canada (excluding Quebec and Ontario), the Australian colonies[66] and some of the West Indies; (ii) recognition by the Crown, as British territory, of unauthorised settlements

---

[60] Sovereignty long disputed by Argentina. The British Government insists that the United Kingdom title is derived from early settlement, reinforced by formal claims in the name of the Crown, and completed by open, continuous, effective and peaceful possession, occupation and administration of the islands since 1833 (save for the ten weeks of forcible Argentine occupation in 1982). Further, the exercise of sovereignty has consistently been shown to accord with the wishes of the islanders: *Fifth Report from Foreign Affairs Committee*, Session 1983–84; *Falkland Islands: Observations by Her Majesty's Government* (H.M.S.O., 1985).

[61] Settled in 1659; recaptured from the Dutch after short interruption in 1673.

[62] Settled in 1790 by mutineers from *H.M.S. Bounty*.

[63] *Winfat Enterprise (H.K.) Co. Ltd.* v. *Att.-Gen. of Hong Kong* [1985] A.C. 733 (P.C.).

[64] See, *e.g. Calvin's Case* (1709) 7 Co.Rep. 1; *Blankard* v. *Galdy* (1693) 2 Salk. 411.

[65] As this topic is now mainly of historical interest, no distinction is made in the examples given between existing colonies and territories that have acquired independence since the last war.

[66] Penal settlements may have constituted a separate kind of colony: see *per* Eggleston J. in *Newbery* v. *The Queen* [1965] 7 F.L.R. 34, 39; and see (1965) 11 A.L.J. 409 *et seq.*

by British subjects, *e.g.* British Honduras, the Pitcairn Islands and Tristan da Cunha; or (iii) formal annexation of uninhabited islands or uninhabitable Arctic or Antarctic areas, *e.g.* some of the Pacific Islands, the Isles of Northern Canada, the Ross Dependency of New Zealand, the Falkland Islands and the British Antarctic Territory.

British settlers took with them the common law of England[67] and the statute law as existing at the time of settlement. Subsequent Acts of Parliament did not apply to the colony unless they were expressed to apply to that colony or to colonies generally.[68] The law, whether enacted or unenacted, that the settlers carried with them was only such as was applicable to their new situation and suitable to the condition of a young colony.[69]

Conquered and ceded colonies[70]

Cession was usually the result of conquest. The varieties of acquisition by these two means were: (i) conquest only; (ii) conquest on terms of surrender; (iii) cession by treaty with a civilised state, *e.g.* Grenada; (iv) voluntary cession by the inhabitants, *e.g.* Malta, Fiji. The Privy Council in *Sammut* v. *Strickland*[71] said that colonies acquired by voluntary cession, or by cession after conquest, were in the same position in British constitutional law as colonies acquired by conquest merely.

In conquered or ceded colonies the existing legal system was retained unless and until it was altered or abrogated by the Crown (*Campbell* v. *Hall per* Lord Mansfield C.J.[72]). The legal system might, for example, be Roman-Dutch law, customary French law, the Code Napoléon, Hindu law, Mohammedan (Islamic) law or native African custom. Existing laws were abrogated if they were: (i) contrary to Acts of Parliament, whether general or particular, extending to the colony[73]; (ii) contrary to British constitutional principles[74]; or (iii) repugnant to the fundamental religious or ethical principles of Europeans.[75]

English law was introduced by Act of Parliament or local legislation

---

[67] *Pictou Municipality* v. *Geldert* [1893] A.C. 524. *Tito* v. *Waddell (No. 2)* [1977] Ch. 106, 132, *per* Sir Robert Megarry V.-C. "The English concept of perpetuities arrived at Ocean Island with the flag, a blessing that the Banabans may not then have appreciated"; (*ibid.* at p. 220).

[68] *Memorandum* (1722) 2 P.Wms. 74; *New Zealand Loan Co.* v. *Morrison* [1898] A.C. 349.

[69] *Whicker* v. *Hume* (1858) 7 H.L.C. 124, 161, *per* Lord Cranworth. In settled colonies where there was a small indigenous population, the native law might still be applied to the natives, *e.g.* the Maoris of New Zealand: see *Hoani Te Heuheu Tukino* v. *Aotea District Maori Land Board* [1941] A.C. 308 (P.C.). New Zealand should perhaps be regarded as having been voluntarily ceded by the inhabitants.

[70] As this topic is now mainly of historical interest, no distinction is made here between existing colonies and territories that have acquired independence since the last war.

[71] [1938] A.C. 678.

[72] (1774) 1 Cowp. 204 (Grenada); following *Calvin's Case* (1609) 7 Co.Rep. 1 and *Blankard* v. *Galdy* (1693) 2 Salk. 411.

[73] *Campbell* v. *Hall* (1774) *ante.*

[74] *Union Government Minister of Lands* v. *Whittaker's Estate* [1916] App.D.(S.A.) 203.

[75] *Calvin's Case* (1609) 7 Co.Rep. 1a 17; *Blankard* v. *Galdy* (1693) 2 Salk. 411; *Memorandum* (1722) 2 P.Wms. 75; *Campbell* v. *Hall, supra.* And see *R.* v. *Picton* (1804–10) 30 St.Tr. 225, 529, 883–955 (torture in Trinidad); *Fabrigas* v. *Mostyn* 20 St.Tr. 175, 181; (1773) 1 Cowp. 161 (Minorca); *Khoo Hooi Leong* v. *Khoo Chong Yeoh* [1930] A.C. 346 (P.C.) (legitimacy of children of second wife).

into some colonies acquired by conquest or cession. This refers to the common law and statute law as they existed at the date of the application of English law to the colony or at some specified date.[76]

Legislation by the United Kingdom Parliament

There has never been any real doubt in British constitutional law about the competence of Parliament to legislate for the colonies, nor, in view of the doctrine of the supremacy of Parliament, are there any legal restrictions on this power. From the middle of the nineteenth century, however, there was a convention against Parliament legislating without their consent for the self-governing colonies that became Dominions in 1931.[77] A similar convention came to apply in the present century to a newer group of self-governing colonies, including Southern Rhodesia, Malta and the Gold Coast (now Ghana). Any doubt there may have been as to how far Acts of Parliament passed after the foundation of a given colony applied to that colony were set at rest by section 1 of the Colonial Laws Validity Act 1865, which states that "an act of Parliament, or any provision thereof, shall . . . be said to extend to any Colony when it is made applicable to such Colony by the *express words or necessary intendment* of any Act of Parliament."

Where parliamentary authority is necessary or desirable for legislation in respect of colonies, Parliament usually prefers to authorise the issue of Orders in Council by the Crown. British Acts are used for matters of general concern, such as Admiralty jurisdiction, aerial navigation, armed forces, copyright, currency, extradition, foreign enlistment, fugitive offenders, international treaties, merchant shipping, nationality and citizenship, official secrets, reciprocal enforcement of judgments, and territorial waters jurisdiction; and also for constitutional changes such as grant of independence or where more than one colony are concerned.

Legislation by the Crown

This may take the form of Orders in Council, proclamations or letters patent. Here it is necessary to distinguish between settled colonies on the one hand and conquered or ceded colonies on the other.

For settled colonies

The prerogatives of the Crown, and the rights and immunities of British subjects, in colonies established by occupancy and settlement are similar to those that obtain in this country (*Kielley* v. *Carson*[78]). The Crown may constitute the office of Governor, and an Executive Council; appoint a Governor and issue royal instructions to him; establish courts of justice; and provide for the summoning of a legislature[79] with power to legislate and tax. In this way constitutions were first granted to Bermuda (1620) and most of the early American colonies. Any other form of

---

[76] *Att.-Gen.* v. *Stewart* (1815) 2 Mer. 143, 160; *R.* v. *Vaughan* (1769) 4 Burr. 2494.

[77] *Post*, Chap. 37.

[78] (1842) 4 Moo.P.C. 63, 84–85 (Newfoundland).

[79] Roberts-Wray, *op. cit.* p. 152, points out that there is little judicial authority for the common opinion that would limit the prerogative to the setting up of a *repesentative* legislature.

constitution was thought to require at common law an Act of Parliament, as with the Australian colonies in the early nineteenth century. Apart from its constituent power, the Crown could not at common law legislate for settled colonies.[80]

As the Crown had no direct lawmaking power at common law, legislation by the Imperial Parliament was also necessary to empower the Crown to make laws for such sparsely populated settlements as the Falkland Islands and those on the West Coast of Africa. General statutory powers, exercisable by Order in Council, were given to the Crown for this purpose by the British Settlements Act 1887.[81] The Act applied in effect to settled colonies that had not already been granted representative institutions, such as the Straits Settlements.[82]

For conquered or ceded colonies

The Crown has a prerogative (common law) power to legislate for conquered or ceded colonies, exercisable by Order in Council, proclamation or letters patent. This includes the power to establish any kind of constitution. When a representative legislature[83] has been granted to a colony, the prerogative power to legislate cannot be exercised while such grant is in force, as that would be repugnant to the grant, unless (as is now almost invariably the case) such power is expressly reserved in the grant.[84] Where the power to amend a colonial constitution by prerogative is reserved, it may be exercised retrospectively.[85] If, however, the representative government is *revoked*, whether by Imperial Act or by a valid exercise of the prerogative (*i.e.* in the latter case, where power to revoke was reserved), the prerogative power to legislate revives, even though such power of resumption has not been expressly reserved.[86]

Powers of colonial legislatures

Colonial legislatures are subordinate lawmaking bodies, and their powers depend on the statute, Orders in Council or letters patent granting them. They are invariably given a general power to make laws "for the peace, order and good government" of the colony. A colonial legislature is restricted as to the area of its powers, but within that area it is unrestricted and does not act as an agent or delegate.[87] No decision on

---

[80] *Re Lord Bishop of Natal* (1865) 3 Moo.P.C.(N.S.) 115, 148, *per* Lord Chelmsford L.C.

[81] Consolidating the settlements and coasts of Africa and Falkland Islands Act 1843 and the West coast of Africa and Falkland Islands Act 1860, and amended in 1945.

[82] Singapore, Penang and Malacca.

[83] A representative legislature is defined for the purposes of the Colonial Laws Validity Act 1865 as a colonial legislature comprising a legislative body of which (at least) one-half are elected by the inhabitants of the colony.

[84] *Campbell* v. *Hall* (1774), 1 Cowp. 204; Lofft 655; 20 St.Tr. 239 (K.B., *per* Lord Mansfield C.J.); duty on sugar exported from Grenada, a colony ceded by France.

[85] *Abeyesekara* v. *Jayatilake* [1932] A.C. 260 (P.C.).

[86] *Sammut* v. *Strickland* [1938] A.C. 678 (P.C.); imposition of customs duties in Malta, a ceded colony, whose representative institutions had been revoked by Act of Parliament. And see *Newbery* v. *The Queen* [1965] 7 F.L.R. 34: power of Crown to place Norfolk Island under authority of Australia: Norfolk Island was occupied by the inhabitants of Pitcairn Island, who were descended from the mutineers of the *Bounty*.

[87] *Hodge* v. *R.* (1883) 9 App.Cas. 117, 131 (Ontario); *Powell* v. *Apollo Candle Co.* (1885) 10 App.Cas. 282 (New South Wales); *Bribery Commissioner* v. *Ranasinghe* [1964] A.C. 172 (P.C.), *per* Lord Pearce.

the validity of colonial legislation appears to have turned on this expression, and the courts have never analysed the words. The expression is tautologous because "peace" and "order" come under "government," and "good" is not justiciable.[88] Such restrictions as there are on the making of laws with extraterritorial operation[89] are a deduction from the power to make laws "for" the territory, or perhaps for the government "of" the territory.[90]

Colonial Laws Validity Act 1865

The early common law rule was the rather vague one that a colonial Act was invalid if repugnant to English law, and so some of the colonial constitutions that were enacted before 1865 provided that the legislative assembly should not pass legislation repugnant to (i.e. inconsistent with) the law of England. A controversy arose in the early 1860s when Boothby J. of South Australia passed adverse judgments on certain Acts passed by the South Australian legislature. Some he held contrary to English law, and others invalid because the Governor had not reserved them for the royal pleasure. The two Houses of the South Australian Parliament passed addresses asking for his removal. The matter went, in accordance with constitutional practice, to the Secretary of State for the Colonies, who asked the Law Officers (Sir Roundell Palmer and Sir Robert Collier) to advise. Their opinion was that the colonial Acts were invalid if contrary to United Kingdom Acts; that royal instructions to reserve assent to certain classes of Bills were instructions to the Governor only, not affecting the validity of such Acts if he gave his assent; but that, as regards repugnance to English law, a distinction was to be drawn between the "fundamental" principles and the non-fundamental rules of English law.[91] Such a distinction, if it ever existed, was complicated and no longer practicable.

The result was the passing of the Colonial Laws Validity Act 1865, which applied to all Her Majesty's dominions except the Channel Islands, the Isle of Man and India.[92] The Act was intended to be declaratory.

The Colonial Laws Validity Act 1865, s.2, provides that: "Any Colonial Law which is or shall be in any respect repugnant to the provisions of any *Act of Parliament* extending to the Colony to which such Law may relate, or repugnant to any Order or Regulation made under authority of such Act of Parliament, or having in the Colony the force and effect of such Act, shall be read subject to such Act, Order or Regu-

---

[88] Cf. Riel v. R. (1880) 10 App.Cas. 675 (Canada); *D'Emden* v. *Pedder* (1904) 1 C.L.R. 91, 109 (Tasmania); *Croft* v. *Dunphy* [1933] A.C. 156 (Canada); R. v. *Fineberg* [1968] N.Z.L.R. 443 (New Zealand).

[89] *Post*, p. 742.

[90] See Roberts-Wray, *op. cit.* 369–370.

[91] Keith, *Responsible Government in the Dominions*, I, pp. 339–341. D. P. O'Connell and A. Riordan, *Opinions on Imperial Constitutional Law* (1971), Section IV. Addresses to remove Boothby J. were presented in 1862 and 1866, but the Law Officers did not advise his removal, especially as some of the Acts held invalid by him were so. In 1867 he was removed by the Governor in Council under the Colonial Leave of Absence Act 1782: Keith, *op. cit.* II, pp. 1072–1073.

[92] Similar principles applied to India. The Act still applies to the Australian States, although they are no longer colonies.

lation, and shall, *to the extent of such repugnancy, but not otherwise,* be and remain absolutely void and inoperative."

Section 3 provides that: "No Colonial Law shall be or be deemed to have been void or inoperative on the ground of repugnancy to the Law of England unless the same shall be repugnant to the provisions of some such Act of Parliament, Order or Regulation as aforesaid."

A "colonial law" is defined in section 1 as including laws made for a colony by the Queen in Council (whether statutory or prerogative) as well as by the colonial legislature. It will be seen from the words we have put in italics in section 2, that a colonial law is only void for repugnancy if it is repugnant to an Act of Parliament or statutory order, etc. made thereunder, and that it is only void to the extent of such repugnancy. Section 3 makes the matter quite clear by expressing it in a different way.[93]

The validity of colonial laws may be tested in actions brought before the courts of the colony, and on appeal to the Privy Council.[94]

Section 4 provides that: "No Colonial Law, passed with the concurrence of or assented to by the Governor of any Colony, or to be hereafter so passed or assented to, shall be or be deemed to have been void or inoperative by reason only of any Instructions with reference to such law or the subject thereof which may have been given to such Governor by or on behalf of Her Majesty, by any Instrument other than the Letters Patent or Instrument authorising such Governor to concur in passing or to assent to Laws for the peace, order and good government of such Colony, even though such Instructions may be referred to in such Letters Patent or last-mentioned Instrument." Thus failure to observe royal instructions does not invalidate the Governor's assent to a Bill, unless such instructions are actually embodied—not merely referred to—in the principal instrument defining his general legislative authority, so as in effect to form part of the constitution of the colony. Apart from this exception, the Governor's failure to regard royal instructions is a matter between him and the Crown, which—though it might result in his recall—does not affect the validity of colonial laws assented to by him.

Section 5 of the Colonial Laws Validity Act 1865 provides that: "*Every Colonial Legislature* shall have, and be deemed at all times to have had, full power within its jurisdiction to establish *Courts of Judicature*, and to abolish and reconstitute the same, and to alter the constitution thereof, and to make provision for the administration of justice therein." Such laws must be passed in the appropriate manner and form, as mentioned below in connection with constitutional amendments.

Section 5 of the Act further provides that: "Every *Representative* Legislature shall, in respect to the Colony under its jurisdiction, have, and be deemed at all times to have had, full power to make laws respecting the *constitution, powers and procedure of such Legislature*; provided that such Laws shall have been passed *in such manner and form* as may

---

[93] See *Phillips* v. *Eyre* (1870) L.R. 6 Q.B. 1.

[94] A colonial legislature may debate, pass and present a Bill to the Governor—without being impeded by declaration or injunction—although it would, if enacted, be void under the Colonial Laws Validity Act as being repugnant to United Kingdom statute; *Rediffusion (H.K.) Ltd.* v. *Att.-Gen. of Hong Kong* [1970] A.C. 1136 (P.C.). See O. Hood Phillips, "Judicial Intervention in the Legislative Process" (1971) 87 L.Q.R. 321.

from time to time be required by any Act of Parliament, Letters Patent, Order in Council, or *Colonial Law* for the time being in force in the said Colony." This part of section 5 applies to a *representative* legislature, which is defined in section 1 of the Act as being "any Colonial Legislature which shall comprise a Legislative Body of which [at least] one half are elected by the inhabitants of the Colony." The expression "constitution" here refers to the composition of the legislature, not the general constitution of the colony. It was held by the Privy Council in *Att.-Gen. for New South Wales* v. *Trethowan*[95] that a representative colonial legislature can bind its successors. In that case an Act passed by the legislature of New South Wales[96] in 1929 providing that no Bill to abolish the Legislative Council (the upper house) should be presented to the Governor for his assent unless it had been approved by a referendum, and that this provision should apply to any Bill repealing or amending the Act, was effective after a change of government in 1930 to present the abolition of the Legislative Council without a referendum having been held.

Such a colonial legislature probably has to remain representative.[97] It cannot enlarge its own powers so as to make a unilateral declaration of independence. In *Madzimbamuto* v. *Lardner-Burke*,[98] an appeal from Southern Rhodesia, (a self-governing colony since 1923), after the Unilateral Declaration of Independence (UDI), the Privy Council stated that: (i) The nature of the sovereignty of the Queen in the United Kingdom Parliament over a British colony must be determined by the constitutional law of the United Kingdom; (ii) the Queen in the United Kingdom Parliament was still sovereign in Southern Rhodesia at the relevant time (1965), and therefore the Southern Rhodesia Act 1965 and Orders in Council passed thereunder were of full legal effect in Southern Rhodesia; and the convention under which the United Kingdom Parliament did not legislate without the consent of the Government of Southern Rhodesia, although important as a convention, had no effect in limiting the powers of the United Kingdom Parliament.

A colonial statute by describing itself as a Constitution Act does not *ipso facto* require any special procedure for its amendment. Thus it was held by the Judicial Committee in *McCawley* v. *The King*[99] that the Constitution Act 1867, passed by the Queensland legislature under the

---

[95] [1932] A.C. 526; *ante*, p. 87. And see *Att.-Gen.* (*N.S.W.*) v. *Trethowan* (1931) 44 C.L.R. 394 (High Ct. Austr.) *per* Dixon J. at pp. 425–427; Mr. Justice Owen Dixon "The Law and the Constitution" (1935) 51 L.Q.R. 590, 602–604.

[96] Not a colony then, but still subject to the Colonial Laws Validity Act 1865.

[97] *Taylor* v. *Att.-Gen.* (*Queensland*) (1917) 23 C.L.R. 457, 477, *per* Gavan Duffy and Rich JJ.

[98] [1969] 1 A.C. 645. Lord Pearce based his dissenting opinion on the doctrine of "necessity"; *cf. per* Sir Jocelyn Simon P., in *Adams* v. *Adams* (*Att.-Gen. intervening*) [1971] P. 188; validity of English woman's divorce in Rhodesia after U.D.I. See Roberts-Wray, *op. cit.* pp. 991–993; L. H. Leigh, "Rhodesia after UDI" [1966] P.L. 148; "Rhodesian Crisis— Criminal Liabilities" by B. A. Hepple, P. O'Higgins and C. C. Turpin [1966] Crim.L.R. 5, and O. Hood Phillips, *ibid.* p. 68. See also Leslie Wolf-Phillips, *Constitutional Legitimacy: a study of the doctrine of necessity.* (Third World Foundation, 1979) pp. 45–69; P. Mirfield, "When is a Judge not a Judge" [1978] P.L. 42.

Southern Rhodesia became the independent Republic of Zimbabwe by the Zimbabwe Act 1979.

[99] [1920] A.C. 691, *per* Lord Birkenhead L.C. See Mr. Justice Owen Dixon, "The Law and the Constitution" (1935) 51 L.Q.R. 590, 602–604.

authority of an Imperial Act, could be amended in the ordinary way and did not require a special Amendment Bill, since it did not prescribe any specific manner or form. The constitutions of the Australian states (formerly colonies) were in this sense "uncontrolled" and not "controlled."

Extra-territorial legislation[1]

The power of a colonial legislature extends to the making of laws for the peace, order and good government *of the colony*, including its territorial waters. Special powers to legislate beyond these limits are conferred by the United Kingdom Parliament in such matters as defence and merchant shipping. Whether, apart from any special powers expressly conferred by Imperial Act, a colonial law purporting to have extra-territorial effect is for that reason necessarily void is uncertain. The Colonial Laws Validity Act 1865 does not deal with this question. There are dicta by the Privy Council in *Macleod* v. *Attorney-General for New South Wales*[2] and other cases[3] to the effect that such legislation is void; but some of the later cases, notably *Croft* v. *Dunphy*,[4] throw doubt on the principle thought to have been established in *Macleod's* case.[5]

These Privy Council cases concerned Canada, Australia and New Zealand when they were self-governing colonies progressing towards independence. A similar latitude was allowed to the Indian legislature under the Government of India Act 1935 in *Wallace* v. *Commissioners of Income Tax, Bombay*,[6] where an Act imposing income tax on income accruing to any company if the greater part of its income arose in British India, was held validly to extend to a company registered in the United Kingdom, apparently on the principle that a subordinate legislature may legislate with extra-territorial effect if there is a sufficient "territorial connection" with the person affected or with a thing in which he is concerned. As regards a person, the territorial connection would extend at least to his presence, residence, domicile or carrying on of business in

[1] See D. P. O'Connell, "The Doctrine of Colonial Extra-Territorial Legislative Incompetence" (1959) 75 L.Q.R. 318; *cf.* Sir John Salmond, "The Limitations of Colonial Legislative Power" (1917) 33 L.Q.R. 117. The question remained of importance also with regard to the Australian states: D. P. O'Connell, "Problems of Australian Coastal Jurisdiction" (1958) 34 B.Y.I.L. 199, 248 *et seq.*

[2] [1891] A.C. 455: New South Wales Act penalising bigamy, "whosoever" and "whatsoever."

[3] *e.g. Ashbury* v. *Ellis* [1893] A.C. 339 (New Zealand Act allowing judicial proceedings where defendant outside the jurisdiction); *Peninsular and Oriental Steam Navigation Co.* v. *Kingston* [1903] A.C. 471 (Australian Act penalising the breaking of customs seals on the high seas); *Att.-Gen. for Canada* v. *Cain* [1906] A.C. 542 (Canadian Act impliedly authorising restraint of alien immigrant outside territorial limits).

[4] [1933] A.C. 156: Canadian Act (passed before the Statute of Westminster) defining Canadian territorial waters in case of vessels registered in Canada as extending to twelve marine miles, at a time when according to the English law view of international law territorial waters extended only to three marine miles. Lord Sankey L.C. in *British Coal Corporation* v. *The King* [1935] A.C. 500 (P.C.) referred to the doctrine forbidding extra-territorial legislation as "a doctrine of somewhat obscure extent."

[5] In *R.* v. *Lander* [1919] N.Z.L.R. 305, the Court of Appeal of New Zealand (Stout C.J. dissenting) followed *Macleod* v. *Att.-Gen. for New South Wales* in the case of a British subject who, while a member of the New Zealand Expeditionary Force, committed bigamy in England. See D. P. O'Connell, "The Doctrine of Colonial Extra-Territorial Legislative Incompetence" (1959) 79 L.Q.R. 318; O'Connell and Riordan, *op. cit.* section V.

[6] (1948) 75 I.A. 86 (P.C.); *per* Lord Uthwatt.

the legislating territory, but not to the ownership of shares in a foreign company which carried on only part of its business in that country.

The Report of the Inter-Imperial Relations Committee of the Imperial Conference, 1926,[7] referred to "the difference between the legislative competence of the Parliament of Westminster and of the Dominion Parliaments, in that Acts passed by the latter operate, *as a general rule*, only within the territorial area of the Dominion concerned." The Report of the Conference on the Operation of Dominion Legislation (1929)[8] said: "It would not seem to be possible in the present state of the authorities to come to definite conclusions regarding the competence of Dominion Parliaments to give their legislation extra-territorial operation."

Rejection, reservation and disallowance

A colonial Governor, as representative of the Queen and a constituent part of the colonial legislature, has power to *refuse his assent to Bills* submitted to him by the legislature, or may in some cases return Bills to the legislature with proposed amendments. The classes of cases in which the Governor should refuse his assent are commonly set out in his instructions.

A colonial Governor has power to *reserve* Bills submitted to him by the colonial legislature, by withholding his assent until Her Majesty's pleasure be taken thereon. The exercise of this power by the Governor may, according to royal instructions, be either obligatory in the case of certain topics, or discretionary in all cases. Her Majesty's pleasure would be made known on the advice of the Secretary of State.[9]

The Crown, acting on the advice of the Secretary of State, has the power to *disallow* or annul a colonial Act. The power exists at common law, but is embodied in most constituent Acts—especially in non-self-governing colonies—usually with a time limit of one or two years. Modern means of speedy communication have deprived this power of its former usefulness. Its continued existence is inconvenient, as lawyers and others in the colony cannot be certain until the prescribed period has elapsed whether the ordinance will continue in force. The power would rarely, if ever, be exercised in relation to a colony possessing fully responsible government unless general Commonwealth interests were involved.

Composition of colonial legislatures

There have been colonies with no legislative body, the sole lawmaking power in the colony being vested in the Governor or High Commissioner. Where there is a legislative body—as there will be nowadays if there is a substantial population—it may be composed in varying proportions of one or more of the following elements: *ex officio* members, *i.e.* senior executive officers who are members by virtue of their office; nominated members, official or unofficial, appointed by the

[7] Cmd. 2768.
[8] Cmd. 3479. Hence section 3 of the Statute of Westminster 1931, relating to the Dominions.
[9] For the Governor's converse "reserved power" of certifying laws against the will of the legislature, see *post*, p. 744.

Crown or the Governor; elected members, chosen by an electorate whose franchise varies from colony to colony.

There have been almost as many varieties of colonial legislatures as of colonies, and their constitutions have been subject to frequent change. Post-war constitution-making tendencies prior to full self-government have been to confer Legislative Councils on colonies that had no legislative body; to turn official majorities into unofficial majorities, elected minorities into elected majorities, and Assemblies with elected majorities into Assemblies wholly elected; to substitute universal adult suffrage (with racial quotas in mixed populations) for property or educational franchise qualifications; and to confer some degree of responsible government, especially as regards internal affairs, on colonies with wholly or mainly elected Assemblies.

The powers of the Governor

Executive government in the colonies is carried on in the name of the Crown by Governors.[10] Governors are appointed by the Crown on the advice of the Secretary of State; and they are responsible to the Crown, although in most colonies the executive depends on the local legislature for supply. The powers of Governors vary; but generally they are empowered by their commission, to appoint members of the Legislative and Executive Councils; to issue writs for the election of members to representative bodies, and to summon or dissolve such bodies; to appoint and dismiss Ministers (if any); to appoint officials; to assent or refuse assent to Bills, or to reserve them for the Crown's assent[11]; to authorise the expenditure of public funds; to remit penalties and pardon offenders.[12] If there is no representative government, they initiate taxation and appropriation measures and usually other Bills.

Where the legislature is representative but the colony is not self-governing, the Governor usually has a *reserved power* (commonly known as his "reserve power" or power of "certification"[13]), if he considers it expedient in the interests of public order, public faith or good government that a Bill introduced into the legislature but not passed by it within a reasonable time shall have effect, to declare that such Bill shall have effect as if it had been passed by the legislature. "Public order," etc. is defined to include the responsibility of the colony as a territory within the Commonwealth, and all matters pertaining to public officers. The Governor is required to report to a Secretary of State any such declaration and the reasons therefor, together with any written objections by members of the legislature.

In addition to these powers, commonly granted by the instruments appointing them, Governors have extensive and detailed authority con-

---

[10] In some colonies the representative of the Crown is called Lieutenant-Governor or High Commissioner, but for the present purposes it is convenient to describe them all as Governors.

[11] *Ante,* p. 743.

[12] On this last point, see O. R. Marshall, "The Prerogative of Mercy" [1948] C.L.P. 104, 116–126; Roberts-Wray, *op. cit.* pp. 341 *et seq.* There is statutory authority for the removal of persons sentenced to inprisonment from a colony to the United Kingdom: Colonial Prisoners Removal Act 1884.

[13] No certificate is in fact issued.

ferred on them by various statutes in respect of customs, defence works, naturalisation of aliens, and many other matters.

The prerogative powers in relation to foreign affairs, war and peace are not delegated to the Governor of a colony.[14] "The prerogative of the Queen, when it has not been expressly limited by local law or statute," it has been stated,[15] "is as extensive in Her Majesty's colonial possessions as in Great Britain."

Executive council and ministers

Executive Councils consisted at first of officials serving in this capacity *ex officio* or nominated by the Governor. At an early stage of development, nominated unofficial members are introduced. The unofficial element grows, and nomination may be made on the recommendation of the Legislative Council. The functions of an Executive Council in non-self-governing colonies (formerly known as "Crown colonies") is advisory only. The Governor may be required to consult the Council on certain matters, but he is not bound by its advice. When the legislature becomes representative (*i.e.* has an elected majority) the unofficial members of the Executive Council will probably be members of the legislature and leaders of opinion there, so that the Governor will try to avoid acting against their unanimous advice.

The introduction of the ministerial system is the next stage[16] in the development of a colony towards self-government. Departments are assigned by the Governor to unofficial members of the Executive Council as Ministers, who are also elected members of the legislature. The Governor is now instructed to act normally on the advice of the Executive Council, and the elected Ministers will by convention depend on the confidence of the legislature. Certain departments are retained by officials, including defence and external affairs. Finance will tend to be among those departments entrusted to Ministers. The Attorney-General's department and internal security may be retained by officials for a time. The Governor's reserved power in matters involving public order, public faith and good government[17] will be available in an emergency. The leader of the majority in the elected House may now be styled Chief Minister.

Development of internal self-government[18]

The last transitional stage before independence within (or outside) the Commonwealth is usually internal self-government, the United Kingdom retaining control only over defence and external affairs,[19] and the power to suspend the constitution in an emergency, for which the

---

[14] See J. E. S. Fawcett, "Treaty Relations of British Overseas Territories" [1949] B.Y.I.L. 86.

[15] *Per* Lord Watson in *Liquidators of Maritime Bank of Canada* v. *Receiver-General of New Brunswick* [1892] A.C. 441.

[16] Sometimes a "membership system" has intervened, responsibility for certain government departments being assigned to unelected members of the Executive Council.

[17] *Ante,* p. 744.

[18] See further, S. A. de Smith, *The New Commonwealth and its Constitutions* (1964) Chap. 2.

[19] Responsibility for defence and external affairs may be entrusted to a United Kingdom Commissioner, as in the pre-independence constitutions of Singapore and Malta. Also, a limited treaty-making power may be delegated under the authority of statute to a self-governing colony.

Secretary of State remains responsible to Parliament. All the other departments are now administered by elected Ministers holding the confidence of the legislature. A Public Service Commission and a Judicial Service Commission will be set up, and provision made for the independence of the judiciary, the Auditor-General and the Director of Public Prosecutions.

The Executive Council now becomes the Council of Ministers or Cabinet, operating as far as possible the conventions of the British Cabinet system, and the Chief Minister is styled Prime Minister. At some stage the Governor no longer summons or presides over the Executive Council.

The description given above must be taken merely as typical. It may not exactly fit any particular territory. These developments in executive government should be considered alongside the typical development of colonial legislatures[20] in order to obtain a general picture of the growth of internal self-government in dependent territories since the Second World War. The chief remaining limitations are the subordination of the colonial legislature to the United Kingdom Parliament, and the lack of international personality.[21]

[20] *Ante*, p. 743.

[21] The pre-independence constitutions of Singapore and Malta, although they retained the legal status of colonies, gave them the name of "States": see O. Hood Phillips, "The Constitution of the State of Singapore" [1960] P.L. 50.

CHAPTER 37

INDEPENDENCE WITHIN THE COMMONWEALTH

I. THE DOMINIONS AND THE STATUTE OF WESTMINSTER

Development of Dominion status[1]

The development of responsible government in the colonies originated in the report sent from North America by Lord Durham in 1839 to
the British Government. Upper and Lower Canada already had representative assemblies. The gist of Lord Durham's Report was that it
was a necessary consequence of the grant of representative institutions
that the Governor should entrust the administration to such men as
could command a majority. In other words, responsible Cabinet
government should be introduced, and this could be effected simply by
a change in the Governor's instructions. Responsible government was
accordingly introduced into the united colonies of Ontario and Quebec
under Lord Elgin in 1848. Full autonomy in internal affairs was gradually supplemented by a degree of autonomy in external affairs. The
British North America Act 1867 implied the existence of responsible
government in the new federal Dominion of Canada. The same principles came to be extended to Newfoundland, the Australian colonies
(now states), New Zealand and the South African colonies during the
latter part of the nineteenth century, to the federal Commonwealth of
Australia in 1900, the Union of South Africa in 1909 and the Irish Free
State when granted Dominion status in 1922. The autonomy of the
Dominions received further impetus by the recognition of Canada,
Australia, New Zealand and South Africa as separate members of the
League of Nations after the 1914–18 war.

The Balfour Declaration of 1926[2] described the position and mutual
relations of the United Kingdom and the Dominions at that time as:
"*autonomous Communities within the British Empire, equal in status, in no
way subordinate one to another in any aspect of their domestic or external
affairs, though united by a common allegiance to the Crown, and freely
associated as members of the British Commonwealth of Nations.*" The principles of equality and similarity appropriate to status, however, did not
universally extend to function, *e.g.* diplomacy and defence. The Crown

---

[1] A. B. Keith, *Responsible Government in the Dominions* (2nd ed., 1928); *The Dominions as
Sovereign States* (1938); *Speeches and Documents on the British Dominions, 1918–1931*;
Dawson, *The Development of Dominion Status, 1900–1936*; R. T. E. Latham, "The Law
and the Commonwealth," in Hancock, *Survey of Commonwealth Affairs*, I (1937), pp. 595
et seq.; *The Round Table*, No. 240 (Diamond Jubilee Special number, 1970). H. Duncan
Hall, *Commonwealth: A History of the British Commonwealth of Nations* (1971); N. Mansergh, *The Commonwealth Experience* (1982); H. H. Marshall, *From Dependence to State-
hood*.

[2] *Report of Imperial Conference, 1926*, Cmd. 1768. This has nothing to do with Balfour's
statement about Zionism.

was the symbol of the free association of the members of what was then called the British Commonwealth of Nations, and they were united by a common allegiance to the Crown, based on the common status of British subjects. It was resolved at the Imperial Conference of 1926[3] that a treaty applying only to one part of the Empire should be made on the advice of the government of that part, and should be stated to be made by the Sovereign on behalf of that part. Dominions might have their own seals for authenticating treaties if they wished. The mutual relations among the self-governing members of the Commonwealth were regarded as being governed, not by international law, but largely by conventions whose character was something between international law and constitutional law (the "inter se doctrine").[4]

The principle that a Dominion might exchange diplomatic representatives with a foreign country was recognised in 1920 in the case of Canada and the United States. The Dominions had come to possess their own armed forces. Although a Dominion could not be compelled without its consent to give active assistance in a war in which the Crown was engaged, it was not generally admitted before 1939 that a Dominion could remain technically neutral in such a war.

The Imperial Conferences of 1926 and 1930[5] resolved that the Sovereign should act on the direct advice of the Dominion Ministers in relation to the appointment of the Governor-General, who was the representative of the Sovereign and not of the British Government. The power of reserving Bills of a Dominion legislature, which had been rarely exercised, ought not to be exercised against the wishes of that Dominion. The power of disallowing Dominion legislation was by convention not exercised.

Conventions were formulated that any alteration in the law touching the succession to the Throne or the Royal Style and Titles should require the assent of the Parliaments of all the Dominions as well as of the Parliament of the United Kingdom[6]; and that laws thereafter made by the United Kingdom Parliament should not extend to any of the Dominions as part of the law of that Dominion otherwise than at the request and with the consent of that Dominion.[7] Further, uniformity of legislation as between the United Kingdom and the Dominions in such matters as the law of prize, fugitive offenders and extradition, could best be secured by the enactment of reciprocal statutes based on consultation and agreement.[8]

---

[3] Ante.

[4] See J. E. S. Fawcett, The British Commonwealth in International Law (1963), Chap. 15; The Inter Se Doctrine of Commonwealth Relations (1958); R. Y. Jennings. "The Commonwealth and International Law" (1953) B.Y.I.L. 320; cf. R. T. E. Latham, "The Law and the Commonwealth" in Hancock's Survey of British Commonwealth Affairs, Vol. I, pp. 602 et seq.

[5] Cmd. 3717.

[6] Report of the Conference on the Operation of Dominion Legislation, 1929, Cmd. 3479.

[7] (1930) Cmd. 3717.

[8] (1926) Cmd. 2768; (1949) Cmd. 3479.

The Statute of Westminster 1931[9]

The Statute of Westminster[10] dealt only with *legislative* powers, and not exhaustively with them. The chief matters with regard to which legislation of the United Kingdom Parliament was required in order to reconcile the law relating to legislative powers with the conventional status of the Dominions were: (i) the operation of the Colonial Laws Validity Act 1865, which nullified Dominion legislation repugnant to United Kingdom statute law; (ii) the doubtful rule that the Dominions could not pass legislation having extra-territorial effect; and (iii) the legally unfettered power of the United Kingdom Parliament to legislate for the Dominions. Attention was drawn to these matters by the Imperial Conference, 1926.[11] They were fully considered by the Conference on the Operation of Dominion Legislation, 1929,[12] whose resolutions were adopted by the Imperial Conference, 1930.[13] They determine the contents of the most important sections of the Statute of Westminster, which was passed by the Imperial Parliament in 1931 on the recommendation of the Imperial Conference, 1930, after the communication of resolutions of the Parliaments of the six Dominions.

The preamble recites: (i) the fact that the Imperial Conferences of 1926 and 1930 concurred in making certain declarations and resolutions; (ii) the convention relating to the law touching the succession to the Throne and the Royal Style and Titles; (iii) the convention with regard to legislation by the United Kingdom Parliament for the Dominions; (iv) that "it is necessary for the ratifying, confirming and establishing of certain of the said declarations and resolutions of the said Conferences that a law be made and enacted in due form by authority of the Parliament of the United Kingdom"; and (v) the request and consent of each of the six Dominions to the passing of the statute.

The expression "Dominion" in section 1 was defined as meaning any of the following: Canada, the Commonwealth of Australia, New Zealand, the Union of South Africa,[14] the Irish Free State,[15] and Newfoundland.[16] Section 11 provided that, notwithstanding the Interpretation Act 1889, the expression "colony" should not, in any subsequent Act of the

---

[9] K. C. Wheare, *The Statute of Westminster and Dominion Status* (5th ed.); *Constitutional Structure of the Commonwealth* (1960) Chap. 2. See also Sir Ivor Jennings. *op. cit.* Beaglehole (ed.,), *New Zealand and the Statute of Westminster*; W. P. M. Kennedy, "The Imperial Conferences, 1926–1930: The Statute of Westminster" (1932) 48 L.Q.R. 191.

[10] The title of the Statute was suggested by Sir Maurice Gwyer, then Treasury Solicitor and a member of the Conference on the Operation of Dominion Legislation, and later Chief Justice of India.

[11] Cmd. 2768.

[12] Cmd. 3479.

[13] Cmd. 3717. These Reports have been referred to by the Judicial Committee; see W. Ivor Jennings, "The Statute of Westminster and Appeals to the Privy Council" (1936) 52 L.Q.R. 173, 175–177.

[14] South Africa became a republic and seceded from the Commonwealth in 1961. The provisions of the Statute of Westminster as affecting South Africa had been enacted as part of the law of the Union by the Status of the Union Act 1934.

[15] The Irish Free State, called Eire after 1937, seceded from the Commonwealth in 1949, and now calls herself the Republic of Ireland. See Republic of Ireland Act 1948 (Ir.); Ireland Act 1949 (U.K.); *In re Article 26 of the Constitution and the Criminal Law (Jurisdiction) Bill, 1975* [1977] I.R. 129.

[16] The Statute never came into operation as regards Newfoundland, which is now a province of Canada.

United Kingdom Parliament, include a Dominion or any province or state forming part of a Dominion.[17]

Repugnance of Dominion legislation to United Kingdom statutes

Section 2 provides as follows:

"(1) *The Colonial Laws Validity Act 1865 shall not apply to any law made after the commencement of this Act by the Parliament of a Dominion.*

(2) No law and no provision of any law made after the commencement of this Act by the Parliament of a Dominion shall be void or inoperative on the ground that it is repugnant to the law of England, or to the provisions of any existing or future Act of Parliament of the United Kingdom, or to any order, rule or regulation made under any such Act, and the powers of the Parliament of a Dominion shall include the power to amend or repeal any such Act, order, rule or regulation in so far as the same is part of the law of the Dominion."

Subsection (2) was inserted in case the mere repeal of the Colonial Laws Validity Act[18] as affecting the Dominions should leave them in the position in which they would have been at common law before 1865. It applies only to Dominion legislation passed after the commencement of the Statute, but any void Act previously passed could be given validity by re-enactment. It covers "any existing or future Act" of the United Kingdom Parliament, but it is doubtful whether it extends to the amendment or repeal of the statute itself.

Extraterritorial operation of Dominion legislation

Section 3 states: "It is hereby declared and enacted that the Parliament of a Dominion has full power to make laws having extraterritorial operation." This set at rest, so far as Dominion legislation was concerned, any doubts that might have existed as a result of the dicta in *Macleod* v. *Attorney-General for New South Wales*.[19] In practice, territorial limitations on the operation of legislation of all legislatures are quite common, and arise from the express terms of statutes or from rules of construction applied by the courts as to the presumed intention of the legislature, regard being had to the comity of nations and other considerations. What this section was designed to get rid of was any constitutional limitations there may have been which placed Acts of Dominion Parliaments in a different position in this respect from Acts of the Imperial Parliament. It did not mean that a Dominion could alter the law of the United Kingdom or of other Dominions or of foreign countries, but that it could pass legislation (for example) in criminal matters, "which attaches significance for courts within the jurisdiction of facts and events occurring outside the jurisdiction."[20]

Extension of United Kingdom legislation to the Dominions

Section 4 provides as follows: "*No Act of Parliament of the United Kingdom passed after the commencement of this Act shall extend, or be deemed to*

---

[17] See now, Interpretation Act 1978, s.5 and Sched. 1. Section 11 of the Statute of Westminster was repealed by section 25 of the Interpretation Act 1978.

[18] *Ante*, Chap. 36.

[19] [1891] A.C. 455. See *ante*, p. 742.

[20] Wheare, *The Statute of Westminster and Dominion Status*, p. 167.

extend, to a Dominion as part of the law of that Dominion, unless it is expressly declared in that Act that that Dominion has requested, and consented to, the enactment thereof."

The request and consent required is that of the *government* of the Dominion concerned, except that in the case of Australia section 9(3) required also the request and consent of the Commonwealth Parliament as the Senate might not be in agreement with the government. Actual request and consent are not required: merely an express declaration of request and consent in the United Kingdom Act would be sufficient.[21] The significance of the words "as part of the law of that Dominion" has been discussed in Chapter 4 concerning the legislative power of the United Kingdom Parliament. Whether the Courts of a Dominion would enforce a United Kingdom Act which was clearly inconsistent with section 4, is another matter. Dixon C.J. said in *Copyright Owners Reproduction Society* v. *E.M.I. (Australia) Pty. Ltd.*[22] that there was a strong presumption that the United Kingdom Parliament would not legislate for a Dominion without its consent even before 1931, and there is therefore a rule of construction in the Australian High Court that, in the absence of evidence of such consent, a United Kingdom Act is not intended to apply to that country. The preamble to His Majesty's Declaration of Abdication Act 1936[23] recited that "the Dominion of Canada, pursuant to the provisions of section 4 of the Statute of Westminster 1931, has requested and consented to the enactment of this Act, and the Commonwealth of Australia, the Dominion of New Zealand, and the Union of South Africa have assented thereto." The Abdication Act made an alteration in the law touching the succession to the Throne which could, with the necessary consents, have been made to extend to the Dominions.

The Statute of Westminster did not recite or provide that the United Kingdom Parliament *would* legislate for a Dominion whenever it requested and consented. A general convention probably existed or developed to that effect, though the matter could have raised difficulties with regard to federal Dominions such as Canada and Australia.

Application to Canada[24]

Canada was the only Dominion that had no power to amend its Constitution Act. This limitation is to be accounted for partly by the relatively early date of the British North America Act 1867 and partly by the federal nature of its Constitution. When the Conference on the Operation of Dominion Legislation reported in 1929 the provinces had not been consulted about the proposed Imperial Act, and the Report of the Imperial Conference, 1930, shows that certain of the provinces protested against the proposed legislation—in particular, section 2—until they

---

21 *Manuel* v. *Att.-Gen.* [1983] Ch. 77, 106, *per* Slade L.J.

22 (1958) 100 C.L.R. 597; (1958) 32 A.L.J.R. 306.

23 N. Mansergh, *Documents and Speeches on British Commonwealth Affairs, 1931–52*, I, pp. 179 *et seq.; Survey of British Commonwealth Affairs, 1931–39*, pp. 41–46; R. T. E. Latham, Appendix to "The Law and the Commonwealth"; K. H. Bailey in *Politica*, March and June 1938; Wheare, *op. cit.* pp. 278–290.

24 P. Hogg, *Constitutional Law of Canada : Canada Act 1982* (1982). B. Laskin, *Canadian Constitutional Law.*

had had an opportunity to determine whether their rights would be adversely affected. The saving clause relating to legislation by the Canadian Parliament (s.7) reads: "(1) Nothing in this Act shall be deemed to apply to the repeal, amendment or alteration of the British North America Acts 1867 and 1930, or any order, rule or regulation made thereunder . . . (3) The powers conferred by this Act upon the Parliament of Canada. . . . shall be restricted to the enactment of laws in relation to matters within the competence of the Parliament of Canada . . . " If Canada wished for constitutional amendments, or to have constituent power, it was free—(semble) subject to consultation with the provinces—to ask the United Kingdom Parliament to pass the necessary legislation. This in fact occurred when the British North America (No. 2) Act 1949 conferred on the Canadian Parliament a power of constitutional amendment by means of ordinary legislation, with certain important exceptions such as matters assigned exclusively to the provincial legislatures.

The "patriation" of the Canadian Constitution[25]

For more than twenty years successive Canadian Prime Ministers tried to bring about the "patriation" of the Canadian Constitution by obtaining agreement among the Provinces, which did not want to lose control over natural resources in their territories, to a formula for constitutional amendment. The Canadian Supreme Court gave an advisory opinion that there was no legal requirement for the Provinces to be consulted before the Queen was requested to lay before the United Kingdom Parliament a Bill to amend the Canadian Constitution where provincial rights or the relations between the Federation and the Provinces would be affected, but the majority thought that convention required there to be at least a substantial measure of provincial agreement.[26] While the Canada Bill was before the United Kingdom Parliament an unsuccessful attempt was made to obtain a declaration from the English courts that, in view of treaties made with the Indians by George III, Indian rights ought to be excluded from the effects of the proposed legislation. The English Court of Appeal held that the obligations of the Crown to the Indian peoples were now those of the Crown in right of Canada and not in right of the United Kingdom.[27]

The Preamble to the Canada Act 1982 recites that Canada (i.e. The Canadian Government) requested and consented to its enactment by the United Kingdom Parliament, and that the Canadian Parliament submitted an address to Her Majesty requesting her to cause a Bill to be

---

[25] D. C. M. Yardley, "The Patriation of the Canadian Constitution," (1982) 7 Holdsworth Law Rev. 84; G. Marshall, Constitutional Conventions (1984) Chap. XI.

[26] Re Amendment of the Constitution of Canada (1981) 125 D.L.R. (3d) 1. See First Report from the Foreign Affairs Committee, Session 1980–81: British North America Acts: The Role of Parliament, H.C. 42 (Kershaw); Second Report on the British North America Acts; the Role of Parliament (1981). See also O. Hood Phillips, "Constitutional Conventions in the Supreme Court of Canada" (1982) 98 L.Q.R. 194; cf. Rodney Brazier and St. John Robilliard, "Constitutional Conventions. The Canadian Supreme Court's View Reviewed" [1982] P.L. 28.

[27] Manuel v. Att.-Gen. [1983] Ch. 77 (C.A.); Noltcho v. Att.-Gen. [1983] Ch. 77 at 89 (Megarry V.-C.), following R. v. Secretary of State for Foreign and Commonwealth Affairs ex p. Indian Association of Alberta [1982] Q.B. 892 (C.A.); (pet. dis.) 937 (H.L.).

laid before the United Kingdom Parliament for that purpose. Section 1 enacts the draft (Canadian) Constitution Act 1982, set out in Schedule B. Section 2 provides that no Act of the United Kingdom Parliament passed after the Constitution Act 1982 comes into force shall extend to Canada as part of its law, and section 4 of the Statute of Westminster is repealed so far as Canada is concerned. The Constitution Act provides a complicated procedure for amendment by the Canadian Parliament of the Canadian Constitution, including the federal distribution of powers. A Charter of Rights and Freedoms, applicable to the legislatures and governments of the Federation and the Provinces, is contained in Part I. This Charter, unlike the Canadian Bill of Rights of 1960, is judicially enforceable, though federal or provincial legislation may expressly override the four "fundamental freedoms."[28] The Constitution, which includes the Canada Act 1982, the Constitution Act 1982 and the scheduled "Constitution Acts" (including the series of British North America Acts) is to be the supreme law of Canada.[29]

The Queen in person signed the Proclamation in Ottawa inaugurating the new Canadian Constitution.

Application to Australia[30]

Sections 2–6[31] of the Statute of Westminster were adoptive with respect to Australia, and Australia adopted them after Japan entered the war in 1942, as from the commencement of the war with Germany.[32]

The Commonwealth of Australia Constitution Act 1900 provides the legal basis of federation under the Crown, which the recital states was intended to be indissoluble. Sections 1–8 of the Act, which involve the federal principle, make no provision for their amendment by the Australian Parliament.[33] The *Constitution*, which is contained in section 9 of the Constitution *Act*, can be altered by the Commonwealth Parliament, but only after a referendum.[34] This position was reserved by sections 8 and 9(1) of the Statute of Westminster, which provided that: "8. Nothing in this Act shall be deemed to confer any power to repeal or alter the Constitution or the Constitution Act of the Commonwealth of Australia . . . otherwise than in accordance with the law existing before the commencement of this Act. 9. (1) Nothing in this Act shall be deemed to authorise the Parliament of the Commonwealth of Australia

---

[28] See *Canadian Charter of Rights and Freedoms*, eds., Tanapolsky and Baudouin (Toronto, 1982); G. L. Peiris, "Legal Protection of Human Rights: The contemporary Canadian experience" (1985) 5 L.S. 261.

[29] See further, Peter Hogg, *The Canada Act 1982 Annotated* (Toronto, 1983).

[30] W. A. Wynes, *Legislative, Executive and Judicial Powers in Australia*; C. Howard, *Australian Federal Constitutional Law*; L. Zines, *The High Court and the Constitution* (Sydney 1981); G. Winterton, *Parliament, the Executive and the Governor-General* (Melbourne, 1983).

[31] Section 5 concerned merchant shipping and section 6 Admiralty courts.

[32] Not from the passing of the Statute of Westminster: *Ex p. Bennett; Re Cunningham* (1967) 86 W.N. (Pt. 2) (N.S.W.) 323.

[33] See G. Sawer, "The British Connection" (1973) 47 A.L.J. 113.

[34] The proposed amendment must be approved not only by a majority of all the votes, but also by a majority of the votes in a majority of the states; and any amendment diminishing the proportionate representation of a State in the House of Representatives requires the approval of the majority of voters in that State: Constitution of the Commonwealth s.128.

to make laws on any matter within the authority of the States of Australia, not being a matter within the authority of the Parliament or Government of the Commonwealth of Australia."[35]

Australia Act 1986

The provisions of the virtually identical Australia Acts passed by the United Kingdom and Commonwealth[36] Parliaments in 1986 were agreed to by the Queen, the Commonwealth Government, all the State Governments and the United Kingdom Government after extensive consultations between the Commonwealth and State Governments over a period of several years. The Commonwealth Parliament enacted its Act under section 51 (xxxviii) of the Constitution. The legislation was designed to remove the residual constitutional links between Australia and the United Kingdom Parliament, Government and judicial system, but the position of the Queen as Queen of Australia is not changed.

The preamble to the United Kingdom Act recites that the Parliament and Government of the Commonwealth of Australia have, with the concurrence of the States of Australia, requested and consented to the enactment of an Act of the United Kingdom Parliament in the terms therein set forth (thus fulfilling the requirements of sections 4 and 9(3) of the Statute of Westminster).

The Act deals first with legislative powers by providing that no future Act of Parliament of the United Kingdom shall extend, or be deemed to extend, to the Commonwealth or a State or Territory of Australia as part of its law (section 1). It goes on to deal with State legislation by declaring that the legislative powers of the Parliament of each State include full power to make laws for the peace, order and good government of that State having extra-territorial operation (following section 3 of the Statute of Westminster), and that the legislative powers of each State include all legislative powers that the United Kingdom Parliament might have exercised for that State before the commencement of the Act, but not including the capacity to engage in relations with countries outside Australia (section 2). The provisions of the Colonial Laws Validity Act 1865 so far as they applied to State Parliaments are repealed (section 3, modelled on section 2 of the Statute of Westminster applying to Commonwealth legislation); but the removal of restrictions on State Parliaments does not affect the Statute of Westminster, the Commonwealth Constitution Act or the Commonwealth Constitution (section 5). Certain restrictions on merchant shipping legislation[37] by State Parliaments are repealed (section 4, corresponding to section 5 of the Statute of Westminster applying to Commonwealth Acts). State legislation respecting the constitution, powers and procedure of the State Parliament must be made in the manner and form (if any) required from time to

---

[35] The constitutions of the Australian states, though written (based largely on United Kingdom statutes), are largely flexible (subject to retaining such fundamentals as the monarchy); see *McCawley* v. *The King* [1920] A.C. 591 (P.C.); R. D. Lumb, *The Constitutions of the Australian States* (2nd ed., Brisbane, 1965).

[36] "The Commonwealth" in the context of the Australia Act means the Commonwealth of Australia.

[37] Merchant Shipping Act 1894, ss.735 and 736.

time by the law of that State (section 6, continuing the effect of section 5 of the Colonial Laws Validity Act).

The Act then deals with executive powers and functions. Instead of the Queen being formally advised on State matters as hitherto by United Kingdom ministers following recommendations from State Premiers to the Foreign and Commonwealth Office, it is provided that Her Majesty's representative in each State shall be the Governor and all the Queen's powers and functions in respect of a State shall be exercisable only by him, except that the appointment and dismissal of the Governor will be done on the advice of the State Premier. While Her Majesty is personally present in a State, however, she may, following mutual and prior agreement, exercise any of her State functions on the advice of the State Premier (section 7). Any powers to disallow, suspend, reserve or withhold assent to Acts or Bills of State Parliaments are abolished (sections 8 and 9); and the United Kingdom Government will have no responsibility for the government of any State (section 10).

All appeals from Australian courts[38] to the Privy Council, whether under statute or prerogative, are terminated, thus making the High Court of Australia the final court of appeal from Australian courts (section 11).

Sections 4, 9(2) and (3) and 10(2) of the Statute of Westminster,[39] in so far as they were part of the law of the Commonwealth or of a State or Territory, are repealed (section 12). This Act or the Statute of Westminster in so far as it is part of the law of the Commonwealth or of a State or Territory, may be repealed or amended only by a Commonwealth Act passed at the request or with the concurrence of all the State Parliaments (section 15).[40]

There was no need for honours, which are awarded by virtue of the prerogative, to be dealt with in the Act; but the Queen has agreed, with the approval of the United Kingdom and Australian Governments, that the Premier of any State whose Government wishes to do so may make recommendations direct to Her Majesty for awards of Imperial Honours.

Application to New Zealand

Sections 2–6[41] of the Statute of Westminster were adoptive with respect to New Zealand, which adopted them after the last war without retrospective effect.

The Constitution of New Zealand was to a very considerable extent alterable by the Parliament of New Zealand; but the powers of alteration conferred by the Constitution Acts were subject to certain qualifications, and it was a matter of doubt whether those qualifications had been removed by section 5 of the Colonial Laws Validity Act. As in the

---

[38] "Australian courts" in this Act do not include the High Court of Australia, from which all appeals to the Privy Council had already been abolished, subject to s.74 of the Constitution (*Inter se* questions certified by the High Court) which had no longer any practical operation: *Kirmani* v. *Captain Cook Cruises Pty. Ltd.* (*No. 2*), *ex p. Att.-Gen. of Queensland* (1984) 58 A.L.R. 108.

[39] *Ante*, p. 749.

[40] This does not apply to a repeal of amendment made in exercise of powers conferred on the Commonwealth Parliament by any future amendment of the Constitution.

[41] See note 31 *supra*.

case of Canada and Australia, it was for New Zealand to make representations to the Imperial Parliament if it wished for further constituent
power. Section 8 of the Statute of Westminster therefore provided that:
"Nothing in this Act shall be deemed to confer any power to repeal or
alter . . . the Constitution Act of the Dominion of New Zealand otherwise than in accordance with the law existing before the commencement of this Act." When New Zealand adopted sections 2–6 in 1947 she
asked for and obtained an Imperial Act that gave her complete constituent powers.[42]

In *Fitzgerald* v. *Muldoon*[43] Wild C.J. adopted Dicey's definition of
sovereignty in relation to the New Zealand Parliament.

II. THE COMMONWEALTH AT THE PRESENT DAY[44]

Grant of independence[45]

Whereas the grant to British dependent territories of responsible self-
government within the Commonwealth, or of independence, is a matter
for the United Kingdom Government and the territory concerned, the
question of the admission of a territory to full membership of the Commonwealth is one on which all existing members are consulted. From
the Indian Independence Act and the Ceylon Independence Act of
1947,[46] the grant of independence has been effected by Act of Parliament.[47] Independence involves, first, the acquisition of international
personality which is recognised by other countries. It leads to application, sponsored by the United Kingdom, for membership of the
United Nations, which is invariably accepted. Independence also gives
rise to complex problems of state succession.[48] Secondly, independence
involves the freedom of the country concerned from dependence on the
Parliament and Government of the United Kingdom.

---

[42] New Zealand Constitution (Amendment) Act 1947. See J. C. Beaglehole (ed.), *New Zealand and the Statute of Westminster* (1944); A. E. Currie. *New Zealand and the Statute of
Westminster, 1931* (1944); J. L. Robson (ed.), *New Zealand, Development of its Laws and
Constitution* (2nd ed., 1967); New Zealand Constitution Amendment Act 1973 (N.Z.):
(extraterritorial legislation).

[43] [1976] 2 N.Z.L.R. 615, 622.

[44] Sir William Dale, *The Modern Commonwealth* (1983); Sir Kenneth Roberts-Wray, *Commonwealth and Colonial Law* (1966) K. C. Wheare, *The Constitutional Structure of the Com-
monwealth* (1960); S. A. de Smith, *The New Commonwealth and its Constitutions* (1964);
The Vocabulary of Commonwealth Relations (1954). Heather J. Harvey, *Consultation and
Co-operation in the Commonwealth* (1952); J. E. S. Fawcett, *The British Commonwealth in
International Law* (1963); *Changing Law in Developing Countries* (ed. J. N. D. Anderson,
1963); *Parliament as an Export* (ed. Sir Alan Burns, (1966); L. Wolf-Phillips, "Post-
Independence Constitutional Change in the Commonwealth" (1970) XVII *Political
Studies*, p. 18.

[45] The gradual acquisition of independence by Canada, Australia and New Zealand is
described in the previous section.

[46] Sri Lanka (Ceylon) adopted an autochthonous republican Constitution in 1972. The
Constitution of 1978 provides for an executive President: see M. J. A. Cooray, *Judicial
Role under the Constitutions of Ceylon/Sri Lanka* (Colombo, 1982).

[47] The Ireland Act 1949 recognised a *fait accompli*.

[48] See Roberts-Wray, *op. cit.* pp. 267–269; Fawcett, *op. cit.* Chap. 18. And see *The Effect of
Independence on Treaties* (International Law Association, 1966).

Independence Acts

The Independence Act will therefore remove, in the manner of sections 2, 3 and 4 of the Statute of Westminster,[49] the three legislative limitations of repugnancy, extra-territoriality and the powers of the United Kingdom Parliament. The doctrine of repugnancy[50] is abolished by a provision on the lines of section 2 of the Statute of Westminster, whereby no future law made by the Parliament of the territory concerned shall be void on the ground that it is repugnant to any existing or future Act of Parliament. This would probably include the Independence Act itself, even if it is not specifically mentioned. Section 3 of the Statute of Westminster, authorising legislation with extra-territorial operation, was needed in relation to the Dominions in 1931, as that Statute did not make a definite break between dependence and independence: it was a statutory declaration of existing facts that had been brought about by gradual evolution. In the post-war Independence Acts this provision may not be necessary as the power of extra-territorial legislation is probably implied by independence, but it may be inserted *ex abundante cautela*.

The provision that future Acts of the United Kingdom shall not apply to the country concerned has been modelled on section 4 of the Statute of Westminster. That section was followed closely in the case of Ceylon (now Sri Lanka) and Ghana (formerly the Gold Coast). The Indian Independence Act, however, omitted the "request and consent" and substituted "unless it is expressly extended thereto" by a law of the Indian legislature. The Nigerian, Sierra Leone and later Acts merely omit the contingency that they might request and consent to United Kingdom legislation.

The powers of disallowance and reservation and the reserved power of certification were abolished by the Indian Independence Act 1947. The power of disallowance survived in theory in relation to Canada until 1982 and Australia until 1986 and has not been formally abolished in relation to New Zealand, but by convention it was never exercised after they became "self-governing." In other cases of independence these extraneous powers will have been abolished by amendment to the pre-independence constitution.

Independence in the case of former colonies, *e.g.* Ghana, Nigeria and Malta, which involves the transfer of sovereignty to territories that previously had no international personality, is usually described in the Act as "fully responsible status" within the Commonwealth. Protectorates (*e.g.* Uganda) and trust territories (*e.g.* Tanganyika, now part of Tanzania) were not within Her Majesty's dominions, and therefore Independence Acts have technically annexed them to the Crown in order that on the withdrawal of protection they might be granted independence within the Commonwealth. In the case of trust territories this process required the approval of the United Nations. The independent Federation of Malaya (now Malaysia) was formed by agreement between the United Kingdom and the rulers of the protected Malay states, prior approval having been given by Act of Parliament.

[49] *Ante*, pp. 750–751.
[50] Colonial Laws Validity Act 1865, s.2.

The Statute of Westminster did not deal with executive powers, because their exercise was adequately governed by constitutional conventions, and the Statute was not intended at the time it was passed actually to confer independence.[51] The Indian Independence Act 1947 provided that the United Kingdom Government should cease to be responsible for the government of India, and this has been followed in Acts granting independence to former colonies. Acts conferring independence on protectorates either do the same or provide that Her Majesty shall cease to have jurisdiction over the territory.

There is usually an Agreement between the United Kingdom and the territory concerned that the latter shall succeed to the rights and obligations affecting it arising out of international agreements.[52] Other countries appear to accept this. Sometimes the grant of independence has been accompanied by an Agreement with the United Kingdom on external affairs, defence and public officers. This was so, for example, with Ceylon,[53] Malaya, Nigeria, Singapore and Malta.[54]

It is also necessary for Parliament to pass an Act continuing the law of the United Kingdom in force here in relation to the territory so far as it is applicable to its new constitutional status,[55] and to modify certain existing Acts of Parliament, e.g. British Nationality Acts (countries whose nationals are Commonwealth citizens), the Army and Air Force and Naval Discipline Acts (Commonwealth forces); and Acts relating to visiting forces and diplomatic immunities.[56]

A special kind of non-colonial though dependent status was devised for certain small islands in the Caribbean by the West Indies Act 1967[57] following the break-up of the Federation of the West Indies in 1962 and the independence of Jamaica and Trinidad and Tobago. The islands concerned were to be "States in association with the United Kingdom." The United Kingdom retained responsibility for defence, external affairs and citizenship, while the Associated States each had control of internal affairs including constitutional amendments, the Colonial Laws Validity Act ceasing for these purposes to apply to them. The association could be terminated by either side. This "Caribbean Arrangement" did not last long, and one by one the Associated States were granted independence.[57a]

Independence constitutions

The constitution of the newly-independent country will have been drafted by agreement between the Secretary of State and the local party

[51] But see now: *Noltcho v. Att.-Gen.* [1983] Ch. 77, 89 *per* Sir Robert Megarry V.-C., following *R. v. Secretary of State for Foreign and Commonwealth Affairs ex p. Indian Association of Alberta* [1982] Q.B. 892 (C.A.); (pet.dis) 937 (H.L.).

[52] *e.g.* Cmnd. 2633 (Malta).

[53] Sir Ivor Jennings, *The Constitution of Ceylon* (3rd ed., 1953); "The Making of a Dominion Constitution" (1949) 65 L.Q.R. 456.

[54] Cmnd. 2423; Cmnd. 2410.

[55] *e.g.* Ghana (Consequential Provisions) Act 1960.

[56] The latest is the Brunei and Maldives Act 1985.

[57] *Constitutional Proposals for Antigua, St Kitts, Nevis, Anguilla, Dominica, St. Lucia, St. Vincent, Grenada* (1965) Cmnd. 2865; *Report of Antigua Constitutional Conference 1966,* Cmnd. 2963.

[57a] See Sir Fred Phillips, *West Indian Constitutions: Post-Independence Reform* (1985).

in power, sometimes in consultation with opposition or minority parties. It is often contained in a statutory Order in Council separate from the Independence Act, as this is a quicker and more flexible way of getting parliamentary approval. When the constitution has come into operation in what is now an independent country, provisions made thereunder by Order in Council cannot be challenged in the English courts.[58]

In addition to Canada and Australia, a number of post-war constitutions of Commonwealth members have some kind of federal form. These include India, Nigeria,[59] Malaysia, Uganda and Kenya.

Fundamental rights in the Commonwealth, though traceable ultimately to natural law and influenced in their formulation by the European and other regional conventions had their immediate origin in the principles of English law. The earliest example in the Commonwealth of a Bill of Rights in the modern sense is the Constitution of Tonga of 1875, which was probably inspired by Methodist missionaries. Most of the post-war constitutions include an entrenched declaration of fundamental rights, with power of judicial review.[60] The first was the Indian Constitution,[61] which came into force in 1950. The Nigerian declaration of fundamental rights (1960) formed the model for several later formulations in other Commonwealth countries, being derived not only from those in the Constitutions of Pakistan (1956) and Malaya (1957), which themselves borrowed extensively from India, but also from the European Convention.

Amendment of the constitutions of Commonwealth countries usually requires some special procedure at least for altering provisions relating to a federal distribution of powers, fundamental rights, and communal or minority guarantees. In *Bribery Commissioner* v. *Ranasinghe*,[62] an appeal from Ceylon, the Privy Council said: "a legislature has no power to ignore the conditions of lawmaking that are imposed by the instrument which itself regulates the power to make law. This restriction exists independently of the question whether a legislature is sovereign." These special provisions, however, may later be repealed by means of their own special procedure, as was done in the case of Ghana.

Commonwealth countries, a little time after achieving independence, often wish to base a revised constitution on a local *grundnorm*: they assert the principle of constitutional "autochthony," that is, that their constitution is sprung from their native soil and not derived from a United Kingdom statute. Strictly, autochthony requires a breach in legal

---

[58] *Buck* v. *Att.-Gen.* [1965] Ch. 745 (C.A.), affirming Wilberforce J. [1964] 3 W.L.R. 850. And see *Manuel* v. *Att.-Gen.*; *Noltcho* v. *Att.-Gen.* [1983] Ch. 77; applying *R.* v. *Secretary of State for Foreign and Commonwealth Affairs ex p. Indian Association of Alberta* [1982] Q.B. 892 (C.A.), and *Buck* v. *Att.-Gen. supra.*

[59] The Nigerian Federation, which has gone through a number of changes since independence, was said to be unique in that it was not formed from units that were previously separate countries. The divisions were mainly tribal.

[60] Dale *op. cit.* Ch. 12; see Sir K. Roberts-Wray, "Human Rights in the Commonwealth" (1968) 17 I.C.L.Q. 908.

[61] H. M. Seervai, *Constitutional Law of India* Vol. I (3rd ed., Bombay, 1983).

[62] [1965] A.C. 172.

continuity, an actual or technical revolution.[63] A complete breach in legal continuity is attended by some risk if the local courts are independent and impartial. The notion of autochthony is hardly applicable at any rate to Canada, Australia or New Zealand.[64]

Dependent peoples usually want at first to adopt British methods of parliamentary and Cabinet government, adapted to suit local conditions. The main constitutional conventions are commonly formulated or incorporated by reference. The balance of power between conflicting ethnic, religious, linguistic or regional interests needs to be settled before independence.[65] An independent country should be economically viable. It must provide for its own defence and the handling of external affairs. The governmental structure should not be too complex in relation to the population. Literacy is not essential for the franchise. Capable leaders can usually be found to fill the ministerial posts; but beyond this there is the urgent need for an honest and efficient civil service. The dearth of administrators is largely a question of education, and the main obstacle in the way of providing education is the cost.

The desire for independence is itself stimulated by British political ideas, and nationalism marks the later stage in the development of a dependent territory. There is in effect only one party, whose aim is to end "colonialism"; but the British political system presupposes two main parties or groups, one being an effective opposition capable of providing an alternative government. The one-party principle may be introduced before long, especially after the country has become a republic with a strong Presidential system.[66] Thus the "Westminster model"[67] of parliamentary democracy was soon abandoned in Pakistan and Ghana, and later in Nigeria, Uganda, and a number of other Commonwealth countries.

Full membership of the Commonwealth

The Commonwealth was based on conventions which grew out of practice, relating largely to the acquisition and discontinuance of membership. Although it is not an international person it has become an association of an international kind, for it has developed an organisation, acquired a headquarters and developed the beginnings of a constitution, including instruments agreed by Heads of Government such as the London Declaration of 1949 (Head of the Commonwealth), the Agreed Memorandum on the Commonwealth Secretariat of 1965, the

---

[63] Wheare, The Constitutional Structure of the Ccommonwealth, Chap. 4; cf. Kenneth Robinson, "Constitutional Autochthony in Ghana" (1961) 1 Journal of Commonwealth Political Studies, 41; "Constitutional Autochthony and the Transfer of Power," in Essays in Imperial Government (ed. Robinson and Madden, 1963), p. 249; The Canadian Constitution of 1982 was as nearly autochthonous as practicable.

[64] Roberts-Wray, op. cit. pp. 289–295; ante, pp. 751–756.

[65] See S. A. de Smith, "Mauritius: Constitutionalism in a Plural Society" (1968) 31 M.L.R. 601; Claire Palley, "Constitutional Devices in multi-racial and multi-religious societies" (1969) 19 N.I.L.Q. 377.

[66] See N. O. Nwabueze, Presidentialism in Commonwealth Africa (1974). One-party republics in the Commonwealth at present are Bangladesh, Kenya, Malawi, Seychelles, Sierra Leone, Tanzania and Zambia. Zimbabwe looks like going the same way.

[67] See per Lord Diplock in Hinds v. The Queen [1977] A.C. 195 (P.C.); D. C. M. Yardley, "The Effectiveness of the Westminster Model of Constitution," Year Book of World Affairs 1977, Vol. 31, p. 342.

Singapore Declaration of 1971 (description of the association, its membership and objectives) and the Lusaka Declaration of 1979 (human rights).[68] Other agreements are the Gleneagles Agreement of 1977 (apartheid in sport) and the Melbourne Declaration of 1981 (economic aid to developing countries). These instruments, however, can hardly be said to create legal, as opposed to political and moral, obligations.

In order that a country may be admitted to full membership of the Commonwealth it must be: (i) independent; (ii) willing to recognise the Queen as Head of the Commonwealth; and (iii) willing to co-operate.[69] The Singapore Declaration begins by describing the Commonwealth of Nations as a voluntary association of independent sovereign states, each responsible for its own policies, consulting and co-operating in the common interests of their peoples and in the promotion of international understanding and world peace. Membership of the Commonwealth, it continues, is compatible with the freedom of member Governments to be non-aligned or to belong to any other grouping, association or alliance. We may notice that political democracy and economic viability no longer appear to be requisite for membership, emphasis being placed rather on racial equality.

The decision to grant independence, as has been said, is made by the United Kingdom.[70] Then, if the government of the country concerned so wishes, the United Kingdom invites the governments of the other full members of the Commonwealth, because they have equality of status, to agree to the full membership of that country. If they, or a majority of them, did not agree, the country concerned would become independent within the Commonwealth, but it would not be a *full* member. On the other hand, there appears to be no rule that the members must be unanimous: a minority probably cannot prevent its becoming a full member, although they might ignore it or even secede.

The number of independent members of the Commonwealth is now about fifty. Those in existence at the time of the passing of the British Nationality Act 1981, about 45 in number, are listed in Schedule 3 of that Act.

While both sentiment and self-interest may be said to operate in keeping the older Dominions in the Commonwealth, self-interest predominates in determining new countries to join the Commonwealth; although even in them sentiment is not absent, especially among administrators, lawyers and educated persons generally. The advantages of the association to new members include continued financial aid; the secondment of skilled personnel, such as administrators and teachers; mutual trade; and co-operation of many kinds, such as the provision of diplomatic information and help in time of trouble. There are also unofficial links such as are formed by associations of Members of Parliament, lawyers, doctors, scientists and technologists. No disadvantages or limitations are involved in membership.

[68] Dale, *op. cit.* Ch. 2; "Is the Commonwealth an international organisation"? (1982) 31 I.C.L.Q. 451.
[69] The only independent country to have entered the Commonwealth from outside is Cyprus, and that took place six months after the termination of its colonial status in order to emphasise the voluntary nature of its membership.
[70] Or Australia, etc., in relation to dependencies of other Commonwealth countries.

It has been recognised since the last war that an independent member may leave the Commonwealth by voluntary secession. Secession, to be fully effective, requires not only local legislation but also an act of the United Kingdom Parliament for such purposes as amending legislation relating to nationality. The secession of Eire in 1948 was recognised by the other members,[71] that of South Africa in 1962[72] and that of (West) Pakistan in 1972.[73]

The Monarchy in the Commonwealth[74]

The symbol of Commonwealth association is the Queen and Head of the Commonwealth. The Queen has adopted a personal flag—initial E and Crown within a chaplet or roses—for use where the royal standard (especially associated with the United Kingdom) is inappropriate.

The convention recited in the preamble to the Statute of Westminster[75] still requires that an alteration by the United Kingdom Parliament in the law touching *the succession to the Throne* should have the assent of the Parliaments of all the Dominions (or realms owing allegiance to the Crown).[76] They would presumably also need to pass their own legislation in order to make such an alteration in the law effective in their own countries. It is suggested that the republics and separate monarchies (such as Malaysia) in the Commonwealth need only be informed of the change made in the law identifying the Head of the Commonwealth, although as a matter of courtesy they would probably be kept informed of any preliminary discussions.

On the other hand, as regards a change made by one member in *the Royal Style and Titles* used by that member—at least within the bounds set by recent precedent—it seems that convention since 1952 no longer requires the assent of any of the other members. On the accession of Queen Elizabeth II in February 1952 proclamations of the Royal Style and Titles were issued in the independent countries of the Commonwealth which, except in the case of New Zealand, differed from that issued in the United Kingdom. Later that year discussions were held among the members, and it was agreed that each one should adopt a title to suit its own circumstances but including a common element. As a result Canada, Australia and New Zealand in 1953 adopted the same royal titles as the United Kingdom, but incorporated a specific reference to their own territory, thus: "Elizabeth II, by the Grace of God of the United Kingdom, Canada [Australia, New Zealand] and Her other

---

[71] Ireland Act 1949: but the Republic of Ireland is not to be regarded as a foreign country nor are its citizens to be regarded as aliens in the United Kingdom.

[72] South Africa Act 1962: South Africa became a foreign country, and its citizens became aliens unless they were also citizens of the United Kingdom and Colonies or of some other Commonwealth country.

[73] Pakistan Acts 1973 and 1974; *R. v. Chief Immigration Officer, Heathrow Airport, ex p. Salamat Bibi* [1976] 1 W.L.R. 979 (C.A.). The former East Pakistan (renamed Bangladesh) remained in the Commonwealth: Bangladesh Act 1973. Burma (1947) and Somaliland (1960) left the Commonwealth on obtaining independence.

[74] Dale, *op. cit..* pp. 35–39. Sir Ivor Jennings, *Constitutional Laws of the Commonwealth* (3rd ed.,). Vol. I pp. 18–25; J. E. S. Fawcett *The British Commonwealth in International Law* pp. 79–85; D. P. O'Connell, "The Crown in the British Ccommonwealth" (1957) 61 I.C.L.Q. 103.

[75] *Ante*, p. 749.

[76] Suppose they do not all agree?

Realms and Territories, Queen, Head of the Commonwealth, Defender of the Faith."[77] In the republics and separate monarchies (*e.g.* Malaysia) the Queen is recognised only as Head of the Commonwealth.[78]

The Queen is a part of the legislature in each of her realms, and the government of each is carried on in her name on the advice of the Ministers in that country. The extent to which prerogative powers in relation to external affairs were transferred to the Governor-General in the former Dominions varied.[79]

Her Majesty during her tours of the Commonwealth has personally opened sessions of Commonwealth Parliaments, presided over Executive Councils and meetings of the Privy Council, administered the oath of office to Ministers and signed letters of credence of Commonwealth ambassadors.

Following the dismissal of the Australian Prime Minister (Mr. Gough Whitlam) and the appointment of the Leader of the Opposition (Mr. Fraser) as caretaker Prime Minister by the Governor-General (Sir John Kerr) in 1975, the Speaker of the House of Representatives wrote to the Queen asking her to intervene. Her Majesty replied; "The written Constitution, and accepted constitutional conventions, preclude the Queen from intervening personally in those functions [given to the Governor-General by the Constitution] once the Governor-General has been appointed, and from interfering with His Excellency's tenure of office except upon advice from the Australian Prime Minister." It is not clear who advised Her Majesty on that occasion, or who drafted her letter.[80]

Some controversy arose early in 1984 out of the Queen's Christmas broadcast to the Commonwealth (in which Her Majesty spoke of her recent visit to India and her meeting with Mrs. Gandhi, the Indian Prime Minister) over the question whether convention requires the Head of the Commonwealth to take advice from ministers of the United Kingdom or of the Commonwealth countries concerned, or whether she may act without such advice. Statements were made by both Buckingham Palace and Mrs. Thatcher, the Prime Minister, in the House of Commons to the effect that as Head of the Commonwealth the Queen may act without formal advice, and these statements were consistent with the opinion expressed by a former legal adviser to the Commonwealth Office.[81]

That does not, however, mean that she may, as Head of the Common-

---

[77] All the overseas countries described her as "Elizabeth the Second," although she was the first Elizabeth to reign over them as distinct Kingdoms: *cf. MacCormick* v. *Lord Advocate*, 1953 S.C. 396 (Scotland). In 1973 Her Majesty personally signed an Australian Act giving her the title of Queen of Australia, instead of Queen of the United Kingdom and Australia.

[78] *Post*, p. 764.

[79] Further prerogative powers, extending to war and peace, were transferred at the beginning of 1978 to the Governor-General of Canada. *Cf.* now, Canada Act 1982 and Australia Act 1986, *ante.*

[80] See D. P. O'Connell, "The Dissolution of the Australian Parliament: 11 November, 1975," (1976) 57 *The Parliamentarian*, p. 1; and letter from D. P. O'Connell and J. M. Finnis to *The Times*, 25 November, 1975.

[81] Sir William Dale, letter to *Daily Telegraph* January 31, 1984. *Cf.* Mr. Enoch Powell, M.P.: "ministerial advice that ministerial advice is not requisite is also ministerial advice": letter to *The Times*, January 26, 1984. See further, R. W. Blackburn, "The Queen and Ministerial Responsibility" [1985] P.L. 361.

wealth, differ publicly from the views of the Government on a matter on which the Government has formed a particular view. In July 1986 there was speculation in a newspaper article that the Queen, as Head of the Commonwealth, did not agree with the Prime Minister on the wisdom of applying (or not applying) economic sanctions against South Africa.[82] Whatever the truth of that story, it would obviously be constitutionally improper for the Queen to express in public a view which was contrary to that of Her Ministers as the United Kingdom on a matter concerning the policy of the United Kingdom.

"The Crown" usually means the central government,[83] and as there are as many independent governments as there are independent countries of the Commonwealth, "the Crown" in any of these will usually mean the government of that country. This is especially so where statute has expressly or impliedly designated a particular fund to meet a debt.[84] Further, disputes between member nations of the Commonwealth are possible, such as the dispute between India and Pakistan on the status of Kashmir. The Crown may at the same time be at war in respect of some Commonwealth territories and at peace in respect of others. In the Second World War not only did some Commonwealth countries make separate declarations of war against Germany and Japan, but Eire remained neutral throughout. Since the war the members of the Commonwealth have not pursued a common foreign policy. They differed, for example, over the Suez Canal intervention in 1956 and on the question of recognising Communist China. Some have entered into regional treaties with non-members to the exclusion of other members.

The conclusion is that the common law doctrine of the indivisibility of the Crown[85] has been modified, from the English law point of view, by legislation and constitutional convention. The Queen holds several offices as Head of State. The legal systems of other Commonwealth countries generally regard the Crown as divisible, but within the federations it is indivisible for certain purposes. In international law the Crown is clearly divisible. Some writers would describe the relation of the Crown to the various realms in the Commonwealth as a new kind of personal union, but no formula yet devised is adequate to cover all the facts.

Republics in the Commonwealth

The India (Consequential Provisions) Act 1949[86] recognised that India[87] was a republic while remaining a member of the Commonwealth. Since its new Constitution came into force in 1950, India no longer owes allegiance to the Crown. The Queen is not Queen of India, but India recognises the Crown as the Head of the Commonwealth with which it is associated and of which it is a full member. The desire of

---

[82] *The Sunday Times,* July 20, 1986, *ante,* p. 316.

[83] *Ante,* p. 267.

[84] *Att.-Gen.* v. *Great Southern and Western Ry. of Ireland* [1925] A.C. 754.

[85] *Ante,* p. 730.

[86] And see Statute Law (Repeals) Act 1976, Pt. VII.

[87] *i.e.* the former British India excluding Pakistan, but including most of the former Indian states.

India to remain a full member of the Commonwealth after the coming into force of her republican Constitution was discussed at a meeting of Commonwealth Prime Ministers in 1949, which issued a declaration[88] to the effect that the Governments of the other Commonwealth countries, the basis of whose membership of the Commonwealth was not thereby changed, accepted and recognised India's continuing membership. This declaration modified the Balfour declaration of 1926,[89] and dropped the term "British" as applied to the Commonwealth. A similar process was gone through in 1956 in relation to Pakistan which has since left the Commonwealth.[90]

The existence of republics within the Commonwealth marks the end of that "common allegiance" which featured so prominently in the Balfour declaration; but the concept of allegiance, now divorced from British nationality, appears to have no legal significance except in the law of treason.

Differences over the wisdom of applying economic sanctions to South Africa led in 1986, to threats by some states to leave the Commonwealth but none has, so far, done so.

Citizenship[91]

As has been seen in Chapter 23, there is no longer a common code of British nationality. The first sign of divergence was the Canadian Nationals Act 1921, and crisis came with the Canadian Citizenship Act 1946. This led to a conference of legal experts on Commonwealth nationality and citizenship in 1947. Their proposal was that the United Kingdom and the other Commonwealth countries should each define their own citizenship, and that the citizens of the various Commonwealth countries should be recognised in every part of the Commonwealth as "British subjects" or "Commonwealth citizens."

This "common clause" was adopted by the United Kingdom, Canada, Australia and New Zealand. It does not necessarily mean, however, that British citizens (formerly citizens of the United Kingdom and Colonies) have in those other three countries the same citizenship and political rights as their citizens have in the United Kingdom.[92] Other Commonwealth countries recognise "Commonwealth citizens" in various ways.

Consultation and co-operation

After the Imperial Conference of 1937 the practice of holding more or less regular Imperial Conferences, with fixed agenda and full published reports, was discontinued. There have since been ad hoc meetings of Commonwealth heads of government to review the state of the war and to discuss post-war settlements; to discuss international relations, economic affairs and defence; to answer the question of India's continued

---

[88] For the negotiations leading to this declaration, including recognition by India of the King as "Head of the Commonwealth," see J. W. Wheeler-Bennett, *King George VI*, pp. 719–731.

[89] *Ante*, p. 747.

[90] The number of republics (with either constitutional or executive Presidents) within the Commonwealth had risen by 1985 to 25, compared with 17 Realms acknowledging the Queen as Head of State and 6 native monarchies.

[91] Dale, *op. cit.* pp. 187–189.

[92] *Ante* p. 458 for the application of the Immigration Act 1971 to Commonwealth citizens.

membership of the Commonwealth after adopting a republican constitution; to discuss South Africa; to discuss the Common Market; the
world political situation; the progress of British territories towards
independence, and membership of the Commonwealth; the means of
promoting closer co-operation between the peoples of the Commonwealth; world economic affairs; disarmament; trade and immigration.
Meetings of all the member states are now held biennially: in 1983 in
Delhi; in 1985 in Nassau (Bahamas).[93]

There have also been other Conferences from time to time below
heads of government level, for example, the British Commonwealth
Conference on Nationality and Citizenship, 1947; and the Conference of
Commonwealth Foreign Ministers at Colombo in 1950, which recommended the establishment of a Commonwealth Consultative Committee to plan developments for South and South-East Asia ("the
Colombo Plan").

Since the war, treaty relations among members of the Commonwealth
no longer appear to differ from those existing between other states. In
the absence of any provision to the contrary, they would be governed
by international law. When members of the Commonwealth have
accepted the compulsory jurisdiction of the International Court of Justice, they have tended to reserve disputes with Commonwealth countries. The United Kingdom no longer excludes such disputes arising
after 1968. No formal machinery had been devised for settling disputes
between members of the Commonwealth. An advisory opinion of the
Privy Council has been sought twice in disputes between Commonwealth members.[94] Settlement through the machinery of the United
Nations has also been resorted to twice: between India and South
Africa in 1946 over the treatment of Indians in the latter country, and
between India and Pakistan over the future status of Kashmir in 1954.

Commonwealth High Commissioners in the United Kingdom now
take precedence with ambassadors of foreign states and are accorded
the title of "Excellency." Republican members of the Commonwealth
may send ambassadors rather than High Commissioners to other Commonwealth countries. These representatives of Commonwealth governments in the United Kingdom were granted immunities similar to those
of foreign diplomatic representatives in 1952.[95]

Consultation, exchange of information and co-operation among
Commonwealth countries are found mainly in the fields of external
affairs, defence, finance and economics, education and law.[96] There is
also a fair degree of mutual help. The obligation to consult, however, is
not clearly defined, and consultation tends to be a one-way traffic. The
United Kingdom would not change any law affecting citizens of Com-

[93] The Nassau meeting was followed by a Seven member Summit in London in 1986 in an
unsuccessful attempt to secure an agreed Commonwealth policy on economic sanctions
against South Africa.
[94] Re Cape Breton (1846) 5 Moo.P.C. 259 (annexation of Cape Breton to Nova Scotia); Re
Labrador Boundary Dispute (1927) 137 L.T. 187.
[95] Diplomatic Immunities (Commonwealth Countries and Republic of Ireland) Act 1952;
Diplomatic Privileges Act 1964; ante, p. 292.
[96] The Secretariat collaborates with the Commonwealth Legal Advisory Service of the
British Institute of International and Comparative Law; see H. H. Marshall, "Commonwealth Legal Advisory Service," (1972) 21 I.C.L.Q. 403.

monwealth countries, such as the Fugitive Offenders Acts, without consulting the other members, and in this case probably trying to effect reciprocal arrangements. The principle obtains of non-intervention in each other's domestic affairs. Apart from express agreements, no positive obligations are involved in Commonwealth membership. Generally, there is no definite Commonwealth policy. In particular, there is no common foreign policy. The experience of Eire in the last war shows that a member of the Commonwealth—even one of the Queen's realms (as Eire was then)—may remain neutral in a war in which the Crown is engaged. Eire's neutrality was recognised by the enemy belligerents, and by the neutral countries.

The media for consultation include the Crown and the Governors-General, meetings of Prime Ministers, other Ministers and officials, the exchange of High Commissioners or Ambassadors, and regular communication between the Foreign and Commonwealth Office and the Departments of External Affairs of Commonwealth countries.[97]

There are also a number of official organs for co-operation covering such matters as agriculture and forestry, education, air transport, economics, scientific liaison, shipping, statistics and telecommunications. Assistance of various kinds is provided by the Commonwealth Development Corporation.[98] Collective defence has been a major preoccupation both in war and peace, but the recent tendency is for regional international arrangements such as the North Atlantic Treaty Organisation. The Commonwealth Foundation administers a fund for increasing interchanges between Commonwealth organisations in professional fields. The Foundation is an autonomous body, maintaining a close liaison with the Commonwealth Secretariat, and is financed by contributions from Commonwealth governments.

The Commonwealth Secretariat[99]

The Commonwealth Secretariat, established in 1965 as a visible symbol of the spirit of co-operation animating the Commonwealth, is at the service of all Commonwealth governments. The Secretariat derives its functions from the authority of Commonwealth heads of government, and the Secretary-General has access to heads of government. The Secretariat has no executive functions. Among its chief purposes are to disseminate factual information to all member countries on matters of common concern; to assist existing agencies in the promotion of Commonwealth links; and to help to co-ordinate preparations for future meetings of Commonwealth heads of government and of other Commonwealth Ministers.

The Commonwealth Secretariat Act 1966 provides that the Secretariat shall have the legal capacity of a body corporate, and it and its staff have the privileges and immunities conferred by the Schedule. The certificate of a Secretary of State is conclusive as to any relevant fact.

---

[97] The United Kingdom temporarily broke off diplomatic relations with Uganda in 1976, British interests being looked after by France.

[98] Commonwealth Development Corporation Acts, 1978 and 1982.

[99] Cmnd. 2713, *Agreed Memorandum on the Commonwealth Secretariat; The Commonwealth Relations Office Year Book 1966*, Chap. 3; Margaret Doxey, "The Commonwealth Secretariat," *Year Book of World Affairs 1976*, p. 69.

CHAPTER 38

APPEALS TO THE PRIVY COUNCIL[1]

I. APPEALS FROM DEPENDENT TERRITORIES

THE abolition of the jurisdiction of the Council in the seventeenth century did not extend to appeals from overseas territories, *e.g.* the Channel Islands, the Isle of Man, colonies ("plantations"), and later India. The remaining jurisdiction rested on the prerogative of the King as the fountain or reservoir of justice; but its exercise came to be regulated by the Judicial Committee Acts of 1833 and 1844, which created the judicial Committee of the Privy Council to hear all Privy Council appeals.[2] The Crown has the prerogative to determine what is the jurisdiction of the Judicial Committee.[3] The Colonial Courts of Admiralty Act 1890 provided for the continued hearing of appeals by the Privy Council from courts in any British possession invested with Admiralty jurisdiction where there was no right of appeal to a local court or on appeal from a local court. There is power to make rules of court.

Privy Council Precedents

A Privy Council decision (technically an opinion) is binding on the courts of the country from which the appeal came. The Judicial Committee said in the *Bakhshuwen* case[4] that decisions of the Board on Islamic law in appeals from India bound the Court of Appeal for Eastern Africa, and there are older dicta to the effect that the Boards' decisions are binding throughout the Privy Council's overseas jurisdiction[5]; but the statement should probably be restricted, first to cases where the relevant parts of the legal systems concerned are the same and, secondly to appeals from dependent territories. Decisions of the House of Lords on United Kingdom legislation which has been adopted in similar terms in a colony should be treated by colonial courts as binding, according to the Board in *Delasala* v. *Delasala*,[6] although in juristic theory such decisions are persuasive only.

Appeals lie from the Channel Islands, the Isle of Man and the colonies, and by virtue of the Foreign Jurisdiction Act 1890 they formerly lay from protectorates, protected states and British trust territories.

---

[1] N. Bentwich, *Privy Council Practice* (3rd ed., 1937); Sir Kenneth Roberts-Wray, *Commonwealth and Colonial Law*, pp. 433–463; Sir William Dale, *The Modern Commonwealth* pp. 128–129; Loren P. Beth "The Judicial Committee: Its Development, Organisation and Procedure" [1975] P.L. 219; E. McWhinney, *Judicial Review in the English-Speaking World.* For the early history, see J. H. Smith, *Appeals to the Privy Council from the American Plantations* (1950).

[2] *Ante,* p. 295.

[3] *Australian Consolidated Press* v. *Uren* [1969] 1 A.C. 590 (P.C.).

[4] *Fatuma Bin Salim Bakhshuwen* v. *Mohamed Bin Salim Bakhshuwen* [1952] A.C. 1; *Australian Consolidated Press* v. *Uren, supra.* See H. H. Marshall, "The Binding Effect of Decisions of the Judicial Committee of the Privy Council" (1968) 17 I.C.L.Q. 743; G. W. Bartholomew in (1952) 1 I.C.L.Q. 392; Roberts-Wray, *op.cit.* pp. 572–575.

[5] *e.g. Robins* v. *National Trust Co.* [1927] A.C. 515.

[6] [1980] A.C. 546.

Appeals to the Judicial Committee from overseas territories fall into two main classes:
(1) Appeals by "right of grant.'
(2) Appeals by "special leave" of the Privy Council.

1. Appeals by "right of grant"

These are called appeals "by right of grant" because the limits are defined by Imperial Act, Order in Council or local statute, although fundamentally the appeal is founded on "the prerogative right and, on all proper occasions, the duty, of the Queen in Council to exercise an appellate jurisdiction" (*R.* v. *Bertrand*[7]). They fall into two groups: (a) appeals "as of right" in the narrow sense, and (b) appeals at the discretion of the local court. In so far as these appeals rest on Act of Parliament or Order issued thereunder, they cannot be limited or abolished by the colonial legislature.[8] Leave to appeal to the Privy Council must be obtained from the local court, usually the Supreme Court of the territory. Neither group of appeals by right of grant now in fact includes criminal cases.[9]

(a) Appeals "as of right"

Although this kind of appeal is called "as of right," application for leave to appeal has to be made to the local court; but the latter must grant leave to appeal if certain conditions are fulfilled. These conditions vary in different territories, although there is now a fair degree of uniformity. Generally speaking, an appeal lies "as of right" where the decision complained of is a final judgment, the subject-matter involved is worth a specified minimum sum, and the appellant fulfils the prescribed conditions, *e.g.* as to the time within which application is to be made.[10]

(b) Appeals at the discretion of the local court

If these conditions are not fulfilled, *e.g.* because the sum involved is below the prescribed minimum or the judgment is not a final one, the local court may have a discretion to grant leave to appeal if it considers that the question is one which by reason of its great general or public importance or otherwise ought to be submitted to Her Majesty in Council. It commonly requires security for costs.

2. Appeals by "special leave" of the Privy Council

These are sometimes still called "prerogative" appeals, although they are now regulated by the Judicial Committee Act 1844. The Judicial Committee may grant special leave to appeal where:
(i) there is no grant of the right of appeal from the court; or

---

[7] (1867) L.R. 1 P.C. 520.
[8] Colonial Laws Validity Act 1865, s.2. But *cf.* Associated States under the West Indies Act 1967; *ante*, p. 758.
[9] *Falkland Islands Co.* v. *R.* (1863) 1 Moo.P.C.(N.S.) 299; and see *Chung Chuck* v. *The King* [1930] A.C. 244.
[10] *Royal Hong Kong Jockey Club* v. *Miers* [1983] 1 W.L.R. 1049.

(ii) the local court has no power to grant leave to appeal in the particular case, that is, generally in criminal cases; or

(iii) the local court has power to grant leave to appeal in the particular case, but has refused leave[11]; or

(iv) appeal lies directly to the Privy Council under the Judicial Committee Act 1844 from a court which is not a court of final appeal.

The power to grant special leave to appeal cannot be limited or abolished by the legislature of a dependent territory except under the authority of an Act of Parliament, first, because that would be repugnant to the Judicial Committee Acts of 1833 and 1844 and therefore void under the Colonial laws Validity Act 1865; and, secondly, because it could only be effective if construed as having an extraterritorial operation, and a colonial Act cannot in general have extraterritorial operation. The decision of the Privy Council in *Nadan* v. *The King*[12] was explained in this way in *British Coal Corporation* v. *The King*,[13] although it would have been sufficient to base it on repugnancy to Imperial statute.

Special leave to appeal may be granted in criminal cases as well as civil cases, but different principles are applied.

(a) *Civil cases*

The Judicial Committee will grant special leave to appeal in civil cases only "where the case is of gravity involving a matter of public interest or some important question of law, or affecting property of considerable amount, or where the case is otherwise of some public importance or of a very substantial character."[14] Thus special leave was granted where the question was whether gold and silver minerals discovered in British Columbia in the nineteenth century were vested in the Crown as represented by the Government of Canada or that of British Columbia.[15] Special leave has been granted on important questions of law even though the amount involved was below the prescribed minimum for an appeal by right of grant[16]; in constitutional cases such as the interpretation of a colonial Act[17]; where the revenue rights of the Crown are concerned[18]; and where the colonial court acted without jurisdiction.[19] Cases where special leave is likely to be granted although the matter is not of great public importance include questions affecting status, the validity of marriage, the legitimacy of children and injury to character or professional reputation.[20]

On the other hand, special leave will not be granted to determine

---

[11] *Davis* v. *Shaughnessy* [1932] A.C. 106.

[12] [1926] A.C. 482.

[13] [1935] A.C. 500 (P.C.); and see *Att.-Gen. for Ontario* v. *Att.-Gen. for Canada* [1947] A.C. 127 (P.C.).

[14] *Prince* v. *Gagnon* (1882) 8 App.Cas. 103, 105 *Caldwell* v. *McLaren* (1883) 9 App.Cas. 295.

[15] *Att.-Gen. of British Columbia* v. *Att.-Gen. of Canada* (1889) 14 App.Cas. 295.

[16] *Sun Fire Office* v. *Hart* (1889) 14 App.Cas. 98.

[17] *Ex p. Gregory* [1901] A.C. 128.

[18] *Re Att.-Gen. of Victoria* (1866) 3 Moo.P.C.(N.S.) 527.

[19] *The Queen* v. *Price* (1854) 8 Moo.P.C. 203.

[20] e.g. *Le Mesurier* v. *Le Mesurier* [1895] A.C. 517; *Att.-Gen. of the Gambia* v. *N'Jie* [1961] A.C. 617. And see *Re Dillet, infra.*

merely abstract right, or purely hypothetical questions; or in election petitions; nor generally on questions of fact.

(b) Criminal cases

In *Re Dillet*[21] Lord Blackburn said of appeals in criminal cases: "the rule has been repeatedly laid down, and has been invariably followed, that Her Majesty will not review or interfere with the course of criminal proceedings, unless it is shown that, by a disregard of the forms of legal process, or by some violation of the principles of natural justice, or otherwise, substantial and grave injustice has been done." These principles were restated by the Board in 1914 in *Arnold* v. *The King-Emperor*.[22] "It is not guided by its own doubts of the appellant's innocence or suspicion of his guilt. It will not interfere with the course of the criminal law unless there has been such an interference with the elementary rights of an accused as has placed him outside of the pale of regular law, or unless, within that pale, there has been a violation of the natural principles of justice so demonstratively manifest as to convince their Lordships, first, that the result arrived at was opposite to the result which their Lordships would themselves have reached, and, secondly, that the same opposite result would have been reached by the local tribunal also if the alleged defect or misdirection had been avoided."[23] It may be noted that these principles were laid down at a time when there was no system of criminal appeals in this country. They have, however, continued to be applied in more recent times: *Ragho Prasad* v. *The Queen*.[24]

Where the Privy Council has jurisdiction, whether civil or criminal, it may hear an appeal from either party. Thus in *Attorney-General of Ceylon* v. *K. D. J. Perera*[25] the Judicial Committee allowed an appeal by the Crown against the decision of the Court of Criminal Appeal of Ceylon ordering a new trial (not an acquittal) of a person who had been convicted of murder by the court of first instance.

The Judicial Committee follow the usual practice of appellate courts in not granting leave to appeal in criminal cases on questions of fact. A misdirection to the jury is not by itself a sufficient ground for interference if either the local Appeal Court or the Judicial Committee itself is satisfied that the facts nevertheless indicate the guilt of the accused. Appeals will not be heard from a military tribunal administering martial law (*Tilonko* v. *Attorney-General of Natal*[26]), or from courts-martial administering military law.[27] The petitioner will generally be expected

---

[21] (1887) 12 App.Cas. 459; Chief Justice of colony acted in effect as prosecutor, witness and judge.

[22] [1914] A.C. 644.

[23] See, *e.g. Chang Hang Kiu* v. *Piggot* [1909] A.C. 312 (grossly improper procedure), *Knowles* v. *The King* [1930] A.C. 366 (jury in murder trial not told they could return verdict of manslaughter); *Ras Behari Lal* v. *The King-Emperor* (1933) 60 Ind.App. 354 (juryman had insufficient knowledge of English).

[24] [1953] A.C. 200; following *R.* v. *Bertrand* (1867) L.R. 1 P.C. 520.

[25] *Attygale* v. *The King* [1936] A.C. 338.

[26] [1907] A.C. 93, 461.

[27] *Mohammad Yakub Khan* v. *R.* (1947) 63 T.L.R. 94.

to have availed himself of any right of appeal to the local courts before approaching the Privy Council.[28]

II. Appeals from Independent Commonwealth Countries

Appeals and the Statute of Westminster

Immediately before the passing of the Statute of Westminster 1931, appeal lay by *right of grant* from the Court of Appeal of New Zealand, and in some cases directly from the Supreme Court of New Zealand with the leave of that court. Appeal by right of grant also lay from the superior courts of the Canadian provinces, and (in relation to their state jurisdiction) from the Supreme Courts of the Australian states. As has been pointed out, such right of appeal could be altered or abolished by a Dominion legislature, subject to the provisions of the Colonial Laws Validity Act 1865.[29]

Before the passing of the Statute of Westminster the Dominions could not restrict or abolish the jurisdiction of the Privy Council to grant *special leave* to appeal: (i) by reason of the Colonial Laws Validity Act 1865, s.2, because the jurisdiction of the Judicial Committee rested on— or was regulated by—the Judicial Committee Acts 1833 and 1844; and (ii) because they could not legislate with extraterritorial effect, except for the peace, order and good government of their territory (*Nadan* v. *The King*[30]).

The general principles on which special leave from the Dominions was at that time granted were explained by Viscount Haldane in *Hull* v. *McKenna*.[31] Generally, he said, the jurisdiction of Dominion courts should be regarded as final: only in exceptional cases would the Judicial Committee use its discretion to grant leave to appeal. Leave was very sparingly granted in criminal cases. Otherwise, leave was more freely granted in *inter se* disputes from federal Dominions (except in so far as limited by statute in the case of Australia) and from India than in cases from unitary dominions. This practice followed the wishes of the various Dominions themselves.

The question of appeals to the Judicial Committee was discussed by the Imperial Conference of 1926, but no proposal was made beyond recording the understanding that "it was no part of the policy of His Majesty's Government in Great Britain that questions affecting judicial appeals should be determined otherwise than in accordance with the wishes of the part of the Empire primarily affected." The Imperial Conference, 1930, did not agree on any solution to the question of appeals from the Dominions to the Privy Council, and it seems fairly clear that the Statute of Westminster 1931 was not intended to affect them.

After the passing of that Statute, however, the Judicial Committee held that sections 2 and 3 enabled the Dominions to which the Statute applied to abolish all appeals to the Privy Council, criminal[32] and

---

[28] *Kenyatta* v. *R.* [1954] 1 W.L.R. 1053.

[29] Though it was doubtful whether the Australian Parliament could abolish such appeals from the States even with their concurrence.

[30] [1926] A.C. 482 (P.C.): Canada.

[31] Reported in [1926] Ir.R. 402: the first appeal from the Irish Free State.

[32] *British Coal Corporation* v. *The King* [1935] A.C. 500. See W. Ivor Jennings, "The Statute of Westminster and Appeals" (1936) 52 L.Q.R. 173.

civil,[33] including appeals by special leave. The same consequence followed without any doubt from the Indian Independence Act 1947 and subsequent Independence Acts affecting other territories. Since the legislature of an independent Commonwealth country may at any time modify or terminate appeals to the Privy Council, said Viscount Radcliffe in *Ibralebbe* v. *The Queen*,[34] true independence is not in any way compromised by continuance of such appeals.

Privy Council precedents

The courts of an independent Commonwealth country are probably not bound by Privy Council decisions on appeal from another country, even where the laws in force in the countries concerned are similar. The attainment of independence, involving an independent legal system and the voluntary nature of the retention of appeals to the Privy Council, may be said to sever the previously undivided jurisdiction of the Privy Council.[35] Such decisions, on the other hand, would be strongly persuasive, apart from the probability that the Privy Council would decide the question in the same way.

Waning jurisdiction of the Privy Council[36]

Appeals to the Privy Council, as we have seen, have now been abolished by the "older" Commonwealth countries of Canada[37] and Australia.[38] Such appeals may be abolished by the legislation establishing the constitution of a newly independent Commonwealth country,[39] but they are usually retained at least for a time on attainment of independence. The tendency has been to abolish the Privy Council's jurisdiction, however, on assuming republican status, as with India, Pakistan, Cyprus,[40] Ghana, Nigeria, Sri Lanka and Malta.

From the New Zealand Court of Appeal appeal lies in most cases, and in exceptional cases directly from the Supreme Court.[41]

As Malaysia (formerly Malaya) became a monarchy not owing

---

[33] *Att.-Gen. for Ontario* v. *Att.-Gen. for Canada* [1947] A.C.127. See C. G. Pierson, *Canada and the Privy Council* (1960).

[34] [1964] A.C.900 (P.C.). And see *Geelong Harbour Trust Commrs.* v. *Gibbs* [1974] A.C. 810; the Privy Council does not think it proper to interfere with matters of legal policy, *e.g.* whether or not to follow a previous decision of the courts of the country concerned, as opposed to substantive law.

[35] There are dicta to the effect that the Judicial Committee is part of the hierarchy of each system of courts from which appeal lies, *e.g. British Coal Corporation* v. *The King* [1935] A.C. 500, 52, *cf. ante*, p. 768.

[36] See H. H. Marshall, "The Judicial Committee of the Privy Council; a Waning Jurisdiction" (1964) 13 I.C.L.Q. 697; Enid M. Campbell, "The Decline of the Jurisdiction of the Judicial Committee of the Privy Council" ((1959) 33 A.L.J. 196; Lord Normand, "The Judicial Committee of the Privy Council" [1950] C.L.P. 1.

[37] *Ante*, n. 32 and n.33.

[38] *Ante*, p. 755.

[39] *Cf. Ibralebbe* v. *The Queen* [1964] A.C. 900 (P.C.); attainment of independence of itself does not abrogate jurisdiction of Privy Council.

[40] Except appeals from the Senior Judges' Court of the Sovereign Base Areas.

[41] *e.g. Lee* v. *Lee's Air Farming Ltd.* [1961] A.C. 12; *Boots Chemists (New Zealand)* v. *Chemists Service Guild of New Zealand* [1968] A.C. 457. In *Thomas* v. *The Queen* [1980] A.C. 125 the Judicial Committee held that no appeal lay from an "opinion" given by the New Zealand Court of Appeal on a reference to the Court by the Governor General under s.406(6) of the Crimes Act 1961 which allows the Governor General, if he desires the assistance of the Court, to refer a point for the Court's opinion.

allegiance to the Queen, an arrangement was made whereby the Head of State should refer appeals, or applications for special leave to appeal, to the Judicial Committee in certain cases; the opinion of the Judicial Committee being then reported direct to the Head of State.[42] The Judical Committee thus became part of the judicial system of Malaysia. Another device has been to make appeals lie from a republic to the Judicial Committee itself, and not to the Queen in Council.[43]

Despite its waning jurisdiction the Privy Council has in recent years been faced with a variety of interesting and often controversial questions[44] concerning, for example, general constitutional principles such as the separation of powers.[45] It has considered whether the normal presumptions and guides applicable to the interpretation of legislation should apply to written constitutions.[46] Fundamental rights before the Board have included the right not to be deprived of property without compensation,[47] the right to bail[48]; and right of a detained person to communication with a lawyer;[49] the right to a fair hearing of a criminal charge within a reasonable time[50]; and the right to legal representation.[51] A number of cases has concerned the constitutional legality of the death penalty.[52]

---

[42] Agreement of 1958. See *Hussien (Shaabin Bin)* v. *Kam (Chong Fook)* [1970] A.C. 492; *Ningkan (Stephen Kalong)* v. *Government of Malaysia* [1970] A.C. 379; *Teh Cheng Poh* v. *Public Prosecutor, Malaysia* [1980] A.C. 458.

[43] *e.g.* Malawi Independence Act 1964, s.5; Kenya Independence Act 1963, s.6. These provisions are no long in force.

[44] Not always confined to constitutional matters: *e.g. Candlewood Navigation Corporation* v. *Mitsui O.S.K. Lines Ltd.* [1985] 3 W.L.R. 381; negligence and financial loss. (Appeal from New South Wales).

[45] *Hinds* v. *R.* [1977] A.C. 195 (Jamaica); *ante*, p. 30. See also *Att.-Gen. of Fiji* v. *D.P.P.* [1983] 2 A.C. 672; *John* v. *D.P.P.* [1985] 1 W.L.R. 657 (Dominica).

[46] *Minister of Home Affairs* v. *Fisher* [1980] A.C. 319 (Bermuda); *Att.-Gen. of St. Christopher, Nevis and Anguilla* v. *Reynolds* [1980] A.C. 637; *Société United Docks* v. *Govt. of Mauritius* [1985] A.C. 585; "less rigidity" and "greater generosity" required in interpreting constitutions than statutes.

[47] *Société United Docks* v. *Govt. of Mauritius, supra*.

[48] *Att.-Gen. of the Gambia* v. *Jobe* [1984] A.C. 689. (Constitutionality of Special Criminal Court also in issue). For a critical note see, Barbara de Smith, "The Judicial Committee as a Constitutional Court" [1984] P.L. 557.

[49] *Thornhill* v. *Att.-Gen. of Trinidad and Tobago* [1981] A.C. 61.

[50] *Bell* v. *D.P.P.* [1985] 3 W.L.R. 73 (Jamaica).

[51] *Robinson* v. *The Queen* [1985] 3 W.L.R. 84 (Jamaica). On the right to a hearing generally see also *Att.-Gen. of Hong Kong* v. *Ng Yuen Shiu* [1983] 2 A.C. 629; *Winfat Enterprise (H.K.) Co. Ltd.* v. *Att.-Gen. of Hong Kong* [1985] A.C. 733; *supra*, p. 674.

[52] *de Freitas* v. *Benny* [1976] A.C. 239 (Trinidad and Tobago); death penalty for murder not a "cruel and unusual punishment." Nor did delay in carrying out sentence of death render punishment "cruel and unusual": in any case sentence imposed before Constitution came into effect; *Riley* v. *Att.-Gen. of Jamaica* [1983] 1 A.C. 719 (Lord Scarman and Lord Brightman dissenting); *Ong Ah Chuan* v. *Public Prosecutor* [1981] A.C. 648 (Singapore); mandatory death penalty for trafficking in drugs over a certain quantity not a violation of constitutional guarantee of equality before the law. (It has been suggested that whatever the juristic theory (to use the phrase of Lord Diplock when considering the position of the House of Lords *vis a vis* colonial courts; *Delasala* v. *Delasala* [1980] A.C. 546) in practice and reality there is something unattractive in a court, sitting in London, deciding appeals concerning death sentences when capital punishment has, to all intents and purposes, disappeared from the laws of England, Scotland and Northern Ireland.

Suggested Commonwealth Court of Appeal[53]

We have noticed the tendency for Commonwealth countries to abolish appeals to the Privy Council on assuming republican status, if not before. This is no criticism of the objective impartiality of the Judicial Committee, as may be seen from the use made of that body as part of the machinery for the removal of judges in some independent Commonwealth countries. But the criticisms of the Judicial Committee as a court of appeal are that it appears to be virtually a British Court sitting in London; it cannot fully understand the background of the legal system it is applying; and its jurisdiction, based as it is largely on the prerogative to grant special leave to appeal to colonies, is inconsistent with independence, and especially with republican status. It is a harmless anomaly that the form of procedure is advisory rather than judicial; and this could be obviated by the method devised by Kenya and Malawi.[54]

The Commonwealth Prime Ministers' Conference in 1962 expressed the hope that the regular appointment of judges from other Commonwealth countries would strengthen the Judicial Committee and emphasise its importance as a Commonwealth link. Such appointments are made from time to time on a temporary basis. A later proposal, which had a good deal of support, was to set up a peripatetic Commonwealth Court composed of judges from various Commonwealth countries. Its jurisdiction would be twofold: (i) as a final court of appeal in certain cases from the courts of the Commonwealth countries, and (ii) to determine justiciable disputes between Commonwealth countries. Some would add the jurisdiction of a Supreme Court for the enforcement of a Commonwealth Bill of Rights.

Procedural problems would have to be solved. Should appeal to the Commonwealth Court always be as of right? If not, on what principles should leave to appeal be granted? And on what principles should decisions of the courts of Commonwealth countries be upset—for any error, or only for a gross miscarriage of justice? Questions such as these could no doubt be settled by legal experts without undue difficulty. But there are more formidable obstacles to be overcome. One is that the United Kingdom would be expected to abolish the appellate jurisdiction of the House of Lords[55] and to accept for herself the new Commonwealth Court as the final court of appeal, at least in some cases, from British courts. Another question is the composition of the court. How would the judges be selected? Would some countries be willing to spare senior judges for this purpose? Would the composition be scrutinised by the country visited? Would the country visited always supply one of its own judges? Lastly, the question of the expense of a court going on circuit round the world is usually raised in discussion of this proposal; and certainly the fares and subsistence allowances would amount to a

[53] See Gerald Gardiner and Andrew Martin, *Law Reform Now* (1963) p. 16; Nwabueze, *The Machinery of Justice in Nigeria* (1963) Chap. 10; H. H. Marshall, "A Commonwealth Court" (1965) *Round Table* No. 221, p. 6.

[54] *Supra*, p. 774n.

[55] The merger of the judicial functions of the House of Lords with those of the Privy Council was often discussed in the nineteenth century: Robert Stevens, "The Final Appeal: Reform of the House of Lords and Privy Council 1867–1876" (1964) 80 L.Q.R. 343.

significant item. On the other hand, we should also take into account the cost to litigants of the present system of appeals going to the Privy Council in London.

A Commonwealth Law Ministers' Meeting in 1966 under the chairmanship of Lord Gardiner, the Lord Chancellor, considered a proposal for a Commonwealth Court of Appeal. Some countries expressed their approval, but the majority have not shown themselves interested. Support came from the smaller Commonwealth countries that still used the Judicial Committee, but little has been heard of this suggestion recently.

ANGLO-IRISH AGREEMENT ON NORTHERN IRELAND

The following sets out in substance the terms of the Agreement between the Government of the United Kingdom and the Government of the Republic of Ireland which was signed on November 15, 1985 at Hillsborough.

Status of Northern Ireland

Article 1: The two Governments (a) affirm that any change in the status of Northern Ireland would only come about with the consent of a majority of the people of Northern Ireland . . . ;

(c) declare that, if in the future a majority of the people of Northern Ireland clearly wish to and formally consent to the establishment of a united Ireland, they will introduce and support in the respective Parliaments legislation to give effect to that wish.

The Intergovernmental Conference

Article 2: Establishes, within the framework of the Anglo-Irish Intergovernmental Council set up in November 1981, an Intergovernmental Conference ("the Conference") concerned with Northern Ireland and with relations between the two parts of the island of Ireland to deal on a regular basis with:

(i) political matters;

(ii) security and related matters;

(iii) legal matters, including the administration of justice;

(iv) the promotion of cross-border co-operation.

The Irish Government will put forward proposals on matters relating to Northern Ireland which are not the responsibility of a devolved administration in Northern Ireland. Some of the matters considered by the Conference will involve co-operative action in both parts of the island of Ireland, and possibly also in Great Britain. There is no derogation from the sovereignty of either the United Kingdom Government or the Irish Government.

Article 3: The Conference will meet at ministerial or official level, as required. Regular and frequent ministerial meetings will be held, when the Secretary of State for Northern Ireland and the Permanent Irish Ministerial Representative will be joint chairmen. Other British and Irish Ministers may hold or attend meetings as appropriate, including Attorneys-General. Ministers may be accompanied by officials and professional advisers: for example, when questions of security are discussed, they may be accompanied by the Chief Constable of the Royal Ulster Constabulary and the Commissioner of the Garda Siochana. A secretariat will be established to service the Conference on a continuing basis.

Article 4: (a) The Conference will be a framework within which the two Governments work together

(i) for accommodating the rights and identities of the two traditions which exist in Northern Ireland; and

(ii) for promoting reconciliation, respect for human rights, co-operation against terrorism, and developing economic, social and cultural co-operation.

(b) It is the policy of the United Kingdom Government that responsibility for certain matters should be devolved within Northern Ireland on a basis which would secure widespread acceptance throughout the community; and the Irish Government may put forward views and proposals for this purpose in so far as they relate to the interests of the minority community.

Political matters

Article 5: (a) The Conference will concern itself with measures to recognise and accommodate the rights and identities of the two traditions in Northern Ireland, to protect human rights and to prevent discrimination; including the consideration of electoral arrangements, the use of flags, and the advantages and disadvantages of a Bill of Rights in some form in Northern Ireland.

(c) If it should prove impossible to achieve and sustain devolution on a basis which secures widespread acceptance in Northern Ireland, the Irish Government may, where the interests of the minority community are significantly or especially affected, put forward views on proposals for major legislation and on major policy issues.

Article 6: The Irish Government may put forward views and proposals concerning such bodies appointed by the Secretary of State as the Fair Employment Agency, the Equal Opportunities Commission and the Police Authority for Northern Ireland.

Security and related matters

Article 7: (a) The Conference will consider

(i) security policy;

(ii) relations between the security forces and the community;

(iii) prisons policy.

(c) The programme may include the establishment of local consultative machinery, training in community relations, and crime prevention schemes involving the community.

Legal matters, including the administration of justice

Article 8: The Conference will deal with issues of concern to both countries relating to the enforcement of the criminal law. In particular it will consider whether there are parts of the criminal law applying in the North and in the South respectively, which might with benefit be harmonised. The Conference will consider the possibility of mixed courts in both jurisdictions for the trial of certain offences.

Cross-border co-operation on security, economic, social and cultural matters

Article 9: (a) With a view to enhancing cross-border co-operation on security matters, a programme of work will be undertaken by the Chief Constable of the Royal Ulster Constabulary and the Commissioner of the Garda Siochana on such matters as exchange of information and liaison structures. The Conference will have no operational responsibilities.

Article 10: The two Governments will co-operate to promote the economic and social development of those areas of both parts of Ireland which have suffered most severely from the instability of recent years.

Arrangements for review

Article 11: At the end of three years, or earlier if requested by either Government, the working of the Conference will be reviewed to see whether any changes in the nature and scope of its activities are desirable.

Interparliamentary relations

Article 12: It will be for parliamentary decision in Westminster and in Dublin whether to establish an Anglo-Irish Parliamentary body of the kind adumbrated in the Anglo-Irish Studies Report of November 1981. The two Governments agree that they would give support to such a body, if it were to be established.

DEVOLUTION WITHIN THE UNITED KINGDOM

I. INTRODUCTION[1]

The concept of "devolution" is used to mean the delegation of central government powers without the relinquishment of supremacy.[2] Devolution may be legislative or administrative or both, and in its more advanced forms involves the exercise of powers by persons or bodies who, although acting on authority delegated by Parliament, are not directly answerable to it or to the central government.[3] It should be distinguished from "decentralisation," which is a method whereby some central government powers of decision-making are exercised by officials of the central government located in various regions.[4]

Nationalism in Scotland and Wales first became a considerable electoral factor at the general election of 1966, when the Nationalist parties received the votes of 20 per cent. of the electors in those countries. While the Kilbrandon Commission was at work Scottish nationalism was quiescent, but it revived on the discovery of North Sea oil, most of which is located nearer to Scotland than to the rest of the United Kingdom and installations related to which are mainly in Scotland. The Liberals have long favoured federalism. In a federal system, however, supremacy is *divided* between the federal legislature and government on the one hand and the legislatures and governments of the constituent units on the other, and the basic terms of a federal constitution (notably the distribution of powers) are *entrenched* so that they cannot be amended at the sole discretion of the federation or of any province or

---

[1] For the background see: (1973) Cmnd. 5460, *Report of Royal Commission on the constitution* (Kilbrandon); Cmnd. 5460–61, *Memorandum of Dissent*: (1974) Cmnd. 5732, *Democracy and Devolution: Proposals for Scotland and Wales*; (1975) Cmnd. 6348, *Our Changing Democracy: Devolution to Scotland and Wales*; (1976) Cmnd. 6585, *Devolution to Scotland and Wales: Supplementary Statement*; (1977) Cmnd. 6890, *Devolution: Financing the Devolved Services*; 936 H.C.Deb. col. 313 (July 26, 1977) Lord President's statement on devolution; (HMSO December 9, 1976) *Devolution: The English Dimension* (Consultative Document). And see J. P. Mackintosh, *The Devolution of Power* (1968): *Devolution* (ed. H. Calvert, 1975); *Independence and Devolution: The Legal Implications for Scotland* (ed. J. P. Grant, 1976); Lord Kilbrandon, "A Background to Constitutional Reform" (Holdsworth Club, University of Birmingham, 1975); T. Daintith, "Kilbrandon: The Ship that Launched a Thousand Faces?" (1974) 37 M.L.R. 544; Isobel Watson, "The Royal Commission on the Constitution" (1974) 3 Anglo-Am. L.Rev., 290; J. E. Trice, "The Kilbrandon Report on the Constitution and Wales" [1974] 5 Cambrian Law Rev., 72; O. Hood Phillips, "Devolution within the United Kingdom" (1977) 8 Id-Dritt 67 (University of Malta).

[2] This Appendix does not deal with Northern Ireland, which had a devolved Parliament and executive for about 50 years from 1922, because at the time of writing the province is being governed directly from Westminster. The collapse of devolution in Northern Ireland may be said to have been the result of the grave emergency there, and not due to defects inherent in its system of devolution save to the extent that it involved virtual one-party rule. See further H. Calvert, *Constitutional Law in Northern Ireland (1968); ante* p. 18.

[3] Cmnd. 5460, p. 165.

[4] Cmnd. 6348, pp. 55–56.

combination of provinces.[5] It has not been shown how—even if federation were thought desirable—we could have a federation in which the federal Parliament is subject to no legal limitations and is unable to limit itself, and in which one unit (England) has four fifths of the population, whose representatives would always be able to outvote those of all other units in the federal legislature.

A Royal Commission on the Constitution was set up in 1969 under the chairmanship, first, of the late Lord Crowther and then under that of Lord Kilbrandon, formerly a Scottish Lord of Appeal. Its terms of reference were "to examine the present functions of the central legislature and government in relation to the several countries, nations and regions of the United Kingdom; and to consider . . . whether any changes are desirable . . . in the present constitutional and economic relationships. . . . " Although the terms of reference were wide enough to cover almost any aspect of the Constitution, the Commission limited its review almost entirely to the question of national feelings and devolution. The terms of reference insisted on the preservation of the political and economic unity of the United Kingdom. The Kilbrandon Commission issued majority and minority reports in 1973.[6] The Government did not accept either report in its entirety, but held further discussions and issued several White Papers. In particular the Government pointed out that there are few parallels anywhere for dividing between two levels of government powers and functions long exercised centrally in a unitary State, and that after devolution to Scotland and Wales each part of the United Kingdom would have a different form of government. To this we may add the system of local government (which would, however, no doubt be modified) on the one hand and European Community laws and regulations on the other. It was also pointed out that, since national financial resources are distributed according to need, public expenditure for Scotland would not be based on revenues arising there. Control of oil revenues by those parts of the United Kingdom off whose shores oil is found would mean the break-up of the United Kingdom. The argument about national resources applies conversely to the large coal deposits found recently in England and to natural gas found off the English shores.

Devolution to parts of the United Kingdom would not affect the unity of the United Kingdom or the power of Parliament to legislate (even in devolved matters) for all or any part of the United Kingdom, or to repeal or amend the devolution arrangements themselves.

The impetus to introduce legislation devolving power to Scottish and Welsh assemblies was the parlous position of Mr. Callaghan's minority government from 1976 onwards and his wish to secure political allies wherever they could be found. Initially one bill to deal with both countries was introduced in the 1976–77 Session of Parliament but was abandoned after the government's defeat when it attempted to introduce a guillotine motion. Two separate bills were introduced in the 1977–78

---

[5] Cmnd. 5460, pp. 152–154.

[6] Of 13 Commission members, eight favoured a scheme of legislative as well as executive devolution to Scotland, six favoured a similar devolution to Wales, and eight members were in favour of co-ordinating and advisory Regional Councils for England, partly indirectly elected by the local authorities and partly nominated.

Session. In the course of their progress through the House of Commons the government, in the words of one commentator suffered "numerous actual and moral . . . defeats as the woolly thinking and shabby opportunism underlying the proposals became ever more apparent."[7]

The possibility of attempts to introduce further devolution proposals cannot be ignored and, while it must be hoped that future legislation would be drafted with more of an eye to principle the details of the unsuccessful Callaghan attempt obviously retain some interest and importance.

II. SCOTLAND

Scottish Assembly

The Scotland Act 1978 provided for a directly elected Assembly for Scotland, established the constitutional and financial machinery for its operation and set out the powers which it would exercise. There was to be a single-chamber Scottish Assembly, elected initially in multi-member constituencies, each Parliamentary constituency returning two or three Assembly members according to size, except that Orkney and Shetland would return one member each. An amendment to introduce a form of proportional representation was rejected by the Commons. For later elections the Boundary Commission for Scotland was to divide Parliamentary constituencies into single-member Assembly constituencies. Everyone entitled to vote in Parliamentary elections, and also peers who have the local government franchise, would be entitled to vote in Assembly elections. The standard duration of any Assembly was to be four years, although an Assembly could be dissolved by order of the Secretary of State within that period if two-thirds of the Assembly members so resolved. Members of the Assembly were not to be disqualified from being members of the House of Commons. Disqualifications from membership of the Assembly were similar to those for the House of Commons, except that peers and ministers of any religious denomination were not disqualified.

The Scottish Assembly was given power to make laws, to be called Scottish Assembly Acts (which might amend or repeal Acts of Parliament), within its legislative competence, *i.e.* relating to a devolved matter.[8] A Bill was not within the legislative competence of the Assembly if it extended to any part of the United Kingdom other than Scotland, if it would impose or abolish any tax, or if its effect would be to amend the Scotland Act. An amendment to insert a Bill of Rights, incorporating the European Convention and adapted to Scotland's devolved powers, was rejected by the Commons. Assembly Bills were to become law when approved by Order in Council.

If the Secretary of State were of opinion that a Bill passed by the Assembly was not within the legislative competence of the Assembly,

---

[7] G. Drewry, *The Commons Today* (ed. by S. A. Walkland and Michael Ryle, 1981), Chap. 4, *Legislation*, p. 115.
[8] *Post*, p. 785.

he was to refer the question of competence to the Judicial Committee of the Privy Council for decision (pre-assent judicial scrutiny). The decision of the Judicial Committee was to be stated in open court, and if the decision were that the Bill was *ultra vires* the Secretary of State could not submit it for approval by Order in Council. If the Secretary of State was of opinion that a Bill passed by the Assembly was not compatible with European Community obligations or any other international obligations of the United Kingdom, or that responsibility for legislating to comply with any such obligation should be with Parliament, he was to certify to the Assembly that he was of that opinion and could not submit the Bill for approval by Order in Council.

Scottish Executive

There was to be a Scottish Executive consisting of a First Secretary and other Scottish Secretaries, appointed by the Secretary of State. The Assembly could nominate one of its members for appointment as First Secretary and, in appointing the other Scottish Secretaries, the Secretary of State was to act on the advice of the First Secretary. The First Secretary could also appoint assistants to Scottish Secretaries. Scottish Secretaries would exercise the executive powers of the Crown and of Ministers in devolved fields, and would carry out existing duties imposed on Ministers in those fields. Provision was similarly made for the making of subordinate legislation by Scottish Secretaries. Certain powers were exercisable concurrently with, or with the consent of, a Minister. The recommendation of a Scottish Secretary was required for an Assembly Bill proposing any expenditure out of public funds. Officers and servants of a Scottish Secretary or of the Scottish Comptroller and Auditor General were to be regarded as members of the home civil service of the State, though their salaries were payable out of the Scottish Consolidated Fund.

Reserved powers of the Secretary of State

If it appeared to the Secretary of State that a Bill passed by the Scottish Assembly contained provisions which would or might affect a reserved matter, whether directly or indirectly, *and* that its enactment would not be in the public interest, he might lay the Bill before Parliament. A "reserved matter" for this purpose was one which concerned Scotland (whether exclusively or not) but was not within the legislative competence of the Scottish Assembly. A Bill so laid would be subject to a negative resolution passed by each House within 28 days, or passed by the Commons within that period and confirmed by a further resolution of the Commons passed within ten days of the Lords rejecting or failing to pass a resolution.

If it appeared to the Secretary of State that any action proposed to be taken, or capable of being taken, by a Scottish Secretary would or might affect a reserved matter, then, if it appeared to him desirable in the public interest to do so, he might direct that the proposed action should not be taken or that the action capable of being taken should be taken. A "reserved matter" for this purpose was one which concerned Scotland (whether exclusively or not) but which was beyond a Scottish Secretary's powers. Such a direction was subject to an affirmative resolution by each House of Parliament, or confirmation by the Commons alone if the Lords rejected or failed to pass a resolution. The Secretary of State had a similar power to issue a direction, not subject to Parliamentary approval, if it appeared to him that such action or inaction would be incompatible with Community obligations or any other international obligations of the United Kingdom. The Secretary of State in similar circumstances could revoke a subordinate instrument made by a Scottish Secretary, with or without Parliamentary approval as the case may be.

Financial provisions

A block grant was to be allocated by Parliament for the devolved services. The Secretary of State would pay into the Scottish Consolidated Fund and the Scottish Loans Fund sums of money voted each year by Parliament. The amounts to be paid were to be determined by the Secretary of State with the consent of the Treasury by order, subject to affirmative resolution of the House of Commons. Separate accounting and auditing arrangements were provided. Thus there was to be a Scottish Comptroller and Auditor General, appointed by the Crown and holding office during good behaviour, who would be responsible to the Scottish Assembly. Responsibility for the payment of rate support and other grants to local authorities was transferred to the Scottish Executive.

A strong Scottish lobby failed to persuade the Government to allow the Scottish Assembly separate tax-raising powers as a means of supplementing the block grant; though the Scottish people were not canvassed as to whether they were eager to be subject to a third kind of direct tax, in addition to United Kingdom income tax and local rates. Among the methods rejected by the Government on grounds of administrative difficulties and costs were a supplementary income tax, a supplementary value-added tax or sales tax, a tax on the occupation of property and supplementary taxes on companies. Concern was felt, however, that annual discussions of levels of block grants would lead to detailed scrutiny by government departments of items of devolved expenditure, and perhaps acrimonious arguments. The Government therefore suggested that the total of devolved spending in Scotland should be related to comparable expenditure elsewhere in the United Kingdom on the basis of relative needs, and then expressed as a percentage of comparable expenditure in the country as a whole, though it would not be practicable to incorporate such a formula in the legislation. It suggested further that such a formula should be settled for a period of, say, four years, a period corresponding to the term of the Assembly. However, if the Scottish administration should wish to have available a limited supplementary tax power and was ready to meet its administrative cost, the Government would be willing to consider any such proposal, other than in relation to offshore oil. Such supplementary tax would have to be operable as a marginal supplement, capable of being turned on and off as needed, and cheap to collect; it should fall on Scotland only, and not be paid indirectly by English taxpayers; it must be compatible with European Community requirements; it should be seen by those paying it as a tax imposed by the Scottish Assembly and not be lost in the mass of general taxation; and it must be politically possible.

Devolved matters

Devolution to Scotland was to be of responsibility in various fields which the United Kingdom Government had hitherto looked after. Functions and powers of local authorities were not reduced by the devolution Act, though they might be affected later by Assembly legislation. Devolved matters within the legislative competence of the Scottish Assembly (subject to limitations and exceptions), fell into the following groups: (1) Health; (2) Social welfare; (3) Education; (4) Housing; (5) Local government and local finance; (6) Land use and development, including town and country planning; (7) Pollution; (8) Erosion and flooding; (9) Countryside; (10) Transport; (11) Roads and bridges; (12) Marine works, especially harbours required for the fishing industry; (13) Agricultural land; (14) Fisheries, in particular, salmon and fresh water fisheries; (15) Water supply and inland waterways; (16) Fire services; (17) Tourism; (18) Ancient monuments and historic buildings; (19) Registration of births, marriage and deaths; (20) Miscellaneous, including charities, public holidays and liquor licensing; (21) Court jurisdiction and procedure, the legal profession and legal aid, advice and assistance; (22) Tribunals and inquiries, including the Lands Tribunal for Scotland; (23) Public records; (24) Civil law matters, including obligations, heritable and moveable property, conveyancing, trusts, bankruptcy, succession, remedies, evidence, diligence, arbitration, and private international law; (25) Crime, including the principles of criminal liability, offences against the person, sexual offences, offences against property, offences of dishonesty, offences against public order, criminal penalties, treatment of offenders, criminal evidence, criminal procedure, including arrest, search and custody, and the recognition and enforcement of court orders.

Among matter *not* included in the above groups were the control of drugs; universities; the continued existence of the High Court of Justiciary and the Court of Session as courts of first instance and of appeal, and of sheriff courts, and their existing jurisdictions; appeals to the House of Lords from the Court of Session; powers of the High Court of Justiciary and the Court of Session to regulate their own procedure and the civil procedure of sheriff courts; Courts-Martial and the Courts-Martial Appeal Court; the Restrictive Practices Court and the Employment Appeal Tribunal; insurance, banking and legal tender; trade unions and employers' associations, trade disputes and labour relations; terms and conditions of employment of the home civil service of the State; the right to prosecute for any offence; and deportation and extradition.

Matters devolved to Scottish Secretaries were the matters devolved to the Assembly, and certain other matters relating to grants to universities, local authority guarantees of housing loans, grants for expenditure due to the immigrant population, land use and development, road traffic and race and sex discrimination. The prerogative of mercy was not a devolved matter, nor was the conduct of relations with any country outside the United Kingdom. If it appeared to a Minister that implementation of a Community obligation or any other international obligation of the United Kingdom required the exercise of any power to make a subordinate instrument, and that the power could be exercised by a Scottish Secretary but it was desirable that it should be exercised by a Minister, he might exercise the power as if it were not a devolved matter.

Legal proceedings involving devolution issues

Provisions were made for post-assent judicial review of Scottish Assembly Acts, and for application of the *ultra vires* doctrine to acts of the Scottish executive, including delegated legislation. A "devolution issue" was defined as a question whether a Scottish Assembly Act or any provision thereof was within the legislative competence of the Assembly; or whether a matter with respect to which a Scottish Secretary had purported to exercise or proposed to exercise a power was a devolved matter. In Scotland proceedings for the determination of a devolution issue might be instituted by the Lord Advocate and defended by any person who as a Scottish Secretary or assistant to a Scottish Secretary, performed functions corresponding to those performed by a Law Officer of the Crown. Where a devolution issue arose in litigation the court or tribunal had to order intimation of it to be given to the Lord Advocate and to any person performing functions corresponding to those of a Law Officer, and they might take part as parties so far as the proceedings related to a devolution issue. In civil proceedings (other than those before the House of Lords or a court consisting of three or more judges of the Court of Session) the court or tribunal might refer the devolution issue to the Inner House of the Court of Session. In criminal proceedings (other than those before a court consisting of three or more judges of the High Court of Justiciary) the court might refer the issue to the High Court of Justiciary. Appeal in such cases lay from the superior courts to the Judicial Committee of the Privy Council, though in criminal cases the leave was required of the High Court of Justiciary or, failing such leave, the special leave of the Judicial Committee.

In England and Wales proceedings for the determination of devolution issues might be instituted by the Attorney-General and defended by any person who, as a Scottish Secretary or assistant to a Scottish Secretary, performed functions corresponding to those of a Law Officer. Where a devolution issue arose in litigation, the court or tribunal had to order notice to be given to the Attorney-General and to a person performing the functions of a Law Officer in Scotland, and they might take part as parties so far as the proceedings related to a devolution issue. In civil proceedings below the Court of Appeal the court or tribunal might refer the issue to the Court of Appeal. In criminal proceedings below the Court of Appeal the court might refer the issue in summary proceedings to the High Court, and in proceedings on indictment to the Court of Appeal. Appeal in such cases lay from the Court of Appeal or the High Court to the Judicial Committee of the Privy Council, but only with leave of the court concerned or, failing such leave, with special leave of the Judicial Committee.

Corresponding provisions were made for the determination of devolution issues arising in proceedings in Northern Ireland. If at devolution issue arose in judicial proceedings in the House of Lords it was to be referred to the Judicial Committee of the Privy Council, unless the House considered it more appropriate, having regard to all the circumstances, they they should determine the issue.

Commencement and referendum

The Act was not to come into operation until such day as the Secretary of State might by order appoint. A draft of the order was to be laid before Parliament and approved by a resolution of each House, or by a resolution confirmed by the Commons if the Lords rejected or failed to pass a resolution. Before such draft order was laid before Parliament, a referendum was to be held on a day to be appointed by Order in Council. Under an amendment passed against the wishes of the Government, the Secretary of State was required to lay an order for the repeal of the Act unless 40 per cent. of those entitled to vote in the referendum indicated their support for the Act. The electors of Orkney and Shetland could vote to stay out of Scottish devolution, in which case a Commission would be appointed to make recommendations on the future of the Islands, though there was nothing to prevent the Commission from recommending that they should after all be included in devolution. In the event a majority of those voting in Scotland supported devolution but the number of votes in favour represented less than a third of the total electorate and the Act was accordingly repealed by Order.

III. WALES

Welsh Assembly

The Wales Act 1978 provided for a directly elected Assembly for Wales, established the constitutional and financial machinery for its operation and set out the powers which it would exercise. The single-chamber Welsh Assembly was to have substantial policy-making and executive, but not legislative, powers. It was to operate through committees responsible for particular subjects rather than through a body modelled on the Cabinet. This scheme was similar to that recommended for Scotland, Wales and five English Regions by the minority report of the Kilbrandon Commission. The provisions for constituencies, the normal duration of the Assembly, disqualification from membership, remuneration of members, the franchise, election of presiding officer, financing of devolved services, accounting and auditing, a Welsh Comptroller and Auditor General and a Welsh Consolidated Fund and Loans Fund, the status and payment of the staff of the Welsh Assembly and of the Welsh Comptroller and Auditor General, commencement of the Act and referendum in Wales, were similar to those relating to Scotland.

Principal functions of the Welsh Assembly

Certain functions hitherto exercised by ministers were transferred to the Welsh Assembly. These included (subject to detailed exceptions): supervision of local government; education; landlord and tenant and housing; fire services; health and social services; pollution; planning and land use; development; forestry; water and land drainage; freshwater fisheries; countryside; ancient monuments and historic buildings; tourism; transport; roads and bridges; road traffic; registration of births, marriages and deaths; tribunals and inquiries. The Assembly was to be responsible for payment of rate support and other grants to local authorities. Some powers were to be exercisable concurrently with, or with the consent of, a Minister. The Assembly could do anything it considered appropriate to support cultural and recreative matters, including the Welsh language. It was to review the structure of local government in Wales, and to report its conclusion to the Secretary of State. It could also exercise such functions given to Ministers by local Acts as the Secretary of State might specify by order, subject to annulment by either House of Parliament. Responsibility for the operations of the Welsh National Water Development Authority and the Severn-Trent Water Authority was divided between the Secretary of State and the Welsh Assembly, and the Secretary of State remained responsible for England/Wales national water policy.

The Attorney-General could institute, and the Assembly could defend, proceedings for the determination of any question whether anything done or proposed to be done by the Assembly was within its powers. Provision could be made by Order in Council for the Parliamentary Commissioner for Administration to investigate administrative action taken by or on behalf of the Welsh Assembly.

The Assembly might institute in its own name, or appear in, any civil proceedings; and generally it might do anything incidental to the discharge of its functions. It might not conduct relations with any country outside the United Kingdom, and Ministers had overriding powers to implement Community or other international obligations.

Subject committees and other committees

The Assembly was required to appoint committees with functions relating at least to its principal powers (subject committees), but the Assembly was not prevented from exercising itself the powers assigned to such committees. Each subject committee was to have a chairman and a leader ("executive member") appointed by the Assembly. A subject committee might arrange for its leader or a sub-committee to exercise the powers with which it was charged, but it was not prevented thereby from exercising such powers itself.

The Assembly could appoint other committees, and it had to appoint an Accounts Committee to examine the report of the Welsh Comptroller and Auditor General, a committee to scrutinise subordinate legislation and also an Executive Committee. The Assembly was to secure that membership of subject committees, the scrutiny committee and the Accounts Committee (but not the Executive Committee) reflected, as far as practicable, the balance of parties in the Assembly.

Executive Committee

The members of the Executive Committee had to include the leaders of the subject committees. The Assembly was to appoint the chairman of the Executive Committee, who was to also be its leader and would be known as the Chief Executive. The recommendation of the Executive

Committee was required before an instrument was made involving the payment of any sum out of the Welsh Consolidated Fund or Loan Fund.

Reserve powers

The Secretary of State for Wales had the same reserve powers as the Secretary of State for Scotland to prevent or require action by the devolved executive, and to revoke subordinating instruments.

Commencement and referendum

As in the case of the Scotland Act, the Wales Act was not to come into effect unless approved by 40 per cent. of the electorate. Of those electors who voted, 79 per cent. voted against the Act which was accordingly repealed by Order.

IV. THE PROSPECT FOR ENGLAND[9]

The case for change in the structure of government in England has been argued on various grounds—the need to lighten the work of the central government so that it can concentrate more on matters of really national importance; remoteness of the central government from the ordinary citizen; the desirability of subjecting important nominated bodies, such as water and health authorities, to local democratic control; and the need for an intermediate layer of government smaller than national but larger than existing local authorities.

Certain options were ruled out of further consideration by Mr. Callaghan's Government. The creation of a separate English Parliament with the same legislative powers for England as the Scottish Assembly was to have Scotland would have involved four separate Assemblies each with its own executive, because it would not be appropriate for the United Kingdom Parliament to act both as the legislature for the United Kingdom and also as the domestic legislature for Wales (and for the time being Northern Ireland) but not for England and Scotland. This would not only diminish greatly the role of Parliament but also truncate the functions of central government. The Consultative Document accepted the opinion of the Kilbrandon Commission that no federal structure in the United Kingdom is feasible. England contains about 85 per cent. of the population and has a correspondingly overwhelming proportion of wealth. A number of English Regional Assemblies with legislative powers similar to those of the Scottish Assembly would have a cumulative effect similar to that which would result from a single English legislative Assembly, and such a structure would lead to possibly marked differences over short distances within England.

Among other "radical" changes the Consultative Document considered the possibility of creating a number of English elected Regional Assemblies with the same executive and subsidiary policy-making powers as the Welsh Assembly. It is objected that this scheme would involve the creation of major new units of administration and an inevitable need for substantial numbers of extra staff and large additional costs; though it may be said that the additional cost in manpower and money would be offset largely by the rationalisation of the decentra-

[9] *Devolution: The English Dimension* (Consultative Document, HMSO, December 9, 1976).

lised regional offices of government and amalgamation of the various nominated *ad hoc* bodies, and perhaps also by a reduction in the number of local authorities. Alternatively, instead of the devolution of central government powers, a number of elected regional bodies might be created drawing their powers from local government and nominated *ad hoc* bodies such as health and water authorities. About a dozen directly elected regional authorities might be responsible for planning, infra-structure development, and community land, water and sewerage, health and economic planning functions. These might be accompanied by "multi-purpose" district authorities responsible for housing, education, social services and other major functions below the regional tier. This would involve yet another reorganisation of local government, squeezing out the counties.

A limited change might be to strengthen the regional advisory bodies, which would continue to be without executive powers, and whose primary functions would be to represent regional interests to the central government and to advise on regional needs. Their members might continue to be appointed, or some might be appointed and others elected indirectly by members of the local authorities in the region. Other options for limited change are at local government level, involving a process of further local government reform, including a review of the tiers at which local government functions are performed, consequential boundary changes and an examination of the scope for democratising nominated *ad hoc* bodies.

Finally, but of fundamental importance, any future attempt to introduce devolution, based on anything other than party political advantage, would also have to address itself to the present over-representation of Scotland and Wales in the United Kingdom Parliament.[10]

---

[10] In 1981 the average electorate in an English constituency was 67,961, in a Welsh constituency 58,753 and in a Scottish constituency, 54,725.

INDEX